W9-CTW-174

DATE DUE

			PRINTED IN U.S.A.

Literature Criticism from 1400 to 1800

Guide to Gale Literary Criticism Series

For criticism on	Consult these Gale series
Authors now living or who died after December 31, 1959	*CONTEMPORARY LITERARY CRITICISM (CLC)*
Authors who died between 1900 and 1959	*TWENTIETH-CENTURY LITERARY CRITICISM (TCLC)*
Authors who died between 1800 and 1899	*NINETEENTH-CENTURY LITERATURE CRITICISM (NCLC)*
Authors who died between 1400 and 1799	*LITERATURE CRITICISM FROM 1400 TO 1800 (LC)* *SHAKESPEAREAN CRITICISM (SC)*
Authors who died before 1400	*CLASSICAL AND MEDIEVAL LITERATURE CRITICISM (CMLC)*
Black writers of the past two hundred years	*BLACK LITERATURE CRITICISM (BLC)*
Authors of books for children and young adults	*CHILDREN'S LITERATURE REVIEW (CLR)*
Dramatists	*DRAMA CRITICISM (DC)*
Hispanic writers of the late nineteenth and twentieth centuries	*HISPANIC LITERATURE CRITICISM (HLC)*
Native North American writers and orators of the eighteenth, nineteenth, and twentieth centuries	*NATIVE NORTH AMERICAN LITERATURE (NNAL)*
Poets	*POETRY CRITICISM (PC)*
Short story writers	*SHORT STORY CRITICISM (SSC)*
Major authors from the Renaissance to the present	*WORLD LITERATURE CRITICISM, 1500 TO THE PRESENT (WLC)*

ISSN 0740-2880

Volume 38

Literature Criticism from 1400 to 1800

Critical Discussion of the Works
of Fifteenth-, Sixteenth-, Seventeenth-, and
Eighteenth-Century Novelists, Poets, Playwrights,
Philosophers, and Other Creative Writers

Jelena O. Krstović, Editor

GALE

DETROIT • NEW YORK • TORONTO • LONDON

STAFF

Jelena O. Krstović, *Editor*

Dana Barnes, Gerald R. Barterian, *Contributing Editors*
Michelle Lee, *Associate Editor*

Aarti Stephens, *Managing Editor*

Susan M. Trosky, *Permissions Manager*
Kimberly F. Smilay, *Permissions Specialist*
Sarah Chesney, *Permissions Associate*
Steve Cusack, Kelly A. Quin, *Permissions Assistants*

Victoria B. Cariappa, *Research Manager*
Laura C. Bissey, Julia C. Daniel, Tamara C. Nott, Tracie A. Richardson, Cheryl L. Warnock, *Research Associates*

Mary Beth Trimper, *Production Director*
Deborah Milliken, *Production Assistant*

Pamela A. Reed, *Photography Coordinator*
Randy Bassett, *Image Database Supervisor*
Mike Logusz, Robert Duncan, *Scanner Operators*

This book is printed on acid-free paper that meets the minimum requirements of American National Standard for Information Sciences—Permanence Paper for Printed Library Materials, ANSI Z39.48-1984.

Library of Congress Catalog Card Number 94-29718
ISBN 0-7876-1132-8
ISSN 0740-2880
Printed in the United States of America

10 9 8 7 6 5 4 3 2 1

Contents

Preface vii

Acknowledgments xi

Preface

L *iterature Criticism from 1400 to 1800 (LC)* presents critical discussion of world authors of the fifteenth through eighteenth centuries. The literature of this period reflects a turbulent time of radical change that saw the rise of modern European drama, the birth of the novel and personal essay forms, the emergence of newspapers and periodicals, and major achievements in poetry and philosophy. Many of these historical forces continue to influence modern art and society. *LC*, therefore, provides valuable insight into the art, life, thought, and cultural transformations that took place during these centuries.

Scope of the Series

LC provides an introduction to the great poets, dramatists, novelists, essayists, and philosophers of the fifteenth through eighteenth centuries, and to the most significant interpretations of these authors' works. Because criticism of this literature spans nearly six hundred years, an overwhelming amount of scholarship confronts the student. *LC* organizes this material into volumes addressing specific historical and cultural topics, for example, "Literature of the Spanish Golden Age," or "Literature and the New World." Every attempt is made to reprint the most noteworthy, relevant, and educationally valuable essays available.

Readers should note that there is a separate Gale reference series devoted exclusively to Shakespearean studies. Although belonging properly to the period covered in *LC,* William Shakespeare has inspired such a tremendous and ever-growing corpus of secondary material that the editors have deemed it best to give his works extensive coverage in a separate series, *Shakespearean Criticism.*

Each author entry in *LC* presents a survey of critical response to a topic or an author's oeuvre. Early criticism is offered to indicate initial responses, later selections document any rise or decline in literary reputations, and retrospective analyses provide students with modern views. The size of each author entry is a relative reflection of the scope of criticism available in English. Every attempt has been made to identify and include the seminal essays on each author's work and to include recent commentary providing modern perspectives.

The need for *LC* among students and teachers of literature and history was suggested by the proven usefulness of Gale's *Contemporary Literary Criticism (CLC), Twentieth-Century Literary Criticism (TCLC),* and *Nineteenth-Century Literature Criticism (NCLC),* which excerpt criticism of works by nineteenth- and twentieth-century authors. There is no duplication of critical material in any of these literary criticism series. Major authors may appear more than once in one or more of the series because of the great quantity of critical material available and because of their relevance to a variety of thematic topics.

Thematic Approach

Beginning with Volume 12, the authors in each volume of *LC* are organized around such themes as specific literary or philosophical movements, writings surrounding important political and historical events, the philosophy and art associated with eras of cultural transformation, and the literature of specific social or ethnic groups. Each volume contains a topic entry providing a historical and literary overview, and several author entries which examine major representatives of the featured period.

Organization of the Book

Each entry consists of the following elements: author or thematic heading, introduction, list of principal works, annotated works of criticism (each preceded by a bibliographical citation), and a bibliography of further reading. Also, most author entries contain author portraits and other illustrations.

- The **Author Heading** consists of the author's name (the most commonly used form), followed by birth and death dates. (If an author wrote consistently under a pseudonym, the pseudonym is used in the author heading, with the real name given in parentheses on the first line of the biographical and critical introduction.) Also located here are any name variations under which an author wrote, including transliterated forms for authors whose native languages use nonroman alphabets. Uncertain birth or death dates are indicated by question marks. Topic entries are preceded by a **Thematic Heading,** which simply states the subject of the entry.

- The **Biographical and Critical Introduction** contains background information that concisely introduces the reader to the author or topic.

- Most *LC* author entries include **Portraits** of the author. Many entries also contain illustrations of materials pertinent to an author's career, including author holographs, title pages, letters, or representations of important people, places, and events in an author's life.

- The **List of Principal Works** is ordered chronologically, by date of first book publication, identifying the genre of each work. In the case of foreign authors whose works have been translated into English, the title and date (if available) of the first English-language edition are given in brackets following the foreign-language listing. Unless otherwise indicated, dramas are dated by first performance, not first publication.

- **Criticism** is arranged chronologically in each author entry to provide a useful perspective on changes in critical evaluation over time. For the purpose of easy identification, the critic's name and the date of first composition or publication of the critical work are given at the beginning of each piece of criticism. Unsigned criticism is preceded by the title of the source in which it appeared. All titles by the author featured in the critical entry are printed in boldface type. Publication information (such as publisher names and book prices) and some parenthetical numerical references (such as footnotes or page and line references to specific editions of works) have been occasionally deleted to provide smoother reading of the text. Footnotes that appear with previously published pieces of criticism are reprinted at the end of each essay or excerpt. In the case of excerpted criticism, only those footnotes that pertain to the excerpted text are included.

- Critical essays are prefaced by **Annotations** as an additional aid to students using *LC*. These explanatory notes provide information such as the importance of a work of criticism, the commentator's individual approach to literary criticism, and a brief summary of the reprinted essay. In some cases, these notes cross-reference the work of critics within the entry who agree or disagree with each other.

- A complete **Bibliographical Citation** of the original essay or book precedes each piece of criticism.

- An annotated bibliography of **Further Reading** appears at the end of each entry and suggests resources for additional study. In some cases, significant essays for which the editors could not obtain reprint rights are included here.

Cumulative Indexes

Each volume of *LC* includes a cumulative **Author Index** listing all the authors that have appeared in the following sources published by Gale: *Contemporary Literary Criticism, Twentieth-Century Literary Criticism, Nineteenth-Century Literature Criticism, Literature Criticism from 1400 to 1800,* and *Classical and Medieval Literature Criticism,* along with cross-references to the Gale series *Short Story Criticism, Poetry Criticism, Children's Literature Review, Authors in the News, Contemporary Authors, Contemporary Authors Autobiography Series, Contemporary Authors Bibliographical Series, Dictionary of Literary Biography, Concise Dictionary of Literary Biography, Something about the Author, Something about the Author Autobiography Series,* and *Yesterday's Authors of Books for Children.* Readers will welcome this cumulative author index as a useful tool for locating an author within the various series. The index, which includes authors' birth and death dates, is particularly valuable for those authors who are identified with a certain period but whose death dates cause them to be placed in another, or for those authors whose careers span two periods. For example, F. Scott Fitzgerald is found in *TCLC,* yet a writer often associated with him, Ernest Hemingway, is found in *CLC.*

Beginning with Volume 12, *LC* includes a cumulative **Topic Index** that lists all literary themes and topics treated in *LC, NCLC, TCLC,* and the *CLC* Yearbook. Each volume of *LC* also includes a cumulative **Nationality Index** in which authors' names are arranged alphabetically under their respective nationalities and followed by the numbers of the volumes in which they appear.

Each volume of *LC* also includes a cumulative **Title Index,** an alphabetical listing of all literary works discussed in the series. Each title listing includes the corresponding volume and page numbers where criticism may be located. Foreign-language titles that have been translated followed by the tiles of the translation—for example, *El ingenioso hidalgo Don Quixote de la Mancha (Don Quixote).* Page numbers following these translated titles refer to all pages on which any form of the titles, either foreign-language or translated, appear. Titles of novels, dramas, nonfiction books, and poetry, short story, or essays collections are printed in italics, while individual poems, short stories, and essays are printed in roman type within quotation marks.

A Note to the Reader

When writing papers, students who quote directly from any volume in the Literary Criticism Series may use the following general format to footnote reprinted criticism. The first example pertains to material drawn from periodicals, the second to material reprinted from books.

T. S. Eliot, "John Donne," *The Nation and the Athenaeum,* 33 (9 June 1923), 321-32; excerpted and reprinted in *Literature Criticism from 1400 to 1800,* Vol. 10, ed. James E. Person, Jr. (Detroit: Gale Research, 1989), pp. 28-9.

Clara G. Stillman, *Samuel Butler: A Mid-Victorian Modern* (Viking Press, 1932); excerpted and reprinted in *Twentieth-Century Literary Criticism,* Vol. 33, ed. Paula Kepos (Detroit: Gale Research, 1989), pp. 43-5.

Suggestions Are Welcome

Since the series began, features have been added to *LC* in response to various suggestions, including a nationality index, a Literary Criticism Series topic index, and thematic organization of entries.

Readers who wish to suggest new features, themes or authors to appear in future volumes, or who have other suggestions or comments are cordially invited to write to the editor (fax: 313 961-6599).

Acknowledgments

The editors wish to thank the copyright holders of the excerpted criticism included in this volume and the permissions managers of many book and magazine publishing companies for assisting us in securing reproduction rights. We are also grateful to the staffs of the Detroit Public Library, the Library of Congress, the University of Detroit Mercy Library, Wayne State University Purdy/Kresge Library Complex, and the University of Michigan Libraries for making their resources available to us. Following is a list of the copyright holders who have granted us permission to reproduce material in this volume of *LC*. Every effort has been made to trace copyright, but if omissions have been made, please let us know.

COPYRIGHTED EXCERPTS IN *LC*, VOLUME 38, WERE REPRODUCED FROM THE FOLLOWING PERIODICALS:

The American Historical Review, v. LXXV, June, 1970 for "Underlying Themes in Witchcraft of Seventeenth-Century New England," by John Demos. Copyright (c) The American Historical Association 1970. All rights reserved. Reproduced by permission of the author.—*American Literature*, XLII, January, 1971. Copyright (c) 1971 Duke University Press, Durham, NC. Reproduced with permission.—*American Quarterly*, v. XX, Winter, 1968; v. 34, Summer, 1982. Copyright 1968, 1982, American Studies Association. Both reproduced by permission of The Johns Hopkins University Press.—*Early American Literature,* v. VII, Winter, 1973 for "Cotton Mather and the Puritan Transition into the Enlightenment" by Pershing Vartanian. Copyrighted, 1973, by the University of Massachusetts. Reproduced by permission of the publisher and the author.—*ELH*, v. 33, September, 1966. Copyright (c) 1966 by The Johns Hopkins University Press. All rights reserved. Reproduced by permission of The John Hopkins University Press. *Journal of American Culture,* v. 8, Winter, 1985. Copyright (c) 1985 by Ray B. Browne. Reproduced by permission.—*Massachusetts Studies in English,* v. I, Fall, 1967 for "Cotton Mather Revisited" by John P. Duffy. Copyright (c) 1967 by the author. Reproduced by permission of the author.—*Proceedings of the American Antiquarian Society*, v. 87, 1978; v. 95, 1985. Copyright (c) 1978, 1985 by American Antiquarian Society. Both reproduced by permission.—*Science,* v. 192, April 2, 1976 for "Ergotism: The Satan Loosed in Salem?" by Linnda R. Caporael; v. 194, December, 1976 for "Ergotism and the Salem Village Witch Trials" by Nicolas P. Spanos and Jack Gottlieb. Copyright 1976 by AAAS. Both reproduced by permission of the publisher and the respective authors.—*The William and Mary Quarterly,* v. XXIX, April, 1972. Copyright, 1972, by the Institute of Early American History and Culture. Reproduced by permission of the Institute.

COPYRIGHTED EXCERPTS IN *LC*, VOLUME 38, WERE REPRODUCED FROM THE FOLLOWING BOOKS:

Bercovitch, Sacvan. From "Cotton Mather," in *Major Writers of Early American Literature*. Edited by Everett Emerson. The University of Wisconsin Press, 1972. Copyright (c) 1972 The Regents of the University of Wisconsin System. All rights reserved. Reproduced by permission.—Boyer, Paul and Stephen Nissenbaum. From *Salem Possessed: The Social Origins of Witchcraft*. Cambridge, Mass.: Harvard University Press, 1974. Copyright (c) 1974 by the Presidents and Fellows of Harvard College. All rights reserved. Excerpted by permission of the publishers and the authors.—Demos, John Putnam. From *Entertaining Satan: Witchcraft and the Culture of Early New England*. Oxford University Press, 1982. Copyright (c) 1982 by Oxford University Press, Inc. Reproduced by permission of Oxford University Press, Inc.—Erikson, Kai T. From *Wayward Puritans: A Study in the Sociology of Deviance*. John Wiley & Sons, 1986. Copyright (c) 1986 by Allyn and Bacon. All rights reserved. Reproduced by permission.—Gay, Peter. From *A Loss of Mastery: Puritan Historians in Colonial America*. University of California Press, 1966. Copyright (c) 1966 by The Regents of the University of California. Renewed 1994 by Peter Gay. Reproduced by permission.—Godbeer, Richard. From *The Devil's Dominion: Magic and Religion in Early New England*. Cambridge University Press, 1992. (c) Cambridge Universi ELH, v. ty Press 1992. Reproduced with the permission of the publisher and the author.—Hanson, Chadwick. From "Andover Witchcraft and the Causes of the Salem Witchcraft Trials," in *The Occult in America: New Historical Perspectives*. Edited by Howard Kerr and Charles L. Crow. University of Illinois Press, 1983. (c) 1983 by the Board of Trustees of the University of Illinois. Reproduced by permission of the publisher and the author.—Hoffer, Peter Charles.

From *The Devil's Disciples: Makers of the Salem Witchcraft Trials.* Johns Hopkins University Press, 1966. Copyright (c) 1966 Peter Charles Hoffer. All rights reserved. Reproduced by permission.—Kagle, Steven E. From *American Diary Literature: 1620-1799.* Twayne Publishers, 1979. Copyright (c) 1979 by G. H. Hall & Co. All rights reserved. Reproduced with the permission of the author.—Kittredge, George Lyman. From *Witchcraft in Old and New England.* Cambridge, Mass.: Harvard University Press, 1929. Copyright 1929 by the President and Fellows of Harvard College. Copyright renewed, 1957, by Henry Crocker Kittredge. All rights reserved. Excerpted by permission of the publishers and the author.—Koehler, Lyle. From *A Search for Power: The "Weaker Sex" in Seventeenth-Century New England.* University of Illinois Press, 1980. (c) 1980 by the Board of Trustees of the University of Illinois. Reproduced by permission of the publisher and the author.—Levin, David. From an introduction to *Bonifacius: An Essay Upon the Good by Cotton Mather.* Edited by David Levin. Cambridge, Mass.: Harvard University Press, 1966. Copyright (c) 1966 by the Presidents and Fellows of Harvard College. Excerpted by permission of the publishers.—Loggins, Vernon. *The Hawthornes.* Columbia University Press, 1951. Copyright (c) 1951 Columbia University Press, New York. All rights reserved. Reproduced with the permission of the publisher.—Lowance, Mason I., Jr. From *Increase Mather.* Twayne, 1974. Copyright (c) 1974 by Twayne Publishers, Inc. All rights reserved. Reproduced by permission of the author.—Middlekauff, Robert. From *The Mathers: Three Generations of Puritan Intellectuals, 1596-1728.* Oxford University Press, 1971. Copyright (c) 1971 by Oxford University Press, Inc. Reproduced by permission of Oxford University Press, Inc.—Miller, Perry. From *The New England Mind: From Colony to Province.* Cambridge, Mass.: Harvard University Press, 1953. Copyright 1953 by the President and Fellows of Harvard College. Reprinted by permission of the publisher.—Murdock, Kenneth Ballard. From *Increase Mather: The Foremost American Puritan.* Cambridge, Mass.: Harvard University Press, 1925. Copyright 1925 by the Presidents and Fellows of Harvard College. Renewed 1977 by Mrs. Kenneth Ballard Murdock. Reproduced by permission of the publisher.—Parrington, Vernon Louis. From *Main Currents in American Thought, An Interpretation of American Literature from the Beginninng to 1920: The Colonial Mind, 1620-1800, Vol. 1.* Harcourt Brace & Company, 1927. Copyright, 1927, by Harcourt Brace & Company. Copyright renewed, 1954, by Vernon L. Parrington, Jr., Louise P. Tucker, Elizabeth P. Thomas. Reproduced by permission.—Robinson, Enders A. From *Salem Witchcraft and Hawthorne's House of the Seven Gables.* Heritage Books, 1992. Copyright (c) 1992 Enders A. Robinson. All rights reserved. Reproduced by permission. —Robinson, Enders A. From *The Devil Discovered: Salem Witchcraft 1692.* Hippocrene Books, 1991. Copyright (c) 1991 Enders A. Robinson. All rights reserved. Reproduced by permission.—Shea, Daniel B. From *Spiritual Autobiography in Early America.* The University of Wisconsin Press, 1988. Copyright (c) 1968, 1988, by Daniel B. Shea, Jr. All rights reserved. Reproduced by permission.—Thomas, M. Hasley. From a preface to The *Diary of Samuel Sewall, Vol. I.* Farrar, Straus and Giroux, 1973. Copyright (c) 1973 by Farrar, Straus and Giroux, Inc. All rights reserved. Reproduced by permissin of Farrar, Straus and Giroux, Inc.—Trask, Richard B. From an introduction to *The Devil Hath Been Raised: A Documentary History of the Salem Village Witchcraft Outbreak of March 1692; Together With a Collection of Newly Located and Gathered Witchcraft Documents.* Yeoman Press, 1997. Copyright (c) 1997 by Richard B. Trask. All rights reserved. Reproduced by permission of the author.--Weisman, Richard. From *Witchcraft, Magic, and Religion in 17th-Century Massachusetts.* Amherst: The University of Massachusetts Press, 1984. Copyright (c) 1984 by The University of Massachusetts Press. All rights reserved. Reproduced by permission.—Winslow, Ola Elizabeth. From *Samuel Sewall of Boston.* The Macmillan Company, 1964. (c) Ola Elizabeth Winslow, 1964. Reproduced by permission of The Macmillan Company, a division of Simon & Schuster, Inc.—Wish, Harvey. From *The Diary of Samuel Sewall.* Revised editon, 1967. Copyright (c) 1967 by Harvey Wish. All rights reserved. Reproduced by permission of The Putnam Publishing Group.

PHOTOGRAPHS AND ILLUSTRATIONS APPEARING IN *LC*, VOLUME 38, WERE RECEIVED FROM THE FOLLOWING SOURCES:

Mather, Increase, illustration. Archive Photos, Inc. Reproduced by permission.—Stoughton, William, illustration. Archive Photos, Inc. Reproduced by permission.—Witchcraft at Salem Village, illustration. The Library of Congress.

Salem Witch Trials

1692-1693

INTRODUCTION

An infamous episode in American history, the Salem witch trials of 1692 resulted in the execution by hanging of fourteen women and five men accused of being witches. In addition, one man was pressed to death by heavy weights for refusing to enter a plea; at least eight people died in prison, including one infant and one child; and more than one hundred and fifty individuals were jailed while awaiting trial. Due to the survival of many relevant records, including notes, depositions, and official rulings, the main facts of the accusations, arrests, trials, and executions are known. What has always engaged scholars is the search for the causes of the "witch hysteria." The proffered explanations for the witchcraft occurrence are many and conflicting.

On January 20, 1692, in Salem Village, the Reverend Samuel Parris' nine-year-old daughter, Elizabeth, and his eleven-year-old niece, Abigail Williams, began exhibiting odd behavior, including shouting blasphemies and entering into trances. Parris eventually called in the local physician, William Griggs, who found the girls experiencing convulsions and scurrying around the room and barking like dogs. The doctor was puzzled and unable to offer a medical explanation, but suggested that it might be the work of evil forces. Parris consulted with local ministers, who recommended he wait to see what happened. But word of the unexplained fits had already spread around Salem Village, and soon several other girls, including three from the home of Thomas Putnam, Jr., were exhibiting similar behavior. Pressured to explain what or who had caused their behavior, the girls named three Village women as witches. One named was Tituba, the Rev. Parris' slave, who had enthralled many local girls with fortune-telling in her master's kitchen. Another named as a witch was Sarah Good, an unpopular woman who had reportedly muttered threats against her neighbors; the third was Sarah Osborne, who had allowed a man to live with her for some months before they were married. Warrants for the three were issued on February 29. The next day Salem Town magistrates John Hathorne and Jonathan Corwin examined the women in the Village meeting house. Good and Osborne declared that they were innocent and knew nothing of witchcraft, but Tituba exuberantly confessed, claiming that witchcraft was practiced by many in the area. Her confession excited the villagers. On March 21 Martha Corey became the fourth woman of Salem Village to be arrested. While she was examined in the meeting house in front of hundreds of people, the afflicted girls cried out in what appeared to be extreme agony. More individuals were accused and jailed as the weeks passed, but no trials could legally take place because, for the first three months of the witchcraft uproar, Massachusetts was without a legally-established government. On May 14, 1692, Governor William Phips arrived with a new charter and soon created a special Court of Oyer (to hear) and Terminer (to determine). The chief justice for the Court of Oyer and Terminer was William Stoughton, and the others serving included John Hathorne and Samuel Sewall. The court's first session, held on June 2, resulted in a death sentence for the accused witch Bridget Bishop; she was hanged on June 10. (She was not the first accused to die, however; Sarah Osborne died of natural causes in a jail in Boston on May 10.) Cotton Mather of Boston's First Church wrote privately to the court expressing reservations on questions of evidence. On June 15 a group of ministers including Cotton Mather, wrote Governor Phips urging that special caution be taken in the use of evidence in the trials, but the ministers said no more publicly in July, August, or September. The court next met on June 29 and heard the cases of five accused women. When the jury tried to acquit one of them, Rebecca Nurse, Stoughton sent the jury back to deliberate some more. When they returned they had changed their verdict to guilty. The women were hanged on July 19. By this time the witchcraft hysteria had spread not only to Salem Town but to Andover. August and September brought more convictions and hangings. The last eight accused witches were hanged on September 22, in what would turn out to be the final executions. On October 3, Increase Mather, father of Cotton Mather, delivered a sermon at a gathering of ministers in Cambridge. The sermon was soon published as *Cases of Conscience Concerning Evil Spirits Personating Men* (1692). The elder Mather insisted that proper evidence should be used in witchcraft cases just as in any other capital cases. He strongly opposed spectral evidence, or evidence based on ghost sightings. As accusations mounted against people of higher and more respectable positions, skepticism grew in the public as to the appropriateness of witchcraft charges. Thomas Brattle wrote an insightful letter to Governor Phips highly criticising the trials. On October 12, Phips, whose own wife had been accused of witchcraft, forbade any further imprisonments for witchcraft, and on the 29th dissolved the Court of Oyer and Terminer. When a new special court convened in early 1693, with several of the same members and William Stoughton once more as chief justice, forty-nine accused persons were acquitted. The difference was in no small part due to the governor not permitting spectral evidence to be heard. When three prisoners were convicted, Phips immediately granted reprieves. Three months later Phips freed all the remaining prisoners and issued a general pardon. Soon many jurors and judges apologized, and Judge Sewall attempted to take full responsibility for the trials and hangings.

A central problem in the trials themselves was the use of spectral evidence. Because the actual crime involved an agreement made between the accused witch and the devil, in which the devil was given the right to assume the witch's human form, and because, by its very nature, this compact would not have witnesses, finding acceptable evidence was difficult. Spectral evidence included testimony by the afflicted that they could see the specters of the witches tormenting their victims; the evil deeds were not perpetrated by the accused themselves, but by the evil spirits who assumed their shapes. One problem with spectral evidence was that apparitions of demons were invisible to other people in the same room; only the afflicted girls could see the shapes. Another concern was the possibility that Satan could appear in the shape of an innocent person. To overcome these obstacles, confessions were vigorously sought. The Salem cases are unusual in that the defendants who confessed were generally not executed, while those who were hanged adamantly maintained their innocence. Considered trustworthy was testimony to some supernatural attribute of the accused. George Burroughs was accused by six persons of performing superhuman feats of strength. One witness claimed Burroughs could read his thoughts. Another test made on the accused was for any "supernatural weaknesses" such as the inability to recite prayers correctly. Yet another criterion was the presence of a "witch's tit"— any small, unusual physical appendage, ordinarily quite small, through which the witch would give suck to the devil when he appeared in the form of some small animal or creature. Anger followed by mischief also indicated a person was a witch, especially when a curse uttered against a neighbor or his property came immediately before the misdeed occurred.

Many factors must be considered in examining the causes of the witchcraft hysteria. Fundamental is the recognition that among the settlers of New England, belief in witchcraft was prevalent. Additionally, Salem was beset with political problems and internal strife. Land disputes and personal feuds were common. Some scholars maintain that the Puritan villagers felt they had failed God and deserved to be punished for their sins. The role of the clergy has also been much debated; some historians see them as largely responsible for stirring up the people and making them expect retribution. Others credit the clergy with ending the trials. The afflicted girls have been variously described as outright liars and frauds, children looking for excitement, victims of disease, and sincere believers in the idea that they were victims of witchcraft.

OVERVIEWS

Kai T. Erikson (essay date 1966)

SOURCE: "The Shapes of the Devil," in *Wayward Puritans: A Study in the Sociology of Deviance,* John Wiley & Sons, Inc., 1966, pp. 65-160.

[In the following excerpt, Erikson discusses the factors that prepared the village of Salem for the witchcraft hysteria, summarizes the events of the trials, and concludes that the year 1692 marked the end of the Puritan experiment in Massachusetts.]

. . . The witchcraft hysteria that began in Salem Village (a town some miles away from Salem itself) is probably the best known episode of Massachusetts history and has been described in a number of careful works. In the pages which follow, then, the story will be sketched in rather briefly: readers interested in a fuller account of those unusual events are urged to consult *The Devil in Massachusetts* by Marion L. Starkey, a book that captures all the grim drama of the period without losing any of its merit as a scholarly work.[66]

Between the end of the Quaker persecutions in 1665 and the beginning of the Salem witchcraft outbreak in 1692, the colony had experienced some very trying days. To begin with, the political outlines of the commonwealth had been subject to sudden, often violent, shifts, and the people of the colony were quite uncertain about their own future. The King's decrees during the Quaker troubles had provoked only minor changes in the actual structure of the Puritan state, but they had introduced a note of apprehension and alarm which did not disappear for thirty years; and no sooner had Charles warned the Massachusetts authorities of his new interest in their affairs then he dispatched four commissioners to the Bay to look after his remote dominions and make sure that his occasional orders were being enforced. From that moment, New England feared the worst. The sermons of the period were full of dreadful prophecies about the future of the Bay, and as New England moved through the 1670's and 1680's, the catalogue of political calamities grew steadily longer and more serious. In 1670, for example, a series of harsh arguments occurred between groups of magistrates and clergymen, threatening the alliance which had been the very cornerstone of the New England Way. In 1675 a brutal and costly war broke out with a confederacy of Indian tribes led by a wily chief called King Philip. In 1676 Charles II began to review the claims of other persons to lands within the jurisdiction of Massachusetts, and it became increasingly clear that the old charter might be revoked altogether. In 1679 Charles specifically ordered Massachusetts to permit the establishment of an Anglican church in Boston, and in 1684 the people of the Bay had become so pessimistic about the fate of the colony that several towns simply neglected to send Deputies to the General Court. The sense of impending doom reached its peak in 1686. To begin with, the charter which had given the colony its only legal protection for over half a century was vacated by a stroke of the royal pen, and in addition the King sent a Royal Governor to represent his interests in the Bay who was both an Anglican and a man actively hostile to the larger goals of New England. For the moment, it looked as if the holy experiment was over: not only had the settlers lost title to the very land they were standing on, but they ran the very real risk of witnessing the final collapse of the congregational churches they had built at so great a cost.

The settlers were eventually rescued from the catastrophes of 1686, but their margin of escape had been extremely narrow and highly tentative. In 1689 news began to filter into the Bay that William of Orange had landed in England to challenge the House of Stuart, and hopes ran high throughout the colony; but before the people of the Bay knew the outcome of this contest in England, a Boston mob suddenly rose in protest and placed the Royal Governor in chains. Luckily for Massachusetts, William's forces were successful in England and the Boston insurrection was seen as little more than a premature celebration in honor of the new King. Yet for all the furor, little had changed. At the time of the witchcraft hysteria, agents of Massachusetts were at work in London trying to convince William to restore the old charter, or at least to issue a new one giving Massachusetts all the advantages it had enjoyed in the past, but everyone knew that the colony would never again operate under the same autonomy. As the people of the Bay waited to hear about the future of their settlement, then, their anxiety was understandably high.

Throughout this period of political crisis, an even darker cloud was threatening the colony, and this had to do with the fact that a good deal of angry dissension was spreading among the saints themselves. In a colony that depended on a high degree of harmony and group feeling, the courts were picking their way through a maze of land disputes and personal feuds, a complicated tangle of litigations and suits. Moreover, the earnest attempts at unanimity that had characterized the politics of Winthrop's era were now replaced by something closely resembling open party bickering. When John Josselyn visited Boston in 1668, for instance, he observed that the people were "savagely factious" in their relations with one another and acted more out of jealousy and greed than any sense of religious pur-

pose.[67] And the sermons of the day chose even stronger language to describe the decline in morality which seemed to darken the prospects of New England. The spirit of brotherhood which the original settlers had counted on so heavily had lately diffused into an atmosphere of commercial competition, political contention, and personal bad feeling.

Thus the political architecture which had been fashioned so carefully by the first generation and the spiritual consensus which had been defended so energetically by the second were both disappearing. At the time of the Salem witchcraft mania, most of the familiar landmarks of the New England Way had become blurred by changes in the historical climate, like signposts obscured in a storm, and the people of the Bay no longer knew how to assess what the past had amounted to or what the future promised. Massachusetts had become, in Alan Heimert's words, "a society no longer able to judge itself with any certainty."[68]

In 1670, the House of Deputies took note of the confusion and fear which was beginning to spread over the country and prepared a brief inventory of the troubles facing the Bay:

> Declension from the primitive foundation work, innovation in doctrine and worship, opinion and practice, an invasion of the rights, liberties and privileges of churches, an usurpation of a lordly and prelatical power over God's heritage, a subversion of the gospel order, and all this with a dangerous tendency to the utter devastation of these churches, turning the pleasant gardens of Christ into a wilderness, and the inevitable and total extirpation of the principles and pillars of the congregational way; these are the leaven, the corrupting gangrene, the infecting spreading plague, the provoking image of jealousy set up before the Lord, the accursed thing which hath provoked divine wrath, and doth further threaten destruction.[69]

The tone of this resolution gives us an excellent index to the mood of the time. For the next twenty years, New England turned more and more to the notion that the settlers must expect God to turn upon them in wrath because the colony had lost its original fervor and sense of mission. The motif introduced in this resolution runs like a recurrent theme through the thinking of the period: the settlers who had carved a commonwealth out of the wilderness and had planted "the pleasant gardens of Christ" in its place were about to return to the wilderness. But there is an important shift of imagery here, for the wilderness they had once mastered was one of thick underbrush and wild animals, dangerous seasons and marauding Indians, while the wilderness which awaited them contained an entirely different sort of peril. "The Wilderness thro' which we are passing to the Promised Land," Cotton Mather wrote in a volume describing the state of New England at the time of the witchcraft difficulties, "is all over fill'd with Fiery flying serpents. . . . All our way to Heaven, lies by the Dens of Lions, and the Mounts of Leopards; there are incredible Droves of Devils in our way."[70] We will return to discussion of this wilderness theme at the conclusion of the chapter, but for the moment it is important to note that Massachusetts had lost much of its concern for institutions and policies and had begun to seek some vision of its future by looking into a ghostly, invisible world.

It was while the people of the colony were preoccupied with these matters that the witches decided to strike.

I

No one really knows how the witchcraft hysteria began, but it originated in the home of the Reverend Samuel Parris, minister of the local church. In early 1692, several girls from the neighborhood began to spend their afternoons in the Parris' kitchen with a slave named Tituba, and it was not long before a mysterious sorority of girls, aged between nine and twenty, became regular visitors to the parsonage. We can only speculate what was going on behind the kitchen door, but we know that Tituba had been brought to Massachusetts from Barbados and enjoyed a reputation in the neighborhood for her skills in the magic arts. As the girls grew closer together, a remarkable change seemed to come over them: perhaps it is not true, as someone later reported, that they went out into the forest to celebrate their own version of a black mass, but it is apparent that they began to live in a state of high tension and shared secrets with one another which were hardly becoming to quiet Puritan maidens.

Before the end of winter, the two youngest girls in the group succumbed to the shrill pitch of their amusements and began to exhibit a most unusual malady. They would scream unaccountably, fall into grotesque convulsions, and sometimes scamper along on their hands and knees making noises like the barking of a dog. No sooner had word gone around about this extraordinary affliction than it began to spread like a contagious disease. All over the community young girls were groveling on the ground in a panic of fear and excitement, and while some of the less credulous townspeople were tempted to reach for their belts in the hopes of strapping a little modesty into them, the rest could only stand by in helpless horror as the girls suffered their torments.

The town's one physician did what he could to stem the epidemic, but he soon exhausted his meagre store of remedies and was forced to conclude that the problem lay outside the province of medicine. The Devil had come to Salem Village, he announced; the girls

were bewitched. At this disturbing news, ministers from many of the neighboring parishes came to consult with their colleague and offer what advice they might. Among the first to arrive was a thoughtful clergyman named Deodat Lawson, and he had been in town no more than a few hours when he happened upon a frightening exhibition of the devil's handiwork. "In the beginning of the evening," he later recounted of his first day in the village,

> I went to give Mr. Parris a visit. When I was there, his kinswoman, Abigail Williams, (about 12 years of age,) had a grievous fit; she was at first hurried with violence to and fro in the room, (though Mrs. Ingersoll endeavored to hold her,) sometimes making as if she would fly, stretching up her arms as high as she could, and crying "whish, whish, whish!" several times. . . . After that, she run to the fire, and began to throw fire brands about the house; and run against the back, as if she would run up the chimney, and, as they said, she had attempted to go into the fire in other fits.[71]

Faced by such clear-cut evidence, the ministers quickly agreed that Satan's new challenge would have to be met with vigorous action, and this meant that the afflicted girls would have to identify the witches who were harassing them.

It is hard to guess what the girls were experiencing during those early days of the commotion. They attracted attention everywhere they went and exercised a degree of power over the adult community which would have been exhilarating under the sanest of circumstances. But whatever else was going on in those young minds, the thought seems to have gradually occurred to the girls that they were indeed bewitched, and after they had been coaxed over and over again to name their tormentors, they finally singled out three women in the village and accused them of witchcraft.

Three better candidates could not have been found if all the gossips in New England had met to make the nominations. The first, understandably, was Tituba herself, a woman who had grown up among the rich colors and imaginative legends of Barbados and who was probably acquainted with some form of voodoo. The second, Sarah Good, was a proper hag of a witch if Salem Village had ever seen one. With a pipe clenched in her leathery face she wandered around the countryside neglecting her children and begging from others, and on more than one occasion the old crone had been overheard muttering threats against her neighbors when she was in an unusually sour humor. Sarah Osburne, the third suspect, had a higher social standing than either of her alleged accomplices, but she had been involved in a local scandal a year or two earlier when a man moved into her house some months before becoming her husband.

A preliminary hearing was set at once to decide whether the three accused women should be held for trial. The girls were ushered to the front row of the meeting house, where they took full advantage of the space afforded them by rolling around in apparent agony whenever some personal fancy (or the invisible agents of the devil) provoked them to it. It was a remarkable show. Strange creatures flew about the room pecking at the girls or taunting them from the rafters, and it was immediately obvious to everyone that the women on trial were responsible for all the disorder and suffering. When Sarah Good and Sarah Osburne were called to the stand and asked why they sent these spectres to torment the girls, they were too appalled to say much in their defense. But when Tituba took the stand she had a ready answer. A lifetime spent in bondage is poor training for standing up before a bench of magistrates, and anyway Tituba was an excitable woman who had breathed the warmer winds of the Caribbean and knew things about magic her crusty old judges would never learn. Whatever the reason, Tituba gave her audience one of the most exuberant confessions ever recorded in a New England courtroom. She spoke of the creatures who inhabit the invisible world, the dark rituals which bind them together in the service of Satan; and before she had ended her astonishing recital she had convinced everyone in Salem Village that the problem was far worse than they had dared imagine. For Tituba not only implicated Sarah Good and Sarah Osburne in her own confession but announced that many other people in the colony were engaged in the devil's conspiracy against the Bay.

So the hearing that was supposed to bring a speedy end to the affair only stirred up a hidden hornet's nest, and now the girls were urged to identify other suspects and locate new sources of trouble. Already the girls had become more than unfortunate victims: in the eyes of the community they were diviners, prophets, oracles, mediums, for only they could see the terrible spectres swarming over the countryside and tell what persons had sent them on their evil errands. As they became caught up in the enthusiasm of their new work, then, the girls began to reach into every corner of the community in a search for likely suspects. Martha Corey was an upstanding woman in the village whose main mistake was to snort incredulously at the girls' behavior. Dorcas Good, five years old, was a daughter of the accused Sarah. Rebecca Nurse was a saintly old woman who had been bedridden at the time of the earlier hearings. Mary Esty and Sarah Cloyce were Rebecca's younger sisters, themselves accused when they rose in energetic defense of the older woman. And so it went—John Proctor, Giles Corey, Abigail Hobbs, Bridgit Bishop, Sarah Wild, Susanna Martin, Dorcas Hoar, the Reverend George Burroughs: as winter turned into spring the list of suspects grew to enormous length and the Salem jail was choked with people awaiting trial. We know nothing about conditions of life in prison, but it is easy to imagine the tensions which must have echoed within those grey walls. Some of the prisoners had cried out against their relatives and friends in a desperate effort to divert attention from themselves, others were witless persons with scarcely a clue as to what had happened to them, and a few (very few, as it turned out) were accepting their lot with quiet dignity. If we imagine Sarah Good sitting next to Rebecca Nurse and lighting her rancid pipe or Tituba sharing views on supernatural phenomena with the Reverend George Burroughs, we may have a rough picture of life in those crowded quarters.

By this time the hysteria had spread well beyond the confines of Salem Village, and as it grew in scope so did the appetites of the young girls. They now began to accuse persons they had never seen from places they had never visited (in the course of which some absurd mistakes were made),[72] yet their word was so little questioned that it was ordinarily warrant enough to put respected people in chains.

From as far away as Charlestown, Nathaniel Cary heard that his wife had been accused of witchcraft and immediately traveled with her to Salem "to see if the afflicted did know her." The two of them sat through an entire day of hearings, after which Cary reported:

> I observed that the afflicted were two girls of about ten years old, and about two or three others, of about eighteen. . . . The prisoners were called in one by one, and as they came in were cried out of. . . . The prisoner was placed about seven or eight feet from the Justices, and the accusers between the Justices and them; the prisoner was ordered to stand right before the Justices, with an officer appointed to hold each hand, lest they should therewith afflict them, and the prisoner's eyes must be constantly on the Justices; for if they looked on the afflicted, they would either fall into their fits, or cry out of being hurt by them. . . . Then the Justices said to the accusers, "which of you will go and touch the prisoner at the bar?" Then the most courageous would adventure, but before they had made three steps would ordinarily fall down as in a fit. The Justices ordered that they should be taken up and carried to the prisoner, that she might touch them; and as soon as they were touched by the accused, the Justices would say "they are well," before I could discern any alteration. . . . Thus far I was only as a spectator, my wife also was there part of the time, but no notice taken of her by the afflicted, except once or twice they came to her and asked her name.

After this sorry performance the Carys retired to the local inn for dinner, but no sooner had they taken seats than a group of afflicted girls burst into the room and "began to tumble about like swine" at Mrs. Cary's feet, accusing her of being the cause of their miseries. Remarkably, the magistrates happened to be sitting in the adjoining room—"waiting for this," Cary later decided—and an impromptu hearing took place on the spot.

> Being brought before the Justices, her chief accusers were two girls. My wife declared to the Justices that she never had any knowledge of them before that day; she was forced to stand with her arms stretched out. I did request that I might hold one of her hands, but it was denied me; then she desired me to wipe the tears from her eyes, and the sweat from her face, which I did; then she desired she might lean herself on me, saying she should faint. Justice Hathorne replied, she had strength enough to torment those persons, and she should have strength enough to stand. I speaking something against their cruel proceedings, they commanded me to be silent, or else I should be turned out of the room. An Indian . . . was also brought in to be one of her accusers: being come in, he now (when before the Justices) fell down and tumbled about like a hog, but said nothing. The Justices asked the girls, "who afflicted the Indian?", they answered "she" (meaning my wife). . . . The Justices ordered her to touch him, in order of his cure . . . but the Indian took hold of her in a barbarous manner; then his hand was taken off, and her hand put on his, and the cure was quickly wrought. . . . Then her mittimus was writ.[73]

For another example of how the hearings were going, we might listen for a moment to the examination of Mrs. John Proctor. This record was taken down by the Reverend Samuel Parris himself, and the notes in parentheses are his. Ann Putnam and Abigail Williams were two of the most energetic of the young accusers.

> JUSTICE: Ann Putnam, doth this woman hurt you?
>
> PUTNAM: Yes, sir, a good many times. (Then the accused looked upon them and they fell into fits.)
>
> JUSTICE: She does not bring the book to you, does she?[74]
>
> PUTNAM: Yes, sir, often, and saith she hath made her maid set her hand to it.
>
> JUSTICE: Abigail Williams, does this woman hurt you?
>
> WILLIAMS: Yes, sir, often.
>
> JUSTICE: Does she bring the book to you?
>
> WILLIAMS: Yes.
>
> JUSTICE: What would she have you do with it?
>
> WILLIAMS: To write in it and I shall be well.
>
> PUTNAM TO MRS. PROCTOR: Did you not tell me that your maid had written?

> MRS. PROCTOR: Dear child, it is not so. There is another judgment, dear child. (Then Abigail and Ann had fits. By and by they cried out, "look you, there is Goody Proctor upon the beam." By and by both of them cried out of Goodman Proctor himself, and said he was a wizard. Immediately, many, if not all of the bewitched, had grievous fits.)
>
> JUSTICE: Ann Putnam, who hurt you?
>
> PUTNAM: Goodman Proctor and his wife too. (Some of the afflicted cried, "there is Proctor going to take up Mrs. Pope's feet"—and her feet were immediately taken up.)
>
> JUSTICE: What do you say Goodman Proctor to these things?
>
> PROCTOR: I know not. I am innocent.
>
> WILLIAMS: There is Goodman Proctor going to Mrs. Pope (and immediately said Pope fell into a fit).
>
> JUSTICE: You see, the Devil will deceive you. The children could see what you was going to do before the woman was hurt. I would advise you to repentance, for the devil is bringing you out.[75]

This was the kind of evidence the magistrates were collecting in readiness for the trials; and it was none too soon, for the prisons were crowded with suspects. In June the newly arrived Governor of the Bay, Sir William Phips, appointed a special court of Oyer and Terminer to hear the growing number of witchcraft cases pending, and the new bench went immediately to work. Before the month was over, six women had been hanged from the gallows in Salem. And still the accused poured in.

As the court settled down to business, however, a note of uncertainty began to flicker across the minds of several thoughtful persons in the colony. To begin with, the net of accusation was beginning to spread out in wider arcs, reaching not only across the surface of the country but up the social ladder as well, so that a number of influential people were now among those in the overflowing prisons. Nathaniel Cary was an important citizen of Charlestown, and other men of equal rank (including the almost legendary Captain John Alden) were being caught up in the widening circle of panic and fear. Slowly but surely, a faint glimmer of skepticism was introduced into the situation; and while it was not to assert a modifying influence on the behavior of the court for some time to come, this new voice had became a part of the turbulent New England climate of 1692.

Meantime, the girls continued to exercise their extraordinary powers. Between sessions of the court, they were invited to visit the town of Andover and help the local inhabitants flush out whatever witches might still remain at large among them. Handicapped as they were by not knowing anyone in town, the girls nonetheless managed to identify more than fifty witches in the space of a few hours. Forty warrants were signed on the spot, and the arrest total only stopped at that number because the local Justice of the Peace simply laid down his pen and refused to go on with the frightening charade any longer—at which point, predictably, he became a suspect himself.

Yet the judges worked hard to keep pace with their young representatives in the field. In early August five persons went to the gallows in Salem. A month later fifteen more were tried and condemned, of which eight were hung promptly and the others spared because they were presumably ready to confess their sins and turn state's evidence. Nineteen people had been executed, seven more condemned, and one pressed to death under a pile of rocks for standing mute at his trial. At least two more persons had died in prison, bringing the number of deaths to twenty-two. And in all that time, not one suspect brought before the court had been acquitted.

At the end of this strenuous period of justice, the whole witchcraft mania began to fade. For one thing, the people of the Bay had been shocked into a mood of sober reflection by the deaths of so many persons. For another, the afflicted girls had obviously not learned very much from their experience in Andover and were beginning to display an ambition which far exceeded their credit. It was bad enough that they should accuse the likes of John Alden and Nathaniel Cary, but when they brought up the name of Samuel Willard, who doubled as pastor of Boston's First Church and President of Harvard College, the magistrates flatly told them they were mistaken. Not long afterwards, a brazen finger was pointed directly at the executive mansion in Boston, where Lady Phips awaited her husband's return from an expedition to Canada, and one tradition even has it that Cotton Mather's mother was eventually accused.[76]

This was enough to stretch even a Puritan's boundless credulity. One by one the leading men of the Bay began to reconsider the whole question and ask aloud whether the evidence accepted in witchcraft hearings was really suited to the emergency at hand. It was obvious that people were being condemned on the testimony of a few excited girls, and responsible minds in the community were troubled by the thought that the girls' excitement may have been poorly diagnosed in the first place. Suppose the girls were directly possessed by the devil and not touched by intermediate witches? Suppose they were simply out of their wits altogether? Suppose, in fact, they were lying? In any of these events the rules of evidence used in court would have to be reviewed—and quickly.

Deciding what kinds of evidence were admissible in witchcraft cases was a thorny business at best. When the court of Oyer and Terminer had first met, a few ground rules had been established to govern the unusual situation which did not entirely conform to ordinary Puritan standards of trial procedure. In the first place, the scriptural rule that two eye-witnesses were necessary for conviction in capital cases was modified to read that any two witnesses were sufficient even if they were testifying about different events—on the interesting ground that witchcraft was a "habitual" crime. That is, if one witness testified that he had seen Susanna Martin bewitch a horse in 1660 and another testified that she had broken uninvited into his dreams twenty years later, then both were witnesses to the same general offense. More important, however, the court accepted as an operating principle the old idea that Satan could not assume the shape of an innocent person, which meant in effect that any spectres floating into view which resembled one of the defendants must be acting under his direct instruction. If an afflicted young girl "saw" John Proctor's image crouched on the window sill with a wicked expression on his face, for example, there could be no question that Proctor himself had placed it there, for the devil could not borrow that disguise without the permission of its owner. During an early hearing, one of the defendants had been asked: "How comes your appearance to hurt these [girls]?" "How do I know," she had answered testily, "He that appeared in the shape of Samuel, a glorified saint, may appear in anyone's shape."[77] Now this was no idle retort, for every man who read his Bible knew that the Witch of Endor had once caused the image of Samuel to appear before Saul, and this scriptural evidence that the devil might indeed be able to impersonate an innocent person proved a difficult matter for the court to handle. Had the defendant been able to win her point, the whole machinery of the court might have fallen in pieces at the magistrates' feet; for if the dreadful spectres haunting the girls were no more than free-lance apparitions sent out by the devil, then the court would have no prosecution case at all.

All in all, five separate kinds of evidence had been admitted by the court during its first round of hearings. First were trials by test, of which repeating the Lord's Prayer, a feat presumed impossible for witches to perform, and curing fits by touch were the most often used. Second was the testimony of persons who attributed their own misfortunes to the sorcery of a neighbor on trial. Third were physical marks like warts, moles, scars, or any other imperfection through which the devil might have sucked his gruesome quota of blood. Fourth was spectral evidence, of the sort just noted; and fifth were the confessions of the accused themselves.

Now it was completely obvious to the men who began to review the court's proceedings that the first three types of evidence were quite inconclusive. After all, anyone might make a mistake reciting the Lord's Prayer, particularly if the floor was covered with screaming, convulsive girls, and it did not make much sense to execute a person because he had spiteful neighbors or a mark upon his body. By those standards, half the people in Massachusetts might qualify for the gallows. This left spectral evidence and confessions. As for the latter, the court could hardly maintain that any real attention had been given to that form of evidence, since none of the executed witches had confessed and none of the many confessors had been executed. Far from establishing guilt, a well-phrased and tearfully delivered confession was clearly the best guarantee against hanging. So the case lay with spectral evidence, and legal opinion in the Bay was slowly leaning toward the theory that this form of evidence, too, was worthless.

In October, Governor Phips took note of the growing doubts by dismissing the special court of Oyer and Terminer and releasing several suspects from prison. The tide had begun to turn, but still there were 150 persons in custody and some 200 others who had been accused.

In December, finally, Phips appointed a new session of the Superior Court of Judicature to try the remaining suspects, and this time the magistrates were agreed that spectral evidence would be admitted only in marginal cases. Fifty-two persons were brought to trial during the next month, and of these, forty-nine were immediately acquitted. Three others were condemned ("two of which," a contemporary observer noted, "were the most senseless and ignorant creatures that could be found"),[78] and in addition death warrants were signed for five persons who had been condemned earlier. Governor Phips responded to these carefully reasoned judgments by signing reprieves for all eight of the defendants anyway, and at this, the court began to empty the jails as fast as it could hear cases. Finally Phips ended the costly procedure by discharging every prisoner in the colony and issuing a general pardon to all persons still under suspicion.

The witchcraft hysteria had been completely checked within a year of the day it first appeared in Salem Village.

II

Historically, there is nothing unique in the fact that Massachusetts Bay should have put people on trial for witchcraft. As the historian Kittredge has pointed out, the whole story should be seen "not as an abnormal outbreak of fanaticism, not as an isolated tragedy, but as a mere incident, a brief and transitory episode in the biography of a terrible, but perfectly natural, superstition."[79]

The idea of witchcraft, of course, is as old as history; but the concept of a malevolent witch who makes a compact with Satan and rejects God did not appear in Europe until the middle of the fourteenth century and does not seem to have made a serious impression on England until well into the sixteenth. The most comprehensive study of English witchcraft, for example, opens with the year 1558, the first year of Elizabeth's reign, and gives only passing attention to events occurring before that date.[80]

In many ways, witchcraft was brought into England on the same current of change that introduced the Protestant Reformation, and it continued to draw nourishment from the intermittent religious quarrels which broke out during the next century and a half. Perhaps no other form of crime in history has been a better index to social disruption and change, for outbreaks of witchcraft mania have generally taken place in societies which are experiencing a shift of religious focus— societies, we would say, confronting a relocation of boundaries. Throughout the Elizabethan and early Stuart periods, at any rate, while England was trying to establish a national church and to anchor it in the middle of the violent tides which were sweeping over the rest of Europe, increasing attention was devoted to the subject. Elizabeth herself introduced legislation to clarify the laws dealing with witchcraft, and James I, before becoming King of England, wrote a textbook on demonology which became a standard reference for years to come.

But it was during the Civil Wars in England that the witchcraft hysteria struck with full force. Many hundreds, probably thousands of witches were burned or hung between the time the Civil Wars began and Oliver Cromwell emerged as the strong man of the Commonwealth, and no sooner had the mania subsided in England than it broke out all over again in Scotland during the first days of the Restoration. Every important crisis during those years seemed to be punctuated by a rash of witchcraft cases. England did not record its last execution for witchcraft until 1712, but the urgent witch hunts of the Civil War period were never repeated.

With this background in mind, we should not be surprised that New England, too, should experience a moment of panic; but it is rather curious that this moment should have arrived so late in the century.

During the troubled years in England when countless witches were burned at the stake or hung from the gallows, Massachusetts Bay showed but mild concern over the whole matter. In 1647 a witch was executed in Connecticut, and one year later another woman met the same fate in Massachusetts.[81] In 1651 the General Court took note of the witchcraft crisis in England and published an almost laconic order that "a day of humiliation" be observed throughout the Bay,[82] but beyond this, the waves of excitement which were sweeping over the mother country seemed not to reach across the Atlantic at all. There was no shortage of accusations, to be sure, no shortage of the kind of gossip which in other days would send good men and women to their lonely grave, but the magistrates of the colony did not act as if a state of emergency was at hand and thus did not declare a crime wave to be in motion. In 1672, for example, a curious man named John Broadstreet was presented to the Essex County Court for "having familiarity with the devil," yet when he admitted the charge the court was so little impressed that he was fined for telling a lie.[83] And in 1674, when Christopher Brown came before the same court to testify that he had been dealing with Satan, the magistrates flatly dismissed him on the grounds that his confession seemed "inconsistent with truth."[84]

So New England remained relatively calm during the worst of the troubles in England, yet suddenly erupted into a terrible violence long after England lay exhausted from its earlier exertions.

In many important respects, 1692 marked the end of the Puritan experiment in Massachusetts, not only because the original charter had been revoked or because a Royal Governor had been chosen by the King or even because the old political order had collapsed in a tired heap. The Puritan experiment ended in 1692, rather, because the sense of mission which had sustained it from the beginning no longer existed in any recognizable form, and thus the people of the Bay were left with few stable points of reference to help them remember who they were. When they looked back on their own history, the settlers had to conclude that the trajectory of the past pointed in quite a different direction than the one they now found themselves taking: they were no longer participants in a great adventure, no longer residents of a "city upon a hill," no longer members of that special revolutionary elite who were destined to bend the course of history according to God's own word. They were only themselves, living alone in a remote corner of the world, and this seemed a modest end for a crusade which had begun with such high expectations.

In the first place, as we have seen, the people of the colony had always pictured themselves as actors in an international movement, yet by the end of the century they had lost many of their most meaningful contacts with the rest of the world. The Puritan movement in England had scattered into a number of separate sects, each of which had been gradually absorbed into the freer climate of a new regime, and elsewhere in Europe the Protestant Reformation had lost much of its momentum without achieving half the goals set for it. And as a result, the colonists had lost touch with the background against which they had learned to assess their own stature and to survey their own place in the world.

In the second place, the original settlers had measured their achievements on a yardstick which no longer seemed to have the same sharp relevance. New England had been built by people who believed that God personally supervised every flicker of life on earth according to a plan beyond human comprehension, and in undertaking the expedition to America they were placing themselves entirely in God's hands. These were men whose doctrine prepared them to accept defeat gracefully, whose sense of piety depended upon an occasional moment of failure, hardship, even tragedy. Yet by the end of the century, the Puritan planters could look around them and count an impressive number of accomplishments. Here was no record of erratic providence; here was a record of solid human enterprise, and with this realization, as Daniel Boorstin suggests, the settlers moved from a "sense of mystery" to a "consciousness of mastery,"[85] from a helpless reliance on fate to a firm confidence in their own abilities. This shift helped clear the way for the appearance of the shrewd, practical, self-reliant Yankee as a figure in American history, but in the meantime it left the third generation of settlers with no clear definition of the status they held as the chosen children of God.

In the third place, Massachusetts had been founded as a lonely pocket of civilization in the midst of a howling wilderness, and as we have seen, this idea remained one of the most important themes of Puritan imagery long after the underbrush had been cut away and the wild animals killed. The settlers had lost sight of their local frontiers, not only in the sense that colonization had spread beyond the Berkshires into what is now upper state New York, but also in the sense that the wilderness which had held the community together by pressing in on it from all sides was disappearing. The original settlers had landed in a wilderness full of "wild beasts and wilder men"; yet sixty years later, sitting many miles from the nearest frontier in the prosperous seaboard town of Boston, Cotton Mather and other survivors of the old order still imagined that they were living in a wilderness—a territory they had explored as thoroughly as any frontiersmen. But the character of this wilderness was unlike anything the first settlers had ever seen, for its dense forests had become a jungle of mythical beasts and its skies were thick with flying spirits. In a sense, the Puritan community had helped mark its location in space by keeping close watch on the wilderness surrounding it on all sides; and now that the visible traces of that wilderness had receded out of sight, the settlers invented a new one by finding the shapes of the forest in the middle of the community itself.[86]

And as the wilderness took on this new character, it seemed that even the Devil had given up his more familiar disguises. He no longer lurked in the underbrush, for most of it had been cut away; he no longer assumed the shape of hostile Indians, for most of them had retreated inland for the moment; he no longer sent waves of heretics to trouble the Bay, for most of them lived quietly under the protection of toleration; he no longer appeared in the armies of the Counter-Reformation, for the old battlefields were still and too far away to excite the imagination. But his presence was felt everywhere, and when the colonists began to look for his new hiding places they found him crouched in the very heart of the Puritan colony. Quite literally, the people of the Bay began to see ghosts, and soon the boundaries of the New England Way closed in on a space full of demons and incubi, spectres and evil spirits, as the settlers tried to find a new sense of their own identity among the landmarks of a strange, invisible world. Cotton Mather, who knew every disguise in the Devil's wardrobe, offered a frightening catalogue of the Devil's attempts to destroy New England.

> I believe, there never was a poor Plantation, more pursued by the wrath of the Devil, than our poor New-England. . . . It was a rousing alarm to the Devil, when a great Company of English Protestants and Puritans, came to erect Evangelical Churches, in a corner of the world, where he had reign'd without control for many ages; and it is a vexing Eye-sore to the Devil, that our Lord Christ should be known, and own'd and preached in this howling wilderness. Wherefore he has left no Stone unturned, that so he might undermine his Plantation, and force us out of our Country.
>
> First, the Indian Powawes, used all their Sorceries to molest the first Planters here; but God said unto them, Touch them not! Then, Seducing spirits came to root in this Vineyard, but God so rated them off, that they have not prevail'd much farther than the edges of our Land. After this, we have had a continual blast upon some of our principal Grain, annually diminishing a vast part of our ordinary Food. Herewithal, wasting Sicknesses, especially Burning and Mortal Agues, have Shot the Arrows of Death in at our Windows. Next, we have had many Adversaries of our own Language, who have been perpetually assaying to deprive us of those English Liberties, in the encouragement whereof these Territories have been settled. As if this had not been enough; the Tawnies among whom we came have watered our Soil with the Blood of many Hundreds of Inhabitants. . . . Besides all which, now at last the Devils are (if I may so speak) in Person come down upon us with such a Wrath, as is justly much, and will quickly be more, the Astonishment of the World.[87]

And this last adventure of the Devil has a quality all its own.

> Wherefore the Devil is now making one Attempt more upon us; an Attempt more Difficult, more Surprising, more snarl'd with unintelligible Circumstances than any that we have hitherto Encountered. . . . An Army of Devils is horribly

broke in upon the place which is the center, and after a sort, the First-born of our English Settlements: and the Houses of the Good People there are fill'd with the doleful shrieks of their Children and Servants, Tormented by Invisible Hands, with Tortures altogether preternatural.[88]

The witchcraft hysteria occupied but a brief moment in the history of the Bay. The first actors to take part in it were a group of excited girls and a few of the less savory figures who drifted around the edges of the community, but the speed with which the other people of the Bay gathered to witness the encounter and accept an active role in it, not to mention the quality of the other persons who were eventually drawn into this vortex of activity, serves as an index to the gravity of the issues involved. For a few years, at least, the settlers of Massachusetts were alone in the world, bewildered by the loss of their old destiny but not yet aware of their new one, and during this fateful interval they tried to discover some image of themselves by listening to a chorus of voices which whispered to them from the depths of an invisible wilderness.

Notes

. . . [66] Marion L. Starkey, *The Devil in Massachusetts* (New York: Knopf, 1949).

[67] John Josselyn, "An Account of Two Voyages to New-England," *Collections of the Massachusetts Historical Society,* Vol. III, Third Series, p. 331.

[68] Alan Heimert, "Puritanism, The Wilderness and The Frontier," *New England Quarterly,* XXVI (1953), p. 381.

[69] Hutchinson, *History,* I, p. 232. The page number here was taken from a later edition of Hutchinson's work than the one cited in other footnotes in the present study. See the Lawrence S. Mayo edition (Cambridge, Mass.: Harvard University Press, 1936).

[70] Cotton Mather, "Wonders of the Invisible World," Boston and London, 1693, found in Samuel G. Drake, editor, *The Witchcraft Delusion in New England* (Roxbury, Mass.: W. Elliot Woodward, 1866), pp. 80-81.

[71] Deodat Lawson, "A Brief and True Narrative of Witchcraft at Salem Village," 1692, in *Narratives of the Witchcraft Cases, 1648-1706,* edited by George Lincoln Burr (New York: Scribner's, 1914), p. 154.

[72] John Alden later reported in his account of the affair that the girls pointed their fingers at the wrong man when they first accused him of witchcraft and only realized their mistake when an obliging passer-by corrected them. See Robert Calef, "More Wonders of the Invisible World," Boston, 1701, in Burr, *Narratives,* p. 353.

[73] Reproduced in Calef, "More Wonders," in Burr, *Narratives,* pp. 350-352.

[74] The "book" refers to the Devil's registry. The girls were presumably being tormented because they refused to sign the book and ally themselves with Satan.

[75] Hutchinson, *History,* II, pp. 27-28.

[76] Burr, *Narratives,* p. 377.

[77] Cotton Mather, "Wonders of the Invisible World," in Drake, *The Witchcraft Delusion,* p. 176.

[78] Calef, "More Wonders," in Burr, *Narratives,* p. 382.

[79] George L. Kittredge, *Witchcraft in Old and New England* (New York: Russell E. Russell, 1956), p. 329.

[80] Wallace Notestein, *History of Witchcraft in England* (Washington, D.C.: The American Historical Society, 1911).

[81] Winthrop, *Journal,* II, pp. 323, 344-345. Altogether, five or possibly six persons were executed for witchcraft in New England prior to the outbreak of 1692.

[82] Massachusetts Records, IVa, pp. 52-53.

[83] Essex County Records, I, p. 265.

[84] Essex County Records, V, pp. 426-427.

[85] Daniel Boorstin, *The Genius of American Politics* (Chicago: University of Chicago Press, 1953).

[86] See, again, the very interesting paper "Puritanism, The Wilderness and the Frontier" by Heimert.

[87] Cotton Mather, "Wonders of the Invisible World," in Drake, *The Witchcraft Delusion,* pp. 94-95.

[88] *Ibid.,* pp. 16-17.

Paul Boyer and Stephen Nissenbaum (essay date 1974)

SOURCE: "Prologue: What Happened in 1692," in *Salem Possessed: The Social Origins of Witchcraft,* Cambridge, Mass.: Harvard University Press, 1974, pp. 1-21.

[*In the following excerpt, Boyer and Nissenbaum comment on the initial witch arrests in Salem, the delay before the trials, the desire for verifiable evidence, and the influence ministers had on the trials.*]

It began in obscurity, with cautious experiments in fortune telling. Books on the subject had "stolen" into the land; and all over New England, late in 1691, young people were being "led away with little sorceries." Fearful of the future, they began to cast spells and to practice "conjuration with sieves and keys, and peas, and nails, and horseshoes."[1]

In Essex Country, Massachusetts, and particularly in the little community of Salem Village, it was mainly young girls who met in small informal gatherings to discuss the future. Their concern came to focus on that point where curiosity about future love merged with curiosity about future status: the nature of their own marriage, "what trade their sweethearts should be of." One of the girls devised a primitive crystal ball—the white of an egg suspended in a glass—and received a chilling answer: in the glass there floated "a specter in the likeness of a coffin."[2] What had begun as fearful curiosity was turning to sharp panic. The magic they had tried to harness was beginning, instead, to ride them: visibly, dramatically, ominously.

Nobody knew then, or knows now, precisely what it was the girls were experiencing. They never told; perhaps they did not know themselves. By February 1692 it was the grownups who began to try to put into words what was happening to their children: "odd postures," "foolish, ridiculous speeches," "distempers," "fits."[3]

Witchcraft

At first, the Villagers tried through informal and quiet means to bring this strange behavior under control. It was the local minister, the Reverend Samuel Parris, father of one of the first two girls to be afflicted and uncle of the other, who took the initiative. (He considered it "a very sore rebuke, and humbling providence," Parris would admit a few years afterward, " . . . that the Lord ordered the late horrid calamity . . . to break out first in my family.") Parris first called in a local physician, one William Griggs. But Griggs was at a loss to understand the behavior of nine-year-old Betty Parris or her eleven-year-old cousin, Abigail Williams, and warned Parris that he suspected the "Evil Hand" or, in more technical parlance, malefic witchcraft.[4]

If this were indeed the case, the problem was not medical at all, but legal. Those who suffered from witchcraft, after all, were the victims of a crime, not a disease. Still Parris did not turn to the civil authorities. Instead, he took counsel with several nearby ministers who, sharing Griggs's fears, advised him to "sit still and wait upon the Providence of God, to see what time might discover."[5]

But rumors had already coursed through Salem Village, and not everybody was content with such a passive response. At the suggestion of one young Village matron named Mary Sibley, a witch cake—rye meal mixed with the urine of the afflicted girls—was baked by Tituba and John Indian, a West Indian slave couple in Parris's household. The cake was then fed to a dog, evidently in the belief that if the girls *were* bewitched, the animal would experience torments similar to their own. A few weeks later, Parris denounced Mary Sibley from the pulpit for suggesting such a "diabolical" stratagem.[6]

By this time, more than a month had elapsed since the girls' strange behavior began, and still no legal action had been taken. By this time, too, the afflictions were beginning to spread ("plague-like," as Parris later put it) beyond the minister's house; soon they would come to affect about seven or eight other girls as well, ranging in age from twelve to nineteen, and including three from the household of Thomas Putnam, Jr. For a time, even several young married women became afflicted. At last the troubled Village resorted to the law. On February 29, 1692, warrants went out for the arrest of three Village women whom the girls, under the pressure of intense adult questioning, had finally named as their tormenters: Sarah Good, Sarah Osborne, and Tituba herself.

The next day, Jonathan Corwin and John Hathorne, the nearest members of the upper house of the provincial legislature, made the five-mile trip out from Salem Town to conduct a public examination of the three women in the Village meetinghouse. Osborne and Good denied that they were witches, but Tituba confessed, volubly and in great detail, even volunteering a description of the devil as "a thing all over hairy, all the face hairy, and a long nose." After their examination, all three women were committed to Boston jail—where, on May 10, Sarah Osborne would die of natural causes.[7]

At this point, anyone familiar with the pattern of earlier witchcraft outbreaks in New England—one or two accusations, arrests, and perhaps convictions—would surely have predicted that the matter was now at an end. But, for once, the pattern did not hold. Even with the three women in prison, the bizarre behavior of the girls continued. Once again, the Village strove to deal with the crisis in its own way. Parris held several "private fasts" in his own household, and on March 11 he invited the neighboring ministers for a day of prayer. But in the very presence of these men of God, the children began to behave "strangely and ridiculously"; one even suffered a "convulsion fit, her limbs being twisted several ways, and very stiff."[8]

Several days later, the Reverend Deodat Lawson, a former minister in the Village, came out from Boston to observe things for himself and to give what help he could to his erstwhile parishioners. Stopping at the inn of Nathaniel Ingersoll in the Village center, Lawson by

candlelight examined a mysterious set of teeth marks on the arm of one of the troubled girls, seventeen-year-old Mary Walcott. Later that evening, as Lawson was visiting with Samuel Parris, Abigail Williams raced through the house, arms outstretched, crying "Whish! Whish! Whish!" Next she began to pull burning logs from the fireplace and toss them about the room.[9]

In the face of such a display, Parris had no difficulty in recruiting Lawson to help bring these manifestations to an end. On Sunday, March 20, the visiting clergyman delivered an earnest anti-witchcraft sermon in the Village meetinghouse. But even as he prepared to speak, Abigail Williams shouted out, "Now stand up and name your text." When Lawson did so, she added mockingly, "It is a long text." Another Village girl, twelve-year-old Ann Putnam, chimed in too, despite the efforts of those nearby to hush her, crying out that she could see a yellow bird perched on Lawson's hat as it hung from a hook by the pulpit. That Wednesday, when Deodat Lawson paid a call on the Putnams, it was to find young Ann's *mother* prostrate on the bed, "having had a sore fit a little before."[10] Adults as well as children were falling victim to the spell.

Mrs. Putnam rallied somewhat after Lawson read a passage of scripture, but despite such temporary respites it was increasingly clear that prayers and sermons were not the answer. The community was by now intensely agitated, and once again recourse to the law seemed unavoidable. On the Monday following Lawson's sermon, the fourth person to be arrested, Martha Cory of Salem Village, was examined by Hathorne and Corwin before a throng of several hundred in the Village meetinghouse. As she was led into the room, the afflicted girls, sitting together at the front, cried out in "extreme agony"; when she wrung her hands, they screamed that they were being pinched; when she bit her lips, they declared that they could feel teeth biting their own flesh. In the general hubbub, a Village woman named Bethshaa Pope flung first her muff and then her shoe at Martha, striking her on the head.[11]

Martha Cory joined the three other women in jail, but still the outbreak showed no signs of abating, and now the arrests began to accelerate. On March 23 Dorcas Good, the four-year-old daughter of accused witch Sarah Good, was sent to Boston prison, where for nine months she remained in heavy irons. (Eighteen years later her father would declare: "She hath ever since been very chargeable, having little or no reason to govern herself.") The day after Dorcas was jailed, at the packed examination of still another Village woman, Rebecca Nurse, the torments of the afflicted produced near pandemonium: Deodat Lawson, walking some distance from the meetinghouse, was amazed by the "hideous screech and noise" that poured from the open window.[12] When it was all over, Goody Nurse, too, was committed to jail in Salem Town.

By this time it had become impossible any longer to treat the outbreak as a local Salem Village matter. The next examinations, on April 11, were held not in the Village but in Salem Town, and not before Hathorne and Corwin only, but before the deputy governor, six magistrates, and a "very great assembly" which included several ministers. Ten days later, Thomas Putnam, Jr., whose daughter and wife were both among the afflicted, dispatched a letter to the magistrates in Salem Town hinting at "high and dreadful" news—a "wheel within a wheel, at which our ears do tingle." The news was dreadful indeed: Abigail Williams had charged that George Burroughs, a former minister in the Village who had moved away to a frontier parish in Maine, was himself a wizard—indeed, that he was the mastermind behind the entire outbreak. In a matter of days, an officer was on his way to Maine with a warrant for Burroughs's arrest. A few days after that, the Massachusetts legislature, the General Court, ordered that a public fast be observed through the length and breadth of the colony.[13]

It was now early spring. The prisons were overflowing; exhausting demands were being placed upon magistrates, jailers, sheriffs, and constables; and the entire apparatus by which the accused had been arrested, examined, and imprisoned was showing distinct signs of strain. The basic problem was that while more and more suspected witches and wizards were being arrested, not one trial had yet been held. Indeed, there *could* be none, for during these months Massachusetts was in the touchy position of being without a legally established government! Eight years earlier, in 1684, its original form of government had been abrogated by the English authorities, and in 1689 the administration with which the King had replaced it was overthrown in a bloodless *coup d'état*. Between 1689 and 1691 the colonists had lobbied vainly at court for a restoration of their original pre-1684 charter.

Finally, early in 1692 the colony learned that a new governor, Sir William Phips, would arrive shortly, bearing with him a new charter. But until Phips—and the new charter establishing the future form of government—were physically present in Massachusetts it would be illegal (and quite possibly fruitless) to proceed with formal prosecution of the accused witches.[14] Ironically, then, the most severe challenge to confront the judicial system of Massachusetts during the entire colonial period came at a moment when that system was nearly immobilized. For the crucial first three months of the Salem witchcraft outbreak, the authorities had no official recourse except to throw suspects into jail without a trial.

Such was the crisis that confronted Sir William when he sailed into Boston harbor from England on May 14, 1692, new charter in hand. Phips's response was swift and bold, if of somewhat dubious legality. Within a few days of his arrival he constituted six members of his advisory council as a special Court of Oyer and Terminer to "hear and determine" the enormous backlog of witchcraft cases. As chief justice of this court, Phips named his lieutenant governor, William Stoughton.[15]

On Friday, June 2, after what must have been a rather hectic two weeks of preparation, the Court of Oyer and Terminer held its first session in Salem Town. The first trial produced the first sentence of death. On June 10, Bridget Bishop, a Salem Village woman who had been in prison since April 18, was hanged.[16] The place of execution—it would come to be called "Witches' Hill"—was a barren and rocky elevation on the western side of the town.

The court sat a second time on June 29. By now it had firmed up its procedures and was able to try the cases of five accused women in a single day. All five were sentenced to die. The jury at first acquitted one of them, Rebecca Nurse, but Chief Justice Stoughton sent it back for further deliberation, and this time it returned with a verdict of guilty. On July 19 the five condemned witches went to their deaths. (When the assistant minister of the Salem Town church urged one of them, Sarah Good, to confess, she shot back from the scaffold: "I am no more a witch than you are a wizard, and if you take away my life, God will give you blood to drink.")[17]

Six more trials on August 5 produced six more convictions. Only five of these resulted in executions, however; Elizabeth Proctor was reprieved by reason of pregnancy, the authorities being unwilling to snuff out an innocent life along with a guilty one. At the execution of the five, two weeks later to the day, the Reverend George Burroughs solemnly protested his innocence and concluded with a recitation of the Lord's Prayer. Afterwards, the bodies (four female, two male) were thrown into a nearby crevice and partially covered with dirt.[18]

And the trials went on. In early September Stoughton's court passed sentence of death upon another half dozen persons. This time, however, two of the condemned managed to cheat the hang-man: one was reprieved and the other, the wife of a Salisbury ship captain, was helped to escape from prison. Not so fortunate was Rebecca Nurse's sister Mary Easty, despite the moving appeal to the court she composed after her trial. "I petition your honors not for my own life," she wrote, "for I know I must die, and my appointed time is set; but . . . , if it be possible, that no more innocent blood be shed."[19]

On the seventeenth of the month, at what would prove to be the final sitting of the Court of Oyer and Terminer, nine more persons were condemned. Five of them, however, confessing to the charges, were reprieved. Two days later, Giles Cory of Salem Village (the husband of Martha), was pressed to death by heavy weights progressively piled upon his body. An accused wizard, Cory had stood mute before the authorities, his refusal to plead to the charges constituting an implicit denial of the court's right to try him. His torture, known as *peine forte et dure,* was an established English procedure designed to force recalcitrant prisoners to enter a plea so their trials might proceed.[20]

On September 22 the little company of eight who had been convicted at the two September sittings of the court went together to the gallows. As the cart in which they were riding creaked up the hill, one of its wheels lodged in a rut; at once a hovering cluster of "afflicted girls" cried out that the devil was trying to save his servants. And when one of the condemned, Samuel Wardwell of Andover, choked on the smoke from the hangman's pipe while making a final appeal to the crowd, the taunting girls shouted that it was the devil who was hindering him from speaking.[21] With these final small dramas, the hangings came to an end—not for that day alone, but for good.

Stopping the Trials: Ministers and the Question of Evidence

But just as prayers and sermons in Salem Village had failed to check the outbreak at its start, so the stern justice of the Court of Oyer and Terminer failed to check it once it had become a matter of colony-wide concern. Even in late September, after nineteen hangings, and with the jails still bursting with more than 100 suspected witches, the accusations and arrests went on. What finally *did* put a stop to the whole process was the direct and organized intervention of the principal ministers of eastern Massachusetts.

From the outset, to be sure, both within Salem Village and beyond, there had been a strong undercurrent of opposition to the arrests, examinations, and trials. Testimony and petitions had been introduced on behalf of several of the accused, and other evidence had called into question the character or veracity of some of the bewitched girls. Daniel Elliot, for example, testified that late in March one of the girls had boasted to him that "she did it for sport; they must have some sport." And after the hanging of Bridget Bishop in June, one member of the Court of Oyer and Terminer itself, Nathaniel Saltonstall, had resigned.[22]

But it was the ministers, at first hesitantly, and finally with a telling stroke, who levied the decisive pressure. Cotton Mather of Boston's First Church, while publicly supporting the trials, throughout the summer addressed a succession of private communications to friends on the Court of Oyer and Terminer mingling encouragement with cautious reservations. On a somewhat more public level, a group of Boston ministers on June 15 submitted a brief letter of advice to Governor Phips and his council. This letter, also from the pen of Cotton Mather, urged "vigorous prosecution" of proven witches but also recommended "a very critical and exquisite caution" in the use of evidence. With this message, the ministers lapsed into an all but total silence that would persist through July, August, and September, while the trials and the hangings went on.[23]

In early October, finally, they acted. They did so under the leadership of Increase Mather of Boston, father of Cotton Mather and himself one of the most influential men in Massachusetts. (It was Increase who had been the colony's chief lobbyist in London between 1689 and 1692, and who had more or less hand-picked William Phips as the new governor; when Phips sailed for Boston, Increase Mather had been on the ship with him.) In a sermon which he preached to a formal gathering of ministers in Cambridge, Massachusetts, on October 3 and which was soon published as *Cases of Conscience Concerning Evil Spirits Personating Men,* Increase Mather delivered an open and forceful challenge to the Court of Oyer and Terminer. The overriding point of the sermon was conveyed in a single sentence: "It were better that ten suspected witches should escape, than that one innocent person should be condemned."[24]

The specific concern of *Cases of Conscience,* as of the ministers' June letter, was a legal one: what constitutes admissible evidence in witchcraft cases? "It is . . . exceeding necessary," declared the preface, "that in such a day as this, men be informed what is evidence and what is not." The fourteen ministers who signed this preface (thereby endorsing the work) did not deny the Biblical injunction that witches must be "exterminated and cut off," but at the same time (and with considerably more passion) they emphasized that every conviction must be based on water-tight proof of guilt.[25] And Mather reiterated the point in the sermon proper, asserting without qualification that in witchcraft cases "the evidence . . . ought to be as clear as in any other crimes of a capital nature."[26]

In thus focusing his discussion on the issue of evidence, Mather was picking up on a matter that had worried many educated men—the court included—since the first pre-trial examinations half a year before. For although witchcraft was indisputably a crime according to the word of God, the common law of England, and the statutes of Massachusetts, it was, for those concerned with the law, the most maddening and frustrating crime imaginable. This was because the evil deeds on which the indictments rested were not physically perpetrated by the witches at all, but by intangible spirits who could at times assume their shape. The crime lay in the initial compact by which a person permitted the devil to assume his or her human form, or in commissioning the devil to perform particular acts of mischief. And yet these private and secret transactions, conducted, really, in the mind of the witch, were exceptionally difficult to prove.

The voluminous examination records of 1692 constitute a remarkable testament to the magistrates' efforts to seek out proofs that would conform to the established rules of courtroom evidence—that is to say, evidence that was empirically verifiable and logically relevant. While much of the testimony accepted by the magistrates seems today naive or superstitious at best, it becomes more comprehensible if viewed as part of the attempt to fit this ancient crime into a rational intellectual framework.

Of the various kinds of evidence the magistrates sought, the simplest and most desirable was outright confession. Over and over again, the record shows the examiners almost frantically trying to draw a confession from the lips of a person whose guilt they clearly do not doubt but against whom they recognize they do not yet have a legal case.[27]

A confession was particularly weighty when buttressed by corroborating detail, and it was the effort to secure such corroboration which led the magistrates to probe for those vivid minutiae which comprise the popular image of what witchcraft was all about: broomsticks, blasphemous rituals, signatures in blood. When the Reverend John Hale of nearby Beverly visited one of the confessing witches in prison, he took care to quiz her closely on such matters: "I asked her if she rode to the meeting on a stick. She said yea. I enquired what she did for victuals. She answered that she carried bread and cheese in her pocket."[28] In a community where the reality of witchcraft was universally accepted, the persuasive power of such homely little details must have been very great.

Ranking just behind confession in the arsenal of damaging evidence was trustworthy testimony to some supernatural attribute of the accused. No fewer than six persons, for example, testified that George Burroughs, the wizard-minister, had performed such superhuman feats of strength as lifting a heavy gun at arm's length with a single finger thrust into the barrel. Another man revealed that Burroughs could "tell his thoughts."[29]

Along with these supernatural abilities went certain compensating supernatural weaknesses believed to characterize a witch, notably the inability to recite prayers, even of the simplest sort, with perfect accuracy. Thus Sarah Good, when so required, could only "mutter . . . over some part of a psalm" and appeared reluctant to

"mention the word God." Recitation of the Lord's Prayer became a favorite test in 1692. One unfortunate, upon reaching the words "hallowed be thy name," said "hollowed" instead. And thus, when George Burroughs ended his final speech from the scaffold by delivering a perfect rendition of the Lord's Prayer, the assembled spectators grew restive. Only a forceful counter-speech by Cotton Mather, who was in attendance that day, enabled the authorities to proceed with Burroughs's hanging.[30]

A somewhat different form of supernatural attribute was the "witch's tit"—an abnormal physical appendage, ordinarily quite small, through which the witch or wizard was thought to give suck to the devil in the form of a bird, a turtle, or some other small creature. While the "witch's tit" was part of the vulgar lore which the authorities generally tried to suppress in 1692, it did have the advantage, like supernatural strength or the inability to pray, of being empirically verifiable, and thus it, too, figured prominently in the evidence. The accused were subjected to exhaustive and conscientious bodily examinations by physicians or midwives searching for this evidence of guilt. On the morning of June 2, for example, a committee of nine reputable women (probably midwives) administered physical examinations to five accused women and reported that on three of them they had discovered "a preternatural excrescence of flesh between the pudendum and anus, much like to teats, and not usual in women." But to confirm their finding they re-examined the three that afternoon, and this time reported that all of them appeared normal.[31]

These two categories of evidence, direct confession and empirical proof of supernatural attributes, were by far the strongest and most acceptable. Indeed, they are the only two which Increase Mather unqualifiedly endorsed as sufficient to justify conviction and execution.[32]

But although Mather was unwilling to accept it, there was another form of empirical evidence which, at least to magistrates caught up in the press of actual examinations, seemed only slightly less persuasive: anger followed by mischief. Typically, such testimony would recount how the accused witch, at some point in the past, had become angered at a second party—so angered as to express or imply a threat—and how this encounter had been shortly followed by some misfortune befalling the threatened party. Sometimes the damage was to his property—livestock which took sick, most often[33]—but just as frequently it was to his person or to the person of a relative.

One elderly Salem Villager, Bray Wilkins, reported a particularly painful instance of such personally directed mischief. His granddaughter's husband, John Willard, finding himself accused of witchcraft, had come to visit Wilkins to ask for prayer; but the latter, pleading the press of other responsibilities, had denied the request. When the two men next met, Willard had given Wilkins a piercing glance and almost at once, the old man later testified, "my water was suddenly stopped and I had no benefit of nature, but was like a man on a rack."[34] This bladder difficulty persisted until Willard was safely in irons, when Bray Wilkins finally had relief.

At its most serious, such demonic mischief actually took the life of the victim. It was, for example, doubly damning to John Willard when, a few days after his encounters with Bray Wilkins, another kinsman, Daniel Wilkins, died an unexpected and agonizing death at the age of seventeen. Thus the protean crime of witchcraft could involve murder itself, sometimes even mass murder: Mrs. Ann Putnam accused Rebecca Nurse of bewitching to death no fewer than fourteen people![35]

But powerful as such evidence might be, it was flawed, and Increase Mather for one recognized the flaw. For although two steps in the process could be empirically verified—the anger and the mischief—the third (that is, the actual performance of the evil deed by the accused), was extremely hard to prove since it was carried out through a supernatural intermediary. Accordingly, in the examinations, evidence of anger followed by mischief was clearly most weighty when the connection was most direct: the piercing glance or its equivalent followed *immediately* by the evil consequences. It was widely noted that as Bridget Bishop was led into the Salem Town courthouse for her trial, she cast her eye on the place of worship across the square and *at that very moment* a heavy roof timber inside the meetinghouse came crashing to the floor. John and Hannah Putnam testified that at just the time John was accusing Rebecca Nurse of witchcraft, their eight-week-old infant, "as well and as thriving a child as most," fell into "strange and violent fits" and within forty-eight hours was dead. And Samuel and Mary Abbey, after describing what seemed to them a long-standing correlation between their relations with Sarah Good and the health of their livestock, concluded with a clinching piece of evidence: at the very hour of Sarah Good's arrest, a cow which had lain dying that very morning suddenly recovered "and could rise so well as if she had ailed nothing."[36]

In their effort to establish a probable connection between instances of misfortune and the malefic will of particular persons, the authorities introduced the practice of stationing the afflicted girls together in the examination room and observing them closely for signs of pain when an accused witch was brought in. (In an extension of this process, the accused witch would then be required to touch the sufferers, and their response—usually instant recovery—would again be noted and entered as part of the record.)[37]

While these public tests helped create the bedlam which emerges so vividly from surviving accounts of the examinations, and although these tests ultimately did much to discredit the entire proceedings, they were, in fact, rooted in the magistrates' determination to accept only evidence which they could verify or which, as in this instance, they could observe with their own eyes. It was consistent with their larger effort to cope with this most baffling of all crimes without betraying their sense of due process and empirical method.

But once again, Increase Mather emphatically rejected such tests. In the first place, they involved a dangerous toying with Satan's power; but also, and equally important, they too easily lent themselves to fakery and deception. *Cases of Conscience* called attention to an obvious fact that had become blurred in the quest for empirical proof: central to the validity of any evidence was the trustworthiness of its source and the circumstances under which it was secured. Thus Mather repeatedly emphasized the importance of relying only upon "credible" witnesses who were willing to testify under oath, and he pointedly related the story of a 1664 English witchcraft case in which a supposedly bewitched child had practiced blatant deception.[38]

There remained one final category of evidence, and it was the one which caused by far the greatest difficulty to the authorities in 1692. This was spectral evidence: testimony about supernatural visitations from some demonic creature—perhaps Satan himself?—who appeared in the specter (that is, shape) of an accused witch. At times these specters attempted actual bodily harm, as they did when "afflicting" the bewitched girls, and as one did against John Cook: "One morning about sun rising, as I was in bed before I rose, I saw Goodwife Bishop [that is, her specter] . . . stand in the chamber by the window. And she looked on me and grinned on me, and presently struck me on the side of the head, which did very much hurt me. And then I saw her go out under the end window at a little crevice about so big as I could thrust my hand into."[39]

In a variant form of spectral testimony, the witness would describe how the images of recently deceased persons had appeared and identified the individual who had caused their death. In early May 1692, for example, young Ann Putnam testified that a pair of female figures had appeared to her: "The two women turned their faces towards me, and looked as pale as a white wall, and told me that they were Mr. Burroughs's first two wives, and he had murdered them. And one told me that she was his first wife, and he [had] stabbed her under the left arm and put a piece of sealing wax on the wound. And she pulled aside the winding sheet and showed me the place."[40] In its dense specificity—the precise time of day, the grin, the left arm, the sealing wax, the shroud—such testimony possessed a superficial resemblance to firm empirical evidence. Yet this kind of evidence was, for two reasons, especially tenuous and uncertain. First, how could anyone be certain that Satan would not appear in the shape of an innocent or even a godly person? (After all, what would more satisfy his demonic purposes than to besmear the reputations of his enemies, God's pious servants?)

Second, even if it could be agreed that Satan lacked the power to deceive in this way, spectral evidence remained almost impossible to verify. For the specters were usually visible only to the person or persons for whom the visitation—vision, really—was intended. Others might be present, but they could see nothing. For example, Benjamin Hutchinson was with young Abigail Williams at eleven o'clock on the morning of April 21, 1692, when Abigail spotted the figure of a short, dark man. It turned out to be George Burroughs, who was in Maine at the time. When Hutchinson asked her "whereabout this little man stood," she replied: "Just where the cart wheel went along." Hutchinson went on to report:

> I had a three-tined iron fork in my hand and I threw it where she said he stood. And she presently fell in a little fit, and when it was over she said, "You have torn his coat, for I heard it tear." "Whereabouts," said I. "On one side," said she. Then we came into the house of Lieut. Ingersoll, and I went into the great room and Abigail came in and said, "There he stands." I said, "Where? Where?" and presently drew my rapier. But he immediately was gone, as she said. Then said she, "There is a gray cat." Then I said, "Whereabouts doth she stand?" "There!" she said, "There!" Then I struck with my rapier. Then she fell in a fit, and when it was over she said, "You killed her."[41]

No issue was more troublesome in 1692 than that of spectral evidence. In actual practice, spectral testimony was included as part of the dossier assembled before the trials, but it was clearly considered somewhat suspect, and the magistrates always took pains to buttress it where they could with other, more empirical, forms of evidence.

To Increase Mather, however, even this compromise was unpalatable. In *Cases of Conscience,* Mather condemned without qualification the use of spectral evidence. Like the tests by which the sufferings of the afflicted were turned on or off with a glance or a touch, it was a dangerous dependence on the devil himself for evidence. To those who contended that spectral evidence could be trusted because a just God would surely not allow innocent persons to suffer because of it, *Cases of Conscience* pointed out that such assumptions implied a restraint upon God's absolute power and were thus "bold usurpations upon [His] spotless sovereignty."[42] The God of John Calvin would not be held accountable to the requirements of merely human justice.

And so, with the inexorable logical thoroughness of the Puritan sermon form, Increase Mather examined each of the kinds of evidence being used in the witchcraft cases—and found most of them wanting.

This is not to portray Mather as a lone and heroic figure battling for a return to reason in a society gone mad with witch hysteria. He was speaking soberly and calmly to men who shared his fundamental concerns, pointing out to them where they had gone off the track. It was this core of shared assumptions about the legal process and the nature of evidence which gave such great force to *Cases of Conscience.* Nobody disputed its conclusions, for it was simply the summing up and clarification of an intellectual process that was already well underway when it appeared. Throughout 1692, under implacable and unrelieved pressure to act, successive levels of authority in Massachusetts had been trying to formulate procedures and standards of evidence for dealing with an unprecedented social and legal crisis. Their effort has sometimes been portrayed as little more than thinly disguised hysteria and superstition bent on extinguishing as many lives as possible.

By twentieth-century standards, of course, the entire episode was simply a matter of "superstition." Undeniably, too, there were instances of gross injustice—injustice by the standards of that day as well as those of our own. But when all this has been conceded, what emerges most strongly from the record is the sense of a society, confronted with a tenacious outbreak of a particularly baffling crime at a time of severe political and legal disruption, nevertheless striving, in an equitable way, to administer justice and to restore order. The sober conclusion of the Reverend John Hale, in a work written shortly after the episode and in fact sharply critical of some of its legal aspects, cannot be ignored: "I observed in the prosecution of these affairs that there was in the justices, judges, and others concerned, a conscientious endeavor to do the thing that was right."[43]

Since the trial records have not survived, no one knows how much weight the Court of Oyer and Terminer gave to the spectral testimony gathered by the magistrates in their preliminary investigations. But as the summer wore on, a general uneasiness emerged, especially as it became apparent that executions were no more successful than fasting and prayer in putting a stop to things.

Cases of Conscience crystallized that growing uneasiness. On October 12 Phips informed the Privy Council that he had forbidden any further imprisonments or trials for witchcraft. On the twenty-sixth a bill was introduced in the Massachusetts legislature calling for a formal convocation of ministers to advise the civil authorities on the best way to deal with the accused witches who were still in prison. The bill passed by a vote of thirty-three to twenty-nine. Coming when it did, this motion was presumably intended to lay the framework for a formal endorsement of Mather's position, with its emphasis on leniency, restraint, and a scrupulous regard for due process. Three days later, Phips dissolved the Court of Oyer and Terminer.[44] In November some of the bewitched girls were sent for by a man who believed that his ailing sister was under an evil spell; but "the validity of such accusations being much questioned, they found not the encouragement they had done elsewhere, and soon withdrew."[45]

Early in the new year a special court of judicature convened at Salem to dispose of the remaining cases. Although four of its five members had served on the Court of Oyer and Terminer, and although William Stoughton was again chief justice, its mandate was sharply circumscribed by Governor Phips: no one was to be convicted by spectral evidence. Forty-nine of the remaining prisoners were acquitted outright. The jury convicted three others, but these three were immediately reprieved by Phips. In a letter to the Earl of Nottingham in February 1693, Governor Phips struck a generally sanguine note: "People's minds, before divided and distracted by different opinions concerning this matter, are now well composed." Three months later Phips felt free to discharge all the remaining prisoners and issue a general pardon.[46]

Notes

[1] Cotton Mather, *The Life of His Excellency, Sir William Phips, Knt., Late Captain General and Governor in Chief of the Province of the Massachusetts Bay, New England* (Boston, 1697; reissued, New York, Covici-Friede, 1929), pp. 130-131.

[2] John Hale, *A Modest Inquiry into the Nature of Witchcraft, and How Persons Guilty of That Crime May Be Convicted: And the Means Used for Their Discovery Discussed, Both Negatively and Affirmatively, According to Scripture and Experience* (Boston, 1702), pp. 132-133; testimony of Sarah Cole of Lynn, WPA, I ("what trade their sweethearts should be of"). These occult experiments are sensitively described in Chadwick Hansen's *Witchcraft at Salem* (New York, George Braziller, Inc., 1969).

[3] Robert Calef, *More Wonders of the Invisible World: Or, The Wonders of the Invisible World Display'd in Five Parts* (London, 1700), excerpted in George Lincoln Burr, ed., *Narratives of the Witchcraft Cases, 1648-1706* (New York, Charles Scribner's Sons, 1914; reissued, New York, Barnes and Noble, 1968), p. 342; Hale, *Modest Enquiry*, pp. 23, 133.

[4] Calef, *More Wonders,* in Burr, *Narratives,* p. 342; Hale, *Modest Enquiry,* p. 23; Samuel Parris, "Meditations for Peace," Church Records, Nov. 26, 1694.

[5] Hale, *Modest Enquiry,* p. 25.

[6] Deodat Lawson, *A Brief and True Narrative of Some Remarkable Passages Relating to Sundry Persons Afflicted by Witchcraft, at Salem Village Which Happened from the Nineteenth of March, to the Fifth of April, 1692* (Boston, 1692), reprinted in Burr, *Narratives,* pp. 162-163; Church Records, March 27, 1692.

[7] W. Elliot Woodward, *Records of Salem Witchcraft Copied from the Original Documents,* 2 vols. (Roxbury, Mass., Privately printed, 1864; reissued, New York, Da Capo Press, 1969), I, 11, 17-23, 41-42 (warrants), 43-48 (examinations); II, 215 (jailing in Boston); Samuel G. Drake, *The Witchcraft Delusion in New England: Its Rise, Progress, and Termination* (Roxbury, Mass., 1866), III, 187-195 (Tituba's examination as recorded by Jonathan Corwin; quoted passage on p. 191); Charles W. Upham, *Salem Witchcraft,* 2 vols. (Boston, 1867), II, 32 (death of Sarah Osborne). A note on our form of citation for the witchcraft testimony: although Woodward's edition of the witchcraft documents is incomplete and often inaccurate, we nevertheless cite it where possible, simply because it is more accessible and more easily usable than the unpublished and unpaginated WPA volumes at the Essex Institute, Salem, Massachusetts. But while our citations are to Woodward, we have in fact checked most of the quotations in the carefully edited WPA typescript, and sometimes silently corrected Woodward's version.

[8] Hale, *Modest Enquiry,* p. 25; Calef, *More Wonders,* in Burr, *Narratives,* p. 342.

[9] Lawson, *Brief and True Narrative,* in Burr, *Narratives,* p. 153.

[10] *Ibid.,* pp. 154, 157.

[11] *Ibid.,* pp. 154-156; see also Woodward, *Records of Salem Witchcraft,* I, 50-51, for the arrest warrant.

[12] *Ibid.,* I, 74-75 (Dorcas Good warrant); II, 215 (jailing); Calef, *More Wonders,* in Burr, *Narratives,* pp. 345 (Dorcas's age) and 349n (irons); 35 *New England Historical and Genealogical Register* (1881), 253 (William Good's 1710 statement); Lawson, *Brief and True Narrative,* in Burr, *Narratives,* p. 159 (Nurse examination). In this period, "Goodwife," usually shortened to "Goody," was the term most generally applied to married women. The more honorific "Mrs." was reserved for those of higher social standing.

[13] Woodward, *Records of Salem Witchcraft,* I, 101 (the April 11 examination); II, 125-126 (testimony of Benjamin Hutchinson *vs.* George Burroughs, reporting Abigail Williams's charges); Calef, *More Wonders,* in Burr, *Narratives,* p. 346; Samuel Sewall diary entry,

April 11, 1692 ("very great assembly"), Massachusetts Historical Society, *Collections,* fifth series, 5 (1878), 358; Upham, *Salem Witchcraft,* II, 139-140 (Thomas Putnam letter), 150 (arrest of Burroughs); Hale, *Modest Enquiry,* pp. 25-26 (the colony-wide fast).

[14] Emory Washburn, *Sketches of the Judicial History of Massachusetts from 1630 to the Revolution in 1775* (Boston, Charles C. Little and James Brown, 1840), pp. 132-136. See also, for a more general survey of these developments, Wesley Frank Craven, *The Colonies in Transition, 1660-1713* (New York, 1968), pp. 223-225, 244-246.

[15] Washburn, *Judicial History of Massachusetts,* pp. 140-141. Phips's arrival and the creation of the Court of Oyer and Terminer are also dealt with in Calef, *More Wonders,* in Burr, *Narratives,* p. 348; William Phips to William Blathwayt, clerk of the Privy Council, Oct. 12, 1692, 9 *EIHC,* part II (1868), 86-88; Samuel Sewall, diary entry, May 14, 1692, Mass. Hist. Soc., *Coll.,* fifth series, 5 (1878), 360. Since, as Washburn points out, the new Massachusetts charter authorized only the provincial legislature to establish judicial courts, Phips was clearly exceeding his legal authority when he set up the Court of Oyer and Terminer.

[16] Calef, *More Wonders,* in Burr, *Narratives,* pp. 355-356 (first session of the court); Woodward, *Records of Salem Witchcraft,* I, 140, 170-172 (Bridget Bishop death warrant). The actual records of the Court of Oyer and Terminer have for the most part disappeared; what are now generally characterized as the "records of Salem witchcraft" are the preliminary examinations of accused persons and the subsequent testimony and depositions presumably submitted in evidence at the trials. (We cannot, however, be sure that all the testimony taken was in fact offered in evidence.)

[17] Calef, *More Wonders,* in Burr, *Narratives,* pp. 357-358; Woodward, *Records of Salem Witchcraft,* II, 214-215 (death warrants); Upham, *Salem Witchcraft,* II, 268 (date of the Court's sitting).

[18] Calef, *More Wonders,* in Burr, *Narratives,* pp. 360-361.

[19] *Ibid.,* pp. 366-367 and 368-369 (Easty petition). Abigail Faulkner of Andover was reprieved, like Elizabeth Proctor, because of pregnancy.

[20] *Ibid.,* pp. 366-367.

[21] *Ibid.,* p. 367.

[22] Thomas Brattle to "Reverend Sir," Oct. 8, 1692, in Burr, *Narratives,* p. 184 (resignation of Saltonstall); Woodward, *Records of Salem Witchcraft,* I, 115-116 (Daniel Elliot testimony). For petitions on behalf of accused witches, see Upham, *Salem Witchcraft,* II, 272 (Rebecca Nurse) and Woodward, I, 115 (John and Eliz-

abeth Proctor). For a number of testimonies casting doubt on the character or veracity of one or more of the accusers, see Paul Boyer and Stephen Nissenbaum, eds., *Salem-Village Witchcraft: A Documentary Record of Local Conflict in Colonial New England* (Belmont, Calif., Wadsworth Publishing Co., 1972), pp. 92-94.

[23] The ministers' letter first appeared in print as part of a "Postscript" attached to *Cases of Conscience Concerning Evil Spirits Personating Men* (Boston, 1693), a work written by Cotton Mather's father Increase. For the younger Mather's other, more private, comments on the witchcraft outbreak while it was still in progress, see Cotton Mather to John Richards, May 31, 1692, and Cotton Mather to John Foster, Aug. 17, 1692, in *Selected Letters of Cotton Mather,* compiled with commentary by Kenneth Silverman (Baton Rouge, Louisiana State University Press, 1971), pp. 35-40, 41-43. On August 1, 1692, a group of eight ministers, including Increase Mather, did gather at Cambridge and unanimously endorse the following cautiously phrased statement: "The Devil may sometimes have a permission to represent an innocent person as tormenting such as are under diabolical molestations. But . . . such things are rare and extraordinary, especially when such matters come before civil judicatures." Quoted in Increase Mather, *Cases of Conscience,* p. 32. This statement seems to have been kept private, however, and not until October did Mather or the other ministers take a further public stand on the trials.

[24] I. Mather, *Cases of Conscience,* p. 66. As was usual for important and timely works, *Cases of Conscience* circulated in manuscript before publication.

[25] *Ibid.,* [p. ii].

[26] *Ibid.,* p. 52.

[27] See for example, in Woodward, *Records of Salem Witchcraft,* the examinations of Sarah Good (I, 17-19); Sarah Osborne (I, 36-38); Dorcas Hoar (I, 237-240); Elizabeth How (II, 69-71); George Jacobs, Senior (I, 255-258); and Susannah Martin (I, 196-203).

[28] Hale *Modest Enquiry,* p. 31. See also, in Woodward, *Records of Salem Witchcraft,* the confessions of Abigail Hobbs (I, 173-176); Samuel Wardwell (II, 148-150); Richard Carrier (II, 198-199); Rebecca Eames (II, 143-146); Ann Foster (II, 136-138); Mary Lacey (II, 140-141), and, of course, that of the first confessing witch, Tituba Indian (I, 44-48).

[29] *Ibid.,* II, 113, 119-120, 123-124, 127-128. For another example of alleged mind-reading, see Elizabeth Balch's testimony against Edward and Sarah Bishop (*ibid.,* I, 167-168), mistakenly included by Woodward

and others as part of the Bridget Bishop case.

[30] *Ibid.,* I, 19 (Sarah Good); Calef, *More Wonders,* in Burr, *Narratives,* pp. 347 ("Hallowed be thy name") and 361 (Burroughs' execution).

[31] Woodward, *Records of Salem Witchcraft,* I, 146-148. For an interesting discussion of this form of medical evidence, relating it to the current state of gynecological knowledge, see Sanford J. Fox, *Science and Justice: The Massachusetts Witchcraft Trials* (Baltimore, The Johns Hopkins University Press, 1968), pp. 75-90.

[32] I. Mather, *Cases of Conscience,* pp. 59, 65-66. The one 1692 conviction Mather explicitly endorsed was that of George Burroughs, the only executed person against whom non-spectral testimony of supernatural strength figured prominently. "I was not myself present at any of the trials, excepting one, *viz.,* that of George Burroughs; had I been one of the judges, I could not have acquitted him." *Ibid.,* unpaginated "Postscript." Interestingly, however, while Mather cited "conjuring," the use of "spells and charms," and the performance of feats "which are above human strength" as examples of empirically verifiable proofs (p. 66), he did not include the "witch's tit" in this category. On the other hand, he neglected to refer to unusual physical appendages when discussing the various "tests" he did not consider sufficient for conviction. It would appear that Mather made a deliberate decision, in composing *Cases of Conscience,* to pass in silence over this troublesome and controversial issue.

[33] See, for example, the testimony of Samuel and Mary Abbey against Sarah Good in Woodward, *Records of Salem Witchcraft,* I, 25.

[34] Wilkins' account of his ordeal is in *ibid.,* II, 8-10; quoted passage on p. 9.

[35] *Ibid.,* II, 6-8, 11-18 (the death of Daniel Wilkins). Mrs. Putnam's testimony (*ibid.,* I, 94-95) is worth quoting: "[T]he apparition of Rebekah Nurse told me she had killed Benjamin Holton and John Fuller and Rebekah Shepard, and she also told me that she and [two other witches] . . . had killed young Jno. Putnam's child. . . . And immediately there did appear to me six children in winding sheets . . . and they told me that they were my sister Baker's children of Boston, and that Goody Nurs and [two other witches] . . . had murdered them, and charged me to go and tell these things to the magistrates or else they would tear me to pieces, for their blood did cry out for vengeance. Also there appeared to me my own sister Bayley and three of her children in winding sheets, and told me that Goody Nurs had murdered them."

[36] Cotton Mather, *The Wonders of the Invisible World. Observations as well Historical as Theological, upon the Nature, the Number, and the Operations of the Devil* (Boston, 1693), excerpted in Burr, *Narratives,* p. 229 (Bridget Bishop and the crashing timber); Woodward, *Records of Salem Witchcraft,* I, 95-96 (testimony of John and Hannah Putnam), and 25 (testimony of Samuel and Mary Abbey).

[37] See, for example, the account of Captain John Alden (an accused wizard) in Calef, *More Wonders,* in Burr, *Narratives,* p. 354.

[38] I. Mather, *Cases of Conscience,* pp. 43-45. Other instances of false and malicious accusations are cited by Mather on pp. 27 and 64. In addition to stressing the danger of malicious deception and the hazard of relying on Satanically-inspired displays as evidence (pp. 49, 50), Mather also pointed out (p. 51) that the seizures experienced by the afflicted in the presence of the accused might "proceed from nature and the power of imagination." In developing these ideas, and in stressing the importance of relying only on "credible" witnesses, Mather came very close (though only by inference) to repudiating entirely the testimony of the afflicted girls of Salem Village. Individuals suffering from such fits and visions, he says (p. 41), are "Daemoniacks" and "no juror can with a safe conscience look on the testimony of such as sufficient to take away the life of a man."

[39] Woodward, *Records of Salem Witchcraft,* I, 165.

[40] *Ibid.,* II, 115-116.

[41] *Ibid.,* II, 125-126.

[42] I. Mather, *Cases of Conscience,* [p. ii]. (This quoted passage is from the preface signed by the fourteen ministers, but Mather himself makes the same point on p. 17 of *Cases of Conscience.*) Robert Middlekauff develops this idea in his *The Mathers: Three Generations of Puritan Intellectuals, 1596-1728* (New York, 1971), pp. 154-155. Interestingly enough, the Mathers' opponent, Robert Calef, makes a similar point in challenging the trials: Robert Calef to Cotton Mather, November 24, 1693, quoted in Calef, *More Wonders,* in Burr, *Narratives,* p. 331. While the attack on spectral evidence is Mather's concern throughout much of *Cases of Conscience,* his position is perhaps most forcibly and succinctly stated on p. 34: "This then I declare and testify, that to take away the life of anyone, merely because a spectre or devil in a bewitched or possessed person does accuse them, will bring the guilt of innocent blood on the land."

[43] Hale, *Modest Enquiry,* p. 27. One modern legal historian, commenting generally on the decisions in all the witchcraft cases in colonial Massachusetts (acquittals as well as convictions) goes so far as to call them "the product of self-conscious and progressive lawmaking

Wood carving entitled "Accusation of the Witch" (Essex Institute, Salem, Mass.).

by a deeply ethical and religious people in an era of unparalleled scientific accomplishment." Fox, *Science and Justice: The Massachusetts Witchcraft Trials,* p. 8.

[44] Samuel Sewall, diary entries, Oct. 26 and Oct. 29, 1692, Mass. Hist. Soc., *Coll.,* fifth series, 5 (1878), 367, 368; William Phips to William Blathwayt, clerk of the Privy Council, Oct. 12, 1692, 9 *EIHC,* part II (1868), 87.

[45] Calef, *More Wonders,* in Burr, *Narratives,* p. 373.

[46] William Phips to Earl of Nottingham, Feb. 21, 1693, in Mass. Hist. Soc., *Proceedings,* second series, I (1884), 341-342.

Richard P. Gildrie (essay date 1985)

SOURCE: "Visions of Evil: Popular Culture, Puritanism, and the Massachusetts Witchcraft Crisis of 1692," in *Journal of American Culture,* Vol. 8, No. 4, Winter,

1985, pp. 17-34.

[*In the following excerpt, Gildrie outlines three distinct phases in the witchcraft investigations: the first, centering on Salem Village; the second, on suspicious characters; and the last, on the town of Andover.*]

. . . In 1692 the nightmares of magistrates, the clerical campaign for "reformation," and popular witchlore collided in a crisis complicated by local social tensions. Given this complexity, interpreting the event, then or now, has not been simple. The timing is the easiest thing to understand. King Williams' War, the first serious contest with the French and their Indian allies, was in its third year and was going poorly in northern New England. The Maine and New Hampshire frontier had virtually collapsed. There were rumors of impending attacks on the exposed Essex County towns. The fishing and commercial fleets of the coastal towns, particularly Salem and Marblehead, had been decimated. The entire economy of the region was disrupted. After the overthrow of the Dominion of New England in 1689 the provincial government was weak and uncertain as it coped with war and awaited the King's pleasure on new political forms for the colony. Early in 1692 the populace of Essex County, the colony's magistrates, and ministers all faced an uncertain, turbulent future. Hysteria was near the surface.

That panic first erupted in Salem Village rather than in one of the more exposed frontier towns or disrupted ports is something of a mystery. Perhaps paradoxically, people require relative safety to initiate hysteria. But, be that as it may, rural Salem Village, with its entrenched factionalism and its long ambivalent but contentious relationship with highly commercialized Salem Town, was certainly prone to disturbance.[41] The fact that many of those early accused were respectable folk around whom clung no aura of the occult was a source of great confusion and played no small part in accelerating the crisis.

Yet there is risk in concentrating exclusively on the Village. Accusations spread quickly through most of the County and into nearby areas. Once launched in the Village, the 1692 witchcraft investigations had a dynamic, a logic, which transcended the peculiar social and political configurations of Salem Village.[42] One way to approach this inner logic is to note the geographical and chronological phases of the investigation.

Essentially the investigation came in three phases. The first, February 29 to April 22, centered on Salem Village with strong attention being paid to Salem Town and Topsfield. Village factionalism was at the heart of the disturbance. In Salem Town the focus was on the Proctor family and other connections which straddled the Village-Town boundary, while in Topsfield interest was on the Hobbs family whose deviant family life was notorious. The first phase culminated in the accusation of George Burroughs, which, as we shall see, gave this stage a certain coherence satisfying to the clerics and magistrates committed to versions of learned witchlore.

In the second phase, April 20 to July 2, the populace and the magistrates collaborated in a general investigation of suspicious characters, many of whom had established occult reputations before 1692. Zeal was fueled by suspicions rekindled in the earlier phase and by preparations for the opening of formal trials in the Court of Oyer and Terminer early in June.

The third phase centered strongly on Andover. This least studied aspect of the 1692 crisis is in many ways the most perplexing. The pattern of accusation and investigation was controlled not so much by the afflicted as by the accused of Andover, most of whom (thirty-five of forty-three) made lurid confessions that blended popular and learned witchlore in ways which, taken together, fit none of the contemporary paradigms. Through all three phases the interplay between learned and popular witchcraft was crucial. In 1692 the perennial Puritan struggle against England's traditional popular culture got out of hand as clerics, magistrates and the populace grappled with their various visions of the evils which afflicted their society.

Fittingly, the Salem Village stage began with some elementary cunning lore that went awry. A band of girls, habitually meeting in the Reverend Samuel Parris' house for conjuring, became "afflicted." After a baffled physician suggested witchcraft, Mary Sibley, a churchmember and aunt of the girls, had Parris' servants, Tituba and John Indian, bake "a cake of rye meal, with the children's water" and feed it to a dog. According to popular lore, this was to allow the victims to "see" their afflicters. It worked, and Tituba herself with two others who fit the stereotype, Sarah Good and Sarah Osborne, were duly named.[43]

Once accusations arose out of popular witchlore, recourse was to learned investigation. Warrants were sworn on February 29 and two magistrates from Salem Town, John Hathorne and Jonathan Corwin, came out the next day to examine the accused. Their approach was, of course, strictly learned. Hathorne's first question to Sarah Good was, "Who do you serve?" She knew the routine and responded, "I serve God," but she felt the stereotype of malice perfectly: "her answers were in a very wicked, spiteful manner, reflecting and retorting against the authority with base and abusive words, and many lies she was taken in." Sarah Osborne, too, said little to disrupt normal expectations. For instance, she avoided worship, she said, because "a voice" told her she "should go no more to meeting."[44]

With the arrest of these three the episode should have ended. Instead Tituba made a confession which triggered the worst nightmare of learned witchlore: explicit satanic pacts made by a group of witches including, beyond Good and Osborne, at least two unknown women and a man who met in the Village. Satan himself had appeared to Tituba, "he tell me he god, and I must believe him and serve him six years and he would give me many fine things."[45] Here was the theme of inversion in its starkest form: Satan, claiming to be God, was seeking worshippers through promises of material reward.

Tituba's vision was probably influenced by her master, Samuel Parris, a minister who had played a strong supporting role in the crusade for "reformation." A pastor of mediocre talents, Parris was floundering in the complexities of Salem Village factionalism. Now his own household was "afflicted." Lacking the sophistication of an Increase Mather and being personally embroiled, he leapt quickly to the worst conclusions of the pact theory. Tituba's confession may have been her translation of his worries, not only about witchcraft but also about apostasy.[46] Indeed, her statement seems prime evidence of the extent to which the clerical crusade for "reformation" had been assimilated by the lowliest into their witchlore.

Despite the signs that this was an uncommon case, the magistrates refused to panic. Tituba's alarming confession seemed confirmed by the fact that the afflictions continued even after the examinations, which was unusual in Massachusetts. Nonetheless Hathorne and Corwin were wary. Even after the girls in their hallucinations settled on Rebecca Nurse and Martha Cory on March 12 the court waited a week to issue warrants. Nurse and Cory apparently attracted the girls' fears for local factional reasons and decidedly not because they fit any witch image.[47] That pattern of accusing the probably innocent was not unknown and so the magistrates waited for clarification, undoubtedly hoping the problem would resolve itself.

Meanwhile during March the techniques developed by the clergy were tried and failed, which of course compounded the fear. On the 11th a prayer service led by "several neighboring ministers" held in the presence of the afflicted only stimulated them to "act and speak strangely and ridiculously."[48] Martha Cory, a pious churchwoman certain that witches "were idle, slothful persons and minded nothing good," determined "to open the eyes of the magistrates and ministers" by following the common remedy of visiting and praying with her chief accuser, young Ann Putnam. The result was worse affliction. The unfortunate Rebecca Nurse, when later asked by Hathorne why she did not try the same technique, answered "Because I was afraid I should have fits too."[49]

On March 19, the day a warrant for Cory was issued, Deodat Lawson, a former Village minister, arrived hoping to calm the situation. Instead he became convinced, as had Parris, that Satan, aided by witches, had opened an assault on Christian society. Lawson witnessed a part of the attack when he tried to preach at the regular Sunday services. "In the beginning of the sermon, Mrs. Pope, a woman afflicted, said to me, Now there is enough of that. And in the afternoon, Abigail Williams, upon referring to my doctrine, said to me, I know no doctrine you had. If you did name one, I have forgot it."[50] Pandemonium at Martha Cory's examination the next day indicated that Satan was disrupting courts as well as churches.

These demonstrations of satanic power went beyond previous clerical experience. Lawson worked out his analysis in a lecture day sermon, given the 24th.[51] The Village had become "the rendezvous of devils, where they muster their infernal forces." The fact that "visible members of the church are under the awful accusations and imputations of being the instruments of Satan" triggered his worst fears. Satan "insinuates into the society of the adopted Children of God, in their most solemn approaches to him, in sacred ordinances . . . for it is certain he never works more like the Prince of Darkness than when he looks most like an angel of light." Even so, Lawson refused to panic. He was certain that some of the accused were innocent and he suspected Village animosities played

a role. "Give no place to the Devil by rash censuring of others, without sufficient grounds, or false accusing any willingly." He reminded the faction-ridden Village church that "Surely his design is that Christ's Kingdom may be divided against itself." Lawson was giving symbolic clarity to their experience.

Even yet, amidst a flood of accusatory visions and rumors, restraint was the rule. By the end of March only Cory, Nurse and Rachel Clinton[52] of Ipswich were newly indicted. But the element of subversion by parody was growing. The afflicted had hinted at witch meetings resembling church services almost from the beginning, but on March 31 and April 1 their premonitions blossomed into explicit visions. On the 31st, while a "public fast," another clerical staple for dampening disturbances, was "kept at Salem," Abigail Williams claimed "that the witches had a sacrament that day at an house in the Village, and that they had red bread and red drink." While the people of God moaned, the people of Satan held communion! The next day Mercy Lewis explained that she had spurned the "red bread like man's flesh" and was rewarded with a vision of heaven, "a glorious place, which had no candles nor sun, yet was full of light and brightness where there was a great multitude in white glittering robes."[53]

The indictments increased markedly after April 11 when Deputy Governor Thomas Danforth and other magistrates joined the proceedings. The persons accused throughout the remainder of the phase generally fit the factional alignment within the Village. But the logic of the hallucinations was governed by visions of a witch church, an alternative society. Sarah Cloyse and Elizabeth Proctor, for instance, "were their deacons" at the witch sacrament. To end the crisis a convincing agent of the Devil capable of raising such havoc had to be identified.

Who better to perpetuate subservice parodies of church order, complete with sacraments and deacons, than an alienated cleric? The magistrates found their man in the Reverend George Burroughs, a former Village pastor, who, Cotton Mather came to believe, "had the promise of being a King in Satan's Kingdom, now going to be erected."[54] On April 21, two fathers of the afflicted, Jonathan Walcott and Thomas Putnam, wrote to the magistrates "of what we conceive you have not heard, which are high and dreadful." Ann Putnam had a vision explicitly of Burroughs. The warrant was drawn on April 22.

His examinatoin early in May rendered the Salem Village outbreak comprehensible within the learned tradition. Burroughs was treated with the close attention his place in the drama required. Once arrested and brought to Salem, he was questioned privately by four magistrates at length before he was brought into court where the heightened sufferings of the afflicted confirmed all suspicions. In camera the magistrates concentrated on Burrough's religious indifference. He was pastor at Wells, Maine, and yet, despite the great distance, he remained "in full communion at Roxbury." Maine, the area most thoroughly devastated by Indian attack, was also noted for its religious laxity. To those who feared God's judgment, the conclusion was obvious.

Yet Burroughs made no attempt to allay suspicion. When asked when last he took communion, "he answered it was so long since he could not tell." He also admitted "that none of his children, but the eldest was baptised." Burroughs' behavior was indeed odd for a Puritan cleric. The magistrates had what they needed, but they did not forbear asking questions out of popular witchlore. "He denied that his house at Casco was haunted, yet he owned there were toads." Having uncovered their apostate, their mentioning of spirits and familiars was just icing on the cake. Also there was strong evidence that Burroughs had been dabbling in the occult and that he had made claims to magical powers in order to intimidate others, particularly his wives and their friends and relatives.

Burroughs was executed in August. All through the crisis and even in death, he continued to play his assigned role which further confirmed the leaders' assessment of his significance. The theme of parody deepened as Burroughs became the witches' surrogate Christ. Several confessing witches claimed "that the night before Mr. Burroughs was executed that there was a great meeting of witches . . . that Mr. Burroughs was there and they had the sacrament and after they had done he took leave and bid them stand to their faith and not own anything."[55]

The arrest of Burroughs marked the climax of the first phase of the investigations. The crisis now made sense within the context of learned lore. Together with some continuing echoes of the Village phase, the logic governing the second phase from April 30 to July 2, 1692 was largely that of popular witch belief which greatly expanded both the numbers and geographic spread of the accusations.

Generally those accused in this phase fit well into the "collective portrait" of reputed witches emerging in recent scholarship.[56] Most were women, middle-aged or older, of quarrelsome disposition who had histories of conflict with neighbors or relations. Some were deranged. Susannah Roots, for instance, was an impoverished Beverly widow placed in a household of another family for support. She had gained a reputation prior to 1692 as a "bad woman" by pointedly refusing to join in family prayers and by wandering about alone in the night speaking "as if there were five or six persons with her."[57] Such persons taxed the charitable resources of their communities and generated feelings of guilt among those who felt obligated to assist but also resented the burden. Witchcraft accusations could discharge the guilt. Apparently this was a common situation in both Old and New England.[58]

Yet alongside and within this general rubric of struggle between communal and individualistic impulses the accusations reveal something of the diversity of these conflicts and the complexity of the popular culture through which they were expressed. Both Dorcas Hoar of Beverly and Wilmot Reed of Marblehead, for instance, were aggressive women living on the edge of subsistence.[59] Yet they were hardly innocent victims. Both cultivated occult reputations in order to intimidate others and to cover fencing operations. Wilmot Reed, the fiftyish wife of a fisherman, encouraged servants to steal linen, a practice tolerated, however grudgingly, by those who knew her. But when a woman newly arrived in Salem Town threatened to charge her before the magistrates the fisherwife "told her . . . that she wished she might never mingere, nor cacare." The unfortunate newcomer naturally developed "the distemper of dry bellyache" and could not relieve herself "so long as she was in Town." Dorcas Hoar, a widow, ran an illegal tavern, practiced fortune-telling to intimidate as well as to amuse, and developed a reputation for maleficium in order to encourage young people to steal and to prevent them from divulging the crimes. She had an unsavory reputation stretching back twenty years prior to 1692. Clearly for some witchlore and popular magic was a career that opened into wider realms of criminality.

Other cases of persons with established reputations prior to 1692 indicate the variety of occult activity and suspicion that dominated this phase of the investigations.[60] Ann Pudeator, a widow of Salem Town who used "threatenings" to gain services she could not afford, may also have been experimenting, judging from the collection of strange "ointments" found in her home, and what was called "the Devil's grease" in Europe. Then too there had been swirling about her since 1680 suspicions that she aided her late husband in poisoning his first wife.[61] Arrested as well was Alice Parker, a reputed "sea witch" able to control weather, founder ships and forecast the fate of voyages. Given her reputation along the waterfront, it would have been a hardy captain who refused her husband a berth.[62] An occult reputation was at times cultivated by those who simply had little other claim to influence. For instance, Job Tookey, a chronically poor but profligate laborer and sailor, sought status by claiming "that he had some learning and could Raise the Devil." The court, more impressed with his talents as a braggart than a wizard, turned him loose.[63]

Nor were all of the accused in this second phase poorer people. Mary Bradbury was a churchmember, the wife of one of Salisbury's leading citizens and, among the mariner population, a reputed seawitch. First accused in 1679, Bradbury fought the designation and earned among many a reputation as "a goodly, godly wife." Stout denials and strong support from the members of her church eventually led to her vindication.

Meanwhile suspicions that she violated communal economic ethics helped fuel the long-standing rumors. A sailor testified that in 1681 she had sold spoiled butter to the captain of a vessel bound for Barbados "which made the men very much disturbed about it and would often say that they had heard Mrs. Bradbury was a witch and that they verily believed she was or else she would not have served the Captain so." To her malignancy they attributed the storms and apparitions that plagued them. Among some landsmen of Salisbury her occult reputation arose out of rumors about love potions, frustrated courtship and the remark of a physician-cum-cunningmam "that Mrs. Bradbury was a great deal worse than Goody Martin," Salisbury's most stereotypical witch who, incidentally, was also arrested in this second phase.[64] Mrs. Bradbury clearly was more victim than exploiter of the witch designation.

Philip English, a wealthy Salem merchant, was another whose unsought occult reputation was tied to perceptions of sharp economic practice. A supporter of the Andros regime, English was engaged in challenging the old town grants on Marblehead during the Dominion of New England. Because of his "threatenings" and attempts to suborn witnesses, some of the fishermen became convinced that he was responsible for various accidents which befell them. When the afflicted of the Village mentioned him in their fits the Marblehead fishing folk brought their suspicions to court and English fled the colony.[65]

Worries about maleficium and the conflicts between communal and individualist impulses governed the second phase of the witch-hunt. Old suspicions and quarrels crystallized into formal accusations. Candidates likely and not so likely were examined and imprisoned to await trial or released as the evidence seemed to dictate. The authorities were no longer uncovering a satanic conspiracy but rather were sifting through Essex County's accumulated local witchlore.[66] By July 2 the process of examination seemed to be concluding as the trials before the Court of Oyer and Terminer were already underway.

But in mid-July the situation changed dramatically. The Andover phase erupted and before it ended nearly one person of every fifteen resident in the town had confessed to or been formally accused of practicing witchcraft. It began as had the Village phase, with an exercise in popular counter-witch magic. Joseph Ballard, a substantial Andover farmer worried over his wife's ailments, suspected witchcraft, an understandable suspicion in 1692. Yet Andover's most likely suspect, Martha Carrier, had been arrested during the second phase. Perplexed, Ballard went to the afflicted Salem Village to determine if maleficium was involved, and, if so, to uncover the culprits. Two of the girls came to Andover to apply the traditional "touch test": if the afflicted relaxed their "fits" when touched by another, then that person was probably a witch. That large numbers of persons quickly became suspect by this method is hardly surprising.[67]

According to learned witchlore, the device was anathema. In similar circumstances Increase Mather berated a Bostonian who had sought out the afflicted girls, "asking him whether there was not a God in Boston, that he should go to the Devil in Salem for advice" on illness in his family. The Andover magistrate, Dudley Bradstreet, seeing the scope of the accusations, refused to sign warrants which rested merely on that evidence. In his view he was seconded by the town's pastors.[68]

Learned skepticism, however, did not dampen popular hysteria. Rather some of the magistrates came to share the fear. The preliminary hearings on the new Andover cases began with a spectacular four day confession by Ann Foster, a widow, that revived the learned nightmare. Foster claimed that Martha Carrier had coerced her into joining the witches, numbering over three hundred, who sought "to set up the Devil's Kingdom." The conspiracy was led, she hinted, by other satanically apostate clergy "besides Mr. Burroughs . . . and one of them had gray hair." One of the Andover ministers, Francis Dane, was an elderly man with an impressive mane of gray.[69]

Thus the Andover phase, animated by a renewed convergence of learned and popular lore, developed two major facets. First, its direction came more from confessions than from hallucinatory accusations, and, second, its logic dictated the search for at least one other leader of a demonic conspiracy as convincing as Mr. Burroughs. The latter effort was futile. The confessions pushed closer and closer to Mr. Dane, implicating a deacon's wife, then his own daughters and granddaughters.[70] Several of these women confessed as well, but no one explicitly accused the minister. The process obviously reflected the tension between Dane and his people, or even within his own family. An autocratic man, Dane had been pastor at Andover since 1649. In 1681 a dispute over his "maintenance" had been serious enough to be settled by the General Court which ordered the town to render adequate support but also suggested the hiring of an assistant.[71] Yet in 1692 Francis Dane could not credibly be accused of witchcraft, even if that had been a conscious wish of any of the confessors. The weakening patriarch, however cantankerous and defensive he may have been, did not have about him the aura of an occult apostate that so readily doomed George Burroughs. Thus the investigation whirled about with no clear point of culmination. Finally all had to settle for the substitute first suggested in one of the early confessions, that Martha Carrier had been promised that "she would be Queen in Hell."[72]

The other major facet of this final phase, the confessions themselves, provide insight into the psychological impact, first, of the long-standing clerical campaign for moral reform and, second, of the preceeding witchcraft investigations. The people of Andover, a relatively isolated farming town in the northwest corner of the country, was particularly vulnerable to a communal and personal sense of impending judgment. Unlike other Essex towns, Andover suffered Indian attacks in King Philip's War and again in 1689-90. The villagers knew they would see more. Also they were experiencing the first signs of land shortage. To compound the sense of unease, the community faced internal divisions. Having two pastors and a growing population, the town was debating forming two precincts, a move Mr. Dane and his supporters stoutly resisted. Meanwhile they were disturbed by a militia reorganization that separated them from the neighboring unit at Boxford, a move which some felt left both towns even more open to attack.[73]

Rather than strike out at each other, as had the people at Salem Village, the people of Andover turned on themselves and confessed en masse to "discontent" and "temptations" which recent events and old pressures had flamed into guilts and fears. Confession allowed communal purgation of anxieties about "impiety."[74] Ann Foster, who began the process, hungered improperly for "prosperity." But more than that, "she formerly frequently the public meeting to worship God, but the Devil had such power over her that she could not profit there and that was her undoing." If not Puritan worship, then Satan's. Mary Lacey, St., cried out on the last day of Foster's marathon confession. "We have forsaken Jesus Christ, and the devil hath got hold of us. How shall we get clear of this evil one?"[75]

Satan, his deeds, and the ceremonies he enjoined were metaphors for temptations, attitudes and practices they felt were separating them from Puritan standards and endangering their lives and souls. Mary Toothaker, Martha Carrier's sister and wife of the "French Doctor," was plagued by nightmares about Indians and devastated by her inability to internalize Puritan religious experience. Her baptism, which Satan desired her to renounce, was a burden "because she had not improved it as she ought to have done." She failed at private prayer "but sometimes she had been helped to say, Lord be merciful to me, a sinner." Even the Bible was a snare, for the Devil "deludes also by Scripture." Having no place in God's Kingdom, she was certain that she had joined Satan's.[76] In contrast Hannah Bromage of Haverhill, being urged to confess by an Andover confessor, "that being the way to eternal life," could only uncover "some deadness with respect to the ordinances for the matter of six weeks." Not being directly involved with Andover passions, she, in her perplexity, came close to the problem: "She being asked what shape the devil appeared to her, answered, she believed the devil was in her heart."[77]

Evil wishes, malice, guilt for past deeds and present hopes that threatened the standing order were what had to be confessed. Learned and popular witchlore

became a kind of Rorschach test to elicit inner visions. One of Francis Dane's daughters, Abigail Faulkner, being angry that "folks laughed" at pious families brought low, admitted that "she did look with an evil eye. . . . She knew not but what the Devil might take that advantage." Rebecca Eames feared her son was a wizard "because he used dreadful bad words when he was angry and bad wishes." She came to suspect that she herself had been a witch "for twenty-six years" because in 1666: "She was then in such horror of conscience that she took a rope to hang herself and razor to cut her throat by reason of the great sin in committing adultery and by that the Devil gained her, he promising she should not be brought out or ever discovered." William Barker, a middle-aged Andover farmer, was discontented. "He said he had a great family, the world went hard with him." Satan promised to pay his debts "and he should live comfortably." The Devil explained that his "design was to set up his own worship, abolish all the churches in the land . . . that his people should live bravely, that all persons should be equal, that there should be no day of resurrection or of judgment, and neither punishment nor shame for sin." Barker's dream was as old as Piers Plowman and an integral part of traditional English radicalism. But in Massachusetts in 1692 the farmer, certain that Puritan standards came from God, was forced to conclude that his visions were from Satan.

From the confessions that marked the Andover phase a multitude of similar examples could be elaborated ranging from the use of "Venus glasses" to attempted murder and swimming nude in front of persons of the opposite sex, but through them all the underlying point was the same. Within the rubric of pacts, witches' sabbaths and afflictions, the people of Andover were confessing their deepest, most personal worries and temptations. They were under enormous pressure to do so. The afflicted cried out at them. Their own neighbors, friends and kin who had earlier confessed urged them to do likewise. Magistrates assumed that they had something to confess. And so most confessed. They were admitting to the "provoked evils" the clergy had been pointing to since the Reforming Synod. The drama of the last phase of the Salem investigations was that the confessing witches were delivering their own personal Jeremiads, and purging themselves the same way those sermons purged the society at large.

Yet the drama had to end, even if the magistrates could find no logical denouement. Judicial institutions were exhausted. There were too many accusations, examinations and incarcerations. The Court of Oyer and Terminer, which opened June 2, spent its first week on Bridget Bishop alone. Even though the pace increased markedly, the Court was unable to try persons as expeditiously as they were being examined and imprisoned from late April through mid-October.

Even more important was the exhaustion of the witch paradigms used in the investigations. The chief weaknesses were the pact and conspiracy aspects of learned witchlore which once triggered by Tituba's confession and abundantly confirmed by disruption and hallucinations, undermined the moderate prescriptions earlier developed by the clergy. Also some of the only accused, most notably Martha Cory, Rebecca Nurse and the Procters who were "cried out at" for reasons peculiar to Village factionalism, did not fit the standard learned or popular emphasis on "malice." The only acceptable explanation was a deeper satanic plot to subvert church and society than the leaders had theretofore encountered. As if to confirm that view, both Cory and Nurse failed the clergy's favorite test of innocence. That failure helped cast doubt on the whole clerical position. In fact, William Stoughton, the chief judge on the Court of Oyer and Terminer, became convinced that the clergy, led by Samuel Willard and Increase Mather, had misinterpreted witchlore consistently since the 1670s.[79]

Thus the full blown conspiracy theory dominated the investigation. But this explanation too had potent critics who were vocal at least as early as May when Cotton Mather privately complained to a magistrate about abuses of the pact theory and warned against hallucinatory evidence. On June 15, their confidence restored by Increase Mather then newly returned from England, the ministers rallied and publicly attacked both the theory and practice of the investigations in a statement urging that in "prosecution . . . there is need of a very critical and exquisite caution."[80] Particularly the magistrates were admonished to show "an exceeding tenderness towards those that they may be complained of; especially if they have been persons formerly of an unblemished reputation." In court they recommended "as little as is possible of such noise, company and openness, as may too hastily expose them that are examined." If these procedures had been followed the Andover phase would not have occurred. In the Court of Oyer and Terminer the jury too had initial problems with the magistrates' approach. On June 30 in the first set of trials after the easy condemnation of Bishop, the jury at first found Rebecca Nurse not guilty, a verdict William Stoughton could not accept. Even so the jury might have stood by their decision had not the ever unfortunate Nurse made a cryptic remark that seemed a near confession.[81]

The conspiracy theory worked only so long as it was confirmed by the example of Burroughs (whose execution, incidentally, was the only one Increase Mather ever explicitly condoned[82]), and by the "confessing witches." Mather and other clerics undermined the latter by visiting the confessors in prison and eliciting accounts of how they had come to confess.[83] The magistrates' interpretation finally collapsed when they failed to find anyone in the latter phase who resembled Burroughs.

The theory of popular witchlore, operative throughout the crisis, was also unable to sustain the investigations. Long before 1692 the popular approach had been badly compromised through its gradual assimilation of learned lore. Traditionally it had held that suppression of occult evil by counter-magic or court action was effective and legitimate. But to conclude, and have abundantly confirmed in confessions, even the desire to defend oneself or others against witch attacks by counter-magic or prosecution could be "a devil's snare." The only solution was a general purge of guilt and a wholesale defection to the ministers' position on the dangers of popular magic.[84]

Briefly put, the Salem crisis erupted when the carefully forged clerical interpretation of witchlore failed to account adequately for what was happening in Salem Village and the crisis ended when the magistrates and populace concluded that they had no intelligible substitute.

The theory leads finally to the question of significance. Recent studies of European witch hunts tend to interpret them as parts of a more general "learned" assault on traditional populaar culture.[85] As a general interpretation it also fits Massachusetts' experience. It is particularly apt as a description of the clerical campaign against "provoking evils" and helps explain the widespread denunciation of cunning lore by both confessing witches and ministers. The temptation, however, is to reduce this several cultural conflict to an expression of social tensions engendered by the rise of commercial economies and "rationalized" bureaucratic states.[86] This view has also been recently applied to Salem Village with success.[87] But in the end it is too narrow a perspective. Even if Western Europe and, more dubiously, Massachusetts towns as various as Salem Town and Andover, were undergoing in 1692 a transition from a "traditional peasant" order to a modern one, that process cannot explain the specific forms the witchcraft theories and accusations took. As Stuart Clark observed, such social explanations of witchlore bypass "the problem of their meaning by reducing them to epiphenomena." Nor can social strain theories comprehend "the extent to which contemporaries found reassurance" in such lore.[88] Nothing is more obviously present in the Salem investigations thatn the hunger for a comprehensible, reassuring explanation.

Hewing closer to a broader cultural approach, the best explanation is, ironically, the one used by the ministers and the confessing witches who sought meaning within the Jeremiad tradition. There is comfort in the notion that God unleashes Satan not only to punish sin but also to give people an opportunity to clarify and purge, individually and corporately, all the multifarious "evils to which flesh is heir." That is more than a social explanation; it is a cultural one. The Salem witchcraft investigations were ceremonies about evil and the greatest of the evils was the inability of people who so badly wished to embrace Puritan experience to do so. In the end, the witchcraft experience contributed to the gradual mutual accomodation of Puritan idealism and Massachusetts reality.

Notes

. . . [41] Paul Boyer and Stephen Nissenbaum have provided an excellent analysis of the Village's internal animosities and why so many of those accusatins conformed to neither popular nor learned stereotypes. See their *Salem Possessed,* esp. pp. 80-109, 179-216.

[42] Breen, "War, Taxes, and Political Brokers," p. 238, note 99.

[43] SR Calef, *More Wonders,* p. 342; Charles W. Upham, *Salem Witchcraft* (2 vols., Boston, 1867), II, 95-96. For background on Osborne, God and Tituba, see Boyer and Nissenbaum, *Salem Possessed,* pp. 193-94, 203-206, 206-208.

[44] Boyer and Missenbaum, *Witchcraft Papers,* II, 357, 611.

[45] Boyer and Nissenbaum, *Witchcraft Papers,* III, 746, 747, 753-54.

[46] Larry D. Gragg, "Samuel Parris: Portrait of a Puritan Clergyman," *Essex Institute Historical Collections* 119 (1983), 228-29; James E. Kences, "Some Unexplored Relationships of Essex County Witchcraft to the Indian Wars of 1675 and 1689," *Essex Institute Historical Collections* 120 (1984), 187; Boyer and Nissenbaum, *Witchcraft Papers,* I, 607. Marion L. Starkey, *The Devil in Massachusetts: A Modern Enquiry into the Salem Witch Trials* (New York, 1949), pp. 57-61, gives a simplistic version of this argument.

[47] Boyer and Nissenbaum, *Salem Possessed,* pp. 146-47, 173-74.

[48] Calef, *More Wonders,* p. 342.

[49] Boyer and Nissenbaum, *Witchcraft Papers,* I, 262, 264-65; II, 586.

[50] Deodat Lawson, "A Brief and True Narrative," in Burr. *Narratives,* pp. 145-46.

[51] Paul Boyer and Stephen Nissenbaum, eds., *Salem-Village Witchcraft: A Documentary Record of Local Conflict in Colonial New England* (Belmont, Ca., 1972), pp. 124-28.

[52] Clinton had an established witch reputation. See Demos, *Entertaining Satan,* pp. 19-35.

[53] Lawson, "Narrative," pp. 160-61. Mercy Lewis' vision seems another reflection of Parris' concerns. He was particularly inclined to castigate the Mass and stress the importance of communion. See Gragg, "Samuel Parris," pp. 213, 221-22.

[54] Mather, *Wonders,* p. 120. Hansen, *Witchcraft in Salem,* pp. 74-77, notes Burroughs' occult reputation and suggests that he was a worshipper" of the "Prince of Lies." See also Weisman, *Witchcraft, Magic and Religion,* p. 138. Boyer and Nissenbaum, *Salem Possessed,* p. 212, suggests Burroughs may have been a "surrogate" for Parris. Despite these differences, few doubt his centrality to the crisis. For the trial evidence see Boyer and Nissenbaum, *Witchcraft Papers,* I, 151-78.

[55] Boyer and Nissenbaum, *Witchcraft Papers,* II, 624-28.

[56] See especially Demos, *Entertaining Salem,* pp. 57-94, and his "Underlying Themes in the Witchcraft of Seventeenth-Century New England," in Stanley Katz, ed, *Colonial America: Essays in Politics and Social Development* (Boston, 1971), pp. 113-33.

[57] Boyer and Nissenbaum, *Witchcraft Papers,* III, 722.

[58] Alan Macfarlane, *Witchcraft in Tudor and Stuart England: A Regional and Comparative Study* (London, 1970), esp. pp. 172-76; Demos, *Entertaining Satan,* pp. 292-329.

[59] Boyer and Nissenbaum, *Witchcraft Papers,* II, 389-404 (Hoar); III, 711-17 (Reed). See also *Essex Quararterly Court Records* VI, 81; VIII, 41-55, for indications of Hoar's reputation.

[60] "Established reputations" were determined by selecting cases from Boyer and Nissenbaum, *Witchcraft Papers,* passim, in which there was evidence from persons other than the "afflicted" and referred to suspicions of occult activity prior to 1691. Twenty-six cases met these criteria. (Compare with Demos, *Entertaining Satan,* p. 66).

Phase I (8 persons): Bridget Bishop, Sarah Bishop, George Burroughs, Rachel Clinton, Mary Esty, Sarah Good, Abigail Hobbs, Sarah Wilds.

Phase II (13 persons): Mary Bradbury, Martha Carrier, Ann Doliver, Philip English, Dorcas Hoar, Elizabeth How, Susannah Martin, Alice Parker, Ann Pudeator, Wilmot Reed, Susannah Roots, Roger Toothaker, John Willard.

Phase III (5 persons): Sarah Coile, Mary Parker, Margaret Scott, Mary Taylor, Samuel Wardwell.

[61] Boyer and Nissenbaum, *Witchcraft Papers,* III, 702-703, 709, Hugh R. Trevor-Roper, "The European Witch-

Craze of the Sixteenth and Seventeenth Centuries," in his *Religion, the Reformation, and Social Change* (London, 1967), p. 94; *Essex Quarterly Court Records*, VIII, 59-60. For the importance of the "Devil's Grease," see Edward Bever, "Old Age and Witchcraft in Early Modern Europe," in *Old Age in Preindustrial Society* (New York, 1982), p. 168.

[62] Boyer and Nissenbaum, *Witchcraft Papers,* II, 624-28.

[63] QUR Boyer and Nissenbaum, *Witchcraft Papers,* III, 759-62; *Quarterly Court of Essex,* VIII, 331.

[64] Boyer and Nissenbaum, *Witchcraft Papers,* I, 117-20, 125-26. For Susannah Martin, see Samuel Drake, *Annals of Witchcraft in New England* (Boston, 1869), pp. 128-29, and Demos, *Entertaining Satan,* pp. 58, 66, 74.

[65] Boyer and Nissenbaum, *Witchcraft Papers,* I, 313-21. For English's "French" background and entanglements, see David T. Konig, "A New Look at the Essex 'French': Ethnic Frictions and Community Tensions in Seventeenth-Century Essex County, Massachusetts," *Essex Institute Historical Collections* 110 (1974), 167-80.

[66] For a different interpretation which attributes more consistency, initiative and intentionality to the magistrates throughout the crisis, see Weisman, *Witchcraft, Magic, and Religion,* pp. 132-35, 148-59.

[67] Claude M. Fuess, *Andover: Symbol of New England* (Andover, 1959), pp. 86-87; Marion L. Starkey, *The Devil in Massachusetts: A Modern Enquiry into the Salem Witch Trials* (New York, 1949), pp. 180-83; Philip J. Greven, Jr., *Four Generations: Population, Land, and Family in Colonial Andover, Massachusetts* (Ithaca, 1970), pp. 84-85.

[68] "Letter of Thomas Brattle," in Burr, *Narratives,* pp. 180-82; Fuess, *Andover,* p. 87.

[69] Boyer and Nissenbaum, *Witchcraft Papers,* II, 341-44; Fuess, *Andover,* p. 91.

[70] Sarah Loring Bailey, *Historical Sketches of Andover* (Boston, 1880), p. 199. The cases in Boyer and Nisenbaum, *Witchcraft Papers,* are Eunice Fry. II, 347-48; the three Faulkner women, I, 327-34, II, 335-37; the two Elizabeth Johnsons, II, 499-506.

[71] Fuess, *Andover,* p. 39-80; Nathaniel B. Shurtleff, ed., *Records of the Governor and Company of the Massachusetts Bay in New England* (Boston, 1853-54, 5 vols., in 6), V, 343-44. For a similar dispute over his fitness to run a proper grammar school, see *Essex Quarterly Court Records,* VIII, 100.

[72] Boyer and Nissenbaum, *Witchcraft Papers* II, 523

(Marcy Lacey, Jr.): Mather, *Wonders,* p. 159

[73] Fuess, *Andover,* pp. 51-56, 19-74, 114; Greven, *Four Generations,* pp. 103-124; Kinces, "Some Unexplored Relationships," pp. 197-98.

[74] Chadwick Hansen argued in "Salem Witchcraft and DeForest's 'Witching Times'," *Essex Institute Historical Collections* 104 (1968), 100 that the "majority" were "hysterics" as were the "afflicted" girls and thus had the initiative, at least by implication. Richard Weisman, on the other hand, believes that the "afflicted" controlled the character of the Andover cases which "no longer bore any discernible relationship to local discontents." For the wording of the confessions the latter seems unlikely. Yet he is astute on the symbolic importance of confession in the campaign for moral regeneration. See *Witchcraft, Magic, and Religion,* pp. 97, 144, 159.

[75] Boyer and Nissenbaum, *Witchcraft Papers,* II, 513. On the purgative possibilities of witchcraft confessions in particular, see Thomas, *Religion and the Decline of Magic,* pp. 520-21.

[76] Boyer and Nissenbaum, *Witchcraft Papers,* II, 767-68.

[77] Boyer and Nissenbaum, *Witchcraft Papers,* I, 143-44. . . .

[79] "Letter of Thomas Brattle," in Burr, *Negatives,* pp. 183-84.

[80] "The Return of Several Ministers . . ." (June 15, 1692), reprinted in Murdock, *Increase Mather,* pp. 405-06.

[81] Calef, *More Wonders,* pp. 358-59; Boyer and Nissenbaum, *Witchcraft Papers,* II, 607-08.

[82] Hansen, *Witchcraft at Salem,* p. 138, Boyer and Nissenbaum, *Witchcraft Papers,* II, 607-08; *Salem Possessed,* p. 13n.

[83] See, for instance, Boyer and Nissenbaum, *Witchcraft Papers,* I, 132, wherein Mather reported that Mary Bridges "was brought to her confession by being told that she certainly was a witch, and so made to believe it."

[84] Compare with H. C. Erik Midelfort, "Witch Hunting and the Domino Theory," in Obelkevich, ed., *Religion and the People,* p. 281.

[85] See, most explicitly, Muchembled, "The Witches of Cambresis," pp. 256-76 and Horsley, "Further Reflections," pp. 71-95, esp. p. 91.

[86] See Alan Macfarlane, *Origins of English Individ-*

ualism: The Family, Property and Social Transis-tion (New York, 1979), p. 59 for a recantation of this view. See also Larner, "Crimen Exceptum?" pp. 72-74, and Trevor-Roper, "European Witch Craze," pp. 115-31.

[87] Boyer and Nissenbaum, *Salem Possessed,* passim, and especially their *Witchcraft Papers,* I, 14.

[88] Clark, "Inversion," pp. 98-99.

Longfellow on witchcraft in Salem:

Delusions of the days that once have been,
Witchcraft and wonders of the world unseen,
Phantoms of air, and necromantic arts
That crushed the weak and awed the stoutest hearts,—
These are our theme tonight; and vaguely here,
Through the dim mists that crowd the atmosphere,
We draw the outlines of weird figures cast
In shadow on the background of the Past.
   Who would believe that in the quiet town
Of Salem, and amid the woods that crown
The neighboring hillsides, and the sunny farms
That fold it safe in their paternal arms,—
Who would believe that in those peaceful streets,
Where the great elms shut out the summer heats,
Where quiet reigns, and breathes through brain and breast
The benediction of unbroken rest,—
Who would believe such deeds could find a place
As these whose tragic history we retrace?...
   Upon this simple folk "with fire and flame,"
Saith the old Chronicle, "the Devil came;
Scattering his firebrands and his poisonous darts,
To set on fire of Hell all tongues and hearts!
And 't is no wonder; for, with all his host,
There most he rages where he hateth most,
And is most hated; so on us he brings
All these stupendous and portentous things!"
   Something of this our scene to-night will show;
And ye who listen to the tale of Woe,
Be not too swift in casting the first stone,
Nor think New England bears the guilt alone.
This sudden burst of wickedness and crime
Was but the common madness of the time,
When in all lands, that lie within the sound
Of Sabbath bells, a Witch was burned or drowned.

*Henry Wadsworth Longfellow, "Prologue," in
his The New-England Tragedies, Ticknor and
Fields, 1868.*

HISTORICAL BACKGROUND

George Lyman Kittredge (essay date 1929)

SOURCE: "Witchcraft and the Puritans," in *Witchcraft in Old and New England,* 1929. Reprint by Russell & Russell, 1958, pp. 329-74.

[*In the following excerpt, Kittredge asserts that belief in witchcraft was common throughout history and points out that the witchcraft trials in the American colonies were remarkably limited in number.*]

. . . It is frequently stated, and still oftener assumed, that the outbreak at Salem was peculiar in its virulence, or, at all events, in its intensity. This is a serious error, due, like other misapprehensions, to a neglect of the history of witchcraft as a whole. The fact is, the Salem excitement was the opposite of peculiar,—it was perfectly typical. The European belief in witchcraft, which our forefathers shared without exaggerating it, was a constant quantity. It was always present, and continuously fraught with direful possibilities. But it did not find expression in a steady and regular succession of witch-trials. On the contrary, it manifested itself at irregular intervals in spasmodic outbursts of prosecution. Notable examples occurred at Geneva from 1542 to 1546;[102] at Wiesensteig, Bavaria, in 1562 and 1563;[103] in the Electorate of Trier from 1587 to 1593;[104] among the Basques of Labourd in 1609;[105] at Mohra in Sweden in 1669 and 1670.[106] In the district of Ortenau, in Baden, witchcraft prosecution suddenly broke out, after a considerable interval, in 1627, and there were seventy-three executions in three years.[107] From the annals of witchcraft in Great Britain one may cite the following cases:—1581, at St. Osyth, in Essex;[108] 1590-1597, in Scotland;[109] 1612, at Lancaster,[110] and again in 1633;[111] 1616, in Leicestershire;[112] 1645-1647, the Hopkins prosecution;[113] 1649-1650, at Newcastle-on-Tyne;[114] 1652, at Maidstone, in Kent;[115] 1682, at Exeter.[116] The sudden outbreak of witch-trials in the Bermudas in 1651 is also worthy of attention.[117]

It is unnecessary for us to consider how much of the evidence offered at witch-trials in England was actually true. Some of the defendants were pretty bad characters, and it would be folly to maintain that none of them tried to cause the sickness or death of their enemies by maltreating clay images or by other arts which they supposed would avail. Besides, now and then an injury is testified to which may well have been inflicted without diabolical aid. Thus Ann Foster, who was hanged for witchcraft at Northampton in 1674, confessed that she had set a certain grazier's barns on fire, and there is much reason to believe her, for she was under considerable provocation.[118] As to occult or super-normal powers and practices, we may leave their discussion to the psychologists. With regard to this aspect of the Salem troubles, we must accept, as substantially in accordance with the facts, the words of Dr. Poole: "No man of any reputation who lived in that generation, and saw what transpired at Salem Village and its vicinity, doubted that there was some influence then exerted which could not be explained by the known laws of matter or of mind."[119] Even Thomas Brattle, in speaking of the confessing witches, many of whom he says he has "again and again seen and heard," cannot avoid the hypothesis of demoniacal action. They are, he feels certain, "deluded, imposed upon, and under the influence of some evil spirit; and therefore unfit to be evidences either against themselves, or any one else."[120]

One common misapprehension to which the historians of witchcraft are liable comes from their failure to perceive that the immediate responsibility for actual prosecution rests frequently, if not in the majority of instances, on the rank and file of the community or neighborhood. This remark is not made in exculpation of prosecutors and judges,—for my purpose in this discussion is not to extenuate anybody's offences or to shift the blame from one man's shoulders to another's. What is intended is simply to remind the reader of a patent and well-attested fact which is too often overlooked in the natural tendency of historians to find some notable personage to whom their propositions, commendatory or damaging, may be attached. A prosecution for witchcraft presupposes a general belief among the common people in the reality of the crime. But this is not all. It presupposes likewise the existence of a body of testimony, consisting of the talk of the neighborhood, usually extending back over a considerable stretch of years, with regard to certain persons who have the reputation of being witches, cunning men, and so on. It also presupposes the belief of the neighborhood that various strange occurrences,—such as storms, bad crops, plagues of grasshoppers and caterpillars, loss of pigs or cattle, cases of lunacy or hysteria or chorea or wasting sickness,—are due to the malice of those particular suspects and their unknown confederates. These strange occurrences, be it remembered, are not the fictions of a superstitious or distempered imagination: they are—most of them—things that have really taken place; they are the *res gestae* of the prosecution, without which it could never have come about, or, having begun, could never have continued. And further, in very many instances of prosecution for witchcraft, there have been, among the accused, persons who believed themselves to be witches,—or who had, at any rate, pretended to extraordinary powers and—in many instances—had either used their uncanny reputation to scare their enemies or to get money by treating diseases of men and cattle. And finally, the habit of railing and brawling, of uttering idle but malignant threats, and, on the other hand, the habit of applying vile epithets—including that of "witch"—to one's neighbors in the heat of anger—customs far more prevalent in former times than now—also resulted in the accumulation of a mass of latent or potential testimony which lay stored up in people's memories ready to become kinetic whenever the machinery of the law should once begin to move.[121]

Nobody will ask for evidence that railing and brawling went on in colonial New England, that our forefathers sometimes called each other bad names, or that slander was a common offence.[122] That suspicion of witchcraft was rife in various neighborhoods years before the Salem outbreak, is proved, not only by the records of sporadic cases that came before the courts,[123] but by some of the evidence in the Salem prosecution itself.

That the initial responsibility for prosecution usually rested with the neighborhood or community might further be shown by many specific pieces of testimony. The terrible prosecution in Trier toward the close of the sixteenth century is a case in point. "Since it was commonly believed," writes Linden, an eyewitness, "that the continued failure of the crops for many years was caused by witches and wizards through diabolical malice, the whole country rose up for the annihilation of the witches."[124] To like purpose are the words of the admirable Jesuit, Friedrich Spee, in the closing chapter of the most powerful and convincing protest against witch-trials ever written—that chapter which the author begged every magistrate in Germany to mark and weigh, whether he read the rest of the book or not:—"Incredible are the superstition, the envy, the slanders and backbitings, the whisperings and gossip of the common people in Germany, which are neither punished by magistrates nor reproved by preachers. These are the causes that first rouse suspicion of witchcraft. All the punishments of divine justice with which God has threatened men in the Holy Scriptures are held to come from witches. God and nature no longer do anything,—witches, everything. Hence it is that all demand, with violent outcry, that the magistracy shall proceed against the witches, whom only their own tongues have made so numerous."[125]

As for England, the annals of witchcraft are full of instances which show where the initial responsibility rests in particular prosecutions. Two examples will serve as well as many.

Roger North, the distinguished lawyer, who was at Exeter in 1682, when a famous witch-trial occurred,[126] gives a vivid account of the popular excitement:—[127] "The women were very old, decrepit, and impotent, and were brought to the assizes with as much noise and fury of the rabble against them as could be shewed on any occasion. The stories of their acts were in everyone's mouth, and they were not content to belie them in the country, but even in the city where they were to be tried miracles were fathered upon them, as that the judges' coach was fixed upon the castle bridge, and the like. All which the country believed, and accordingly persecuted the wretched old creatures. A less zeal in a city or kingdom hath been the overture of defection and revolution, and if these women had been acquitted, it was thought that the country people would have committed some disorder."[128]

Our second example is a very notable case, which occurred in 1712,—that of Jane Wenham, the last witch condemned to death in England. Jane Wenham had a dispute with a neighboring farmer, who called her a witch. She complained to the local magistrate, Sir Henry Chauncy. He referred the dispute to the parson of the parish, who, after hearing both sides, admonished the wranglers to live at peace and sentenced the farmer to pay Jane a shilling. The old crone was not pleased. Shortly after, one of the clergyman's servants, a young woman, was strangely afflicted. Jane was brought to trial. Every effort seems to have been made by the court to put a stop to the affair, but the local feeling was so strong, and the witnesses and complainants were so many (including the clergymen of two parishes) that nothing could be done. The official who drew up the indictment endeavored to make the whole affair ridiculous by refusing to use any other phraseology in describing the alleged crime than "conversing with the devil in the form of a cat." But the well-meant device only intensified the feeling against the witch. Mr. Justice Powell, who presided, did what he could to induce the jury to acquit, but in vain. They brought in a verdict of guilty, and he was obliged to pass sentence of death. He suspended the execution of the sentence, however, and secured the royal pardon,—to the intense indignation of the neighborhood. Here we have a jury of the vicinage, accurately reflecting the local sentiment, and insisting on carrying out its belief in witchcraft to the bitter end, despite all that the judge could do.[129] It is well to note that the clergymen involved in the prosecution were not New England Puritans, and that the whole affair took place just twenty years after the last execution of a witch in Massachusetts. Of itself, this incident might suffice to silence those who ascribe the Salem outbreak to the influence of certain distinguished men, as well as those who maintain that the New Englanders were more superstitious than their fellow-citizens at home, that their Puritanism was somehow to blame for it, and that witchcraft was practically dead in the Mother Country when the Salem outbreak took place.[130]

Yet Thomas Wright—never to be mentioned without honor—speaks of the New England troubles as "exemplifying the horrors and the absurdities of the witchcraft persecutions more than anything that had occurred in the old world,"[131] and Dr. G. H. Moore,—in an important article on The Bibliography of Witchcraft in Massachusetts—declares that the Salem outbreak "was the *epitome* of witchcraft! whose ghastly records may be challenged to produce any parallel for it in the world's history!"[132] In further refutation of such reckless statements I need add but a single instance. In 1596 there was an outbreak of some pestilence or other in Aberdeen. The populace ascribed the disease to the machinations of a family long suspected of witchcraft. A special commission was appointed by the Privy Council, "and before April, 1597, twenty-three women and one man had been burnt, one woman had died under the torture, one had hanged herself in prison, and four others who were acquitted on the capital charge, were yet branded on the cheek and banished from the sheriffdom."[133]

There was a very special reason why troubles with the powers of darkness were to be expected in New England,—a reason which does not hold good for Great Britain or, indeed, for any part of Western Europe. I refer, of course, to the presence of a considerable heathen population—the Indians. These were universally supposed to be devil-worshippers,—not only by the Colonists but by all the rest of the world,—for paganism was held to be nothing but Satanism.[134] Cotton Mather and the Jesuit fathers of Canada were at one on this point.[135] The religious ceremonies of the Indians were, as we know, in large part an invocation of spirits, and their powwaws, or medicine men, supposed themselves to be wizards,— *were* wizards, indeed, so far as sorcery is possible.[136] The Colonial government showed itself singularly moderate, however, in its attitude toward Indian practices of a magical character. Powwawing was, of course, forbidden wherever the jurisdiction of the white men held sway, but it was punishable by fine only, nor was there any idea of inflicting the extreme penalty[137]—although the offence undoubtedly came under the Mosaic law, so often, quoted on the title-pages of books on witchcraft, "Thou shalt not suffer a witch to live."

The existence of all these devil-worshipping neighbors was a constant reminder of the possibility of danger from witchcraft. One is surprised, therefore, to find that there was no real outbreak until so late in the century. It argues an uncommon degree of steadiness and common sense among our forefathers that they held off the explosion so long. Yet even this delay has been made to count against them, as if, by 1692, they ought to have known better, even if they might have been excusable some years before. In point of fact, the New Englanders, as we have seen, made an end of trying witches nearly twenty years earlier than their English fellow-citizens. But we shall come back to this question of dates presently.

Much has been written of the stupendous and criminal foolishness of our ancestors in admitting "spectral evidence" at the Salem trials. Nothing, of course, can be said in defence of such evidence in itself; but a great deal might be said in defence of our ancestors on this score. The fact is,—and it should never be lost sight of,—there was nothing strange in their admitting such evidence. It was a matter of course that they should admit it. To do so, indeed, was one of the best established of all legal principles. Spectral evidence was admitted, for example, in England, either in examinations or in actual trials, in 1593,[138] 1612,[139] 1616,[140] 1621,[141] 1633,[142] 1645,[143] 1650,[144] 1653,[145] 1654,[146] 1658,[147] 1660,[148] 1661,[149] 1663,[150] 1664,[151] 1665,[152] 1667,[153] 1670,[154] 1672,[155] 1673,[156] 1680,[157] 1682,[158] 1683,[159] Even Chief Justice Holt, whose honorable record in procuring the acquittal of every witch he tried is well-known, did not exclude spectral evidence: it was offered and admitted in at least two of his cases,—in 1695 and 1696,[160]—both later than the last witch-trial in Massachusetts. In the 1697 edition of that very popular manual, Michael Dalton's Country Justice, spectral evidence ("Their Apparition to the Sick Party in his Fits") is expressly mentioned as one of the proofs of witchcraft.[161] What may fairly be called spectral evidence was admitted by Mr. Justice Powell, anxious as he was to have the defendant acquitted, in the trial of Jane Wenham in 1712.[162] The question, then, was not whether such evidence might be heard, but what weight was to be attached to it. Thus, in Sir Matthew Hale's case, Mr. Serjeant Keeling was "much unsatisfied" with such testimony, affirming that, if it were allowed to pass for proof, "no person whatsoever can be in safety."[163] He did not aver that it should not have been admitted, but only protested against regarding it as decisive, and in the end he seems to have become convinced of the guilt of the defendants.[164] It is, therefore, nothing against our ancestors that they heard such evidence, for they were simply following the invariable practice of the English courts. On the other hand, it is much to their credit that they soon began to suspect it, and that, having taken advice, they decided, in 1693, to allow it no further weight. We may emphasize the folly of spectral evidence as much as we like.[165] Only let us remember that in so doing we are attacking, not New England in 1692, but Old England from 1593 to 1712. When, on the other hand, we distribute compliments to those who refused to allow such evidence to constitute full proof, let us not forget that with the name of Chief Justice Holt we must associate those of certain Massachusetts worthies whom I need not specify. It is not permissible to blame our ancestors for an error of judgment that they shared with everybody, and then to refuse them commendation for a virtue which they shared with a very few

wise heads in England. That would be to proceed on the principle of "heads I win, tails you lose,"—a method much followed by Matthew Hopkins and his kind, but of doubtful propriety in a candid investigation of the past. We shall never keep our minds clear on the question of witchcraft in general, and of the Salem witchcraft in particular, until we stop attacking and defending individual persons.

Sir John Holt, Chief Justice of the King's Bench from 1682 to 1710, has a highly honorable name in the annals of English witchcraft. A dozen or twenty cases came before him, and in every instance the result was an acquittal.[166] Chief Justice Holt deserves all the credit he has received; but it must be carefully noted that his example cannot be cited to the shame and confusion of our ancestors in Massachusetts, for most of his cases,—all but one, so far as I can ascertain,—occurred after the release of the New England prisoners and the abandonment of the prosecution here. As to that single case of acquittal, we must not forget that there were also acquittals in Massachusetts,—in 1673, 1675, 1676, 1680, and 1683.[167] As to acquittals in England *after* 1693, let it be remembered that there were *no trials at all for witchcraft* in New England subsequent to that year. If Chief Justice Holt is to be commended for procuring the acquittal of a dozen witches between 1693 and 1702, what is to be ascribed to our forefathers for bringing no cases to trial during that period?

The most remarkable things about the New England prosecution were the rapid return of the community to its habitually sensible frame of mind and the frank public confession of error made by many of those who had been implicated. These two features, and especially the latter, are without a parallel in the history of witchcraft. It seems to be assumed by most writers that recantation and an appeal to heaven for pardon were the least that could have been expected of judge and jury. In fact, as I have just ventured to suggest, no action like Samuel Sewall's on the part of a judge and no document like that issued by the repentant Massachusetts jurymen have yet been discovered in the witch records of the world.[168]

But it is not for the sake of lauding their penitential exercises that I lay stress upon the unexampled character of our forefathers' action. There is another aspect from which the outcome of the Salem trials ought to be regarded. They fell at a critical moment, when witchcraft was, for whatever reason, soon to become a crime unknown to the English courts. They attracted attention instantly in the Mother Country.[169] Can there be any question that the sensational recovery of the Province from its attack of prosecuting zeal, accompanied as that recovery was by retraction and by utterances of deep contrition, had a profound effect in England? The mere dropping of the prosecution would not have had this effect. In 1597, James I, alarmed at the extent to which witch-trials were going in Scotland, revoked all the existing special commissions that were engaged in holding trials for this offence.[170] But the evil was soon worse than ever. What was efficacious in the New England instance was the unheared-of action of judge and jury in recanting. This made the Salem troubles the best argument conceivable in the hands of those reformers who, soon after 1700, began to make actual headway in their opposition to the witch-dogma.

I am not reasoning *a priori*. By common consent one of the most effective arraignments of the superstition that we are discussing is the Historical Essay on Witchcraft of Dr. Francis Hutchinson, which appeared in 1718 and again in 1720. Now Hutchinson, who gives much space to the New England trials, refers to Sewall's action, and prints the recantation of the jurors in full. Nor does he leave us in doubt as to the purpose for which he adduces these testimonies. "And those Towns," he writes, "having regained their Quiet; and this Case being of that Nature, that Facts and Experience are of more Weight than meer rational Arguments, it will be worth our while to observe some Passages that happened after this Storm, when they had Time to look back on what had passed."[171]

Whatever may be thought of these considerations, one fact cannot be assailed. In prosecuting witches, our forefathers acted like other men in the seventeenth century. In repenting and making public confession, they acted like themselves. Their fault was the fault of their time; their merit is their own.

We must not leave this subject without looking into the question of numbers and dates. The history of the Salem Witchcraft is, to all intents and purposes, the sum total of witchcraft history in the whole of Massachusetts for a century. From the settlement of the country, of course, our fathers believed in witchcraft, and cases came before the courts from time to time, but, outside of the outbreak in 1692, not more than half-a-dozen executions can be shown to have occurred.[172] It is not strange that there should have been witch-trials. It is inconceivable that the Colony should have passed through its first century without some special outbreak of prosecution—inconceivable, that is to say, to one who knows what went on in England and the rest of Europe during that time. The wonderful thing is, not that an outbreak of prosecution occurred, but that it did not come sooner and last longer.

From the first pranks of the afflicted children in Mr. Parris's house (in February, 1692) to the collapse of the prosecution in January, 1693, was less than a year. During the interval twenty persons had suffered death, and two are known to have died in jail.[173] If to these we add the six sporadic cases that occurred in Massachusetts before 1692, there is a total of twenty-eight; but this is the whole reckoning, not merely for a year

or two but for a complete century. The concentration of the trouble in Massachusetts within the limits of a single year has given a wrong turn to the thoughts of many writers. This concentration makes the case more conspicuous, but it does not make it worse. On the contrary, it makes it better. It is astonishing that there should have been only half-a-dozen executions for witchcraft in Massachusetts before 1692, and equally astonishing that the delusion, when it became acute, should have raged for but a year, and that but twenty-two persons should have lost their lives. The facts are distinctly creditable to our ancestors,—to their moderation and to the rapidity with which their good sense could reassert itself after a brief eclipse.[174]

Let us compare figures a little. For Massachusetts the account is simple—twenty-eight victims in a century. No one has ever made an accurate count of the executions in England during the seventeenth century, but they must have mounted into the hundreds.[175] Matthew Hopkins, the Witchfinder General, brought at least two hundred to the gallows from 1645 to 1647.[176] In Scotland the number of victims was much larger. The most conscientiously moderate estimate makes out a total of at least 3,400 between the years 1580 and 1680, and the computer declares that future discoveries in the way of records may force us to increase this figure very much.[177] On the Continent many thousands suffered death in the sixteenth and seventeenth centuries. Mannhardt reckons the victims from the fourteenth to the seventeenth century at millions,[178] and half a million is thought to be a moderate estimate. In Alsace, a hundred and thirty-four witches and wizards were burned in 1582 on one occasion, the execution taking place on the 15th, 19th, 24th, and 28th of October.[179] Nicholas Remy (Remigius) of Lorraine gathered the materials for his work on the Worship of Demons,[180] published in 1595, from the trials of some 900 persons whom he had sentenced to death in the fifteen years preceding. In 1609, de l'Ancre and his associate are said to have condemned 600 in the Basque country in four months.[181] The efforts of the Bishop of Bamberg from 1622 to 1633 resulted in six hundred executions; the Bishop of Würzburg, in about the same period, put nine hundred persons to death.[182] These figures, which might be multiplied almost indefinitely,[183] help us to look at the Salem Witchcraft in its true proportions,— as a very small incident in the history of a terrible superstition.

These figures may perhaps be attacked as involving a fallacious comparison, inasmuch as we have not attempted to make the relative population of New England and the several districts referred to a factor in the equation. Such an objection, if anybody should see fit to make it, is easily answered by other figures. The total number of victims in Massachusetts from the first settlement to the end of the seventeenth century was, as we have seen, twenty-eight,—or thirty-four for the whole of New England. Compare the following figures, taken from the annals of Great Britain and Scotland alone. In 1612, ten witches were executed belonging to a single district of Lancashire.[184] In 1645 twenty-nine witches were condemned at once in a single Hundred in Essex,[185] eighteen were hanged at once at Bury in Suffolk[186] "and a hundred and twenty more were to have been tried, but a sudden movement of the king's troops in that direction obliged the judges to adjourn the session."[187] Under date of July 26, 1645, Whitelocke records that "20 Witches in Norfolk were executed," and again, under April 15, 1650, that "at a little Village within two Miles [of Berwick], two Men and three Women were burnt for Witches, and nine more were to be burnt, the Village consisting of but fourteen Families, and there were as many Witches," and further that "twenty more were to be burnt within six Miles of that place."[188] If we pass over to the Continent, the numbers are appalling. Whether, then, we take the computation in gross or in detail, New England emerges from the test with credit.

The last execution for witchcraft in Massachusetts took place in 1692,[189] as we have seen; indeed, twenty of the total of twenty-six cases fell within the limits of that one year. There were no witch-trials in New England after 1693. The annals of Europe are not so clear. Six witches were burned in Renfrewshire in 1697.[190] In England, there were trials, one or more, in almost every year from 1694 to 1707, though always with acquittal.[191] Then, in 1712 Jane Wenham was condemned to death for witchcraft, but she was pardoned. Two clergymen of the Church of England, as well as a Bachelor of Arts of Cambridge,[192] gave evidence against her. Just before the arrest of Jane Wenham, Addison in the Spectator for July 11, 1711, had expressed the creed of a well-bred and sensible man of the world: "I believe in general that there is, and has been such a thing as Witch-craft; but at the same time can give no Credit to any particular Instance of it." Blackstone, it will be remembered, subscribed to the same doctrine, making particular reference to Addison.[193] The last witch-trial in England was apparently Jane Wenham's. In 1717 three cases came before the grand jury at Leicester, but no bill was found.[194] Prompted, one may conjecture, by the stir which the Wenham trial made, the Rev. J. Boys, of Coggeshall Magna, in Essex, transcribed, in this same year, from his memoranda, "A Brief Account of the Indisposition of the Widow Coman." This case had occurred in his own parish in 1699, and he had given it careful investigation. Both in 1699, when he jotted down the facts, and in 1712, Mr. Boys was clearly of the opinion that his unfortunate parishioner was a witch. His narrative, which remained in manuscript until 1901,[195] may be profitably compared with Cotton Mather's account of his visit to Margaret Rule in 1693.[196] Such a comparison will not work to the disadvantage of the New England divine. Incidentally

it may be mentioned that the mob "swam" the widow Coman several times, and that "soon after, whether by the cold she got in the water or by some other means, she fell very ill, and dyed." Let it not be forgotten that this was six years after the end of the witchcraft prosecutions in Massachusetts. In 1705, a supposed witch was murdered by a mob at Pittenween in Scotland.[197] In 1730, another alleged witch succumbed to the water ordeal in Somersetshire.[198] The English and Scottish statutes against witchcraft were repealed in 1736,[199] but in that same year Joseph Juxon, vicar, preached at Twyford, in Leicestershire, a Sermon upon Witchcraft, occasioned by a late Illegal Attempt to discover Witches by Swimming,[200] and in 1751 Ruth Osborne, a reputed witch, was murdered by a mob in Hertfordshire.[201] The last execution for witchcraft in Germany took place in 1775. In Spain the last witch was burned in 1781. In Switzerland Anna Göldi was beheaded in 1782 for bewitching the child of her master, a physician. In Poland two women were burned as late as 1793.[202]

That the belief in witchcraft is still pervasive among the peasantry of Europe, and to a considerable extent among the foreign-born population in this country, is a matter of common knowledge.[203] Besides, spiritualism and kindred delusions have taken over, under changed names, many of the phenomena, real and pretended, which would have been explained as due to witchcraft in days gone by.[204]

Why did the Salem outbreak occur? Of course there were many causes—some of which have already suggested themselves in the course of our discussion. But one fact should be borne in mind as of particular importance. The belief in witchcraft, as we have already had occasion to remark, was a constant quantity; but outbreaks of prosecution came, in England—and, generally speaking, elsewhere—spasmodically, at irregular intervals. If we look at Great Britain for a moment, we shall see that such outbreaks are likely to coincide with times of political excitement or anxiety. Thus early in Elizabeth's reign, when everything was more or less unsettled, Bishop Jewel, whom all historians delight to honor, made a deliberate and avowed digression, in a sermon before the queen, in order to warn her that witchcraft was rampant in the realm, to inform her (on the evidence of his own eyes) that her subjects were being injured in their goods and their health, and to exhort her to enforce the law.[205] The initial zeal of James I in the prosecution of witches stood in close connection with the trouble he was having with his turbulent cousin Francis Bothwell.[206] The operations of Matthew Hopkins (in 1645-1647) were a mere accompaniment to the tumult of the Civil War; the year in which they began was the year of Laud's execution and of the Battle of Naseby. The Restoration was followed by a fresh outbreak of witch-prosecution,—mild in England, though far-reaching in its consequences, but very sharp in Scotland.

With facts like these in view, we can hardly regard it as an accident that the Salem witchcraft marks a time when the Colony was just emerging from a political struggle that had threatened its very existence. For several years men's minds had been on the rack. The nervous condition of public feeling is wonderfully well depicted in a letter written in 1688 by the Rev. Joshua Moodey in Boston to Increase Mather, then in London as agent of the Colony. The Colonists are much pleased by the favor with which Mather has been received, but they distrust court promises. They are alarmed by a report that Mather and his associates have suffered "a great slurr" on account of certain over-zealous actions. Moodey rejoices in the death of Robert Mason, "one of the worst enemies that you & I & Mr. Morton had in these parts." Then there are the Indians:—"The cloud looks very dark & black upon us, & wee are under very awfull circumstances, which render an Indian Warr terrible to us." The Colonists shudder at a rumor that John Palmer, one of Andros's Council, is to come over as Supreme Judge, and know not how to reconcile it with the news of the progress their affairs have been making with the King. And finally, the writer gives an account of the case of Goodwin's afflicted children, which, as we know, was a kind of prologue to the Salem outbreak:—"Wee have a very strange th[ing] among us, which we know not what to make of, except it bee Witchcraft, as we think it must needs bee."[207] Clearly, there would have been small fear, in 1692, of a plot on Satan's part to destroy the Province, if our forefathers had not recently encountered other dangers of a more tangible kind. . . .

Notes

. . . [102] Sigmund Riezler, Geschichte der Hexenprozesse in Bayern, Stuttgart, 1896, p. 143.

[103] Ibid.

[104] Soldan, Geschichte der Hexenprozesse, revised by Heppe, II, 37; cf. G. L. Burr, The Fate of Dietrich Flade, 1891 (reprinted from the Papers of the American Historical Association, V).

[105] Jean d'Espaignet and Pierre de l'Ancre, the special commissioners, are said to have condemned more than 600 in four months (Soldan, ed. Heppe, II, 162; cf. Baissac, Les Grands Jours de la Sorcellerie, 1890, p. 401). I do not find that de l'Ancre makes a distinct statement of the number convicted. He makes various remarks, however, which seem to show that 600 is no exaggeration. Thus he says that the Parliament of Bordeaux, under whose authority he acted, condemned "an infinity" of sorcerers to death in 1609 (Tableau de

l'Inconstance des Mauvais Anges et Demons, Paris, 1613, p. 100). "On fait estat qu'il y a trente mille ames en ce pays de Labourt, contant ceux qui sont en voyage sur mer, & que parmy tout ce peuple, il y a bien peu de familles qui ne touchent au Sortilege par quelque bout" (p. 38). The commission lasted from July to November (pp. 66, 456, 470); besides those that the two commissioners tried during this period, they left behind them so many witches and wizards that the prisons of Bordeaux were crowded and it became necessary to lodge the defendants in the ruined château du Hâ (pp. 144, 560). Cf. pp. 35 ff., 64, 92, 114, 546. The panic fear that witchcraft excites is described by de l'Ancre in a striking passage:—"Qu'il n'y ayt qu'vne seule sorciere dans vn grand village, dans peu de temps vous voyez tant d'enfans perdus, tant de femmes enceintes perd s leur fruit, tant de haut mal donné à des pauures creatures, tant d'animaux perdus, tant de fruicts gastez, que le foudre ni autre fleau du ciel ne sont rien en comparaison" (pp. 543-544).

[106] An Account of what Happened in the Kingdom of Sweden, in the Years 1669, 1670 and Upwards, translated from the German by Anthony Horneck, and included in Glanvil's Saducismus Triumphatus, ed. 1682 (ed. 1726, pp. 474 ff.). Horneck's version is from a tract entitled, Translation . . . Der Königl. Herren Commissarien gehaltenes Protocol über die entdeckte Zauberey in dem Dorff Mohra und umbliegenden Orten, the Hague, 1670. Cf. Thomas Wright, Narratives of Sorcery and Magic, II, 244 ff.; Soldan, ed. Heppe, II, 175 ff.; Vilhelm Bang, Hexevæsen og Hexeforfølgelser især i Danmark, Copenhagen, 1896, pp. 48 ff. This is what Mr. Upham calls Cotton Mather's "favorite Swedish case" (Salem Witchcraft and Cotton Mather, Morrisania, 1869, p. 20). It was, in a manner, "Leonato's Hero, your Hero, every man's Hero" toward the end of the seventeenth century, since it was one of the most recent instances of witchcraft on a large scale. The good angel in white who is one of the features of the Mohra case appears much earlier in England: see Potts, Wonderfull Discoverie of Witches, 1613, sig. L (a reference which may serve as a note to Mr. Upham's essay, just cited, p. 34).

[107] Franz Volk, Hexen in der Landvogtei Ortenau und Reichsstadt Offenburg, Lahr, 1882, pp. 24-25, 58 ff.

[108] Scot, p. 543; Hutchinson, Historical Essay, 2d ed., p. 38; A True and Iust Recorde, of the Information [etc.] of all the Witches, taken at S. Oses (London, 1582).

[109] F. Legge, The Scottish Review, XVIII, 261 ff.

[110] Thomas Potts, The Wonderfull Discoverie of Witches in the Countie of Lancaster (London, 1613); Thomas Wright, Narratives of Sorcery and Magic, Chap. xxiii.

[111] Whitaker, Whalley, I (1800), 184 ff; Baines, History of the County Palatine of Lancaster, I (1836), 605-606; Crossley, Chetham Society reprint of Potts, pp. lix ff.; Wright, chap. xxiii; Heywood and Brome's play, The Late Lancashire Witches, 1634; Calendar of State Papers, Domestic Series, 1634-1635, pp. 77-79, 98, 129-130, 141, 152; Historical Manuscripts Commission, 10th Report, Appendix, Part IV, p. 433; 12th Report, Appendix, Part II, p. 53, cf. p. 77; Notes and Queries, 3d Series, V, 259, 385.

[112] Nichols, History and Antiquities of the County of Leicester, II, 471.

[113] See . . . note 176, below.

[114] Whitelocke's Memorials, December 13, 1649, ed. 1732, p. 434; Brand, Popular Antiquities, ed. Hazlitt, III, 80; Ralph Gardner, England's Grievance Discovered, in Relation to the Coal-Trade, 1655 (reprinted, 1796, chap. 53, pp. 114 ff.).
[115] A Prodigious & Tragicall History of the Arraignment [etc.] of Six Witches at Maidstone . . . Digested by H. F. Gent, 1652 (reprinted in an Account, etc., London, 1837).

[116] A True and Impartial Relation of the Informations against Three Witches, 1682.

[117] Sir J. H. Lefroy, Memorials of the Discovery and Early Settlement of the Bermudas or Somers Islands, II, 601 ff.

[118] A Full and True Relation of the Tryal [etc.] of Ann Foster, London, 1674 (Northampton, reprinted by Taylor & Son, 1878); Relation of the Most Remarkable Proceedings at the late Assizes at Northampton, 1674. Cf. W. Ruland, Steirische Hexenprozesse, in Steinhausen's Zeitschrift für Kulturgeschichte, 2. Ergänzungsheft, Weimar, 1898, pp. 45 ff.

[119] New England Historical and Genealogical Register, XXIV, 382.

[120] Thomas Brattle, Letter of October 8, 1692, Massachusetts Historical Society Collections, V, 65. Compare, on the whole question, the remarks of Professor Wendell in his interesting paper, Were the Salem Witches Guiltless? (Historical Collections of the Essex Institute, XXIX republished in his Stelligeri and Other Essays concerning America, New York, 1893) and in his Cotton Mather, pp. 93 ff.

[121] A long and curious list of cases of defamation may be seen in a volume of Depositions and other Ecclesiastical Proceedings from the Courts of Durham, extending from 1311 to the Reign of Elizabeth, edited by James Raine for the Surtees Society in 1845 (Publications, XXI). Thus, in 1556-57, Margaret Lambert ac-

cuses John Lawson of saying "that she was a chermer" (p. 84); in 1569-70 Margaret Reed is charged with calling Margaret Howhett "a horse goodmother water wych" (p. 91); in 1572. Thomas Fewler deposed that he "hard Elizabeth Anderson caull . . . Anne Burden 'crowket handyd wytch.' He saith the words was spoken audiently there; ther might many have herd them, beinge spoken so neigh the crose and in the towne gait as they were" (p. 247). So in 1691 Alice Bovill complained of a man who had said to her, "Thou bewitched my stot" (North Riding Record Society, Publications, IX, 6). See also Historical Manuscripts Commission, Report on Manuscripts in Various Collections, I, 283; Lefroy, Bermudas or Somers Islands, II, 629 (No. 15).

[122] See, for example, Mr. Noble's edition of the Records of the Court of Assistants, II, 43, 72, 85, 94, 95, 104, 131, 136,—all between 1633 and 1644.

[123] See Drake's Annals of Witchcraft in New England; Noble's Records, as above, I, 11, 31, 33, 159, 188, 228, 229, 233.

[124] "Quia vulgo creditum, multorum annorum continuatam sterilitatem à strigibus et maleficis diabolicâ invidiâ causari; tota patria in extinctionem maleficarum insurrexit" (as quoted from the autograph MS. in the Trier Stadt-Bibliothek by G. L. Burr, The Fate of Dietrich Flade, p. 51, Papers of the American Historical Association, V).

[125] "Incredibile vulgi apud Germanos, & maxime (quod pudet dicere) Catholicos superstitio, invidia, calumniæ, detractationes, susurrationes & similia, quæ nec Magistratus punit, nec concionatores arguunt, suspicionem magiæ primum excitant. Omnes divinæ punitiones, quas in sacris literis Deus minatus est, à Sagis sunt. Nihil jam amplius Deus facit aut natura, sed Sagæ omnia. 2. Unde impetu omnes clamant ut igitur inquirat Magistratus in Sagas, quas non nisi ipsi suis linguis tot fecerunt" (Spee, Cautio Criminalis, seu de Processibus contra Sagax Liber, 2d ed., 1695, pp. 387-388; cf. Dubium xv, pp. 67-68, Dubium xxxiv, pp. 231-232). Spee's book came out anonymously in 1631, and, unlike most works on this side of the question, had immediate results. Spee had no doubt of the existence of witchcraft (Dubium i, pp. 1 ff., Dubium, iii, pp. 7-8); his experience, however, had taught him that most of those condemned were innocent.

[126] The case is reported in A True and Impartial Relation of the Informations against Three Witches [etc.], 1682, which is reprinted in Howell's State Trials, VIII, 1017 ff.

[127] Roger North, Autobiography, chap. x, ed. Jessopp, 1887, pp. 131-132. North gives a similar account of the same trial, with some general observations of great interest, in his Life of the Lord Keeper Guilford, I,

267-269 (ed. 1826). It is not clear whether North was present at the trial or not. It is important to notice that North wrote his biographies late in life and that his death did not take place until 1734, only two years before the statute against witchcraft was repealed.

[128] North remarks that Guilford (then Francis North, Chief Justice of the Common Pleas) "had really a concern upon him at what happened; which was, that his brother Raymond's passive behavior should let those poor women die" (Life of the Lord Keeper Guilford, I, 267). Raymond was, to be sure, the judge who presided at the trial, but Francis North cannot be allowed to have all the credit which his brother Roger would give him, for he refused to reprieve the convicted witches (see his letter, quoted at p. 334, above).

[129] There was a fierce war of pamphlets over Jane Wenham's case. See the bibliography in Notestein, pp. 373-375. Cf. Memoirs of Literature, 1722, IV, 357; Wright, Narratives of Sorcery and Magic, 1851, II, 319-326. Jane Wenham lived nearly twenty years after her trial; she died in 1730 (Clutterbuck, History and Antiquities of the County of Hertford, II, 461; W. B. Gerish, A Hertfordshire Witch, p. 10).

[130] I refer to such remarks as the following: "As the devil lost his empire among us in the last age, he exercised it with greater violence among the Indian Pawwaws, and our New England colonists" (Richard Gough, British Topography, 1780, II, 254, note[P]); "The colonists of [Massachusetts] appear to have carried with them, in an exaggerated form, the superstitious feelings with regard to witchcraft which then [at the time of the settlement] prevailed in the mother country" (Introduction to the reprint of Cotton Mather's *Wonders of the Invisible World*, in the Library of Old Authors, 1862); "In the dark and dangerous forests of America the animistic instinct, the original source of the superstition, operated so powerfully in Puritan minds that Cotton Mather's *Wonders of the Invisible World* and the Salem persecution surpassed in credulity and malignity anything the mother country could show" (Ferris Greenslet, Joseph Glanvill, New York, 1900, pp. 150-151); "The new world, from the time of its settlement, has been a kind of health resort for the worn-out delusions of the old. . . . For years prior to the Salem excitement, European witchcraft had been prostrate on its dying bed, under the watchful and apprehensive eyes of religion and of law; carried over the ocean it arose to its feet, and threatened to depopulate New England" (George M. Beard, The Psychology of the Salem Witchcraft Excitement, New York, 1882, p. 1).

[131] Wright, Narrative of Sorcery and Magic, II, 284.

[132] Proceedings American Antiquarian Society, New Series, V, 267.

[133] F. Legge, Witchcraft in Scotland, in The Scottish Review, October, 1891, XVIII, 263.

[134] On modern savages as devil-worshippers, see, for example, Henry More, Divine Dialogues, 1668, I, 404 ff. (Dialogue, iii, sections 15-16).

[135] Mather, Magnalia, Book i, chap. i, 2, ed. 1853, I, 42; Book, vi, chap. vi, 3, III, 436; Jesuit Relations, ed. Thwaites, I, 286; II, 76; VIII, 124, 126. See also Thomas Morton, New English Canaan, 1637, chap. ix, ed. Adams (Prince Society), p. 150, with the references in Mr. Adams's note. Cf. Hutchinson, History of Massachusetts, chap. vi, ed. 1795, I, 419 ff.; Diary of Ezra Stiles, June 13, 1773, ed. Dexter, I, 385-386. Captain John Smith says of the Virginia Indians: "Their chiefe god they worship is the Diuell" (A Map of Virginia, 1612, p. 29).

[136] Mayhew's letter of October 22, 1652, in Eliot and Mayhew's Tears of Repentance, 1653 (Massachusetts Historical Society Collections, 3d Series, IV, 203-206); Gookin, Historical Collections of the Indians in New England (Massachusetts Historical Society Collections, I, 154). See the references in Mr. Adams's note to Morton's New English Canaan, Prince Society edition, p. 152, and compare the following places in the Eliot Tracts (as reprinted in the Massachusetts Historical Society, Collections, 3d Series, IV),—pp. 17, 19-20, 39, 50-51, 55-57, 77, 82, 113-116, 133-134, 156, 186-187. See, for the impression that Indian ceremonies made on a devout man in 1745, David Brainerd's Journal, Mirabilia Dei inter Indicos, Philadelphia, [1746,] pp. 49-57:—"I sat," writes Brainerd, "at a small Distance, not more than Thirty Feet from them, (tho' undiscover'd) with my Bible in my Hand, resolving if possible to spoil their Sport, and prevent their receiving any Answers from the *infernal* World" (p. 50).

[137] Gookin, Historical Collections (Massachusetts Historical Society, Collections, I, 154); Massachusetts Records, ed. Shurtleff, II, 177; III, 98.

[138] The Most Strange and Admirable Discoverie of the Three Witches of Warboys, 1593, sigg. B2 r[o], P v[o].

[139] Thomas Potts, The Wonderfull Discoverie of Witches, 1613, sig. S; The Arraignment and Triall of Iennet Preston, of Gisborne in Craven, in the Countie of York, London, 1612 (in the same, sig. Y2).

[140] Mary Smith's case, Alexander Roberts, A Treatise of Witchcraft, 1616, pp. 52, 56, 57; the Husbands Bosworth case, Letter of Alderman Robert Heyrick, of Leicester, July 18, 1616, printed in Nichols, History and Antiquities of the County of Leicester, II, 471.

[141] Edward Fairfax, Dæmonologia, 1621 (ed. Grainge, 1882).

142 Chetham Society Publications, VI, lxiv.

143 A True and Exact Relation of the Severall Informations [etc.] of the late Witches, London, 1645, p. 20; T. B. Howell, State Trials, IV, 846.

144 Depositions from the Castle of York, [edited by James Raine,] Surtees Society, 1861 (Publications, XL), pp. 28-30.

145 The same, p. 58.

146 The same, pp. 64-65, 67.

147 Glanvil, Saducismus Triumphatus, ed. 1682, Relations, pp. 96, 98, 100 (ed. 1726, pp. 286, 288, 289).

148 York Depositions, p. 82.
149 The same, pp. 88-89, 92.

150 The same, pp. 112-114; Glanvil, ed. 1682, pp. 160-161 (ed. 1726, pp. 328-329).

151 A Tryal of Witches . . . at Bury St. Edmonds . . . 1664, London, 1682, pp. 18, 20, 23, 26, 29, 34, 38 (Sir Matthew Hale's case); York Depositions, pp. 124-125.

152 Glanvil, ed. 1682, pp. 103-104, 109 (ed. 1726, p. 291).

153 Calendar of State Papers, Domestic, 1667-1668, p. 4; York Depositions, p. 154.

154 York Depositions, p. 176.

155 Ann Tilling's case, Gentleman's Magazine for 1832, Part I, CII, 489 ff.; Inderwick, Side-Lights on the Stuarts, 2d ed., 1891, pp. 171-172, 191.

156 York Depositions, pp. 192, 202-203.

157 The same, p. 247.

158 An Account of the Tryal and Examination of Joan Butts, 1682.

159 Margaret Stothard's case, The Monthly Chronicle of North-Country Lore and Legend, [II,] 1888, p. 395.

160 Hutchinson, Historical Essay, 1718, pp. 44-45 (ed. 1720, pp. 61-62). There is a very interesting account of the second of these trials (that of Elizabeth Horner or Turner) in a letter to the Bishop of Exeter from Archdeacon (?) Blackburne, who attended at the bishop's request. This letter, dated September 14, 1696, has been printed by Mr. T. Quiller-Couch in Notes and Queries, 1st Series, XI, 498-499, and again in Brand's Popular Antiquities, ed. Hazlitt, III, 103-104. The spectral evidence comes out clearly. Of Holt, Blackburne remarks: "My Lord Chief Justice by his questions and manner of summing up the Evidence seem'd to me to believe nothing of witchery at all."

161 Dalton, Country Justice, chap. 160, 5, p. 384. "The court justified themselves from books of law, and the authorities of Keble, Dalton and other lawyers, then of the first character, who lay down rules of conviction as absurd and dangerous, as any which were practised in New England" (Hutchinson, History of Massachusetts, ed. 1795, II, 27).

162 James Burvile testified "That hearing the Scratchings and Noises of Cats, he went out, and saw several of them; that one of them had a Face like *Jane Wenham*; that he was present several Times when *Anne Thorn* said she saw Cats about her Bed; and more he would have attested, but this was thought sufficient by the Court" ([F. Bragge,] A Full and Impartial Account of the Discovery of Sorcery and Witchcraft, practis'd by Jane Wenham, London, 1712, p. 29). After the conviction of the witch, Ann was still afflicted: "*Ann Thorn* continues to be frequently troubl'd with the Apparition either of *Jane Wenham* in her own Shape, or that of a Cat, which speaks to her, and tempts her to destroy her self with a Knife that it brings along with it" ([Bragge,] Witchcraft Farther Display'd, 1712, Introduction). In 1711 spectral evidence was admitted at the trial of eight witches at Carrickfergus, in Ireland (A Narrative of some Strange Events that took place in Island Magee, and Neighbourhood, in 1711, by an Eye Witness, Belfast, 1822, Appendix, pp. 49-50).

163 A Tryal of Witches, as above, p. 40.

164 "The Judge and all the Court were fully satisfied with the Verdict" (A Tryal, etc., p. 58).

165 For a learned discussion of spectral evidence, see J. B. Thayer, Atlantic Monthly, April, 1890, LXV, 471 ff.

166 Dr. Hutchinson, who acknowledges his indebtedness to Holt, mentions six witches as tried by the Chief Justice from 1691 to 1696, and adds, "Several others in other Places, about Eleven in all, have been tried for Witches before my Lord Chief Justice *Holt,* and have all been acquitted. The last of them was *Sarah Morduck,* accused by *Richard Hathaway,* and tried at *Guilford* Assize, *Anno* 1701" (Historical Essay, 2d ed., pp. 58-63). It is not clear whether the "eleven in all" includes the seven previously mentioned. On the Morduck-Hathaway case, cf. Howell, State Trials, XIV, 639 ff.

167 Drake, Annals of Witchcraft in New England, pp. 136, 138; Noble, Colonial Society Publications, X (1907), 21-23.

[168] Compare Goodell's remarks on the reversal of attainder, in his Reasons for Concluding that the Act of 1711 became a Law, 1884. I have not considered here the bearing of this reversal, or of the attempt to pay damages to the survivors or their heirs, because these things came somewhat later. It must be noted, however, that all such measures of reparation, whatever may be thought of their sufficiency, were unexampled in the history of witch-trials the world over, and that they came before the last condemnation for witchcraft in England (1712). See the references appended by Goodell to the Act of 1703 in The Acts and Resolves of the Province of the Massachusetts Bay, VI, 49-50.

[169] See p. 338, above.

[170] Legge, as above, p. 264; Register of the Privy Council of Scotland, V (1882), 409-410.

[171] Hutchinson, p. 83; 2d ed., p. 108.

[172] See W. F. Poole in Winsor's Memorial History of Boston, II, 133; cf. Noble, Colonial Society Publications, X (1907), 20-23.

[173] See Poole, II, 133. Dr. Poole finds twelve executions in New England before 1692. This makes the total for all New England, from 1620 to the present day, 34 (including two who died in jail). Cf. C. W. Upham, Salem Witchcraft, Boston, 1867, II, 351; S. G. Drake, Annals of Witchcraft, 1869, pp. 191 ff. In this part of the chapter I have made a few quotations from a book of my own, The Old Farmer and his Almanack (Boston, 1904).

[174] "They were the first of all people," writes Mr. Goodell, "to escape the thraldom" (Reasons for Concluding that the Act of 1711 became a Law, 1884, p. 21).

[175] See Hutchinson, Historical Essay, 2d ed., 1720, pp. 45 ff.

[176] John Stearne, Hopkins's associate, speaks of what he has himself "Learned and observed since the 25. of March 1645 as being in part an agent in finding out or discovering some of those since that time, being about two hundred in number, in Essex, Suffolke, Northamptonshire, Huntingtonshire, Bedfordshire, Norfolke, Cambridgeshire, and the Isle of Ely in the County of Cambridge, besides other places, justly and deservedly executed upon their legall tryalls" (A Confirmation and Discovery of Witch-craft, London, 1648, To the Reader). Stearne wrote his book after the death of Hopkins, which took place in 1647. In the life of Hopkins in the Dictionary of National Biography, the Witch-Finder is said to have begun operations in 1644. This is a manifest error. Hopkins himself (Discovery of Witches, 1647, p. 2, see be-

low) says that his experiences began at Manningtree "in *March* 1644," but Stearne's statement makes it clear that this is Old Style, for Stearne was also concerned in the Manningtree business, and the year is completely established by the report of the proceedings,—A True and Exact Relation of the severall Informations [etc.] of the late Witches, London, 1645 (cf. T. B. Howell's State Trials, IV, 817 ff.). The traditional statement that Hopkins was hanged as a wizard (cf. Hudibras, Part II, canto 3, ll. 139 ff.) is disproved by the following passage in Stearne: "I am certain (notwithstanding whatsoever hath been said of him) he died peaceably at Manningtree, after a long sicknesse of a Consumption, as many of his generation had done before him, without any trouble of conscience for what he had done, as was falsly reported of him" (p. 61). For the record of his burial, August 12, 1647, see Notes and Queries, 1st Series, X, 285. The notion that Hopkins was "swum" and, since he floated, was subsequently hanged, most likely originated in a document criticising his performances which was brought before the Norfolk judges in 1646 or (more probably) in 1647. Hopkins printed a reply to this document shortly before his death,—The Discovery of Witches: in Answer to severall Queries, lately delivered to the Judges of Assize for the County of Norfolk. And now published by Matthew Hopkins, Witch-finder (London, 1647). The first "querie," as printed by Hopkins, was this:—"That he must needs be the greatest Witch, Sorcerer, and Wizzard himselfe, else hee could not doe it." Cf. Wright, Narratives of Sorcery and Magic, II, 145 ff.; Lives of Twelve Bad Men, edited by Thomas Seccombe, London, 1894, p. 64; Ady, A Candle in the Dark, 1656, pp. 101-102; James Howell, as above (note 7); Gough, British Topography, 1780, II, 254.

[177] Legge, Scottish Review, XVIII, 273-274. Ady (A Candle in the Dark, 1656, p. 105) says: "A little before the Conquest of *Scotland* (as is reported upon good intelligence) the Presbytery of *Scotland* did, by their own pretended authority, take upon them to Summon, Convent, Censure, and Condemn people to cruel death for Witches and (as is credibly reported) they caused four thousand to be executed by Fire and Halter, and had as many in prison to be tried by them, when God sent his conquering Sword to suppress them." The "conquest" to which Ady refers is Cromwell's, in 1650. It is well known that from 1640 to Cromwell's invasion, witch prosecution ran riot in Scotland, but that during his supremacy there were very few executions in that country (see Legge, pp. 266-267).

[178] Mannhardt, Die Praktischen Folgen des Aberglaubens, p. 34.

[179] Soldan, Geschichte der Hexenprozesse, ed. Heppe, I, 492.

[180] Remy, Daemonolatreia, Lugduni, 1595.

[181] See note 105, above.

[182] Soldan, Geschichte der Hexenprozesse, ed. Heppe, II, 38 ff.

[183] See the extraordinary enumeration in Roskoff, Geschichte des Teufels, Leipzig, 1869, II, 293 ff.; cf. S. Riezler, Geschichte der Hexenprozesse in Bayern, pp. 141 ff., 283 ff.

[184] Potts, The Wonderfull Discoverie of Witches, 1613.

[185] Matthew Hopkins, Discovery of Witches, 1647, p. 3.

[186] John Stearne, A Confirmation and Discovery of Witch-craft, 1648, p. 14.

[187] Wright, Narratives of Sorcery and Magic, chap. xxv.
[188] Memorials, 1732, pp. 163, 450.

[189] Hugh Hare, Justice of the Peace, in his charge at the General Quarter Sessions for Surrey, at Dorking, on April 5, 1692, spoke as follows: "Besides these Crimes which are so frequently and so imprudently perpetrated, there are some others also which may not improperly be ranked among the offences against Moral Justice. But, Gentlemen, the proof of some of them is so difficult, and they are so seldom practised, that I shall but just put you in mind of them, and that you are to enquire and present all Persons that have invocated, entertained or employed any wicked Spirit, or have used any Witchcraft, Charm, or Sorcery; this is a sin of a very deep die, being directly against the first Commandment, and is punished with Death both by the Law of God, and by a Statute made in the first Year of King *James* the First; but it is so hard a matter to have full proof brought of it, that no Jury can be too cautious and tender in a prosecution of this Nature. However, where the evidence is clear and undeniable, you must proceed according to your Oaths." (Surrey Archæological Collections, XII [1895], 128-129.) Coincidence in date justifies the quotation.

[190] A Relation of the Diabolical Practices of above Twenty Wizards and Witches, 1697; Sadducismus Debellatus, 1698; A History of the Witches of Renfrewshire, 1877. A seventh committed suicide in prison.

[191] See Inderwick, Side-Lights on the Stuarts, 2d ed., 1891, pp. 193-194; Notestein, pp. 313-333, 418-419.

[192] That is, Francis Bragge, who was also a clergyman, being Curate of Biggleswade according to W. B. Gerish (A Hertfordshire Witch, p. 8). . . .

[193] Blackstone, Commentaries, Book iv, chap. 4, sec. 6

(4th ed., 1770, IV, 60-61); cf. Dr. Samuel A. Green, Groton in the Witchcraft Times, 1883, p. 29. In 1715 and 1716 there appeared, in London, A Compleat History of Magick, Sorcery, and Witchcraft, in two volumes, which asserted the truth, and gave the particulars, of a long line of such phenomena, from the case of the Witches of Warboys (in 1592) to the Salem Witchcraft itself. The book was the occasion of Dr. Francis Hutchinson's Historical Essay, published in 1718, and in a second edition in 1720. Richard Boulton, the author of the Compleat History, returned to the charge in 1722, in The Possibility and Reality of Magick, Sorcery, and Witchcraft, Demonstrated. Or, a Vindication of a Compleat History of Magick, etc. The Compleat History came out anonymously, but Boulton, who describes himself as "sometime of Brazen-Nose College in Oxford," acknowledges the authorship in his reply to Hutchinson.

[194] British Museum, Additional MS. 35838, fol. 404; Notestein, pp. 330-331, 419; Summers, The Geography of Witchcraft, 1927, pp. 160-161. I leave in suspense the statement that Jane Clarke of Great Wigston and her son and daughter were tried at Leicester in 1717 (Leicestershire and Rutland Notes and Queries, I [1891], 247). I suspect this is the same case. On the alleged executions at Northampton in 1705 and Huntingdon in 1716 see Notestein, pp. 375-383, who makes out a very strong case for the fictitious character of the pamphlets that profess to record them. In the Proceedings of the American Antiquarian Society, New Series, XVIII (1907), 206, I accepted the 1705 case and rejected (though not decidedly) that of 1716.

[195] The Case of Witchcraft at Coggeshall, Essex, in the year, 1699, being the Narrative of the Rev. J. Boys, Minister of that Parish. Printed from his Manuscript in the possession of the Publisher. London, A. Russell Smith, 1901 (50 copies only).

[196] In Calef, More Wonders of the Invisible World, 1700, pp. 3 ff.

[197] An Answer of a Letter from a Gentleman in Fife, 1705; cf. also A Collection of Rare and Curious Tracts on Witchcraft and the Second Sight, Edinburgh, 1820, pp. 79 ff.

[198] Daily Journal, January 15, 1731, as quoted in the Gentleman's Magazine for 1731, I, 29.

[199] Daines Barrington points with pride to this early abolition of penalties: "It is greatly to the honour of this country, to have repealed all the statutes against this supposed crime so long ago as the year 1736, when laws of the same sort continue in full force against these miserable and aged objects of compassion, in every other part of Europe" (Observations on

the More Ancient Statutes, 3d ed., 1769, p. 367, on 20 Henr. VI).

200 Gough, British Topography, 1780, I, 517.

201 Gentleman's Magazine for 1751, XXI, 186, 198; Wright, Narratives of Sorcery and Magic, II, 326 ff.; Gough, as above, I, 431.

202 Soldan, ed. Heppe, II, 314, 322, 327.

203 See, for example, A. Löwenstimm, Aberglaube und Strafrecht, Berlin, 1897; W. Mannhardt, Die Praktischen Folgen des Aberglaubens, 1878 (Deutsche Zeit- und Streit-Fragen, ed. by F. von Holztendorff, VII, Nos. 97, 98); Wuttke, Der Deutsche Volksaberglaube der Gegenwart, 2d ed., 1869; the chapter on Hexerei und Hexenverfolgung im Neunzehnten Jahrhundert, in Soldan, Geschichte der Hexenprozesse, ed. by Heppe, II, 330 ff.; cf. The Monthly Chronicle of North-Country Lore and Legend, [II,] 1888, p. 394; North Riding Record Society, Publications, IV, 20, note; History of Witchcraft, sketched from the Popular Tales of the Peasantry of Nithsdale and Galloway (R. H. Cromek, Remains of Nithsdale and Galloway Song, 1810, pp. 272 ff.); H. M. Doughty, Blackwood's Magazine, March, 1898, CLXIII, 394-395; Brand's Popular Antiquities, ed. Hazlitt, III, 71, 95, 96, 100 ff.; The Antiquary, XLI, 363; W. G. Black, Folk-Medicine, 1883; Miss Burne, Shropshire Folk-Lore, chap. xiii; W. Henderson, Notes on the Folk-Lore of the Northern Counties, 1879, chap. vi; J. G. Campbell, Witchcraft and Second Sight in the Highlands and Islands of Scotland, 1902; Notes and Queries, 1st Series, VII, 613, XI, 497-498; 3rd Series, II, 325; 4th Series, III, 238, VII, 53, VIII, 44; 5th Series, V, 126, 223, IX, 433, X, 205, XI, 66; 6th Series, II, 145, IV, 510; 7th Series, IX, 425, XI, 43; 8th Series, IV, 186, 192, V, 226, VI, 6, VII, 246; 9th Series, II, 466, XII, 187; the journal, Folk-Lore, *passim.*

204 Cf. Allen Putnam, Witchcraft of New England explained by Modern Spiritualism, Boston, 1880.

205 See pp. 251 ff., above. On the prevalence of occult phenomena in troublous times cf. Froude, History of England from the Fall of Wolsey to the Death of Elizabeth, II (1856), 182-183.

206 Legge, The Scottish Review, XVIII, 262. See also Newes from Scotland declaring the Damnable Life of Dr. Fian, 1591 (Roxburghe Club reprint).

207 Mather Papers, Massachusetts Historical Society Collections, 4th Series, VIII, 366-368. This was the same Joshua Moodey, it will be remembered, who afterwards assisted Philip English and his family to escape from jail in Boston, and thus saved them from

being executed as guilty of witchcraft (Sibley, Harvard Graduates, I, 376-377). . . .

Frederick C. Drake (essay date 1968)

SOURCE: "Witchcraft in the American Colonies, 1647-62," in *American Quarterly,* Vol. XX, No. 4, Winter, 1968, pp. 694-725.

[*In the following excerpt, Drake examines pre-1692 witchcraft cases in the American colonies and finds them to have followed a different pattern from what would later occur in Salem.*]

The witchcraft events that shattered Salem society in 1692 led directly to nineteen human executions by hanging, one by pressing with heavy weights, and the imprisonment of scores of people. Since that date they have also inspired a multitude of narrative accounts and stimulated at least three different controversies among historians.

The first of these controversies dealt with the role of Cotton and Increase Mather in the trials of 1692. Attacks upon the Mathers have varied from insinuations of responsibility for guiding the hysteria, in order to drive people back to church, to open condemnation for being slow to speak out against spectral evidence, a charge of ignoring the rules in judging the presence of witchcraft.[1] During the last quarter of the 19th century a second argument developed over the legality of the courts which dealt with the indictments of 1692 and the adequacy of the compensation awarded to the dependents of those who suffered in the trials. Two of the foremost witchcraft historians of the 1880s, George H. Moore and Albert Goodell Jr., were the chief protagonists in this debate.[2] Yet a third dispute, which arose in the first decade of the 20th century, between George Lyman Kittredge of Harvard and George Lincoln Burr of Cornell, concentrated more intently upon establishing the significance of witchcraft in America. The echoes of this debate, which evaluated the Salem outburst of 1692 within the overall context of European witchcraft, can still be heard today.

Professor Kittredge pointed out that belief in witchcraft was a constant quality in mankind; it was "the common heritage of humanity."[3] Professor Burr dissented sharply from this view, claiming that witchcraft rose and fell in less than five centuries during "the greatest burst of Christian civilization."[4] For Burr witchcraft meant the practice of worshiping the Devil thrown down from Heaven, and using powers gained from him to work evil. As the witch hunters justified their activities by reference to chapters from the Old Testament, it followed that witchcraft was a phenomenon within the Christian religion embracing both New and Old Testament doctrine. Necromancing, spiritualism and types of voodoo lay beyond the scope of this definition, and Burr accordingly rejected Kittredge's more universal view of witchcraft. Obviously, these respective definitions of the phenomenon led toward totally different conclusions. When both historians examined the New England record on witchcraft they differed considerably. Kittredge drew up a list of 21 theses on the subject, the twentieth of which stated: "the record of New England in the matter of witchcraft is highly creditable, when considered as a whole and from the comparative point of view."[5] Burr, however, was unable to acquit his own ancestors upon the grounds that their belief in witchcraft was universal, or was more logical than disbelief. He affirmed that:

> it was superstitious and bigoted and cruel, even by the standards of their own time . . . their final panic [Salem] was the last on such a scale in any Christian land. Their transatlantic home I cannot think an excuse. . . . One thing is sure: we must not blow hot and cold with the same breath. If our fathers were the helpless victims of circumstance, then they were not its masters.[6]

The multiple effect of these three controversies has been to elevate Salem to a position of being the only significant point of reference in colonial witchcraft literature. The prelude to the hysteria of 1692 is usually acknowledged to be the Goodwin case of 1688, when Goodwife Glover was executed in Boston after accusations that she had bewitched four young Goodwin children suffering from convulsions.[7] Cases of witchcraft prior to 1692 have generally served merely as introductory material for the main discussion on Salem. John M. Taylor, an historian who provided evidence of early cases in Connecticut, nevertheless clung to this approach.[8] References to earlier cases are often incorrect on numbers and important details. For example, W. N. Gemmill wrote of "over twenty trials for witchcraft" before 1692, when "many people were convicted and several hung [*sic*]."[9] This estimate alone reduced the numbers indicted to 25% of the actual total and vaguely underestimated the numbers convicted and executed. Rossell Hope Robbins in the excellent *Encyclopedia of Witchcraft and Demonology* concentrated so intently upon Salem that he termed it "the best known name in the entire history of witchcraft." He asserted that the colonial witchcraft delusion was "sporadic and mild and, compared with the holocausts in sixteenth and seventeenth century Europe," it was largely "insignificant." Robbins affirmed, moreover, that the "relative freedom" from witchcraft for the 40 preceding years made the Salem trials overshadow everything else to such an extent that "it may be said the history of American witchcraft is Salem."[10]

In some cases a tendency has developed to dismiss the crisis of 1692 as "a mere bubble in Massachusetts history."[11] Thus Ola E. Winslow in her biography of Samuel Sewall, Salem judge in 1692, has commented that the "sporadic" witchraft cases before the Salem troubles, were "surprisingly few in comparison with the disasters that might so naturally have been attributed to evil spirits in human flesh."[12] A further example can be found in an essay by Stuart Henry upon Puritan character displayed in the Salem crisis. Henry generalized about the entire Puritan response to witchcraft from the one example at Salem. Closely following Kittredge's arguments to exonerate Puritanism, he flatly asserted that "the first vibration of the acute, high-strung Puritan mind to the demons of the spirit world was in Boston, 1688." Consequently, the Salem story polarizes as "one of the few chapters of American history which seems to have a definite beginning, middle and end." In searching for the source of the Salem story Henry observed that some English cases in 1683, "were instances of witchcraft, not in America, but in England, the memory of which might have been in the minds of the American colonists."[13]

Salem has thus become the focal point of historical analysis of colonial witchcraft. The outburst of 1692 has been effectively separated from its American ancestry, and its origins located somewhere in the 1680s. Earlier cases have been ignored and miscounted. For there were over 95 incidents involving colonial people with witchcraft before 1692. Nearly 60 of these incidents occurred between the adoption of the Cambridge platform of 1648 and the acceptance of the Half-Way Covenant of 1662. These incidents led to at least 83 trials between 1647 and 1691 in which 22 people were executed, and many others suffered banishment, whipping and financial loss. Yet, of the 22 executions 20 had taken place between 1647 and 1662, and the first eight occurred in less than four years. . . .

The two questions . . . are, firstly, why did so many cases occur and, secondly, what characteristics did they possess? Both questions may be approached through an analysis of the three factors most likely to contribute to the occurrence of witchcraft activity in a society, namely the theological (or ideological) background of the people suspecting witchcraft, the presence of external stimuli and evidence of internal pressures in society likely to produce an active awareness of witches.[14]

In his monumental survey of the theological framework of Puritan New England, Perry Miller wondered why no more cases of witchcraft had occurred before 1692, "for it was axiomatic that the Devil would try hard to corrupt regions famous for religion." He accepted without reservation, however, that cases of witchcraft before 1692 were "sporadic" but speculated that:

> Perhaps the reason there were so few witches in

New England . . . is . . . the people were good enough Calvinists to resist temptation. They might not always be able to refuse an extra tankard of rum, but this sin—although it was the most plausible and the most enticing—they withstood.[15]

Many of those indicted for witchcraft were judged to have failed in withstanding the sin. This was relatively easy to do for a covenant could be applied with equal diligence to a relationship with the Devil or with God, and the American Puritans were openly confronted with the Indians as positive instruments of Satan's power and determination to conquer New England for himself, permitted to torment all because of God's terrible judgements against his wayward people. Once it had been decided that the assumption of redemption through God's grace no longer applied to an individual, the twin assumption of original sin worked against him with devastating effect. The next step backward was seduction by the Devil, then open covenanting with him. For example, the indictments against Mary Johnson indicated that she was an allegedly lazy servant girl who prayed to the Devil for aid, and "by her own confession shee is guilty of familliarity with the Deuill." The evidence against her cited the fact that she had been able to command the services of a goblin to perform her household duties. When she was chastised for not carrying out the ashes "a Devil afterwards would clear the Hearth of Ashes for her," and when she was sent into the fields to chase out marauding hogs "a Devil would scowre the Hogs away, and make her laugh to see how he scared them." In her confession she admitted uncleanness "both with men and with Devils." At Wethersfield, Connecticut, the indictment against the Carringtons claimed they had "Intertained familiarity with Sathan, the Great Enemy of God and Mankinde," and in the Mary Parsons case the indictment accused her of not having fear of God before her eyes, nor in her heart, seduction by the Devil, familiarity and covenanting with the Devil while having used several devilish practices by witchcraft "to the hurt of the persons of Martha and Rebeckah Moxon," and yielding to the Devil's instigations and "malitious motion." Similarly, in the cases where people were released they were warned, generally, that they were "suspitious of witchcraft." These warnings were given to Mrs. Godman, the Baylys and the Jennings. . . .

Evidence of witchcraft was accumulated in three ways: by confession, by searchings for witchmarks and by the collection of testimonies and accusations of witchcraft. The first two alone meant automatic proof of guilt followed by execution. Margaret Jones was examined and found to possess a Devil's mark, "a teat, as fresh as if [it] had been newly sucked." This revealed where an imp or animal of the Devil had fastened on to her, a physical affirmation of the reversal of the covenant. Both the Staplies and Knapp cases in Connecticut were concerned with the discovery of witch-

marks on Mrs. Knapp's body, and her fate was sealed by seven neighbors who claimed to have seen them. Mrs. Staplies refused to believe Goodwife Knapp was a witch, and suspicion fell on her also. As Mrs. Knapp's body was brought off the gallows, Mrs. Staplies examined it for the alleged witchmarks and found none. Mrs. Lockwood, one of the seven accusers, declared that they had been there; "she had them, and she confessed she was a witch; that is sufficient."[17]

The majority who did withstand the sin of witchcraft did not do so merely as a passive exercise. As the Elect they were presented with Biblical evidence of the existence of witchcraft. They would hardly be good Calvinists if they did not seek out witches, for Calvin stood explicitly by the Old Testament book of Exodus which declared "Thou shalt not suffer a witch to live" and this decree was written into the laws of Massachusetts, Connecticut, New Haven and Plymouth. Upon witchcraft itself Calvin had declared: "now the Bible teaches that there are witches and that they must be slain. God expressly commands that all witches and enchantresses be put to death, and this law of God is a universal law." For this reason the early colonists of New England were good Calvinists precisely because they did search out witches. Witchcraft was not only a "temptation" to resist; it was an evil requiring positive eradication before God.[18]

Consequently, colonial leaders became increasingly concerned during the 1640s with the emergence of witchcraft activity as a manifestation of the Devil's desire to subvert God's Commonwealth. Puritan, Anglican, Pilgrim and Catholic alike took steps to arm themselves with legal protection against his agents. In 1636 Plymouth included in its Summary Offences "lyable to Death," the action of "Solemm Compaction or conversing with the devil by way of Witchcraft, conjuration or the like." The 1641 Massachusetts Bay Body of Liberties and the 1642 Connecticut Capital Code both included, as their second law: "Yf any man or woman be a witch (that is) hath or consulteth with a familiar spirit, they shall be put to death." All three colonies re-enacted these laws in 1646. Rhode Island accepted a witchcraft law on May 19th, 1647, after its charter had been granted. The law stated that "witchcraft is forbidden by this present Assembly to be used in this colony, and the penalty imposed by the authority that we are subjected to, is felony of death." New Haven possessed a law similar to Connecticut's. Armed thus, the colonies were prepared to deal with outbreaks of witchcraft, as well as conform to the laws of England on the subject. By 1662 they had made good use of their legal provisions in a fifteen-year campaign against the Devil's agents in nearly all of the colonies.[19]

While New England laws and religion attempted to undermine the "Great Enemy of God and Mankind," the pressure for an outbreak of witchcraft activity came from overseas. In England, against a background of mounting tension, and later warfare, between King and Parliament, hundreds of witchcraft accusations were made. Between 1645 and 1647 over two hundred witches were executed. The period of greatest slaughter was in the summer of 1645 when Matthew Hopkins, Witch Finder General, was at the height of his campaign to find witches. Altogether, the decade between 1637 and 1647 produced the greatest percentage of hangings per. indictment, 42%, of any period in English witchcraft history. Later still, outbreaks were recorded in Scotland, 1643-50; East Anglia, 1645; Newcastle, 1648; Kent, 1652 and Scotland, 1661. In Europe, the Swedish case of bewitched children, sometimes referred to as the possible inspiration for the Goodwin case of 1688 and the Salem episode of 1692, occurred in 1661.[20]

These persecutions undoubtedly troubled the colonists in New England. Certainly the colonial magistrates knew of English methods of examining suspected witches. In their search for "familiars," witchmarks and imps they were adopting the same practices as Matthew Hopkins. In the very first case brought before the bench at Boston, the Court was "desireows that the same course which hath ben taken in England for the discouery of witches, by watchinge, may also be taken here with the witch now in question." Thus for Margaret Jones the Court ordered that "a strict watch be set about her every night, & that her husband be confined to a priuat roome, & watched also." In Hartford, in 1662, William Ayres and his wife were given the water test, a common European method of determining witchcraft. They failed the test which was sufficient evidence of guilt to warrant execution, and they were in prison after it when they escaped with the aid of friends. The executions at sea in 1654, 1658 and 1659 indicated not only common denominators in the search for witches, but also stimulated witchcraft incidents in the colonies where the vessels landed.[21]

As a series of distressing internal upheavals combined with Old Testament theology in England to generate the witchcraft cases, so too in the colonies did Puritan theology serve as a catalyst to the extraordinary number of distressing events which affected colonial society in the 1640s. A similar state of affairs had prevailed in Salem before the outburst of 1692. Samuel E. Morison has observed that the 1692 episode needed little clerical belief in witchcraft for it arose, "as witchcraft epidemics had usually arisen in Europe, during a troubled period, the *Decennium Luctuosum* of New England History."[22] Morison noted the uneasiness of the people with rebellions, changes of government, fear of Indian attacks, and factional strife within the community. The unsettled state of the colony was further agitated when Increase Mather, after long negotiations, failed to win back the old charter revoked by James II; the colony had to accept a Royal Governor; a boundary dispute broke out with neighboring Topsfield;[23] and the new Governor had to leave for the frontier to lead an expedition against the Indians.

This unrest of the 1692 period was a replica of the distress in the 1640s, particularly in Massachusetts, Connecticut and Plymouth. William Bradford commented upon the wickedness that had grown and broken forth "in a land wher the same was so much witnessed against, and so narrowly looked into, and severly punished." Despite these punishments, Bradford observed "sundrie notorious sins" prevailed in Plymouth, "oftener than once." In analyzing the outbreak of wickedness, he feared that:

> The Divell may carrie a greater spite against the churches of Christ and the gospell hear, by how much the more the indeaour to preserve holynes and puritie amongst them. . . . I would rather thinke thus, then that Satane hath more power in these heathen lands, as some have thought, then in more Christian nations espetially over God's servants in them.[24]

Even greater evidence of unrest existed in Massachusetts. On September 22, 1642, the year after the colony's promulgation of its witchcraft law, John Winthrop drew attention in his journal to the "unsettled frame of spirit" which had led many people to emigrate to the West Indies, to New Amsterdam, Long Island or even back to England. He blamed the "sudden fall of land and cattle"; the scarcity of money and foreign commodities, and people fleeing from the colony, for the unrest in Massachusetts.[25] From that date forward evidence of Satanic intervention in the colony's affairs fills his pages. The corn crop of 1643 was spoiled by pigeons and mice; a great storm swept over Newberry, darkening the air with dirt on July 5, 1643; lights were seen near Boston and over the North East point in January 1644, at the place where Captain Chaddock's pinnace had been blown up, reputedly by a necromancer. A voice was heard calling across the water several times. At Hingham, a man named Painter, who turned Anabaptist and prevented his wife from baptizing their child, even though she was a member of the church, disturbed the Church leaders sufficiently in July for them to have the man whipped for "reproaching the Lord's ordinance." Out of just such small beginnings arose the great tensions leading to the Half-Way Covenant as a solution for the baptismal problems of the children of non-church members. In 1645 the wife of Hartford's Governor, Mrs. Hopkins, lost her reason and understanding. Externally, preparations were made for a second war against the Pequot Indians, for "Sathan may stir up & combine many of his instruments against the Churches of Christ." The Hingham militia had to be lectured by Winthrop on the meanings of liberty to obey their leaders. On August 28, 1645, a day of fasting and humiliation for troubles in Old and New England was held, the third such day to be set aside since 1643. By 1646 the General

Court of Massachusetts was inundated with petitions of grievances. Then came two monumental calamities in 1646-47. The colonies were just struggling back to prosperity after the depression of 1642-43 when the corn, wheat and barley crops were ruined by black worms and caterpillars, which ate the blades and tassels and left the rest to wither. The churches held a day of humiliation. Secondly, in 1647, an epidemic swept the country among Indians, English and Dutch. It weakened the people so much that the gathering of the remaining crops was lost for want of help, even though few died in Massachusetts and Connecticut.[26]

The pessimism that was generated by these plagues was aptly described in the almanacs of a young Harvard intellectual, Samuel Danforth. In 1647 the Harvard "philomathemat" recorded the ordinary occurrences in the colony—the arrival of ships, the coming of winter, and the debilitating effects of the late sickness—in epigrammatic verse. To his first almanac was appended a list of events which optimistically expressed the hopes of the settlers in converting the Indians, and illustrated the expansion of New England towns. In 1648, however, the contents of his verse underwent a marked change. With a painstaking tribute to classical allusion and allegory he ran through all the blessings of the New England scene; a pleasant land in which the Puritan plant, tended by a faithful husbandman, could survive. All of the advantages of Justice, Liberty, Peace, Unity, Truth, Plenty, a Nursery [Harvard College], and the conversion of the Indians, were meticulously spelled out. On the surface this appears to be a hymn of praise to a beneficent providence. But the verses should be examined alongside the chronological table of "some few memorable occurrences" that are listed at the end of the almanac. There Danforth summarized every melancholy event and disaster that had hit the colonies from 1636 to 1647. Nothing was omitted, and the whole checks off exactly with Winthrop's observations. Far from being a hymn of praise, Danforth's verses of 1648 represent an antidote to social, economic and religious distress by referring to classical abstract virtues. With the issue of the 1649 almanac he even removed this escapist cloak. Both his verse content and his table of occurrences list one long series of unhappy events. With intended irony, the young intellectual informed his readers that, even in the midst of their host of troubles, things could still be worse. With England, Ireland, Scotland and Barbadoes racked by war and pestilence, "the worthless Orphan may sit still and blesse, That yet it sleeps in peace and quietness."[27]

In the presence of so many other troubles, the absence of war may have seemed small consolation to New Englanders. For when the synod of 1648 met at Cambridge to settle "such errors, objections, and scruples as had been raised about it by some young heads in the country," the barriers of resistance to the realities of the Devil's work were going down in Connecticut and

Massachusetts. While Winthrop glorified the synod as the triumphant representative of the churches of Christ in New England, his fellow magistrates in Boston and Hartford were finding fresh confirmation of the Devil's malignant concern. As Mary Johnson and Margaret Jones went to their respective scaffolds the whole formula of religious ferment added to social distress and natural disasters, which later characterized the Salem episode, was present in 1647.[28]

Once underway, the witchcraft cases of 1647 to 1662 added to the tension from which they sprang. They did this in a steady stream of cases, year by year, rather than in one frenzied outburst such as occurred in 1692. Yet many of the characteristics of the Salem trials were in evidence in the earlier trials. The indictments were often concerned with the bewitchment of children and animals. Mary Johnson and Mary Parsons were accused of killing their own children by witchcraft. The former had smothered her child, and before execution left another baby, born in prison, to the care of Nathaniel Rescew, the jailer. Mary Parsons, after marrying Hugh Parsons on October 27, 1645, had two sons to him, born October 4, 1649, and October 26, 1650. Both died in less than a year of their births, and the evidence suggests that after the death of the second one, on March 1, 1651, the mother lost her reason. Although denunciations of witchcraft were leveled against Hugh Parsons by his neighbors, it was Mary Parsons who was imprisoned at Boston on May 1, and her case came before the General Court six days later. Later still the cases involving Mrs. Kendal and Goodwife Garlick concerned the deaths of other people's children. Mrs. Kendal was executed for bewitching to death a young child belonging to Goodman Genings of Watertown. The child's nurse testified that Mrs. Kendal had fondled the child, that soon afterward it changed color and died. The Court received this evidence without bothering to call the child's parents. After Mrs. Kendal's execution the parents testified that the child had died of exposure caused by the neglect of the nurse. By this time the latter was in prison for adultery, and she died there. The case ended with no further recantations; striking evidence of how the stigma of witchcraft tainted the innocent and muted inquiry. Further afield, in Easthampton, in the winter of 1657-58, Goodwife Garlick escaped from an identical accusation by a fellow servant, who claimed she had bewitched her child. The head of the household, Lion Gardiner, gave evidence that the baby died from the neglect of the mother, yet the magistrates at Easthampton ordered two men, Thomas Baker and John Hand, to go "into Kenicut for to bring us under their government . . . and also to carry Goodwife Garlick, that she may be delivered up into the authorities there for the triall of the cause of witchcraft [of] which she is suspected."[29]

Some of the evidence in many of the cases concerned the illnesses of witnesses and animals, and accidental occurrences. In Maryland, Peter Godson and his wife alleged that he became lame after seeing the wife of Richard Manship. In the first Mrs. Godman case of 1653, in New Haven, she was accused on May 21, of knowing whatever was done at church meetings, muttering to herself, being responsible for the sickness of the Rev. Mr. Hooke's son, and for the "verey strang fitts wch hath continewed at times ever since," of Mrs. Bishop, who had lost her own children. Later Mrs. Godman quarreled with the wife of the Colonial Treasurer, Mrs. Atwater, who then blamed her when she found Betty Brewster, a servant, ill "in a most misserable case, heareing a most dreadfull noise wch put her in great feare and trembling, wch put her into such a sweate . . . and in ye morning she looked as one yt had bine allmost dead." Three days later, on May 24, 1653, further depositions were made regarding the cause of Mrs. Bishop's fainting fits. As early as 1648 this type of evidence had brought about the conviction of Margaret Jones, blamed when her neighbor's children fell ill.[30]

Illness among animals was often blamed upon the activities of witches. In New Haven, during the first Mrs. Godman case, Mrs. Thorp swore that after she had refused to sell or give some chickens to Mrs. Godman she feared they would be struck down by witchcraft:

> she thought then that if this woman was naught as folkes suspect, may be she will smite my chickens, and quickly after one chicken dyed, and she remembred she had heard if they were bewitched they would consume wthin, and she opened it and it was consumed in ye gisard to water & wormes, and divers others of them droped, and now they are missing and it is likely dead, and she neuer saw either hen or chicken that was so consumed w'hin wth wormes.[31]

Later, in the second and third Godman cases, the testimonies of new witnesses included similar examples. Allen Ball spoke of strange happenings with his calf; Mrs. Thorp added fresh complaints about her cow; and others mentioned troubles with pigs and calves. In Hartford, the Mary Johnson case involved the frightening of hogs by a goblin. During 1659 a deposition was made before Governor Bradstreet of Massachusetts that the Tyler family in Andover had received a visitation from the Devil in the form of a "Thing like a Bird" six years earlier. In 1665 the Tylers renewed their testimonies. The second case in New Hampshire, involving Eunice Cole, was brought before the courts by Goodman Robe who had lost a cow and a sheep. . . .

Even more trivial evidence was accepted as proof of the Devil's evil influences on his agents. Part of the charges against Mrs. Godman dealt with her ability to smell figs in the pockets of Mrs. Atwater when no one else could. The main evidence against Hugh Parsons was given by his wife after she had confessed to witchcraft in May 1651. Her charges included his knowing all of the secrets that she had revealed only to her intimate friend Mrs. Smith; being out late at night; his arrival in a bad temper; putting out the fire; throwing peas about; talking in his sleep and fighting with the Devil. The Jury convicted him on this testimony, but he was acquitted by the General Court. In the Lydia Gilbert case execution followed evidence that she had caused the accidental death of Henry Stiles, two years previously. Any strange occurrence could thus be laid at the witches' doors. In 1657, Thomas Mullener's use of a witchcraft charge, in an attempt to gain personal revenge upon William Meaker, backfired upon the accuser, but the potentialities of the charge remained. Dissatisfaction with a neighbor could easily be converted into accusations of witchcraft. . . .

As the evidence presented to the courts covered a wide range of accusations it also concerned a large number of people. In the trial of Hugh Parsons 39 testimonies were presented to Edward Rawson, clerk of the court. Only nine of these bore the same surname as other witnesses, and at least 30 families were involved in this case at Springfield in 1651. During 1653 and 1654, the Staplies and Knapp trials recorded the names of at least seven people who had accused Mrs. Knapp and then accused Mrs. Staplies of witchcraft. For the latter case 18 more added their contributions to the evidence. In addition five people went to see Mrs. Knapp in prison. Altogether 30 people were involved in this case, 22 of whom possessed different surnames. Two of the witnesses, Deborah Lockwood and Bethia Brundish were seventeen and sixteen years old respectively. In New Haven, Nicholas Bayly and his wife were called before a court and informed that "sundrie passages taken in writing . . . doth render them both, but especially the woman, very suspitious in poynt of witchcraft. . . . "

With large numbers in small communities that were closely clustered, the news of witchcraft was carried from one region to another on the wings of gossip. This gossip was often sufficient to stimulate a search for other witches. Mary Parsons' charges against her husband included a declaration that "you tould her that you were at a Neighbor's Howse a little before Lecture, when they were speaking of Carrington and his Wife, that were now apprhended for Witches," thus establishing a direct link with the execution of the Carringtons of Wethersfield. In the Staplies' case, Goodwife Sherwood's written testimony against Staplies revealed much of the preoccupation with witchcraft, as well as intercommunity awareness:

> so the next day she went in againe to see the witch with other neighbours, there was Mr. Jones, Mris. Pell & her two daughters, Mris. Ward and goodwife Lockwood . . . Elizabeth [Mrs. Pell's daughter] bid

her [Knapp] doe as the witch at the other towne [Bassett] did, that is, discouer all she knew to be witches.[35]

The spread of tragic examples from New England implicated other areas in witchcraft activity. Virginia experienced the first effects of the dangers inherent in gossiping over witches in May 1655. At a private court in Linhaven, the following resolution was passed:

Whereas divrs dangerous & scandalous speeches have been raised by some psons concerning sevrall women in this Countie, termeing them to be Witches, whereby their reputacons have been much impaired and their lives brought in question (ffor avoydeing the like offence). It is by this Cort ordered that what pson soever shall hereafter raise any such like scandall, concerninge any partie whatsor, and shall not be able to pve the same, both upon oath, and by sufficient witness, such pson soe offending shall in the first place paie a thousand pounds of tob: and likewise by lyable to further Censure of the Cort.[36]

It was in the face of this resolution that the Rev. David Lindsaye proved his case against William Harding in 1656, and Ann Godby failed to prove her case against Mrs. Nicholas Robinson in 1659. Virginia and Maryland's first cases followed immediately after the excitements of the shipboard hangings that were brought to light in their courts, but the cases resembled New England cases so closely that it is difficult to say which was the major cause of witchcraft spreading to these areas. From the colonists' point of view it was not important. What had occurred was an extension of the Devil's activities. While still interested primarily in Puritan New England, the "Great Enemy" was conducting flanking operations along the shores of Catholic Maryland and Anglican Virginia. He also appeared across the New Hampshire border. . . .

In addition to large numbers of people generating the searches for witches in their own communities, leading to inquiries in other towns, many of these cases reveal a curious comparison with the Salem outburst of 1692. That frenzy had occurred in the absence of the Governor, away fighting the Indians. Similarly, the cases of 1647-62 often developed in the absence of the colonial governors, and were directly connected with the Deputy Governors, leading officials and prominent clergymen. In 1653, all of the eminent citizens of New Haven society were implicated when Elizabeth Godman, a woman possessing a quick temper and the ability to antagonize her own sex, became the subject of malicious gossip by a clique gathered around the wives of Deputy Governor Stephen Goodyeare, Colonial Treasurer, Mr. Atwater, and the Rev. Mr. Hooke. As she was attached to the Goodyeare household, Mrs. Godman was easily accessible as the center of attraction and the rumors spread. After being locked out of the Atwater house one day, Mrs. Godman proceeded to alarm the Rev. Mr. Hooke by maintaining that witches should not be provoked but, instead, brought into the church. This doctrine shocked Hooke, and as he was troubled in his sleep about witches at the time of his son's sickness he centered his uneasiness upon Mrs. Godman. She proved as resourceful as her adversaries, and won the day by carrying the fight to them by summoning all of her tormentors before the magistrates, and complaining of them for suspecting her of being a witch. After reviewing all of the evidence, which included a claim that "Hobbamocke" [the Indian Devil] was her husband, the Court pointed out that Mrs. Godman was known as a liar, and it found the defendants not guilty. Moreover, it warned her that she had "vnjustly called heither the seuerall psons before named, being she can proue nothing against them, and that her cariage doth justly render her suspitious of witchcraft, wch she herselfe in so many words confesseth." The Court warned her to watch her conduct afterward, for in the event of further proof being presented, "these passages will not be forgotten." Credit has been given to the Court of Magistrates for its forbearance in withstanding the force of contemporary pressure, and to Governor Eaton for judiciously distinguishing between "a cross grained temper and possession by a devil," but Mrs. Godman also deserves credit for her astute legal move as opinion began to build against her. It became exceedingly difficult to find her guilty of witchcraft when she was the plaintiff, however much the Court might pass opinions upon her. . . .

The Knapp and Staplies cases developed in New Haven and Connecticut in 1653 when Deputy Governor Roger Ludlow of Connecticut accused the two women. In the course of the trial Ludlow reported that Goodwife Knapp had revealed that Mrs. Staplies was her accomplice. Mrs. Knapp had refused to incriminate anyone, especially when seven of her neighbors constantly placed Mrs. Staplies' name before her. Mrs. Staplies refused to believe that Knapp had witchmarks, or was a witch. When she protested against the searchings for witchmarks she was howled down by the seven old harridans, and then accused by Ludlow. Her husband, Thomas, cross-sued for defamation. Before the court met at New Haven, May 29, 1654, Mrs. Staplies gained an ally, the Rev. Mr. Davenport, who testified that Ludlow had told him that Mrs. Knapp had come down from the gallows and revealed Mrs. Staplies as a witch. Ludlow protested that he had told this to Davenport in strictest confidence, but Davenport testified on oath that he had been careful to make no unlawful promises to Ludlow to keep any confidences and secrets, and that with God's help he would keep only lawful promises. His evidence thus meant that Ludlow had been guilty of defaming Mrs. Staplies. Even though Ludlow marshaled impressive evidence that Mrs. Staplies admitted to possessing witchmarks if Goodwife Knapp did, the Court, pressed by Staplies' lawyer, would not accept unsworn testimony for Ludlow, and the case went against him. But it had needed the active intervention of one of the founding fathers of New Haven, invoking the righteousness of his oaths before God, to thwart Ludlow's charges.[39]

In other areas witches were not as fortunate. Deputy Governor Richard Bellingham of Salem was powerless to save his sister, Anne Hibbins, in 1656. But the Hartford case of 1662, when a whole coven of witches was condemned, proved the most disastrous for the accused, when Governor Winthrop was absent in England gaining a charter. The case had a further similarity to Salem in 1692, for the accusations were inspired by two young children. In spring 1662, the eight-year-old daughter of John Kelley cried out in delirium before she died that Goodwife Ayres had bewitched her. William Ayres and his wife were arrested and given the water test. Then James Walkley fled to Rhode Island. The net gathered in Judith Varleth, sister-in-law of the Governor of New Amsterdam, Peter Stuyvesant. On May 13, 1662, Nathaniel Greensmith filed suit against the Ayres for slander of witchcraft, but then the Greensmiths were arrested. Mary Sanford was indicted for the same offense. Nathaniel Greensmith had a criminal record for stealing, and his wife, married twice previously, was described by the Rev. John Whiting as a "lewd, ignorant and considerably aged woman." After the daughter of John Kelley died, the accusations were maintained by Ann Cole, daughter of John Cole, a neighbor of the Greensmiths. She was afflicted with fits, muttering in a Dutch tongue when she did not know the language, and cried out that a company of devils was conspiring to ruin her. She then denounced Goodwife Seager for bewitching her. This woman was indicted for witchcraft three times between 1662 and 1665, and was only released when Governor Winthrop postponed a death sentence upon her, releasing her in 1666. Rebecca Greensmith, under the promptings of the Rev. Mr. Hooke of Farmington, admitted the charges against her, implicated her husband, and set in motion the train of events that led to the executions of four people, the fleeing of several others and the disruption of Hartford society. . . .

Why the Deputy Governors and more prominent religious leaders should be active as participants within the witchcraft cases, and not merely concerned with stamping them out, is difficult to discern. One possibility is that the frustrations attached to a position one level removed from actual power in the colonies concerned may have spilled over into energetic involvement with witch searches. The absence of superior authorities would have given them their chances. Furthermore, they had a compelling desire to prove their worthiness to lead the colonists at a time when

the first-generation leaders were dying.[41] They were being called on to lead at a time of spiritual depression. As liberty of conscience was becoming a subject for acrimonious debate, Charles Chauncey complained in 1665 that there was to be found in New England "the contempt of the word of God and his Ordinancies, and listening to lying books & pamphlets, that are brought over into the country whereby multitudes are poysoned amongst us." The next year Thomas Shepherd Jr. worried that "this land which sometimes flourished: Shall in a dying state be found." By 1662, Michael Wigglesworth was ready to condemn, among the hosts who trembled on the day of judgment, those "Witches, Inchanters and Ale-House-haunters" who faced their final doom. In offering reasons for the Truth of the Doctrine of God, John Higginson, pastor at Salem, warned his audience that "Satan from the beginning hath had an old grudge against the seed of the Woman, and he never wanted instruments, who either by force or fraud or both, have done what mischief they could against the Church and cause of God." Well might Edward Johnson declare, therefore, that "now N. E. that had such heaps upon heaps of the riches of Christ's tender compassionate mercies, being turn'd off from his dandling knees, began to read their approaching rod in the bend of his brows and frowns of his former favourable countenance toward them."[42]

From 1647 to 1662 witchcraft incidents and cases spread across the colonies into Maryland, New Hampshire, New Haven, old Plymouth Colony and Virginia, from the original bases in Connecticut and Massachusetts. After 1663 there was still a steady progression of cases, year by year, and they spread still further into New York. Pennsylvania, North and South Carolina.[43] But only two executions took place between 1662 and 1691, and it is evident that the colonial magistrates and governors seriously questioned the wisdom of executions as a remedy for control after 1662. Before 1662, however, it is equally evident that they used executions as a legitimate weapon against the Devil's handmaidens. Their aim was to suppress the work of those covenanting with the Devil. Consequently, this sixteen-year period from 1647 to 1662 produced over 50 indictments and 20 executions, three banishments, three people fleeing to Rhode Island, two water tests, three long-term imprisonments, and at least two whippings, one of which could be prevented by paying a fine. In terms of executions alone, the percentage returns of 40% compare as highly as the witchcraft execution rate in England at the height of the 1637-47 period. By 1662 the English percentage rate was well below that figure.

This period of witchcraft has several obvious similarities with the Salem episode. But two differences also stand out. By 1692 evidence of witchcraft had been before the public eye for 45 years. The Devil had a solid footing, and to rout him it would require a tremendous effort. In 1647, by contrast, there was no colonial reservoir of cases and prosecutions. The Great Enemy of God and Mankind was then attempting to gain a footing in order to subvert God's Commonwealth in the wilderness, and the early leaders were just as grimly determined that he would not succeed. That they failed is evident from the chain of events culminating in 1692. But in documenting the Devil's advance, the New England ministers, especially the Mathers, went out of their way to record some, though not all, of the earlier cases. To them the urge to provide some background for their own dilemma was compelling. Yet they started out with the Ann Cole case involving the Greensmiths in 1662, in order to illustrate the wonderful providences of the invisible world. Nathaniel Mather chided Increase in 1684 for omitting earlier examples as evidence, but the authors were more concerned with presenting earlier cases merely as evidence that the Devil did exist; thus atheists would be refuted. Consequently, historians relying upon them have accepted their intention and missed an opportunity to demonstrate that their ancestors were faced with an outbreak before 1692, and that they dealt with it severely. Salem should be studied as part of the witchcraft in America, and not as an isolated example. The background, as well as the peculiarities of 1692, is worth examining. Because Salem judges were to deal with their witches in the strange way of hanging those protesting their innocence and releasing those admitting their guilt, the reverse logic of covenant theology applied in 1692 has always attracted historians. The cases of 1647-62 followed a more normal pattern; confession was followed by execution. From that point of view the earlier period of witchcraft was the more orthodox one in the colonies, and Salem was the aberration.

Notes

[1] The Mathers have been charged with much more than this. Robert Calef, *More Wonders of the Invisible World,* in *Narratives of the Witchcraft Cases: 1647-1706,* ed. George Lincoln Burr (New York, 1914), pp. 296-393; George Bancroft, *History of the United States* (Boston, 1857), III, 75-99; Vernon Louis Parrington, *Main Currents of American Thought* (New York, 1927), I, 115-17; and C. W. Upham, *Salem Witchcraft* (Boston, 1867), *passim,* all placed the Mathers in the forefront of those who contributed to the hysteria of the time. For the whole controversy see Charles W. Upham, *Salem Witchcraft with an Account of Salem Village, and a History of Opinion on Witchcraft and Kindred Subjects* (Boston, 1867) and his *Salem Witchcraft and Cotton Mather: A Reply* (Morrisana, N.Y., 1869); W. F. Poole, "Cotton Mather and Salem Witchcraft," *North American Review,* CVIII (Apr. 1869), 337-97; Poole, *Cotton Mather and Salem Witchcraft: two Notices of Mr. Upham his Reply* (1870); Poole, "Witch-

craft at Boston," in *The Memorial History of Boston: 1630-1880,* ed. Justin Winsor (Boston, 1881) II, 131-72; *Narratives,* ed. Burr, pp. 291-93; and G. H. Moore's review of the respective parts played by Calef and the Mathers in "Bibliographical Notes on Witchcraft in Massachusetts," American Antiquarian Society, *Proceedings,* n. s., V (1888), 245-73. For more recent sympathetic views of Mather see Clifford K. Shipton, "New England Clergy of the 'Glacial Age,'" Colonial Society of Massachusetts, *Publications,* XXXII (Dec. 1933), 23-54; M. L. Starkey, *The Devil in Massachusetts* (New York, 1949), chap. 20. On Calef one should consult W. S. Harris, "Robert Calef, Merchant of Boston," *Granite Monthly,* n. s., XXXIX (May 1907), 157-63.

[2] George H. Moore, "Notes on the History of Witchcraft in Massachusetts," American Antiquarian Society, *Proceedings,* n. s., II (Oct. 1882), 162-92; Moore, "Supplementary Notes on Witchcraft in Massachusetts: a Critical Examination of the Alleged Law of 1711 for Reversing the Attainder of the Witches of 1692," Massachusetts Historical Society, *Proceedings,* 2nd ser., I (1884), 77-98; Moore, *Final Notes on Witchcraft in Massachusetts: a Summary Vindication of the Laws and Liberties concerning Attainders with Corruption of Blood, Escheats, Forfeitures for Crime, and Pardon of Offenders in Reply to the "Reasons," etc. of A. C. Goodell* (New York, 1885); Abner C. Goodell Jr., "The Trial of the Witches in Massachusetts," Massachusetts Historical Society, *Proceedings,* XX (June 1883), 280-326; Goodell, *Further Notes on the History of Witchcraft in Massachusetts* (Cambridge, 1884) and his rebuttal to Moore's "Supplementary Notes . . ." in Massachusetts Historical Society, *Proceedings,* 2nd ser., I (1884), 99-118. The meeting of the Massachusetts Historical Society in Sept. 1883 had several letters and a debate upon Goodell's paper, *Proceedings,* XX (Sept. 1883), 327-33. There is a survey of the controversy in Justin Winsor, "The Literature of Witchcraft in New England," American Antiquarian Society, *Proceedings,* n. s., X (Oct. 1895), 371-73. With it should be read Henry W. Belknap, "Philip English, Commerce Builder," American Antiquarian Society, *Proceedings,* n. s., XLI (Apr. 1931), 17-24.

[3] G. L. Kittredge, "Notes on Witchcraft," American Antiquarian Society, *Proceedings,* n. s., XVII (Apr. 1907), 210.

[4] G. L. Burr, "New England's Place in the History of Witchcraft," American Antiquarian Society, *Proceedings,* n. s., XXI (Oct. 1911), 186-87, 217.

[5] Kittredge, American Antiquarian Society, *Proceedings,* XVII, 211-12.

[6] Burr, American Antiquarian Society, *Proceedings,* XXI, 215-16.

[7] For estimates of the importance of this case for the Salem trials see the works cited above, or Samuel E. Morison, "Charles Morton," Colonial Society of Massachusetts, *Publications,* XXXII (1940), xxvi.

[8] John M. Taylor, *The Witchcraft Delusion in Colonial Connecticut: 1647-1697* (New York, 1908), pp. 24-25.

[9] W. N. Gemmill, *The Salem Witch Trials, a chapter of New England History* (Chicago, 1924), p. 45. Compare also with Caroline E. Upham, *Salem Witchcraft in Outline* (Salem, 1891), p. 6.

[10] Rossell H. Robbins, *The Encyclopedia of Witchcraft and Demonology* (New York, 1959), pp. 519-20.

[11] John Noble, "Some Documentary Fragments touching the Witchcraft Episode of 1692," Colonial Society of Massachusetts, *Publications,* X (Dec. 1904), 12-26.

[12] Ola Elizabeth Winslow, *Samuel Sewall of Boston* (New York, 1964), p. 115, wrote also that not one of the earlier cases "aroused widespread hysteria." A similar comment was made by Perry Miller, *The New England Mind from Colony to Province* (Cambridge, 1953), p. 179.

[13] Stuart C. Henry, "Puritan Character in the Witchcraft Episode of Salem," in *A Miscellany of American Christianity: Essays in Honor of H. Shelton Smith,* ed. Stuart C. Henry (Durham, N. C., 1963), pp. 148, 165, 142.

[14] There is another area of witchcraft analysis based upon the collection of colorful tales, legends and folklore of witches and witchcraft, rather than court records, in the manner of the epic songs examined by A. B. Lord, *The Singer of Tales* (Cambridge, 1960). The best examples are Joseph F. Folsom, "Witches in New Jersey," New Jersey Historical Society, *Proceedings,* n. s., VII (1922), 293-305; Tom Peete Cross, *Studies in Philology,* XVI, 217-87; Mary L. Deaver, "Witchcraft in Buttermaking," *Ross County Historical Society* Pamphlet (Chillicothe, Ohio, 1958); Nelson E. Jones, "Witchcraft in Lawrence Country," from his book *The Squirrel Hunters of Ohio, or, Glimpses of Pioneer Life* (Ohio Valley Folk Publications, n. s., p. 100); Albert Douglas, "Ohio's only Witchcraft Case," *Ohio Archaeological and Historical Publications,* XXXIII (1924), 205-14.

[15] Perry Miller, *The New England Mind: From Colony to Province* (Cambridge, 1953), p. 179. . . .

[17] Readers familiar only with the procedure at Salem in 1692, where confession was followed by release should note that confession by witches was proof of guilt, and led to execution under the Statute of James, 1604. Salem judges reversed this process. Witchmarks revealed where a witch had allowed a devil or an imp to "fasten" on to her, a physical reaffirmation of the reverse covenant. See Joseph Glanvil, *Saducisimus Triumphant* (London, 1689), pp. 75-76. . . .

[18] Calvin's pronouncements upon witchcraft are clearly analyzed in Burr, American Antiquarian Society, *Proceedings,* XXI, 198-99.

[19] *Records of the Colony of New Plymouth in New England,* ed. David Pulsifer (Boston, 1861), XI, 12, 95, 172; *The Public Records . . . Connecticut,* ed. Trumbull, I, 77; Drake, *Annals of Witchcraft,* p. 56; Taylor, *Witchcraft Delusion,* pp. 23.24; "Laws of Rhode Island," Massachusetts Historical Society, *Collections,* 2nd ser., VII (Boston, 1818), 79, n2. Samuel G. Drake believed that early activity led to the Plymouth laws. John Winthrop in 1639 noted that "the Indians near Aquiday being pawwawing in this tempest, the devil came and fetched away five of them." See John Winthrop, *Journal,* 1, 297; Edward Johnson. *Wonder-Working Providence,* p. 237; Josiah Gilbert Holland, *History of Western Massachusetts. The Counties of Hampden, Hampshire, Franklin and Berkshire* (Springfield, 1885), I, pt. I 40-41; Cross, *Studies in Philology,* XVI, 221, n9, who pointed out that "accusations of witchcraft are found in Virginia records as early as 1641." James R. Jacob, *"The Phantastick Air": The Idea of the Praelernatural in Colonial New England* (Master's thesis, Rice University, May 1964), gives an excellent treatment of the bases and assumptions of colonial attitudes to witchcraft theory, especially pp. 21-22, 47-67 and 69-87.

[20] For the European background see *Narratives,* ed. Burr, pp. xv-xvi; Burr, "The Literature of Witchcraft," *Papers of the American Historical Association,* IV (July 1890), 37-66 and American Antiquarian Society, *Proceedings,* XXI, 185-217; Kittredge, American Antiquarian Society, *Proceedings,* XVII, 8, 148-212 and his *Witchcraft in Old and New England* (New York, 1928); *Materials toward a History of Witchcraft,* ed. Henry C. Lea (Philadelphia, 1939) gives great detail of cases all over Europe and C. L'Estrange Ewen, *Witch Hunting and Witch Trials: the indictments for Witchcraft from the Records of 1373 Assizes held for the Home Circuit, A. D. 1559-1736* (London, 1929), pp. 1-115, esp. 31, 42, 100, 112-13. Ewen's statistical tables will cause many revisions of witchcraft estimates, especially in the corrections of exaggerated claims of witch executions in the Commonwealth period.

[21] The water test, whereby a suspected witch was thrown into a pond with the thumbs cross-tied to the opposite big toes, was a common European method of determining witchcraft. It was based upon the assumption that the pure element would not receive an

agent of the devil. If one floated one was regarded as a witch, and if one sank one was innocent, though often drowned! . . .

[22] Samuel E. Morison, *The Puritan Pronaos* (New York, 1963), p. 259.

[23] Abbie W. Towne, "William Towne, his daughters and the Witchcraft Delusion," Topsfield Historical Society, *Collections,* I (1895), 12-14; Abbie Peterson Towne & Marietta Clark, "Topsfield in the Witchcraft Delusion," *ibid.,* XIII (1908), 23-38; George Francis Dow, "Witchcraft Records Relating to Topsfield," *ibid.,* pp. 39-143.

[24] William Bradford, *History of Plymouth Plantation* (Boston, 1912), II, 308-9.

[25] John Winthrop, *Journal,* II, 82, 83-84. He noted "they fled from fear of want, and many of them fell into it, even to extremity, as if they had hastened into the misery which they feared and fled from."

[26] *Ibid.,* II, 92, 126, 155-56, 177, 225, 229-39. See also John Winthrop, *A Declaration of Former Passages and Proceedings Between the English and the Narragansets* (Boston, 1645), p. 7; George Parker Winship, *The Cambridge Press: 1638-1692* (Philadelphia, 1945), pp. 64-65; Edward Johnson, *Wonder-Working Providence,* p. 237, n2, p. 238, n1, pp. 240-41 and Samuel Danforth, *An Almanac for 1647* (Cambridge, 1647), list of notable events for the years 1646 and 1647; Danforth, *An Almanac for 1648* (Cambridge, 1648), A chronological table of some few memorable instances, years 1646 and 1647.

[27] Danforth, *Almanacs* for 1646, 1647, 1648 and *An Almanac for 1649* (Cambridge, 1649), lines 87-88.

[28] John Winthrop, *Journal,* II, 347. There is a remarkable observation by Charles Francis Adams in *Massachusetts: Its Historians and Its History* (Boston, 1893), pp. 85-86. Writing upon the witch cases at Salem in 1692, he noted, "The New England historians have usually regarded this curious and interesting period as an isolated phenomenon, to be described as such, and then palliated it by references to the far more ferocious and unthinking maniacal outbreaks of like nature in other lands at about the same time. . . . The mania of 1691-92 in Massachusetts was no isolated or inexplicable manifestation . . . given John Winthrop's journal in 1630-40, Salem witchcraft at a somewhat later period might with safety be predicted. The community was predisposed to the epidemic. . . . " This single reference to Salem and Winthrop's *Journal* indicated that Adams had made the connection between witchcraft and the unrest of the 1640s. All he lacked was the specific information of the cases in these years.

[29] In 1651 Massachusetts held a solemn day of prayer "to consider how far Satan prevails amongst us in respect of witchcraft." See Robbins, *Encyclopedia of Witchcraft,* p. 520. Exactly the same decision was made in 1688, following the Goodwin case, but then it was confined only to Boston and Charlestown. See Cotton Mather, *Magnalia Christi Americana,* II, 457. Fifty years after Mary Johnson's death, Cotton Mather concluded with unintended irony that "she dy'd in a frame extreamly to the satisfaction of them that were spectators of it," which meant that she repented under the guidance of the Rev. Mr. Stone, her minister. See *The Public Records . . . Connecticut,* ed. Trumbull, I, 209, 222, 226 and 232. In 1646 Mary Johnson had been whipped for thievery and sentenced at the Particular Court, Aug. 21, 1646, *ibid.,* I, 143. For the reference to Mather see *Magnalia Christi Americana,* II, 456.

[30] For the clique gathered around "Mr. Goodyeare, Mris. Goodyeare, Mr. Hooke, Mris. Hooke, Mris. Bishop, Mris. Atwater, Hanah and Elizabeth Lamberton [sisters of Mrs. Bishop], and Mary Miles, Mris. Atwater's maide," see *Records of New Haven . . . 1653 to the Union,* ed. Hoadley, pp. 31-34.

[31] Complaint of Goodwife Thorp, June 16, 1653, after the examination of Mrs. Godman, May 24, 1653, *ibid.,* p. 36. . . .

[35] Testimony of Mrs. Parsons in Drake, *Annals of Witchcraft,* p. 233. Mrs. Parsons continued "I hope that God will find all such wicked Psons and purge New England of all Witches ere it be long" (p. 234); Taylor, *Witchcraft Delusion,* p. 136, for Goodwife Sherwood's testimony.

[36] "Lower Norff: At a private Cort held the 23 day of May, 1655, at the home of Mr. Edward Hall in Linhaven. . . . " in James, *William & Mary Quarterly,* I, 58-60. . . .

[39] The instances of vindictiveness and crowd consensus about witchcraft and witchmarks are shown clearly in the testimonies of the witnesses presented to the court of magistrates "held at New Hauen, for the Jurisdiction, 29 of May, 1654." . . .

[41] In 1643 Plymouth lost William Brewster, a stalwart of "this poore persecuted church above 36. years in England, Holand, and in this wildernes." William Bradford, *History of Plymouth Plantation,* II, 342; and in 1644 George Philips, pastor of the church at Watertown died. By 1647 the Connecticut Valley flock had been left leaderless by the death of Thomas Hooker, pastor of the church at Hartford. Hooker was soon followed by Mr. Green, pastor of the church at Reading, and by the end of the decade Massachusetts had lost Governor Winthrop and Thomas Shepherd, pastor at Cambridge. The cream of colonial leadership was

skimmed further in the 1650s: John Cotton died in 1652; William Bradford and John Wilson, pastor of the first church in Boston in 1657; and the remote, but still "Lord Protector" Cromwell in 1658.

[42] Charles Chauncey, *God's Mercy Shewed to His People in Giving Them A Faithful Ministry and Schooles of Learning for the Continual Supplyes Thereof* (Cambridge, 1655), p. 19; Thomas Shepherd Jr., *An Almanac for the year 1656* (Cambridge, 1656), verse for February; Michael Wigglesworth, *The Day of Doom*, verse 33; John Higginson, *The Cause of God and His People in New England . . . in a sermon preached before the . . . General Court of the Massachusetts Colony, 27 May 1663* (Cambridge, 1663), p. 7, and Johnson, *Wonder-Working Providence*, p. 252.

[43] Cases and incidents of witchcraft occurred at different places in the colonies for all but the years 1666-67, 1672, 1677-78, 1687 and 1689-90, before Salem.

Richard Godbeer (essay date 1992)

SOURCE: "Rape of a Whole Colony: The 1692 Witch Hunt," in *The Devil's Dominion: Magic and Religion in Early New England*, Cambridge University Press, 1992, pp. 179-222.

[*In the following excerpt, Godbeer explores the ways in which catastrophes and threats of invasion created widespread fear and xenophobia in pre-1692 New England.*]

. . . Until 1675, the northern colonies had enjoyed relative peace, stability, and prosperity. Over the previous fifty years, the English colonists had transformed a patchwork of scattered and vulnerable settlements into a well-organized and seemingly permanent colonial society. The New Englanders lived in peace, albeit an uneasy peace, with the Dutch in New York and the French in Canada. Since 1636, their conflicts with the native Americans had been sporadic and minimally disruptive. The settlers had constructed an efficient and representative political system that gave loyal support to an entrenched but responsive leadership. Religious and civil institutions had succeeded in enforcing at least a facade of Puritan orthodoxy; for all the ministers' concern about the future, New England's spiritual mission was apparently intact. The achievements of the last fifty years were, then, impressive. But the events of the next two decades would demonstrate just how fragile many of those achievements really were.

During the final quarter of the seventeenth century, a series of disasters convulsed the northern colonies and brought New England to the brink of destruction. The first of these disasters was Metacomet's War (sometimes called King Philip's War) of 1675-6. Relations with the native Americans had deteriorated over the two decades previous to the war. Continued English appropriation of native land, the colonial government's insistence that native Americans acknowledge English laws, and the settlement of several thousand native converts to Christianity in "praying Indian" towns had gradually convinced native Americans that the English settlers posed a fundamental threat to their survival as autonomous peoples. In 1675, a court at Plymouth Colony convicted and executed three members of the Wampanoag tribe for the murder of a "praying Indian" called Sassoman. The Wampanoags' chief, Metacomet, responded by ordering his tribesmen to attack the colony. From June to December 1675, native Americans ravaged the interior of Massachusetts and Plymouth Colony. Guerrilla warfare continued through 1676 and at one point Metacomet's forces came within twenty miles of Boston itself. The English eventually defeated and dispersed the Wampanoags and their al ies, but not before they had sustained terrible losses. One in every sixteen men of military age died as a result of the war. Many other men, women, and children were either killed in raids, carried off into captivity by the native Americans, or died of starvation and exposure. Hundreds more fell victim to a smallpox epidemic in 1677-8.[9] By the end of the war, twelve towns had been completely destroyed and half the towns in New England badly damaged. The war cost almost one hundred thousand pounds and all but crippled the colonial economy. By any standards, this was a catastrophe for New England.[10]

If Metacomet's assault brought into question the very survival of the northern colonies, the imperial government in London became a no less fundamental threat to the colonists' way of life during the decade following. In the late 1670s and early 1680s, the English crown tried to establish a closer control over the affairs of its American colonies, particularly in matters of trade. None of the colonies were eager to cooperate with the government's wishes, but Massachusetts was particularly stubborn in its refusal to compromise over the exercise of royal authority within its boundaries. This recalcitrance infuriated the rising imperialist faction within the English government. Eventually, London lost patience with Massachusetts and decided to abandon negotiation in favor of a more radical and draconian solution. In 1684, the English crown revoked Massachusetts' charter. Two years later, it incorporated all eight colonies stretching northward from New Jersey into a new imperial structure, the Dominion of New England.

The Dominion took power away from colonists and placed it in the hands of royal officials. New Englanders would no longer elect their own governor and ruling council; these would now be royal appointments. There would be no representative assembly. Town meetings would take place only once a year, and then only for the election of local officials. Perhaps most ominous of all in light of recent English history, the government could levy taxation without popular consent. The New Englanders had placed democratic procedures at the very center of their public life; the dismantling of representative institutions that now ensued constituted nothing less than a political revolution. The new regime's land policy was no less radical in its implications. Hitherto, each township had itself controlled the distribution of land within its boundaries. Royal officials now announced that all land grants except for those given by the General Court and bearing the colony's official seal were invalid; all those whose deeds were in doubt had to petition the new government for a legitimate patent. In other words, landowners were to become formally dependent upon the crown for the titles to their land.

Edmund Andros, governor of the Dominion, epitomized the authoritarian spirit of the new regime. Andros, a career soldier who had spent many years as governor of New York, was temperamentally as autocratic as his royal master James II. The governor's personal style was domineering and offensive, as was the administration of which he was the head. Andros not only behaved like a Stuart, but he also looked the part. The governor dressed like a London courtier and shocked Bostonians by attending a Harvard commencement wearing a scarlet coat and flowing wig.

Not only did the Andros regime emasculate local government and threaten property rights, but it also failed to protect the frontier settlements from native American attacks. The governor's attempts to negotiate a peace with the native Americans collapsed and his costly military expedition to Maine in the winter of 1688-9 was a dismal failure. Indeed, native American tribesmen were so successful in evading the governor's forces that some colonists began to suspect a secret alliance between their new master and the native Americans. Andros had now lost all credibility. When news of James II's downfall reached northern America in 1689, New Englanders responded with uncharacteristic unanimity and overthrew the Dominion. On 18 April 1689, the people of Boston arrested Andros and his supporters in a bloodless coup. Both the royal fort on Castle Island and the royal frigate moored in Boston harbor surrendered on the following day. A month later, delegates from all over Massachusetts convened in Boston and instructed an interim government to administer the colony according to the old charter. The colonists requested that Increase Mather, who was already in London protesting against the Dominion, now negotiate a permanent settlement with the royal government.[11]

No sooner had New Englanders thrown off the shackles of the Dominion than they had to face another threat in the form of renewed native American attacks. With the accession of William and Mary to the English throne, Louis XIV of France declared war on England and its colonies. The war in northern America took the form of French-inspired native American raids along the New England frontier, no part of which was left unthreatened. These were dark years for the northern colonies. Their expedition against Quebec in 1690 was a disastrous failure. The unruliness of returned soldiers, the heavy losses sustained by merchants who had helped to finance the expedition, and the general economic effects of curtailed trade with France spread fear and despondency throughout New England. In late 1690, another smallpox epidemic ravaged Massachusetts and morale there reached a new low.[12] It was at this point that the native Americans launched a series of attacks on the Massachusetts backcountry. Until 1691, they had concentrated their efforts on the northern reaches of New England, but in the summer of that year, native Americans attacked Lancaster, Brookfield, and Billerica.[13]

The native American assault on Massachusetts in 1691 coincided with the appearance of yet another major threat. The new charter, ratified that year, gave freedom of worship to all dissenters from Congregationalism. During his brief tenure as governor of the colony, Edmund Andros had taken initial steps toward the disestablishment of Congregationalism in New England. Andros had forced the South Church in Boston to let Anglicans hold weekly services there. He also appropriated a plot of common land for the construction of a separate Anglican chapel. These measures scandalized Congregationalists. When the Dominion collapsed in 1689, New England Puritans hoped that they could now put behind them the governor's unwelcome experiment in liberty of conscience. But the charter of 1691 gave its blessing to public heterodoxy and enfranchised dissenting groups such as Quakers and Anglicans. This was a direct blow to the Congregationalists' privileged position within the community.[14]

New England, then, was under attack—physically, politically and spiritually—during the last quarter of the seventeenth century. The degree to which these different threats affected people's lives depended on their geographical location. Those who lived in or around Boston would have been much more aware of the political changes wrought by Andros than those living out on the frontier. Yet colonists settled in outlying areas were in greater danger from native American attacks and the failure of the Andros government to provide adequate defense. Wherever New Englanders lived during these years, they experienced fear and uncertainty. Whereas earlier crises such as the Antinomian controversy and the struggle over the halfway covenant had originated within the colonial community, the dangers that faced New England toward the end of the century intruded upon the colonies as emissaries of a hostile outside world.[15] In close and deadly succession, a series of external forces had assaulted the colonists, imperiling not only their integrity as a political and spiritual community but even their very survival. This chain of crises had a cumulative impact, constituting for New Englanders a common trauma, which they expressed in a common language.

During the months that followed the collapse of the Dominion, "Gentlemen," "Merchants," and other "Inhabitants of Boston" penned and published a number of tracts to justify their rebellion. The language these writers used to describe the Dominion emphasized the alien, invasive, and oppressive character of the Andros regime. The tracts condemned Edmund Andros's policy as "a Treasonable Invasion of the Rights which the whole English Nation lay claim unto."[16] Just as James II's government in England "had invaded both the Liberty and Property of English Protestants," so Andros "did Invade the Property as well as Liberty of the Subject" in New England.[17] Andros had loaded preferments upon "such Men as were strangers to and haters of the People."[18] His high sheriff was "a Stranger in the Country, and one that had no Estate there." He appointed as jurors other "Strangers who had no Freehold."[19] Before Andros came to Boston, he had been governor of New York. The anti-Andros tracts now declared that New Englanders had been "squeez'd by a Crew of abject Persons fetched from New York, to be the Tools of the Adversary."[20] It was surely no coincidence that New England Puritans also called Satan "the Adversary." Nor was Andros the only representative of the imperial government to be described in diabolical terms: according to Samuel Sewall, Boston mariners referred to Colonel Percy Kirke, the ruthless governor of Tangier, whom Charles II had selected as governor of Massachussets in 1685 (but whose appointment was cancelled after the king's death), as "the Devil Kirk[e]."[21]

The Andros tracts located their description of the Dominion within a framework of anti-French and anti-Catholic sentiment. The seventeenth-century English tended to associate autocratic government with the French monarchy and Roman Catholicism. Many believed that any attempt to impose authoritarian government must originate with one or both of these alien powers. There was some empirical basis for such an association. The Stuart monarchs had repeatedly sought French support for their experiments in nonrepresentative government. Charles I was an Arminian and married a Catholic; James II was himself a Catholic. When Charles II had moved to secure James's position as heir, the government's enemies denounced this as the latest stage in a "popish plot." The anti-Andros tracts now claimed that the revocation of the colonial charters had been "one of the most considerable Branches of the late Popish Plot."[22] Andros had insisted on complete liberty of conscience and worship for Anglicans within the Dominion. New Englanders, many of whom saw Anglicanism as crypto-popery, accused Andros and his associates of being "intoxicated with a Bigotry inspired into them by the great Scarlet Whore."[23] According to the pamphleteers, Andros had determined "to destroy the Fundamentals of the English and to Erect a French Government."[24] That "French design" was "an Essay or Specimen of what was intended for the whole English Nation."[25]

Not only did these writers associate Andros with French authoritarianism and the spiritual corruptions of Roman Catholicism, but they also linked him to a much more immediate despoiler of English life and liberty: the Indian. According to his enemies, Andros had supplied native Americans with ammunition and had encouraged them to make war against the colonists.[26] In the past, the French in Canada had often inspired or encouraged native American attacks and there were suspicions that Andros had made a secret pact with the French.[27] Both literally and figuratively, the colonists were in danger of being "given away to a Forreign Power."[28] By invading the liberty and property of the colonists, by usurping control over their affairs, and by imposing an external authority, Edmund Andros and his government had "commit[ted] a Rape on a whole Colony."[29]

A significant symmetry emerges here: the anti-Andros tracts described the Dominion in much the same terms used to characterize witchcraft. In the same year that these political essays began to appear, Cotton Mather published in *Memorable Providences* his account of a 1688 Boston witchcraft case that had resulted in the execution of Goodwife Glover, an Irish Catholic. Glover had apparently bewitched the children of John Goodwin, a pious mason who belonged to Mather's congregation. Mather appended to his account a sermon on witchcraft he had delivered in Boston during the winter of 1688-9. Mather's description of witchcraft in this sermon bore a close resemblance, both in language and tone, to the anti-Andros tracts' description of the Dominion regime. According to Mather, witches and their confederate Devils sought to "break the hedge of . . . Providence" that protected New Englanders against the "Assaults" of Satan's minions. Just as Andros had "Invade[d] the Property as well as Liberty of the Subject," so witches "invaded" and "plunder[ed]" their victims' bodies and possessions, ever anxious to "exert their Devillish and malignant Rage upon their Neighbours."[30] Like Andros's "Crew of abject Persons fetched from New York, to be the Tools of the Adversary," Goodwife Glover was an outsider, marginalized by both ethnicity and religious faith. Alien, invasive, and oppressive: the affinities between the two descriptions are unmistakable.[31]

Native American raids constituted a much more literal form of invasion and were perceived as such by New Englanders. Despite English attempts to convert and acculturate neighboring tribes, most of the native Americans had clung to their own way of life; they remained as alien as ever. In the aftermath of Metacomet's War, English colonists had every reason to see the native Americans as a deadly threat. English accounts of the war described recent hostilities in terms of native American invasion. "The Boar out of the Wood," wrote William Hubbard, "hath broke into the Vineyard."[32] During the war itself, in September 1675, the Council of Massachusetts had called for a day of humiliation,

> we having greatly incensed [God] to stir up many Adversaries against us, not only abroad, but also at our own Doors, causing the Heathen in this wilderness to be as Thorns in our sides, who have formerly been, and might still be a wall unto us therein.

The councilors chose to evoke the war through a series of specific images, each of which related to intrusion. The "Heathen[s]," formerly a "wall" against the French, were now "Thorns" in the "sides" of the English. They threatened English settlers "not only abroad" but even at their "own Doors."[33] Increase Mather, writing in 1676, described the war as a fulfillment of God's warning in Leviticus 26:31:

> I will send wild Beasts among you, which shall rob you of your Children, and destroy your Cattle, and make you few in number, and if you will not be reform'd by these things, I will bring your Sanctuaryes to Desolation, and I will not smell the sweet Savor of your Odours.

To the language of invasion Mather added the potent image of "wild Beasts," violating "Sanctuaryes" and bringing them to utter "Desolation." Mather described the "Epidemical Diseases" that accompanied the war in similar language, as "breaches . . . upon divers of the colonies of New-England."[34]

The twin images of invasion and bestial violation dominate both clerical and lay narratives of native American raids during 1675-6 and after 1689. These narratives often described the attacks as "assaults"[35] and referred to the native Americans themselves as "beasts of prey" and "brutish wolves."[36] The literally invasive character of these attacks surfaces again and again in English accounts. Town after town and, perhaps more significantly, home after home fell to the native Americans. It is through detailed descriptions of raids on individual homes that we can see most clearly the impact of the war on those "assaulted" by native forces. Mary Rowlandson, who was taken captive in February 1676, wrote an account of the attack on her home in Lancaster, Massachusetts:

> It is a solemn sight to see so many Christians lying in their blood, some here, and some there, like a company of Sheep torn by Wolves. All of them stripped naked by a company of hell-

hounds, roaring, singing, ranting, and insulting, as if they would have torn our very hearts out.[37]

Benjamin Tompson's verse narrative of the war, *New England's Crisis* (published in 1676), is equally vivid, though poetically inept, in its evocation of individual responses to native American attack:

> Poor people spying an unwonted light,
> Fearing a martyrdom, in sudden fright
> Leap to the door to fly, but all in vain,
> They are surrounded with a pagan train;
> Their first salute is death, which if they shun
> Some are condemned the gauntlet to run;
> Death would a mercy prove to such as those
> Who feel the rigor of such hellish foes.
>
> . . . . .
>
> Here might be seen the infant from the breast
> Snatched by a pagan hand to lasting rest:
> The mother, Rachel-like, shrieks out "My child."
> She wrings her hands and raves as she were wild.
> The brutish wolves suppress her anxious moan
> By cruelties more deadly of their own.
> Will she or nill the chastest turtle must
> Taste of the pangs of their unbridled lust.
> From farms to farms, from towns to towns they post,
> They strip, they bind, they ravish, flay, and roast.[38]

Tompson was not alone in accusing native American attackers of sexual assault. Nathaniel Saltonstall claimed that raiders "defile[d]" English women, forcing them "to satisfie their filthy lusts" before killing them.[39] Collectively, individually, and sexually, then, the New Englanders saw themselves as having been the victims of native American "invasion" and "assault."

Just as incursions of imperial authority were described by New Englanders in much the same language used to characterize assaults by witchcraft, so colonists linked native Americans to witchcraft. But in this case, the association was explicit. Many of the English settlers had either seen or heard about the native medicinemen and their mysterious rituals. New Englanders tended to equate native American supernaturalism with witchcraft. At a New Haven slander hearing in 1653, Goodwife Atwater was said to have claimed that Elizabeth Godman was a witch and that Habbamock, a native spirit, was her husband.[40] When Nicholas Disborough of Hartford, Connecticut, became afflicted ("things being thrown at him and his boy, night and day, in house and feilde"), the first suspect was a native American who worked for neighbor Richard Lord.[41] In the early 1650s, Mary Staples of Fairfield, Connecticut, came under suspicion for witchcraft partly as a result of a story circulating the neighborhood about a native American who, it was claimed, had visited Staples's house and offered her "two little things brighter than the light of the day . . . Indian gods, as the Indian called them." When questioned by neighbors, Staples apparently admitted that the visit had taken place, but claimed that she had refused the proffered gift, a claim some townsfolk were reluctant to believe.[42] Any association with native Americans, however tenuous and whether or not connected with native religion, could be used to incriminate a witch suspect. As we will see, accusers at the Salem witch trials in 1692 not only detailed the connections between suspects and native Americans as indicative of their guilt, but also claimed that the Devil looked like a native American.

Puritans were convinced that New England and its native inhabitants had belonged to the Devil until the arrival of God's chosen, namely, the English.[43] It is, then, hardly surprising that ministers and godly layfolk referred to the native Americans in diabolical terms. Cotton Mather described them as Satan's "most devoted and resembling children."[44] Writing in 1689, Mather claimed that "Evil spirits" were at work in "the Wigwams of Indians, where the pagan Powaws often raise[d] their masters, in the shapes of Bears and Snakes and fires."[45] These "powaws" were apparently "horrid Sorcerers, and hellish Conjurers, and such as Conversed with Daemons."[46] Mary Rowlandson accused the native Americans of "devilish cruelty to the English" and described one native camp as "a lively resemblance of hell."[47] Benjamin Tompson's verse narrative characterized the native Americans as "hellish foes."[48] Metacomet, like Andros, was described in terms also used to characterize Satan: the sachem was a "grand Rebel" who harbored "inveterate malice and wickedness against the English."[49] Like Satan and his indefatigable minions, the native Americans constituted "an Ever-Approaching and Unapproachable Adversary."[50] Their reputation for witchcraft and diabolism reinforced their impact as an invasive threat. Native American raids during the years following 1689 confirmed and deepened the psychological effects of the Dominion experience.

Many colonists perceived heresy as yet another alien force that had invaded and now threatened to subvert the New England community. In the late 1650s, a number of Quakers had crossed the Atlantic in a bid to purify New England of its spiritual corruption. Needless to say, Congregationalists did not appreciate this attention. The Quakers' refusal to abide by norms of social deference and their generally bizarre behavior made them appear threatening even to those who were less concerned about their spiritual beliefs. The General Court in Massachusetts was not slow to take action against the Quaker mission. In a bid "to prevent the intrusions of the Quakers," the court ordered that all visiting Friends be ejected, and that all resident converts to Quakerism be banished.[51] Initial responses to Quakerism within the colony often used invasive imagery to describe the Friends. John Norton, a Puritan cleric who was commissioned by the General Court to write a tract refuting Quaker doctrine, compared the Friends to "the wolfe which ventures over the wide Sea, out of a ravening desire to prey upon the sheep, when landed."[52] In 1658, twenty-five laymen submitted a petition to the General Court, demanding severer laws against the Quakers, who had, claimed the petitioners, "audaciously intruded themselves" upon the colonists.[53] Governor John Endecott, writing to Charles II on behalf of the General Court in order to explain its punitive actions toward the Quakers, described the Friends as "breaking in upon us."[54] The General Court itself referred to the Quakers' "arrogant, bold obtrusions."[55] The court also used images of disease and even of sexual subversion in describing the Quaker threat: the Friends had "infected and seduced . . . diverse . . . inhabitants."[56]

Images of invasion reappeared in two anti-Quaker tracts published in the early 1690s. Both pieces were written in response to the evangelical efforts of George Keith, an itinerant Quaker preacher who had arrived in New England in June 1688. The first piece, published in 1690 and written by three prominent New England ministers (James Allen, Joshua Moodey, and Samuel Willard), maintained that the Church of God had "in all ages undergone the Batteries of a various assault." Heresy was foremost among these "Batteries." According to Allen, Moodey, and Willard, no heresy posed so grave a threat to the New-English Israel as did Quakerism, "this great Choak-weed of the Christian and Protestant Religion, taking root in the Borders of New England."[57] A year later, Cotton Mather also warned against "the assaults of Quakerism" and recommended that the godly arm themselves with an array of spiritual "Weapons" to "keep off the Quakers with." Mather, like Norton, saw the Friends as "Grievous Wolves" who sought to devour the "Little Flocks" of New England Congregationalists.[58]

Anti-Quaker polemic linked the Friends to threats from the invisible as well as visible world. Puritans believed that there was a close connection between heresy, diabolism, and witchcraft. The Friends were particularly susceptible to such associations, partly as a result of their reliance upon revelation. Congregationalists refused to accept that the Quakers received "inner light" from God: as John Norton put it, Quaker revelation was "in pretence divine, but indeed diabolical."[59] Increase Mather assured his readers that Quakers were "under the strong delusions of Satan" and that "some of them [were] undoubtedly possessed with Evil and Infernal Spirits, and acted [upon] in a more than ordinary manner by the inmates of Hell."[60] The General Court condemned Quaker doctrine as "devilish" and "diabollicall."[61] The Friends' tendency to "quake" when receiving revelation strengthened their association with Satan in Puritan minds, since their physical convulsions bore a close resemblance to possession. "The quaking and shaking motions of the Quakers," wrote Roger Williams, "cannot be imagined to proceed from the Holy Spirit of God, but from Sathan."[62] John Norton claimed that it was Satan's "ancient and known manner . . . when he inspired his Enthusiasts, to afflict the bodyes of his instruments with paines and those often in their bowells, and to agitate them with Antick and uncouth motions, and in particular with this of quaking and trembling."[63] According to Cotton Mather, "Diabolical Possession was the thing which did dispose and encline men unto Quakerism."[64]

In both England and New England, Quakers were vulnerable to accusations of witchcraft.[65] In 1656, when two Quaker missionaries, Ann Austin and Mary Fisher, arrived in Massachusetts, magistrates instructed a group of midwives to search the two women for witch marks.[66] Magistrates and ministers were not alone in associating Quakers with witchcraft. When Friend Mary Thompkins disrupted a church service in Portsmouth, members of the congregation threw her down a flight of stairs; Thompkins survived the fall, and the disappointed townsfolk attributed this to her being a witch.[67] Caleb Powell, the seaman who offered his services as a cunning man to townsfolk in Newbury, Massachusetts, and who was subsequently accused of witchcraft, claimed to have learned his craft from Francis Norwood, a Quaker who lived in Gloucester.[68] In 1688, when John Goodwin's four children became bewitched, they derived great comfort from any mention of Quakerism. One of them was unable to read the bible, but could read "a Quaker's Book." Another fell into fits if his parents tried to take him to a Congregationalist meeting, but felt much better when his father spoke of going to a Quaker assembly. The Goodwin children's attraction to Quaker writings and meetings whilst bewitched horrified those around them, but it cannot have come as a surprise.[69]

As in the case of the native Americans, the Quakers' association with witchcraft intensified the psychological impact of their intrusion into the officially sanctioned community after 1691. Cotton Mather drew a direct connection between the Quaker and native American threats:

> While the Indians have been thus molesting us, we have suffered Molestations of another sort, from another sort of Enemies, which may with very good Reason be cast into the same History with them. If the Indians have chosen to prey upon the Frontiers, and Out-Skirts, of the Province, the Quakers have chosen the very same Frontiers, and Out-Skirts, for their more Spiritual Assaults; and finding little Success elsewhere, they have been Labouring incessantly, and sometimes not unsuccessfully, to Enchant and Poison the souls of poor people, in the very places where the Bodies and Estates of the

people have presently after been devoured by the Salvages.

According to Mather, native American and Quaker "Assaults" could "be cast into the same History." Both had "prey[ed] upon the Frontiers, and Out-Skirts, of the Province." The Quakers had "Labour[ed] . . . to Enchant and Poison the souls" of those very people whose "Bodies and Estates" were then "devoured by the Salvages."[70] Mather was not alone in making this association. John Norton compared Quaker palpitations to "the custome of the Powwows or Indian Wizards, in this Wilderness; whose bodies at the time of their diabolicall practises, are at this day vexed and agitated in a strange, unwonted and dreadfull manner."[71] Edmund Batter, a merchant of Salem Town, testified in court that Elizabeth Kitchen was a Friend, having met her "betim[e]s in the morning comeing as he supposed from a quaking meeting." Batter referred to Quakerism as "apawawing."[72]

All of these interrelated, alien, and intrusive forces, which the colonists equated with witchcraft, converged on a local level in Essex County. In particular, Salem Village and Andover, the two principal sources of which hysteria in 1692, were prey to threatening, invasive forces. When France declared war on England in 1689 and persuaded the native Americans to attack New England, native forces converged initially on the northern areas of English settlement. Not until 1691 did Massachusetts become a target, with one significant exception. On 14 August 1689, native Americans attacked Andover, killing John and Andrew Peters, the sons of a distiller.[73] Andover was the only settled community in Massachusetts to suffer a native raid during the first two years of the war. The anxieties caused by the raid of 1689 revived and intensified in 1691 as the native Americans launched a major attack on western Massachusetts. The following year, Andover produced more cases of witchcraft than any other community.[74]

Salem Village faced less literal but equally disturbing forms of invasion. The village, legally subordinate to nearby Salem Town, had no civil government of its own and no independent church. Salem Town maintained careful control over the village's internal affairs and showed remarkable insensitivity to the villagers' concerns. Some of the villagers were eager to secure legal independence from the town; others, who had economic ties with the town and identified with its interests, resisted independence.[75] The conflict between village and town, which became increasingly bitter as the years passed by, was, in effect, a microcosm of the troubled relationship between Massachusetts and England. In 1689, the same year in which the Dominion collapsed, those in favor of autonomy from the town secured the ordination of Samuel Parris as minister of an independent congregation. Henceforth, Parris and his church became the focus for conflict within the village. In his sermons, Parris translated factional division into a cosmic struggle between the forces of good and evil. Parris made an explicit connection between his enemies and the legions of Hell: there was, he declared in 1690, "a lamentable harmony between wicked men and devils, in their opposition of God's kingdom and interests."[76] Sectarian as well as political forces threatened Salem Village: between the village and Salem Town itself was located the largest Quaker community in all of Essex County.[77] As the villagers looked eastward, they saw a doubly threatening world just beyond the village boundary.[78]

The pattern of witch accusations in 1692 suggests an intense preoccupation with invasion in the minds of Salem Villagers. Of those villagers who became actively involved in witchcraft cases, most accused witches and their defenders lived on the side of the village nearest to Salem Town, whereas most accusers lived on the other side of the village.[79] Many of the accused also lived in close proximity to the Quaker community situated between village and town.[80] In other words, the direction of witch accusations expressed fears aroused by the alien forces, both political and spiritual, which threatened the integrity of the local community.[81]

Salem Villagers were not alone in using witch accusations to express hostility toward Quakers. In Andover, Gloucester, and other towns throughout Essex County, a significant number of the accused had close Quaker associations. In the aftermath of the new charter's imposition of religious toleration, Congregationalists could no longer have Quakers fined for espousing heretical doctrines or refusing to attend orthodox church meetings. Attacking Quakers as witches was equally unacceptable: the beliefs and palpitations that made Friends vulnerable to such accusations were now, at least officially, unexceptionable. However, the direction of witch accusations against the relatives and friends of Quakers offered an alternative way to express anxieties aroused by their invasion of the orthodox community. A significant number of the accused were connected to Quakers by ties of kinship or friendship.[82] Rebecca and Francis Nurse had acted as the guardians of Samuel Southwick, the orphaned son of a local Quaker farmer. Elizabeth Proctor's family, the Bassets, included a large number of Quakers. Thomas Farrar was father of a leading Lynn Friend; the Wardwells and Hawkes also had Quaker connections.[83] Job Tookey, another accused witch, was reputed to be the son of "an Annybaptisticall Quakeing Rogue that for his maintainence went up and down England to delude Soules for the Divell."[84]

Just as the direction of witch accusations reflected a fear of sectarian invasion, so court depositions expressed acute anxiety about native American invasion. Essex County, situated in northern Massachusetts, was uncomfortably close to New Hampshire and Maine, where most of the attacks occurred. The county had suffered heavy losses during the war of 1675-6 and must have feared for the worst now that hostilities had resumed, especially after the raid on Andover in 1689.[85] Since the beginning of the war, refugees from the northern stretches of New England had resettled in Massachusetts; their presence must have intensified local fear and uncertainty. Mercy Short, a seventeen-year-old servant who was afflicted by specters following an argument with one of the accused, had been captured by native American forces in 1690. Until 18 March 1690, Mercy had lived with her family in Salmon Falls, Maine, but that day the native Americans launched a surprise attack against the settlement. Thirty-four people were killed, including Mercy's parents, one brother, and one sister; fifty-four were taken prisoner, including Mercy, who was carried north to Canada by her captors and then brought to Boston after having been redeemed. Perhaps not surprisingly, she described the Devil as being "a Tawney, or an Indian colour."[86] Mary Toothaker of Billerica, an accused witch, also claimed that the Devil appeared to her "in the shape of a Tawny man." Toothaker had recently been "troubled w[it]h feare about the Indians, and used often to dream of fighting with them." The Devil, she confessed on 30 July, persuaded her to become a witch by promising to keep her safe from native Americans.[87] That Toothaker had good reason to be worried about the possibility of an attack was demonstrated six days later, on 5 August, when native American forces raided the Toothaker farm in Billerica.[88] Abigail Hobbs, who confessed to witchcraft, had lived in Maine until driven south by native attacks. In her confession, Hobbs declared that she had first seen the Devil in the woods near Casco, Maine.[89]

Other testimony presented to the court in 1692 linked accused witches and the Devil to native Americans. One confessing witch told the court that French Canadians and native Sagamores had attended the "Cheef Witch-meetings," hoping "to concert the methods of ruining New England."[90] In mid-1692, just after the outbreak of witch hysteria in Andover, a number of townsfolk at nearby Gloucester claimed to have seen native Americans and Frenchmen lurking on Cape Ann.[91] Sarah Osborne, a witch suspect from Salem Village, testified that she "either saw or dreamed that shee saw a thing like an indian all black which did pinch her in her neck and pulled her by the back part of her head to the dore of the house."[92] Yet another accused witch, John Proctor, had been fined in 1678 "for selling cider and strong waters to Indians."[93] One of John Alden's accusers charged that he "[sold] Powder and Shot to the Indians and French, and [lay] with the Indian Squa[w]es, and ha[d] Indian Papooses."[94]

In addition to these specific fears relating to Quakers and native Americans, the witchcraft accusations expressed a general hostility toward outsiders. Not only did most of the accused witches from Salem Village live on the side of the village closest to Salem Town, but some of them were only formally resident within the village. John Proctor had become a resident in 1666, but actually lived on a farm southeast of the village boundary. Martha and Giles Corey lived just over the village line in Salem Town.[95] Bridget Bishop had lived within the village boundary for seven years, but had rarely ventured into the village itself. Nobody contradicted Bishop at her examination when she said, "I never was in this place before . . . I know no man, woman or child here."[96] Sarah and Edward Bishop were outsiders in a figurative sense. Sarah Bishop had turned her house into an unlicensed tavern and exercised a disruptive influence over younger members of the community. According to John Hale, Bishop "did entertaine people in her house at unseasonable houres in the night to keep drinking and playing at shovel-board, whereby discord did arise in other families and young people were in danger to bee corrupted."[97] Long before Sarah Bishop sought to intrude her alien and evil ways into the minds of innocent young villagers, Martha Corey had become an outsider by giving birth to an illegitimate mulatto son who still lived in the Corey household.[98] Sarah Osborne had caused scandal after the death of her first husband, Robert Prince, by committing fornication with her indentured servant, a young Irish immigrant named Alexander Osborne, whom she later married. The Osbornes now threatened traditional patterns of inheritance by conspiring to subvert Robert Prince's will so as to gain full control over his land, which Sarah Osborne was holding in trust for Prince's two sons.[99]

The same pattern of hostility toward outsiders characterized Andover accusations. Eight of the suspects were marginalized by ethnic affiliation. Martha Carrier was Scottish and had married a Welshman: she and four of her children were accused. The Carrier family had been further ostracized as carriers of smallpox and were warned out of Andover in 1690.[100] Ann Foster's husband Andrew was Scottish; her own ethnic background is unclear, but she was accused in 1692 along with a daughter and granddaughter.[101] In 1689, Hannah Foster had been killed by her husband, Hugh Stone, the first case of murder in Andover. The taint of this shocking event may well have stuck to the Foster family and strengthened their marginal status.[102] The Wardwell family's reputation was tarnished by connection with heresy: Samuel Wardwell's father and uncle accompanied the Reverend John Wheelwright into New Hampshire when he was banished from Massachusetts as an Antinomian. His uncle, William Wardwell, became a Quaker, as did his brother Eliakim.[103]

In *Wonders of the Invisible World,* a commentary on the events of 1692, Cotton Mather argued that the various threats that faced New Englanders during these years were not discrete, but constituted a vast, interlocking assault. Mather argued that the witch conspiracy was the latest in a series of diabolical offensives against New England: native American sorceries and raids, the revocation of the charter, the French war, and a succession of heresies. Each of these, wrote Mather, should be understood as part of a larger pattern. Mather described the witch conspiracy itself as an outright invasion:

> such is the descent of the Devil at this day upon our selves, that I may truly tell you, The Walls of the whole World are broken down! The usual Walls of defence about mankind have such a Gap made in them that the very Devils are broken in upon us . . . [104]

By no means everybody saw their predicament in diabolical terms, but Mather had captured effectively the general state of mind in Massachusetts. Royal officials, native Americans, and dissenters had all threatened the well-being of the community in much the same way that a witch threatened the well-being of an individual; many people believed that native Americans and Quakers were witches. Alien, invasive, and oppressive: these associations provided the context for witch hysteria.

In the light of their experience since 1675, the people of Essex County were only too willing to blame misfortune on alien malefactors. This predisposition, under the pressure of recent events, to locate evil outside the self is the key to understanding what happened in 1692. An accusation of witchcraft involved a decision to blame suffering on a malevolent, external force. There were alternatives: victims could interpret suffering as divine punishment for their own sinfulness, or they could just accept it as an inexplicable misfortune. Ministers urged their congregations to look inward for the source of their troubles, yet clerical descriptions of the ordeals that faced New England in the late seventeenth century magnified the threat from without and so reinforced the literal impact of native American warriors and other invasive forces. Furthermore, ambiguity within Puritan theology enabled even godly colonists to displace responsibility for sin and suffering, should they be inclined to do so, without any clear sense of violating orthodoxy. The likelihood of individuals deciding to blame their troubles on witchcraft would depend on their own psychological inclinations, their mood at the time of misfortune, and the broader influences being exerted upon them by their cultural environment. The latter was crucial in 1692.[105] The Andros regime, the renewal of native American attacks, and the imposition of religious toleration each encouraged the people of Massachusetts to associate external forces with some kind of threat. Andover and Salem Village, where over half of the 1692 cases originated, underwent additional and analogous ordeals that accentuated this cast of mind. When Samuel Parris decided to pursue those responsible for the mysterious "distempers" in Salem Village and so began the witch panic, townsfolk in nearby communities recalled recent misfortunes and readily blamed them on witch suspects. The torments undergone by the afflicted girls in Salem Village touched a raw nerve exposed and sensitized by the ordeals of the last decade. The psychological impact of these ordeals spawned the witch hunt of 1692.

The traumatic events of the previous two decades had affected the entire community, clerical and lay, Puritan and non-Puritan. The witch hunt provided an opportunity to release pent-up fears and to root out persons who seemed threatening to the community. Ministers and magistrates sought to locate this process within a religious context. The Salem judges saw themselves as fulfilling an almost priestly function: under their guidance, the accused were to confess their sins, renounce the Devil, and rejoin the church of God. The New-English Israel would emerge from that process cleansed and spiritually reinvigorated. Yet most of those who gave testimony against witch suspects in 1692 had no desire to locate their experience within a theological framework. Just as invasions by native Americans, imperial officials, and iconoclastic dissenters were not perceived by all those who feared them as diabolical, so witchcraft itself impinged upon many people's lives as maleficium rather than as diabolical heresy. Thus, problems of evidence plagued the Salem trials just as they had plagued other New England witch prosecutions. Court officials demanded proof of a direct link between the accused and the Devil, but most witnesses did not interpret witchcraft in diabolical terms and saw no reason to mention the Devil in their testimony. The trials of 1692, although atypical in their scale and intensity, were consistent with other seventeenth-century New England trials in embodying the tension between magical and theological perceptions of witchcraft. . . .

Notes

. . . [9] See John Demos, *Entertaining Satan,* p. 521 n17.

[10] The most detailed account of the 1675-6 war remains Douglas Edward Leach, *Flintlock and Tomahawk: New England in King Philip's War* (New York, 1958). For contemporary narratives of the war, see John Easton, "A Relacion of the Indyan Warre," in Charles Lincoln, ed., *Narratives of the Indian Wars* (1913; New York, 1952), pp. 7-17; Nathaniel Saltonstall, *The Present State of New-England with Respect to the Indian War* (London, 1675); Saltonstall, *A Continuation of the State of New-England* (London, 1676); Saltonstall, *A New and Further Narrative of the State of New-England* (London, 1676); Increase Mather, *A Brief History of the War with the Indians in New-England* (Boston, 1676); Benjamin Tompson, *New England's Crisis, or, A Brief Narrative of New-England's Lamentable Estate at Present, Compar'd with the Former (but Few) Years of Prosperity* (Boston, 1676; reprinted in Richard Slotkin and James K. Folsom, eds., *So Dreadfull a Judgment: Puritan Responses to King Philip's War, 1676-7* [Middletown, Conn., 1978],

pp. 213-33); Thomas Wheeler, *A Thankefull Remembrance of God's Mercy to Several Persons at Quabaug or Deerfield* (Cambridge, Mass. 1676); William Hubbard, *A Narrative of the Troubles with the Indians* (Boston, 1677); Richard Hutchinson, *The War in New-England Visibly Ended* (London, 1677); Mary Rowlandson, *The Sovereignty and Goodness of God, Together with the Faithfulness of His Promises Displayed* (Cambridge, 1682); and Thomas Church, *Entertaining Passages Relating to Philip's War* (Boston, 1716).

[11] For more detailed accounts of the Dominion and its downfall, see Richard Johnson, *Adjustment to Empire: The New England Colonies, 1675-1715* (New Brunswick, N.J., 1981), chaps. 1 and 2; David Lovejoy, *The Glorious Revolution in America* (New York, 1972); Timothy Breen, *The Character of a Good Ruler* (New Haven, Conn., 1970), chap. 4; Michael G. Hall, *Edward Randolph and the American Colonies 1676-1703* (Chapel Hill, 1960); Viola F. Barnes, *The Dominion of New England: A Study in British Colonial Policy* (New York, 1923).

[12] John Demos, *Entertaining Satan,* p. 522 n22.

[13] Philip Haffenden, *New England in the English Nation, 1689-1713* (Oxford, 1974), chap. 3. See also Cotton Mather's account of these years in *Decennium Luctuosum* (Boston, 1699).

[14] For studies of Quakerism in early New England, see Carla Gardina Pestana, *Quakers and Baptists in Colonial Massachusetts* (New York, 1991); Jonathan Chu, *Neighbors, Friends, or Madmen* (Westport, Conn., 1985); Christine Heyrman, *Commerce and Culture: The Maritime Communities of Colonial Massachusetts, 1690-1750* (New York, 1984), chap. 3; Arthur Worrall, *Quakers in the Colonial Northeast* (Hanover, N.H., 1980); George Selleck, *Quakers in Boston: 1656-1964, Three Centuries of Friends in Boston and Cambridge* (Cambridge, Mass., 1976); J. William Frost, *The Quaker Family in Colonial America: A Portrait of the Society of Friends* (New York, 1973); Frederick Tolles, *Quakers and the Atlantic Culture* (New York, 1960); Rufus Jones, *The Quakers in the American Colonies* (London, 1911); Richard Hallowell, *The Quaker Invasion of Massachusetts* (Boston, 1883).

[15] See John Demos, *Entertaining Satan,* p. 380. Kenneth Silverman also argues that "a mentality of invasion" took hold in New England during the last quarter of the century (Kenneth Silverman, *The Life and Times of Cotton Mather* [New York, 1984], chap. 3). The discussion that follows lends support to the interpretations put forward by Demos and Silverman. See also James E. Kences, "Some Unexplored Relationships of Essex County Witchcraft to the Indian Wars of 1675 and 1689," *Essex Institute Historical Collections,* 120

(1984): 194.

[16] "An Account of the Late Revolutions in New-England" (1689), in William Whitmore, ed., *The Andros Tracts,* 3 vols. (Boston, 1868-74), II: 192.

[17] "The Revolution in New-England Justified" (1691), in *The Andros Tracts,* I: 72, 87.

[18] "Declaration of the Gentlemen, Merchants and Inhabitants of Boston" (1689), in *The Andros Tracts,* I: 13.

[19] "The Revolution in New-England Justified," in *The Andros Tracts,* I: 112.

[20] "Declaration of the Gentlemen, Merchants and Inhabitants of Boston," in *The Andros Tracts,* I: 13.

[21] Samuel Sewall, *Diary,* ed. M. Halsey Thomas, 2 vols. (New York, 1973), I: 108, 15 April 1686.

[22] "An Appeal to the Men of New-England" (1689), in *The Andros Tracts,* III: 192.

[23] "Declaration of the Gentlemen, Merchants and Inhabitants of Boston," in *The Andros Tracts,* I: 12.
[24] "The Revolution in New-England Justified," in *The Andros Tracts,* I: 79-80.

[25] Ibid., I: 87; "An Appeal to the Men of New-England," in *The Andros Tracts,* III: 194.

[26] See especially "The Revolution in New-England Justified," in *The Andros Tracts,* I: 101-11.

[27] Timothy Breen, *The Character of a Good Ruler,* p. 149.

[28] "Declaration of the Gentlemen, Merchants and Inhabitants of Boston," in *The Andros Tracts,* I: 19.

[29] "The Revolution in New-England Justified," in *The Andros Tracts,* I: 128.

[30] Cotton Mather, *A Discourse on Witchcraft* (Boston, 1689), pp. 6, 10, 18, 21.

[31] John Demos notes that "untoward and unwanted intrusiveness" was a recurring element in descriptions of witches (John Demos, *Entertaining Satan,* pp. 178-9).

[32] William Hubbard, *A Narrative of the Troubles with the Indians,* The Epistle Dedicatory, p. ii. Hubbard was minister at Ipswich, Massachusetts.

[33] Declaration of Massachusetts Council, 17 September 1675, quoted by Increase Mather in *A Brief History of the War,* pp. 15-16.

[34] Increase Mather, *A Brief History of the War,* pp. 17, 32.

[35] See, for example, Mary Rowlandson, *The Sovereignty and Goodness of God,* p. 13; Josiah Winslow and Thomas Hinckley, "A Brief Narrative of the Begining and Progresse of the Present Trouble between Us and the Indians," in Nathaniel Shurtleff and David Pulsifer, eds., *Records of the Colony of New Plymouth in New England,* 12 vols. (New York, 1968), X: 364; Nathaniel Saltonstall, *A New and Further Narrative,* pp. 2, 3, 4, 10; Increase Mather, *A Brief History of the War,* pp. 12, 23, 24, 29, 30, 33, 37, 41, 48; and Cotton Mather, *Decennium Luctuosum* (Boston, 1699), pp. 33, 45, 90, 91, 144.

[36] Nathaniel Saltonstall, *A New and Further Narrative,* p. 8; Benjamin Tompson, *New England's Crisis,* p. 219. See also Increase Mather, *An Earnest Exhortation to the Inhabitants of New-England to Hearken to the Voice of God in His Late and Present Dispensations* (Boston, 1676), p. 6; and Cotton Mather, *Decennium Luctuosum,* pp. 25, 123.

[37] Mary Rowlandson, *The Sovereignty and Goodness of God,* p. 5.

[38] Benjamin Tompson, *New England's Crisis,* pp. 219, 221. "Turtle" refers to turtledove.

[39] Nathaniel Saltonstall, *The Present State of New-England,* p. 6; Saltonstall, *A New and Further Narrative,* p. 14.

[40] Charles J. Hoadly, ed., *Records of the Colony or Jurisdiction of New Haven,* 2 vols. (New Haven, Conn., 1857-8), II: 31, 4 August 1653. The native Americans believed that Habbamock entered certain individuals and resided in their bodies as guardian and familiar. Habbamock was not the only spirit to do this; sometimes, several spirits would occupy the same person. Humans into whom spirits entered derived special powers from their guardians and became "pow-wows," or shamans. Puritans claimed that Habbamock and the other guardian spirits were devils, and that pow-wows were possessed witches (see William S. Simmons, "Cultural Bias in the New England Puritans' Perceptions of Indians," *William and Mary Quarterly,* 38 [1981]: 60-2).

[41] John Russell to Increase Mather, 2 August 1683, *Collections of the Massachusetts Historical Society,* 4. ser., 8 (1868): 86-7.

[42] Charles J. Hoadly, ed., *Records of the Colony or Jurisdiction of New Haven,* II: 80, 86.
[43] See, for example, Cotton Mather, *Wonders of the Invisible World* (1693; Amherst, Wisc., 1862), p. 74.

44 Cotton Mather, *Magnalia Christi Americana,* 2 vols. (1702; New York, 1967), I: 213.

45 Cotton Mather, *Memorable Providences* (Boston, 1689), Introduction, p. ii.

46 Cotton Mather, *Decennium Luctuosum,* p. 103. See also Increase Mather, *Angelographia* (Boston, 1696), To the Reader, p. x.

47 Mary Rowlandson, *The Sovereignty and Goodness of God,* pp. 6, 62.

48 Benjamin Tompson, *New England's Crisis,* p. 221.

49 William Hubbard, *A Narrative of the Troubles with the Indians,* pp. 103-4.

50 Cotton Mather, *Decennium Luctuosum,* p. 79. English commentators often complained that the native Americans' stealth and tendency to attack at night made them as inscrutable as they were deadly (see, for example, Nathaniel Saltonstall, *A New and Further Narrative,* p. 8).

51 Nathaniel Shurtleff, ed., *Records of the Governor and Company of Massachusetts Bay,* IV. pt 1, 346, 19 October 1658; and pt 2, 2-3, 22 May 1661.

52 John Norton, *The Heart of New-England Rent at the Blasphemies of the Present Generation, or, A Brief Tractate Concerning the Doctrine of the Quakers* (Cambridge, Mass., 1659), p. 54.

53 "Petition for Severer Laws against the Quakers," October 1658, Massachusetts Archives, X: 246.

54 *Records of the Governor and Company of Massachusetts Bay,* IV: pt. 1, 451, 19 December 1660.

55 Ibid., IV: pt. 1, 346, 19 October 1658. See also IV: pt. 1, 383, 18 October 1659.

56 Ibid. IV: pt. 1, 346.

57 James Allen, Joshua Moodey, and Samuel Willard, *The Principles of the Protestant Religion Maintained* (Boston, 1690), Preface, pp. i, iii.

58 Cotton Mather, *Little Flocks Guarded against Grievous Wolves* (Boston, 1691), p. 100. See also ibid., p. 57. For more references to Quakers as wolves, see James Allen et al., *The Principles of the Protestant Religion Maintained,* Preface, p. vi; p. 152.

59 John Norton, *The Heart of New-England Rent,* p. 6.
60 Increase Mather, *An Essay for the Recording of Illustrious Providences,* (Boston, 1684), pp. 345, 347.

61 *The Records of the Governor and Company of Massachusetts Bay,* IV (pt 1): 278, 321.

62 Roger Williams, "George Fox Digg'd Out of His Burrowes," ed. J. Lewis Diman, in *The Complete Writings of Roger Williams* (New York, 1963), pp. 44-5.

63 John Norton, *The Heart of New-England Rent,* pp. 5-6.

64 Cotton Mather, *Memorable Providences,* p. 67.

65 See Keith Thomas, *Religion and the Decline of Magic* (1971; Middlesex, England, 1973), pp. 580-1; and Amelia Mott Gummere, *Witchcraft and Quakerism: A Study of Social History* (Philadelphia, 1908), pp. 30-5.

66 Humphrey Norton, *New England's Bloody Ensigne* (London, 1659), p. 7; George Bishop, *New England Judged by the Spirit of the Lord,* Part One (London, 1661), p. 12.

67 George Bishop, *New England Judged by the Spirit of the Lord,* Part Two (London, 1667), p. 82.
68 *Records and Files of the Quarterly Courts of Essex County,* 9 vols. (Salem, Mass., 1911-78), VII: 357.

69 Cotton Mather, *Memorable Providences,* pp. 22, 43.

70 Cotton Mather, *Decennium Luctuosum,* p. 162.

71 John Norton, *The Heart of New-England Rent,* p. 6.

72 *Records and Files of the Quarterly Courts of Essex County,* II: 219, 26 June 1660.

73 Sarah Loring Bailey, *Historical Sketches of Andover* (Boston, 1880), p. 179.

74 The Andover cases are often underplayed in historical accounts of the 1692 crisis. See Chadwick Hansen, "Andover Witchcraft and the Causes of the Salem Witchcraft Trials," in Howard Kerr and Charles Crow, eds., *The Occult in America: New Historical Perspectives* (Urbana, Ill., 1983), pp. 38-57.

75 See Paul Boyer and Stephen Nissenbaum, *Salem Possessed.* Boyer and Nissenbaum argue that the divisions within Salem Village over the issue of autonomy were closely bound up with economic circumstance. As Salem Town became more prosperous, the farmers who lived in the surrounding countryside were encountering serious economic difficulty. Population growth and the diminished availability of land led to smaller units of ownership and a consequent decline in individual wealth. Those Salem Village farmers who lived closest to the town were in a much stronger position than those who lived at the other end of the village: not only was their land of a higher quality, but their proximity to the town

gave easier access to its markets. These farmers tended to see the growth of the town as an exciting opportunity, whereas those who lived further west feared and resented the town.

[76] Samuel Parris, "Sermons 1689-1695" (Connecticut Historical Society), 12 January 1690.

[77] See Richard Gildrie, *Salem, Massachusetts, 1626-1683: A Covenant Community* (Charlottesville, N.C., 1975), pp. 117, 130-7. See also Jonathan Chu, *Neighbors, Friends, or Madmen.*

[78] John Demos notes that the "strains" that engendered a "sense of crisis" throughout New England in the early 1690s were "powerfully evident at Salem, perhaps more so than in any other New England community" (John Demos, *Entertaining Satan,* p. 385).

[79] See Paul Boyer and Stephen Nissenbaum, *Salem Possessed,* p. 34.

[80] See Christine Heyrman, *Commerce and Culture,* p. 114.

[81] David Konig argues that the people of Massachusetts were particularly sensitive to the violation of boundaries during the years leading up to the witch hunt; the depositions of 1692 referred frequently to animals intruding on private property. Konig places this sensitivity in the context of general insecurity caused by the breakdown of the legal system during the political crisis of 1684-92. According to Konig, fences and other boundaries "stood as symbols of local regulation" (David Konig, *Law and Society in Puritan Massachusetts: Essex County 1629-92* [Chapel Hill, 1979], p. 180). Kai Erikson pursues a similar line of argument in *Wayward Puritans: A Study in the Sociology of Deviance* (New York, 1966). Social and political change had removed many of the boundaries according to which the colonists had defined themselves: "Most of the familiar landmarks of the New England Way had become blurred by changes in the historical climate, like signposts obscured in a storm . . ." (p. 140). The colonists, "bewildered by the loss of their old destiny but not yet aware of their new one," used the witch hunt "to discover some image of themselves . . ." (159). See also Larzer Ziff, *Puritanism in America: New Culture in a New World* (New York, 1973), pp. 244-5.

[82] This paragraph is much indebted to Christine Heyrman, *Commerce and Culture,* chap. 3. Heyrman argues that "the witchcraft outbreak . . . constituted in part a counteroffensive against the Quaker heresy under the conditions imposed by the new Massachusetts charter" (p. 123).

[83] These examples are drawn from Christine Heyrman,

Commerce and Culture, pp. 112-14.

[84] *Records and Files of the Quarterly Courts of Essex County,* VIII: 336, 27 June 1682.

[85] James E. Kences, "Some Unexplored Relationships of Essex County Witchcraft to the Indian Wars of 1675 and 1689," p. 181.

[86] Douglas Leach, *Arms for Empire: A Military History of the British Colonies in North America, 1607-1763* (New York, 1973), p. 88; Cotton Mather, "A Brand Pluck't Out of the Burning," in George L. Burr, ed., *Narratives of the Witchcraft Cases,* pp. 259, 261.

[87] Paul Boyer and Stephen Nissenbaum, eds., *The Salem Witchcraft Papers: Verbatim Transcripts of the Legal Documents of the Salem Witchcraft Outbreak,* 3 vols. (New York, 1977), III: 767-8.

[88] Samuel Adams Drake, The Border Wars of New England (1897; Williamstown, mass., 1973), p. 107.

[89] *Salem Witchcraft Papers,* II: 405.

[90] Cotton Mather. "A Brand Pluck't Out of the Burning," pp. 281-2. Cotton Mather suspected that the witch conspiracy had "some of its Original among the Indians" (Cotton Mather, *Decennium Luctuosum,* p. 103).

[91] Ibid., pp. 243-7. See also Christine Heyrman, *Commerce and Culture,* p. 105 n11.

[92] *Salem Witchcraft Papers,* II: 611.

[93] *Records and Files of the Quarterly Courts of Essex County,* VII: 135, 26 November 1678.

[94] *Salem Witchcraft Papers,* I: 52.

[95] Paul Boyer and Stephen Nissenbaum, *Salem Possessed,* pp. 146, 200.

[96] *Salem Witchcraft Papers,* I: 83, 86.

[97] Ibid., I: 95.

[98] Paul Boyer and Stephen Nissenbaum, *Salem Possessed,* p. 146.

[99] Ibid., pp. 193-4.

[100] Sarah Loring Bailey, *Historical Sketches of Andover,* p. 202; Charlotte Helen Abbott, "Early Records of the Allen Families of Andover" (Andover Historical Society, Andover, Mass.), p. 1.

[101] Charlotte Helen Abbott, "Early Records of the

Foster Families of Andover" (Andover Historical Society, Andover, Mass.), p. 1; Frederick Clifton Pierce, *Foster Genealogy* (Chicago, 1899), p. 1032.

[102] John Noble and John F. Cronin, eds., *Records of the Court of Assistants of the Colony of Massachusetts Bay, 1630-1692,* 3 vols. (Boston, 1901-28), I: 303-4.

[103] Anders Robinson, "Wardwell and Barker Families of Andover in the Seventeenth Century" (Andover Historical Society, Andover, Mass.), 3.10-3.12, 4.10.

[104] Cotton Mather, *Wonders of the Invisible World,* pp. 74-5, 80.

[105] As John Demos points out, it was because "the social climate of New England as a whole was then unusually strained" that fears of witchcraft "spread well beyond Salem, and adjacent communities produced responsive accusations of their own" (John Demos, *Entertaining Satan,* p. 385). . . .

JUDICIAL BACKGROUND
Thomas Fisk et al. (essay date 1692)

SOURCE: "The Penitance of the Jurors," in *Narratives of the Witchcraft Cases, 1648-1706,* edited by George Lincoln Burr, 1914. Reprint by Barnes & Noble Books, 1972, pp. 387-88.

[In the following excerpt from a document written in the year of the trials, Fisk, representing the Salem jurors, admits that they were deluded and mistaken in convicting the accused witches, and humbly asks forgiveness.]

. . . We whose names are under written, being in the Year 1692 called to serve as Jurors, in Court at Salem, on Tryal of many, who were by some suspected Guilty of doing Acts of Witchcraft upon the Bodies of sundry Persons:

We confess that we our selves were not capable to understand, nor able to withstand the mysterious delusions of the Powers of Darkness, and Prince of the Air; but were for want of Knowledge in our selves, and better Information from others, prevailed with to take up with such Evidence against the Accused, as on further consideration, and better Information, we justly fear was insufficient for the touching the Lives of any, Deut. 17. 6, whereby we fear we have been instrumental with others, tho Ignorantly and unwit-

tingly, to bring upon our selves, and this People of the Lord, the Guilt of Innocent Blood; which Sin the Lord saith in Scripture, he would not pardon, 2 Kings 24. 4, that is we suppose in regard of his temporal Judgments. We do therefore hereby signifie to all in general (and to the surviving Sufferers in especial) our deep sense of, and sorrow for our Errors, in acting on such Evidence to the condemning of any person.

And do hereby declare that we justly fear that we were sadly deluded and mistaken, for which we are much disquieted and distressed in our minds; and do therefore humbly beg forgiveness, first of God for Christ's sake for this our Error; And pray that God would not impute the guilt of it to our selves, nor others; and we also pray that we may be considered candidly, and aright by the living Sufferers as being then under the power of a strong and general Delusion, utterly unacquainted with, and not experienced in matters of that Nature.

We do heartily ask forgiveness of you all, whom we have justly offended, and do declare according to our present minds, we would none of us do such things again on such grounds for the whole World; praying you to accept of this in way of Satisfaction for our Offence; and that you would bless the Inheritance of the Lord, that he may be intreated for the Land.

Foreman, THOMAS FISK,   THOMAS PERLY, *Senior*

WILLIAM FISK,	JOHN PEBODY,
JOHN BATCHELER,	THOMAS PERKINS,
THOMAS FISK, *Junior*	SAMUEL SAYER,
JOHN DANE,	ANDREW ELLIOTT,
JOSEPH EVELITH,	HENRY HERRICK, *Senior.* . . .

Perry Miller (essay date 1953)

SOURCE: "The Judgment of the Witches," in *The New England Mind: From Colony to Province,* 1953. Reprint by Beacon Press, 1961, pp. 191-208.

[In the following excerpt, Miller examines the impact made on the witchcraft trials by jeremiads, or Puritan sermons, which emphasized that God brings affliction on sinners and stressed the need for confession and repentance.]

The most curious of all the facts in that welter we call Salem witchcraft is this: if you expunge from the record those documents that arise directly out of the affair, and those which treat it historically, like the

Magnalia or Hale's and Calef's accounts, and a few twinges of memory such as appear in Sewall's *Diary,* the intellectual history of New England up to 1720 can be written as though no such thing ever happened. It had no effect on the ecclesiastical or political situation, it does not figure in the institutional or ideological development. Aside from a few oblique lamentations in election sermons (briefly noted amid the catalogue of woes), for twenty-eight years this cataclysm hardly appears in the record—until summoned from the deep by opponents of inoculation as a stick to beat the clergy for yet another "delusion." Only in 1721 does it begin to be that blot on New England's fame which has been enlarged, as much by friends as by foes, into its greatest disgrace.

To this statement, there is one qualification: after 1692, not only is the episode seldom referred to, but the very word witchcraft almost vanishes from public discourse. While the clergy were steadily expanding the list of possible afflictions which would surely befall the community, the place reserved by Cotton Mather's *Memorable Providences* for the threat of demonic intervention is suddenly vacated. This silence speaks volumes: although new and fascinating abuses are relentlessly explored, no one any longer tries to induce a confession of sinfulness by predicting a spate of witches.

I do not need to demonstrate that belief in witchcraft was, for the seventeenth century, not only plausible but scientifically rational. No more tedious pages exist than those devoted to the thankless task of exonerating the Puritans, on this score, from the charge of superstition. Despite such efforts, thousands of Americans are still persuaded that Cotton Mather "burned" witches in Salem; further refutation becomes a bore. Still, it is difficult to see clearly and objectively just what was involved; language itself proves treacherous, and analysis rebounds upon the analyst. Critics of the Puritan priesthood—often children of that caste—have wrenched the story from its context; sober historians, trying to restore the true setting, slide into the accents of apology and gloss over a crime. One may appreciate that witchcraft was as real an offense in 1692 as murder or treason and yet remain profoundly convinced that what went wrong at Salem is something for which Puritanism and New England are justly to be indicted, not in terms of a more "enlightened" age, but specifically in their own terms—in those of the covenant.

I dislike dissociating myself from previous scholarship, but many students, including some who strive to place these occurrences within the intellectual frame of the period, fail to consider them in relation to the whole scheme of thought. They have read the contemporaneous literature of witchcraft, but not the

weekly sermons. We shall avoid confusing ourselves by an irrelevant intrusion of modern criteria only when we realize that what struck Salem Village was intelligible to everybody concerned—instigators, victims, judges, and clergy—within the logic of the covenant. That in the end the irruption nearly wrecked this intellectual structure—that it left the scaffolding dangerously shaken and out of kilter—is its deepest meaning in the actual language of the community.

Let us remember, without concerning ourselves about the psychosis of the hysterical girls who precipitated the panic by their reckless accusations of an array of tormentors, that an appearance of witchcraft among the afflictions of New England was from the beginning as much to be anticipated as Indian raids; by 1692 several instances had been encountered, and a more organized assault was altogether predictable. Some in Salem Village may have read *Memorable Providences,* but they needed no book to set them off. Accusations and interrogations were already in train when the former minister, Deodat Lawson, came back to the town from Scituate to deliver a Thursday lecture, on March 24; he knew something of what was going on, and had even heard that victims complained of being tormented by specters of his wife and daughter, both three years dead. Charles Upham, writing from the point of view of 1867, felt that Lawson must have prepared his sermon in advance and have come to the village deliberately intending to blow up the flames. But Upham had not studied the jeremiads. Lawson did not require preparation: the formula, with its neatly boxed heads of argument and application, with its rhetorical tags already minted, was as ready to be wheeled into action as a loaded fieldpiece. Of course his sermon did nothing to allay the panic, but what Lawson applied to the situation was not malicious incendiarism; it was traditional federal wisdom. What other wisdom was there?

He made the standard points: afflictions come upon a people from God (or by His permission) because of their sins; the only relief is prayer and repentance, to be manifested by confession of the provoking deeds; meanwhile, the duty of civil magistrates, in the interest of public welfare, is vigorously to suppress disorders and to punish criminals, above all those who refuse to repent and confess. He used customary artifices of style to "improve" the present distress, exactly as every preacher enhanced military disasters or epidemics. In the light of accumulated experience, his discourse was no more "irrational" than the speech of Edward Everett at Gettysburg. So recognizable an exercise of the type was Lawson's *Christ's Fidelity the only Shield against Satan's Malignity* that upon its publication in Boston, masters of the form—the Mathers, Willard, James Allen, Baily, Charles Morton—happily endorsed it. That it reënforced the resolve of the magistrates to ferret out evildoers cannot be questioned: since 1689 clerical leaders, worried lest the royal charter should prevent magistrates from coöperating, had redoubled the effort to exhort them; Lawson followed precedent, and besought Hathorne not to bear a sword in vain.

But, as we know, the list of sins and their afflictions was long and daily becoming longer; no single offense stood by itself, for all were interconnected. The pattern of depravity was so subtle that an exclusive concentration upon one vice easily became encouragement of another. Lawson knew that already the specter of his dead (and sainted) wife was being accused; this was a highly suspect piece of witchcraft which might the more readily be explained on the grounds of a disordered "phansie"—as Increase Mather in the *Essay* had accounted for previous apparitions in New England. For decades the ministers had been denouncing—without effect—an increase of backbiting, talebearing, and rash censuring; Lawson recognized that a vigorous prosecution of real witches might offer the temptation, to a people exacerbated by a series of peculiarly acrimonious village quarrels, to imagine that the specters of any or all their neighbors were let loose. So, even thus early, he delivered the momentous caution: the Devil may represent good and decent citizens as afflictors of others; therefore, to accuse any without sufficient grounds will have a pernicious influence, will bring in confusion and an abundance of evil.

This much we may say the jeremiad (as developed up to 1692) could do: on the one hand exhort to action and on the other caution against headlong zeal. But what Lawson saw with his own eyes, the day before he spoke, was as real as any Indian rush upon a frontier town; the situation did not require subtle discriminations concerning the role of specters. Gestures of the accused produced physical and visible effects upon the afflicted, "so that they are their own Image." This was as welcome to the investigating authorities as first-hand evidence would be to a modern prosecuting attorney eager not to have to rely on circumstantial testimonies.

Through the next weeks and months doubt spread, more slowly than we might wish, but at about the pace we ought to expect. The Court of Oyer and Terminer, with Stoughton presiding, and with Sewall, Richards, Gedney, Wait Winthrop, Sargent, Corwin on the bench, was trusting far too much to "spectral evidence." It was not insisting upon the solid common-law principle that an act must be seen by two witnesses. The doctrine of the specter was as old as the science of witchcraft itself: as Cotton Mather summarized it, once a witch signs the book and covenants with hell (the special heinousness of this crime was the fact that it, like regeneration, took the form

of a covenant), Satan delegates to him a devil who, taking on the likeness of the witch, executes his behests, such chores as pinching his enemies, blinding them, burning their houses or wrecking their ships. True, the specter, like the sorcerer's apprentice, might gain mastery over the master and compel him to molest those with whom he had no quarrel; but still, the specter belongs to the culprit and, if seen, is a fair presumption against him, just as a dog may lead the police to its owner.

Nonetheless, experience had shown that spectral evidence must be handled with care. New England intellectuals probably had not heard, "The spirit that I have seen may be the Devil"; but in more authoritative works they had learned that he might assume a pleasing shape and abuse the credulous in order to damn them. Wherefore not every specter was to be taken for the person he resembled. But the court at Salem—mainly because of Stoughton's conviction—committed itself to the proposition that no innocent person could, under the providence of God, be represented by a specter, and that therefore those who were manifested were guilty. That the accused should deny their confederacy was only to be expected: having become the Devil's children, they could confess only with his permission. Upon these (as Cotton Mather called them) "philosophical schemes of witchcraft," they proceeded, as juries have been known to act upon a settled pre-conviction that no white woman can possibly offer sexual provocation to a Negro.

There is no evidence that any minister ever taught this doctrine, or that more than three accepted it; both Mathers, the principal theorists in the country, had explicitly warned against it. As early as May 31, Cotton was begging John Richards not to lay too great stress on this sort of testimony, because—here was the issue—"It is very certain that the divells have sometimes represented the shapes of persons not only innocent, but also very virtuous." Indeed, the riddle of Cotton Mather's part in the business is bound up with his prophecy that if once unrestricted credit were yielded to diabolical representations, "The Door is opened!" Had the court heeded his recommendation, there would have been no executions; if, having made it, he had thereafter kept his mouth shut, he would be a hero today.

By June 15, doubt was spreading rapidly, and a puzzled Phips, trying his level best to be a pious magistrate, asked advice from the local association of ministers. In the *Magnalia* Cotton says, with that unction which infects even his most worthy actions, that the answer "was drawn up at their desire by Mr. Mather the younger, as I have been informed." *The Return of Several Ministers,* by whomever written, is a significant document in the history of New England because, first, it acknowledges that the ministers were in a quandary of their own making, and, second, it shows that even in a regime where they had contrived to seat their own governor and a Council of their own choosing, and where the court at Salem was made up of professing brethern, they really no longer had any power. The court was proceeding on a principle of its own; the clergy might counsel otherwise, but were prisoners of their own reiterations; they were obliged by their previous utterances to conclude with the familiar exhortation that civil authority should press forward to a vigorous prosecution of the obnoxious—which Stoughton was heartily doing without their encouragement. At that moment, nobody quite heard the crash, but a central pillar of the jeremiad, shored up after 1689, tumbled to earth. This was the last time that a ruler of Massachusetts, in an hour of hesitation, formally and officially asked advice of the churches.

In the eyes of posterity, *The Return* is vitiated by its concluding paragraph. This must be read as a formality which the ministers were obliged to observe. The really important paragraph is the sixth, which asserts positively that a demon can appear in the shape of an innocent person, and that therefore a mere charge of representation does not constitute adequate grounds for conviction. On August 17, Cotton Mather was again insisting, this time to John Foster, that spectral evidence is fallacious; during the summer he so far admitted his awareness of the court's incompetence as to propose the remedy he had proved efficacious in the case of Martha Goodwin: he offered to take six or more of the afflicted into his house and cure them by prayer, without any trials or executions. Finally, on October 3 Increase Mather—and he alone—brought the murders to an end by issuing *Cases of Conscience,* which so unequivocally condemned spectral evidence that Phips at last saw his duty clear and terminated the court—although by that time twenty persons had been executed and a raging Stoughton, as his final gesture, signed a warrant (which Phips annulled) for eight more.

We may imagine—though there is no way of telling—that had *The Return* spoken as emphatically on June 15 as *Cases of Conscience* did on October 3, the frenzy would have been arrested. Lacking such guidance, between these dates the madness had to work itself out: a reckless use of spectral evidence gave rein to the seething passions and festering animosities of New England. Prisons became crowded, every man's life lay at the mercy of any accuser, brother looked sidewise at brother, and the friend of many years' standing became a bad security risk: said Gedney from the bench to John Alden, "that truly he had been acquainted with him these many years; and had always accounted him a good man; but indeed now he should be obliged to change his opinion." If the ministers are to be blamed—as they must—for not aggressively combating Stoughton's insensate dogmatism, still only three let themselves become open supporters: Samuel Parris (who appears

utterly contemptible), Nicholas Noyes of Salem (who lived to repent), and John Hale of Beverly, who abruptly altered his mind when his wife was accused. Otherwise a fair number of them ventured at least as far as offering testimonials to the good character of several of the accused—an act which required courage. We become convinced that behind these attestations lies more than readily meets the eye when we find a petition from Chebacco parish on behalf of John Proctor headed with the name of John Wise. The mania had, to almost everybody's perception except Stoughton's, run its course when at last Samuel Willard of the Old South was cried upon. Out of the dungeon of the condemned, John Proctor sent an appeal to Increase Mather, Willard, Allen, Baily (endorsers of Lawson's sermon), which told them of the "Popish cruelties" the court was employing in order to extract confessions; the ministers were the last hope. And Thomas Brattle is convincing proof that, aside from the misguided three, throughout the country the elders were dissatisfied, and that, above all, Increase Mather and Samuel Willard were aghast.

Thomas Brattle's *Letter,* purportedly addressed to someone in England, is dated October 8, five days after Increase's *Cases;* that it was ever sent is doubtful, and the presumption is that, like Cotton's *Political Fables,* it circulated through the proper quarters in manuscript. Phips put an end to the court because Increase gave him the signal; Brattle's *Letter* was not a factor in that decision, but it represents a response to the deteriorating situation which, independent of the ministers, was in step with them—although chronologically no earlier. Brattle was a merchant, a mathematician, and an amateur astronomer whose contributions won him the gratitude of Sir Isaac Newton. The *Letter* is a milestone in American literature if only for its free-and-easy, its highly literate and satirical tone; in New England it is the first treatment of disaster that steps outside the scheme of the jeremiad. Considered merely stylistically, it may be interpreted as a more open expression than any provincial had yet undertaken of the mentality that had slowly been taking shape in "moderate" circles. Certainly its style was the more accessible to Brattle because, after 1689, through contact with the capital new England had become aware of the revolutions wrought in prose discourse since the days of Cromwell. He did not trouble to wrestle with the problem of how a covenanted nation could make so manifest a gaff as that at Salem. Striking a new note in American polemics, he plunged directly into ridicule of the court, calling its doctrine not a "new philosophy" but "Salem superstition and sorcery." If rhetorical tricks would serve, he would goad his countrymen into the Enlightenment with the sneer that such nonsense was "not fitt to be named in a land of such light as New-England is."

Hence it is all the more instructive to discover Brattle's reason for delaying until October his blast against

Stoughton's court: he was reluctant to besmear authority. He did not want to appear as one notoriously given to a "factious spirit." In 1692, this meant only Elisha Cooke's anti-charter party (one has to remember that the witchcraft issue did not, at least at this time, become entangled in the acrimonious political division, and that Cooke's "patriots" did not use it against the Mathers—which shows that they were no clearer in their own minds, and that at this moment no such charge against the clergy would have stuck). But now, as bitter experience made clear that the court, through its fanatical adherence to an idiotic principle of jurisprudence, had shed "the innocentest blood imaginable," Brattle excoriated the "Salem Gentlemen" because, having submitted to the Devil's stratagem, they imperiled that "liberty" which "was evermore accounted the great priviledge of an Englishman." At no point suggesting the slightest disagreement with Increase Mather—rather making clear his full accord—Brattle concluded his *Letter* with one of the great sentences of the time, which, eschewing the jargon of the covenant, reveals how much the theme of the jeremiads had become, if only through the discipline of disillusion, a secular patriotism: "I am afraid that ages will not wear off that reproach and those stains which these things will leave behind them upon our land."

Perhaps I make too much of Brattle's omission of any covenantal consideration. Nevertheless, brief as his *Letter* is, not only does it fail to summon up that conception, not only does it take the land to be simply "our land" instead of one plighted to God, but it assumes two radical positions: it declares that the (by then) glib confessions of guilt are not to be trusted; and it flatly asserts that the court has perpetrated a disastrous mistake.

One fact the record does indeed make clear: in this situation that very course of action so resoundingly trumpeted in the jeremiads as the only remedy for social ills—confession and repentance—became a dodge. It did not heal the grievance, but compounded the evil. For decades the logic of the covenant had been clear, whether applied to individuals or to nations: one enters into the bond, he sins, and is afflicted, according to explicit terms; he confesses his sin, the affliction is removed, he is restored to the covenant (as a church member under censure is fully restored to the church after public confession). But on August 20, Margaret Jacobs, who had acknowledged the crime and whose accusations hanged her grandfather, recanted her admission, "Having, through the magistrates' threatenings, and my own vile and wretched heart, confessed several things contrary to my conscience and knowledge." At Andover, whither the accusations spread, the whole mechanism became a shambles as six women promptly confessed, only to explain that they had not known what else to say. By the time Brattle and Mather wrote, the jails were full of confessors; several fled, but

others confessed wholesale—and were safe. The hunt could have become such a horror as to outrun the worst imaginings of the time had not the very weight of the confessions broken down every effort to secure them; their value depreciated spectacularly (as did the bills of credit) as they became patently devices for eluding what Brattle called the "rude and barbarous methods" of the court. But in this case, what was left, in the midst of such merely politic humiliations, of that sincere repentance called for in the enduring covenant of Abraham?

According to federal theory, an afflicted but unrepenting people invite further affliction. In the opinion of many unprejudiced spectators, said Brattle, the condemned "went out of the world not only with as great protestations, but also with as good shows of innocency, as men could do." By strictly and conscientiously applying the doctrine of the jeremiad, the court created a situation in which meretricious confession went free and sincere denial automatically became guilt. There is no more poignant testimony to the hold of the conception upon the minds of ordinary New Englanders than the fact that those who died because of it remained to the end faithful to it. Records of the court were not published, and so few actually heard the words of Mary Easty, but such "considerate" observers as Brattle were bound to sense the logical impasse to which she had come:

> I petition to Your Honors not for my own life, for I know I must die, and my appointed time is set; but the Lord he knows it is that, if it be possible, no more innocent blood may be shed, which undoubtedly cannot be avoided in the way and course you go in. I question not but Your Honors do to the utmost of your powers in the discovery and detecting of witchcraft and witches, and would not be guilty of innocent blood for the world. But, by my own innocency, I know you are in the wrong way.

Her dilemma was precisely her inability to do what, had she been guilty, she would gladly have done; and she could not, like so many others, prostitute the federal theology by cynically confessing. "They say myself and others have made a league with the Devil, we cannot confess." Hordes of reformed witches, instead of testifying to the mercy of the covenant, were becoming an embarrassment, while Mary Easty simply said, "I cannot, I dare not, belie my own soul." Good citizens, caught in the mesh of accusation, had no way to escape except by a deed more evil than any bargain with the Black Man, while repentant witches could smear whomever they pleased with impunity. In a remarkably short time (all things considered) it was borne upon even John Hale that had all twenty of the executed ("some of them were knowing persons") been guilty, a few of them would surely have saved their lives by doing the expected. Whereas for the mass who did confess—"we had no experience whether they would ("some of them were knowing persons") been guilty, a few of them would surely have saved their lives by doing the expected. Whereas for the mass who did confess—"we had no experience whether they would stand to their Self-condemning confessions, when they came to dye." For Mary Easty, having worked herself through the labyrinth with no other guide than her native wit, said to the court, "I would humbly beg of you, that Your Honors would be pleased . . . to try some of these confessing witches"—which the court never dared do. Indeed, had it come to that extremity, there was reason to suspect that many of them, instead of standing to their profession of evil, would have recanted to virtue!

Cases of Conscience is as important a document in the history of the American mind as Brattle's *Letter*, not so much because it was effective as because it sprang from the same recognitions. Fourteen ministers signed the preface, making it even more a manifesto of solidarity than Lawson's sermon; they showed their comprehension of the issue by declaring that unless there was convincing proof for any crime, whether witchcraft or murder, God does not then intend that the culprit be discovered. Whereupon Increase denounced spectral evidence, and skillfully turned the possibility that a good man should be so represented into a trial of faith. Those who supposed that the malice of Satan is so constrained that he is incapable of this feat were now accused of being the Sadducees! Confession itself, at least in these realms, was no longer a safe rule; the only reliable ground was such as would obtain "in any other Crime of a Capital nature"—the credible testimony under oath of two actual witnesses.

But—and it is a large but—Increase added a postscript: he did not intend any reflection on members of the court! "They are wise and good Men, and have acted with all Fidelity according to their Light, and have out of tenderness declined the doing of some things, which in our Judgments they were satisfied about." He himself had attended the trial of Burroughs, and could declare it fair. The judges must be believed when they say that none was convicted "meerly on the account of what Spectres have said." Without the postscript, *Cases of Conscience* would be a bold stroke; with it, the book is a miserable species of double-talk.

We grasp its import only to the extent that we appreciate the habit of speech that grew up in New England as an inevitable concomitant of the jeremiads: references had to be phrased in more and more generalized terms, names never explicitly named, so that we are obliged to decipher out of oblique insinuations what to contemporaries were broad designations. When ministers denounced "oppression" and "luxury," they meant certain people whom they did not have to specify.

The controversy between moderates and the charter party must be deduced from what seem like platitudes in election sermons, where minor shifts of emphasis betrayed party maneuvers. This habit of ambiguity, de

---

Beard on contemporary theories about witchcraft:

. . . The leading idea all through witchcraft was that the devil entered into people; and that persons of high position and noted for piety sometimes entered into covenant with Satan to do evil work, such as tormenting or killing their neighbors and friends, or injuring the earth in many ways. It was claimed that the devil would appear as a "black man," or in any other shape he chose to assume; he presented a book and made a bargain with those who consented to act as his agents; and he, on his part, promised to confer upon his allies riches, eloquence, and strength, and bestow upon them amazing powers, and they could go to do his will in the form of a dog, a cat, a hog, mouse, or toad, or a bird. . . .

It was part of the theory of the witchcraft delusion that the devil used the spectres of some persons to affect other persons. Some contended that the devil could employ only spectres of persons "who were in league with him;" others that he could employ the specters of "innocent persons, without their knowldege or consent." The former idea–that he could only employ the spectres of persons who were in voluntary league with him– was the dogma on which the Salem tricks were founded, and the dogma which convicted all who were accused; just as the dogma of the ability to know right from wrong would condemn nearly every lunatic who is arraigned for murder.

In Salem village, the suspected witches, male and female, were subjected, as the custom for ages had been, to examination with pins, all over the body, in order to detect the shriveled and callous and nonsensitive places, which were supposed to be diagnostic of bewitchment. . . .

George M. Beard, The Psychology of the Salem Witchcraft Excitement of 1692, *John E. Edwards, 1882.*

---

veloped out of New England's insecurity, out of its inability to face frankly its own internal divisions, out of its effort to maintain a semblance of unity even while unanimity was crumbling—which became more elaborate and disingenuous as internecine passions waxed— was to cling to the New England mind for centuries.

were proud that their sermons never indicated any awareness of controversy. In Boston society today, matters may be fully discussed which, to an outsider, seem never to be mentioned at all. Such tribal reticence only an occasional Thoreau was to defy or an Emily Dickinson to turn into secret triumph.

Hence, for contemporaneous ears, *Cases of Conscience* was actually a blast against the court. Early the next year, Increase was circulating a letter from an English correspondent expressing surprise that so learned a man as Stoughton "should take up a persuasion, that the devil cannot assume the likeness of an innocent, to afflict another person." Increase Mather would stand in American history with a Zenger or a Lovejoy had he said what was in his mind, had he publicly repudiated the court. But neither he nor any of the clergy could do so—the friendship of the judges and all they stood for was too valuable. A modern political party will write into its platform a plank which in effect disowns the conduct of Congressional leaders—and then support the reëlection of exactly those discredited members. The virtuous act would be to split the party, but Increase shrank from that nobility. He wrote a treatise which by every implication—and in historical fact—proscribed the court, but which still preserved a show of unity among leading citizens by praising what it censured. He may honestly have persuaded himself (as at the trial of Burroughs) that the court was not sentencing "meerly" on spectral evidence, but he could not have written the *Cases* had he not known otherwise. It is a carefully designed book—courageous but also dishonest. Once his arguments were accepted, the court became (as Increase knew it would) infamous; group loyalty—or, if you will, class loyalty—kept him from saying so outright, and still more distressingly, kept him trying to avoid saying so for the rest of his life. Still, there is honesty in his book, enough to make it a matter of record that the supervisors of the covenant—the ruling class of Massachusetts—had been stampeded into a barbarism as gross, fundamentally, as anything they charged against Louis XIV. And as he defined it, the error consisted not in any charge which later generations would levy, but solely in violation of the standards professed by the Puritan jeremiad.

Increase had long since become a tactician: he had learned much in London that he had not known when preaching on the woes of Philip's War. He was capable of writing his postscript to the *Cases* even while acknowledging to his journal that innocent blood had been shed. His son Cotton never left the vicinity of Boston, never served apprentice in a wider, a less scrupulous world. Upon him fell the weight of contradiction, and we must say to the credit of provincial morality that he was the one to suffer. Pressed into service by those already apprehensive that things had gone wrong, he was commissioned to absolve them; to his undying infamy, he accepted the assignment. He knew of only

one device through which the deed might be justified—the theology of the national covenant. If the Salem Gentlemen (which meant all gentlemen) were to preserve their self-respect—or their solidarity—they must have not so much a defense as a demonstration; whatever had happened had still, by some stretch of ingenuity, to be translated into a proof that New England was the chosen people. He undertook the task when he knew better, and composed that apologia for insincerity which, entitled *The Wonders of the Invisible World,* has ever since scarred his reputation, even among those who have no notion wherein its actual dishonesty consists.

He had put himself into the position from which he could not retreat by becoming the peerless penman of the colony. In the middle of September, poor Phips was under fire from the home government; he needed help. He asked—Cotton says "commanded"—that Mather prepare a plausible record of some, if not all, of the trials. On September 20, Cotton, who seems not to have known exactly what his father was pondering, wrote an abject letter to Stephen Sewall, brother of Samuel, clerk of the court in Salem, beseeching a transcript of the record; even then he betrayed the paralyzing doubt that hung over the composition of his most deplorable utterance. "You should imagine me as obstinate a Sadduce and Witch-advocate as any among us," he begged of Sewall: "Address mee as one that Believ'd Nothing Reasonable." Propagandists put to an impossible task commence with the prayer that they may first of all manage to propagandize themselves.

On September 22, the final day of the court, after the last executions, Samuel and Stephen Sewall, with Stoughton and Hathorne (who had conducted the high-handed preliminary interrogations), rode down to Boston; they met with Cotton Mather and sealed his fate. Stephen promised to go back to Salem and get the records; Stoughton and Sewall promised to stand by him; Cotton went to his study and, in fear and trembling, began to write. Leaving a blank page for the endorsement Stoughton was to supply him, this tortured soul blurted out his first sentence: "I live by Neighbours that force me to produce these undeserved Lines." If ever there was a false book produced by a man whose heart was not in it, it is *The Wonders*.

Once started, this man whose pen raced across blank paper at breakneck speed could not stop. His mind was bubbling with every sentence of the jeremiads, for he was heart and soul in the effort to reorganize them. And for days Stephen Sewall did not send the records. Cotton might have waited; a man secure of himself would have waited; he was insecure, frightened, sick at heart (at the end of his manuscript he was again to betray himself: he had done "the Service imposed upon me"). He wrote an introduction, hoping that it would anticipate the records; like a criminal who protests his innocence, the more he scribbled, the more he disclosed.

Still no word from Salem: he put in an extract from Perkins; he redacted a sermon (in the vein of Lawson's) he had delivered on August 4; he devised a further jeremiad-like address to the country—and still nothing from Salem. He ransacked his library for stories of apparitions, hoping that they might substantiate what he was about to receive. The book was already swelling much too big—he had to admit—and he had just transcribed the report of a trial before Sir matthew Hale, when, to his immense relief, Stephen's packet arrived. He worked out a version of five of the twenty trials, wrote a few wearied and confused observations, and rushed the monstrous collection to a printer. The book was on the streets about October 15. (Meanwhile, Increase had read *Cases of Conscience* to the associated ministers on October 3; though it was not published for another month, Phips and the General Court had acted upon it; and Stoughton, who raged against Phips and was never to retract his conviction that a specter is proof of witchcraft, had written his foreword of full approbation for Cotton Mather's zeal and vigor—which he would never have done had the book managed to convey, except by its utter confusion, what Cotton Mather had really believed about spectral evidence.)

Cotton evidently finished his redaction of Stephen Sewall's notes on October 11, for on that day Stoughton and Samuel Sewall attested that it was a true report of matters of fact and evidence. Why did the poor devil not leave well enough alone, publish the reports, and throw into the fire everything he had poured out during the days of waiting? He suffered from a monstrous lust for publication, that much is certain; but the fuller explanation, accounting for the discharge of both his conscious and unconscious motivations, is the compelling force of the jeremiad. He had to find a rationale for his country's ordeal and at the same time a modicum of peace with himself; he did both by forcing this wretched business into the traditional scheme of sin and retribution, which to him was the only form that would give conceivable significance either to New England's tragedy or to his own comprehension of it. He could not let a word he had written out of his trance go to waste; hence he, a stylist who kept even the sprawling *Magnalia* under some coherent control, published the most incoherent jumble he ever allowed to appear between covers.

In the helter-skelter of prefatory material he made once again every point which in the previous two chapters have emerged as themes in the reconstituted jeremiads. The first part—a good two-thirds of the book—is an epitome of all pronouncements since 1689. We New Englanders, he says, are the most loyal of subjects: hence Their Majesties' people should not be tormented by witches. We fully accept the principle of toleration, and make no distinction among Christians, whether Congregationalists, Presbyterians, or Episcopalians. Somehow at stake in all this are our "English Liberties" and our charter, which is attended "with singular Priviledges," such as choosing our own Council. Cotton could not cope with witches unless he first explained once more that New England was not so bad as the jeremiads had sometimes said: the body of the people were honest and industrious, multitudes here grew ripe for heaven, and were such as could make a right use of stupendous and prodigious occasions. Therefore New England should not have "an Unsavoury and a Sulpherous Resentment in the Opinion of the World abroad." At the same time, this community—founded by a chosen generation of saints and at first "a true Utopia"—was abysmally degenerated; it had become a nest of swearing, Sabbath-breaking, whoring, drunkenness. Consequently it had suffered in increasing severity a series of judgments—Antinomians, crop failures, sickness, revocation of the charter, Indian wars, fires, losses at sea, and now this climax, a descent of devils *in propribus personibus*. There is something both appealing and repulsive in Cotton's frantic clutching at the old array of sins in order to explain this affliction, at those village vices so long since arraigned: back-biting, scandal-mongering, talebearing, suits-at-law—precisely that cave of winds into which anthropologists of today would search for "causes" of the saturnalia that overwhelmed Salem Village.

Cotton Mather made all he could of the manifest stepping up of the scale of suffering, which would in itself certify New England's special position in the universe: "A Variety of Calamity has long follow'd this Plantation," even unto "a more than ordinary affliction." Against all these there was in 1692, as from the beginning, only one preservation: "REFORMATION! REFORMATION! has been the repeated Cry of all the Judgments that have hitherto been upon us." But, according to formula, because we have hitherto been as deaf as adders, "the Adders of the Infernal Pit are now hissing about us." Here at last was the long-sought, the long-desired consummation of the catalogue.

Except that there was—or there might be—a climax beyond even this: that dreadful culmination which for the Mathers (if not for all their colleagues) would be the truly final resolution. We cannot begin to comprehend this curious volume without perceiving that on page after page, whenever the tension becomes unbearable, the discourse plunges into Chiliastic ecstasy. The witches are signs of the times, of the death-pangs of the Devil; mischievous powers prevail for the moment, but only because his rule is nearing extinction. "The Devils Whole-time, cannot but be very near its End."

In the pressure of these packed moments, on the tenterhooks of anxiety, Cotton Mather made a syllabus for the new jeremiad. In his feverish concentration, everything pointed to one conclusion—the one he had striven for three years to make—that because Satan was gathering his forces for the ultimate assault, the civil magistrates were especially required to suppress any and all disorders, to punish every offender. (However, oddly enough, even in his delirium he kept his recently acquired sense of proportion, and though he termed New England the "center," hastily added, "and after a sort, the First-born of our English Settlements.") Whatever cautions he had studied during the summer, in throwing together these words he went with the tide of his rhetoric and found himself exhorting the magistrates "to do something extraordinary in promoting what is laudable, and in restraining and chastising of Evil Doers."

All of this was in the pattern; and Salem judges, having done their duty, endorsed *The Wonders.* There was only one hitch, and Cotton revealed it: the convictions had been secured "notwithstanding the Great and Just Suspicion, that the Daemons might Impose the Shapes of Innocent Persons in their Spectral Exhibitions upon the Sufferers (which may perhaps prove no small part of the Witch-Plot in the issue)." Every day he waited for Stephen's transcripts, Cotton heard that this had become "a most agitated Controversie among us," until he was shrieking that the Devil has pushed us "into a Blind Mans Buffet, and we are even ready to be sinfully, yea, hotly, and madly, mauling one another in the dark." This sentence is, obviously, a prime example of that peculiar kind of revelation without explicit admission that had become an acquired characteristic of the New England mind.

What he could not conceal from himself was that the formula of covenant reformation had miscarried. As all good jeremiads had said, the preliminary to release from affliction is confession; now there were confessions aplenty, the jails were full and "there is extream Hazard, lest the Devil by Compulsion must submit to that Great Work, may also by Permission, come to Confound that Work," lest he "intertwist some of his Delusions." Knowing that every moment he delayed, "a common Stream of Dissatisfaction" was mounting to which Phips would have to yield, putting the best face possible upon that prospect by prophesying that a wise magistrate may leave undone things he can no longer do "when the Publick Safety makes an Exigency," Cotton salvaged what defense he could for a court in which he did not believe by the pitiful remonstrance: "Surely, they have at worst been but the faults of a well-meaning Ignorance." We avert our gaze while he, having made what he could of Stephen's notes, fled up the ladder of the jeremiad and soothed himself with fresh dreams of the New Jerusalem, "from whence the Devil shall then be banished, there shall be no Devil within the Walls of that Holy City."

Mather did all this harm to himself after the trials were over, at the very moment sanity was returning. There is no need to apologize for him, for what he did deserves no apology; but we need accuse him only of what he actually did do. He is not responsible for killing Rebecca Nurse or George Burroughs. But he tried to make those killings legitimate when he knew they were murders by dressing them in the paraphernalia of the federal doctrine ("When this is done, Then let us own the Covenant"). He tried it even though he knew that the covenant remedy of confession had become a farce. By gathering the folds of that prophetic mantle around the gaping hypotheses of Stoughton's court, he fatally soiled it. The consequences were not to be fully realized for several years, but the damage was done. Samuel Eliot Morison says that Robert Calef tied a tin can to Cotton Mather which has rattled and banged through the pages of superficial and popular historians. My account is not popular, and I strive to make it not superficial; assuredly, if by tin can is meant the charge that Mather worked up the Salem tragedy, it does not belong to him; but what Calef was actually to charge was that he prostituted a magnificent conception of New England's destiny to saving the face of a bigoted court. In that sense, the right can was tied to the proper tail, and through the pages of this volume it shall rattle and bang.

Sometime during this fatal week, while Increase Mather was seeking a way to stop the court without discrediting it, while Cotton was being forced into defending the indefensible and Thomas Brattle was sickening of the Salem Gentlemen, a wit in Boston wrote a, sixteen-page dialogue between *S* (obviously Salem) and *B* (by the same token, Boston), entitled *Some Miscellany Observations on òur Present Debates respecting Witchcrafts,* and got it printed as though by William Bradford in Philadelphia. It purports to be issued for Hezekiah Usher, and to be written by "P. E." (everybody knew this meant Philip English) and "J. A." (John Alden)—three of the accused who had fled instead of confessing. Scholars say that the type bears no relation to anything in Bradford's cases. A remarkable achievement of the native intelligence, this neglected essay is perhaps a greater indication of the tendency of the society than either of the Mathers'.

Who wrote it? Immemorial tradition says Samuel Willard; in 1695 Calef addressed him as "the suppos'd Author." He has a good record: at Groton in 1671 Elizabeth Knapp put on an exhibition which anticipated the antics of the possessed girls in Salem Village, and Willard (then the pastor) stifled the furor and wrote a clinical report which, had it been studied, might have cured the Salem wenches. He helped Usher, English, and Alden to escape, and he signed Increase's *Cases.* True, he also signed Lawson's tirade, but, as we have seen, early in the business that had seemed just another jeremiad. At his funeral, in 1707, his successor said that he should be honored for discovering the cheats and delusions of Satan—which undoubtedly meant something more specific to a congregation in the Old South than it does to us. It is difficult to recognize evidences of Willard's Style in the *Observations*—unless, under the pressures of this terrible moment, and writing secretly, he divested himself of his polemical mode and addressed himself to a more conversational manner.

For the *Observations* is a masterful analysis of how, in this model for all witch-hunts, confession became acquittal and an opportunity to besmirch others, while denial *ipso facto* became guilt. *B* does not doubt the existence of witches; neither does he deny that magistrates should hang them—but cautions should be observed: there must be clear proof. Whereupon *S,* good federal theologian that he is, asks the crucial question: can you maintain the "Rectoral Holiness" of God in governing the world if the specter of an innocent person be allowed to make mischief? *B* replies that God in His infinite wisdom may permit even this. Step by step, *B* drives *S* to conceding that the evidence of a renegade witch is not to be taken seriously, because even if he be sincere, he cannot be trusted. But when rational argument has all but stripped *S* of his defenses, he turns upon *B* with a snarl which comes down the years like a bullet: "You are an admirable Advocate for the Witches." After this, it becomes indeed difficult for *B* to protest that he is sound on the subject.

For modern ears, an equally dramatic moment comes when *S* protests that if a trial is to be hampered by too many safeguards, no witches will ever be caught; hence, he says, it is better to convict upon presumption. To which *B* replies,

> This is a dangerous Principle, and contrary to the mind of God, who hath appointed that there shall be good and clear proof against the Criminal; else he is not Providentially delivered into the hands of Justice, to be taken off from the earth. Nor hath God exempted this Case of Witchcraft from the General Rule. Besides, reason tells us, that the more horrid the Crime is, the more Cautious we ought to be in making any guilty of it.

One's admiration goes further out to *B* (who, let us remember, signifies Boston) as he explains, in the face of spectral accusations, "This is no light matter to have mens names for ever Stigmatized, their Families ruined, and their Lives hazarded," and so concludes that if such creatures as specters are to be believed, then the Devil himself has turned informer, and all good men shall forever be hoodwinked.

To comprehend the predicament of the Puritan intellect in 1692, we should note that earlier in the crisis Cotton Mather preached one of his most stirring jeremiads, *A Midnight Cry,* in which he trounced New England with the gory threat of Indian atrocities: they "have taken our Brethren, and binding them to a Stake, with a Lingring Heat, Burned and Roasted them to Death; the Exquisite Groans and Shrieks of those our Dying Bretheren should Awaken us." In the intoxication of such external dangers, he publicly committed himself to the thesis that internal traitors had been convicted "by so fair and full a process of Law, as would render the Denyers thereof worthy of no Reasonabler Company than that in Bedlem." But his *Diary* shows him wrestling with the doubt that corrodes the pages of the *Wonders;* by June 7, 1694, he had openly to declare that the affliction consisted not so much in a descent of evil angels as in "unheard of DELUSIONS." At the election of May 27, 1696, he was simply nonplussed: "It was, and it will be, past all Humane Skill, Exactly to Understand what Inextricable Things we have met withal." In 1697 he had the honesty in his life of Phips (and later the integrity to incorporate the passage into the *Magnalia*) to acknowledge that the court had operated upon an erroneous notion; he still, though lamely, insisted that there had been other proofs, but in a last agony could not prevent himself from recording: "Nevertheless, divers were condemned, against whom the chief evidence was founded in the spectral exhibitions."

In the privacy of his *Diary,* Cotton Mather could simultaneously tell himself, even in 1692, that he always testified against spectral evidence and that the judges were "a most charming Instance of Prudence and Patience." Because he spoke "honourably" of their persons (at least according to his own account), "the mad people thro' the Countrey . . . reviled mee, as if I had been the Doer of all the hard Things, that were done, in the Prosecution of the Witchcraft." Considering that there is ample evidence in the *Diary* (all the more remarkable because it is studiously composed) that he never succeeded in persuading himself he had done the right thing (in 1697, after Sewall had repented, he grew panicky lest the Lord take revenge upon his family "for my not appearing with Vigor enough to stop the proceedings of the Judges"), it is the more striking that there are no respects in which one can say that the clergy suffered any immediate diminution of prestige or influence because of witchcraft. Nor did the judges lose standing in the community: neither Stoughton, who never admitted error, nor Samuel Sewall, who, in one of the noblest gestures of the period, took the shame of it upon himself before his church. The real effect of the tragedy is not to be traced in the field of politics or society, but in the intangible area of federal theory, and in the still more intangible region of self-esteem.

Henceforth there was, although for a time desperately concealed, a flaw in the very foundation of the covenant conception. The doctrine that afflictions are punishments to be dispelled by confession had produced at least one ghastly blunder; repentance had been twisted into a ruse, and the civil magistrate, by a vigorous exercise of his appointed function, had become guilty of hideous enormities. Nineteen years later, Cotton Mather was still keeping vigils to inquire of the Lord "the meaning of the Descent from the Invisible World," and was obliged repeatedly to discharge his sense of guilt by advertising, as a fundamental tenet of New England along with liberty of conscience, "That Persons are not to be judg'd Confederates with Evil Spirits, meerly because the Evil Spirits do make possessed People cry out upon them." The meaning of New England had been fixed, by Winthrop and the founders, in the language of a covenant; if henceforth there was so much as a shadow of suspicion upon that philosophy, in what realm of significance could the land hold its identity?

John Hale, we have seen, was one of three ministers who committed themselves; in his revulsion, he went so far to the other extreme that Sewall feared he would deny witchcraft itself. He wrote *A Modest Enquiry Into the Nature of Witchcraft* in 1698; it is a sad, troubled, and honest book, which he could not bring himself to publish, so that it appeared two years after his death, in 1702. It passed unnoted, and is of importance mainly for the light it sheds upon the working of many minds obliged to live with perplexity. For the fact could not be got round: Hale had been trained to a belief in certain articles, and precisely these fundamentals "I here question as unsafe to be used." Nobody in New England had yet uttered such a sentence. Once the process of "a more strict scanning of the principles I had imbibed" was started, once it led to a rejection of any of the principles of aged, learned, and judicious persons, where would it stop? We followed (with a "kind of Implicit Faith") the "traditions of our fathers," and now see that they, "weighed in the balance of the Sanctuary, are found too light." The whole edifice of the New England mind rocked at the very thought that it might be based, not upon a cosmic design of the covenant, but merely upon fallible founders; yet Hale forced himself to recognize the power of conditioning: "A Child will not easily forsake the principles he hath been trained up in from his Cradle."

Frightened by his own audacity, Hale turned back at the end of his soliloquy: because our fathers did not see deeply into these mysteries, let us not undervalue the good foundations they did lay. They brought the land into an engagement with God, and He may even yet not entirely "cut off the Entail of his Covenant Mercies." In 1720, Samuel Sewall had his memories come thick upon him as he read the account in Neal's *History,* and cried out, "The good and gracious God be pleased to save New England and me, and my family!" The onus of error lay heavy upon the land; realization of it slowly but irresistibly ate into the New England conscience. For a long time dismay did not translate itself into a disbelief in witchcraft or into anticlericalism, but it rapidly became an unassuageable grief that the covenanted community should have committed an irreparable evil. Out of sorrow and chagrin, out of dread, was born a new love for the land which had been desecrated, but somehow also consecrated, by the blood of innocents.

Works Cited

The bibliography on witchcraft, and on Salem in particular, is, of course, enormous (see Miller and Johnson, *The Puritans,* pp. 826-827). The principal documents used in this chapter are conveniently assembled in George Lincoln Burr, *Narratives of the Witchcraft Cases* (New York, 1914), and William E. Woodward, *Records of Salem Witchcraft* (2 volumes; Roxbury, 1864). See also the analysis of *Cases of Conscience* and *The Wonders of the Invisible World* by Thomas J. Holmes in his *Bibliography* of Increase Mather (Cleveland, 1931) and of Cotton Mather (Cambridge, 1940). Holmes's dissection of Cotton Mather's processes in composing *The Wonders*—the desperate filling up of blank paper while awaiting documents from Salem—marks an epoch in the study of Salem witchcraft; however, the book itself, in terms of "internal evidence," yields up the meaning which for centuries has been staring scholars in the face. Perhaps too many of them have written with inadequate understanding of how an author—or at any rate such a nervous author as Cotton Mather—writes a book.

Richard Weisman (essay date 1984)

SOURCE: "Witchcraft in Historical and Sociological Perspective," in *Witchcraft, Magic, and Religion in 17th-Century Massachusetts,* Amherst: The University of Massachusetts Press, 1984, pp. 184-89.

[*In the following excerpt, Weisman compares the Salem witchcraft prosecutions with those that took place before them, finding notable differences in the types of individuals accused and in the approaches taken at the trials.*]

This study differs from previous investigations of New England witchcraft in that it attempts to deal systematically not just with the Salem prosecutions but with the entire history of witchcraft prosecutions in Massachusetts Bay. From this perspective, the events of 1692 become comprehensible neither as a sudden, aberrational manifestation of witchcraft belief nor as a simple amplification of earlier patterns of prosecution. The difference between the pre-Salem and the Salem prosecutions in terms of both the scale of operation and the social distribution of witches was indeed the outcome of different expressions of the idiom of witchcraft. But to acknowledge this difference does not require that one pattern be defined as normal and the other as abnormal or pathological. The two periods of legal action generated different patterns because they were produced by different audiences who proceeded according to different interpretations of witchcraft.

In the pre-Salem prosecutions, the witch emerged as the living embodiment of those attributes that were most despised by her neighbors. She was not only the agent of misfortune and disaster in the lives of those around her; she was also someone who contravened local norms of propriety and neighborliness. By her violent and intemperate outbursts, she disturbed the tranquillity of the community. In her open defiance of authority, she challenged the very assumptions that made orderly social transactions possible. Typically, she was described as quarrelsome, scornful of her neighbors, contemptuous of her near relations, and vengeful if her unreasonable demands were not met. In short, the pre-Salem witch was a destructive presence in both her worldly and her otherworldly activities.

In contrast, the Salem witches were notable for other qualities. Not infrequently, they were persons who commanded respect both from their family and from members of their community; indeed, several were renowned in the colony as models of Christian virtue. Such worldly displays of good character, however, rendered their activities all the more sinister, for what defined the Salem witches was their involvement in an organized conspiracy against God and the state—and what better way was there of pursuing their real objectives in the invisible world than by inspiring trust and confidence in their dealings in the visible world? As one confessor revealed late in the proceedings, "And the design was to Destroy Salem Village, and to begin at the Ministers House, and to destroy the Church of God, and to set up Satans Kingdom, and then all will be well."[1] Where the pre-Salem witch emerged as the enemy within the community, the Salem witch was above all the enemy within the church.

That the pre-Salem and the Salem prosecutions embodied approaches to the problem of witchcraft that were divergent and even conflicting is of historical and sociological significance. Once it is recognized that unified collective action against witchcraft was increasingly difficult to achieve throughout the seventeenth century in New England, the decline of witchcraft prosecutions after 1692 appears not so much a sudden reversal in public policy as an understandable resolution to a longstanding predicament. The coexistence of competing conceptions of witchcraft furnished the ideal conditions for the emergence of doubt and disbelief. The believers who embraced the popular version of witchcraft as rep-

resented in the pre-Salem prosecutions eventually came to perceive the actions of the Court of Oyer and Terminer as illegitimate and unwarranted. At the same time, the attitude of clergy and magistrates toward the pre-Salem witch was one of growing skepticism over the sources of village suspicion.

From a historical standpoint, New England witchcraft emerges not as a prime illustration of the idiom of witchcraft belief but as a manifestation of this belief just prior to its disappearance. Sociologically, it presents the unusual spectacle of a form of deviance in which collective mobilization against a perceived problem proved to be more divisive than unifying. Some brief remarks on how the two perspectives complement each other are in order.

The Social Sources of Disbelief

To suggest that the different approaches to witchcraft were ultimately socially divisive is not to overlook their potential utility for the groups that advanced them. In directing accusations toward particular members of the community, the villagers of pre-Salem Massachusetts were able to define norms of neighborly conduct and, at the same time, to tacitly condone the breaching of these norms when the responsibilities of neighborliness appeared too onerous. Similarly, the activities of the Court of Oyer and Terminer were also responsive to the social conditions that produced them. The Salem prosecutions are more accurately described as a witch-finding movement than as a witch hunt—the goal of the magistrates was not so much to execute witches as to bring about their conversion.[2] By gathering together suspects from the different villages of the colony under strong pressure both to confess their guilt and to rededicate themselves to the church, the actions of the court can be seen as a device to reintegrate the community during a period of pronounced political uncertainty.

Whether as doer of malefic deeds or as arch-conspirator, the witch served the interests of the groups that mobilized against her. In the socially and culturally differentiated society of seventeenth-century New England, however, this harsh utilitarianism was not enough to insulate proponents of either conception of evil from public challenge. The witch may have helped to define the priorities of one group, but attempts to impose these priorities on other groups by intimidation, by force, by threat of extralegal action, or even by judicial fiat were likely to encounter some form of public resistance. It is under these circumstances that the laws against witchcraft became politically dangerous to enforce.

Against this background of conflict, members began to divest witchcraft of its status as an objectively knowable crime with enforceable sanctions. The stages of this process are most readily discerned in the recurring debates over the problem of proof. Efforts by expert diagnosticians such as clergy and jurists to transform the volatile issue of whose interests the courts would serve into the safer technical issue of which tests to apply to the discovery of witchcraft were never entirely successful. In New England, the political problem of deciding whose definition would prevail kept intruding upon the legal problem of how to apply either definition.

In the pre-Salem prosecutions, the cross-pressures generated by popular and theological audiences were a constant source of embarrassment for the court. On the one hand, popular definitions had to be taken seriously if only because of the aggressive manner in which they were advanced. By the time the suspect came to the attention of legal authorities, villagers were likely to have already convinced themselves of her guilt. It required years of tense relationships to produce the malefic witch, and the villagers who appeared in court were prepared to exert strong pressure for a quick and decisive resolution to this tension.

On the other hand, the theological requirements for adequate proof virtually ruled out conviction on the basis of popular testimony. Because the one sure proof from the theological standpoint—the confession—was only rarely obtained, efforts were made to meet the exacting 'tandards of the clergy in other ways. An abundance of texts was produced in seventeenth-century England to assist in the translation of popular allegations into terms compatible with theological criteria, but the manuals with which the New England clergy were most familiar tended rather to widen the gap between popular and theological definitions than to reduce it.

Richard Bernard's influential guide, for example, ostensibly a work of mediation in order to ease the judicial predicament, did not conceal the author's skepticism toward the popular version of the crime. What villagers perceived as the evil deeds of the witch, Bernard interpreted as the product of their own suspicions. Just as the devil could corrupt the witch, so also could he deceive the accuser.

1. [The devil works] a slavish feare.

2. Upon this fear, he suggesteth a suspition of this or that party to be a witch.

3. The suspition a little settled, hee then stirreth the man or woman to utter the suspition of this or that neighbor.

4. The Divell worketh credulity in those neighbors, and withal sets them on worke to second the relation, with openings of these suspicious thoughts to the same partie: and withall, to tell what they have either heard from others, or observed from themselves.

5. Through this credulity, this relation, and

rumouring this suspition, from one talking group to another, it is taken for granted that such an one is a witch.[3]

Such an analysis did more than challenge the validity of village accusations. It justified a categorical devaluation of the legal weight to be given to the popular version of the crime. For Bernard, Perkins, and others, evidences that conformed to popular understandings were granted the status of mere presumptions and evidences that conformed to theological understandings were treated as convictions. The problem of how to elicit convictive proofs from presumptive evidences remained disturbingly unresolved, however. Other attempts to simplify the problem of translation by means of quasi-objective tests such as witch's marks, swimming the witch, and so forth, were rejected either on theological grounds as judicial magic or on medical grounds as unreliable.

The official disposition of the pre-Salem cases well reflected the stalemate between popular demands and theological strictures. After years of equivocal and indecisive verdicts in which defendants were neither convicted nor cleared of suspicion, the magistrates finally arrived at a policy in which they would repudiate popular definitions of witchcraft but respect popular demands for legal protection. Such a compromise yielded verdicts in which the suspect was released from confinement on condition that she leave the community that despised her. In effect, the pre-Salem witch was cleared of charges of witchcraft but convicted on grounds of gross unpopularity.

That accusations of witchcraft generated convictions in the Salem prosecutions should not be taken as an indication that the magistrates who presided in these legal actions were any less scrupulous in the weighing of evidence than were their predecessors who rendered judgments in the pre-Salem prosecutions. To the contrary, the methods employed during the Salem trials represented perhaps the most conscientious attempt in the history of Anglo-American prosecutions to reconcile the conflicting directives of popular and theological audiences. A thorough search was made for evidences that were compatible with both orientations to witchcraft. The allegations of maleficia and other village testimonies were supplemented with examinations for witch's marks as well as evidence of competence in magical arts. Confessions were obtained and the testimony of confessors was used to provide information on other suspects. The spectral evidence that figured so crucially in the prosecution was validated by means of tests and experiments derived from contemporary doctrines of spiritual causation. Throughout the investigation, the magistrates sought to follow legal precedent and authoritative opinion in the formulation of the rules of evidence, to make these rules explicit, to apply the rules consistently, and to collect corroborative evidence wherever possible. As the minister John Hale observed, the Court of Oyer and Terminer approached the prosecution of witchcraft far more systematically than did any previous judicial commission on witchcraft in New England.

It is one of the ironies of New England witchcraft that this most systematic of prosecutions was also the most socially disruptive. For all its rigor, the official solution to the problem of proof was compatible with neither popular nor theological approaches to witchcraft. The replacement of allegations of maleficia with impartially administered tests applied to spectral evidence rendered the actions of villagers, whether for or against the suspect, utterly irrelevant to the outcome of the case. As a result, the magistrates managed to imprison and convict precisely those persons who would have been least vulnerable to suspicion in village-initiated legal actions. The validation of spectral evidence by means of experiments in court did violence to theological understandings about the availability of the invisible world to human perceptions. The consequence of this innovation was to usurp the prerogative of the clergy to define the terms in which God communicated his intentions to humanity. The eventual alliance of popular and theological audiences in opposition to the findings of the court constituted one of the very few occasions in the history of witchcraft prosecutions in Massachusetts in which these two groups were able to find a point of agreement.

Ultimately, Increase Mather's conclusion that the activities of the devil were too elusive for human understanding may be read not only as theology but also as sociology. Human perceptions could not be trusted to reveal the truth about witchcraft, and the rules of evidence that invested these perceptions with validity would have to be revoked. Mather had interviewed a number of the confessors just after publishing *Cases of Conscience* and, as he listened to their recantations, he learned that the magistrates had been deceived. Just as the villagers had not foreseen that it was their "rumouring" that generated the context of suspicion out of which accusations would later arise, so the magistrates had not perceived that it was their aggressive policies that had induced the large number of confessors.

It was a mark of Satan's subtlety that he did not need miracles to accomplish his evil; the materials of the visible world would suffice. The devil could achieve his goal in the invisible world because the villagers and magistrates could not see how their actions in the visible world affected the actions of others. The invisible world of witchcraft derived from that part of the social world that somehow escaped awareness. Given the human susceptibility to being deceived by this world, the best response to the mystery of witchcraft was silence.

Notes

[1] Burr, George Lincoln, ed., *Narratives of the Witchcraft Cases* (New York: Barnes & Noble, 1959), p. 420. See also confession of Mary Toothaker, *The Salem Witchcraft Papers,* Paul Boyer and Stephen Nissenbaum, eds. vol. 3. New York: Da Capo Press, 1977.

[2] I have drawn upon R. G. Willis, "Kamcape: An Anti-Sorcery Movement in South-West Tanzania," pp. 1-15, and "Instant Millennium" by the same author in *Witchcraft Confessions and Accusations,* pp. 129-39 for a general characterization of witch-cleansing or witch-finding movements.

[3] Bernard, Richard, *A Guide to Grand-Jury Men,* pp. 76-79. Published 1629.

THE SEARCH FOR CAUSES

Linnda R. Caporael (essay date 1976)

SOURCE: "Ergotism: The Satan Loosed in Salem?" in *Science,* Vol. 192, No. 4234, April 2, 1976, pp. 21-6.

[*In the following excerpt, Caporael suggests that convulsive ergotism (an illness caused by a rye fungus) may have initiated and furthered the Salem witchcraft delusion.*]

Numerous hypotheses have been devised to explain the occurrence of the Salem witchcraft trials in 1692, yet a sense of bewilderment and doubt pervades most of the historical perspectives on the subject. The physical afflictions of the accusing girls and the imagery of the testimony offered at the trials seem to defy rational explanation. A large portion of the testimony, therefore, is dismissed as imaginary in foundation. One avenue of understanding that has yet to be sufficiently explored is that a physiological condition, unrecognized at the time, may have been a factor in the Salem incident. Assuming that the content of the court records is basically an honest account of the deponents' experiences, the evidence suggests that convulsive ergotism, a disorder resulting from the ingestion of grain contaminated with ergot, may have initiated the witchcraft delusion.

Suggestions of physical origins of the afflicted girls' behavior have been dismissed without research into the matter. In looking back, the complexity of the psychological and social factors in the community obscured the potential existence of physical pathology, suffered not only by the afflicted children, but also by a number of other community members. The value of such an explanation, however, is clear. Winfield S. Nevins best reveals the implicit uncertainties of contemporary historians (*1; 2*, p. 235).

> . . . I must confess to a measure of doubt as to the moving causes in this terrible tragedy. It seems impossible to believe a tithe of the statements which were made at the trials. And yet it is equally difficult to say that nine out of every ten of the men, women and children who testified upon their oaths, intentionally and wilfully falsified. Nor does it seem possible that they did, or could invent all these marvelous tales; fictions rivaling the imaginative genius of Haggard or Jules Verne.

The possibility of a physiological condition fitting the known circumstances and events would provide a comprehensible framework for understanding the witchcraft delusion in Salem.

Background

Prior to the Salem witchcraft trials, only five executions on the charge of witchcraft are known to have occurred in Massachusetts (*3, 4*). Such trials were held periodically, but the outcomes generally favored the accused. In 1652, a man charged with witchcraft was convicted of simply having told a lie and was fined. Another man, who confessed to talking with the devil, was given counsel and dismissed by the court because of the inconsistencies in his testimony. A bad reputation in the community combined with the accusation of witchcraft did not necessarily insure conviction. The case against John Godfrey of Andover, a notorious character consistently involved in litigation, was dismissed. In fact, soon after the proceedings, Godfrey sued his accusers for defamation and slander and won the case.

The supposed witchcraft at Salem Village was not initially identified as such. In late December 1691, about eight girls, including the niece and daughter of the minister, Samuel Parris, were afflicted with unknown "distempers" (*1, 4-6*). Their behavior was characterized by disorderly speech, odd postures and gestures, and convulsive fits (*7*). Physicians called in to examine the girls could find no explanation for their illness, and in February one doctor suggested the girls might be bewitched. Parris seemed loath to accept this explanation at the time and resorted to private fasting and prayer. At a meeting at Parris's home, ministers from neighboring parishes advised him to "sit still and wait upon the Providence of God to see what time might discover" (*6*, p. 25).

A neighbor, however, took it upon herself to direct Parris's Barbados slave, Tituba, in the concocting of a "witch cake" in order to determine if witchcraft was present. Shortly thereafter, the girls made an accusation of witchcraft against Tituba and two elderly women of general ill repute in Salem Village, Sarah Good and Sarah Osborn. The three women were taken into custody on 29 February 1692. The afflictions of the girls did not cease, and in March they accused Martha Corey and Rebecca Nurse. Both of these women were well respected in the village and were convenanting members of the church. Further accusations by the children followed.

Examinations of the accused were conducted in Salem Village until 11 April by two magistrates from Salem Town. At that time, the examinations were moved from the outlying farming area to the town and were heard by Deputy Governor Danforth and six of the ablest magistrates in the colony, including Samuel Sewall. This council had no authority to try accused witches, however, because the colony had no legal government—a state of affairs that had existed for 2 years. By the time Sir William Phips, the new governor, arrived from England with the charter establishing the government of Massachusetts Bay Colony, the jails as far away from Salem as Boston were crowded with prisoners from Salem awaiting trial. Phips appointed a special Court of Oyer and Terminer, which heard its first case on 2 June. The proceedings resulted in conviction, and the first condemned witch was hanged on 10 June.

Before the next sitting of the court, clergymen in the Boston area were consulted for their opinion on the issues pending. In an answer composed by Cotton Mather, the ministers advised "critical and exquisite caution" and wished "that there may be as little as possible of such noise, company and openness as may too hastily expose them that are examined" (*2*, p. 83). The ministers also concluded that spectral evidence (the appearance of the accused's apparition to an accuser) and the test of touch (the sudden cessation of a fit after being touched by the accused witch) were insufficient evidence for proof of witchcraft.

The court seemed insensitive to the advice of the ministers, and the trials and executions in Salem continued. By 22 September, 19 men and women had been sent to the gallows, and one, Giles Corey, had been pressed to death, an ordeal calculated to force him to enter a plea to the court so that he could be tried. The evidence used to obtain the convictions was the test of touch and spectral evidence. The afflicted girls were present at the examinations and trials, often creating such pandemonium that the proceedings were interrupted. The accused witches were, for the most part, persons of good reputation in the community; one was even a former minister in the village. Several notable individuals were "cried out" upon, including John Alden and Lady Phips. All the men and women who were hanged had consistently maintained their innocence; not one confessor to the crime was executed. It had become obvious early in the course of the proceedings that those who confessed would not be executed.

On 17 September 1692, the Court of Oyer and Terminer adjourned the witchcraft trials until 2 November; however, it never met again to try that crime. In January 1693 the Superior Court of Judicature, consisting of the magistrates on the Court of Oyer and Terminer, met. Of 50 indictments handed in to the Superior Court by the grand jury, 20 persons were brought to trial. Three were condemned but never executed and the rest were acquitted. In May Governor Phips ordered a general reprieve, and about 150 accused witches were released. The end of the witchcraft crisis was singularly abrupt (*2, 4, 8*).

Tituba and the Origin Tradition

Repeated attempts to place the occurrences at Salem within a consistent framework have failed. Outright fraud, political factionalism, Freudian psychodynamics, sensation seeking, clinical hysteria, even the existence of witchcraft itself, have been proposed as explanatory devices. The problem is primarily one of complexity. No single explanation can ever account for the delusion; an interaction of them all must be assumed. Combinations of interpretations, however, seem insufficient without some reasonable justification for the initially afflicted girls' behavior. No mental derangement or fraud seems adequate in understanding how eight girls, raised in the soul-searching Puritan tradition, simultaneously exhibited the same symptoms or conspired together for widespread notoriety.

All modern accounts of the beginnings of Salem witchcraft begin with Parris's Barbados slave, Tituba. The tradition is that she instructed the minister's daughter and niece, as well as some other girls in the neighborhood, in magic tricks and incantations at secret meetings held in the parsonage kitchen (*2, 4, 8, 9*). The odd behavior of the girls, whether real or fraudulent, was a consequence of these experiments.

The basis for the tradition seems two-fold. In a warning against divination, John Hale wrote in 1702 that he was informed that one afflicted girl had tried to see the future with an egg and glass and subsequently was followed by a "diabolical molestation" and died (*6*). The egg and glass (an improvised crystal ball) was an English method of divination. Hale gives no indication that Tituba was involved, or for that matter, that a group of girls was involved. I have been unable to locate any reference that any of the afflicted girls died prior to Hale's publication.

The other basis for the tradition implicating Tituba seems to be simply the fact that she was from the West Indies. The Puritans believed the American Indians worshiped the devil, most often described as a black

man (*4*). Curiously, however, Tituba was not questioned at her examination about activities as a witch in her birthplace. Historians seem bewitched themselves by fantasies of voodoo and black magic in the tropics, and the unfounded supposition that Tituba would inevitably be familiar with malefic arts of the Caribbean has survived.

Calef (*7*) reports that Tituba's confession was obtained under duress. She at first denied knowing the devil and suggested the girls were possessed. Although Tituba ultimately became quite voluble, her confession was rather pedestrian in comparison with the other testimony offered at the examinations and trials. There is no element of West Indian magic, and her descriptions of the black man, the hairy imp, and witches flying through the sky on sticks reflect an elementary acquaintance with the common English superstitions of the time (*9-11*).

Current Interpretations

1) *Fraud.* Various interpretations of the girls' behavior diverge after the discussion of its origins. The currently accepted view is that the children's symptoms of affliction were fraudulent (*4, 8, 12*). The girls may have perpetrated fraud simply to gain notoriety or to protect themselves from punishment by adults as their magic experiments became the topic of rumor (*2*). One author supposes that the accusing girls craved "Dionysiac mysteries" and that some were "no more seriously possessed than a pack of bobby-soxers on the loose" (*8, p. 29*). The major difficulty in accepting the explanation of purposeful fraud is the gravity of the girls' symptoms; all the eyewitness accounts agree to the severity of the affliction (*6, 10, 11, 13*).

Upham (*4*) appears to accept the contemporaneous descriptions and ascribes to the afflicted children the skills of a sophisticated necromancer. He proposes that they were able ventriloquists, highly accomplished actresses, and by "long practice" could "bring the blood to the face, and send it back again" (*4, vol. 2, p. 395*). These abilities and more, he assumes, the girls learned from Tituba. As discussed above, however, there is little evidence that Tituba had any practical knowledge of witchcraft. Most colonists, with the exception of some of the accused and their defenders, did not appear even to consider pretense as an explanation for the girls' behavior. The general conclusion of the New Englanders after the tragedy was that the girls suffered from demonic possession (*2, 6, 9*).

2) *Hysteria.* The advent of psychiatry provided new tools for describing and interpreting the events at Salem. The term hysteria has been used with varying degrees of license (*2, 8, 9, 14*), and the accounts of hysteria always begin in the kitchen with Tituba practicing magic. Starkey (*8*) uses the term in the loosest

sense; the girls were hysterical, that is, overexcited, and committed sensational fraud in a community that subsequently fell ill to "mass hysteria." Hansen (*9*) proposes the use of the word in a stricter, clinical sense of being mentally ill. He insists that witchcraft really was practiced in Salem and that several of the executed were practicing witches. The girls' symptoms were psychogenic, occasioned by guilt at practicing fortune-telling at their secret meetings. He states that the mental illness was catching and that the witnesses and majority of the confessors became hysterics as a consequence of their fear of witchcraft. However, if the girls were not practicing divination, and if they did indeed develop true hysteria, then they must all have developed hysteria simultaneously—hardly a credible supposition. Furthermore, previous witchcraft accusations in other Puritan communities in New England had never brought on mass hysteria.

Psychiatric disorder is used in a slightly different sense in the argument that the witchcraft crisis was a consequence of two party (pro-Parris and anti-Parris) factionalism in Salem Village (*14*). In this account, the girls are unimportant factors in the entire incident. Their behavior "served as a kind of Rorschach test into which adults read their own concerns and expectations" (*14*, p. 30). The difficulty with linking factionalism to the witch trials is that supporters of Parris were also prosecuted while some nonsupporters were among the most vociferous accusers (*2, 14*). Thus, it becomes necessary to resort to projection, transference, individual psychoanalysis, and numerous psychiatric disorders to explain the behavior of the adults in the community who were using the afflicted children as pawns to resolve their own personal and political differences.

Of course, there was fraud and mental illness at Salem. The records clearly indicate both. Some depositions are simply fanciful renditions of local gossip or cases of malice aforethought. There is also testimony based on exaggerations of nightmares and inebriated adventures. However, not all the records are thus accountable.

3) *Physiological explanations.* The possibility that the girls behavior had a physiological basis has rarely arisen, although the villagers themselves first proposed physical illness as an explanation. Before accusations of witchcraft began, Parris called in a number of physicians (*6, 7*). In an early history of the colony, Thomas Hutchinson wrote that "there are a great number of persons who are willing to suppose the accusers to have been under bodily disorders which affected their imagination" (*12*, vol. 2, p. 47). A modern historian reports a journalist's suggestion that Tituba had been dosing the girls with preparations of jimsonweed, a poisonous plant brought to New England from the West Indies in the early 1600's (*8*, footnote on p. 284). However, because the Puritans identified no physiological cause, later historians have failed to investigate such a possibility.

Ergot

Interest in ergot (*Claviceps purpura*) was generated by epidemics of ergotism that periodically occurred in Europe. Only a few years before the Salem witchcraft trials the first medical scientific report on ergot was made (*15*). Denis Dodart reported the relation between ergotized rye and bread poisoning in a letter to the French Royal Académie des Sciences in 1676. John Ray's mention of ergot in 1677 was the first in English. There is no reference to ergot in the United States before an 1807 letter by Dr. John Stearns recommending powdered ergot sclerotia to a medical colleague as a therapeutic agent in childbirth. Stearns is generally credited with the "discovery" of ergot; certainly his use prompted scientific research on the substance. Until the mid-19th century, however, ergot was not known as a parasitic fungus, but was thought to be sunbaked kernels of grains (*15-17*).

Ergot grows on a large variety of cereal grains—especially rye—in a slightly curved, fusiform shape with sclerotia replacing individual grains on the host plant. The sclerotia contain a large number of potent pharmacologic agents, the ergot alkaloids. One of the most powerful is isoergine (lysergic acid amide). This alkaloid, with 10 percent of the activity of D-LSD (lysergic acid diethylamide), is also found in ololiuqui (morning glory seeds), the ritual hallucinogenic drug used by the Aztecs (*15, 16*).

Warm, damp, rainy springs and summers favor ergot infestation. Summer rye is more prone to the development of the sclerotia than winter rye, and one field may be heavily ergotized while the adjacent field is not. The fungus may dangerously parasitize a crop one year and not reappear again for many years. Contamination of the grain may occur in varying concentrations. Modern agriculturalists advise farmers not to feed their cattle grain containing more than one to three sclerotia per thousand kernels of grain, since ergot has deleterious effects on cattle as well as on humans (*16, 18*).

Ergotism, or long-term ergot poisoning, was once a common condition resulting from eating contaminated rye bread. In some epidemics it appears that females were more liable to the disease than males (*19*). Children and pregnant women are most likely to be affected by the condition, and individual susceptibility varies widely. It takes 2 years for ergot in powdered from to reach 50 percent deterioration, and the effects are cumulative (*18, 20*). There are two types of ergotism—gangrenous and convulsive. As the name implies, gangrenous ergotism is characterized by dry gangrene of the extremities followed by the falling away of the affected portions of the body. The condition occurred in epidemic proportions in the Middle Ages and was known by a number of names, including *ignis sacer*, the holy fire.

Convulsive ergotism is characterized by a number of symptoms. These include crawling sensations in the skin, tingling in the fingers, vertigo, tinnitus aurium, headaches, disturbances in sensation, hallucination, painful muscular contractions leading to epileptiform convulsions, vomiting, and diarrhea (*16, 18, 21*). The involuntary muscular fibers such as the myocardium and gastric and intestinal muscular coat are stimulated. There are mental disturbances such as mania, melancholia, psychosis, and delirium. All of these symptoms are alluded to in the Salem witchcraft records.

Evidence for Ergotism in Salem

It is one thing to suggest convulsive ergot poisoning as an initiating factor in the witchcraft episode, and quite another to generate convincing evidence that it is more than a mere possibility. A jigsaw of details pertinent to growing conditions, the timing of events in Salem, and symptomology must fit together to create a reasonable case. From these details, a picture emerges of a community stricken with an unrecognized physiological disorder affecting their minds as well as their bodies.

1) *Growing conditions.* The common grass along the Atlantic Coast from Virginia to Newfoundland was and is wild rye, a host plant for ergot. Early colonists were dissatisfied with it as forage for their cattle and reported that it often made the cattle ill with unknown diseases (*22*). Presumably, then, ergot grew in the New World before the Puritans arrived. The potential source for infection was already present, regardless of the possibility that it was imported with English rye.

Rye was the most reliable of the Old World grains (*22*) and by the 1640's it was a well-established New England crop. Spring sowing was the rule; the bitter winters made fall sowing less successful. Seed time for the rye was April and the harvesting took place in August (*23*). However, the grain was stored in barns and often waited months before being threshed when the weather turned cold. The timing of Salem events fits this cycle. Threshing probably occurred shortly before Thanksgiving, the only holiday the Puritans observed. The children's symptoms appeared in December 1691. Late the next fall, 1692, the witchcraft crisis ended abruptly and there is no further mention of the girls or anyone else in Salem being afflicted (*4, 9*).

To some degree or another all rye was probably infected with ergot. It is a matter of the extent of infection and the period of time over which the ergot is consumed rather than the mere existence of ergot that determines the potential for ergotism. In his 1807 letter written from upstate New York, Stearns (*15*, p. 274) advised his medical colleague that, "On examining a granary where rye is stored, you will be able to procure a sufficient quantity [of ergot sclerotia] from among that grain." Agricultural practice had not advanced, even by Stearns's time, to widespread use of methods to clean or eliminate the fungus from the rye crop. In all probability, the infestation of the 1691 summer rye crop was fairly light; not everyone in the village or even in the same families showed symptoms.

Certain climatic conditions, that is, warm, rainy springs and summers, promote heavier than usual fungus infestation. The pattern of the weather in 1691 and 1692 is apparent from brief comments in Samuel Sewall's diary (*24*). Early rains and warm weather in the spring progressed to a hot and stormy summer in 1691. There was a drought the next year, 1692, thus no contamination of the grain that year would be expected.

2) *Localization.* "Rye," continues Stearns (*15*, p. 274), "which grows in low, wet ground yields [ergot] in greatest abundance." Now, one of the most notorious of the accusing children in Salem was Thomas Putnam's 12-year-old daughter, Ann. Her mother also displayed symptoms of the affliction and psychological historians have credited the senior Ann with attempting to resolve her own neurotic complaints through her daughter (*8, 9, 14*). Two other afflicted girls also lived in the Putnam residence. Putnam had inherited one of the largest landholdings in the village. His father's will indicates that a large measure of the land, which was located in the western sector of Salem Village, consisted of swampy meadows (*25*) that were valued farmland to the colonists (*22*). Accordingly, the Putnam farm, and more broadly, the western acreage of Salem Village, may have been an area of contamination. This contention is further substantiated by the pattern of residence of the accusers, the accused, and the defenders of the accused living within the boundaries of Salem Village. Excluding the afflicted girls, 30 of 32 adult accusers lived in the western section and 12 of the 14 accused witches lived in the eastern section, as did 24 of the 29 defenders (*14*). The general pattern of residence, in combination with the well-documented factionalism of the eastern and western sectors, contributed to the progress of the witchcraft crisis.

The initially afflicted girls show a slightly different residence pattern. Careful examination reveals plausible explanations for contamination in six of the eight cases.

Three of the girls, as mentioned above, lived in the Putnam residence. If this were the source of ergotism, their exposure to ergotized grain would be natural. Two afflicted girls, the daughter and niece of Samuel Parris, lived in the parsonage almost exactly in the center of the village. Their exposure to contaminated grain from western land is also explicable. Two-thirds of Parris's salary was paid in provisions; the villagers were taxed proportionately to their landholding (*4*). Since Putnam was one of the largest landholders and an avid supporter of Parris in the minister's community disagreements, an ample store of ergotized grain would be anticipated in Parris's larder. Putnam was also Parris's closest neighbor with afflicted children in residence.

The three remaining afflicted girls lived outside the village boundaries to the east. One, Elizabeth Hubbard, was a servant in the home of Dr. Griggs. It seems plausible that the doctor, like Parris, had Putnam grain, since Griggs was a professional man, not a farmer. As the only doctor in town, he probably had many occasions to treat Ann Putnam, Sr., a woman known to have much ill health (*2, 4*). Griggs may have traded his services for provisions or bought food from the Putnams.

Another of the afflicted, Sarah Churchill, was a servant in the house of a welloff farmer (*25*). The farm lay along the Wooleston River and may have offered good growing conditions for ergot. It seems probable, however, that Sarah's affliction was a fraud. She did not become involved in the witchcraft persecutions until May, several months after the other girls were afflicted, and she testified in only two cases, the first against her master. One deponent claimed that Sarah later admitted to belying herself and other (*11*).

How Mary Warren, a servant in the Proctor household, would gain access to grain contaminated with ergot is something of a mystery. Proctor had a substantial farm to the southeast of Salem and would have had no need to buy or trade for food. Both he and his wife were accused of witchcraft and condemned. None of the Proctor children showed any sign of the affliction; in fact, three were accused and imprisoned. One document offered as evidence against Proctor indicates that Mary stayed overnight in the village (*11*). How often she stayed or with whom is unknown.

Mary's role in the trials is particularly curious. She began as an afflicted person, was accused of witchcraft by the other afflicted girls, and then became afflicted again. Two depositions filed against her strongly suggest, however, that at least her first affliction may have been a consequence of ergot poisoning. Four witnesses attested that she believed she had been "distempered" and during the time of her affliction had thought she had seen numerous apparitions. However, when Mary was well again, she could not say that she had seen any specters (*11*). Her second affliction may have been the result of intense pressure during her examination for witchcraft crimes.

Ergotism and the Testimony

The utmost caution is necessary in assessing the physical and mental states of people dead for hundreds of years. Only the sketchiest accounts of their lives remain in public records. In the case of ergot, a substance that affects mental as well as physical states, recognition of the social atmosphere of Salem in early spring 1692 is basic to understanding the directions the crisis took. The Puritans' belief in witchcraft was a totally accepted part of their religious tenets. The malicious workings of Satan and his cohorts were just as real to the early colonists as their belief in God. Yet, the low incidence of witchcraft trials in New England prior to 1692 suggests that the Puritans did not always resort to accusations of black magic to deal with irreconcilable differences or inexplicable events.

The afflicted girls' behavior seemed to be no secret in early spring. Apparently it was the great consternation that some villagers felt that induced Mary Sibley to direct the making of the witch cake of rye meal and the urine of the afflicted. This concoction was fed to a dog, ostensibly in the belief that the dog's subsequent behavior would indicate the action of any malefic magic (*14*). The fate of the dog is unknown; it is quite plausible that it did have convulsions, indicating to the observers that there was witchcraft involved in the girls' afflictions. Thus, the experiments with the witch cake, rather than any magic tricks by Tituba, initiated succeeding events.

The importance of the witch cake incident has generally been overlooked. Parris's denouncement of his neighbor's action is recorded in his church records. He clearly stated that, until the making of the cake, there was no suspicion of witchcraft and no reports of torturing apparitions (*4*). Once a community member had gone "to the Devil for help against the Devil," as Parris put it, the climate for the trials had been established. The afflicted girls, who had made no previous mention of witchcraft, seized upon a cause for their behavior—as did the rest of the community. The girls named three persons as witches and their afflictions thereby became a matter for the legal authorities rather than the medical authorities or the families of the girls.

The trial records indicate numerous interruptions during the proceedings. Outbursts by the afflicted girls describing the activities of invisible specters and "familiars" (agents of the devil in animal form) in the meeting house were common. The girls were often stricken with violent fits that were attributed to torture by apparitions. The spectral evidence of the trials appears to be the hallucinogenic symptoms and perceptual disturbances accompanying ergotism. The convulsions appear to be epileptiform (*6, 13*).

Accusations of choking, pinching, pricking with pins, and biting by the specter of the accused formed the standard testimony of the afflicted in almost all the examinations and trials (*26*). The choking suggests the involvement of the involuntary muscular fibers that is typical of ergot poisoning; the biting, pinching, and pricking may allude to the crawling and tingling sensations under the skin experienced by ergotism victims.

Complaints of vomiting and "bowels almost pulled out" are common in the depositions of the accusers. The physical symptoms of the afflicted and many of the other accusers are those induced by convulsive ergot poisoning.

When examined in the light of a physiological hypothesis, the content of socalled delusional testimony, previously dismissed as imaginary by historians, can be reinterpreted as evidence of ergotism. After being choked and strangled by the apparition of a witch sitting on his chest, John Londer testified that a black thing came through the window and stood before his face. "The body of it looked like a monkey, only the feet were like cock's feet, with claws, and the face somewhat more like a man's than a monkey . . . the thing spoke to me . . ." (*25*, p. 45).

Joseph Bayley lived out of town in Newbury. According to Upham (*4*), the Bayleys, en route to Boston, probably spent the night at the Thomas Putnam residence. As the Bayleys left the village, they passed the Proctor house and Joseph reported receiving a "very hard blow" on the chest, but no one was near him. He saw the Proctors, who were imprisoned in Boston at the time, but his wife told him that she saw only a "little maid." He received another blow on the chest, so strong that he dismounted from his horse and subsequently saw a woman coming toward him. His wife told him she saw nothing. When he mounted his horse again, he saw only a cow where he had seen the woman. The rest of Bayley's trip was uneventful, but when he returned home, he was "pinched and nipped by something invisible for some time" (*11*). It is a moot point, of course, what or how much Bayley ate at the Putnams', or that he even really stayed there. Nevertheless, the testimony suggests ergot. Bayley had the crawling sensations in the skin, disturbances in sensations, and muscular contractions symptomatic of ergotism. Apparently his wife had none of the symptoms and Bayley was quite candid in so reporting.

A brief but tantalizing bit of testimony comes from a man who experienced visions that he attributed to the evil eye cast on him by an accused witch. He reported seeing about a dozen "strange things" appear in his chimney in a dark room. They appeared to be something like jelly and quavered with a strange motion. Shortly, they disappeared and a light the size of a hand appeared in the chimney and quivered and shook with an upward motion (*27*). As in Bayley's experience, this man's wife saw nothing. The testimony is strongly reminiscent of the undulating objects and lights reported in experiences induced by LSD (*28*).

By the time the witchcraft episode ended in the late fall 1692, 20 persons had been executed and at least two had died in prison. All the convictions were obtained on the basis of the controversial spectral evidence (*2*). One of the commonly expressed observations about the Salem Village witchcraft episode is that it ended unexpectedly for no apparent reason (*2, 4*). No new circumstances to cast spectral evidence in doubt occurred. Increase Mather's sermon on 3 October 1692, which urged more conclusive evidence than invisible apparitions or the test of touch, was just a stronger reiteration of the clergy's 15 June advice to the court (*2*). The grounds for dismissing the spectral evidence had been consistently brought up by the accused and many of their defenders throughout the examinations. There had always been a strong undercurrent of opposition to the trials and the most vocal individuals were not always accused. In fact, there was virtually no support in the colonies for the trials, even from Boston, only 15 miles away. The most influential clergymen lent their support guardedly at best; most were opposed. The Salem witchcraft episode was an event localized in both time and space.

How far the ergotized grain may have been distributed is impossible to determine clearly. Salem Village was the source of Salem Town's food supply. It was in the town that the convictions and orders for executions were obtained. Maybe the thought processes of the magistrates, responsible and respected men in the Colony, were altered. In the following years, nearly all of them publicly admitted to errors of judgment (*2*). These posttrial documents are as suggestive as the court proceedings.

In 1696, Samuel Sewall made a public acknowledgment of personal guilt because of the unsafe principles the court followed (*2*). In a public apology, the 12 jurymen stated (*9*, p. 210), "We confess that we ourselves were not capable to understand nor able to withstand the mysterious delusion of the Powers of Darkness and Prince of the Air . . . [we] do hereby declare that we justly fear that we were sadly deluded and mistaken. . . . " John Hale, a minister involved in the trials from the beginning, wrote (*6*, p. 167), "such was the darkness of the day . . . that we walked in the clouds and could not see our way."

Finally, Ann Putnam, Jr., who testified in 21 cases, made a public confession in 1706 (*2*, p. 250).

> I justly fear I have been instrumental with others though ignorantly and unwittingly, to bring upon myself and this land the guilt of innocent blood; though what was said or done by me against any person I can truly and uprightly say before God and man, I did it not for any anger, malice or ill will to any person, for I had no such things against one of them, but what I did was

ignorantly, being deluded of Satan.

One Satan in Salem may well have been convulsive ergotism.

Conclusion

One could reasonably ask whether, if ergot was implicated in Salem, it could have been implicated in other witchcraft incidents. The most cursory examination of Old World witchcraft suggests an affirmative answer. The district of Lorraine suffered outbreaks of both ergotism (*15*) and witchcraft persecutions (*4*) periodically throughout the Middle Ages until the 17th century. As late as the 1700's, the clergy of Saxony debated whether convulsive ergotism was symptomatic of disease or demonic possession (*17*). Kittredge (*3*), an authority on English witchcraft, reports what he calls "a typical case" of the early 1600's. The malicious magic of Alice Trevisard, an accused witch, backfired and the witness reported that Alice's hands, fingers, and toes "rotted and consumed away." The sickness sounds suspiciously like gangrenous ergotism. Years later, in 1762, one family in a small English village was stricken with gangrenous ergotism. The Royal Society determined the diagnosis. The head of the family, however, attributed the condition to witchcraft because of the suddenness of the calamity (*29*).

Of course, there can never be hard proof for the presence of ergot in Salem, but a circumstantial case is demonstrable. The growing conditions and the pattern of agricultural practices fit the timing of the 1692 crisis. The physical manifestations of the condition are apparent from the trial records and contemporaneous documents. While the fact of perceptual distortions may have been generated by ergotism, other psychological and sociological factors are not thereby rendered irrelevant; rather, these factors gave substance and meaning to the symptoms. The content of hallucinations and other perceptual disturbances would have been greatly influenced by the state of mind, mood, and expectations of the individual (*30*). Prior to the witch cake episode, there is no clue as to the nature of the girls' hallucinations. Afterward, however, a delusional system, based on witchcraft, was generated to explain the content of the sensory data (*31*, p. 137). Valins and Nisbett (*31*, p. 141), in a discussion of delusional explanations of abnormal sensory data, write, "The intelligence of the particular patient determines the structural coherence and internal consistency of the explanation. The cultural experiences of the patient determine the content—political, religious, or scientific—of the explanation." Without knowledge of ergotism and confronted by convulsions, mental disturbances, and perceptual distortions, the New England Puritans seized upon witchcraft as the best explanation for the phenomena.

Notes

[1] I have attempted to use sources that would be readily available to any reader. The spelling of quotations from old documents has been modernized to promote clarity.

[2] W. S. Nevins, *Witchcraft in Salem Village* (Franklin, New York, 1916; reprinted 1971).

[3] G. L. Kittredge, *Witchcraft in Old and New England* (Harvard Univ. Press, Cambridge, Mass., 1929).

[4] C. W. Upham, *Salem Witchcraft* (Wiggins & Lunt, Boston, 1867; reprinted by Ungar, New York, 1959), vols. 1 and 2.

[5] The number of afflicted girls varies between 8 and 12, depending on the history consulted. I have restricted the "afflicted girls" to those eight whose residence in or near Salem Village is known. They are Ann Putnam, Jr., Mary Warren, Mercy Lewis, Sarah Churchill, Betty Parris, Abigail Williams, Elizabeth Hubbard, and Mary Walcott.

[6] J. Hale, *A Modest Inquiry Into the Nature of Witchcraft* (Boston, 1702; facsimile reproduction by York Mail, Bainbridge, N.Y., 1973).

[7] R. Calef, in *Narratives of the Witchcraft Cases 1648-1706*. G. L. Burr, Ed. (Scribner's, New York, 1914).

[8] M. L. Starkey, *The Devil in Massachusetts* (Knopf, New York, 1950).

[9] C. Hansen, *Witchcraft at Salem* (Braziller, New York, 1969).

[10] S. G. Drake, *The Witchcraft Delusion in New England* (Franklin, New York, 1866; reprinted 1970).

[11] W. E. Woodard, *Records of Salem Witchcraft* (privately printed, Roxbury, 1864; reprinted by Da Capo, New York, 1969).

[12] T. Hutchinson, *The History of the Colony and Province of Massachusetts Bay*. L. S. Mayo, Ed. (Harvard Univ. Press, Cambridge, Mass., 1936), vols. 1 and 2.

[13] D. Lawson, in *Narratives of the Witchcraft Cases 1648-1706*. G. L. Burr. Ed. (Scribner's, New York, 1914).

[14] P. Boyer and S. Nissenbaum, *Salem Possessed: The Social Origins of Witchcraft* (Harvard Univ. Press, Cambridge, Mass., 1974) (a map indicating the geography of the witchcraft is on p. 35).

[15] F. J. Bove, *The Story of Ergot* (Barger, New York, 1970).

[16] A. Hoffer, *Clin. Pharmacol. Ther.* 6. 183 (1965).

[17] G. Barger, *Ergot and Ergotism* (Gurney & Jackson, London, 1931).

[18] C. E. Sajous and J. W. Hundley, *The Cyclopedia of Medicine* (Davis, Philadelphia, 1937), vol. 5, pp. 412-416.

[19] Ergot has been used to induce and hasten labor in childbirth; however, it is generally unsuccessful in procuring abortion. Also, there is no evidence that epidemics of chronic convulsive ergotism of the type hypothesized to have occurred in Salem have produced abortions (*17*).

[20] C. M. Gruber, *The Cyclopedia of Medicine, Surgery, Specialties* (Davis, Philadelphia, 1950), vol. 5, pp. 245-248.

[21] W. C. Cutting, *Handbook of Pharmacology: Action and Uses of Drugs* (Appleton-Century-Crofts, New York, 1972).

[22] L. Carrier, *The Beginnings of Agriculture in America* (McGraw-Hill, New York, 1923).

[23] R. E. Walcott, *N. Engl. Q.* 9. 218 (1936).

[24] M. H. Thomas, Ed., *The Diary of Samuel Sewall 1674-1729* (Farrar, Straus & Giroux, New York, 1973).

[25] P. Boyer and S. Nissenbaum, Eds., *Salem Village Witchcraft: A Documentary Record of Local Conflict in Colonial New England* (Wadsworth, Belmont, Calif., 1972). The editors publish an extremely useful map adapted from Upham (*4*).

[26] A random selection of almost any testimony in Woodard (*11*) will attest to this.

[27] Essex County Archives, Salem Witchcraft. Elizer Keysar's testimony from the Thomas F. Madigan photostats as transcribed in the Works Progress Administration verbatim report, vol. 2, p. 9.

[28] S. H. Snyder, *Madness and the Brain* (McGraw-Hill, New York, 1974).

[29] D. van Zwanenber, *Med. Hist.* 17, 204 (1973).

[30] A. Goth, *Medical Pharmacology* (Mosby, St. Louis, 1972).

[31] S. Valins and R. Nisbett, in *Attribution: Perceiving the Causes of Behavior,* E. Jones *et al.,* Eds. (General Learning Press, Morristown, N.J., 1972).

[32] I thank C. F. Paul and M. B. Brewer for their helpful comments on the manuscript.

Nicholas P. Spanos and Jack Gottlieb (essay date 1976)

SOURCE: "Ergotism and the Salem Village Witch Trials," *Science,* Vol. 194, No. 4272, December, 1976, pp. 1390-94.

[In the following excerpt, Spanos and Gottlieb offer a rebuttal to Linda R. Caporael's thesis, examining the symptoms of the participants in the Salem witchcraft trials, but finding no evidence that convulsive ergotism played a role in the crisis.]

In a recent article in *Science* (*1*) it was suggested that the residents of Salem Village, Massachusetts, who in 1692 charged some of their neighbors with witchcraft did so because of delusions resulting from convulsive ergotism. The author of the article, L. R. Caporael, argued that (i) the general features of the Salem crisis corresponded to the features of an epidemic of convulsive ergotism, (ii) symptoms manifested by the girls who were the principal accusers were those of ergot poisoning, (iii) the symptoms shown by other accusing witnesses were also those of convulsive ergotism, and (iv) the abrupt ending of the Salem crisis suggests ergot poisoning. We shall attempt to show that these arguments are not well founded.

Features of Convulsive Ergotism Epidemics

Ergot is a fungus (*Claviceps purpurea*) that under some conditions infests rye and other cereal grains. When ingested the ergotized grain may produce a variety of cardiovascular effects leading, among other things, to gangrene (gangrenous ergotism), or neurological effects leading, among other things, to convulsions (convulsive ergotism) (*2-5*). Epidemics of convulsive ergotism have a number of general features that differ substantially from the events that occurred in Salem.

According to Barger (*2*), epidemics of convulsive ergotism have occurred almost exclusively in locales where the inhabitants suffered severe vitamin A deficiencies. Ergot poisoning in individuals with adequate vitamin A intakes leads to gangrenous rather than convulsive symptoms. Vitamin A is found both in fish and in dairy products. Salem Village was a farming community and Salem Town, which bordered the village, was a well-known seaport; cows and fish were plentiful. There is no evidence to suggest a vitamin A deficiency in the diet of the inhabitants, and it would be particularly unlikely for the so-called "afflicted girls," some of whom came from well-to-do farming families. The absence of any instance of gangrenous symptomatology makes it highly unlikely that ergot played any role in the Salem crisis.

Young children are particularly susceptible to convulsive ergotism. Barger states (*2*, p. 39):

> All accounts of convulsive ergotism agree that children were more liable to convulsive ergotism than adults; thus 56 percent in the Finnish epidemic were under 10 years of age; 60 percent of Scrinc's cases were under 15 years of age. . . .

Only 3 of the 11 afflicted girls at Salem were under 15 years of age and only one of those was under 10 (*6*, p. 57). There is no evidence either in the trial records or in eyewitness accounts to indicate a high rate of convulsive symptoms in the young children of Salem Village during the witch crisis (*7-11*). In fact we could find references to only two cases of convulsions in children under ten during the period of the crisis. One of these was the afflicted girl mentioned above. The other was an 8-week-old infant that convulsed before it died (*11*, vol. 1, p. 95). An 8-week-old infant would not yet have been weaned, and nursing infants do not suffer ergot poisoning even if their mothers have a very severe case of the disease (*2*, p. 38); it is therefore unlikely that this infant died from ergotism.

The fact that most of the individuals (including young children) living in the same households as the afflicted girls showed no symptoms is attributed by Caporael to wide individual differences in susceptibility to ergot poisoning. While there are wide individual differences in susceptibility to gangrenous ergotism, convulsive ergotism is another matter. According to Barger it was common for all members of a family to develop symptoms of convulsive ergotism during epidemics (*2*, p. 27). This tendency was so pronounced that convulsive ergotism was long (but erroneously) thought to be infectious.

Symptoms of the Afflicted Girls

Convulsive ergotism characteristically produces the following symptoms: (i) vomiting, (ii) diarrhea, (iii) a livid skin color, (iv) sensations of heat and cold in the extremities, (v) spastic muscular contractions in the extremities, which in severe cases may become permanent sequelae, (vi) severe itching and tingling sensations, (vii) convulsions, (viii) a ravenous appetite following convulsions, (ix) death in severe cases (*2, 3, 5, 12*). Permanent dementia may also be a symptom in severe cases. Perceptual disturbances may occur, but such disturbances would not be expected to occur independently of the other symptoms (*12*).

Caporael says that "complaints of vomiting and 'bowels almost pulled out' are common in the depositions of the accusers" (*1*, p. 25). This statement is incorrect. *Records of Salem Witchcraft* (RSW) (*11*) contains 117 depositions by the afflicted girls and 79 depositions in which other witnesses describe the behavior of the girls. There are also eyewitness accounts by Mather (*10*), Lawson (*9*), Brattle (*7*), and Hale (*8*) which are not contained in RSW. We examined all these sources and were unable to find any reference to the occurrence of vomiting or diarrhea among the afflicted girls. In all these sources we found only three instances of gastrointestinal complaints among the girls (*11*, vol. 1, p. 106; vol. 2, p. 31). In one of these cases (*11*, vol. 1, p. 106) the girl making the complaint (Mary Warren) lived outside the area that Caporael suggested was exposed to ergot (*13*). Thus 8 of the 11 afflicted girls did not report any gastrointestinal symptoms. Those who did reported only a single instance. None of them reported vomiting or was observed to vomit, and there is no indication that any of them suffered from diarrhea.

We found no indication in any of the works examined that the afflicted girls manifested a livid color of the skin. We found no reference to cold sensations in the extremities, and only two references to burning sensations. In one of those cases an afflicted girl slowly reached out and touched the hood of an accused witch, then immediately pulled back her hand and "cried out, her fingers, her fingers burned" (*14*, vol. 2, p. 110). In the second case the judges had obtained a rag puppet which they believed had been used by a witch to afflict people at a distance. They burned the puppet in the presence of the afflicted girls with the following results: "A bit of one of the rags being set on fire (the afflicted) cried out dreadfully (that they were burned)" (*14*, vol. 2, p. 216). Rather than ergot poisoning, these descriptions suggest that the afflicted girls were enacting the roles that would sustain their definition of themselves as bewitched and that would lead to the conviction of the accused.

According to Caporael, the afflicted girls' convulsions "appear to be epileptiform" and their reports of being bitten, pinched, and pricked by specters "may allude to the crawling and tingling sensations under the skin experienced by ergotism victims" (*1*, p. 25). There is no question that the girls frequently convulsed and reported being bitten and pinched. However, a careful look at the social context in which these symptoms were typically manifested belies the notion that they resulted from an internal disease process. The trial testimony indicates very clearly that the girls convulsed and reported being bitten and pinched when an accused person's behavior provided them with a social cue for such acts.

For example, when one of the accused was ordered to look at an afflicted girl, "he looked back and knocked down all (or most) of the afflicted who stood behind him" (*11,* vol 2, p. 109). In another case, "As soon as she [the accused witch] came near all [the afflicted] fell into fits" (*11,* vol. 1, p. 140). The courtroom testimony contains a great many instances of the afflicted girls' convulsing en masse when the accused entered the room, looked in their direction, moved his chair, and so on (*11*). The afflicted girls' reports of being pinched, choked, and bitten are described thus by Lawson, an eyewitness (*9,* p. 156):

> It was observed several times, that if she [the accused witch] did but bite her underlip in time of examination the persons afflicted were bitten on their arms and wrists and produced the marks before the magistrates, Ministers and others.

The afflicted also produced the pins with which the accused purportedly pinched them (*9,* p. 156).

The afflicted girls were responsive to social cues from each other as well as from the accused and were therefore able to predict the occurrence of each other's fits. In such cases one of the girls would cry out that she saw the specter of an accused witch about to attack another of the afflicted. The other girl would then immediately fall into a fit (*11,* vol. 1, p. 183). Termination of the girls' convulsions was also cued by social-psychological factors. In some cases convulsions would cease when a certain Biblical passage was read (*9,* p. 158). More commonly the girls' convulsions would cease as soon as they were touched by the accused (*7,* p. 171).

Convulsions at the sight of a witch, alleviation of convulsions by the witch's touch, prediction of their own and others' convulsions, and production by the afflicted of bite marks and the pins used to pinch them were all considered standard symptoms in 16th and 17th century cases of demonic possession (*15*). Taken together, these facts indicate that the afflicted girls were enacting the role of demoniacs as that role was commonly understood in their day.

Caporael points out that one ergot alkaloid, isoergine (lysergic acid amide), has 10 percent of the activity of LSD and might therefore produce perceptual disturbances. She remarks that "the spectral evidence of the trials appears to be hallucinogenic symptoms and perceptual disturbances accompanying ergotism" (*11,* p. 25). The term "hallucination" is, unfortunately, very unspecific, and in the psychological literature is used to refer to a wide variety of distinct experiences (*16*). Although LSD is commonly referred to as a hallucinogen, Barber has correctly pointed out that "subjects who have ingested [LSD] very rarely report, when their eyes are open, that they perceive formed persons or objects which they believe are actually out there" (*17,* p. 109). Instead, they tend to report perceptual distortions such as persistent afterimages, rainbow-like colors, halos on the edges of

objects, changes in depth perception, contours that appear to undulate, and the like. None of the testimony given by the afflicted girls indicates perceptual distortions of that kind. Instead, they reported seeing "formed persons"—the specters of the accused—attacking, biting, pinching, and choking them and others.

As to the remaining symptoms of ergot poisoning, none of the work we studied indicates that the girls experienced ravenous appetites after their convulsions, suffered permanent contractures of the hands or feet or other signs of permanent neurological damage, suffered permanent dementia, or died. It should be noted that the girls often appeared to be quite healthy outside the courtroom. Even in the courtroom they did not exhibit the signs of chronic malaise and debilitation that might be expected after months of chronic poisoning. Thus, Brattle wrote (*7,* p. 187):

> Many of these afflicted persons, who have scores of strange fits in a day, yet in the intervals of time are hale and hearty, robust and lusty, as tho' nothing had afflicted them. I remember that when the chief Judge gave the first Jury their charge, he told them, that they were not to mind whether the bodies of the said afflicted were really pined and consumed, as was expressed in the indictment; but whether the said afflicted did not suffer from the accused such afflictions as naturally *tended* to their being pined and consumed, wasted etc.

In summary, while the afflicted girls exhibited rather dramatic behavior, none of them displayed the syndrome of convulsive ergotism. Instead, they showed symptoms of "demonic possession," a phenomenon that was fairly common among 16th- and 17th-century Puritans in both England and Colonial America (*18, 19*).

It is worth noting that the initial symptoms of the afflicted girls were rather ambiguous, and that they began to correspond more closely to popular stereotypes of demonic behavior as the girls gained increasing exposure to information about those stereotypes. The initial symptoms included "getting into holes, and creeping under chairs and stools, and [using] sundry odd postures and antic gestures, uttering foolish and ridiculous speeches" (*20,* p. 342). About 2 weeks after these symptoms began a neighbor had a "witch cake" baked in order to determine whether the girls were bewitched. Only after this event did the girls begin convulsing and reporting the specters of witches (*20,* p. 342). As the witchcraft trials progressed, the girls added to the repertoire. They collapsed en masse when looked at by the accused during the first trial (*11,* vol. 1, p. 18). During the fourth examination they began complaining of being bitten whenever they observed the accused nervously bite her lip and of being pinched when she moved her hand (*14,* vol. 2, p. 48). In later examinations they began to mimic the accused; they held their heads in the same position as that of the accused (*11*, vol. 1, p. 87) and rolled their eyes up after the accused did so (*11*, vol. 1, p. 142). This temporal pattern suggests that the demonic manifestations were learned, that the girls' behavior was gradually (although perhaps unwittingly) shaped to fit the expectations for demonic behavior held by the community.

In Caporael's view, there is a "major difficulty in accepting the explanation of purposeful fraud . . . [namely] the gravity of the girls' symptoms" (*1*, p. 22). The implication of this statement is that the girls' performances somehow transcended the volitional capacities of normal, physically healthy people. Therefore it should be pointed out that numerous 16th-century English demoniacs who displayed all the symptoms manifested by the Salem girls later confessed that they had faked these displays (*21*). They confirmed their confessions by publicly enacting all of their supposedly involuntary symptoms. These facts certainly do not prove that the performances of the Salem girls consisted entirely of conscious faking, but they do indicate that the girls' behavior can be accounted for without recourse to explanations based on unusual diseases.

Symptoms of Other Witnesses

Twenty-nine of the accused witches lived in or on the fringes of Salem Village or had moved from the village within a few years of the crisis (*22*, p. 375). Boyer and Nissenbaum (*23*) have pointed out that most of the accused lived in one half of the village and most of the witnesses who testified against them lived in the other half. They hypothesize that this geographical split in the pattern of accusations was to a large extent a function of political and social factionalism within the village. Caporael postulates that the accusing witnesses were exposed to ergot poisoning by their location while the accused were not exposed by theirs. She suggests that not only the girls but "many of the other accusers" had physical symptoms such as are "induced by convulsive ergot poisoning" (*1*, p. 25).

Records of Salem Witchcraft contains 111 depositions made by 80 different witnesses (not including the afflicted girls) against the 29 accused village residents. Trial records compiled by Boyer and Nissenbaum (*22*) include a deposition made by one of these witnesses that is not included in RSW. We examined these 112 depositions looking for behavior that, even in a broad sense, might possibly represent symptoms of convulsive ergotism. . . . Witnesses were excluded if they reported that their symptoms occurred a year or more before the Salem crisis began (five cases), or while they were out of Salem and therefore not exposed to the supposedly ergotized grain (one case), or for some other reason could not have been exposed to ergot (one case—that of the 8-week-old infant referred to earlier). One of these excluded witnesses, John Londer, gave a colorful ac-

count of seeing a "thing" with a monkey's face and cock's feet (*11*, vol. 1, p. 160). Caporael specifically cites this testimony as a probable example of ergot poisoning (*1*, p. 25) despite the fact that Londer stated explicitly that he had experienced the apparition 7 or 8 years before the outbreak of the Salem crisis.

The first fact uncovered by our examination was that 78 percent of the witnesses did not report suffering even a single symptom; only 18 reported suffering one or more symptoms after the ergotism is hypothesized to have begun. Most of the testimony consisted of observations made on the afflicted girls or other factual information (such as that the witness's cow died three days after the accused passed by his barn). Three witnesses testified about the death of one man and several testified about symptoms of three other individuals. Altogether, the testimony examined contained symptoms for 21 individuals other than the afflicted girls.

The first thing to note is that none of the witnesses reported a pattern of symptoms characteristic of convulsive ergotism. There is no evidence that any of them suffered vomiting, diarrhea, a livid skin color, permanent contractures of the extremities, a ravenous appetite, or perceptual disturbances (other than apparitions). In 10 of the 21 cases only a single symptom was reported. G. Cory reported a short-lived inability to say his prayers, and W. Putnam mimicked the gestures of one of the accused (he clenched his fist when she clenched hers and held his head in the same position as she did hers). These are obviously not cases of ergotism. In a third case, J. Putnam suffered briefly from "strange fits." The timing of these fits makes ergot an unlikely possibility. Caporael reasons that the village was exposed to ergotized rye by December 1691. Putnam reported having his fits in April 1692. It is unlikely that he would have been so late in succumbing to its effects.

In a fourth monosymptomatic case two of the afflicted girls testified that J. Holton was "tormented" by specters and that while they observed him the specters left him and began attacking them instead. Holton testified that he was immediately cured as soon as the girls reported that the specters had left him to attack them. Such an immediate alleviation of symptoms is obviously not characteristic of ergot poisoning.

In the other six monosymptomatic cases the witnesses each reported an apparition. These individuals all stated that on one or more occasions they saw a specter of some sort, usually the vivid image of an accused witch, a dead person, or an animal. All indicated belief that these imaginings were real events rather than dreams (some occurred while they were in bed) or flights of fancy. However, none of these witnesses also reported perceptual disturbances (such as halos around objects). As was pointed out above, apparitions or perceptual distortions in the absence of other symptoms are not characteristic of ergot poisoning (*13*). . . .

The remaining 11 witnesses . . . each exhibited more than one symptom. In two of these cases (Bittford and Gould) the witnesses' experiences consisted primarily of what were probably dreams or hypnagogic experiences. Both men reported being in bed at night when they saw apparitions of accused witches. Bittford testified that his experience was accompanied by a stiffness in his neck that lasted several days, and Gould said that he was pinched twice on his side. Gould also reported a second apparition, which was followed by a pain in his foot lasting 2 or 3 days.

Daniel Wilkins died after an illness that lasted about 2 weeks. The only symptom reported about his illness was that he appeared to be choking shortly before he died, and this was reported only after the afflicted girls testified that they saw specters choking him. Wilkins did not show any sign of illness before the beginning of May 1692. For ergot to explain these events he would have had to be eating poisoned rye for 4 months without exhibiting any symptoms and then suddenly to have fallen ill and died in 2 weeks—a highly improbable occurrence.

Several symptoms are recorded for Wilkins's sister Rebecca, but she had not exhibited any of them until after a physician had diagnosed her brother's illness as preternatural and after the afflicted girls had reported seeing specters attack his body.

Another brother, S. Wilkins, reported an array of symptoms which included a pain in his hand, specters of a witch and of a black hat, falling off his horse, and a strong urge to run. None of them were experienced before June 1692.

Four persons, J. Doritch, J. Indian, T. Indian, and Mrs. Pope, displayed symptoms during the trials similar to those displayed by the afflicted girls. All convulsed and reported seeing specters that afflicted them or others. Mrs. Pope convulsed whenever an afflicted girl "saw" her about to be attacked by specters (*14,* vol. 2, p. 109), and J. Indian's convulsions could be terminated by the touch of a witch (*14,* vol. 2, p. 241). On one occasion Mrs. Pope also reported pain in her stomach whenever an accused witch "did but lean her Breast against the Seat" (*9,* p. 156). T. Indian eventually confessed that she had reported apparitions and enacted other symptoms because her master had beaten her and otherwise threatened her until she agreed to do so (*20,* p. 343).

E. Keysar is the only witness in all the Salem records whose testimony includes symptoms even vaguely resembling the perceptual distortions associated with LSD. Keysar reported that, while in a darkened room, he saw

"strange things" that quivered (*22,* p. 75). This was immediately followed by seeing a quivering hand in his fireplace. Testimony of this type may be associated with acute anxiety and a host of other factors as well as with hallucinogenic substances. There are at least three reasons to infer that Keysar's experience was due to anxiety and expectation rather than to ergot: (i) he reported no other symptoms, (ii) the experience occurred in May 1692, five months after the time he would have begun ingesting ergot, and (iii) earlier that same day he had been severely frightened because he believed that an accused witch "did steadfastly fix [his] eyes upon me."

The final case, and the only one to exhibit as many as four . . . symptoms . . . , is that of J. Bayley, who as Caporael points out did not live in Salem Village. He and his wife had spent one evening there and left the next day. On their way out of the village they passed the house of a man and wife accused of witchcraft. Bayley reported that at this point he felt a blow to his chest and a pain in his stomach. He also thought he saw the accused witches (who were jailed at the time) near the house and then became speechless for a brief period of time. Shortly thereafter he experienced another blow to the chest and thought he saw a woman in the distance. When he looked again he saw a cow rather than a woman. After arriving at his home he reported feeling pinched and bitten by something invisible. His wife experienced no symptoms. Caporael says Bayley's testimony "suggests ergot" (*1,* p. 25). It seems far more plausible, however, that being a fervent believer in witchcraft he experienced an upsurge of anxiety as he approached the house of two convicted witches than that he ingested ergot during his stay in the village and by coincidence experienced the first symptoms of his poisoning as he happened to pass the witches' house.

Thus, the testimony of the witnesses who testified against the Salem Village witches does not support the ergot poisoning hypothesis. On the contrary, it tends to disconfirm it.

The End of the Salem Crisis

Caporael says that "the Salem witchcraft episode was an event localized in both time and space" (*1,* p. 25). The implication of this statement is that the episode was confined to the geographical area hypothesized to be affected by ergotized grain. However, by midsummer of 1692 individuals were being accused of witchcraft not only in Salem but also in the neighboring towns of Amesbury, Andover, Beverly, Billerica, Boxford. Charlestown, Gloucester, Ipswich, Salisbury, and Topsfield (*11*). The Salem crisis even spurred on witch accusations in Connecticut (*24*). No one has proposed that the spreading panic resulted from a concurrent spread of ergotized rye. It is therefore worth noting that the witnesses from neighboring towns who testified against their own local witches provided the same kinds of spectral testimony that are found in the Salem records. Andover even produced its own afflicted girl.

Caporael cites a "commonly expressed observation" that the Salem witch hunt, after escalating through the summer of 1692, ended abruptly "for no apparent reason" (*1*, p. 25). Her own view is, apparently, that it ended abruptly because the village was no longer exposed to ergotized rye. She points out that, after the crisis had passed, some of the magistrates and jurymen experienced deep remorse and had difficulty comprehending their own behavior. She suggests that ergot may have altered their thought processes during the crisis and after they regained their senses they could not understand what had happened to them (*1*, p. 25).

It is important to point out that abrupt endings to large-scale panics about witchery were the rule rather than the exception. Midelfort, who has studied the many large-scale witch crises that occurred in 16th- and 17th-century Germany (*25*), describes the process. These crises commonly began with accusations against socially deviant and lower-class individuals. Accusations escalated quickly, and more and more prominent individuals who did not fit the popular social stereotype of a witch were accused. Inevitably, many people, including some of the prosecuting judges, became increasingly skeptical of the validity of the judicial procedures and the spectral evidence, and persons of standing took steps to bring the persecutions to an abrupt end. These crises were often followed by remorse and second thoughts on the part of some magistrates and other officials. The course of the Salem crisis was the same as that of the typical German crisis.

In summary: The available evidence does not support the hypothesis that ergot poisoning played a role in the Salem crisis. The general features of the crisis did not resemble an ergotism epidemic. The symptoms of the afflicted girls and of the other witnesses were not those of convulsive ergotism. And the abrupt ending of the crisis, and the remorse and second thoughts of those who judged and testified against the accused, can be explained without recourse to the ergotism hypothesis.

Notes

[1] L. R. Caporael, *Science* 192, 21 (1976).

[2] G. Barger, *Ergot and Ergotism* (Gurney & Jackson, London, 1931).

[3] F. J. Bove, *The Story of Ergot* (Barger, New York, 1970).

[4] W. C. Cutting, *Handbook of Pharmacology: Action and Uses of Drugs* (Appleton-Century-Crofts, New York, 1972).

[5] C. E. Sajous and J. W. Hundley, *The Cyclopedia of Medicine* (Davis, Philadelphia, 1937).

[6] C. Hansen, *Witchcraft at Salem* (Braziller, New York, 1969).

[7] Letter of Thomas Brattle, F.R.S., 1692, in *Narratives of the Witchcraft Cases 1648-1706*, G. L. Burr, Ed. (Scribner's, New York, 1914).

[8] J. Hale, "A Modest Inquiry into the Nature of Witchcraft" (originally published in 1702), in *Narratives of the Witchcraft Cases 1648-1706*, G. L. Burr, Ed. (Scribner's, New York, 1914).

[9] D. Lawson, "A Brief and True Narrative" (originally published in 1693), in *Narratives of the Witchcraft Cases 1648-1706*, G. L. Burr, Ed. (Scribner's, New York, 1914).

[10] C. Mather, "The Wonders of the Invisible World" (originally published in 1693), in *Narratives of the Witchcraft Cases 1648-1706*, G. L. Burr, Ed. (Scribner's, New York, 1914).

[11] W. E. Woodward, *Records of Salem Witchcraft* (privately printed, Roxbury, Mass., 1864; reprinted by DaCapo, New York, 1969).

[12] A. Cerletti, in *Proceedings of the First International Congress of Neuropharmacology*, P. B. Bradley, P. Deniker, C. Radauco-Thomas, Eds. (Elsevier, Amsterdam, 1959), pp. 117-123.

[13] Four of the afflicted girls, S. Bibber, S. Churchill, E. Hubbard, and M. Warren, lived outside of the area supposedly exposed to ergot, and the place of residence of two others is uncertain. Caporael (*1*, p. 24) offers post hoc speculations concerning how three of these girls might have been exposed to ergot, but provides no unambiguous evidence to support her views. For instance, she cites a document indicating that Mary Warren stayed overnight in the village and might, therefore, have eaten ergotized food. She does not mention, however, that the same document (*11*, vol. 1, pp. 63-64) clearly indicates that Mary was experiencing her symptoms before spending the night in the village. In short, there is no evidence that 6 of the 11 afflicted girls were exposed to the supposedly ergotized grain before they began exhibiting symptoms.

[14] C. W. Upham, *Salem Witchcraft* (Wiggins & Lunt, Boston, 1867; reprinted by Ungar, New York, 1959), vols. 1 and 2.

[15] T. K. Oesterreich, *Possession; Demoniacal and Other* (University Books, Hyde Park, N.Y., 1966; originally published in German in 1921); N. P. Spanos, paper read at the annual meeting of the American Psychological Association, Chicago, 1975.

[16] T. R. Sarbin, *J. Pers.* 35, 359 (1967).

[17] T. X. Barber, in *Imagery: Current Cognitive Approaches,* S. J. Segal, Ed. (Academic Press, New York, 1971), pp. 102-124.

[18] F. Hutchinson, *An Historical Essay Concerning Witchcraft* (London, 1720).

[19] The great popularity of Increase Mather's "Illustrious Providences" may be cited as an example of the widespread Colonial interest in demonic possession. In this work Mather discussed the case of Ann Cole of Connecticut in 1662 and that of Elizabeth Knapp of Groton, Mass., in 1671. He also discussed numerous other "preternatural happenings" in both old and New England ["An Essay for the Recording of Illustrious Providences" (originally published in 1684), in *Narratives of the Witchcraft Cases 1848-1706,* G. L. Burr, Ed. (Scribner's, New York, 1914)].

More or less stimultaneous occurrences of "demonic possession" in a group of children or adolescents were by no means rare in the 16th and 17th centuries. The most famous of such cases in England involved about a dozen afflicted youths and led to the execution of three alleged witches [*The Most Strange and Admirable Discovery of the Witches of Warboys . . .* (London, 1593)].

[20] R. Calef, "More Wonders of the Invisible World" (originally published in 1700), in *Narratives of the Witchcraft Cases 1648-1706,* G. L. Burr, Ed. (Scribner's, New York, 1914).

[21] S. Harsnett, *Declaration of Egregious Popish Impostures* (London, 1603); *Discovery of the Fraudulent Practices of John Darrel* (London, 1599).

[22] P. Boyer and S. Nissenbaum, Eds., *Salem Village Witchcraft: A Documentary Record of Local Conflict in Colonial New England* (Wadsworth, Belmont, Calif., 1972).

[23]_____, *Salem Possessed: The Social Origins of Witchcraft* (Harvard Univ. Press, Cambridge, Mass., 1974).

[24] M. L. Starkey, *The Devil in Massachusetts* (Knopf, New York, 1950).

[25] H. C. E. Midelfort, *Witch Hunting in Southwestern Germany 1562-1684* (Stanford Univ. Press, Stanford, Calif., 1972).

[26] We thank B. Jones, D. K. Chambers, M. E. Marshall, and A. B. Laver for their helpful comments on the manuscript.

Ann Kibbey (essay date 1982)

SOURCE: "Mutations of the Supernatural: Witchcraft, Remarkable Providences, and the Power of Puritan Men," *American Quarterly,* Vol. 34, No. 2, Summer, 1982, pp. 125-48.

[*In the following excerpt, Kibbey explores how the concept of* maleficia, *or harm-doing by occult means, influenced the social roles of adult males and played a central role in the Salem prosecutions.*]

On April 19, 1692, Mary Warren appeared before the court convened to try suspected witches at Salem. Having testified initially as a victim of witchcraft, the twenty-year-old woman now stood accused of it herself. After altering her plea several times over a period of several weeks, she finally confessed she had signed the "Devil's Book." Strangely, this yielding to Satan did not damage Warren's credibility as a star witness for the court. Self-confessed witch though she was, the court continued to take depositions from her and she continued to be "afflicted," paradoxically performing the legal roles of accuser and accused simultaneously. Warren's capacity to be at once both agent and victim of the devil's power was only a particular instance of her capacity to offer contradictory views of witchcraft, for she was just as inconsistent when she ventured into non-religious explanations. When it was deposed that she had accused her peers of fraud, that "she the Said Mary said that the afflicted girls did but dissemble," Warren paradoxically responded by falling into a "fit" herself. She continued to experience numerous other seizures during her testimony, despite her own assessment of fraud. Warren also resorted to the belief that the afflicted were merely insane, that "the Majestrates Might as well Examine Keysars Daughter that has Bin Distracted Many Yeares And Take Noatice of what Shee said: as well as any of the Afflicted pe'sons." Presumably she included herself in this repudiation, for some of her fellow prisoners testified that Mary was well aware of her own self-contradiction, that she had explained to them in the jail:

> When I was Afflicted I thought I saw the Apparission of A hundred persons: for Shee said hir Head was Distempered [so] that Shee Could not tell what Shee Said, And the Said Mary tould us that when Shee was well Againe Shee Could not Say that Shee saw any of [the] Apparissions at the time Aforesaid.

Nonetheless, Warren was never so self-disparaging or skeptical in court. Before the judges, she agreeably testified at length of "apparissions" who had appeared to her and threatened her.[1]

More than any other witness, Mary Warren appears to be a totally unreliable source on the Salem witchcraft trials, someone who did not even understand herself, much less anyone else. Yet her case record is unusually interesting because, ironically, in her mental wanderings she managed to delineate the whole range of interpretations that historians have since offered to explain the Salem afflicted. From the earliest, Robert Calef's charge of fraud in 1697, through Chadwick Hansen's 1969 analysis of hysteria (coupled with his belief in "real witches"), to Paul Boyer and Stephen Nissenbaum's recent assertion that the behavior of the "afflicted girls" is interpretively insignificant—Mary Warren had already suggested these conflicting possibilities, albeit not in such finished form.[2] Pleading both innocence and guilt, both insane hallucinations and belief in witches and, as it were, both fraud and fits, Warren was admirably comprehensive in her incoherence. Perhaps, then, this servant woman's nonsense was also unwitting insight.

Although Warren seems nearly unintelligible as an individual subject, she makes much more sense from a cultural perspective. Her sense of interchangeable, opposing views was tacitly corroborated by the reversal of legal opinion in 1711, when the legislature formally exonerated most of those who had been convicted in 1692. Declaring these defendants innocent, official authority then changed sides itself, blaming "the Influence and Energy of the Evil Spirits so great at that time *acting in and upon those who were the principal accusers and Witnesses* proceeding so far as to cause a Prosecution to be had of persons of known and good reputation."[3] The dualist opposition between divine power and witchcraft seems to have been much more fragile, much more vulnerable to reversal, than the occurrence of the trials and executions might otherwise suggest. Even before 1692, there was obvious evidence of deep confusion about the nature of supernatural influence in Increase Mather's *Essay for the Recording of Illustrious Providences* (1684). Mather, a Boston minister and politician, had collected narratives from his fellow colonists to demonstrate that, despite the Indian wars and loss of the colony's original charter, the deity had consistently singled out New Englanders for special benevolence. However, this collection of "remarkable and very memorable events" in New England included not only the narratives of providences, but also numerous accounts of sorcery, apparitions, demonic possession, magic, and witchcraft—many of them culled from English collections. In short, Mather included every form of supernatural power he knew of, good or evil, and inexplicably offered them all under one cover as the "illustrious providences" of the Puritan deity. Moreover, many providences of the divinity were more bizarre and horrifying than clearly benevolent: among the more impressive close calls, people survived being captured by Indians, burned by gunpowder, shot in the head, struck by lightning, and having houses fall down on them. Even in the 1690s Mather's book was viewed by some as an irresponsible incitement to the Salem tragedy, mainly because he had introduced a wealth of occult tales to the American Puritan imagination and lent his prestige to their circulation. In retrospect, however, it seems equally significant that Mather implicitly attributed occult power and apparently hostile acts to the Puritan deity as well as to the witch. Mather's editing seems just as fickle as Warren's testimony, and from a close perspective, just as idiosyncratic.

Warren's testimony, Mather's book, the reversal of legal opinion—taken singly, each appears to be an atypical moment of emotional indulgence. Taken together, they begin to imply that a confusing similarity between divine and occult power was actually characteristic of Puritan thought. Indeed, if we step back from the immediacy of the Salem witchcraft decade, and take a secular view of Puritan beliefs about supernatural power as they developed in the seventeenth century, the confusion surrounding Salem looks very different. From this broader perspective, the stark, dualist opposition between divine power and witchcraft appears to have been superimposed over a chronic similarity in the acts attributed to the deity and the witch. As I will show, the Puritan concept of divine power, particularly among American Puritans, developed in part by appropriating the powers attributed to sorcerers and witches in pre-Reformation Europe. Beginning in the late 1500s the Puritan deity steadily acquired these powers, so much so that the power of the medieval *wicche* came to characterize divine power.

The startling resemblance between the Puritan deity and the witch has been obscured by considerable misunderstanding in our own century about the history of witchcraft beliefs. Although the diabolic image of the witch has long been presumed to be as old as Christianity itself, historians have recently proved this to be false. Actually, belief in the diabolic witch developed on the Continent sometime in the fifteenth century, when the Church's attack on magicians and heretics was expanded to include witches *per se*. Christian society concomitantly began to believe that most witches were women, despite the fact that it continued to accuse and convict significant numbers of men. (At Salem, about one-third of the accused, and one-third of those tried and convicted, were men.) Adapting already existing beliefs about magicians and heretical sects, and further incorporating symbolic images of women and reports of pagan religious practices among women, Continental clerics and lawyers of early modern Europe produced a synthetic nightmare of powerful, dangerous, numerous, and distinctly female witches who paid homage to Satan and threatened all of society. At the height of prosecution in Europe, roughly 1550-1650, this new diabolic, sexualized image of the witch was a staple of Continental trials. People were convicted as much—or more—for spiritual and sexual relations with the devil as for any particular harm to their neighbors.[4]

The typical emphasis placed on the symbolic female witch has done more than just distort the chronology of witchcraft beliefs. It has also made it easy to overlook the significance of the most obvious fact of witchcraft prosecution: that men were responsible for the public articulation of the concept of the symbolic witch and for the social fact of widespread prosecution and execution. While many women also believed in witches, the court authorities who initiated and conducted the prosecutions were men; they were sanctioned by laws created by men, defended in tracts written by men, and their court convictions led to executions conducted by men. Nonetheless, men have been a neglected subject in analyses of witchcraft prosecutions, hidden from history (as perhaps they wished to be) by the impressive diabolic witch. Even Boyer and Nissenbaum, whose study of Salem has done much to correct the imbalance, fall back at crucial points on conventional symbolic images of female witches to explain the dynamics of specific charges.[5] Furthermore, while they describe at length the jealousies, hatreds, and rivalries that fueled the Salem trials, they never explain why these hostile emotions took the particular form of *witchcraft* accusations. The purpose of this essay is to explore the social as well as the religious significance of the concept of witchcraft in the thought of Puritan men.

As Alan MacFarlane and Keith Thomas have shown, witchcraft accusations in the courts of Elizabethan and Stuart England differed significantly from the accusations of diabolism that inundated Continental courts in early modern Europe. Although Englishmen shared the new Continental predilection for prosecuting women, they were preoccupied with witchcraft as a material, much more than a spiritual crime. Despite the warnings of a few English authors (such as William Perkins) who shared the Continental terror of diabolic compacts and devil-worship, English judges and accusers rarely gave their attention to Sabbats, covens, or pacts with the devil. According to MacFarlane's analysis of Essex prosecutions, ninety-two percent of witchcraft charges in Assize Court indictments were for injuring or killing people or livestock, or damaging property. While Continental indictments included these crimes, they were typically interwoven with the more volatile charge of heretical devil-worship. By contrast, English courts prosecuted witches in small numbers and principally for deeds that intervened in the material world of the ordinary person's life in a direct and obvious way. How the witch acquired her power was not very important to the magistrates. Instead, they sought proof of malice and tangible harm. The relation between the individual witch's own hostility and the victim's material misfortune was the focus of the trial.[6]

By concentrating almost exclusively on material crimes and the motive of malice, the English courts clearly maintained an older image of the witch's powers, one found in European sources antedating the concept of the diabolic witch. Medieval authors indentified the witch by his or her capacity and desire to perform *maleficia*. *Maleficium* originally meant "an evil deed or mischief," but from the fourth century on, it appeared in official documents meaning "harm-doing by occult means." *Maleficia* were ascribed to witches and sorcerers alike, and authors writing in English or French similarly made no distinction between witchcraft and sorcery. The Old English *wicca,* the etymological root of "witch," simply meant a man who practiced magic and divination. The Old French equivalent was *sorcier.* Not all harm-doing was ascribed to magic, and certainly magic had a broad range of common uses, many of them benevolent. *Maleficium* denoted only one kind of deed within a wide range of occult possibilities, and certain adversities were believed to be especially typical *maleficia*: natural disasters such as storms and fires that damaged grain, livestock, or household, or killed or injured people; and diseases in human beings or animals, particularly if they resulted in death. Unlike the later image of the diabolic witch, the concept of *maleficium* drew attention to a concrete event and its effect (harmful), the supposed means (preternatural, but not diabolic), and the implied motive (malice), but it did not stereotype the characteristics of the person who did it. Anyone with malicious intent and occult knowledge was capable of *maleficium,* and terminology suggests that both men and women were believed to be culpable. The agents of these evil deeds were called, in Latin, *maleficus/malefica;* in Old English, *wicca/wicce;* and in Old French, *sorcier/ sorciére.* The Middle English *wicche* was used for both men and women and so, initially, was the modern English "witch."[7]

It was the medieval sorcerer-witch, not the later diabolic witch, that the Puritan deity came to resemble. Drawing on the general credence of *maleficia,* Puritans imagined a deity who performed the same deeds as the medieval *wicche,* intervening in the natural course of events in the same ways. Of course the Puritans gave these supernatural acts a different name and a different motive, variously calling them "afflictions," "remarkable providences," and "memorable deliverances." However adverse events seemed to be, when Puritans believed them to be special acts of their divinity, they reinterpreted the motive as the correcting hand of divine love, the deity's edifying intervention meant to instruct erring souls and provoke repentance. In retrospect, what really seems remarkable about "remarkable providences" was the capacity of Puritan imaginations to transform bad fortune into good fortune. . . .

Although theologically the divinity was not limited to any particular means or ends, in their daily lives the Puritans applied the criteria of *maleficia* to identify the special providences of their deity. Colonial narratives yield many more examples like the illustrations I have given above. They are equally numerous in the writings of clerics and laymen, and indeed it is difficult to find a colonial narrative that does not employ this concept of the deity. Strange as it seems, what for centuries had been the evil deeds of witches and sorcerers became, for American Puritans, the benevolent signs of divine love. Whether this was also true for other Protestant sects is difficult to assess, since studies of European witchcraft do not address this question. What evidence can be gleaned from existing interpretations strongly suggests, however, that the Puritans were by no means unique. In Thomas's study of beliefs about supernatural power in early modern England, the chapter on providences and the chapter on witchcraft describe very similar kinds of events. In his detailed study of Essex for the same period, MacFarlane concludes in perplexity, "Yet, as a method of explaining misfortune and evil, witchcraft beliefs to some extent overlapped with religious explanations," and adds further that "the difference between the Puritans and those they castigated was merely in the details." MacFarlane makes nothing of this, but his own evidence indicates that the "details" were crucial to contemporary writers because the "overlap" was very substantial. The minister George Gifford complained that his congregation constantly confused the deity with the witch: "They can by no means see, that God is provoked by their sinnes to give the devill such instruments to work withall, but rage against the witch." Reginald Scot likewise viewed witchcraft accusations as mere delusions of impious souls who could not bear to see divine power for what it really was:

> The fables of witchcraft have taken so fast hold and deepe root in the heart of man, that fewe or none can (nowadaies) with patience indure the hand and correction of God. For if any adversitie, greefe, sicknesse, losse of children, corne, cattell, or libertie happen to them; by & by they exclaime uppon witches. As though there were no God in Israel that ordereth all things according to his will.

Neither a Puritan nor a cleric, Scot nevertheless derided those Englishmen who did not yet understand Reformation religion, who mistook the Protestant deity's providences for *maleficia*.[17]

In general, European authors and judges consistently suggested a significant resemblance between the power of the new Protestant deity and the traditional powers of the sorcerer-witch. Sometimes the resemblance was expressed unwittingly, as in the English account of Elizabeth Jackson's "prophesying threatenings, ever taking effect, which Judge Anderson observed as a notable property of a witch."[18] The charwoman's curses were described in the same terms used for the Old Testament prophecy of Jeremiah. Moreover, Puritan ministers called their own conventicles "prophesyings." In the writings of the French political theorist, Jean Bodin, the similarity between his concepts of the deity and the witch made his argument for witchcraft prosecution nearly unintelligible. Believing that witchcraft

was an "insult" to the "majesty of God," Bodin contended that witches should be executed not so much to punish malicious harmdoing as to appease the deity's wrath. He confusedly warned that those "who let the witches escape, or who do not punish them with the utmost rigor, may rest assured that they will be abandoned by God to the mercy of the witches. And the country which shall tolerate this will be scourged with pestilences, famines, and wars."[19] But who would cause all this harm? The escaped witches, or the enraged and "insulted" deity? To judge from Bodin's reasoning, the deity and the witch were equally capable of such vengeful attacks. German Protestant theologians at Württemberg, far more aware of the possible confusion between the powers of the deity and the witch, argued that such confusion was itself the work of the devil. In 1613 Johann Sigwart, a Professor of Scripture at Tübingen and a follower of the Württemberg school, explained that the hailstorm near his city of Tübingen was not witchcraft, but that the devil had tried to maske it seem so: "For when Satan . . . notices that according to nature a storm may arise, he suggests to his witches . . . to work their magic, and to cook and stir this or that together in their hail pot." But the apparent power of *maleficia* was the devil's delusion, for "at the same time it thunders and hails, not because they [the witches] caused it, but because it was already about to happen without them, either by nature or at God's decree."[20] Only deluded witches, Sigwart argued, could fail to see that the hailstorm was the work of an all-powerful deity.

For Sigwart, as for Scot and Gifford in England, the concept of divine power as the author of disaster had become important enough to make it an act of bad faith if one believed in the witch's power to perform *maleficia* at all. Regardless of whether they supported or opposed the prosecution of witches, European authors searched urgently for ways to distinguish their deity as the sole perpetrator of misfortune. The ideological threat of resemblance, not misfortune itself, was what they feared. Historians have speculated that the Protestant lack of techniques for combating witchcraft may have weakened their struggle against Catholicism, that pious prayers and counsels to endure must have seemed dangerously inadequate when compared to the battery of Catholic ritual.[21] However, this hypothesis altogether misses the nature of the major threat presented by witchcraft beliefs: the Protestant deity was communicating his presence in the same way that sorcerers and witches had traditionally communicated theirs. And it misses, as well, the Protestants' real "defense" against Catholicism. We are accustomed to interpreting the Reformation as an effort to eradicate traditional beliefs in Europe, but when we consider the growth of Protestantism in light of traditional beliefs about witches and sorcerers, the influence seems rather to have gone the other way. Far from eliminating these older beliefs, Protestantism appropriated them for its own cause.

The Puritan injunction to endure any affliction, any harm or misery, as a just punishment meted out by the deity was not theologically innovative. What was new was the significance afflictions received from the Puritan theory of history. Sacvan Bercovitch has shown how English Protestantism assigned religious significance to contemporary events by discovering, they believed, parallels between Israel's history and English history. As he explains, American Puritans tipped the balance of the analogy decisively in favor of contemporary events, producing a "wholesale inversion of traditional hermeneutics" that "transferred the source of meaning from Scripture to secular history."[22] Restricting the relevance of Israel's history to themselves alone, American Puritans treated the events of their own lives as types prophecying the millenial, definitive revelation that would vindicate their interpretation of their own importance in the world. It was not that pre-Reformation Christians had never read the book of nature, but they had never read it in this way. While typological interpretation had been applied to the history of the Catholic Church, and while any medieval theologian would readily have agreed that history was providential, they did not read the ordinary, material events of their own lives as a divine prophecy with an unprecedented message to convey to the rest of the world. The Puritans, well aware of the novelty of their perspective (that was exactly the point), advertised it with such phrases as "remarkable providences," "wonder-working providences," and "remarkable deliverances" to announce the deity's interventions in the world on their behalf.

Puritan hermeneutic theory claimed that significant events in Puritan lives had clear biblical equivalents, but in practice the analogy with Israel's history was difficult to discern beyond the initial emigration/exodus from England/Egypt and the crossing of the Atlantic/Red Sea. For the most part, the hermeneutics intended to reveal their own history instead tended to conceal it in suggestive biblical symbolism. Puritans made this biblical analogy credible to themselves not so much through parallels to Scriptural chronicles, but by appropriating the Old Testament prophetic jeremiad, the anxious warning of Jeremiah that an elect people must expect warning chastisements from the deity whenever they lost their sense of spiritual purpose. Unlike specific events of Israel's history, the "prophesying threatenings" of Jeremiah were extremely versatile, for the general logic maintained an abstract connection with Israel's history, while the indefiniteness of the threat freed interpretation from the necessity to argue any particular parallels between Puritans and Israelites. Short of the whole society being utterly "consumed out of the land," any adverse events were an oblique confirmation of their elect status.[23] Thus affliction became a convoluted divine sanction, however much it might appear to the uninitiated to be a sign of rejecting wrath. Since the deity's blessing could take apparently hostile forms, the gracious blows of the correcting hand of affliction, "remarkable providences" could be anything as long as the event was considered extraordinary, an intrusion of supernatural power into their otherwise ordinary lives. What made an event a sign of election was the perceptible disruption *per se,* not the consequences of it. Destruction, disease, and death, if they seemed unusual, could be just as persuasive as health and prosperity.

Preternatural events, disrupting ordinary life, and expressing a personal, vengeful anger, causing harm and promising the possibility of more harm—for the Puritans these events proved to be, not surprisingly, the same ones European culture had recognized as such for centuries. Under the aegis of the jeremiad, however, the whole range of *maleficia* acquired a new importance and a new meaning as the Puritans' means of religious self-identification. In between the biblical metaphors and public histories, and tucked away in the privacy of journals and diaries, Puritan narrators had their moments of "remarkable" clarity in which they detailed the particular storms, fires, diseases, premature deaths, and destruction of property that marked their lives—not now as *maleficia,* but as the crucial signs of the Puritan deity's loving displeasure. Conversely, the tradition of *maleficia* lent credence to Puritanism, for Puritan narrators felt no need to prove, to themselves or to others, that these events were preternatural, or even that they were expressions of a personally directed anger: *maleficia* bore the sanction of centuries of custom declaring them to be just that. And because these misfortunes had long been interpreted as the expression of someone's displeasure at someone else, they resembled biblical types as purposeful communications carrying semantic value. When the English witches performed *maleficia,* they acted out of anger, seeking vengeance against those who had denied or offended them. And so did the deity of the jeremiads, promising the vengeance of destruction for the sins that offended and denied him.

Because the Puritan deity's "signs" were also the witch's *maleficia,* and because both were motivated by angry vengeance, the Puritans were threatened by belief in witchcraft as they never were by official religions such as Catholicism and Anglicanism. Arguments with these latter opponents were always concerned with what constituted a proper religious practice, an efficacious invocation of supernatural power—the the Catholic Mass or the Puritan Lord's Supper? The Anglican Prayer Book or the Puritan sermon? Dismissing these official religious opponents as frauds, the Puritans saved their credulity for the witch. Since Puritanism and witchcraft came to focus on the same set of events, in effect agreeing on what constituted a spiritual intervention in the natural world, the contention with respect to the witch was not what constituted a properly supernatural event, but rather, who was producing it? From this perspective, the image of the deity as the author of remarkable providences, and the image of the witch as the author of *maleficia,* were positive and negative forms of a single idea about supernatural power.

That the image of a deity is a projected image of power in human society is a long-standing, if not very well-understood, argument. What I would like to consider here instead is the way in which the negative form, the image of the witch, is similarly a projection. (The psychological phenomenon of projection is the location in another person of qualities or feelings which the subject does not recognize in the self.[24] As a social relation, projection paradoxically permits the subject to enact prohibited behavior while still treating it as prohibited, for the projected qualities in turn become the rationale for the subject's own acts.) There is, of course, an important difference in the displacement: where the projected image of the deity is displaced on an imagined anthropomorphic being, the image of the witch is, in the act of accusation, displaced on a real human being. MacFarlane has shown how projection describes the actions of accusers in English courts: when someone accused another person of angry and hostile acts of witchcraft, that is, *maleficia,* the accusation was an expression of hostility that was in turn justified by the projected hostility. Moreover, the accuser's hostility was easy to discern, for it had already surfaced in some previous altercation. Accusers regularly produced explanations for why witchcraft had been practiced against them in particular, and their explanations followed a consistent pattern. Prior to the occurrence of some *maleficium,* the accused witch had asked for some trivial act of charity, or simply begged outright, and the accuser had refused them. Angry at this refusal, the accused witch sought reprisal through acts of witchcraft.[25] The case against the accused witch, then, was not that the accused had acted with complete illogicality, without any provocation. Rather, the crime of the accused witch was that he or she had retaliated with grossly disproportionate anger and hostility. Sarah Good, the first person accused at Salem, fits the archetype of English cases, for she was an indigent villager who, according to the many witnesses testifying against her, was a chronic beggar in the town and was easily angered by refusals. According to MacFarlane's model, the Salem Villagers, angry at her continual begging because they were guilt-ridden by their own uncharitable refusals, expressed that anger in accusations of witchcraft. Mac-Farlane's interpretation is viable as far as it goes, but he neglects to show the importance of the specific accusation of witchcraft itself. The accused witch was not accused of hostile anger in the abstract, but

of hostile anger expressed through particular *maleficia.* For example, when Sarah Gadge testified against Sarah Good, she first recounted Good's entreaty, her own refusal, and Good's subsequent anger at being refused, all as MacFarlane's model predicts. But Gadge then went on to couple this sequence with another story of the sudden death of the Gadge cow, which the Gadges believed (and the court agreed) had been killed by Good's retaliatory witchcraft.[26] The projection offered by the witness and acted upon by the court was not just a general image of unjustified or disproportionate anger, but the image of Sarah Good as author of *maleficium.* How, then, can we interpret the attribution of *maleficia* as a projection?

We can begin to answer this question by considering the one *maleficium* of medieval tradition we have not yet considered with respect to Puritanism: mysterious illnesses that often resulted in death. Over the course of the seventeenth century, this *maleficium* became an increasingly important indictment and seems to have focused on dependent family members as victims. As greater numbers of witches were accused of it, greater numbers of dependents appeared in court as afflicted accusers, like the "afflicted girls" of Salem. The murder of children was a relatively frequent accusation at Salem. In the precedent-setting case against Bridget Bishop, the first person tried and executed at Salem, witnesses related numerous stories of local children's deaths, many occurring before 1692 but all attributed to her supposed witchcraft. For instance, one married man testified he did "verily believe that the said Bridget Bishop was instrumental to his daughter Precilla's death about two years ago. The child was a likely, thriving child, and suddenly screeched out and so continued in an unusual manner for about a fortnight, and so died in that lamentable manner." Samuel Gray also believed that his child had died of witchcraft, recounting how he had seen the apparition of Bishop in his house at night, "standing between the cradle and the bedside." The apparition vanished, and then returned,

> and the child in the cradle gave a screech out, as if it was greatly hurt, and she disappeared. . . . From which time, the child, that before was a very likely, thriving child, did pine away and was never well, although it lived some months after, yet in a sad condition, and so died.

Samuel Shattoch, a middle-aged father like Samuel Gray, blamed his child's insanity on Bishop, whose frequent visits to his house seemed to him to coincide with his son's mental deterioration. As these narratives suggest, Salem residents saw the fits of the "afflicted girls" in the same light. They were, contemporaries observed, very like the fits and strange experiences other children had had before dying or becoming insane.[27]

The Puritan deity shared this *maleficium,* too, for deaths of dependents were among the most frequent of his remarkable providences. Although the doctrine of affliction has usually been understood as punishment of the *self* for the self's own sins, the deaths of Puritan children show that the idea was more complicated—and more painful—than this. Thomas recounts the Puritan Ralph Josselin's grief and anguish over Josselin's son's death:

> When the infant son of Ralph Josselin, vicar of Earl's Colne, Essex, died of diphtheria in 1648, his bereaved father sought to know which of his faults God was punishing, and concluded that the judgment must have partly been provoked by his vain thoughts and unseasonable playing at chess.[28]

The ambiguity in Thomas's pronouns arises from the social ambiguity in Josselin's head concerning who had died for what. Only when we realize that the infant son could not himself have played the chess games that killed him do we then understand that the *father's* sins caused the *son's* death—or so Josselin believed. The son's death was supposed to be "edifying" to the father, a mode of instruction that would reveal to Josselin the gravity of his, the father's, sins, and encourage him, the father, to repent. Thus the Puritan father was meant to "profit from affliction." Thomas Shepard, a minister in Cambridge, Massachusetts, arrived at the same explanation for John Shepard's death: "My son John, after sixteen weeks departed on the Sabbath-day morning, a day of rest, to the bosom of rest to him who gave it, which was no small affliction and heartbreaking to me that *I should provoke the Lord to strike at my innocent children for my sake.*" Shepard similarly explained his wife's death:

> But the Lord hath not been wont to let me live long without some affliction or other . . . he took away my dear, precious, meek and loving wife in childbed. . . . This affliction was very heavy to me, for in it the Lord seemed to withdraw his tender care for me and mine which he graciously manifested by my dear wife. . . . And I saw that if I had profited by former afflictions of this nature I should not have had this scourge.[29]

Men like Shepard interpreted their personal histories in the same way they understood the history of the Puritan community as a whole. Unusual events disrupting their personal lives were similarly interpreted as signs of the Puritan deity's disposition toward them as individuals. Thus, in the context of events in a Puritan man's individual life, the death of his wife or child became one more index to the state of his soul. Shepard, writing his autobiography, described his son as "innocent" and his wife as far more saintly than himself, but as he tells it, their grace did not outweigh the importance of his sin in the eyes of the Puritan deity. Both these dependents died, according to Shepard, for the instruction of their father's and husband's soul. These narratives imply there were limits to the concept of the Puritan father's power, that each father was held responsible only for deaths of dependents in his immediate family. Anthony Thacher's story of his disastrous voyage to Marblehead bears this out. He blamed himself for the deaths of his own children, but not for the deaths in his cousin Avery's family. In commemorating the tragedy, he named each of the fathers on the voyage and, of course, only them: "In a boat that came that way, we went off the desolate island, which I named after my name, Thacher's Woe; and the rock, Avery his Fall: to the end that their fall and loss, and mine own, might be had in perpetual remembrance."[30] To be an unnamed dependent, in this story as in others, meant that the wife's or child's very life was only a function of the husband's or father's moral condition in the eyes of the deity, a sacrifice toward the education of someone else's soul. When Thomas Shepard himself died in 1649, just a few years after his son and first wife, no one related *his* death to the sins of his surviving sons or second wife. He was thought to have died autonomously, just as Avery had died in his own right in the storm.

Insofar as the deaths of wives and children were believed to be the result of the husband's or father's sins, the Puritan adult male, if he married, acquired a power commensurate with the witch's. Within this religious framework the nature of his relationship to his dependents was in effect the same as the witch's relationship to other members of the community. This likeness is particularly important because it suggests a perspective for the whole pattern of resemblance between the acts of the deity and the witch. The *maleficium* that resulted in personal injury or death emphasizes an aspect of Puritan thought that is less obvious, but still present, in other accounts of remarkable providences: the belief in the indirect power of the Puritan adult male's own moral acts to literally destroy the lives of people around him.

Ironically, despite a man's theological guilt before the deity, the Puritan father and husband whose sins supposedly caused the destruction of property, or worse, the deaths of his wife and children, received no blame from society; his grief and guilt were his double testimony of his social innocence and his spiritual grace. As for his dependents, their grace consisted in their willingness to be sacrificed. As Thomas Shepard observed of his wife, "She was a woman of incomparable meekness of spirit, toward myself especially," and "she was fit to die long before she did die."[31] Despite the power Puritan men assigned to themselves, such as Shepard believed he held over his wife, it would be erroneous to presume that a Puritan man was enjoined by his religion to feel guilt for the death of a dependent *per se.* These deaths were the consequences of the soul's sin, of his offense against the deity, and in order to "profit from affliction" the Puritan father or husband had to repent to the deity for the sin that had led the deity to punish him by the death of his wife or child. The sin, not the death, was the theological source of guilt. . . .

The resemblance between witchcraft beliefs and remarkable providences, between the power of the traditional European sorcerer-witch and the power of Puritan husbands and fathers, shows that traditional cultural beliefs about witchcraft strongly influenced the concept of the deity and the concept of the adult male social role in seventeenth-century Puritan culture. It suggests as well that some of our previous assumptions about the history of witchcraft beliefs have diverted us from asking major interpretive questions about witchcraft prosecutions. While I cannot here offer a comprehensive model for interpreting the Salem prosecutions, let me suggest some of the possible implications of this essay and give some examples of what sort of inquiries we might make in constructing such a model.

First, that the concept of *maleficia* continued to inform the concept of the Puritan father's power, but that this concept had become intolerable for many people, is implied in at least two important ways in the Salem trials. When Thomas Putnam journeyed with three other men into Salem town to enter the first charge of witchcraft in February, 1692, setting in motion the infamous trials, in effect he turned his back on the conventional doctrine of affliction as a way to explain the strange, disturbing behavior of his daughter, Ann Putnam, his servant, Mercy Lewis, and his niece who lived with him, Mary Walcott. His wife, Ann Carr Putnam, would soon become "afflicted" too. In effect, his accusation of witchcraft meant that their fits and seizures were not the result of his own sins. They were, rather, caused by someone else—a witch. From the broader perspective of Puritan cultural assumptions, the point is not that there was no explanation for the behavior of the "afflicted girls." Indeed, this way of describing them refers us to it. Nonetheless, that Putnam made the accusations suggests that important changes had occurred in the cultural experience of Puritan fathers and husbands in the late seventeenth century, changes that made the doctrine of affliction so undesirable or implausible that Putnam refused the self-interpretation it offered him, and reverted instead to the older explanation of such events as the *maleficia* of witchcraft. In the assertion that his family members were "afflicted" by witchcraft was the oblique confession of Putnam's own *lack* of power as a Puritan father, and perhaps this aspect of his accusation had something to do with the positive response he received from legal authority. Boyer and Nissenbaum have documented the numerous occasions before 1692 on which Putnam men had made appeals to legal authority and lost, emphasizing the seeming irony of Thomas Putnam's immense success in 1692 from this perspective. But insofar as Putnam was asserting his own *lack* of power, a lack that successful prosecu-

tion would only validate, the positive response of legal authority was quite consistent with its earlier refusals to help Putnam either acquire or recover political and economic power.[33]

That Putnam's individual dilemma and his choice of a solution evoked widely shared attitudes is suggested not only by the large public response in favor of the trials and concern for the "afflicted girls," but also by elements of subsequent accusations. For example, the accusations against George Burroughs, the first Puritan man accused at Salem, are a mirror image in negative form of the powers of Puritan fathers and husbands. In the initial deposition, Ann Putnam's, Burroughs was accused of killing his first two wives. Other "witnesses" corroborated her testimony, Susanna Sheldon elaborating that "He appeared to me at the house of Nathanniel Ingolson and told me he had been the death of three children at the eastward and had killed two of his wives, the first he smothered and the second he choked, and killed two of his own children." Burroughs, like other defendants, was also accused of causing the fits of the "afflicted girls," but more severely in his case, "almost choking them to death." The "witchcraft" Burroughs practiced, however, was none other than a diabolic version of Puritanism itself. His case record contains the first deposition on Black Sabbaths at Salem, a staid parody of a Congregational service that the Salem judges construed as witchcraft. Burroughs, a former minister of Salem village, was accused of returning to hold illicit diabolic services at night—in the pasture *next to* the parish house of the current minister, an appropriate metaphor for displacement. A minister as well as a husband and father who had suffered the deaths of spouses and children, Burroughs was a particularly apt "place" to project the power attributed to adult men by the deity of remarkable providences. Boyer and Nissenbaum show that the accusations against Burroughs were an important turning point in the development of the Salem trials, that after these charges were made accusations increased rapidly and the Salem trials assumed major proportions. It is also true that, relative to preceeding accusations, this watershed case focused with unusual clarity on the power of adult men in relation to the deaths of family dependents, and associated that power with an organized sect and formal religious thought that is easily recognizable as a parodic inversion of Puritan church ordinances.[34]

A second dimension of relevance concerns the power of figurative "father," how the Puritan concept of a literal father's power influenced concepts of public authority. In a colony where the public authority of men was explicitly justified by analogy with the structure and character of power in the literal family, how far did the concept of *maleficia*/remarkable providences also define the power of public "patriarchs?" Historians have long argued that the effects of the Glorious Revolution on the colony government were an important influence on the Salem prosecutions, that it was not sheer coincidence that prosecutions occurred at a time of instability and confusion about the character of legal authority in the colony. Since the Salem court was convened for the sole purpose of trying witchcraft cases, it seems plausible that its contribution to changing concepts of legal power would especially reflect the importance of *maleficia*. That is, what the figurative "fathers" of the court borrowed through the analogy of the family was not just a general notion of partriarchy, but rather the more specific concept of the Puritan father's power over his dependents as it resembled *maleficia*. Since the case records repeatedly show that the judges were hardly impartial observers and frequently adopted an accusatory stance themselves, we could well begin to explore this question by extending MacFarlane's model to the court itself. Did the capacity to intentionally cause sudden death as an act of revenge, an expression of disproportionate anger, describe the social character of the Salem court's power? If we set aside the concept of the deity/witch as the cause of events, the concept that overtly justified the prosecutions, then the projection becomes apparent: although the defendants were the ones accused of exacting revenge, it was the court—and the witnesses through the power of the court—who actually got it. Without the concealment of supernatural intervention, the discernable social facts in the Salem testimony show only the occurrence of petty offenses to which the court responded by sanctioning legal murder. In Sarah Good's case, for example, her acts of begging were punished with execution, surely a grossly disproportionate response to such trivial social offenses. In short, what legal authority condemned in the accused it also enacted in the very process of condemnation.

What the legal process seems to have offered witnesses was the vicarious satisfaction of a new mutation of *maleficia* in a systematically "true" projection produced at the will of the court but guided by the "requests" for specific targets named in witnesses' accusations: the gratuitous execution (sudden death) of "witches" and the confiscation (destruction) of their property. Indeed, the court delivered with unerring accuracy, for the conviction rate at Salem was astonishingly high, even by Continental standards—one hundred percent.[35] Unlike literal fathers, the figurative fathers of judicial authority possessed a real social power to intentionally cause death and destruction by secular means. However much Puritan fathers such as Shepard may have believed that the deaths of their dependents were the intentional punitive consequences of their own sins, from a secular point of view this is no more plausible than the capacity of accused witches to actually accomplish *maleficia*. From a secular point of view, the court's version of themselves as the cause of death and destruction is much more persuasive. Moreover, the court claimed a conscious intention: it did not simply offer retroactive explanations for unwitting death and destruction, but intentionally produced such events through the

purportedly rational mechanism of the legal process. In this sense, the judicial authority of the Salem court freed itself from the accidents of remarkable providences as the unpredictable occasions for the expression of its "fatherly" power, and consequently freed itself in a crucial way from the power of the Puritan deity.[36]

Extending MacFarlane's model in this way shifts the primary point of tension away from the relation between witnesses and the accused and toward the relation between court authority and the accused. This is exactly where the history of witchcraft beliefs indicates the focus really was, however, for the century of great persecution was marked first and foremost by the widespread execution of people for witchcraft *through the mechanism of the legal process of the state*. After all, people had believed in witches for centuries, and private citizens had made informal accusations of witchcraft and punished witches for just as long. What was new in early modern Europe, and what distinguished Salem in the New England history of witchcraft beliefs, was the massive intervention of state authority to prosecute witchcraft—and the subsequent epidemic of accusations and executions that intervention produced.

The Salem trials may also have been an expression of new conflicts among men about different versions of figurative fatherly power. Did the court in effect assert a new superiority of the figurative "fathers" of state power, attacking men who refused to be obedient "sons" in the new patriarchy of the new charter? That the figurative dimension of fatherly power was important in the Salem trials is suggested by the fact that the figurative "fathers" of the court found very cooperative witnesses in women and girls who, as servants or slaves, knew well how to live by this analogy: Mary Warren, servant of John Proctor; Mercy Lewis, servant of Thomas Putnam; Sarah Churchill, servant of George Jacobs; Tituba, slave of Samuel Parris; and Elizabeth Hubbard, servant of William Griggs. Two more major witnesses, Abigail Williams and Mary Walcott, were living in the households of their uncles at the time of the trials. Of all the "afflicted" who were consistently the center of attention and the main source of testimony, only two, Ann Putnam and Elizabeth Parris, were living in the households of their literal fathers—and both these fathers were among the most ardent public supporters of the court. The depositions of female servants include complaints of mistreatment by their employers, suggesting that young women like Mary Warren and Sarah Churchill exploited the power of one father-figure to retaliate against another. The court in turn exploited the grievances of the "afflicted" servants to punish men like Proctor and Jacobs who expressed disdain for the court's power. Whatever the individual antagonisms here, the struggle between the figurative "fathers" of the court and the figurative "fathers" of private households seems to have been an important dimension of the Salem trials.[37]

Finally, understanding the importance of *maleficia* for the Puritan concept of adult male power enables us to ask different kinds of questions about the accusations made against women at Salem. Since the power of *maleficia*/remarkable providences had been attributed throughout the seventeenth century to a deity invariably described as male, or to adult men by means of their sins, how can we explain the accusations against *women* at Salem? That women should be prone to accusations of witchcraft has always been taken for granted, but since Puritan culture so strongly associated the power of *maleficia* with adult males, we need to ask seriously why and how were women accused of witchcraft at Salem at all? The research of Boyer and Nissenbaum is an instructive point of departure insofar as it interprets the wider social context of conflicts between women expressed in court depositions. Boyer and Nissenbaum, analyzing economic conditions in Salem Village, argue that traditionalist agrarians such as Thomas Putnam, whose status was declining, were extremely jealous of arrived, newly successful men like Daniel Andrew and Philip English, who were accused of witchcraft. What Boyer and Nissenbaum ignore is the relevance of these same economic tensions to accusations among married women. For example, their lengthy discussion of Thomas Putnam, the leading male accuser, culminates very oddly—in speculation about his *wife's* grievances with other wives in order to explain her accusations against such women as Rebecca Nurse. What their own evidence most clearly suggests, however, is that Thomas Putnam, through his wife, attacked Francis Nurse, through his wife. Francis Nurse was an economically successful late arrival in Salem Village, just the sort of enterprising upstart who, Boyer and Nissenbaum argue, was vulnerable to accusation.[38] In a society where the experiences of wives and children, indeed their very lives, were mere signs of an adult male's own personal success or failure, where the identity of family dependents was a mere extension of their father/husband, conflicts between women could easily be exploited to express conflicts between the men with/by whom they were identified. That Puritan culture still very strongly associated the power of witchcraft with the power of adult men, to the point that Puritan men were actually hesitant to ascribe *maleficia* to women alone—despite centuries of custom that would have supported such accusations—is suggested by the impact of the accusations against Burroughs. Reportedly, the Black Sabbaths of the diabolical Burroughs were initially attended by the women who had already been accused of witchcraft, and only when these already accused women were further accused of having acquired their power of *maleficia* from an adult male did the Salem trials begin to take on major proportions. Conceivably, the crime of which women were accused at Salem was really two-fold: not only that they were engaging in *maleficia*, but that they were *women* gaging in *maleficia*, attempting to take

for themselves a power that Puritan culture had come to associate with adult male sexual identity.

Notes

[1] Paul Boyer and Stephen Nissenbaum, eds., *The Salem Witchcraft Papers: Verbatim Transcripts of the Legal Documents of the Salem Witchcraft Outbreak of 1692*, 3 vols. (New York: DaCapo Press, 1977), 793, 802-03, 795. See also 103, 680 for descriptions of Warren.

[2] Robert Calef. *More Wonders of the Invisible World* (London, 1700). Marion L. Starkey, *The Devil in Massachusetts* (New York: Knopf, 1949), tends to follow Calef. Modern historians share Warren's credulity as well as her incredulity. Chadwick Hansen, *Witchcraft at Salem* (New York: Braziller, 1969), analyzes the "afflicted" in terms of Freud's studies of hysteria and anthropological studies of voodoo, concluding that "at least two of the persons still attainted as witches under Massachusetts law—Bridget Bishop and Mammy Redd—actually were witches" (219). In the most recent study of Salem, Paul Boyer and Stephen Nissenbaum. *Salem Possessed: The Social Origins of Witchcraft* (1974; rpt. Cambridge: Harvard Univ. Press, 1977), the authors explain, "Oddly enough, it has been through our sense of 'collaborating' with [the Salem minister] Parris and [the main family of accusers] the Putnams in their effort to delineate the larger contours of their world, and our sympathy, at least on the level of metaphor, with certain of their perceptions, that we have come to feel a curious bond with the 'witch hunters' of 1692" (180).

[3] "Reversal of Attainder, October 17, 1711," in Boyer and Nissenbaum, *Witchcraft Papers,* 1015-156 (italics added). A few attainders were not reversed.

[4] Severe problems with chronology were first noted by Charles Edward Hopkin, *The Share of Thomas Aquinas in the Growth of the Witchcraft Delusion* (Philadelphia: Univ. of Pennsylvania Press, 1940), 174-84, but the forgeries were not exposed until Norman Cohn, *Europe's Inner Demons: An Enquiry Inspired by the Great Witch-hunt* (New York: Basic Books, 1975). Cf. Richard Keickhefer, *European Witch Trials: Their Foundation in Popular and Learned Culture, 1300-1500* (Berkeley: Univ. of California Press. 1976), who independently confirms Cohn; and Edward Peters, *The Magician, the Witch, and the Law* (Philadelphia: Univ. of Pennsylvania Press, 1978). Cohn, Keickhefer, and Peters agree that pre-Reformation trials were overwhelmingly concerned with magic and heresy, not witchcraft, and that massive witch-hunts were a phenomenon of early modern Europe. For basic statistics on Salem, see John Demos, "Underlying Themes in the Witchcraft of Seventeenth Century New England," *American Historical Review*. 75 (1970), 1311-26. Clarke Garrett. "Women and Witches: Patterns of Analysis," *Signs,* 3 (1977),

461-70, greatly oversimplifies available European data. See instead H. C. Erik Midelfort, *Witch-hunting in Southwestern Germany, 1562-1684: The Social and Intellectual Foundations* (Stanford: Stanford Univ. Press, 1972), 179-81; and E. William Monter, *Witchcraft in France and Switzerland: The Borderlands During the Reformation* (Ithaca: Cornell Univ. Press, 1976), 119-23.

5 Boyer and Nissenbaum, *Salem Possessed,* 147-51. The highly speculative descriptions of two wealthy women, Elizabeth Carr and Mary Veren, 135-44, markedly resemble fairy-tale portraits of evil stepmothers, as the authors admit, 144. The description of Sarah Good, 203-06, accepts at face value the stereotypic image of the symbolic witch in forming accusations against her, offering no alternative interpretation of Good's behavior. These are only a few examples from a book marred throughout by recourse to symbolic images of women.

6 American historiography assumes, erroneously, that Perkins was representative of English thought. See Alan MacFarlane, *Witchcraft in Tudor and Stuart England: A Regional and Comparative Study* (New York: Harper and Row, 1970), 23-25, 134-39, 189; Keith Thomas, *Religion and the Decline of Magic* (New York: Scribner's, 1971), chs. 5-6, 9, 15; John L. Teall, "Witchcraft and Calvinism in Elizabethan England: Divine Power and Human Agency," *Journal of the History of Ideas,* 23 (1962), 21-36.

7 On *maleficia* and their agents, see Cohn, *Europe's Inner Demons,* 147-224; Peters, *Magicians, the Witch, and the Law,* xvii, 17, 139, 145, 154, 160-61, 165, 168-69; The *Oxford English Dictionary; Stratmann's Middle-English Dictionary.* On magic, see Thomas, *Religion and the Decline of Magic,* chs. 7-9; Peters, *Magicians, the Witch, and the Law,* chs. 1-3; MacFarlane, *Witchcraft in Tudor and Stuart England,* 67, 128; D.P. Walker, *Spritual and Demonic Magic: Ficino to Campanella* (London: Warburg Institute, 1958). . . .

17 Thomas, *Religion and the Decline of Magic,* chs. 4, 14; MacFarlane, *Witchcraft in Tudor and Stuart England,* 189, 194, cites Gifford, 194, and Scot, 192.

18 On the Jackson case, see Thomas, *Religion and the Decline of Magic,* 511. On prophesying, see Irvonwy Morgan, *The Godly Preachers of the Elizabethan Church* (London: Epworth Press, 1965).

19 Jean Bodin, *De la Démonomanie des Sorciers* (Paris, 1850), quoted in Alan C. Kors and Edward Peters, eds., *Witchcraft in Europe 1100-1700: A Documentary History* (Philadelphia: Univ. of Pennsylvania Press, 1972), 215.

20 Midelfort, *Witch-hunting in Southwestern Germany,* 44.

21 For a recent statement of this view, see Thomas, *Religion and the Decline of Magic,* chs, 1-9.

22 Sacvan Bercovitch, *The Puritan Origins of the American Self* (New Haven: Yale Univ. Press, 1975.) See esp. 109, 113.

23 On the jeremiad in American thought, see Sacvan Bercovitch, *The American Jeremiad* (Madison: Univ. of Wisconsin Press, 1978).

24 See J. Laplanche and J.-B. Pontalis, *The Language of Psychoanalysis,* trans. Donald Nicholson-Smith (New York: W. W. Norton, 1973), 349 (def. II).

25 MacFarlane, *Witchcraft in Tudor and Stuart England,* 158-64, 192-209. Demos and Boyer and Nissenbaum use MacFarlane's model.

26 Paul Boyer and Stephen Nissenbaum, eds., *Salem-Village Witchcraft: A Documentary Record of Local Conflict in Colonial New England* (Belmont, Calif.: Wadsworth, 1972), 14.

27 On Continental cases, see Monter, *Witchcraft in France and Switzerland,* 100, 198. On Salem cases, see Boyer and Nissenbaum, *Salem-Village Witchcraft,* 42-43, 30.

28 Thomas, *Religion and the Decline of Magic,* 83.

29 Thomas Shepard, "Autobiography," in Michael McGiffert, ed., *God's Plot* (Amherst: Univ. of Massachusetts Press, 1972), 69, 70 (italics added).

30 "Thacher's Narrative," 494.

31 Shepard, "Autobiography," 70-71. . . .

33 On Thomas Putnam and the Putnam family, see Boyer and Nissenbaum, *Salem Possessed,* 5-6, 110-52.

34 Boyer and Nissenbaum, *Salem Village Witchcraft,* 68-69, 73-74, 77, 79, 70, 82.

35 On European conviction rates, see Midelfort, *Witch-hunting in Southwestern Germany,* 179-81; Monter, *Witchcraft in France and Switzerland,* 119-23.

36 No wonder, then, that the clergy for the most part opposed the trials. On ministerial opposition, see Hansen, *Witchcraft at Salem,* passim; and Perry Miller, *The New England Mind: From Colony to Province* (1953; rpt. Boston: Beacon Press, 1961), 191-208.

37 Boyer and Nissenbaum, *Salem Possessed,* 5-6, 35n. The "girls" are also identified in arrest war-

rants in Boyer and Nissenbaum, *Salem Witchcraft Papers,* passim. Further information appears in depositions against their employers, among which see esp. the George Jacobs and John Proctor case records.

[38] Boyer and Nissenbaum, *Salem Possessed,* 80-109, 120-22, 131-32, 147, 181-82, 192, 210; and *Salem-Village Witchcraft,* 148-54. Nurse may have symbolized a new style of agrarianism in buying his farm on a mortgage.

Chadwick Hansen (essay date 1983)

SOURCE: "Andover Witchcraft and the Causes of the Salem Witchcraft Trials," in *The Occult in America: New Historical Perspectives,* edited by Howard Kerr and Charles L. Crow, University of Illinois Press, 1983, pp. 38-57.

[*In the following essay, Hansen emphasizes some differences between the Andover and the Salem witchcraft cases in an exploration of why the latter "got out of hand."*]

I

Over the past thirteen years American scholars have offered an extraordinary number of explanations of that most grotesque episode in our colonial history, the Salem witchcraft trials. John Demos has suggested that generational hostility was the "underlying" cause. Richard Slotkin has suggested that it was racial hostility: demonic possession in his view becomes merely a neurotic parody of the experience of Indian captivity. Paul Boyer and Stephen Nissenbaum have suggested factional hostility. Linnda R. Caporael has suggested that ergotism, a kind of food poisoning occasioned by a fungus infestation of the rye from which bread was made, was responsible for the seizures, hallucinations, and other symptoms of the "afflicted" persons. David Thomas Konig has seen malefic witchcraft as one of several means by which "opponents of law" might take the law into their own hands, and has suggested that servants constitute a class to which such extralegal power might seem particularly attractive. Lyle Koehler has suggested sexual hostility and the resulting anxieties as the cause of much feminine hysteria, including the hysterical seizures at Salem. And Cedric B. Cowing has suggested hostilities between persons with origins in the southeast of England and those from the northwest as "the roots" of Salem witchcraft.[1]

There is considerable merit in some of these explanations. Konig's view of witchcraft as one of several extralegal avenues to power is particularly illuminating. If Cowing's regional characterizations are valid, his

statistics are impressive. Certainly there was abundant factional hostility in Salem Village. And sexual hostility, or at least conjugal hostility, is very clearly present in many of the more important cases. Bridget Bishop was alleged to have bewitched her first husband to death. Edward Bishop accused his wife Sarah of being "familiar with the Devil." Martha Corey's, Sarah Good's, and Sarah Osburn's husbands testified against them at their hearings. "Indeed," said Sarah Good's husband, in one of the more memorable lines in the legal testimony, "I may say with tears that she is an enemy to all good." John Procter was alleged to have contemplated suicide because of his wife's quarreling with him, and he left her out of the will that he made in prison. George Burroughs was alleged to have been cruel to his wives, and John Willard to have beaten his wife.[2]

With any single explanation, however, there is always the temptation to see it as comprehensive and sufficient in itself. Witchcraft is so alien to the experience of twentieth-century American scholars, so medieval, so primitive a matter, that it is tempting to dismiss all the evidence of folk belief and folk behavior at Salem and to account for the events there in terms that are modern, and thus comfortable and familiar, to say, for example, "Oh, so that's all it was—just something they ate." Boyer and Nissenbaum, among others, yield temporarily to this temptation. Having described the two main Salem Village factions as allied to the mercantile-capitalist economy of Salem Town on the one hand and to the agrarian economy of Salem Village on the other, they announce that "a superhuman force" was loose in Essex County and conclude, "We have chosen to construe this force as emergent mercantile capitalism. Mather, and Salem Village, called it witchcraft."[3]

The purpose of this essay, however, is less to review the recent scholarship than to return to the documents in the light of it, to see whether there is anything more that they can tell us about the causes of the Salem trials. Such a return has been made more convenient by Boyer and Nissenbaum, chiefly by their publication of *The Salem Witchcraft Papers,*[4] which is a much more comprehensive collection of the basic legal documents than Woodward's nineteenth-century collection, but also by their various lists and maps, which make it easier to find one's way around in the documents. Here their "List of All Persons Accused of Witchcraft in 1692"[5] will be particularly useful. It gives the names of the accused, the town in which they were living at the time of the trials, and the date of the complaint against them or the warrant for their arrest. It is not complete, but of course no modern list could be. And it does contain a number of inaccuracies.[6] But it is complete enough, and accurate enough, for the present purposes.

There are 141 names on the list. One each come from Amesbury, Boston, Chelmsford, Marblehead, Rumney Marsh, Salisbury, Wells (Maine), and Wenham. Two each come from Billerica, Charlestown, Ipswich, Malden, Manchester, and Piscataqua (Maine). Three come from Woburn and four from Beverly. Five each come from Haverhill, Lynn, and Reading. Six each come from Gloucester, Rowley, and Topsfield. Nineteen come from Salem Town (now Salem). Twenty come from Salem Village (now Danvers). Forty-three come from Andover.

One's first reaction to this simple analysis of the list of the accused is that we have been remiss in talking about the Salem witchcraft. If we want to be geographically comprehensive, we ought to call it the Essex County, Middlesex County, Suffolk County, and Maine witchcraft. Or if we want to name it after the town where it was at its worst, we ought to call it the Andover witchcraft, relegating to a subtitle or a footnote the information that it began in Salem Village and that the trials were held in Salem Town, the Essex County seat.

These statistics are all the more surprising because recent studies of seventeenth-century New England communities have portrayed Salem Town and Salem Village as subject to extraordinary social stress of one kind or another, and thus as thoroughly unstable,[7] while Andover has been seen as virtually devoid of stress. Richard P. Gildrie, the author of a recent community study of Salem (both Town and Village), contrasted Dedham and Andover to his own stress-torn subject as "Puritan utopia[s]," "organic and stable agricultural commune[s]."[8] Philip J. Greven, Jr., the author of the groundbreaking demographic study of Andover, said of that community in the second half of the seventeenth century that "during this period, the evidence reveals that people were extraordinarily healthy, lives were unusually long, and women were exceedingly fecund. . . . . What the basic demographic characteristics of life in seventeenth-century Andover imply . . . seems clear enough: stability and health. . . . [T]he small rural agricultural towns like Andover probably proved to be excellent places in which to realize the [Puritan] goals of order, hierarchy, and the closely-knit community." He adds that "in no significant sense were the lives of the first and second generations in disorder, once their permanent roots had been firmly established in early Andover."[9] Yet Andover, at the height of its second generation, produced 30 percent of the accused persons during the witchcraft trials, more than Salem Village (14 percent) and Salem Town (13 percent) put together. What had gone wrong in this orderly agricultural utopia?

II

It is more difficult to tell what happened at Andover than what happened at Salem Village and Salem Town. In part this is because so many of the accused persons from Andover confessed. When the magistrates had obtained a confession, they seem to have stopped looking for further evidence. As a consequence it is generally impossible to tell, with confessors, what brought them under suspicion in the first place. With most of them one has only the confession (or the report of it) and the names of some of the accusers. Another difficulty is that many of the Andover accused were first examined in Andover by Dudley Bradstreet, the local magistrate. The accounts of these examinations are much more sketchy than the accounts of examinations at the county seat in Salem.[10] Andover is poorly documented in the contemporary narratives as well as in the surviving legal evidence. Nevertheless, it is possible to sketch at least a broad outline of what took place there.

The witchcraft proceedings began with the issuing of warrants for three Salem Village women on February 29, 1692. It was not until almost three months later, on May 28, when matters were well underway and dozens of persons had been arrested, that the first warrant was issued for a resident of Andover. It was for Martha Carrier. Her accusers were several of the afflicted girls of Salem Village, and at her examination they went into convulsive seizures and began hallucinating, complaining that her "specter" was biting, pinching, pricking, and choking them, and accusing her of looking "upon the black man." When the examining magistrate (presumably John Hathorne) asked her, "What black man did you see?" her reply was, "I saw no black man but your own presence." Twentieth-century readers are bound to applaud such words, but they may have struck seventeenth-century hearers as impudent or even malicious. Shortly afterward she said to Hathorne one of the most sensible things, from a twentieth-century point of view, that he was to hear during the entire proceedings: "It is a shameful thing that you should mind these folks that are out of their wits." Her defiance evoked even more violent seizures from the afflicted girls. According to the anonymous court reporter, "The tortures of the afflicted was so great that there was no enduring of it, so that she was ordered away and to be bound hand and foot with all expedition, the afflicted in the meanwhile almost killed, to the great trouble of all spectators, magistrates, and others." "Note," he added, "As soon as she was well bound they all had strange and sudden ease."[11]

By the time of her trial in August there were other kinds of testimony against her, and some of it, from her former neighbors, suggests why she first came under suspicion. John roger of Billerica testified, "That about seven years since, Martha Carrier, being a nigh neighbor unto this deponent, and there happening some difference betwixt us she gave forth several threatening words, as she often used to do." Shortly afterward Roger missed two of his sows. One he never found. The other he found "dead, nigh the said Carrier's house, with both ears cut off." During the same summer one of his cows for no apparent reason suddenly stopped giving milk in the mornings for about a month's time. Roger concluded by saying, "I did in my conscience believe, then in the day of it, and have so done ever since, and do yet believe, that Martha Carrier was the occasion of those ill accidents by means of witchcraft, she being a very malicious woman."[12]

The importance of the dead sow with the ears cut off is that taking a part of the body, or a body product, and subjecting it to occult manipulation was one of the commonest means of working either white or black magic on a person or an animal. With a person you took some of their hair, or their nail parings, or their urine or feces. The hair and nail parings and urine were most commonly boiled; the urine and feces might also be stopped up tight in a container. With an animal it was most common to cut off one or both ears, and boil or burn them. (For a proposal to cut a piece off of a sick mare and burn it, as white magic, see the hilarious affair of the mare's fart.)[13]

There were others of her neighbors who thought that Martha Carrier was a witch. Samuel Preston testified that "about two years since I had some difference with Martha Carrier, which also had happened several times before, and soon after I lost a cow [i.e., it died] in a strange manner. . . . Within about a month after this the said Martha and I had some difference again, at which time she told me I had lost a cow lately, and it would not or should not be long before I should lose another, which accordingly came to pass."

The implication here, of course, is that Martha Carrier predicted the death of the cow because she intended to kill it with a charm or a spell. A similar implication is present in the threats she made against human beings. Benjamin Abbott testified that a little over a year before, when the town of Andover had granted him some land next to Goodman Carrier's,

> Goodwife Carrier was very angry, and said that she would stick as close to Benjamin Abbott as the bark stuck to the tree, and that I should repent of it afore seven years came to an end, and that Doctor Prescott could never cure me. . . . Presently after I was taken with a swelling in my foot, and then was taken with a pain in my side, exceedingly tormented, which bred to a sore which was lanced by Dr. Prescott, and several gallons of corruption did run out, as was judged, and so continued about six weeks very bad. And then one other sore did breed in my groin which was lanced by Doctor Prescott also and continued very bad a while. And then one other sore bred in my groin which was also cut, and put me to very great misery, so that it brought me almost to death's door, and continued until Goodwife Carrier was taken and carried away by the constable. And that very day I began to grow better. My sores grew well and I grew better every day, and so have been well ever since, and have great cause to think

that the said Carrier had a great hand in my sickness and misery.

It should be kept in mind that Goodwife Carrier's threat would have been understood as something more than an ill wish in the seventeenth century. Such words were a curse. In and of themselves they were believed to be a dangerous weapon. One would not utter them lightly. It is most unlikely, of course, that they had anything to do with Benjamin Abbott's actual physical condition. But that is not the point. Benjamin Abbott believed they did, and the chances are that so did Martha Carrier. Martha Carrier's own nephew, Allen Toothaker, testified that he had been a witness to her cursing of Benjamin Abbott. She had once cursed Toothaker as well: "I was wounded in the war. Martha Carrier told me I would never be cured. Afore she was apprehended I could thrust in my wound a knitting needle four inches deep, but since she have been taken I am thoroughly healed." He was so afraid of his aunt that once, during a fight with her son, Richard Carrier, he had suffered an attack of hysterical paralysis, followed by a hallucination: "I fell down flat upon my back to the ground, and had not power to stir hand nor foot. Then I told said Richard I would yield to him and own him the best man. And then I saw Martha Carrier go off from my breast, but when I was risen up I saw none of her." The sudden appearance and disappearance of his aunt's shape meant, of course, to Allen Toothaker, that it was her "specter" that had been restraining him. He concluded by saying that several of his animals had died after his aunt had threatened him. "And I know not of any natural causes of the death of the abovesaid creatures, but have always feared it hath been the effect of my Aunt Martha Carrier her malice."

Toothaker was not the only Andover resident whose fear of Martha Carrier produced psychogenic disorders. Phoebe Chandler, "aged about twelve years," testified that

> about a fortnight before Martha Carrier was sent for to Salem to be examined, upon the Sabbath Day when the psalm was singing, said Martha Carrier took me, said deponent, by the shoulder and shaked me, in the Meeting House, and asked me where I lived. But I made her no answer (not doubting but that she knew me, having lived some time the next door to my father's house, on one side of the way). And that day that said Martha Carrier was seized, my mother sent me to carry some beer to the folks that were at work in the lot, and when I came within the fence there was a voice in the bushes (which I thought was Martha Carrier's voice, which I know well) but saw nobody. And the voice asked me what I did there and whither I was going, which greatly frighted me, so that I run as fast as I could to those at work and told them what I had heard. About an hour and [a] half, or two hours after, my mother sent me again upon the same occasion, to the workmen abovesaid. Coming home, near the place

abovesaid where I heard that voice before, I heard the same voice, as I judged, over my head, saying I should be poisoned within two or three days, which accordingly happened, as I conceive. For I went to my Sister Allen's farm the same day, and on Friday following about one half of my right hand was greatly swollen and exceeding painful, and also part of my face, which I can give no account how it came, and continued very bad some days. And several times since I have been troubled with a great weight upon my breast, and upon my legs when I have been going about, so that I could hardly go, which I have told my mother of. And the last Sabbath Day, was seven night, I went to meeting very well in the morning and went to my place where I used to sit (the ministers not being come). And Richard Carrier, son of abovesaid Martha, looked very earnestly upon me and immediately my hand, which had formerly been poisoned, as abovesaid, began to pain me greatly, and I had a strange burning at my stomach, and then was struck deaf, that I could not hear any of the prayer nor singing till the two or three last words of the singing.

She believed, of course, that Richard Carrier had "over-looked" her, given her the evil eye. Her hysterical deafness was one consequence. The "strange burning" in her stomach was probably the lower body pain with which the *globus hystericus* typically begins. And since the pain in her hand followed so immediately on Richard Carrier's look, one wonders whether it too may not have been psychogenic. One wonders even to what extent her earlier pains may have been a consequence of her aural hallucination of Martha Carrier. In any case, it is clear that some of the citizens of Andover had been living in fear of the supposed occult powers of Martha Carrier for a period of up to seven years before her trial.

A little over two weeks after Martha Carrier's arrest, on July 15, another Andover woman, Ann Foster, was arrested, but little is known about her except for her confessions.

It was John Ballard, an Andover constable, who had served the warrant and warned the witnesses in the Martha Carrier case, and although the documents are missing he may have done the same in the Foster case. At any rate, Ballard's wife had been "this several months sorely afflicted and visited with strange pains and pressures."[14] He thought her bewitched, and thus had several of the hallucinating girls of Salem brought to Andover to see whose specters were afflicting her.[15] As a consequence Mary Lacey, Sr., and Mary Lacey, Jr., the daughter and granddaughter of Ann Foster, were arrested on July 20. Both confessed. The next day three sons of Martha Carrier were arrested, and they confessed as well.

It was a week later, on July 28, that a warrant was issued for the next citizen of Andover, Mary Bridges,

Sr. This time the accuser was not one of the afflicted girls of Salem but Timothy Swan, of Andover. From that time on the names of the Salem girls are only infrequently found in indictments against citizens of Andover. That town had developed its own group of hallucinating afflicted persons, who were responsible for the overwhelming majority of the Andover accusations. The names one sees most often in the indictments, besides that of Timothy Swan, are Rose Foster, of Andover; Abigail Martin, of Andover, "aged about sixteen years";[16] Sarah Phelps, of Andover; and Martha Sprague, alias Tyler, of neighboring Boxford, "aged sixteen years."[17] Among them they accused an extraordinary number of persons, and most of those whom they accused confessed. But before we look at the confessors we should look at two more cases in which, because the persons did not confess, the magistrates accumulated sufficient evidence so that we can tell what had brought them under suspicion.

The first is that of Mary Parker, who was arrested toward the end of August. Besides the behavior of afflicted persons, who went into seizures at the mention of her name and were "recovered . . . out of their fits"[18] by the touch of her hand, and besides the evidence given by confessors, there were three witnesses against her. John Westgate testified that "about eight years since" he had been at the public house of Samuel Beadle when John Parker was among those present. Goodwife Parker then

> came into the company and scolded at and called her husband all to naught, whereupon I, the said deponent, took her husband's part, telling of her it was an unbeseeming thing for her to come after him to the tavern and rail after that rate. With that she came up to me and called me rogue, and bid me mind my own business, and told me I had better have said nothing. Sometime afterwards I, the said deponent, going from the house of Mr. Daniel King, when I came over against John Robinson's house I heard a great noise coming from towards Mr. Babbidge his house. Then there appeared a black hog running towards me with open mouth as though he would have devoured me.

He fell on his hip, driving his knife into it, and had to crawl home with the hog worrying him all the way. He had a "stout" dog with him that ran from the hog, "leaping over the fence and crying much, which at other times used to worry any hog well or sufficiently, which hog I then apprehended was either the Devil or some evil thing, not a real hog, and did then really judge or determine in my mind that it was either Goody Parker or by her means, and procuring fearing that she is a witch."

It seems an idle tale, or would seem so in most contexts. But it shows how little it took for a colonial American to convince himself that his neighbor's wife was a witch, and how his fear of her, festering over eight years, would be enough to bring him into court to testify that she was what he had feared her to be.

The second witness, John Bullock, had helped to get Goodwife Parker home when she had been lying out of doors in winter in what was apparently a catatonic state, since the man carrying her "let her fall upon a place of stones, which did not awake her, which caused me to think she was really dead." But when they got her home and "were taking off her clothes to put her into bed, she rises up and laughs in our faces." Martha Dutch confirmed Bullock's testimony and added "that I have seen said Parker in such a condition several other times." Again, it seems an idle tale, and one's first reaction is to wonder why it was offered as testimony in a witchcraft case. Apparently Bullock and Dutch believed that Mary Parker's catatonic seizures were evidence that she possessed occult powers. Once more one has to be impressed at how little it took to make people afraid of their neighbors.

The third witness was Samuel Shattuck, a Quaker who was a hatter and dyer in Salem Town. He testified

> that in the year 1685 Goodwife Parker, wife to John Parker, Mariner, came to my house and went into the room where my wife and children were and fawned upon my wife with very smooth words. In a short time after, that child which was supposed to have been under an ill hand for several years before was taken in a strange and unusual manner, as if his vitals would have broke out, his breast bone drawn up together to the upper part of his breast, his neck and eyes drawn so much aside as if they would never come to right again. He lay in so strange a manner that the doctor and others did believe he was bewitched. Some days after some of the visitors cut some of his hair off to boil, which they said, although they did [it] with great tenderness, the child would shriek out as if he had been tormented. They put his hair in a skillet over a fire which stood plain on the hearth, and it was thrown down, and I came immediately into the room as soon as they were gone out of the room, and could see no creature in the room. They put it on again, and after it had boiled some time the abovesaid Goodwife Parker came in and asked if I would buy some chickens.

Shattuck's visitors had themselves been practicing malefic witchcraft here, since boiling the victim's hair was a charm intended either to harm the witch or compel her presence. Since it turned out on later investigation that Goodwife Parker had had no chickens to sell, it must have been considered a success, in spite of the spectral casting down of the skillet on the first attempt.

Here as elsewhere it should be noted that New England witchcraft cannot be considered a temporary insanity confined to 1692. Shattuck's suspicions of Mary Parker dated back seven years, to a time when she had lived in Salem Town. Why hadn't he prosecuted her then? Perhaps he was one of Professor Konig's "opponents of law"; certainly he had been willing to take the law into his own hands. Or perhaps he had realized that although his suspicions were strong his evidence was incomplete. Nobody had heard Mary Parker curse the child, or seen her work a charm against it, or even look at it fixedly with an evil eye. And if you took a witch to court, and the court did not put her to death, surely she would find some way to have her revenge. But in 1692, when the Court of Oyer and Terminer was doing its best to rid the country of witches, and when the afflicting specter of Mary Parker had appeared in the hallucinations of three of her present neighbors (Sarah Phelps of Andover, Hannah Bigsby of Andover, and Martha Sprague of Boxford), Samuel Shattuck was willing to come forward and offer his testimony.

Our third case is that of Samuel Wardwell, and in some ways it is the most interesting, if only because it is so very insubstantial. His specter had appeared in several persons' hallucinations, afflicting Martha Sprague of Boxford. He had been "much addicted" to fortune telling, so much so that several of his neighbors were clearly in awe of his supposedly occult abilities in predicting the future. And he had boasted "that he could make cattle come to him when he pleased."[19] When he was first examined he confessed "that he had been foolishly led along with telling of fortunes, which sometimes came to pass. He used also when any creature came into his field to bid the Devil take it, and it may be the Devil took advantage of him by that." He went on to provide an account of meetings with the Devil, and of making a covenant with him. But he later repudiated his confession. Whether he had ever actually practiced malefic magic remains in doubt, of course. But the evidence we have seen against him so far is "specter" evidence and evidence about his practicing white magic. So it would be a little surprising to learn that he, Mary Parker, and Martha Carrier were the three citizens of Andover who were executed for witchcraft if it were not for the fact that there was another kind of evidence against him. His name, like that of Martha Carrier and Mary Parker, turns up repeatedly in the testimony of the Andover confessors.

John Hale, whose *Modest Enquiry into the Nature of Witchcraft* is the most reliable contemporary account of the Salem trials, tells us that the "matter was carried on . . . chiefly by the complaints and accusations of the afflicted . . . and . . . by the confessions of the accused, condemning themselves and others."[20] Of the forty-three Andover names on Boyer and Nissenbaum's life of accused witches, it is not known how seven pled. Of the remaining thirty-six, only six denied the accusations; thirty confessed. If Hale and Calef are correct in saying that there were "about fifty"[21] confessors altogether, that would mean that Andover supplied at least 60 percent of them. Whether they are correct or not, it is clear that the number of Andover confessors is out of all proportion both to the relative size of the community and to the number of the Andover accused.

One can find several motives for the Andover confessions in the surviving documents. Two of the confessors clearly enjoyed the attention paid them in their hearings. Mary Lacey, Jr., responded readily to the magistrates in her several examinations, frequently supplying colorful details for which she had not been asked. It was she who volunteered that "Goody Carrier told me the Devil said to her that she should be a queen in Hell,"[22] a detail that so impressed the Massachusetts magistrates and ministers that it found its way into Cotton Mather's account of the Carrier case in *Wonders of the Invisible World*. She later joined the ranks of the afflicted persons, although she does not seem to have initiated any accusations. William Barker, Sr., also enjoyed confessing, so much so that courtroom appearances were not enough for him: John Hale prints a confession "which he wrote himself in prison, and sent to the magistrates to confirm his former confession to them."[23]

A very different motive for confession is found in the case of Sarah Wilson, Sr. When the Reverend Increase Mather interviewed several of the confessing Andover women in prison, she told him "that, knowingly, she never had familiarity with the Devil; that, knowingly, she never consented to the afflicting of any person, &c. However, she said that truly she was in the dark as to the matter of her being a witch. And being asked how she was in the dark, she replied that the afflicted persons crying out of her as afflicting them made her fearful of herself."[24]

Neither her examination nor her confession survives, but it is easy to reconstruct what happened. Affliction took two main forms. In the first, the afflicted person went into seizures and hallucinations at the glance of the accused person, and could be recovered by her touch. The cause of the affliction was then believed to be the evil eye. In the second form the afflicted also went into seizures and hallucinations, complaining that the "specter" or spirit of the accused was the cause of her convulsions, or was pinching, pricking, biting, or choking her. Goodwife Wilson had seen the awe-inspiring behavior of the afflicted persons in her presence, and, hearing their accusations and unable to think of any other cause, was afraid that she might possess the evil eye without being aware of it, or that her spirit might be responsible for the afflictions without her knowledge.

A third motive for confession was that by the time arrests became general in Andover, it was clear that confessors were not being executed. As the Reverend Francis Dane, the senior minister of Andover, wrote to an anonymous "reverend sir," "I fear the common speech that was frequently spread among us, of their liberty if they would confess, have brought many into a snare" (i.e., of false confession).

But by far the greatest reason for the large number of confessions at Andover appears to have been the bullying of the accused by their own friends and relatives. A particularly chilling instance was discovered by Increase mather when he interviewed Martha Tyler in prison. She told him

> that when she was first apprehended she had no fears upon her, and did think that nothing could have made her confess against herself. But since she had found, to her great grief, that she had wronged the truth and falsely accused herself. She said that. when she was brought to Salem her brother Bridges rode with her, and that all along the way from Andover to Salem her brother kept telling her that she must needs be a witch, since the afflicted accused her and at her touch were raised out of their fits, and urging her to confess herself a witch. She as constantly told him that she was no witch, that she knew nothing of witchcraft, and begged him not to urge her to confess. However, when she came to Salem she was carried to a room where her brother on one side, and Mr. John Emerson on the other side, did tell her that she was certainly a witch, and that she saw the Devil before her eyes at that time (and accordingly the said Emerson would attempt with his hand to beat Him away from her eyes); and they so urged her to confess that she wished herself in any dungeon rather than to be so treated. Mr. Emerson told her, once and again, "Well, I see you will not confess! Well, I will now leave you, and then you are undone, body and soul, forever." Her brother urged her to confess, and told her that in so doing she could not lie, to which she answered, "Good brother, do not say so, for I shall lie if I confess, and then who shall answer unto God for my lie?" He still asserted it, and said that God would not suffer so many good men to be in such an error about it, and that she would be hanged if she did not confess, and continued so long and so violently to urge and press her to confess that she thought, verily, that her life would have gone from her, and became so terrified in her mind that she owned, at length, almost anything that they propounded to her; that she had wronged her conscience in so doing; she was guilty of a great sin in belying of herself, and desired to mourn for it so long as she lived. This she said, and a great deal more of the like nature; and all with such affection, sorrow, relenting, grief, and mourning, as that it exceeds any pen to describe and express the same.[25]

Indeed, Andover became notorious for the ease and thoroughness with which family and community bonds were broken in the face of witchcraft accusations. Brattle speaks of the "husbands who, having taken up that corrupt and highly pernicious opinion that whoever were accused by the afflicted were guilty, did break charity with their dear wives upon their being accused and urge them to confess their guilt."[26] Calef says of Andover, "Here it was that many accused themselves of riding upon poles through the air, many parents believing their children to be witches, and many husbands their wives."[27] And Andover's senior minister, Francis Dane, lamented that "the conceit of specter evidence as an infallible mark did too far prevail with us. Hence we so easily parted with our neighbors of honest and good report, and [church] members in full communion. Hence we so easily parted with our children, when we knew nothing in their lives, nor any of our neighbors to suspect them. And thus things were hurried on, hence such strange breaches in families. . . . "[28]

Why did Andover's family and community loyalties break down so thoroughly in the face of witchcraft accusations? It may not be possible, of course, to find a fully satisfactory explanation. Perhaps it was their very devotion to Puritan ideals of communal unity which made Andover citizens prefer to think their wives, children, and neighbors witches rather than accept the idea that, as Martha Tyler's brother put it, God would permit "so many good men to be in such an error about it."

Factional hostility has been the most persuasive of the recent explanations of the Salem trials. But it does seem clear, in the light of Andover's experience, that we cannot account for those trials by suggesting that Salem had a history of factional hostility and Andover had not. Even without the Andover experience, it ought to be clear that factional hostility does not in itself provide a comprehensive explanation for the Salem trials. There are departments in twentieth-century American universities with as long and as vicious a history of factional hatreds as any to be found in Salem, and the parties to these hatreds accuse each other of all sorts of absurdities, but witchcraft is not one of them. If we want to understand what happened at Salem, we shall have to begin by acknowledging as causes of the trials some of the ways in which seventeenth-century American culture was different from our own.

III

The first, or one might say the underlying, cause was that seventeenth-century Americans, like seventeenth-century Europeans, believed in witchcraft. That is to say, they believed it possible to affect the course of events, including doing good or evil to other persons, through occult means. Belief in witchcraft was virtually universal, but the practice of it was limited, because it was seen not simply as an appeal to occult forces but to specifically anti-Christian occult forces. Therefore it was practiced only by certain kinds of

people: the ignorant, who did not understand that their charms or spells were anti-Christian, and the powerless, the desperate, and the malicious, who did not care. None of these kinds of people are apt to put themselves on the historical record, and most of them are apt to try to keep themselves off it, so we hear of colonial American witchcraft only when it reached the attention of the authorities. But this happened far more frequently than most American historians, or even most historians of American witchcraft, have recognized. Frederick C. Drake lists fifty-eight "cases and incidents" of witchcraft in the American colonies in the eighteen years from 1645 to 1662,[29] and when we remember that colonial records, especially outside New England, are very incomplete, it seems clear that witchcraft cases were a regular feature of American colonial experience. Only some of these cases, of course, were instances of the actual practice of witchcraft; many of them were instances of the fear of it. But if we keep in mind that the "cases and incidents" in the surviving records must be only a very small proportion of the total number, it seems clear that belief in and fear of witchcraft were endemic in the American colonies. From the evidence of the surviving documents it also seems clear that white witchcraft was commonly practiced and that black witchcraft was not uncommon. We have one instance of openly avowed black witchcraft above, in the boiling of the Shattuck child's hair. Without the near-universal belief in witchcraft and the regular practice of it, it is hard to see how witchcraft could have remained a capital crime, as it did in both England and English America until a generation after the Salem trials.[30]

But in the typical colonial witchcraft trial only one or two persons were accused. What distinguishes the Salem trials from all the others is their scale. The total number of the accused is unknown, but a conservative estimate would put the figure over 200. Calef claims that it was more than 350.[31] Nineteen people were hanged, and one was pressed to death for refusing to plead to his indictment. In one sense, then, when we ask the causes of the Salem trials, we are really asking why, on this occasion, a fairly common kind of judicial proceeding got out of hand. Community studies will not help us much here because the accused, the accusers, and the judges of the Court of Oyer and Terminer came from many different communities. Nor will the various hostility theories help us, although servile hostility, sexual hostility, regional hostility, and factional hostility may all be useful in an analysis of why particular persons were accusers or accused. A number of explanations can be found, however, all of them more or less familiar.

Let us start with John Hale's statement that the "matter was carried on . . . chiefly by the complaints and accusations of the afflicted . . . and . . . by the confessions of the accused, condemning themselves and others." "The complaints and accusations of the afflicted" depended chiefly on their hallucinations of the "specters" of the accused, that is, on so-called spectral evidence. The Boston clergy advised the court early, and throughout the proceedings, not to place too much weight on spectral evidence, and it is clear that the court did not take this advice seriously enough. Why they did not do so can only be a matter for conjecture, because no record was kept and no report made of the court's deliberations.[32] One possible explanation may lie in the characters of the magistrate who conducted most of the preliminary examinations, John Hathorne, and of the chief justice, William Stoughton. Both of them, through most of the proceedings, seem to have been much more anxious to obtain evidence of guilt—any kind of evidence of guilt—than to weigh the evidence impartially. It is not only possible but probable that with a different leadership the proceedings would have turned out very differently.

As for confessions, it was here that the Salem court's procedure differed from that of all other colonial American courts, as Drake has pointed out,[33] and from all English courts as well. The ordinary procedure was to execute confessors, since confession was often the best possible proof of guilt in witchcraft cases. The Salem court did not bring them to trial; it even stayed the executions of condemned witches who subsequently confessed. Again we do not know the reasons for the court's procedure. They may have been following Cotton Mather's early advice that "lesser criminals be only scourged with lesser punishments, and also put upon some solemn, open, public and explicit renunciation of the Devil."[34] Or they may have been attracted to the drama of redemption that the confession presented, and reluctant to execute those they had redeemed. Or they may have been hungry for guilt, and pleased that the confessors incriminated not only themselves but others. In any case, the court's policy toward confessors was a major cause of the escalation of accusations.

And of course, as many scholars have pointed out, 1692 was a time of extraordinary troubles for Massachusetts. She had finally and irrevocably lost her Old Charter, which had been the very basis of her identity. There were serious troubles with the French and the Indians on the frontier. It was precisely the sort of time in which even the best of men are apt to feel that unnamed evils are abroad in the land, and that it would be a public service to root them out.

We cannot know, in our present state of knowledge, which of these causes were the more compelling. But we can recognize that the causes of the Salem trials were extraordinarily complex. No single explanation is going to sweep them under the historical rug; we can expect the debate over them to continue.

Notes

[1] John Demos, "Underlying Themes in the Witchcraft of Seventeenth-Century New England," *American Historical Review,* 75 (1970): 1311-26; Richard Slotkin, *Regeneration through Violence* (Middletown, Conn.: Wesleyan University Press, 1973), ch. 5; Paul Boyer and Stephen Nissenbaum, *Salem Possessed* (Cambridge, Mass.: Harvard University Press, 1974); Linnda R. Caporeal, "Ergotism: The Satan Loosed in Salem?" *Science,* 192 (Apr. 2, 1976): 21-26; David Thomas Konig, *Law and Society in Puritan Massachusetts* (Chapel Hill: University of North Carolina Press, 1979), chs. 6 and 7; Lyle Koehler, *A Search for Power* (Urbana: University of Illinois Press, 1980), chs. 10-13; Cedric B. Cowing, "The Roots of Salem Witchcraft." I am indebted to Professor Cowing for his kind permission to read his essay in typescript and to refer to it here.

[2] Paul Boyer and Stephen Nissenbaum, *The Salem Witchcraft Papers,* 3 vols. (New York: Da Capo, 1977), pp. 83; 112; 249, 259-60; 357; 611; 797-98, 963; 162-63, 176; 824, 842. This collection is cited hereafter as *SWP.*

[3] Boyer and Nissenbaum, *Salem Possessed,* p. 209.

[4] See n. 2.

[5] Boyer and Nissenbaum, *Salem-Village Witchcraft* (Belmont, Calif.: Wadsworth, 1972), pp. 376-78.

[6] If one takes the table of contents of *SWP* as a revised list, some omissions and errors are corrected there, but new omissions and errors are introduced. Either list would do for the present purposes, but the later one would have to be corrected.

[7] Richard P. Gildrie, *Salem, Massachusetts, 1626-1683* (Charlottesville: University of Virginia Press, 1975), and Boyer and Nissenbaum, *Salem Possessed.*

[8] Gildrie, *Salem,* p. 179.

[9] Philip J. Greven, Jr., *Four Generations: Population, Land, and Family in Colonial Andover, Massachusetts* (Ithaca, N.Y.: Cornell University Press, 1970), pp. 269-71.

[10] See, for example, the Andover and Salem examinations of Elizabeth Johnson, Jr. (*SWP,* pp. 503-5).

[11] *SWP,* pp. 185-86. Because of the extreme irregularity of spelling, punctuation, and capitalization in the legal documents, I have modernized all three.

[12] The testimony of Martha Carrier's neighbors is in *SWP,* pp. 189-94.

[13] *SWP,* pp. 444-46.

[14] Ibid., p. 513.

[15] The account of Ballard's sending to Salem for witch-finders is to be found both in Thomas Brattle's "Letter" and in Robert Calef's *More Wonders of the Invisible World,* in George Lincoln Burr, ed., *Narratives of the Witchcraft Cases* (New York: Barnes & Noble, 1959), pp. 180-81 and 371-72. Both Brattle and Calef seem to have been working from very incomplete evidence, as their brief accounts of Andover demonstrate.

[16] *SWP,* p. 788.

[17] Ibid., p. 786.

[18] The legal documents of the Mary Parker case are in *SWP,* pp. 629-37.

[19] The legal documents of the Samuel Wardwell case are in *SWP,* pp. 783-89.

[20] Burr, *Narratives,* p. 421.

[21] Ibid., pp. 416, 373.

[22] The legal documents of the Mary Lacey, Jr., case are in *SWP,* pp. 520-29.

[23] Hale, *Modest Enquiry* in Burr, *Narratives,* p. 419.

[24] An account of Mather's visit, presumably from Thomas Brattle's papers, is in the *Massachusetts Historical Society Collections,* 2d ser., 3: 221-25.

[25] Ibid.

[26] Burr, *Narratives,* p. 181.

[27] Ibid., p. 372.

[28] *SWP,* p. 882.

[29] Frederick C. Drake, "Witchcraft in the American Colonies, 1647-62," *American Quarterly,* 20 (1968): 694-725. A recent article on the widespread existence of various kinds of occultism in colonial America is Jon Butler, "Magic, Astrology, and the Early American Religious Heritage, 1600-1760," *American Historical Review,* 84 (1979): 317-46.

[30] For the Old Charter law, see Section 94 of the *Body of Liberties,* reprinted in Edwin Powers, *Crime and Punishment in Early Massachusetts* (Boston: Beacon, 1966), pp. 533-48. The English law in effect at the time is 1 *Jacob.* Cap. 12.

[31] Burr, *Narratives,* p. 373.

[32] For a discussion of the court's and the clergy's disagreements on this issue, see Chadwick Hansen, *Witchcraft at Salem* (New York: George Braziller, 1969), especially those passages indexed under "spectral evidence."

[33] Drake, "Witchcraft," p. 725.

[34] Cotton Mather, "Letter to John Richards," *Collections of the Massachusetts Historical Society,* 4th ser., 8: 397.

Richard B. Trask (essay date 1992)

SOURCE: An introduction to *The Devil Hath Been Raised: A Documentary History of the Salem Village Witchcraft Outbreak of March 1692,* Yeoman Press, 1992, pp. ix-xvii.

[*In the following excerpt, Trask outlines the conflicts between Salem Village and Salem Town and the controversies surrounding the Village's minister, Samuel Parris.*]

"The Devil hath been raised amongst us, & his Rage is vehement & terrible, & when he shall be silenc'd the Lord only knows." So wrote Samuel Parris, the pastor of Salem Village, in his church record book in late March 1692 when confronted with what was discovered to be a diabolical occurrence taking place in this small Massachusetts hamlet.

What at first seemed only a localized witchcraft outbreak soon would spread rapidly and by the end of May 1692 people from communities as distant and diverse as Salem, Billerica, Andover, Charlestown, Marblehead, Lynn, Reading, Topsfield, Gloucester, Malden, and Beverly would be accused by various "afflicted persons" of using witchcraft upon them. By the fall of 1692 over 150 people had been examined and sent to prison. Men and women, both rich and influential as well as poor and hapless, were enmeshed in frightening legal confrontation. Some 50 falsely confessed to being witches who, in exchange for special powers and favors, had made a covenant with the Devil to assist in his assault upon the people of the colony. Nineteen persons who staunchly maintained their innocence were tried, found guilty and hanged, while one old man was tortured to death, and at least five others died in prison succumbing to harsh conditions and treatment.

the Devil to assist in his assault upon the people of the colony. Nineteen persons who staunchly maintained their innocence were tried, found guilty and hanged, while one old man was tortured to death, and at least five others died in prison succumbing to harsh conditions and treatment.

The story of the Salem Village witch hysteria is a minor, though well-known footnote in American colonial history. Its popular fascination has continued to make it the subject of innumerable scholarly as well as superficial books and articles. In our own time the expression "A Salem Witch Hunt" is often used as a universal phrase which points to a scapegoating position taken by people or groups emphasizing hysterical, blindly illogical and intolerant actions or expressions.

What was the cause of the historical 1692 Salem witch hunt, the largest witch outbreak in America, that occurred at a time when the earlier, massive witch hunts of Europe were on the wane? Writers and researchers since the last decade of the 17th century down to the present time have been trying to find a theory or an explanation to this question. Colonial clerics, including John Hale and Cotton Mather, saw these events as the direct intervention of the Devil attacking the Puritan Commonwealth and being partially successful as the result of a religious backsliding of New Englanders and the use by civil authorities of ill-conceived traditions and non-biblical principles to discover who was a witch. Later authors would come up with a wealth of hypotheses to describe the causes, postulating among other explanations that it resulted from the pranks of bored adolescents, the influence of oligarchical and power-hungry clergy, local petty jealousies and land grabs, mental aberrations, spiritualist goings-on, political instability, a conspiratorial holding action against the disintegration of Puritanism, mass clinical hysteria, a clash between agrarian and emerging commercial interests, a continuation of the suppression of certain types of women, and even physical reactions to ingested fungus. Besides the mysterious quality of the subject matter, the Salem cases have always afforded the researcher a fairly extensive accumulation of primary source documents representing a diversity of people, yet combined with a body of knowledge that is manageable enough to be examined in microcosm.

The ordinary English Puritan settler in 17th century New England believed, as did his European counterpart, in the existence of a literal Devil and the possibility of witchcraft affecting his everyday life. Witches were thought to be humans, typically women, who had agreed to serve the Devil. In return for favors and certain amazing powers from the Devil, they attempted to help "The Old Deluder" bring ruin upon the Christian community.

On continental Europe beginning in the 15th century, literally tens of thousands of "witches" had been discovered and put to death. There, witchcraft was considered a heresy against the church, and heretics were burned at the stake. Because of geography and

---

Rosenthal on the search for explanations regarding Salem:

. . . Few topics in American culture have received the broad attention received by the Salem witch trials. The subject of scholarly tomes, television shows, folklore, and newspaper cartoons, and the vehicle for countless metaphors of oppression and persecution, Salem has had a powerful hold on American imagination. An event that by some European standards of witchcraft persecutions would be relatively minor in its magnitude has achieved an archetypal status in our own country and in others. . . .

A common explanation for the "witchcraft" outbreak spreading beyond Salem Village centers on the political and social turmoil facing the colony, particularly in view of its lack of a charter. That is, the colony's charter had been revoked in 1684, and although Increase Mather was soon expected to arrive with a new one, a situation of instability and anxiety prevailed. In addition to this uncertainty about the charter, itself a symptom of ongoing political disputes with England, were persistent threats from "Indians" (i.e., Native Americans) against the colony and a decline of power among orthodox clergy—all ingredients for broad social instability, providing fertile ground for the discovery of enemies in the invisible world. . . .

This traditional explanation centering on political and social turmoil is plausible but not satisfying. . . . Attempts to explain by a single theory what happened in 1692 distort rather than clarify the events of that year, although anyone who offers to adjudicate once and for all the various competing theories about the Salem witch trials should be a soldier rather than a scholar.

Different conclusions about Salem follow from different questions asked about the event and from different methodologies applied in answering those questions. . . .

Bernard Rosenthal, Salem Story: Reading the
Witch Trials of 1692, *Cambridge University
Press, 1993.*

out and hanged. In England witchcraft was considered a felony against the state, and felons were hanged. Major English witch outbreaks typically occurred during those periods of social or political strife as, for example, during the Civil War when in less than two years in the mid 1640s about 200 witches were executed following their discovery by a merciless and deceitful man named Matthew Hopkins, who was dubbed the "Witch Finder General."

The English settlers of 17th century New England did on occasion find witchcraft at work within their various communities, and although a large-scale witch outbreak did not occur prior to 1692, over 90 individual complaints and accusations took place before that date.

One of the larger Massachusetts Bay towns was Salem, first occupied by Englishmen in 1626. Soon a large migration of people followed from the mother country. By the mid 1630s with the available land of this coastal community quickly diminishing and the desire for larger and better farmland, a group of settlers established homesteads to the west of Salem some five to ten miles from the town center. This area soon became known as Salem Village, and by the 1660s included a substantial collection of widely scattered farms.

Once established, the farmers or "villagers," as they began to refer to themselves, saw that they had less and less in common with Salem and began to look towards their own self-interests. Many resented their subservient position to the more mercantile and distant townspeople, and beginning in 1667 with a group of villagers petitioning to be exempt from the Salem military watch, "considering how remote our dwellings are from the Town," the farmers pressed towards becoming independent from their mother community. Salem, having previously lost significant territory to other developing settlements, was not eager to grant any such new request. For the major part of a century through delaying counter-proposals, political clout and obstinacy the town staved-off losing the valuable and taxable village territory.

Turning to the General Court for possible relief, the villagers petitioned for permission at least to build their own meeting house and hire a minister to preach among them. In 1672 Salem relented to the religious argument, and the village was allowed to establish a parish.

A parish was not an independent church, however, and although the villagers could choose from among themselves a five-man committee to assess support for a minister and a building, the chosen minister was not an ordained pastor and theirs was not an independent, covenant church. Villagers who desired full church membership and participation in communion at the Lord's Table would continue to be required to travel the many miles to the Salem church. Though the villag-

ers were free from paying Salem church rates, for all other purposes, taxing and political, they were legally part of Salem Town. Many but not all of the approximately 550 villagers still desired full independence, both ecclesiastical and political, from the town, and they pressed the issue on numerous occasions. It would not be until the 1750s, however, that Salem Village would be finally granted its full independence with the establishment of the Town of Danvers.

Even while they possessed a semblance of ecclesiastical independence, a divisive inter-village religious factionalism emerged resulting in much controversy during the three, short term, successive ministeries which served the village from 1672 to 1688. Ministers James Bayley, George Burroughs, and Deodat Lawson seemed never to gain the endorsement and support of more than a simple majority of the villagers, and typically found themselves entangled in heated, uncharitable controversy with a vocal minority. Upon finding the situation not worth the fight, each would unhappily depart the village.

In a 1682 letter villager Jeremiah Watts complained concerning the local factionalism, "Brother is against brother and neighbors against neighbors, all quarreling and smiting one another." Still later in the 1680s during a dispute involving Rev. Lawson, a committee of arbitrators from Salem commented in their written advice to the village that "uncharitable expressions and uncomly reflections tost [sic] to and fro . . . have a tendency to make such a gap as we fear, if not timely prevented, will lett out peace and order and let in confusion and every evil work." Among the arbiters in this February 1687 communication were future witchcraft judges John Hathorne and Bartholomew Gedney.

Although much of the contentiousness and quarreling over village ministers was indeed homegrown, Salem Town shared part of the blame in its heavy-handed dealings with the village. Salem Village was in an unenviable position. It sorely lacked those traditional institutions meant to assist in the governing and the stability of New England communities. The village church could congregate, tax itself, and worship, but was denied performing its own sacraments or holding its own covenant. The Village Committee could be elected and meet, but it was a governing body in name only, not able to act on its own or the inhabitants' self-interest and forced to appeal to the town selectmen on any substantive issues. Though by no means the only explanation for the village's problems with factionalism, this vacuum of power greatly exacerbated its difficulties. A not inconsequential number of villagers also had a vision and an empathy more in keeping with the mercantile interests of Salem Town rather than with the agrarian outlook of Salem Village. With these significant political, religious, social, and economic differences existing from without and from within the village society, it is not difficult to understand why the area had acquired a regional reputation for provincialism and ill-feeling.

By 1689 the villagers in a seemingly unusual spirit of cooperation pushed hard for a completely independent church, while at the same time hiring their fourth successive minister, Samuel Parris. By a chance of circumstances, the request was granted from the Salem mother church and on November 19, 1689, the Rev. Mr. Samuel Parris was ordained pastor of the newly created and independent Church of Christ at Salem Village, with twenty-seven adults joining together in full covenant.

What at first seemed a fresh and positive beginning, soon took on the same old attitudes and style of former controversies. Thirty-five-year-old Rev. Parris was a novice to the ministerial calling, having engaged for much of his adult life in the mercantile field. After over a decade of attempting to make a successful living in the Barbados, West Indies, and then in Boston, Parris gradually changed his life's course to become a minister for Christ. Through truncated negotiations in 1688 and 1689 with various small committees purporting to fully represent the will of the village inhabitants, Parris eventually acquired for himself what he felt to be adequate terms for his calling among the farmers. Though his salary was smaller and included less hard currency than he had initially desired, he concluded that it was sufficient for him and his family. He had also wrangled the major concession of full ownership of the village-built 1681 parsonage and its two-acre lot.

Unfortunately everyone had not been privy to the full terms of the agreement, or at least later claimed this to be the case. A vociferous minority, primarily of non-church member inhabitants, saw the settlement agreement as unwarrantable and an illegal give-away of their village-owned parsonage. As a contemporary chronicler of the witchcraft events, Robert Calef, would write of the parsonage dispute, "This occasioned great Divisions both between the Inhabitants themselves, and between a considerable part of them and their said Minister, which Divisions were but the beginning or Praeludium to what immediately followed." Slowly festering, the controversy continued to build until by October 1691 the opposition faction made its move. In the annual election of the Village Committee, the old committee made up of the minister's church supporters was ousted and a new committee composed of Joseph Porter, Francis Nurse, Joseph Putnam, Daniel Andrews, and Joseph Hutchinson, most if not all strong opponents of Parris, was installed. When called upon by the church in November 1691 to begin the gathering of taxes to support the ministry, the committee, whose primary duty this was, chose instead inaction. Thereupon, the church voted to sue the committee in court. The two village institutions had set their course of confrontation, and villagers were placed in the unenviable position of choosing sides.

Meanwhile, his firewood supply virtually depleted, the minister entreated his congregation to provide him with wood for heating and cooking. Even this request was tinged with controversy. Parris expected the wood to be brought forth and stacked upon his wood pile by his respectful congregation. Most villagers, however, believed Parris's salary included a wood allotment payment and that he should not presume to be above making arrangements for his own wood.

From the scant written sources which survive, Parris appears to have been a man of strong will who expected the deference from his people which was customarily given to respected community ministers. A good portion of the inhabitants were unwilling to give Parris, both as to his personal comfort among them and in their acknowledgment of him as their spiritual guide, either their generosity of spirit or of purse. An examination of Parris's surviving sermon outlines, particularly those written during the last quarter of 1691, seem to include thinly veiled references to his dissatisfaction with his lot among them. He often preached on the theme of conflict between good and evil, Christ and Satan, and enemies who are both within and without the church.

Besides these ever-present conflicts within the village and between the village and the town, the inhabitants of Salem Village were part of the larger community of the Massachusetts Bay and New England. The times were full of uncertainty and apprehension. Many clergy spoke of the backsliding of the current generation of New Englanders into a less God-fearing and righteous-living society, and suggested that in answer to these sins God might allow tribulation to befall His wayward people. Indians and the French to the north were a constant threat. In early 1692 Abenaki Indians had resumed bloody warfare by viciously attacking settlements in Maine, killing or carrying off inhabitants at York and Wells and burning many houses. These attacks led Essex County people to fear that this was the beginning of another war on the scale of the King Philip's War of the mid 1670s when many Salem Village soldiers had died and when the village had erected a watch house and fortified the meeting house. Indeed not too long before 1692 several young village men on duty elsewhere had died in Indian attacks.

The political scene in Massachusetts was also a matter of concern. In 1684 the colony had lost its self-governing charter and the Crown's newly appointed governor, Sir Edmund Andros, arrived in 1686. It was unclear during this period if the land granted under the old charter would be considered valid by the new power. With the excuse of the "Glorious Revolution" in England, Massachusetts in 1689 revolted against Andros and set up its own commonwealth based on the old charter. Rev. Increase Mather had been sent to England as advocate for Massachusetts concerning a new charter. The success or failure of his venture was unknown and the cause of much apprehension. Thus the bleak midwinter of 1691-1692 was a period of uneasiness in the colony. Little Salem Village with its divisive social structure and scattered population faced not only consternation from without, but also a continuation of the institutional difficulties with Salem and significant internal stress over its own religious community.

Just when a strange malady first struck several children in the minister's house and that of several of his neighbors' homesteads is unclear. By late January and early February of 1692, a number of locals knew that something was amiss, however. Two of the youngsters in the Parris household, daughter Betty, age 9, and niece Abigail Williams, age 11, together with Ann Putnam, Jr., the daughter of staunch Parris supporter Thomas Putnam, who lived less than a mile from the parsonage, were affected. Putnam's wife's niece, Mary Walcott, the 17-year-old daughter of Jonathan Walcott who lived within a stone's throw of the parsonage, was also " . . . afflicted by they knew not what distempers." While it would later be speculated that these adolescent girls and perhaps others were dabbling in unhealthy and sinful games of divination, attempting to find out by means of white witchcraft their future fate, what caused their fits is not clearly known. Though presumed by later writers, it is unclear if Tituba, Rev. Parris's Indian slave, had any hand in letting the impressionable girls have their forbidden sport and encouraged or at least did not prevent their irreligious games.

An undoubtedly chagrined Parris must have seen these young girls' actions as extremely dangerous signs. The fits they exhibited were not simply playful; and instead of diminishing over time, they seemed to intensify and infect others. Rev. John Hale of Beverly, an observer of many of these early happenings, would in later years, describe the symptoms:

> These children were bitten and pinched by invisible agents; their armes, necks, and backs turned this way and that way. . . . Sometimes they were taken dumb, their mouths stopped, their throats choked, their limbs wracked and tormented so as might move an heart of stone, to sympathize with them, with bowels of compassion for them.

As these torments continued, they became the talk of the village, and many saw a clear comparison of what was presently occurring in Salem Village with the reported afflictions of the Goodwin children who had been tormented by a witch in Boston in 1689. Other classic English bewitchment cases were also brought to mind.

Rather than separating the affected children as had been done with successful results in the Boston case by Rev. Cotton Mather, the village parents seem to have allowed the children to keep together. This did not quiet the situation, but rather encouraged its festering. The anxious elders, undoubtedly guided by Rev. Parris, held prayer meetings with the children present. They also held private fasts and called upon the neighborhood ministers to visit and pray over the girls at the parsonage and elsewhere.

A local physician, most probably William Griggs, was also called to offer his assistance and advice. Finding no physical malady he could identify as to the cause, he suggested that their afflictions were likely to be the result of bewitchment, an explanation that others quickly embraced as logical considering the evidence. The teenage maid living with the Griggs family also became an early sufferer of this same strange affliction.

Once it was recognized that these were no epileptic-like seizures or anything of that type and that the problem was spreading to others, many felt that firm action had to be taken. The various private and public fasts and the patient, continual praying and the waiting upon Providence was too ineffectual for some. Concerned adults began pressing the young ones to discover who or what agent was hurting them.

Some sincere but meddling neighbors dabbled in white witchcraft in an attempt to discover the cause of the afflictions. Mary Sibley directed Parris's slaves to concoct a witch cake utilizing the children's urine, and when the minister later learned of this abomination occurring under his roof, he severely and publicly chastised the woman, and identified this occurrence as what he perceived to be the new and dangerous plateau of allowing the Devil entry into this sad and now horrific calamity.

Finally the girls, under now unknown pressures and from unclear sources, named three tormentors. The accused were the safe kind of victims to cry out upon. One, the minister's slave, another a destitute woman of ill repute possessing a sharp tongue, and the third a sickly woman who had avoided church attendance for over a year and whose unsavory marital past had been the occasion for much gossip, were safe choices. With the swearing out of warrants for their arrest issued on February 29, 1692, Tituba, Sarah Good and Sarah Osburn would become the first to be examined in relation to the girls' afflictions. The events, the words and the actions that would transpire at their examination, and the testimony and evidence that would result would significantly transform this seemingly typical and local witch incident. And it would be during the critical first thirty-one days of the witchcraft outbreak that the course would be set, the confrontation joined and the community hysteria stoked, leading into the most dramatic, far reaching and deadly witch hunt in all of American history.

THE ROLE OF WOMEN IN THE TRIALS

John Demos (essay date 1970)

SOURCE: "Underlying Themes in Witchcraft of Seventeenth-Century New England," in *The American Historical Review*, Vol. LXXV, No. 5, June, 1970, pp. 1311-26.

[*In the following excerpt, Demos comments on the significance of the fact that most of the accused Salem witches were eccentric and / or anti-social, middle-aged women, while their accusers were girls a generation younger.*]

It is faintly embarrassing for a historian to summon his colleagues to still another consideration of early New England witchcraft. Here, surely, is a topic that previous generations of writers have sufficiently worked, indeed overworked. Samuel Eliot Morison once commented that the Salem witch-hunt was, after all, "but a small incident in the history of a great superstition"; and Perry Miller noted that with only minor qualifications "the intellectual history of New England can be written as though no such thing ever happened. It had no effect on the ecclesiastical or political situation, it does not figure in the institutional or ideological development."[1] Popular interest in the subject is, then, badly out of proportion to its actual historical significance, and perhaps the sane course for the future would be silence.

This assessment seems, on the face of it, eminently sound. Witchcraft was not an important matter from the standpoint of the larger historical process; it exerted only limited influence on the unfolding sequence of events in colonial New England. Moreover, the literature on the subject seems to have reached a point of diminishing returns. Details of fact have been endlessly canvassed, and the main outlines of the story, particularly the story of Salem, are well and widely known.

There is, to be sure, continuing debate over one set of issues: the roles played by the persons most directly involved. Indeed the historiography of Salem can be viewed, in large measure, as an unending effort to judge the participants—and, above all, to affix blame. A number of verdicts have been fashionable at one time or another. Thus the ministers were really at fault; or Cotton Mather in particular; or the whole culture of Puritanism; or the core group of "afflicted girls" (if their "fits" are construed as conscious fraud).[2] The most

recent, and in some ways most sophisticated, study of the Salem trials plunges right into the middle of the same controversy; the result is yet another conclusion. Not the girls, not the clergy, not Puritanism, but the accused witches themselves are now the chief culprits. For "witchcraft actually did exist and was widely practiced in seventeenth-century New England"; and women like Goody Glover, Bridget Bishop, and Mammy Redd were "in all probability" guilty as charged.[3]

Clearly these questions of personal credit and blame can still generate lively interest, but are they the most fruitful, the most important questions to raise about witchcraft? Will such a debate ever be finally settled? Are its partisan terms and moral tone appropriate to historical scholarship?

The situation is not hopeless if only we are willing to look beyond the limits of our own discipline. There is, in particular, a substantial body of interesting and relevant work by anthropologists. Many recent studies of primitive societies contain chapters about witchcraft, and there are several entire monographs on the subject.[4] The approach they follow differs strikingly from anything in the historical literature. Broadly speaking, the anthropological work is far more analytic, striving always to use materials on witchcraft as a set of clues or "symptoms." The subject is important not in its own right but as a means of exploring certain larger questions about the society. For example, witchcraft throws light on social structure, on the organization of families, and on the inner dynamics of personality. The substance of such investigations, of course, varies greatly from one culture to another, but the framework, the informing purposes are roughly the same. To apply this framework and these purposes to historical materials is not inherently difficult. The data may be inadequate in a given case, but the analytic categories themselves are designed for any society, whether simple or complex, Western or non-Western, past or contemporary. Consider, by way of illustration, the strategy proposed for the main body of this essay.

Our discussion will focus on a set of complex relationships between the alleged witches and their victims. The former group will include all persons accused of practicing witchcraft, and they will be called, simply, witches.[5] The category of victims will comprise everyone who claimed to have suffered from witchcraft, and they will be divided into two categories to account for an important distinction between different kinds of victims. As every schoolchild-knows, some victims experienced fits—bizarre seizures that, in the language of modern psychiatry, closely approximate the clinical picture of hysteria. These people may be called accusers, since their sufferings and their accusations seem to have carried the greatest weight in generating formal proceedings against witches. A second, much larger group of victims includes people who attributed to witchcraft some particular misfortune they had suffered, most typically an injury or illness, the sudden death of domestic animals, the loss of personal property, or repeated failure in important day-to-day activities like farming, fishing, and hunting. This type of evidence was of secondary importance in trials of witches and was usually brought forward after the accusers had pressed their own more damaging charges. For people testifying to such experiences, therefore, the shorthand term *witnesses* seems reasonably appropriate.

Who were these witches, accusers, and witnesses? How did their lives intersect? Most important, what traits were generally characteristic and what traits were alleged to have been characteristic of each group? These will be the organizing questions in the pages that follow. Answers to these questions will treat both external (or objective) circumstances and internal (or subjective) experiences. In the case of witches, for example, it is important to try to discover their age, marital status, socioeconomic position, and visible personality traits. But it is equally important to examine the characteristics attributed to witches by others—flying about at night, transforming themselves into animals, and the like. In short, one can construct a picture of witches in fact and in fantasy; and comparable efforts can be made with accusers and witnesses. Analysis directed to the level of external reality helps to locate certain points of tension or conflict in the social structure of a community. The fantasy picture, on the other hand, reveals more directly the psychological dimension of life, the inner preoccupations, anxieties, and conflicts of individual members of that community.

Such an outline looks deceptively simple, but in fact it demands an unusual degree of caution, from writer and reader alike. The approach is explicitly cross-disciplinary, reaching out to anthropology for strategy and to psychology for theory. There is, of course, nothing new about the idea of a working relationship between history and the behavioral sciences. It is more than ten years since William Langer's famous summons to his colleagues to consider this their "next assignment";[6] but the record of actual output is still very meager. All such efforts remain quite experimental; they are designed more to stimulate discussion than to prove a definitive case.

There is a final point—about context and the larger purposes of this form of inquiry. Historians have traditionally worked with purposeful, conscious events, "restricting themselves," in Langer's words, "to recorded fact and to strictly rational motivation."[7] They have not necessarily wished to exclude non-rational or irrational behavior, but for the most part they have done so. Surely in our own post-Freudian era there is both need and opportunity to develop a more balanced picture. It is to these long-range ends that fur-

ther study of witchcraft should be dedicated. For witchcraft is, if nothing else, an open window on the irrational.

The first witchcraft trial of which any record survives occurred at Windsor, Connecticut, in 1647,[8] and during the remainder of the century the total of cases came to nearly one hundred. Thirty-eight people were executed as witches, and a few more, though convicted, managed somehow to escape the death penalty. There were, of course, other outcomes as well: full-dress trials resulting in acquittal, hung juries, convictions reversed on appeal, and "complaints" filed but not followed up. Finally, no doubt, many unrecorded episodes touching on witchcraft, episodes of private suspicion or public gossip, never eventuated in legal action at all.[9]

This long series of witchcraft cases needs emphasis lest the Salem outbreak completely dominate our field of vision. Salem differed radically from previous episodes in sheer scope; it developed a degree of self-reinforcing momentum present in no other instance. But it was very similar in many qualitative aspects: the types of people concerned, the nature of the charges, the fits, and so forth. Indeed, from an analytic standpoint, all these cases can be regarded as roughly equivalent and interchangeable. They are pieces of a single, larger phenomenon, a system of witchcraft belief that was generally prevalent in early New England. The evidence for such a system must, of course, be drawn from a variety of cases to produce representative conclusions. For most questions this is quite feasible; there is more evidence, from a greater range of cases, than can ever be presented in a single study.

Yet in one particular matter the advantages of concentrating on Salem are overwhelming. It affords a unique opportunity to portray the demography of witchcraft, to establish a kind of profile for each of the three basic categories of people involved in witchcraft, in terms of sex, age, and marital status. Thus the statistical tables that follow are drawn entirely from detailed work on the Salem materials.[10] The earlier cases do not yield the breadth of data necessary for this type of quantitative investigation. They do, however, provide many fragments of evidence that are generally consistent with the Salem picture.

There is at least minimal information about 165 people accused as witches during the entire period of the Salem outbreak. . . . [The] witches were predominantly married or widowed women, between the ages of forty-one and sixty. While the exceptions add up to a considerable number, most of them belonged to the families of middle-aged, female witches. Virtually all the young persons in the group can be identified as children of witches and most of the men as husbands of witches. In fact this pattern conformed to an assumption then widely prevalent, that the transmission of witchcraft would naturally follow the lines of family or of close friend-ship. An official statement from the government of Connecticut included among the "grounds for Examina-tion of a Witch" the following:

> if ye party suspected be ye son or daughter the servt or familiar friend; neer Neighbor or old Companion of a Knowne or Convicted witch this alsoe a presumton for witchcraft is an art yt may be learned & Convayd from man to man & oft it falleth out yt a witch dying leaveth som of ye aforesd. heirs of her witchcraft.[12]

In short, young witches and male witches belonged to a kind of derivative category. They were not the prime targets in these situations; they were, in a literal sense, rendered suspect by association. The deepest suspicions, the most intense anxieties, remained fixed on middle-aged women.

Thirty-four persons experienced fits of one sort or an-other during the Salem trials and qualify thereby as accusers. . . . The vast majority of the accusers were single girls between the ages of eleven and twenty. The exceptions in this case (two boys, three males of un-determined age, and four adult women) are rather difficult to explain, for there is little evidence about any of them. By and large, however, they played only a minor role in the trials. Perhaps the matter can be left this way: the core group of accusers was entirely composed of adolescent girls, but the inner conflicts so manifest in their fits found an echo in at least a few persons of other ages or of the opposite sex.

Eighty-four persons came forward as witnesses at one time or another during the Salem trials. . . . Three-fourths of the witnesses were men, but a close exam-ination of the trial records suggests a simple reason for this: men were more likely, in seventeenth-centu-ry New England, to take an active part in legal pro-ceedings of any type. When a husband and wife were victimized together by some sort of witchcraft, it was the former who would normally come forward to tes-tify. As to the ages of the witnesses, there is a fairly broad distribution between twenty and sixty years. Probably, then, this category reflects the generalized belief in witchcraft among all elements of the com-munity in a way that makes it qualitatively different from the groupings of witches and accusers.

There is much more to ask about external realities in the lives of such people, particularly with regard to their social and economic position. Unfortunately, however, the evidence is somewhat limited here and permits only a few impressionistic observations. It seems that many witches came from the lower levels of the social structure, but there were too many ex-ceptions to see in this a really significant pattern. The first three accused at Salem were Tituba, a Ne-gro slave, Sarah Good, the wife of a poor laborer, and Sarah Osbourne, who possessed a very consid-erable estate.[13] Elizabeth Godman, tried at New Haven in 1653, seems to have been poor and per-haps a beggar;[14] but Nathaniel and Rebecca Green-smith, who were convicted and executed at Hartford eight years later, were quite well-to-do;[15] and "Mis-tress" Ann Hibbens, executed at Boston in 1656, was the widow of a wealthy merchant and former magistrate of the Bay Colony.[16]

What appears to have been common to nearly all these people, irrespective of their economic posi-tion, was some kind of personal eccentricity, some deviant or even criminal behavior that had long since marked them out as suspect. Some of them had pre-viously been tried for theft or battery or slander;[17] others were known for their interest in dubious ac-tivities like fortunetelling or certain kinds of folk-healing.[18] The "witch Glover" of Boston, on whom Cotton Mather reports at some length, was Irish and Catholic, and spoke Gaelic; and a Dutch family in Hartford came under suspicion at the time the Green-smiths were tried.[19]

More generally, many of the accused seem to have been unusually irascible and contentious in their per-sonal relations. Years before her conviction for witchcraft Mrs. Hibbens had obtained a reputation for "natural crabbedness of . . . temper"; indeed she had been excommunicated by the Boston church in 1640, following a long and acrimonious ecclesiasti-cal trial. William Hubbard, whose *General History of New England* was published in 1680, cited her case to make the general point that "persons of hard favor and turbulent passions are apt to be condemned by the common people as witches, upon very slight grounds." In the trial of Mercy Desborough, at Fair-field, Connecticut, in 1692, the court received nu-merous reports of her quarrelsome behavior. She had, for example, told one neighbor "yt shee would make him bare as a bird's tale," and to another she had repeatedly said "many hard words." Goodwife Claw-son, tried at the same time, was confronted with testimony like the following:

> Abigail Wescot saith that as shee was going along the street goody Clasen came out to her and they had some words together and goody Clason took up stones and threw at her: and at another time as shee went along the street before sd Clasons dore goody Clason caled to mee and asked mee what was in my Chamber last Sabbath day night; and I doe afirme that I was not there that night: and at another time as I was in her sone Steephens house being neere her one hous shee folowed me in and contended with me becase I did not com into her hous caling of me proud slut what—are you proud of your fine cloths and you love to be mistres but you neuer shal be and several other provoking speeches.[20]

The case of Mary and Hugh Parsons, tried at Springfield in 1651, affords a further look at the external aspects of our subject. A tax rating taken at Springfield in 1646 records the landholdings of most of the principals in the witchcraft prosecutions of five years later. When the list is arranged according to wealth, Parsons falls near the middle (twenty-fourth out of forty-two), and those who testified against him come from the top, middle, and bottom. This outcome tends to confirm the general point that economic position is not, for present purposes, a significant datum. What seems, on the basis of the actual testimonies at the trial, to have been much more important was the whole dimension of eccentric and anti-social behavior. Mary Parsons, who succumbed repeatedly to periods of massive depression, was very nearly insane. During the witchcraft investigations she began by testifying against her husband and ended by convicting herself of the murder of their infant child. Hugh Parsons was a sawyer and brickmaker by trade, and there are indications that in performing these services he was sometimes suspected of charging extortionate rates.[21] But what may have weighed most heavily against him was his propensity for prolonged and bitter quarreling; many examples of his "threatening speeches" were reported in court.

One other aspect of this particular episode is worth nothing, namely, the apparent influence of spatial proximity. When the names of Parsons and his "victims" are checked against a map of Springfield in this period, it becomes very clear that the latter were mostly his nearest neighbors. In fact nearly all of the people who took direct part in the trial came from the southern half of the town. No other witchcraft episode yields such a detailed picture in this respect, but many separate pieces of evidence suggest that neighborhood antagonism was usually an aggravating factor.[22]

We can summarize the major characteristics of the external side of New England witchcraft as follows: First, the witches themselves were chiefly women of middle age whose accusers were girls about one full generation younger. This may reflect the kind of situation that anthropologists would call a structural conflict—that is, some focus of tension created by the specific ways in which a community arranges the lives of its members. In a broad sense it is quite probable that adolescent girls in early New England were particularly subject to the control of older women, and this may well have given rise to a powerful underlying resentment. By contrast, the situation must have been less difficult for boys, since their work often took them out of the household and their behavior generally was less restricted.

There are, moreover, direct intimations of generational conflict in the witchcraft records themselves. Consider a little speech by one of the afflicted girls during a fit,

a speech meticulously recorded by Cotton Mather. The words are addressed to the "specter" of a witch, with whom the girl has been having a heated argument:

> What's that? Must the younger Women, do yee say, hearken to the Elder?—They must be another Sort of Elder Women than You then! they must not bee Elder Witches, I am sure. Pray, do you for once Hearken to mee.—What a dreadful Sight are You! An Old Woman, an Old Servant of the Divel![23]

Second, it is notable that most witches were deviant persons—eccentric or conspicuously anti-social or both. This suggests very clearly the impact of belief in witchcraft as a form of control in the social ordering of New England communities. Here indeed is one of the most widely-found social functions of witchcraft; its importance has been documented for many societies all over the world.[24] Any individual who contemplates actions of which the community disapproves knows that if he performs such acts, he will become more vulnerable either to a direct attack by witches or to the charge that he is himself a witch. Such knowledge is a powerful inducement to self-constraint.

What can be said of the third basic conclusion, that witchcraft charges particularly involved neighbors? Very briefly, it must be fitted with other aspects of the social setting in these early New England communities. That there was a great deal of contentiousness among these people is suggested by innumerable court cases from the period dealing with disputes about land, lost cattle, trespass, debt, and so forth. Most men seem to have felt that the New World offered them a unique opportunity to increase their properties,[25] and this may have heightened competitive feelings and pressures. On the other hand, cooperation was still the norm in many areas of life, not only in local government but for a variety of agricultural tasks as well. In such ambivalent circumstances it is hardly surprising that relations between close neighbors were often tense or downright abrasive.

"In all the Witchcraft which now Grievously Vexes us, I know not whether any thing be more Unaccountable, than the Trick which the Witches have, to render themselves and their Tools Invisible."[26] Thus wrote Cotton Mather in 1692; and three centuries later it is still the "invisible" part of witchcraft that holds a special fascination. Time has greatly altered the language for such phenomena—"shapes" and "specters" have become "hallucinations"; "enchantments" are a form of "suggestion"; the Devil himself seems a fantasy—and there is a corresponding change of meanings. Yet here was something truly remarkable, a kind of irreducible core of the entire range of witchcraft phenomena. How much of it remains "unaccountable"? To ask the question is to face directly the other side of our subject: witchcraft viewed as psychic process, as a function of internal reality.

The biggest obstacles to the study of psycho-history ordinarily are practical ones involving severe limitations of historical data. Yet for witchcraft the situation is uniquely promising on these very grounds. Even a casual look at writings like Cotton Mather's *Memorable Providences* or Samuel Willard's *A briefe account* etc.[27] discloses material so rich in psychological detail as to be nearly the equivalent of clinical case reports. The court records on witchcraft are also remarkably full in this respect. The clergy, the judges, all the leaders whose positions carried special responsibility for combatting witchcraft, regarded publicity as a most important weapon. Witchcraft would yield to careful study and the written exchange of information. Both Mather and Willard received "afflicted girls" into their own homes and recorded "possession" behavior over long periods of time.

A wealth of evidence does not, of course, by itself win the case for a psychological approach to witchcraft. Further problems remain, problems of language and of validation.[28] There is, moreover, the very basic problem of selecting from among a variety of different theoretical models. Psychology is not a monolith, and every psycho-historian must declare a preference. In opting for psychoanalytic theory, for example, he performs, in part, an act of faith, faith that this theory provides deeper, fuller insights into human behavior than any other. In the long run the merit of such choices will probably be measured on pragmatic grounds. Does the interpretation explain materials that would otherwise remain unused? Is it consistent with evidence in related subject areas?

If, then, the proof lies in the doing, let us turn back to the New England witches and especially to their "Trick . . . to render themselves and their tools Invisible." What characterized these spectral witches? What qualities were attributed to them by the culture at large?

The most striking observation about witches is that they gave free rein to a whole gamut of hostile and aggressive feelings. In fact most witchcraft episodes began after some sort of actual quarrel. The fits of Mercy Short followed an abusive encounter with the convicted witch Sarah Good. The witch Glover was thought to have attacked Martha Goodwin after an argument about some missing clothes.[29] Many such examples could be accumulated here, but the central message seems immediately obvious: never antagonize witches, for they will invariably strike back hard. Their compulsion to attack was, of course, most dramatically visible in the fits experienced by some of their victims. These fits were treated as tortures imposed directly and in every detail by witches or by the Devil himself. It is also significant that witches often assumed the shape of animals in order to carry out their attacks. Animals, presumably, are not subject to constraints of either an internal or external kind; their aggressive impulses are immediately translated into action.

Another important facet of the lives of witches was their activity in company with each other. In part this consisted of long and earnest conferences on plans to overthrow the kingdom of God and replace it with the regin of the Devil. Often, however, these meetings merged with feasts, the witches' main form of self-indulgence. Details are a bit thin here, but we know that the usual beverage was beer or wine (occasionally described as bearing a suspicious resemblance to blood), and the food was bread or meat. It is also worth noting what did not happen on these occasions. There were a few reports of dancing and "sport," but very little of the wild excitements associated with witch revels in continental Europe. Most striking of all is the absence of allusions to sex; there is no nakedness, no promiscuity, no obscene contact with the Devil. This seems to provide strong support for the general proposition that the psychological conflicts underlying the early New England belief in witchcraft had much more to do with aggressive impulses than with libidinal ones.

The persons who acted as accusers also merit the closest possible attention, for the descriptions of what they suffered in their fits are perhaps the most revealing of all source materials for present purposes. They experienced, in the first place, severe pressures to go over to the Devil's side themselves. Witches approached them again and again, mixing threats and bribes in an effort to break down their Christian loyalties. Elizabeth Knapp, bewitched at Groton, Massachusetts, in 1671, was alternately tortured and plied with offers of "money, silkes, fine cloaths, ease from labor"; in 1692 Ann Foster of Andover confessed to being won over by a general promise of "prosperity," and in the same year Andrew Carrier accepted the lure of "a house and land in Andover." The same pattern appears most vividly in Cotton Mather's record of another of Mercy Short's confrontations with a spectral witch:

> "Fine promises!" she says, "You'l bestow an Husband upon mee, if I'l bee your Servant. An Husband! What? A Divel! I shall then bee finely fitted with an Husband: . . . Fine Clothes! What? Such as Your Friend Sarah Good had, who hardly had Rags to cover her! . . . Never Dy! What? Is my Life in Your Hands? No, if it had, You had killed mee long before this Time!—What's that?—So you can!—Do it then, if You can. Come, I dare you: Here, I challenge You to do it. Kill mee if you can. . . . "[30]

Some of these promises attributed to the Devil touch the most basic human concerns (like death) and others reflect the special preoccupations (with future husbands, for example) of adolescent girls. All of them imply a kind of covetousness generally consistent with the pattern of neighborhood conflict and tension mentioned earlier.

But the fits express other themes more powerfully still, the vital problem of aggression being of central importance. The seizures themselves have the essential character of attacks: in one sense, physical attacks by the witches on the persons of the accusers and in another sense, verbal attacks by the accusers on the reputations and indeed the very lives of the witches. This points directly toward one of the most important inner processes involved in witchcraft, the process psychologists call "projection," defined roughly as "escape from repressed conflict by attributing . . . emotional drives to the external world."[31] In short, the dynamic core of belief in witchcraft in early New England was the difficulty experienced by many individuals in finding ways to handle their own aggressive impulses. Witchcraft accusations provided one of the few approved outlets for such impulses in Puritan culture. Aggression was thus denied in the self and attributed directly to others. The accuser says, in effect: "I am not attacking you; you are attacking me!" In reality, however, the accuser is attacking the witch, and in an extremely dangerous manner, too. Witchcraft enables him to have it both ways; the impulse is denied and gratified at the same time.

The seizures of the afflicted children also permitted them to engage in a considerable amount of direct aggression. They were not, of course, held personally responsible; it was always the fault of the Devil at work inside them. Sometimes these impulses were aimed against the most important—and obvious—figures of authority. A child in a fit might behave very disobediently toward his parents or revile the clergy who came to pray for his recovery.[32] The Reverend Samuel Willard of Groton, who ministered to Elizabeth Knapp during the time of her most severe fits, noted that the Devil "urged upon her constant temptations to murder her p'rents, her neighbors, our children . . . and even to make away with herself & once she was going to drowne herself in ye well." The attacking impulses were quite random here, so much so that the girl herself was not safe. Cotton Mather reports a slight variation on this type of behavior in connection with the fits of Martha Goodwin. She would, he writes, "fetch very terrible Blowes with her Fist, and Kicks with her Foot at the man that prayed; but still . . . her Fist and Foot would alwaies recoil, when they came within a few hairs breadths of him just as if Rebounding against a Wall."[33] This little paradigm of aggression attempted and then at the last moment inhibited expresses perfectly the severe inner conflict that many of these people were acting out.

One last, pervasive theme in witchcraft is more difficult to handle than the others without having direct recourse to clinical models; the summary word for it is orality. It is helpful to recall at this point the impor-

tance of feasts in the standard imaginary picture of witches, but the experience of the accusers speaks even more powerfully to the same point. The evidence is of several kinds. First, the character of the "tortures" inflicted by the witches was most often described in terms of biting, pinching, and pricking; in a psychiatric sense, these modes of attack all have an oral foundation. The pattern showed up with great vividness, for example, in the trial of George Burroughs:

> It was Remarkable that whereas Biting was one of the ways which the Witches used for the vexing of the Sufferers, when they cry'd out of G.B. biting them, the print of the Teeth would be seen on the Flesh of the Complainers, and just such a sett of Teeth as G.B.'s would then appear upon them, which could be distinguished from those of some other means.[34]

Second, the accusers repeatedly charged that they could see the witches suckling certain animal "familiars." The following testimony by one of the Salem girls, in reference to an unidentified witch, was quite typical: "She had two little things like young cats and she put them to her brest and suckled them they had no hair on them and had ears like a man." It was assumed that witches were specially equipped for these purposes, and their bodies were searched for the evidence. In 1656 the constable of Salisbury, New Hampshire, deposed in the case of Eunice Cole,

> That being about to stripp [her] to bee whipt (by the judgment of the Court att Salisbury) lookeing upon hir brests under one of hir brests (I thinke hir left brest) I saw a blew thing like unto a teate hanging downeward about three quarters of an inche longe not very thick, and haveing a great suspition in my mind about it (she being suspected for a witche) desiered the Court to sende some women to looke of it.

The court accepted this proposal and appointed a committee of three women to administer to Goodwife Cole the standard, very intimate, examination. Their report made no mention of a "teate" under her breast, but noted instead "a place in her leg which was proveable wher she Had bin sucktt by Imps or the like." The women also stated "thatt they Heard the whining of puppies or such like under Her Coats as though they Had a desire to sucke."[35]

Third, many of the accusers underwent serious eating disturbances during and after their fits. "Long fastings" were frequently imposed on them. Cotton Mather writes of one such episode in his account of the bewitching of Margaret Rule: "tho she had a very eager Hunger upon her Stomach, yet if any refreshment were brought unto her, her teeth would be set, and she would be thrown into many Miseries." But also she would "sometimes have her Jaws forcibly pulled open, whereupon something invisible would be poured down her throat . . . She cried out of it as of Scalding Brimstone poured into her."[36] These descriptions and others like them would repay a much more detailed analysis than can be offered here, but the general point should be obvious. Among the zones of the body, the mouth seems to have been charged with a special kind of importance for victims of witchcraft.

In closing, it may be appropriate to offer a few suggestions of a more theoretical nature to indicate both the way in which an interpretation of New England witchcraft might be attempted and what it is that one can hope to learn from witchcraft materials about the culture at large. But let it be said with some emphasis that this is meant only as the most tentative beginning of a new approach to such questions.

Consider an interesting set of findings included by two anthropologists in a broad survey of child-rearing practices in over fifty cultures around the world. They report that belief in witchcraft is powerfully correlated with the training a society imposes on young children in regard to the control of aggressive impulses.[37] That is, wherever this training is severe and restrictive, there is a strong likelihood that the culture will make much of witchcraft. The correlation seems to suggest that suppressed aggression will seek indirect outlets of the kind that belief in witchcraft provides. Unfortunately there is relatively little concrete evidence about child-rearing practices in early New England; but it seems at least consistent with what is known of Puritan culture generally to imagine that quite a harsh attitude would have been taken toward any substantial show of aggression in the young.[38]

Now, some further considerations. There were only a very few cases of witchcraft accusations among members of the same family. But, as we have seen, the typical pattern involved accusations by adolescent girls against middle-aged women. It seems plausible, at least from a clinical standpoint, to think that this pattern masked deep problems stemming ultimately from the relationship of mother and daughter. Perhaps, then, the afflicted girls were both projecting their aggression and diverting or "displacing" it from its real target. Considered from this perspective, displacement represents another form of avoidance of denial; and so the charges of the accusers may be seen as a kind of double defense against the actual conflicts.

How can we locate the source of these conflicts? This is a more difficult and frankly speculative question. Indeed the question leads farther and farther from the usual canons of historical explanation; such proof as there is must come by way of parallels to findings of recent psychological research and, above all, to a great mass of clinical data. More specifically, it is to psychoanalytic theory that one may turn for insights of an especially helpful sort.

The prominence of oral themes in the historical record suggests that the disturbances that culminated in charges of witchcraft must be traced to the earliest phase of personality development. It would be very convenient to have some shred of information to insert here about breast-feeding practices among early New Englanders. Possibly their methods of weaning were highly traumatic,[39] but as no hard evidence exists we simply cannot be sure. It seems plausible, however, that many New England children were faced with some unspecified but extremely difficult psychic tasks in the first year or so of life. The outcome was that their aggressive drives were tied especially closely to the oral mode and driven underground.[40] Years later, in accordance with changes normal for adolescence, instinctual energies of all types were greatly augmented; and this tended, as it so often does, to reactivate the earliest conflicts[41]—the process that Freud vividly described as "the return of the repressed." But these conflicts were no easier to deal with in adolescence than they had been earlier; hence the need for the twin defenses of projection and displacement.[42]

One final problem must be recognized. The conflicts on which this discussion has focused were, of course, most vividly expressed in the fits of the accusers. The vast majority of people in early New England—subjected, one assumes, to roughly similar influences as children—managed to reach adulthood without experiencing fits. Does this pose serious difficulties for the above interpretations? The question can be argued to a negative conclusion, in at least two different but complementary ways. First, the materials on witchcraft, and in particular on the fits of the accusers, span a considerable length of time in New England's early history. It seems clear, therefore, that aggression and orality were more or less constant themes in the pathology of the period. Second, even in the far less bizarre testimonies of the witnesses—those who have been taken to represent the community at large—the same sort of focus appears. It is, above all, significant that the specific complaints of the accusers were so completely credible to so many others around them. The accusers, then, can be viewed as those individuals who were somehow especially sensitive to the problems created by their environment; they were the ones who were pushed over the line, so to speak, into serious illness. But their behavior clearly struck an answering chord in a much larger group of people. In this sense, nearly everyone in seventeenth-century New England was at some level an accuser.

Notes

[1] S. E. Morison, *The Intellectual Life of Colonial New England* (Ithaca, 1956), 264; Perry Miller, *The New*

England Mind: From Colony to Province (Boston, 1961), 191.

[2] Examples of these varying interpretations may be found in Charles W. Upham, *Salem Witchcraft* (Boston, 1867); Winfield S. Nevins, *Witchcraft in Salem Village* (Salem, 1916); John Fiske, *New France and New England* (Boston and New York, 1902); W. F. Poole, "Witchcraft in Boston," in *The Memorial History of Boston,* ed. Justin Winsor (Boston, 1881); Marion L. Starkey, *The Devil in Massachusetts* (Boston, 1950); Morison, *Intellectual Life of Colonial New England,* 259 ff.

[3] Chadwick Hansen, *Witchcraft at Salem* (New York, 1969). See especially x, 22 ff., 64 ff., 226-67.

[4] Those I have found particularly helpful in developing my own approach toward New England witchcraft are the following: Clyde Kluckhohn, *Navajo Witchcraft* (Boston, 1967); E. E. Evans-Pritchard, *Witchcraft, Oracles, and Magic Among the Azande* (Oxford, 1937); M. G. Marwick, *Sorcery in its Social Setting* (Manchester, 1965); *Witchcraft and Sorcery in East Africa,* ed. John Middleton and E. H. Winter (London, 1963); Beatrice B. Whiting, *Paiute Sorcery* (New York, 1950).

[5] This usage is purely a matter of convenience, and is not meant to convey any judgment as to whether such people actually tried to perform acts of witchcraft. Chadwick Hansen claims to show, from trial records, which of the accused women were indeed "guilty"; but in my opinion his argument is not convincing. The testimony that "proves" guilt in one instance seems quite similar to other testimony brought against women whom Hansen regards as innocent. There may indeed have been "practicing witches" in colonial New England, but the surviving evidence does not decide the issue one way or another.

[6] William L. Langer, "The Next Assignment" (*AHR,* LXIII [Jan. 1958], 283-304), in *Psychoanalysis and History,* ed. Bruce Mazlish (Englewood Cliffs, N. J., 1963).

[7] *Ibid.,* 90.

[8] See John M. Taylor, *The Witchcraft Delusion in Colonial Connecticut* (New York, 1908), 145 ff.

[9] Some of these episodes are mentioned, in passing, among the records of witchcraft cases that came before the court. See, for example, the references to Besse Sewall and the widow Marshfield, in the depositions of the Parsons case, published in Samuel G. Drake, *Annals of Witchcralt in New England* (Boston, 1869), 218-57. It is clear, too, that many convicted witches had been the objects of widespread suspicion and gossip for years before they were brought to trial.

[10] These findings are based largely on materials in the vital records of Salem and the surrounding towns. . . .

[12] An early copy of this statement (undated) is in the Ann Mary Brown Memorial Collection, Brown University.

[13] The proceedings against these three defendants are included in the typescript volumes, *Salem Witchcraft, 1692,* compiled from the original records by the Works Progress Administration in 1938. These volumes—an absolutely invaluable source—are on file in the Essex County Courthouse, Salem.

[14] See *Records of the Colony of New Haven,* ed. C. J. Hoadly (Hartford, 1858), II, 29-36, 151-52, and *New Haven Town Records 1649-1662,* ed. Franklin B. Dexter (New Haven, 1917), I, 249-52, 256-57.

[15] Some original records from this trial are in the Willys Papers, Connecticut State Library, Hartford. For good short accounts see Increase Mather, *An Essay for the Recording of Illustrious Providences, in Narratives of the Witchcraft Cases,* ed. G. L. Burr (New York, 1914), 18-21, and a letter from John Whiting to Increase Mather, Dec. 10, 1682, entitled "An account of a Remarkable passage of Divine providence that happened in Hartford, in the yeare of our Lord 1662," in *Massachusetts Historical Society Collections,* 4th Ser., VIII (Boston, 1868), 466-69.

[16] See *Records of Massachusetts Bay,* ed. Nathaniel B. Shirtleff, IV, Pt. I (Boston, 1854), 269; William Hubbard, *A General History of New England* (Boston, 1848), 574; Thomas Hutchinson, *The History of the Colony and Province of Massachusetts Bay,* ed. Lawrence S. Mayo (Cambridge, Mass., 1936), I, 160-61.

[17] For example, Giles Corey, executed as one of the Salem witches, had been before the courts several times, charged with such offenses as theft and battery. Mary Parsons of Springfield was convicted of slander not long before her trial for witchcraft.

[18] For example, Katherine Harrison, prosecuted for witchcraft at Weathersfield, Connecticut, in 1668, was reported to have been given to fortunetelling; and a group of ministers called to advise the court in her case contended that such activity did "argue familiarity with the Devil." See John M. Taylor, *The Witchcraft Delusion in Colonial Connecticut* (New York, 1908), 56-58. Evidence of the same kind was offered against Samuel Wardwell of Andover, Massachusetts, in 1692. See the proceedings in his case in the typescript volumes by the Works Progress Administration, *Salem Witchcraft, 1692,* in the Essex County Courthouse, Salem. Margaret Jones, convicted and executed

at Boston in 1648, was involved in "practising physic." See Winthrop's *Journal,* ed. J. K. Hosmer (New York, 1908), II, 344-45. Elizabeth Morse, prosecuted at Newbury, Massachusetts, in 1679, was alleged to have possessed certain occult powers to heal the sick. See the depositions published in Drake, *Annals of Witchcraft,* 258-96.

[19] Cotton Mather, *Memorable Providences, Relating to Witchcraft and Possessions, in Narratives,* ed. Burr, 103-06; Increase Mather, *An Essay* etc., 18.

[20] Hutchinson, *History of the Colony and Province of Massachusetts Bay,* I, 160; Hubbard, 574. There is a verbatim account of the church proceedings against Mrs. Hibbens in the journal of Robert Keayne, in the Massachusetts Historical Society, Boston. I am grateful to Anita Rutman for lending me her transcription of this nearly illegible document. Manuscript deposition, trial of Mercy Desborough, Willys Papers; manuscript deposition, trial of Elizabeth Clawson, Willys Papers.

[21] The tax list is published in Henry Burt, *The First Century of the History of Springfield* (Springfield, Mass., 1898), I, 190-91; a long set of depositions from the Parsons case is published in Drake, *Annals of Witchcraft,* 219-56; see also 224, 228, 242. Mary Parsons herself offered some testimony reflecting her husband's inordinate desire "for Luker and Gaine."

[22] See Burt, *First Century of the History of Springfield,* I, for just such a map; see Increase Mather, *An Essay* etc., 18 ff., on the case of the Greensmiths. Also Richard Chamberlain, *Lithobolia,* in *Narratives,* ed. Burr, 61, on the case of Hannah Jones at Great Island, New Hampshire, in 1682.

[23] See Cotton Mather, *A Brand Pluck'd Out of the Burning,* in *Narratives,* ed. Burr, 270.

[24] See, for example, Whiting, *Paiute Sorcery;* Evans-Pritchard, *Witchcraft, Oracles, and Magic Among the Azande,* 117 ff.; and *Witchcraft and Sorcery in East Africa,* ed. Middleton and Winter.

[25] For material bearing on the growth of these acquisitive tendencies, see Philip J. Greven, Jr., "Old Patterns in the New World: The Distribution of Land in 17th Century Andover," *Essex Institute Historical Collections,* CI (April, 1965), 133-48; and John Demos, "Notes on Life in Plymouth Colony," *William and Mary Quarterly,* 3d Ser., XXII (Apr. 1965), 264-86. It is possible that the voluntary mechanism of colonization had selected unusually aggressive and competitive persons at the outset.

[26] Cotton Mather, *The Wonders of the Invisible World,* in *Narratives,* ed. Burr, 246.

[27] Cotton Mather, *Memorable Providences* etc., 93-143; Samuel Willard, *A briefe account of a strange & unusuall Providence of God befallen to Elizabeth Knap of Groton,* in Samuel A. Green, *Groton in the Witchcraft Times* (Groton, Mass., 1883), 7-21.

[28] The best group of essays dealing with such issues is *Psychoanalysis and History,* ed. Mazlish. See also the interesting statement in Alexander L. George and Juliette L. George, *Woodrow Wilson and Colonel House* (New York, 1964), v-xiv.

[29] See Cotton Mather, *A Brand Pluck'd Out of the Burning,* 259-60, and *Memorable Providences* etc., 100.

[30] Willard, *A briefe account* etc., in *Groton in the Witchcraft Times,* ed. Green, 8; deposition by Ann Foster, case of Ann Foster, deposition by Andrew Carrier, case of Mary Lacy, Jr., in Works Progress Administration, *Salem Witchcraft, 1692;* Cotton Mather, *A Brand Pluck'd Out of the Burning,* in *Narratives,* ed. Burr, 269.

[31] This is the definition suggested by Clyde Kluckhohn in his own exemplary monograph, *Navajo Witchcraft,* 239, n. 37.

[32] See, for example, the descriptions of the Goodwin children during the time of their affliction, in Cotton Mather, *Memorable Providences* etc., 109 ff., 119.

[33] Willard, *A briefe account* etc., 9; Cotton Mather, *Memorable Providences* etc., 108, 120.

[34] Cotton Mather, *Wonders of the Invisible World,* 216-17.

[35] Deposition by Susannah Sheldon, case of Philip English, in Works Progress Administration, *Salem Witchcraft, 1692;* manuscript deposition by Richard Ormsbey, case of Eunice Cole, in Massachusetts Archieves, Vol. 135, 3; manuscript record, case of Eunice Cole, in *ibid.,* 13.

[36] Cotton Mather, *Memorable Providences* etc., 131.

[37] John W. M. Whiting and Irvin L. Child, *Child Training and Personality* (New Haven, 1953), Chap. 12.

[38] John Robinson, the pastor of the original "Pilgrim" congregation, wrote as follows in an essay on "Children and Their Education": "Surely there is in all children . . . a stubbornness, and stoutness of mind arising from natural pride, which must be broken and beaten down. . . . . Children should not know, if it could be kept from them, that they have a will in their own: neither should these words be heard from them, save by way of consent, 'I will' or 'I will not'" Robinson, *Works* (Boston, 1851), I, 246-47. This point of view

would not appear to leave much room for the free expression of aggressive impulses, but of course it tells us nothing certain about actual practice in Puritan families.

[39] However, we can determine with some confidence the usual time of weaning. Since lactation normally creates an impediment to a new conception, and since the average interval between births in New England families was approximately two years, it seems likely that most infants were weaned between the ages of twelve and fifteen months. The nursing process would therefore overlap the arrival of baby teeth (and accompanying biting wishes); and this might well give rise to considerable tension between mother and child. I have found only one direct reference to weaning in all the documentary evidence from seventeenth-century New England, an entry in the journal of John Hull: "1659, 11th of 2d. My daughter Hannah was taken from her mother's breast, and, through the favor of God, weaned without any trouble; only about fifteen days after, she did not eat her meat well." American Antiquarian Society, *Transactions,* III (Boston, 1857), 149. Hannah Hull was born on February 14, 1658, making her thirteen months and four weeks on the day of the above entry. Hull's choice of words creates some temptation to speculate further. Was it perhaps unusual for Puritan infants to be "weaned without any trouble"? Also, does it not seem that in this case the process was quite abrupt—that is, accomplished entirely at one point in time? (Generally speaking, this is more traumatic for an infant than gradual weaning is.) For a longer discussion of infancy in Puritan New England see John Demos, *A Little Commonwealth: Family-Life in Plymouth Colony* (New York, 1970), Chap. 8.

[40] I have found the work of Melanie Klein on the origins of psychic conflict in infancy to be particularly helpful. See her *The Psycho-Analysis of Children* (London, 1932) and the papers collected in her *Contributions to Psycho-Analysis* (London, 1950). See also Joan Riviere, "On the Genesis of Psychical Conflict in Earliest Infancy," in Melanie Klein *et al., Developments in Psycho-Analysis* (London, 1952), 37-66.

[41] See Peter Blos, *On Adolescence* (New York, 1962). This (basically psychoanalytic) study provides a wealth of case materials and some very shrewd interpretations, which seem to bear strongly on certain of the phenomena connected with early New England witchcraft.

[42] It is no coincidence that projection was so important among the defenses employed by the, afflicted girls in their efforts to combat their own aggressive drives. For projection is the earliest of all defenses, and indeed it takes shape under the influence of the oral phase. On this point see Sigmund Freud, "Negation," *The Standard Edition of the Complete Works*

of Sigmund Freud, ed. J. Strachey (London, 1960), XIX, 237, and Paula Heimann, "Certain Functions of Introjection and Projection in Early Infancy," in Klein *et al., Developments in Psycho-Analysis,* 122-68.

Lyle Koehler (essay date 1980)

SOURCE: "The Salem Village Cataclysm: Origins and Impact of a Witch Hunt, 1689-92," in *A Search for Power: The "Weaker Sex" in Seventeenth-Century New England,* University of Illinois Press, pp. 383-417.

[*In the following excerpt, Koehler discusses the issues of empowerment and non-traditional behavior in examining why a disproportionate number of the accused witches and their accusers were female.*]

An Epidemic of Witchcraft

. . . The Salem Village witch mania began easily enough, when several young girls experimented with fortune-telling and read occult works. In late January 1692, these girls began creeping under chairs and into holes, uttering "foolish, ridiculous speeches," assuming odd postures, and, on occasion, writhing in agony. Their antics soon became full-fledged hysterical fits. Their tongues extended out to "a fearful length," like those of hanged persons; their necks cracked; blood "gushed plentifully out of their Mouths." A local physician named William Griggs, unable to explain the girls' behavior in medical terms, warned that it must be due to an "Evil hand." The fits quickly spread to other youngsters ranging in age from twelve to nineteen, as well as to married women like Ann Pope, Sarah Bibber, Ann Putnam, and "an Ancient Woman, named Goodall."[28]

The afflicted girls initially charged Sarah Good, Sarah Osborne, and the minister's Indian slave Tituba with practicing *maleficium* upon them. Local magistrates served warrants on these designated witches, who faced a courtroom examination on March 1. Twenty days later, Deodat Lawson, an ex-Salem Village pastor visiting from Boston, delivered a rousing anti-witchcraft sermon after observing the convulsive fits of Mary Walcott and Abigail Williams.[29] A week later, Samuel Parris called his congregation to search out the many devils in the church.[30] Parris was an old-line Puritan—a man anxious about his declining ministerial power, intensely suspicious of his neighbors, obsessed with thoughts of his own filthiness, and fearing the subversion of the Biblical Commonwealth.[31]

The half-dozen afflicted girls had accused only three

witches in February and four in March, but after the ministers' warnings no fewer than fifteen girls and women of Salem Village accused witches—at least twenty-five additional during April, and fifty-one in May. "Witch" Martha Corey warned the authorities in March, "We must not believe all these distracted children say," but prosecutions continued.[32] More persons from areas outside Salem Village were added to the list of accused witches—thirteen from Topsfield, most of whom had previously quarrelled with the Putnam family over land boundaries;[33] twelve others from Gloucester; thirteen from the port of Salem; and fifty-five from Andover, a locale torn by land stress.[34] Twenty-eight different persons, including four Andover women, fell subject to hysterical attacks in five outlying towns. Altogether, these ostensibly betwitched persons denounced almost all of the 56 men and 148 women accused of practicing witchcraft in 1692-93. Not only were three-quarters of the accused persons females, but of the 56 men half were singled out only after a close female relative or a wife had been accused—a sort of guilt by association. The reverse pattern holds true for only one, or possibly three, of the remaining male witches. Thus the traditional notion of the witch as a specifically female type held true for most Essex County accusations—even during times of severe stress, when virtually anyone might suffice as a scapegoat. Estimates of the actual number of witches at large ranged from 307 (by confessed witch William Barker) to 500 (Susannah Post, Thomas Maule).[35] Sir William Phips, the newly appointed royal governor who arrived in May, soon established a Special Court of Oyer and Terminer to try the many recently imprisoned witches. This court included Salem magistrate John Hathorne, Sam Sewall, the stringent chief justice William Stoughton, Dorchester merchant John Richards, Salem physician Bartholomew Gedney, Cavalier Waitstill Winthrop, the wealthy Peter Sargent, and Nathaniel Saltonstall of Haverhill—all members of the coalition government, who, in Roger Thompson's words, "were very much on trial themselves."[36] Although Saltonstall soon disapproved of the proceedings, resigned, and was replaced by Salem magistrate Jonathan Corwin, the justices listened to testimony against witch after witch, usually presuming that the accused was guilty before the trial began.[37] In court, the afflicted girls pointed to imaginary specters, and officials flailed away at such witches until the floor was "all covered" with invisible blood.[38] As the frenzy escalated, ten persons broke out of prison to hide in other locales, and eight or ten more fled "upon rumor of being apprehended." One of these, sixteen-year-old Elizabeth Colson, outraced the Reading constable and his dog in a wild chase through thick bushes, while Philip English escaped a group of searchers by hiding behind a bag of clothing.[39]

The Court of Oyer and Terminer sentenced Bridget Bishop to be hanged on June 10. Five more women followed her to the gallows on July 19, four men and a woman on August 19, and seven women and a man on September 22. On September 16 the authorities ordered Giles Corey pressed to death under a pile of stones when he refused to plead.[40] All these witches, Cotton Mather related, faced execution "impudently demanding of God, a Miraculous Vindicacion of their Innocency."[41]

Faced with the awful possibility of their own deaths, other accused witches began propitiously confessing their wrongdoings. After the July 19 hangings, five accused Andover witches "made a most ample, surprising, amazing Confession, of all their Villanies and declared the Five newly Executed to have been of their Company." Such "witches" may have observed the immediate leniency extended to self-confessed offenders like Tituba and Sarah Churchill. In August and September fifty-five other "witches" confessed—many, if not all of them, under extreme duress.[42]

Accused witches clogged the prisons of eastern Massachusetts, where they suffered from the biting cold of winter and sometimes from a lack of sufficient food. Often jailors held them in irons for long periods, to prevent them from afflicting their accusers by moving their bodies.[43] The Salem jailor tied each of three boys neck and heels together "till the blood was ready to come out of their Noses" (and did, in fact, gush out of William Proctor's).[44] Thirteen or fourteen accused witches at Ipswich prison petitioned the General Court for release on bail as winter approached, asserting they were "all most destroyed with soe long an imprisonment."[45] By October six "witches," including Sarah Osborne, had died in jail. Two, Abigail Faulkner and Elizabeth Proctor, gave birth under such atrocious conditions.[46]

Witchcraft accusations diminished during the summer (eight in June, seven in July), but after a council of eight ministers at Cambridge affirmed the reality of specter evidence on August 1, charges again boomed—twenty-five in August and twenty-seven in September, mostly from Andover.[47] Throughout 1692 people intently scrutinized their neighbors' behavior, being especially watchful of those against whom they had some personal grievance. In court, "it was usual to hear evidence of matter foreign, and of perhaps Twenty or Thirty years standing, about over-setting Carts, the death of Cattle, unkindness to Relations, or unexpected Accidents befalling after some quarrel." The accusatory tone established in the trials helped activate animosities existing within families as well, with many parents therefore "believing their Children to be Witches, and many Husbands their Wives, etc."[48]

The Accusers

For many people who were already struggling against spiritual, political, and economic deprivation, and against the force of late seventeenth century changes, making a witchcraft accusation expressed their anxiety while it reasserted a sense of their own potency. Sociologist Dodd Bogart's conclusion that demon or witch charges are attempts to restore "self worth, social recognition, social acceptance, social status, and other related social rewards" is pertinent to the Salem Village situation.[49] Accusations allowed the angry, the helpless, and sometimes the sensitive to fight the imagined malign powers that frustrated them by scapegoating suitable incarnations of evil. By testifying against a witch, they not only exposed but also conquered their own feelings of powerlessness in a changing world. By blaming witches, men and women attempted to reestablish some feeling of order, of control, when confronted by the discomforting effects of threats both external (e.g., Indians, political anarchy, urban materialism) and internal (e.g., the inability to achieve assurance of justification before God, or to understand, if assured, why God had chosen to "providentially" destroy a given animal or person).

The sixty-three men and twenty-one women who testified as corroborating witnesses against accused witches had much in common with the six males and thirty-seven females whose hysterical fits initiated proceedings. In specifically sex-role-defined ways, members of each sex responded to an apparent condition of helplessness. Men primarily appeared before the magistrates and, in typically straightforward fashion, gave accounts of the witches' *maleficium;* women usually made their accusations more circuitously, behind the cover of a fit. Men revealed their feelings of fear and impotence by describing how witches had pressed them into rigid immobility; bewitched women demonstrated dramatically, before the very eyes of the justices, how that—and far worse—could happen.[50]

Women, particularly those adolescents who experienced fits, used the witchcraft accusation as a viable form of self-expression in 1692-93. Burdened by the restrictive contingencies of the ideal feminine role, with its dictum (reinforced in church and school) that good girls must control their longings for material joy and submit to stronger adult authority figures, many young females probably felt a great deal of frustration as they searched for gaiety, attention, accomplishment, and individual autonomy. This was especially true considering the recent fits of the Goodwin children in Boston (1688), the occupational assertiveness of female innkeepers and school dames, and the patent examples of so many women who violated Puritan laws—all of which had an impact upon the consciousnesses of developing adolescents.

After studying spirit possession and shamanism in primitive societies, I. M. Lewis concluded that accusatory fits are "thinly disguised protest movements directed against the dominant sex. They thus play a significant part in the sex-war in traditional societies and cultures where women lack more obvious and direct means of forwarding their aims. To a considerable extent, they protect women from the exactions of men and offer an effective vehicle for manipulating husbands and male relatives."[51] Lewis's conclusion is equally applicable to Salem Village. There, in the paranoid atmosphere of 1692, girls used the fit—although not necessarily consciously—as a vehicle to invert the traditional social status hierarcy. Similarly, adult women, those perpetual children, expressed, through the fit, a need for excitement and dominion. For females, such assertion entailed, symbolically and on occasion literally, the elimination of the immediate oppressing force—the adult, the husband, or, in Mercy Short's case, the Indians. The bewitched parties, through their accusations, did help to eliminate authority figures—if not actual parents or husbands, whose destruction would be *too* discomforting or would deprive them of necessary support, then surely "representative" substitutions. A female figure suggestive of parental authority by her mature years, or one closely associated with a male of high position, was frequently chosen as a safer but still satisfactory surrogate.[52] Later, as the afflicted girls achieved more self-confidence, they actually attacked men, including at least two ministers.

All of the afflicted women, most particularly the Salem Village girls, exercised fantastic power. The public watched spellbound while the girls contorted their bodies into unbelievable shapes. Magistrates hung on their every word, believing them even when the girls were caught in outright lies.[53] At least one justice changed his opinion of a prominent friend after that man came under accusation.[54] Accused witches hardly knew what to say, save to maintain their innocence, when confronted by the awesome spectacle of girls throwing themselves about the courtroom, pulling four-inch-long pins and broken knife blades out of their own flesh. Some accused witches even became confused as to their own complicity in such goings on.[55] Anyone who criticized the court proceedings or the afflicted quickly fell under accusation as another witch, including even defecting members of the girls' own group.[56]

As early as March 20 the afflicted proved they could also, on occasion, assume a more self-consciously assertive stance. When Deodat Lawson prepared to give a Sabbath lecture, eleven-year-old Abigail Williams shouted out, "Now, stand up, and Name your Text." In the beginning of his sermon Goodwife Ann Pope told him, "Now there is enough of that," and after it was finished, Williams asserted, "It is a long Text." Twelve-year-old Anne Putnam shouted out that an invisible yellow bird, a witch's familiar, sat on Lawson's hat as it hung on a pin. In the afternoon sermon Williams again spoke up: "I know no Doctrine you had," she informed the minister, "If you did name one, I have forgot it."[57] Such outspokenness dumbfounded the congregation. Here three females had violated the biblical injunction against women speaking in church; furthermore, a little girl had criticized the minister. Obviously witches were to blame!

Not only had such females assumed the power to speak in church, and to designate men and women as witches; they also claimed the ability to vanquish supernatural creatures. They asserted that they could see and talk to the Devil, yet emerge unscathed from those encounters. Tituba, powerless both as servant and as woman, told imaginative tales of her own fearless contact with frightening spectral creatures—hairy upright men and great black dogs.[58] Another "very sober and pious woman," uncowed by a malign specter's appearance, disputed with it about a scriptural text.[59] Mercy Short, a fifteen-year-old Boston girl who two years before had watched while Indians cut down her frontier family, in her fits dared the Devil (interestingly enough, a man "of Tawny, or an Indian colour") to kill her: "Is my Life in Your Hands? No, if it had, You had killed me long before this Time!—What's that?—So you can!—Do it then if You can.—Poor Fool!. . . . What? Will you Burn all Boston and shall I bee Burnt in that Fire?—No, tis not in Your Power." Although "Satan" was able to cause her much physical pain, she ultimately emerged victorious in their confrontations by relying upon the transcendent power of God. Always assertive while in her fits (although she did not blame witches for them), Mercy Short hardly hesitated to call one onlooker a fool when that person objected to singing a psalm which Mercy had requested.[60]

Power and influence were not the only deep-seated impulses revealed by the fit. Filled with what Marion Starkey has called "repressed vitality, with all manner of cravings and urges for which village life afforded no outlet," the bewitched girls of Salem Village danced and sang for several hours at Job Tyler's house. Ephraim Foster's wife also danced at her home, and Martha Sprague sang for nearly an hour—both ostensibly under the influence of witchcraft.[61] Mercy Short's torments sometimes "turned into Frolicks; and she became as extravagant as a Wild-Cat." Margaret Rule laughed much and would drink nothing but rum in her fits. When Sarah Ingersoll accused one girl of lying about Goody Proctor's witchcraft, that girl placed this need for joy on an overtly conscious level by declaring simply, "they must have some sport."[62]

Repressed sexuality also emerged as a theme in the behavior of some of the afflicted, in the charges levied, and in the confessions of "witches." In her fits Ann Pope suffered a "grievous torment in her Bowels as if they were torn out,"[63] which may have been a manifestation of her sexual fears, since the bowels were considered the seat of passion. Mary Warren, age twenty, believed that a spectral nineteen-year-old male witch sat on her stomach, and she sometimes crossed her legs together so tightly that "it was impossible for the strongest man ther to [uncross] them, without Breaking her

Leggs."[64] Such behavior is frequently observed in sexually repressed hysterical women. Margaret Rule reacted with obvious sensual appreciation when Cotton Mather rubbed her stomach to calm her, but she greeted a similar well-meaning effort by a female attendant with the words "don't you meddle with me." In her fits she loved being "brush'd" or "rub'd," as long as it was "in the right place." Sometimes she wished only men to view her afflictions; once "haveing hold of the hand of a Young-man, said to have been her Sweet-heart formerly, who was withdrawing; She pull'd him again into his Seat, saying he should not go to Night."[65]

At times the sexual theme was even more explicit, although not as much as it often was in European witchcraft proceedings. One girl cried out that witch John Alden "sells powder and shot to the Indians and lies with Indian squaws and has Indian papooses."[66] Two "witches," Bridget Bishop and Elizabeth Proctor, reportedly afflicted while dressed only in their shifts—by Puritan standards, a most seductive approach.[67] "Witch" Rebecca Eames admitted giving the Devil her "soul & body"; then, in "horror of Conscience," she took a rope to hang herself and a razor to cut her throat "by Reason of her great sin in committing adultery." Mercy Wardwell, daughter of the hanged "witch" Samuel Wardwell, confessed to having sexual relations with Satan after "people told her yt she should Neuer hath such a Young Man who loved her." Abigail Hobbs also admitted giving herself "body and soul to the Old Boy."[68]

In the increasingly secular world of the 1690s, Satan reputedly offered alluring temptations to Puritan women—"Carnal and Sensual Lusts," wine, "pretty handsome apparell," a horse to facilitate physical mobility, "a piece of money," "a pair of French fall shoes," "gold and many fine things." When asked how Satan had approached them, many confessed "witches" explained that they were "Discontent at their mean Condition in the World" and wished to sample the many joys he offered. They asserted that feasting, dancing, and jollity were the rule at witch meetings.[69] Witches indulged in all those pleasures that good Puritans detested—the same pleasures that had gained so many adherents in these changing times. Regardless of whether they were sincere or merely prompted by the desire to escape execution, such confessions helped fuel both the spreading panic of the general community and the fervor of the most active accusers—not only because they *were* confessions, but also because their details echoed the same forbidden impulses with which their accusers, as well as many of the courtroom spectators, were grievously "afflicted."

The nine ringleaders of the Salem Village accusations included the daughter and niece of the minister, the daughter of a church deacon, and the wife and daughter of the parish clerk. Since material luxuries, expressions of vitality, and power impulses were not completely acceptable, especially to women who had grown up in very religious families, the psychosomatic pain experienced in fits, and the afflicted's obsession with imagining "Coffins, and bodies in shrouds" calling out for vengeance against their witchmurderers,[70] manifested the accusing women's guilt at the unacceptability of their own disowned impulses. Caught between their training and their desires, there was no resolution, save in laying the blame for the latter on someone who by definition epitomized, in a fully malign way, those same impulses. Condemning the witch purged the self. Projecting the self into accusations of witchcraft helped religious women and envious adolescents to deal with the change in the female sex role which began occurring gradually after 1665. They were able to resist such change, while on another level giving explosive expression to it behind the fit's veil.

The choice of victims, many of them eccentrics, suggests that the bewitched females were most discomforted by those women who had acted upon their own inner needs to ignore or defy the ideal feminine sex role; i.e., those women who best illustrated the projected desires of the afflicted. Unable to be similarly assertive, the accusers turned instead to equally unfeminine, but disguised and purely destructive, aggression in punishing those nontraditional women. The psychoanalyst Merell Middlemore appears correct when he writes that the Salem Village girls could not "consolidate a female identification"—but only if his remark is qualified to read Puritan, or perhaps seventeenth-century, female identification.[71]

Scapegoating witches did not always work for the individual accuser, as the shocking inhumanity of sending people to the gallows sometimes became too much for the afflicted girls to handle. Some initial accusers ceased to have fits or to denounce witches long before the frenzy abated. Mary Warren, after actively accusing a number of witches, suddenly began to charge that the "afflicted children did but dissemble." Immediately she was cried out upon as a witch, but in prison she continued to speak out against the proceedings, asserting several times that the magistrates "might as well examine Keysar's daughter that had been distracted many years." She explained, "when I was afflicted, I thought I saw the apparitions of a hundred persons," but then added that her head had been "distempered." In court, however, the other girls, Ann Pope, and John Indian attributed their violent fits to her, and under stringent cross-examination Mary Warren fell once again into fits. Imprisoned for a month, she finally retracted her criticism, admitted her own witchcraft, and once more began accusing others.[72] Similarly, when Deliverance Hobbs wavered from her accusatory afflictions, the bewitched girls denounced her. She, like Mary Warren, denied signing the Devil's book, but then, under the magistrates' relentless questioning, also admitted her

witchcraft.[73] Another of the girls, Sarah Churchill, fell under suspicion of practicing witchcraft, probably for the same reason. After her examination she cried and appeared "much troubled in spirit." She explained to Sarah Ingersoll that she had confessed her *maleficium* only "because they threatened her, and told her they would put her into the dungeon."[74]

The line between witch and bewitched was dangerously thin, both on the psychological level and in terms of the social distribution of power which an accuser manipulated. Once a woman began having fits in which she declared herself afflicted by agents of Satan, she could afford no second thoughts, however sane and humane. Once she had "sold her soul"—that is, disavowed responsibility for her own deepest impulses—she could not recover it without sharing the fate of her accused victims, without becoming as powerless as they in the grip of the larger Puritan community.

The Accused: Innocent Victims of Circumstance

Many of the alleged witches fell under suspicion not for any personal deviance, but because friction existed between families who contended over land. When some failed to secure satisfaction from the county courts or town meetings, they themselves, or women in their families, could easily accuse opponents of witchcraft in order to get even. In this respect, the 1692 outbreak represented a new departure in the history of seventeenth-century New England witchcraft. Previous witch-scapegoat accusations had been hurled at community eccentrics; in Essex County, however, because of the extreme level of anxiety prevailing, the witch's character in many instances became irrelevant. The Salem Village bewitched included at least three females who would have been privy to the antagonisms between the Putnams and their neighbors. As Boyer and Nissenbaum have pointed out, the Putnams, a fairly well-to-do family with old roots, envied the prosperity of the *nouveau riche* Porters, who had close ties to Salem mercantile interests. Accusations followed, not of patriarch Israel Porter—perhaps because he was related by marriage to Judge John Hathorne—but of persons more distantly connected to the family. The bewitched girls charged Daniel Andrews, who was the husband of Sarah Porter, a schoolmaster, an ex-deputy to the General Court, the owner of a Salem apothecary shop, and one of the four wealthiest men in Salem Village.[75] Another "witch," Philip English, a confederate of the Porters, owned an imposing house in Salem, fourteen town lots, and twenty sailing vessels. He fled with his wife, Mary, rather than appear before the Court of Oyer and Terminer.[76] Andrews's brother-in-law George Jacobs, Jr., and Jacobs's wife and daughter faced prosecution, as did Andrews's tenant Peter Cloyse, his wife, and the wife of a servant in John Porter's household.[77] Francis Nurse, the brother-in-law of Cloyse, had long antagonized the Putnams, by living on land which Nathaniel Putnam claimed and by his ties to Salem, where he had served as constable. Despite her reputation as a holy and God-fearing person, Nurse's wife, Rebecca, was hanged for practicing *maleficium*.[78] Altogether, twelve of fourteen accused Salem Village witches lived in the eastern part of the village, near Salem, as did twenty-four of twenty-nine witch defenders, whereas thirty of thirty-two accusers lived in the west. . . .[79]

Because the Putnams had also become involved in land disputes with some inhabitants of Topsfield, the afflicted girls and the Putnams accused the most economically and politically important persons at Topsfield—those most able to injure the Putnam cause. Charges were filed against Isaac Easty, who was a selectman, tithing-man, surveyor of highways, and member of many different town committees, as well as against his wife, Mary. The latter was hanged on September 22, two months after her sister Rebecca Nurse. Sarah Wilds, mother of the Topsfield town constable, was also hanged, on July 19.[80]

Antagonism over land existed on a more local level in Topsfield as well. The Hows and Perleys had argued over property boundaries; ten-year-old Hannah Perley accused the entire How family of afflicting her, and on July 19 Elizabeth How was hanged. Mistress How's brother and her nephew were also accused.[81] Similar antagonisms affected the Wild and Gould families. After John Wild's first wife, Rebecca Gould, died, inheritance problems arose between the two families, both of whom were in the wealthiest one-fifth of Topsfield's taxpayers. John Wild testified against John Gould in a treason case in 1686; subsequently Gould's sister too began spreading witchcraft stories about Sarah Wild. These tales stopped when Wild threatened to sue Gould for slander. In 1692 such charges resurfaced, along with accusations against Wild's daughter and son-in-law, Sarah and Edward Bishop. The Goulds were aided in their accusations by the Putnams, to whom they were related by marriage. John Gould had earlier become co-owner, with Nathaniel Putnam, of the Rowley iron-works.[82]

Local friction also erupted at Andover, where no fewer than fifty-five "witches" faced accusations. Philip Greven has reported a heightened concern over Andover land titles after 1662, the result of first-generation monopolization of community land. In the 1660s the townsmen reduced the amount of realty available to those newcomers who wished to take up estates. Notwithstanding this, "outsiders" purchased 67.8 percent of all lots offered for sale between 1668 and 1686; still, they never enjoyed much status in the community. Joseph Ballard, one of these "outsiders," brought the Salem Village girls into Andover to point out his ill wife's afflicters. The resultant accusations soon came to reflect the "great Controversie in ye

towne, about giving out land," as charges were levied against nine of Andover's thirteen wealthiest families (in terms of land allotted before 1662). Twenty-nine of the fifty-five accused witches were either nuclear family members, descendants, or related by marriage to these nine, who belonged to the Bradstreet, Osgood, Parker, Fryer, Stevens, Barker, Dane, Faulkner, and Tyler families. . . .[83]

The Accused: Nontraditional Women

While many witches served as scapegoat-victims of various men's land greed, others more clearly fitted the image of social deviants. Women who did not toe the ideal feminine line offered the afflicted females a superb opportunity to work out their own projected aggressions and needs for dominion—those unacceptable urges which the afflicted found desirable yet incompatible with their Puritan training. In what was probably an overstatement, Thomas Maule estimated that two-thirds of the accused were either guilty of rebellion against their parents (who included, in Puritan terms, husbands and magistrates) or of adultery.[84] One, Sarah Osborne, had lived in a common law relationship with her "wild" Irish servant; another, Martha Corey, had given birth to a mulatto child.[85] "Witch" Susannah Roots had earned a reputation as a "bad woman" who entertained company late at night.[86]

Those women who had openly flouted the ideal role in the changing world of the late century received quick convictions. One of the first three persons accused, Sarah Good, was such a woman. Born into a wealthy family, she had been cheated out of her inheritance after her father's suicide in 1672. She married twice, both times to men who became debt ridden. By 1689 her second husband, William Good, had lost all of his land and seventeen head of cattle to his creditors. Too poor to own a house, he lived with Sarah and their infant daughter in neighbors' houses, barns, and sometimes open ditches. Turbulent and vitriolic, Sarah Good often scolded and "fell to muttering" when people extended charity to her. When one neighbor refused her lodging, she was not above setting his cattle loose. In court she answered the magistrates "in a very wicked spiteful manner, reflecting and retorting against the authorities with base and abusive words." After the minister Nicholas Noyes urged her to confess, since "she knew she was a witch," Sarah pulled no punches in lashing out, "you are a liar; I am no more a Witch than you are a Wizard; and if you take away my Life, God will give you Blood to drink." She died on July 19, protesting to the end.[87]

Bridget Bishop, the first "witch" hanged, would not be dominated by her three husbands. She operated an unlicensed tavern where visitors congregated late at night to play the illegal game of shuffleboard, and she dressed provocatively—some of her contemporaries might say whorishly—in a red paragon bodice. Once she had driven an accusatory stranger off her porch with a spade. Like so many other alleged witches, she protested her innocence, asserting, "I know not what a witch is."[88]

Martha Carrier, accused of no less than thirteen witchly murders at Andover, had actively disputed with neighbors over land, physically shaken up one twelve-year-old girl in church, and threatened a male opponent by saying that "She would hold his Nose close to the Grindstone as ever it was held since his Name was Abbot." Her interrogator asked at the witch trials, "What black man did you see?" She retorted, "I saw no black man but your own presence." She charged the magistrates with not listening to what she said, while they "shamefully" paid attention to every little utterance of the bewitched girls. Cotton Mather, detesting her outspokenness, termed her "this rampant hag."[89]

Many other witches revealed their deviance both in and out of court. Abigail Hobbs expressed no fear of lying out in the woods at night, explaining that "she was not afraid of any thing." Disobedient to her parents, she had once sprinkled water in her mother's face, saying she "baptised hir in the name of the Father Son and Holy Ghost."[90] Susannah Martin of Amesbury, long accounted a witch, spoke harshly to neighbors, accused the girls of "dealing in the Black Art," and pointed out (to the magistrates' chagrin) that the Old Testament described Satan's appearance in the shape of an innocent, one "glorified Saint."[91] Mary Parker had once shocked her associates by coming to the tavern after her husband and there "railing" at him.[92] Ann Pudeator possessed a long-standing reputation as "an ill-carriaged woman," while Mary Obinson several times abused Thomas Hill, calling him "cuckold & old foole." Mammy Read had the gall to tell Mistress Symmes, after an argument, that she wished her antagonist "might never piss, nor shit, if she did not goe [*i. e.,* leave]."[93] Read, Pudeator, Martin, Carrier, and Bishop all swung from the gallows, but Hobbs received a reprieve after her conviction. No further record exists of Obinson's case. Whether any of these women actually practiced witchcraft cannot now be determined, but it is unlikely.[94] The fact that women in 1692 had more freedom than ever before—a reality produced in part by the lack of witchcraft prosecutions after 1665—would presumably have decreased the need for "rebels" against the feminine ideal to assume the totally malign inversion of the proper role. The clarity and force of the earlier typologies of Witch and Whore, as well as Virgin and Wife, had considerably weakened by the 1690s, only to dramatically resurface in 1692.

Despite their realizations that they faced a death sentence, most of the accused women refused to insure their own releases by concocting confessions. Instead, they "would neither in time of Examination, nor Trial, Confess any thing of what was laid to their Charge;

some would not admit of any Minister to Pray with them, others refused to pray for themselves."[95] Nineteen women died protesting their innocence, including five in prison. One of the hanged "witches," Mary Easty, knowing that she could not save her own life, wished to save those "that are going the same way with myself." She urged the Salem Court to examine carefully all confessing witches who accused others, for, she explained, they "have belyed themselves and others."[96]

Those women who walked bravely to the gallows may have summoned strength from their religious faith, or from recognition of the integrity of their own personhood. Other women signed petitions supporting accused witches, even though such petitioners should have been aware that the afflicted girls quickly accused their critics. Two Putnam opponents, Israel and Elizabeth Porter, headed a petition signed by sixteen other women and twenty-one men on behalf of Rebecca Nurse. Another thirteen men and seven of their wives requested leniency for the Proctors. At Salisbury fifty-eight women and fifty-seven men, neighbors of "witch" Mary Bradbury, asserted they had never heard that Bradbury "ever had any difference or falleing oute wth any of her neighbors man woman or childe but was always, readie and willing to doe for them wt laye in her power night and day, though wth hazard of her health or other danger more." Twelve women and forty-one men of Andover also petitioned for the release of their accused neighbors.[97] No one, however, argued on behalf of the nontraditional women accused.

During the trials, from time to time an occasional unaccused woman went so far as to attack the character of one or more of the afflicted. For example, Lydia Porter charged Goody Bibber with mischief-making and lying.[98] Mary Phips, the wife of the governor, expressed her own disagreement by pardoning one convicted witch in the governor's absence, although she had no legal power to do so.[99] Lady Phips, Lydia Porter, and the almost one hundred female petitioners, as well as many of the "witches," were acting assertively in varying degrees, reflecting and contributing to the style of the nontraditional woman.

An End to Witchcraft

As witchcraft accusations increased in number, protests also mounted, from men as well as from women. Husbands spoke up in defense of their wives.[100] Ex-deputy Robert Pike told Justice Corwin that "diabolical visions, apparitions or representations" were "more commonly false and delusive then real," also pointing out that the afflicted women raised the dead, like the Witch of Endor in biblical times.[101] A Salem Quaker named Thomas Maule anonymously blasted the Puritans for murdering one another under the Devil's influence, and as early as June the Anabaptist William Milbourne protested to the General Court against the use of "bare specter testimonie" to convict "persons of good fame and of unspotted reputations."[102] A Boston merchant by the name of Thomas Brattle, in an October letter, penned a scathing criticism of the Salem proceedings.[103] At about the same time Samuel Willard published a disapproving analysis of the arguments used against witches, in *Some Miscellany Observations on our Present Debates Respecting. Witchcraft, In a Dialogue between S[alem] and B[oston].* Cotton Mather had begun to doubt the reality of specter evidence, while other ministers, including Joshua Moody, John Hale, John Wise, Francis Dane, James Allen, and John Baily, raised objections to the proceedings. Willard and Moody took occasion to preach the text, "they that are persecuted in one city, let them flee to another," and then counselled four "witches" to escape from prison.[104]

The afflicted girls ultimately insured that the witchcraft proceedings would halt—by accusing the most prestigious members of Puritan society. The girls had first charged contentious, penniless Sarah Good, disreputable Sarah Osborne, and the exotic Barbadian Indian slave Tituba. Sensing their own power in the court's response, they subsequently broadened their attack by clamoring not only against low-status eccentrics, but also against virtuous women like Rebecca Nurse, and even against men. On May 31 attorney Thomas Newton would assert that they "spare no person of what quality so ever."[105] By November the bewitched had charged the wives of critics Moody, Hale, and Dane, as well as several members of Boston's ruling elite. However, the authorities were reluctant to prosecute. Margaret Thatcher, the widow of Boston's wealthiest merchant and mother-in-law of Judge Jonathan Corwin, who presided at witchcraft trials, escaped apprehension, even though she was much complained about by the afflicted. So did Mary Phips, Samuel Willard, and Mistress Moody. The magistrates did issue a warrant for the arrest of a prominent merchant named Hezekiah Usher, but he received lodging in a private house and then was permitted to leave the colony.[106]

Bostonians had less respect for the orders of the Salem Court than did the citizenry of any other area; their constables ignored warrants. Accused witches broke out of prison altogether too easily, suggesting complicity on the part of the jailor. In fact, the keeper had no apparent hesitancy about releasing one "witch" upon receipt of Lady Phips's pardon.[107] Other Bostonians hid "witches" who had escaped from prison or fled apprehension.

The Salem Village girls who accused proper Bostonians quite possibly exploited the resentment of many rural Salem Villagers for those alien yet very powerful urbanites who often valued capital over land, commerce over husbandry, ornamentation over simplicity, and new ideas over old. The Putnams, in particular, facing diminishing land resources and declining status, had a good deal to resent; they listened with open ears while the girls accused nine prominent Bostonians and denounced Nathaniel Saltonstall, the Haverhill Councillor who had resigned his seat on the witch court.[108] Those with Boston connections also faced prosecution. In Andover, for example, three prominent Bradstreets—a family with close marital and political ties to Boston's ruling elite—fled prosecution.[109] Before the witchcraft frenzy had abated, even the secretary of Connecticut had been denounced.[110]

Perhaps nothing better illustrates many people's dislike for the merchant class than the destruction wrought against the property of the wealthy French Huguenot, Philip English. (There was undoubtedly some anti-French feeling involved in English's case as well.) After English and his "aristocratic" wife, Mary, escaped from Salem prison, an irate group of citizens sacked their "great house" at Salem, destroying or carrying away various old family portraits and furniture and robbing storehouses of goods valued at £2,683. When English later returned, he found a single servant's bed the only furniture remaining in the house.[111]

The colony's economic and political leaders objected to the accusations levied against so many of their friends and wives. Quite probably their objections were crucial in bringing the frenzy to a halt. Robert Calef credited one prominent Bostonian with stopping proceedings at Andover by threatening to sue his accusers there in a £1,000 defamation action.[112] Governor William Phips initially left all witchcraft affairs to the Court of Oyer and Terminer, but after returning to Boston from an expedition against the Maine Indians he found "many persons in a strange ferment of disatisfaction." Soon the royal governor forbade the issuance of any new literature on the subject, asked the Crown for counsel, and dissolved the Court of Oyer and Terminer. In the winter of 1692-93 Phips pardoned some convicted witches, caused some to be let out on bail, and "put the Judges upon considering a way to relieve others and prevent them from perishing in prison." The General Court on December 16, 1692, directed the newly created Superior Court to try the "witches" still in custody within Essex County. The Superior Court, meeting on January 3, 1692/3, acquitted forty-nine "witches," and convicted three. Deputy Governor Stoughton, the chief justice, ordered the execution of those three, as he had of other "witches," but Phips pardoned these and five other convicted persons.[113] Stoughton, enraged, refused to sit on the bench of the next court at Charlestown. That body released all the accused persons tried before it.[114]

Before the Superior Court met at Salem, the bewitched girls had ceased their afflictions. Perhaps by then they had realized that their reach exceeded their grasp. Perhaps they felt guilty over precipitating the deaths of twenty-five persons. Perhaps their power impulses had been satiated. (After all, for some time people as far away as Boston, Andover, and Gloucester had sought their advice in pointing out witches.) Perhaps they were drained by the physical and emotional strain which attended fits. Perhaps they felt purged, for a time, of their own unfeminine longings. For whatever reasons, they *had* had their day; now it seemed only appropriate that they return to their status as unobtrusive members of the Puritan community. Only in Boston did two girls, Mary Watkins and Margaret Rule, continue to have fits during 1693.[115]

More than forty Massachusetts residents had suffered from hysterical fits in 1692 and 1693, accusing over two hundred persons of witchcraft. While Massachusetts was not the only colony to experience such an outbreak, the events in Connecticut, where for the first time in three decades the courts also began trying several "witches," ultimately produced a very different outcome. In late 1692 and early 1693, a seventeen-year-old French maidservant at Fairfield assumed the hysterical fit pattern of the Bay Colony's afflicted persons. Catherine Branch sometimes acted as one struck dumb, "put out her tong to a great extent," and experienced "a pinching & pricking at her breast." Like many at Salem Village, she sought the joys of "Singing, Laughing, Eating, [and] Rideing" in her fits. As she threw herself convulsively about, she complained of six different witches afflicting her.[116] The accused included among their small numbers both the virtuous and the unholy. Mercy Disborough, the only one of these "witches" to receive the death sentence, had the worst reputation; she had tossed harsh words at many men in the community and had earned a general reputation as a witch before 1692.[117] Elizabeth Clawson, on the other hand, never spoke threatening words. Believing in the motto "we must liue in pease," she often served as a mediator whenever her neighbors argued.[118]

Unlike many Essex County inhabitants, those in Fairfield Country had a more skeptical attitude about witchcraft. Some thought Catherine Branch "desembled." Abigail Wescott, her mistress, said none of the girl's accusations held any validity; she reportedly claimed that Branch "was such a Lying girl that not any boddy Could belieue one word what she said." Sarah Betts wished to treat the young woman's bewitchment through medicinal bloodletting, while Sarah Ketcham expressed disbelief that any witches at all existed in Fairfield.[119] Men also objected to Branch's charges, and the special Court of Oyer and Terminer held at Fairfield on September 15, 1692, freed all the accused save Mercy Disborough; she received a death sentence, but later (in May 1693) the Connecticut General Assembly granted her a reprieve. On October 17, 1692, a meeting of Connecticut ministers held the water test to be "unlawfull and sinfull," rejected special evidence, considered "unusuall excresencies" or teats no proof of witchcraft, dismissed strange accidents as no evidence whatsoever,

and expressed the view that Catherine Branch was deluded by the Devil.[120] Two successive trials of "witches" resulted in acquittals. Like the Salem Village girls, Branch had made a play for power, but she could not convince her associates of the legitimacy of her claims.

Connecticut was not ripe for a witch hunt. A progressive ministry helped to undercut any accusatory zeal there. Although the colony's residents certainly experienced much tension between 1689 and 1692, their general anxiety level did not equal that of their Bay Colony neighbors. Political affairs were volatile, but the relative isolation and independence of towns defused the political turmoil. Land antagonisms, although emergent, had not reached serious proportions.[121] The conflict between rural and urban lifestyles, so clear at Salem Village, was insignificant in this almost completely agrarian colony. The concern over moral decay was somewhat less extreme than in Massachusetts. Connecticut did not have to suffer the frightening effects of a witch hunt; instead, residents could cope with stress through less harsh actions, such as voting to catechize all "Bachelors and boys from eight years ould and upwards . . . once a fortnight on the Lords Daye in Ye meeting house."[122]

The inhabitants of Maine, New Hampshire, and Plymouth had no concern about witches. In Maine, the Indian problem diverted attention from any occult concerns, while both the "red devils" and political factionalism had the same effect in New Hampshire. In both areas real enemies abounded, and neither had a history of witchcraft accusations. In Plymouth, the basic problem—a high tax rate—was alleviated through incorporation into the Bay Colony.

Only in eastern Massachusetts, with its intense and numerous frustrations, could a sustained witch hunt be mounted. There the reality of the nontraditional woman loomed larger, helping to precipitate fits in powerless adolescents and religious Puritan wives, as well as aggravating the already established tendency to view unfeminine behavior as witchlike. Those independent-spirited women who faced prosecution as witches were the victims of other, more conservative women's unconscious search for power.

Notes

. . . [28] Lawson, *Brief & True Narrative,* pp. 153-55: Calef, *More Wonders of Invisible World,* p. 342.

[29] Lawson, *Brief & True Narrative,* pp. 151-54.

[30] Samuel Parris, "Christ Knows How Many Devils There Are," in Boyer & Nissenbaum, eds., *Salem-Village Witchcraft,* pp. 129-31.

[31] For a good description of Parris's character, see Boyer & Nissenbaum, *Salem Possessed,* pp. 153-78.

[32] Corey quoted in Upham, *Salem Witchcraft,* II, 45.

[33] Towne & Clark, "Topsfield in the Witchcraft Delusion."

[34] Lockridge, "Land, Population & Evolution," supplies general information on the declining size of estates throughout Massachusetts.

[35] Barker in "Salem Witchcraft—1692," I, n.p.; Post in "Ct. Files—Suffolk Co.," XXXII (1692-93), no. 2705; [Maule,] *N. Eng. Persecutors Mauled,* p. 181.

[36] Thompson, "Review Article: Salem Revisited," p. 322.

[37] Whether the judges presumed a witch guilty before examining him or her depended, to a large extent, on the witch's respectability. Hathorne and Corwin asked the low-status Sarah Good such questions as "Why do you hurt these children?" "Sarah Good, do you not see now what you have done?" "Why do you not tell us the truth?" However, with saintly Rebecca Nurse, the tone was much more tentative: "You see these accuse you. Is it true?" "Are you an innocent person, relating to this witchcraft?" "You would do well, if you are guilty, to confess." Cf. examinations in Boyer & Nissenbaum, eds., *Salem-Village Witchcraft,* pp. 5-6, 23-25.

[38] Calef, *More Wonders of Invisible World,* p. 355.

[39] Foxcroft, "Letter"; Noble, "Doc. Fragments Touching Witchcraft Episode of 1692," pp. 15, 19; Upham, *Salem Witchcraft,* II, 457.

[40] Corey refused to enter a plea, apparently to avoid the confiscation of his property upon being found guilty.

[41] C. Mather, *Diary,* I, 142.

[42] Brattle, "Letter," p. 189. Later, Many "witches" repudiated their confessions, explaining that their own fear of execution and the urging of their friends had convinced them to admit to untrue charges. Tituba testified "her master did beat her and other-ways abuse her to make her confess and accuse (such as he called) her sister-witches, and that whatever she said by way of confessing or accusing others was the effect of such usage; her master refused to pay her fees unless she would stand to what she had said." Even before the trials had ended, Sarah Ingersoll, "crying and wringing her hands," repudiated the earlier confession she had made for fear of being tossed into the "dungeon" (Calef, *More Wonders of Invisible World,* pp. 374-75; Upham, *Salem Witchcraft,* II, 169-70).

[43] Fowler, "Biog. Sketches of Green, Clark, & Wadsworth," p. 58; Foxcroft, "Letter," p. 80.

[44] Calef, *More Wonders of the Invisible World,* p. 363.

[45] "Salem Witchcraft—1692," III, n.p.

[46] Starkey, *Devil in Mass.,* p. 239.

[47] The Cambridge Council stated that Satan "may sometimes have a Permission to represent an Innocent Person as Tormenting such as are under Diabolical Molestations. But such things are rare and extraordinary, especially when such Matters come before Civil Judicatures." See I. Mather, *Cases of Conscience,* pp. 32. 63.

[48] Calef, *More Wonders of Invisible World,* pp. 372-74.

[49] Bogart, "Demonism as Function of Status Certainty Loss," pp. 41-42.

[50] See ch. 6 for a full treatment of the hysterical fits' psychological dynamics.

[51] I. Lewis, *Ecstatic Rel.,* p. 31, also pp. 66-99.

[52] John Demos writes that "it is quite probable that adolescent girls in early New England were particularly subject to the control of older women, and this may well have given rise to a powerful underlying resentment. By contrast, the situation must have been less difficult for boys, since their work often took them out of the household and their behavior generally was less restricted." This historian stresses the importance of the defense mechanism of projection in that process, but connects the resentment to severe breast-weaning trauma and not explicitly enough to the position of women in Puritan society. After all, if weaning occurred early, boys and girls would presumably be similarly affected. See Demos, "Underlying Themes in Witchcraft of N. Eng.," pp. 1318-19, 1322-26.

[53] Robert Moulton pointed out discrepancies in Susannah Sheldon's stories, asserting that whereas she had once told him that witches had hauled her upon her belly through the yard and over a stone wall, later she contradicted herself by saying she came over the wall through her own power. However, the magistrates ignored Mouton's evidence, as they earlier had ignored the more convincing testimony presented by a young man at Sarah Good's trial. One of the afflicted girls had pulled out half of a knife blade, which she claimed Good had been using to stab her; but the young man produced the remainder of the knife and said the girl had been present when he had thrown away the other half. The Court bade him "not to tell lyes." The judges also swept aside the skepticism of some male jurors and failed to note that most persons who criticized the proceedings were all too readily designated witches (Woodward, ed., *Rec. of Salem Witchcraft,* II, 208; Calef, *More Wonders of Invisible World,* pp. 357-58).

[54] Calef, *More Wonders of Invisible World,* pp. 353-54.

[55] Sarah Wilson stated "that the afflicted persons crying out of her as afflicting them made her fearfull of herself" and caused her to feel "in the dark as to the matter of her being a witch." Mary Bridges was "told that she certainly was a witch and so made to believe it, though she had no other grounds so to believe" ("Recantation of Confessors of Witchcraft").

[56] See pp. 398-99.

[57] Lawson, *Brief & True Narrative,* p. 154.

[58] Woodward, ed., *Rec. of Salem Witchcraft,* I, 45-47.

[59] *Ibid.,* I, 105.

[60] C. Mather, *Brand Pluck'd Out of Burning,* pp. 261, 269, 275.

[61] Starkey, *Devil in Mass.,* p. 13; "Salem Witchcraft—1692," II, n.p.

[62] C. Mather, *Brand Pluck't Out Burning,* p. 271; Calef, *More Wonders of Invisible World,* p. 327; Woodward, ed., *Rec. of Salem Witchcraft,* I, 115.

[63] Lawson, *Brief & True Narrative,* p. 156.

[64] Woodward, ed., *Rec. of Salem Witchcraft,* I, 105-6; "Salem Witchcraft—1692," II, III, n.p.

[65] Calef, *More Wonders of Invisible World,* pp. 325, 327.

[66] *Ibid.,* p. 353.

[67] "Salem Witchcraft—1692," I, n.p.; Nevins, *Witchcraft in Salem Village,* p. 170.

[68] "Salem Witchcraft—1692," II, III, n.p.; Upham, *Salem Witchcraft,* II, 128-29.

[69] Lawson, *Christ's Fidelity the Only Shield,* pp. 116-18; Boyer & Nissenbaum, *Salem Possessed,* p. 210.

[70] I. Mather, *Further Account of Tryals,* p. 10.

[71] Middlemore unfortunately brings in the "cause" of allegedly deep-seated, subconscious "castration anxiety" in the girls to explain a complex phenomenon in a chauvinistic way. Another psychoanalyst's observation that witch hunters become inquisitors to avoid probing their own painful inner assumptions and desires appears more accurate. See Middlemore, "Treatment of Bewitchment in a Puritan Community," p. 57; Rosenman, "Witch Hunter."

[72] Upham, *Salem Witchcraft,* II, 114-20.

[73] Woodward, ed., *Rec. of Salem Witchcraft,* II, 188.

[74] Upham, *Salem Witchcraft,* II, 169-70.

[75] Boyer & Nissenbaum, *Salem Possessed,* pp. 120-22, 130-31.

[76] *Ibid.,* pp. 131-32.

[77] *Ibid.,* p. 182. In 1674 Nathaniel Putnam complained to the magistrates that George Jacobs had driven Putnam's horses into the Ipswich River, threatening to "drown them if he could." Jacobs argued that the horses had trespassed on his property. The justices directed only that Jacobs pay court costs (G. Dow, ed., *Essex Ct. Rec.,* IV, 428).

[78] Boyer & Nissenbaum, eds., *Salem-Village Witchcraft,* pp. 48-54; G. Dow, ed., *Essex Ct. Rec.,* V, 117; VI, 8.

[79] Boyer & Nissenbaum, *Salem Possessed,* p. 35.

[80] Towne & Clark, "Topsfield in the Witchcraft Delusion," pp. 34-36.

[81] *Ibid.*

[82] W. Davis, "Wildes Family."

[83] For description of interfamilial friction at Andover, see Greven, *Four Generations,* pp. 41-65.

[84] [Maule,] *N. Eng. Persecutors Mauled,* p. 184.

[85] G. Dow, ed., *Essex Ct. Rec.,* III, 5, 402; VI, 374-75; IV, 237; Boyer & Nissenbaum, *Salem Possessed,* pp. 193-94, 146.

[86] Woodward, ed., *Rec. of Salem Witchcraft,* II, 52-3.

[87] *Ibid.,* I, 12-29; Calef, *More Wonders of Invisible World,* pp. 357-58; Boyer & Nissenbaum, *Salem Possessed,* pp. 203-5.

[88] Boyer & Nissenbaum, eds., *Salem-Village Witchcraft,* pp. 155-62.

[89] Woodward, ed., *Rec. of Salem Witchcraft,* II, 56-66; "Salem Witchcraft—1692," n.p.; C. Mather, *Wonders of Invisible World,* pp. 125-28.

[90] Woodward, ed., *Rec. of Salem Witchcraft*, II, 177-78.

[91] C. Mather, *Wonders of Invisible World*, pp. 113-20.

[92] *Ibid.*, p. 156.

[93] Woodward, ed., *Rec. of Salem Witchcraft*, II, 15-16; "Photostatic Copy of Suffolk Ct. Rec., 1680-92," pt. 1, p. 192; "Salem Witchcraft—1692," III, n.p.

[94] All evidence of actual witchcraft being practiced in Essex County in 1692 is dubious, at best. Those women who confessed did so only under great psychological, if not physical, duress. Chadwick Hansen makes much of John and William Bly's testimony that they once found "several puppets made up of rags and hogs' bristles, with headless pins in them" upon tearing down the wall of Bridget Bishop's house, but such evidence is worthless. In the hallucinatory climate of mid-1692, the Blys may have misconstrued their earlier find, converting harmless dolls into pin-laden puppets. If not, then we are left wondering why John Bly had not reported such awesome evidence to the authorities. (Obviously William Bly could not, because he was only eight years old.) At a time when so many persons were imagining specters and strange beasts, it is difficult to accept the Bly testimony and other accounts at face value. (See Hansen, *Witchcraft at Salem*, pp. 95-96.)

[95] Lawson, *Christ's Fidelity the Only Shield*, p. 112.

[96] Calef, *More Wonders of Invisible World*, p. 368.

[97] Upham, *Salem Witchcraft*, II, 272, 307; T. Hutchinson, *Hist. of Mass.*, II, 32-33; Woodward, ed., *Rec. of Salem Witchcraft*, I, 115; II, 172-74.

[98] Woodward, ed., *Rec. of Salem Witchcraft*, II, 203-4.

[99] T. Hutchinson, *Hist. of Mass.*, II, 46n.

[100] Other husbands, however, such as Giles Corey, William Good, and Edward Bishop, testified against their wives.

[101] "Robert Pike to Jonathan Corwin, August 9, 1692," in Pike, *New Puritan*, pp. 149-57.

[102] [Maule,] *N. Eng. Persecutors Mauled*, p. 56; G. Burr, ed., *Narratives of Witchcraft*, pp. 196-97n.

[103] Brattle, "Letter," pp. 169-90.

[104] Drake, *Witchcraft Delusion in N. Eng.*, pp. 179-81; Woodward, ed., *Rec. of Salem Witchcraft*, II, 66-68; Upham, "Salem Witchcraft & C. Mather," p. 212, and *Salem Witchcraft*, p. 364; G. Burr, ed., *Narratives of Witchcraft*, p. 187n.

[105] Quoted in Boyer & Nissenbaum, *Salem Possessed*, p. 32.

[106] Brattle, "Letter," pp. 177-78.

[107] T. Hutchinson, *Hist. of Mass.*, II, 46n.

[108] Sewall, *Diary*, I, 373.

[109] Dudley Bradstreet, the son of Massachusetts Governor Simon Bradstreet (1679, 1689-92) and an ex-Councillor, imprisoned 40 "witches" at Andover, then refused to sit in judgment on any more, and fled the colony to avoid apprehension himself. His brother John with his own wife, Ann, ran away to New Hampshire. The afflicted girls thereafter accused the Bradstreets of assailing dogs in spectral form, and two such dogs were executed. Amazingly enough, the family patriarch was not accused even though he had criticized the witchcraft proceedings and had weathered sharp criticism himself as an ineffectual governor. See Calef, *More Wonders of Invisible World*, p. 372; Brattle, "Letter," p. 184; Breen, *Character of the Good Ruler*, pp. 171-72.

[110] T. Hutchinson, *Witchcraft Delusion of 1692*, p. 41n; Woodward, ed., *Rec. of Salem Witchcraft*, II, 53.

[111] Clever, "Sketch of P. English," I, 160-61. English, after his return, reportedly constructed a secret room in the garret of his house which might serve as a place of temporary concealment in the event of another witchcraft frenzy.

[112] Calef, *More Wonders of Invisible World*, pp. 372-73.

[113] Phips, "Letters," pp. 196-202. Phips meant well by his pardons, but one "witch" so freed indicated that even a pardon could not restore her good name. Abigail Faulkner, of Andover, complained in 1700; "The pardon so far had its effect so that I am as yet suffered to live, but this only as a malefactor, convicted upon record of ye most heinous crimes, that mankind can be suffered to be guilty, which, besides its utter Ruining and Defaming my Reputation, will certainly expose myself to Iminent Danger by new accusations, which will thereby be ye more readily believed, and will remain a perpetual brand of Infamy upon my family." She requested that the General Court "order the Defacing of ye record against me." See Fowler, "Biog. Sketches of Green, Clark, & Wadsworth," p. 59.

[114] Calef, *More Wonders of Invisible World*, pp. 382-83.

[115] Mary Watkins, once a servant to Dame Swift at Salem and often reportedly "distracted," denounced her ex-mistress, but was threatened with punishment if she persisted in such accusations. Then, "falling into Melancholly humours she was found strangling her self . . . and immediately accused her self of being a Witch." The Superior Court, however, acquitted her on April 25, and she was thereafter sold into servitude in Pennsylvania. The other girl, Margaret Rule of Boston, after an argument with one woman "who had frequently Cured very painfull Hurts by muttering ouer them certain Charms," fell into fits in which her joints became "strangely distorted," mysterious black and blue marks appeared on her body, pins were stuck in her back and neck, blisters raised on her skin, and she experienced "exorbitant Convulsions." See *ibid.*, pp. 308-23, 383-84; Watkins, "Discolored Hist. of Witchcraft."

[116] Wyllys, "Wyllys Col. Suppl. Witchcraft in Conn. 1662-93," pp. 7-8; J. Taylor, *Witchcraft Del. in Conn.*, pp. 109-12.

[117] J. Taylor, *Witchcraft Del. in Conn.*, pp. 63-71. John Barlow testified that, in one argument with Mercy Disborough, the alleged witch had sworn "if shee had but the strength shee would tear me in peses." She threatened to make Thomas Benit "as bare as a birds taile" and spoke harsh words to others. Often neighbors accused her of afflicting their cattle, and Thomas Benit, Jr., told her to "unbewitch" his uncle's child "or else he would beat her hart out."

[118] Wyllys, "Wyllys Papers. Depositions on Witchcraft," pp. 19-21.

[119] *Ibid.*, p. 32; J. Taylor, *Witchcraft Del. in Conn.*, pp. 102-5.

[120] J. Taylor, *Witchcraft Del. in Conn.*, pp. 73, 75; J. Trumbull, ed., *Conn. Rec.*, IV, 76-77.

[121] A treatment of the gradual development of Connecticut land difficulties appears in Bushman, *From Puritan to Yankee.*

[122] J. Burr, ed., *Lyme Rec.*, p. 20.

John Putnam Demos (essay date 1982)

SOURCE: "Accusers, Victims, Bystanders: The Innerlife Dimension," in *Entertaining Satan: Witchcraft and the Culture of Early New England,* Oxford University Press, Inc., 1982, pp. 153-212.

[*In the following excerpt, Demos explores the role of female autonomy, menopause, menarche, and anorexia nervosa in the Salem witchcraft crisis.*]

"Every man is in certain respects: (a) like all other men, (b) like some other men, (c) like no other man."[1]

This simple yet profound observation, offered many years ago by two eminent social scientists, can be pressed into service in the present context. In certain respects the disposition of individual New Englanders toward witchcraft was quite idiosyncratic. In others it was common to particular groups, large or small. And in still others it touched matters of species-wide significance.

The present chapter deals with psychological issues at the group level. For the most part it speaks to the entire New England "group"—in short, to those preoccupations which all (or, at any rate, most) people of that time and place effectively shared. Still, at some points it reaches out toward the realm of "universals," while at others it explores distinctions within the population. For example, one cannot overlook the presence of sub-groups which occupied rather different positions in relation to witchcraft. The ranks of accused witches were (as noted already) disproportionately filled with women in the middle years. And there was also some imbalance in the proportions of witchcraft-victims—those who saw themselves as objects of attack (and who, in their turn, supplied most of the testimony against the accused). . . .

By and large, it was middle-aged women and younger men who supplied the most detailed and keenly felt testimony against accused witches. The qualitative materials also spotlight one other group whose importance is not evident in the numbers alone: girls in the agerange ten to nineteen. In the popular lore of witchcraft this has, of course, been the victim-group *par excellence*. The lore exaggerates, but it does not falsify. When a teen-aged girl succumbed to "fits," other manifestations of witchcraft were usually overshadowed. Among the known prosecutions less than half included this particular feature; but wherever present its impact was extreme.

Here, then, were the leading groups in witchcraft proceedings. In fact, each one has received some special attention in the case-study chapters immediately preceding. Elizabeth Knapp was in most respects a prototype of the teen-aged girl "under affliction"; while the victim/accusers of Goody Morse came predominantly from the ranks of younger men and middle-aged women. There is, however, something more to be said about these three groups. Disproportionately represented among the victims of witchcraft, they must in some sense have felt disproportionately vulnerable. The sources and meanings of such vulnerability belong, indisputably, to the "innerlife dimension."

Women in Midlife

It is easy enough to label the first group as "menopausal women," but the label itself demands special consideration. When such women complained about the witchcraft of Goody Morse, they showed a marked preoccupation with body-states, with illness and injury, with morbidity and mortality in children. And the same tendency appeared in other cases where women in mid-life came forward as witchcraft victims.[2] If this seems implicitly "menopausal," then some of it is attributable to biological processes shared by women of comparable age everywhere. But other elements were added by the context—both demographic and cultural. New England wives of the seventeenth century bore children, at quite regular intervals, for as long as they were able;[3] most had their last child after the age of forty.[4] The pregnancies came again and again, until suddenly they stopped, which is to say that menopause was vividly demarcated in terms of personal experience. At the same time childbearing was an assumed and vital function of such women—in their minds, literally "God-given." No matter what the difficulties and perils involved, New Englanders accepted the Biblical command to "be fruitful and replenish the earth"; indeed, the bearing of children shaped their very definition of womanhood.

How, then, would individual women react to the loss of this central, life-giving capacity? Unfortunately, the extant records are not of a sort to answer such questions, but they do allow certain inferences. As always, menopause was a life-stage of painful transition, but probably more so *then* than nowadays.[5] Its core was a sense of sudden and profound loss, perhaps even of "robbery." The flow of inner (and outward) experience broke sharply; life henceforth must proceed in new channels. The forces that made the change were hard to understand and impossible to control, obscure yet deeply felt, unseen in their origins but most palpable in their results. Given all these circumstances, New England women of middle age might well cast themselves as sufferers, as victims—even as targets of witchcraft.

There is another, still more speculative point to raise about the vulnerability of such women. Recent research on aging has noticed a pattern of midlife "crossover"—a tendency in men and women over forty to reverse, or at least to diminish, their conventional sex-roles.[6] Men give increasing play to traits and impulses hitherto considered "feminine"—to "nurturance," to "dependency," to sentiment of all kinds. Women, on the other hand, move in an opposite direction—toward increasing autonomy and self-assertion. Since this phenomenon appears in a variety of otherwise different cultural settings, it lays claim to universal developmental significance. And if the claim is accepted, there are intriguing implications for the present study. New England values were, by and large, notably uncongenial to personal expressions of self.[7] Yet New England women in midlife experienced deep, inner promptings of precisely that sort. Individual response must have varied—from greater to lesser compliance, and even to outright repression. Perhaps the witches were recruited disproportionately from the former group (those who yielded most fully to assertive impulse). The victims, by contrast, may have been those who struggled against the trend—but experienced a sense of danger, of exposure to unseen forces, in doing so.

Men in Young Adulthood

Autonomy was more obviously a central issue for another category of victims. Most New England men would, in their twenties and thirties, assume the status of independent householders.[8] They must take a wife and begin to father children. At the same time, and as part of the same process, they must assume control of their own livelihoods (whether in farming, in a trade, in commercial enterprise, or, more rarely, in an ecclesiastical "calling"). The process was neither rapid nor entirely smooth. Average age at marriage, for New England men, was over twenty-five years; and cultural convention made "youth" last until thirty. Moreover, it was not always easy to establish the economic underpinnings of independence. The property of young men came, most typically, from their families of origin (in short, from their fathers), and sometimes it was given grudgingly, or late, or on terms that fell short of outright control. There is enough evidence here for one scholar to propose the term "patriarchalism" as a way of describing the family system of early New England.[9]

But there was more to all this than the adjustment of property relations vis-à-vis potentially witholding fathers. Young men everywhere, as they assume an independent status, must break from an emotional matrix in which they have been sustained and guided through their early years. Expressed in formal terms, this means the relinquishment—or at least the drastic realignment—of underlying "infantile" ties. And among such ties none is more powerful, and ultimately compromising, than the one which pulls (back) toward mother. The danger is of doublebarreled "regression," to infantile dependence and infantile sexuality. (Our highly pejorative term "mother's boy" captures both elements. Such a person continues too long and too much to rely on the support and approval of his mother, while also retaining her as his primary "love object." As a result he does not—inwardly—grow up.) The opportunity, on the other hand, is to act by and for oneself, to move ahead toward new (age-appropriate and "non-incestuous") loves. Therein lies the route to maturity.

The possible connections to witchcraft are not far to seek. Young men supplied a far larger number of victims than any other category. Moreover, their sense of liability to attack can be interpreted as expressing several convergent strands of inner concern with women of their mothers' generation. In the first place, the witch commands extraordinary power over them and their possessions. (They continue to feel the strength of the "maternal object.") At the same time, they strike postures of resistance and repudiation—refusing the witch's requests for cooperation in routine aspects of everyday experience, and leading the charge against her in the courts of law. (They wish, however they can, to break the "incestuous" tie.) For this the witch grows angry with them, and punishes them severely. (They feel guilty, and deserving of punishment, for what they are about.) But when the witch attacks them, she does so indirectly, i.e. through familiars, or by striking down their cattle. (Distance is still maintained; in fantasy, as in social reality, the "maternal object" must not come too close.) The entire situation is complex and keenly felt—and *vulnerability* is right at the heart of it.

Girls in Adolescence

The third of the leading victim-groups, girls between the ages of ten and nineteen, presents special problems of interpretation. On the one hand, the evidence of their involvement in witchcraft proceedings is remarkably full and vivid; on the other, there is hardly any evidence about their experience apart from such involvement. Girls in their teens left fewer tracks for historians than any other group (young children alone excepted). Boys of comparable age can (sometimes) be followed in schools or colleges; and at least a few older men left autobiographies which made reference to their early years. For girls, however, there is virtually nothing. One imagines them growing up in a family-centered context and absorbed in a conventional round of domestic chores. They certainly assisted their mothers—in tending to gardens and orchards and domestic animals, in cooking and spinning, and in the care of still younger children. Their average age at menarche can be estimated at fourteen to sixteen.[10] Shortly afterward they began to be drawn into courtships, though most would not marry before twenty. Did they form "peer-groups" or some equivalent thereof? Where they much involved with older persons outside their immediate families? What was the balance between internal and external restraints in their everyday experience? On these points the record is mute.

Of course, there are vast differences between adolescence then and adolescence now. The whole context of growth between childhood and adulthood has been transformed, with corresponding changes of inner experience. One result, for example, is a greatly increased emphasis on issues of adolescent "identity." Modern-day teenagers confront a bewildering variety of pathways into adult life (e.g. alternative careers, geographic and social environments, value systems, etc.). And the reality, or illusion, of choice is frequently painful. In this respect the young people of seventeenth-century New England were differently situated. Their choices

were relatively few, and some elements of "identity" came to them almost ready-made.[11]

The biological dimension of adolescence is, however, much less liable to change. From the standpoint simply of hormonal and biochemical process, the experience of this age-group cannot have differed very substantially across the centuries. Assuming, moreover, that psychological process is rooted in biology, then it too must show elements of invariance. And it is in exploring such elements that one may reasonably look for help from current scientific theory. The evidence of participation in witchcraft cases is itself compelling. To "interpret" this material is to build a long and admittedly shaky bridge toward what is known of adolescent psychology in general.

The fits of Elizabeth Knapp (see Chapter 4) were in many respects typical for teenaged girls under the influence of witchcraft. Still, no one experience was *entirely* typical, so it is well to review the main, i.e. the most commonly noted, features.

> *Preliminaries:* The victim becomes anxiously preoccupied with her spiritual condition. She discovers ominous signs of God's displeasure toward her—this in spite of her manifest involvement in religious devotions and her outwardly faultless behavior.

> *Onset:* Her fits begin with spells of fainting, hysterical crying, disordered speech, and disturbances of sight and hearing.

> *Intensification:* The fits become longer, more frequent, and more bizarre in their substantive features. This phase often includes a delusionary confrontation with spectral witches, who seek to tempt, trick, or terrorize the victim into signing "the Devil's book" (that is, making a pact of perpetual allegiance). The victim offers desperate resistance, herself reviling the witches in the most outspoken terms.

> *Acute Phase:* The fits at peak intensity may include the following elements: (1) excruciating sensations of "pricking" and "pinching" (as if by numberless pins and nails), also of "burning" (by invisible flames); (2) bizarre contortions of body parts: twisting, stretching, unusual postures of extreme rigidity and limberness by turns; (3) frenzied motor activity: rolling on the ground, running about aimlessly, simulated "flying" and "diving"; occasional "barking" or other animal imitation; some impulse to injury of self or others; (4) periods of extreme immobility, amounting to paralysis; feelings of extraordinary pressure on the chest or elsewhere; (5) anorexia: more or less complete inhibitions of eating (sometimes accompanied by a strong wish to eat, but with clenching of mouth whenever food is brought); (6) occasional forced consumption of

invisible (and painful or poisonous) liquids when overpowered by the witch; (7) "frolicsome" intervals, mostly without pain; cavorting in a "ludicrous" way, babbling impertinent nonsense; insults and gestures of physical assault toward bystanders, friends, and family.

Intermissions: The victim experiences "quiet" periods, lasting hours or days, and characterized by lassitude, a "melancholy" air, and feelings of self-reproach.

These behaviors constitute a package, a syndrome, a composite picture of a considerable group, which partly reflects the individual experience of each victim, while entirely representing none of them. As such, it does not lend itself to full-fledged diagnostic or "genetic" interpretation of the sort possible in a single case-study. Nonetheless certain themes do come clear, and some of them are very close to the surface.

In the first place, "fits" invariably conveyed a sharp challenge to conventional standards and received authority. The victim might do or say almost anything, no matter how shocking. ("She frequently told us that if she might but steal or be drunk she should be well immediately.")[12] Parental commands were ignored or rejected. ("Upon the least reproof of their parents . . . most grievous, woeful, heart-breaking agonies would they fall unto. If any useful thing were to be done to them, or by them, they would have all sorts of troubles fall upon them.")[13] A minister's prayers brought ingratitude and scorn. ("Her whole carriage to me was with a sauciness that I had not been used to be treated with. . . . She would call to me with multiplied impertinences . . . and hector me at a strange rate.")[14] Ordinary human constraints were rejected, and mocked, when the victims simulated animals. ("They would bark at one another like dogs, and again purr like so many cats.")[15]

A second aspect of these episodes was attention-seeking—or outright exhibitionism. The routines of a household, a neighborhood, even an entire village were temporarily reorganized around the sufferings of the victim. Ministers came from near and far to pray over her; magistrates prepared other forms of public action in her behalf. Her fits were endlessly recounted in local gossip; they might, in addition, yield material for sermons and books. Affliction of this sort was, in sum, a route to instant fame.[16]

To challenge authority, to court fame: these, presumably, were wishes for which the fits provided ample gratification. But we must also credit the painful side—the hurts, both physical and psychological—of much afflictive experience. Viewed from the standpoint of clinical theory, such hurts look extremely "primitive." They seem random and disorganized, and unmodified by any rational or "censoring" process. Indeed, the fits

epitomize an infant's world of sensation. The extreme orientation to body surfaces, the pricks, the pinches, the sudden changes of body temperature: here are the (sometimes inevitable) discomforts of the first period of life. And yet the infant is not merely a recipient of such "torments"; he (she) wishes, in fantasy, to respond in kind. Consider the ingredients of "infantile sadism" as observed by a clinical psychoanalyst:

> All physical functions . . . are drawn in . . . [to] the attack. . . . Limbs shall trample, kick, and hit; lips, fingers, and hands shall suck, twist, pinch; teeth shall bite, gnaw, mangle, and cut; mouth shall devour, swallow, and kill (annihilate); eyes kill by a look, pierce, and penetrate; breath and mouth hurt by noise, as the child's oversensitive ears have experienced. . . .[17]

Virtually every one of these attacking modes could be matched to particular points in seventeenth-century accounts of fits: in effect, the modern psychoanalytic theorist and the premodern observer of witchcraft have discovered the same thing. Of course, the fits reflected the viewpoint of victims, not agents, of attack; but in the world of unconscious process such postures are readily turned around. Indeed, the infant cannot tolerate his (her) own "sadism"; there is less danger in attributing these impulses to other "objects." And so they are "projected" outside the self, where they join company with the actual discomforts mentioned previously and then return to attack. [In fact, the matter is more complicated still. Infants can only sporadically maintain the boundaries between "self" and "non-self"; and "objects" from their environment frequently obtain a place in their internal representational world. A "bad object," in short, may be experienced as being "inside" as well as "outside." Consider once again, the words of the psychoanalyst: "In our earliest days, but later in life too, when the self feels full of ruthless egoism or hate, . . . intense anxiety arises; the violence . . . raging within, and felt to be uncontrollable, is unutterably terrifying. It is then omnipotently denied and dissociated from the self, but is attributed instead to the persons inside who are the objects of the hate or greed, and are then felt to have provoked hate by their hate. It is they who are felt as bad: envious, robbing, ruthless, murderous. Thus it happens that a good helping person . . . changes shape and turns into a terrifying and dangerous enemy inside one; *one is felt to be possessed of a devil inside* [emphasis added]. . . . The bad objects within thus take their origin from our own dangerous and evil tendencies, disowned by us; characteristically, therefore, they are felt as 'foreign objects,' as an incubus, a nightmare, an appalling, gratuitous, and inescapable persecution."[18]]

In most of us these "primitive" images and fantasies lie dormant far below the threshold of consciousness. Revised and reworked into new structures after infancy, their connection to any actual behavior seems remote indeed. There is, however, one subsequent period of life when they may gain new energy and find new pathways to expression. This is the period of adolescence. Again, in most of us the developmental residues of earliest life remain largely suppressed (or modified and controlled) *even* during adolescence. But for a few with psychic "deficits" of one sort or another, the odds of a breakthrough are much increased.[19]

The central tasks of adolescence, as understood by current psychoanalytic theory, are twofold: first, to shift from the original "infantile" object-ties toward more mature levels of psycho-sexual functioning, and, second, to rework the "nuclear self" around goals, ideals, and a sense of inner "identity" appropriate to the adult life-situation. Both of these tasks, however, entail some return to earlier developmental positions: one must first go backward in order ultimately to be free to move forward. As a leading theorist has put it: "The significant emotional needs and conflicts of early childhood must be recapitulated before new solutions with qualitatively different instinctual aims and ego interests can be found." Thus, "adolescent regression not only is unavoidable, it is obligatory . . . [and] phase specific."[20]

On the side of psychosexual development this means, more specifically, a renewal of both oedipal and *pre-*oedipal issues. And the latter are of special interest here. Adolescent *girls,* in particular, experience a powerful regressive pull toward the "pre-oedipal mother." This, in turn, calls forth resistances and defenses (to avoid "remaining attached to a homosexual object and thus fatally rupturing the development of femininity").[21] The ensuing tug-of-war may generate all manner of behavioral and emotional stress: the (nowadays) familiar mother-daughter conflicts are only its most visible manifestation.

Our own culture accords a measure of tolerance to such conflicts; but in early New England the situation was probably quite different. The "regressive pull" and its defensive counterparts would obtain fewer chances for expression in everyday behavior; the "phase-specific" struggles were, for the most part, confined to the nether regions of the unconscious. Yet in some few cases they could not be so confined. Outward circumstance (such as a heightened level of public anxiety about witchcraft) and unusually severe inward pressures (in one or more individual persons) combined to "convert" them into behavior: hence the fits of the "afflicted girls." The fits bear the stamp of pre-oedipal regression at virtually every point. The "dependency" theme is unmistakable: the victim lies helpless before the whims of her witch-tormentor. The prevalence of "oral" imagery is another powerful indicator. The mouth becomes a prime conduit of attack (as with biting, but also, by way of implicit referents, the pricking and pinching so commonly mentioned) and of succor (the witch and her imps).

The witch, as represented in these fits, has an entirely negative coloration; but this, too, seems consistent with well-known inner processes. The relation to the pre-oedipal mother is always highly ambivalent; love and need mix uncomfortably with rage and resentment.[22] Moreover, the revival of this relation in adolescence necessarily spotlights the negative side; the victim seeks to ward it off, to repudiate it, or at all events to overcome it. [No doubt the figure of the witch was invested with some "oedipal" anger as well (i.e. in the adolescent girl, vis-à-vis her mother as possessor of the paternal "love object"). Indeed, the antagonism expressed here included at least three different psychodynamic undercurrents: (1) pre-oedipal rage; (2) a "reaction formation" against pre-oedipal love; and (3) direct oedipal rivalry. The present interpretation accords primacy to the first two elements, owing to the highly "primitive" nature of the symptom-formations. In fact, many young people experience preoedipal regression when faced with the (developmentally appropriate but always frightening) revival of oedipal issues near the onset of adolescence.] Her behavior has the characteristic structure of many such symptomatic outcomes in that it expresses a compromise between the original wish and the main line of defense. Occasionally the wish itself, with its loving connotations, rises near to the surface: the witch offers blandishments of one sort or another (for example, "a table spread with a variety of meats and . . . asked her to eat"),[23] and the victim describes herself as feeling "tempted." More often, though, the positive side of the ambivalence is suppressed—converted, indeed, to its opposite. This process, which theory calls "reaction formation," is recognizable in the compulsive and exaggerated character of its result. "Oh, you horrid wretch! You make my very heart grow cold within me!" says a victim to her spectral tormentor, in announcing a theme that she will endlessly belabor.[24] The cold heart, the scorn, the hatred are so emphatically expressed as to invite skepticism: she protests too much. Here, once again, she defends herself against the strength of her own underlying yearnings. [A version of these same inner processes is commonly observed among adolescents of our own day—as witness the following comment by Anna Freud: "Instead of displacing libido from the parents—or, more likely, after failing to do so—the adolescent ego may defend itself by turning the emotions felt toward them into their opposites. This changes love into hate, dependence into revolt, respect and admiration into contempt and derision. . . . The behavioral picture that emerges at this stage is that of an uncooperative and hostile adolescent. . . . The hostility and aggressiveness, which serve as a defense against object love in the beginning, soon become intolerable to the ego, are felt as threats, and are warded off in their own right. This may happen by means of projection; in that case the aggression is ascribed to parents who, consequently, become the adolescent's main oppressors and persecutors. In the clinical picture this appears first as the adolescent's suspiciousness and, when the projections increase, as paranoid behavior."[25] To this familiar sequence the "afflicted girls" of early New England seem to have added one further measure of defense—a "displacement" of the unaccepted impulses (both of the original object-love and the projected aggression) away from the true objects, i.e. the parental figures themselves, onto "witches," spectral and otherwise.]

The biological and biochemical changes which usher in the psychosexual conflicts of adolescence have a similar triggering effect in the realm of the "self"-system.[26] A rapid growth-spurt, the evident signs of sexual maturation, the emergence of new emotional experiences (especially in relation to the opposite sex) combine to foster a sense of inner discontinuity. There are, too, unsettling aspects of *psychosocial* development—a new awareness of the larger human community beyond the home of one's childhood, the community which holds one's ultimate fate. Hence a measure of "diffusion," even in a previously "cohesive self," is normal for adolescence. There is some revival of earlier narcissistic structures, which find outward manifestation in flights of blatantly "grandiose fantasy" and intense episodes of idealization (adolescent hero worship). An optimal passage through this period leads in the end to reintegration of the self, around the "push" of more realistic ambitions and the "pull" of mature ideals. But where development is less than optimal, the adolescent regression carries a threat of severe pathology. "Diffusion" amounts then to full-blown "fragmentation"; and the clinical picture may verge on psychosis.

The fits allegedly caused by witchcraft always implied fragmentation in their most characteristic features—the violent frenzies, the sudden surges of pain in widely separated parts of the body, the disorganization of functions such as speech, sight, and hearing. There were also implicit elements of "grandiosity" (the victim as *special* target for the forces of evil), demands for "mirroring" (from excited onlookers), "idealizing" attachments to figures of eminence (ministers come to offer counsel and prayers), and periods of "melancholy" intermission (between fits). In different but convergent ways these were the signs of a deeply disordered self.

One additional feature of some (not all) fits was an inability, over long periods, to *eat.* (The problem was sufficiently common for Cotton Mather to conclude: "It seems that long fasting is not only tolerable but strangely agreeable for such as have something more than ordinary to do with the invisible world.")[27] What makes this especially interesting is its apparent similarity to the clinical syndrome known today as *anorexia nervosa.* Here, indeed, is a rare opportunity for directly bridging the centuries with a single piece of symptomatic behavior. The modern-day victims of *anorexia* are also, for the most part, adolescent girls.

According to current authority, anorexic disorders are rooted in a desperate "struggle for individuation." The typical sufferer/patient attempts through her illness to throw off underlying (and initially unconscious) feelings of "being enslaved, exploited, and not . . . permitted to lead a life of . . . [her] own."[28] This feeling derives, in turn, from a long sequence of developmental experience. Outward impressions of the family setting are often quite favorable: the patient has been "obedient, . . . helpful, . . . eager to please, . . . precociously dependable, . . . excelling in school work"—indeed "the pride and joy of her parents." Closer inspection, however, reveals a broad pattern of overcontrol on the one side and overconformity on the other. One or both parents have been "overly helpful" and "overly rigid" in supervising all aspects of the patient's development, and "overly proud" of her accomplishments. The child has reacted with a sunny show of "pleasing compliance," while experiencing an inward sense of ineffectiveness, suffocation, and (deeper still) resentment and rage. The *anorexia* expresses a covert declaration of independence: by not eating, the patient declines further control, and, in real terms, precipitates an agonizing struggle with "authority" (parents and doctors).[29]

This short summary necessarily oversimplifies a large corpus of clinical writing, and the parts relating to familial interaction could not in any case be applied in witchcraft studies. (The data on the families of particular victims are simply too thin.) However, the diagnostic categories do make an interesting approach to certain of the leading themes found in the experience of the "afflicted" girls. As noted above, the fits conveyed a challenge to authority—and so, now, does *anorexia.* Behind the fits lay much "narcissistic" pathology—and in this respect as well *anorexia* seems broadly parallel. Anorexic patients are described as having especially "fragile self-esteem," as feeling "helpless" and "ineffectual"; and these are the most generalized symptomatic features of narcissistic disorders. The patient, in effect, has been used as an extension of the parent's own narcissism (hence the exaggerated elements of control and pride);[30] as a result, her own sense of self, and more especially of *body* self, is precarious. And this, too, is a plausible way of viewing the afflicted. [There is, in most anorexics, a manifest defect in "the perception, or cognitive interpretation, of stimuli arising in the body." In this connection an "inability to recognize hunger" is the "most pronounced deficiency"; however, the pattern extends to other areas as well (e.g. an indifference to changes in temperature, even of a quite extreme sort). It appears "that such patients experience their bodily sensations in a way that is bewildering and foreign to them"; and they have similar difficulty "in identifying [their own] emotional states."[31] A sense of self that includes seemingly "foreign" elements is the common *residuum* in both anorexic patients and witchcraft victims troubled with fits.]

The discussion has reached, by a very roundabout route, an area of convergence in the experience of the three leading sub-groups of witchcraft victims. The women in midlife, the cohort of younger men, and now the afflicted girls seem—in different ways and for different reasons—to have marked out a common center of preoccupation. It is not altogether easy to characterize, but such terms as control, autonomy, and self have appeared again and again. . . .

Notes

1 "The Determinants of Personality Formation," in Clyde Kluckohn and Henry A. Murrays, eds., *Personality in Nature, Society, and Culture,* 2nd ed. (New York, 1953), 53.

2 See pp. 144-45.

3 See John Demos, *A Little Commonwealth* (New York, 1970), 68-69.

4 In one sample of seventeenth-century New England women, 65 percent had their last child after the age of forty. See Patricia Trainor O'Malley, "Rowley, Massachusetts, 1639-1730: Dissent, Division and Delimitation in a Colonial Town" (unpublished Ph.D. diss., Boston College, 1975), 211.

5 See, for example, B. L. Neugarten, V. Wood, R. J. Kraines, and B. Loomis, "Women's Attitudes toward Menopause," in B. L. Neugarten, ed., *Middle Age and Aging* (Chicago, 1968), 195-200; K. Stern and M. Prados, "Personality Studies in Menopausal Women," *American Journal of Psychiatry,* CIII (1946), 358-67; and P. Weideger, *Menstruation and Menopause* (New York, 1976). For a survey of the literature on this subject see S. M. McKinlay and J. B. McKinlay, "Selected Studies of the Menopause: An Annotated Bibliography," in *Journal of Biosocial Science,* V (1973), 533-55.

6 For an especially interesting discussion of this phenomenon see David Gutmann, "The Cross-Cultural Perspective: Notes toward a Comparative Psychology of Aging," in J. E. Birren and K. W. Schaie, eds., *Handbook of the Psychology of Aging* (New York, 1977), 302-26.

7 See Sacvan Bercovitch, *The Puritan Origins of the American Self* (New Haven, Conn., 1975), ch. 1; Richard L. Bushman, *From Puritan to Yankee: Character and the Social Order in Connecticut, 1690-1765* (New York, 1967), ch. 1; Philip J. Greven, Jr., *The Protestant Temperament: Patterns of Child-Rearing, Religious Experience, and the Self in Early America* (New York, 1977); and Emory B. Elliott, *Power and the Pulpit in Puritan New England* (Princeton, N.J., 1975), chs. 1-2.

8 Demos, *A Little Commonwealth,* ch. 10.

9 Philip J. Greven, Jr., "Family Structure in Seventeenth-Century Andover, Massachusetts," *William and Mary Quarterly,* 3rd ser., XXIII (1966), 234-56.

10 There are scattered references to the everyday activities of adolescent girls in court records from early New England. On average age at marriage, see Demos, *A Little Commonwealth,* 151, and Philip J. Greven, Jr., *Four Generations: Population, Land, and Family in Colonial Andover, Massachusetts* (Ithaca, N.Y., 1970), 121. On age at menarche see Peter Laslett, "Age at Menarche in Europe Since the Eighteenth Century," in Theodore K. Rabb and Robert I. Rotberg, eds., *The Family in History: Interdisciplinary Essays* (New York, 1976), 28-47.

11 These issues are discussed at some length in Demos, *A Little Commonwealth,* 145-50. For a different line of interpretation, see Ross Beales, "In Search of the Historical Child: Miniature Adulthood and Youth in Colonial New England," in *American Quarterly,* XXVII (1975), 379-398.

12 The reference is to Martha Goodwin, a girl of thirteen who experienced severe fits in and around her home at Boston in the year 1688. A long account of this case was published by Cotton Mather in his "Memorable Providences, Relating to Witchcrafts and Possessions," and reprinted in Burr, ed., *Narratives,* 111.

13 *Ibid.,* 109.

14 *Ibid.,* 119.

15 *Ibid.,* 107.

16 The experience of Elizabeth Knapp makes an obvious case in point. But no less was true of the Goodwin children of Boston (see *ibid.,* 99-131), Ann Cole of Hartford (*ibid.,* 18-21), and of course the various "afflicted children" at the Salem trials in 1692-93.

17 Joan Riviere, "On the Genesis of Psychical Conflict in Earliest Infancy," in M. Klein, P. Heimann, S. Isaacs, and J. Riviere, *Developments in Psychoanalysis* (London, 1952), 50.

18 Joan Riviere, "The Unconscious Phantasy of an Inner World Reflected in Examples from Literature," in M. Klein *et al., New Directions in Psychoanalysis* (London, 1955), 364-65.

19 The overall view of adolescence presented here draws heavily on the work of Peter Blos—especially his book *On Adolescence: A Psychoanalytic Interpretation* (New York, 1962). See also his essays "Character Formation

in Adolescence," in *The Psychoanalytic Study of the Child,* XXIII (1968), 245-63, and "The Second Individuation Process of Adolescence," in *ibid.,* XXV (1970), 162-86.

[20] Blos, *On Adolescence,* 11; Blos, "Character Formation in Adolescence," 253.

[21] Blos, *On Adolescence,* 68.

[22] *Ibid.,* 28ff.

[23] Examination of Mercy Disborough and Elizabeth Clawson (Stamford, Connecticut, May 27-28, 1692), manuscript paper in the Willys Papers, W-19.

[24] The words are those of Mercy Short, as quoted by Cotton Mather; see Burr, ed., *Narratives,* 268.

[25] Anna Freud, "Adolescence," in *The Psychoanalytic Study of the Child,* XIII (1958), 270-71.

[26] On adolescence and the development of the self, see E. Wolf, J. Gedo, and D. Terman, "On the Adolescent Process as a Transformation of the Self," in *Journal of Youth and Adolescence,* I (1972), 257, 272, and Philip C. Gradolph, "Developmental Vicissitudes of the Self and the Ego-Ideal during Adolescence" (unpublished paper, presented at the Central States Conference of the American Society for Adolescent Psychiatry, October 1976).

[27] Among the victims of witchcraft who experienced this particular form of affliction were Mercy Short (see Burr, ed., *Narratives,* 266ff.), Margaret Rule (see *ibid.,* 312ff.), and Winifred Holman (see Middlesex Court Files, folder 25). The comment by Cotton Mather is included in his treatise "A Brand Plucked Out of the Burning," as reprinted in Burr, ed., *Narratives,* 266.

[28] Hilda Bruch, *Eating Disorders: Obesity, Anorexia Nervosa, and the Person Within* (New York, 1973), 85, 250. The work of Bruch and her colleagues has generally been regarded as definitive for *anorexia;* however, see also a recent study by Salvador Minuchin, Lester Baker, and Bernice Rosman, *Psychosomatic Families: Anorexia Nervosa in Context* (Cambridge, Mass., 1978).

[29] Bruch, *Eating Disorders,* 82ff.

[30] Some sufferers from *anorexia* seem, as children, to have been powerfully encouraged to "perform" in various public settings (e.g. family gatherings); the parents in one instance declared pride in their daughter for being a "complete exhibitionist." The element of narcissistic enhancement seems patent here; however, it must be set alongside the equally obvious tendency to narcissistic insult (deflation). Presumably it is the stop-and-go combination of enhancement and deflation which so distorts the experi-

ence of archaic "grandiosity." On these and related points see *ibid.,* 329ff.

[31] Ibid., 254.

FURTHER READING

Booth, Sally Smith. "The Law and Trial of Witchcraft," pp. 141-67. In *The Witches of Early America*, New York: Hastings House, 1975.

    Describes the laws and procedures involved in the witchcraft trials.

Boyer, Paul and Stephen Nissenbaum, eds. *Salem-Village Witchcraft.* Belmont, Cal.: Wadsworth Publishing, 1972, 416 p.

    Reference work of primary material that contains trial records, sermons, deeds, wills, depositions, petitions, maps, and genealogies.

———. *The Salem Witchcraft Papers.* 3 vols. New York: Da Capo Press, 1977.

    Essential reference work that contains historical documents pertaining to the trials, including testimony of the accused, letters, petitions, and official court judgments. Also features an introduction and extensive notes by Boyer and Nissenbaum.

Breslaw, Elaine G. *Tituba, Reluctant Witch of Salem.* New York: New York University Press, 1996, 243 p.

    Biography of the slave woman accused of launching the Salem witchcraft hysteria with her vivid confessions. Breslaw maintains that Tituba was an American Indian.

Gragg, Larry. *The Salem Witch Crisis.* New York: Praeger, 1992, 228 p.

    General overview that relates the events of the Salem crisis in a chronological narrative; includes a chapter on prison conditions.

Hall, David D. "Witchcraft and the Limits of Interpretation." *The New England Quarterly* 58, No. 2 (June 1985): 253-81.

    Assesses the individual works of several historians who wrote about witchcraft in New England.

———. *Witch-Hunting in Seventeenth-Century New England.* Boston: Northeastern University Press, 1991, 332 p.

    Focuses on many individual pre-1692 cases of witch persecution.

Hansen, Chadwick. *Witchcraft at Salem.* New York: George Braziller, 1969, 252 p.

    A controversial work which asserts that witchcraft did exist in Salem, that those afflicted behaved pathologically and not fraudulently, and that the clergy have been unfairly blamed for their role in the crisis.

Levin, David, ed. *What Happened in Salem?* New York: Harcourt, Brace & World, 1960, 238 p.

  Contains trial evidence, contemporary comments, court declarations, and two pieces of historical fiction, including Hawthorne's "Young Goodman Brown."

Mappen, Marc, ed. *Witches and Historians.* Malabar, Fla.: Kreiger Publishing, 1980, 120 p.

  Wide-ranging collection of essays by noted scholars.

Nelson, Mary. "Why Witches Were Women." In *Women: A Feminist Perspective,* edited by Jo Freeman, pp. 335-50. Palo Alto, Cal.: Mayfield Publishing, 1975.

  Discusses the belief in witchcraft during the middle ages as a response to certain problematic behaviors of women.

Robinson, Enders A. *The Devil Discovered.* New York: Hippocrene Books, 1991, 382 p.

  Provides a biography for each of the first seventy-five individuals accused of being witches at Salem.

Rosenthal, Bernard. *Salem Story.* Cambridge: Cambridge University Press, 1993, 286 p.

  Compares original documents with the myths that have grown out of the trials and concludes that much of the behavior in Salem was, in context, rational.

Cotton Mather

1663-1728

American minister, philosopher, historian, and essayist.

INTRODUCTION

Cotton Mather is one of the best known Puritans in American history. Born to two distinguished Massachusetts families, he served as a prominent minister at the Old North Church in Boston, as did his father, Increase Mather, and became an influential leader in the Puritan community. His scholarship was praised in both North America and Europe; he was elected a fellow of the Royal Society of London; and he published more than four hundred works. These have allowed scholars a better understanding of Puritan ideology and offer a rare glimpse into the daily life of seventeenth-century America. Mather is often remembered for his role in the Salem witch trials, primarily because he lent his support to the persecution of witches. However, Mather was not a high-profile player in the trials. He never attended them and his attention to witchcraft was slight considering his many other concerns. Still, his significance to the trials lies in the fact that he was an important figure in the New England church establishment who later admitted that persecution of alleged witches was wrong.

Biographical Information

Mather was born in Boston on 12 February 1663 to Increase Mather and Maria Cotton Mather. Both the Mather and Cotton families occupied positions of influence and prestige within the Puritan community and Mather enjoyed such privileges as a Harvard University education (AB 1678, MA 1681.) With these privileges also came responsibility; the Mathers saw themselves in a position of religious and intellectual leadership. Although he stuttered throughout his life, Mather served as minister of the Old North Church in Boston, under his more popular and charismatic father. He married three times and suffered the deaths of two wives and thirteen children—two in adulthood and nine as children. In 1688 Mather became involved in a witch trial in Boston. Long after the accused woman had confessed to witchcraft and been executed, Mather continued to work with the victims to insure their recovery and salvation. In 1692 Mather became interested in the famed witch trials in Salem, during which twenty people were executed and more than one hundred arrested. Mather publicly supported the state's

investigation into witchcraft but he warned judges to exercise caution and restraint in the prosecution of those accused. During the smallpox epidemic of 1720-21 Mather encouraged the people of Boston to be inoculated against the disease, a rare and progressive stand for the times. He never traveled beyond Massachusetts and died on 13 February 1728, five years after his father's death.

Major Works

Mather published more than four hundred works during his lifetime and left many other works in manuscript form. He wrote on subjects as varied as the weather, children, drunkenness, and political reform. He published fifty-one funeral sermons, sixteen histories of New England, ten works on medicine, and ten biographies, among other works. He is best known for four works: *Magnalia Christi Americana* (1702), *Bonifacius. An Essay Upon the Good* (1710), *Manuductio ad Ministerium* (1726), and *The Christian Philosopher*

(1720). In *The Christian Philosopher* Mather attempted to explain the connection between scripture, the teachings of God, and events in the natural world, the actions of God. In *Magnalia Christi Americana*, a history of Puritan America, Mather discusses his belief that the Puritans were analogous to the Israelites under Moses's leadership. The Puritans also had a covenant with God, one that had to be maintained with strict accordance to God's laws. God showed his anger and disappointment with the transgressions of the Puritans through physical acts such as storms and disease. The Devil attempted to thwart God's plans through witches. During his lifetime, Mather published two complete works, three portions of larger works, and one open letter to the governor on the subject of witchcraft. In addition, he wrote five letters, three manuscripts, and a proclamation. Mather was firm and unapologetic in his belief that witches existed, that they were doing the work of the Devil, and that if proven guilty (preferably through their confession) they should be put to death.

Critical Reception

Although Mather's writing on witchcraft comprises only sixteen of his more than four hundred works, it has drawn a majority of the scholarly attention. This interest began soon after Mather published *The Wonders of the Invisible World* (1692), an account of the witch trials. Robert Calef subsequently wrote *More Wonders of the Invisible World* (1700), an attack on Cotton and Increase Mather and their roles in the trials. Nineteenth-century historians, with a strong dislike for religious fervor, took up Calef's criticism of Mather, finding him to be the chief scapegoat for the witch hunts. Charles W. Upham claimed that Mather not only failed to stop the witch hunts but in fact helped orchestrate them. Upham's view, echoed by many other nineteenth-century historians, shaped popular opinion of Mather and the Puritans. However, scholars in the twentieth century have reconsidered Mather's intent and the extent to which he was involved. Like many other scholars, Richard H. Werking has argued that Mather's writings must be considered within the context of the Puritan ideology and concerns of the time. He argues that Mather tried to maintain a balance between protecting the lives of the accused and the spiritual safety of the community. A. Warren and Thomas J. Holmes have stressed the limited degree to which Mather concerned himself with witches and have argued that scholars have focused too much on Mather's connections to the trials. Warren has asserted that the witch trial was just one episode "in a busy life and scarcely touch[ed] him at center."

PRINCIPAL WORKS

Military Duties, Recommended to an Artillery Compa- *ny; A Their Election of Officers, in Charls-Town* (nonfiction) 1687
Memorable Providences, Relating to Witchcrafts and Possessions (nonfiction) 1689
Work upon the Ark: Meditations upon the Ark as a Type of the Church (sermon) 1689
The Wonderful Works of God Commemorated: Praises Bespoke for the God of Heaven, in a Thanksgiving Sermon (sermon) 1690
The Triumphs of the Reformed Religion, in America: The Life of the Renowned John Eliot; A Person justly Famous in the Church of God, Not only as an Eminent Christian and an Excellent Minister, among the English, but also, as a Memorable Evangelist among the Indians, of New-England (biography) 1691
Preparatory Meditations upon the Day of Judgement (sermon) 1692
†*The Wonders of the Invisible World: Observations as well Historical as Theological, upon the Nature, the Number, and the Operations of the Devils* (nonfiction) 1692
Early Religion, Urged in a Sermon, upon the Duties Wherein, and the Reasons, Wherefore, Young People Should Become Religious (sermon) 1694
Brontologia Sacra: The Voice of the Glorious God in the Thunder Explained and Applyed (nonfiction) 1695
Johannes in Ermo: Memoirs, Relating to the Lives, of the Ever-Memorable Mr. John Cotton, Who dyed, 23.d. 10.m. 1652. Mr. John Norton, Who Dyed 5.d. 2.m. 1663. Mr. John Wilson, Who Dyed, 7.d. 6.m. 1667. Mr. John davenport, Who Dyed, 15.d. 1.m. 1670 (biography) 1695
Piscator Evangelicus. Or, The Life of Mr. Thomas Hooker (biography) 1695
Humiliations follow'd with Deliverences: A Brief Discourse on the Matter and Method of that Humiliation which would be an Hopeful Symptom of our Deliverance from Calamity. Accompanied and Accommodated with a Narrative of a Notable Deliverance lately Received by some English Captives from the Hands of Cruel Indians (nonfiction) 1697
Pietas in Patriam: The Life of His Excellency Sir William Phips, Knt. Late Captain General, and Governour in Chief of the Province of the Massachusetts-Bay, New England (biography) 1697
The Bostonian Ebenezer: Some Historical Remarks, on the State of Boston, the Chief Town of New-England, and of the English America (history) 1698
Eleutheria: Or, An Idea of the Reformation in England: And a History of Non-Conformity in and since that Reformation, with Predictions of a more glorious Reformation and Revolution at hand (nonfiction) 1698
Magnalia Christi Americana; Or, the Ecclesiastical History of New-England, from Its First Planting in the Year 1620, unto the Year of our Lord, 1698 (history) 1702

The Best Ornaments of Youth. A Short Essay, on the Good Things, Which are found in Some, and should be found in All, young people (essay) 1707

A Memorial of the Present Deplorable State of New-England, With the many Disadvantages it lyes under, by the Male-Administration of their present Governour, Joseph Dudley (nonfiction) 1707

The Deplorable State of New-England, By Reason of a Covetous and Treacherous Governour, and Pusillanimous Counsellors (nonfiction) 1708

Bonifacius: An Essay Upon the Good, that is to be Devised and Designed, By Those Who Desire to Answer the Great End of Life, and to Do Good While they Live (essay) 1710

Nehemiah. A Brief Essay on Divine Consolations (essay) 1710

Theopolis Americana. An Essay on the Golden Street of the holy City: Publishing, A Testimony against the Corruptions of the Market-Place. With Some Good Hopes of Better Things to be yet seen in the American World (nonfiction) 1710

Perswasions from the Terror of the Lord. A Sermon Concerning The Day of Judgement; preached on a solemn occasion (sermon) 1711

Psalterium Americanum. The Book of Psalms, In a Translation Exactly conformed unto the Original; But All in Blank Verse (poetry) 1718

The Christian Philosopher: A Collection of the Best Discoveries in Nature, with Religious Improvements (nonfiction) 1720

India Christiana. A Discourse, Delivered unto the Commissioners, for the Propagation of the Gospel among the American Indians (nonfiction) 1721

A Father Departing. A Sermon on the Departure of the Venerable and Memorable Dr. Increase Mather, Who Expired Aug. 23, 1723. In the Eighty Fifth Year of his Age (sermon) 1723

The Voice of God in a Tempest. A Sermon Preached in the Time of the Storm; Wherin many and heavy and unknown Losses were Suffered at Boston (sermon) 1723

Manuductio ad Ministerium (theology) 1726

Ratio Disciplinae Fratrum Nov Anglorum: A Faithful Account of the Discipline Professed and Practised in the Churches of New-England (nonfiction) 1726

The Vial poured out upon the Sea. A Remarkable Relation Of certain Pirates Brought unto a Tragical and Untimely End (nonfiction) 1726

Agricola. Or, The Religious Husbandman: The Main Intentions of Religion, Served in the Business and Language of Husbandry (nonfiction) 1727

Boanerges. A Short Essay to preserve and strengthen the Good Impressions Produced by Earth-quakes (essay) 1727

The Terror of the Lord. Some Account of the Earthquake That Shook New-England In the Night, Between the 29 and the 30 of October. 1727 (nonfiction) 1727

*Also published as *Late Memorable Providences Relating to Witchcrafts and Possessions,* 1691.
†Also published as *The Wonders of the Invisible World: Being an Account of the Tryals of Several Witches, Lately Executed in New-England.*

CRITICISM

Cotton Mather (essay date 1693)

SOURCE: "The Author's Defense," in *Narratives of the Witchcraft Cases: 1648-1706,* edited by George Lincoln Burr, 1914. Reprint by Barnes & Noble Books, 1972, pp. 210-15.

[*Here, Mather defends the actions taken against those conspiring in the "Plot of the Devil against New England." His text was written in 1693.*]

'Tis, as I remember, the Learned Scribonius, [1] who Reports, that One of his Acquaintance, devoutly making his Prayers on the behalf of a Person molested by Evil Spirits, received from those Evil Spirits an horrible Blow over the Face: And I may my self Expect not few or small Buffetings from Evil Spirits, for the Endeavours wherewith I am now going to Encounter them. I am far from Insensible, That at this Extraordinary Time of the Devils Coming down in Great Wrath upon us, there are too many Tongues and Hearts thereby Set on Fire of Hell; that the various Opinions about the Witchcrafts which of Later Time have Troubled us, are maintained by some with so much Cloudy Fury, as if they could never be sufficiently Stated, unless written in the Liquor wherewith Witches use to write their Covenants; and that he who becomes an Author at such a Time, had need be Fenced with Iron, and the Staff of a Spear. The unaccountable Frowardness, Asperity, Untreatableness, and Inconsistency of many persons, every Day gives a Visible Exposition of that passage, *An Evil Spirit from the Lord came upon Saul;* and Illustration of that Story, *There met him two Possessed with Devils, exceeding Fierce, so that no man might pass by that way.* To send abroad a Book, among such Readers, were a very unadvised Thing, if a man had not such Reasons to give, as I can bring, for such an Undertaking. Briefly, I hope it cannot be said, They are all so; No, I hope the Body of this People, are yet in such a Temper, as to be capable of Applying their Thoughts, to make a Right Use of the Stupendous and prodigious Things that are happening among us: and because I was concern'd, when I saw that no Abler Hand Emitted any Essayes to Engage the Minds of this People in such Holy, Pious, Fruitful Improvements, as God would have to be made of His Amazing Dispensations now upon us, Therefore it is, that One of the Least among the Children of New-England, has here done, what is done. None, but the Father, who sees in Secret, knows the Heart-breaking Exercises, wherewith

I have Composed what is now going to be Exposed, Lest I should in any One Thing miss of Doing my Designed Service for His Glory, and for His People; But I am now somewhat comfortably Assured of His favourable Acceptance; and, I will not Fear; what can a Satan do unto me!

Having Performed Something of what God Required, in labouring to suit His Words unto His Works, at this Day among us, and therewithal handled a Theme that has been sometimes counted not unworthy the Pen, even of a King, it will easily be perceived, that some subordinate Ends have been considered in these Endeavours.

I have indeed set my self to Countermine the whole Plot of the Devil against New-England,[2] in every Branch of it, as far as one of my Darkness can comprehend such a Work of Darkness. I may add, that I have herein also aimed at the Information and Satisfaction of Good men in another Countrey, a Thousand Leagues off, where I have, it may be, More, or however, more Considerable Friends, than in My Own;[3] And I do what I can to have that Countrey, now as well as alwayes, in the best Terms with My Own. But while I am doing these things, I have been driven a little to do something likewise for My self; I mean, by taking off the false Reports and hard Censures about my Opinion in these matters, the Parters Portion, which my pursuit of Peace has procured me among the Keen. My hitherto Unvaried Thoughts are here Published; and, I believe, they will be owned by most of the Ministers of God in these Colonies; nor can amends be well made me, for the wrong done me, by other sorts of Representations.

In fine, For the Dogmatical part of my Discourse, I want no Defence; for the Historical part of it, I have a very Great One. The Lieutenant-Governour of New-England, having perused it, has done me the Honour of giving me a Shield,[4] under the Umbrage whereof I now dare to walk Abroad.

Reverend and Dear Sir,

You Very much Gratify'd me, as well as put a kind Respect upon me, when you put into my hands, Your Elaborate and most seasonable Discourse, entituled, *The Wonders of the Invisible World*. And having now Perused so fruitful and happy a Composure, upon such a Subject, at this Juncture of Time, and considering the Place that I Hold in the Court of Oyer and Terminer, still Labouring and Proceeding in the Trial of the persons Accused and Convicted for Witchcraft, I find that I am more nearly and highly concerned than as a meer Ordinary Reader, to Express my Obligation and Thankfulness to you for so great Pains; and cannot but hold my self many ways bound, even to the utmost of what is proper for me, in my present Publick Capacity, to

declare my Singular Approbation thereof. Such is Your Design, most plainly expressed throughout the whole; such Your Zeal for God, Your Enmity to Satan and his Kingdom, Your Faithfulness and Compassion to this poor people; Such the Vigour, but yet great Temper of your Spirit; Such your Instruction and Counsel, your Care of Truth, Your Wisdom and Dexterity in allaying and moderating that among us, which needs it; Such your Clear Discerning of Divine Providences and Periods, now running on apace towards their Glorious Issues in the World; and finally, Such your Good News of The Shortness of the Devils Time, That all Good Men must needs Desire the making of this your Discourse Publick to the World; and will greatly Rejoyce that the Spirit of the Lord has thus Enabled you to Lift up a Standard against the Infernal Enemy, that hath been Coming in like a Flood upon us. I do therefore make it my particular and Earnest Request unto you, that as soon as may be, you will Commit the same unto the Press accordingly. I am,

Your Assured Friend,

WILLIAM STOUGHTON

I Live by Neighbours that force me to produce these Undeserved Lines. But now, as when Mr. Wilson,[5] beholding a great Muster of Souldiers, had it by a Gentleman then present said unto him, "Sir, I'l tell you a great Thing: here is a mighty Body of People; and there is not Seven of them all but what Loves Mr. Wilson;" that Gracious Man presently and pleasantly Reply'd, "Sir, I'll tell you as good a thing as that; here is a mighty Body of People, and there is not so much as One among them all, but Mr. Wilson Loves him." Somewhat so: 'Tis possible that among this Body of People there may be few that Love the Writer of this Book; but give me leave to boast so far, there is not one among all this Body of People, whom this Mather would not Study to Serve, as well as to Love. With such a Spirit of Love, is the Book now before us written: I appeal to all this World; and if this World will deny me the Right of acknowledging so much, I Appeal to the Other, that it is Not written with an Evil Spirit: for which cause I shall not wonder, if Evil Spirits be Exasperated by what is Written, as the Sadducees doubtless were with what was Discoursed in the Days of our Saviour. I only Demand the Justice, that others Read it, with the same Spirit wherewith I writ it.[6]

. . . . .

But I shall no longer detain my Reader, from His expected entertainment, in a Brief Account of the Trials which have passed upon some of the Malefactors Lately Executed at Salem, for the Witchcrafts whereof they stood Convicted. For my own part, I was not Present at any of Them,[7] nor ever Had I any personal prejudice at the persons thus brought upon the Stage; much less at the Surviving Relations of those persons, with and for whom I would be as Hearty a mourner as any man Living in the World: The Lord Comfort them! But having Received a Command so to do,[8] I can do no other than shortly Relate the Chief Matters of fact, which occurr'd in the Trials of some that were Executed, in an Abridgment collected out of the Court-Papers, on this occasion put into my Hands.[9] You are to take the Truth, just as it was; and the Truth will hurt no good man. There might have been more of these, if my Book would not thereby have been swollen too big; and if some other worthy hands did not perhaps intend something further in these Collections;[10] for which cause I have only singled out Four or Five, which may serve to Illustrate the way of dealing, wherein Witchcrafts use to be concerned; and I Report matters not as an Advocate but as an Historian.

They were some of the Gracious Words inserted in the Advice, which many of the Neighbouring Ministers did this Summer humbly lay before our Honorable Judges, "We cannot but with all thankfulness acknowledge the success which the Merciful God has given unto the Sedulous and Assiduous endeavours of Our Honourable Rulers, to detect the abominable Witchcrafts which have been committed in the Country; Humbly Praying that the discovery of those mysterious and mischievous wickednesses, may be perfected."[11] If in the midst of the many Dissatisfactions among us, the publication of these Trials may promote such a pious Thankfulness unto God, for Justice being so far executed among us, I shall Rejoyce that God is Glorified; and pray that no wrong steps of ours may ever sully any of His Glorious Works. . . .

Notes

[1] Wilhelm Adolf Scribonius, a Hessian scholar, is best known in the literature of witchcraft as the chief advocate of the water ordeal. . . for the detection of witches. This story is told on ff. 82-83 of his *Physiologia Sagarum* (Marburg, 1588—the full title is *De Sagarum Natura et Potestate, deque his recte cognoscendis et puniendis Physiologia*), and in English by Baxter, *Worlds of Spirits,* p. 104.

[2] As to this "plot of the Devil," see Mather's own words (*Wonders,* pp. 16-19, 25, not here reprinted): "we have been advised . . . that a Malefactor, accused of Witchcraft as well as Murder, and Executed in this place more than Forty Years ago, did then give Notice of An Horrible Plot against the Country by Witchcraft, and a Foundation of Witchcraft then laid, which if it were not seasonably discovered would probably Blow up, and pull down all the Churches in the Country." "We have now with Horror," he adds, "seen the Discovery of such a Witchcraft!" and from the confessions at Salem he learns that "at prodigious Witch-Meetings the Wretches have proceeded so far as to

Concert and Consult the Methods of Rooting out the Christian Religion from this Country" and setting up instead of it a "Diabolism." Not even this is all: "it may be fear'd that, in the Horrible Tempest which is now upon ourselves, the design of the Devil is to sink that Happy Settlement of Government wherewith Almighty God has graciously enclined Their Majesties to favour us."

[3] It is of England, of course, that he speaks.

[4] As to Lieutenant-Governor Stoughton, head of the court which had tried the witch cases, see above, . . . note 2. . . . His "shield" means the following letter.

[5] Doubtless the Rev. John Wilson (d. 1667), the first minister of Boston.

[6] There now follow the miscellaneous matters described in the introduction, making up more than half of his volume.

[7] He must at least have been present at some of the examinations (like those described by Lawson) preceding the trials; for in his *Diary* (I. 151), commending the judges, he adds, "and my Compassion, upon the Sight of their Difficulties, raised by my Journeyes to Salem, the chief Seat of these diabolical Vexations, caused mee yett more to do so." From attending the trials he had excused himself (see the letter mentioned on p. 194, note 5) on the score of ill health.

[8] From the governor; see above, p. 194, and p. 250.

[9] See introduction.

[10] Meaning, doubtless, Hale and Noyes. See p. 206, above.

[11] This is the second paragraph in the reply of the ministers of Boston, June 15, 1692, to the request of the governor and Council for advice. (See p. 194, above.) It was drawn up by Cotton Mather himself.

Robert Calef (essay date 1697)

SOURCE: "Criticism of Cotton Mather's *Life of Phips* (1697)," in *Narratives of the Witchcraft Cases: 1648-1706,* edited by George Lincoln Burr, 1914. Reprint by Barnes & Noble Books, pp. 388-93.

[*In the following excerpt, written in 1697, Calef attacks Mather's views on witchcraft.*]

. . . Mr. C. M. having been very forward to write Books of Witchcraft, has not been so forward either to explain or defend the Doctrinal part thereof, and his belief (which he had a Years time to compose) he durst not venture so as to be copied.[1] Yet in this of the Life of Sir William he sufficiently testifies his retaining that Heterodox belief, seeking by frightfull stories of the sufferings of some, and the refined sight of others, etc., P. 69 to obtrude upon the World, and confirm it in such a belief, as hitherto he either cannot or will not defend, as if the Blood already shed thereby were not sufficient.

Mr. I. Mather, in his *Cases of Conscience*, P. 25, tells of a Bewitched Eye, and that such can see more than others. They were certainly bewitched Eyes that could see as well shut as open, and that could see what never was, that could see the Prisoners upon the Afflicted, harming of them, when those whose Eyes were not bewitched could have sworn that they did not stir from the Bar. The Accusers are said to have suffered much by biting, P. 73. And the prints of just such a set of Teeth, as those they Accused, had, but such as had not such bewitch'd Eyes have seen the Accusers bite themselves, and then complain of the Accused. It has also been seen when the Accused, instead of having just such a set of Teeth, has not had one in his head. They were such bewitched Eyes that could see the Poisonous Powder (brought by Spectres P. 70.) And that could see in the Ashes the print of the Brand, there invisibly heated to torment the pretended Sufferers with etc.

These with the rest of such Legends have this direct tendency, *viz.* To tell the World that the Devil is more ready to serve his Votaries, by his doing for them things above or against the course of Nature, shewing himself to them, and making explicit contract with them, etc., than the Divine Being is to his faithful Servants, and that as he is willing, so also able to perform their desires. The way whereby these People are believed to arrive at a power to Afflict their Neighbours, is by a compact with the Devil, and that they have a power to Commissionate him to those Evils, P. 72. However Irrational, or Inscriptural such Assertions are, yet they seem a necessary part of the Faith of such as maintain the belief of such a sort of Witches.

As the Scriptures know nothing of a covenanting or commissioning Witch, so Reason cannot conceive how Mortals should by their Wickedness arrive at a power to Commissionate Angels, Fallen Angels, against their Innocent Neighbours. But the Scriptures are full in it, and the Instances numerous, that the Almighty, Divine Being has this prerogative to make use of what Instrument he pleaseth, in Afflicting any, and consequently to commissionate Devils: And tho this word commissioning, in the Authors former Books, might be thought to be by inadvertency; yet now after he hath been caution'd of it, still to persist in it seems highly Criminal. And therefore in the name of God, I here charge such belief as guilty of Sacriledge in the highest Nature, and so much worse than stealing Church Plate, etc., As it is a higher Offence to steal any of the glo-rious Attributes of the Almighty, to bestow them upon Mortals, than it is to steal the Utensils appropriated to his Service. And whether to ascribe such power of commissioning Devils to the worst of Men, be not direct Blasphemy, I leave to others better able to determine. When the Pharisees were so wicked as to ascribe to Beelzebub, the mighty works of Christ (whereby he did manifestly shew forth his Power and Godhead) then it was that our Saviour declar'd the Sin against the Holy Ghost to be unpardonable.

When the Righteous God is contending with Apostate Sinners, for their departures from him, by his Judgments, as Plagues, Earthquakes, Storms and Tempests, Sicknesses and Diseases, Wars, loss of Cattle, etc. Then not only to ascribe this to the Devil, but to charge one another with sending or commissionating those Devils to these things, is so abominable and so wicked, that it requires a better Judgment than mine to give it its just denomination.

But that Christians so called should not only charge their fellow Christians therewith, but proceed to Tryals and Executions; crediting that Enemy to all Goodness, and Accuser of the Brethren, rather than believe their Neighbours in their own Defence; This is so Diabolical a Wickedness as cannot proceed, but from a Doctrine of Devils; how far damnable it is let others discuss. Tho such things were acting in this Country in Sir Williams time, yet p. 65, there is a Discourse of a Guardian Angel, as then over-seeing it, which notion, however it may suit the Faith of Ethnicks,[2] or the fancies of Trithemius;[3] it is certain that the Omnipresent Being stands not in need as Earthly Potentates do, of governing the World by Vicegerents. And if Sir William had such an Invisible pattern to imitate, no wonder tho some of his Actions were unaccountable, especially those relating to Witchcraft: For if there was in those Actions an Angel super-intending, there is little reason to think it was Gabriel or the Spirit of Mercury, nor Hanael the Angel or Spirit of Venus, nor yet Samuel the Angel or Spirit of Mars; Names feigned by the said Trithemius, etc. It may rather be thought to be Apollyon, or Abaddon.

Obj.[4] But here it will be said, "What, are there no Witches? Do's not the Law of God command that they should be extirpated? Is the Command vain and Unintelligible?" *Sol.*[5] For any to say that a Witch is one that makes a compact with, and Commissions Devils, etc., is indeed to render the Law of God vain and Unintelligible, as having provided no way whereby they might be detected, and proved to be such; And how the Jews waded thro this difficulty for so many Ages, without the Supplement of Mr. Perkins and Bernard thereto, would be very mysterious. But to him that can read the Scriptures without prejudice from Education, etc., it will manifestly appear that the Scripture is full and Intelligible, both as to the Crime and means to detect the culpable. He that shall hereafter see any person, who to confirm People in a false belief, about the power of Witches and Devils, pretending to a sign to confirm it, such as knocking off of invisible Chains with the hand, driving away Devils by brushing, striking with a Sword or Stick, to wound a person at a great distance, etc., may (according to that head of Mr. Gauls, quoted by Mr. C. M. and so often herein before recited, and so well proved by Scripture) conclude that he has seen Witchcraft performed.

If Baalam became a Sorcerer by Sacrifizing and Praying to the true God against his visible people; Then he that shall pray that the afflicted (by their Spectral Sight) may accuse some other Person (whereby their reputations and lives may be indangered) such will justly deserve the Name of a Sorcerer. If any Person pretends to know more then[6] can be known by humane means, and professeth at the same time that they have it from the Black-Man, *i.e.* the Devil, and shall from hence give Testimony against the Lives of others, they are manifestly such as have a familiar Spirit; and if any, knowing them to have their Information from the Black-Man, shall be inquisitive of them for their Testimony against others, they therein are dealing with such as have a Familiar-Spirit.

And if these shall pretend to see the dead by their Spectral Sight, and others shall be inquisitive of them, and receive their Answers what it is the dead say, and who it is they accuse, both the one and the other are by Scripture Guilty of Necromancy.

These are all of them crimes as easily proved as any whatsoever, and that by such proof as the Law of God requires, so that it is no Unintelligible Law.

But if the Iniquity of the times be such, that these Criminals not only Escape Indemnified,[7] but are Incouraged in their Wickedness, and made use of to take away the Lives of others, this is worse than a making the Law of God Vain, it being a rendring of it dangerous, against the Lives of Innocents, and without all hopes of better, so long as these Bloody Principles remain.

As long as Christians do Esteem the Law of God to be Imperfect, as not describing that crime that it requires to be Punish'd by Death;

As long as men suffer themselves to be Poison'd in their Education, and be grounded in a False Belief by the Books of the Heathen;

As long as the Devil shall be believed to have a Natural Power, to Act above and against a course of Nature;

As long as the Witches shall be believed to have a Power to Commission him;

As long as the Devils Testimony, by the pretended afflicted, shall be received as more valid to Condemn, than their Plea of Not Guilty to acquit;

As long as the Accused shall have their Lives and Liberties confirmed and restored to them, upon their Confessing themselves Guilty;

As long as the Accused shall be forc't to undergo Hardships and Torments for their not Confessing;

As long as Tets for the Devil to Suck are searched for upon the Bodies of the accused, as a token of guilt;

As long as the Lords Prayer shall be profaned, by being made a Test, who are culpable;

As long as Witchcraft, Sorcery, Familiar Spirits, and Necromancy, shall be improved to discover who are Witches, etc.,

So long it may be expected that Innocents will suffer as Witches.

So long God will be Daily dishonoured, And so long his Judgments must be expected to be continued.

Notes

[1] In a part of his book not here reprinted (pp. 85 ff.) Calef speaks more fully of this paper, lent him early in 1695, but on condition of its return within a fortnight and uncopied. It was perhaps the MS. described by Poole (*Memorial History,* II. 152, note) as now in the possession of the Massachusetts Historical Society, and called "Cotton Mather's belief and practice in those thorny difficulties which have distracted us in the day of temptation"—having "marginal reflections in another hand." [Since the foregoing words were written, this conjecture has been proved true.]. . . .

[2] Pagans.

[3] A German abbot and scholar who in the early sixteenth century wrote most credulously about witches and angels.

[4] *Objection.*

[5] *Solution.*

[6] *I.e.,* than.

[7] Unpunished.

Barrett Wendell (essay date 1891)

SOURCE: "Witchcraft," in *Cotton Mather: The Puritan Priest,* Dodd, Mead, and Company, 1891, pp. 88-123.

[*In the following excerpt, Wendell provides a detailed account of Mather's role in the witchcraft trials and surveys the author's writings on witchcraft.*]

What happened in the next two years was of less consequence to New England than the matters we have been considering. To Cotton Mather, however, and to the cause which throughout his life he had most at heart,—the preservation, the restoration, of the pure polity of the fathers,—these two years were fatal. It was the great tragedy of witchcraft, I think, that finally broke the power of theocracy: it was almost surely the part Cotton Mather played in it that made his life, for the five and thirty years that were left him, a life—at least publicly—of constant, crescent failure. Tragic even if we join with those who read in the records left us no more worthy story than that of frustrated ambition, his career takes an aspect of rare tragic dignity if in his endless, undiscouraged efforts to do God's work we can honestly see what he tells us was there,—an all-mastering faith that the fathers were divinely right, that all which tended away from their teaching was eternally wrong, and that his own failure meant nothing less than the failure of the kingdom of Christ in a land whither Christ's servants had come with high hopes that here, as nowhere else on earth, Christ's kingdom should prevail.

Sir William Phipps, the new Governor, is in certain aspects a most romantic figure. The obscure son of a settler in the wilds of Maine, he was first an apprentice to a ship-carpenter: coming to Boston early in manhood, he learned there to read and write, and soon married a widow of position and fortune decidedly above his own. Prospering for a while as a shipbuilder, he soon took to the sea; and by the year 1684 he had so distinguished himself that he was put in command of a frigate, in which he sailed to the West Indies in search of a wrecked Spanish treasure-ship. After various adventures and mutinies, he actually discovered the wreck. He brought back to England treasure to the amount of three hundred thousand pounds, in return for which feat he was knighted by James II. And in Sir Edmund Andros's time he came home to Boston with a comfortable fortune of his own and the office of High Sheriff of New England. By no means in sympathy with the Governor, he soon went back to England for a while, where he had more or less to do with Increase Mather. In 1690 he was again in Boston, where, as we have seen before, he took command of the successful expedition against Port Royal. The first real rebuff in the career of this archetype of self-made Yankees was the failure of the expedition which, too

late in the same year, he led against Quebec. Undiscouraged, he went back to England with plans for a fresh expedition against the French. This came to nothing; but Increase Mather, who saw much of him in London, pitched on him, and obtained the approval of King William for him, as the man of men to be the first Governor of the royal Province of Massachusetts.

It would have been hard to find a governor who should promise more for the polity to which the Mathers gave every energy of their lives. A man of the people, conspicuous above any one else of his time for just that kind of material success which most touches the popular imagination, Sir William, though hotheaded and full of the pompous tyranny of the quarterdeck, seems to have had one of those big, hearty, human natures which command liking even where one cannot approve. He might be expected at once to command the sympathy of the people, who would see in him an example of what any one of them might become, and to be very firm in his determination to have his own way. If such a man be on the right course, he will carry things farther than any other kind. And, like most self-made Yankees, Sir William was on exactly the right course, from the point of view of the clergy. As a class, self-made men to this day grow up with a rather blind faith in the superiority to other men of ministers of the Gospel: in worldly moments they may smile at their spiritual advisers as impractical; but they go to church, and when it comes to spending their money they are very apt to spend it as the minister tells them to. And more than most self-made men Sir William looked up to the clergy, and most of all the clergy to the Mathers. It was Increase Mather's sermon on "The day of trouble is near," in 1674,[1] that first made him sensible of his sins; it was by Cotton Mather, just before the expedition to Port Royal, in 1690, that he was baptized and received into the communion of the faithful; it was to Increase Mather that he owed the office which crowned his worldly ambition. Clearly such a man as this might be trusted, if anybody might, to do the will of God as the Mathers expounded it. And the Mathers meant to expound it in the good old orthodox way; and the new Charter gave the Governor more power than he had ever had under the old; so there was never a moment when the hopes of Christ's kingdom looked brighter.

To understand what followed, we may well recall some things at which we have glanced already. In the view of the Puritans, the continent of America, whither they came to live in accordance with no laws but those of Scripture, had been until their coming the special territory of the Devil. Here he had ruled for centuries, unmolested by the opposing power of the Gospel: whoever doubted this had only to look at the degradation of his miserable subjects, the native Indians, to be pretty well convinced. The landing of the Puritans was a direct invasion of his territories. He fought it in all manner of ways,—material and spiritual. The physical hardship of the earlier years of the settlement was largely his work; so were the disturbances raised within the Colonies by heretics and malcontents; so, more palpably still, were the Indian wars in which his subjects rose in arms against the servants of Christ; so, too, were certain phenomena that every one at the present day would instantly recognize as natural: more than once Cotton Mather remarks as clearly diabolical the fact that the steeples of churches are oftener struck by lightning than any other structures. And from the very earliest days of the settlement the Devil had waged his unholy war in a more subtle way still: appearing in person, or in the person of direct emissaries from the invisible world, to more than a few hapless Christians, he had constantly striven with bribes and threats to seduce them to his service. Whoever yielded to him was rewarded by the possession of supernatural power, which was secretly exerted for all manner of malicious purposes; these were the witches: whoever withstood him was tortured in mind and body almost beyond the power of men to bear; these were the bewitched. There was no phase of the Devil's warfare so insidious, so impalpable, so dangerous, as this: in the very heart of the churches, in the pulpits themselves, witches might lurk. Their crime was the darkest of all,—deliberate treason to the Lord; but it was the hardest of all to detect and to prove,—the most horrible, both in its nature and in its possibility of evildoing. Mysterious, horrible, inevitable, it demanded every effort of Christians to withstand its subtle power.

To the Mathers, I believe, all this was very real. In 1684 Increase Mather had written a book against witchcraft. Two years later, as we have seen, Cotton Mather had had what he might well have believed a special message from Heaven that his chief mission for the moment was to fight the witches. The sins of the Colonists had brought on them the most terrible of their misfortunes: the Charter was gone, and Kirk was coming with his red-coats; and, in the deep agony of secret prayer, Cotton Mather was beseeching God to show mercy to New England, and promising, when such mercy came, what special services the Lord might see fit to demand. The good news came, at a moment when the Lord was rewarding his prayers by visions of a white-robed angel from whose lips he heard assurances of Divine favour. King Charles was dead, Kirk was coming no longer. His prayers had availed to save New England from the worst of her dangers. What should he do for the Lord? At that very moment, as we have seen, witchcraft was abroad. It was his duty to collect testimony against it, to denounce it, to fight it with all his might. From that moment, apparently, he began. And the more he studied it, the more real and terrible he found it. In 1688 there was a sad outbreak of it in Boston: Cotton Mather took into his own house one of the afflicted children, whose behaviour as he relates it was in all respects such as to increase his belief both in the reality of the Devil's work, and in the divine sanction of his own efforts against it. And now, in 1692, when the prayers of New England for a righteous charter had been granted, when the best of governors was come, ready to put into execution the best of policies, when at last the material prospects of Christ's kingdom were fairer than for years before, the Devil began such a spiritual assault on New England as had never before been approached.

The story of Salem Witchcraft has been told by Upham with a fulness and a fairness that leave nothing to be added. But he fails, I think, sympathetically to understand a fact which he emphasizes with characteristic honesty,—the tremendous influence on human beings of that profound realizing sense of the mysteries that surround us, to which those who do not share it give the name superstition.

At various periods of history epidemics of superstition have appeared, sometimes in madly tragic forms, sometimes, as in modern spiritualism, in grotesquely comic ones. These are generally classed as pure delusions, based on no external facts. But for my part, though I may claim none of the authority which would come from special study of the subject, I am strongly inclined to believe that from the earliest recorded times a certain pretty definite group of mysterious phenomena has, under various names, really shown itself throughout human society. Oracles, magic, witchcraft, animal magnetism, spiritualism,—call the phenomena what you will,—seem to me a fact. Certain phases of it are beginning to be understood under the name of hypnotism. Other phases, after the best study that has been given them, seem to be little else than deliberate fraud and falsehood; but they are fraud and falsehood, if this be all they are, of a specific kind, unchanged for centuries. The evidence at the trial of the Maréchal de Rais, a soldier of Joan of Arc and the original of the tale of Blue-Beard, relates phenomena that anybody can see to-day by paying a dollar to a "materializing medium." And some of them are very like what are related in the trials of the Salem witches. So specific is the fraud, if only fraud it be, that it may well be regarded, I think, as a distinct mental, or perhaps rather moral disorder.

With no sort of pretension to scientific knowledge, I have found that a guess I made in talk some years ago throws what may be a little light on many of the mysterious phenomena that in Cotton Mather's time were deemed indisputably diabolical. I shall venture, then, to state it here, to be taken for no more than a layman's guess may be worth. If, as modern science tends to show, human beings are the result of a process of evolution from lower forms of life, there must have been in our ancestral history a period when the intelligence of our progenitors was as different from the modern human mind—the only form of intelligence familiar to our experience or preserved in the records of our race—as were their remote aquatic bodies from the human form we know to-day. To-day we can perceive with any approach to distinctness only what reveals itself to us through the medium of our five senses; but we have only to look at the intricate wheelings of a flock of birds, at the flight of a carrier pigeon, at the course of a dog who runs straight home over a hundred miles of strange country, to see more than a probability that animals not remote from us physically have perceptions to which we are strangers. It seems wholly conceivable, then, that in the remote psychologic past of our race there may have been in our ancestors certain powers of perception which countless centuries of disuse have made so rudimentary that in our normal condition we are not conscious of them. But if such there were, it would not be strange that, in abnormal states, the rudimentary vestiges of these disused powers of perception might sometimes be revived. If this were the case, we might naturally expect two phenomena to accompany such a revival: in the first place, as such powers of perception, from my very hypothesis, belong normally to a period in the development of our race when human society and what we call moral law have not yet appeared, we should expect them to be intimately connected with a state of emotion that ignores what we call the moral sense, and so to be accompanied by various forms of misconduct; in the second place, as our chief modern means of communication—articulate language—belongs to a period when human intelligence has assumed its present form, we should expect to find it inadequate for the expression of facts which it never professed to cover, and so we should expect such phenomena as we are considering to be accompanied by an erratic, impotent inaccuracy of statement, which would soon shade into something indistinguishable from deliberate falsehood. In other words, such phenomena would naturally involve in whoever abandons himself to them a mental and moral degeneracy which any one who believes in a personal devil would not hesitate to ascribe to the direct intervention of Satan.

Now what disposes me, scientifically a layman I must repeat, to think that my guess may have something in it is that mental and moral degeneracy—credulity and fraud—seem almost invariably so to entangle themselves with occult phenomena that many cool-headed people are disposed to assert the whole thing a lie. To me, as I have shown, it does not seem so simple. I am much disposed to think that necromancers, witches, mediums,—what not,—actually do perceive in the infinite realities about us things that are imperceptible to normal human beings; but that they perceive them only at a sacrifice of their higher faculties—mental and moral—not inaptly symbolized in the old tales of those who sell their souls.

If this be true, witchcraft is not a delusion: it is a thing more subtly dangerous still. Such an epidemic of it as came to New England in 1692 is as diabolical a fact as human beings can know: unchecked, it can really work mischief unspeakable. I have said enough, I think, to show why I heartily sympathize with those who in 1692 did their utmost to suppress it; to show, too, why the fatally tragic phase of the witch trials seems to me, not the fact that there was no crime to condemn, but the fact that the evidence on which certain wretched people were executed proves, on scrutiny, utterly insufficient. It was little better than to-day would be the ravings of a clairvoyant against one accused of theft. And yet, if there be anything in my guess, this too is just what we might expect. Not knowing what they did, the judges would strain every nerve—just as in their rapt ecstasies the Mathers strained every nerve, along with their Puritan fellows, and the saints of every faith—to awaken from the lethargy of countless ages those rudimentary powers which can be awakened only at the expense of what we think the higher ones that have supplanted them. The motive may make a difference: he who strives to serve God may end as he begun, a better man than he who consents to serve the Devil. But, for all that, bewitched and judges alike, the startled ministers to whom the judges turned for counsel, and perhaps not a few of the witches too, who may well have believed in themselves, vie with one another in a devil's race, harking back to mental and moral depths from which humanity has taken countless centuries to rise.

Whoever cares to know in detail the story of 1692 may read it in Upham, or in Palfrey. In brief, the children of Mr. Parris, minister of Salem Village, were seized early in the year with disorders which seemed of no earthly origin. They accused certain neighbours of bewitching them; the neighbours were arrested. The troubles and the accusations spread with the speed of any panic. By the time Sir William assumed the government, the whole region was in an agony of superstitious terror; and whoever raised his voice against the matter fell under suspicion of league with the Devil. At that moment, as the old judicial system had fallen with the Charter, there were no regular courts. Within a few weeks, Sir William, full of the gravity of the situation, and probably under the direct advice of the Mathers, appointed a special Court of Oyer and Terminer to try the witches. William Stoughton, the Deputy Governor, was made Chief Justice: his six associates were gentlemen of the highest station and character in the Province: among them was Samuel Sewall, whose Diary I have so often quoted. On the 2d of June this court condemned one Bridget Bishop: on the 10th she was executed for witchcraft. Before proceeding further, the court consulted the ministers of Boston and the neighbourhood. The answer of the ministers is said to have been drawn up by Cotton Mather: in general terms it urged "the importance of caution and cir-

cumspection in the methods of examination," but "earnestly recommended that the proceedings should be
vigorously carried on."[2]

It is largely on this document that the charge against
Cotton Mather rests: he is believed by many deliberately to have urged the judicial murder of innocent
people for the simple purpose of establishing and main
taining his own ascendency in the state. To me, and
what I have written already should show why, the paper
seems the only possible thing for an honest, superstitious man—himself in direct communication with the
blessed part of the invisible world—to have written.
Witchcraft was to him the most terrible of realities; not
to proceed against it would have been to betray the
cause of Christ; but the Devil stood ready to beguile
the courts themselves; the evidence must be carefully
scrutinized, or who could tell what mischief might
come?

Thus encouraged, the Court proceeded. How many
wretched people were committed can never be quite
known: Upham thinks several hundreds.[3] Nineteen were
hanged; one was pressed to death for refusing to plead
to his indictment; at least two died in jail. By the end
of September, a revulsion of popular feeling had come.
The accusations had spread too far: the evidence on
which the witches were executed was beginning to
seem too flimsy. On the 22d of September came the
last executions. In January, 1693,[4] the special Court of
Oyer and Terminer was supplanted by a regular Superior Court, consisting of much the same men. It threw
out "spectral evidence,"—that is, it declined to consider the ravings of the bewitched: only three out of fifty
indicted for witchcraft were condemned, and none of
these was executed. In May, 1693, the panic was over.
By proclamation, Sir William Phipps discharged all
the accused. "Such a jail delivery," says Hutchinson,
"has never been known in New England."

In all this matter Increase Mather seems to have played
no conspicuous part. Four years of diplomacy in the
capital of the British empire had perhaps taught him
practical lessons of prudence not to be learned in any
less arduous school. But while these were learning, his
son, not yet thirty years old, had been surrounded by
influences diametrically different. In the provincial
Boston, which was at once the greatest city in America
and the only home he ever knew, Cotton Mather had
found himself, at an age when most men are still passed
by as young, among the chiefs of the leaders. And
then, as later, it had been his lot to meet hardly anybody whom he could honestly deem by his own standards superior to himself. As we shall see by and by,
his later career was marked by what has often seemed,
particularly when we remember his constant failure to
achieve the public ends he strove for, a ridiculous and
overweening vanity. But I think that few can rise from
a careful study of his diary without feeling that this

vanity was no blind self-approval; but at most a conviction, in his happier moments, that, far as he was
from the attainment of his ideals, there were none
about him who were any nearer the attainment of
theirs, and that there were many—and year by year
more—who were falling away from the ancestral traditions that he never gave up. In 1692 he was still in
the flush of youth and of success. No one was more
active in fighting the Devil's works as revealed in
witchcraft. No one, for well on to two centuries, has
borne so much of the odium of what was done as he.

We have seen how his books and his conduct in 1688
tended to stir up public feeling against the witches;
we have seen how the letter of the ministers which he
drew up encouraged the puzzled Court of Oyer and
Terminer to proceed with its deadly work. On the
19th of August, 1692, the most eminent of the victims of the proceedings was hanged; this was the Rev.
George Burroughs, a graduate of Harvard College,
and for something like twenty years a minister of the
Gospel. Four others died with him. One of Sewall's
very few notes of this period describes this day.

> A very great number of Spectators . . . present. Mr
> Cotton Mather was there. . . . All of them said
> they were inocent. . . . Mr. Mather says they all
> died by a Righteous sentence. Mr. Burroughs, by
> his Speech, Prayer, protestation of his Innocence,
> did much move unthinking persons, which
> occasions their speaking hardly concerning his
> being executed." In the margin Sewall has written
> "Dolefull Witchcraft!"[5]

Calef, of whom we shall hear more by and by, gives
a fuller account of the scene:—

> When [Mr. Burroughs] was upon the ladder, he
> made a speech for the clearing of his innocency,
> with such solemn and serious expressions, as were
> to the admiration of all present: his prayer (which
> he concluded by repeating the Lord's prayer[6]) was
> so well worded, and uttered with such
> composedness, and such (at least seeming) fervency
> of spirit, as was very affecting, and drew tears
> from many, so that it seemed to some that the
> spectators would hinder the execution. The
> accusers[7] said the black man stood and dictated to
> him. As soon as he was turned off, Mr. Cotton
> Mather, being mounted upon a horse, addressed
> himself to the people, partly to declare that . . .
> [Burroughs] was no ordained minister, and partly to
> possess the people of his guilt, saying that the devil
> has often been transformed into an angel of light; and
> this somewhat appeased the people, and the executions
> went on. When he was cut down, he was dragged by
> the halter to a hole . . . between the rocks, about two
> feet deep, his shirt and breeches being pulled off, and
> an old pair of trowsers of one executed put on his
> lower parts; he was so put in . . . that one of his hands
> and his chin . . . were left uncovered.[8]

Just a month later, Giles Corey was pressed to death for refusing to plead to his indictment,—the solitary instance in America of this terrible barbarity of the old English criminal law.

> Sept. 20, [writes Sewall], Now I hear from Salem that about 18 years agoe he was suspected to have stamped and press'd a man to death, but was cleared. Twas not remembered till Ane Putnam was told of it by said Corey's Spectre the Sabbath-day night before the Execution.[9]

On this very day, the 20th of September, two days before the last of the executions, Cotton Mather wrote to Stephen Sewall, clerk of the court at Salem, a letter which Upham deems conclusive of his artful dishonesty.[10]

> That I may bee the more capable to assist, in lifting up a standard against the Infernal Enemy, [it runs,] I must Renew my most IMPORTUNATE REQUEST, that you would please quickly to perform, what you kindly promised, of giving me a Narrative of the Evidences given in at the Trials of half a dozen, or if you please a dozen, of the principal Witches, that have been condemned. . . . I am willing that when you write, you should imagine me as obstinate a Sadducee and Witch-advocate as any among us: address mee as one that Believ'd Nothing Reasonable; and when you have so knocked mee down, in a spectre so unlike mee, you will enable mee, to box it about, among my Neighbs, till it come, I know not where, at last.

Two days later, on that very 22d of September when the last witches were hanging, Sewall notes that "William Stoughton, Esqr., John Hathorne, Esqr., Mr. Cotton Mather, and Capt. John Higginson, with my brother St., were at our house, speaking about publishing some Trials of Witches."[11] The results of this letter and conference seems to have been Cotton Mather's well known "Wonders of the Invisible World," published the next year both in Boston and in London.

A few of Sewall's notes show the course of popular feeling meanwhile. On the 15th of October he went to Cambridge to discourse with Mr. Danforth about witchcraft: Mr. Danforth

> "thinks there ca ot be a procedure in the Court except there be some better consent of Ministers and People." On the 26th, "A Bill is sent in about calling a Fast, and Convocation of Ministers, that may be led in the right way as to the Witchcrafts. The reason and ma er of doing it, is such, that the Court of Oyer and Terminer count themselves thereby dismissed. 29 Nos and 33 yeas to the Bill." On the 28th, Sewall, "as had done several times before, desired to have the advice of the Governour and Council as to the sitting of the Court of Oyer and Terminer next week: said should move it no more;

great silence, as if should say, do not go." Next day, "Mr. Russell asked whether the Court of Oyer and Terminer should sit, expressing some fear of Inconvenience by its fall. Governour said it must fall. Lieut.-Governour[12] not in Town."

It was nearly a year later, in September, 1693, that Cotton Mather, in Upham's phrase,[13] "succeeded in getting up" the case of witchcraft that cost him dearest. One Margaret Rule, a young woman of Boston whose character seems to have been none of the best, was seized with all the symptoms of possession. One symptom, mentioned I think only in her case, throws considerable light on her disorder: the devils prevented her from eating, but permitted her occasionally to swallow a little rum. Both of the Mathers visited her, surrounded by her startled and credulous friends; they listened with full faith to her tales of black spirits and white who haunted her; they examined her person with what in less holy men might have savoured of indiscretion; they prayed with her and for her. And finally, the discouraged devils fled away; and she, returning perfectly to herself, though extremely weak and faint and overwhelmed with vapours, most affectionately gave thanks to God for her deliverance.[14] This case, portending such a diabolical descent on Boston as had passed over Salem, attracted the attention among others, of one Robert Calef, a merchant of the town. He visited Margaret Rule when the Mathers were with her. A perfect matter-of-fact man, thoroughly honest and equally devoid of imagination, he saw in her sufferings only a vulgar cheat, and in the conduct of the Mathers something which seems to have impressed him as deliberate and not wholly decent connivance in her imposture. He made notes of what he had seen, and submitted them to Cotton Mather. The controversy that followed, which has been admirably summarized by Sibley,[15] lasted in one form or another for six years. In 1700, Calef's book on the subject was published in London, and soon found its way to Boston.[16]

Calef's temper was that of the rational Eighteenth Century: the Mathers belonged rather to the Sixteenth,—the age of passionate religious enthusiasm. To me, both sides seem equally honest; and the difference between them seems chiefly due to the fact that, as in a thousand other cases in human history, a man of the future can rarely so rise above himself as to understand men of the past. In such a controversy, it is the man of the future that the future holds right. In the time that has passed since the Mathers and Calef have lain in their graves, the world has seen an age of reason, and not of imaginative emotion. And most of those who have concerned themselves about these dead men have deemed Calef all in the right, and the Mathers foolish, if not worse. But did Calef see all? Is there, after all, in a great epidemic of superstition nothing beyond what those who escape the contagion perceive? Are we not to-day beginning to guess that there may be in heaven and earth more things than are yet dreamt of in your philosophy? If there be, it may in the end prove the verdict of men that neither honest Calef nor the honest Mathers saw all that passed before their eyes; but that each in his own way caught a glimpse of truth, and that each believed that all the truth was comprised in the bit he saw.

But we are come now to a point where we must turn to Cotton Mather himself; where we must look to the diaries he has left us, and to the works he wrote later, for an account of what these critical years meant to him. The substance of his later writings seems to me adequately represented by the passages about witchcraft in the *Magnalia* and the *Parentator*. A few words of these, and we will pass to his diaries for 1692[17] and 1693.[18]

The substance of his final view of the case, as shown in his published works, seems to have been this: The witchcraft was a real attack of the Devil, permitted perhaps as a punishment for dabblings in sorcery and magical tricks which people had begun to allow themselves.[19] The afflictions of the possessed, which he details in all their petty absurdities, that seem nowadays as monstrously trivial, were really diabolical.

> Flashy people may burlesque these things, but when hundreds of the most sober people in a country where they have as much *mother-wit* certainly as the rest of mankind, know them to be *true,* nothing but the absurd and froward Spirit of Sadducism can question them.[20]

The only doubtful question was whether the Devil had the power of assuming before the eyes of his victims the shape of innocent persons. The assumption on the part of the judges that he had no such power led to the conviction on spectral evidence of not a few victims of the court. The abandonment of this assumption led to the cessation of the prosecutions, and to the jail delivery of 1693. Mather asserts in substance that he always opposed spectral evidence; and it is certain that Increase Mather's *Cases of Conscience,* published in 1694, clearly condemns it. It is certain, too, that Cotton Mather's letter to John Richards, dated May 31, 1692,[21] warns the judge in the most specific terms against the dangers of spectral evidence. Cotton Mather's own position, as he finally states it, then, seems to have been a persistent belief in witchcraft, a persistent determination to keep the public alive to all the horrors of the crime, and to oppose it by every means in his power, but a growing doubt as to how far so mysterious and terrible an evil can be dealt with by so material an engine as the criminal law. On the whole he inclines more and more to reliance on fasting and prayer. This was undoubtedly the view taken, when the panic was once over, by even the most strenuous advocates of the reality of witchcraft, and Cotton

Mather undeniably takes to himself the credit of having held and urged it all along.

The part of the *Magnalia* in which these facts appear is the Life of Sir William Phipps, first published separately and anonymously in 1697. On the fact that this book was anonymous, Calef bases much of his charge that Mather wrote it dishonestly to praise himself, and to delude people into believing him free from the responsibility of having urged on the prosecutions. On this fact, on the feebleness of the caution addressed by the ministers to the Court of Oyer and Terminer, and on the letter to Stephen Sewall, rests most of the charge of dishonesty from which Mather's name has never been cleared to the satisfaction of his opponents. It seems to me that the anonymous publication—by no means the only example of it in Mather's voluminous works[22]—may well have been due to no worse motive than a wish for a fair hearing, which might not have been accorded to a name which was held up to public execration. It seems to me, too, that the letter of the ministers may be taken for just what it purports to be,—an honest warning of a danger, in spite of which the Court has no moral right to hesitate in the performance of its official duty. And in the letter to Stephen Sewall I can see nothing inconsistent with the conclusion that what Cotton Mather wished to maintain unshaken was not the fatal penalty of the law, but that belief in the reality of witchcraft which he certainly never abandoned. Calef and posterity seem to me to have confused two distinct things,—this belief in the reality of witchcraft, and insistence on the validity of spectral evidence. But, when all is said, I think two facts against Mather remain: his conduct and his words had as much as any one man's could have to do with the raising of the panic; and in his final presentation of the matter, both in his diaries and in his published works, he never grants or meets the full strength of the case against him.

But before we agree with those who believe him to have been deliberately dishonest, it will be only fair to read what his diaries tell us of these troubled years; and to read it, too, with certain facts in mind that seem to me too little considered. In the first place, as we have seen, Cotton Mather had for years been a religious enthusiast whose constant ecstasies brought him into such direct communication with Heaven as he believed the witches to maintain with Hell; in other words, he had for years been, what he remained all his life, a constant victim of a mental or moral disorder whose normal tendency is towards the growth of unwitting credulity and fraud. In the second place, I grow to believe more and more that the ceaseless activity of mind and body, of thought, of emotion, of action, into which he never ceased to lash himself,—the activity which produced in actual words and deeds a lifework whose bulk to-day seems almost incredible,—never permitted him, in any act or word, to be really deliberate at all. Striving with all his might to do the Lord's work, believing that the Lord's will forbade him for a moment to relax a particle of his energy, he went through this world from beginning to end in a state of emotional exaltation, of passionate afflation and reaction, which left him in all the sixty years of his conscious life hardly an hour of that cool thoughtfulness without which any deliberation is impossible. It has been his fate—a man whose whole career was a storm of passion—to be judged, in the seclusion of libraries, by unimaginative, unimpassioned posterity. So cool sympathizers with old Calvinism who have sought to defend him, and cooler Protestants who have constantly condemned him, have alike failed to understand.

They have failed, too, adequately to emphasize what seems to me the most notable piece of contemporary evidence. On May 31st, 1692, we have seen,—three days before Bridget Bishop, the first victim of the Court, was sentenced,—Cotton Mather wrote to John Richards, one of the judges, a letter in which he takes, with the utmost decision, exactly the ground he occupied to the end of his life.

> 'Do not lay more stress upon pure Spectre evidence than it will bear," he writes. . . . "It is very certain that the divells have sometimes represented the shapes of persons not only innocent, but also very vertuous."

There should be confession, or unmistakable signs: he believes in witch-marks, to be sure, and in the water-ordeal. But at the very end he adds this caution:—

> It is worth considering whether there be a necessity alwayes by Extirpacons by Halter or fagott [to punish] every wretched creature that shall be hooked into some degrees of Witchcraft. What if some of the lesser Criminalls, be only scourged with lesser punishments, and also put upon some solemn, . . . Publike . . . renunciation of the Divel? I am apt to thinke that the Divels would then cease afflicting the Neighbourhood.

So we come back to the diary for 1692.[23] As I have said already, this is far more abridged and less specific than most of his diaries. But I do not believe it untrue. The last entry I quoted was made in May, when his father had just returned, and the new Charter was just passing into operation. "And now," he wrote, "I will call upon the Lord as long as I live."

The rest of his entries for the year bear no date. He notes briefly that he has preached against temporal persecution of heresy; "And I hope the Lord will own me with a more Singular Success in the suppression of Haeresy by Endeavours more Spiritual and Evangelical." He notes that in his public ministry he has been largely handling the Day of Judgment, from texts in the 25th chapter of Matthew. Then comes a long note beginning, "The Rest of the Summer was a very doleful Time unto the whole Countrey." He tells how devils possessed many people, how witches were accused in the visions of the afflicted, how he himself testified both publicly and privately against the dangers of spectral evidence, and how it was he who drew up the letter from the ministers to the Court of Oyer and Terminer.

> Nevertheless, [he goes on,][24] I saw in most of the Judges a most charming Instance of prudence and patience, and I knew their exemplary pietie, and the Anguish of Soul with which they sought the Direction of Heaven: above most other people, whom I generally saw enchanted into a Raging, Railing, Scandalous and unreasonable disposition as the distress increased upon us. For this cause, though I would not allow the Principles, that some of the Judges had espoused, yet I could not but speak honourably of their Persons, on all occasions: and my Compassion upon the Sight of their Difficulties Raised by my Journeys to Salem, the Chief Seat of these Diabolical Vexations, caused me yett more to do so. And merely, as far as I can Learn, for this Reason, the mad people thro' the Countrey under a fascination on their Spirits equal to what the Energumens had on their Bodies, Reviled *mee,* as if I had been the Doer of all the Hard Things that were done in the prosecution of the Witchcraft.

He goes on to note how he offered to provide in his own family for six of the possessed, that he might try whether prayer and fasting "would not putt an End to their Heavy Trials"; how throughout the summer he prayed and fasted weekly for this heavy affliction to the country; how he visited witches in prison and preached to them; and how he wrote his "Wonders of the Invisible World." And at the end of this passage is a note in brackets, apparently made at some later time:—

> [Upon the severest Examination, and the Solemnest Supplication, I still think, that for the main, I have *Written Right.*]

Later come less coherent notes. One remarks that the spectres brought books in which they urged the possessed to sign away their souls. Now, as Cotton Mather worked for God largely by writing books, this looked as if "this Assault of the Evil Angels upon the Countrey was intended by Hell as a particular Defiance unto *my* poor Endeavours to bring the Souls of men unto Heaven." Whereupon, he wrote "Awakenings for the Unregenerate," which he resolved, if he lived, to give away at the rate of two a week for two years. In the margin he notes that the evil angels, through a possessed young woman, reproached him for never having preached on Rev. 13. 8.[25] "I to oppose them," he goes on, "and yett not follow them, chose to preach on

Rev. 20. 15."[26] Later he makes a memorandum: as the devils bid Energumens sign books, he will sign the best of books. On the fly-leaves of his favourite Bibles he wrote professions and confessions of his faith: for example, "Received as the Book of God and of Life by Cotton Mather."

> "The Hearty Wishes of Cotton Mather," come next. "I have ever now and then gone to the good God with the most Solemn Addresses *That I may be altogether delivered from* Enchantments: *that no* Enchantment on my *mind may hinder mee from seeing or doing any thing for the glory of God, or dispose mee to anything whereat God may be displeased.* The Reason of this Wish is Because I beleeve, that a Real and proper *Enchantment* of the Divels do's blind and move the minds of the most of men: even in Instances of every sort. But I remember, That much Fasting as well as prayer is necessary to obtain a Rescue from Enchantments."

The last entry I have noted for the year, when I remember all the circumstances of the man's life, has for me real pathos: he would carefully avoid personal quarrels,

> "Because no man can manage a personal Quarrel against another without Losing abundance of precious Time. . . . And one Likely to Live, so little a *Time,* as i, had need throw away, as Little of his Time, as ever he can."

The diary for 1693[27] is a little more full than that for 1692; but, like that, is an abridgement of the original, and omits most of the dates. On his birthday, he preached from the text, "O my God, take me not away in the midst of my days." Then he set to preaching over the whole Epistle of Jude,[28] "intermingled with occasional texts." A little later he notes that a young woman possessed of devils has been delivered after he has held three fasts for her. He holds a thanksgiving accordingly; but, her possession being renewed, falls again to fasting and prayer:—

> "And unto my amazement, when I had kept my *Third Day* for her, shee was finally and forever delivered from the hands of the *Evil Angels:* and I had afterwards the satisfaction of seeing, not only *Her* so brought home unto the Lord that she was admitted into the *Church,* but also many others, even some scores, of young people Awakened by the picture of *Hell* exhibited in *her* Sufferings, *to flee from the wrath to come.*"

The next note I have copied tells more than any other I have found of Cotton Mather's pastoral methods:—

> The church having hitherto extended a *Church Watch* unto none but Communicants, and confined *Baptism* unto *Them* and *Their Children,* I was

desirous to bring the church into a posture more Agreeable unto the Advice of the *Synod,* in the year, 1662." So he preached on the subject, and allowing no disputation, proceeded to circulate among the brethren of the church "an instrument containing my Sentiments and purposes." The brethren "generally signed a Desire and Address unto myself thereto annexed that I would act accordingly. As for the few . . . who were Disaffected unto my proceedings. I carried it so peaceably, and obligingly, and yett resolutely, towards them, that they patiently Lett me take my way: and some of them told mee, they thought I did well to *do* as I did: tho' they could not yett come to *see* as I did. . . . Thus was the church quietly brought unto a point, which heretofore cost no Little Difficulty. But my Charge of such as now submitt themselves to my *Ecclesiastical Watch* was exceedingly increased.—Lord, LETT THY GRACE BEE SUFFICIENT FOR ME.

He notes that during the spring his days of fast and humiliation were so frequent that he lost record of them; that he kept, too, one or two days of Thanksgiving in his study. On one of these days, he goes on,—

> "My Special Errand unto the Lord was this: That whereas His Good *Angels,* did by *His Order,* many good offices for His people, Hee would please to grant unto mee the Enjoyment of all those *Angelical Kindnesses,* which are to bee done by *His Order,* for His *Chosen Servants* . . . in a manner and measure more *Transcendent,* than what the great *Corruptions* of the generalty of *Good Men,* permitted them to be made partakers of. Now that I might bee *Qualify'd* for this Favour, I . . . Entreated that I *may* not, and Engaged that I *will* not, on the Score of any *Angelical Communications,* forsake the Conduct of the Lord's *Written Word.*"

He goes on to state certain lines of conduct which he proposes to follow, with the hope of making his behaviour as agreeable to that of angels as he can. And his closing purpose is this:—

> 'To *Conceal* with all prudent Secrecy whatever *Extraordinary Things* I may perceive done for mee, by the *Angels,* who love *Secrecy* in their Administrations. I do now believe," he adds, 'That some Great Things are to be done for mee by the *Angels* of God.'"

On the 28th of March his first son was born. The child had a malformation beyond the reach of contemporary surgery. On the 1st of April it died unbaptized. It was buried beneath the epitaph, "Reserved for a glorious Resurrection."

> I had great reason," writes the bereaved father, "to suspect a *Witchcraft,* in this praeternatural Accident; because my Wife, a few weeks before her

Deliverance, was affrighted with an horrible *Spectre,* in the porch, which fright caused her Bowels to Turn within her; and the *Spectres* which both before and after, Tormented a young woman in the Neighbourhood, brag'd of their giving my Wife that Fright, in hopes, they said, of doing mischief unto her *Infant,* at Least, if not unto the *Mother:* and besides all this the child was no sooner Born but a suspected Woman sent unto my Father a Letter full of Railing against myself, wherein shee told him *Hee little knew what might quickly befall some of his posterity.* However, I made little *Use* of, and laid little *Stress* on, this Conjecture: desiring to submitt unto the will of my Heavenly Father without which, *Not a sparrow falls unto the Ground.*

He notes how during the summer he testified against the sin of uncleanness, on the occasion of the execution of two young women for child murder. "I accompanied the wretches to their execution," he writes, "but extremely fear all the Labours were lost upon them: however sanctify'd unto many others." He notes how his preaching at Reading started a revival there; how he conceived the idea of writing the Church History which, under the name of **Magnalia Christi Americana,** remains by far the most notable of his publications; how in July a fleet arrived, and he started down the harbour to preach to it, but fell so ill that he had to go home; and how he recovered in the afternoon to find that there was yellow-fever aboard the ships, and to be convinced that an Angel of the Lord had upset his stomach for the purpose of preserving him from infection. He notes how he has prayed and preached against vices which are bringing judgments on the community, "and such of these vices as called for the Correction of the Magistrates, I hope, I did effectually stir up some of the Justices to prosecute." Then, very ecstatically, he notes how in these dying times he feels himself quite ready for death: yellow-fever was abroad now. He notes a resolution to visit widows and the fatherless: he tells how he wrote a "True and Brief Representation of the Country," which was transmitted "with all the Secrecy desirable, unto the KING's own hand: who Read it with much Satisfaction, and I hope, formed from thence, in His own Royal Mind, those Characters of the Countrey whereof we shall reap the good Effects for many a day." He notes how he wrote a book called **Winter Mediations,** which when winter came on was published; and how towards the end of the summer he began his great commentary on the Bible,—a collection of every scrap of learning he can discover which has any bearing on Scripture. He worked at this for twenty years: it still remains in manuscript, under the name of **Biblia Americana.**[29]

Early in September, he went to preach at Salem, where he sought "Furniture" for his Church History, and endeavoured "that the complete *History* of the Late *Witchcrafts and Possessions* might not be Lost." The notes from which he intended to preach were stolen

"with such Circumstances, that I am . . . satisfy'd, the Spectres, or Agents in the *Invisible World,* were the Robbers." But he preached from memory, "so the Divel gott nothing." He had an interview with a pious woman, lately visited by shining spirits. Along with some things "to be kept secret," she prophesied a new "Storm of Witchcraft . . . to chastise the Iniquity that was used in the wilful Smothering . . . of the Last." On his return home, he found Margaret Rule down.

> "To avoid gratifying of the *Evil Angels,* . . . I did . . . concern myself to *use,* and *gett* as much *prayer* as I could for the afflicted Young Woman; and at the same time, to forbid, either her from *Accusing* any of the Neighbours, or others from *Enquiring* anything of her. [30] Nevertheless, a Wicked Man wrote a most Lying Libel to revile my Conduct in these Matters, which drove me to the Blessed God with my supplications. . . . I did at first, it may bee, too much Resent the Injuries of that Libel; but God brought *good* out of it: it occasioned the multiplication of my *prayers* before Him: it very much promoted the works of *Humiliation* and *Mortification* in my Soul."

He resisted the temptation to desert, in consequence of the libel, the lecture at the Old Meeting-House. As for his missing notes, he adds, the spectres bragged to the possessed girl that they had stolen them, but confessed that they could not keep them. Sure enough,

> "On the fifth of October following Every Leaf of my Notes. . . . tho' they were in eighteen separate . . . sheets, . . . were found drop't here and there about the Streets of Lyn; but how they came to bee so Dropt I cannot Imagine, and I as much wonder at the Exactness of their preservation."

On the 3d of October, his little daughter Mary [31] was ill. He prayed for her

> "With such Rapturous Assurances of the Divine Love unto *mee* and *mine,* as would richly have *made Amends for the Death of more Children, if God had then called for them.* I was Unaccountably Assured, not only that *this child* shall be Happy forever, but that I never should have *any Child,* except what should bee an everlasting Temple to the Spirit of God: Yea, *That I and Mine should bee together in the Kingdome of God, World without End.*"

On the 6th, the child died: next day she was buried: her epitaph was "Gone but not Lost." On the 8th, in spite of his bereavement, he administered the sacrament;

> "And, I hope, that I now so exemplify'd such a Behaviour as not only to embolden my Approaches to the Supper of the Lord, but also to

direct and instruct my Neighbourhood, with what frame to encounter their Afflictions."

On the 10th, a military training day, he prayed and fasted, particularly for a possessed girl,—doubtless Margaret Rule. A white spirit appeared to her, with word that God had made Cotton Mather her father, and thereupon she was delivered.

He notes in detail how he drew up a plan for a Negro meeting, in which he carefully attended both to the spiritual welfare of the Africans and to their temporal duties in the station of slavery to which it had pleased God to call them; and how he prayed and preached at the almshouse. He tells then how he was himself accused of witchcraft: the tormentors of a possessed young woman made

> "my Image to appear before her, and they made themselves Masters of her tongue so far, that she began in her Fits to complain that I Threatened her, . . . tho' when shee came out of them, shee owned that They could not so much as make my *Dead Shape* do her any Harm. . . . Her greatest outcries when shee was *herself,* were for my poor prayers."

Aware of the terrible danger to his influence, if these rumours should gain credence,

> "I was putt," he writes, "upon . . . Agonies, and Singular . . . Efforts of Soul, in the *Resignation* of my *Name* unto the Lord; content that if Hee had no further Service for my *Name,* it should bee torn to pieces. . . . But I cried unto the Lord as for the Deliverance of my *Name* from the Malice of Hell, so for the Deliverance of the Young Woman whom the powers of Hell had seized upon. And behold! . . . the possessed person . . . was Delivered . . . on the *very same day;* and the whole *plott of the Divel* to Reproach a poor Servant of the Lord Jesus Christ was Defeated."

In January, his only surviving child, Katharine, was very ill; praying for her, he was assured that she should recover, and presently she did. His last note for the year tells how he offered to give up a part of his salary to some members of his church who lived at a distance, and were for starting a new meeting nearer home: but nothing came of it.

Meanwhile he had published nine works: two,—a volume of sermons, and some meditations on the last judgment,—in 1692; and seven,—a preface to Mosten's *Spirit of Man,* two volumes of sermons, his warnings against uncleanness, his **Winter Meditations,** a letter on Witchcraft, and his **Wonders of the Invisible World,** which was printed both at home and abroad,—in 1693.

Title page of Cotton Mather's The Wonders of the Invisible World *(1693).*

I have cited with perhaps tedious detail his account of himself during these years that proved the most critical of his life, because I have not found it much noticed elsewhere, and without it he cannot, I think, be fairly judged. I have told enough, I hope, to enable whoever cares, to pass honest judgment on him. There remain two or three facts, without which our notion of the great tragedy of witchcraft would be incomplete.

Sewall, it will be remembered, was one of the judges who accepted spectral evidence. In the years that followed, he suffered many afflictions. In his diary for January, 1696-7, is this note:—

> Copy of the Bill I put up on the Fast day; giving it to Mr. Willard as he pass'd by, and standing up at the reading of it, and bowing when finished; in the Afternoon.

> Samuel Sewall, sensible of the reiterated strokes of God upon himself and family; and being sensible, that

as to the Guilt contracted upon the opening of the late Comission of Oyer and Terminer at Salem (to which the order for this Day relates) he is, upon many accounts, more concerned than any that he knows of, Desires to take the Blame and shame of it, Asking pardon of men, And especially desiring prayers that God, who has an Unlimited Authority, would pardon that sin and all other his sins; personal and Relative: And according to his infinite Benignity, and Sovereignty, Not Visit the sin of him, or of any other, upon himself or any of his, nor upon the Land: But that He would powerfully defend him against all Temptations to Sin, for the future; and vouchsafe him the efficacious, saving Conduct of his Word and Spirit.

It is said that when Stoughton, the Chief Justice of the Court of Oyer and Terminer, heard what Sewall had done, he declared that he had no such confession to make, having acted according to the best light God had given him.[32]

In Cotton Mather's diaries for later years[33] are two entries that belong here. The first was made at this very time, January 15th, 1696-7.

'Being afflicted last Night," it runs, "with Discouraging Thoughts as if unavoidable *marks* of the *Divine Displeasure* must overtake my Family, for my not appearing with *vigour* enough to stop the proceedings of the Judges, when the Inextricable Storm from the *Invisible World* assaulted the Countrey, I did this morning in prayer with my Family, putt my Family into the merciful Hands of the Lord. And with Tears I Received Assurance of the Lord that *marks* of His Indignation should not follow my Family, but that having the *Righteousness* of the Lord Jesus Christ pleading for us, *Goodness and Mercy* should follow us and Signal Salvation of the Lord."

The other entry comes years later. On the night between the 15th and 16th of April, 1713, he held a vigil: in it he prayed that many books which he had published might do the good in the hope of which he had written them; and finally, in the troubled perplexity of spirit that had been growing during these long years, when his public influence and the public power of the church had been constantly waning, he wrote these words:—

"I also entreated of the Lord, that I might understand the meaning of the Descent from the Invisible World, which nineteen years ago produced in a Sermon from me, a good part of what is now published."

Notes

[1] Cf. page 26.

[2] Upham, II. 268.

[3] Upham, II. 351.

[4] Ibid., II. 349.

[5] *Diary*, I. 363.

[6] It was believed that no witch could repeat the Lord's prayer without error.

[7] The bewitched: a capital example of spectral evidence.

[8] Page 213.

[9] *Diary*, I. 364. Upham, II. 341, *seq.*, shows the charge against Corey to have been groundless. There is no more notable example of the popular infatuation.

[10] Upham, II. 487, *seq.* Cf. Sibley, III. 11.

[11] *Diary*, I. 365. Stoughton, Hathorne, and Sewall were judges of the Court of Oyer and Terminer; Stephen Sewall, clerk of the Court, was the man to whom Cotton Mather had written on September 20.

[12] Stoughton.

[13] Upham, II. 489.

[14] Calef, p. 34.

[15] Harvard Graduates, III. 12-18.

[16] Cf. pages 150, 186.

[17] In possession of the American Antiquarian Society.

[18] In possession of the Massachusetts Historical Society.

[19] *Parentator,* XXVIII.

[20] *Magnalia,* II. App. 16.

[21] Mather Papers, 392, *seq.* See page 110.

[22] What is more, he acknowledged the book in 1702, when the *Magnalia* was published.

[23] In possession of the American Antiquarian Society.

[24] This passage, and indeed the diaries concerning this matter in general, have been studied and cited by Peabody: Sparks's American Biographies, Vol. VI.

[25] "And all that dwell upon the earth shall worship him [the beast], whose names are not written in the book of life of the Lamb slain from the foundation of the world."

[26] "And whosoever was not found written in the book of life was cast into the lake of fire."

[27] In possession of the Massachusetts Historical Society.

[28] A most minatory scripture.

[29] In possession of the Massachusetts Historical Society.

[30] In Calef himself I find nothing to contradict this.

[31] Born in 1691.

[32] Sewall's Diary, I. 446, note.

[33] Both diaries are in possession of the American Antiquarian Society.

Thomas J. Holmes (essay date 1924)

SOURCE: "Cotton Mather and His Writings on Witchcraft," in *The Papers of the Bibliographical Society of America,* Vol. 18, 1924, pp. 31-59.

[*In the essay below, Holmes surveys Mather's works and contends that his writings on and role in the witchcraft trials hold a relatively minor place in his career.*]

Cotton Mather's entrance into the world's annals of witchcraft, in the character in which some of our historians have portrayed him, did not come about primarily through his two major works on that subject nor through the relative importance of his witchcraft writings as compared with his other works. It came about through that inconsiderable manuscript of his concerning the comparatively insignificant "witchcraft" case of Margaret Rule, and by his contact over it with Robert Calef.

Mather opponents have tuned their fiddles to Calef's key. Many a tune have they fiddled, out of harmony with truth, respecting Cotton Mather and the witch tragedies at Salem in 1692. It therefore may not be amiss to contribute our little aid toward the correction, if that is possible, of two minor strains among those errors.

First, I would invite you to a very brief survey of Mather's works, to effect a comparison of the whole of them with that portion of his writings devoted to the subject of witchcraft. Second, I hope to indicate evidence tending to show that, however the reaction from the witch frenzy first manifested itself, whatever were the immediate causes, the nature and extent of that reaction, which came all too slowly and too timidly— the development of which no one to this day has quite fully delineated—that reaction, did *not* involve Cotton Mather in any serious loss of public following, or in any serious diminution of his personal prestige. The

contrary of this has been many times reiterated, as by W. R. Bliss, *Side glimpses from the Colonial meeting house* (Boston, 1894), page 199.

Before writing his trifle of a paper on Margaret Rule, Cotton Mather, then thirty years old, had published approximately 38 separate works. After it, and before he ceased his labor at the age of sixty-five, he published at least 399 more. A total of no less than 437 published works are to his credit, exclusive of reprints, prefaces, and unprinted manuscripts. The editors of the *Cambridge History of American Literature,* by including posthumous works, prefaces, etc., have compiled a list of 475 items. These probably could still be augmented.

Without attempting the difficult task of an exhaustive classification of these at this time, a hasty examination shows that among them are works on the following subjects:

For the popular light reading of the day, funeral sermons take the lead with fifty-one examples. Sixteen works deal with various aspects of New England history. On medicine there are ten, five of which are on small-pox, exclusive of three contributed papers and one circulated MS on that subject. There were ten biographies, five issued singly and five in one work. Of these there were eight reprinted in the **Magnalia,** which contains over sixty biographies as well as a large number of short memoirs. At least four works were devoted to psalms, hymns, singing. There were two elegies.

On each of the following themes he wrote one, two, or on some subjects three books: pirates, captives, criminals, thieves, impostors, evil customs, murder, drinking, taverns, dancing, cursing, anger, idolatry, hypocrisy, slothfulness, slander, the ark, the tabernacle, sacrifices, adversity, prosperity, fifth of November, new year, winter, summer heat, change, time, heavenly world, terrors of hell, natural science, Sabbath-keeping, antinomianism, arianism, quakerism, rules for right living, civic affairs, society to suppress disorders, commerce and trading, debtor and creditor, fidelity in engagements, masters, servants, parents, children, widows, orphans, youth, catechisms, oaths, calamitous fires, earthquakes, storms, rainbow, aurora borealis. No subject of possible interest in his day escaped his attention.

Books were especially addressed to farmers, soldiers, sailors, fishermen, negroes, Indians.

A great many of these works, though not all, were originally sermons, containing a good mixture of homily and theology. They were printed in small books varying from about twenty-four to one hundred and eight pages each. Some of the sermons were printed by request of some of the auditory. Some of the issues were simply tracts; though others were considerable works of two to three hundred pages, a few of which retain interest and value even to this day. Among such are his ***Manuductio ad ministerium, directions for a candidate of the ministry,*** and his ***Ratio disciplinae, a faithful account of the discipline professed and practised in the churches of New England.*** His ***Christian philosopher, a collection of the best discoveries in nature with religious improvements*** still has its usefulness in the history of science. The works just mentioned, though less known, are probably in some ways superior to the ***Magnalia,*** by which Mather's name is still best known in literature.

His works were in great measure the reflection of passing events, and the moods of that public of which Cotton Mather was popular preacher, writer, and idol. The works are not only formidably numerous but the originals are now rare and widely scattered. Some titles exist only in a single copy still remaining, so that their perusal is attended with no little difficulty. Therefore I have not minutely examined the entire contents of all of his works but have judged some of them by photographs of their titlepages only. I do not assume any dogmatic bellicose attitude in regard to my conclusions. The witch trials have already resulted in the fruitless shedding of much ink.

So far, then, I might say I have found that on witchcraft Mather published two complete works only, three chapters or portions of other works, and the text of a letter of advice to the governor. He probably also supervised the compilation and aided in the publication of one other complete work written in his defense. In addition to publishing these, he wrote on this subject five letters and three manuscripts that he did not publish, and the text of an unpublished proclamation. The list is given at the end of this paper, and comprises a total of 16 items on witchcraft as against over 475 on all subjects.

I think it is safe to say that if Cotton Mather had been the active, interested, conscious promoter of the persecutions that some historians seem to have thought and others still think he was, there should have been a much larger deposit from that sort of mental activity seen in his writings than the remains of his work now show.

In the twelve years from 1688 to 1700, during which the subject of witchcraft is commonly supposed to have eaten up Mather's mind almost completely, he wrote on other subjects than witchcraft a total of eighty-eight works.

During the four years from about the autumn of 1693 to that of 1697, in which Robert Calef and his sev-

eral aids were engaged in distracting Mather with their activities and in concocting their book, *More wonders of the invisible world,* the harried one published twenty-six works, and did much toward preparing for the press his largest, his bestknown, and still useful work, the ***Magnalia.***

In the five years or a little more immediately preceding this period, occurred those two chief groups of witchcraft cases that Mather recorded in his two books on the subject, and the books themselves were written and printed within this span of years. Yet we may safely assign to this period not less than thirty publications on other subjects; among them the ***Life of John Eliot,*** afterward four times reprinted.

Nor should it be forgotten that these five years embraced the greater part of the intercharter period, the revolution, and the two expeditions—one that gained Port Royal and the other that failed against Quebec and caused Sir William Phips, who led them, to seek aid in London.[1] It was a time of nerve-racking anxiety for all public men in the colony; which, in a triple sense, affected Cotton Mather. He was concerned about his father, then in London working for the charter. Upon him also rested added responsibilities and work of the North Church by reason of the father's absence.

That he carried his share, too, of the general public anxiety, and aided to some extent in the Revolution when the people took arms against Andros, is shown by the fact that it was he who wrote the rousing ***Declaration of the Gentlemen Merchants and Inhabitants of Boston and Country adjacent,*** which was read on April 18, 1689, from the gallery of the council-chamber to a "vast concourse of people." This ***Declaration*** gave voice to the provisional government, and justified the arrest of Andros and his minions.[2]

If we can obtain a correct impression of Cotton Mather during the development and passing of the witchcraft craze, busy on his pastoral visits, preaching his sermons in Boston and occasionally in adjacent towns and villages, conducting private meetings, and, in his turn, Thursday lectures, keeping fasts even to the endangering of his health, engaging in omnivorous reading and in the writing of his many books,[3] and never once attending any of the witchcraft trials, we cannot but conclude that he gave comparatively little of his mind and time to the subject of witchcraft, and that it interested him far, far less than is usually supposed.

Then later, during the reaction from the witchcraft persecutions, when "Calef and the Brattles. . . . seized Mather by the throat," as Brooks Adams expressed it, and when Leverett, the Brattles, Coleman, and the young liberals were working against him at Harvard and elsewhere, and the diaries on various accounts were recording those humiliations before the Lord that nearly two centuries later were to be so helpful to the traducers of his good name[4] how did Mather during those years stand with his public? After the witch trials and during the Margaret Rule affair was "public opinion. . . . arrayed solidly against him," as James T. Adams[5] says it was? Let us see.

It has been usual to enlarge gleefully on Mather's quarrel with Governor Dudley, and on the loss by Increase Mather of the presidency of Harvard after the council order of 1701 required the president to live at Cambridge, and on the closing of the door to that office also against Cotton Mather. It has been usual to enlarge on these points, and to fortify them with confessions of disappointment from Mather's diaries and fulminations from his letters, in order to prove Mather's loss of public esteem. It is true that Cotton Mather was denied complete fulfilment of some of his ambitions, spiritual as well as temporal. He strove for that which in the changing times, perhaps even at any time, was unattainable.

In his personal inner life—and that must be noticed in the case of a man of Cotton Mather's type—in his inner life, he sought to realize and to perpetuate that mystical ecstasy which is possible for human beings to know if at all only in brief trances.[6] The reaction from such efforts, like those of the saints of old, was a sense of sin, of great personal imperfection, which found its expression in utter self-abasement in many an overwrought passage in the diaries[7]—passages that too often have been misread and misused by the enemies of his good name.

In a temporal and outward sense, his success in life was not always and in all places as great as were his hopes—a common-enough human experience that should not have been counted against him as it has been. His disappointment reacted in many a hasty word and in more than one undignified letter that has since told to his disadvantage. He experienced rebuffs, and, in common with the best of men, met an occasional defeat, but that he suffered no great failure, no serious loss of public esteem, I hope to show presently.

Cotton Mather was not a traveled man. He probably never ventured from his native Boston farther, perhaps, than New Haven. His views might pardonably be provincial. His father had stood before kings and had nominated William Phips to be the first royal governor under the new charter. Such a son, who had in addition intimately consulted with God, the King of Kings, might easily make the mistake of offering advice or even reproof to Joseph Dudley, a mere governor of Massachusetts, whose very appointment was in

some measure due to Mather's earlier and at that time friendly influence. Especially was Cotton Mather, the born teacher, liable to such error when the inner root and motive of the quarrel with Dudley concerned the government, not of Massachusetts, but of Harvard College.

Cotton Mather had no talents for diplomacy and skilful scheming. In his tilts with the self-seeking, intriguing, worldly wise Dudley he was worsted. But there was perhaps a more subtle force than Dudley working against the Mathers, father and son. It was the implacable Elisha Cooke, protagonist of the lost old charter and foe of the new charter that had been secured by the elder Mather's agency.

Then there were young men among the overseers of Harvard who held views about the Lord's Supper and church administration that were less strict than those taught by the early Fathers and held by the Mathers. The Mathers would prevent the sowing of what they thought was the seed of pernicious doctrine in the young minds at Harvard; but the temper of the times being less strict than at an earlier day, fostered perhaps by the liberal conditions under the new charter, seemed to favor the new ideas enough to give them a trial.

But these changes were fruiting after 1700—over seven years after the events of Salem. The changes were at heart almost wholly political in character. Even the ecclesiastical changes had their political aspects. They had nothing to do with the reaction from the witch frenzy, and they had apparently no great bearing on the personal popularity of either teacher Increase, or pastor Cotton Mather.

This paper concerns Cotton Mather. If Harvard, then, was lost to him, as he himself finally saw, was his public lost to him? Fortunately on this there exists unbiased, trustworthy evidence, that of experts in measuring public esteem, those who convert that esteem into cold unsentimental business. If Mather fell from public favor, the fall would be instantly reflected in loss of demand for his publications. If his public deserted him, his publishers—in spite of financial help on special occasion from father-in-law Phillips or friends like Thomas Bradbury and John Winthrop or his own ample purchases and his solicited subscriptions—if his public deserted him, his publishers must, by inexorable necessity, very speedily follow. To undertake the publication of even one book in those days of limited capital was a matter of consideration for the publisher. If composition by hand was relatively cheaper then than it is today, type, paper, ink, and presswork were expensive. Real money must come in from one book, or be fairly assured, before the next could be undertaken.

No author's works can be sold to, or successfully

unloaded, in any period by any ruse, device, or stratagem known to the publishing craft, by title after title during year after year, upon a public that is arrayed solidly against him. A publisher's business thrives solely upon the popularity of his authors.

To judge how busy, impetuous, witty, outwardly cheerful though often inwardly despondent, generous, loquacious, pedantic, egoistic, yet in many ways adaptable and tolerant and withal mystical, Cotton Mather stood in his day with his public it should be necessary only to glance briefly at his published titles.

To afford a rapid survey, the following summary is grouped in five-year periods:

> From 1682 to 1686, he published 4 titles
> From 1687 to 1691, he published 23 new titles
> From 1692 to 1696, he published 26 new titles
> From 1697 to 1701, he published 51 new titles
> From 1702 to 1706, he published 60 new titles
> From 1707 to 1711, he published 46 new titles
> From 1712 to 1716, he published 77 new titles
> From 1717 to 1721, he published 68 new titles
> From 1722 to 1726, he published 66 new titles
> In 1727 and 1728, he published 16 new titles

Many of these works, first printed in Boston, were reprinted in London; some of them were reprinted more than once. ***Ornaments for the daughters of Zion*** had six editions, as also had his ***Monitor for communicants***. The ***Family religion excited*** appeared at least seven or eight times. His ***Essays to do good,*** which proved helpful even to the practical-minded Benjamin Franklin, though not reprinted in Mather's lifetime, had eighteen editions, three of them published over a century after the author's death, two editions appearing as late as 1842 (London) and 1845 (Boston).

This unbroken cataract of new publications pouring forth to the last of Mather's days shows no diminution during the reaction from the witchcraft episode, no indications of serious defections of patronage contemporary with the liberal movement centered about Coleman and the Brattles from 1700 onward, no indications of a stampede from the ranks of his readers at any time. Whatever were the political or ecclesiastical developments of his time, whatever enemies he may have had—and who is without these?—we might even say whatever were his views over or connections with the witch persecutions, Cotton Mather, if continued avidity for his writings indicates anything, carried his great personal popularity during the whole of his life. How great that popularity was, may be conjectured from Increase Mather's statement[8] that ordinarily fifteen hundred persons attended services in their church. If this is not acceptable as a proof of popularity, it could be confirmed in several other ways; perhaps most readily by Mather's ***Diary,***[9] if we care to accept that

authority when quoted in his favor as it has been so often cited against him:

On Monday, September 5, 1698, he journeyed to Salem; on the next day, with a council of five churches, he went to Chebacco (i.e., Ipswich), where, on the day following, the council sat and rendered decision on a case before it. Thursday he "preached the Lecture at Ipswich." On Friday he returned to Salem, where on the following Sunday he preached in both the forenoon and afternoon, with a sense of great success. This in Salem, the center, six years earlier, of those tragedies and terrors by which the town had "lost, in one year, a quarter of its whole population."[10]

Upon his return to Boston after his few days' sojourn in Salem and in Ipswich, Mather records the following impression:

> Finding that whenever I go abroad, the *Curiosity* and *Vanity* of the people discovers itself, in their *great Flocking* to hear mee; with no little Expectation; it still causes mee aforehand, exceedingly to *humble* myself before the Lord. . . . By this Method, I not only am in a comfortable measure kept from the foolish *Taste* of *popular Applause* in my own Heart, but also from the humbling Dispensations of Heaven, whereunto the Fondness of the People might otherwise expose mee.

It probably is no exaggeration to say that Cotton Mather as an entertainer was the seventeenth-century New England prototype of the present-day matinée idol. Granted that the compliments he received made him vain, may not a little vanity be allowed him as a professional perquisite?

The favorable view of Cotton Mather's character entertained by the public of his time did not die with him. "A fragrant memory of him remains to this day," said his biographer, Marvin (p. 218), and adds: "Among the many eulogies of Cotton Mather no immortelle cast upon his grave was sweeter or brighter than that of Benjamin Colman."

Even concerning the witchcraft frenzy, there are not wanting in earlier and in recent times studiously and carefully written accounts, having the cogency of truth, that exhibit sympathetic views of Mather's relation to the events of 1692; or in which his responsibility is held to have been of very minor importance. Among such accounts are those of John Fiske, *New France and New England;* E. B. Andrews, *History of the United States,* Volume I; D. Neal, *History of New-England,* chapter xii; W. F. Poole, *Salem Witchcraft;* W. S. Nevins, *Witchcraft in Salem Village;* A. P. Marvin, *Cotton Mather;* and B. Wendell, *Cotton Mather.* The most recent and perhaps most comprehensive discussion of the relationship of the Mathers, Cotton and

Increase, to Salem witchcraft, however, is in K. B. Murdock, *Life and Work of Increase Mather,* chapter xvii, a doctoral thesis (1923) published by the Harvard University Press.

It will be seen, then, that concerning the historical figure of Cotton Mather there have flowed across two-centuries of his country's literature two utterly divergent streams of criticism; and it is not easy for the average reader, or even the busy writer of history, to decide which contains the water of truth and which the mud of error.

One of Mather's biographers, W. B. O. Peabody (1836), confessed:

> It is very difficult to form a satisfactory estimate of a character like Cotton Mather's which abounds in contradictions; to tell the precise amount of blame due to his faults, which were many, and how heavily they should weigh against the credit due his virtues [p.345].

Peabody's quandary indicates how thoroughly the old Puritan's character has been slandered—not always with wilful malice—and how early the aspersion began.

The adverse criticism in literature concerning Cotton Mather goes back through C. W. Upham and Francis Hutchinson, diminishing at each remove toward its source in Robert Calef's *More Wonders.* Though Calef's conclusions were drawn as much from his theories, which can be seriously questioned, as from his reports of local facts which are his best title to credibility, still his chief criticism concerning the Salem tragedies—throughout his letters and Preface, the only portions ascribable with certainty to his pen—was directed against the underlying doctrines, the "Heathenish notions" and "the Slavery of a corrupt Education" whence he believed the evils had sprung.

He traces these pernicious witchcraft doctrines back to Perkins, Gaul, and Bernard—writing in England since the Reformation. "The Doctrine of the power of Devils, and Witchcraft as it is now, and long has been understood" he finds among the "pernicious weeds" that came into the church from the "Fables of Homer, Virgil, Horace and Ovid &c."[11]

Calef speaks of "the *received* Opinions about Witchcraft,"[12] which I take to mean the opinions commonly held by people around him whom he knew and saw and conversed with daily. This would indicate that the people, the public, of Calef's day, held to a very wide extent those opinions that he criticized. Palfrey says:

> The people of Massachusetts in the seventeenth century, like all other Christian people at that time,— at least, with extremely rare individual exceptions,—

believed in the reality of a hideous crime called witchcraft.[13]

Rev. William Bentley, D.D., Harvard, 1777, minister of the Second Church in Salem, 1783-1819, states:

> Mr. Noyes. . . . believed in witchcraft, and so did every other person. . . . The doctrine of invisible agency, no one was bold enough utterly to deny. . . . The Salem judges. . . . were over ruled by the madness which was universal around them.[14]

The necessary support of that dreadful tribunal, said Dr. George H. Moore, "had been in the madness of the people, the poisoned breath of the mob."[15] A mob spirit that has left its definite trace in history in the plundering by the multitude of the home of Mr. Philip English after first his wife then he himself had been accused of witchcraft and arrested.[16]

C. W. Upham says: "The whole force of popular superstition, all the fanatical propensities of the ignorant and deluded multitude, united with the best feelings of our nature to heighten the fury of the storm."[17]

Then, after the storm was over, said Dr. Bentley, "Few dared to blame other men, because few were innocent. They who had been most active, remembered that they had been applauded."[18]

Against some features of those generally diffused, popular conceptions of witchcraft of his time, Calef, then, worked out his ideas, embodied them in what he called his "doctrinals,"[19] and with these opposed the "received opinions" of his day. If we read Calef aright, he set himself to pillory the witchcraft beliefs, held generally by the intellectual leaders, the ministers and writers, the magistrates and judges, and the public of his time, that had made possible the blind fury of 1692.

Though heat was generated and personalities involved, as was certain to be in any clash with popular notions, and though Calef said Mather's "Strenuous and Zealous asserting his opinions, has been one cause of the dismal Convulsions,"[20] he never regarded Mather as the singly responsible source.

It was during the nineteenth century that the idea gained force for holding Cotton Mather chiefly blamable for the Salem calamity of 1692—an idea that developed currency out of the strong bias of Upham's work as it relates to Cotton Mather, and that found ready reception in that critical, iconoclastic, realistic spirit of the nineteenth century that had very little sympathy with the ideals, very little patience with the faults, of the fervently religious, believing, seventeenth century—which in many ways Cotton Mather typified and represented.

In recapitulation, then, of the foregoing, I would submit for the consideration of any who may think it worth while, that Cotton Mather's works show that he was much less interested in witchcraft than is sometimes supposed, and that the time he is considered to have been giving to the study of that subject he was very strenuously devoting to quite different undertakings. Also I would submit that the statement occasionally repeated by Cotton Mather's opponents, that he was discredited by his public over and following the witch trials, cannot be true when the ever growing volume of his publications indicate an increasing popularity throughout the period of the witch trials, straight through the attacks by Calef and the differences with the liberals and with Dudley, and on down the years of his life.

With the fuller understanding of the underlying causes, character, and nature of the phenomena of witch persecutions in past ages[21]—which persecutions, sad though they were, were but one aspect of that universal woe and travail through which humanity has suffered and labored into partial enlightenment—and with a dispassionate examination of the original sources of the history of the New England outbreak, the present writer believes that those charges made against Cotton Mather concerning the originating and the promoting of the lamentable proceedings at Salem in 1692 will ultimately fall away. Then Mather will bear, in the work not only of some but of all future reputable writers of Massachusetts history, no more than his just small fractional share of indirect responsibility with the men of his time for the shortcomings of his community under the darkness of the age in which they lived.

Notes

[1] Palfrey, IV, 49-59.

[2] Neal, *History of New England*, pp. 430-42; Palfrey, III, 579.

[3] See *Diary*, I, 147, and B. Wendell, *Cotton Mather*, pp. 79-87.

[4] E.g., W. R. Bliss, *Side Glimpses*, pp. 199-203, and Upham, *Salem Witchcraft*, II, 503-5.

[5] *Founding of New England*, p. 455.

[6] *Diary*, I, 5-11, 187, 192-93, 254-55, 477-79; C. A. Bennett, *Philosophical Study of Mysticism*, pp. 10, 47, 48, etc.; B. Wendell, *op. cit.*, p. 304.

[7] *Diary*, I, 479.

[8] Letter to Stoughton (December 16, 1698), in Sewall, *Diary*, I, 493.

[9] I, 272-73.

[10] Bentley, *Description of Salem*, p. 234, in *M.H.S. Coll.*, Vol. VI.

[11] Preface.

[12] Pp. 64, 83. Italics mine.

[13] *Op. cit.*, IV, 96.

[14] "Description and History of Salem," *Massachusetts Historical Society Collections*, VI, 266.

[15] *Final Notes on Witchcraft in Massachusetts* (New York, 1885), p. 81.

[16] Bentley, *Description of Salem*, p. 270.

[17] *Salem Witchcraft*, II, 370-71.

[18] *Op. cit.*, p. 271.

[19] *More Wonders* (1700), pp. 17, 18, 34, 42.

[20] *Ibid.*, p. 33.

[21] Professor George L. Kittredge has pointed the way to that understanding in his "Notes on Witchcraft," *Amer. Antiq. Soc. Proc.*, XVIII (N.S., 1907), especially in his summary in twenty-one brief theses of his conclusions (pp. 210-12). Professor George L. Burr made reply to this in his paper in *Amer. Antiq. Soc. Proc.*, Vol. XXI (N.S.). In connection with Professor Burr's paper should be read an earlier one by him, "The Literature of Witchcraft," *Papers of the Amer. Hist. Assoc.*, Vol. IV. See also Preface, introductions, and notes to his *Narratives of the Witchcraft Cases*, New York, 1914. On the whole question, of course, see W. E. H. Lecky, *Rationalism*, chapter on "Magic and Witchcraft."

A new view of the question of witchcraft is set forth by Margaret Alice Murray, *The Witch-Cult in Western Europe*, Oxford, 1921. See also Ian Ferguson, *The Philosophy of Witchcraft*, New York, 1925.

Mather's account of Margaret Rule is discussed in "The Surreptitious Printing of one of Cotton Mather's Manuscripts," by Thomas J. Holmes, *Bibliographical Essays, A Tribute to Wilberforce Eames* (1924), pp. 149-60.

Vernon Louis Parrington (essay date 1927)

SOURCE: "The Mather Dynasty," in *Main Currents in American Thought, An Interpretation of American Literature from the Beginning to 1920: The Colonial*

Mind, 1620-1800, Vol. 1, Harcourt Brace & Company, 1927, pp. 99-118.

[In the following excerpt, Parrington attempts an examination of Mather's psychology and argues that the Puritan theocracy, whose virtues and glories Mather celebrated, was already crumbling when Mather was in his prime.]

. . . Of the unpopularity that gathered about the name of Mather after the fall of the theocracy, the larger portion fell to the lot of the son, the eccentricities of whose character made him peculiarly vulnerable to attack. In his youth the spoiled child of Boston, in middle life he was petulant and irritable, inclined to sulk when his will was crossed. In the career of no other New England Puritan is the inquisitorial pettiness of the Genevan system of theology and discipline revealed so disagreeably. The heroic qualities of an earlier age had atrophied in an atmosphere of formalism, and Boston Calvinism of the year 1690 had become a grotesque caricature of a system that in its vigor had defied the power of Rome and laid kingdoms at its feet. Embodied in Cotton Mather it was garrulous, meddlesome, scolding, an echo of dead voices, a shadow of forgotten realities. The common provincialism had laid its blight upon it. The horizons of the New England imagination grew narrow, and Puritan anthropomorphism unconsciously reduced the God of the Hebrew prophets to the compass of a village priest, clothed in stock and gown, and endowed with the intellect of a parish beadle. In the egocentric universe wherein Cotton Mather lived and labored the cosmos had shrunk to the narrow bounds of a Puritan commonwealth, whereof Boston was the capital and the prosperity of the North Church the special and particular object of divine concern. The mind of Increase Mather had been enlarged by contact with English life; the mind of the son was dwarfed by a village world.

Cotton Mather is an attractive subject for the psychoanalyst. Intensely emotional, high-strung and nervous, he was oversexed and overwrought, subject to ecstatic exaltations and, especially during his celibate years, given to seeing visions. In the carefully edited *Diary* which he left for the edification of his natural and spiritual children, at the beginning of his twenty-third year, is an apologetic entry—*"Cum Relego, Scripsisse Pudet!"*—that Professor Wendell has put into English thus:

> A strange and memorable thing. After outpourings of prayer, with the utmost fervor and fasting, there appeared an Angel, whose face shone like the noonday sun. His features were as those of a man, and beardless; his head was encircled by a splendid tiara; on his shoulders were wings; his garments were white and shining; his robe reached to his ankles; and about his loins was a belt not unlike the girdles of the peoples of the East. And this Angel said that he was sent by the Lord Jesus to bear a clear answer to the prayers of a certain youth, and to bear back his words in reply. Many things this Angel said which it is not fit should be set down here. But among other things not to be forgotten he declared that the fate of this youth should be to find full expression for what in him was best; . . . And in particular this Angel spoke of the influence his branches should have, and of the books this youth should write and publish, not only in America but in Europe. And he added certain special prophecies of the great works this youth should do for the Church of Christ in the revolutions that are now at hand. Lord Jesus! What is the meaning of this marvel? From the wiles of the Devil, I beseech thee, deliver and defend Thy most unworthy servant.[14]

The passage throws a good deal of light on the psychology of Cotton Mather. Such visions were clearly the result of abnormal stimuli, acting on a neurotic temperament. From both sides of his family he inherited a tense nervous system that was aggravated by precocity and an unnatural regimen. The inevitable result was a hothouse plant of Puritan forcing. His religious exaltation flowered from the root of egoism. His vanity was cosmic. He esteemed himself a beacon set on a hill, a divine torch which the very hand of God had lighted. The success or failure of God's plan for New England, he believed, rested on his shoulders; and with such heavy responsibilities devolved upon him he was driven, hot-haste, by the prick of urgency. The king's business requireth haste. The work of the Lord cannot wait upon sluggards. "O then *To work* as fast as you can," he wrote in *The Magnalia,* "and of soul-work and church-work as much as ever you can. Say to all *Hindrances* . . . 'You'll excuse me if I ask you to be short with me, for my work is great and my time is but little.'" And so with an amazing activity that was little short of neurosis, he gave himself over to the great business of managing the affairs of New England in accordance with God's will.

In undertaking so difficult a job, he frequently came into conflict with other interpreters of God's plan for New England, and partisan venom gathered about him wherever he passed. Tact was never a Mather virtue, and Cotton made two enemies to his father's one. His quarrels trod on each other's heels, and a downright vindictiveness breathes through his private records of them. He railed at whoever disagreed with him, and imputed silly or malignant motives. The pages of his diary are filled with epithets that he flung privately at his enemies; one marvels that so many in the little town of Boston could be singled out as "strangely and fiercely possessed of the Devil." Robert Calef, whose *More Wonders of the Invisible World* was an inconvenient reply to his *Wonders of the Invisible World,* was set down as "a very wicked sort of a Sadducee in this Town, raking together a crue of Libels . . . an abominable Bundle of Lies, written on purpose, with a Quil under a special Energy and Management of Satan, to damnify my precious Opportunities of Glorifying my Lord Jesus Christ."[15] When an anti-Mather group of Cambridge men set up the Brattle Street Church, and invited Benjamin Colman, who had received Presbyterian ordination in England, by way of reply to the Mather group, to become their pastor, Cotton wrote in his diary:

> A Company of Head-strong Men in the Town, the cheef of whom, are full of malignity to the Holy Waye of our Churches, have built in this Town, another Meeting-house. To delude many better-meaning Men in their own Company, and the Churches in the Neighbourhood, they past a Vote . . . that they would not vary from the Practice of these Churches, except in one little Particular. . . . But a young Man, born and bred here, and hence gone for England, is now returned hither, at their Invitation, equip'd with an *Ordination,* to qualify him, for all that is intended.

On his "returning and arriving here, these fallacious People" gave themselves over, in short, to "Their violent and impetuous Lusts, to carry on the Apostasy," and Cotton Mather prayed God to make him an instrument to defeat the "Designs that Satan may have in the Enterprise."[16] Similar passages of extravagant abuse of men so wicked as to disagree with him flowed from his pen in copious abundance, Although he constantly prayed that his daily life might be "a trembling walk with God," he was clearly a difficult fellow to get on with; and in the opinion of many he was justly described by a contemporary, as a "malecontent priest," consumed with an "Hereditary rancour" that made him "everlastingly opposite" to every will but his own.

The diary of Cotton Mather is a treasure-trove to the abnormal psychologist. The thing would be inconceivable if the record were not in print. What a crooked and diseased mind lay back of those eyes that were forever spying out occasions to magnify self! He grovels in proud self-abasement. He distorts the most obvious reality. His mind is clogged with the strangest miscellany of truth and marvel. He labors to acquire the possessions of a scholar, but he listens to old wives' tales with greedy avidity. In all his mental processes the solidest fact falls into fantastic perspective. He was earnest to do good, he labored to put into effect hundreds of "Good devices," but he walked always in his own shadow. His egoism blots out charity and even the divine mercy. Consider his account of an "execution sermon" preached to a nameless girl condemned for killing her natural child, and the light it throws on both minister and congregation:

> The Execution of the miserable Malefactor, was ordered for to have been the last Week, upon the Lecture of another. I wondred then what would

become of my *Particular* Faith, of her condition being so ordered in the Providence of God, that it should furnish me, with a *special Opportunity* to glorify Him. While I was entirely resigning to the wisdome of Heaven all such Matters, the Judges, wholly without my seeking, altered and allow'd her Execution to fall on the Day of *my Lecture.* The *General Court* then sitting, ordered the Lecture to bee held in a larger and a stronger House, than that *old* one, where 'tis usually kept. For my own part, I was weak, and faint, and spent; but I humbly gave myself up to the *Spirit* of my Heavenly Lord and Hee assured mee, that Hee would send His good Angel to strengthen mee. The greatest Assembly, ever in this Countrey preach'd unto, was now come together; It may bee four or five thousand Souls. I could not gett unto the *Pulpit,* but by climbing over *Pues* and *Heads:* and there the Spirit of my dearest Lord came upon mee. I preached with a more than ordinary Assistance, and enlarged, and uttered the most awakening Things, for near two hours together. My Strength and Voice failed not; but when it was near failing, a silent Look to Heaven strangely renew'd it. In the whole I found Prayer answered and Hope exceeded, and Faith encouraged, and the Lord using *mee,* the vilest in all that great Assembly, to glorify Him. Oh! what shall I render to the Lord![17]

Straightway thereafter, he rendered the Lord another characteristic service. No sooner was the girl hanged—for whose safekeeping no good angel seems to have been available after the minister had bespoken his—than he hastened to the printer to arrange for printing the sermon, and "annexed thereunto, an History of Criminals executed in this Land, and effectually, an Account of their dying Speeches, and of my own Discourses with them in their last Hours. . . . I entitled the Book, PILLARS OF SALT." Clearly this was the time to peddle his wares, when all Boston was talking of the great event; and with a nose for publicity as keen as Defoe's, he flung together a jumble of material, and trusted to its timeliness to sell. Some such origin, no doubt, accounts for a good many of the small library of titles that bore his name, an output that seems to have justified the angelic prophecy of "the books this youth should write and publish." With a very lust for printer's ink, he padded his bibliography like a college professor seeking promotion; but in spite of all the prayers poured out in behalf of them, they would seem for the most part to have been little more than tuppenny tracts, stuffed with a sodden morality, that not even an angel could make literature of.

Holding so strong a conviction of apostleship, Cotton Mather would certainly play the politician, and quite as certainly blunder and go wrong. Far more than his father he was a bookman, who believed that all knowledge was shut up between pigskin covers. He was as lacking in worldly wisdom as a child, and in his ecstatic contemplation of the marvels wrought by God in primitive New England he never discovered that that older world had passed away. Another age was rising, with other ideals than ecclesiastical, which the three thousand books in his library told him nothing about. He was an anachronism in his own day. Living in an earlier age, when the hierarchy was in its prime, he would have been carried far on the tide of theocratic prestige; a generation later, when lay-power had definitely superseded clerical, he would have taken his place as a stout defender of Tory ways. But at the moment when a critical realignment of parties was under way in Massachusetts; when the villagers were becoming democratized and the gentry toryized; when even the clergy were dividing—Cotton Mather was a general without an army. He was a primitive Puritan in a Boston that was fast becoming Yankee, and his love for the theocracy grew stronger with every defeat.

The judgment of after times finds little in his political activities to approve and much to condemn. After all allowances are made the fact remains that he was a leader of reaction; and no protestations can obscure the motive of personal ambition. His own prestige was involved with that of the theocracy. It was due to the traditional authority of the ministry that he enjoyed the distinction of being a "Person, whom the Eye and the Talk of the People is very much upon," and any lessening of that authority would hurt him cruelly in his vanity. This remains the sufficient explanation of his varied political activities in the course of which he trimmed his sails to different winds He first essayed a frontal attack on the secular power, but suffering a personal slight, he shifted and struck in the dark at an exposed flank; and finally, receiving only further mortification, he made overtures of peace and found his way back to the tables of the great. It was against the administration of the wily and unscrupulous Dudley that he waged his bitterest warfare. Failing to make headway by open hostility, he seized upon a current trade scandal, poured out his grievances in an anonymous pamphlet sent to London to be published, and awaited the result. It was a slashing attack, done in the tone of a lover of the ancient rights and privileges of New England, and it must have cut Dudley to the quick. A quotation or two will suffice to reveal the nature of the charges:

> But, when the President [Dudley] was pleased, out of an Active and Passive Principle, to tell our Countreymen, in open Council, *That the People in New-England were all Slaves; and that the* only *Difference between Them and Slaves, was their not being* Bought *and Sold: And that they must not think the Privileges* of Englishmen *would follow them to the end of the World.* I say, when the People heard this, they lookt upon themselves in a manner Lost. . . .

> All the People here are Bought and Sold, betwixt the Governour and his son Paul. . . .

This is the *Third Time* that he has been Trusted with Power from the *Crown* in *America,* and he has constantly Abus'd it, to the Dishonour of the Government, and almost Ruin of the People he was sent to Govern.[18]

There was enough truth in the charges to make them serious, but the spleen was quite too evident. The author was at once discovered and Cotton Mather suffered a vigorous counter-attack that damaged a reputation already undermined. Perhaps even worse was the social slight put upon him by those in government. What it cost him to be left out of the invitations of the great he reveals in the *diary:*

> 2 *d.* 7m. [September] Friday. [1709] The other Ministers of the Neighbourhood, are this Day feasting with our wicked Governour; I have, by my provoking Plainness and Freedom, in telling this *Ahab* of his wickedness, procured myself to be left out of his Invitations. I rejoiced in my Liberty from the Temptations, with which they were encumbred, while they were *eating of his Dainties* and durst not reprove him. And, considering the Power and Malice of my Enemies, I thought it proper of me, to be this day Fasting, in Secret, before the Lord.

Ten years later there is a different story to tell. The minister has left the opposition bench and gone over to the government. A note in Sewall's diary tells the tale:

> March, 12. [1718/19] Dr. Cotton Mather prays again [in Council]. Preaches the Lecture from Prov. 29: 18. no Vision. [*Where there is no vision, the people perish: but he that keepeth the law, happy is he.*] The Govr., Lt. Govr., Mr. Dudley, Mr. Belcher press'd hard that there might be an order of the Govr. and Council to print it. Col. Tailor, Clark, Davenport, Sewall and others opposed it. For my part, the Dr. spake so much of his visions of Convulsion and Mutiny, mentioning our being a dependent Government, and the Danger of Parliamentary Resentments: that I was afraid the printing of it might be an Invitation to the Parliament to take away our Charter. Govr. would have it put to the vote: but when he saw how hardly it went, caused the Secretary to break off in the midst.[19]

Here is a party alignment that tells its own story, and it needs no very lively imagination to fill out the meager note and reënact the little drama. The minister, eager to make overtures of peace, falls into the Tory note, talks about mob-rule and the sinfulness of popular unrest, calls upon authority to maintain law and order, and hints at the expediency of preserving due colonial subservience in view of possible resentments on the part of certain great men in England. Sewall, as a "true New-England man," squirms somewhat under the implications, but the little group of Tories are loud in praise. Such a sermon, from so eminent a servant of God, would aid wonderfully in strengthening the spirit of loyalty to the crown, and it must be printed and circulated amongst the people. But the opposition proved too spirited, and the manuscript was not dispatched to the printer, no doubt to Cotton Mather's chagrin.

It was easy for so reactionary a nature to slide over into the Tory. There was not a grain of liberalism in his make-up. His antipathy to all popular movements was deep-rooted, for he knew no other political philosophy than that of the obsolete theocracy in which he had grown up. He was a bourgeois soul who loved respectability and was jealous of his social position; no fraternizing with the poor and outcast for him, no profitless excursions into the realms of Utopian justice. Though he might play to popular prejudices to serve his political ends, he had scant regard for popular rights. The highest privilege of the New England people, he believed, was the privilege of being ruled by the godly. His real attitude towards the plain people is revealed in a note by his son, that refers to the days following the overturn of the Andros government:

> Upon Discoursing with him of the Affairs he has told me that he always pressed *Peace* and *Love* and *Submission* unto a legal Government, tho' he suffered from some tumultuous People, by doing so; and upon the whole, has asserted unto me his *Innocency* and Freedom from all known Iniquity in that time, but declared his Resolution, from the View he had of the fickle Humors of the Populace, that he would chuse to be concern'd with them as little as possible for the future.[20]

As he grew older and the shadow of failure fell across his life, his bitterness towards a people that had rejected his admonitions is revealed on many a page of his diary. It was a "silly people," a "foolish people," "insignificant lice"—"The cursed clamour of a people strangely and fiercely possessed of the Devil"—"My aged father laies to heart the withdrawal of a vain, proud, foolish people from him in his age"—"It is the Hour of . . . Darkness on this Despicable Town." He could not easily forgive those who had wounded his love of power and lust of adulation, and he was too aloof from the daily life of men to understand the political and social movements of the times, too self-centered to understand his fellow villagers. He possessed none of the sympathetic friendliness that made Samuel Sewall a natural confidant to every one in trouble. He loved the people when they honored and obeyed him, but when they hearkened to other counsels he would fall to scolding like a fishwife. Doubtless he was sincere in thinking he would gladly die to save his people from their sins, but he had no mind to neighbor with them or humor their wicked love of power. He immured himself so closely within the walls of the old

theocratic temple that he never took the trouble to examine the groundsills, and when the rotten timbers gave way and the structure came tumbling about his ears, he was caught unprepared and went down in its ruins.

Happily most of the printed output of Cotton Mather has fallen into the oblivion it deserved. It is barren of ideas, and marred by pedantic mannerisms that submerge the frequent felicities of phrase—old-fashioned on the day it came from the press. "In his *Style,* indeed," wrote his friend Thomas Prince, "he was something singular, and not so agreeable to the Gust of the Age. But like his *manner of speaking,* it was very emphatical." Yet he possessed very considerable gifts and under happier circumstances he might have had a notable literary career; but he was the victim of a provincial environment. He was the most widely read man of his generation in America, and one of the few who followed sympathetically the current scientific movement in England. Like old Increase he dabbled in science; he was proud of his membership in the Royal Society, to which he forwarded his characteristic *Curiosa Americana*—a hodgepodge of those marvels in which his generation delighted. It was from an English source that he got the idea of inoculation for smallpox, which he urged upon Boston so insistently that a war of scurrilous pamphlets broke out. He made use of the method in his own family, incurring thereby much stupid abuse and at least one attack of violence. It was an intelligent and courageous experiment, that is not to be forgotten in casting up the accounts of Cotton Mather.

Of his major works two only call for brief consideration: the celebrated ***Magnalia Christi Americana; or, The Ecclesiastical History of New England;*** and the less known ***Wonders of the Invisible World.*** The latter is suggestive for the light it throws on the psychology of the witchcraft mania. The fantastic devil-fear, which bit so deeply into the imagination of Puritan New England, has already been commented on. In that common seventeenth-century delusion, Cotton Mather not only ran with the mob, but he came near to outdistancing the most credulous. His speech and writings dripped with devil-talk. The grotesqueries that marked the current marvel-tales crop out nakedly in his writings. "I have set myself," he wrote in the ***Diary,*** "to countermine the whole *Plot* of the Devil, against New-England, in every branch of it, as far as one of my *darkness* can comprehend such a *Work* of Darkness." His conviction of the malignant activities of Satan was so vivid, that in delivering a carefully prepared sermon on the *Wiles of the Divil,* he was fain, he tells us, to pause and lift up his eyes and cry "unto the Lord Jesus Christ, that he would rate off Satan," who "all the Time of my Prayer before the Lecture" had "horribly buffeted me"—by inflicting on the fasting priest certain qualms of the stomach. How tremendous he conceived to be the battle over a human soul, he describes thus:

> The *Wilderness* through which we are passing to the Promised Land is all over fill'd with Fiery flying serpents. But, blessed be God, none of them have hitherto so fastned upon us as to confound us utterly! All our way to Heaven lies by *Dens of Lions* and the *Mounts of Leopards;* there are incredible Droves of Devils in our way. . . . We are poor travellers in a world which is as well the Devil's Field, as the Devil's *Gaol;* a world in which every Nook whereof, the Devil is encamped with *Bands of Robbers* to pester all that have their Faces looking Zionward.[21]

In the light of Mather's logic, "That there is a *Devil,* is a thing Doubted by none but such as are under the influence of the Devil," and "God indeed has the *Devil* in a *Chain,* but has horribly lengthened out the Chain," his private comment on the work—"that reviled book"—becomes comprehensible.

The *Magnalia* is a far more important work, the repository of a vast miscellany of information concerning early New England that his pious zeal saved from oblivion. It is the *magnum opus* of the Massachusetts theocracy, the best and sincerest work that Cotton Mather did. The theme with which it deals, and about which he accumulates marvels and special providences together with historical facts, was the thing which next to his own fame lay nearest his heart—the glory of that theocracy which men whom he accounted foolish and wicked were seeking to destroy. The purpose of the book has nowhere been better stated than by Professor Wendell:

> Its true motive was to excite so enthusiastic a sympathy with the ideals of the Puritan fathers that, whatever fate might befall the civil government, their ancestral seminary of learning should remain true to its colours. . . . The time was come, Cotton Mather thought, when the history of these three generations might be critically examined; if this examination should result in showing that there had lived in New England an unprecedented proportion of men and women and children whose earthly existence had given signs that they were among the elect, then his book might go far to prove that the pristine policy of New England had been especially favoured of the Lord. For surely the Lord would choose His elect most eagerly in places where life was conducted most according to His will.[22]

When old Increase was near the end of his many years, a friend wrote to ask if he were still in the land of the living. "No, Tell him I am going to it," he said to his son; "this Poor World is the land of the Dying." The bitter words were sober truth. The New England of the dreams of Increase and Cotton Mather was sick to death from morbid introspection and ascetic inhibitions; no lancet or purge known to the Puritan pharmacopeia could save it. Though father and son walked the streets of Boston at noonday, they were only twilight figures, communing with ghosts, building with shadows. They were not unlike a certain mad woman that Sewall tells of, who went crying about the town, "My child is dead within me." The child of Cotton Mather's hopes had long been dead within him, only he could not bring himself to acknowledge it. The fruit of the vine planted by the fathers was still sweet to him, and when other men complained of its bitterness, and fell to gathering from other vines, he could only rail at their perversity. He would not believe that the grapes were indeed bitter and the vine blighted; that the old vineyard must be replowed and planted to fresh stock. All his life he had set marvels above realities and in the end his wonder-working providence failed him. Prayers could not bring back a dead past; passionate conjurations could not strike the living waters from the cold granite of Puritan formalism. A New England flagellant, a Puritan Brother of the Cross, he sought comfort in fasts and vigils and spiritual castigations, and—it is pleasant to learn—in ways far more natural and wholesome. Incredible as it may seem, the following record is authentic, and it falls like a shaft of warm sunshine across the path of the morbid priest: "Augt, 15. [1716]. . . . Now about Dr. C. Mather Fishing in Spy-pond, falls into the Water, the boat being ticklish, but receives no hurt.[23] The restless minister who had fished overmuch in troubled waters, sometimes, it would appear, ventured for perch in Spy Pond.

Notes

. . . [14] *Cotton Mather, Puritan Priest*, p. 64.

[15] *Diary,* Vol. I, p 271.

[16] *Ibid.,* pp. 325-326.

[17] *Diary,* Vol. I, p. 979.

[18] *A Memorial of the Present Deplorable State of New-England . . . by the Male-Administration of their Present Governour, Joseph Dudley, Esq., and his Son Paul,* London, 1707, in *Massachusetts Historical Society Collections,* Fifth Series, Vol. VI.

[19] Vol. II, p. 214.

[20] Wendell, *Cotton Mather, etc.,* p. 82.

[21] *Wonders of the Invisible World,* p. 63.

[22] *Literary History of America,* pp. 48-49.

[23] Sewall, *Diary,* Vol. III, p. 98.

Marion L. Starkey (essay date 1949)

SOURCE: "The Devil and Cotton Mather," in *The Devil in Massachusetts: A Modern Inquiry into the Salem Witch Trials,* Alfred A. Knopf, 1949, pp. 240-57.

[In the excerpt below, Starkey explores Mather's role in the Salem witch trials.]

1.

What had actually been accomplished on the spiritual plane by the wholesale jail delivery of 1693 was a point which at the time could only be described as moot. In spite of the relief which many communities felt at the lifting of the nightmare, the eagerness with which husbands welcomed back their witches, repenting that they had ever distrusted them, people farther removed from the scene could look on the whole process as a monstrous miscarriage of justice, boding no good to the future of Massachusetts. These agreed with Stoughton, "We were in a way to have cleared the land of the witches. . . . Who it is that obstructs the course of justice I know not."

It was true that some of the most obvious symptoms of witchcraft were disappearing. Little was heard from the afflicted girls once the jail delivery got under way. Though logically the return of so many witches to civilian life should have afflicted them even unto death, none of the girls did die; they remained well enough. A few, notably Mary Walcott and Elizabeth Booth, presently settled down and got married. Some of the others, still manless, and apparently at a loss how to put in their time in these duller, flatter days, turned, it was rumored, to coarser pleasures; certain of them, never explicitly named in history, went unmistakably bad.

In Salem Village where this development could be watched at close range, there was said to be a general revulsion against them. It was not good to watch a wench at her harlotries and remember that on that harlot's word the good and chaste had been hanged. But at a farther remove other interpretations were possible. The girls were being slandered, and the judges with them; would the likes of William Stoughton have been taken in by harlots? Also it was by no means certain that the girls had come out of their fits; it was more probable that these were being callously ignored when they fell into them. Look what had happened in the fall of 1692 when the girls had tried in vain to warn Ipswich of a malefactor. God was punishing an unworthy, half-hearted people by so hardening their hearts that they were incapable of receiving further revelation.

The plain truth was for those who had eyes to see

that the devil was by no means bound up, had not lost his battle against New England, but was well on his way to bringing the entire community under his power. Of this there were unmistakable signs.

2.

What was the devil? To the Puritan the question was no less important than the question, what is God. A surprising variety of answers were possible. Some in Massachusetts were still reading an English best seller two decades old, John Milton's *Paradise Lost,* in which the poet in defeat and blindness had all unconsciously created Satan in his own image, doomed, but not without his grandeur. Such a being could be abhorred but not despised; one might pity, even respect the enemy of mankind. In his contest with Omnipotence he showed a perverse nobility of spirit; there was something almost Promethean in the tragic Satan who from hell defied the lightning of heaven and reached out to make mankind his own.

Yet how far was such a concept understood in provincial Massachusetts whose own tastes were represented not by the organ music of Milton's blank verse but by the jigging and jingling of Wigglesworth's *Day of Doom?* Certainly Cotton Mather, who had his own copy of *Paradise Lost,* did not associate Satan with the grandeur of lost but not ignoble causes. His Satan had more the spirit of the poltergeist, or of the comic devil of the early miracle plays. The fellow was ubiquitous, and as such damnably dangerous and eternally a nuisance, but as little dignified as the worm that eats up the garden.

Still a third concept was possible, the strange Adversary who presented himself before God in the time of Job and was received with courteous attention. What manner of devil was this who did not stoop to laying petty ambush for his enemy, but came openly into God's presence to challenge him; and what meaning could be read into God's acceptance of a challenge from such a source? Could it be that such was the omnipotence of God that the very devil worked for him to examine the hearts of men and test the limits of their faith? Was it even possible that God made use of the devil to bring a new thing on earth, that out of ill good would come?

Yet what good would come out of what the devil had done in Massachusetts? The phase of the colony's martyrdom had been not single but multiple. Not the witchcraft only but the new charter had delivered the faithful into the devil's hand. Now that people outside the faith could vote and shape the course of government, the power of theocracy had been forever broken. No longer would it be possible to get rid of perversely creative minds—the Ann Hutchinsons and Roger Williamses—by exile or death. Demoniac energies had been loosed now, and God alone could foresee the outcome. Was it possible that what the devil had promised William Barker of Andover would come to pass under God's providence, that there would be no more sin or shame or judgment, "that all men should be equal and live bravely"?

Well, it was God's will. God had delivered them if not to the devil, at least to an adversary. God save the Commonwealth of Massachusetts.

3.

If symptoms of diabolism had faded at last in Salem Village—so odd a site for God to choose as the battle-ground between hell and heaven—there was deviltry aplenty in Boston. Even while the judges were dismissing the witches, Cotton Mather's own wife, she who had once had to smother a laugh at the sight of diabolic manifestation as observed in the person of little Martha Goodwin, had been affrighted on her porch by a diabolic vision and had in consequence given birth to a malformed, short-lived child.

And as if that were not enough, Mather himself, because of his charitable interest in certain afflicted maids of Boston, was about to be given to drink of the vinegar of mockery by what he called "the witlings of the coffee houses." The devil had lately discovered to Boston a new brew which sharpened the wit and incited it to skepticism. Here in the waning days of the witchcraft were wont to sit several of the devil's own who made it their business to keep a derisive eye on the current activities of Cotton Mather and to publish them to the town.

Until lately there had been little occasion to connect the younger Mather with the witchcraft. He who had been so active in the Glover affair, and whose record of the case had helped prepare Massachusetts for the new outbreak, had nevertheless remained surprisingly aloof from the latter. Not that the aloofness had been by intention; it was simply a matter of living far from Salem and having much to detain him in Boston.

Early in the day he had written the Salem authorities offering to receive any six girls into his home for observation and treatment; had the magistrates responded it is probable that they would have exchanged a major calamity for yet another quaint, archaic monograph. The segregation of the girls would have served to localize the psychic infection, and the girls themselves, exposed to the wayward streak of poetry in Mather's composition, would almost certainly have found their fantasies deflected to the more normal preoccupations of adolescence. They would, in short, like a large proportion of the female members of his congregation at any given time, have fallen in love with him. Infatuation is not any guarantee against hysteria; quite the contrary. But in this case such a development might have diverted the antics of the girls to less

malignant forms. Young Ann Putnam might, like Martha Goodwin, have ridden an airy horse up and down the stairs and into the pastor's study, to find her catharsis there rather than before the gallows.

It had not been given Mather thus to experiment; he had watched the case from afar and had only thrice taken positive action. One of these occasions had been his drafting of the advice of the ministers to the judges, cautioning them against too great reliance on spectral evidence, though praising their zeal. Even before then Mather had unofficially written in the same vein to Judge John Richards, not only warning him against spectral evidence but against uncritical acceptance of such confessions as might come from a "delirious brain or a discontented heart." He specifically denounced torture as a means of getting confessions.

His only dramatic intervention in the witchcraft had been the speech he had made to the crowd at the hanging of Burroughs. This speech was the only real complaint that his enemies could make against him. There were some who thought that Mather had shown small charity to a fellow minister in his hour of need. Yet not much could be fairly made of the incident. Had not Mather spoken another must, for the crowd before the gallows was fast deteriorating into a mob. Mather who had seen mobs in Boston in 1689 had acted instinctively and without premeditation to do what was necessary to quiet this one. Control of the crowd and not slander of Burroughs had been his purpose.

In any case the incident was now well in the past. It would not have been held a serious count against Mather, nor could his name have been fairly connected with the witchcraft but for what happened after it was all over.

4.

On September 22, 1692, a kind of council-of-war had been called at Samuel Sewall's house in Boston. Present were Samuel's brother Stephen of Salem, Captain John Higginson, John Hathorne, William Stoughton and Cotton Mather. The subject under discussion was the propriety of making public some of the evidence in the witch trials. Not since Lawson's *Brief and True Narrative* of last spring had there been any authoritative published statement, and the latter had been written months in advance of the sitting of the Court of Oyer and Terminer. Now with so much irresponsible talk going on, it seemed clear that the time had come for an official report on what the judges had accomplished for Massachusetts. It would be an interim report. As of this date the judges expected to go forward with the trials in October. In spite of the rising tide of protest none could know that the seven women and one man who that day hung on the gallows in Salem would be the very last witches to hang in Massachusetts.

Mather stood ready to take on this assignment, and had been anticipating it for some time. To this end he had been accumulating some of his own sermons, notably his "Hortatory and Necessary Address" with its charge upon the conscience of New England. "'Tis our Worldliness, our Formality, our Sensuality and our Iniquity that has helped this letting of the Devils in." In addition he had been after Stephen Sewall to copy out such of the documents in Salem as could be used in a history of the witchcraft. Some of this material—not quite so much as he had hoped—was now available. If it was the will of his colleagues he would gladly do his best with a subject, which had been, he modestly reminded them, "sometimes counted not unworthy the pen, even of a king."

Whatever the faults of the younger Mather, procrastination was not one of them. By early October when Phips returned, the manuscript was not only complete, awaiting the latter's approval, but had already had some circulation among dignitaries of the colony. That he had also done his work well, had achieved what could be regarded as the authoritative version of the affair, was indicated not only by a laudatory preface by Stoughton, but by the fact that Sir William borrowed whole paragraphs for incorporation into his first report to England.

Phips did not, however, encourage publication. Brattle's letter, which denounced the entire premises of the trials, was circulating as far and as fast as Mather's defense. At a time of such diversity of opinion so hotly expressed the governor found it wise to suppress any publicity whatsoever. It was not until 1693 when the trials had been resumed on a new basis and the "general jail delivery" begun that he judged it wise to let Mather publish his *Wonders of the Invisible World.*

Mather's narrative was the nearest equivalent Massachusetts was to get to a full newspaper report of the mysterious events in court. The public fell on it with avidity and got their money's worth. Mingled in with sermons and philosophizings, Mather had presented a full and accurate account of the examination and trials of five representative witches, George Burroughs, Bridget Bishop, Susanna Martin, Elizabeth How, and Martha Carrier. He had followed the records in painstaking detail, summarizing competently when he did not quote in full. Not even his worst enemies were ever to find fault with his court reporting, and compared with the chapbooks of such cases put out to entertain the English public, it was a journalistic masterpiece.

Yet this document, so well planned and executed, so invaluable to the historian, was to serve the reputation of Mather ill. It had two conspicuous defects: its omissions and its tone. Those who really knew the trials read a significance into the fact that Mather had carefully avoided several of their most embarrassing aspects, Rebecca Nurse's brief acquittal, the powerful reasoning of John Procter and Mary Esty. The avoidance, to be sure, was by no means necessarily Mather's doing; what to include and what to omit had certainly been one of the subjects of discussion at the editorial meeting at Sewall's house. These circumstances could not, however, negate the fact that Mather had lent his hand to fabricating that most dangerous of falsehoods, the half truth.

The tone of the book was another thing again, and wholly Mather's. It suggested that the Dutch divines had spoken against spectral evidence in vain, and that Mather himself in recommending caution in this direction had not meant it. For he had written throughout in a spirit of childlike, marveling credulity.

Yet how could Mather, given his temperament, have written otherwise of his witches? As well ask Shakespeare to revise *Macbeth* without mentioning the Weird Sisters, or Milton to erase all reference to Satan in *Paradise Lost* as to ask Mather to do other than what he had done. There was in him much of the artist, and artistry in his austere position in theocratic Massachusetts found only such wayward expression as this. To such a temperament—and some of the afflicted girls probably resembled him in this—the details of the witchcraft, of horns that sounded across Essex County at midnight, the airborne excursions to Parris' pasture, the folklore that gaudily embroidered the life of Susanna Martin, were less a horror and an abomination than part of the suppressed color and drama of life. Mather's righteous indignation that such things could be was unconsciously submerged in the thrill of having been present as spectator at a collision between heaven and hell. The witchcraft was one experience that Mather would not willingly have foregone; it was the scarlet thread drawn through the drab of New England homespun.

But men who had been painfully involved in the crisis were little likely to respond to so artless and unconsciously poetic a viewpoint. What impressed them was that in his zeal for discovering witches an eminent Boston divine had stultified his capacity to see human beings and their very real agonies, that in short, to judge by the tone of his record, he had learned nothing at all from experience. So far as he was concerned, the delirium might begin again full force tomorrow.

5.

Indeed the delusion had by no means spent itself. While the afflicted of Andover and Salem were falling one by one into silence, dampened by the lack of a responsive audience, new voices were being heard in Boston. To two of these Mather was giving all the attention he could spare from his parochial duties. He was, in fact, launched on a whole new cycle of psychic research.

The first case to come to his attention was that of Mercy Short, seventeen-year-old servant maid of Boston, recently back from captivity among the Indians, who, as natural creatures of the devil, had probably had not too wholesome an influence on the girl. It was Mercy who in the course of a call on the Boston Prison in the summer of 1692 had mocked Sarah Good's plea for tobacco and had been afflicted since.

One would have supposed that the hanging of Sarah would have released Mercy, but not at all. Sarah must have delegated the torture of the girl to her surviving confederates, for it went right on through the summer and fall and became a favorite subject of speculation among the frequenters of the coffee houses. On December 4 Mercy achieved the attention of Cotton Mather by falling into such convulsions during a sermon that she had to be carried out. Naturally Mather looked her up afterwards, both he and a "little company of praying neighbors." He had long been itching to study at close range the type of case responsible for the Salem outbreak; now at last he had one in his own precinct.

From his interviews with this medium he got a first hand description of the devil, "a short and black man—a Wretch no taller than an ordinary Walking Staff; hee was not a Negro but of a Tawney or an Indian color; he wore a high crowned hat with straight hair; and he had one Cloven Foot." The eyes of this creature flamed unbearably, resembling according to Mercy, the glass ball of the lantern Mather took with him through the dim streets of Boston on his nocturnal rambles.

Sometimes Mercy's affliction took the form of long fasts, during which she could force herself to take nothing but hard cider. Sometimes she was seared by flames, and her visitors could smell the brimstone and see the burns on Mercy's flesh, though "as 'tis the strange property of many witch marks," these were "cured in perhaps less than a minute." Sometimes the devil forced white liquid down her throat. Sometimes she had fits of wild frolic when she was deaf to all prayers.

It was not for want of name calling on Mercy's part that these investigations did not result in arrests. She cried out against all sorts of people, especially some with whom she had recently quarreled. But Mather, acting with a discretion for which he was not to be thanked, decided that most of these were devil's delusions and charged his "praying company" not to report them. Among Mercy's more oblique accusa-

tions was Mather himself; this fact gave him more gratification than otherwise, for he gathered from the context that the devil feared and hated him more than any other minister in New England, a very pretty compliment.

Mercy, responding to fasting, prayer, and the invisible ministrations of an angel who sometimes fended the devils off, finally came out of her trance in March, 1693, and Mather wrote up his observations under the title of *A Brand Pluck'd out of the Burning*. Somehow he did not publish it. The jail delivery was in progress, and friends and relatives of released witches would not appreciate yet another starry-eyed report of this sort, especially so soon after the *Wonders,* from whose philosophies some of them were cringing. Or perhaps it was the development of Mercy herself which restrained him. The sad truth was that when the devil was cast out of her, seven others took its place, these being devils of the more common and carnal sort. Martyrs are impressive in the long run only when they are also saints; since Mercy was plainly nothing of the sort, Mather's pious account of her sufferings would be oddly received in Boston's coffee houses, places much more productive of skepticism than the ale houses had ever been. Mather did not risk it.

6.

Mather was, however, by no means done with the devil. In September, 1693, he made a trip to Salem to get "furniture" for the completion of the work now nearest to his heart, his *Magnalia Christi Americana*. This was to be his epic in somewhat the same way that *Paradise Lost* was Milton's. His purpose was cognate, though whereas Milton had undertaken to justify the ways of God to man, Mather would seek to justify the ways of man to God, particularly man as represented by the leaders of Puritan theocracy. He would eschew the sonorities of blank verse for the plainer sense of English prose, albeit richly embellished by latinisms, and the somber glory of such characters as Beelzebub and Lucifer for the more unassuming personnel to be found in New England parsonages; the *Magnalia* was indeed to be primarily a history of the churches in New England. Lucifer, however, would not be ignored in Mather's work; he would again give himself the luxury of describing the Fiend's descent on Salem Village.

To such an end he came to Salem. He delivered two sermons and between them pursued his inquiries. He was much interested in a Mrs. Carver and her viewpoint on late events. This lady was in direct communication with "shining spirits" who told her that "a new storm of witchcraft would fall upon the country and chastise the iniquity that was used in the wilful smothering and covering of the last."

This news Mather received about as a genera might receive intelligence that he would soon be called upon to march again. There had indeed been something abrupt, something questionable about the end of the witchcraft. The case had not been so much disposed of as allowed to collapse. It was as if an army of occupation had been called home without awaiting the signing of a peace treaty. It would be little wonder if the devil were to begin a new assault against a people so little capable of sustained effort.

These reflections were reinforced by evidence that the devil was interfering directly in his own affairs. He had prepared two sermons to deliver in Salem and the devil stole them both. Luckily he was able to give them from memory "so the devil got nothing." The story did not end there. When he got home to Boston he found that affliction had started again in his own neighborhood in the person of another seventeen-year-old, one Margaret Rule. From Margaret's lips he learned what had happened in Salem. The eight spectral shapes that tormented her had stolen his sermons and were bragging about it. Yet it was not given to creatures covenanted to the devil to keep a hold on a thing so holy as a sermon by Cotton Mather. In October the spirits relaxed their grip and dropped the missing manuscripts leaf by leaf about the streets of Lynn. Every page was recovered in a perfect state of preservation.

After such portents Mather could not deny his time and prayers to the new victim of the invisible world. Margaret was indeed a pitiful case. Her present physical tortures had been preceded by a spiritual phase in which she was prey to a belief that she was damned. Now she was the victim of witches who desired her to sign the Book. She was resisting heroically and before a cloud of witnesses. For Margaret was yet another who had had to be carried shrieking from meeting; since that had first happened on September 10, she had become the major theatrical attraction in Boston. If Mather wanted to minister to her privately he must first clear the room of a company—by no means a praying company—of thirty or forty spectators. Frequently he did not take this precaution, with the result that a fraction of the population of Boston was entertained not only by the antics of Margaret but by the measures taken by Mather to exorcize her demons.

Margaret's affliction had begun with an involuntary fast. For nine days her teeth had set against food, though occasionally it was possible to get her mouth open just wide enough to admit a sip of rum. ("That's the devil all over," commented a seaman.) Sometimes it was the devil who forced open her mouth in order to pour scalding brimstone down her throat so that people in the room could hardly bear the smell of the stuff or the sound of the girl's screams.

Marvels happened right under the eyes of the beholders. Some of them saw the woman stuck full of pins. Six men signed affidavits that they had seen her pulled to the ceiling by invisible hands and that it took their concerted might to pull her back to bed again. Mather himself once made a grab for something stirring on her pillow and felt an imp in his hand, tangible and yet invisible, and so startling in that combination that he let it get away.

She dreamed dreams and saw visions. She forecast the drowning of a young man and exactly as she spoke it happened—almost; that is, by God's providence the man wasn't actually drowned but was fished out of the water into which sundry devils had impelled him to leap. She saw the thieving of an old man's will. She saw the faces of her tormenters, or anyway of some of them, particularly that of an evil old woman who had been taken in the recent witchcraft and incontinently released again when the judges lost their heart for proper prosecution. Some witches she could not identify because they, having learned a thing or two, now went about their business veiled. Veiled or no, when Mather got to her, he prevailed on her to "forbear blazing their names lest any good person come to suffer any blast of reputation." He was willing that she name them to him privately and was reassured, for they were "the sort of wretches who for these many years have given over as violent presumption of witchcraft as perhaps any creatures yet living on this earth." Even so he did not report them.

He got small thanks for his self-sacrificing labors in behalf of Margaret Rule. His efforts had been observed by a motley company come off the streets of Boston to see the show, merchants, seamen, scholars, goodwives, everybody. These behaved decorously enough in his presence and on the whole he thought it well that a variety of observers witness the agonies of the girl the better to combat the skepticism of the coffee houses. What he did not know was that one of these "coffee house witlings" had not only got in with the rest but was taking copious notes of the seances and preparing to publish.

This observer was Robert Calef, an obscure merchant of Boston. He was a friend of Thomas Brattle and agreed with the skeptical viewpoint expressed in Brattle's letter, and had therefore come to watch Mather in none-too-reverent a frame of mind. What his cold eye noted in the afflicted Margaret was her craving for the attentions of men. She visibly liked being stroked across face and naked breast and belly by the Mathers, father and son, this being a kind of laying on of hands by which they tried to relieve her, but let a woman touch her and she cried out sharply, "Don't you meddle with me!"

When the ministers withdrew, Margaret told the women to clear out altogether, saying "that the company of men was not offensive to her, and having hold of the hand of a young man said to have been her sweetheart . . . she pulled him again into his seat saying he should not go tonight."

Six days later Calef found her enjoying what Mather had explained to observers as "her laughing time; she must laugh now." Mather having already gone for the evening, she was free to make eyes at yet another young man and to fuss with her attendants because they "did not put her on a clean cap but let her lie so like a beast, saying she would lose her fellows."

There was talk, to be sure, about her frightful affliction earlier in the day, and there were symptoms of a recurrence when one or two of the women got a whiff of brimstone. Everyone sniffed with them, but Calef and others couldn't pick up the scent and said so. The women became less sure of themselves; they could smell something, they said; they were not sure what.

Calef, in short, was less than impressed with the martyred Margaret. Even less had he been impressed in the still recent past by what he called a "Bigotted Zeal stirring up a Blind and most Bloody Rage" against innocent people by such media as these. He resented the credulous interest of the Mathers, particularly Cotton; this sort of thing had led to public disaster only two years earlier. Calef did not propose to stand by and watch the engineering of a second outbreak. Accordingly he copied out his notes and let them circulate from hand to hand.

Never in his life had Mather been so rudely handled or so affronted as he was by the talk to which these notes gave rise. He was enraged by the description of his stroking the half-naked Margaret so as "to make people believe a Smutty thing of me." His first impulse was to bring suit for "scandalous libel"; his second not to risk so public an appearance on so delicate an issue. The warrant was issued against Calef, but when the latter appeared before court, none came against him and the case was dismissed.

The larger case was not at all dismissed, however. The controversy between minister and merchant went on for years and culminated at the turn of the century in a book called *More Wonders of the Invisible World,* a work by Calef with the involuntary collaboration of Mather and a probable but disguised contribution by Brattle. Its core was the later witch writings of Mather, including his unpublished account of Margaret Rule. To this Calef added his own appendix to Mather's **Wonders,** furnishing full details on cases which Mather had neglected, notably that of Rebecca Nurse, and adding reports by such survivors as the Carys and John Alden.

Its publication was one of the most afflicting things that had ever happened to Mather, his sorrow's crown of sorrow. And indeed, though Calef's work was a valuable addition to the history of witchcraft, it did inflict an injustice on Mather in connecting his name inseparably with a tragedy with which he actually had had little to do.

Increase Mather, who himself had drawn Calef's fire, owing to his proposal to New England ministers in 1695 that they continue to collect "Remarkables," among them evidence of the agency of the invisible world, stood loyally by his son and made a spectacle of the infamy of the book—or so the story goes—by having it burned in the Harvard Yard. This fine symbolic gesture had oddly little effect in preventing its circulation.

7.

Margaret Rule had in the meantime come out of her fits long since. It was well that Calef never heard of her last seance with Mather, for during it she dreamily named the wizard whose Shape was currently afflicting her, and it was none other than Cotton's.

Mather was terrified. Superstition played little part in his fright, nor did he anticipate taking a place by Burroughs on the gallows. What unmanned him was the derision of the coffee houses if this accusation ever got around.

Heroic measures were necessary, heights of prayer to which he had never won before. He won them now. Finally, after Mather had spent several hours in the dust before his God, the "shining spirit" that had intermittently appeared to Margaret came again and informed her that Mather was now her father in Christ and that through God's providence he had saved her. The angel also opened her eyes to the actual demons crowded around her. They were rather pitiful; the devil himself stood over them lashing them to further effort, for all the world like an overseer whipping his slaves. Indeed the demons were fainting under the punishment and under the strain of their hopeless endeavor. At last they cried out to Margaret, "Go and the devil go with you. We can do no more." Then they fled the place. Nor did they come again, at least in that guise. Margaret's affliction and Boston's best show were both a thing of the past; hereafter Margaret had no more difficulty in getting privacy for her interviews with her "fellows."

Mather for his part learned to keep strictly away from her. His "spiritual daughter" did not turn out to be a very nice girl.

Works Cited

1.

It is irritating not to know exactly which of the afflicted girls "went bad." Certainly they did not include Ann Putnam, Elizabeth Parris, and probably not Abigail Williams, Mary Walcott, or Elizabeth Booth. That they did include others is indicated by a statement in the reversal of the attainder in 1711 which speaks of "some of the principal accusers" as having "discovered themselves to be persons of profligate and vicious conversation." (*Historical Collections* of the Topsfield Historical Society, XIII, pp. 135-137). . .

3.

Cotton Mather's letter to Judge Richards is in Barrett Wendell's *Cotton Mather,* p. 110.

4.

The text of Mather's "Hortatory Address" is printed in Samuel P. Fowler's *Salem Witchcraft,* pp. 394-414.

5.

Cotton Mather's story of Mercy Short, "A Brand Pluck'd out of the Burning," is printed from the manuscript in the possession of the American Antiquarian Society in Burr, pp. 259-287.

6.

The trip to Salem is described in Cotton Mather's *Diary,* September, 1693. Mather's interviews with Margaret Rule are from "Another Brand Pluckt out of the Burning" as incorporated in Calef's "More Wonders," Burr, pp. 307-323.

The seaman is quoted by Calef, *Ibid.,* p. 327; Mather's injunction to Margaret, *Ibid.,* p. 311; Calef's story of Margaret's ways with men, *Ibid.,* pp. 325-327.

Calef's attack on Mather and the latter's reaction are described in *Ibid.,* pp. 305, 335; the correspondence between the two, pp. 339-341.

7.

Mather's successful resolution of the Margaret Rule affair is described in Wendell's *Cotton Mather,* pp. 104 ff.

William Reid Manierre (essay date 1961)

SOURCE: "Verbal Patterns in Cotton Mather's *Magnalia,*" in *The Quarterly Journal of Speech,* Vol. XLVII, No. 4, December, 1961, pp. 402-13.

[*In the essay below, Manierre focuses on the* Magnalia *in his analysis of Mather's writing style and suggests some of the consequences of "appropriating to the written language techniques apparently more suited to the spoken."*]

In 1702, at the age of thirty-nine. Cotton Mather, champion of Puritan orthodoxy ("Puritan Priest," Barrett Wendell called him), third and last of Boston's great ministerial triumvirate of Mather,[1] indefatigable preacher of sermons, most prolific of all American writers and a conscious stylist in all that he wrote, enjoyed, after more than four years of nervous anticipation, his first sight of the published version of his masterpiece, the monumental church history of New England, the **Magnalia Christi Americana.**[2] In this vast work, which covers in seven books the settlement of New England, the lives of its governors and ministers, the establishment of its college, the codification of its theological principles and ecclesiastical practices, and concludes with a record of divine mercies vouchsafed and of dangers overcome, Mather chants a sustained paean to the virtues of "primitive" New England and of its founding saints. His purpose was to create a moral renaissance in a "backsliding" generation. The historical intention is, therefore, strongly qualified by the desire to move and to persuade. The method is largely biographical, and biography for Mather meant the "narration of an exemplary man's exemplary deeds, written to glorify God, honor the memory of his faithful servants, and stimulate readers to admiration and imitation."[3] Biography, then, as conceived by Mather, involved principles closely allied with epideictic—that branch of rhetoric concerned with praise or blame and most often associated with highly ornamented and extravagant style.

In the **Manuductio,**[4] twenty-four years later, Mather cautions against "Squandering . . . Time on the RHETORIC[5] . . . and upon all the *Tropes* and *Schemes,* . . . the very Profession whereof usually is little more than to furnish out a *Stage-Player.*" But he qualifies this advice by advocating careful observation of the "Flowres and Airs of such *Writings,* as are most in Reputation for their *Elegancy*" and by recommending the "agreeably ingenious" employment in the *"Pulpit-Oratory,"* of "The *Sublime . . . Beautiful . . .* [and] *. . . Affectuous . . . Rhetoric*[al] *. . . Figures . . .* in our *Sacred Scriptures*" (p. 34). Thus, the "flowers of rhetoric" out one window are back in through another; and the **Magnalia,** written in the "grand" manner, generously exemplifies this permissiveness. In this work, rhetorical ornament and verbal ingenuity, involving studied play on the sounds and/or meanings of words, constitute the most striking characteristics of Mather's heightened use of language.

To be fully appreciated Mather's prose must be read aloud. This fact suggests both the ultimately oratorical nature of his stylistic strategies, and the close relationship between spoken and written word in an age and place in which the sermon was the dominant literary form. The style points forward to the near fusion of rhetoric with poetic in the eighteenth century, and to the politically oriented rhetoric of America's early national period.[6] But so too does it point back to the glories of an earlier baroque in the works of Sir Thomas Browne, Jeremy Taylor and Thomas Fuller—and beyond these to the source of Renaissance styles in the Middle Ages.

As a means of distinguishing Mather's style from that of others. I have attempted to indicate some of the ways in which his use of various "schemes" differs from that of his contemporaries. It is hoped that the following analysis of Mather's verbal patterns will illuminate his methodology, partly define his style, and suggest some of the possible consequences of appropriating to the written language techniques apparently more suited to the spoken.

At its least conspicuous level, sound play in the *Magnalia* stems from the customary seventeenth-century practice of using words in pairs: "Bent and Aim" (III, 18),[7] "Erroneous and Heretical" (III, 22). Though other New England writers sometimes coupled words in similar fashion, Mather used the device far more frequently than they, and he alone repeatedly combined it with paromoion (repetition of sound). Because of the presence of more striking verbal ingenuities, one might well miss the two sets of word pairs contained in the following passage from "The LIFE of JOHN NORTON":

> But he had the Privilege to enter into *Immortality,* without such a Formal and Feeling Death, as the most of *Mortals* encounter with; for though in the *Forenoon* of *April 5, 1663,* it was his Design to have Preached in the *Afternoon,* he was that *Afternoon* taken with a sudden *Lypothymie,* which presently and easily carried him away to those Glories, wherein the *Weary are at Rest;* but it was a *Dark Night,* which the Inhabitants of *Boston* had upon the Noise of his Death: Every Corner of the Town was filled with Lamentations, which left a Character upon that *Night,* unto this *Day,* not forgotton (III, 38).

The paired adjectives, "Formal and Feeling," and adverbs, "presently and easily," are unobtrusive, but they exemplify one of Mather's favorite stylistic devices, which coupled noun with noun, verb with verb, or, as here, adjective with adjective or adverb with adverb.

When others combined paromoion with word pairs, it was usually in the form of simple alliteration (repetition of sound at the beginning of words). This form often appears in the *Magnalia: "forget* or *forgive"* (I,

9); "Seasonable and Sufficient" (I, 31); *"shaken* and *shatter'd"* (II, 58). With equal, if not greater frequency, however, such pairs in the *Magnalia* involve repetition of sound at the end of words (homoioteleuton): "Killing and Wounding" (I, 9); *"Liberty* and *Property"* (II, 197); "Temptations and Afflictions" (III, 16).

Almost as frequent, and far more noticeable, are the word pairs involving repetition of sounds at both end and beginning. This form (paronomasia)[8] often combines a play on sound with a play on sense, but, when in conjunction with word pairs such as those described here, paronomasia in Mather's prose tended to be primarily a figure of sound. It is, however, less likely than the simpler forms to be merely additive: *"Conviction . . . Confession"* (III, 7); "encouraging and enlivening" (III, 53); "Passion and Poison" (III, 72); *"Pathetical* and *Prophetical"* (III, 62). The punning possibilities of this figure are sufficiently obvious, but since the pun does not necessarily involve repetition of sound, being primarily a figure of sense, it will be dealt with later.

Another form of paromoion that constantly appears in the *Magnalia* consists of the repetition in a modified word of a sound initially introduced in the modifier: "most memorable" (I, 2); "unseasonable Freezing" (I, 24); "Troublesome Time" (II, 20). Like the less elaborate word pairs, this variety of sound play is quite unobtrusive when occurring by itself. Locutions, however, that incorporate pairs of modifiers with pairs of words modified, particularly when each word contains sounds identical or similar to those contained in the other three, convey effects considerably more striking: "comfortable Dwellings and considerable Demesnes" (III, 87); "terrible *Temptations,* and horrible *Buffetings"* (III, 121). Frequently, the modifier is simply repeated: "several Deliverances from several Distresses" (III, 87). Less frequently, the modified words, although themselves containing similar sounds, do not contain sounds present in the reiterated modifier: "of Good Estate, and of Good Esteem" (III, 33).

But Mather, not satisfied with the coupling of merely two words, extended the technique to include combinations of three or more words in series. Inordinately aware of sounds, he usually incorporated paromoion with such structures: "Little, Idle, Angry" (I, 25); *"Colonies, Counties,* and *Congregations"* (I, 27); "Provoking, Pernicious, and Perillous" (VII, 23). Frequently the series consists of three or more phrases of various types rather than of single words: "with what *Holiness,* with what *Watchfulness,* with what *Usefulness"* (III, 40); "their Love to, and Zeal for, and Care of these *Churches"* (II, 21); "broke up, went off, and came to nothing" (I, 12).[9] Sometimes the series is interrupted by qualifying words or phrases which partly break the otherwise symmetrical pattern. Sometimes not all the words or phrases contain similar sounds, and, time after time, words placed in conjunction with each other are presented in such a way as to stress contrast or antithesis. And sometimes sets of words and phrases are not simply presented in series but are incorporated into more complex structures.

When modification is combined with sets of three or more words, the effect is conspicuous. It will be noted that, in some of the following examples, Mather varies his structure in order to avoid absolute symmetry, to make additional modification possible, or to add still another "member" to the series. Regardless of variations, however, the overall pattern remains the same—an extension and elaboration of the relatively simple device of using words in pairs: "an extraordinary *Invention,* Curious *Disposition,* and Copious *Application*" (IV, 173); "the *Gravity,* the *Majesty,* the Scriptural and Awful *Pungency* of these his Dispensations" (IV, 174); "most Exemplary *Piety,* Extraordinary *Ingenuity,* Obliging Affability, join'd with the Accomplishments of an Extraordinary Preacher did render him truly Excellent" (IV, 200); "*Prayers* and *Praises,* and in Inexpressible *Joys*" (II, 25); "It is an *Honest,* and a *Lawful,* tho' it be not a very *Desirable* Employment" (I, 36). It would be a pointless task to categorize in detail the many variations which patterns of this kind can and do take in Mather's prose. Consider, for instance, the following passage, which, although it belongs to the same general category as do the examples already cited, is identical with none of them: "the Ministers and Passengers constantly served God, Morning and Evening; *Reading, Expounding* and *Applying* the Word of God, *singing* of His Praise, and *seeking* of His Peace" (I, 17). The possible combinations are inumerable, but all of them fit into the same general pattern of conscious verbal manipulation for stylistic effect.

Verbal patterns such as those described here illustrate the copia of Mather's style. He was seldom satisfied with one word if he could use two, or with two if he could use three. His theory of style does not advocate concision, nor does his prose exemplify this characteristic. These facts may partly result from the customary Puritan desire for exactness and precision, even at the expense of brevity. Much New England prose consisted of precise Biblical exegesis and the drawing of fine distinctions between theological points. In order to combine clarity with precision, the Puritan author frequently resorted to what can only be called superfluity of modification. Mather, who combined with these motives the desire to present everything in its strongest colors, delighted in piling adjective on adjective and adverb on adverb: "he was Affable, Courteous, and generally *Pleasant,* but *Grave* perpetually; and so Cautelous and Circumspect in his Discourses, and so Modest in his Expressions" (II, 28): "this our Learned, Able, Holy, and no less *Considerate,* than *Considerable* MITCHEL" (IV, 180); "One of the most Eminent and Judicious Persons that ever lived in this World,

was *Intentionally* a *New-England Man,* tho' not *Eventually,* when that *Profound,* that *Sublime,* that *Subtil,* that *Irrefragable,* yea that *Angelical Doctor*" (III, 3). There were simply not enough words in the English, or any other language, to express adequately the extremity of Mather's reverence for the leaders of primitive New England.

Closely related to the repetition of sound in groups of two or more different words is the repetition of the same word within a single sentence.[10] Play on the concepts of night and day is probably the most conspicuous feature of the passage on Norton (*"Dark Night";* "upon that *Night";* "unto this *Day"*). Mather here calls attention to his own ingenuity by repeating the same word in different contexts and by placing it, toward the close of the sentence, in emphatic contrast with the antithetic word "*Day.*"[11] Repetition of a single key word for stylistic effect (ploce) is one of Mather's favorite devices: "a very diminutive kind of Boat . . . [which] . . . they made a shift . . . to lengthen it so far, that they could therein form a *little Cuddy,* . . . and they set up a *little Mast,* whereto they fastened a little Sail, and accommodated it with some other *little Circumstances,* according to their present poor Capacity" (II, 54).[12] Sometimes, as here, the purpose is to emphasize a single descriptive point. Although this passage is somewhat atypical in that Mather usually emphasizes bigness, abundance, excess, rather than diminutiveness or paucity,[13] the same technique could serve either purpose. There were no words strong enough to express Mather's detestation of idleness other than the very word itself, which, by repetition, constitutes its own superlative: "*Idleness,* alas! *Idleness* increases in the Town exceedingly: *Idleness,* of which there never came any *Goodness; Idleness,* which is a *reproach to any People*" (I, 37). Equally emphatic is Mather's denunciation of sin: "Let us beware of every *Sin;* for *Sin* will turn a *Man* into a *Devil.* Oh! Vile SIN, horrid SIN, cursed SIN; or, to speak a more pungent Word, than all of That; Oh, SINFUL sin!" (IV, 198).

Repetition of key words is a standard characteristic of the New England sermon. In order to keep their listeners' attention on the Biblical text, or particular thesis, New England ministers were not averse to using the same words over and over again in different contexts. They did so primarily in order to gain clarity, precision, and less often, emphasis. Mather, as usual, carried the device to extremes, and in his sermons its effect is less that of clarity and precision than of exaggerated emphasis—and, at times, of pure ingenuity. In his sermon entitled "What the Pious Parent Wishes For,"[14] Mather repeats the key word "heart" more than one hundred and sixty times. The number of exclamation marks is staggering, and the unutterable excess of his emotion is conveyed by no fewer than thirty-four instances of the exclamatory interjection "OH!"[15] Mather's reliance on this characteristically oratorical stratagem is simply another indication of his overpowering compulsion to magnify, to exaggerate, to present every subject in superlative terms.

Such studied repetition of an individual word provided him with a suitable means of attaining "elegant," "charming," and "agreeably ingenious" rhetorical turns: "It was not on the *Lord's Day* only, but *every Day*, that this good Man was usually, *In the Fear of the Lord all the Day long*" (III, 79).[16] More striking are passages which involve the repetition of more than one key word or phrase. These structures usually point verbal contrasts and always involve balance of one kind or another; their witty effect sometimes results from reversal of the original word order, and, less often, from violation of natural word order. Here are examples:

> There was nothing more *Observable* in his *Temper*, than such a Study of a *Temper* in all Difficult Matters, as renders a Person *aimable* [sic], wherever 'tis *Observable* (IV, 477).

> *He was a Burning and a Shining Light*. In the Tabernacle of Old . . . there were those Two Things, a Candlestick and an Altar; in the One a *Light* that might never go out, in the other a *Fire* that might never be extinguished; and yet such an Affinity between these, that there was a *Fire* in the *Light* of the one, and a *Light* in the *Fire* of the other (III, 32).

Mather was fond of attaining antithetic and surprising verbal relationships by altering prefixes[17] or the elements of compound words: "this *False-dealing* proved a *Safe-dealing*" (I, 7); "I was my Self an *Ear-witness*, that one, who was an *Eye-witness*" (II, 67). Usually, however, this figure consists of the repetition of a single root in different inflectional forms (polyptoton): "his Abstinence had more *Sweetness* in it, than any of the *Sweets* which he abstained from" (III, 179). Here the root word "sweet" appears with two different endings but each time as a noun. Metathetic change is illustrated by the noun "Abstinence" and the verb "abstained from." The device enabled him to use what was essentially a single word as more than one part of speech within a single sentence, and to combine ingenious patterns of sound play with varying degrees of semantic antithesis.

Clearly a development of the simpler device of repeating the same word within a given passage, polyptoton is the most distinctive form of Mather's sound play.[18] In its possibilities for emphasis, for elaboration of similar or antithetic concepts, for variety, and for ingenious verbal twists, this form of paromoion was ideally suited to the purposes Mather set for himself as an author, and like his other stylistic characteristics, it is an extreme form of customary Puritan literary techniques. The examples which follow will give some notion of the many variations which this figure can take:

> (1) he was loth to *see*, and yet fear'd he *saw* . . . (III, 189).

> (2) though a Great Person for *Stature*, yet a Greater for *Spirit*, he was greatly serviceable for the Good of the Church . . . (III, 214).

> (3) Governour *Phips* . . . must have, his *Envious Enemies*; but the palest Envy of them, who turned their worst Enmity upon him . . . (II, 58).

> (4) After *Him* we have had, besides those, whose *Lives* are anon to be Written, many others that by *Writing* have made themselves to *Live* . . . (IV, 135).

> (5) He was a very *Lively Preacher*, and a very *Preaching Liver*. He lov'd his *Church* as if it had been his *Family*, and he taught his *Family*, as if it had been his *Church* (III, 114).

> (6) The Faults of the *Penitent*, indeed, should be *Concealed*; but these pretended *Preachers* of *Repentance* are not known to *Practice* the *Repentance* which they *Preach* (VII, 32).[19]

In these examples, polyptoton, in combination with balanced structures, not only serves to accentuate various degrees of semantic contrast, but to emphasize the decidedly rhythmical qualities inherent in such structures.[20]

Our progression has been from the simpler forms of sound repetition, relatively divorced from plays on meaning, to those in which semantic relationships are at least equal in importance to sound play. Ploce and polyptoton, for instance, particularly when combined with balanced structures, serve to emphasize contrasts in sense; but one often feels that Mather used such figures as much for their own sake as for their contribution to meaning. In passages such as those quoted in the last paragraph it is impossible to distinguish so precisely as to state dogmatically that polyptoton is primarily a figure of sound or of sense. It serves both functions about equally and so constitutes the turning point of this essay; the remainder deals with verbal ingenuities, which, although they may involve paromoion, are primarily plays on meaning rather than sound.[21]

In the following passage, play on differing meanings of "stand" results in paradox: "sometimes he could not *stand before it;* but it was by *not standing* that he most effectually *withstood it*" (II, 10). Apparent contradiction is also the initial impression conveyed by the following play on *"Falling Down"* and *"Flying up"*; "his Labours were so fervent and eager, that he would sometimes *Preach* till he *fell down*. . . . His last *Falling Down* was a *"Flying up"* (III, 217). As in these instances, the apparent contradiction of a Mather paradox is apt to be metaphorical or verbal rather than actual. *"Flying up"* is a metaphor for the ascension of the soul to heaven;[22] "stand," in the verb "to withstand," means something decidedly different from when used by itself. Because of this characteristic, Mather's verbal paradoxes are actually a kind of pun instead of the expression in words of concepts or situations that are themselves paradoxical.

The "punning paradox" constitutes a culmination of the various verbal patterns previously identified. It represents the setting up of words or phrases in balanced and antithetic relationship with each other carried to its extreme form—that of implied contradiction. Although it does not always illustrate paromoion, it frequently involves balance, antithesis, symmetry, inversion and contrast to which paromoion, in its various forms, draws attention:

(1) But what is now become of *New-Haven* Colony? I must Answer, *It is not*: And yet it has been growing ever since it first *was* (I, 26).

(2) he was chosen a *Magistrate* of *New-England* before *New-England* it self came into *New-England* (II, 19).

(3) having been taught by the Affliction to *Die Daily*, as long as he *Lived* (II, 24).

(4) Hitherto we have seen the *Life* of Mr. *Cotton*, while he was not yet *Alive!* (III, 15).

(5) he became a *Father* to the *Colledge*, which had been his *Mother* (IV, 181).

(6) Wo to us, if we are not *Born Twice* before we *Die Once!* (III, 230).

Mather also indulged in the pun pure and simple. In the **_Magnalia_,** the pun usually consists of a repetition of the same word in two different senses, but, on occasion, one use of the word sufficed: "when he judg'd that he had kept them on their *Knees* long enough, he having first secur'd their *Arms*, received them aboard" (II, 40). Here, without repetition, Mather expressed both the anatomical and the military meanings of the single word. Similarly, repetition was unnecessary to an ingenious play on animadversions: "It will not be so much a Surprise unto me, if I should live to see our *Church-History* vexed with *Anie-mad-versions* of Calumnious Writers" ("General Introduction"). Usually, however, the effect was gained by repeating homonyms in their different senses:

He did not put off his *Charity*, to be put in his *last Will*, as many who therein shew that their *Charity* is *against their Will* (III, 181).

. . . the *Ministers* . . . used all due Pains to *Charm* these *Adders* with convincing Disputations, when they were in the *Bay*, and indeed often drove them to a *Bay* with Argument (VII, 12).

. . . to be oft, or long in your *Visits* of the *Ordinary*, 'twill certainly expose you to Mischiefs more than ordinary (I, 36).

Mather's desire to be ingenious is even more apparent in his discussion of certain *"Private Meetings* [at which] good People [concluded] their more Sacred Exercises with Suppers; [but now, although the meetings] do still abound among us; . . . the *Meals* that made *Meatings* of them, are generally laid aside" (III, 6). Puns on common nouns, usually combined with some form of repetition, are frequent in Mather's prose, but his special delight was in the metaphorical possibilities afforded by personal names.

In contrast to his other verbal ingenuities, Mather's puns on personal names rarely depend on repetition of sound or on balanced structure. Their distinguishing feature is their metaphorical quality—easy metaphors, to be sure, but not used frivolously:

[Henry Flint] was a Solid *Stone*, in the Foundations of *New-England* (III, 122).

Thomas Shepard . . . escaped those, *to whom such a Shepherd was an Abomination* (III, 87).

. . . even that *Hooker*, who having *Angled* many Scores of Souls into the Kingdom of Heaven (III, 174).

. . . for all the Fires of Martyrdom which were kindled in the Days of Queen *Mary*, [Yorkshire] afforded no more *Fuel* than one poor *Leaf*; namely, *John Leaf*, an apprentice (II, 2).

Sometimes, as in the following pun on the name of John Cotton, the effect is ludicrous: "One would have thought the Ingenuity of such a Spirit should have broke the *Hearts of Men*, that had indeed the *Hearts of Men* in them; yea, that the hardest *Flints* would have been broken, as is usual, upon such a soft Bag of *Cotton!* (III, 26). It is, perhaps, all for the best that Mather closed this sentence with an exclamation point.

Play on the meanings of personal names often appears in conjunction with Mather's use of knowledge derived from books. The name of Samuel Stone was, like those of Hooker and Shepard, ideally suited for the simple pun. "Indeed the Foundation of

New-England had a precious *Jem* laid in it, when Mr. *Stone* arrived" (III, 116). "He was a *Man of Principles,* and in the Management of those Principles, he was both a *Load stone* and a *Flint stone*" (III, 117). In the following passage, however, the simple pun, in which Samuel Stone gave "sparks" in the form of a theological work, introduces equations between Samuel Stone, the "*Stone* from the *Sling of David*" (I Samuel, 17:49) and the "*Stone* of *Bohan*" (Joshua, 15:6; 18:17):

> But certain Strokes of Mr. *Hudson* and Mr. *Cowdrey,* fetch'd one Spark out of this well compacted *Stone;* which was, *A Discourse about the Logical Notion of a Congregational Church;* wherein some thought, that as a *Stone* from the *Sling* of *David,* he has mortally wounded the Head of that *Goliah, A National Political Church.* At least, he made an Essay, to do what was done by the *Stone* of *Bohan,* setting the *Bounds* between Church and Church, as *That* between Tribe and Tribe (III, 118).

The puns here refer not only to Biblical matters but to controversies over the relationship between church and state. The knowledge derived from books also contributes its share to a pun on the illness that did not cause Samuel Stone's death: "As for Mr. *Stone,* if it were *Metaphorically* true (what they *Proverbially* said) of Beza, that *he had no Gall,* the Physicians that opened him after his Death, found it *Literally* true in this worthy Man" (III, 118).[23] And a Latin aphorism concludes yet another pun on the apposite subject of stones: "'Tis not easy to *comprehend,* and I wish no such Faithful Servant of God may *experience* it; how much the *Spirit* of Mr. *Stone,* was worn by the *Continual Dropping* of this Contention.—*Gutta Cavat Lapidem*" (III, 118).[24] In fact, "The LIFE of Mr. SAMUEL STONE" opens with a learned, biographical parallel based on the identity of meanings of the English word "stone" and the Latin word "lapis."

"The LIFE of Mr. ADAM BLACKMAN" consists largely of a play on contrasts between name and character, combined with appropriate comments on a famous teacher who "had the Name of *Niger*" and that "Great Person among the Reformers in *Germany,* . . . [Melanchthon] . . . who had almost the same Name with our *Blackman*" (III, 94). Although the name of Partridge is less obviously suited to puns on character and calling than are Shepard, Hooker, Stone, or Blackman, Mather discovered a parallel that thoroughly pleased him. "The LIFE of Mr. RALPH PARTRIDGE" consists almost entirely of an extended, punning metaphor that conveys, in little, the essence of the Puritan migration to New England.[25] This particular divine was described (III, 99):

> *an hunted Partridge* . . . , distress'd by . . .

Ecclesiastical *Setters* . . . [Having] Defence, neither of *Beak,* nor *Claw,* . . . [he took] *Flight* over the Ocean . . . [and] . . . Covert [in] the Colony of *Plymouth.* . . . [He had] the Innocency of the *Dove* [and] . . . , in the great Soar of his intellectual Abilities . . . , the Loftiness of an *Eagle.* . . . [He was], notwithstanding the *Paucity* and the *Poverty* of his Congregation, so afraid of being any thing that look'd like *a Bird wandring from his Nest,* that he remained with his poor People, till he *took Wing* to become a *Bird of Paradise,* along with the winged *Seraphim* of Heaven.

EPITAPHIUM

Avolavit—

This is not great literature, but surely it is a pleasure to read. Doubtless, the formula is mechanical; neither intuitive perception nor artistic sensitivity is requisite to its use. The pun and the fanciful conceit are out of date and have lost their seriousness, but for Mather they provided a perfect means of combining variety and ingenuity with edification. His delight in developing such figures communicates itself to the sympathetic reader—but this is beyond the reach of analysis.

Personal names were not, for Mather, mere tags, of use only to distinguish one man from another.[26] They, like everything else, were full of meaning. What may be called the etymological pun was another device by means of which Mather utilized such meaning: to "bedeck" his prose, to characterize his subject, to advocate desirable personal "attributes," and, ultimately, to profit his readers. This variety of the pun consists of the pointed use, in English translation, of the original meanings conveyed by personal names in their parent languages. Sometimes, as with the name of Thomas Allen, Mather underscores his linguistic knowledge. "The Name of *Allen* being but our Pronunciation of the *Saxon* Word, *Alwine,* which is as much as to say *Beloved of All,* expressed the Fate of this our *Allen,* among the Generality of the welldisposed. And being a *Man greatly Beloved* . . ." (III, 215).[27] Sometimes Mather used his knowledge of ecclesiastical history to introduce his etymological puns. The result is a variety of the biographical parallel. "One of the First *English* Arch-bishops *assumed* the Name of *Deus dedit,* and the Historian says, he *answered* the Name that he *assumed.* Our *Nathanael* was not in the Rank of Arch-bishops; but *as was his Name,* a GIFT OF GOD, *so was he!*" (III, 104). Usually, however, as in the two following examples, Mather's use of this learned device was unobtrusive. "His *Benjamin* was made the *Son of his Right Hand* . . ." (III, 174). "Her Name was *Anne,* and *Gracious* was her Nature" (III, 173). Somehow less obnoxious to modern tastes than the pun pure and simple, the etymological pun reflects, and partly defines, Mather's learned background.

The anagram, like the pious pun, and itself a kind of pun, provided Mather with still another means of extracting significance from personal names. ". . . an End, whereat JOHN NORTON went, according to the Anagram of his Name INTO HONOR" (III, 38). ". . . our *Eliot* (the Anagram of whose Name was TOILE . . ." (III, 193). Mather himself described the anagram as "a certain little *Sport of Wit*" (III, 49)—a phrase indicative of low esteem. He recognized, however, that it, like the pun, could be used for edification. Sometimes it "has afforded Reflections very *Monitory*, as *Alstedius* by his just Admirers changed into *Sedulitas;* or very *Characterizing*, as *Renatus Cartesius,* by his Disciples turn'd into, *Tu scis res Naturae;* or very *Satyrical*, as when *Satan ruleth me*, was found in the Transposed Name of a certain Active Persecutor"[28] (III, 49). Since anagrams could be at the same time instructive and ingenious, Mather had every reason for using them in the *Magnalia,* but few of those that appear in the work are of his own devising. Almost all are qualified by the remark that someone else made them up. "Mr. Wilson's anagrammatising of JOHANNES NORTONUS into *Nonne is Honoratus?* Will give him his deserved Character" (III, 38). John Allin "was indeed one of so sweet a Temper, that his Friends *Anagrammatised* [his name] into this: IN HONI ALL" (III, 133).

Anagrams and pious puns are forms of the same general technique, which results from a search for significance over and above mere literal import. They are also indicative of the importance attached by New England Puritans to the meanings of words and, in particular, of those most meaningful of all words—personal names. J. F. Jameson remarks:

> The punning habit . . . crops out in all [of Mather's] writings, and indeed a general habit of verbal jingles and ingenuities which might justify one in applying to [Mather] what he in the *Magnalia* says in praise of Rev. John Wilson, in commending
>
> "His care to guide his *Flock* and feed his *lambs,*
>
> By words, works, prayers, psalms, alms, and anagrams."[29]

Mr. Jameson's comment introduces the final point of this essay. Play on the sound and/or meaning of words is unquestionably characteristic of the *Magnalia's* style, but to what extent is it a distinguishing feature?

What distinguishes Mather's sound play is less the nature of the techniques used than the excessive use to which he put them. Many of the patterns described at the beginning of this paper occasionally appear in the prose of other New England authors. William Bradford, John Cotton, Edward Johnson, and John Norton, for instance, utilized word pairs and sometimes combined them with repetition of sound.[30] Others, such as John Winthrop, Increase Mather, and William Hubbard, rarely used such pairs either with or without sound play. Repetition of the same word within a single sentence was not uncommon, but the purpose was, almost invariably, clarity or emphasis rather than ingenuity. Repetition of the same stem with inflectional variation[31] was, however, extremely rare. Play on two key words in antithetic relationship was also uncommon, but does, on occasion, appear. Structures involving antithetic and balanced relationships between clauses or phrases are far more frequent, but, with the exception of Mather, few authors brought attention to them by paromoion. Other writers, when they wished to make a passage particularly striking, had at their disposal the same techniques that Mather used. But he wanted everything to be striking and, consequently, used exorbitantly what others used with restraint.

The passage in which William Hubbard remarks that "the foolishness of the sons and daughters of men makes them choose sin rather than shame, till at last they are covered with sin for their shame,"[32] is virtually indistinguishable from innumerable passages in the *Magnalia*. So too with isolated passages in the writings of John Norton, Thomas Hooker, and Increase Mather. In the prose of these authors, however, such rhetorical turns are isolated, tending to occur no more than three or four times in a given work. Furthermore, by the 1690's, Cotton Mather was almost alone in continuing to use them at all.[33] They reflect an earlier period, during which a restrained play with words was a legitimate form of decoration, during which a limited use[34] of verbal ingenuity was not regarded as entirely frivolous. By the 1690's, however, literary standards were changing, and spokesmen for a new age—the Stoddards, Calefs, Colmans, and Wises—had no use for such "outworn devices." What distinguishes Mather's use of sound play from that of earlier New England writers is that he utilized it so frequently and in such a variety of contexts. What rarely appears in the prose of others is constantly present in the *Magnalia*. Few of its paragraphs are without rhetorical turns of one kind or another, and, when missing, their place is usually taken by ingenious displays of learning. When, as so often happens, the two appear in combination, the effect is distinctly Matherian.

The abundance of "verbal jingles,"[35] rather than their mere presence, distinguishes Mather's prose from that of New Englanders who wrote prior to the last decade of the seventeenth century. Their presence or absence alone, however, helps to distinguish "early" New England prose from that produced after the turn of the century. But verbal ingenuity stemming primarily from the studied play on multiplicity of meanings, rather than on repetitive sound patterns, is, regardless of date, a major feature in the prose of but two New England authors—Cotton Mather and Nathaniel Ward.

Before the close of the century, the pious pun had been a thoroughly reputable ingredient of elegiac verse. "Since nothing in the life of a good man could be unordained by Providence, one's name—either in its pristine form, or anagrammatically rearranged—or the disease one suffered from, or one's profession, or the mode of one's death: all were motifs not adventitious."[36] Except for Mather and Ward, however, New Englanders tended to restrict the pun, whether on common noun or personal name, to the funeral elegy.[37] The anagram, too, was ordinarily limited to obituary verse; although it occasionally appeared in prefatory poems.[38] These were techniques that the generality of New Englanders considered somehow less suitable to prose than to poetry, Cotton Mather and Nathaniel Ward dissenting.

The "punning habit" perfectly exemplifies Mather's custom of putting to use every rhetorical device available to him. Others used the pun in their poetry; Mather used it in his prose as well. Others occasionally used antithetic structures in their prose, and, less often, combined it with simple and unobtrusive forms of sound play; Mather incorporated seeming contradiction with such structures, and the result is the punning paradox. Others, interested in exegetical precision, worked out the etymology of words; Mather combined etymological study with plays on double meanings, and the result is the etymological pun. Others tended to limit the anagram to obituary verses; Mather utilized it in his prose. In short, whatever had proved useful to other writers, Mather appropriated to his own purposes; verbal techniques that others used seldom, unobtrusively, and with restraint, Mather used without restraint, extravagantly, and in exaggerated form.

Notes

[1] Richard (1596-1669); Increase (1639-1723); Cotton (1662/63-1727/28).

[2] Printed in London by Thomas Parkhurst. All quotations from the *Magnalia* are taken from this edition.

[3] Reginald E. Watters, "Biographical Technique in Cotton Mather's *Magnalia*," *William and Mary College Quarterly—Historical Magazine*, 3rd Series, II (1945), 155.

[4] *Manuductio ad Ministerium* (Boston, 1726).

[5] I have retained the original capitals, spellings, and italics throughout.

[6] Gordon E. Bigelow, "Rhetoric and American Poetry of the Early National Period," University of Florida Monographs, *Humanities*, No. 4 (Spring, 1960).

[7] Each of the seven books of the 1702 folio has separate pagination.

[8] The minute differences between paronomasia, agnomination, syllabic antithesis, etc. need not concern us. What is desired here is to give some idea of the general patterns that characterize Mather's use of language.

[9] The symmetry in this and the preceding example is the result of isocolon and parison rather than of paromoion. Mather ordinarily relied more on similarity of sound than of form or length, although quite often all three are involved.

[10] Sometimes Mather would repeat a key word over and over again throughout passages extending to a paragraph or more. In his sermons, key words are repeated throughout.

[11] The effect is all the more pronounced because of the earlier play on *"Forenoon"* and *"Afternoon."*

[12] The four locutions in which *"little"* is repeated, each time with a different noun, may be considered an elaboration of Mather's use of three or more words in series. Note also that "diminutive" and "poor" are roughly synonymous with *"little."*

[13] In fact, when applied to human beings, "little" was one of Mather's favorite terms of disparagement. To magnify was to praise; to diminish, to condemn.

[14] Included in *A Course of Sermons on Early Piety* (Boston, 1721). This is a delightful little collection of sermons by various New Englanders. A reading of the sermons contained in it will give, as no description can, a feeling for the difference between Mather's characteristic frenzy and the more restrained tone of his contemporaries.

[15] Appearing entirely by itself, rather than in such apostrophes as "Oh God!," with which the sermon is also liberally endowed.

[16] The play on *"Night"* and *"Day"* in the passage on Norton is, like the just quoted example, more ingenious than emphatic. Usually, the two qualities are about equal: "gave *Thanks* unto the God of Heaven, so they sent an Address of *Thanks* unto Their Majesties, with other Letters of *Thanks* unto some Chief Ministers" (II, 58).

[17] As in the play on *"Forenoon"* and *"Afternoon"* in

the passage on Norton.

18 Both ploce and polyptoton are important features of Edward Taylor's poetry. See my forthcoming "Verbal Patterns in the Poetry of Edward Taylor," *College English.*

19 This and the preceding example illustrate another trait of style frequently encountered in the *Magnalia*: the ending of a sentence with a word (usually with inflectional variation) that has previously appeared in it. As a result of Mather's. fondness for repetitive patterns (isocolon. parison, and, above all, paromoion), his sentences tend to be more symmetrical than those of most New England authors. Unlike Ciceronian (or euphuistic) sentences, however, Mather's are almost never perfectly circular or symmetrical in structure. They are, rather, characterized by symmetry of the part and asymmetry of the whole, and are far more apt to involve intraclausal than interclausal balance. They conform to Senecan, not Ciceronian, patterns; on occasion, repetition of words in terminal position tends to obscure the fact.

20 The emphatic rhythms of Mather's prose are further accentuated by his preference for polysyllabic diction: "As his Diligence was indefatigable, so his *Proficiency* was proportionable: And he was particularly considerable there, for his Disputations upon the Points then most considerably controverted" (III, 143). But this is an extreme example.

21 *Schemata sententiae* as opposed to *schemata verborum;* roughly synonymous with the terms "puns" and "jingles," which have often been used—most often pejoratively—to describe Mather's verbal ornaments.

22 The apparent contradiction results from Mather's intentional omission of the distinction between body and spirit.

23 Note the explicit distinction between metaphorical and literal meanings. Note also the equation drawn, in the preceding quotation, between *"Goliah"* and *"A National Political Church."* Analogical, metaphorical, and symbolical (no less than typological) interpretation of the Scriptures was responsible for much that appears in New England (as in Medieval) literature.

24 One cannot fail to note how Mather's verbal devices appear again and again. In this example, there is the pointed contrast between *"comprehend"* and *"experience;"* in the preceding example, between *"Metaphorically,"* *"Proverbially,"* and *"Literally,"*

25 As Austin Warren says in *New England Saints* (Ann Arbor, 1956), p. 15: "Cotton Mather, commemorating the Reverend Ralph Partridge, . . . finds a

life in a name. . . ."

26 Nor did other orthodox New England Puritans consider them as mere tags. See the first chapter of Warren (above).

27 For a more extended example, which combines display of linguistic knowledge with Biblical exegesis, see Mather's discussion of "the signification of the word Azazel" (VI, 66).

28 Mather, in discussing John Wilson's penchant for the anagram, points out the didactic values of this form of wit: " . . . there could scarcely occurr the Name of *any* Remarkable *Person,* at least, on *any* Remarkable *Occasion* unto him, without an *Anagram* raised thereupon; and he made this *Poetical,* and *Peculiar* Disposition of his Ingenuity, a Subject whereon he grafted *Thoughts* far more Solid, and Solemn, and Useful, than the *Stock* it self" (III, 49).

29 J. Franklin Jameson, *The History of Historical Writing in America* (Boston, 1891), p. 5. Jameson quotes from "The LIFE of Mr. JOHN WILSON," *Magnalia,* III, 51.

30 Usually in the form of alliteration. Johnson was fond of using series of three or more nouns or noun phrases. Such series, in Johnson, frequently involve either alliteration or homoioteleuton.

31 Or with metathetic change or varied prefix.

32 William Hubbard, *A General History of New England from the Discovery to MDCLXXX,* Vols. V and VI, MHS Collections, 2nd Series (Boston, 1848), VI, 530.

33 They continue to appear sporadically in the prose of Increase Mather, and one occasionally encounters them in that of Benjamin Wadsworth.

34 Cotton Mather's generous use of such techniques would always have conflicted with the negative requirements of the plain style.

35 Those that consist of sound play rather than play on meaning.

36 Warren, *loc. cit.*

37 This is not to say that puns never appear in the prose of others than Ward or Mather; only, that they are rare.

38 See, for instance, the anagrams on the name of Cotton Mather that precede the text of the *Magnalia.*

. . . [Historians] have called the *Magnalia* the last work of its kind, a monumental elegy to a defunct corporate ideal. . . . By all accounts, the *Magnalia* was an anachronism on the day of its publication. . . . [Its] summons fell on deaf ears; it scarcely aroused the antagonism its author anticipated. When in 1820 the Reverend Thomas Robbins, librarian of the Connecticut Historical Society, persuaded a publisher of antiquarian curiosities to venture the first American edition, he expected a small sale at best. By that time, the name Cotton Mather had become a catchall for puritan hypocrisy and repression. As for the *Magnalia* itself, "a small part of the community," Robbins sighed, "even knew of [its] existence." To his suprise, the edition sold steadily though slowly, and a second was called for in 1853. Robbins speculated, accurately, that the interest centered not so much in the church history as in the general fascination with the growth of America. The Puritans, he noted, quoting Virgil, had dedicated themselves to a holy labor—"And now we may say, by the favour of HEAVEN, THE WORK IS DONE. The world looks with amazement on a great Countrey. . . more extensive than Rome," inhabited by an equally "great population . . . all looking for Salvation in the name of the DIVINE NAZARENE."

Sacvan Bercovitch, *The Puritan Origins of the American Self*, Yale University Press, 1975.

Sacvan Bercovitch (essay date 1966)

SOURCE: "New England Epic: Cotton Mather's *Magnalia Christi Americana*," in *ELH*, Vol. 33, No. 3, September, 1966, pp. 337-50.

[*In the essay below, Bercovitch describes Mather's* Magnalia Christi Americana *as a metaphoric account of life in Puritan New England and compares the work to those of Vergil and John Milton.*]

On July 4, 1700, in the solitude of his diary, the heir to the dispossessed dynasty of Puritan New England lamented the emergence of a new era in America. "I saw, to my Sorrow," he wrote,

> that there was hardly any but my Father, and myself, to appear in Defence of our invaded Churches. Wherefore I thought I must cry mightily unto the Lord, that He would mercifully direct my feeble, but faithful, Endeavors in an evil Generation.

I also thought, that since it be the Purpose of Heaven that the *Apostasy* shall go on [I] may be in danger of a Stroke from the *Angel of Death,* that so *a Way may be made for the Anger of God.* Hereupon, the Lord sent into my Spirit a Sweet Meditation and Consolation that my *Life* shall the rather be prolonged; and my *Name* shall be the more precious [to posterity].[1]

The Lord did not, on this occasion, deceive His feeble but faithful servant. Cotton Mather lived twenty-eight years longer into the yankee apostasy, and the Church History he had just bundled off for publication in England, his largest and greatest book, remains perhaps the supreme achievement of American Puritan literature.

The **Magnalia Christi Americana** is an important work of the figural imagination. Puritan scholars have discussed it either as a "historical *omnium gatherum*" or, in terms of church tradition, as the *magnum opus* of New England jeremiads.[2] Their view, which assumes the strict subordination of literature to theology throughout the period, has in general stunted a proper literary appreciation of early colonial writing; in particular, their approach is inadequate for the **Magnalia**. Mather's arguments here are not, as they would have it, "theology clothed in metaphor." His arguments *are* metaphor. Written in defiance of "an evil Generation," not for it, the **Magnalia** recasts fact into image and symbol, and raises the story of New England into a heroic world, in which, as Hawthorne recognized, "true events and real personages move before the reader with the dreamy aspect which they wore in Cotton Mather's singular mind."[3]

Mather himself suggests that he *intended* a transformation of this kind. In the **Magnalia,** he often likens the process of its composition to that of artistic creation, speaks of it in terms of sculpture, painting, music, and drama, and refers continually to literary works, from Sophocles to Cervantes.[4] Especially, he shows familiarity with *The Aeneid* and *Paradise Lost.* From the latter—where he found his great example of the Puritan literary imagination—Mather quotes at length, "taking the colours of Milton to describe our story" (II, 566); and throughout the work he alludes numerous times, directly and indirectly, to *The Aeneid,* in which he saw the pagan counterpart of his undertaking. Predictably enough, the great majority of his references come from the Bible; but it is the Bible seen through the eyes of a seventeenth-century Puritan: not only as a historical document—nor even, in our sense, as a source for ecclesiastical doctrine—but also, in Mather's words, as "a Book of Mysteries" (I, 33) awaiting typological interpretation. For him, its "open metaphors"—over which he had labored almost twenty years (I, 33-34)[5]—subsumed history in a complex system of archetypes, and, in effect, formed out of theology an all-encompassing myth shared by the whole Puritan community. The climax of the "histories of all ages," he believed, lay in the American church-state; with the aid of the Bible's "figures or types," he wished to show New England's punctual and surprising *fulfilments* of the divine Prophecies" (I, 33)—fulfillments which had been adumbrated in the lives of Adam and Aeneas.

Within this framework, Mather's allusions to Virgil and Milton—and to Du Bartas, Tasso, and Blackmore—provide a clue to the nature of his work. Like *The Aeneid* and *Paradise Lost*, the **Magnalia** celebrates a great legend in the form of an epic. To be sure, Mather never says so explicitly. Sharing the Puritan distrust of all poetic modes, he adopted the role of historian; harassed at the time by "imployments multifarious" (I, 34), he did not even strive for any kind of formal perfection. His immense work—packed with narratives, sermons, church decrees, and biographies—has seemed to its readers "a mighty chaos," "flung together" and "heaped up huge and undigested."[6] And viewed as theology or history, it warrants such criticism. Mather himself anticipates this, and begs indulgence on the grounds that "the book hath been a sort of rhapsody made up . . . with many little rags" (I, 34). Yet as a rhapsody, as a work of passion and imagination, the **Magnalia** shows a coherent development. Its "mighty chaos" is welded together by the intrinsic unity of its vision and by a number of carefully sustained literary techniques.

Following epic convention, Mather begins, in a suitably "elevated" style, by describing his subject and invoking his muse:

> I write the   WONDERS of the   CHRISTIAN RELIGION, flying from the depravations of Europe, to the American Strand; and, assisted by the Holy Author of that Religion, I do with all conscience of Truth, required therein by Him, who is the Truth itself, report the wonderful displays of His infinite Power, Wisdom, Goodness, and Faithfulness, wherewith His Divine Providence hath irradiated an Indian Wilderness.

> I relate the Considerable Matters, that produced and attended the First Settlement of COLONIES . . . erected in those *ends of the earth.* . . .

> The reader will doubtless desire to know, what it was that

> —*tot Vovere casus*
> *Insignes Pietate Viros, tot adire Labores,*
> *Impulerit.*
>   [Virgil's *Aeneid*, I. 9-11; altered]

And our History shall . . . satisfy him. (I, 25)

Through its pointed parallels with the opening of the *Aeneid,* this invocation suggests that the New England epic surpasses as well as resembles its Latin predecessor. Inspired by Christ, not the pagan muse, it reveals the truth rather than dealing in fables, and glorifies not an Aeneas but a convenanted theocracy. In short, in the terms Mather would have preferred, the founding of Rome prefigures that of New England and Virgil's poem finds its antitype in his Church History. Mather strengthens these implications—gathers them into the pattern of "Divine Providence"—by the italicized scriptural reference. The *"ends of the earth"* (which here, and recurrently in the *Magnalia,* means America) "signifieth the victory of the Blessed Remnant over Sathan's world," according both to his own *Biblia Americana* and to his uncle's authoritive *Figures or Types.*[7] For the seventeenth-century Puritan, that is, who understood that the "Blessed Remnant" was a "figure" simultaneously for the Chosen Hebrews and the elect, the phrase links the "pious" Trojans and New Englanders in a great providential movement, now at the verge of fulfillment. "He shall have dominion . . . unto the ends of the earth," writes the Psalmist. "They that dwell in the wilderness shall bow before him" (Psalms 72:8-9; cf. Psalms 98:3). Or again:

> The adversaries of the LORD shall be broken to pieces . . . the LORD shall judge the ends of the earth; and he shall give strength unto his kind, and exalt the horn of his anointed. (I Samuel 2:10; cf. Luke I: 46-55)

> . . . . .

> Assemble yourselves and come; draw near together, ye *that are* escaped of the nations. . . . Look unto me, and be ye saved, all the ends of the earth. . . . In the LORD shall all the seed of Israel be justified, and shall glory. (Isaiah 45:20-25; cf. Isaiah 43:1-6 and Zechariah 9:9-15)

This implicit mythicizing of history extends throughout the **Magnalia,** and supports the explicit design of the work. The theme formulated in the opening lines combines every aspect of the Puritan view of New England as this had developed through the earlier histories from Bradford to Scottow and, in its essentials, has left a lasting imprint on the American imagination: the renunciation of Europe, the effort at a new beginning, and the "great works" providentially attained through "affliction" and "temptation." But Mather at once proceeds to translate all this into legend. The American Puritans, he writes, have created another *"golden* Age. . . . there are golden candlesticks (more than twice times seven!) in the midst of this 'outer darkness'" (I, 27). The phrase, which looks back to paradise and early Christianity and forward to the millenium (Rev. 1:12, 8:2), grows into an emblem of the theocracy, maintained through all seven books of the *Magnalia*.[8] Speaking of the emigrants' achievements, Mather exults that "in one or two years' time, there were to be seen *seven* Churches . . . all of them *golden candlesticks*" (I, 79); and he later applies the image also to the next generation, whose *"two sevens"* of Harvard graduates assure New England that its *"aetas aurea"* was not "a *business of one age*" (I, 237; II, 8). Finally, in the last sections, he carries legend into prophecy—"a time of wondrous *light*" heralded by the seven golden trumpets (I, 509, II, 57)—fusing the colony's past and future into an aesthetic whole.

No one knew better that all this belied the course of history than did Cotton Mather. His sermons after 1690 occasionally still urge a renascence of the Good Old Way;[9] his diary, the mirror of his inmost convictions, asserts again and again that the effort was futile, that the colony had strayed beyond recall.[10] And in the *Magnalia* itself, he turns at times to the actual world—generally in epilogues and appendixes[11]—only to reject it for the world of his creation. These insertions (which form a very small part of the work) all too clearly reveal that the second generation was backsliding into worldliness; that the enemies of the Mather dynasty stood in control of Harvard College; that, in sum, New England had irrevocably abandoned the founders' principles. Mather's shift of focus serves only to enhance his imaginative achievement. He refers to the present in order more fully to define the ideal: in separating one from the other he can, as it were, rescue from "the *Anger of God*" the "Utopia that was"—and, within the *Magnalia* itself, still is—"NEW-ENGLAND" (I, 103). With the "stones they throw at this book . . . I will build myself a monument," he exclaims in the General Introduction; " . . . whether New-England may *live* [historically] any where else or no, it must *live* [spiritually] in our History!" (I, 36, 27).

The *Magnalia*'s New England, then, transcends all material boundaries. The setting becomes, as with Milton's Eden, the focal point for a cosmic war that will decisively alter human history. Of course, the change in the *Magnalia* stands at the opposite extreme from that described in *Paradise Lost;* it precisely reverses Satan's errand into Eden. And its structure, corresponding to its theme, presents something like an inversion of Milton's epic.[12] Satan's anti-heroic actions (though we first see him in hell) begin with his fall from heaven, and proceed in three stages: his ascent from hell, his conquest of earth, and, briefly, the summoning of his legions to their new home. The New England theocracy, the collective epic hero of the *Magnalia* (as are the chosen people in the Bible), accomplishes its mission in what may be called equal but opposite actions. Mather opens, *in medias res,* with a description of America, to which "in the fulness of time the Church of our Lord Jesus Christ . . . is *victoriously* sailing," changing geography into *"Christiano-graphy"* (I, 42-43). The narrative itself progresses from Europe, across the Atlantic, and into the wilderness where the Puritans plant the colony (Books I, II, and III),[13] establish the church-state (Books IV and V), and, in a series of triumphs over Satan (Books VI and VII) prepare for "the descent of . . . CHRIST from Heaven [to a] . . . *renovated world*" (I, 46).

The first part of the narrative, concerning the old world and the Atlantic passage, is dominated by images of depravity and chaos. Mather portrays Europe as the counterpart of pagan Rome, Babylon, Egypt, Ur.[14] He compares the several "removals" from England and Holland to the Israelite exodus, to Abraham's "leaving the Chaldean territories" (I, 48) and to the flight of the "primitive Christians" from "the kingdom of Anti-Christ" (I, 584). Throughout this section his phrases and epithets echo the biblical descriptions of fallen civilizations;[15] and amplifying his meaning, he extracts prophecies of doom from the sermons of every important emigrant divine. "'Is not England ripe?'," he quotes Thomas Hooker. "'Is she not weary of God? Nay, she is fed fat for the slaughter . . . [and] shall be abased and brought down to hell'" (I, 341).[16] "Flying the deprivations of Europe," the Puritans shut behind them the gates of a lost world—only to encounter "*Chaos* and *ancient* Night."[17] The Atlantic, in the *Magnalia,* becomes magnified to epic proportions. As described in most of the emigrants' biographies, it is another "river of Lethe" (I, 529) on which the voyagers "were surprised with horrible tempests . . . wherein they saw not sun, moon, or star . . . [while] doleful shrieks gave all over" (I, 109). These elemental storms, surpassing those Aeneas encountered in his sea-journies, together with the "divine deliverances" which accompany them, give the ocean-crossing a legendary, almost supernatural quality, and through this double focus provide a symbolic link between the old hell and the New World. The God that had carried them through the "Flames, worse than hell's . . . [of] PERSECUTION," Mather comments, was now with them on a worse than *"unpassable ocean"* in their passage toward "the *pure enjoyment* of *all his ordinances*" in America (I, 65, 69).

The *Magnalia* portrays the founding of the theocracy through the metaphor of the garden of God. At first, as I have suggested, the country appears as a *devils'* paradise, "where Satan alone had reigned without controul in all former ages" (I, 332). Mather devotes some space to the Puritans' early hardships;[18] primarily, however, he stresses how the settlers, purified by the *"wilderness*-condition," transform the "desart" into a second Eden. The triumph of Milton's Satan all at once lays waste the world (*PL,* X. 1063-75); Christ's Church fulfills the first part of its mission when the country, as in a dream or legend, springs almost immediately into full bloom. "Never," Mather exclaims, "was any plantation brought unto such a considerableness, in a space of time so inconsiderable! an *howling wilderness* in a few years became a *pleasant land*" (I, 80). He presents this metamorphosis through images of "*great farms . . . protected by a guard of angels*," of "clusters of *rich grapes,*" and of a "*vine*" that took "deep root and filled the land" (I, 62-63, 163, 81). The magistrates and the clergy he characterizes as being themselves gardens of the Lord, microcosms of the whole plantation. Abraham Pierson, he writes, was "become (what Paradise was called) 'an island of the innocent'"; Richard Denton's "speech distilled as the dew, as the small rain upon the tender herb, and as the showers upon the grass" (I, 398). In this mythical-green glow,[19] Mather unfolds the second major action of his epic.

"THE HISTORY OF HARVARD COLLEDGE" extends and enlarges the garden metaphor. Founded by the settlers and continued by their sons, the college becomes at once a symbol of fructification and fruition. Mather calls it "a river without the streams whereof these regions would have been meer unwatered places for the devil" (II, 7). But equally it represents the harvest of that cultivation. "The death of those brave men that first planted New-England," he adds, "would have rendered a fit emblem for the country—a beech tree with its top lopt off (which tree withers when its top is lopt off!)—if Harvard Colledge had not prevented it. But now . . . [we have] another set, who indeed had their whole growth in the soyl of New-England: persons, whom I may call *cedars* . . . [that] 'beautifie the place of my [God's] sanctuary'" (II, 34). This idealized harmony between generations forms the real subject of the fourth book. The biographies of all the ten "exemplary" Harvard graduates abound in allusions to biblical filiopietism and assert, often through the analogy of vegetation, the undisturbed succession from father to son. The "lives" of Samuel and Nathaniel Mather both begin with a disquisition on Saul's question, "Whose son in this youth?" (II, 39, 156); in the Shepard household, "the *father* was the *brightness* of the *son,* [and] . . . the *son* was the *brightness* of the *father;* such a lustre did father and son mutually reflect upon one another. . . . [Thus] the *root* gives verdure to the *branches,* and the flourishing *branches* again commend the *root*" (II, 142).[20] For Mather, this "growth" of Harvard College proves that the New England commonwealth has superseded all the holy communities of the past: "where God had before planted his church[es] . . . 'lo, they were all overgrown with thorns and nettles.' . . . [But now] the proverb 'That vinegar is the son of wine' and 'That the sons of heroes are trespassers' has been contradicted in [our] . . . happy experience" (II, 66-67).[21]

New England's happy experience receives its fullest affirmation, according to the *Magnalia,* in its ecclesiastical "Acts and Monuments" (Book V). For his purposes, Mather organizes these documents thematically rather than chronologically. He opens in 1680 with the "Confession of Faith," which he claims represents a

clerical thanksgiving for half a century of "*rest and growth*" (II, 207). He then turns to the Cambridge Platform (1648), the main document of the orthodoxy, exulting that "the churches have cheerfully embraced it, practised it, and been prospered in it, unto this very day" (II, 237); and upon the basis of this uniformity, he proceeds to the church decrees of the second generation. The Half-Way covenant (1660), which actually marked the failure of the orthodoxy,[22] for him fulfills the expectation of "our *seers,*" binding fathers and sons in a "*combination* . . . [that] might not easily be broken" (II, 277-78). By its principles, a long procession of synods guides the colony to "an exactest unity," a "vigorous unanimity" in which every "breach was healed . . . unto the general joy" (II, 313, 181, 312-13).[23] New England's garden, presented earlier in physical terms, appears here in its brightest spiritual aspect, against the background of a total harmony of belief which Mather likens to "the fabulous *musick* of the *spheres*" (II, 180).

Though the theocracy prospects both physically and spiritually, it never quite becomes a "sanctuary." To the end, the natural perils of the new world hinder its progress; and even its "guard of angels" cannot prevent the outbreak of witchcraft and of Indian warfare. Milton's epic concludes with paradise lost; but the "*magnalia Christi Americana*" form only the road, as it were, to the New Jerusalem. Christ's Church advances by overcoming a series of obstacles; the closer it approaches to its final triumph, the more dangerous these obstacles become. Its most glorious battle, Mather reiterates over and over, will be the most dire of all, one in which "the *devils* and the *damned* [are] . . . let loose to make a furious but a fruitless attempt" against the saints (I, 46). Accordingly, the last action of the *Magnalia* deals with the conflicts between the Puritans and the forces of evil: "Wars of the Lord" by which the theocracy increasingly nears the realization of its "original design" and destiny.

Book VI presents these conflicts through an assortment of case histories, each one of which illustrates in miniature the experience of the colony. The first chapter, "CHRISTUS SUPER AQUAS," recalls on a diminished scale the images of the ocean-crossing. The next chapter evokes the planting of the wilderness through vignettes of farming life; and the third, "THE RETURNING PRODIGAL," lists various instances of filial devotion. Whether or not Mather here intended a broad thematic development, as I am implying, his tales of suffering and regeneration, occurring as they do in an already established colony, together accent the theocracy's victory over Satan in every area of life. The victory takes on still greater import in the fourteen "*sad examples*" of witchcraft which follow. Mather claims that the very ferocity of Azazel's rage on these occasions shows that New England had made things "very uneasie unto the devils," that its saints, "the 'heirs of salvation'," were literally "treading Satan underfoot" (II, 447, 470). And he underscores his meaning by relating the whole witchcraft episode to the temptation in the wilderness: "The assaults that Satan then . . . made," he states summarily, " . . . producing a most horrible anguish in his [Christ's] mind, made such a figure in his conflicts for us, that they were well worthy of a most particular prefiguration" (II, 447) for these events. It is no less than "Christ's Combate and Conquest over the Dragon," which, typology tells us, at once foreshadow and embody the Second Coming.[24]

The last book of the *Magnalia* brings these millenial overtones to a climactic pitch. The *"Ecclesiarum Praelia"* against the heretics, with which the book begins, are told with a swelling note of triumph, from Roger Williams, a minor irritation to the colony, through the more dangerous Antinomians, to the Quakers, who for Mather represent all "the *vomit* cast out in the by-past ages . . . lick'd up again for a *new digestion*" (II, 522). Their banishment, a major defeat for the powers of darkness, fortifies the theocracy for its greatest "temptation," the Indian wars.

For several reasons, these battles (entitled "ARMA VIROSQUE CANO" to emphasize their superiority to those before Virgil's Latium) provide the right conclusion to Mather's epic. First, they had not yet reached a decisive end—unlike the heresies and witchcraft—and could thus be used to symbolize the theocracy's continuing victories over Satan. Second, the Indians—again unlike the witches and heretics—were an integral part of America; their destruction would more clearly demonstrate that the Puritan mission stood at the verge of completion. Most important, the Indian conflicts afforded a striking *finale* to two dominant motifs of the *Magnalia*. As a series of "Wars of the Lord" with primitive tribes, they enforce the resemblance between the colonists and the children of Israel. In this last section Mather most frequently affirms the "biblical parallel," uncovering precedents for every Puritan action,[25] from the Pilgrims' troubles with the Pequots, whom he identifies with the "Emim, those terrible giants" (II, 553), to Phips' crucial victory over the Indian King Philip, in which he recreates the Hebrews' entrance into the promised land. But the New Englanders do not therefore simply duplicate the progress of the "erratick church of Israel" (I, 249). Above and beyond this, the covenanted saints are an army of Christ. As soon as Mather completes the parallel between King Philip and Og, "the king of the woody Bashan encountered and conquered by Joshua, the Lord General of Israel with his armies passing into Canaan," he declares:

> I am sure New-England has a true church to people it; for all the *serpents,* yea or giants . . . have found themselves engaged in a fatal enterprize. We have by a true and plain history secured the story of our

success against all the Ogs [here interpreted as "the serpent, Python destroyed by Apollo"] . . . from falling under the disguises of mythology . . . And we will not conceal [that] . . . 'tis our Lord Jesus Christ, worshipped according to the rules of his blessed gospel, who is the great Phoebus, that "SUN of righteousness," who hath so saved this church from the designs of the "generations of the dragon." (II, 579)

The "true church," Mather is saying, having secured its Canaan, is advancing into the New Jerusalem. And in this light, the "fatal enterprize" undertaken by the Indian "serpents" and "giants"—and foreshadowed, Mather intimates (II, 566), by the War in Heaven—becomes part of the great assault of "the *devils* and the *damned*": for the "serpent Python" which the Puritans are defeating is none other than Satan himself.

At the end of the work, in a section called "THINGS TO COME," Mather infers the outcome of this assault in all its chiliastic significance. Throughout the narrative he had hinted at the proximity of the millenium, affirming that "the *reigning* of the saints a thousand years [becomes] within the last few sevens of years nearer to accomplishment" (I, 330-31). Now, as his epic draws to a close, he sets the theocracy's continuing success directly before the backdrop of the New Jerusalem. Quoting in part from the sermons of Nicholas Noyes, he announces that "there is a REVOLUTION AND A REFORMATION at the very door [cf. Mat. 24: 33, Mark 13: 29], which will be more wonderful than any of the deliverances yet seen by the church of God from the beginning of the world. . . . [And we may well] live to see it. These things will come on with horrible commotions . . . [My] *fancies* and *juggles*," he concludes, "have their foundations laid in *realities*" (II, 653-54). Mather's vision is of course theological in origin. But as an intrinsic part of his epic its foundations stand primarily in esthetic realities. Binding the great actions by which the colony was planted with the "happy period" which awaits the saints, his "fancies and juggles," far from covering the truth from "the disguises of mythology," transforms the "plain history" of New England into myth.

They serve, further still, to distinguish Mather's epic from those of either Vergil or Milton. Latium and Eden come to us from an irrevocable past; the Magnalia's New England is at once a vanished garden of God and a golden age which remains perpetually "near, even at the door," requiring one last great act in order to realize itself. In this respect, as Roy Harvey Pearce has noted, [26] the *Magnalia* may be seen to be the first in a long line of distinctively American epics, which continues in Barlow's *Columbiad* and Whitman's *Leaves of Grass*. More broadly, its main theme, its central metaphors, even perhaps its structure (the apparent chaos controlled by a vision which looks always beyond the present) can all be traced throughout subsequent American literature, and suggest that the **Magnalia** is a germinal work of symbolic art. Long after its theology fades, after the historiography it favors gives place to different and alien methods, after New England as a whole loses its national influence, its most important legacy lies in the realm of the imagination.

Notes

[1] *Diary,* ed. Worthington Chauncy Ford. *Massachusetts Historical Society Collections,* 7th ser. (Boston, 1911), VII, 358. (Ellipses omitted).

[2] For example: Barrett Wendell, *Cotton Mather, The Puritan Priest* (New York, 1963; first published, 1891), pp. 116 ff.; Perry Miller, *The New England Mind: Colony to Province* (Cambridge, Mass., 1953), pp. 189-90; Kenneth B. Murdock, *Literature and Theology in Colonial New England* (New York, 1963), p. 129; William Reid Manierre, "Verbal Patterns in Cotton Mather's *Magnalia,*" *Quarterly Journal of Speech,* XLVII (1961), 402. In spite of my basic disagreements with Miller and Murdock, I am indebted to their pioneering work on typology in colonial America. See respectively: Introduction to Jonathan Edwards, *Images or Shadows of Divine Things* (New Haven, 1948), pp. 1-41; and "Clio in the Wilderness: History and Biography in Puritan New England," *Church History,* XXIV (1955), 221-38.

[3] *Grandfather's Chair,* in *Complete Works,* ed. George P. Lanthrop (Boston and New York, 1900), XII, 103. This is not to deny that Mather had a great many yankee traits—which, indeed, have recently received a good deal of attention—but these generally lie in areas of intellectual interest; emotionally and imaginatively, Mather adhered to the former age.

[4] See: I, 25, 31-32, 34, 37-39, 40, 58, 65, 107, 125, 142, 261, 337, 386, 390, 399, 436, 482, 479, 504, 603, 608; II, 15-16, 48, 92, 116, 124, 174, 179, 256, 343-44, 363, 392, 514, 529, 535, 566-67, 569, 574, 586, 588, 620, 635. All references (giving volume and page number) are to the *Magnalia,* ed. Thomas Robbins, 2 vols. (Hartford, Conn. 1853), though they have been checked with the first edition published in London, 1702.

[5] The result of this twenty-year labor is the valuable but still unpublished *Biblia Americana,* now at Massachusetts Historical Society. See further, regarding Mather's interest in typology, Ursula Brumm, *Die Religiöse Typologie im Amerikanischen Denken* (Leiden, 1963), pp. 38-48.

[6] John Greenleaf Whittier, quoted in Austin Warren's "Grandfather Mather and his Wonder Book," *Sewanee Review,* LXXII (1964), 116; Wendell, *Cotton Mather,* p. 117; Miller, *Colony to Province,* p. 104.

[7] Samuel Mather, *The Figures or Types of the Old Testament . . . Shadowed to the People of GOD of Old* (London, 1683), p. 118; see also the commentary on the seventy-second Psalm in the (unpaginated) *Biblia Americana,* vol. IV. William Guild discusses at length the typological meaning of the phrase, as the final "*Calling of the Gentiles . . . according to Noahs wish and the Promise made to Abraham,*" in *The Harmony of the Gospels* (London, 1926), pp. 40-41.

[8] In addition to the references given below, see: I, 43, 235, 286, 328-29, 372, 479, 585; II, 66, 72. The "figure" of the golden candlesick extends beyond even the associations noted above. It represents also the faith of the Chosen People (e.g., Exod. 25:31, 37:17), the Jerusalem of the Gentiles which Zachariah portrays as "a candlestick all of gold . . . [with] seven lamps thereon" (4:2), and finally, in the well-known passage explicated by John Winthrop, the universal mission of Christ's Church: "Ye are the light of the world. A city that is set on an hill cannot be hid. Neither do men light a candle, and put it under a bushel, but on a candlestick . . ." (Mat. 5:14-15; cf. Mark 4:21 and Luke 8:16, 11:33). Undoubtedly, Mather was well aware of all these implications, which support the idea of America as "the ends of the earth," and intended them, as he states in the General Introduction, "for the observation of the attentive" (I, 31). Undoubtedly, too, he intended the seven-fold division of the *Magnalia* to evoke the significance of seven as a "perfect" and "typical" number; in this connection see Arthur Dent's *Exposition Upon the Revelation* (Amsterdam, 1611) which—recalling the popular doctrine of the seven stages of mankind's development from Adam to the Second Coming—"proves" that seven is "a *type*" linking the Israelite state and "the churches among the Gentiles" and foreshadowing the New Jerusalem (pp. 6 ff.).

[9] See for example: *Batteries upon the Kingdom of the Devil* (London, 1695); *Durable Riches* (Boston, 1695); *Fair Weather* (Boston, 1692); *The Faith of the Fathers* (Boston, 1699); *The Good Old Way* (Boston, 1698), and *The Serious Christian* (London, 1699).

[10] *Diary,* ed. Ford, VII, 160-360, *passim.*

[11] Sermons are added at the end of Books I, VI and VII; and an appendix is added to Book V. Exceptions to this pattern occur in Book III (I, 249) and in Book V (II, 316-17). At the end of Book III, Mather appends a funeral sermon for John Baily which enlarges upon man's sinfulness, but in a traditional way rather than with specific application to the colony. In addition to this, Mather dissociates the theocracy's accomplishments from the present by quoting occasionally from its leaders' jeremiads, and these scattered excerpts have

the effect of caustic theatrical asides which indirectly assert the drama's superiority to, and independence of, its degenerate audience. See: I, 63 (Bradford); I, 147 (Edward Hopkins); I, 143 (Hooker); II, 117 (Urian Oakes). These instances, containing in total about twenty lines, represent all the comments of this nature in the *Magnalia,* with the exception of those in Increase Mather's introduction to the Harvard history, II, 70, 72-73, 78-79.

[12] In the subsequent analysis I draw several general parallels between *Paradise Lost* and the *Magnalia,* and I should perhaps note that no evidence exists that Mather was particularly influenced by Milton's work and that I do not assume any such influence. Regarding the knowledge of Milton's works in early New England see Perry Miller, *The New England Mind: The Seventeenth Century* (Cambridge, Mass., 1939), pp. 118-19 and George F. Sensabaugh, *Milton in Early America* (Princeton, 1964), pp. 7, 38-41, 303.

[13] In the discussion below, I treat the first three books of the *Magnalia* in what might be called spatial, rather than linear, terms: by way of the themes carried through all three books, rather than simply dealing with each book in succession (or in Mather's own words, by "*affinity* rather than *chronology*" [II, 504]). All three books portray the first-generation settlers and hence return with every action and every biography to the same basic experiences: the persecutions in Europe, the ocean-crossing, and the conquest of the wilderness. However, these three books also show a coherent structure from a "linear" viewpoint: Books I and II describe the secular triumphs which lead to the founding of New England, in an orderly procession of set-pieces which itself conveys the impression of a successful state organization. This development culminates in Book III, with the biographies of the fifty divines, the most important members of the theocracy.

[14] In addition to the instances cited below, see I, 48, 79, 114, 119, 152, 166, 263, 323, 461, 464, 478, 504, 519. With regard to England, Mather several times expresses a contradictory attitude. While on the whole his attitude is strongly negative, he sometimes makes self-conscious obeisances to "our dear Mother England," perhaps because he was submitting the work to an English publisher (see I, 26, 74-76 and II, 179-80). These instances have been, it seems to me, far overstressed in Peter H. Smith's "Politics and Sainthood: Biography by Cotton Mather," *William and Mary Quarterly,* XX (1963), 186-207.

[15] I, 65, 81, 263-64, 396, 429, 461, 465-66, 468, 511-12, 519, 531, 584.

[16] See also: I, 326 (John Davenport); I, 361 (Francis Higginson); I, 372 (Jonathan Burr); I, 377 (George Phillips); I, 409 (Ezekiel Rogers); I, 448 (Richard

Mather). Mather supports these comments in two places outside of Book III: once in the first book, where he prophecies that England's "*fall* will become like that of the house which our Saviour saw built upon the sand" (K, 65); and again in Book IV, where he quotes his uncle, Samuel Mather: Christ "'will bring you [England] to a swift destruction . . . and in the day when God shall visit you, the guilt of all the righteous blood . . . will come down the hill upon your heads'" (II, 50).

[17] *Paradise Lost,* II. 969-70. All quotations are from Merritt Y. Hughes' edition of the poem in *John Milton, Complete Poems and Major Prose* (New York, 1957). For examples of the descriptions of ocean-crossing other than those noted below, see: I. 146-47 (William Bradford); I, 283-85 (John Cotton); I, 336-37 (John Avery); I, 384 (Thomas Shepard); I, 389 (John Norton); I, 450 (Richard Mather); I, 512 (John Sherman).

[18] See for example: I, 50-55, 77-79, 238-39, 302, 363-64. The Indians are infrequently mentioned in the first three books (I, 55-59, *passim*); Mather deliberately leaves the Indian wars for Book VII.

[19] See also, for example: I, 288, 296 (John Norton); I, 388 (Thomas Shepard); I, 429 (Samuel Newman); I, 470 (Charles Chauncey); I, 529 (John Eliot).

[20] See further: II, 40, 42, 61, 88, 114, 155, 164.

[21] For further assertions in Book IV of this superiority of New England to other attempts at establishing a holy commonwealth, see: II, 39-40, 60, 116, 119, 127, 142-43, 146.

[22] See Miller, *Colony to Province,* pp. 232-33.

[23] See also: II, 210, 331-34, 512.

[24] See for example: Thomas Taylor, *Christs Combate and Conquest; or the Lyon of the Tribe of IVDAH, Vanquishing the Roaring Lyon, assaulting him in three most fierce and hellish Temptations* (London, 1618), *passim;* Benjamin Keach, *Tropologia, or a Key to Open Scripture Metaphors* (London, 1681-82), II, 9-40; and Samuel Mather, *Figures or Types,* pp. 213 ff. For a general view of the European background of this prophetic-millenarian method, see C. A. Patrides, *The Phoenix and the Ladder: The Rise and Decline of the Christian View of History* (Berkeley, 1964), pp. 7-9, 47-51.

[25] In addition to the examples given below, see especially: II, 553, 556, 561, 572, 587, 627.

[26] *The Continuity of American Poetry* (Princeton, 1961), pp. 60, 62. See also Marion L. Starkey's brief but astute comments on the *Magnalia* in *The Devil in*

Massachusetts: A Modern Inquiry into the Salem Witch Trials (Garden City, N. Y., 1961), p. 242. The *Magnalia* is not, of course, the first New England work to outline a myth of the colonial venture—it is foreshadowed in this by earlier histories, such as Edward Johnson's *Wonder-Working Providence* (1651)—but it is the major statement of its kind in Puritan America.

David Levin (essay date 1966)

SOURCE: "Essays to Do Good for the Glory of God: Cotton Mather's *Bonifacius*," in *The American Puritan Imagination: Essays in Revaluation,* edited by Sacvan Bercovitch, Cambridge University Press, 1974, pp. 139-55.

[*In the essay below, Levin examines the themes of Mather's* Bonifacius, *also known as* Essays to Do Good, *and argues that the book is historically relevant to an understanding of American philosophers and reformers of the eighteenth, nineteenth, and twentieth centuries. Levin's essay was first published in 1966.*]

Bonifacius—usually known by its running title, *Essays to Do Good*—has always had a better reputation than the author who published it anonymously in 1710. It is Cotton Mather's historical fate to be considered largely as a transitional figure whose prodigious but narrow mind stretched inadequately between the zealous founding of the Bible Commonwealth and the enlightened struggle for the Republic. His efforts to retain the old Puritan values along with the old Puritan power have tended to diminish him in contrast to the giants who had first established that power in Boston. His advanced ideas on medicine, botany, education, philanthropy, and family discipline look like minor departures from reactionary principles when they are set beside the beliefs of eighteenth-century secular thinkers.

The habit of viewing Mather in the shadow of his potent ancestors began with his parents, who named him for his maternal grandfather, John Cotton, and it continued to affect his life until, in his sixtieth year, he wrote the life of his distinguished father, Increase Mather. When Cotton Mather was an eleven-year-old freshman at Harvard in 1674, his father became embroiled with other members of the Board of Overseers in a public battle that nearly destroyed the college. When the boy became at fifteen the youngest Harvard graduate, the president reminded him publicly of his duty to emulate not only his father but Richard Mather and John Cotton, his two famous grandfathers. Cotton Mather eventually devoted his entire life as a pastor to the very congregation that his father served as teacher. For forty years he worked closely with his father in various political controversies and social crises, from the loss

of the colony's original charter, the rebellion against Sir Edmund Andros, the acceptance of a new charter, and the witchcraft trials, through debates about church government and membership and control of Harvard and Yale early in the new century. As a prolific historian, moreover, he wrote the lives of the first governors, the first ministers, the first Harvard presidents—the monumental church-history of New England, *Magnalia Christi Americana.*

Thus Mather unhappily observed the dissolution of the old theocracy even while he cheerfully did his best to extend pious influence in the community through his retrospective writings and his schemes for social action. At the same time, he labored enthusiastically in behalf of the new science. He sent reports of American phenomena to the Royal Society in London, which elected him a Fellow. He collected and published in New England the discoveries of European scientists. He persuaded a medical doctor to try inoculation during a smallpox epidemic in Boston. By the time he died in 1728, it was clear that the millennium he had so confidently predicted thirty years earlier was not yet to be expected. New England would have to settle instead for the imperfect Enlightenment.

For three centuries both Cotton Mather and his works have been discussed almost exclusively in this context of change. The churchhistory, we say, looks backward to Mather's grandfathers; *The Christian Philosopher* and *Bonifacius* look forward to Benjamin Franklin. Indeed, it was Franklin himself who first stressed the value of *Essays to Do Good* as a transitional document. In his very first published work Franklin paid Mather the tribute of parody by adopting the pseudonym of Mrs Silence Dogood (counting on his Bostonian readers to know that the author of *Essays to Do Good* was rarely silent). Half a century later[1] Franklin told Samuel Mather that *Bonifacius* had turned his own youthful thoughts to methods of doing good, and again in his autobiography he acknowledged *Bonifacius* along with the works of Daniel Defoe and John Bunyan as one of the most valuable influences on his early thought. The relationship would be evident even if Franklin had not written so explicitly. Commentators have repeatedly cited it ever since George Burder quoted Franklin's letter to Samuel Mather in an English edition of *Essays to Do Good* (London, 1807).

Insistence on such historical relationships has taught us much about the changes from pious Puritanism to moralism, from striving in the world for the glory of God to striving for enlightened self-interest. But this perspective has also done considerable harm. Students of historical change have often blurred our understanding of Franklin's and Mather's individual minds and books. The intense light focused on one set of eighteenth-century statements has left others in the darkness. Mather, especially, has been projected so rigidly against what he looked back to, or what he anticipated, that it is unusually difficult to discover what he was.

The modern reader of **Bonifacius** must be prepared to recognize two influential versions of this distortion. The first concerns Puritan piety; the second, Puritan commercial ethics and benevolence.

Perry Miller's magnificent volumes on *The New England Mind* argue that the earliest New England Puritans temporarily united pious faith and reasoned, vigorous action under a grand modification of Abraham's Covenant. The second volume dramatizes the inevitable separation of faith from thought and the inevitable subordination of faith as the Covenant dissolves under the pressure of seventeenth-century events in Europe and America. Cotton Mather is the pivotal figure in Miller's narrative of historical change. At first he preaches jeremiads, long sermons condemning the sins of the land. But as he and other clergymen lose political power in the early decades of the eighteenth century, Mather resorts to new devices, both social and psychological. Now he abandons the jeremiad. Renouncing hope of political power, he tries instead to influence events by publishing 'pietist' instructions for communal life, including proposals for voluntary associations to reform morals. Privately, moreover, he takes emotional refuge from the religious decline of New England by retreating often to his study; there, according to Miller, Mather tries to 'stimulate' his overwrought nervous system to a factitious piety that seeks explicit, divine assurances and demands prostrate, methodical prayer and fasting. In this analysis his correspondence with such foreign reformers as Auguste Francke of Halle is an accidental consequence of Mather's compulsive scribbling and of his response to New England's needs and his own. It has nothing to do with international pietist movements of the time. Mather, indeed, is astonished to find himself in the vanguard, an agent of the new pietism.

Miller presents **Bonifacius** as a milestone on the downward road from John Winthrop to Dickens' caricature of nineteenth-century utilitarianism, Thomas Gradgrind, and he contends that Cotton Mather was further from Winthrop than from Gradgrind. **Bonifacius,** he concedes, is 'not quite a surrender of piety to business', but he declares that Mather found in **Bonifacius** 'a new form of marketing religion'. He describes Mather's appeal to the inherent reward of doing good as a sentimental invitation to luxuriate in the 'delicious swooning joy of the thing itself'. He sees Mather's voluntary associations not as part of an effort to liberate New Englanders but as an attempt to reassert clerical control, and he associates Mather with those service clubs (from the Y.M.C.A. to the Rotary) that work for conformity of various kinds in modern America.[2]

The chief trouble with this interpretation is that it is almost completely subservient to a generalization about the decline in piety. It cannot admit the possibility that Cotton Mather was as pious as his ancestors; it insists on explaining his piety as a neurotic, belated reaction to historical events that occurred when he was past thirty.

The consequent distortion of **Bonifacius** begins at the beginning, with Mather's title. Because of our modern interest in placing Mather on the line from Puritanism to utilitarianism, scholars have customarily shortened the original title of **Bonifacius** in a way that changes its significance. **Bonifacius,** they have called it; *an Essay upon the Good that is to be Devised and Designed by Those who Desire . . . to Do Good While they Live.* This seems in any case a strangely illogical title—as if there were others, *besides* those who desire to do good, who should devise and design good! The important distortion, however, is the change in Mather's purpose. He did not really write for those who desire to do good but for those who desire 'to Answer the Great End of Life', and who *therefore* desire to do good while they live.

The great end of life, for Cotton Mather as for John Winthrop before him and Jonathan Edwards after, was not to do good but to glorify God. Mather had made this plain from the beginning of his career as a preacher, and at the height of his political power. Just after he had served as one of the chief conspirators to overthrow the tyrant Sir Edmund Andros in 1689, he published a volume of sermons at the request of his wealthy father-in-law, John Phillips, who on recovering from a serious illness had offered to subsidize the publication of four sermons on 'Practical Godliness'. None of these sermons is a jeremiad. All relate devotional piety to doing good:

> The chief end of man is to *glorify* Good . . . To praise God is to *render* and *procure* a due acknowledgment of His excellence . . . This, this *praise* of the LORD is the *end* of our *life* in the world.

> This is the *end* of our *being*. We are told that *we have our* being *in God*. Of all things whatever this is then most reasonable, *that we should have our* being *for* God; and our being *for* Him, is not expressed without our praising of Him . . . Every man should say: 'I *live* that God who is worthy to be *praised,* may have the *praises* of my obedience to Him.'

The saints in Heaven, Mather says in the same sermon, have their appropriate way of praising God, by 'shouting Hallelujah, Hallelujah, before the Throne'; but men living on earth have special, additional ways of praising Him here: 'by the discharge of many *relations,* which the dead saints are strangers unto. We may *now* praise God as *parents,* as *masters,* as *officers* in the Church or Common-wealth. All those capacities shall *die* with us.'[3]

In these sermons there is no tension between doing good and praising God. Doing good is one way of praising Him. Of course, we can find sentences that support the emphasis on practical striving in the world: 'To *serve God* was the very errand which we were brought into the wilderness upon'; 'the service of God is His worship'; 'there are two things incumbent upon us, to do good and to get good'. But the good we are to get is the capacity to enjoy God. Lifting such statements out of their pious context is a serious error. Although it may indicate those subtle changes of emphasis that eventually prevailed in American life when the idea of God's sovereignty had been weakened, it can misrepresent not only individual books and the condition of individual minds, but at last the very history that such abstractions were meant to serve.

As early as 1689, then, Cotton Mather had set forth the principle on which he would organize **Bonifacius** twenty years later.[4] He would begin with the reformation of the self and would then move outward into the community, suggesting methods of service in the various 'relations' of life. In the intervening years he often followed this procedure in composing biographies. Thus his life of John Eliot opens outward from personal piety to family government to preaching in the church, and finally to Eliot's evangelism among the Indians.

The organization communicates the central purpose: to praise God in every act of life. By 1688 Mather had adopted the 'delightful and surprising way of thinking' that he attributed to his deceased younger brother Nathanael. His language suggests that he was perhaps as close to Jonathan Edwards and to Emerson, Thoreau, and Whitman as he was to Thomas Gradgrind: Nathanael Mather, Cotton Mather wrote, 'considered that the whole *Creation* was full of God; and that there was not a leaf of *grass* in the field, which might not make an observer to be sensible of the Lord. He apprehended that the *idle minutes* of our lives were many more than a short liver should allow: that the very filings of *gold,* and of time, were exceeding precious; and, that there were little *fragments of hours* intervening between our more stated businesses, wherein our *thoughts* of God might be no less pleasant than frequent with us.'[5] Just as Henry Thoreau would later tell New England's time-passing knitters that it is impossible to kill time without injuring eternity, Mather warned busy Bostonians that God would 'find an *eternity* to *damn* the man that cannot find a *time* to *pray*'.[6]

The terms in which Mather implored Christians to 'redeem time' show that his pietism was in full vigor in 1682, before he was twenty and before the original charter of Massachusetts Bay had been revoked. He

was taking John Winthrop's original message to the community but with a new emphasis on method, on the deliberate saturation of one's life in pious action, and especially on ingenuity. 'Thus be *zealous of good works, work for God*', he said in 1689. 'Let even your *eating,* your *trading,* your *visiting,* be done as a *service* for the Lord, and let your *time,* your *strength,* your *estates,* all the *powers* of your spirits and all the *members* of your bodies be ingeniously laid out in that *service.* Often ask your own souls, *What is there that I may do for God?* Even court, and hunt advantages to be serviceable.'[7]

The origins of Mather's interest in such hunting lie deep in seventeenth-century Protestant pastoral work. To understand his career we must remember that Cotton Mather was the *pastor* in the Boston church which his father served as teacher, and that he therefore had a special duty to attend to the people's daily needs. From the beginning of his professional life, he had a remarkable opportunity to apply his great energy over the whole range of Bostonian life. His social action began with secluded meditations in which, with the occasional aid of specific assurances from an angel, he prayed for divine support of afflicted parishioners and of Massachusetts battles against the Devil and the French; it extended to the writing of histories and biographies, to joining the leadership of a revolution, to advising governors, addressing the legislature, offering medical advice, curing the bewitched child of a parishioner, making pastoral visits, catechizing children, administering church discipline to offending members of the congregation, and writing books to teach the most ordinary people methods of becoming Christians and then practicing Christianity in their daily lives.

For some of this work a number of English writers had provided valuable guides. Cotton Mather and his brother Nathanael were especially fond of Joseph Hall's *Occasional Meditations* (3rd edition, 1633), William Waller's *Divine Meditations* (1680), Henry Scudder's *The Christian's Daily Walk* (1628). Cotton Mather also borrowed from Richard Baxter's immense folio *Christian Directory* (1673) and *How to Do Good to Many; or, the Public Good is the Christian's Life* (1682).

All these books have in common with Mather's efforts a determination to bring the common into touch with the divine. Hall's meditations, which both Nathanael and Cotton Mather emulated, drew religious lessons from such conventional earthly experiences as 'the sight of a grave digged up', 'gnats in the sun', 'the sight of a drunken man', 'bees fighting', 'the sight of a piece of money under water', 'a defamation dispersed'. Ready to let every leaf of grass make him sensible of the Lord, Nathanael Mather notes that a kettle of water taken from the fire in a cold New England room is quickly 'seized with lukewarmness'. So, he concludes, are Christians after they have been warmed by some awareness of God's glory. When John Winthrop interprets the killing of a snake during a synod meeting or Nathanael Mather jumps from his 'bed of security', braving the cold to put on 'Christ's garments' and walk to the fire, the lesson in this literary form is always made explicit, and the value of the meditation depends on the aptness of explicit parallels. This is a principle Benjamin Franklin kept in mind when he perfected a quite different kind of anecdote a century later in his autobiography.

In a book like **Bonifacius** the method is reversed. The pastor, accustomed to studying minor events for evidence of God's will, now uses his ingenuity to find explicit ways in which a Christian can express the benevolence with which grace has endowed him. Christians need to be told *how* to do good, especially when they live outside the traditional authority of a hierarchical church and in a swiftly changing society. Yet the movement should not be seen simply as a weakening of old Calvinist reliance on faith and predestination. It seems instead a natural extension of the kind of impulse that led Puritans to establish the New England colonies in the first place. Once the community of saints has established its right to exist, it must set about expanding God's work in the world. 'Though God set up lights so small as will serve but for one room, and though we must begin at home, we must far more esteem and desire the good of multitudes', Baxter said, and we must set 'no bounds to our endeavors, but what God and disability set'. **Bonifacius** echoes: the magistrate is 'the *Minister of God for good. His empty name* will produce a *cruel crime,* if he don't set himself to do good, as far as ever he can extend his influences.' Americans in the second half of the twentieth century have seen this kind of rhetoric applied to vast proposals for a Great Society at home and for aid to multitudes in Asia.

For Cotton Mather, moreover, the millennium was not a metaphor for secular achievement. It was literally imminent. He wrote quite seriously, on the one hand, about exactly how the righteous in America might be spared from the fires sweeping the earth before the establishment of the Kingdom here.[8] And he did his best, in the year he wrote **Bonifacius,** to see that Bostonians accepted 'the true doctrine of the Chiliad' so that, by eliminating all 'base dealing'— all 'dirty ways of dishonesty'—from the market place, they might make their street as golden as the one promised in the Book of Revelations from which he had taken his text. He preached this sermon to the General Assembly of the colony, before whom he 'proclaimed unto all the world' that 'ill-dealings are not at all countenanced; no, they are vehemently disallowed, by the religion of NEW-ENGLAND'. The gold he referred to was not profit but precept: 'The street of the city is pure gold' meant to him that 'the business of the CITY, shall be managed by the *Golden*

Rule. The things that use to be done in the marketplace, shall be done without *corruption.*'[9]

It is in this context that we must consider the second historical distortion of Mather's ideas. Just as emphasis on the decline of piety may overlook his concentration on divine glory, so efforts to trace the Protestant Ethic can ignore not only the divine object of human striving but also his thorough conviction of community. A. Whitney Griswold, in an important essay published more than thirty years ago,[10] cited impressive evidence to show that Mather stressed the Christian's obligations to work diligently in his calling; Mather repeated the biblical promise (so effective with Benjamin Franklin) that the young man who was diligent would stand before kings, and he urged the young man who wished to rise *by* his business to rise *to* his business. But although Griswold scrupulously links this personal calling with the general vocation of a Christian, his interest in linking Mather's advice to the 'rugged individualism' of a later time ignores the perfectly explicit condemnation of all sharp dealing and dishonesty in financial affairs. Mather insisted that New England's professions of extraordinary religion would be worthless if its 'dealing' should be 'defective in honesty . . . Let a man be never such a professor and pretender of *religion,* if he be not a *fair-dealer,* THAT MAN'S RELIGION IS VAIN. A noise about *faith and repentance,* among them that forget MORAL HONESTY, 'tis but an empty noise. The men are utter strangers to *faith* and *repentance . . .* Woe, woe, woe, to you professors, and HYPOCRITES, who can make a show of this and that piety, and *purity;* but can *cheat,* and *cozen,* and *oppress,* and wrong other people in your dealing with them!'[11]

Far from supporting rugged individualism, Mather declared that the golden rule should have its application to business through the scriptural command of Paul (I Corinthians 10:24): '*Let no man seek his own, but every man another's wealth.*' Lying was to be forbidden, all dealings were to be 'transparent glass', and neither the foolish nor the poor were to be exploited: 'For men to *overreach* others, because they find them *ignorant,* or screw grievously upon them, only because they are poor and low, and in great necessities; to keep up the *necessaries* of human life (I say the necessaries, which I always distinguish from the *superfluities*) at an immoderate price, merely because other people want them, when we can easily spare them; *'tis an abomination!*' For necessities, at least, the law of supply and demand was not supreme.[12]

Thus, although Mather confessed that he knew neither the niceties nor the mysteries of the market place, he did not rest content with prescribing the golden rule. Stating that imperative even in its most positive form[13] would hardly forbid ruthless competition if the individual merchant should be willing to have his neighbor compete just as fiercely as himself. Mather did not supply an ethic fit for the mysteries and niceties, but he did condemn many commercial 'abominations', from the slave trade ('one of the worst kinds of thievery in the world') to the adulteration or misrepresentation of a large number of specified products.[14]

It was a theological principle that gave Mather's sense of community its importance in practical affairs, in his day as well as through the later teachings of Franklin. To consider the principle we must enter that dizzy world of circular argument and begged questions in which Puritans struggled to distinguish faith from works without becoming either antinomians or (to use a word from *Bonifacius*) meritmongers.

In that world a Christian must recognize a central paradox: his assurance of salvation depends on his renouncing all claims to salvation that place any confidence or value in himself. He must become convinced that he does not deserve salvation and that he cannot earn it. If convinced of his inadequacy but unable to attain a conviction of faith, he may fall into the sin of despair, a beginning of hell on earth. If he does find a conviction of Christ's power and willingness to redeem him, he must test the conviction by regularly examining his attitude and his conduct. Good works cannot save him—indeed, no works are truly good unless they proceed from a justifying faith—but the consequence of true faith is a benevolence that impels the converted sinner to praise God through obedient service. *Bonifacius* declares, therefore, that 'a workless faith is a worthless faith'.

Historians gain some value from turning this process around (as some busy, conscientious sinners must have done) to mean not only that worklessness proved worthlessness but also that works proved worth. Often, however, the reversal costs too much, for it blocks appreciation of the great power in one of the chief articles of American faith. The great power comes from the conviction that what is right, works. Both Mather and Franklin worked to propagate this conviction, and both appealed to the reader's self-interest, but neither man ever contended that whatever works is right. Mather and other Puritans actually believed that prosperity could be as threatening a providential judgment as calamity. Merciful dispensations, Mather said, 'are so many trials whether we will hear God speaking in our prosperity; or whether when we wax fat we will kick against the Lord'.

For many people, at least, the drama of guilt, self-doubt, and self-accusation was a terrible reality, and so, too, was the kind of faith that Mather preached. (Even Franklin recognized it during the Great Awakening.) Once that reality stands at the center of our attention, we need not be religious to understand Mather's declaration that good works are a part of, as

well as prescribed steps along the way to, 'the great salvation'. The penitent sinner who wanted to join the church might be crushed (in Edward Taylor's phrase) between desire and fear—between a longing to profess his conversion and fear that it is delusory. Having experienced this kind of paralysis, the conscientious sinner might well be grateful for rescue, even in this world, from the psychological self-torture of futility. The ability to act might well be the worldly consequence of such faith.

Not only the motive but the social consequence, too, is a principle or a power rather than a quantitative fact. Just as Mather and Franklin, despite their obvious differences, worked outward from the idea of virtue, gratitude, duty, and wisdom to acts of service, so they conceived of the good done to others as a beginning rather than as charity in the limited sense of alms. *Bonifacius* cites the primitive church's doctrine that the sin of a Christian's neighbor is a sin by the Christian himself. As Richard Baxter ordered Christians to succor poor men's bodies in order to make it possible to save their souls,[15] Mather argues that the American Indians must be 'civilized' so that they can be 'Christianized'. He praises the English philanthropist Thomas Gouge for finding work for the poor, and he commands his own readers to 'find 'em work, set 'em to work, keep 'em to work'. Benjamin Franklin says it is hard for an empty sack to stand upright.

In these years both Old and New England had need of the ingenuity to which Mather appealed. The vigorous new capitalist organizations in 'this projecting age' gave such different authors as Richard Baxter, Daniel Defoe, Jonathan Swift, Cotton Mather, and (by the early 1720s) Benjamin Franklin examples of mutual cooperation that might be used for the public good. Baxter's *Christian Directory* directed Christians 'How to Improve all Helps and Means' toward a Christian life in the world. Defoe's *Essay on Projects* (1697) proposed Friendly Societies for several kinds of life and medical insurance; Swift's ironic *A Project for the Advancement of Religion and the Reformation of Manners* (1709) suggested a scheme for institutionalizing virtue through the Queen's power of preferment and the Court's leadership of fashion.

In England the Societies for the Reformation of Manners had already come under suspicion as petty meddlers by the time Swift published this proposal, but the social need for such organizations seems more interesting than the modern temptation to think of their motives as simply repressive. Systematic welfare programs were of course unknown. Widespread drunkenness seems to have been a relatively new problem, and it existed in a context that may now be difficult to imagine. Wine was often poisonously adulterated; alcoholic and other debtors and petty criminals were locked up indiscriminately in prisons in which conditions were far more abominable than the worst kind of do-gooding. Epidemics in these foul places sometimes made the punishment for civil offenses as lethal as the capital penalty officially attached to so many crimes. There was no effectively organized, properly trained, or trustworthy police force to prevent the growing number of violent crimes on city streets, which were generally unlighted. Private citizens armed to defend themselves. Two years after *Bonifacius* was published, a group of drunken young men who called themselves Mohocks terrorized London with atrocious beatings and mutilations that seemed the more terrible because they were apparently unmotivated.

I do not mean to contend that life in Queen Anne's London was a nightmare. The point is that specific needs in the society, needs unmet by government or other established organizations, encouraged the new techniques for organized benevolence and that in the absence of better preventive methods religious writers naturally encouraged Christians to set an individual example. Nor should we forget, even when considering the restrictive nature of some actions, the disastrous consequences of indiscretions that may seem minor today. Under the prevailing Canon Law, for example, it was easy to find oneself entrapped in a virtually indissoluble marriage, and many Londoners— sailors and young gentlemen alike—suffered from a lucrative conspiracy of clergyman, landlord, prostitute, and lawyer. In such circumstances advice against drinking, which neither Cotton nor Increase Mather ever opposed in its moderate form, and advice against falling into debt need not be officious. Meddlesomely repressive though they might become, societies like Mather's Young Men's Associations, Count Zinzendorf's Slaves of Virtue, and Benjamin Franklin's projected Society of the Free and Easy grew out of a positive desire to free men for the practice of virtue in this world.

What we need to remember, then, is the firmness with which Mather's good-doing is tied to the praise of God, the certainty with which his exhortations to be diligent rely on traditional ethics. *Bonifacius* is addressed to Christians; Mather invites unbelievers to close the book until, by repentance, they begin to live. He is not marketing religion but bringing religion into the market.

Besides a few specific ideas, which deserve separate attention, the key value of *Bonifacius* lies in the resourceful application of methodical ingenuity to pious affairs. Christians, Mather says, should employ their wits for God's service. As Thoreau will later complain that farmers speculate in herds of cattle in order to acquire shoestrings, Mather charges New Englanders with wasting grand capacities on trivial ends. He exhorts them to apply to good works the same ingenuity noted in their business affairs, to equal the degree of

contrivance (without the deception) employed by the Devil and the wicked in pursuit of evil ends.

Bonifacius thus appeals simultaneously to one of the most powerful traits in the New England character and to one of the strongest intellectual forces of the eighteenth century. Mather invokes for his divine purpose the desire to invent new means, to contrive, devise, experiment. Nor does he content himself with precepts. He repeatedly sets the example, for the impulse has come from one of the most powerful sources of his own conduct.

Scholarship has rarely found a less appropriate figure than the cliché that says Cotton Mather's knowledge was undigested. Ever since the early 1680s Mather had been scribbling in private as well as for publication, and he worked hard to reduce his experience and his knowledge to usable form. In his *Quotidiana,* copybooks in which he recorded scraps of quotations, scientific curiosities, and historical anecdotes, he laboriously compiled indexes so that he would be able to call on the information in his sermons and other works. In his conversation, moreover, he was remarkably quick to apply his diverse knowledge with an ingenuity that was sometimes startling. His diary, *'Paterna',*[16] and *Bonifacius* demonstrate that this quality was more than a natural aptitude. He hunted advantages for pious service in conversation, in idle moments of dinner parties, in the observance of various people as he walked the streets. And of course he wrote down the suggestions, which ranged from prayers to be said on seeing a beautiful woman, and resolutions to drop the name of a poor parishioner when visiting a rich one, to planning the conversation at his family's meals so that the children would be instructed.

It is easy to treat this carefully nurtured habit as comically tasteless by selecting one detail, such as Mather's resolution to meditate while urinating. Even when we supply the context for this example and notice that Mather feared the excruciating pain of kidney stones, which had tortured his grandfather, many of us will find it difficult to accept his resolution to offer up thanks, while urinating, for the grace that has spared him from his grandfather's affliction. Such a meditation can be defended, too, but the criticism misses the point. What matters is the total concentration on developing the discipline of pious resourcefulness. For every ludicrous example there is a passage that seems successful. Benjamin Franklin reports that when he accidentally hit his head on a beam in Mather's house, Mather told him to stoop always as he walked through life, so that he would save himself many a hard thump. Mather resolves in *'Paterna'* never to offer his children play as a reward for hard work, lest they come to consider diversion better than diligence. Instead he contrives to punish them by refusing to teach them something, and he resolves to reward them by teaching them 'some curious thing'.

Nor was there any hesitation to work out a much more elaborate meditation relating to recent scientific theories. A long paragraph from 'Paterna' will illustrate the kind of personal resolution that led Mather to write his **Christian Philosopher**. Here he comes very close to using eighteenth-century science in precisely the way that ennobles the works of Jonathan Edwards:

> I am continually entertained with *weighty body,* or *matter* tending to the *center of gravity;* or attracted by matter. I feel it in my own. The *cause* of this *tendency,* 'tis the glorious GOD! *Great GOD, Thou givest this matter such a tendency; Thou keepest it in its operation!* There is no other cause for *gravity,* but the *will* and *work* of the glorious GOD. I am now effectually convinced of that ancient confession, and must effectuously make it, 'He is not far from every one of us.' When I see a thing moving or settling that way which its *heavy nature* carries it, I may very justly think, and I would often form the thought, 'It is the glorious GOD who now carries this matter such a way.' When *matter* goes *downward,* my spirit shall therefore mount *upward,* in acknowledgment of the GOD who orders it. I will no longer complain, 'Behold, I go forward, but He is not there; and backward, but I cannot perceive Him: on the left hand, where He does work, but I cannot behold Him: He hideth Himself on the right hand, that I cannot see Him.' No, I am now taught where to meet with Him; even at every turn. *He knows the way that I take;* I cannot stir forward or backward, but I *perceive* Him in the *weight* of every *matter. My way* shall be to improve this as a *weighty argument* for the being of a GOD. I will argue from it, 'Behold, there is a GOD, whom I ought forever to love and serve and glorify.' Yea, and if I am tempted unto the doing of any wicked thing, I may reflect, that it cannot be done without some *action,* wherein *the power of matter* operates. But then I may carry on the reflection: 'How near, how near am I to the glorious GOD whose commands I am going to violate! Matter keeps His laws; but, O my soul, wilt thou break His laws? How shall I do this wickedness and therein deny the GOD, who not only is above, but also is exerting His power in the very matter upon which I make my criminal misapplications!'[17]

The very repetitiousness of Mather's inexhaustible pen demonstrates the persistence of his search for advantages to do good methodically, ingeniously. Besides recording his resolutions, drawing up proposals, preparing indexes, he completely revised his annual diaries so that they might be useful to other readers. Then he copied the relevant portions of these revised versions into **'Paterna',** for his son, and he copied relevant incidents, some of them extensive, into **Bonifacius,** making appropriate revisions. At his death he left two

grand unpublished books, **'The Angel of Bethesda'** and **Biblia Americana,** which form part of this same resolute plan. **'The Angel of Bethesda'** is a collection of medical advice and cures incorporating the kind of spiritual usefulness proposed' in **Bonifacius,** and **Biblia Americana** condenses, with Mather's own contributions, centuries of commentary on the Bible.

The energy that performed such prodigies undoubtedly drew some strength from vanity as well as from piety. Although **Bonifacius** was published anonymously, Mather's effort to seem expert in varied professional subjects will seem amusingly pretentious to modern readers, especially when he alludes to legal authors. Yet the conscious purpose of such allusions is to win the respect of those to whom the author offers moral advice useful in their professions, and to exemplify the kind of ingenuity he has been prescribing. The author of **Bonifacius** has taken the trouble to inform himself of at least a few good books and a few specific means for lawyers to do good. In medicine, Mather had no less training and was better read than many practicing physicians.

The pastor's concern with social health leads Mather to express in **Bonifacius** a number of ideas that would be interesting to modern readers even outside the context I have tried to establish. He declares that none but a good man really lives, and that one becomes more alive as one acts for good. Concern for the soul and interest in method led him to encourage rewards rather than punishment in educating children. He opposes beating except for the most serious offenses. He condemns tyrannical schoolmasters as a curse. He advises ministers to preach on subjects of particular use to their congregations and to ask the people to suggest topics for sermons. He favors the practical education of girls. He advises physicians to treat the poor without charge and to attend not only to the patient's soul but also to the 'anxiety' that may be causing his illness. He tells lawyers never to appear in a dirty cause, always to eschew sharp tricks, and to defend the principle of restitution. He condemns that usury which charges interest for money that the debtor never gets to use. He tells the rich to use their money for good while they live, rather than leave large estates.

All these proposals issue from the same pious concern that asks landlords to oblige their tenants to pray, pious societies to look out for their neighbors' sins, schoolmasters to teach Duport's verses on Job instead of Homer. What we must seek if we wish to know Mather is the man who could believe in both these kinds of proposals at once. For him witches, devils, angels, remarkable interventions of Providence, and the certainty of eternal judgment were as real as gravity. For his mind there was no contradiction between working for social justice and spending two or perhaps three days a week in secret fasts; no conflict between hail-ing Copernicus and Newton and preaching the imminence of the millennium, now that the seven last plagues of the Vial are about to be poured out on the Papal Empire; no conflict between studying the Talmud and preaching the Covenant of Grace.

Evaluation of Mather's literary achievement ought to profit from the same kind of attention to his prose style, which has too often been dismissed as fervid and pedantic. The remarkable quantity of his work, the cleanness of his manuscripts, and the testimony of his son all indicate that he wrote very rapidly, but the charge that his writing is fervid seems superficial. Although a small portion of his work fits the description, its importance has been exaggerated by the typographical devices used in his books and by the dubious belief that he was 'neurotic' and therefore unable to control his rhetoric.

The prevalence of learned allusions and foreign quotations has also been exaggerated, partly because Mather defended these useful ornaments and partly because readers of his history of New England must traverse an unusually thick jungle of classical fact and lore, with a name dropping from every tree, before they can escape from his self-conscious introduction into the history itself. All this may be of little comfort to readers of **Bonifacius,** who will find that Mather studded some pages with what he liked to consider jewels of Latin and Greek. Those who are not completely antagonized may take some comfort in noting how aptly many of these come forth from the index of Mather's *Quotidiana* or the electronic computer of his extraordinary mind. Repeatedly, the quotation is apt, and Mather's comment repeatedly makes it so.

Notice, too, how much of the prose in **Bonifacius** is plain, forceful, precise. Mather's speed makes his paragraphs repetitious, and it is difficult for us to avoid overemphasizing his italics, but I am convinced that much of Mather's writing is plainer than any by Thomas Hooker or John Cotton. Even in **Bonifacius** this passage on brutal schoolmasters seems as representative as the more elaborate classical quotations:

> *Ajax Flagellifer* may be read at the school. He is not fit for to be the master of it. Let it not be said of the scholars, 'They are brought up *in the school of Tyrannus.' Pliny* says that *bears* are the fatter for beating. Fitter to have the conduct of *bears* than of ingenuous *boys,* are the masters, that can't give a *bit* of learning, but they must give a *knock* with it. Send 'em to be tutors of the famous *Lithuanian* school, at *Samourgan.* The harsh, fierce, *Orbilian* way of treating the children, too commonly used in the *school,* is a dreadful *curse* of God upon our miserable offspring, who are *born children of wrath.* It is boasted now and then of a *schoolmaster,* that such and such a *brave man* had his education under him. There is nothing said, how many that might

have been *brave men,* have been destroyed by him; how many *brave wits,* have been dispirited, confounded, murdered, by his *barbarous* way of managing them.

Bonifacius is an important historical document because it brings to bear on the world of affairs all the piety and ingenuity that New England Puritanism had been nourishing, despite theological and political troubles, for eighty years. Without wavering from the central conviction of Puritans that man exists to glorify God, Cotton Mather exhorts all Christians to hunt opportunities to do good in the world. It is from this perspective, rather than by focusing on practical rewards, that we can best understand Puritan influences on Benjamin Franklin, later reformers, and American benevolence in the twentieth century. We continue to say, with the author of **Bonifacius,** that the ways of honest men are simple and the ways of the wicked are subtle, but we seek to devise a similar ingenuity for doing good around the world. We may also find it especially interesting that Mather the American, unlike his English predecessor Richard Baxter, says not a word about the danger that our efforts to do good may lead to disaster.

Notes

[1] 12 May 1784.

[2] Perry Miller, *The New England Mind: from Colony to Province* (Cambridge, Mass., 1953), pp. 402-16.

[3] Cotton Mather, *Small Offers toward the Service of the Tabernacle in the Wilderness. Four Discourses accommodated unto the Designs of Practical Godliness* (Boston, 1689), pp. 108-11.

[4] Here Mather seems clearly to have been following Richard Baxter's *How to Do Good to Many: or, the Publick Good is the Christian's Life. Directions and Motives It* (London, 1682), p. 5: 'But as all motion and action is first upon the nearest object, so must ours; and doing good must be in order: First we must begin at home with our own souls and lives, and then to our nearest relations, and friends, and acquaintance, and neighbors, and then to our societies, church, and kingdom, and all the world. But mark that order of execution, and the orders of estimation and intention differ. Though God set up lights so small as will serve but for one room, and though we must begin at home, we must far more esteem the desire and good of the multitude, of city and church and commonwealth; and must set no bounds to our endeavours, but what God and disability set'.

[5] Cotton Mather, *Early Piety, Exemplified in the Life and Death of Mr. Nathanael Mather . . .* (London, 1689), p. 39.

[6] Mather, *Small Offers*, p. 37.

[7] *Ibid.*, pp. 19ff.

[8] See *Theopolis Americana. An Essay on the Golden Street of the Holy City: Publishing a* TESTIMONY *against the* CORRUPTIONS *of the Market-Place. With some Good* HOPES *of Better Things to be yet seen in the* AMERICAN *World* (Boston, 1710), p. 48.

[9] *Ibid.*, p. 5. The text was Revelations 21:21. The sermon was preached on 3 November 1709.

[10] See A. Whitney Griswold, 'Three Puritans on Prosperity', *New England Quarterly,* VII (1934), 475-93.

[11] *Theopolis Americana,* pp. 13-14.

[12] *Ibid.,* p. 21.

[13] He did not say, 'Do unto others as you would have them do unto you', but rather: '*All things whatsoever* ye would, that men should do to you, do ye even so unto them.' He cited Matthew 7:12. See *Theopolis Americana,* pp. 14-16.

[14] *Ibid.,* pp. 18-22.

[15] Baxter, *How to Do Good to Many,* p. 15.

[16] A book-length autobiographical manuscript addressed to Mather's son and concentrating on the father's devices for piety. The manuscript is in the Alderman Library, University of Virginia. Many of these passages had been copied in turn from Mather's Reserved and Revised Memorials, which have since been published as *The Diary of Cotton Mather,* two vol., ed. Worthington C. Ford, in *Massachusetts Historical Society, Collections,* seventh ser., VII-VIII (Boston, 1911-12).

[17] This passage is quoted, with the permission of the University of Virginia, from the manuscript 'Paterna', pp. 304-5. I have modernized the spelling and capitalization.

Peter Gay (essay date 1966)

SOURCE: "Cotton Mather: A Pathetic Plutarch," in *A Loss of Mastery: Puritan Historians in Colonial America,* University of California Press, 1966, pp. 53-87.

[*In the following excerpt, Gay examines Mather's* Magnalia Christi Amricana *and argues that it has played a significant role in shaping modern views on Puritan New England.*]

I

The Founding Fathers of New England had written their histories under the pressure of great events, with all the passionate immediacy of the participant. But by the 1660's, their day was over. William Bradford died in 1657; Edward Winslow had preceded him by two years, John Winthrop by eight. Edward Johnson lived on to 1672, but after publishing his *Wonder-Working Providence of Sions Saviour in New England*—that naive military bulletin reporting Christ's victories against Satan in America—he allowed his official duties to engross his time, and wrote no more.

They had all been devout chroniclers, looking up to heaven as their dearest country, but significantly they had all been laymen, public servants who composed their annals from a found of political experience. The generation of historians that took their place were all clerics. They were scarcely less active in public affairs than the statesmen who had preceded them, and no more fanatical, but as the appointed guardians of the Puritan conscience, they turned the writing of history into a self-conscious pursuit. Intermittent warfare with the Indians in the 1670's and 1680's produced some splendidly artless chronicles, narratives alive with terror and the pious thirst for blood, but for the most part the production of history became a tribal rite, almost a religious act.

The historians of the second generation drew heavily on the first for their documentation, their standards of excellence, their mode of historical thinking. Their derivative mentality was not wholly regrettable; what they lost in originality, they gained in professional piety for the work of the Founders, notably for Bradford. This was only reasonable: Bradford's authority was deservedly high, and Bradford had recorded the critical events from which the New England myth was to be constructed. But while *Of Plimmoth Plantation* deserved its eminence, the loneliness of that eminence called attention to the flatness of the surrounding landscape. New England historians from Nathaniel Morton to Thomas Prince, from Cotton Mather to Thomas Hutchinson, diligently consulted and generously copied Bradford's manuscript: to check colonial historians of New England against one another is all too often to check Bradford against Bradford. Piety for Bradford was indeed reasonable, but it was also a symptom of resignation, a demonstration of the very decay that would be the dominant theme of the histories written in the second half of the seventeenth century.

The very purpose of these histories was borrowed from the Founders. Bradford had made it plain that he was filling his history with circumstantial detail so that the Puritans' "children may see with what difficulties their fathers wrastled in going through these things in their first beginnings, and how God brought them along notwithstanding all their weaknesses and infirmities."[1] By the 1670's, the call for didactic history had become general, and its reasons were Bradford's reasons. But the tone had a new pathos. In 1672, the General Court of Massachusetts Bay Colony voted to encourage the collecting of special providences, of events "beyond what could in reason have binn expected," so that Puritans might be led to serve their Lord.[2] In the following year, Urian Oakes said in a famous plea: "It is our great duty to be the Lords *Remembrancers* or *Recorders*." God had been good to his children, and "it were very well if there were a memorial of these things faithfully drawn up, and transmitted to Posterity." Such a history of New England would register in men's hearts now, and remind later generations, how much the Lord had done for his elect. "It is a desirable thing, that all the loving kindnesses of God, and his singular favours to this poor and despised out cast might be Chronicled and communicated (in the History of them) to succeeding Ages; that the memory of them may not dy and be extinct, with the present Generation."[3] And three years later, in 1676, Increase Mather pleaded the utility of history, the encouragement Scripture gives to its writing, and the propriety of divines to write it, as weighty support to his earnest wish that "some effectual Course may be taken (before it is too late) that a just *History of New England* be written and published to the World. That," he added, forgetful or disdainful of the histories already available, "is a thing that hath been often spoken of, but was never done to this day, and yet the longer it is deferred, the more difficulty will there be in effecting of it."[4]

Considering the frequency and solemnity of such calls for history, the response was tepid: if the American Puritans had any special vocation for history, they did not show it. Nathaniel Morton, Bradford's nephew and a diligent official in his own right, anticipated much of the public demand with his *New Englands Memoriall,* published in 1669, a compilation drawn largely from his uncle's manuscript. William Hubbard, the learned and urbane minister of Ipswich, discovered his historical talents with an effective history of the Indian wars, published in 1677, and then turned to a *General History of New England from the Discovery to MDCLXXX;* it closely followed Morton's *Memoriall* and Winthrop's *Journal,* but took its own course with its relatively skeptical view of providential intervention in history. In 1682, the General Court voted to pay Hubbard £50 in support of this history, but it remained in manuscript: neither its intellectual dependence nor its theological independence, it seems, appeared an adequate answer to New England's need for a reliable past. The most alert, most obedient response to Increase Mather's invitation came from his son, Cotton Mather, who always responded to his father's invitations.

II

Cotton Mather's *Magnalia Christi Americana,* written between 1693 and 1697, and published in London in 1702, is an erudite, informative, sprawling, and puzzling book. It is extraordinarily ambitious: its subtitle, "The Ecclesiastical History of New England," though suggestive of its orientation, falls markedly short of its scope. In seven books, the *Magnalia* offers a cursory outline of New England's history from the Plymouth settlement to the end of the seventeenth century; a set of brief biographies of governors and other officials; a far larger set of far more massive biographies of "Famous Divines"—for, Mather said, "of all History it must be confessed, that the palm is to be given unto Church History; wherein the dignity, the suavity, and the utility of the subject is transcendent";[5] a history of "Harvard-College" complete with the lives of some prominent ministers who graduated from it; the "Acts and Monuments" of the Puritan churches in America; a "Faithful Record" of "many Illustrious, Wonderful Providences" as they fell upon God's children in New England; and, in conclusion, a history of *"The Wars of the Lord,"* of Antinomians, Quakers, clerical impostors, and other plagues that beset the elect in the wilderness. Of all the Puritan intellectuals in New England in his time, only Cotton Mather could have written this history.

Cotton Mather has been widely, and often justly, maligned. If he had never existed, no village atheist would have had the wit to invent him. He was a seeker who drove the Puritan habit of self-examination, and the Puritan affliction of self-doubt, to morbid lengths: he writhed in the dust for his loathsome idleness after spending the day in exhausting charitable endeavor; weeping and praying, day after day, he looked for sure signs of grace; he performed in public as the omniscient guardian of morality while in private he moaned over his unclean soul; he tried to do justice to the leading role that his powerful father had assigned to him and, in a sense, acted out for him in his own versatile career, but, in the midst of success, surrounded by the trophies of his power, the son saw himself as a pathetic failure. Cotton Mather was singularly unfortunate in these symptoms: they display so much self-deception, so much self-indulgence, that they invite psychoanalytical probing, but without the clinical benevolence that the psychoanalyst extends to his patients. Cotton Mather lusted all his life for the presidency of Harvard, a post his father had held, and which the son affected to despise, especially after others were chosen; he was a prig and a meddler; an unscrupulous ideologue and a windy orator; a scribbler who praised simplicity in flowery circumlocutions, so anxious to see his productions in print that it might be said of him, with little fear of exaggeration, that he would rather lose his soul than misplace a manuscript.

Yet this same man, and without any apparent sense of strain, was also a patient husband and affectionate father; a responsible clergyman who gave generously of his time to counsel young people and new churches; an intelligent bibliophile and often discriminating reader; a curious observer of God's handiwork, interested enough in science to become a Fellow of the Royal Society—or, at least so eager for the right to bear the initials F.R.S. that he made extensive, if sometimes absurd, inquiries into nature. He was less responsible, and less courageous, in the witchcraft episode than some of his fellow Puritans, but also less credulous, and far less sadistic, than most of his fellow divines. He was, in sum, a cultivated man with a good mind and an international reputation. His stature, and his oddities, make him remarkable, but he was neither unique nor eccentric among the Puritans; what gives him significance is precisely that he was characteristic of his time and of his tribe.

It is Mather's representative quality that makes his *Magnalia* such an informative witness to the Puritan mind in America. Yet, though informative, it is also a reluctant witness: its meaning lies concealed in the maze of its organization and the tangled wilderness of its prose. Its opening line—"I write the WONDERS of the CHRISTIAN RELIGION, flying from the depravations of *Europe,* to the *American Strand,*"—evokes Vergil, but the rest of the book bears no resemblance to Vergil's classical balance and lovely melody. The *Magnalia* displays learning as Othello displayed love, not wisely but too well. No American writer has been called pedant more often than Cotton Mather, no American writer has deserved the epithet more than he. As early as 1708, the hostile English historian John Oldmixon recognized, and proclaimed, the literary limitations of the *Magnalia:* the book, he wrote, is "cramm'd with Punns, Anagrams, Acrosticks, Miracles and Prodigies."[6] Oldmixon was right: the *Magnalia* is a showcase of pedantry and elephantine wit. It is overloaded, and often overwhelmed, with expansive and irrelevant introductory passages, with far-fetched parallels, embarrassing puns, fatiguing alliterations, puerile anagrams; the writing is prolix, arch, involuted, imprecise, repetitive, and hysterical. It is also reactionary, a retreat to the ornate Mandarin writing fashionable half a century before. The *Magnalia,* as Oldmixon shrewdly observed, was like one of those "School Boys Exercises" of "Forty Years Ago."[7]

For all that, Mather prided himself on his style—another instance of his failure to achieve self-knowledge. He claimed that he had written his *Magnalia* in a "simple, submiss, humble style," and he never ceased to express his affection for Puritan simplicity. In the *Magnalia* he promises to record the lives of Puritan divines without "figure of rhetorick";[8] he enjoys retelling the story of young John Cotton giving up metaphysical preaching and embracing the plain style after

his conversion; and he holds up his grandfather Richard for his "way of preaching," which was "very plain, studiously avoiding obscure and foreign terms, and unnecessary citations of Latin sentences."[9] As the reader of the *Magnalia* knows, the grandson did not imitate his grandfather, at least not in this.

Yet there were times when Cotton Mather actually wrote well; in some of his scientific letters and didactic pamphlets, in several narrative passages in the *Magnalia* itself, he was direct, economical, even dramatic. But these felicitous passages only arouse the suspicion that Mather's style was more a symptom than a policy. His modes of writing appear not as the result of deliberate choices, but of irrational forces; Mather is not in control of his materials. His vacillations, his incoherence, like his profusion of words and deluge of allusions, suggest—it is no more than an impression—that Mather had something to hide, some besetting uncertainty, some fear of an unpalatable or unbearable truth, perhaps some doubt about the vocation of the Mather dynasty in God's New England.

The organization of the *Magnalia* strengthens this impression. Its seven books, as I have said, proceed from topic to topic, each in roughly chronological order. Hence decisive events, like the expulsion of the Antinomians, the troubles at Harvard College, the execution of the Quakers, may be reported several times, or reported only in passing. Mather offers much documentary evidence—he reprints the Statutes of Harvard, and the resolutions of Synods, in full—and he does not shun narration: he gives detailed descriptions of rescues at sea and battles with Indians. But over and over again Mather interprets critical moments in Puritan society as personal crises, social conflicts as the struggles of individual Christians with Satan. Mather dissolves history into biography.

The result is strangely soothing, especially since the lives that Mather celebrates appear as almost wholly admirable. Samuel Clark, the prolific English biographer whom Mather read with much interest though not without some reservations, had laid it down that the biographer "must eye" his subjects "not to observe their weaknesses, to discover their shame, for this is a poysonous disposition"; but "eye them, as we look into Glasses, to dress, and adorn ourselves thereby." He "must eye them for imitation": he must "look upon the best, and the best in the best."[10] Cotton Mather cheerfully agreed. "How can the *lives* of the commendable be written without commending them?"[11] he asked, and answered his rhetorical question in 1,400 pages.

The scores of biographies that populate the *Magnalia* are indispensable to Mather's irenic strategy. They were a sound choice: in the seventeenth century, biographies enjoyed enormous popularity. They were the kind of history everyone could understand, and they permitted readers to measure themselves against giants or identify themselves with sufferers. Biography, wrote John Norton in his life of John Cotton, gave witness to "many full and glorious triumphs over the World, Sin and Satan, obtained by persons in like temptations, and subject to like passions with ourselves."[12] Such a genre simply could not fail. "When many excellent Lives are collected into one or more Volumes," Samuel Clark said confidently, "they do continue, and will do so, till Printing shall be no more."[13] Cotton Mather's *Magnalia Christi Americana* was a collection of excellent lives.

Cotton Mather was too great an admirer of his "incomparable Plutarch" to reduce his biographies to mere eulogies.[14] Mather knew everyone of consequence in New England, and he used his position intelligently: he secured private letters and intimate diaries, sought out eye-witnesses, and then wove his precious materials into a coherent narrative. At the same time, Mather subordinated the individuality of his lives to their pedagogic purpose. He strove to entertain, but to entertain for the sake of giving instruction, and to instruct—as Samuel Clark, and before him, many other biographers, had said—for the sake of inducing imitation.

The biographies in the *Magnalia* are, therefore, exemplary lives, cut from a single pattern. A typical life runs somewhat like this: One: the young man converts to a religious walk of life, and his conversion is attended with deep misery and high illumination, lengthy turmoil and a tormenting conviction of unworthiness. Two: close study of Scriptures convinces him that Anglican ceremonies are affected with popish pomp, and Anglican beliefs laden with popish trash; the true Christian, he discovers, must be a Puritan, living, as all Puritans do, in the primitive simplicity of the early Church. Three: this conviction subjects him to harassment by hardened sinners, Satan's minions in England, and leads to his decision to flee to the American strand. Four: Laud's dreaded pursuivants try to capture the convert that they may torment him, but they are miraculously diverted from their prey. Five: the young Congregationalist crosses to America, and his passage is beset by dreadful storms and near disaster, but a special Providence—secured after fervent prayers—calms the sea and eases the voyage (at this point, the pattern provides an alternative: God grants his saint smooth passage to America). Six: once in New England, the saint performs wonderfully well in his calling, securing conversions, guarding the churches, keeping peace in the colony. Seven: when the time for settling down is ripe, the saint contracts a marriage that is a model of mutual devotion and Christian love, with husband cherishing wife and wife obeying husband—all marriages in New England, at least all marriages in the *Magnalia,* are blissfully happy. Eight: as he grows older, the saint leads an unspotted private life, bringing up grave—Mather's word is "old"—young men

and women who are filled with concern for their salvation and the love of death, and showing worldly men the road to sobriety and devotion. Nine: since Satan never sleeps, the saint suffers repeated assaults of temptation, but fights them all off. Ten: the saint grows rich in years and honors, and dies an edifying death, commemorated by the poems of his friends, celebrated by the eulogy of his pastor, and witnessed by his tearful, unconsolable wife. Eleven: widow remarries.

This, Cotton Mather tells his readers over and over again, this is how men lived in New England, this is how they should live, but this is how they live no longer. Mather was the Plutarch of Puritan America, but he was a pathetic Plutarch. In an age of Jeremiads the *Magnalia Christi Americana* is the greatest Jeremiad of them all.

III

The second generation of American Puritans lived under the doom of divine displeasure. They were certain of it, largely because they incessantly confirmed each others' apprehensions. In 1662, "in the time of the great drought," Michael Wigglesworth found an appropriate designation for the Puritans' malaise; it was a sign, he said, of "God's Controversy with New-England."[15] To us, such a controversy appears as a projection, a sign of inner uncertainty. But to Wigglesworth, as to his fellow Puritans, it was an objective reality: Puritans had planted New England and prospered there, but now they were declining, living in the daily expectation of divine punishment. To be sure, New England still harbored "many praying saints"—to appeal to them was, after all, the point of Wigglesworth's poetic effort—but the saints must act before it was too late:

> Beware, O sinful land, beware;
>   And do not think it strange
> That sorer judgments are at hand,
>   Unless thou quickly change.

Wigglesworth was a pastor, but devout laymen echoed his judgment. "*New-England* is not to be found in *New-England,* nor *Boston* in *Boston*," Joshua Scottow, a prosperous businessman, wrote mournfully in 1691. "We must now cry out, our *Leanness,* our *Leanness,* our *Apostacy,* our *Atheism, Spiritual Idolatry, Adultery, Formality in Worship, carnal and vain Confidence* in Church-Privileges, forgetting of GOD our Rock, and Multitude of other Abominations."[16] Everyone articulate enough to publish tracts or sermons agreed that spiritual decay was a pervasive rot, attacking New England at its roots, and inviting the most dreadful disasters; the cheerful remnant was silent. The General Court proclaimed official Days of Humiliation, and in its call compiled appalling lists of military defeats, bad harvests, epidemic outbreaks, interchurch rivalries, and untimely deaths. Puritan preachers above all, who had always found portentous warnings an entertaining theme for their sermons, specified for their parishioners the counts of the great indictment under which they all lay. Boston is the new Babylon, its fair face pock-marked with alehouses and whorehouses; merchants dream of profits and imperil their immortal souls; the rising generation forgets its obedience; shameless daughters of Zion parade about with naked arms and naked breasts; sinners drunk with prosperity imitate English fashions and invite the lightning by wearing periwigs. All these evils, and others, Increase Mather said in 1679, are "a sad sign that we have in great part forgotten our *Errand* in this Wilderness."[17]

The function of these laments was plain to performer and audience alike. The Jeremiad was a stylized history, designed to shame the present generation out of its erring ways by recalling the surpassing virtues of its fathers. The modern Jeremiah prayerfully expected that the celebration of the Founders would change the course of affairs and prepare a future worth celebrating.

There was nothing new about this purposeful scolding; in fact, it derived much of its strength from its respectable ancestry. The prophets of the Old Testament—and not Jeremiah alone—had reminded their flocks of a heroic time when men walked with God; urbane Greek poets had composed their nostalgic pastorals to move their readers to a purer life; Roman orators, historians and poets had sought to cure the corruption and decadence of an imperial city by constructing Republican fantasies about courageous, simple men, and chaste, dutiful women. Like their secular ancestors, the New England Jeremiahs astutely mixed historical fact with edifying fiction; like their religious ancestors, they impregnated their tirades with mythical thinking. God, they insisted, was angry, and manifested his anger with dire visitations. One way—the Puritan divines thought the best, probably the only way—of reconciling him to his children was to acknowledge the visitations, to dwell on them with the kind of pleasure that only self-punishment can give, to accept them humbly, with real repentance, and to resolve to do better. Doubtless there were some practicing Congregationalists who listened to these Jeremiads and enjoyed them as a conventional ceremony; doubtless there were others who used them unscrupulously to score debating points against political opponents: it was all too easy to see the hand of Satan in the maneuvering of a rival minister, and to interpret his prosperity as a visible token of New England's decline. There were some, too, who took the Jeremiad as a rite of propitiation, hoping to avert the jealousy of higher powers by dramatizing the Puritans' afflictions, on the age-old principle that God humbles the happy. But most of the Jeremiads—and there were many—bear the unmistakable mark of absolute sincerity. They speak of decay because they see decay; they

say that God's hand is on his sinful children because they see God's hand in Indians winning battles and beloved relatives dying young. The Jeremiad was a ritual and a remedy, but the ritual was grounded in the Puritans' most intimate convictions and most pressing anxieties, and the remedy was not prescribed lightly. For the devout Puritan in Cotton Mather's day, the enterprise of New England was sick unto death; the dismay of the aging John Winthrop and William Bradford had become the dominant temper of the orthodox.

The Jeremiads were implicit histories, the histories were explicit Jeremiads. Cotton Mather was perfectly clear about this. *"De tristibus,"* he said, "may be a proper title for the book I am now writing."[18] The book he wrote began with triumphant settlements, and with that magnificent invocation of Vergil; it ended with an account of afflictions, and a quotation from the most pathetic book of the Old Testament: "We have been under the lamentable punishments of our sins for two lustres of years together, 'tis time for every man, and for all of us as one man, to say, as in Lamentations iii, 40, 'Let us search and try our ways, and turn again unto the Lord.'"[19] To ask men to turn again unto the Lord suggests, plainly enough, that they have turned away from him. "I saw a fearful *degeneracy,*" Mather intoned, adjusting the mantle of the Old Testament prophet around his shoulders, "creeping, I cannot say, but rushing in upon these churches; I saw to multiply continually our dangers, of our losing no small points in our *first faith,* as well as our *first love,* and of our giving up the *essentials* of that church order, which was the very end of these colonies; I saw a visible *shrink* in all orders of men among us, from that *greatness,* and that *goodness,* which was in the *first grain* that our God brought from *three sifted kingdoms,* into this land, when it was a *land not sown.*"[20]

With the sure instinct of a trained polemicist, Mather couched his warnings in the commonplaces current among his peers: there was grave danger, he said, that New England might forget its *"errand into the wilderness"*;[21] it is "very certain," he said, that "the God of heaven had (and still hath!)" a "controversie" with New England.[22] In this emergency, Mather saw his duty. Obviously, *"speedy* care" must "be taken to preserve the memorables of our first settlement," lest the "laudable *principles* and *practices* of that first settlement" be utterly "lost in our apostasies." Mather resolves to recall, and by recalling revive primitive worship: "To advise you of your dangers," he tells the churches of Connecticut, "and uphold the *life* of *religion* among you, I presume humbly to lay before you the life of that excellent man," Thomas Hooker. "What should be done for the stop, the turn of this degeneracy?" Mather asks himself, and replies: "I'll shew them the graves of their dead fathers."[23]

Obviously Mather's readers liked nothing better; the *Magnalia* soon acquired and long retained great authority. It was valuable enough to be stolen: in 1720, a burglar ransacking Jonathan Belcher's well-stocked warehouse included in his booty "a Book Entituled, Magnalia Christi Americana."[24] Approval such as this did not rest on shared necrophilia alone; the *Magnalia* told the Puritans what they wanted to hear. It told them, to begin with—and it was edifying to hear it from a philosopher who corresponded with savants in Europe—that the old theology, the theology of William Bradford and, indeed, St. Augustine, need not be revised in the light of modern knowledge. Moses still was, as he had always been, "the first and the best historian in the world."[25] God himself had cast "a long *series* of preserving and prosperous smiles" on the early settlers of New England, and now that "the enchantments of *this world*" had "caused the rising generation" to "neglect the primitive designs and interests of *religion* propounded by their fathers," God was blasting harvests, drowning sailors, burning houses, and filling the air with pestilence.[26] The marvelous stories about pious divines rescued at sea by a special Providence, the affecting stories about dying children converting their unregenerate fathers with the Lord's help, the fitting last words of convicted criminals led by God to say the appropriate thing, the poetic justice dealt out to blasphemers by a watchful and vengeful Lord—all these were true. The visible world, like the invisible world, was full of wonders.

This was reassuring enough. But the *Magnalia* did not stop here. It also told its readers that Puritan New England was important, its cause just, and its conduct irreproachable. Doubtless there were scoffers—there were always scoffers. "But whether *New-England* may Live any where else or no," Cotton Mather wrote, with slightly tremulous pride, "it must *live* in our *History*." Admittedly, "a war between *us* and a handful of Indians" may "appear no more than a *Batrachomyomachie* to the world *abroad*." But to New Englanders "*at home* it hath been considerable enough to make an history."[27] Thinking of his own *Magnalia,* Mather could feel confident that his modesty was misplaced: New England was considerable enough to make a history abroad as much as at home.

It deserved to live in history because it was fulfilling a great calling. Like other New England Jeremiahs, Cotton Mather had two masks: tragedy for domestic, comedy for foreign consumption. Of course, New England was decaying: that was the point of the Jeremiads; of course, New England was imperfect: that was the nature of man. Still, New England remained a city upon a hill: "I perswade myself," Mather suavely observed, "that *so far as they have attained,*" the Congregational churches in America "have given great examples of the methods and measures wherein an Evangelical Reformation is to be prosecuted." To be sure, "I do not say, that the Churches of New-England are the most *regular* that can be; yet I do say, and am sure, that they are very like unto those that were in the first ages of Christianity."[28] It was the highest praise Mather could bestow.

These complex judgments confirm the impression that Cotton Mather had something to hide. The *Magnalia* proves the Puritans guilty, and pronounces them innocent. Mather reaches this gratifying verdict by emphasizing consensus at the expense of conflict: he forgets inconvenient facts, refuses to call things by their right names, and defends the indefensible. It is possible to reconstruct the battles among the churches of New England by reading the *Magnalia* with infinite care, but infinite care is needed, for Mather calls this vicious internecine warfare, "little *controversies*."[29] In 1668, John Davenport, a founder of New Haven and pastor there, accepted a call from the First Church in Boston, despite his advanced age and despite the reluctance of his parishioners to let him go. His supporters in Boston suppressed vital evidence to secure his appointment; Davenport himself, eager to sit in the place once graced by John Cotton, gave it as his opinion that "whither it be from errour in judgment" or from "designe," it was "evident Satan hath a great hand" in the resistance of his opponents.[30] The parishioners of the First Church, and with them the city of Boston, divided into vituperative factions; before it was all over, the minority had walked out and formed a congregation of their own—Old South Church. Of these proceedings, known to all, ugly in tone, unprecedented in acrimony, there is scarcely a trace in the *Magnalia;* Mather omits all specific details and instead says airily that Davenport's "removal from New Haven was clogged with many temptatious difficulties"—but then, would it not be a miracle if on so long a journey one did not meet some stumbling stones? And in any event, Davenport "broke through them all, in expectation to do what he judged would be a more comprehensive service unto the churches of *New-England,* than could have been done by him in his now undistinguished colony."[31] And so, an old man's ambition, and an undignified squabble, are transmuted into glorious service to God.

Vagueness is a favorite weapon of apologists, and Cotton Mather uses it with admirable deftness. He waves aside the fierce contentions among the Connecticut churches: "There arose at length some unhappy contests in one town of the colony, which grew into an alienation that could not be cured" without a bitter parting. Still, all was for the best: "These little, idle, angry *controversies,* proved occasions of *enlargements* to the church of God; for such of the inhabitants as chose a *cottage in a wilderness,*" just moved "peaceably higher up the river, where a whole county of holy churches has been added unto the number of our congregations."[32] After this, it comes as no surprise to read Mather's bland biography of the subtle John Cotton, and Mather's expansive account of the Antinomian crisis, in which Cotton's prevarications are disguised behind a few portentous phrases and dissolved in a cheerful denouement: "An happy *conclusion of the whole matter.*"[33] Retelling the career of William Bradford, obviously with the manuscript of *Plimmoth Plantation* before him, Mather has no difficulty seeing Reverend Lyford as a hypocrite, a liar, and a plotter—that, after all, is what Bradford had called him. But when it comes to Bradford's interception and opening of Lyford's letters to England—an illegal action which Bradford justifies in considerable detail—Mather improves on his source in the interest of making his saint more saintly: "At last there fell into the hands of the governour" Lyford's letters "home to England."[34]

What Mather does not achieve with dilution, he achieves with suppression. Mather is uncomfortably aware that the treatment of the Quakers has given the American Puritans a bad name: "A great clamour hath been raised against New-England for their 'persecution of the Quakers.'" He refuses to defend it—"if any man will appear in the vindication of it, let him do as he please; for my part, I will not"—and then proceeds to defend it. He regrets the executions: *"Haereticide"* is not an *"evangelical way* for the extinguishing of heresies"; neglect, or contempt, would have been sufficient. Yet they were madmen, these Quakers, lunatics, energumens, enemies to the civil and sacred order of Massachusetts: the authorities, he is sure, would "gladly" have released them.[35] This is not unreasonable: the Quakers who came back to Massachusetts with full knowledge that their return would lead to their death were courting a martyr's fate. But Mather's account, though reasonable, is not candid: it is wholly silent about the poignant sufferings of the miserable sectaries, about the insults, the bloody whippings, the brutal legislation enacted expressly against them; it is largely silent about Governor John Endicott, that tight-lipped fanatic, who of all the Quakers' scourges in New England was the worst. Cotton Mather's impulse to decency was strong, but he could not afford to indulge it to the full. The Puritans wanted their myth, and Cotton Mather, obliging as always, supplied the demand.

IV

The *Magnalia Christi Americana* was tribal history, expressing Puritan sentiments, feeding Puritan anxieties, and sustaining Puritan pride. But it was also something more specific: it was family history constructed on the single principle that the Mathers were always right.

This principle is not as parochial as it may sound; in New England, as in old England, party history was family history writ large. The Mathers were a potent and far-flung dynasty—Cotton Mather never forgot that he was the grandson of Richard Mather and John Cotton—and while they were wrong to identify family wishes with the public good, they had every right to claim that their private interests were inextricably interwoven with public policy. There were no modern political parties in the New England of Cotton Mather's day; there were stable groupings and shifting coalitions, confused contests for power, for status and rewards, in which alliances were formed, dissolved, and reorganized. The alignments were as varied as the issues, and largely depended on them: they arose from struggles for grants of land, competition for profitable intimacy with English officials, quarrels within congregations, and, on occasion, abstract questions like toleration. Politics in Mather's day, as in our own, was a serious game in which suppressed passions found their outlet: ambitious men exercised their energies, and quarrelsome men gratified their lust for trouble, by competing for office. It was also a religious game: to say, as we must say, that Puritan politics was interest politics is not to say that it was secular politics. Most New Englanders, urbane Anglicans and plain Congregationalists alike, were deeply religious men, and could contest religious issues with as much fervor as economic ones—and more.

By the time Cotton Mather wrote his *Magnalia,* New England had transformed itself from a collection of rude settlements into a civilized, diversified community, complete with social and political conflict. New England was still underpopulated: by 1700, it had about 100,000 inhabitants—Boston, its commercial and intellectual capital, had about 7,000—and most of this population were simple farmers and craftsmen. Yet, hard as the orthodox Puritans tried to retain traditional simplicities, New England society was too large, too complex, too prosperous, too civilized, to resist the need for change. England, in those days of slow and hazardous travel, still seemed far away, but more and more as the century went on, it influenced affairs in its American dependencies. The great traumatic events in New England's history all occurred, or were all caused by events in England.

The early settlers had been singularly fortunate. They had built their Utopia with practically no interference from the home government—they had violated their charter, disregarded instructions from England, and in general conducted themselves like an independent power. But after the Restoration of Charles II, in 1660, this was no longer possible, and, to many New Englanders, no longer desirable. Merchants who developed extensive interests in international trade, gentry hungry for land and status, Anglican settlers who resented the Puritan monopoly of civic rights and political power, looked to England for protection, for profits, for comforts, for symbols of distinction. Merchants might be restive under the restrictions of the English

Navigation Acts, but they preferred a remote monarchy that limited their profits to a watchful oligarchy that kept them politically impotent and socially insecure. The stirring events of the 1680's, culminating in a rather belated Glorious Revolution in New England in the Spring of 1689, realigned political alliances for a while: Puritan oligarchs, prosperous merchants, ambitious politicians found it expedient to make compromises, to cooperate under the new Protestant monarchy, and to work for the restoration of their Charter.

But while social groupings found uneasy peace in their demand for partial self-government and their search for a social organization capable of coping with new realities, the Puritan oligarchy itself was fatally divided. Protestantism has an irrepressible tendency toward fission; as Roman Catholics had argued since the sixteenth century, the exercise of private judgment must lead to the splintering of sects. The Puritan leadership in America had fully recognized this danger and had sought, at times desperately, to find the right middle way—some of the *Magnalia's* denials of trouble in paradise read like a frantic attempt to wish it out of existence. Yet, as the synods show by their Resolutions—by the very need to call them—the tensions inherent in Congregationalism could not be permanently kept down. Puritans prized religious experience but abhorred the chaos of private inspiration and unchecked enthusiasm; Puritans wished an orderly church but disliked the centralized authority of the Presbyterians. Puritans thought a church should be a gathering of saints, but they needed to insure its survival by admitting the saints' descendants: the uneasy and unenforceable compromise of the Half-Way Covenant, which they devised in the early 1660's—a procedure granting to children of church members who had had no saving religious experience of their own the right to all privileges of membership save only the Lord's Supper—was a symptom of their embarrassment. Puritans wanted no nonsense about toleration: why tolerate Satan? Yet there were many among them, and not among Cromwell's men alone, who hated persecution and thought many theological disagreements "indifferent," which is to say, harmless. Puritans accepted Calvin's uncompromising teachings about God's absolute sovereignty and man's total depravity, but their experience taught them that virtuous and vicious actions have their effect in the world and even on God: the Jeremiads were intended to have results, to change the mind of the Lord and the course of events.

Tentatively in the first generation, vigorously in the second, an increasing number of Puritans tried to resolve these tensions in what they liked to call a "Catholick spirit," a flexible attitude toward questions of doctrine, church polity, and the relations of the sacred to the secular power. They remained good Congregationalists; they believed in divine Providence, miracles, witches, and Satan. But their temper was tolerant and expansive, and by the 1690's they were a distinct party, powerful enough to be recognized by Cotton Mather. "In my own country," he wrote in the *Magnalia,* there is "a number of eminently godly persons, who are for a larger way, and unto these my Church-History will give distaste."[36] It was not for this group that Mather wrote his history. "I have endeavoured, with all good conscience, to decline this writing meerly for a party,"[37] he proclaimed, but he was in fact writing for a party, and its head was named Mather.

This required some judicious navigation, for the Mathers had changed their minds. Increase Mather had first opposed, and then supported, the Half-Way Covenant; both Increase and Cotton Mather had accepted toleration with reluctance: it was imposed on them partly by developments in the New England churches, largely by the Glorious Revolution. In the *Magnalia,* Cotton Mather reports the first reversal as a blessing, and antedates the second reversal to give the Mathers credit they did not deserve.[38] The *Magnalia* was more than an apology for the Mather clan—it derived its persuasiveness from the excellence of much of its research and documentation. But in the end, the apologetic aim of the *Magnalia* overwhelms its historical scholarship, and it becomes a Jeremiad in the service of a tribe in retreat.

V

This interpretation of Cotton Mather and his most famous book may seem uncharitable. Did not the *Magnalia* itself show traces of a Catholick temper? Was it not, besides, a young man's work? Did not Mather's conduct, in the thirty years that remained to him, reveal a flexible spirit? Was it not a manifestation of admirable tolerance to have Mather preach at the ordination of a Baptist minister? Did he not show a progressive mentality during the inoculation controversy of 1721-1722, when he bravely stood by science and reason? Did he not write *The Christian Philosopher,* a pioneering work in natural theology which (in Kenneth Murdock's words) expounded an "advanced intellectual position" that looked forward to Emerson, offered "proof positive of his intellectual development," and proved "him to have been far more 'modern' than his times"?[39]

The facts are true enough, but they will not bear the strain that our historical piety places on them. To be sure—I have insisted on it—Cotton Mather was civilized, intelligent, and often reasonable. He had nothing but distaste for the more egregious forms of fanaticism; especially in his mature years, his pronouncements on religious toleration were irenic for temperamental, not merely for political reasons. He abhorred heresy, but he preferred combating it by persuasion to stamping it out by force. His cultivation, the fruit of wide reading and high ambition, compelled him into a certain breadth of view. But none of these qualities made him a modern man. Not even his celebrated appearance in a Baptist church in 1718 justifies our calling him more modern than his times: he went to perform his good deed mainly to gratify his vanity; he was eager to bear "a Testimony to the grand Intention of an Union for good Men upon the Maxims of Piety" by ordaining a Baptist pastor, but he luxuriated in the awareness that his action would "cause much Discourse and Wonder," and "occasion various Discourse in the world."[40]

There was nothing that caused more discourse in the world of Boston than Cotton Mather's defense of inoculation. When the smallpox visited New England in 1721, Boylston inoculated a number of Bostonians, and Cotton Mather, to the dismay of many, supported him. Someone threw a bomb into Mather's house, and this bomb—which did not go off—has made him into a martyr to progress.[41] But the issue was not between science and superstition: most of the leading physicians, and many educated Puritans, thought inoculation an absurd and dangerous fad: Dr. William Douglass, who led the medical opposition, likened Mather's support of inoculation to Mather's support of the witchcraft trials thirty years before—another instance of "mistaken Notions." Mather was on the right side, and for good reasons: he had first read of inoculation in the *Philosophical Transactions*. But he supported the practice in the spirit of a Christian virtuoso, certain that to cure a great evil by enduring a lesser one was to obey the ways of Providence: Increase Mather had discovered, and Cotton Mather rejoiced to see, that among those who approved of inoculation, only a few were men of "a Prophane Life and Conversation," while on the contrary, "it cannot be denied, but that the known Children of the Wicked one, are generally fierce Enemies to Inoculation."[42] To support inoculation under these circumstances was not to advance secularism but to combat Satan.

Cotton Mather wrote his **Christian Philosopher** in the same combative mood. If the book was indeed the first defense of natural theology in Puritan America, this reflects not the modernity of Mather but the provinciality of the Puritans. To prove the existence, the goodness, the glory, and the omnipotence of God by pointing to his manifestations in nature, to suggest that God had revealed himself first by his works and then by his words, was to utter an antique commonplace of Christian apologetics—and a safe one: Mather was at one with other apologists in insisting that natural religion taught not naturalism but humble submission to God's splendid decrees: "A PHILOSOPHICAL RELIGION: And yet how *Evangelical!*"[43]

Such philosophical religion had deep roots in the books that the Puritans studied with unwearied devotion. "The heavens declare the glory of God; and the firmament sheweth his handy-work. Day unto day uttereth speech, and night unto night sheweth knowledge."[44] Thus the Psalmist. "For the invisible things of him from the creation of the world are clearly seen, being understood by the things that are made, even his eternal power and Godhead; so that they"—the ungodly and the unrighteous—"are without excuse."[45] Thus St. Paul to the Romans. The great Reformers, for all their insistence on divine sovereignty and inscrutability, all their preachment of the arbitrariness of Providence, commented on these Biblical passages with pious approval. Calvin above all insisted that "the knowledge of God shines forth in the fashioning of the universe and the continuing government of it," so that everyone must see his splendor: "The clarity of God's self-disclosure strips us of every excuse" for denying his "wonderful wisdom." It is not only astronomy, medicine, and other sciences intended to elucidate "recondite matters" that declare God's handiwork, but common, ordinary experiences, "which thrust themselves upon the sight of even the most untutored and ignorant person."[46] In 1728, in their obituary sermons, polite Catholick preachers like Benjamin Colman found much to praise in Cotton Mather; but after all, there was much to praise, and besides, he was safely dead.[47] Yet the politeness of the eulogies could not conceal the distance of the new Congregationalists from the Mather faction. Far from looking ahead to Emerson's transcendentalism, Mather's thought looked back to the Church Fathers.

Cotton Mather had known this. He had found it expedient to reach an accommodation with the Colmans and the Brattles, but in December 1699, when the Brattle Street Church was being founded, the irreconcilable conflict found expression in Mather's diary. The Brattle Street group, he wrote, are "Head-strong Men," filled with "malignity to the Holy Wayes of our Churches"; these "fallacious people" delude "many better-meaning Men," and "invite an ill Party thro' all the Countrey, to throw all into Confusion." It was necessary to take strong action against these innovators, though even the most loving reproof only "enrages their violent and impotent Lusts, to carry on the *Apostasy*." These were strong words, but more was to come. In January of 1700, Cotton Mather confided to his diary that he saw "*Satan* beginning a terrible Shake unto the Churches of *New England*"; a "*Day of Temptation*" has come, brought by men who are "ignorant, arrogant, obstinate, and full of Malice and Slander," men who "fill the Land with *Lyes*."[48]

These are the rages of a defeated man, and indeed, Cotton Mather lost battle after battle. The merchants who put profits before piety, built lavish establishments, and married their daughters to Anglicans, founded the commercial empires that moved the colonies into active competition with European traders. The politicians who discounted religious considerations in their struggle for office or their zeal for good administration broke the tribal mould of Puritan society. The Catholick Congregationalists who founded Brattle Street Church, seized Harvard College from the Mathers, and moved, however timidly, toward Arminianism, opened the windows of a provincial society to the breezes of intellectual change, and prepared educated Americans for a fruitful reunion with enlightened Europe.

Yet Cotton Mather and, through him, Puritan orthodoxy, had their revenge. For two centuries and even longer, Americans, even those who criticized the **Magnalia** or professed to despise its author, have seen the great struggle for New England's soul through Cotton Mather's eyes. Everyone owned his history, everyone read it, everyone, consciously or not, absorbed its views and employed its categories. For whatever the liberals and rebels in Massachusetts did—and they did much—there was one thing they neglected to do. They did not write history.

Notes

1 Bradford, *Of Plymouth Plantation,* I, 120.

2 Kenneth B. Murdock, "William Hubbard and the Providential Interpretation of History," *Proceedings of the American Antiquarian Society,* LII (1942), 23.

3 *New-England Pleaded With* (1673), quoted in Miller and Johnson, *The Puritans,* I, 81.

4 *A Brief History of the War with the Indians in New-England,* ed. Samuel G. Drake (1862), p. 37.

5 Cotton Mather, *Magnalia Christi Americana,* I, 28.

6 Quoted by Perry Miller, *The New England Mind: From Colony to Province* (1953), p. 360.

7 *Ibid.*

8 *Magnalia Christi Americana,* I, 31.

9 *Ibid.,* I, 452.

10 *Lives of Ten Eminent Divines* (1662), A3, quoted in Donald A. Stauffer, *English Biography Before 1700* (1930), p. 253.

11 *Magnalia Christi Americana,* I, 30.

12 Kenneth B. Murdock, "Clio in the Wilderness: History and Biography in Puritan New England," *Church History,* XXIV (1955), 227. God himself, the American Puritans believed, had enjoined them to write history—had he not said, in the 140th Psalm, "He hath made his wonderful works to be remembered"? Murdock, *ibid.,* 222.

13 See Stauffer, *English Biography Before 1700,* p. 305.

14 Mather calls Plutarch "incomparable" in *Magnalia Christi Americana,* I, 29. In his life of Governor William Phips, Mather announces that he intends to imitate Plutarch's method as a biographer. *Ibid.,* I, 166.

15 A sizable selection from the poem is reprinted in Miller and Johnson, *The Puritans,* II, 611-616. My quotation below is at p. 616.

16 *Old Men's Tears for their own Declension mixed with Fears of their and Posterities Falling off from New England's Primitive Constitution,* quoted in Bernard Bailyn, *The New England Merchants in the Seventeenth Century* (1955), p. 123.

17 Bailyn, *New England Merchants,* p. 141.

18 *Magnalia Christi Americana,* II, 537.

19 *Ibid.,* II, 681.

20 *Ibid.,* I, 249.

21 *Ibid.,* I, 64.

22 *Ibid.,* II, 318.

23 *Ibid.,* I, 249-252; I, 332.

24 Clifford K. Shipton, *New England Life in the 18th Century,* p. 48, life of Jonathan Belcher.

25 *Magnalia Christi Americana,* II, 109.

26 *Ibid.,* II, 316.

27 *Ibid.,* I, 27; II, 581.

28 *Ibid.,* I, 26-27.

29 *Ibid.,* I, 63.

30 See Hamilton Andrews Hill, *History of the Old South Church (Third Church) Boston, 1669-1884,* 2 vols. (1890), I, 24.

31 *Magnalia Christi Americana,* I, 328-329.

32 *Ibid.,* I, 83.

33 *Ibid.,* II, 515. This incident had already been noted by Perry Miller in *The New England Mind: From Colony to Province,* p. 61.

34 *Magnalia Christi Americana,* I, 60. Bradford's original account is in *Of Plymouth Plantation,* I, 382-388.

[35] See especially, *Magnalia Christi Americana,* I, 298; II, 523-525.

[36] *Ibid.,* I, 36.

[37] *Ibid.,* I, 29.

[38] See Perry Miller, *The New England Mind: From Colony to Province,* pp. 103, 108.

[39] Kenneth B. Murdock, ed., *Cotton Mather, Selections* (1926), pp. l-lii.

[40] Cotton Mather, *Diary,* II, 531-536.

[41] See *ibid.,* II, 657-658.

[42] John B. Blake, "The Inoculation Controversy in Boston: 1721-1722," *New England Quarterly,* XXV (1952), 497, 503.

[43] *The Christian Philosopher,* Introduction, in Murdock, *Cotton Mather, Selections,* p. 286.

[44] Psalm 19:1; see also Psalms 104 and 145.

[45] Romans 1:20.

[46] Calvin, *Institutes of the Christian Religion,* transl. by Ford Lewis Battles, ed. John T. McNeill, 2 vols. (1960), I, 51-53. In his exposition, Calvin relies mainly on Romans 1:20, Psalm 104, and Psalm 145.

[47] In his laudatory essay on Cotton Mather (Introduction to *Cotton Mather, Selections*), Kenneth Murdock quotes the opinions of Benjamin Colman, Thomas Prince, and Joshua Gee, all favorable, but all uttered upon Cotton Mather's death. It is well to remember Samuel Johnson's observation that "In lapidary inscriptions a man is not upon oath."

[48] Cotton Mather, *Diary,* I, 325-326, 330.

John P. Duffy (essay date 1967)

SOURCE: "Cotton Mather Revisited," in *Massachusetts Studies in English,* Vol. I, No. 2, Fall, 1967, pp. 30-8.

[*In the essay below, Duffy reviews Mather's treatment by historians and argues that modern scholars should reconsider the unattractive stereotype that has prevailed.*]

One may rummage around among the characters of American history for a good long time without finding a figure who has been so badly treated as Cotton Mather, that old New England puritan divine about whom Barrett Wendell said, "There is still good ground for believing that it was a good man they buried on Copp's Hill one February day in the year 1728."[1] But those who have written about Cotton Mather during the past one hundred years have cut that good ground right out from under him in what might almost appear to be a conspiracy of unkindness or even malice. But in his own time, the late seventeenth and early eighteenth centuries, Cotton Mather was, as a puritan minister, a man of great force and influence. In and around Boston during his lifetime, no event of importance could occur without his participation, opposition, or considered acquiescence: when the Royal governor, Edmund Andros, was deposed in 1689, Cotton Mather led the rebellion; when the new governor, William Phips, was inaugurated in 1691, he led the prayers. In all this he was loved and admired, feared and respected by his contemporaries at home and honored in Europe. But in the twentieth century, hear with what apparent glee the historian Samuel Eliot Morison joins in the hazing of the twelve-year-old Harvard freshman: "We may feel confident that normal college life was completely restored, if that insufferable young prig Cotton Mather was being kicked about as he so justly deserved." So wrote Morison in *Harvard College in the Seventeenth Century,* and there is a sound basis to think that Morison may be completely wrong in his appraisal of the hazing of young Mather; he may very well have oversimplified a complex case of church and college politics.[2]

If Morison is wrong in this particular, the whole stereotype of Cotton Mather's puritan meddling, self-righteousness, credulity, pedantry, and reaction may call for a reexamination. Not that Mather has received much attention from those writing about American literature and history; he has been given only three brief mentions in Commager and Morison's standard two-volume history, *The Growth of the American Republic,* and the most substantial of these is the little anecdote about Benjamin Franklin's visit to him. When these writers do write about him, they are likely to speak of him as Perry Miller does in *The New England Mind* as a "frantic character who boasts, blurts, sneers, gloats, and shrieks in retrospective adulation of the Old Order,"[3] then is reluctant, later opportunistic, in surrendering to the New Order. Some writers have dealt with him sympathetically, especially Barrett Wendell, but they have had little effect on prevailing opinion, either in the scholarly community or among the people. Perhaps because he is portrayed as unattractive, or perhaps because he does not merit more attention, very few biographies have been written about Cotton Mather (only one in this century), and none of these is satisfactory.

Although one commentator says, "Barrett Wendell's *Cotton Mather* is so excellent a study of its difficult subject as to make quite superfluous any attempt to rewrite the tale,"[4] and many others seem to be in agreement, I fail to see that there is still not needed a good biography of Cotton Mather. Wendell's biography, published in 1891, and reissued three years ago, attempted to tell the story in Mather's own words from his diary and other writings. The treatment given Mather is as sympathetic as he gets anywhere, but the result is dull—a dull book about an interesting man. This dullness stems in part from Wendell's leaning too heavily on Mather's own words; at times it appears that Wendell is publishing his notecards.

Two more recent biographies are poorly done. *The Life and Times of Cotton Mather* by Abijah P. Marvin, a Congregationalist minister, was published the year after Wendell's. It is strong in New England church history but weak everywhere else. It is offensively pietistic toward the puritans, especially the clergy and their families, and defensive about Cotton Mather. In addition, the book seems to have no plan other than chronological, the life is not focused, and nothing leads up to or away from anything else. Even the paragraphs are not unified. The other, *Cotton Mather: Keeper of the Puritan Conscience* by Ralph and Louise Boas, is a kind of fictionalized biography. At the very outset, for example, we see the death of Richard Mather, Cotton's grandfather, through young Cotton's eyes: "In his childish mind he stored up the picture of a pious son exhorting a pious father; and with the normal child's love of imitation he projected himself into the years ahead, seeing himself a learned minister speeding his father's journey into the unknown Presence. . . . He, too, would be a learned man; he, too, would preach to multitudes; he, too, when he was a man, would guide his father's footsteps on the path to heaven." And in another place, "There is every reason to believe that this pamphlet was written by Cotton Mather. It may be assumed, therefore, that he was aware of the plan to present a petition to the Queen."[5] So, an assumption is based on a reason to believe. These are the accustomed techniques of this book, which was probably expected to be known as a "popular" biography: guesswork, imagination and assumption, but no footnotes. It did not turn out to be popular, nor is it a dependable biography.

Many short sketches of Cotton Mather's life have been written, and most of them have been unkind. He received the worst treatment at the hands of twentieth-century writers with a strong liberal view of our history and a readiness to let their political opinions color their critical judgment. This is not true of Kenneth Murdock, who wrote a number of short sketches of Mather's life, including the one in *Dictionary of American Biography,* and another typical Murdock sketch in the Introduction to *Selections from Cotton Mather* where he makes this balanced observation: "He was human in his shortcomings, deservedly famous for his good works, and to know him well is to understand a man whose nature abounds in baffling inconsistencies, and who is the more interesting because he defies reduction to the limits of type." With this view, Murdock could have written the needed biography of Cotton Mather on the order of his *Increase Mather,* that excellent biography of Cotton Mather's father, though we can be grateful for his doing justice to the younger Mather by editing his great **Magnalia**.

Like many of the others who have written about Mather, Murdock does not always deal kindly with him but accuses him of hypocrisy and questions his integrity. This is the nub of the criticism here where Murdock makes it appear that Mather prays and fasts only to prove something: "He knew how his grandfathers had fasted and prayed, and he strove to outdo them, in a rather too conscious effort to prove that in him the fire burned as brightly as in the saints of the past."[6] In every particular his action is challenged or his integrity questioned. Those who have written of him in the past one hundred years say, and Mather would readily admit it, that in leading the 1689 rebellion he was not really concerned with traditional English liberties, but with traditional puritan religion. They say that when he became an advocate of religious toleration, he did so only because it became expedient; that his conduct during and after the witchcraft trials was dishonorable; that his efforts to restore theocracy were tireless and offensive; and that his diary (which he edited and revised for others to see) reveals a person of the greatest vanity. In addition these writers find everywhere in his writing a discrepancy between the motives he claims and those which, they say, are his obvious real motives.

It is not surprising then, given these beliefs, to find these writers saying some most intemperate things about Cotton Mather. Parrington, in the short chapter he contributes to Mather in *Main Currents of American Thought,* is vituperative. Of course for Parrington good and bad writers are easy to differentiate: good writers contributed to the liberal social and economic development of the United States, while bad writers opposed it. Mediocre writers ignored it. Cotton Mather must have opposed this development vigorously to cause Parrington to say:

> What a crooked and diseased mind lay back of those eyes that were forever spying out occasions to magnify self! He grovels in proud self-abasement. He distorts the most obvious reality. His mind is clogged with the strangest miscellany of truth and marvel. He labors to acquire the possessions of a scholar, but he listens to old wives' tales with greedy avidity. In all his mental processes the solidest fact falls into fantastic perspective. He was earnest to do good, he labored

to put into effect hundreds of "Good devices," but he walked always in his own shadow. His egotism blots out charity and even the divine mercy.[7]

Such pictures of Cotton Mather are not accurate, yet it is hard to see how the record became so confused. However it began, it began early. In his own time Cotton Mather was a controversial man. He was involved in the politics of the Bay Colony and the politics of Harvard College. Either of these activities could assure a man some enemies, and Mather probably made more than his share, for he was hot-tempered and quick to say what he thought. There were other controversies, too, and he seemed to be drawn to them. The most violent of them he started, and it brings only honor to him. During an epidemic of smallpox he inoculated his children, advocated inoculation for everyone, and introduced this medical innovation into the New World. The controversy boiled, and he demonstrated great courage in the face of it. The fever this issue created was greater than that caused by the smallpox. It even caused someone to throw a *granado,* a bomb, through his window with a note attached which sounded almost as if it had been written by one of his twentieth-century critics: "Cotton Mather, you Dog; Dam you: I'll inoculate you with this, with a pox to you."[8] It also caused someone, two centuries later, to write a little book, a fine but very specialized study published in 1954, called *Cotton Mather: First Significant Figure in American Medicine.* The bomb did him little harm, the book did him little good, but the controversy made for Cotton Mather a bitter enemy. This enemy, Dr. William Douglas, during the rest of Mather's life and for twenty years after his death dedicated himself to reviling every aspect of Mather's public life. Douglas, the only man in the colony with a medical degree, had opposed inoculation and lost, but he succeeded during the eighteenth century in getting his view of Cotton Mather accepted as the record.

In the eighteenth century and after, those who did not wish Cotton Mather well can be found in another and somewhat surprising place. Harvard men, and we must remember that they dominated the literary scene in New England for a long time, looked upon Mather as one who had done a disservice to their alma mater. He was a stalwart advocate of orthodoxy at Harvard, and when he was sure that it had gone finally wrong, he shifted his allegiance to Yale. He solicited funds for that institution from the wealthy merchant, Elihu Yale, and succeeded in getting the college named after him. Harvard men to the time of Wendell held the position that Mather was an alumnus in whom they took little pride.

During the nineteenth century interest in Mather as a literary figure tended to decline, although some of

his writings were still available. Alan Heimert has this to say about the view of Mather in the last century: "James Russell Lowell had in 1860 set down Mather as the most 'pedantic' representative of a New England which had become soon after the Restoration 'narrow in thought, in culture, in creed.'"[9] Little has been done to this day to alter that judgment among those writing about literature, although in the *Literary History of the United States,* Kenneth Murdock speaks with respect of Cotton Mather's control and versatility of style in his various writings.

When *The Diary of Cotton Mather* was published by the Massachusetts Historical Society, a derogatory essay was written as a preface by the editor, Worthington Chauncey Ford, in which he says of Mather that there is "much to repel and little to attract."[10] Ford is critical of Mather's efforts to get his work published which he refers to as a "regular manufacture of matter for the press." But to see Mather thoroughly rebuked for his publishing, we must turn to Parrington again: "With a very lust for printer's ink, he padded his bibliography like a college professor seeking promotion; but in spite of all the prayers poured out in behalf of them, they would seem for the most part to have been little more than tuppenny tracts, stuffed with a sodden morality, that not even an angel could make literature of."[11] Mather was a prolific writer; more than four hundred of his works were published, most of them sermons or collections of sermons. His detractors criticize him for the number of his publications, his artful method of getting some of them published, and his practice of giving his books away, often without identifying the giver.

Cotton Mather's propensity for seeing visions also disturbed Ford and others. Here is how Ford speaks of them: "Believing himself to be a favorite of God, he established communication with Deity, either through agency of an angel or even more directly, and received encouragements which fortunately he was unable to express in human language, and which became little less than ridiculous in his attempts to express them, unless allowance is made for his physical and mental condition."[12] Ford and others are not at all sure that Mather did see visions, and even if he did, they feel it only served to feed an already overdeveloped vanity. Most of the writers attribute the visions to the severe strain he put on an emotional and physical system not strong enough to stand up under it. Some writers attribute Mather's visions to oversexuality coupled with a puritan repression. Whatever it was, Cotton Mather made much less of the visions than do those who write of him.

Two honors which pleased Cotton Mather very much came to him in his late forties, but about both of them he was much abused in his own time. Those who abused him were his opponents in church, colony, and college politics, and the written attacks then made have been used by later writers to belittle his achievements. The first honor was the awarding of a degree of Doctor of Divinity by Glasgow University, and even before he had become accustomed to seeing the D.D. after his name someone had written a poem beginning, "The mad enthusiast, thirsting after fame." The degree was followed two years later by his election to the Royal Society. He had begun as a medical student and had maintained an interest in science, evident in his position on inoculation. Through some bungling his name was left off Royal Society membership lists, though he was a member, and this fact was used by his enemies to discredit him as though he had falsely claimed the honor. The Royal Society called a special meeting to rectify the error.

It may be said that in our time little has been written about him, and that what has been written has been unfair to Cotton Mather, and in addition, that his biographies are not particularly well done. One reason for all this might be that, despite the great number of things he wrote, Cotton Mather left little of value to a biographer. His biographers must rely heavily on Samuel Sewall's *Diary* and other records for basic facts about his life. Mather's own diary does not tell the biographers what they need to know.

Cotton Mather began keeping the diary in 1681 and continued it for forty-four years. He began each year on February 12, his birthday, and recorded throughout the year pious thoughts, good intentions, references to personal and family problems, and allusions to events of local or historical importance. All thoughts, intentions, references, and allusions are of equal importance in the diary, for all are concerned with the war between God and Satan in which Cotton Mather is very much concerned, and in which he sees himself as a central figure.

The diary was in manuscript until 1911 and 1912, and at that time the Massachusetts Historical Society published all known manuscripts. That publication contained the diaries for twenty-three years and was published again in 1957. Neither of these publications included the diary for 1712 which was thought to be lost until it turned up at a book sale in 1919. It was published separately in 1964.[13]

Cotton Mather's intention in keeping the diary seems to have been to leave a record of his times for his children, and doubtless he fully expected others to read what he had written. He left a record of what he was and what he wanted to be, but not a record of what he did. Nor did he leave a record, as historians are chagrined to learn, which sheds much light on his time. His references to people and events are vague and abstract. He seems to have an aversion to writing down people's names, substituting "my kinsman in the Indian service" or "my wife's brother's eldest nephew" and for specific events refers to "catastrophes" and "enormities." Some of these "enormities" can be understood from a reading of Sewall's *Diary* for the same period.

A criticism often made of Cotton Mather is that he wrote in a style fantastically ornate, loaded down in some grotesque way with puns and rhetorical flourishes. This criticism cannot be made of the diary, however, which is direct and unadorned, even telegraphic. Nor for that matter can it be said of some of his other writing; **The Christian Philosopher,** for example, is in a fine eighteenth-century style. Some of his critics also make much of the fact that Mather copied the diary over, as though his purpose was to expurgate. Actually only the diary for the years before 1711 was copied over, and what comes later differs little. He wrote less after 1711, but only because he felt the diary took more time than it deserved.

An increasingly large part of the later diary is devoted to "Goods Devised." Each day Cotton Mather recorded an intention to perform some good action according to a formula which assigns to each day of the week a beneficiary for this attention. For Sunday (labeled 1 G. D. in his diary), his good devised will benefit his flock; Monday (2 G. D.), his family; Tuesday (3 G. D.), alternating between relatives abroad and personal enemies; Wednesday, benefit to other people or in the country; Thursday, the societies; Friday, objects of compassion; and Saturday he devotes himself to the question: What remains for the Kingdom of God in my own heart and life?[14]

Despite its inadequacies the diary would seem to be a chief resource for the biographer, as it was for Barrett Wendell; but William Manierre, editor of *The Diary of Cotton Mather for the Year 1712,* says that it is "precisely in his diary that Mather looks least attractive." Manierre says that this results from the changing "world view" in which Mather looks unattractive from the "perspective of that newer complex of chilling thought and disillusion which Joseph Wood Krutch calls 'the modern temper.'"[15]

To see Mather in an attractive perspective, then, would require of us a sweeping historical adjustment. We may not in the twentieth century be capable of understanding Cotton Mather's "world view." Without questioning his sincerity, integrity, or motives, we would have to sympathize, to use an older meaning of that word, with a man who believed in a very strenuous Christian religion, not only on Sunday, but all day—all week; who believed in visions and witches; and in a very real black man with a black book. And he believed all this along with many other intelligent and educated people.

In many ways he had a very uncomfortable religion; this makes it hard for us to understand the religion or the man.

If one can make the historical adjustment, he may find Cotton Mather more attractive. The prayers for his enemies, for instance, and they have disturbed many of his critics, might not seem like hypocrisy. Here is a typical one:

> An horrid fellow, who is one of the wickedest of men, formerly made me the object of his malice, and his fury, and his libels. He has lately endeavored a cursed slander, and a subornation of mischief, against a pious and faithful magistrate, my very good friend Mr. Bromfield. . . . Having him with me in my study, we together entered before the Lord, our complaint concerning that child of Belial. We first forgave him and renounced with abhorrence all thoughts of a personal revenge upon him. We asked the Lord to forgive him and make him a new creature.[16]

The writers so critical of Cotton Mather think the intemperate language used on his enemies while praying for them is hypocrisy, but one wonders how many pray for their enemies in any language. Cotton Mather also made a practice of praying for people who did not know he was praying for them. He prayed for people sitting at a meeting, or at dinner, or just walking along the street. When he saw a tall man he said, "Lord, give that man high attainments in Christianity; let him fear God above many," or a lame man, "Lord, help that man to walk upright," or a Negro, "Lord, wash that poor soul white in the blood of thy Son."[17]

There can be seen here and elsewhere a kind of generous spirit and a readiness to do God's work that does not come through in his biographies and does not correlate with the abuse heaped upon Cotton Mather by Parrington and others. Nor do the biographers portray a man who was obviously a successful pastor genuinely liked by his congregation and much in demand as as preacher. He was often requested by condemned murderers to preach their last sermon to them. His biographers never describe him as a pleasant companion, although several of his contemporaries say he was good company. He is painted as a man unsympathetic to the aspirations of youth and intolerant of their feelings, but this is not Benjamin Franklin's picture of him, or his own picture of his relationship with his children and others. He was apparently most successful in instructing children and popular enough with them to be prevailed upon by a Society of Pious Children to permit them to meet in his library.

So then, let us put Cotton Mather down as one who loved God and his neighbors, but loved God more. Under the puritan rubrics there was no alternative to this, for man was depraved. This puritan view led Cotton Mather to acts of uncharitable piety, but to many more acts of pious charity, and to countless acts of good plain generosity. At one time he was giving financial assistance to as many as ninety charity cases among his relatives, friends, church members, and even those he considered enemies of God. If this generosity is dimmed by what the writers call boasting, blurting, sneering, gloating and shrieking in retrospective adulation of the old order, it is because he thought the old order was the way of God. As a puritan pastor it was his duty to exert a leadership in every facet of the colony's life to insure that he and others found that way. His uncharitable piety is the quality most often remembered by those who write of him. This is not surprising; in any time those who loved God more than they loved their neighbors are misunderstood by their neighbors and probably misinterpreted by history.

Notes

[1] Barrett Wendell, *Cotton Mather, The Puritan Priest* (New York, 1963), p. 4.

[2] Samuel Eliot Morison, *Harvard College in the Seventeenth Century* (Cambridge, 1936), I, 82-83. For another view of the matter see David Levine, "The Hazing of Cotton Mather," *New England Quarterly* XXXVI (June, 1963), 147-171.

[3] Perry Miller, *The New England Mind: From Colony to Province* (Cambridge, 1953), p. 357.

[4] Kenneth B. Murdock, ed., *Selections from Cotton Mather* (New York, n.d.), p. ix.

[5] Ralph and Louise Boas, *Cotton Mather, Keeper of the Puritan Conscience* (New York, 1928), pp. 2-3.

[6] Murdock, xiv.

[7] Vernon L. Parrington, *Main Currents of American Thought*, I, (New York, 1927), 110-111.

[8] Murdock, xxii.

[9] Alan Heimert, in Wendell p. xvi. Heimert adds that this judgment was upheld by M. C. Tyler in his *A History of American Literature: 1607-1765*.

[10] Worthington Chauncey Ford, ed., *Diary of Cotton Mather,* 2 vol. (Boston, 1911-12), xix.

[11] Parrington, 112.

[12] Ford, xix.

[13] William R. Manierre II, ed., *The Diary of Cotton Mather for the Year 1712* (Charlottesville, 1964).

[14] *Diary* II, 24-28.

[15] Manierre, xvii.

[16] *Diary for 1712,* 29.

[17] *Diary* II, 481.

Richard H. Werking (essay date 1972)

SOURCE: "'Reformation Is Our Only Preservation': Cotton Mather and Salem Witchcraft," in *The William and Mary Quarterly,* Vol. XXIX, No. 2, April, 1972, pp. 281-90.

[*In the following essay, Werking discusses Mather's role in a Boston witchcraft case of 1688 and explores the role Mather sought to play in the "Puritan mission in late seventeenth-century Massachusetts."*]

Accounts of Cotton Mather's connection with the Salem witchcraft episode are hardly new. From Robert Calef's denunciations of the younger Mather in the 1690s to Chadwick Hansen's efforts in the 1960s to vindicate him, historians have expended considerable effort either attacking or defending his behavior in the Salem affair.[1] Charles W. Upham, politician and Unitarian minister at Salem in the mid-nineteenth century, was particularly vociferous in his attacks on the Puritan clergy in general and Cotton Mather in particular. He accused Mather of "getting up" the Salem tragedy by publicizing a case of witchcraft that occurred in Boston in 1688; attempting to revive the matter after the Salem trials had ended by zealously and credulously attempting to cure persons allegedly victimized by witches; urging the magistrates to continue the prosecution of witches when he drafted the advice of the clergy to the judges; and failing to put forth effort to stop the witch trials, instead writing an exoneration of the judges in October 1692. Other historians, among them George Bancroft, George L. Burr, Justin Winsor, George Moore, and James Truslow Adams, have been sympathetic to Upham's charges.[2]

As Chadwick Hansen has recently pointed out, such has remained the popular view of Mather's place in the history of Salem witchcraft, due largely to the influence of Bancroft's work.[3] This view has persisted in the face of repeated attempts by historians to place Mather in a more favorable light. W. F. Poole challenged Upham's accounts on more than one occasion in the nineteenth century, and others have followed him, among them Josiah Quincy, Barrett Wendell, Kenneth B. Murdock, Samuel Eliot Morison, and, of course, Hansen himself.[4] Hansen in particular successfully defends Mather against the greater number of the accusations, showing that witchcraft was frightfully real to virtually all the residents of New England and not

just to Cotton Mather, that Mather was not responsible for the outbreak of the witchcraft incidents in the first place, that he advised the judges to be extremely cautious in the use of the all-important "spectral evidence," and that he used considerable caution in his own dealings with persons whom he was attempting to cure of witchcraft's effects.[5]

Despite the considerable heat generated by debate over the degree of Cotton Mather's "guilt" or "innocence," something remains less than fully clarified.[6] We still do not know just what Mather intended his connection with the witchcraft episode to be, or why it was what it was. In other words, why did this Boston minister, who managed not to attend a single witch trial at Salem, insinuate himself so actively into the affair in the manner that he did?[7] An explanation lies in his experience with the Boston witchcraft case of 1688 and in the way he viewed his role within the context of the Puritan mission in late seventeenth-century Massachusetts.

In the eyes of the Puritan clergy, the latter decades of the century were a troubled time for the colony of Massachusetts Bay. Perry Miller has demonstrated very well the anxiety of the ministers and their increasing reliance upon the jeremiad to steer the straying colonists onto God's path.[8] King Philip's War in 1675-1676 and the crown's attacks upon the colony's charter appeared as examples of divine wrath turned upon a spiritually declining people. "The countrey is Distress'd in many points," wrote Cotton Mather in 1686. "Wee are in great Hazard of losing our Colledge. . . . The Charters of our Colonies are in Extreme Danger also to be lost."[9]

According to the clergy, the great danger—and the cause for divine displeasure—was increasing secularization in the life of the colony and the consequent loss of religious zeal.[10] In order to reverse this trend a number of the clergy stressed the necessity of continually reminding the people of the existence of the spiritual world and of its close connection with the material world. Joseph Glanvill and other English writers had been calling for the collection of remarkable occurrences in order to confound the secularists. "Modern relations" of such events, Glanvill wrote in 1661, "being fresh, and near, . . . it may be expected they should have more success upon the obstinacy of Unbelievers."[11] At a conference of the ministers in Cambridge, Massachusetts, in 1681, Increase Mather and others repeated Glanvill's plea. Three years later, Increase published his *An Essay for the Recording of Illustrious Providences.* . . . (better known as *Remarkable Providences*), in which he recorded, among other things, miraculous sea rescues, "strange apparitions," "witchcrafts," [and] "diabolical possessions."[12] He intended it to be only the first in a succession of similar projects, for he explained: "In this essay I design no more than a specimen; and having (by the good hand of God upon me) set this wheel a going, I shall leave it unto others, whom God has fitted and shall incline thereto, to go on with the undertaking."[13]

Although the story thus far is familiar to anyone acquainted with the Salem episode, the activity that had occurred is important in explaining Cotton Mather's interest in and behavior toward the witchcraft cases, for the younger Mather would be most industrious in keeping the "wheel a going." In March 1681 he had already recorded in his diary his five most important daily duties which involved not only prayer and meditation but also the duty "to be diligent in *observing* and *recording* of *illustrious Providences*"[14] Then, in 1688, he became prominent in the handling of the Boston witchcraft case, another well-known story. Briefly, Mather and several other ministers prayed with and for the children of John Goodwin, who had become subject to hysterical fits. When Goodwin swore out a complaint against an old woman in the neighborhood, Goody Glover, the authorities searched her house and found small images made of rags and goat hair, which in their eyes furnished evidence that she was a practicing witch.[15] She confessed her guilt and received a sentence of death after being declared *compos mentis* by several doctors. Cotton Mather attempted to pray with her, but she refused to repent and embrace the covenant.[16]

Glover's execution did not halt the afflictions of the Goodwin children—an important point. They continued to suffer for some time, while Mather diligently prayed and fasted with them. He did not feel it necessary to seek out possible suspects, since he thought "we should be tender in such Relations, lest we wrong the Reputation of the Innocent by stories not enough enquired into."[17] Eventually the fits left the children, and Mather gave the credit to particular techniques. "Prayer and Faith," he concluded, "was the thing which drove the Divils from the Children."[18]

Mather's account of the case, entitled ***Memorable Providences,*** consciously followed the work of other recorders of the spirit world's manifestations, including his father and Joseph Glanvill:

> I can with a Contentment beyond meer Patience give these . . . Sheets unto the Stationer, when I see what pains Mr. Baxter, Mr. Glanvill, Dr. More, and several other Great Names have taken to publish Histories of Witchcrafts and Possessions unto the world. I said, Let me also run after them; and this with the more Alacrity because, I have tidings ready. Go then, my little Book, as a Lackey to the more elaborate Essayes of those learned men. Go tell Mankind, that there are Devils and Witches. . . . Go tell the world, What Prayers can do beyond all Devils and Witches. . . . [19]

Seemingly his propensity to witness and record evidence of witchcraft made Mather more zealous than the other ministers in his efforts to help the Goodwin children.[20]

This twin desire to seek out and register examples of witchcraft while at the same time using the techniques of prayer, fasting, and caution also motivated Cotton Mather during the witchcraft outbreak at Salem in 1692. As he had done in the Goodwin case, he asked that he might take some of the afflicted children into his own home.[21] This time he was not permitted to handle matters as he wished, and after October 1692, when he wrote the defense of a court which had tried the accused witches, his reputation suffered a blow from which it has not yet recovered.

Historians have since debated Mather's responsibility for the Salem tragedy without emphasizing the dual nature of his conduct. Defenders have continually pointed to Mather's frequent advice for caution, especially regarding the crucial question of spectral evidence. Accusers have denounced what they consider to have been his credulity in believing in witches, his zeal in seeking them out (including two communications to the judges urging them to be zealous), and his defense of the court. That both interpretations are possible suggests an ambiguity that has often gone unnoticed.[22] If people were to renew the covenant, they had to be reminded of the nearness of the spiritual world, and no opportunity should be lost in doing so.[23] But at the same time, a good deal of caution had to be used toward those accused of witchcraft. Here was a delicate balance, which Mather was able to maintain when he himself was investigating presumed witchcrafts, but which disintegrated when he was not. His obsession with this balance is evident in a number of his writings connected with the witch trials.

Cotton Mather's letter to his friend Judge John Richards on May 31, just before the trials began, is a most revealing document. As historians have repeatedly shown, he urged Richards to be very cautious regarding spectral evidence. At the same time, he told the judge that "the indefatigable paines that are used for the tracing [of] this Witchcraft are to be thankfully accepted, and applauded among all this people of God." The most direct proof of guilt for Mather was a confession, and toward the end of the letter he suggested:

> It is worth considering, whether there be a necessity always by Extirpations by Halter or fagott, [ ] every wretched creature, that shall be hooked into some degrees of Witchcraft. What if some of the lesser Criminalls, be onely scourged with lesser punishments, and also put upon some solemn, open, Publike and Explicitt renunciation of the Divil? I am apt to thinke that the Divels would then cease afflicting the neighbor-hood. . . . Or what if the death of some of the offenders were either diverted

or inflicted, according to the success of such their renunciation.

> But I find my free thoughts, thus freely layd before your Honour, begin to have too much freedome in them. I shall now therefore adde no more. . . . [24]

It was evidently more important to Mather that the reality of witches be made apparent and the covenant renewed than that witches be executed. He later returned to this theme.

In mid-June *The Return of Several Ministers* . . . was delivered to the court, which had paused to ask the advice of the clergy. One accused witch had been tried and executed, and the court was recessed temporarily. The **Return,** written by Cotton Mather,[25] is probably the best-known document dealing with the Salem episode and has been reprinted frequently. Yet virtually every historian who has commented on it has ignored the subtlety of some key paragraphs in it.[26] After discussing the suffering of the afflicted in the first paragraph, Mather wrote:

> We cannot but with all Thankfulness acknowledge, the Success which the merciful God has given unto the sedulous and assiduous Endeavours of our honourable Rulers, to detect the abominable Witchcrafts which have been committed in the Country; humbly praying that the discovery of these mysterious and mischievous Wickednesses may be perfected.

> We judge that in the prosecution of these, and all such Witchcrafts, there is need of a very critical and exquisite Caution, lest by too much Credulity for things received only upon the Devil's Authority, there be a Door opened for a long Train of miserable Consequences, and Satan get an advantage over us, for we should not be ignorant of his Devices.

Paragraphs four through seven continued the emphasis on caution, but Mather concluded:

> Nevertheless, We cannot but humbly recommend unto the Government, the speedy and vigorous Prosecution of such as have rendred themselves obnoxious, according to the Direction given in the Laws of God, and the wholesome Statutes of the *English* Nation, for the Detection of Witchcrafts.

It is apparently the second and final paragraphs which have been the basis of the charge that Mather and the other clergymen "approved, applauded, and stimulated the prosecutions."[27] But the second paragraph did no such thing. What Mather praised was the effort to "detect" and "discover" witchcrafts. The third paragraph began the discussion of prosecution, which was something else again, and the language was that of

extreme caution. The final paragraph did urge the prosecution of persons, but only "such as have rendred themselves obnoxious," i.e., "liable to punishment or censure; guilty, blameworthy."[28] Cotton Mather was praising the zealous investigation of the spiritual world in order to confound atheists and inject religious zeal, but he was simultaneously urging great caution in the handling of suspected witches encountered in the course of such activity.[29]

A letter in August to John Foster, member of the governor's council, demonstrates the same pattern. Cotton Mather, although more complimentary toward the judges than the language in his two communications to them might indicate, offered a way out of the increasingly bloody business at Salem.[30] He suggested that perhaps "a famous divine or two" might be appointed to the court, as had occurred during an outbreak of witchcraft in England in 1645. One of the ministers, Mather told Foster, "did preach two sermons to the court before his first sitting on the bench, wherein having first proved the existence of witches he afterwards showed the evil of endeavoring the conviction of any upon defective evidence. The sermon had the effect that none were condemned who could be saved without an express breach of the law. And then, though 'twas possible some guilty did escape, yet the troubles of those places were, I think, extinguished."[31] As when he had offered to take some of the afflicted children into his home, Mather was very anxious to keep his own hand on affairs.

Nevertheless, the desire for caution did not slow Mather's own quest for evidence of the diabolical. The next year he went to Salem to collect as much information as he could on the witchcrafts, because such an account "might in a while bee a singular Benefit unto the Church, and unto the World."[32] By this time he had already been investigating similar phenomena in Boston. First Mercy Short, and later Margaret Rule, seemed to be victims of witchcraft. Circumstances allowed Mather to repeat the procedure he had followed with the Goodwin children: praying and fasting with the young women, suppressing as unfounded the accusations against various persons, and writing accounts of both cases. He himself published neither account but merely circulated them among his friends.[33] Toward the conclusion of the Margaret Rule narrative, Mather spelled out what he viewed as the result of his activity: "The Devil got just nothing; but God got praises, Christ got subjects, the Holy Spirit got *Temples,* the Church got *Addition,* and the Souls of Men got everlasting *Benefits;* I am not so vain as to say that any *Wisdome* or *Vertue* of mine did contribute unto this good order of things: But I am so just, as to say I did not hinder this Good."[34]

This essentially was Mather's goal, and it was not necessary that witches be apprehended and executed in order to carry it out. Glover's execution did not end the Goodwin children's torment, but it seemed that prayer and fasting did. If witches happened to be apprehended, Mather hoped they would confess. Indeed, he wrote Richards that it was not so great a crime for these "wretched creatures" to be "hooked in" by the Devil as it was to fail to confess.[35] If the accused were to confess and renounce the Devil "openly and publicly," perhaps the people would be made aware of their reliance upon God, the churches, and the ministers. Mather outlined the procedure in *The Wonders of the Invisible World:*

> With a *Great Zeal,* we should lay hold on the *Covenant* of God, that we may secure *Us* and *Ours,* from the *Great Wrath,* with which the Devil Rages. Let us come into the *Covenant of Grace,* and then we shall not be hook'd into a *Covenant with the Devil,* nor be altogether unfurnished with *Armour,* against the Witches that are in that *Covenant.* . . . While others have had their Names Entred in the *Devils Book;* let our Names be found in the *Church Book. . . .* So many of the *Rising Generation,* utterly forgetting the Errand of our Fathers to build Churches in this Wilderness, . . . 'tis as likely as any one thing to procure the swarmings of *Witch Crafts* among us.[36]

Such a renewal of the covenant was presumably the colony's only hope. As Mather put it more succinctly a few pages earlier, "*Reformation* is . . . our only *Preservation*."[37]

We can, then, understand Cotton Mather's role at Salem only within the context of the temper of Massachusetts in the late seventeenth century and of Mather's own feeling that the spirit of the people was in decline. Not only did he feel constrained to protect the judges' reputations, but he also tried to keep the spiritual world a reality by reporting instances of witchcraft at the same time that he sought to protect persons accused in the process. Others were either less interested or less successful in maintaining that balance.

Notes

[1] Robert Calef, *More Wonders of the Invisible World* . . . (1700), in Samuel G. Drake, comp., *The Witchcraft Delusion in New England* . . . (Roxbury, Mass., 1866), II and III, *passim;* Chadwick Hansen, *Witchcraft at Salem* (New York, 1969), esp. ix-xiv, 95-102, 171-172, 194-195.

[2] Charles W. Upham, *Lectures on Witchcraft, . . .* (Boston, 1831), 103, 106-115, 184; Upham, *Salem Witchcraft; With An Account of Salem Village . . . ,* II (Boston, 1867), 366-369, 487, 503; Upham, "Salem Witchcraft and Cotton Mather," *Historical Magazine,* 2d Ser., VI (Sept. 1869), 129-219; George Bancroft, *History of the United States of America . . . ,* rev. ed.,

II (New York, 1891), 53-54, 62; George L. Burr, ed., *Narratives of the Witchcraft Cases, 1648-1706* (New York, 1914), 141n, 379n; Justin Winsor, "The Literature of Witchcraft in New England," American Antiquarian Society, *Proceedings,* N. S., X (1895), 351-373; George H. Moore, "Notes on the Bibliography of Witchcraft in Massachusetts," *ibid.,* V (1887-1888), 262-267; James Truslow Adams, *The Founding of New England* (Boston, 1921), 454-455.

[3] Hansen gives a good general outline of the evolution of the anti-Mather line. *Witchcraft at Salem,* xi-xiv.

[4] W. F. Poole, "Cotton Mather and Salem Witchcraft," *North American Review,* CVIII (Apr. 1869), 337-397; Poole, "Witchcraft at Boston," in Justin Winsor, ed., *The Memorial History of Boston . . . ,* II (Boston, 1886), 131-172; Josiah P. Quincy, "Cotton Mather and the Supernormal in New England History," Massachusetts Historical Society, *Proceedings,* 2d Ser., XX (1906-1907), 439-453; Barrett Wendell, *Cotton Mather, The Puritan Priest* (New York, 1891), Chap. 6; Kenneth B. Murdock, *Increase Mather: The Foremost American Puritan* (Cambridge, Mass., 1925), Chap. 17; Samuel Eliot Morison, *The Intellectual Life of Colonial New England* (New York, 1956; publ. in 1936 as *The Puritan Pronaos: Studies in the Intellectual Life of New England in the Seventeenth Century*), 258-259, 263-264. Perry Miller's analysis, whose conclusions correspond with many of my own, falls between the two "schools." See *The New England Mind: From Colony to Province* (Cambridge, Mass., 1953), Chaps. 10, 11, 13.

[5] More than once Mather received the names of suspected witches, but he kept such information to himself. Hansen, *Witchcraft at Salem,* 23-24, 179.

[6] As John Demos has observed recently, the historiography of Salem has been devoted principally to judging the participants and affixing blame. "Underlying Themes in the Witchcraft of Seventeenth-Century New England," *American Historical Review,* LXXV (1969-1970), 1311-1312.

[7] Although he was not in attendance at the trials, some historians have speculated that he may have attended one or more of the pretrial examinations. Upham, "Salem Witchcraft," *Hist. Mag.,* 2d Ser., VI (Sept. 1869), 162; Burr, ed., *Narratives,* 214n.

[8] Miller, *New England Mind,* Chap. 2.

[9] *The Mather Papers* (Massachusetts Historical Society, *Collections,* 4th Ser., VIII [Boston, 1868]), 389. Hereafter cited as *Mather Papers.* An editorial note gives 1686 as the "probable" date of this paper.

[10] Miller, *New England Mind,* 49; Worthington C. Ford,

ed., *Diary of Cotton Mather, 1681-1708* (Mass. Hist. Soc., *Collections,* 7th Ser., VII [Boston, 1911]), xviii. Hereafter cited as Mather, *Diary.*

[11] Burr, ed., *Narratives,* 5. English writers engaged in this activity included Richard Baxter, Henry More, and Matthew Poole. See also George L. Burr, "New England's Place in the History of Witchcraft," Amer. Antiquarian Soc., *Proceedings,* N. S., XXI (1911), 185-217.

[12] (Boston, 1684; reprinted London, 1856, as *Remarkable Providences Illustrative of the Earlier Days of American Colonisation*), Preface, n.p. See also Robert Middlekauff, *The Mathers: Three Generations of Puritan Intellectuals* (New York, 1971), 143-148.

[13] *Ibid.*

[14] Mather, *Diary,* 4-5. Hansen in particular tends to see Cotton as more the dispassionate observer than the Puritan minister investigating for a vital purpose. While he is certainly correct in pointing out that Mather was not "a witch hunter" and that he was "a witchcraft scholar," a more precise term would be "witchcraft hunter." *Witchcraft at Salem,* 172. As Perry Miller wrote some time ago, to call Mather's work an "inductive investigation . . . allows us to suppose the incredible: that, at the moment Mather and his colleagues were engaged in a struggle for existence, they idly embarked upon a collection of curiosal" *New England Mind,* 143.

[15] One of Hansen's chief points is that there were at least several women in the colony actually practicing witchcraft through image-magic. He argues that, like voodoo, this often worked, since the target of the witch's ill will believed that it did. *Witchcraft at Salem,* x, xiv-xv, 10-11, 22-23, 70, 81-86, 219, 226.

[16] As Mather related, "I Sett before her the Necessity and Equity of her breaking her Covenant with Hell, and giving her self to the Lord Jesus Christ, by an everlasting Covenant; To which her Answer was, that I spoke a very Reasonable thing, but she could not do it." Mather, *Memorable Providences, Relating to Witchcrafts and Possessions . . .* (1689), in Burr, ed., *Narratives,* 106.

[17] *Ibid.,* 107.

[18] *Ibid.,* 126.

[19] *Ibid.,* 98-99.

[20] John Goodwin related how "Mr. Mather particularly . . . not only pray's with us, and for us, but he taketh one of my Children home to his own house; . . . a troublesome guest, for such an one that had so much work lying upon his hands and heart." Goodwin went on, in the classic pattern of the jeremiad, to thank God for the affliction which had cleansed him of sin and had effected a renewal of the covenant. The lesson was plain: "The Lord help us to see by this Visitation, what need we have to get shelter under the wing of Christ, to hast to the Rock, where we may be safe." *Ibid.,* 129-131.

[21] Mather, *Diary,* 151-152.

[22] Perry Miller's account of Mather's activity is the one which most successfully pinpoints his agonizingly ambiguous situation. *New England Mind,* Chap. 13.

[23] Cotton observed in his diary for early 1692 that a great "Lethargy" lay on the land, and that the churches needed to be awakened. Mather, *Diary,* 144-146.

[24] Cotton Mather to John Richards, May 31, 1692, *Mather Papers,* 392, 393, 396-397. Cf. Mather's opinion some three years earlier: "That the Grace of God may be admired, and that the worst of Sinners may be encouraged, Behold, Witchcraft also has found a Pardon. . . . From the Hell of Witchcraft our merciful Jesus can fetch a guilty Creature to the Glory of Heaven. Our Lord hath sometimes Recovered those who have in the most horrid manner given themselves away to the Destroyer of their souls." *Memorable Providences,* in Burr, ed., *Narratives,* 135. Burr himself quoted a portion of the above passage of the letter to Richards, remarking that the failure to execute a single confessing witch was "the most striking feature of the Salem trials." *Ibid.,* 374n.

[25] Mather, *Diary,* 151.

[26] Kenneth B. Murdock was an exception. *Increase Mather,* 295n. The text of the *Return* is taken from David Levin, ed., *What Happened in Salem? Documents Pertaining to the 17th-Century Witchcraft Trials* (New York, 1952), 160-162.

[27] Upham, *Salem Witchcraft,* II, 368. Barrett Wendell felt that it was this document more than anything else which had prompted historians to burden Mather with the charge of urging "judicial murder." *Cotton Mather,* 98-99.

[28] *Oxford English Dictionary.*

[29] For obvious reasons, I cannot agree with Hansen when he says that paragraphs three through seven constituted "the heart of this document." *Witchcraft at Salem,* 125. This communication was considerably more cautious than the author's letter to Richards. In that document Mather had allowed several methods of inquiry that were specifically rejected in the *Return,* as well as the infamous water test for witches. Hansen

contends that it was the presence of Increase at the meeting of the clergy (which authorized the document) that made for the yet more cautionary tone. *Ibid.* He may be correct, but another explanation suggests itself as well. By mid-June, a witch trial had been held and the accused executed without a confession forthcoming. Perhaps the younger Mather now had less confidence in the judges' ability and wisdom than he had possessed previously and thus sought to limit the methods he had then sanctioned more freely.

[30] When addressing themselves solely to the judges, the clergy were more outspoken in their advice for caution than they were when addressing others. As Mather recorded in his diary, "Tho' I could not allow the *Principles,* that some of the Judges had espoused, yett I could not but speak honourably of their *Persons,* on all Occasions." Mather, *Diary,* 151. Similarly, in early August the ministers appeared to be backing away from their stronger stand of June, again in a message meant for persons other than the judges. As Hansen very perceptively observes, the pursuit of consensus by the ministers and magistrates was all-important. Real differences had to be glossed over, for if such dissension broke out, it would be an admission that "the Massachusetts way of life was . . . a failure." *Witchcraft at Salem,* 137.

[31] Hansen, *Witchcraft at Salem,* 143. Cf. Mather's account of a sermon he had delivered the previous May concerning religious dissenters, in which he had cautioned against "the *Persecution* of erroneous and conscientious Dissenters, by the *civil Magistrate,*" because he "feared, that the *Zeal* of my Countrey had formerly had in it more *Fire* than should have been." Mather, *Diary,* 149.

[32] Mather, *Diary,* 171.

[33] *A Brand Pluck'd Out of the Burning* (1693), in Burr, ed., *Narratives,* 253-287; *Another Brand Plucked Out of the Burning . . .* (1693), in Drake, comp., *Witchcraft Delusion,* II, 23-48.

[34] Mather, *Another Brand,* in Drake, comp., *Witchcraft Delusion,* II, 47.

[35] George L. Haskins has emphasized that confession and repentance were an important part of legal theory in 17th-century Massachusetts. He argues that the most important and striking influence of the Puritans upon the law can be found in their emphasis on "moral persuasion in order to reform the offender" rather than on retribution. *Law and Authority in Early Massachusetts, A Study in Tradition and Design* (New York, 1960), 204. See also 91-92, 121, 209-212; Hansen, *Witchcraft at Salem,* 123; Miller, *New England Mind,* 180, 197, 199. One critical observer of the witch trials noted, too, that the judges were upset when the accused showed no tears of remorse. Thomas Brattle to—, Oct. 8, 1692, Mass. Hist. Soc., *Collections,* 1st Ser., V (Boston, 1798), 67. But the importance of a confession of guilt and a reaffirmation of established values has not been confined solely to residents of colonial Massachusetts. Witness the amount of praise that has been heaped on Samuel Sewall, one of the trial judges, for his public confession in 1697. Bancroft, *History of the U. S.,* II, 66; Morison, *Intellectual Life,* 164-165; Marion Starkey, *The Devil in Massachusetts, A Modern Inquiry into the Salem Witch Trials* (New York, 1949), 272-274; Charles A. and Mary R. Beard, *The Rise of American Civilization,* I (New York, 1927), 150.

[36] Cotton Mather, *The Wonders of the Invisible World . . .* (London, 1862), 101-102; Middlekauff, *The Mathers,* 160.

[37] Mather, *Wonders of the Invisible World,* 95.

Sacvan Bercovitch (essay date 1972)

SOURCE: "Cotton Mather," in *Major Writers of Early American Literature,* edited by Everett Emerson, The University of Wisconsin Press, 1972, pp. 93-150.

[*In the excerpt below, Bercovitch discusses Mather's ideas on piety and science as expressed in* Bonifacius *and* The Christian Philosopher.]

> *. . . Throw a stone into the stream, and the circles that propagate themselves are the beautiful type of all influence.*
>
>   Emerson, *Nature*

To interpret Mather's shifts of perspective as a slackening of Puritan principles overlooks his meaning; much less should we read them as a covert capitulation to Arminianism or as a conscious transition from piety to moralism. Undoubtedly, they were so adapted later in the eighteenth century, but we ought not to burden the author with the sins of his readers. He held adamantly to Orthodox Calvinism, the system erected by the master's Swiss, Dutch, and English disciples, which, despite basic modifications, built upon the notions of man's depravity and impotency. A year before his death, Mather denounced the Arminians as vigorously as had his grandfathers. Deism he regarded as a front organization for the atheist conspiracy. He respected the intellect, like the earlier Puritans, as a dignified but decisively limited faculty. With his father, he supported the Half-Way Covenant because he believed it carried forward the theocracy's original design. When he directed the saints' unconverted heirs to will themselves to heaven, he was articulating what he considered, with good reason, to be a theory indigenous to the New England Way. Virtually every major first-generation theoretician (as Increase argued impressively in 1675) had assumed that church-membership tests reliably segregated the sheep from the goats, and that, for the most part, the line of election ran "through the loins of godly parents." Virtually all of them believed that the spiritual seed passed genetically from father to son. By this logic (a consequence or extension of the doctrines of preparation, visible sainthood, and providential-teleological historiography), the unconverted-but-baptised children were saved in all ways but one, their unthawed wills, just as their once-repentant-but-backsliding parents were already redeemed, though in need of corrective affliction, and just as the colonial errand, which by God's time was long since accomplished, demanded their present services.

To that unique community, and not to the world at large, Mather thundered the duty actively to seek after salvation. For them alone he stressed social responsibilities in sermons on *Free-Grace Maintained* (1706) and *The Salvation of the Soul* (1720); only before an American Puritan congregation did he claim that baptism indicates that God "has *Praeingaged* those Children for Himself." What elsewhere would be flat self-contradiction, what had in fact been denounced abroad as well-nigh heretical presumption, became a paradox of faith in the pulpit of Boston's North Church: "it is *Grace,* pure *Grace* that helps us; *God is with you, while you are with Him*"; or again: "there is a COVENANT OF GRACE; And by our *Consent* unto this most gracious *Covenant,* we are to *make choice* of the Great GOD for *Our God,* and [thereby] *make sure* of His being so"; or once again, at the close of a covenant-renewal ceremony: "Let us Request for, and Rely on, the Aids of Grace for a Self-Reformation" *and* for "ALL the [outward] Designs of *Reformation; the Land mourns and fades because we have broken the everlasting Covenant.* Wherefor if we would be recovered," one and all, now and *ad aeternum,* "tis the *Covenant* that must Recover us, the *Covenant of Grace,* which is Brought unto us all as have been Admitted unto any [!] *Ecclesiastical Priviledges among us.*"

Mather's approach varies not so much in thought as in expression from that of his forebears: in the confident, easy sweep of his language. Yet here too the variance betokens a qualitative distinction. Transferred to the domain of letters, the struggle for a Holy Commonwealth issues in the foregone triumph of the absolute over the temporal. By means wholly of rhetoric Mather subdued reality in his political sermons and accredited himself as prophet-watchman; by those means elsewhere, especially after 1700, he integrated that role with his functions as pastor. Forced back from the political arena, he absorbed himself in the possibilities for public awakening provided in his vocation, turned increasingly to the "watchfulness in particulars" which led Sam-

uel to say that "the Ambition and Character of my Father's life was Serviceableness," and Ben Franklin to acknowledge Mather as an inspiration for his own way to wealth, benevolence, and moral self-improvement. This tendency also underlies the familiar charge that Mather launched the national success ethos, with its unsavory alliance of grace and cash, and the popular definition of the Puritan as an inveterate meddler, driven by the fear, as Mencken put it, that someone, somewhere, might be enjoying himself.

Whatever justification these charges may have in Mencken's America, they belie the character of Mather's writings. In the first place, insofar as doing good expresses an immemorial Christian attitude (reinforced anew by the Reformation), Mather's preoccupation reveals him as a conservative rather than an innovator. He modeled his views, as he takes pains to point out, upon scores of earlier authorities, and in this sense his sermons on serviceableness stand with his political sermons as an effort to recover the theocratic ideal. "We live in faith in our vocations," said John Cotton, "in that faith in serving God serves men, and in serving men, serves God." Secondly, judged from a practical standpoint, Mather's well-doing is genuinely well-meant. When we read of him as "a Man of *Whim* and *Credulity,*" dangerously eager "to make Experiments on his Neighbours," we should remember that those phrases originated during the smallpox epidemic with the opponents of immunization. His own words suggest at least a different motivation: "They have lived longest in the world, who have done the most good in the world; whatever contributes unto the welfare of mankind, and a relief of their miseries, is to glorify God." His pastoral advice follows his precept. In sermon and treatise he urges the practice (not merely the profession) of charity, denounces the slave trade, extols the benefits of ecumenism. He instructs parents to look to their own ways before mending those of their children, and to discipline, when necessary, by example rather than brute authority. So, too, he would have teachers attend to "not only the *brains,* but also the *souls*" of their pupils, supplementing instruction with tutorials designed to bolster the student with *"expectations and encouragements"*. He applies similar strictures to the relations between master and servant, ruler and subject, minister and layman, lawyer and client, physician and patient.

Bonifacius (1710) is Mather's classic formulation of the nature and meaning of these "essays to do good." At some level, predictably, he intended the book as an advertisement for himself. His exhortations about rising to an *"afflatus* that will conquer *temptations,"* about being such "a son that the best surname for the glad father would be, *the father of such an one,"* about responding with Christ's meekness to "vile INGRATITUDE from Communities as well as *individuals*"—these and many other imperatives (buttressed by quotations from his previous writings) unmistakably mirror his most private aspirations. Most telling of all in this respect is the tree image which grows into the controlling metaphor of the work. According to its preface, "to *plant trees of righteousness* is the hope of the book now before us"; its first section argues that "we begin to bring forth *good fruit* by lamenting our own *unfruitfulness*"; the next section explains how "to live fruitfully" for others; subsequent sections make the obligations specific: ministers must seek "pardon for *unfruitfulness,*" the prosperous must remember that "gathering the fruit relieves the tree," the educated must share their learning like "a *tree that brings forth fruit.*" In every instance, the delegated function becomes the means of replanting oneself, in unity with all men, within the garden of God, like the Second Adam "abounding in the fruits of *well-doing.*"

The harvest, Mather promises, will yield blessings both in this world and the next. In light of current criticism, it needs to be re-emphasized that the promise does not mark a departure from orthodoxy. It was standard fare in the early colonial churches, intrinsic to the rationale for corporate calling and for preparation for salvation. Like his forebears, Mather circumscribed the discussion by positing first that sanctification is not a means to redemption (*"Woe unto us if it were!"*) and then by limiting it effectually to the visible saints. "Though we are *justified,* yet good works are demanded of us to *justify* our *faith,*" he puns; the agency of free grace compels us (in time) and, simultaneously, disposes us (from eternity) to the outward forms of Christianity. To be sure, the staggering difference between the principle and its local application—and the problematic distinction in the latter context between the virtues and vices of wealth—required delicate exposition to the world at large; his predecessors had tread warily in the realm of theory. Like them, he sought to hedge his position with traditional denunciations: "Riches are a Fine, Gay, speckled Bird; but it is a Bird in the *Bush*"; he who *"has nothing but Gold & Silver in his mouth"* is a fish swimming into *"the Nets of Perdition"*. But because he knew that prosperity might follow the labor of the convenanted (in the New Israel above all other lands), he set his sights upon its positive ramifications; and because he could not resolve the tension between dogma and practice, between a flourishing New England as it should be and as it was, he turned as usual to rhetoric in order to dissolve it. With an effortless fluency which has shocked later theologians, he elaborated on the metaphor that the righteous are the trustees of God's world, on the parable of the bread thrown upon the waters, and on the prophecies concerning the blessed remnant. In these terms he measured the distance between the saintly rich and those who rise by fraud, and, affirming the correspondence between God's providential and absolute aid, he urged parents never to *"Concern themselves more to get the World than Grace for their Children,"* since "if God giveth them Grace, Earthly blessings shall never fail."

In **Bonifacius** he incorporates these various explanations into an imaginatively more heightened and more comprehensive approach, one which absorbs the transitory, at all levels, into the eschatological. As he develops his argument, every good work becomes magnified into a momentaneous demonstration of the judgment to come. When he states that "the more good any man does, the more he really *lives,*" he means "life" as an emblem of eternity, wherein "the only wisdom of man" lies in his union with God. When he terms "GOOD DEVICES the most *reasonable religions,*" he does so to persuade the reader to embrace them "with *rapture,* as enabling him directly to answer the great END of his being." On these foundations he proposes beneficence as a bridge between the visible and the invisible. "To do *good,* is a thing that brings its own *recompense,*" he writes; it stands of itself as "your powerful, and perpetual vindication." It must begin, like conversion, in the soul-struggle to be perfected in the image of God. Subsequently, of its own accord it leads outward to others; but its essential motive, "the *greatest* and *highest* of its glories," remains first and last atemporal. Thus morality seeks no worldly remuneration (in fact, "your conformity unto Him, yet *lacks one thing*" if you are not *"despised and rejected of men"*); thus also it may be said to win heaven ("the more you consider the *command* in what you do, the more assurance you have" of redemption); and thus, finally, the elect may find material recompense. As the saint in solitude prepares himself for life by meditating upon death, so conversely the well-doer, by eschewing the *gloria mundi,* shows himself worthy of the earthly blessings vouchsafed to certain servants of the Lord.

Even on a practical level Mather's notions merit our respect. They signify a wholesome if chimerical reaction against the *"Private Spirit"* he had long lamented, an effort to impose some spiritual cohesion upon a community that was disintegrating under the "liberating" ruthlessness of enlightened self-interest. Appropriately, one of the key terms in **Bonifacius** is *relatedness*. The section on "Home and Neighbourhood," for example, reminds us that not only family members but "*Neighbours* stand *related* unto one another," and that in both spheres the relationship entails duties: "relieving the afflicted with all agreeable kindnesses," assisting the destitute with gifts or loans (the latter to be repaid not on a certain day but when the borrower should find himself able to repay it, without inconvenience). Emanating from the center of one's concern for his soul, such circles of relatedness, as Mather conceived them, would widen progressively to envelop the whole body social. His most ambitious conception devolved upon "reforming societies." None of his projects has come under sharper attack, and none more unjustly. His intent was neither repression nor prurience but the desire to curb expediency by attaching the mean to an ideal—without, however, discarding the notion of the mean: he asked for temperance, not prohibition, and taught his "sodalities" (the prototypical graduate seminars he inaugurated) "rather *Socratically than Dogmatically*," aware that "what is now most in vogue may anon be refuted like its Predecessors." If he required zeal of his "Societies of Young Men Associated," he sought to temper excess through compassion and discretion. What he envisioned at most was a "blessed concord" of visible saints, "bound up in one *bundle of love*," "charitably watchful over one another" and rejoicing in "*opportunities to do good*."

His scheme had immediate precedents in Augustan England; more important for him, certainly, was the parallel it offered with the bonds of church-covenant which knit together, "as one man with one soul," the citizens on a hill. To the degree that we grant him the validity of the parallel, *Bonifacius* stands, Janus-faced, as a crucial document in the continuity of the culture. Hopelessly nostalgic from one perspective, it looks forward from another not only to Franklin's "Clubs for Mutual Improvement" but to Edwards's "Blessed Unions." Its connection with the Great Awakening, indeed, appears to be the more basic of the two. I refer to *Bonifacius*'s consuming eschatological thrust, personal and social, its emphasis alike upon conversion and upon groups animated by "the wondrous force of *united prayers*," with "the *savor* on them of the saints" of old, seeking to revivify a dead land by doing that only, in Edwards's words, which added to "the glory of God or the good of men." Above all, I refer to the book's pervasive millennial expectations. That Mather never abandoned those expectations is evident everywhere in his published and unpublished works; and if after 1700 he had little or no following at home he found support abroad. Through his enormous European correspondence, to which he increasingly gave his energies, he aligned himself with the millenarians in Scotland. In 1709 he came into contact with August Hermann Francke and German Pietism, whose influence was extending through many regions of Europe, including England and Scotland, and whose missions had reached across the Atlantic to the East Indian Islands.

The full impact of Franckean Pietism upon colonial thought remains to be explored. It may be gleaned in different ways from Samuel Mather's *Vita Franckii* (1733) and from Edwards's tribute in his *History of the Work of Redemption* to Francke's leading role in the events which led to the Revival. Cotton Mather was especially affected by Francke as a kindred spirit whose efforts (unlike his own) met with "amazing" success. To further their "Marvellous Effects" he contributed to Pietist enterprises at Halle and advocated their emulation in America. He had himself urged similar enterprises often before. Now, however, he felt emboldened by the support of a gathering international movement, one that based its social beneficence on the same chiliastic Reformed historiography as that which informed the Great Migration (though transferred to a *spiritual* migration from local corruption). Like Edwards, he carefully insisted on the priority in all this of the New World theocracy; the American church, he pointed out, was "*pulcherrima inter mulieres*," the most beautiful of Christ's brides, and so had "the Honour of making the *First,* Right, Fair and Genuine *Beginning*."[1] But he was eager to express his gratitude and solidarity. He did so most notably by assimilating the Pietists' techniques and terminology: their integration of homilectic "uniting maxims," for instance, with the neo-Joachite "Everlasting Gospel," their emphasis on the "prophecy of Joel" in conjunction with the emergent "Age of the Holy Spirit," and, in general, their shifting sense of the apocalypse, from the premillenarianism of the New England planters toward something approaching the postmillenarianism that characterizes American thought from the Great Awakening onwards—toward a view, that is, which sees the chiliad *within* history rather than as the result of a cataclysmic, supernatural break with history.

The shift was not a radical one. With the other Franckean concepts he espoused, it was consonant with the emigrants' gradualistic-typological soteriology, in which the church-state served both as antitype of the Old Testament Jerusalem and as *figura* of the Jerusalem-to-be. What German Pietism offered Mather was in essence what Coleridge and Carlyle offered Emerson: the potential for a renewed activism within an established national mythos, as well as a means of reaffirming the mythos within a contemporaneous intellectual-spiritual *Zeitgeist*. It was too late in life, too far into the Yankee apostasy, for Mather to recall his political ambitions. (Though he continued to interfere in public affairs, he recognized that he would never command the authority he once dreamed of, and exercised momentarily two decades before, in his father's absence). But he could transfer the momentum of Pietism's burgeoning success into literary summons and "Goods Devised." "I am dismissed from any expectation of much encouragement," he confessed in 1717 to an English correspondent. "And the truth is, I have dismissed and even divorced myself in a great measure from every party, but one which is now going to be formed." Yet that party of the future, *already* combining as it did the best of the past and the present (the New England Way and the Franckean revival) provided encouragement enough.

Its impact upon his schemes for doing good appears in his revived enthusiasm for local reform, particularly in the ministry and in education.[2] It is evident, too, in his reanimated call for missionary endeavors, to awaken not only the Indians but the Jews. Through the 1690s he had made several gestures, as another "Evangelical Elias," toward bringing about the restitution of Israel. A ten-year silence on the issue followed. When he then returned to it, his new-found fervor, he explained, stemmed from the "Tokens for Good" at Halle, and the "miraculous" conversion of several Jewish children in Berlin. He set forth his convictions in 1718 in **Faith Encouraged,** an expanded version of the Berlin miracle, and, most dramatically, in **Psalterium Americanum,** whose preface and commentary magnify the enterprise of translation into a concerted missionary service, preparatory to the Marriage of the Lamb with His first-and still-beloved spouse at the altar of the apocalypse.

Of course, Mather stresses that the Psalms also pertain to every *spiritual* Israelite. Insofar as they continuously invoke Christ, they may ensure the Christian reader "here the Character of those who are to be admitted into the *Messiah's* glorious Kingdom." And insofar as they contain the *"Key of David"* to "the *Mysteries* of the *Great Salvation,"* they illuminate the contours of Christian history, from the church's persecution under Antichrist to its victory on the fields of Gog and Magog. But beyond such private aids, they may also provoke the reader to a sublime serviceableness, one that concerns the mightiest of the end-time events. Nowhere, cries Mather, is the progress of the Jews more vividly depicted and (metaphorically) enacted than in the Psalter. Indeed, "the Design of the PROPHETIC SPIRIT in the PSALMS all along has been to describe the Sufferings" and "predict the Recovery of the *Jewish Nation.*" What nobler service, therefore, could a second Baptist aspire to, what surer means for making way for the City of God, than to render their meaning intelligible? What time could be more suitable than the present, when "the condition of the *Jewish Nation* is like to be"—by that very nation—"more considered than in the former Ages"? What place, finally, could be more advantageous for the task than the New World, since the Psalms specifically hold out "Hopes for *Americans,*" predicting (Ps. 18:43) that after "Our Saviour had seen and known *Asians, Africans, Europeans,*" He would turn, at the close of history, to the unknown continent at the world's fabled fourth corner? Taking all this into account, "the Psalms put into the hands of the *Jews* with so Entertaining a *Commentary* thereupon, may be a powerful and perswasive Engine" for guiding them into "the Grand Revolution which concludes our Bible."

To that end Mather gears the whole machinery of translation and commentary, recasting the Psalter into a divine comedy of the wandering House of Israel. Substantiating his figural and Christological readings by way of rabbinical opinions (his most frequently used source), he expands the poetry into a prophetic saga of decline and recovery: the destruction of Jerusalem and Babylonian captivity; the Hebrews' stiff-necked disobedience, culminating in their rejection of Christ; their subsequent pitiful persecution, wonderful preservation, and happy restoration. Threading the narrative is the theme of National Conversion; over one-third of the Psalms (by Mather's account) center on this concept. The focus alternates, between linear advance and vertical revelation, in what becomes a dialectic of human action and divine will, promise and fulfillment. The process itself takes several forms. Sometimes it shapes the meaning of an individual set of verses, as in Psalm 69, which is said to relate the *agones* of Christ and the Jews. More often it evolves by juxtaposition, so that the Jews' songs of praise upon their rejuvenation (Psalms 96 and 97) seem to flow logically into the cosmic jubilee at the Second Coming (Psalm 98).

Characteristically, the process unfolds in separable series or blocks of poems, all built around the same theme, though following one another with rising intensity. Thus Psalms 125 through 136 describe successively the grounds of Israel's perseverance, its retrospective lament for sins past, and its thankful devotions to the Lord of its salvation; the next series (137-50) opens by recapitulating the sorrows of the dispersed Jews, then recounts their prayers for help, announces their redemption, and ends in an extended encomium to the New Jerusalem. In every case the movement proceeds from the urgency for conversion; and through the book as a whole the reiterated "Miracles to be wrought when *Israel* shall be returned from Exile" increasingly broaden to encompass the well-doer, beneficent societies, and, in the "transcendent efficacy" of the end-time wedding-ritual, "the supreme and final true PIETY" whose signs have already appeared:

> DOUBTLESS, *the Day approaches* wherein the *Kingdom of* GOD will appear in brighter displays than the World has ever yet been Enlightened withal. There are certain MAXIMS OF PIETY wherein all Good *Men* and *United.* GOD will bring *His People to receive one another* upon these generous MAXIMS. An admirable *Peace* and *Joy* will arise from the operations of the *Holy Spirit;* and *Joels* Prophecy will be accomplished. ANGELS shall *Fly thro' Heaven,* having the *Everlasting Gospel.* That cry *Babylon is fallen* will ensue upon it; and wondrous Changes upon the World [reflecting in grander form the accomplishments of New England] will turn an horrid and howling *Wilderness* into a *Paradise.*[3]

The strains of *Psalterium Americanum* thus lead back to *Bonifacius*, as do most other aspects of Mather's pietism. Written in the first flush of his contact with Halle, *Bonifacius* unites his earlier concepts of doing good with the possibilities newly opened by the Franckean revival. His proposals here for missionary undertakings extol those of the Pietists—they should "animate us, to imitate them"—and affirm New England's superiority in this respect by a detailed summary of the work *"formerly done* for the Christianizing of our *Indians."* Now, he promises, our missions will extend much further. The Holy Spirit will clear our path, as it did in the infancy of Christendom, with irresistible influences which will "cause whole *nations* to be *born at once"* and "render this world like a *watered garden."* A century before, the Bay emigrants had carried those influences to a new continent; the children of that exodus are to amplify the joyful sound to all peoples. As for the Hebrews, Mather would seem here to summon them primarily by the example of the reborn New World garden (as Increase did in 1669, in *The Mystery of Israel's Salvation,* and Edward Johnson in 1654, in *Wonder-Working Providence).* In general, he refers over and again to rabbinical dicta: partly to prod the colonists to "outdo *Judaism,"* as a rule to remind all his readers of the way of living which the rabbis foretell for "the *generation wherein the Messiah comes,"* the perfect serviceableness which will characterize that *"illustrious state of the Church of God, which is to be expected, in the conversion of the Jews."*

This millennial way of living most fully embodies Mather's essays to do good. It also serves most lucidly to explain his position as precursor of Franklin and Edwards. The rags-to-riches stories he recounts (in a number of biographies as well as in *Bonifacius)* become "charming examples" of godliness chiefly in terms of his pietistic eschatology. It is a distinction which separates him from the conventional Protestant apologists for laissez-faire; and it is a distinction which applies, in different ways, to the spirit of the Great Awakening, and, later, to the concept of national mission. For Mather's vision of well-doing, beyond the material benefits it brought, beyond its excellence per se, beyond even its value as a private passport to heaven, carried forward the standard of the Everlasting Gospel. The chosen heirs of the uttermost parts of the earth could hardly consider their redemption merely as single, separate persons; assuredly, too, their "relatedness," under the ascending sun of the Holy Spirit, would never stop short at secular goals. "In engaging as many others as we can, to join with us," *Bonifacius* insists, we are "promoting His Kingdom among the children of men." The *"springs of usefulness"* we dig open by each act, "having once begun to run, will spread into *streams,* which no *human foresight* can comprehend"; each proposal realized, "like a *stone* falling into a *pool,"* will cause "one *circle* (and *service)* to produce another, until they extend" ad infinitum. So our magistrates

will enact solely those laws by which the reign of holiness may be advanced; so our universities, charged with *"collegia pietatis,* like those of our excellent *Franckius,"* will accomplish *"wonders* in the world"; so our societies, "Propagating the *Maxims* wherein His *Will* shall *be done on Earth as it is in Heaven,"* will by that "blessed symptom be together associated in the *Heavenly City"*; and so, comprehensively, we will reconstitute ourselves, what once we were, what God wishes us to be again, a serviceable light to the world, a knot of saints associated whose *"works of the day* fall in with the designs of *Divine Providence."*

In this perspective, as in subsequent American millenarianism, secular employment contrasts as unequivocally with the "work of the day" as does the house built upon sands with the stone cast upon the waters of eternity. The one stands self-contained, trapped in the limits of space and time; the other swells *sui generis* into an image of the entire human-divine order, dilating concentrically, ineluctably, from the personal sphere to the "federal" and the universal, imaging simultaneously the Neo-Platonic circle of salvation and the spiralling movement of Christian teleology.[4] By the same dynamic the work of the day comes also to image the order of nature. "Serious and shining *Piety,"* Mather writes in *Bonifacius,* "will glorify the *God of Nature.* Nothing so *unnatural* as to be *irreligious."* He notes that the concept derives from Thomas Browne's *Religio Medici* (1643); its larger context is the "natural theology" which developed in the seventeenth century, the belief that creation, as the New Science revealed it in all its majestic, intricate symmetry, embodied God's goodness and wisdom. Mather was the first American actively to espouse the belief, in league with European religious scientists and scientifically minded clerics: William Derham, for example, author of *Physico-Theology* (1713), and Halle's Philip Spener, and, of course, Sir Isaac Newton, physicist and chiliast (as he was popularized in Richard Bentley's *Confutation of Atheism* [1693]). In *Bonifacius* Mather projects as part of this tradition his own *Angel of Bethesda,* designed to "instruct people how to improve in agreeable points of piety; and at the same time, inform them of the most experimental, natural, specific *remedies* for diseases." He might already have included his *Wonderful Works of God* (1690), his eloquent *Winter-Meditations* (1693), and perhaps the **"Declamations on Natural Philosophy"** he delivered as a student at Harvard. His most important undertaking of this kind, begun within a few months of *Bonifacius,* was published a decade later as *The Christian Philosopher: A Collection of the Best Discoveries in Nature, With Religious Improvements.*

In his scientific pursuits, Cotton Mather (again like Edwards and Franklin) was an avid dilettante, with an encyclopaedic range of interests and a predisposition toward the experimental and the pragmatic. His manuscript **"Curiosa Americana,"** together with his communications to the Royal Society, reveal an amusing credulity. As historians of the subject have recognized, they also display a "striking ability to select, from the maze of 'natural philosophy,' those discoveries and problems which were eventually to prove of major importance." *The Christian Philosopher* unites this ability with his still more striking ingenuity in extracting "religious improvements" from the selections, drawing upon the discoveries and problems to erect a monument to the God of his fathers. The discoveries celebrate the reaches of man's mind; the problems teach him not to exceed his grasp: demonstrate that his "*Reason* is too feeble, too narrow a thing to comprehend the *infinite*," leave him "so transcended" that he will not "cavil, but adore" the "*Mysteries* altogether beyond [his] *Penetration*." The interaction between the two strains, resembling the theocracy's blend of mysticism and rationalism, conveys Mather's purpose. As in *Bonifacius,* he was not so much adapting Puritanism to the Enlightenment as trying to dam up the excesses of the latter by recourse to orthodoxy: in effect, updating the Ptolemaic providential-natural theology that ran from (say) Augustine's *Confessions* to John Cotton's *Briefe Exposition upon Ecclesiastes*. And as in *Bonifacius,* his contributions to the humanitarian-scientific outlook of Franklin and Jefferson forms the lesser aspect of his legacy. In its quality of imagination at least, *The Christian Philosopher* belongs to a different national tradition—meta-scientific and at some level counter-rationalistic—which includes Edwards's *Images or Shadows of Divine Things* and Emerson's *Nature*.

This is not to deny *The Christian Philosopher* its transitional importance in the transformation of the earlier cosmology. Unquestionably, it is a crucial expression (in the New World) of the configuration of Puritanism, Pietism, and science which has been identified as a mainstream of American thought. Unquestionably, too, Edwards's epistemology, insofar as it derived from either Berkeley or Locke, is as difficult to reconcile with Mather's spiritualizations as it is with Emerson's transcendentalism. The similarity between the three preachers hinges on the fact that their subordination of science proper to divinity resulted in comparable symbolic modes. In part, this manifests itself in terms of natural theology: in certain common sources, for example, such as Thomas Browne; or in the effort to restrain the tide of materialism stirred up by the New Science; or in the "feeling akin to the poet's" which their passages evoke (for one critic, Mather's "artistic effects" recall the method of many of Walt Whitman's poems); or in the anachronistic inconsistencies which insinuate themselves into their technical expositions (Edwards's strangely medieval notes, Mather's obstinate belief in discrete providences). But such parallels may be found in scores of European works. What distinguishes *The Christian Philosopher,* and what seems specifically to relate it to later American works, is the

theocratic confluence of personal and social eschatology, transferred now to the mind of the awakened observer of Nature. "The whole *World,*" writes Mather, "is a *Temple* of GOD," where "Every thing about me Preaches unto me" concerning "the grand End of man's Being," the "*Evangelical* Spirit of *Charity,*" and "the Blessedness of the *future State*." This threefold pattern, integrating salvation, serviceableness, and history, informs Edwards's response to the Newtonian universe; it appears, in one secular guise or another, in Emerson's (as well as Whitman's and Thoreau's) internalization of the meaning of America; to a large extent it defines the method of *The Christian Philosopher*.

Mather's fundamental assumption is the correspondence between the Book of Nature and the Book of God. "We will now for a while read in the *Former* of these *Books,*" he explains, "'twill help us in reading the *Latter*." But of course he means equally that (in Edwards's words) "the Book of Scripture is the interpreter of the Book of Nature," and he organizes his material in accordance with Genesis 1, proceeding from light to the celestial bodies to the elements to the forms of life on earth, and concluding, in the longest section, with man. Hermeneutically and rhetorically, the creation story conveys his meaning on all of its three levels. Its literal-naturalistic aptness allows him to set the progress of science within the biblical framework. On a figural plane, the first seven days shadow forth the seven ages of man, so that the natural wonders he records bespeak the impending Judgment Day and the Sabbatism to follow, when "our Saviour may *feast* His *Chosen People* with Exhibitions of all these Creatures, in their various *Natures*." Anagogically, the mystery of creation, like the mystery of the Scriptures, stands revealed in the Incarnation; all things refer ultimately to Christ, from the magnet to the laws of gravity a "shadow" of His parturient love. Man's cognitive process follows this paradigm in that it recreates the individual in harmony with the cosmos. The principles of plant growth or of light are bare statistics "unto him that has no Faculty to discern *spiritually*." Granted that agency of inner renewal, he finds the light to be correlative to his own reason, his capacity (in Christ) to overcome the powers of darkness, and his claims to the inheritance of the saints in light; he discerns in the plants' physical structure "the Analogy between their States and ours" and, spiritually, in their revival in the Spring an emblem of the resurrection and "of the *Recovery* which the Church will one day see from a *Winter of Adversity*."

Right perception, then, reconciles man simultaneously with Creation, with history, and with his Redeemer. And in so doing it unites him with himself as paragon both of Nature and of the Bible: as "a *Machine* of a most astonishing Workmanship," which is also "the most exquisite Figure for an *holy Temple*"; as "the highest link in the *golden chain,* whereby *Heaven* is joined to *Earth,"* who is at the same time "the *Microcosm"* of all being. *"Opera Creationis externae habent in se Imaginem Creationis internae,"* Mather declares, anticipating Emerson's "every appearance in nature corresponds to some state of mind." Our inner and outer worlds are synonymous: "he that speaks to MAN, speaks to *every Creature";* the Me and the Not-Me reflect one another through their common generative divinity. But beyond both, for Mather, circumscribing and delimiting their linked analogies, stand the Scriptures and ecclesiastical authority. As though he divined the anarchic subjectivism, the "imperial selfhood," potential in his outlook, he requires the observer to uncover meaning rather than invent it, to guage his spiritualizing faculty by an objective hierarchy of values which lies beyond his understanding and yet communicates itself to him through concrete, restrictive obligations: the maxims of piety that "the whole creation of GOD would mind us of," the good works that result from his homage to the sun as *"An Image of the Divine Goodness,"* the services he will render when he can feel toward his neighbor the *"Law of Attraction,* whereby all the Parts of *Matter* embrace one another."

The Christian Philosopher fails in this attempt to bridge science and pietism. Its inadequacies have been discussed from a scientific or a theological standpoint. They seem to me most glaring in the haphazard proliferation of literary modes. Allegory and analogy, sacred and secular similitude, *figura* and trope follow indiscriminately from one another, often within the same context. Some such confusion appears in every Bible culture; but here it tends conspicuously toward chaos, palpably betokens a dissolution of external controls (in contrast to medieval Catholicism with its boggling excess of imposed categories). It issues in a kind of democratic blur of traditionally distinct forms: a universal levelling (not unlike a Whitmanesque catalogue) which (unintentionally) discards the differences between wit, metaphor, and hermeneutic, and invokes moral authority equally through the notion that faith is a telescope to the heavenly world, that ornithology affords a norm of filial devotion, and that typology highlights the botanical *curiosa* of a well-tended garden. It is this collapse of rhetorical distinctions, I believe, that most clearly marks the cultural significance of the book. For one thing, it offers an interesting perspective on the failure of natural theology and, more broadly still, on the aesthetic revolution implicit in Reformed thought, which cleaved literal from spiritual, set man vis-à-vis God without an officially sanctioned intermediary network of human-divine meaning, and so opened the road to modern symbolism. In particular, it serves—precisely in its levelling of symbolic dimensions as reality is ingested and "improved" in the microcosmic imagination—to highlight the beginnings of a movement which continues through Ed-

ward's "subjective idealism" to mid-nineteenth-century "American romanticism." The continuity here should not obscure the many differences between Mather and later writers. But neither should the differences discourage us from tracing the lines of development, especially, perhaps, through the affinity Mather draws, in the metaphor of creation, between Nature, the symbolic observer, and the exemplary American, the book's autobiographical-suprapersonal protagonist who explores himself in exploring the world, and for whom, as for Emerson's Poet, the world-self "is a temple whose walls are covered with [hermeneutic] emblems, [aesthetic] pictures and [moral] commandments of the Deity."

It is true that *The Christian Philosopher* does not have a pronounced American setting. It does not, like (say) Thoreau's "Walking," apply the individual's spiritual rebirth in Nature to the "true tendencies" of the renovated, or renovating, wilderness. Its historiographic implications emerge in context of related undertakings, as those in Emerson's *Nature* may be discerned in "The American Scholar," and as those in Edwards's *Images or Shadows* reveal themselves by way of *Thoughts on the Revival* and *The History of the Work of Redemption.* Probably the relevant texts in this particular connection are the passages (in **Bonifacius** and elsewhere) dealing with American Pietism, and the manuscript "Biblia Americana," which Mather advertised in a concluding appendix to **Bonifacius,** and within which he intended to incorporate *The Christian Philosopher.* As the advertisement describes the organization of "Biblia Americana," the sixth and central section deals with *"Natural Philosophy,* called in to serve *Scriptural Religion,"* where *"the best thoughts of our times"* on science combine with those concerning the three *"grand revolutions,* the *making,* and the *drowning,* and the *burning* of the world." Surrounding this section are a history of Jerusalem (until its "present and wretched condition, in which it waits *the set time to come on"*), the saga of Israel, concluding with its imminent recovery, a discussion of types and prophecies—all of which (except those pertaining to the chiliad) "have had their most punctual *accomplishment"*—and an exhortation on the advantages of *"experimental piety."* The entire configuration explains Mather's emphasis on "Americana"; his last proud words apply with equal force to **Bonifacius** and *The Christian Philosopher:* "All done By the blessing of CHRIST on the Labors of an *American."* . . .

Notes

[1] The point was crucial to Mather because it allowed him at once to embrace German Pietism and to fit it into the framework of New England historiography. Thus he feels obliged even in his flowery epistles to Francke and Boehme to affirm that "There is not a place in which true Christianity is more cultivated than

here in New England," and to note that *"American Puritanism* is so much of a Peece with the *Frederician Pietism"* that his *Magnalia* would prove "serviceable to [your] glorious intentions." Indeed, he introduced Francke to the "true *American Pietism"* in 1710 as a system which embodied the "Principles and Practices of the Immanuelan People" (adding privately that, "admirable" as they are, the German "Professors are not without their Errours"); and in reprinting Francke's resumé of the Pietist missionary triumphs, he points out that those undertakings followed the lead of the emigrants: of John Eliot in particular ("no One is wronged if it be confessed, that our ELIOT shone as the *Moon among the Lesser Stars"*), and in general of the theocracy's "Pure MAXIMS of the *Everlasting Gospel,"* harbinger of the *"Mighty Showers* to be expected in the *Latter Days."* The relations between German Pietism and American thought merit close study, not only in their direct manifestations (e.g., Mather and Edwards) but in their later indirect influences—through the writings of Schiller (for example)—in the nineteenth century.

² *Manuductio ad Ministerium* (1724), his chief contribution in this area, owes much of its pungent forcefulness to that enthusiasm. Fundamentally, like all his books, it is a personal testament, at once the product of his pastoral experience, an *apologia* for his style, a paean to the persecuted Christ-like servant, and compensation for his failure to attain the Harvard presidency. But the sublimating process is undergirded by the appeal to an immediate historic thrust: specifically to the curriculum in use at Halle; generally, to the "new type of ministerial leadership," admittedly modeled upon Francke's *Manuductio,* which would control "the lives of the people through pietism." The appeal begins with the familiar do-good eschatology (subordinating all studies, actions, and intentions "to an union with God"); it proceeds through the maxims of pietism—seconded by a "dear brother of mine, a professor in the Frederician University"—which raises the well-doing minister into the "state of Paradise"; its crown and essence is proclaimed in the book's running title: *The Angels Preparing to Sound the Trumpets.*

³ *Psalterium Americanum* (Boston, 1718), introduction, pp. xxxii-xxxiv.

⁴ The concept of the circle in these terms needs fuller treatment than the present essay can allow. Briefly: the metaphor of the circle of redemption stems from the philosophy of Plotinus as this was absorbed into Christian thought from the Church Fathers through the Renaissance; the circle-as-spiral comes to symbolize the repetitive yet forward-moving history of redemption, especially as this was expounded by progressivist-typologists from Eusebius and Orosius to the Bay emigrants. Mather's conflation of the two images may be seen in his dual self-concept in the diaries, in the rhet-

oric of his political sermons (such as *A Midnight Cry*), and above all in the notion of "representative men" he set forth in his biographies (discussed below).

Pershing Vartanian (essay date 1973)

SOURCE: "Cotton Mather and the Puritan Transition into the Enlightenment," in *Early American Literature,* Vol. VII, No. 3, Winter, 1973, pp. 213-24.

[*In the following essay, Vartanian argues that Mather was able to rectify his ideas on piety and the relationship between God and reason with the teachings of the Enlightenment, including the concept of a mechanistic world.*]

Caught by the more spectacular public drama of colonial America's "progress" from darkness to enlightenment—a transition as remarkable as the Enlightenment itself—historians have slighted the unprecedented ease with which many Puritans privately stepped across the threshold. Historians, failing to recognize the ease of this accommodation, have sought to explain that larger cultural transition in terms of conflict. Additionally, reading late-nineteenth-century issues back into the eighteenth century has artificially dramatized the tensions between secular and clerical thought over the relationship between religion and science. Though tensions did exist, they were more subtle, for the Puritan clergy had performed a positive role in the transition to the Enlightenment.¹

In certain respects, the problem is complicated by our understanding of Enlightenment and Puritan thought. While each style had its pronounced contours, neither intellectual mode was static; consequently, orthodox Puritan thought is as difficult to delineate as is Enlightenment thought. Though Puritan thought was teleological and Enlightenment thought was naturalistic, in neither epoch was purpose or nature excluded. Moreover, while rationalism in science characterized the Enlightenment, that rationalism had a changing significance throughout the eighteenth century. As a result, while it is necessary to differentiate between the early, middle and later Enlightenment, it must be recognized that each stage flowed into the other and each possessed with differing emphasis the elements of the other.² In its initial phases, the Enlightenment differed more in degree than in substance from late Puritan thought. While Puritan thought could not be confused with Enlightenment rationalism, as Samuel Eliot Morison implies,³ in practice the Puritans had a limited but undeniable respect for reason, a conception of the social compact in their covenantal polity, and saw in nature not simply carnality, but God's first principles in operation.⁴

In many essentials Puritan thought resembled the "Cosmic Toryism" of the early Enlightenment. In the Calvinist tradition, the Puritan God had always been a somewhat remote transcendent entity. If the early Enlightenment pushed God further out, it was more degree than kind. Distance did not divorce God from the universe for the intellectuals of the early Enlightenment any more than it did for the Puritans. While Newton's mathematics needed no metaphysical substructure, nevertheless his mathematics failed to abolish irregularities in the cosmic machine and Newton too found God essential to explain its operations. Gravity, he observed, was God's will manifesting itself as force in the ether. Clocks would lose their energy and bodies in motion required guidance to maintain their regular course. No one in the early Enlightenment could dispense with God to describe the operations of nature as Laplace did in saying, "I have no need for that hypothesis." God's participation in maintaining the cosmic clock was as essential to the early Enlightenment as it was to the teleological universe contemplated by the Puritans.[5]

Neither teleology nor mechanism dissolved the need for God any more than a mechanistic cosmos dispatched the hierarchical order expressed in the Great Chain of Being that linked the natural world with the invisible universe of spirit. Although this hierarchical cosmology rested upon a set of static relationships, it nevertheless gave rise to a subtle, persistent and pervasive optimism which gradually assumed control over human expectations to emerge as an idea of progress. As a conviction, its existence was based upon the augmentation of material, technological and intellectual improvements that were the fruits of the New Science. Science shaped the rationalism, undergirded the optimism, and altered the relationships between God, man and nature throughout the Enlightenment, while providing the era with an internal coherence. Thus, the touchstone to Enlightenment thought lies in the interest in science, and it is possible to describe the Puritan transition into the Enlightenment through such a figure as Cotton Mather, whose scientific interests pushed him, if not always fastest, furthest into the new age.[6]

Just as he was in life, Cotton Mather has been a contentious figure in the historical imagination. Energetic and assertive, he was a vigorous partisan. Occupying a middle position somewhat to the right of the Brattles and Leveretts, he untiringly resisted their latitudinarianism while campaigning against the congregational independence of John Wise and the presbyterianism of Solomon Stoddard. During the inoculation crisis in 1720-21 when Boston was plagued with smallpox, Mather challenged the community, and while his position was vindicated, his life was threatened, his character besmirched and his veracity questioned. His belief in sorcery, witchcraft and possession, and his role in guiding the

Massachusetts colony through its first crisis under the new charter by vindicating the magistrates who presided over the Salem trials, cast an unfading shadow over his life and his historical reputation. To the nineteenth century Mather was an intolerant, illiberal and superstitious bigot whose name became synonymous with "Puritan." Neo-filialpietists like Samuel Eliot Morison and Perry Miller, despite their leadership in renovating Cotton Mather, persist in abusing Mather for allowing political expediency to override his better judgment in composing the 1693 Salem apology. Recently, however, this criticism has been redirected into a fresh perspective by Robert Middlekauff, reflecting the continued reconstruction in Cotton Mather's historical reputation.[7]

The modern American quest for community has contributed significantly to the new interest accorded Cotton Mather, just as it has for the Puritans. Mather, perhaps more than most, provides substance for Richard Hofstadter's exaggerated claim that as a community, the Puritans alone had been most consistently concerned with the life of the mind for its own sake. Mather's breadth of curiosity is borne out by the number and the variety of publications and the volume of unpublished manuscript material he prepared in his three-score years. That the thought which emerged from this curiosity was largely derivative is of minor importance. As Raymond Stearns has observed, Cotton Mather "demonstrated a considerable capacity for growth" and his enormous library is as much a testimony to that intellectual maturation as are his own compositions. Though Mather derived much more than he contributed, historians like Stearns have been drawn to him more for his scientific than for his religious thought.[8]

Cotton Mather's early interest in medicine was balanced by his interest in astronomy, mechanics, and climatology. As an experimental scientist, his enduring contributions were in genetics and preventive medicine, as well as in ornithology, attested to by his observations on corn hybridization, the passenger pigeon and his role in the inoculation issue. In natural philosophy, his role as scientist was more passive. After twenty years of sporadic labor, in 1712 Mather completed his "Biblia Americana" as a study of scripture improved by science. Though he never succeeded in having this work published, Mather extracted portions from it as the basis for his earliest contributions to the London Royal Society, a series of some hundred communiqués which began in 1712 and extended over a decade. Though the first letters to the Society in 1712 drew upon the "Biblia" as well as upon Mather's contributions to the Boston Philosophical Society in the 1680's, the vast majority of his letters thereafter broke new ground. In a sense, the Biblia and the 1712 correspondence which was later formed into the Curiosa

Americana, are the beginnings of Mather's scientific thought, and not the sum, as Middlekauff has implied.[9]

Concurrently with his effort to establish inoculation as a smallpox preventive, Mather in 1720 completed *The Christian Philosopher,* and two years later finished *The Angel of Bethesda.* Though the *Angel* suggests an originality not found in *The Christian Philosopher,* both are intellectually related. Each digested selected aspects of some forty years of Mather's experimentations and observations into a synthesis that included the most current medical and scientific thought then available to him. Moreover, it is evident from these treatises that Mather's biological experiments and observations enriched his appreciation for natural philosophy. As had been his custom in such earlier works as *The Wonderful Works of God Commemorated* (1690) and *Winter Meditations* (1693), Cotton Mather continued to incorporate the New Science into such ostensibly non-scientific tracts as the *Manuductio ad Ministerium* (1726). In this work, his ordering of intellectual priorities for young ministers ranked mastery of the new sciences ahead of such traditional work as holy geography. Despite this, by 1722 Mather was drawing his exploratory and literary interest in science to a close. However, while the intellectual outline of his thought was evident in his youthful exercises, intellectually, as Raymond Stearns has observed, Mather "was not the same in the 1720's that he had been in the 1680's" (p. 405).

While Mather's later thought retained some of his earlier ideas, by the time he completed his "Biblia Americana" his central interests had changed. From 1702 to 1712, as Middlekauff has observed, Mather's interest in the Jeremiad as a religious device declined. Moreover, he abandoned the struggle to maintain organizational unity among the churches and discarded the Federal Theology. His apprehensions about the demonic receded. "'Twas Nature sent these monsters," he said reassuringly, but "nature, too, sent Hercules, the monsters to subdue." At the same time, Mather reconstructed his millennial expectations. He abandoned his many efforts to plot Christ's coming on an historical scale, instead contenting himself with infrequent but periodic descriptions of the event as he contemplated a world ruled by Christ. As Mather's preoccupation with these issues and interests declined, his thought moved in a new direction during the decade before 1712.[10]

In these years, Mather's interest was drawn to the New Piety and the New Science. While both were evident in his sermons from the 1690's, after 1702 his imagination fastened upon them and was transformed by them. Despite their contrary character, however, piety and rationalism never competed for

dominance in Mather's thought. They emerged together and matured together and each was rooted in the other, thereby exerting a reciprocal influence one upon the other. At the same time as Mather's universe became more rational, its mechanical intricacies less mysterious and its operations more orderly and restrained, his religious life became more private and his faith more personal and spontaneous. Consequently, Mather's piety was integral to his rationalism and both were essential ingredients in his intellectual growth. Though both elements moved Mather into the early Enlightenment, only his piety has been properly explored, to the neglect of his rationalism. That rationalism grew out of Mather's interest in the New Science.[11]

By 1720, Mather had completed *The Christian Philosopher,* "a Collection of the Best discoveries in nature with religious improvements." This work was substantially rationalistic in its account of nature.[12] Except for fleeting references to spirits, a rare reference to scripture and a closing affirmation of the Trinity, Mather's religious improvements were simply pious exclamations about creation: "Great GOD, Thou are the Father of all things; even the Father of Insects, as well as the Father of Spirits: And Thy Greatness appears with a singular Brightness in the least of Thy Creatures!" (p. 146). In many instances where scripture or theology could have been conveniently introduced—Jonah with whales, Moses with frogs, the Garden of Eden, Satan and sin with snakes—Mather ignored the opportunity. Such supernatural interruption in nature's regularity was inconsistent with the spirit of *The Christian Philosopher.*

In his synthesis, Mather referred to God as the Divine Artificer. Nature's principles were consistent, he believed, in "that they come at first from a Divine Regulator" who "holds onto the springs" that make the machine function (p. 96). As the first mover, God's periodic involvement was essential for "without His *continual influence* the whole Movement would fall to pieces" (p. 88). Through thunder and lightning, as well as in his mechanical consistency, God often displayed his power. In addition, God, as Mather pointed out, could suspend the laws which governed the cosmic machine. While rainfall had been uniformly distributed over the globe, God withheld it from time to time to indicate his displeasure over human affairs (p. 53). Thus, Mather's belief in divine interposition was limited to such idiosyncratic features as the weather and were intimately related to his mechanistic conception of the universe.

Mather's mechanical cosmology embraced the organic as well as the inorganic. Though he speculated upon the possibility of life on the comets that shot across the heavens and the possibility of a collision with one, he marvelled at the comets' regularity.[13] Living organisms too conformed to mechanical principles from reproduction to respiration: "The Body of Man being most obvious to our view, is that which we will first begin with; a Machine of a most astonishing Workmanship and Contrivance" (p. 222). He applied Harvey's studies on the circulation of blood to demonstrate that the heart cooperated with atmospheric pressure to pump the blood. As if Newton's Third Law were crucial, Mather observed "the weight of the incumbent atmosphere to be the true antagonist for all the muscles" (p. 262). Without it, breathing would be impossible and thus, the organic world responded to God's laws with the same regularity as the sun, moon and planets, and rain and snow.

In *The Angel of Bethesda,* written concurrently with *The Christian Philosopher,* Mather summarized his own inquiries into biology, psychology, and genetics; he incorporated his findings about inoculation as a smallpox preventive and introduced his belief that diseases were communicated by insects and "animaculae"—microscopic life forms which had been observed through the microscope to be on all surfaces.[14] Though he marvelled at the mechanical beauty of the human body, he concluded that "there are indeed many Things in the Humane Body, that cannot be solved by the Rules of Mechanism" (pp. 68, 140)—in particular, foetal formation, infant suckling and emotional disorders or the body's capacity to mobilize itself against internal disorder. "In any other Machine," he stated, "if anything be out of Order it will remain so till some Hand from abroad shall rectify it," but not so with the human body (p. 142). Mather looked for the source of this phenomenon in his hypothesis of the Nishmath-Chajim.

As Mather developed his theory of the Nishmath-Chajim, it emerged as something more than an internal regulator. It was the link between the incorporeal soul and the body and "the Seat of our Diseases, or the Source of them." It was "the Spirit of the several Parts" with "Faculties and Tendencies from God imprinted upon it." It was, therefore, a vital principle, "the Breath of Life" (pp. 143, 139, 142, 137). He also developed this idea in the *Triparadisus* as the mechanism whereby the soul is conducted to heaven. While suggestions for the Nishmath-Chajim could be found among Mather's authorities (Helmont, the Galenists, Heurnius and Fernelius, among others), this was a further refinement of ideas that had first impressed him as a result of his experiments with possession and his observations regarding witchcraft and demonology in the 1690's.

The witchcraft outburst in Puritan New England from 1688 to 1693 provided Mather with an unusual opportunity to study the Satanic world. Though he had little direct contact with those either accused of witchcraft or claiming demonic possession from the accused at Salem in 1692, he had studied the instances of possession among the Goodwin family in 1688-89 and the Mercy Short and Margaret Rule incidents in 1693. Much of his thought about the "pneumatic science," as demonology was then called, was shaped by his experiences with the Goodwin case. Reflecting a spirit of intellectual inquiry, Mather sought to affirm the existence of devils, study them and provide forms of medical treatment for their victims. Mather conceded that Scripture had much to say about demons, but despite the numerous references to them, their behavior was quite mysterious. "The Word of God, having said so little in that particular concerning their way of action," he declared, "all that can be determined is important."[15]

For nearly a year Mather studied the Goodwin case under his own roof. In *Memorable Providences,* published in 1689, Mather reported upon the victim's behavior, the experiments performed and the methods used. He said: "I was not insensible that it might be an easy thing to be too bold and to go too far in making of experiments, nor was I so unphilosophical not to discern many opportunities of giving and solving many problems. I confess, I learnt much more than I sought"; but, he added, some things were not "proper to tell" (p. 31). In his experiments, Mather was interested primarily in the activities of demons, their ability to effect possession, and their limitations, if any. While his experimental procedure, his controls and his approach were simple, his tests led him to several inferential conclusions, among them that devils had finite powers. His experiments demonstrated that they could not read one's thoughts. "We could cheat them," he said, "when we spoke one thing and meant another. This was found when the children were to be undressed" (pp. 122-23). In *Wonders of the Invisible World* (1693), Mather noted that devils did not know all the languages nor did they have a uniform capacity to do mischief. "Some are therefore most suited to one nation than to another," he concluded, and consequently, "there might be some difference in their abilities" (p. 6). If one views the concern of science to be empirical reality, as Bernard Barber has pointed out, Mather's interest in the preternatural was clearly unscientific. Despite this, his controlled experimentation, logical consistency and inferential analysis of spirit behavior were wholly consistent with the scientific rationalism of the early Enlightenment.[16]

While Mather's interest had been focused upon spirit behavior, his therapeutic experiments had drawn his attention away from the devils to the behavior of the victims. "It is one of the chief arts of evil spirits," he had stated in his summary about the Salem witchcraft outburst in the *Magnalia Christi Americana,* "to make things which have no reality seem real to those who witness them" (I, 213). His experiments implied that the body could be affected by the mind and the mind could be treated through the body. He therefore approached the problem of possession as if it were an illness. Seeking appropriate treatment for it, his experiments followed "along the lines of what today would be termed psychosomatic medicine" (Stearns, p. 404). In general, Mather recommended prayer and fasting, as well as dietary changes. In addition, he sought the source of possession in the human psyche and for this he turned to the Nishmath-Chajim.

As an internal regulator, Mather also saw the Nishmath-Chajim as the controlling agent for mental health. Many diseases, Mather believed, were related to "a Weight of Cares, lying on the Minds of Men," thus, "our Nishmath-Chajim will go very far to help us, in the Solution of them" (*Angel,* pp. 145, 140). He prescribed proper diet, rest, "agreeable Conversation," and prayer as the means for revitalizing the Nishmath-Chajim. Suggesting further a relationship between this elusive vital principle, possession and mental health, Mather shifted the problem of witchcraft from external forces to internal, psychic balance. "In the indisputable and indubitable Occurrences of Witchcraft (and Possessions) there are many Things, which, because they are hard to be understood," he declared, "the *Nishmath-Chajim* well understood, would give us a marvellous Key to lett us into the Philosophy of them" (*Angel,* p. 144). Apart from recording his observations and some conclusions respecting the Nishmath-Chajim, Mather had no suggestions for proceeding with this analysis. Nevertheless, he was confident the vital principle could be understood, and through it mental disorders including possession. That confidence reflected Mather's own optimism in reason and progress, elements which had found a place in the early Enlightenment.

As Cotton Mather responded to the experimental science, his thought conformed to the beliefs of the early Enlightenment. His optimism, while reflecting a pale millennialism, derived from a conviction that the world had improved. As a concept, progress through improvement had been implicit in Mather's thought since the 1690's. In *Wonders of the Invisible World,* he celebrated the technological marvels his age had uncovered: the microscope, spectacles, and the lodestone magnet were remarkable achievements. Their discovery, so long in coming, had been delayed by Satan, "who does begrudge us all manner of good" (Sec. 4, p. 10). This negative expression of human progress had disappeared by the time Mather wrote *The Christian Philosopher*. He had turned to a positive explanation of progress in which reason emerged as an active ingredient. As he put it. "the progress which the invention of man had made" was itself divine. Such inventions as the microscope, lodestone magnet, the printing press, and the mechanical clock, were to him only a beginning: "If the *Mathematicks,* which have in the

two last Centuries had such wonderful Improvements, do for two hundred Years more improve in proportion to the former, who can tell what Mankind may come to!" (pp. 289, 291). Though Mather's sense of progress derived from the principle of augmentation, it reflected the excellence of reason.

Mather's conception of reason was more theistic than naturalistic. It was that faculty implanted in man by God and if it did not function independently, it was at every point in harmony with God. "The Light of Reason," he recorded in his diary in 1711, "is the Work of God; the Law of Reason is the Law of God; the Voice of Reason is the Voice of God." The capacity of reason to resolve mysteries was endorsed by Mather not simply in the improvements produced through mathematics, but in his belief that reason could penetrate the mysteries of its own activities as well as those of the Nishmath-Chajim. This was an activism poised against the suspicion that he lived, if not in the best of all possible worlds, clearly in one that had much to recommend it. Reason in all its various activities had directed "that the Business of the World may be all transacted, and with Satisfaction." In this balance between a satisfactory world and one which could be improved by reason, Mather's optimism could not be restrained by the Christian's characteristic sense of a tragic loss. Despite his profound piety, this tragic sense was not the controlling spirit of his natural history.[17] Instead he celebrated the idea of recovery through reason and progress. "O my Soul," Mather sang admiringly of reason in *The Christian Philosopher,* "what a wondrous Being art thou! How capable of astonishing Improvements! How worthy to be cultivated with the best Improvements! How worthy to have all possible endeavors used for thy Recovery from the Depravations which thy Fall from God has brought upon thee!" (pp. 291-92). Mather discounted any idea of loss that might have been implicit in this thought and directed his vision to a future in which mathematics performed its wonders.

As Mather's rationalism took root in his thought, it worked a subtle change in his perception of nature and heaven. No human achievement could replace Mather's sense of heaven. It remained God's exclusive creation, even in *The Christian Philosopher*. Mather's heavenly vision, however, appeared to be a divine form of a world improved by reason. To those who obeyed God, their heavenly reward was to "be fetch'd up into very comfortable Circumstances" (p. 295). It would be "a New Jerusalem," he said in the *Triparadisus,* which appeared the year *The Christian Philosopher* was published, "made of gold and studded with jewels," wherein the saints would possess an incorruptible corporeality (Middlekauff, pp. 330-31). Mather had materialized heaven. As he did so, he quite unconsciously spiritualized nature. Though much less intensely than Jonathan Edwards, Mather pondered nature's beauty, as when he quoted as "wonderful" a description of "the Moon walking in her brightness." Though paradoxical, each of these thoughts reflected the reciprocal relationship between his piety and his rationalism as Mather entered the modern world.[18]

Mather's intense piety has fixed his place, perhaps indelibly, in the historical imagination. Because of this, Mather's receptivity to early Enlightenment thought, his interest in the experimental science and his rationalistic outlook, are admired, but discounted. Though his views ranked in kind, if not in quality, with the men whom he accepted as authorities. in contrast to Cotton Mather, their place in the early Enlightenment has rarely been doubted. Despite this, at his death, Mather had not only attained a new plateau of piety, but that piety had acquired intensity from his acceptance of a mechanistic universe which was comprehensible through reason and which displayed signs of progressive improvement. Mather's piety sustained his optimistic vision of a rational universe and allowed him to respond to nature with a poet's sensitivity. Armed with his piety and his rationalism, between 1702 and 1712, Cotton Mather had crossed the threshold into the early Enlightenment. In his persistence in subordinating reason to God, Mather expressed the opinion of his Enlightenment authorities. No less than they, he regarded natural philosophy as only another, if potent, way to magnify God. Not for Mather, but for another generation would the two be separated and reason set free from divine regulation; but by then another phase in the Enlightenment would have emerged, one which would give birth to the Great Awakening.

Notes

[1] Thomas Jefferson Wertenbaker has interpreted the transformation as a conscious shift from supernaturalism to rationalism, in which the principal actors were unaware of their own intellectual transition. Viewed this way, the witchcraft frenzy at Salem in 1692, otherwise incomprehensible to him, assumes a new vitality and becomes, for him, a necessary stage in the rational development of the New England Puritans: *The Puritan Oligarchy; The Founding of American Civilization* (New York, 1947); see preface and chapter 9, especially pp. 289-90. On the other hand, John Van de Wetering, in his study of Thomas Prince, considers Puritan thought to be still in transition as late as 1750. Nevertheless, Van de Wetering associates the transition into the Enlightenment with a conflict between Prince's scientific rationalism and his Puritan idea of God: "The Christian History of the Great Awakening," *New England Quarterly* (1965), 494-507.

[2] Peter Gay, *The Enlightenment, an Interpretation.* Vol. I: *The Rise of Modern Paganism* (New York, 1966), Ch. 1.

[3] Samuel Eliot Morison, *The Intellectual Life of Colonial New England* (New York, 1956), pp. 241-42.

[4] Stow Persons, *American Minds, A History of Ideas* (New York, 1958), Ch. 1; and Perry Miller, *The New England Mind; The Seventeenth Century* (New York, 1939), pp. 181-206.

[5] Basil Willey, *The Eighteenth Century Background; Studies on the Idea of Nature in the Thought of the Period* (London, 1950), Ch. 3. See also Gerald Stourzh, "Reason and Power in Benjamin Franklin's Political Thought," *American Political Science Review,* 47 (1953), 1092-1115; John Herman Randall, Jr., "The Religious Consequences of Newton's Thought," *Texas Quarterly,* 10 (1967), 279-80; and Randall's introduction to H. S. Thayer, ed., *Newton's Philosophy of Nature* (New York and London, 1953), ix-xvi.

[6] I wish to express my appreciation to my colleague Robert Filner for directing my attention to the subtleties of scientific thought.

[7] Kenneth Murdock, ed., *Selections from Cotton Mather* (New York, 1926); Richard H. Werking, "Reformation is Our Only Preservation: Cotton Mather and Salem Witchcraft," *William and Mary Quarterly,* 3rd Series, 29 (April, 1972), 281-90; Robert Middlekauff, *The Mathers, Three Generations of Puritan Intellectuals,* 1596-1728 (New York, 1971). Middlekauff's reconstruction goes so far as even to ignore, except in a passing reference (pp. 159-60), Mather's role in the witchcraft trials.

[8] Hofstadter, *Anti-Intellectualism in American Life* (New York, 1963), p. 59; Thomas J. Holmes, *Cotton Mather: A Bibliography,* 3 vols. (Cambridge, Mass., 1940); Raymond F. Stearns, *Science in the British Colonies of America* (Urbana, Ill., 1970), p. 404; Otho T. Beall, Jr. and Richard H. Shryock, *Cotton Mather First Significant Figure in American Medicine* (Baltimore, 1954); Theodore Hornberger, "The Date, The Source and the Significance of Cotton Mather's Interest in Science," *American Literature,* 6 (1935), 413-20.

[9] Frederick T. Lewis, "The passenger pigeon as observed by the Rev. Cotton Mather," *The Auk,* 66 (1944), 587-92; Conway Zirkle, *The Beginnings of Plant Hybridization* (Philadelphia, 1935), pp. 91, 97, 100, 199; John T. Barrett, "The inoculation controversy in Puritan New England," *Bulletin of the History of Medicine,* 12 (1942), 169-90; Beall and Shryock, pp. 50-51; Beall, "Cotton Mather's Early Curiosa Americana in the Boston Philosophical Society, 1683," *William and Mary Quarterly,* 3rd Series, 18 (1961), 360-72; Middlekauff's analysis of Mather's scientific thought (Ch. 16) concentrates almost entirely upon the "Biblia Americana" and ignores all Mather's thought related to science composed after 1712.

[10] Middlekauff, p. 407, n. 12 and ch. 14; Cotton Mather, *Magnalia Christi Americana,* 2 vols. (New York, 1962). I, 211; see also II, 361-72: "I say, then, live we thus in the midst of thunders and devils too; and yet live we." In discussing Mather's millennialism, Middlekauff's approach is one of uniformity. Though he fails to stress the chronological development and change in Mather's millennialism, except incidentally, his numerous citations, when organized chronologically, reveal the shift after 1712 indicated; see Ch. 18.

[11] See, for example, *The Man of God Furnished* (1708); *A Man of Reason* (1709); *The Heavenly Conversation* (1710); *Reason Satisfied and Faith Established* (1712); Middlekauff, p. 304.

[12] In spirit and substance, *Philosopher* (rep., Gainesville, Fla., 1968) fails to sustain Stearns' judgment that Mather's naturalism was but "a momentary lapse," p. 424.

[13] Notwithstanding Perry Miller, *The New England Mind: From Colony to Province* (Cambridge, Mass, 1953), p. 443.

[14] Beall and Shryock, *Cotton Mather,* pp. 87-92.

[15] "Memorable Providence Relating to Witchcraft and Possession," in George Burr, ed., *Narratives of the Witchcraft Cases,* 1648-1706 (New York 1914), p. 95; Richard Werking follows Miller's *From Colony to Province* in arguing that as "a witchcraft hunter," Mather deliberately sought possessed persons in order to work a conversion upon them and induce a Christian revival. On the other hand, Chadwick Hansen's highly provocative and quite exciting study, *Witchcraft at Salem* (New York, 1969), follows a narrower line, suggesting that Mather's principal interest in witchcraft was as an object for study, as "a witchcraft scholar." Stearns follows Beall and Shryock in developing Mather's medical interests through his interest in witchcraft along the lines of psychosomatic medicine. William F. Poole integrated all these elements as he discussed Mather's role and interest in the Salem witchcraft controversy, in *The Memorial History of Boston,* 4 vols. (Boston, 1882), II, 131-72.

[16] While Mather composed the *Wonders* (Boston and London) he pursued his experimentation with possession in the Mercy Short and Margaret Rule cases, summarizing his findings in *A Brand Plucked from the Burning* and *Another Brand Plucked from the Burning.* See Barber, *Science and the Social Order* (New York, 1952), p. 33.

[17] *Christian Philosopher,* pp. v, 291, 287.

[18] *Christian Philosopher,* p. 52.

Enders A. Robinson (essay date 1991)

SOURCE: "Cotton Mather," in *The Devil Discovered: Salem Witchcraft 1692,* Hippocrene Books, 1991, pp. 37-55.

[*In the following excerpt, Robinson compares the actions of Increase Mather to those of his son Cotton Mather during the witch trials.*]

. . . The year 1692 had opened as a particularly troubling one in New England. The winter was cruel;[26] taxes were intolerable; pirates were attacking commerce; smallpox was rife. The French were actively supporting the Indians on a bloody warpath.

The armies of the French and the Indians represented a lethal threat to the people of New England. King William's War had been going on for three and a half years. Morale was low, tension high, in the wake of periodic massacres by the Indians. While the heaviest fighting occurred in New Hampshire and Maine, raids had repeatedly been made on the northern towns of Essex County in Massachusetts, Andover, Billerica, and Haverhill, in particular. New England towns were hard pressed to support the war with their tax money and their young men.

On January 25, 1692 one hundred fifty Abanaki Indians attacked "wretchedly secure" York, Maine, fifty miles northeast of Salem. Most of the houses were burned, and the minister and seventy-five other men, women, and children were killed. About one hundred were marched off into captivity. The Rev. George Burroughs, the minister at neighboring Wells, Maine, supplied the authorities in Boston with a description: "Pillars of smoke, the raging of the merciless flames, the insults of the heathen enemy, shouting, hooting, hacking [the bodies], and dragging away 80 others."[27] (George Burroughs was arrested for witchcraft on May 4, 1692 and hanged on August 10, 1692.)

Captain John Floyd of Romney Marsh (now Chelsea), Massachusetts, in command of a militia company which included Salem men, found the town of York in ruins. On January 27, 1692 he wrote to his superiors, "The 25 of this instant, I, having been informed that York was destroyed, made the greatest haste that I could with my Company for their relief, if there were any left, which I did hardly suspect."[28]

Captain John Alden of Boston was given the assignment of redeeming the York captives from the Indians. His instructions read, "It will be necessary that you represent unto them their baseness, treacheries and barbarities practiced in this war, having always declined a fair pitch battle, acting instead like bears and wolves."[29] The Puritans regarded the Indian style of fighting as diabolic; today it is called guerrilla warfare.

Captain John Alden had previously negotiated a truce with the Indians, but unscrupulous traders and land speculators operating from Massachusetts soon violated its conditions, thereby inciting the Indians.[30] Now that the Indians were answering in kind, the same unprincipled men, unwilling to admit their guilt, shifted the blame to Captain Alden for his efforts to reach a peaceful compromise. (Captain John Floyd and Captain John Alden were arrested for witchcraft on May 28, 1692.)

The new royal charter represented a grave threat to the Puritan rulers who saw that their provisional government was nearing its end. Now, for the first time, they would be faced with a situation where the common rabble could vote in political elections. Their Puritan church would no longer hold exclusive control over the lives of the people.

As if these external threats were not enough, the Rev. Cotton Mather found an internal threat, the threat of witchcraft. To understand why the Puritan leaders considered witchcraft such a danger in 1692, it is very instructive to study the lives and characters of the Mathers, father Increase and son Cotton.

Some historians laud the New England Puritans as begetters of the highest American virtues, while others revile them as the source of the deepest American woes. Some cherish them as the symbol of spotless devotion to religious truth; others spurn them as the epitome of icy self-righteousness. In American folklore, the Puritans always seem to fall at one extreme or the other: splendid morality or niggardly repression, religious insight or blind bigotry, political freedom or savage persecution.

Confronted with a myriad of apparent contradictions, writers seldom place a Puritan in the middle ground of history. In all accounts, however, Increase Mather fares better than his more brilliant son. The father usually is placed on the positive side, whereas the son almost invariably is placed on the negative side. Cotton Mather is seen as the one who, through his writings and sermons, triggered the witch hunt of 1692. His father is often credited with using his influence to bring the witch hunt to an end. Their positions in history are chiefly associated with their participation in this tragic story, but at opposite extremes.

The heritage of the Mathers placed them squarely in the elite of Puritan society. Increase Mather (1639-1723) was the son of Richard Mather. Richard (1596-1669) came to America in 1635 and was the minister of the Dorchester church, near Boston. The most revered of the New England Puritans was John Cotton (1585-1652). He emigrated to America in 1633 and was the minister of the First Church in Boston. The Rev. John Cotton and the Rev. Richard Mather were two Moses-like figures among the American Puritans.

Even in youth, Increase Mather demonstrated that he would equal or outshine the eminence of his father Richard. Increase graduated from Harvard in 1656. He preached his first sermon on his eighteenth birthday, and then went to Trinity College in Dublin, Ireland to obtain a Master's degree. He became the minister of the Second Church (Old North Church) in Boston. In 1662, he married the Rev. John Cotton's daughter Maria Cotton.

On February 12, 1663 the couple's first child Cotton Mather was born. Bearing the distinguished names of both *Cotton* and *Mather,* the boy may have felt destined for greatness. By 1674 he had mastered the entrance requirements for Harvard College and was accepted. Entering at the age of eleven and a half, he is the youngest student ever admitted to the college to this day. The normal time spent on the undergraduate degree was three years. When Cotton attended, the total enrollment at Harvard was never more than twenty students; in his own class there were only four. The ages of most of the students ranged from about fifteen to eighteen. As an eleven-year-old boy with a stutter, Cotton was discouraged when some of the students threatened him. After only a month at college he returned home for the rest of the freshman year, studying with his father and on his own.

Early in 1674 his father, Increase Mather, predicted that God would strike New England by the sword. The summer of 1675 fulfilled the prophecy; King Philip's War erupted, a war waged by Indians to drive the white men into the sea.[31] The Indian leader was King Philip; his Indian name was Metacom. King Philip was the son of Massasoit, the Indian chief who had befriended the Pilgrims, making possible their first thanksgiving. The Indians said that "they had been the first in doing good to the English, and the English the first in doing wrong. When the English first came, their King's father [Massasoit] was as a great man, and the English as a little child. He constrained the other Indians from wronging the English and gave them corn, and showed them how to plant, and let them have a hundred times more land than now the King [Philip] has for his own people."[32]

The first attack was made by the Wampanoag Indians against Plymouth Colony in June 1675. As the Indians swept northward into Massachusetts, all the settlements went on the alert, no man leaving his house without a gun. Each settlement had several garrison houses where the populace would assemble for protection, often staying for weeks at a time while under siege.[33]

A combined colonial force was organized to prevent the powerful Narragansett Indians of Rhode Island from joining the other New England tribes. The army met the Indians near Kingston, Rhode Island in December 1675. In what came to be known as the Great Swamp Fight, the Indians' fort was demolished. The Narragansetts fled northward and, joining with other Indians, attacked settlements throughout New England. Of the ninety settlements in New England, fifty-two were attacked and thirteen completely destroyed. The white population was decimated; literally one man out of every ten was killed by the Indians, and like numbers of women and children. In proportion to the population, King Philip's War was the bloodiest war in American history.

The fighting came within twenty miles of Boston. Cotton heard his father's many prayers to God for victory, and believed them efficacious. Increase set apart a special day to beseech God to kill the Indian leader, King Philip, by a stroke of providence. In less than a week the deed was accomplished. On August 12, 1676 King Philip was shot. "This Agag was now cut into quarters, which were then hanged up, while his head was carried in triumph to Plymouth, where it arrived on the very day that the church there was keeping a solemn thanksgiving to God. God sent them the head of a *leviathan* for a *thanksgiving-feast*," wrote Cotton Mather.[34] King Philip, like his father Massasoit before him, provided the Pilgrims with a reason for a thanksgiving celebration, his head instead of corn.

Despite their defeat in King Philip's War, the Indians continued to fight the white man, mostly with guerrilla tactics, in northern New England for nearly another one hundred years.

At age thirteen, Cotton saw the fulfillment of another of his father's prophecies, that Boston would be punished by a judgment of fire. On the morning of November 27, 1676 his family's house burned down along with forty-five others and the Old North Church. After the fire the Mathers lived temporarily with John Richards, a prominent member of the Second Church (Old North Church).[35] (John Richards was one of the witchcraft justices in 1692.)

Cotton Mather graduated from Harvard in 1678 at age fifteen. Still suffering from a speech impediment, he at first believed himself unfit for the ministry and studied medicine. In the seventeenth century, medical practitioners were divided into physicians and surgeons. The surgeons were usually barbers. They performed amputations and phlebotomy (the drawing of blood), as well as extracting teeth. Their sign is used by barbers to this day, a red pole wound with a narrow white bandage.

Physicians of that day had little knowledge of the body or mind. Their training was in certain customary remedies. They had no understanding of the reason behind administering such remedies, nor of what quantities should be used. Among the herbs employed were crude tobacco leaves, fivefinger, brambles, strawberry roots, powdered sumac, powdered elecampane roots, wormwood, wild carrot seeds, sweet fennel seeds, raisins, maiden hair, liverwort, elder buds, knotgrass, shepherd's pouch, pollipod, borrage, buglose root, rosemary, primrose, cowslips, violets, and peony seeds. Other common ingredients were red lead, lead ore, wax, oven-dried horses' livers, and the fillings of a dead man's skull. The most revolting substances, best left unmentioned, comprised many of the remedies. Physicians freely prescribed the medicines, whether or not they knew the physiological effects on the patient.

The following cure for a distracted woman is a specimen of the remedies used in that period. "Take milk of a nurse that gives suck to a male child. Also take a he cat and cut off one of his ears or a piece of it. Let it bleed into the milk and then let the sick woman drink it. Do this three times."

On August 22, 1680 Cotton Mather was invited to preach a sermon at the Dorchester church, and six months later he was made assistant in his father's church, the rebuilt Second Church (Old North Church). Five years later, he was ordained the assistant minister in the church. Apparently there were no more thoughts about violets, horses' livers, and other physic (the old word for medicine).

The Puritans clergy portrayed vivid pictures of the supernatural. They preached that any variation from the known routine of nature, however small or great, was a divine sign. Comets, for example, were supernatural manifestations set in the sky to mark some special event, such as famine, war, or pestilence. "A great and blazing comet" preceded the wheat blight of 1665 in Massachusetts. The comet of 1680 gave Increase Mather inspiration for a sermon entitled "Heaven's Alarm to the World." When John Cotton died, a comet appeared in the heavens as testimony "that God had removed a bright star, a burning and a shining light out of the Heaven of his church here."

In 1681 a group of eminent New England clergymen, after long discussions about the dangers to religion from the growth of rationalism, decided to combat the unwelcome trend with proofs of the supernatural. They set themselves the task of gathering and publishing every instance they could find of "divine judgments, tempests, floods, earthquakes, thunders as are unusual, strange apparitions, or whatever else shall happen that is prodigious, witchcrafts, diabolical possessions, remarkable judgments on noted sinners, eminent deliverances, and answers to prayer."[36]

In 1684 Increase Mather completed his part of the project and published it under the title *An Essay for the Recording of Illustrious Providences*.[37] In his book he relates how certain holy men were preserved at sea, when all others on the ship were lost. He regarded meteorites as missiles hurled from Heaven. He assigned to the sphere of the supernatural every manifestation of nature which could not be explained. He writes, "There is also that which is very mysterious and beyond human capacity to comprehend, in thunder and lightning." He calls lightning "Heaven's arrow" and gives numerous instances in which men were smitten with the fire of God. Not until the next century would his countryman Benjamin Franklin give the scientific explanation of lightning.

On the dark side, Increase Mather promulgated the belief that the world was governed by magic and witchcraft. To him, any ill happenings were caused by the powers of the air, the Devil. A thunderstorm was the work of malignant spirits; persons in league with the Devil sank ships, ruined crops, and caused death and sickness.

In his book, Increase Mather includes essays on: "A remarkable relation about Ann Cole of Hartford." "Several witches of the colony." "Of the possessed maid at Groton." "An account of the house at Newbury lately troubled with a demon." "And of one in Portsmouth lately disquieted by evil spirits." "A woman at Berwick molested with apparitions, and sometimes tormented by invisible agents."

The essay on Anne Cole says that in the year 1662 she "was taken with very strange fits, wherein her tongue was improved by a demon." Various measures were tried, but "after the suspected witches were either executed or fled, Ann Cole was restored to health."

Increase Mather's account of the possessed maid at Groton is fundamental to any study of New England witchcraft. The event took place in 1671; the girl was Elizabeth Knapp, age sixteen. Mather's essay says, "Elizabeth Knapp was taken after a very strange manner, with violent agitations of her body. A demon began manifestly to speak in her. The things uttered by the Devil were chiefly railings and revilings of Mr. [Samuel] Willard, pastor to the church in Groton. She cried out in her fits that [the specter of] a woman, one of her neighbors, appeared to her, and was the cause of her affliction. The person thus accused did visit the poor wretch, and prayed earnestly with and for the possessed creature, after which she confessed that Satan had deluded her, making her believe evil of her good neighbor without any cause. Nor did she after that complain of any apparition from such an one."[38]

The essay on the house at Newbury says that on December 8, 1679, "there were five great stones thrown in while the man's wife was making the bed, the bedstead was lifted up from the floor, and a cat was hurled at her, a long staff danced up and down in the chimney." Such things went on for months, but "all the while the Devil did not appear in any visible shape." In their attempts to catch the Devil, sometimes "they would think they had hold of the hand that scratched them, but it would give them the slip."

His work was an immediate success, widely read in front of the fireplace, at work in the fields, over mugs in the tavern. People started to speak with awe of the magicians, witches, and imps which this eminent author held before them. At one extreme, some historians say that this book planted the seed which sprouted into the rankest harvest of witchcraft in the history of New England.[39] At the opposite extreme, other historians lament that its significance as one of the first scientific writings in America is, for the most part, neglected.[40] Increase Mather describes one notable "experiment" that was used on "suspected persons." Its purpose was to determine "whether the stories of witches not being able to sink under water were true. Accordingly a man and woman had their hands and feet tied, and so were cast into the water, and they both apparently swam after the manner of a buoy, part under, part above the water. Whether this experiment were lawful, or rather superstitious and magical, we shall . . . inquire afterward."[41]

The son of Increase Mather now deserves attention. Of all the Puritans. Cotton Mather is most often singled out as the epitome of their way of life. His lifetime, from 1663 to 1728, represents that period midway between the arrival of the first American settlers and the American Revolution. The object of meager praise and violent blame, Cotton Mather has not fared well in history. His few defenders have concentrated on his religious forms and literary abilities rather than his personality. Most historians hasten to disclaim any favorable interest in him, and have been almost eager to defame him. Yet he remains the best known of the American Puritans.[42]

Modern readers know Cotton Mather most intimately through his profuse writings. In his diary he bared his soul, undertaking to set down how God dealt with him. By putting his thoughts, acts, and spiritual experiences into words, he hoped to unravel the mystery of his fate. His diary became a testimonial to his unremitting quest for personal holiness. Of all of New England's Puritan writers, Cotton Mather appears as the most morbidly introspective. His visions gave rise to intolerable tensions for which he sought relief. The traumatic experience of looking into the pit of Hell, which was the favorite Puritan vista, seemed almost to turn his mind into a chamber of horrors.

Cotton Mather was a man tortured by his Puritanical fears and fantasies. He felt that the cosmos revolved around himself. The theme of his diary is a titanic struggle for his soul between God and Satan. God was fighting so that Cotton Mather could further His work on earth, whereas Satan was fighting to prevent it. The Deity's chief concern in the universe was Cotton Mather, his doings, the state of his soul, and his personal welfare. Repeatedly, Cotton Mather's diary affirms that God wished him well, that mercies for him were being stored up in Heaven pending his arrival, and that everything he did had Heaven's wholehearted approval.

Cotton Mather not only walked with God, but also, on occasion, talked with God. His diary was an expression of his duty to keep a record, for the benefit of posterity, of his "sweet conversation" and "extraordinary intimate communion" with God. In one entry, God told him, "Go into your great chamber and I will speak with you." Doing as directed, he had the gratification of receiving "unutterable communications from the Holy Ghost." In a 1705 entry, on a truly memorable day, he "conversed with each of the three Persons in the Eternal Godhead." Yet curiously, in all the revelations given to Cotton Mather, none offered anything new. No one who was granted the astonishing privilege of looking into Heaven and Hell emerged with a more stereotypical description of those places.

Cotton Mather's war with the Powers of Darkness took the form of an all-out effort to preserve and strengthen the old ways of his ideal Puritanism against what he saw as the corroding effects of worldliness and mercantile prosperity. When he wrestled with the Devil, he complained that a "carnal, giddy, rising generation" cheered loudly whenever Satan seemed on the point of pinning him down. Through his books and sermons he hoped to make people "serious and powerful, and afraid of sin."

The Puritan preachers in New England developed a type of sermon known as a *jeremiad,* with a recognizable literary style. The name comes from the Old Testament Book of Jeremiah; a typical verse is 9:4, "Take ye heed everyone of his neighbor, And trust ye not in any brother." The preachers claimed the "tyranny" of Andros was a punishment for the people's breach of the religious covenant. To sustain their appeal, the clergy needed a succession of evils. But the usual troubles, such as Indian wars, party squabbles, decay of trade, and smallpox, had begun to lose their effect.

The jeremiad labored under the continual need to pile up horrible tales of woe resulting from sin. Cotton Mather, the most expert of its practitioners, was driven to uncover fresh material. In 1689 he preached about the weakened position of European Protestants, and called upon New England to assist them through prayer and by renouncing sin.

Searching for more and more effective means to lash the conscience of New England, Cotton Mather seized on a fear lying ripe for exploitation, witchcraft. Witchcraft was an internal threat of the most insidious sort; a witch could be your neighbor, even your brother or sister, husband or wife. Cotton Mather started preaching, "Satan is marshaling his forces for a final decision." In sermon and pamphlet, he warned that the Prince of Darkness was preparing to exterminate New England. The Devil would return the country to his own children, the Indians, he said. The whole colony began to listen.

So that no one should miss the point, Cotton Mather constantly enlarged upon the sinister threats of witchcraft during the three years (1689-1692) of the existence of the provisional government. He preached that all our sins have been "at least implicit witchcrafts." Cotton Mather feared that New England would become possessed with the Devil. Through his popular writings Cotton Mather had directly influenced the general public. The ruling Board of Assistants, dominated by the old guard, gladly supported his point of view.

His close friend on the Board was Samuel Sewall. Samuel Sewall's father had settled in New England earlier, but had then returned to England, where Samuel was born in 1652. With the Restoration, the whole family fled to New England in 1661. Samuel Sewall graduated from Harvard College in 1671. He became a magistrate, an assistant to the governor, in 1684. In 1692 he was living in Boston, where he had gained a reputation for fairness. Samuel Sewall admired Cotton Mather and often went to hear his sermons. Frequently they dined together and they carried on an active correspondence. (Samuel Sewall was one of the justices in the witchcraft trials of 1692.)

In 1688 in England, Sir Isaac Newton wrote *Principia Matematica,* in which he gave the "System of the World." His book has governed the scientific understanding of the visible universe ever since. In the same year in New England, Cotton Mather wrote **Memorable Providences Relating to Witchcraft and Possessions**. This book, published the next year, was Cotton Mather's first attempt to give a scientific account of the invisible world of the Devil. The book is based on his first-hand observation; he uses as data the experiences of the Goodwin children in the summer and fall of 1688. In Latin, he wrote, "Haec ipse miserrima vidi," or "these things these wretched eyes beheld."

The family of Boston mason John Goodwin was well regarded, and his children had been religiously educated. The eldest, Martha Goodwin, thirteen years old, was a plain girl with long, straight black hair. A pretty young Irish woman with a fair complexion worked as laundress for the Goodwin family. Martha, taking a dislike to her, accused her of stealing some of the family linen. The young woman's mother, Mary Glover, better known as Goody Glover or the Widow Glover, came to her daughter's defense.[43] Goody Glover spoke harshly, perhaps profanely, to Martha. After the encounter, Martha fell into an agitated state, described by Cotton Mather as "odd fits that carried in them something diabolical." One of her sisters and two of her brothers, following her example, also fell into fits.

Cotton Mather learned of this episode soon after his father left for England in May 1688. He visited the children, and became the most active and forward of any minister in the Goodwin case. When it appeared, his book *Memorable Providences* gave the case credibility. Few learned persons expressed any doubt about the "facts" presented in the book, readily accepting the preternatural agency of witchcraft as the cause of the children's afflictions. Mr. Richard Baxter, an eminent English cleric, in a preface to an edition published in London in 1691, says, "The evidence is so convincing that he must be a very obdurate Sadducee who will not believe."[44]

In the spirit of the times, Cotton Mather wrote his book in the guise of a scientific report. He describes the "afflictions" of the children as follows. "Sometimes they were deaf, sometimes dumb, sometimes blind, and often all this at once. Their tongues would be drawn down their throats, and then pulled out upon their chins to a prodigious length. Their mouths were forced open to such a wideness that their jaws went out of joint, and anon clap together again, with a force like that of a spring-lock, and the like would happen to their shoulder blades and their elbows, and hand wrists, and several of their joints. They would lie in a benumbed condition and be drawn together like those who are tied neck and heels, and presently be stretched out, yea, drawn backwards to such an extent that it was feared the very skin of their bellies would have cracked. They would make most piteous outcries that they were cut with knives, and struck with blows that they could not bear." All their afflictions were during the day; they slept comfortably at night.

The Puritan ministers of Boston and Charlestown kept a day of fasting and prayer at the troubled house. Afterwards the youngest child had no more fits. Had not magistrate William Stoughton interposed, the matter might have ended there. Goody Glover, described by Cotton Mather as "a scandalous Irish woman," was arrested, brought to trial, and sentenced to death for witchcraft. Most scandalous of all, the underlying reason for her condemnation was that she was a Roman Catholic. Gallows were erected on Boston Common.

On the day of the hanging, November 16, 1688, the Goodwin children were present in the front row. Cotton Mather, his Bible in hand, said prayers for them, making frequent references to God and Christ. Goody Glover was brought forth. Because of the heavy chain on her legs, the gait of the witch on the way to her execution was difficult and stumbling. The hangman, eager to do his office, tightened the chain clapped about her body as he pulled her along, inflicting excruciating pain. Cotton Mather whispered to Martha that the witch was being pulled to the fire of Hell. The noose of the stiff rope was put around Goody Glover's neck. As she died, she was choked until she was black in the face. When she was cut down, Martha could see the gashing red marks left on her neck.

Goody Glover had declared that the afflicted children would not be relieved by her death because others had a hand in their affliction. According to Cotton Mather, "the three children continued in their furnace as before, and it grew rather seven times hotter than it was." Cotton Mather took Martha Goodwin as a guest into his household. He wrote, "I took her home chiefly that I might be a critical eye-witness of things that would enable me to confute the sadducism of this debauched age." For a few days she behaved normally, but on November 20, 1688 she cried, "Ah, they have found me out," and immediately fell into her fits.

Martha complained that Glover's chain was upon her leg, and, trying to walk, her gait exactly matched that of the chained witch before she died. An invisible chain would be clapped about Martha's body, and she cried out in pain and fear as the specters tightened it around her. Rushing to her aid, Cotton Mather valiantly tried to knock the invisible chain off her as it began to be fastened. He writes, "But ordinarily, when it was on, she would be pulled off her seat with such violence towards the fire, that it was as much as one or two of us could do to keep her out. And if we stamped on the hearth, just between her and the fire, she screamed out, 'That by jarring the chain, we hurt her.' I may add that the specters put an unseen rope, with a cruel noose, about her neck, whereby she was choked until she was black in the face; and though it was got off before it had killed her, yet there were the red marks of it, and of a finger and thumb near it, remaining to be seen for some while afterwards."

He gave her his Bible, the one he had taken to Boston Common, to read some scriptures, but "she said that she sooner die than read them." Yet she had read the same scriptures in the Anglican *Book of Common Prayer*.[45] She could read whole pages of a Roman Catholic book, but always skipped over the names of God and Christ. What more proof of witchcraft could there be?

Combining agility of body and quickness of mind, children are capable of extraordinary behavior. Were the "afflictions" of the Goodwin children the manifestations of witchcraft, or were they fraud, pure and simple? Cotton Mather considered this question. In the scientific spirit of the times, he decided to carry out some experiments. One experiment involved his upstairs study. He knew that the Devil would not dare enter his study, a place of God. He had observed that whenever Martha was brought up to his study, she became well. When her fits came upon her downstairs, only with extreme difficulty could she be dragged upstairs. He wrote, "The demons would pull her out of the people's hands, and make her heavier than perhaps three of herself. With incredible toil (though she kept screaming, 'They say I must not go in!') she was pulled in. She then could stand on her feet, and, with an altered note, say 'I am well.' To satisfy some strangers, the experiment was repeated divers times, with the same success."

After Cotton Mather finished his book, the Goodwin children became well and lived normal lives. One might conclude that his account serves as evidence of his own inattention and strong prejudice. But three centuries later, can such a simple judgment be made? Cotton Mather concluded that his experiments showed that the afflictions of the Goodwin children could only be explained by witchcraft. In the Puritan teaching, supernatural intervention was made to appear as a commonplace event. Behind the witchcraft accusation against Goody Glover lay an element of superstition, even terror. To the Puritan clergy of seventeenth-century America, the Devil was every bit as real as God.

Read by thousands of people in both New England and England, Cotton Mather's book met with much acclaim. Together with his numerous sermons and pamphlets, this book represented a major effort to instill in the minds of the people a belief in the reality of witchcraft and a fear of witches. Although witchcraft was an element in the general belief of the times, it took his aggressive and inflammatory arguments to persuade key authorities that witchcraft was the msajor enemy of New England. With unbounded faith in his own power, Cotton Mather saw himself as divinely appointed to lead in the salvation of New England by driving out the Devil.

To Cotton Mather, New England was a former realm of the Devil, and the Indians inhabitants were Satanic agents. In this fair land, God had enabled the visible saints to gain a foothold, but now the Devil had opened a counter-attack. The present Indian war was only the outward manifestation of the assault; there were also witches who would tear down New England from within. As the young and vigorous acting pastor of the Second Church (Old North Church) in Boston, Cotton Mather skillfully and cunningly had laid the groundwork for the witchcraft delusion which erupted in February 1692.

Notes

. . . [26] *The year 1692, at the center point of the "little ice age," was one of the coldest years in the history of civilization.*

[27] Petition from Wells, January 27, 1692 (*Massachusetts Archives,* 37:259).

[28] *Massachusetts Archives,* 37:257; 37:318.

[29] Instructions to Captain John Alden, February 5, 1692 (*Massachusetts Archives,* 37:305).

[30] Major Richard Waldron of Dover, New Hampshire during King Philip's War had issued "general warrants" to seize every native known to be a "man slayer." Vicious Puritan traders for years used this authority to kidnap Indians and transport them to the West Indies as slaves. Their vessels would lurk in concealed inlets about the harbors of Maine with a view to this traffic. They knew that their business stirred up the Indians, but what was the peace of a few small farmers and fishermen compared to the profits of the slave trade? There were a considerable number of slaves throughout New England, and in Salem and Boston black slaves were bought and sold. Captain John Alden, a long-time trader on the Maine coast, spurned those engaged in these Indian kidnappings, as did the French Huguenots and traders of other backgrounds who had made their home there.

[31] In 1675 the native population of New England was about 20,000, having declined from nearly 100,000 in the year 1600, largely due to the white man's diseases. The white population of New England was over 80,000 by 1675. The Indians had already lost an undeclared economic war, and were suffering continual degradation and loss of territory. King Philip's War, from 1675 to 1676, represented the final attempt of the Indians to retain their hold in Southern New England; they lost decisively. Philip's army had some 3,000 warriors, about 2,500 of whom were either killed or sold into slavery. Because about that many more women and children were killed, nearly one-fourth of the Indian population of New England was destroyed in the war.

[32] Easton, 10.

[33] The American soldiers also took scalps, and were sometimes paid bounties for them by the government. The bounty was equivalent to several thousand dollars today. In major encounters, the Americans indiscriminately killed old men, women, and children. In reporting the interrogation of an Indian woman, Captain Samuel Mosely added, "The aforesaid Indian was ordered to be torn to pieces by dogs, and she was dealt with all." Captive Indians who were not hanged were

sold into miserable slavery in the West Indies. Unable to cope as slaves, many of them were killed trying to escape.

[34] In its so-called mercy, the General Court shipped King Philip's nine-year-old son to Bermuda where he was sold as a slave. This was done against the advice of some ministers who advocated death.

[35] John Richards had become a magistrate, an assistant to the governor, in 1680.

[36] From the preface of Increase Mather, *Providences.*

[37] The running title was *Remarkable Providences.*

[38] In 1671, through prayer and understanding, the Rev. Willard convinced Elizabeth Knapp that her affliction was not due to the witchcraft of her neighbor. This realization not only made her well, but made her love her neighbor. In 1692, the Rev. Willard's approach, however, was decisively rejected by the authorities; they chose to take every accusation, however absurd, of the sanctioned afflicted girls as gospel. The Rev. Willard was an opponent of the Salem witch hunt. In a letter of October 8, 1692 his friend Thomas Brattle wrote, "I cannot but admire that these [sanctioned] afflicted persons should be so much countenanced and encouraged in their accusations. I often think of the Groton woman [Elizabeth Knapp] that was afflicted. There was as much ground to countenance the Groton woman, and imprison on her accusations, as there is now to countenance these afflicted persons, and to imprison on their accusations. It is worthy of our deepest consideration, that in the conclusion, after multitudes have been imprisoned, and many have been put to death, these afflicted persons should admit that all was a mere fancy, as the Groton woman did."

[39] Wertenbaker, 269.

[40] Murdock, *Increase Mather*, 167.

[41] The Greek words . . . mean "with God," i.e., God willing. Unfortunately for Increase Mather, but fortunately for them, "the suspected persons took flight, not having been seen in that part of the world since."

[42] Cotton Mather understood Hebrew, Greek, Latin, Spanish, and Iroquois, and wrote in them all. From his diary, it appears that in one year he kept sixty fasts, and twenty vigils, and published fourteen books, besides discharging the duties of his pastoral office. His publications amount in number to 382. His style abounds with puns and strange conceits, and he makes a great display of learning. So pre-cious did he consider his time that, to prevent long visits, he placed the admonition "BE SHORT" over his study door.

[43] The titles *Mr.* and *Mrs.* were reserved for men and woman of rank, with *Mrs.* used for either married or single women as the title *Miss* did not exist at that time. The common titles for a married man and woman were *Goodman* and *Goodwife*. *Goody* was used as a familiar form of the title *Goodwife*.

[44] Cotton Mather (*Discourse*, 99) wrote, "Since there are Witches, we are to suppose that there are Devils too. It was the heresy of the ancient *Sadducees* in Act. 23:8. *The Sadducees do say, That there is neither Angel nor Spirit*. And there are multitudes of Sadducees yet in our day; fools that say, *Seeing is believing*; and will believe nothing but what they see."

[45] *The Book of Common Prayer* was authorized by the Church of England, and banned by the Puritans. The Church of England is also known as the Anglican church. After the American Revolution, the American branch was named the Episcopal church.

FURTHER READING

Biography

Cole, Franklin P. "Cotton Mather (1663-1728)." In *Mather Books & Portraits Through Six Early American Generations 1630-1831*, pp. 104-68. Portland, Ma.: Casco Printing Company, 1978.

   Biographical overview of Mather's life and career.

Wood, James Playsted. *The Admirable Cotton Mather*. New York: Seabury Press, 1971, 164 p.

   Overview of Mather's life and career with one chapter devoted to Mather's role in the Salem witch trials. Wood argues that despite evidence to the contrary, "the myth of [Mather's] responsibility for the cruel purge . . . has been happily accepted even by those who should know better."

Criticism

Bercovitch, Sacvan. "The Genetics of Salvation." In *The American Jeremiad*, pp. 86-92. Madison: University of Wisconsin Press, 1978.

   Describes the *Magnalia Christi Americana* as the "epitome of the seventeenth-century jeremiad" because of its "sevenfold division" and the "self-conscious isolation of the author from his audience."

Boas, Ralph and Louis Boas. *Cotton Mather: Keeper of the Puritan Conscience*. Hamden, Conn.: Archon Books, 1964, 271 p.

Examines Mather's ideas and place in Puritan society. In the chapter devoted to Mather's part in the Salem witch trials, the critics conclude that Mather should not be condemned for "not being ahead of his generation" but argue that "it is fair to blame him for not making a serious study of both sides of the question."

Bosco, Ronald A. An Introduction to *Paterna: The Autobiography of Cotton Mather,* edited by Ronald A. Bosco, pp. xiii-lxvii. Delmar, N.Y.: Scholars' Facsimiles & Reprints, 1976.

Discusses the composition and history of *Paterna,* Mather's motives for writing it, and the literary methods Mather employed in its composition.

Elliott, Emory. "The Reverend Cotton Mather." In *Power and the Pulpit in Puritan New England,* pp. 186-200. Princeton, N.J.: Princeton University Press, 1975.

Focuses on the themes of Mather's sermons, particularly his depictions of Satan.

Ford, Worthington Chauncey. A Preface to *Diary of Cotton Mather, Volume 1: 1681-1709,* pp. vii-xvii. New York: Frederick Ungar Publishing, 1957.

Remarks on Mather's ambitions and the historical context in which he lived.

Griswold, A. Whitney. "Three Puritans on Prosperity." *The New England Quarterly* 7 (March 1934): 475-93.

Discusses Mather's ideas on the relationship between business and religion.

Kagle, Steven E. "Cotton Mather (1663-1728)." In *American Diary Literature 1620-1799,* pp. 160-70. Boston: Twayne Publishers, 1979.

Discusses Mather's character and ideas through an examination of his diaries. Kagle argues that Mather's "need to question [religion] shows him to have been a more complex individual than one might have expected" from his public writings.

Levy, Babette M. "Witchcraft: Cotton Mather's Part in the 'Sad Errours' of 1692." In *Cotton Mather*, Boston: Twayne, 1979, pp. 56-73.

Examines Mather's role in the witch trials in Boston and Salem and places his beliefs and actions within the historical context of the period.

Lowance, Mason I., Jr. "Typology and the New England Way: Cotton Mather and the Exegesis of Biblical Types." *Early American Literature* IV, No. 1 (Summer 1969): 15-37.

Focuses on Mather's *Work upon the Ark, Magnalia Christi Americana,* and "Biblia Americana" in an examination of Mather's approach to Biblical exegesis and the "significance of exegetical typology to his reading of New England's history."

Manierre, William Reid, II. "Some Characteristic Mather Redactions." *The New England Quarterly* XXXI, No. 4 (December 1958): 496-505.

Discusses Mather's approach to borrowing information and phraseology from other sources and making the material his own, particularly as evidenced in *Magnalia Christi Americana.*

————. "Cotton Mather and the Biographical Parallel." *American Quarterly* XIII, No. 2 (Summer 1961): 153-60.

Examines Mather's use of literary and rhetorical devices in *Magnalia Christi Americana.* Manierre focuses primarily on Mather's use of "biographical parallels," the comparison of a "subject to some historical [or legendary] figure."

————. "A Description of *Paterna*: The Unpublished Autobiography of Cotton Mather." In *Studies in Bibliography: Papers of the Bibliographical Society of the University of Virginia,* Volume 18, edited by Fredson Bowers, pp. 183-205. Charlottesville: University Press of Virginia, 1965.

Argues that the publication and study of the *Paterna* would add little, if anything, to our understanding of Mather's character.

Middlekauff, Robert. "Book III: Cotton Mather (1663-1728): Prophecy." In *The Mathers: Three Generations of Puritan Intellectuals, 1596-1728,* pp. 191-368. New York: Oxford University Press, 1971.

Analysis of Mather's intellectual development, focusing on his efforts to achieve a synthesis of piety and reason.

Murdock, Kenneth B. An Introduction to *Selections from Cotton Mather,* edited by Kenneth B. Murdock, pp. ix-lviii. New York: Harcourt, Brace and Company, 1926.

Provides an overview of Mather's life and remarks on several of his works, including *Magnalia Christi Americana, The Christian Philosopher,* and *Political Fables.*

————. "Cotton Mather" and "The *Magnalia.*" In *Magnalia Christi Americana, Books I and II,* edited by Kenneth B. Murdock, pp. 1-48. Cambridge, Mass.: Belknap Press of Harvard University Press, 1977.

Presents a biographical overview and discusses the style and language of Mather's *Magnalia Christi.*

Poole, William Frederick. "Cotton Mather and Salem Witchcraft." *North American Review* CVIII, No. 223 (April 1869): 337-97.

Proposes to re-examine the "historical evidence on which . . . so large a portion of the culpability for these executions [during the Salem witch been laid upon one individual," Cotton Mather. Poole concludes that Mather was above all else doubtful and hesitant regarding the trials. "Mather believed in witchcraft, but disbelieved in the Salem methods of dealing with it."

Robinson, Enders A. "Cotton Mather, Clergyman." In *Salem Witchcraft and Hawthorne's House of the Seven Gables,* pp. 76-83. Bowie, Md.: Heritage Books, 1992.

Discusses Mather's career as a minister and Puritan leader, noting his efforts to perpetuate the Puritan theocracy and his role in the Salem witch trials.

Shea, Daniel B. "The *Paterna* of Cotton Mather." In *Spiritual Autobiography in Early America,* pp. 163-81. Madison: University of Wisconsin Press, 1988.

Examines Mather's motives, style, and criteria for selection in *Paterna.* Shea argues that "very little of *Paterna* properly belongs to the category of autobiography, if introspection and self-definition are held to be important criteria for the genre."

Silverman, Kenneth. "Letters of Thanks from Hell." In *The Life and Times of Cotton Mather,* pp. 83-137. New York: Harper & Row, 1984.

Detailed account of Mather's role in the Salem witch trials.

Smith, Peter H. "Politics and Sainthood: Biography by Cotton Mather." *William and Mary Quarterly* XX, No. 2 (April 1963): 186-206.

Examines Mather's approach to biographical writing, focusing on *Johannes in Eremo* and *Magnalia Christi Americana.* Smith argues that Mather's efforts followed the "traditional" didactic formula of Puritan biography and were also aimed at furthering various political interests.

Warren, Austin. "Grandfather Mather and His Wonder Book." *The Sewanee Review* LXXII, No. 1 (January-March 1964): 96-116.

Examines Mather's style in *Magnalia Christi Americana,* which Warren describes as "belatedly Baroque, as its author's view of the world is also dominantly . . . belatedly Baroque."

————. "Cotton Mather (1663-1728)." In his *The New England Conscience,* pp. 76-87. Ann Arbor: The University of Michigan Press, 1966.

Focuses on Mather's *Spiritual Diary* in his analysis of the author's consciousness and contends that Mather's interest in witchcraft and his promotion of smallpox vaccinations were minor incidents "in a busy life and scarcely touch him at the center."

Williams, George H. "The Idea of the Wilderness of the New World in Cotton Mather's *Magnalia Christi Americana.*" In *Magnalia Christi Americana, Books I and II,* edited Kenneth B. Murdock, pp. 49-58. Cambridge, Mass.: Belknap Press of Harvard University Press, 1977.

Discusses Mather's use of the wilderness experiences of the Israelites and early Christians in his account and explanation of the Puritan experience in the North American wilderness.

Additional coverage of Cotton Mather's life and career is contained in the following source published by Gale Research: *Dictionary of Literary Biography*, Vol. 24.

Increase Mather

1639-1723

American essayist and theologian.

INTRODUCTION

Increase Mather was a highly influential Puritan minister in seventeenth-century Massachusetts. The Puritans were a branch of the Congregationalist Church, more progressive than Presbyterians but less so than radical Protestants. Puritans wanted to reform the Church of England whereas Separatists, the other branch of Congregationalists, wanted to leave the Church altogether. Mather is the author of many religious, political, and scientific works; many were originally copied by members of his congregation for publication. His writings are studied today more for the historical insights they offer than for their literary merit. An influential church leader, Mather played a central role in the course of the Salem witch trials of the 1690s, using his *Cases of Conscience* (1692) to call for limiting the use of spectral evidence at the proceedings.

Biographical Information

Mather was born the youngest son of the influential Puritan minister Richard Mather and his wife, Katherine, on June 21, 1639. He entered Harvard College at the age of twelve, graduated in 1656, and delivered his first sermon on his eighteenth birthday, in 1657. He sailed for England later that year. His older brother Samuel had a congregation in Dublin, Ireland; Mather stayed there and entered Trinity College, from which he earned a Masters of Arts degree in 1658. He then worked as a preacher in England, serving churches at Devonshire, Gloucester, and Dorchester. He refused to convert to Anglicanism at the time of the Restoration, however, and instead returned to America to preach in 1661. He married his step-sister Maria Cotton the next year, and together they eventually had three sons and seven daughters. Mather also made his first major public appearance in 1662 as a delegate to an ecclesiastical synod. There he opposed his father and the clergy on the Half-Way Covenant, which would have made it easier to become a member of the church, because he believed that less-stringent requirements would weaken the role of the Church in society. Mather later reversed his stance on the issue and, in 1675, wrote *A Discourse Concerning the Subject of Baptisme* and *The First Principles of New England, Concerning the Subject of Baptisme and*

Communion of Churches, supporting the measure. Most historians believe that experience taught Mather that churches would not flourish unless they accepted new members. Mather received invitations from several congregations in New England but decided to stay in Boston and assume teachership of the Second, or North, Church in 1664. Mather had a lively, yet unscholarly, interest in scientific study. He attempted to use "pseudo-science" to explain contemporary natural phenomena in order to illustrate the power of God in all things. This enthusiasm for science prompted Mather to encourage its study while he was president of Harvard, a post he held from 1685 until 1701. During that time, he was chosen by regional Congregational churches to petition King William III for a new charter to replace the one withdrawn by the former monarch in 1683. Mather sailed for England in 1688 and remained there until 1692. With the new charter that Mather helped secure, the colonists lost their right to elect their own governors but retained the power to elect the representative assembly. The king allowed Mather to select the governor and other officers who would serve for the first year of the new government, subject to approval of the king. When Mather and the new governor, Sir William Phips, returned to Boston, many people there were under arrest for suspicion of witchcraft, and Phips appointed a court to try the accused. The court relied heavily on spectral evidence, and the public was divided over using such evidence as the sole basis for conviction and execution. Although Mather was a highly influential person by this time, he took no official stance on the trials until early that fall, when he was asked by several clergymen to render a decision regarding the admission of spectral evidence. By early October he had produced *Cases of Conscience Concerning Evil Spirits Personating Men*, a discourse on the use of spectral evidence in the Salem witch trials. In it, Mather argued that spectral evidence— testimony by a person who claims to have been afflicted by an accused person while the accused was in the form of a witch or ghost—was not sufficient evidence for execution. Mather's statement that it is better for ten witches to go free than for one innocent person to be executed, indicates to some critics that it was Mather's intention only to slow the rate of executions, since he stops short both of calling previous executions a mistake and of condemning the court. Today, critics tend to disagree about the impact of the *Cases of Conscience* on the witch trials. Some argue that Mather wisely used his influence to stop the trials; others believe he reacted too slowly and too passively. Critics also disagree on whether Mather's scientific reasoning helped or hindered his judgement on the trials. Most critics agree that *Cases of Conscience* played a major role in ending the witch trials. After the trials, Mather's political influence declined. He had chosen the governor and agreed to the charter, and when they proved unpopular, Mather became so, too. He resigned his position at Harvard in 1701 when his opponents demanded that he leave Boston and live in Cambridge; Mather chose instead to stay with his church. Maria Mather died in 1714, and in 1715 Increase married his nephew's widow, Ann Cotton. Mather's constant interest in science was again exercised in 1721 when he supported the controversial measure of inoculation for smallpox in *Several Reasons Proving that Inoculating or Transplanting the Small Pox, is a Lawful Practice*. He died in 1722.

Major Works

Mather wrote in several contemporary genres. His biography of his father, *The Life and Death of That Reverend Man of God, Mr. Richard Mather* (1669), is a characteristic Puritan biography, glorifying the life of the subject rather than offering a factual portrayal of it. In 1675, Mather, who had previously opposed the Half-Way Covenant, wrote two books supporting the measure, which called for less-stringent requirements in order to become a member of the church: *A Discourse Concerning the Subject of Baptisme* and *The First Principles of New England*. Both of these writings are considered valuable for their insights into the intellectual battle grounds of New England.

One of the goals of Mather's religious writings was to show that political disorder and natural disturbances such as storms and droughts were visible evidence of sinfulness in the colony. In *The Day of Trouble is Near* (1674), Mather drew correlations between God's wrath as incurred by the second generation of Israelites in the Old Testament, and the spiritual troubles of New England. These similarities, Mather wrote, foretold of imminent, apocalyptical destruction. He also used contemporary events to arouse fear in his congregation in *The Times of Man are in the Hands of God* (1675), when he preached that the recent destruction of a ship in Boston Harbor was an example of fiery destruction that precedes the "general calamity" told of in the Bible. In addition to arousing fear and guilt in church members, Mather used his pulpit to attack the younger generation of Puritans. The sins of youth, Mather argued, were externally apparent in the changing fashions of clothing of young women and hair length of young men.

Mather's interest in science, particularly comets, prompted him to pen several sermons regarding celestial events. Both *Heaven's Alarm to the World* (1681) and *Kometographia. Or a Discourse Concerning Comets* (1683) discuss comets and other cosmic events. In *Heaven's Alarm*, Mather asserted that one of the roles of a minister is to interpret signs seen in stars and comets, which he said were used by God as warnings of coming disasters. *The Latter Sign* (1682) was also a sermon on comets, given during an appearance of what is now known as Halley's comet. Both *Heaven's Alarm* and *Latter Sign* were reprinted in 1683 in a longer book, *Kometographia*. In that book, Mather used the scientific method to illustrate how God's providence is evident in nature.

A less scientific but more literary work is *An Essay For the Recording of Illustrious Providences*, often considered by critics as Mather's greatest literary piece; he used a crude scientific method to reach conclusions about nature that depended on theology. Mather carefully documented dramatic, potentially disastrous stories told to him by both acquaintances and strangers, and concluded that happy outcomes were brought about by the grace of God's intervention. In *Illustrious Providences*, Mather recounted tales of the power of Satan, as well as tales of phenomena that were considered to be events of witchcraft. Mather did not refute witchcraft but instead contended that supernatural events can be inspired by Satan as well as by God. *Illustrious Providences* was written eight years before the witch trials began at Salem, and very few historians link the hysteria of the trials to its publication. Mather did, however, draw upon it eight years later when he wrote *Cases of Conscience* at the height of the Salem trials. In *Cases of Conscience*, Mather again emphasized that Satan can control earthly events to harm man in the same way God can control them to benefit man. Therefore, the accusers could also be afflicted by Satan, and could then condemn innocent people. For this reason, among others, Mather wrote that while spectral evidence may be useful for raising suspicion of witchcraft, it should not be the sole determinate of guilt. *Cases of Conscience* was finished in early October, 1692, and presented to Governor Phips before being published. Public opposition had been growing to the trials, which had led to the executions of twenty people. In late October, Phips dismissed the court he had assigned. Critics widely believe that *Cases of Conscience* heavily influenced Phips's decision.

Critical Reception

To Mather's congregation, he was a well-respected man who could inspire fear, guilt, and loyalty in the people he led. Mather was popular enough to be appointed president of Harvard College and an ambassador to King William III when the colony needed a new charter. But contemporary opponents of Mather charged that he was too rigid and dogmatic and also held him responsible for the unsuccessful administration of Phips, whom Mather had chosen as governor. Mather's writings continue to be important to historians: his disciplined work habits resulted in a voluminous body of writings that record human, natural, and celestial events, and they provide a first-hand look at colonial life of his age.

PRINCIPAL WORKS

The Life and Death of That Reverend Man of God, Mr. Richard Mather. . . (biography) 1669

The Day of Trouble Is Near (theology) 1674

A Discourse Concerning the Subject of Baptisme Wherein the present Controversies, that are agitated in the New England Churches are from Scripture and Reason modestly enquired into (theology) 1675

The First Principles of New-England, Concerning The Subject of Baptisme and Communion of Churches. . . (theology) 1675

The Times of Man are in the Hands of God (theology) 1675

Heaven's Alarm to the World. Or A Sermon Wherein is Shewed, That fearful Sights and Signs in Heaven are the Presages of great Calamities at hand (sermon) 1681

The Latter Sign (sermon) 1682

Kometographia. Or A Discourse Concerning Comets. . . (theology / science) 1683

An Essay For the Recording of Illustrious Providences, Wherein an Account is given of many Remarkable and very Memorable Events, which have happened in this last Age: Especially in New-England (prose) 1684

Cases of Conscience Concerning evil Spirits Personating Men, Witchcraft, infallible Proofs of Guiilt in such as are accused with that Crime. . . (theology / political) 1692

Several Reasons Proving that Inoculating or Transplanting the Small Pox, is a Lawful Practice, and that has been Blessed by God for the Saving of many a life (science / theology) 1721

CRITICISM

Moses Coit Tyler (essay date 1878)

SOURCE: "Virginia: Its Literature During the Remainder of the First Period," in *A History of American Literature*, Vol. I, 1878. Reprint by G. P. Putnam's Sons, 1881, pp. 60-92.

[*In the following excerpt, first published in 1878, Tyler praises Mather for his simple, straightforward literary style.*]

. . . Of the six sons of Richard Mather, four became famous preachers, two of them in Ireland and in England, other two in New England; the greatest of them all being the youngest, born at Dorchester, June twenty-first, 1639, and at his birth adorned with the name of Increase, in grateful recognition of "the increase of every sort, wherewith God favored the country about the time of his nativity."[2]

Even in childhood he began to display the strong and eager traits that gave distinction and power to his whole life, and that bore him impetuously through the warfare of eighty-four mortal years. At twelve, he entered Harvard College, taking his Bachelor's degree at seventeen. His Latin oration, at Commencement, was so vigorous an assault upon the philosophy of Aristotle, that President Chauncey would have stopped him, had not the Cambridge pastor, Jonathan Mitchell—a man of great authority—cried out in intercession, "Pergat, quaeso, nam doctissime disputat." In 1657, on his nineteenth birthday, he preached in his father's pulpit his first sermon,—a sermon so able in matter and in manner, that it greatly added to the general belief that here was a youth from whom more was to be heard by and by. Twelve days afterward, he sailed for Dublin, where his eldest brother, Samuel, was a noted preacher, and where, entering himself as a student of Trinity College, he took, with high reputation, his Master's degree in the following year,—declining a fellowship. During the subsequent three years, he exercised his talents as a preacher, with great effect, in various parts of England and in Guernsey; and in 1661, not deeming the outlook an agreeable one, just then, for dissenters in the mother-country, he abandoned his purpose of making a career there, and returned to his native land.

At once, invitations poured in upon him from "as many places as there are signs for the sun in the Zodiac." Declining to be settled anywhere in haste, he divided his services between his father's church at Dorchester and the North Church of Boston; and at last, in May, 1664, he consented to be made minister of the latter church, which, thenceforward, to the end of his own life, and to the end of the life of his more famous son, continued to be the tower and the stronghold of the Mathers in America.

Thus, before his twenty-sixth birthday, Increase Mather had found the place of his work for life,—a prominent pulpit in the chief town of the New England theocracy. There, wielding the most tremendous weapon of influence known in such a community, he continued to fulminate, to the delight of his adherents, to the great terror of his foes, for almost sixty years; and by force of his learning, his logic, his sense, his eloquence, his tireless energy, his adroitness in intrigue, his sagacity and audacity in partisan command, he became, during the first thirty years of that time, the most powerful man in all that part of the world. In the desperate conflict in which Massachusetts contended with James the Second for its own existence, Increase Mather was a potent counsellor of the people; and for several years, as the representative of his colony at the court of James, and of William and Mary, the Boston pastor proved himself an able and successful diplomate. For sixteen years, also, he filled the high office of president of Harvard College, without ceasing to be pastor of North Church. From about 1694 and until his death in 1723, his political prestige, even his ecclesiastical prestige, greatly declined; yet to the last, he was a sovereign man throughout New England, illustrious for great talents and great services, both at home and abroad.

Here, then, was a person, born in America, bred in America,—a clean specimen of what America could do for itself in the way of keeping up the brave stock of its first imported citizens; a man every way capable of filling any place in public leadership made vacant by the greatest of the Fathers; probably not a whit behind the best of them in scholarship, in eloquence, in breadth of view, in knowledge of affairs, in every sort of efficiency.

As to learning, it has been said[3] that he even exceeded all other New-Englanders of the colonial time, except his own son, Cotton. On the day when he was graduated at our little rustic university, he had the accomplishments usual among the best scholars of the best universities of the old world; he could converse fluently in Latin, and could read and write Hebrew and Greek;

and his numberless publications in after life bear marks of a range of learned reading that widened as he went on in years, and drew into its hospitable gulf some portions of nearly all literatures, especially the most obscure and uncouth.

His habits as a student were those of the mighty theologians and pulpit-orators among whom he grew up. He had the appalling capacity of working in his study sixteen hours a day. One now contemplates with a mixture of admiration and horror—alleviated by incredulity—the picture that has been left us by filial hands, of one of this man's ordinary working-days: "In the morning, repairing to his study (where his custom was to sit up very late, even until midnight and perhaps after it) he deliberately read a chapter, and made a prayer, and then plied what of reading and writing he had before him. At nine o'clock, he came down and read a chapter, and made a prayer with his family. He then returned unto the work of the study. Coming down to dinner, he quickly went up again, and begun the afternoon with another prayer. There he went on with the work of the study till the evening. Then with another prayer he again went unto his Father; after which he did more at the work of the study. At nine o'clock, he came down to his family sacrifices. Then he went up again to the work of the study, which anon he concluded with another prayer; and so he betook himself unto his repose."[4]

His power as a pulpit-orator was very great, and it was bought at a great price. On Monday morning he began his sermons for the next Sunday, and continued to work upon them diligently until Friday night; on Saturday he committed them to memory. Of course, on Sunday, armed thus at every point, he could march into his pulpit with confident tread. Using no manuscript, he spoke without hesitation, "with a grave and wise deliberation," often with impassioned vehemence. He had, like his father, a commanding voice; and he used it with great effect, at times, indeed, "with such a tonitruous cogency that the hearers would be struck with an awe, like what would be produced on the fall of thunderbolts."[5] It was a common saying of his contemporaries, that Increase Mather was "a complete preacher."

From a literary point of view, his writings certainly have considerable merit. His style is far better than that of his son,—simpler, more terse, more sinewy and direct, less bedraggled in the dust of pedantry; it has remarkable energy; in many places it is so modern in tone that it would not seem strange in any pulpit now, except for the numerous quotations from Scripture, as well as for an occasional use of some Latin or Greek or Hebrew phrase. Thus, depicting the victory of Christ over the Devil, the preacher exclaims: "He has led captivity captive. He has disarmed the Devil and all his angels, and, as it were, tied them to his triumphal chariot, and exposed them openly in the sight of heaven and earth."[6] The worth of a human soul—that enticing and ineffable theme of pulpit-rhetoric in every age—he proclaims in this pithy and vivid manner: "One soul is of more worth than all the world. . . . Every man has . . . a body that must die, and shall die, and a soul that shall never die. To save such a soul is a mightier thing than to save all the bodies in the world."[7] In the battle of life, here upon the earth, we are not engaged, he tells us, in an obscure field, or unwatched by throngs of spectators: "Let us always remember what eyes are upon us. There are glorious eyes, which, though we see not them, are observing us in all our motions. The eyes of holy angels are upon us. . . . And the eyes of Jesus Christ, the Son of God, behold us. . . . And the eyes of God behold us. . . . It is reported of a faithful minister of Christ, that there was written on the walls of his study, 'Deus videt, angeli adstant, conscientia testabitur,'—God seeth thee, angels are by thee, thy own conscience will be a witness how thou dost behave thyself."[8] Sometimes, he casts his thought into an illustration so luminous and so shrewd that it makes further argument unnecessary; as when he says of the government of Massachusetts under Sir Edmund Andros: "The Foxes were now made the administrators of justice to the Poultry."

The publications of Increase Mather defy mention, except in the form of a catalogue. From the year 1669, when he had reached the age of thirty, until the year 1723, when he died, hardly a twelvemonth was permitted to pass in which he did not solicit the public attention through the press. An authentic list of his works would include at least ninety-two titles.[9] The most of these works are sermons; but as sermons, they sweep the entire circuit of themes, sacred and secular, on which men employed their thoughts in those days,— divinity, ethics, casuistry, church government, law, English and American politics, history, prophecy, demonology, angelology, crime, poverty, ignorance, dancing, the Indian question, earthquakes, comets, winds, conflagrations, drunkenness, and the small-pox.

Of all the great host of Increase Mather's publications, perhaps only one can be said to have still any power of walking alive on the earth,—the book commonly known by a name not given to it by the author, "*Remarkable Providences*." The origin of this book is worth mention. As early as 1658, a number of Puritan ministers in England and in Ireland combined to put on record, and finally to publish, authentic accounts of extraordinary interpositions of Providence in recent human affairs. After some progress had been made in the work, it was dropped. Subsequently, the manuscript was sent to New England, probably by Milton's friend, Samuel Hartlib. For many years it lay in obscurity in Boston, until, by good fortune, it fell into the energetic hands of Increase Mather. The plan was exactly suited to a mind like his; and after communicating it to his clerical brethren, and receiving their cordial encouragement to go on with it, he sent forth proposals through New England, calling upon ministers and other reputable persons to forward to him written narratives of Providential events that had occurred under their own observation. In 1684, the book was published, under the title of *An Essay for the Recording of Illustrious Providences*.[10] Thus the work is simply a compilation of anecdotes sent to the editor, or culled by him from his own observation and from books, the whole being plentifully decorated with comments and speculations of his own. The materials are classified under these topics: "remarkable sea-deliverances;" "some other remarkable preservations;" "remarkables about thunder and lightning;" "things preternatural which have happened in New England;" "demons and possessed persons;" "apparitions;" "deaf and dumb persons;" remarkable tempests, earthquakes, and floods in New England; remarkable judgments upon Quakers, drunkards, and enemies of the church; finally, "some remarkables at Norwich in New England." It cannot be denied that the conception of the book is thoroughly scientific; for it is to prove by induction the actual presence of supernatural forces in the world. Its chief defect, of course, is its lack of all cross-examination of the witnesses, and of all critical inspection of their testimony, together with a palpable eagerness on the author's part to welcome, from any quarter of the earth or sea or sky, any messenger whatever, who may be seen hurrying toward Boston with his mouth full of marvels. The narratives, often vividly told, are tragic, or amusing, or disgusting, now and then merely stupid; in several particulars they anticipate the phenomena of modern spiritualism; while the philosophical disquisitions of the author are at once a laughable and an instructive memorial of the mental habits of very orthodox and very enlightened people in Protestant Christendom, in the seventeenth century.

Notes

. . . [2] C. Mather, "Parentator," 1-5.

[3] By Enoch Pond, "Life of I. Mather," 142.

[4] C. Mather, "Parentator," 181.

[5] Ibid. 216.

[6] "Several Sermons," 13.

[7] Ibid. 13-14.

[8] Sermon on death of Rev. John Baily, 6-7.

[9] One list is given in W. B. Sprague, "Annals of Am. Pulpit," I. 156-157; another and better list in J.

L. Sibley, "Harv. Grad." I. 438-463.

[10] Reprinted, London, 1856.

Williston Walker (essay date 1901)

SOURCE: "Increase Mather," in *Ten New England Leaders,* Silver, Burnett and Company, 1901, pp. 175-213.

[*In the following excerpt, Walker offers an overview of Mather's life, paying particular attention to the influences on Mather as a young man, and to his conflicts with Harvard College in his later years.*]

. . . Increase Mather was born on June 21, 1639, in that home in Dorchester into which we have already glanced in considering the career of his father, Richard. Popular tradition represents Puritan names as Biblical or fantastically religious to a degree not true of them in general. If one looks over a list of Puritan emigrants or a catalogue of early church members, one finds it made up chiefly, in reality, of the Williams, the Johns, the Edwards, the Henrys, the Richards, the Thomases, in which Anglo-Saxon parents have delighted certainly since the Norman conquest. But occasionally you will meet an odd exception, and the child whose story we are beginning received his name, we are told, "because of the never-to-be-forgotten *Increase,* of every sort, wherewith GOD favored the Country, about the time of his Nativity."[2] The boy whose name was thus bestowed was the youngest of six children,—all sons,—five of whom grew to maturity, and four of whom entered the ministry, doing service of much more than ordinary conspicuity. The household atmosphere into which he was ushered, that subtle environment which determines for so many of us what we are to be, made the path of scholarship and of Christian service easy for him. His father's character and studious habits we have already considered; and his mother had no lower ideals for her boy. "Child," she was wont to say to him, "if GOD make thee a Good Christian and a Good Scholar, thou hast all that ever thy Mother Asked for thee."[3] The mother's desires for his scholarship were early fulfilled, for, at the age of twelve, the son entered Harvard. . . .

In Mather's case, however, his residence at Harvard was interrupted by ill-health, and probably half his college course, if not more, was pursued in the household and under the instruction of that ablest dialectician among the early New England ministers, Rev. John Norton, at first at Ipswich, and then at Boston, where Norton succeeded Cotton in the care of the First Church.[4] Here at Boston, and in Norton's home, occurred, in 1654, the spiritual turning-point in Increase Mather's history. That experience was strenuous enough. Illness had laid its hand on the fifteen-year-

old boy, and turned his thoughts Godward; but a sense of his own sinfulness overcame him. He prayed, he fasted, he wrote out a catalogue of his particular offenses; but he felt no peace of mind. He feared that he "Was Guilty of the Unpardonable Sin." At length in his distress the boy made use of the absence of his fellow pupils from Norton's house on election day, in a way that he later described in the following words:[5]

I took this Opportunity of a Private Chamber; and shutting the Door, I spent all the Day, in Pouring out my Complaints unto the Lord. Towards the Close of the Day, being full of Extremity of Anguish in my Soul because of my Sin, it was put into my Heart, that I must go and throw myself down at the Feet of my Saviour, and see whether He would Accept of me, or no; . . . So I came before Him with those Words of *Esther, If I Perish, I Perish, Yet,* (I said) *Lord, if it must be so, I am resolved to Perish at the Feet of thy Mercy. It is true, I am a Dog, and indeed unworthy of so much as a Crumb; I have been a great Sinner; Yet I am resolved, I will not Offend any more, but be Thine, and be Thine only, and be Thine forever.* And while I was thus Praying and Pleading, those Words of CHRIST were darted into my Mind, *Him that cometh unto me I will in no wise Cast out.* . . . After that I had some *Comfortable Perswasion* that my Sins were Pardoned.

But the poor boy's hard-won peace of mind was soon shaken, for Norton preached a sermon in which he advanced the view often inculcated by the founders of New England, and notably by Thomas Hooker, "That a man might *Forsake* his Sins, and have been in some *Sorrow of Heart* for them, and yet not be *truly Converted* unto GOD." That was a staggering thought, and it was not till he had heard other sermons, from his father and from the "matchless" Jonathan Mitchell, that comfort came to him at last. Nor was there anything unusual in this intensity of struggle, this sense of guilt, or this self-distrust even in a school-boy. We have already observed something similar in the case of others whose story we have considered. The preaching of early New England taught it as the normal mode of entrance into the Kingdom of God, and represented not merely that the path of conversion was difficult and open to but few, but that it was surrounded by pitfalls of self-deception, which only the most rigid scrutiny of the motives and intents of the heart could guard against.

Graduation came in 1656, and on his eighteenth birthday, in 1657, Mather preached his first sermon.[6] But the favor shown to New Englanders by Cromwell made the home country very attractive to Harvard graduates desirous of a career.[7] Many had gone thither; among them Increase Mather's two older brothers, Samuel, who had settled over an important congregation in Dublin, and Nathanael, who had obtained a living at

Barnstaple in Devonshire. At Samuel's invitation, Increase now sailed for England, on July 3, 1657, less than two weeks after the delivery of his first sermon; and, on reaching Dublin, entered Trinity College, where he graduated Master of Arts in 1658.[8] His decided pulpit gifts brought him into notice, and the succeeding winter was spent by Mather in supplying the congregation left temporarily vacant at Great Torrington by the absence of its pastor, John Howe, on chaplain's duty at the court of Richard Cromwell. The spring of 1659 saw his appointment, at less than twenty years of age, as garrison chaplain on the island of Guernsey, a post which he held till the Restoration made it untenable in March, 1661. The young preacher was popular. He was urged to conform, as some of his fellow graduates of Harvard had done. A living of £400, at least fourfold any salary he could hope for in New England, was offered him; but his conscience would not allow him to use the Prayer Book, and on June 29, 1661, he left England, surprising his father by his unheralded arrival in the Dorchester home on August 31st, and his father's congregation by preaching to them the next morning.[9] A sermon before the Second Church in Boston a week later was followed by a call to its charge; but the young minister's deliberations were distracted by invitations from eleven other congregations,[10] and by the strongly cherished hope that the political situation in the home land would permit him to resume his ministry there, so that it was not till May 27, 1664, that he was ordained, by his father, Richard Mather, and his colleague, Rev. John Mayo, to the teachership of the Second, or, as it was generally called, the North, Church in Boston, which was to be his post of influence till his death, fifty-nine years later. The site of this meeting-house, now North Square, is in the densely populated foreign section of modern Boston, where Puritan or even Anglo-Saxon occupants of ancient days have scarcely left a trace behind; but under Mather's leadership, it was then the most largely frequented place of worship in the little colonial seaport.

While Increase Mather was debating this call, he had his first experience of public service for the churches, being sent by his father's church at Dorchester as a delegate to the Synod of 1662, where the Half-Way Covenant was approved, as has already been described in narrating the life of Richard Mather. It will be recalled that the youthful delegate opposed the result reached by the majority, and defended by his father; but on the point at issue he speedily changed his mind, and, certainly from 1671 onward, there was in New England no more devoted champion than Increase Mather of the rather dubious spiritual expedient for benefiting the young which the Synod had approved and he had originally opposed.[11]

It was in this time of waiting, also, on March 6, 1662, that Increase Mather married his stepsister, Mary, daughter of John Cotton, whose widow, the mother of the bride of twenty years of age, had married his father, Richard Mather. She bore him ten children; and when death took her from him, in his old age, after fifty-two years of life together, he married, in 1715, the widow of her nephew, the third to bear the name of John Cotton in the New England ministry.[12]

But, though settled over a growing church, the early years of his ministry were a trying time for the young teacher and his household. As we have already seen was the case with his father, serious religious doubts, even to the extent of questioning the existence of God, assailed him. His ill-paid salary, in the earlier years of his ministry, left him under a constant burden of anxiety by reason of debt. "I could be Content to be *Poor,* I care not how *Poor,*" he wrote in his journal; "But to be *in Debt,* to the Dishonour of the Gospel, is a *Wounding, Killing* Thought to me; Yea, so Grievous as that if it be not Remedied, in a little time it will bring me with Sorrow to my Grave."

But as time went on his spiritual perplexities vanished, and the increase of his congregation under his successful ministry, together with the generosity of a few friends, at length placed him in circumstances of pecuniary comfort.[13]

As a pastor Increase Mather was most laborious; though we should probably think as some did in his own day, disproportionately devoted to his study rather than to the visitation of his flock. But Mather always believed the pulpit the seat of ministerial power, and he made most elaborate preparation for its duties. His son Cotton records,[14] that sixteen hours of the twenty-four were usually devoted to mental labor.

> His *Daily Course* was This. . . . In the Morning repairing to his Study, (where his Custom was to sit up very late, even *until* Midnight, and perhaps *after* it) he deliberately Read a *Chapter,* and made a *Prayer,* and then plied what of Reading and Writing he had before him. At Nine a Clock he came down, and Read a *Chapter* and made a *Prayer,* with his Family. He then returned unto the *Work of the Study.* Coming down to *Dinner,* he quickly went up again, and begun the Afternoon with another *Prayer.* Then he went on with the *Work of the Study* till the Evening. Then with another *Prayer* he went again unto his Father: after which he did more at the *Work of the Study.* At Nine a Clock he came down to his *Family-Sacrifices.* Then he went up again to the *Work of the Study;* which anon he Concluded with another *Prayer;* and so betook himself unto his Repose.

It makes one ache with sympathy to think of this Puritan scholar, toiling over his plain desk, by daylight or by the dim light of a candle, without exercise, and with scanty interruption for the necessary food, the laborious round broken only by his frequent and methodical devotions. No wonder that, under the special strain of his father's death, in 1669, he so fell into what Cotton Mather calls "that Comprehensive Mischief which they call *The Hypocondriac Affection,* that," for a time, "his Recovery to any Service, was by many very much Despaired of."[15]

But perhaps you would like to know a little more in detail how Increase Mather mapped out his toilsome week. He has left a record of its allotment of time.[16] On Sundays he preached, and catechised his family. Monday was dedicated to the study of his coming sermons, with a slight break, devoted to general reading after dinner. Tuesday saw the sermons continued through the morning, while in the afternoon he sought "to *Instruct Personally* some or other"; Wednesday was again devoted to his sermons and his books; a labor which was resumed the next morning; though a respite came on Thursday afternoon by the necessity of attending, and frequently conducting, the Thursday lecture, which was then the sole midweek service of the Boston churches. After the lecture Mather was accustomed to hold, with the other pastors of Boston and vicinity, what would now be called a ministers' meeting. Friday was again spent on the sermons and in general reading; and Saturday was largely devoted to memorizing the discourses to which so large a part of the week had been dedicated, for, though Mather wrote out all that he preached with painstaking minuteness, he left his manuscript behind him when he went into the pulpit. His delivery was clear, his strong, sonorous voice was used with deliberate gravity, and his manner, though powerfully impressive, was extremely simple and non-oratorical. In the pulpit he was deemed a master always.

It would be natural to imagine, from what I have just said, that Increase Mather was a recluse, persuasive in the pulpit, perhaps, but dwelling apart from men, shut away in his study from the concerns of the world about it. No conclusion could be more mistaken. Certain it is that he labored with almost the persistence of a bookworm in the room in which most of his waking hours were spent; but it is equally undeniable that no man in the New England ministry of his day had so great an influence over his professional brethren, the churches that they served, the educational interests that they held dear, or the political fortunes of the commonwealth as Increase Mather, nor could all his weeks have been mapped out like that just recorded. A brief consideration of four or five of the most striking instances of this activity for what he deemed the general good will illustrate the leadership which it was possible for a minister to attain in early New England.

Mather's first conspicuous appearance as the leader of the Massachusetts churches was in connection with the so-called "Reforming Synod" of 1679 and 1680.[17] To a man of his warm spiritual nature, pastoral zeal, and

conservative devotion to the ideals of early New England, the spiritual tendencies of the age in which his ministry was cast were distressing. The old Puritan movement had largely spent its force. The spiritual life of the second New England generation was distinctly lower in vitality than that of its fathers. Men looked back on the years of colonial beginnings with their fresh enthusiasms, their self-sacrifice and their spiritual power as a golden age of better things, and not wholly without reason. The decline was undeniable. Preaching in 1668, for instance, William Stoughton,[18] later Lieutenant-Governor, exclaimed in his election sermon:

> O what a sad Metamorphosis hath there of later years passed upon us in these Churches and Plantations. The first generation have been ripened time after time, and most of them geathred in as shocks of corn in their season. . . . Whilest they lived their Piety and Zeal, their Light and Life, their Counsels and Authority, their Examples and Awe kept us right . . . . but now that they are dead and gone, Ah how doth the unsoundness, the rottenness and hypocrisie of too many amongst us make it self known.

Ten years later Increase Mather told his Boston congregation:[19]

> "Prayer is needful on this Account, in that Conversions are becoming rare in this Age of the World. They that have their thoughts exercised in discerning things of this Nature have had sad apprehensions with reference to this Matter; that the Work of Conversion hath been at a great Stand in the World."

Nor was it only the decay of active piety that caused concern. The rough contact with the wilderness lowered the tone of the sons and daughters of the emigrants; the passion for land led the settlers to spread themselves over the country in a way that made education and the maintenance of religious institutions difficult problems. And the eighth decade of the seventeenth century was marked by losses and distresses heretofore unexampled in colonial history. In 1675 and 1676 the struggle known as Philip's war, which we have noted already in treating of Eliot's missionary activities, took its ghastly toll of property and life; in November, 1676, just after this struggle, Boston had its first great fire, Mather's own church and dwelling, together with the section of the town adjacent, being destroyed. This calamitous loss was followed by an even more disastrous fire in the business portion of the chief colonial seaport three years later. Epidemics of smallpox, failure of crops, and shipwrecks added to the general sense of calamity, and, as the Puritan divines interpreted these things, of divine displeasure.[20]

Under these circumstances Increase Mather persuaded eighteen of his ministerial associates, doubtless those assembled at the annual convention then held at the time of the election, to unite with him in a petition to the Massachusetts legislature for a Synod. The prayer was granted, the summons issued,[21] and on September 10, 1679, the body met at Boston. Though not the moderator at this session, Increase Mather was the life of the assembly. His pen formulated the conclusions, and when those results were presented to the legislature and by it commended to the attention of the churches, his voice preached "a very Potent Sermon, on the Danger of not being *Reformed by these things*."[22] The pamphlet embodying the Synod's conclusions, known as the ***Necessity of Reformation,*** is a most interesting witness to the religious state of New England, and to the questions which then awakened pastoral solicitude. Undoubtedly the picture it presents is too somber. It was designed to awaken and alarm. But enough of truth remains after all necessary deductions are made to make one query whether, indeed, the former days were better than these. Besides the general complaints of the "decay of the power of Godliness," pride, contention, intemperance, profaneness, lack of public spirit, untruthfulness, and "inordinate affection to the world," the catalogue of provocations to divine judgment enumerates certain special offenses, some of which, as charged on our ancestors of those supposedly stern and simple days, sound rather strangely.

> "Pride in respect to Apparel," the Synod through Mather[23] declared, "hath greatly abounded. Servants, and the poorer sort of People are notoriously guilty in the matter, who (too generally) goe above their estates and degrees, thereby transgressing the Laws both of God and man.... There is much Sabbath-breaking.... Walking abroad, and Travelling ... being a common practice on the Sabbath day, which is contrary unto that Rest enjoyned by the Commandment. Yea, some that attend their particular servile callings and employments after the Sabbath is begun, or before it is ended.... There are many Familyes that doe not pray to God constantly morning and evening, and many more wherein the Scriptures are not daily read.... Nay, children & Servants ... are not kept in due subjection; their Masters, and Parents especially, being sinfully indulgent towards them."

The remedies proposed, in order that God's anger might be averted from the suffering land, included a general "Renewal of the Covenant" in the churches, the enforcement of discipline, the better support of schools, a more efficient regulation of the liquor traffic, and "a full supply of Officers in the Churches, according to Christ's Institution." This last-named suggestion of amendment reminds us that, by 1679, the elaborate and supposedly exclusively Scriptural officering of churches with pastor, teacher, ruling elder and deacons, had largely given place to the more economical service of a single paid officer, the pastor, and the assistance of the deacons. In a few churches teachers

and ruling elders were long to survive, but in most they had disappeared already when this Synod met.

The evils against which the Synod labored were too deep-seated to be cured by any such palliative as it had to offer, though undoubtedly some good was accomplished. In general, the same state of religious decline continued till after Mather's death. But one more act of the Reforming Synod must be noted, in which, as in the work already described, Mather bore large share. The Cambridge Synod had approved the doctrinal portions of the Westminster Confession in 1648; but a generation had passed since that event and though no doctrinal discussion had intervened, the Reforming Synod, at its first session in 1679, appointed a committee, of which Mather was a member, to "draw up a Confession of faith," to be reported at a second session in May, 1680.[24] Mather and one other of this committee had been in England, when, in 1658, the representatives of the Congregational churches of that land had adopted a slight modification of the Westminster standard, known from their place of assembly in London as the "Savoy Confession." This creed, with one or two trifling emendations, was now adopted by the ministers and delegates, with a unanimity and an absence of debate which reveal clearly how little of departure from, or indeed of discussion of, the common Calvinism of the Puritan founders had yet developed in New England. Cotton Mather thus records[25] his father's share in its approval:

> Though there were many Elder, and some Famous, Persons in that Venerable Assembly, yet Mr. *Mather* was chosen their *Moderator*. He was then Ill, under the Approaches & Beginnings of a *Fever;* but so Intense was he on the *Business* to be done, that he forgot his *Illness;* and he kept them so close to their *Business,* that in *Two Days* they dispatch'd it: and he also Composed the *Præface* to the *Confession.*

So came into being the creed known usually as the "Confession of 1680," long regarded as the standard of the Massachusetts churches, though never imposed on them by governmental or ecclesiastical authority, and so venerated, in name at least, that it is referred to as one of the standards of Congregational belief in so comparatively recent a symbol as the "Burial Hill Declaration," adopted by the National Council of these churches in 1865.

Already the most conspicuous minister in New England, it was but natural that the trustees of Harvard College should turn to Mather when the presidency of that institution became vacant by the death of Urian Oakes in 1681. He declined at that time. But when death once more emptied the president's chair, he accepted the post; though continuing his Boston pastorate, a labor which was made lighter by the settlement of his eldest son, Cotton Mather, the same year, as colleague pastor of the church of which he was in title "teacher"—an intimate and almost fraternal association that was to last for more than thirty-eight years, and to be broken only by death.

The college of which Increase Mather thus became president was, as we have already seen, but a feeble plant, and his aid, though granted necessarily for but a fragment of his time, seems to have been of real value. Undoubtedly he considered his services to the college more indispensable than they were judged by others; but unquestionably, also, no man in the Massachusetts of that day was so well fitted to carry the institution safely through the troublous fifteen years during which he was its head. The actual work of instruction was largely in the hands of the tutors, John Leverett and William Brattle,[26] with whom, as we shall see later, Mather did not sympathize theologically. But the credit of bringing the college safely, and with increasing classes, through the crisis which deprived the institution, as well as the colony, of its charter, and left it long without a legal basis, as well as of securing for it the important gifts of Thomas Hollis, must be ascribed to Increase Mather. And the influence of this position on the churches can only be estimated when we remember that nearly all ministerial candidates in New England then received the training of the one New England college.

The time of Mather's accession to the presidency of Harvard was, indeed, one of concern for Massachusetts. The charter of 1629, conferring upon it, as interpreted by the colonists, nearly the powers of an independent state, had long been looked upon with disfavor by the Stuart sovereigns; and, in 1683, that opponent of the colonial liberties, Edward Randolph, had a writ served on the Massachusetts government summoning it to defend its charter from annulment by the English courts. Increase Mather vigorously encouraged resistance; and through his influence the lower house of the legislature and the Boston town meeting alike strenuously opposed the royal demand. The blow fell, nevertheless, for in June, 1684, the Court of Chancery at London vacated the charter. All Massachusetts institutions, the legislature, the courts, the college, the churches, even the tenure of private property, were deprived of their legal basis by this decision; and with the reign of James II., which began in February of the next year, Massachusetts soon chafed under the rule of the younger Dudley and of Sir Edmund Andros, and trembled with apprehension or realization at the abolition of personal, political, and property rights long held sacred.

To those in Massachusetts who looked with regret at the passing away of the old order it seemed that something might possibly be effected by a personal appeal to James II., whose undisguised Catholic sympathies disposed him to seek the support of all other English Non-conformists.[27] No man in the colony was so fitted for such a mission as Increase Mather, by reason of his conspicuity in the pulpit, his political principles, his acquaintance in England, where he had been an acceptable preacher, and his capacity to appear to advantage at court. His errand was suspected, and Randolph tried his best to arrest him; but on April 7, 1688, after more than a week of hiding, he got safely on shipboard,[28] and twenty-nine days later landed at the English Weymouth. James received Mather graciously, though he granted none of his requests;[29] but Mather cultivated the friendship of the chief of the Non-conformists and of the Whig leaders with such diligence that when, in the winter of 1688—1689, the throne of England passed to William and Mary he was in a position to present the case of the colonies to the new sovereigns. It needed all the persuasive arts of the colonial ambassador-in-chief, for William was jealous of colonial independence, and the two associates whom the Massachusetts legislature had sent over to assist Mather complicated his efforts by staking all on a restoration of the old charter, to which the King would not agree. So Mather fought out the battle single-handed, and on the whole very successfully. The charter which he obtained in the summer of 1691 was not all that he desired. It gave to the King, instead of to the colony, the right to appoint the highest officers of state; it reserved to him a right to reject distasteful laws; it allowed appeals to his higher English courts, and it granted freedom of worship to all Protestants. But though Mather would gladly have had these provisions other than they were, the new charter united Plymouth colony to Massachusetts, thus permanently preventing its dreaded annexation to New York; it left the legislature under the control of the people; reserved to it the public purse; preserved the local governments of the towns; and, by comfirming all grants heretofore made by the General Court, assured to individuals and the churches the possession of their property, and largely the maintenance of their ancient constitution.

Though Mather could not escape the criticism of those who wished the restoration of the old semi-independent and ecclesiastically exclusive government, many of whom looked upon him as a traitor for not securing more than he did, there can be no doubt that no Massachusetts man of that age could have obtained as much. It is not extravagant to affirm that he did more than any other man of his generation to maintain essentially operative, and to hand down to his successors, the civil and ecclesiastical institutions of New England, which without his efforts could not have escaped far more serious modification than they actually underwent in this trying time.

Mather's influence in this negotiation, and the impression of leadership among the citizens of Massachusetts which he made upon the English authorities is perhaps best illustrated by the fact that the royal government left the crown appointments at the initiation of the new provincial administration largely to his nomination.[30] The extent to which he used this influence to secure office for his friends and parishioners was unwise, and was the source of much later hostility to him. And, in general, it may be said that, while Mather did a work for Massachusetts of almost inestimable importance in this troubled time, he made more enemies than he could possibly have aroused in any other way, and the jealousies and antagonisms now engendered embittered his later life.

Increase Mather was not a man to forget his mission as a minister in the excitement of politics, and one incident of his English sojourn illustrates at once his freedom from ecclesiastical partisanship and his interest in religious affairs. The Toleration Act of 1689, passed during Mather's time of waiting in London, gave to Trinitarian Protestant Non-conformists a legal, though restricted, right to worship. Of the Non-conformist bodies the Presbyterian, of which Richard Baxter and John Howe were the guiding spirits, was the largest, the Congregationalists ranking next in size and counting about one half as many adherents. It was natural that this new-found freedom should awaken desire for the union of bodies so long under persecution, and this desire found expression primarily, it would appear, in London, where Increase Mather labored with his characteristic activity to bring Congregationalists and Presbyterians into confederation. To his efforts, more than to those of any other man, was due the union effected on April 6, 1691, by which these Dissenters in London became one body, and through the efforts of Flavel and others the movement spread rapidly to other parts of England. It had, indeed, no lasting history.[31] Closely related as Presbyterianism and Congregationalism are, they seem impossible of amalgamation, and this confederation was ruptured in 1694, two years after Mather's return to New England; but its written basis, the so-called "Heads of Agreement," crossed the Atlantic by Mather's influence, and, in 1708, was adopted, together with the *Saybrook Platform* of that year, as a legal basis of the churches of Connecticut—a position of political authority which it sustained in that commonwealth till 1784.

One event, closely connected in time with Mather's return from England, cannot be passed by in any estimate of his influence in New England—the grim witchcraft tragedy at Salem. Increase Mather's connection with it was, indeed, much more remote than that of his son Cotton. The excitement in the household of Rev. Samuel Parris, of what is now Danvers, with which the fanatic outburst opened, had begun in March, 1692, two months before Mather's return. But Cotton and Increase Mather were so one in spirit, that, in the public eye, all that the former did carried the sanction of the latter. There can be no doubt, also, that Increase Mather's *Illustrious Providences,* of 1684, contributed

to the popular belief in witchcraft, if not so powerfully as his son's *Memorable Providences, Relating to Witchcrafts and Possessions,* of 1689 and 1691. Increase Mather certainly could have done much, had he been so disposed, to check the witchcraft excitement, and he was enlightened enough to argue against the adequacy of several of the popularly accepted evidences of witchcraft in his *Cases of Conscience Concerning Evil Spirits;* but he as certainly believed in the possibility of compacts with the devil, and, as late as 1694, the Harvard trustees, under his leadership, issued an appeal to the ministers of New England for the collection of narratives of enchantments. He and his son Cotton tried their best to suppress that influential, if exceedingly personal, volume, the *More Wonders of the Invisible World,* of 1700, in which Robert Calef of Boston expressed a skepticism regarding witchcraft which all intelligent persons have since come to share. But there can be no doubt that Mather's belief in the reality of satanic possession was conscientious; and it had the support of many of the best men of his age on both sides of the Atlantic. Such a man as Richard Baxter, for instance, was no less strongly a believer in these supposedly supernatural manifestations. Yet, however we may excuse Increase Mather, the witchcraft episode is not a pleasant page in his story.

Mather may be said to have been at the height of his influence and popularity in 1692, the year of his return from England. In that year, the colonial legislature granted to Harvard College a new charter permitting the bestowment of the higher academic degrees, and under this charter, which was speedily annulled by the King, Harvard gave to Increase Mather the first doctorate of divinity ever granted in New England, and the title of Bachelor of Divinity to the two tutors, Brattle and Leverett, who had been associated with him. Not till 1771 was the doctor's degree given by Harvard again.[32]

But, as has been pointed out, Mather's great services to the colony had given offense no less than satisfaction, and the popular awakening from the witchcraft delusion reacted in considerable measure upon him. His friend and nominee for Governor, Sir William Phips, proved an unsuccessful administrator, and the difficulties of securing a proper charter for Harvard grew rather than decreased as successive efforts to this end were frustrated in 1692, 1696, 1697, 1699, and 1700. Mather's parish and his publications demanded so much of his time that he could only "Visit it [the college] once or twice every Week, and Continue there a Night or two";[33] and his opponents now made the very natural desire that Harvard should have a resident president the basis for an attack upon him. At successive sessions of the legislature, in 1693, 1695, and 1698, the wish was expressed by formal vote,[34] that Mather should remove from Boston to Cambridge; but he did nothing in the way of compliance, being naturally reluctant to leave the pulpit of the largest church in the colony for an exclusive devotion to the headship of a charterless college of two tutors and perhaps sixty students.

As the last decade of the seventeenth century drew to a close, however, the situation was further complicated by the rise of what may be styled a liberal movement in Boston and in Cambridge, though the modifications of usage and thought were so slight that it hardly deserves so pretentious a name.[35] Increase Mather, as has been pointed out, was strongly a conservative. Sincerely alarmed by the declining state of religion in the New England of his time, he considered a return to the old ways, an enforcement of discipline, and the perpetuation of the ideals of his early ministry the true method of fostering the religious life. How dark the situation of New England then seemed to him may be judged from a sentence or two in a sermon[36] preached before Harvard College on December 6, 1696:

> There is call to fear lest suddenly there will be no Colledge in New England; and this is a sign that ere long there will be no Churches there. I know there is a blessed day to the visible Church not far off; but it is the Judgment of very Learned men that in the Glorious Times promised to the Church on Earth, America will be Hell.

But there were others who regarded a modification of the usages of early New England as desirable. Most intimately connected with Mather of any of these were John Leverett and William Brattle, who, we have already seen, were long associated with him as tutors under his presidency, and had become trustees of the college in 1692. Leverett was a political force. In 1698 he had entered the legislature, where he rose to the speakership, and his classes, to accommodate his political duties, had had to meet at five in the morning.[37] William Brattle had become pastor of the Cambridge church in 1696. In hearty sympathy with his brother was Thomas Brattle, the Harvard treasurer, and with them stood Ebenezer Pemberton, a younger tutor at Harvard, and Benjamin Colman, a young ministerial candidate of the class of 1692. Probably the most significant change desired by these innovators was an abandonment of the early New England custom of requiring a public account, or relation, as it was styled, of religious experience from all who united with a church—a requirement consonant enough with the intense and conscious piety of the founders, but which the lowered tone of spiritual life had rendered irksome to many. They also wished that all baptized adults who contributed to a minister's support should share in his selection, and that any children presented by a Christian sponsor, whether parent or not, should be admitted to baptism. They furthermore desired an enrichment of the service by the devotional reading of some portion of the Scriptures, without explanatory comment,—a kind of Prayer-Book-like reading which the early Puritans had stigmatized as dumb reading,—and the occasional liturgical use of the Lord's Prayer. These modifications do not seem very radical to us, but to Mather they appeared full of peril. In 1697, he attacked the innovators' view of the needlessness of relations in a letter to the church at Cambridge of which Brattle was pastor, and to the students of the college; and three months later followed this charge into the enemy's camp by a protest from his church to that of Charlestown, which had chosen its minister in the way the innovators desired.

All this seemed dictatorial, and though undoubtedly conscientious, was none the less irritating. The result was that Thomas Brattle and some Boston sympathizers constructed a new meeting-house in Boston in 1698, called Benjamin Colman home from England to its pulpit, requesting him to procure ordination before sailing from more sympathetic hands than he would find among Mather's friends in Boston, and, on December 12, 1699, organized a new church—Brattle Church—without summoning the advice of any council, to occupy the meeting-house and to practice the innovations. These acts had the approval of the other members of the liberal party, and they called out from Increase Mather, in March, 1700, his most interesting contribution to Congregational history and polity—his *Order of the Gospel*. In this tract he condemned the Brattle Church principles, and declared that to approve them was to "give away the whole Congregational cause at once, and a great part of the Presbyterian Discipline also." He remarked, with pointed reference to Colman's English ordination, that, "to say that a Wandering Levite who has no Flock is a Pastor, is as good sense as to say, that he that has no Children is a Father"; and the allusion to his subordinates at the college was unmistakable in his exhortation, "Let the Churches Pray for the Colledge particularly, that God may ever Bless that Society with faithful Tutors that will be true to Christ's Interests and theirs, and not Hanker after new and loose wayes."[38]

Two ecclesiastical parties had evidently developed, and Mather's opponents were strong enough to have the question of his non-residence reopened by the legislature in July, 1700. Thus alarmed, he actually removed to Cambridge for a few months; but the absence from his family distressed him, and he proposed to the legislature that he continue on the non-residential basis on which his presidency had been actually placed so long. But while the representatives of the country towns supported him loyally in the lower house, sympathetic with his conservative position, the upper house, largely from Boston and vicinity, and hostile to him for many reasons, personal, political, and religious, on September 6, 1701, declined to approve Mather's continuance as president, and thus dropped him from the office which he had filled for sixteen years. How largely personal the action of the legislature was is shown by the fact that it immediately made Samuel Willard of the Boston Old South Church his successor on precisely the same terms of non-residence—the court keeping a show of consistency by calling him vice-president, instead of president.

To Mather the defeat was a bitter disappointment, and its gall and wormwood continued as long as he, and his son Cotton, his associate in the struggle, lived. Nor was it only the pain of a personal discomfiture or the disregard of services which Mather was conscious were well rendered and which seemed to him to deserve a better recompense. For, besides the personal motives which had entered into the struggle, his had been a serious and honest attempt to save the college from what he deemed essential spiritual harm, and defeat seemed the ruin of a cause which he believed to be that of the Gospel. But the defeat was none the less final. When Willard died, in 1707, Mather hoped that the office would come to him or to his son Cotton, but he hoped in vain. His innovating former subordinate, John Leverett, was the choice, and the bitterness of the disappointment was shown in a violent attack by father and son on Governor Joseph Dudley, whom they looked upon as responsible for this second shattering of their hopes.

Increase Mather was sixty-two years of age when he lost the presidency of Harvard, and what was to him far more important, when he saw in his own rejection the defeat of the conservative party for whose predominance in Church and State he labored. He had twenty-two years of life yet before him. Though he was to some extent passed by in the current of the age, though he felt the bitterness of disappointment always, and a sense that his services to the colony had not received the appreciation that their worth deserved, and thus his old age became in some considerable degree one of repining, it was a time of usefulness, fruitfulness, and honor to the end. The estimate in which he was held by his clerical brethren is shown by their unanimous choice of him in April, 1715, to bear the congratulatory address, then expected at the accession of a sovereign, to George I.—an honor which his age compelled him to decline.[39] His church valued his services and listened to him with pleasure so long as he was in physical strength to preach. His wisdom was much sought at councils and other ecclesiastical gatherings. And his activity with his pen was constant. In the case of the other leaders of early Congregationalism whom we have already considered I have attempted to give a fairly complete account of their writings. With Mather their number and variety make such a treatment impossible. Though the productions of his pen are far from equaling in number the four hundred and fifty-one titles attributed to his son, Cotton, they reach the sufficiently remarkable total of one hundred and fifty-nine.[40] Of these, more than one half were written after his retirement from the presidency of Harvard in 1701. Most are small in size, but many are considerable volumes, and the range of topics which they cover is as wide as their number is surprising. Some are sermons on events of public interest, fires, earthquakes, storms, comets, executions. Others are biographical sketches of deceased worthies, or narratives of important public events, like the Indian wars; yet others are political tracts, designed to present the New England cause, as he saw it, to New England's critics. Religious controversy has its ample place, of course, but by far the larger part of these volumes, great and small, have a distinctly edificatory aim, their prime purpose being to upbuild the spiritual life. Increase Mather's style, as compared with the curiously pedantic, whimsical diction of his son Cotton, was simple and direct, though with some tendencies toward the same aberrations that appear in the latter's writings. He reveals himself everywhere the man of learning and of wide observation of the world. Yet much of this literature is trite and uninteresting to modern readers. Much is commonplace. But it did not seem so then. The first New England newspaper that had any duration was not printed till 1704; few non-ministerial households had any volumes, save perhaps a Bible, an almanac, and a few treatises of the older Puritan divines. To such a generation writings like those of Mather came with all the freshness, timeliness, and interest of the modern religious newspaper. They met a real need; and in a way that made the New England of that day truly debtor to him who wrote.

Mather's tolerance grew with his years. In 1679, when he framed the conclusions of the Reforming Synod, he wrote of the Dissenters then in New England:[41]

> Men have set up their Threshold by Gods Threshold, and their Posts by his Post. Quakers are false Worshippers; and such Anabaptists as have risen up amongst us . . . do no better than set up an Altar against the Lords Altar.

But, in 1718, he shared in the ordination of Elisha Callender over the Baptist church in Boston; and in the Preface to the sermon which his son Cotton preached on the occasion he bore testimony that "all of the brethren of that church with whom I have any acquaintance . . . are, in the judgment of rational charity, godly persons."[42] His pecuniary generosity was unfailing. Besides the tenth of his income which he devoted to benevolence as a matter of conscience, he stood ready to render aid to the deserving; and the church over which he was pastor was noted for its liberality in gifts in that day when contributions for other than home expenses were unusual.

On entering the fiftieth year of his ministry, in 1713, Mather proffered his resignation to his people. Its acceptance was refused, though the church speedily voted that he should preach "only when he should feel himself able and inclin'd."[43] So, blessed in the kindly regard of his own congregation, and in the continued association of his son with him in his ministry and labors, whatever disappointments he may have felt over other circumstances of his later life, he gradually relaxed his hold on the world of which he had been so conspicuous a citizen. His enfeebled condition confined him to the house after September, 1719; the thought of his approaching rest in the presence of his Lord seemed increasingly attractive to him. To his London friend, Thomas Hollis, who had inquired if he were still in "the land of the living," he sent the message: "No! Tell him, I am going to it; This Poor World is the Land of the Dying. 'T is Heaven that is the true Land of the Living."[44] But, as in his father's case, his suffering was prolonged, and he died, after a distressing illness, but rejoicing in confidence of entrance into the eternal city, on August 23, 1723, at the ripe age of eighty-five. They honored him, so his son recorded, "with a Greater *Funeral* than had ever been seen for any *Divine*, in *these* . . . parts of the World";[45] and it was fitting that they should, for the Massachusetts of that day had lost its most gifted son.

Notes

. . . [2] Cotton Mather, *Parentator: Memoirs of Remarkables in the Life and the Death of . . . Increase Mather,* p. 5. Boston, 1724.

[3] *Ibid.,* p. 3.

[4] *Parentator,* p. 6.

[5] *Ibid.,* pp. 7-12; Chandler Robbins, *History of the Second Church . . . Boston,* pp. 18-19.

[6] *Parentator,* p. 15.

[7] See letter of Nathanael Mather, March, 1651, in Sibley, i., p. 157.

[8] *Parentator,* pp. 15-17.

[9] *Parentator,* pp. 17-23.

[10] *Ibid.,* pp. 23, 24; Chandler Robbins, *Hist. of the Second Church,* pp. 21, 22.

[11] Though Increase Mather's *First Principles of New England Concerning the Subject of Baptism* was printed in 1675, its Preface is dated 1671.

[12] Sibley, *Graduates of Harvard,* i., p. 437.

[13] On these troubles, see *Parentator,* pp. 26-36, and Chandler Robbins, *Second Church,* pp. 29-31.

[14] *Parentator,* p. 181.

[15] *Parentator,* p. 68.

[16] Quoted, *Parentator,* p. 38.

[17] A more minute account of the Reforming Synod and its work is given in Walker, *Creeds and Platforms,* pp. 409-439.

[18] *New Englands True Interest; Not to Lie,* etc. Cambridge, 1670.

[19] *Pray for the Rising Generation,* etc. Cambridge, 1678.

[20] See Preface to Increase Mather's *Returning unto God . . . A Sermon,* etc., Boston, 1680; and *Magnalia,* ii., p. 316.

[21] *Records . . . of Mass.,* v., p. 215.

[22] *Parentator,* p. 85; *Records . . . of Mass.,* v., p. 244.

[23] *Necessity of Reformation,* pp. 4-15.

[24] See Walker, *Creeds and Platforms,* p. 419.

[25] *Parentator,* p. 87; see also *Magnalia,* ii., p. 180.

[26] Sibley, *Graduates of Harvard,* iii., p. 181.

[27] For Mather's mission to England, see *The Andros Tracts,* ii. (Prince Society), Boston, 1869, edited by W. II. Whitmore. I have described this incident in *Papers of the American Society of Church History,* v., pp. 72-77, and in picturing it here have to some extent reproduced the language in which I have there told the story.

[28] Sewall, *Diary, v. Cell. Mass. Hist. Sec.,* v., pp. 209, 210.

[29] For these requests, see Hutchinson, *Hist. Mass. Bay,* pp. 367-369. London, 1765.

[30] *Parentator,* p. 144.

[31] The story is told at length in Walker, *Creeds and Platforms,* 440-462.

[32] *Parentator,* pp. 170-172; Sibley, *Graduates of Harvard,* i., pp. 424, 425.

[33] So Vice-President Willard summarized the duties, Sibley, ii., p. 22.

[34] Sibley, i., pp. 425-427.

[35] I have told this story at some length in the *Yale*

Review for May, 1892: and in *Creeds and Platforms,* pp. 465-483.

[36] Quoted in Sibley, i., p. 453, from *A Discourse Concerning the Uncertainty of the Times of Men.* Boston, 1697.

[37] Sibley, iii., p. 183.

[38] *Order of the Gospel,* pp. 8,. 11, 12, 102.

[39] *Parentator,* p. 194.

[40] A full list may be found in Sibley, i., pp. 438-469.

[41] *Necessity of Reformation,* p. 3.

[42] Backus, *Hist. of New England,* i., p. 421. 1871.

[43] *Parentator,* p. 197.

[44] *Ibid.,* p. 209.

[45] *Ibid.,* p. 211.

Kenneth Ballard Murdock (essay date 1925)

SOURCE: "Dolefull Witchcraft," in *Increase Mather: The Foremost American Puritan,* 1925. Reprint by Russell & Russell, 1966, pp. 287-316.

[*In the following excerpt from a work first published in 1925, Murdock recounts Mather's involvement in the witch trials and argues that Mather has been unfairly labeled throughout history as a proponent of the executions when he was instead a voice for temperance and moderation.*]

A month after his arrival home, Mather wrote to the Earl of Nottingham, thanking him for his efforts toward securing the charter, and assuring him "that the Generallity of their Maj[ties] Subjects (so far as I can understand) doe with all thank-fulness receive the favours which by the new Charter are granted to them." The General Court ordered a day of thanksgiving for the safe installation of the new government, and the return of "Mr. Increase Mather."[1] Thus far the new régime seemed welcome and secure.

When Phipps and Mather landed, there were, however, grave troubles not far from Boston, and from them grew a series of events which cloud the record of New England history as it is read to-day. In jail were several score of colonists, awaiting final trial on the heinous charge of witchcraft. One of Phipps's first problems was how they should be treated; and his decision, however it may have appeared at the time, has tended in our day to bring discredit on his whole administration.

Nowhere more than in the tale of the "witchcraft delusion" in New England, is it necessary to confine one's self to the few facts surely established in contemporary records. Nowhere are conjectures, opinions, or generalizations of later times more misleading. This is particularly true when we consider the relation of Cotton and Increase Mather to the whole affair; for, with the human tendency to find individual scapegoats for all errors of the past, later history has delighted in laying the "persecution" of the Salem witches at the door of the two Mathers. Cotton has suffered most, for few critics have been so uninfluenced by the facts known in regard to Increase, as not to modify their statements as to his "cruelty" and "superstition," leaving Cotton to the fore as the villain of the piece. Too many writers, however, have found it easiest to link father and son together, to accept the legend that Cotton was a worker of dark deeds, and, accordingly, to tar his father with the same brush.[2] Aside from the fact that the two men differed in temperament, that even their literary styles were unlike, and that their points of view on many questions were variously established, it would still be unjust to transfer Cotton's fancied faults to Increase merely because the two men stood in close blood relation.

For our purpose, fortunately, we may leave Cotton quite out of account, except in so far as Increase was obviously his partner in opinions or acts. Similarly, we may confide to physician, psychologist, or student of religious survivals, the explanation of just what was behind the strange behavior of certain Salem Village children, whose accusations brought many people to jail, and twenty to execution. And, best of all, we need not try to discuss or answer the many judgments passed on this chapter of New England history by writers viewing it from a later standpoint, with eyes opened by generations of scientific advance, except in so far as such judgments are based on facts which could have influenced the actors in the tragedy.

Very briefly, the story is that of a group of children in Salem Village, who, early in 1692, began to show signs of being tormented by agents of the devil. Their actions agreed with what was expected of victims of witchcraft, and their naming of their tormentors, and the popular excitement which ensued, led to the imprisonment of many citizens. These were charged with having entered into a contract with the devil, and with thus having secured power to molest others by the agency of infernal spirits. In May the disturbance was at its height. The jail was full. The ministers were alarmed by clear evidence that Satan was fighting for his erstwhile domain of New England, and had sent his emissaries there in force. From the pulpits came pleas for the detection and prosecution of the witches, and for popular reformation which alone could make the country inaccessible to diabolical attacks. The people, probably, were torn between rage against those they believed to have injured their neighbors' children, fear of this great revelation of the devil's might, and sympathy, growing as time went on, for those of good name who were drawn into the net.

For the twentieth-century mind it is almost impossible to appreciate as clearly as one must to understand what happened at Salem Village, how it was possible for the best-educated men of the day to accept without cavil the belief that witches existed and had power to do such things as were thought to have been done in this latest outbreak of Satanic power. It is even harder for us to realize how any man of reason could for one moment agree to sentence to death any human being on the charge of being a witch.

But the fact remains that, in England and America alike, the belief in witches and witchcraft was general.[3] Witchcraft was a crime punishable by death, not only in the colonies but in England. There were, of course, a few sceptics. Bekker, in Holland, greatest of all, later combatted the delusion.[4] Scot, in England, and Webster, had already argued against it with force. But, curiously enough, the basis of their pleas was hardly better founded in reason than that of the orthodox believers in witchcraft. The latter found in the Bible, in history, and in the phenomena of their own times evidence that witches were real, dangerous to men and to God's rule. This evidence they had to interpret without our present medical and psychological theories, and their opponents too often could not explain the facts observed and recorded. Denial of their reality was the only method the sceptics could rely upon, and they, too, were often forced to argue chiefly from written authority.[5] . . .

There were, however, a few men who did honor to the community by objecting to what was done at Salem, not because the crime was a fancied one, but because they, like the ministers, distrusted the legal methods employed. They agreed with Increase Mather in thinking that "spectral evidence" was not enough to convict a witch. So thought Nathaniel Saltonstall,[23] again one of the "weak fanatics" Mather chose to office; and he refused to sit longer on the court because he disliked its methods. So also Samuel Willard had the courage to write and publish a little tract questioning the use of "spectral evidence."[24] And Thomas Brattle set forth in trenchant terms his opposition to some of the evidence accepted by the judges.[25] It has been said that in so doing he implied scepticism as to the reality of the crime of witchcraft.[26] This is not susceptible of proof, but it is certain that he did give, together with his statement of his own attitude, invaluable evidence as to what the most enlightened New Englanders believed.

The letter in which he expressed his opinions takes

pains to mention several men who were dissatisfied with what the court had done. Saltonstall and Willard are thus named, Bradstreet, Danforth, and Increase Mather.[27] Here is contemporary evidence of the best that the elder Mather held to what he had signed in the ministers' reply of June 15, and that he disapproved the methods of the court. Yet neither he, Saltonstall, Willard, Brattle, nor any one of the objectors spoke out against the executions. Brattle's letter was to a friend, not for publication, and was not printed until 1798.[28] So, if Mather be blamed, as he sometimes has been, for his "delay" in protesting against the "persecution" of the witches,[29] we must number with him those men most praised for their humanity, who kept quite as silent as he. And for the same reasons, no doubt. They knew, as he did, that the judges did what they saw as their duty, and followed accepted legal standards. Willard, Mather, and other divines, in June, protested against their methods, and then, being but private citizens, interfered no more with a constituted court of justice. In any other matter, had they done more, they would have been denounced for trying to restore theocracy by bringing their influence to bear in a case concerned only with the enforcement of the laws of the state. As it is, they cannot be accused of officious meddling in government, and attacks shift to make them into inhumane upholders of superstition. So they seem to-day; but in their time, and for a generation thereafter, they appeared simply as would-be servants and teachers of their congregations, urging the most liberal attitude in witch trials, but not carrying their activity beyond the scope allowed them by the popular view, which still persists, of the place of the minister in public affairs.

Brattle's letter, with its unshakable testimony as to Mather's position, was written October 8, 1692. He not only tells us that Mather disliked the way the court proceeded, but tells how a certain Bostonian went to see one of the "afflicted" in Salem for advice as to strange symptoms observed in his own child. Thus he got "spectral evidence" against an individual, and attempted to secure a warrant for his arrest. This was denied him, and Increase Mather "took occasion severely to reprove the said man; asking him whether there was not a God in Boston, that he should go to the devil in Salem for advice; warning him very seriously against such naughty practices."[30] Mather appears in this incident as a man interested neither in upholding "spectral evidence" nor in keeping the witchcraft excitement alive.

Further testimony as to Mather's feeling during the summer of 1692 is afforded by a letter of John Proctor and others, protesting against the sentence imposed by the court, for it was addressed to several ministers, and Mather's name heads the list. Mr. Upham infers, reasonably, that this points to its having been known that the Teacher of the Second Church was doubtful as to the means by which the court arrived at convictions.[31] We know, too, that in all the fever of excitement about the trials, Mather not only kept silence, refraining from writing or saying anything that might fan the blaze, but also never went to Salem, even as a spectator, except on one occasion.[32] Then George Burroughs, a fellow minister, was on trial, and his colleague came to hear the evidence. In this case there was produced what seemed to Mather, as to the judges, clear evidence that Burroughs had used supernatural powers, so that his conviction was based by no means solely upon "spectral evidence."[33] Mather, therefore, found nothing to criticize in the conduct of the trial, and Burroughs's declaration of his own innocence, appealing as it seems to us, who judge on evidence then unknown, was no more striking to those who heard it, than are similar protestations from more than one legally condemned criminal of the present.

On October 3, the Cambridge Association of ministers met, and to them was read "a manuscript of cases of conscience relating to witchcraft, composed by the President of the College, the epistle commendatory whereunto was then signed by the" ministers at the meeting.[34] The "epistle commendatory," written by Willard, makes it plain that Mather, in accordance with the wishes of the Association, drew up a full statement of the ministers' position in regard to witch trials. It was intended as no shifting of ground, but simply as a fuller exposition of what had already been said by the clergy in June.[35]

Printed promptly, Increase Mather's *Cases of Conscience* gives, as definitely as one can ask, his views and his brethren's.[36] It was the first publicly printed discussion of the methods of the witch court, with the possible exception of Willard's pamphlet, dated in 1692, which appeared in Philadelphia. Mather finished his work, and it was read to his colleagues, five days before Brattle wrote his letter. In other words, no one anticipated his protest unless Willard's little dialogue antedated it. The position of the *Cases of Conscience* in the history of the expression of opinion on New England witchcraft entitles it, therefore, to a detailed examination.

It begins with the question, "Whether it is not Possible for the Devil to impose on the imagination of Persons Bewitched, and to cause them to Believe that an Innocent, yea that a Pious person does torment them, when the Devil himself doth it; or whether Satan may not appear in the Shape of an Innocent and Pious, as well as of a Nocent and Wicked Person to Afflict such as suffer by Diabolical Molestations?" And we are told at once: "The Answer to the Question must be Affirmative" (p. 225). No more explicit denial of the validity of "spectral evidence" can be framed. Mather's views, shared by the Salem judges, would have altered the whole course of the trials.

His main point decisively made, Mather goes on to support it by authorities. But here, as in the *Illustrious Providences,* authority alone could not serve. "Our own Experience hath confirmed the Truth of what we affirm," Mather writes (p. 253), and proceeds to argue from the experience of Bostonians of his own and earlier generations. "Spectral evidence" is thoroughly repudiated. The Scriptures, the writings of scholars, and the observations of New Englanders, all prove that the Devil can disguise his agents in the shapes of the innocent.

Mather continues, taking up a second question of importance in relation to the trials. "If one bewitched is struck down at the Look or cast of the Eye of another, and after that recovered again by a Touch from the same Person, Is not this an infallible Proof, that the Person suspected and complained of is in League with the Devil?" (p. 255). The answer is once more based on the opinions of learned authors, among them, be it noted, John Webster himself (p. 255 n.). The experience of recent investigators in English trials is also adduced. The final answer is clear. Testing witches by the methods discussed "is an unwarrantable Practice" (p. 269).

Mather, having cut the ground from under the advocates of two common proofs of witches' guilt, turns now to the query, "Whether there are any Discoveries of this Crime, which Jurors and Judges may with a safe Conscience proceed upon to the Conviction and Condemnation of the Persons under Suspicion?" He premises, first, that "The Evidence in this Crime ought to be as clear as in any other Crimes of a Capital nature," and, second, that "there have been ways of trying Witches long used in many Nations . . . which the righteous God never approved of." He denounces some superstitious "witch tests" used in "a Neighbor Colony." He argues against "ducking," together with other such popular measures, as contrary to Scripture, redolent of Paganism and the Devil, and as proved fallible by experience. But, leaving aside such unsound tests, "there are Proofs for the Conviction of Witches which Jurors may with a safe Conscience proceed upon, so as to bring them in guilty." These proofs are, first, "A free and voluntary Confession of the Crime made by the person suspected and accused," and, second, the sworn statement of "two credible Persons . . . that they have seen the . . . accused speaking such words, or doing things which none but such as have Familiarity with the Devil ever did or can do." Testimony of one witch against another is not reliable, and its acceptance has caused the shedding of innocent blood. Only the two proofs cited are sufficient to convict.[37]

The book ends with a quotation from Perkins, urging no convictions without adequate proof (p. 283). It is impossible to read the *Cases of Conscience* as anything but a thoroughly documented answer to certain questions raised by the witch trials, and an answer insisting upon a caution which, had it been used in the summer of 1692, would have prevented much bloodshed.

To his book Mather added a Postscript. It has been conjectured that this was appended after the ministers' approval was secured,[38] but there is no evidence that, even if this was done, the brethren failed to approve it. No one of them protested when it appeared in a book commended by them. In it Mather explains that he has written, not "to plead for Witchcrafts, or to appear as an Advocate for Witches." He has, he declares, written a discourse to prove that witches exist, but has not published it, although in "due time" he may do so (p. 285). He has not "designed any Reflection on those worthy Persons who have been concerned in the late Proceedings at *Salem;* They are wise and good Men, and have acted with all Fidelity according to their Light. . . . Pitty and Prayers rather than Censures are their due" (pp. 285ff.). Less could hardly be said in fairness. More approval of the trials Mather never expressed.

He then mentions Cotton's account of some of the doings of the court, condemns once more some of the popular tests for witchcraft, and, finally, writes of his son's book. "I perused and approved of" it "before it was printed; and nothing but my Relation to him hindred me from recommending it to the World" (p. 288). Such approval was entirely reasonable. Cotton Mather had argued that there were witches, had praised the faithfulness of the judges, and had given an account of some of the trials drawn from the records of the court. To this he added an unqualified disapproval of convictions based on the sort of evidence his fellow divines and his father denounced.[39] However they differed in their conduct during the excitement, Increase and Cotton shared certain fundamental beliefs; and the father's endorsement of the son's writings marks no more than his welcoming of one more statement of the position of the more liberal critics of the witch court.

The *Cases of Conscience* stands alone in its careful exposure of the most dangerous fallacies in the legal process by which the witches died.[40] It is far more explicit than Willard's pamphlet on the same subject. It expressed the views of the foremost ministers, and it remains, for us, a landmark. With it at hand, there can be no doubt as to Mather's stand; seen in its pages, he must always be the intelligent critic who found the Bible, scholars, and human observation all in opposition to the court's methods. That he had courage to speak his views was much; that he wrote, "It were better that ten suspected Witches should escape, than that one innocent Person should be Condemned. . . . It is better that a Guilty Person should be absolved, than that he should without sufficient ground of Conviction be condemned. I had rather judge a Witch to be an

honest woman, than judge an honest woman as Witch" (p. 283), proves him to have been mindful of humanity and caution in the face of a popular frenzy. No zeal to stamp out crimes ever drove him from his belief that, whatever the fate of the guilty, the innocent must never be in peril.

By autumn, whether because of this book,[41] the unanimity of the ministers, or a real dawning of light in Massachusetts minds, the opposition to the court's ways made itself heard. Stoughton, undeterred by a letter Mather had received from England denouncing "spectral evidence," uninfluenced by Brattle, Willard, Mather, Danforth, or any of the protesting clergy, persisted in his views of evidence.[42] Sewall significantly remarks that so great was the difference of opinion between the court and the ministers that the proceedings were halted.[43] The General Court had now voted to establish a Supreme Court, so that the temporary witch tribunal was automatically dissolved.[44] Judges for the new court were elected on December 7. Lest one fancy that popular feeling was in advance of the ministers', it is worth while to note that of all the new judges, Stoughton received most votes.[45] Danforth, who shared Mather's cautious views, came next, then John Richards who had also been on the former court, Winthrop, and Samuel Sewall. In other words, of those elected, four were among those who had tried and sentenced the witches, and there was included Stoughton, the man most opposed to the ministerial view. Only one of the new appointees was among those Brattle named as having questioned the proceedings of the summer.

The court did not meet at Salem until January, 1693. In the meanwhile the ministers' views had a chance to do their work, and the bringing of charges against some persons in high place and of unquestioned reputation, coupled with the time the people now had in which to think over more soberly what had been done, led to a decided change in feeling.[46] Governor Phipps was enough of a politician to detect it, and put himself on the side of the opponents of the trials. In so doing he gave as one of his reasons the advice he had received from Increase Mather and the other divines.[47] Thus, when the court met in January, all but three out of fifty were acquitted, and those three won pardons from Phipps.[48]

In England witchcraft trials continued well into the eighteenth century, and in Scotland bloody chapters in the history of witchcraft were still to be written.[49] But New England never again brought a witch to trial, and the "delusion," so far as it imprisoned human beings, brought them to trial, or to the gallows, was dead on her shores. Its tragic outbreak in 1692, however gruesome as a page in human history, was by no means so dreadful as similar occurrences in equally limited districts in older civilizations not under Puritan or "clerical" dominion.[50]

We have seen the facts in regard to Increase Mather's connection with the affair. They give no basis for the somewhat reckless ascription of motives which led to many eighteenth-and nineteenth-century accusations of him as one who fostered the "delusion," or, at least, delayed inexcusably in opposing its excesses. The facts refute such charges. They show that Mather was three thousand miles away from the scene of the tragedy until May, 1692; that, after the first execution, he publicly urged caution in the use of evidence; that he did not attend the trials; that he cautioned a parishioner against spreading the excitement; that he made plain to Brattle his discontent with what was done; that he was chosen to write the full statement of the ministers' position; that the book which resulted was the first detailed argument against the procedure of the trials; and that, after it was printed, no witch was executed in Massachusetts. We know that Phipps, claiming credit for stopping the bloodshed, named Mather as one of those who advised the course he chose. And we know that Increase wrote and published a sentence which does not deserve to be forgotten when his reputation is at stake: "It is better that a Guilty Person should be absolved, than that he should without sufficient ground of Conviction be condemned."

But instead of finding him held up as a leader of the enlightened thought of his time, we have John Wise, Brattle, Pike, Moodey, Hale, and Willard singled out for praise.[51] Now Brattle, however worthy of honor, knew that Mather was liberally minded, and said so. As for Wise, his only public expression in the affair was his endorsement of what Mather wrote.[52] Willard, too, joined in commending the *Cases of Conscience,* and himself criticized the court. But, it is well to remember that neither he nor Moodey doubted the reality of witchcraft, for both had studied and written about cases of diabolical possession.[53] Pike, advanced as were his views, went no further than Mather.[54] Hale wrote nothing till five years after the event, and then was still interested in discovering witches who deserved punishment. Wherever such men as these have a place as clear-sighted thinkers in a time of "delusion," Mather must join them, not as the blind tyrant from whose influence they had emancipated themselves,[55] but as the leader they publicly owned.

There are, however, one or two accusations brought against Increase Mather, which purport to have foundation in the recorded facts of his time. Perhaps it is necessary to say no more in answer to attacks of later generations, than that they are attacks of later generations and not those of Brattle and the men who knew Mather and his deeds. But his position among his contemporaries is important for any biography, and a glance at some of the charges brought against him may not be without use.

First, then, we are told that his *Illustrious Providences,* published, one remembers, eight years before 1692, is shown by evidence from the Mathers' own time to have been largely responsible for the "delusion" centring about Salem Village.[56] This statement has been made again and again since Francis Hutchinson first gave grounds for it in his invaluable essay on witchcraft. But he said no more than that the Mathers' books prepared men's minds to become prey to the "delusion" of 1692.[57] Of course, all such statements are dangerous. To say to-day that moving pictures excite youth to crime, or that this or that book establishes false beliefs, is common, but in every case such statements, perforce, remain unproved. There is no harm in thinking that Increase Mather, who wrote of events which he and other sober citizens believed to have occurred, strengthened in his readers' minds opinions which made it possible for them to see in the Salem Village excitement evidence of a real outbreak of crime.[58] This is well enough, if we are content to accept also what logically follows, and to admit that his responsibility was shared by those ministers who concurred in the idea that narratives of witchcraft cases were an indispensable part of any history of the "remarkable" events of New England. Willard, John Whiting, John Russell, and Joshua Moodey all furnished him material, by writing of cases which had come to their attention.[59] If his book was pernicious, they share with him the reproach of having unwittingly contributed to a tragedy—a reproach applicable also to all men who spoke of witches of which they had seen or heard. With them must be classed, too, the Englishmen who wrote of witches to their American friends, the German and English scientists whom Mather quoted, and the writers of a host of other books written before and after his and accessible to readers in New England. He did no more than edit a historical collection, to which he added his own denunciation of certain superstitions, one of which cost at least one life as late as 1863.[60]

But he did argue that witches existed, and this has excluded all else in the minds of some historians. This doctrine, however, needed no advocate in 1684; no one could have written a history of New England without including the witchcraft cases unless he were deliberately to omit a chapter of what was generally recognized as historical fact, and no one thus writing could have urged disbelief in witchcraft unless he had been a sceptic far in advance of any the colonies knew. Mather wrote history. Witchcraft filled but a small part of his book,[61] and he preached against superstition. If the work was of evil influence, so were most histories of the day, so was much other literature prior to 1700, and so is many a book written to-day in the interest of some theory now accepted but doomed to fall with time.

Yet a careful modern historian writes that Increase Mather deliberately sought to encourage credulity and superstition, and sees no way by which he can be forgiven![62] The reply to this is contained in what has been said above. And, had any man fancied that "superstition," as applied to witchcraft, needed aid from his pen, he could hardly have chosen a worse method than the writing of a book of narratives, which, for the most part, concerned nothing supernatural. He could hardly have been so addle-pated as to forget his aim, and challenge some points of popular credulity, and certainly he would have wasted no time on scientific discussions of magnetism and heat. Had his purpose been to encourage credulity, he could have committed no greater folly than to brand many tales of witchcraft as false! To say that his dark intention is proved by contemporary evidence, is to distort the facts. Baxter said, in 1691, that the *Illustrious Providences* was a sufficient answer to the disbeliever in witchcraft. Of course it was, just as was any standard history, or the Bible. But Baxter never hints that Mather, or Glanvill, or Boyle, or anyone else, wrote in order to egg on the credulous and superstitious. Hutchinson, writing in 1718, is no contemporary, and he, too, was careful to impute no motives. He wrote in a later generation, when belief in witchcraft was waning. His view of a book written thirty-four years before is not good evidence as to its character or its writer's. . . .

Finally, Increase Mather has been accused of responsibility for establishing the witch court and continuing its activities through the summer of 1692.[64] The argument is simple. Mather was influential in making Phipps governor, and Phipps was his disciple. Had he not approved, the court would never have been appointed. Had he wished it, Phipps must have stopped the trials. Had he spoken out, his position as a leader was such that the whole excitement would have died away.

Nothing is more dangerous, of course, than an attempt to define the influence of one man upon another in politics. There can be no shred of proof that Mather approved, or failed to oppose, the establishment of the court. If every act of Phipps is to be ascribed to his pastor, then to Mather belongs the credit for ending the trials, and pardoning the victims. Moreover, Stoughton was as much Mather's appointee as Phipps, and Stoughton, we know, was opposed by the party whose views Mather expressed in the *Cases of Conscience*. Only conjecture can support criticism of the Teacher of the Second Church as the dictator of all Phipps's acts, and if conjecture lays at his door all the governor's bad deeds, it cannot fairly deny him credit for the good works of his disciple. If Phipps was Mather's slave, we may with equal reason say that Stoughton was one, but records prove that this was not the case. Nathaniel Saltonstall, too, was chosen to office by Mather, and if Phipps represented the divine's influence, why not also Saltonstall, whose attitude we praise?

We have facts to prove Mather's position as member and leader of the liberal party in the discussion of legal methods. The charges against him rest on guesswork, and on a hypothesis which makes him, at one and the same time, the mentor of Saltonstall, Stoughton, and Phipps, men who held different views and chose different courses, and gives to him the credit for ending the trials. His reputation has nothing to fear from such conjectures or from the facts.

There remain to be considered the comments made by Robert Calef.[65] Calef is an American of whom we may be proud, because he was "modern" enough to question some commonly accepted beliefs as to witchcraft. True, he argued, like those he criticized, from no purely rationalistic ground, but from his own interpretation of Scripture, and too often he confronted well-attested statements by flat denials, not convincing from a strictly logical point of view. He was no writer, and by no means a scholar, but he did mock some things that we now hold to be "delusions." He was a man of the world, and of common sense. He had definite views, however poorly supported they were. He wrote, unfortunately, too late to deserve any credit for the ending of the witchcraft excitement, and when his book came out, Sewall's public repentance for the methods he had used at Salem had said all that Calef could say.[66] Public opinion was, when his work was printed, as enlightened as he. He did not deny that there were witches, nor did his neighbors; but they had come to see, even before he did, that some innocent blood had been shed in 1692.

Most of his "More Wonders of the Invisible World" was an attack on Cotton Mather. He also found space for a paragraph or two directed against Willard, the clergy and judiciary in general, and against Increase Mather. To him he refers comparatively rarely. He mentions his presence with his son at the bedside of a suspected sufferer from witchcraft in Boston, after the Salem outbreak had passed, but does not record how scrupulously careful we know Cotton Mather to have been in avoiding anything that could lead to fresh accusations or a new stirring of popular superstition.[67] He bases his remarks on a paper written by the younger Mather, but printed without the author's consent.[68] He indulges in innuendoes which led the Mathers to bring an action against him.[69] On his writing an apparently contrite letter, the proceedings were dropped.[70] But, curiously enough, in all this, Calef finds few specific charges to bring against Increase Mather individually, without deserting his subject to go afield in a discussion of the agents' work in England.[71] There are hints that Mather served his own interest rather than his country's. He is strangely silent as to the *Cases of Conscience,* but he refers more than once to the paragraphs of the ministers' reply of June 15, 1692, which spoke of the need for continuing the court's efforts according to the laws of God and England.

On the whole, there is nothing here that needs answer. The book appeared when Increase Mather was opposed by many on grounds other than his views on witches, and such effect as it had in weakening his influence it owed, probably, not to any superior wisdom as to events of 1692 and 1693, but to its timely recapitulation of the arguments most useful to Mather's enemies in the church and in politics. Such a work, as we shall see, offered welcome material to those who sought weapons against the Mathers; but even so, it was quite adequately answered by certain citizens who thought with the leaders of the Second Church. To their reply, Mather himself added a few paragraphs, disposing of the attacks upon his conduct in England.[72] The witchcraft issue was, so far as Increase was concerned, the least important item in Calef's arsenal.

Summing up, we find Increase Mather in 1692 as a believer in witchcraft, an opponent of the methods of the court, and an ally and leader of those whom we see as the most liberal of the time. He wrote the first full statement of their views, and throughout the whole excitement he kept himself from any act or speech that could possibly have increased the harm that was done. His creed he epitomized himself, when he wrote: "It were better that ten suspected Witches should escape, than that one innocent Person should be Condemned."

This much can be shown by the evidence hitherto accessible to all students. To it we may now add Mather's own statement of his position in the witchcraft affair. Like "spectral evidence," what Mather says of himself must be supported by other records in order to pass current to-day, not because the Mather's testimony can be proved to be unsound, but because those historians to whom they have seemed sinister figures have found it necessary to attack their veracity. We have seen how Increase Mather appears in the testimony of his contemporaries, and in the accessible records. With this picture agrees his own description of his attitude.

"I found ye country in a sad condition," he writes in May, 1692, "by reason of witchcraft & possessed persons. The judges & many of ye people had espoused a notion yt ye devill could not personate i ocent persons as afflicting others. I doubt [i. e. fear] yt i ocent blood was shed by mistakes of that nature. I therefore published my Cases of Conscience *de* witchcraft, &c. By wch, (it is sayed) many were enlightened, juries convinced, & the shedding of more i ocent blood prevented."[73] The truth of this document remains unshaken.

The space devoted to Increase Mather's relation to the witchcraft outbreak is not justified, perhaps, by its importance in his life. But later criticism has so often determined its final judgment on inferences wrested from the events of 1692, that no biography can afford to let the matter go uninvestigated. For the purposes of twentieth-century eulogy, it would be possible to regret that he was not a Hutchinson thirty years ahead of his time, or even a Calef; but biography can hope for no more than to attempt a fair estimate of his position. Its verdict must be that, in witchcraft, he was not a radical on the side of what we now see as the truth, but an orthodox educated man, sharing the most liberal of the then orthodox doctrines.

Much has been said of the influence exerted by his stand on witchcraft in bringing down his power from the heights it reached in 1687 or 1692.[74] Nothing is harder to determine than such influences. Mather, in 1692, was open to attack, as we have seen, from opponents of the charter and of the officers he had chosen for the colony, and from all those to whom the government's acts were unwelcome. Nearly ten years later, when his prestige received its first serious blow, other forces than political enmity played a part. It is hardly necessary to feel that the community rebelled against his opinions on witchcraft, and that therein lay the cause of his partial loss of popular favor. Hostility to him can be shown to have many roots, but there is no evidence that any of his foes based their feeling on dislike for his relation to the events in Salem Village.

There is only one bit of evidence bearing on the popular view of those concerned in the witchcraft trials, and this has been curiously neglected by historians. We have a record of the result of the election of 1693. Those voting were not, it is true, the rank and file of the people, but they were their representatives, and as dependent on their favor as legislators of to-day. The issue was determined, of course, by other forces than approval or disapproval of what had been done in the witch court. Men were voted for, then as now, because they were personally liked, or because their decision on this or that question had pleased the voters. At the same time, a few of those who were candidates in 1693 were so involved in the Salem trials that their fate at the polls may reasonably be interpreted as partial evidence, at least, of the popular feeling toward their deeds in combating the wiles of Satan.

Twenty-eight councillors were elected.[75] Of these, eighteen had been chosen to office by Mather in the previous year. Nearly two thirds of his appointments were thus confirmed by the representatives of the people. Of those rejected, one, the aged Bradstreet, was probably unwilling to serve.[76] Of the others, three were men who had held office before Mather appointed them, and the remaining six were men whom he had chosen from those not previously endorsed by the voters. Now, of this class of men he chose but eight, and only two were reelected. In other words, though most of the government he had chosen was confirmed in office, the fortunate candidates were for the most part those who had been office-holders prior to 1692, and of the candidates who may be said to have been selected by him on personal grounds, three quarters failed of popular support. If all his appointees were under his influence, he still controlled the government; but most of those whom he had chosen on his own responsibility were rejected.

Why was this? Not on religious grounds, for but one of the defeated was a member of his congregation. Can we then say that the shift in the membership of the Council represented the voters' views on witchcraft, and their repudiation of Mather and some of his less distinguished friends? No such answer is possible. Of those rejected, not one, so far as we know, played any prominent part in the witch trials, or expressed his views in regard to them. But of the nine judges who sentenced the witches, every one was elected to the Council in 1693. The most liberal of all, Nathaniel Saltonstall, received fewer votes than Sewall, Winthrop, or Richards, and only a few more than Stoughton himself. Danforth, whom Brattle called an opponent of the court's methods, ran behind Winthrop and Sewall. There is here no evidence that the populace and their legislators saw those involved in condemning the witches as deluded or inhumane. Every judge received the stamp of popular approval, and the two who seem most likely to have been liberals did not head the list. The most popular name was that of Samuel Sewall, who felt, in later years, that he had erred enough to make necessary a public recantation.[77]

It is possible to explain the result of this election only by regarding the issue as in no way concerned with witchcraft, but as old charter *versus* new. From this point of view we can see why those men whose claim to office lay only in Mather's favor should fail, if popular opinion to any considerable extent opposed the charter he had brought from England. We can see also why Danforth and Cooke were elected. Both held the old charter view of independence, and clung to a belief in the colony's right to dispense with royal governors. Hutchinson was near enough to 1693 to be able to judge more accurately than we can, and he was far better equipped with records. He gives no hint that the shift in the make-up of the Council was due to any but the obvious political motive.[78] There was, as yet, no overwhelming opposition to the new charter, for some of those retained in office supported the new order; but there was a feeling that a more truly representative character should be given to a body which Mather had composed solely of those who he felt sure would support the government to which he was himself committed.

The election of 1693, then, reveals no trace of a popular reaction against belief in witchcraft or Mather's views upon it, but shows the strength of the old charter party led by Elisha Cooke. The political rift was real, and widened with the passing years. Cooke came home from England in 1692, and kept a "Day of Thanksgiving for his safe Arrival." Neither Mather was there.

Perhaps they were not invited; perhaps they refused to go. In any case, Samuel Sewall scented "Animosities," and prayed that "the Good Lord unite us in his Fear."[79] He was not heard, and the two parties grew away from one another. In the beginnings of this division between the advocates of colonial independence and the adherents of the new charter lies the explanation of the election of 1693, and what we should call to-day its political "rebuke" to Increase Mather.

Voters in May, 1693, saw him as we must see him when we free our minds from the authority of the last two centuries, and study his position as his neighbors knew it. He came through the witchcraft ordeal unscathed. He believed in witchcraft, but he urged moderation and justice, not fanatical zeal. The saving of innocent life interested him more than the hunting down of every guilty witch. Such men as Brattle, clearest sighted of all those who lived through the alarming events at Salem Village, saw him as a wise guide, and his writing was the most complete expression of their views. Once more he proved himself in the front rank of his day, and able to speak clearly and decisively for what he believed to be the right.

Notes

[1] *Acts and Resolves,* vii, 9.

[2] Cf., for example, A. D. White, *A History of the Warfare,* ii, 127.

[3] Cf. G. L. Kittredge, "Notes on Witchcraft," in *American Antiquarian Society Proceedings,* xviii, 148 ff., and W. Notestein, *A History of Witchcraft,* p. 308.

[4] Balthazar Bekker's "most telling attack upon the reality of witchcraft" was published in Dutch in 1691-1693, too late to have influenced the New England trials. The English translation appeared in 1695. Cf. Kittredge, "Notes," pp. 180ff.

[5] *Ibid., passim,* and M. A. Murray, *The Witch-Cult in Western Europe,* p. 11. . . .

[23] Upham, *Salem Witchcraft,* ii, 251; *MHS [Massachusetts Historical Society] Coll.,* Series 1, v, 75.

[24] *Memorial History of Boston,* ii, 164. A reprint is in *Congregational Quarterly* (1869), xi, 400ff.

[25] *MHS Coll.,* Series 1, v, 61ff.

[26] J. A. Doyle, *The Puritan Colonies,* ii, 393ff.

[27] *MHS Coll.,* Series 1, v, 75.

[28] *Ibid.,* v, 61. Doyle (*The Puritan Colonies,* ii, 393) says: "The honour of being the first to speak out fear-

lessly and to brave a mob, cruel with the cruelty of panic," belongs to Brattle. But Brattle did not "speak out publicly," but simply wrote a private letter to a friend, whereas Increase Mather's *Cases of Conscience,* questioning some of the evidence used by the court, was finished and read at a meeting of ministers five days before Brattle wrote.

Neither Mather nor Brattle believed it wise publicly to attack the conduct of the judges. The latter writes: "When errors of that nature are thus detected and observed, I never thought it an interfering with dutifulness and subjection for one man to communicate his thoughts to another thereabout; and with modesty and due reverence to debate the premised failings; at least when errors are fundamental, and palpably pervert the great end of authority and government." *MHS Coll.,* Series I, v, 61, 62.

[29] Cf. G. H. Moore, "Bibliographical Notes on Witchcraft in Massachusetts," in *American Antiquarian Society Proceedings,* v, 265, 266, who says that Increase Mather made no effort to stop the trials, and approved twenty executions before he was heard from. This leaves out of account his signing the answer of the ministers in June, does not explain why Brattle regarded him in October as one who had opposed the court's doings, and neglects the fact that Mather never, during the summer, specifically "approved" a single execution.

[30] *MHS Coll.,* Series I, v, 71.

[31] Upham, *Salem Witchcraft,* ii, 310-312, 308, 309.

[32] I. Mather, *Cases of Conscience Concerning Evil Spirits,*" p. 286: "I was not myself present at any of the Tryals, excepting one, *viz.* that of *George Burroughs.*" If this refers only to the few trials written of by Cotton Mather, the fact remains that we have no record of Increase's presence in Salem Village during the summer of 1692, in Sewall's Diary, or elsewhere, so far as I have been able to discover. Mather did go to Salem on October 19, after the trials were over, to visit the confessors. See *MHS Coll.,* Series 2, iii, 221.

[33] Hutchinson, *History,* ii, 56, 57; Upham, *Salem Witchcraft,* ii, 296-304. The latter gives the facts of the trial, but some of the interpretations and inferences seem unsound.

[34] *MHS Proc.,* xvii, 268.

[35] I. Mather, *Cases of Conscience,* pp. 289-291.

[36] The full title is (from the London edition): "Cases of Conscience Concerning Evil Spirits Personating Men; Witchcrafts, Infallible Proofs of Guilt in such as are Accused with that Crime. All Considered according to the Scriptures, History, Experience, and the Judgment of many Learned Men. . . . Printed at *Boston,* and Reprinted at *London,* for John Dunton, at the *Raven* in the *Poultrey.* 1693." There was an edition in Boston in 1693. The London edition also appeared as the second part of a book, with the title, "A Further Account of the Tryals of the New-England Witches. With The Observations Of a Person who was upon the Place several Days when the suspected Witches were first taken into Examination. To which is added, Cases of Conscience Concerning Witchcrafts and Evil Spirits Personating Men. Written at the Request of the Ministers of *New-England.* By *Increase Mather,* President of *Harvard* Colledge. Licensed and Entred according to Order. *London.* . . . 1693."

This contains, first, "A True Narrative of some Remarkable Passages relating to . . . *Witchcraft* at *Salem* Village in *New-England,*" "Collected by Deodat Lawson." This is followed by "A Further Account of the Tryals of The . . . Witches, Sent in a Letter from Thence, to a Gentleman in London." Then comes, as a separate part of the volume, Increase Mather's "Cases of Conscience."

The whole book has been often credited to Increase Mather, under the title of "A Further Account," etc., but it seems to me that only the "Cases of Conscience" can be called his. The first section was avowedly by Deodat Lawson, and the second, the letter, offers no proof that Mather wrote it. It begins, moreover, "Here were in *Salem,*" suggesting that a resident of Salem, not of Boston, was the author. Probably Increase Mather's connection with the volume included under the title of "A Further Account," etc., was that of a compiler, and even this much instrumentality cannot be proved. It is quite possible that the passage by Lawson and the letter were put together by the publisher.

The *Cases of Conscience* was reprinted in an edition of C. Mather: *The Wonders of the Invisible World,* London, 1862. To this edition all references here are made.

[37] Pp. 269, 270, 275, 276, 279ff., 282.

[38] Cf. I. Mather, *Early History of New England,* etc. (a reprint of an early work of Mather's, given a new title by the editor, S. G. Drake, Boston, 1864), pp. xxii, xxiii. Mr. Drake says here: "Perhaps the Fourteen [signers of the preface] did not include the Postscript in their Commendation. Indeed it is quite probable they knew Nothing of it until after the Book was printed. . . . The Postscript . . . did not probably appear in the original Edition of the *Cases of Conscience.* I have a manuscript copy of it (chiefly in the Autograph of the Author) to which there is no Postscript." The absence of the postscript from the manuscript as it reached Mr.

Drake proves nothing, of course, and I know of no edition from which the Postscript can be proved to have been lacking originally. Moreover, as noted in the text, no one of the signers of the preface seems to have protested against the Postscript when it appeared as part of the book they had commended.

[39] *Memorial History of Boston,* ii, 160, 161, 162.

[40] *Ibid.,* 162.

[41] Cf. *Parentator,* p. 166.

[42] Hutchinson, *History,* ii, 23 n. and 61; *Cal. State Papers, Am. and W. I.,* xiv, #112 (p. 30).

[43] *MHS Coll.,* Series 5, v, 367.

[44] *Ibid.,* 367, 368; Palfrey, iv, 111.

[45] *MHS Coll.,* Series 5, v, 370.

[46] Hutchinson, *History,* ii, 60.

[47] Cf. *Cal. State Papers, Am. and W.I.,* xiv, #112 (p. 30); and *MHS Proc.,* xxi, 340, 341.

[48] Hutchinson, *History,* ii, 60; Doyle, *The Puritan Colonies,* ii, 395.

[49] *Kittredge,* "Notes," pp. 202ff.

[50] *Ibid.,* pp. 205ff.

[51] Upham, *Salem Witchcraft,* ii, 304, 305; Doyle, *The Puritan Colonies,* ii, 393; Winsor, *The Literature of Witchcraft,* p. 363; and J. Quincy, *History,* i, 147, 148. As for Hale, Upham (*Salem Witchcraft,* ii, 475) speaks of his "rational view." In 1697 he wrote an expression of this view in *A Modest Enquiry Into the Nature of Witchcraft,* Boston, 1702. (The preface is dated 1697.) This is reprinted in part in G. L. Burr, *Narratives,* pp. 395ff. Hale, as Mather had done five years before, questions the method used in the trials, citing Mather as one authority, and urges repentance for the errors committed. He regrets that it is necessary to fear "that there hath been a great deal of innocent blood shed," but also, "that there have been great sinful neglects in sparing others, who by their divinings about things future, or discovering things secret, as stollen Goods, &c or by their informing of persons and things absent at a great distance, have implored the assistance of a familiar spirit," etc. He is concerned, not with denying witchcraft, but deciding who are witches, and feels that the Salem prosecution chose the wrong ones, leaving others deserving conviction! Such "rational views" do not compare favorably with Mather's.

[52] Wise signed the commendatory preface to the *Cases of Conscience,* and, so far as we know, published nothing of his own on the subject.

[53] *MHS Coll.,* Series 4, viii, 555, 360, 361, 367ff.

[54] See J. S. Pike, *The New Puritan,* chap. 23. John Pike wrote a letter on August 9, 1692, in which he asserts his belief that there are witches, and recommends the same tests for guilt which were held by Mather to be the only reliable ones. Creditable as his view was to him, it was exactly Mather's; in view of which one wonders why Upham, in *Salem Witchcraft,* devotes so much space (ii, 449ff.) to praise of Pike and so little to commendation of Mather.

[55] Winsor (*The Literature of Witchcraft,* p. 363) says: "There lived at the time o the Mathers some who were not enslaved by their influence," and that this "shows that society could have been saved, but for such misguided leaders. Such was Joshua Moody, who spirited away to a place of safety the accused Philip English and his wife. . . . Such was the outspoken Robert Pike." But Moodey wrote Mather to tell him of a witchcraft case, and we know he furnished for Mather's *Illustrious Providences* (which Mr. Winsor considers to have been instrumental in causing the outbreak of 1692) at least one narrative. Cf. note 53, *ante.* Whether or not they emancipated themselves from Mather's influence, Pike and Moodey shared his views, and never wrote, as he did, to make their liberal attitude public.

[56] Cf. Winsor, *The Literature of Witchcraft,* pp. 355, 356, where, after making the charge referred to, he adds: "It is no merely modern propensity, prompted by a disregard of the tendency of that time, to charge so much upon the baleful misuse of literature, for these books were recognized even in the Mathers' day as an active agency, leading to direful events." In support of this he quotes Baxter, who said that the *Illustrious Providences* would overcome incredulity as to the existence of witches, and Hutchinson, whose essay on witchcraft came out thirty-four years after Mather's book. The same charge appears again and again in the work of other historians, less scholarly and careful than Justin Winsor.

[57] F. Hutchinson, *An Historical Essay,* 2d ed., p. 101.

[58] Cf., for a modern expression of this point of view, J. A. Doyle, *The Puritan Colonies,* ii, 389. Mr. Doyle says, however, that to the *Illustrious Providences* "anyone might contribute an account of anything which sounded like a miracle." This is hardly fair, for one remembers that we have no proof that Mather printed any story simply because it was contributed. Cf. p. 174, *ante.*

[59] Cf. *MHS Coll.,* Series 4, viii, 86ff., 466ff., 360ff., 555ff., and I. Mather, *Essay for the Recording of Illus-*

trious Providences, pp. 96, 99, 113, 114.

[60] *Memorial History of Boston,* ii, 172 and n. Mather, one remembers, in his *Illustrious Providences,* argued against the "water-test" for witches.

[61] In the edition of the *Illustrious Providences,* of London, 1890, 23 pages are devoted to "things Preternatural which have Hapned in New England," 24 to an argument proving "that there are Daemons and Possessed Persons," and 33 to "Apparitions." The book contains 262 pages of text. In other words, less than one third of its space is devoted to witchcraft cases. G. L. Burr (*Narratives,* p. 6 n.) says: "It is true the book of Mather is not wholly on 'the world of spirits': other 'providences' fill half the volume. But it is more largely so than any earlier collection of its sort, and in this the author's interest clearly centres." Two thirds, not half, of the volume, deals with other subjects. If it treats witchcraft more largely than other collections, it may be because witchcraft had been more prevalent in New England. I can find no evidence that Mather's interest centred more on the witchcraft narratives than on any other of his chapters.

[62] Justin Winsor, in *The Literature of Witchcraft,* pp. 355, 356, says: "The systematic efforts of the Mathers, father and son, to engage the superstitious and reckless—and in this nefarious business Increase at a later day used his position as President of Harvard College, the better to accomplish his ends—led to many ministers and others helping, by offering a premium on invention and exaggeration, to pour in upon the expectant credulous, what Mather was pleased to call 'memorable or illustrious providences.'" He then goes on to say that this view is supported by evidence of writers in Mather's lifetime. The facts are that neither of the authorities Winsor cites (one of whom wrote thirty-four years after 1684) suggested that Mather wrote with any design to encourage superstition. Furthermore, as to his desire to "engage the superstitious," Mather writes in *Cases of Conscience,* p. 264, "The Laws and Customs of the Kingdom of darkness, are not always and in all places the same. And it is good for men to concern themselves with them as little as may be." This is a statement quite out of place in the mouth of a man with the motives Winsor ascribes to Mather!. . .

[64] Cf., for example, Winsor, *The Literature of Witchcraft,* p. 360.

[65] There is some doubt as to the identity of Calef. See W. F. Poole, in *Memorial History of Boston,* ii, 165ff.; S. G. Drake, *The Witchcraft Delusion,* ii, xiff.; and G. L. Burr, *Narratives,* pp. 291ff. Calef wrote *More Wonders of the Invisible World,* London, 1700, printed in Drake, *op. cit,* ii, 1ff.

[66] January 14, 1697, Sewall made public statement of his regret for the errors of the court, but did *not* deny the reality of witchcraft. *MHS Coll.,* Series 5, v, 445. Nor did the government, in calling a fast day to atone for the errors at Salem, deny that Satan had been active. See *Ibid.,* 446 n.

[67] Cf. R. Calef, *More Wonders,* ii, 49, 51, 55. As to Cotton Mather's caution, cf. W. F. Poole, in *Memorial History of Boston,* ii, 156, 157.

[68] Of this document Calef writes (*More Wonders,* p. 14): "I received [it] of a Gentleman, who had it of the Author, and communicated it to use, with his express consent." To whom the "his" refers is not easy to decide, and "consent . . . to use" is hardly consent to publish.

[69] Calef, *More Wonders,* p. 55.

[70] W. F. Poole, in *Memorial History of Boston,* ii, 167.

[71] A reading of Calef makes this clear. He does, however, say (*More Wonders,* iii, 157): "It is rather a Wonder that no more Blood was shed, for if that Advice of his [Phipps's] Pastors could still have prevailed with the Governour, Witchcraft had not been so shammed off as it was." Calef seems not to have known that Phipps gave Increase Mather credit for his influence in stopping the trials. There is more excuse for this failure on Calef's part, than on that of later historians. As for Calef's attack on Mather as agent, see *Andros Tracts,* ii, 315-323, where the charges, and Mather's quite adequate reply, are given.

[72] The answer was: *Some Few Remarks,* etc., Boston, 1701, by O. Gill and others. Cf. also, *Andros Tracts,* ii, 315-323.

[73] *Autobiography.*

[74] Cf. J. A. Doyle, *The Puritan Colonies,* ii, 400, 401. J. T. Adams (*The Founding,* p. 455) says that "public opinion was arrayed solidly against" Cotton Mather when, in 1693, he "tried to start another alarm in Boston." Cotton, of course, did not "try to start another alarm" (cf. W. F. Poole, in *Memorial History of Boston,* ii, 146ff.), and his account of the 1693 case was not printed until Calef brought it out. There is no evidence that "public opinion was arrayed solidly against" him, though, seven years later, one man criticized him, making charges most of which he denied. Of course, by 1700, when Increase Mather was attacked on various grounds, and when public opinion had had seven years to develop a more enlightened point of view on witchcraft, an attack, like that of Calef, was useful, and played a part in stirring up feeling against the Mathers. It does not prove that in 1693 any popular reaction against their witchcraft views had occurred, or even that any had occurred in 1700, ex-

cept on the part of one man. Probably it is safe to say that Calef's book in 1700 aroused some feeling against the Mathers' witchcraft attitude, among those who read it without examination of its facts, or memory of what, precisely, the Mathers had done; and so, by 1700, the witchcraft episode may have played a part in weakening Increase and Cotton. But it seems to me to be quite unsafe to say that immediately after the trials popular opinion turned against them, because of their witchcraft views. Such statements, however, are found in many histories. None of these, nevertheless, so far as I know, points to the election results in 1693, which are referred to in the text.

[75] Palfrey, iv, 142; *MHS Coll.,* Series 5, v, 378.

[76] Palfrey, iv, 142.

[77] *MHS Coll.,* Series 5, v, 378.

[78] T. Hutchinson, *History,* ii, 70.

[79] *MHS Coll.,* Series 5, v, 369.

Vernon Louis Parrington (essay date 1927)

SOURCE: "The Mather Dynasty," in *Main Currents in American Thought, Vol. I,* 1927. Reprint by Harcourt Brace & Company, 1954, pp. 99-118.

[*In the following excerpt, first published in 1927, Parrington assesses Mather as a religious and politically influential figure.*]

. . . The Mathers were a singularly provocative family, capable, ambitious, certain to have a finger in every pie baking in the theocratic oven. From the emigrant Richard with the great voice, chief architect of the Cambridge Platform, to the provincial Cotton, the family combativeness and love of publicity put their marks on New England history. Of the three generations, certainly Increase Mather was the most generously endowed with capacity for leadership; an able man, practical and assertive, liking to be in the forefront of affairs, not wanting his light hidden under a bushel. An archconservative, he justified his ways to his conscience by the excellence of the heritage he strove to conserve. A formalist, he satisfied his intellectual curiosity by extolling the sufficiency of the creed of the fathers. He closed the windows of his mind against the winds of new doctrine, and bounded the fields of speculative inquiry by orthodox fences. He was of the succession of John Cotton rather than Thomas Hooker, a priestly theocrat, though never a shuffler like Cotton, less troubled by free inquiry, less by the intellectual. All his life he was inhibited from bold speculation by his personal loyalties and interests. As a beneficiary of things as they were, certain to lose in prestige and power with any relaxing of the theocracy, it would be asking too much of human nature to expect him to question the sufficiency of the established system of which he was the most distinguished representative. Not to have approved it would have been to repudiate his habitual way of thinking, his deepest prejudices, his strongest convictions. He had been molded and shaped by the theocracy; it was the very marrow of his bones; as well demand that pig iron turn molten again after it comes from the matrix. The ore of which he was fashioned was excellent, but once molded it was rigid; there would be no return to fluidity. And so determined by every impact of environment, by every appeal of loyalty, and by a very natural ambition, Increase Mather became a stout upholder of the traditional order, a staunch old Puritan Tory of the theocratic line. How could any promptings of liberalism find nourishment in such a mind?[2] Why should one expect to find in the works of such a man the seeds of new systems of thought or more generous institutions? He was the outstanding figure of the theocracy in the days of its overthrow, but intellectually he was not worthy to unloose the shoe-strings of Roger Williams.

In his professional capacity, Increase Mather was the priest rather than the theologian, a pastor of the flock, an expounder of the creed, rather than a seeker after new light. As a minister his mind was circumscribed by the thinking of John Calvin. He learned nothing from Luther, and was bitterly hostile to those phases of Independency that embodied the more generous Lutheran principles. No man was by temperament better fitted to embrace the coercive spirit of the Genevan discipline. Strong-willed and ascetic, he discovered in discipline the chief end for which the children of Adam are created. A profound admirer of the close-knit Genevan system, he was a Presbyterian in spirit, a man after Calvin's own heart, who clung to the old coercions in an age that was seeking to throw them off. If he counseled innovation it was in the way of strengthening ministerial authority, never in the way of liberalizing either creed or practice. It was the Congregationalism of the Cambridge Platform, and not that of early Plymouth, that he upheld; and to strengthen that order he turned earnestly to the practical work of Presbyterianizing. He was the prime mover in summoning the synod of 1679—80, requested by the Court to consider amongst other things what "may appear necessary for the preventing schismes, haeresies, prophaneness, & the establishment of the churches in one faith & order of the gospell,"[3] and the chief suggestions of the body, of which he was the conspicuous leader, were a return to a stricter discipline, and a strengthening of the passage in the Savoy Confession of faith—adopted by the synod—by borrowings from the Westminster Confession, which "more positively set forth the authority of the state in doctrinal questions."[4]

In 1691, while in London, Mather had been active in the work of uniting the Presbyterian and Congregational churches of England, under articles that would seem to have been more Presbyterian than Congregational; and in 1705, following the curiously spiteful controversy over the Brattle Street Church he joined vigorously in the proposed work of rejuvenating the New England system by engrafting further shoots from the Presbyterian stock. One of these grafts from the London agreement—the principle of licensing ministerial candidates by the association of ministers, thereby effectively preventing the intrusion of undesired members—established itself on the Congregational system; but another—the principle of associational control of the several churches—was blighted by the attack of John Wise.[5] What this desired consolidation of power in the hands of the ministers implied, is suggested by the terms of the Cambridge Platform, which asserted that "the work & duty of the people is expressed in the phrase of obeying their Elders," and that they may not "speak in church, before they have leave from the elders: nor continue so doing, when they require silence, nor may they oppose nor contradict the judgment or sentence of the Elders, without sufficient & weighty cause."[6] Recalling that the elders of a church had been reduced in number to the single minister, one may perhaps venture to suggest that a man ardently working to strengthen the hands of the ministerial oligarchy by further Presbyterianizing was no friend to Separatist-Congregationalism, nor one in whom the spirit of humility would work any lessening of the authority of the Lord's stewards.[7]

In his conception of toleration Mather followed naturally in the footsteps of John Cotton. He would tolerate all views that were not in error, but his criteria of truth were so far from catholic as to lead him into constant and vehement attack upon other sects. As a responsible leader he was careful to clothe his attacks with generous professions; but he never stepped forward to uphold the right of free thought, or to dissuade his brethren from heresy-baiting. His biographer is greatly impressed by the minister's professions, and takes them at somewhat more than face value, forgetting the ancient saying that by the fruits of men's lives they shall be known. Casuistry is useful for purposes of defense, and a skillful apologist can explain away much; but the spirit of toleration revealed in the following passages was certainly no child of liberalism:

> The "Anabaptists" had given trouble in New England. They had installed as minister a man excommunicated from the Congregational church, and, when their meeting-house was closed to them, they persisted in assembling publicly before its barred doors rather than worship unmolested in a private house. To Mather these were attacks upon the true faith, and manifest disturbances of the civil peace. Naturally there is some acidity in his strictures on the "blasted Error" of "Antipedobaptism." . . .

He denounces Baptists roundly enough, points to their kinship with the turbulent Anabaptists in Europe, and writes: "Are they not generally of a bad Spirit? Bitter enemies to the Lords most eminent Servants? yea, to the faithfull Ambassadors, spitting the cruel venome of Asps against them."

He then concludes: "Nor is the modern reader likely to disagree" with the apology by President Oakes, who wrote in an introduction to Mather's screed:

> It is sufficiently known to those that know the Author, that he is none of the Ishmaels of the times, that have their hand against every man and love to be taking a Dog by the Ears . . . or to be dabbling in the waters of strife. . . . They that know his Doctrine and manner of life, cannot but know that the life of his Spirit is in the things of practical Divinity, and the great Design of his ministry is to promote the power and practice of piety in the greatest instances. . . . I dare undertake . . . his design . . . is not to traduce . . . those that are otherwise minded, or expose them to severities & sufferings on the bare account of their opinion.[8]

From these curious passages the unsympathetic realist is likely to draw the conclusions that the spirit of mutual admiration came to early birth in New England, and that it makes a vast difference whose ox is gored. Something of the same casuistry is employed to explain away Increase Mather's unhappy part in the witch-craft mess.[9] The whole matter is involved and rendered difficult by guilty consciences and the need to save reputations, and perhaps the facts are not to be got at; yet it is only another instance to show how quickly candor flies out at the window when a Mather comes in at the door. One may make much or little of the son's statement that Increase grew more tolerant in his later years; it would seem at best to have been only the difference between black and dark gray. A dominating man does not take kindly to differences of counsel. Increase Mather was a stout upholder of the law and order in the shaping of which he had a hand, but he looked with no friendly eye on the architects of a different order; and the bitterness of his later years was the natural consequence of a strong, proud, ambitious man, thwarted in his dearest projects.

If he contributed nothing to a more liberal theology or church organization, it is idle to expect him to have contributed to political speculation. As a leader of the theocracy he meddled much in practical politics, but it would seem that he was quite unread in the political philosophers and wholly ignorant of major principles. The great English liberals of Commonwealth times and later left him untouched. He bought and read many books, but almost none of a political nature.[10] Hobbes, Harrington, Sidney, Milton, Filmer, Locke, were as much out of his intellectual ken as were the speculations of Roger Williams. Interest in political theory had ceased in Massachusetts with the banishment of the great Independent, and the principles of liberal thinkers like Harrington and Milton would have awakened little sympathy in so stalwart a theocrat as Increase Mather. He was a practical man, an administrator and mentor, a stern *castigator morum* to the commonwealth, and as a college president he had been trained in a school little notable for its sympathetic consideration of the views of subordinates. He got on ill with his Harvard tutors, and one of the unseemliest squabbles of his later years grew out of the bitterness sowed between a "strong" administrator and his teaching staff.[11] A man accounted less pious, concerned with ends more patently worldly, might well be reckoned dictatorial and domineering; but Puritan righteousness, perhaps, is not to be judged by profane standards, nor the same severity of judgment applied to politicians laboring in the theocratic vineyard, that is applied to the common breed.

Perhaps the happiest years of Increase Mather's arduous life were those spent in London as agent of the theocratic party to secure such terms as he could for the settlement of New England. It was a congenial task and a congenial field. His love of diplomacy and his fondness for England were both gratified. He mingled there on terms of equality with the intellectual leaders of English Nonconformity, and matched his wit with men high in station. He proved himself a skillful manager, but the threads were too tangled for any Puritan diplomat to smooth out, and he fell short of his hopes. The terms of the charter as finally drafted satisfied few of the Boston theocrats, and his nomination of Sir William Phipps for Governor was certainly ill-judged. Sir William had been converted to the true faith by Increase himself and was recloned by him a chosen vessel of the Lord; but he turned out to be no better than a cracked pot, and with the coming of Dudley the political influence of Increase Mather was finally broken. He was maneuvered out of his position as president of Harvard and later suffered the mortification of seeing the post fall into the hands of Leverett, the old tutor now become an influential politician, with whom he had been bitterly at outs. "Doubtless there is not any government in the world," he wrote, "that has been laid under greater obligations by a greater man than this government has been by me. Nevertheless I have received more discouragement in the work of the Lord, by those in government, than by all the men in the world besides. Let not my children put too much confidence in men."[12] It is not pleasant to be ousted from one's position by politicians, and if one is certain that the slight intended for the servant falls on the Master, it is scarcely to be borne. If waves of black pessimism swept over him in those unhappy later years when his ambitions were hopelessly frustrated, there was provocation enough. He had outlived his age and the ablest of the native-born theocrats had become a byword and a mocking amongst the profane of Boston.

Not a great man, as the world reckons greatness, Increase Mather may scarcely be accounted a great Puritan. As a theologian he was wanting in speculative vigor, and as a pastor he was wanting in self-denying love. It is not necessary to set him over against Roger Williams or Jonathan Edwards or William Ellery Channing, to reveal his intellectual and spiritual shortcomings. One has only to place him beside so rugged and honest a Puritan as Samuel Hopkins, who is true Christian humility, utterly regardless of his own fame, gave his life to theology and the care of the poor and the outcast, to realize how conventional a soul was Increase Mather, how incurious intellectually, how ambitious and self-seeking. Men loved Samuel Hopkins even though they might vigorously reject his doctrine, as they loved Roger Williams and Ellery Channing; but few seem to have loved Increase Mather. One might respect his abilities, but he was too austerely forbidding to like, too overbearing to awaken the spirit of good will. Ideas in the abstract held no interest for him. His biographer has happily recalled Mather's forgotten interest in scientific inquiry, and for this slight relief from the intolerable drab of his life-story one may be grateful. Yet one must not build too high on an insubstantial foundation. In the England that Mather loved, and toward which he was strongly drawn—hoping that opportunity would offer for a pulpit there—pottering over natural philosophy had become a mark of distinction, and a man so envious of repute would have wished to approve himself to those whom he admired. Though he lived in Boston he would not have it thought that he was provincial.

Of the miscellaneous literary output that flowed from his pen in an abundant stream, little need be said. It is of concern only to minute historians of the local. That he was master of an excellent prose style, clear and straightforward, is sufficiently evident; if his matter had been so good, his legitimate fame would have been far greater. The work on which his reputation largely rests is *An Essay for the Recording of Illustrious Providences,* printed at Boston and London in 1684, and twice reissued in the nineteenth century under the title *Remarkable Providences* It is an amusing book of old wives' tales, not singular at all for the times, but characteristic rather; an expression of the naïveté that crops out in Winthrop's *History of New England,* and other writings of the emigrant generation, but now become a fashion amongst the lesser lights of the Royal Academy and English Nonconformists. It suited to a nicety the Mather love of marvels, and Increase constituted himself a generous repository of all the chimney-corner tales of the countryside. To call such a book "a scientific and historical recording of phenomena observed in New England," as his biographer has done, is to gall the back of a thesis with hard riding.[13] In one chapter only does Mather suggest the spirit of scientific inquiry; four out of the twelve deal with witchcraft and kindred topics; and the rest are made up of such instances of divine providence as great fish jumping out of the sea into the boats of starving sailors adrift, of the freaks played by lightning and tornadoes, and of God's punishments on wicked Quakers. At the time it was a harmless enough book, but in the light of after developments it was scarcely so harmless. The emphasis laid upon witchcraft was an unfortunate, if unconsidered, influence in preparing the psychology of New England for the Salem outbreak, and the minister later reaped a bitter harvest from it.

"Not many years ago," he wrote in the preface to **Illustrious Providences,** "I *lost* (and that's an afflictive *loss* indeed!) several moneths from study by sickness. Let every God-fearing reader joyn with me in prayer, that I may be enabled to redeem the time, and (in all ways wherein I am capable) to serve my generation." That Increase Mather sincerely desired to serve his generation according to his lights, none may deny. His labors were appalling, his reputation was great, and when he died the light of the old churches went out. The spirit of Presbyterianism went to its grave in New England, and not till a hundred years later did the new light—which was no other than primitive English Independency—shine out in the life and work of William Ellery Channing. After two centuries Unitarianism recovered for the Massachusetts churches the spirit of early Separatism that had been lost since the days of the Cambridge Platform. Channing finally uprooted the vine that Increase Mather had so laboriously tended. . . .

Notes

. . . ² Compare Murdock, *Increase Mather,* pp. 394-95.

³ Quoted in W. Walker, *A History of Congregational Churches, etc.,* p. 187.

⁴ *Ibid.,* p. 190. His biographer has overlooked the significance of this. See Murdock, *Increase Mather,* p. 151.

⁵ His biographer has somewhat slurred his account of the "Proposals." See p. 282. But his justification is worth noting: "If the original brand of Puritan piety was worth saving, and Mather believed it was, an oligarchic church government was the only means of securing it in an age when men were inclined to change their religious ideas as they changed their thought on other affairs."

⁶ W. Walker, *A History of the Congregational Churches, etc.,* p. 205.

⁷ Compare Murdock, *Increase Mather,* pp. 361-363.

⁸ Murdock, *Increase Mather,* pp. 138-139.

⁹ See pp. 294-295, where he seeks unsuccessfully to refute the position taken by J. T. Adams.

¹⁰ See Murdock, *Increase Mather,* pp. 125-127.

¹¹ "The Brattle-Street Church Controversy," for which see *ibid.,* pp. 258 ff

¹² *Ibid.,* pp. 373-4, note.

¹³ *Ibid.,* p. 170.

William J. Scheick (essay date 1971)

SOURCE: "Anonymity and Art in the Life and Death of That Reverend Man of God, Mr. Richard Mather," in *American Literature,* Vol. XLII, No. 4, January, 1971, pp.457-67.

[*In the following essay, Scheick examines Increase Mather's biography of his father, Richard Mather, paying particular attention to Increase's use of paternal imagery in a familial, spiritual, and communal sense.*]

It is true that in many respects the intention of New England Puritan biographies is identical to that of their sermons. Both reflect an attempt to convey religious instruction regarding the conduct of one's life on earth; both likewise seek to stimulate the reader to the practice of *imitatio Christi,* a practice discussed at length in numerous sermons as well as reflected through the exemplary lives of Puritan biographical subjects.¹ Consequently, seventeenth-century American biographies "aimed less at the modern ideal of accurate revelation of a personality than at the graphic portrayal of the virtues of the Puritan saint."²

Although this attitude toward biography proved rigid and to some extent impeded this genre from flowering into a fully developed art form, apparently it was sufficiently tractable to yield such disparate works as Cotton Mather's prodigious *Magnalia Christi Americana* (1702) and Increase Mather's gentle **The Life and Death of That Reverend Man of God, Mr. Richard Mather** (1670). To be sure, both books share common religious premises as well as manifest orthodox Puritan views of biography. Yet, whereas the *Magnalia* has been described as "a showcase of pedantry and elephantine wit,"³ *Life and Death* has always received a more benign reception, as, for example, when we are told that "we read the little biography to-day without boredom and, often, with admiration for a simple dignity that comes close to art."⁴

A closer look at *Life and Death* suggests that the work does more than merely approach art. There is present in this biography an artistically structuring motif centered around the image of the father. On one level, of course, the motif originates from the fact that Increase is Richard Mather's son; but on another, deeper level this father imagery points beyond a solely natural or secular sense and reveals the more pervasive religious dimension of the relation between spiritual fathers or ministers, such as Richard Mather, and the New England family as a whole.

This underlying framework of father imagery is informed by a fundamental thematic concern in *Life and Death:* that Providence progressively unfolds or reveals the continuity of the divine will through succeeding Puritan generations, particularly through certain individuals in these generations. In the context of the primary motif of the biography, these individuals are fathers; and in the light of their role as agents of God's will, their example and guidance, reviewed *in toto,* contribute to a collective voice, a voice transcending the specifically temporal individuality of each father and deriving from his membership in that spiritual community in which all true Puritan fathers bear witness to immutable essential truths.[5]

Recognition of this theme and the motif stemming from it provides a better appreciation of *Life and Death*. It sheds light on Increase's motivation for publishing the biography anonymously; it also gives insight into the significance of the book's style and techniques which have received such favorable, if evasive, comment. The outcome of such an investigation reveals *Life and Death* to be a New England Puritan biography—unified in theme and method—which deserves acknowledgment as a true literary achievement.

I

The structure of *Life and Death* is based on the image of Richard Mather as a father, as Increase's natural father and Dorchester's spiritual father. This image is established in the opening line of the Preface of the biography: *"You have here presented to your view, and for your Imitation in the Lord, the* Life *of him that was to many of you a* Spiritual *(as to me a* Natural*) Father."*[6] But in order to appreciate the significance of this twofold role, it is necessary to view Richard Mather's life in a larger context: the succession of Puritan fathers, beginning in England, and the continuity of God's design for New England as progressively unveiled in their life and works. It was Increase's fidelity to this theme which dictated the brevity and elliptic nature of *Life and Death;* for in order to avoid any diffusion of focus, Increase relates only those aspects of his father's life and character which are relevant to this theme.

It is appropriate, therefore, that although Richard Mather always remains at the center of attention in the biography, the opening pages concern to a significant extent his parents, especially his father, Thomas Mather. Richard remarked, for instance, that as a child his painful experiences with a schoolmaster would have led to his *"utter undoing, had not the good Providence of God, and the Wisdome and Authority of my Father prevented"* (p. 3). In this passage God is, in accord with common Puritan custom, given primary credit; but in equally typical Puritan fashion God manifests His will through natural agency—in this case, as throughout *Life and Death,* by means of a Puritan father.[7]

In *Life and Death* the word *father* is interchangeable with the terms *minister* and *teacher.* It is not surprising, consequently, that after his natural father the next decisive influence on young Richard's life was exerted by a Mr. Palin, the minister or spiritual father of Leagh. Of Reverend Palin, Richard often said that "the remembrance of that man was Comfortable and Honourable in his thoughts, even in his old Age, though his knowledge of him was in his Childhood" (p. 4).

Eventually, in accordance with God's design, Richard had to prepare for his own vocation as a divine servant in this chain of fathers, and so "he was called to leave his Fathers Family" to teach the children of Toxteth (p. 4). In retrospect Increase sees that this initial stage in Richard's development as a teacher foreshadowed his future career as a famous natural and spiritual father in New England; for "the Lord helped him in those his young years to carry it with such Wisdome and Love and Gravity amongst his Scholars as was to admiration, so as that he was by them both loved and feared, beyond what is usual" (p. 5). If *Life and Death* is to be trusted, similar sentiments were felt in Richard's later years by the laity of Dorchester.[8]

While at Toxteth Richard benefited from still other divinely directed paternal influences:

> The means of his Conversion was partly by seeing a strange difference between himself and sundry in that godly Family, where Divine Providence had cast his Lot in *Toxteth,* viz. the Family of Mr. *Edward Aspinwall,* who was a Learned and Religious Gentleman. Now he observed that the way and walking of that holy man, was such as himself had not as yet been accustomed unto. . . . Also Mr. *Harrison,* then a famous Minister at *Hyron,* Preaching upon *Job.* 3. 3. concerning the necessity of Regeneration, and at the same time reading a Book of Mr. *Perkins.* (pp. 5-6)

After his conversion Richard's future destiny as a Puritan father, particularly as an instrument of God's will to the "children" of the Dorchester "family," became more apparent. While still at Toxteth, "Being thus become a *New Creature,* he was the more eminently a Blessing in the Family, and in the Calling which the Lord had disposed of him in: And such notice was taken of him, as that even from places remote Children were sent unto him for Instruction and Education" (p. 6). Later, as spiritual father and teacher of Dorchester, Richard mirrored the outcome of this preparatory experience at Toxteth in his attitude toward his spiritual children, his parishioners: "*If . . . I preach Learnedly, then onely the Learned and not the Unlearned can understand and profit by me; but if I preach plainly, then Learned and Unlearned both can understand*" (p. 31). To be sure, this idea follows naturally from the traditional Puritan notion of the role of sermons in the experience of conversion;[9] but in the context of *Life and Death* this belief further reinforces the theme that God reveals His will through a succession of spiritual fathers and that Richard Mather indeed received a divine calling to contribute to that succession, to become in fact one of the very founding fathers of New England.

The next important stage in Richard Mather's life was his immigration to the New World, and Increase relates in entirety his father's arguments for the Puritans' departure from England. The inclusion of this document at first strikes the reader as a flaw; it is eight pages in length, seems to interrupt the pace, and is not of the same quality as the rest of the biography. On second thought, however, the imagery in Increase's rationale for including these arguments deserves closer attention: "because they are of weight, and because Posterity may thereby see what were the swaying Motives which prevailed with the First-fathers of *N.E.* to venture upon that unparallell'd Undertaking, even to Transport themselves, their Wives and Little ones, over the rude Waves of the vast Ocean, into a Land which was not sown" (p. 11). The emphasis in this explanation falls not only upon the Puritan view of the promise of New England but also, in regard to the underlying motif of the biography, upon the establishment, by Richard Mather and the other forefathers, of the New England family out of which there will arise in time generations of subsequent natural and spiritual fathers. This focus on the paternal role in the family is, in fact, readily apparent in the document itself. Among Richard's justifications for the emigration, one learns, for instance, that since all families—whether natural, civil, or religious—require fatherly authority, "removing from a Family where is no Government or good order for suppressing of sin and wickedness, to another where is, be necessary for one that is free" (pp. 15-16).[10] Likewise, Richard reasoned that since "Parents and Masters are bound to remove if they were in such Commonwealths, where they might not be suffered to Rule and Govern their own Children and Servants," it follows that "Ministers being free, are bound to remove, if they be in such place where they may not govern their own Flocks" (p. 19). Thus, even this lengthy document actually proves to be an organic part of *Life and Death,* for it sustains the basic motif on which the entire book is structured.

In his mature years, as minister and "Teacher" of Dorchester where "he did (by the help of Christ) set upon the great Work of *Gathering a Church*" (p. 24), Richard Mather fulfilled the promise of his novitiate as schoolmaster by accepting God's call and hence becoming a true elder of the New England family: "Being thus again setled in the Lords Work, he therein continued unto his dying day; the Lord making him an Eminent Blessing not onely to *Dorchester,* but to all the Churches and Plantations round about, for the space of near upon Four and thirty years" (p. 24). Yet, even during the time of his mature ministry and in spite of the fact that he was himself a founding father, Richard Mather still continued to learn from other spiritual fathers in the Puritan community: from Reverend Norton, for example, "then *Teacher* to the Church in *Ipswich,* unto whom (under Christ) God gave the tongue of the Learned to speak a word in season, whereby his [Richard's] Soul was Comforted"; from "Doctor *Goodwins* Discourse about *Patience,* in which Book he read till the very day of his Death" (pp. 25, 29).

In the light of his concentration on this father motif it is consistent for Increase to bypass specific details of his father's life. Hence he next focuses on Richard's old age, especially on a bedside scene which reveals that even while suffering a fatal illness his father thought about the generation to follow him. Of particular concern to him as a spiritual father are the future children of the Puritan household; and so speaking of the Half-Way Covenant he instructed his son Increase, now "*Teacher*" of a Church in *Boston*": "*a speciall thing which I would commend to you, is, Care concerning the Rising Generation in this Country, that they be brought under the Government of Christ in his Church; and that when grown up and qualified, they have Baptism for their Children*" (p. 27).[11] Richard desired that the continuity of Puritan generations, as guided by their spiritual fathers, be maintained. This idea is further mirrored in Increase's frequent references to his father's six natural sons, references which place some of them firmly within the next generation of spiritual fathers (pp. 8, 22): "the Lord was faithful and gracious to him, in respect of his Children. . . . And the Lord cheered the heart of this his Servant in his old Age, by giving him to see most of his Sons imployed in the Ministry many years before their precious Father's decease" (p. 29).

That his sons should carry on, through the practice of *imitatio Christi,* the work of their natural father is further evidenced in Richard Mather's last will and testament. Although it was a seventeenth-century convention to include the will of the biographical subject, that of Richard Mather is appropriate to *Life and Death* because it further emphasizes his role as a father to the "children" of New England, "*in which Imployment if any thing hath been done which hath been pleasing unto him* [God], *or any way beneficiall to any Childe of his, it hath not been I that hath done the same, but the grace of God which was with me"* (p. 35). The will similarly expresses the hope that his sons are truly of the elect, from whom such fathers are drawn: *"I hope God hath already made them partakers, at least Sundry of them, of his saving grace in Christ"* (p. 37). But Richard's hope went deeper than this; it included the possibility that perhaps his sons would contribute to the succession of spiritual fathers, a point Increase discloses just prior to presenting his father's will when he cites from his father's private papers that Richard Mather desired that *"his Sons after him might see by their Fathers Example, what it is to walk before God"* (p. 33).

The closing words of the will center on heaven, where, Richard hopefully anticipated, he and his first wife *"shall see not our selves alone, but those also that have proceeded and come forth out of our own bowels, to have their part and portion in that Eternall Glory"* (p. 38). Then, he hoped, his entire natural family would be reunited in Christ's heavenly family. But in the light of Increase's prefatory designation of Richard as both a natural and a spiritual father, the implication of this, the final passage of the biography, extends beyond the confines of his immediate family; in a sense it brings the biography full circle, for this sentiment doubtless signifies, as does the Preface, an appeal to the spiritual children of Dorchester, indeed of all New England, that they continue under the leadership of their spiritual fathers. Then Richard would eventually be joined in heaven not only by his natural sons but also by the elect of Dorchester and, as well, by all the spiritual children of each succeeding generation of the Puritan fathers—all united eternally in the household of Christ, Himself the Son of God, the Father.

II

The success of *Life and Death* to some degree proceeds from the author's anonymous voice or persona as well as from his style and biographical techniques. In ascertaining the motivation behind Increase's anonymity—he signed the Preface in which he wrote that *"the Composer of this ensuing Relation is not willing that his Name should be published"* (p. iii)—one might point to what he himself describes as his father's best characteristic:

Some have thought that his greatest errour was, that he did not magnifie his Office, as he might and sometimes should have done. If a man must erre, it is good erring on that hand. *Humble enough, and good enough,* was the frequent Saying of a great Divine. And another observeth, *That every man hath just as much and no more true worth in him, as he hath Humility, Austine* being asked which was the most excellent grace, answered, *Humility;* and which was the next, answered, *Humility;* and which was the third, replied again, *Humility.* That indeed is

Comprehensively All, being of great price in the sight of God: And if so, Mr. *Mather* was a man of much Reall Worth. (p. 34)

By suppressing his own identity Increase likewise evidences the virtue of humility, an attribute which Cotton Mather, despite his numerous borrowings, never reflected in the resounding authorial voice of the *Magnalia.* However, this quelling of the author's self may have a more subtle meaning. Increase's anonymity may be directly related to the father motif on which the biography is structured as well as to the theme informing this motif.

The theme of the book, as we have already noted, concerns the progressive unfolding of the divine will through the spiritual fathers of the Puritan community. In order to maintain the continuity of this sequence each father must, in a sense, continue to live on in the following generation; this is especially true when one considers that the revelation to which their lives and works gave testimony remains constant throughout the vicissitudes of time.[12] It therefore follows that if such a continuity is to be preserved, each younger generation must imitate their spiritual parents—hence the Puritan interest in biographies. This idea is expressed in the first sentence of the book when Increase explains that Richard Mather's life is presented *"for your Imitation in the Lord";* shortly thereafter he again remarks: *"your selves know that God made him* Exemplarily *Faithfull, Zealous, Patient, Humble, Holy: Follow him as he followed Christ"* (p. iv). Later in the work not only are we told that his father was *"a Pattern of Patience"* (p. 28) but we are instructed by Richard Mather himself to think in terms of "the imitable and commended Example of Christ, and other faithful Servants of God" (p. 13).

As Richard's deathbed scene makes clear, Increase is to carry on this tradition; he is to imitate his father in his role as a minister and teacher of the Puritan family. Certainly Increase could not have escaped the full impact of his father's wish "that his Sons after him might see by their Fathers Example, what it is to *walk before God."* To imitate his father would mean that, in a sense, his own voice and that of his father would become one and the same, at least regarding theological truth; for although God deals with New England progressively, His timeless design is radically complete from the first.[13] Thus in regard to this design the individual voices of all the Puritan spiritual fathers are transformed into a collective voice, a voice rooted in Christ and stemming from the underlying continuity of truth expressed through the lives and works of His ministerial servants.[14]

Here, I think, lies the deeper dimension of Increase's anonymity. In *Life and Death* he seeks to evidence implicitly what he is expressing explicitly about imitating exemplary figures; that is to say, by subverting the individuality of his voice and thereby keeping the narration of the biography relatively free from authorial intrusions, Increase completely identifies with his father. He wrote the biography during what has been called a "time of stress," when subsequent to his father's death his "mood was one of passionate desire to do some last service before he, too, should be called to face trial by God";[15] and in this work Increase was seeking to merge his voice with that of his father in order to arrive at a sense of sharing in the collective voice of Puritan divines as it had been manifested in Richard Mather's life and work. From this perspective anonymity actually means less a surrender of Increase's self than the achievement of a true self, a self whose identity derives from the collective voice which has been and will continue to be, through generations of Puritan fathers, an instrument of the divine will.

Increase's anonymity is related to the style and techniques he uses in **Life and Death**. The style is characteristically Puritan in that it is a "plain style,"[16] a fact placing it squarely within the traditional voice of most seventeenth-century New England writing. This manner of writing had been advocated by his father, when, for example, "He would often use that Saying, *Artis est celare Artem*" (p. 31). The style of a Puritan father's works, especially in his sermons and other didactic writings such as biographies, should be transparent so that, as a medium of Christ's influence, the light of truth may shine through them. The style and language of **Life and Death** signify Increase's attempt to imitate his father—the language is drawn largely from Richard's own words—and to allow this truth to reveal itself through the biography. Thus it is both appropriate and significant that Increase echoes his father's literary standard when he speaks of the biography as comprised of "words of truth and plainness" (p. 2).

The author's anonymity is similarly related to the techniques employed in the biography. By relying on his father's own words—from his books, sermons, conversations, private meditations, and last will and testament—as well as on anecdotes and others' comments about his father, Increase actively represses any overt emotional response to the loss of his father and assumes a somewhat passive disposition which is concomitant with a transparent style of "truth and plainness." The very technique of allowing details to filter through his prose without embellishing comment arises from Increase's effort to become an instrument of the divine will and thus identify with the collective voice of the Puritan fathers. By means of this identification Increase consciously begins to fulfill his father's wish to be imitated by his sons; and by so doing Increase pays his father the highest compliment he can.[17] Moreover, through this identification with his father in **Life and Death** he achieves a sense of renewal at a time when he is spiritually depressed. Now, symbolically assuming his father's role as a spiritual father, Increase is ready to assert his new self and heed his father's advice about taking *"Care concerning the Rising Generation"*; for in an effort to carry on his father's work and the tradition to which it belongs, Increase resolved in his diary after his father's death to write "some discourses wherein the rising generation should be especially concerned . . . for God's glory, and the good of souls."[18]

Thus, just as his father's funeral speeches were "taken up not with Praising the Dead, but with *Instructing the Living*" (p. 9), so finally is Increase Mather's book. **The Life and Death of That Reverend Man of God, Mr. Richard Mather** is not merely a biography of one father but an attestation to God's continuing call to the New England family through its spiritual fathers, indeed through Increase himself as one of them. As biography, however, it represents a paragon of the genre as it developed in seventeenth-century America. The author's anonymity as well as the book's brevity, underlying motif, pervading theme, simple style, and biographical techniques all contribute to an integrated art work, one which conveys implicitly as a whole what it argues explicitly. It is a true literary achievement, even as judged in the light of modern belletristic standards.

Notes

[1] It has been suggested that the use of a form of character essay in sermons was directly linked to the origin of Puritan biographical works: Josephine K. Piercy, *Studies in Literary Types in Seventeenth Century America* (New Haven, 1939), pp. 168-175.

[2] Kenneth B. Murdock, *Literature and Theology in Colonial New England* (New York, 1963), p. 117.

[3] Peter Gay, *A Loss of Mastery: Puritan Historians in Colonial America* (New York, 1968), p. 60. To this somewhat unfair appraisal Gay further writes: "It is overloaded, and often overwhelmed, with expansive and irrelevant introductory passages, with far-fetched parallels, embarrassing puns, fatiguing alliterations, puerile anagrams; the writing is prolix, arch, involuted, imprecise, repetitive, and hysterical."

[4] Kenneth B. Murdock, *Increase Mather, the Foremost American Puritan* (Cambridge, Mass., 1925), p. 97.

[5] The subject of voice in New England Puritan literature has not received sufficient attention. To the best of my knowledge the only article which treats certain aspects of the matter is Thomas E. Johnston's "A Note on the Voices of Anne Bradstreet, Edward Taylor, Roger Williams, and Phillip Pain," *Early American Literature*, III (Fall, 1968), 125-126.

[6] *The Life and Death of That Reverend Man of God, Mr. Richard Mather* (Cambridge, Mass., 1670), p. iii. Subsequent references to this work will be included in the text.

[7] "The Lord is pleased, not through any *defect of power* in Himself but out of *the abundance of his goodness* to communicate causal power and virtue to his Creatures, & to honour them with that Dignity that they may be his Instruments" (Urian Oakes, *The Soveraign Efficacy of Divine Providence,* Boston, 1682, p. 6).

[8] Murdock comments that for Increase, Richard was "not merely a dear human father but a father of much that to him and his friends was best in New England. Richard Mather remained teacher to the last" (*Increase Mather,* p. 96).

[9] See, for instance, John Cotton, *The Way of Life* (London, 1641), pp. 162-165.

[10] This concept of civil or federal freedom as opposed to natural freedom is explained in detail by John Winthrop in his famous speech to the general court (July 3, 1645); see Perry Miller and Thomas H. Johnson, eds., *The Puritans: A Sourcebook of Their Writings* (New York, 1963), I, 206-207.

[11] For a discussion of the Half-Way Covenant see Perry Miller, *The New England Mind: From Colony to Province* (Boston, 1961), pp. 95-104.

[12] Consider, for instance, the following observation about the Puritans: "To them all human affairs have always been under the continuous direction of God; history is the record of His incessant supervision, and there can be no real decline or fluctuation of God's power. The past is a drama, written, directed, produced, and prompted by God. It must, therefore, be as full of meaning at one time as at another" (*The Puritans,* I, 82).

[13] This idea informed, among other things, the Puritan understanding of typology, according to which "God's revelation was progressive and continuous from one moment in history to another" (Mason I. Lowance, "Typology and the New England Way: Cotton Mather and the Exegesis of Biblical Types," *Early American Literature,* IV, no. 1, 1969, 15).

[14] In his undergraduate oration, "The prayse of Eloquence," Michael Wigglesworth noted that it is "ould truth" which "receivs a new habit" through the power of eloquence, that though truth's "visage" may be "so altered that it may currently pass and be accepted as a novelty," yet "its essence be the same" (Samuel E. Morison, *Harvard College in the Seventeenth Century,* Cambridge, Mass., 1936, I, 180).

[15] *Increase Mather,* p. 97.

[16] Perry Miller discusses the Puritan regard for a "plain style" in *The New England Mind: The Seventeenth Century* (Boston, 1961), pp. 302-304.

[17] "I considered with myself that if I should write & publish my Father's life it would be a service not only honorable to my Father, but acceptable & honorable to the name of God" (as quoted from Increase Mather's "Autobiography" by Murdock, *Increase Mather,* p. 96).

[18] Ibid., p. 98.

Robert Middlekauff (essay date 1971)

SOURCE: "The Invisible World," in *The Mathers: Three Generations of Puritan Intellectuals, 1596-1728,* Oxford University Press, Inc., 1971, pp. 139-61.

[*In the following essay, Middlekauff asserts that while Mather's stated purpose in his scientific writings was to discredit scientific explanations of natural occurances, it was also this interest in science and his knowledge of the difference between appearance and reality that enabled him to help end the witch trials.*]

While the controversy with Stoddard was brewing, but before it reached a boil, Increase Mather was thinking about another matter that affected his ideas about the Church in New England: nature and an arena beyond nature, the invisible world. In fact Mather always pursued his scientific studies in the frame of mind that inspired not only his ecclesiology but all his scholarship. His preoccupations, which were those of his generation of New English divines, remained centered on God's designs—especially as they involved New England. It is true that in Mather's lifetime such concerns lost much of their urgency for him as he turned his attention to the problems of converting the elect, but even then his sense of wonder at the mystery in the world and his love of the power behind it, which had been reinforced by his scientific studies, continued as strong as ever.

Increase approached scientific study with the traditional Puritan assumptions about nature as an extension of God's wisdom and power. His friend Samuel Willard once said that "When God wrought the works of Creation, he had a Design in every Creature."[1] The detection of that design was recommended to all sorts of men, who were told that it was their duty just as poring over the Scriptures was. The divines who urged scientific study were aware of the dangers in what they encouraged. scholarship and natural philosophy might completely absorb a man; they possessed the attractiveness of any of the things of this world. Some men developed an inordinate taste for meat and drink and became gluttons and drunkards; some rich men valued their vanities more than their souls; some scholars failed to see beyond second causes. This last failure was understandable because God chose to work through the laws of His created universe; but to see nothing beyond second causes was atheism nonetheless, for Providence lay behind every natural event. God's power filled the order of the cosmos. So long as men remembered that nature contrived to reconcile order and arbitrary power, they would make natural philosophy a godly enterprise. So long as they regarded nature as John Cotton had, as "a mappe and shaddow of the spirituall estate of the soules of men," they might examine it confident that they did so in the faith.[2]

Accepting these premises, Increase probed into the natural world with the eagerness, if not with the rigor, of the great figures of seventeenth-century science. The range of his interests grew throughout his life and included astronomy, geology and, under the tutelage of his son, Cotton, medicine. His most impressive study was of comets, which he discussed in several sermons and tracts, and in one major book, **Kometographia**, published in 1683. Much in these studies, and especially in the long work, suggests that a powerful curiosity pulled Increase into his investigation of the heavens. He explains in **Heavens Alarm to the World** that he was intrigued by the comet of 1680, the largest one he had ever seen.[3] He took the trouble to measure its "radiant Locks," presumably the blaze of the comet, and found them to be approximately sixty-six degrees long. As was his custom when he became interested in any subject, he read everything he could lay his hands on, but of course the great seventeenth-century works on comets were still to be written. Fortunately for his need of direction, Robert Hooke, the Secretary of the Royal Society, had published his work on the Comet of 1677; and Increase used it as a guide in his investigation of Halley's Comet, which had made one of its periodic visits in 1682.[4]

Hooke dealt with a number of problems long of interest to astronomers. He speculated on the density of comets: the nucleus of a comet was solid, he said, with a density as great as the earth's, while the tail or blaze partook of the nature of flame. He studied the source of a comet's light and finally decided that it was its own source. Hooke also considered the traditional questions about the nature of a cometary movement and distance of comets from the earth. Before Tycho Brahe's work became known, many scientists had argued that comets were sublunary bodies which had been drawn into the air, where they were set on fire. Skeptical of the view, Brahe measured their parallax and, discovering that it was less than the moon's, properly concluded that comets were at a greater distance from the earth. But Brahe made his own mistakes, the most notable one being his assumption that comets followed an orbit around the sun.[5]

The exact course of cometary movements intrigued Hooke, perhaps more than any other issue concerning their character, and much of his study was given to a calculation of their orbits. The proposition he offered on this subject which Increase Mather found intriguing was that if exact observations of a comet's parallax could be obtained, the return of a comet might be accurately predicted.

Mather's reaction to Hooke's formulation reveals more sharply than any other single feature of his work the character of his scientific interests. He agreed with Hooke, Brahe, and Kepler, all of whom he read with care, that comets did not move within the earth's atmosphere. The argument on the basis of parallax convinced him, and he pointed to the need of precise astronomical observations from several parts of the earth. But he did not accept the views of Hooke, Brahe, and Kepler uncritically. The evidence from other astronomers, inexact as their observations were, was taken into his reckonings. He also gave weight to observations which showed the relative movements of the earth, other planets, and comets. At certain times, he noted, planets interpose themselves between comets and the earth. This suggested to Increase that comets moved "in an higher Sphere" than planets.[6]

The evidence of the senses did not carry Increase as far as it did Hooke, however. Hooke described the movement of a comet as corresponding to a natural law; Increase agreed but stopped short of the inference that Hooke found compelling: the path of a comet was predictable and the return of comets could be precisely calculated. This last contention appalled Increase Mather. If it were accepted, how could the doctrine of *concursus*—the faith in a God who sustained every instant of all existence—stand; a created being operating according to its own laws, presumably independent of the Divine, compromised the sovereignty of God. Increase was prepared to believe that comets were generated somewhere beyond the earth's atmosphere, but not that they possessed everlasting (sempiternal) existence. And surely they followed the laws of nature, so far as men could understand these laws, only as long as God decreed. God used comets, as He did all nature for His own purposes; most commonly He chose to employ them as signs of impending events, "Ensigns" held up in Heaven for men to see.[7]

What comets portended depended upon Man's course along the line of time leading to the Day of Judgment. In certain periods their appearance forecast happy events; for example, the birth of Christ had been announced by a blazing star. Eventually, Mather suggested, one might anticipate a shower of comets as the Second Coming approached. But for the most part, comets did not bring happy tidings; rather they served to warn men of disasters which awaited them should they fail to heed divine commands. New England in particular had reason to recognize the dreadful portents of comets. God had often spoken to it through these preachers of divine wrath before sending His afflictions on the land.[8]

If God spoke in comets, He also acted through them, using their mysterious power as a "natural influence upon the Earth." Increase did not presume to explain the naturalness of this "influence"; rather, he contended himself with the assertion that comets "caused" droughts, infestations by caterpillars, tempests, floods, sickness, and perhaps even earthquakes. Besides signifying the coming of afflictions, which might be forestalled by repentance and then causing them when repentance was not forthcoming, they seemed also to predict apocalyptical events. Thus the second woe, the crushing blow upon the Turks, was announced by a comet; and assaults by the sixteenth-century reformers on the Antichrist in Europe were forecast. At times God chose to make their awful messages even clearer by giving comets extraordinary shapes; one in 1627, for example, assumed the form of a man's arm holding a sword about ready to descend in a crushing swipe.[9]

The belief in the grotesque stories of the shape of comets, the insistence that their orbits were unpredictable, the emphasis on their emblematic quality, the belief in their capacity to produce natural disasters, seems to comport uncomfortably with the careful observations, the sane comments about the importance of parallax, the preference for Kepler and Hooke over early superstitious savants. And in fact, Increase Mather's "science" contained jarring inconsistencies. Like the best natural philosophy of the seventeenth century, Mather's *Kometographia* was intended to brighten the glory of God in men's eyes by illuminating His secrets in nature. But Increase sensed the danger that this enterprise of opening God's mind in nature would diminish the awareness of His mysterious power. Hence the crude assertion that explanations from second causes alone constituted atheism. And hence the fact that much of *Kometographia* departed from scientific concern to explain nature on the level of the mysterious. Natural explanations sufficed for limited purposes, but for genuine understanding, the final resort had to be to piety.[10]

Increase offered *Kometographia* as an exercise in natural philosophy as well as in piety, though he inevitably blurred the conventional distinctions between the two. A year later he published *An Essay for the Recording of Illustrious Providences,* which provided additional evidence of his curiosity about nature. Yet this book, too, like his studies of comets, was designed to reinforce a sense of the mystery in life, in this case by emphasizing the power of the demonic as well as the power of the Divine.[11]

The exact beginnings of the book cannot be reconstructed. Such books of God's wonders, of remarkable providences, had appeared for centuries. The possibility of writing a book of this sort apparently first occurred to Increase when, in examining the papers of John Davenport, he discovered a manuscript that had been inspired by Matthew Pool's *Synopsis Criticorum,* an account of God's providences in such matters as storms, apparitions, floods, and possessions. (Whether Davenport had written the stories, or collected the accounts, is not clear.) Sometime in the year 1681, Increase evidently showed the collection to other Boston ministers, who, following his lead, decided to complete and publish the manuscript. Increase took the project over and finished it with the aid of his colleagues, who either contributed accounts of wonders or suggested books he might examine.[12]

The publication of the *Essay* brought to attainment a hope Increase had declared years before in the *Discourse Concerning the Danger of Apostasy.*[13] At that time he had conceived of the collection of special providences to New England, with the intention of using them to demonstrate the special character of the Lord's chosen people in America. The collection would testify to the extraordinary blessings the Puritans had received and would contribute to the rejuvenation of the faith of the fathers.

Increase's purpose survived the passage of the years; the *Essay*'s subtitle—*Wherein, An Account is given of many Remarkable and very Memorable Events, which have happened in this last Age; Especially in New England*—reflects it and the text occasionally refers to the special concern God felt for New England. But for the most part these expressions remain as afterthoughts to the main commentary, which concentrates on God's glory—not the glory of men in New England. Many of the wondrous examples of divine Providence occur outside New England, and do not involve New Englanders in any way. As in *Kometographia* these wonders are types of the Lord's wisdom and power; they are emblems of His goodness.[14]

The book carried the same purposes as Increase's studies of comets did—to undermine the authority of scientific explanation of natural phenomena and to substitute the ancient sense of divine mystery in life. To be sure, the range of subjects taken up in the *Essay* suggests a scientific curiosity which operates impartially over the varieties of nature. Sea deliverances, preservations, thunder and lightning, magnetic variations, witchcraft, demonology, storms, earthquakes are some of the subjects Increase reports on. Within this variety his intention is unvarying: to offer one level of explanation in terms of second causes, but also to insist that the Providence of God whether working through nature or outside its confines is ultimately inexplicable in this world. It is true that every case includes concrete details, suggesting the reliance upon the observation of the senses, calculated to satisfy any natural philosopher. In the accounts of preservations, boards are shattered by lightning, bricks are thrown about, positions of people tossed by wind and sea are minutely described and their injuries tabulated down to the last cut and bruise. Such details give the stories of the *Essay* their remarkable vividness; they intensify their horror and mystery. Increase wrote in the conviction that his readers would be more inclined to believe the implicit propositions about the strength and mystery of the unseen if their observed effects were fully described.[15]

Though the book is offered as observation, it is not genuinely empirical. Most of the illustrious providences were reported by witnesses whose testimony Increase accepts unquestioningly; and "evidence" of all kinds is lumped together indiscriminately. Increase repeats old folk belief—elephants fear mice, the horse abominates the camel, lions tremble at the crowing of a cock; he reports instances of strange antipathies in nature—men who swoon at the sight of eels and frogs or when they smell vinegar—with the same seriousness that he discusses current scientific speculation about magnetic variation. But given his purposes, this lack of sophistication is as it should be. What Increase most hoped for the *Essay* was that it would convince men that "There are Wonders in the Works of Creation as well as Providence, the reason whereof the most knowing amongst Mortals, are not able to comprehend." Hence a story of fish that jumped into the boat of starving sailors drifting on the sea was as important as the properties of magnets—both ultimately were "very mysterious and beyond humane capacity" to understand.[16]

The *Essay on Illustrious Providences* presumed to deal with the problems of nature in its extraordinary guises; and therefore in the four chapters on witches, possessions, and apparitions Increase made no claim that these subjects, surrounded by the occult and embedded in folklore though they were, deserved special treatment. Their study should be pursued in the way of God's illustrious providences and with the expectation that scientific explanation would carry one so far and no farther. Something of witchcraft and apparitions could be explained in terms of secondary causes just as something of magnetic variation could. But the scholar would reach the limit of such investigation soon and eventually would have to retire in the face of the demonic mystery. He could console himself with the knowledge that the Devil and his kind operated within restraints set by God who used the evil spirits for His own purposes.[17]

The method of study, Increase recognized, depended upon the assumptions about the phenomenon studied. Some men insisted upon the total validity of natural investigation because they denied the existence of evil spirits and witches. Increase was concerned to banish these skeptics whose skepticism threatened religion itself. As Joseph Glanvill, one of the compilers of witch stories from whom he drew, said, "*Atheism* is begun in Sadducism: And those that dare not bluntly say, *There* is NO GOD, content themselves . . . to deny there are SPIRITS or WITCHES."[18] Just who the skeptics were in New England is not clear; announcing themselves would have been a dangerous trespass against received opinion. A few years later during the outburst in Salem a few scoffers raised their voices. Martha Cory was one—she did not think there were any witches, she said—and her sniffing at the whole affair helped hasten her way to the gallows.[19]

Increase Mather rarely produced a major book for the local audience alone, and in the *Essay* he hoped to destroy the doubters in cosmopolitan Europe as well as in provincial New England. Not many genuine skeptics published their views in Europe, and Mather was reduced to attacking men who believed as seriously as he in the existence of witches but who had urged that only the most careful and scientific means of detecting them be used. The four Increase mentioned as deserving particular contempt were Reginald Scot, a sixteenth-century English author who inspired other critics for the next two centuries, Thomas Ady, John Wagstaffe, and John Webster, all well known in the seventeenth century. Increase either misread or misunderstood these men, or relied on secondhand information about the content of their books. None of them denied, as he charged, that witches and evil spirits abounded in this world.[20]

The technique Increase used to cashier the "skeptics" throughout the *Essay* and in later studies of the invisible world, relied on a mass of data. His purpose apparently was to present so much evidence—stories, attestations, testimonials, narratives—of the incursion of witches and apparitions in every corner of the world as to leave his reader no choice but to agree. As in the accounts of the remarkable use of thunder and lightning, to say nothing of earthquakes, floods, and storms, he attempted to convey a sense of the mysterious immediacy of the Devil and his dark spirits. The visible, the concrete, the stuff of ordinary existence, paradoxically, was made to suggest the presence of another order of invisible, immaterial and dangerous being. Thus, the stories abound with "evidence" of men being bitten by unseen teeth (the marks appear before the victim's astonished eyes); chairs are lifted into the air despite the best efforts of men to hold them against the floor; burning ashes are flung out of a fireplace by an unseen hand; children sicken and die at the command of a voice from an unseen mouth. Some afflicted men imagine that they have been turned into beasts; others speak in languages they do not know; still others receive dreadful information about the future. The people who endure these tortures all appear as normal Englishmen or Americans. The implication is that the same kinds of things might happen to Increase's readers, should Providence be disposed to lengthen the Devil's leash.[21]

This type of demonstration surely convinced many of the power of the demonic in the world of men and things. It employed the conventional and it connected the visible and the invisible. Still it did not convince everyone, as Increase well knew. And one who doubted the existence of the invisible world might accept the truth of all Increase's descriptions and still insist that they all could be explained in natural terms.

Those savants and skeptics who resorted to science for explanations did not presume to suggest that the laws of physics accounted for the strange levitations reported in many cases; nor did they plot the orbits of witches riding on sticks. Rather they fastened on the extraordinary behavior of the accused witches and their victims. The convulsions, the fits, the Lycanthropia—the delusion of some men that they had been transformed into animals—even the confessions by practicing witches, all took their origin from the same source, they said: disease of the body and brain. These skeptics denied that supernatural creatures inserted themselves into men. Illness could produce all the symptoms of witchcraft and it could lead men to admit crimes they had not committed when they were accused by strong-willed investigators.[22]

This argument baffled Increase who knew that calling it atheism did not constitute refutation. The best he could do was to point to the delusions of afflicted and accused, the terrors, the frightful ideas, their hatreds and enmities. How did these phenomena enter the mind? How could "meer natural Disease" produce them out of nothing, he asked. Consider, for example, the extraordinary capacity of some of the afflicted to speak with tongues, that is, to speak in languages, unknown to them. Surely what they spoke came from the mind; what baffled him was how anyone could explain "how should that be in the mind, which never came there through the outward senses." The conclusion seemed obvious to him: "This cannot be without some supernatural influence." Perhaps recognizing the lameness of his argument, he charged that the "patrons of witchcraft" favored the view that there was no mystery in the behavior that the vulgar attributed to the demonic—disease explained it all. And he added, in an opinion that had dangerous implications, witches themselves often put their godly pursuers off the scent by using this medical argument.[23]

Because the *Essay* proved to be popular, these views must have been widely known. But there is no evidence that they contributed to the venomous atmosphere that swirled around Salem Village when witchcraft appeared there in 1692. Even so, they do help us understand Increase Mather's responses to the incursions of the witches that year.

The witches first appeared in Salem Village, now Danvers, which was a small parish on the edge of the town of Salem, then a small seaport of traders and fishing men. Salem Village did not enjoy much contact with the larger community, or with any other town in New England. Its isolation probably contributed to the propensities of its inhabitants to backbiting and talebearing; and perhaps it encouraged them to resort to the courts for other kinds of satisfaction. At any rate, the petty squabbles there over land and crops and animals often ended with the parties involved appearing before the local justices.[24]

Salem Village also had a history of unhappy relations with its ministers. Two, the Reverend James Bayley and the Reverend George Burroughs, had departed the parish after quarrels with their parishioners over their salaries and a long list of lesser matters. Apparently sharing the local fondness for litigation, both ministers took their people to court in an attempt to collect, and both won judgments. But both had then left, happy to be free of such a tightfisted flock. A third minister, Deodat Lawson, avoided the worst of these struggles but he did not remain long.[25]

The Reverend Samuel Parris who succeeded Lawson late in 1689, did not find his parishioners in a generous or charitable frame of mind. After hassling over his salary, they forced him to accept a meager sixty-six pounds a year, a third in provisions, and they refused to provide his firewood for the winter, a discourtesy that must have soured his coming. Parris was scarcely a sweet-tempered man under the best of conditions, not that he had the opportunity to enjoy the best of anything very often. He was thirty-eight years old in 1692, and he had come to the ministry not from Harvard College but after failure in the West Indian trade. His family in Salem Village included his wife, about whom almost nothing is known, his nine-year-old daughter Betty, his eleven-year-old niece Abigail Williams, and two slaves, John Indian and Tituba, apparently half Carib and half Negro.[26]

The trouble started with Tituba who, in the long winter of 1691-92, began entertaining the two girls and a number of others in the village with stories of the occult. She also instructed them in fortune telling, a forbidden art in any Protestant community. Although historians have assumed that Tituba was innocent of any evil motive in these practices, she doubtless took herself seriously, and so, evidently, did the girls. The problem of how her practices induced the pathological reactions that began appearing in this circle of female adolescents is beyond the scope of this book. Whatever was involved, by January 1692 symptoms of morbidity and soon of hysteria began to appear. Samuel Parris first noticed the abnormalities in his daughter Betty. Early in her illness, Betty seemed withdrawn and preoccupied with her own secret thoughts; she was also forgetful and began to neglect the chores she performed for her mother. She lost interest in almost all her customary activites, including worship, to the point of forgetting prayer and then rejecting the Bible when it was offered to her. Fits began in the same months, dreadful convulsions accompanied by shrieking, screams, tears, and sometimes unconsciousness.

About this time the other girls began displaying similar symptoms. Parris and other frightened parents at first attempted to keep their children's illnesses quiet, consulting the village physician, who was baffled, and then seeking the advice of ministers in Salem proper and nearby Beverly. As one girl after another began to act as if she were possessed, the chances of a rapid cure or of maintaining secrecy disappeared. Like many parents in the village, Parris suspected that the disease had a supernatural origin, but he does not seem to have announced his fear until the village doctor suggested that the girls were suffering from demonic possession. This learned opinion may have emboldened the girls, for soon in answer to the question, "Who torments you?" they named Tituba, and two village women, Sarah Good and Sarah Osborne.[27]

The accusations made during these convulsions by the demented girls were that the spectres, or the shapes of these women, appeared to them demanding that they enter a compact with the Devil by signing his black book. The girls refused with the results visible to everyone. The spectres of the witches kicked and bit them, flung them around like rag dolls, and twisted them into rigid postures. All this suffering, the girls insisted, was their reward for resisting the blandishment of the Devil and his agents, the witches.[28]

When the witches showed up in Salem, Increase was in England at the Court of William and Mary completing a successful appeal for a charter for Massachusetts Bay to replace the old one which had been withdrawn eight years earlier. He finished the last of his business in March 1692, and with the new Governor, Sir William Phips, sailed for home on the twenty-ninth. He had not seen New England since 1688. His ship anchored in Boston on Saturday night, May 14, 1692.[29]

The return brought him joy until he recognized the danger of the distress at Salem. The jails bulged with the accused, whose numbers would certainly grow as the afflicted girls cast their nets more widely each day. The girls drew the sympathy of those who watched their torments, but the accused too had their supporters. Devout families could not comprehend the justice of having pious members snatched out of their houses on nothing more than the charges of the suffering girls.

Of course, the Devil roamed this world; of course hypocrites sat in churches along with the saints. But these families also believed that when the charge of witchcraft was lodged at one's door, some caution and judiciousness had to be exercised. The whole matter belonged before the courts for trial, once and for all. And those who supported the girls agreed, at least they agreed that the courts must proceed against witchcraft and drive the Devil and his cohorts from New England. The supporters, who in the Spring included Lt. Governor Stoughton and most of the Council and a number of ministers outside Salem, did not clamor for the exoneration of the innocent, however. In May when the Governor arrived, they were more interested in discovering the guilty than in freeing the guiltless.[30]

The Governor delayed any action until May 29, when he commissioned a special court to try the cases. The judges, who sat without a jury, included nine distinguished members of the Council. Lt. Governor William Stoughton presided.

Increase certainly approved referring the witch cases to the court; established procedures in England called for judicial decision, as he had noted years before in his studies of witchcraft. But the creation of the court did not assure equitable proceedings, and he watched the first two weeks of the court's actions with a growing sense that long established practices were not being followed. The first trial lasted one day, and the conviction was clearly based on "spectral evidence," testimony by the afflicted girls that the spectre of an accused person was doing the tormenting. Bridget Bishop, the defendant, was not an attractive character; common gossip had it that she was an immoral woman, fond of gambling, prone to keep unusual hours and receive company of doubtful reputation on doubtful business. Her neighbors dredged up stories of unpleasant encounters with her, several going back as far as fifteen years. The most telling evidence was the accounts of the horror her spectre wrought: it had beaten Deliverance Hobbs, mother of one of the girls, with iron rods. Bridget Bishop was also supposed to have murdered several children, and given suck to her familiar, which turned out to be a snake. The judges found this testimony convincing and at the end of the long day of the trial, Stoughton sentenced her to hang. Phips was preparing to leave about this time to lead the fight against the Indians and may not have followed the trial closely; on June 8, six days after the trial, Stoughton ordered the execution for June 10. Bridget Bishop hanged that day.[31]

The trial troubled Nathaniel Saltonstall, one of the magistrates, so much that he resigned from the court as soon as it was over. Perhaps this resignation shocked Phips, for soon after he appealed to the leading ministers in Boston and nearby towns for advice as how best to proceed. The "Return of several ministers" to the Governor, issued from Cotton Mather's pen almost immediately, and was approved by Increase and twelve other ministers.[32] This report reeks of the awful tension the ministers felt between the dangers of convicting the guiltless, and of the opportunities of ridding the land of the witches. The ministers were clearly offended at the bedlam of the pre-trial hearings; such investigations— they urged—should be conducted as quietly and discreetly as possible so that "Noise, Company, and Openness" might be avoided. They were also perplexed by the indiscriminate accusations, commenting especially upon the girls' insensitivity to social status, which is what led to their fear that "persons formerly of an unblemished Reputation" might be lightly accused. Nor, they declared, should the accused be convicted on the basis of spectral evidence, a clear rebuke to the court.[33]

The opportunities presented by the affair were no less on the ministers' minds. And therefore while the disorder of the hearings and the quality of several of the accused dismayed them, they did not hesitate to exhort the Justices to a "*vigorous* Prosecution" of the witches. And if spectral evidence was inadmissible in court, it clearly had its uses in the pre-trial investigation of accused persons, and the ministers were careful to urge only that it not be admitted as convicting evidence.[34]

Increase felt both dispositions which informed the ministers' "Return" and he continued to feel them as the trials resumed, convictions mounted, and executions took a toll. Five witches died on the gallows on July 19; another five on August 19; and eight on September 19, the last day of the hangings. Three days before, Giles Cory, an old man of steadfast courage, was pressed to death in a field by heavy stone in return for his refusal to answer the charges against him. His standing mute before the court protected his property for his heirs, but he experienced the terrible torture prescribed by English common law procedure.[35]

Cory's brave death shook the watchers in the field. Increase did not witness it, nor any of the executions as far as we know. His alarm arose from the knowledge that the court continued to rely on spectral testimony. Governor Phips returned from the Indian Wars about this time to learn that the court and the executions had served neither to purge the land of the witches nor to persuade an increasingly large body of critics that justice was being rendered. No one could deny that the court continued to receive the most doubtful sort of evidence, nor could anyone doubt that a number of those cried out upon by the girls remained at large, untouched by the law, because they came from the best families. Among them were Saltonstalls, Thatchers, and even, it was rumored, Lady Phips, the wife of the Governor.[36]

Bewildered, the Governor did the only thing left for him to do—he went to Increase Mather and several other leading ministers for a way out of this tangle.

Increase delivered his answer almost immediately and in the following year published it as *Cases of Conscience*.[37] While Increase refrained from criticizing Stoughton and the other judges directly, indeed he disavowed "any Reflection on those worthy Persons who have been concerned in the late proceedings at Salem: They are wise and good Men, and have acted with all Fidelity according to their Light," his essay constituted a repudiation of their methods. For Increase insisted once more that the Devil could impersonate persons innocent of witchcraft and denied that evidence based on the claims of the afflicted that they could identify their tormentors' shapes should be admissible in court. He also branded the trial by sight and touch, which the magistrates had resorted to in the preliminary hearings, an inadmissible technique; its efficacy rested on the demonic power, Increase pointed out, and one using it compacted with the Devil. But the problem of what evidence was good remained. The free confessions of witches constituted solid grounds for conviction, Increase argued; there were still confessing witches in jail; and at the time he wrote the *Cases* he believed in their sincerity. But the evidence he found most reliable was the testimony of two credible witnesses, the sort of evidence required for conviction in any capital crime.[38]

This argument persuaded Phips, who trusted Increase and who also was impressed by the array of ministers who subscribed to the views expounded in the *Cases of Conscience*. The Governor dismissed the court on October 29, freed on bail many of the imprisoned, and urged the judges to find other ways of relieving the remaining prisoners. Early in January, a Court of Assize and General Jail Delivery met in Salem and, proceeding along the lines suggested by Mather, exonerated almost fifty accused, and condemned three of witchcraft. Lt. Governor Stoughton regarded these proceedings with disfavor and ordered the "speedy" execution of these three along with five others, who had been convicted through special judicial action. Phips, now seeing the need to act with dispatch, stayed all these judgments, and thereby "inraged" Stoughton who, filled with "passionate anger," left the bench of the court then sitting in Charleston. The special court charged with hearing the witch cases took up again the following year in April but there were no more convictions; and in May 1693 Phips granted a general pardon.[39]

At several times while the hysteria over the witches convulsed New England, Increase Mather had acted to restore sanity. He declared privately that it was better for the witches to escape detection than that one innocent person be punished. He urged the court not to admit spectral testimony as evidence; and he pointed out that the ordeal by sight and touch was no more reliable. On one occasion he was able to discourge a prominent citizen of Boston who was seeking a warrant from the magistrates against a local woman named by the Salem girls. The Boston gentleman had taken his daughter, suffering from an undiagnosed illness, to Salem for treatment by the girls. They obliged him by proclaiming that far from having an ordinary disease, his daughter was bewitched. Increase disagreed with this mode of treatment and berated the gentleman for forsaking the Lord in Boston in favor of the Devil in Salem. The magistrates in Boston may have received some advice from Increase too. The most admirable act, of course, was the advice given to the Governor in *Cases of Conscience*. Increase, more than anyone else, had stopped the whole grisly business.[40]

He did not do so out of scientific skepticism, or because he was a "liberal" in any sense, or because he doubted that witches were tormenting the people of Salem. Indeed, it was precisely because he entertained not a shred of scientific rationalism that he was able to argue that the methods of the court were unreliable. What he, and only a few others realized, was that the rationalists were the ones who had made the dreadful mistakes and perhaps had even shed the blood of the innocent. The court had proceeded on the assumptions that things in this world were what they appeared to be, that the world was orderly and reasonable and susceptible to understandings rooted in common sense. The court had denied that the Devil could take the shapes of men innocent of any compact with him and harm others, precisely because they believed such a situation could not be reconciled with God's government of the world. The judges saw chaos lurking in this doctrine of demonic power, the subversion of government, the "ruine" of society. There "would be no living in the World," if it were true, the court said. Reliance on spectral testimony was the fruit of the belief that the world conformed to men's reason, that things must be what they seemed, that appearances must be trusted. Increase, of course, could not accept it—he knew that appearance must not be confused with reality. Hence in his critique of the court's practices he returned to what he had found so fascinating in his studies of comets—the unpredictability and mystery in life.[41]

He could not rest his case on the simple assertion that the court's view of the demonic badly underestimated the Devil's power. Renewed demonstration was needed and in the *Cases* he provided it, along with a mass of data calculated once more to remind New England of the remarkable providences of the Lord. Therefore he filled the pages of the *Cases* with stories of men gifted with supernatural sight on Tuesdays and Fridays, but not on other days of the week, of fruit on plum and pear trees that shriveled up when the owners became mortally ill, of men who were offended by the stink of the corpses of men not yet dead but who died while apparently in good health a few days later, of an "inchanted pin" which could be run two inches into a

man and not draw blood. This world did not begin to yield all of its secrets, these stories implied—not to natural philosophers, not to judges, not to ministers, nor to the shallow rationalists who denied the Lord because they could not see Him.[42]

The same set of emphases appeared in Increase's selections from the array of scientific and Christian examinations of witchcraft. His preferences in this vast literature, which he studied with his usual dedication, were for the Protestant commentators who, while repudiating Popish superstition, also recommended means for the detection of witches that conceded the full mystery of Providential and demonic power. The "Return" of the ministers of June 15, prescribing methods for the eradication of witchcraft, endorsed the techniques outlined by the great William Perkins and the Reverend Richard Bernard of Batcombe in Somerset. Both Increase and Cotton Mather praised these authorities on several occasions, and explicitly drew from their works.[43]

What Increase found valuable in these writers were the precise prescriptions for the identification and conviction of witches. Both Perkins and Bernard despised the ancient folk practices; no test by water nor by scalding for them (a suspect tossed into water who floated was guilty, as was one who was burned by a hot iron). And neither advised accepting spectral testimony for conviction. Yet each approved devices for detecting demons that seriously compromised seventeenth-century scientific views. Perkins and Bernard both agreed that charges of witchcraft by neighbors should be grounds for investigation; and a single witch in a family brought other members under suspicion, Perkins said, because the practice of demonology could be taught. A curse by one man of another, followed by some calamity, was also grounds for suspicion that ought to be officially probed. And unusual body marks such as those sucked by Satan and his demons should bring a formal probe. A magistrate whose suspicions were aroused by any of these "tests" ought to question the accused vigorously and even to use torture if confessions were not forthcoming, Perkins argued. Medical authorities, such as Dr. John Cotta, a Northampton physician who had taken an A.B. and an M.A. at Cambridge University and who was widely respected in the seventeenth century, were also willing to accept "Common defamation" and family association as grounds for pursuing an investigation of witches. But Cotta urged caution against credulous acceptance of rumor and the findings of unqualified examiners. And he left little doubt that what gave one expertise in such examinations was not a knowledge of theology but medical training. Grand juries, magistrates, town officials, ministers, all, he wrote, should have resort to medical opinion before bringing any charges. The problem in detection—he implied—lay as much with the afflicted as with the accused. The problem was first to identify the bewitched. Since the identification came down to discriminating between natural disease and supernatural possession, a physician ought to be the only one to attempt it. A physician knew that disease sometimes produced horrible fits and delirium that closely resembled the attacks experienced by the bewitched. There were cases in medical records of dreadful symptoms, which seemed to indicate witchcraft; and indeed some suffers rolled, shrieked, and complained that they were being tortured by demons and witches. The credulous considered the symptoms and the claims of the afflicted and agreed that they were witnessing witchcraft. Then, according to Cotta, physicians took over and discovered the natural causes—in one case, a boy who endured such torments and complained of witches was found to be suffering with nothing more than a bad case of worms! And in another case, the true disorder was so mild as to be cured in the most prosaic fashion by a stay at the baths. Increase read Cotta, praised him, and ignored all such deflationary prescriptions. He felt no doubt that the witches were abroad in Salem and that the girls were what they claimed to be, bewitched. To be sure, the girls were deceived by the spectres which did not usually represent the persons they seemed to resemble; but the girls' testimony about their own sufferings was to be trusted. Increase knew, of course, that scientific rationalism suggested skepticism of the girls' statements about both themselves and others. Only the evidence of the senses, rationally construed, could help in the identification of those tortured by demons and spirits, Cotta said. Though the girls' "evidence" was simply not accessible to anyone else's senses and the girls' rational faculties had obviously been disordered by the horror of their experiences, Increase persisted in taking their claims seriously—on the grounds that the inaccessible "evidence" could indicate only one thing in this case, the operations of demonic forces. His opposition to the admission of spectral evidence in court arose not from scientific reasonableness, but from the traditional Christian belief in the Devil's capacity for trickery and deceit.[44]

Still, following the prescriptions of Perkins and Bernard, he was willing to approve of convictions based on the confessions of guilt by witches. Here again he departed from medical opinion as given by Cotta and Merci Casaubon, another seventeenth-century Cambridge scholar, whom he praised and ignored. Casaubon emphasized the connections between disease and such disorders as enthusiasm. Perkins had urged that convictions of witchcraft should be obtained on only two bases: one, the confessions of guilt of suspected witches, and the other, the testimony of at least two witnesses that the accused had made a league with the Devil, or had performed some recognized demonic practice. Calling on the Devil for help constituted evidence, in Perkins' eyes, of a league; and divination, or a supposed conference with the Devil, who most likely appeared as a creature, say a cat or a mouse, provided evidence of the entertaining of a familiar spirit. These grounds satisfied Increase, though the scientific writers he professed to admire agreed that confessions under any condition should not be accepted, and implied that brains deluded by illness might seem to call on the Devil, or hold a conference with his agents.[45]

The doubts about the authenticity of the experience of the afflicted girls that medical opinion introduced shook Increase, but did not persuade him that the meaning of Salem could be explained by scientific rationalism. In the thirty years following, he often returned to the problems of understanding the invisible world, especially the difficulty of separating fancies produced by sickness from genuine apparitions. Though in these years he remained faithful to his first insights, he reread the medical commentators—Cotta and Casaubon—and studied fresh accounts of the appearance of demons and evil spirits. From these authorities he learned that melancholy, epilepsy, an imbalance of the humors, and disease, all might contribute to the delusions of men. But Increase refused to believe that such afflicted persons were suffering from physical disorders alone. Physicians might satisfy themselves that the afflicted were simply deluded, but he would not be so easily convinced; by reducing such cases to physical terms such explanations reduced the power of God. The facts were, he said, that in virtually every report he had received, the Devil had taken advantage of physical weakness to insert himself or his agents into the mind of the sick. The sufferers at Salem had even sometimes been deceived by devils impersonating good angels; the sick—Increase argued—were especially prone to the delusion that they were attended by angelical apparitions, while in fact only their imaginations were affected and then only by diabolical illusions. Increase did not raise the possibility that the Salem girls had only imagined that they were afflicted by the agents of the Devil. That experience had not been illusory.[46]

Increase put most of these truths into print in a book about angels published only five years after Salem.[47] He was not altogether comfortable with them because he knew that they did not remove suspicions that a terrible crime had been committed in the Salem episode. If delusions had physical origins, who was to say that some bodily disorder had not been at the root of the whole business? No one could deny that the judges had made use of spectral testimony at least in their pre-trial examinations; and Increase admitted that they had used it in the trials themselves. Minds disordered by disease—he conceded—sometimes "imagine that they see and hear wonderful things." Increase wrote this line in 1706, when he was clearly still troubled by what had happened almost fifteen years earlier. But by this time he had worked out a view of the actions of spirits that must have eased his mind. Sometime after 1694 he had come across *An Essay upon Reason, and the Nature of Spirits* by Richard Burthogge, an obscure English physician, who was deeply influenced by the Cambridge Platonists.[48] Increase recognized in Burthogge a "master in reasoning" and especially admired his argument that the apparitions of spirits, of which a witch's spectre was one type, did not affect the senses of men however much they seemed to, but struck directly into their imaginations. Burthogge did not "prove" this assertion, nor did Increase, though he pointed out that it agreed with the ancients who called apparitions "Phantasms" and "Images." But he hastened to add they are not "meer Phansies or Imaginations," they are "real."[49]

This was the line that Increase held to for the rest of his life. It was, of course, entirely compatible with all his instincts and his contention announced in *An Essay for the Recording of Illustrious Providences* that some subjects were not susceptible to scientific study. Science, after all, dealt with the evidence of the senses. But Increase, with the assistance of Burthogge, lifted witchcraft out of this realm. For if apparitions and spectres of of witches do not affect the senses but jump across them directly into the imagination, what could science tell men of Salem? In this world the invisible controlled the visible. Men in New England now had been reminded of this fact—that was one meaning of Salem.

There were other meanings. But it was not Increase who made them clear to the land. Cotton Mather took up that task in the *Wonders of the Invisible World,* written as the whole dreadful affair ended in the Fall of 1692.[50] Increase endorsed the book's version of what happened at Salem, and thereby joined his son in the gallery of villains who attempted to excuse the bloody trials. There is no need to defend either Mather for his part in the trials or in the public discussions that followed. Neither of course took part in the judicial proceedings, though Increase observed for himself the trial of George Burroughs who, he reported, was justly convicted on the evidence of two witnesses. And Increase, more than any other man, was responsible for stopping the prosecutions. But he defended the judges for acting according to their lights and he denied that the guilt of innocent blood hung over the land.

It is clear that in 1692 both Mathers *felt,* whatever they *believed* or said they believed, that the judges had made a horrible mistake in permitting the evidence of the spectres to be used against the accused. Both admitted that this testimony was received in court, but argued that it alone was never allowed to convict. They knew better and five years later Cotton Mather said so publicly: "Nevertheless, divers were condemned, against whom the chief evidence was founded in the spectral exhibitions." Increase made no such public confession.[51]

If the Mathers are guilty of not being honest with themselves and the court in time to save the lives of the innocent, they were sincere in proclaiming that the incursion of the witches was a judgment of God sent to punish the land for its violation of the covenant. Neither ever repudiated this interpretation of the outbreak; each continued to believe it as long as he lived. Cotton, who first announced it as he called for reform and repentance in the *Wonders,* has been charged with having "prostituted a magnificent conception of New England's destiny" to save "the face of a bigoted court."[52] Certainly New England's destiny did not shine more brightly as a result of the killing of the witches in Salem. Yet the fault was not the Mathers' who understood the whole miserable affair no more clearly than anyone else. Nor was Cotton Mather the first to conceive of the witches as a judgment of God on the land for its sins. The people in Salem Village reacted almost instinctively in a way that revealed their own convictions on the matter. They held fast days, and days of humiliation, all calculated to move the Lord to forgive them their sins and to lift His judgments. Shortly after these attempts the General Court proclaimed a general day of fasting throughout the colony with the same purposes in mind. Cotton Mather followed this lead in the *Wonders,* and a few years later others, even more profoundly convinced than he that the court had erred, did the same. Eighty-two-year-old John Higginson of nearby Salem Town in 1698 said simply that the witches had been sent by God as an affliction "for the Punishment of a declining People."[53]

Higginson wrote this in a preface to a book by the Reverend John Hale of Beverly. Long a student of witchcraft, Hale had questioned the accused at Salem and studied their judges and the evidence they accepted. He agreed with almost everyone else that the court had tried to do the right thing, but he, more clearly than anyone else, understood the extent of its failure. He did not shrink from saying that the innocent had been destroyed. Nor did he hesitate to say that not only had his generation proceeded on mistaken grounds against witches, but so had the founders. In summing up one meaning of Salem, Hale likened New England to Israel in the Wilderness punished by famine for a breach of the covenant made four hundred years before by the patriarchs. And he asked: "Why may not the Lord visit upon us the misguided zeal of our Predecessors about Witchcraft above forty years ago, even when that Generation is gathered to their fathers?" The children had also sinned according to Hale, and the larger meaning of the witchcraft at Salem lay in this long-standing judgment of God on the land for its sins.[54]

Although Increase Mather could not bring himself to speak so forthrightly, he remained as troubled as Hale was about what the crisis at Salem portended for New England. His generation had created the noble myth of the Puritans' errand into the wilderness. His generation had uncovered the meaning of New England, a magnificent enterprise typifying the purity of the millennium. That meaning had now apparently been seriously challenged by the incursion of the witches. Increase knew better: the corruption of New England had brought on the judgment of the witches and threatened its typological significance. In this knowledge of the evil abroad in the land, Increase dreaded the immediate future and yearned for the conversion of the elect and the coming Kingdom of God.

Notes

[1] Quoted in Perry Miller, *The New England Mind: The Seventeenth Century* (New York, 1939, reissued Cambridge, Mass., 1954), 207.

[2] Quoted in *Ibid.* 212.

[3] Increase Mather, *Heavens Alarm To The World,* "To the Reader." The comet was first noticed in New England on November 14, 1680; it could not be seen after the middle of the following February. Mather gave this sermon January 20, 1681.

[4] *Ibid.* "To the Reader" for the measurement of the comet's "radiant Locks." Increase Mather read the following by Hooke: *Lectures and Collections Made By Robert Hooke, Secretary of the Royal Society* (London, 1678).

[5] Hooke, *Lectures and Collections,* 7-10, 15. Hooke discusses Brahe and Kepler on 17-19.

[6] Increase Mather, *Kometographia, Or A Discourse Concerning Comets* (Boston, 1683), 7, for the quotation. See also 2-6, and *passim.*

[7] *Ibid.* "To the Reader," and 16-17. For Hooke's views on the regularity of cometary movements see *Lectures and Collections,* 27-30.

[8] Increase Mather, *Kometographia,* 129-31; *Heavens Alarm To The World,* 1-16; *The Latter Sign* (Boston, 1682), 25-27.

[9] *Kometographia,* 21, 78, 96, 132. On 132, Mather says that comets may be supposed "to be not only signal but causal" of various natural afflictions.

[10] *Heavens Alarm* and *A Latter Sign* are less critical, of course.

[11] (Boston, 1684).

[12] Mather reconstructs the origins of the book in its Preface. There is a full account in Thomas J. Holmes, *Increase Mather: A Bibliography,* I, 240-49.

[13] (Boston, 1679), 70-72.

[14] Increase Mather, *An Essay For The Recording Of Illustrious Providences,* 32-72, and *passim.*

[15] *Ibid.* 74-75, and *passim.*

[16] *Ibid.* 99-100, 109, for the quotations. The stories fill the book.

[17] For the interesting comments on magnetic variation see *Ibid.* 104-5.

[18] Joseph Glanvill, *Sadducismus Triumphatus* (London, 1681), "Preface."

[19] For Martha Cory, see Marion L. Starkey, *The Devil in Massachusetts* (Garden City, N.Y., 1961), 66-68, 72-75, and *passim.*

[20] For biographical and bibliographical information on these writers, see Holmes, *Increase Mather,* I, 248, notes. I have read their works cited there, and this paragraph is based on my reading.

[21] Increase Mather, *An Essay, passim.*

[22] One such writer, discussed below, was Merci Casaubon, author of *A Treatise Concerning Enthusiasme, As It is An Effect Of Nature: But Is Mistaken By Many For Either Divine Inspiration, Or Diabolical Inspiration* (London, 1655). Casaubon did admit that witches existed, however.

[23] Increase Mather, *An Essay,* 199, 186, for the quotations, and the comments on disease as a source of irrational behavior.

[24] Besides reading the standard collections of documents and records of the Salem episode by George L. Burr, *Narratives of the Witchcraft Cases* (New York, 1914), and William E. Woodward, *Records of Salem Witchcraft* (2 vols., Roxbury, Mass., 1864), I have read much of the secondary literature. The accounts by Miller and Morison are valuable; Marion L. Starkey, *The Devil In Massachusetts* is excellent. Frederick C. Drake, "Witchcraft In The American Colonies," *American Quarterly* (Winter 1968) XX, 694-725, is also useful.

[25] Starkey, *Devil In Massachusetts,* 26-27.

[26] *Ibid.* 24-29.

[27] *Ibid.* 31-51.

[28] *Ibid.* 40-41.

[29] Murdock, *Increase Mather* 284-86, tells of his return home. There is no evidence that Mather had heard in England of the beginnings of witchcraft in Salem.

[30] Early ministerial reaction followed the same lines. See Deodat Lawson, *Christ's Fidelity The Only Shield Against Satan's Malignity* (Boston, 1693), a sermon preached in Salem, March 24, 1692.

[31] Starkey, *Devil in Massachusetts,* 153-56.

[32] "The Return," dated June 15, 1692, was printed in Increase Mather, *Cases of Conscience Concerning Evil Spirits* (London, 1693). A part of the "Postscript;" its pages are unnumbered.

[33] There is no doubt that spectral evidence was used. Virtually everyone connected to the affair admitted it. Other doubtful tests—doubtful by seventeenth-century standards—such as the ordeal by sight and touch were used in pre-trial hearings and in the trials. See Deodat Lawson, *A Brief and True Narrative Of Some Remarkable Passages Relating to . . . Witchcraft* (Boston, 1692), and *A Further Account of the Tryals of the New England Witches* (London, 1693).

[34] "The Return of Several Ministers."

[35] Starkey, *Devil In Massachusetts,* 204-7.

[36] *Ibid.* 219.

[37] (London, 1693). Fourteen ministers, including John Wise, signed it.

[38] *Ibid.*

[39] Phips to Earl of Nottingham, Feb. 21, 1693, in Burr, *Narratives,* 201, for the quotations. See 198-202 for Phips version of the end of the affair. See, too, his letter to William Blathwayt, Oct. 12, 1692, in *Ibid.* 196-98.

[40] There is a careful and sane account of these matters in Murdock, *Increase Mather.* See Starkey, *Devil In Massachusetts* for careful assessments.

[41] The quotations are from *Cases of Conscience, To the Christian Reader,* written by Samuel Willard, and from the body of the text, 8, written by Increase Mather.

[42] *Ibid.* 12-15.

[43] *Ibid.* 18, 34.

[44] Richard Bernard, *A Guide To Grand-Jury Men* (London, 1627), Book 2, 214 (water test); Book 2, 209-10 (spectral evidence); Book 2, 111-12, 219 (sucking marks); Book 2, 240 (use of torture). Bernard used and cited Cotta, discussed below. William Perkins, *A Discourse Of The Damned Art of Witchcraft* (London, 1631), 643 (water and other tests), 643-45 (spectral and other evidence, witch marks, and torture). John

Cotta, *The Triall of Witchcraft* (London, 1616), 70-78, 104, 115-22, and *passim.*

[45] Merci Casaubon, *A Treatise Concerning Enthusiasme,* 90, and *passim;* Perkins, *A Discourse,* 644-45.

[46] Increase Mather, *A Disquisition Concerning Angelical Apparitions* (Boston, 1696), 17-18. Bound with this work, but with separate pagination is another by Mather which deals with some of these matters—*Angelographia, Or, A Discourse Concerning The Nature and Power of the Holy Angels* (Boston, 1696). See 64-66.

[47] There are other references to New England in these works.

[48] The quotation is from Increase Mather, *A Disquisition Concerning The State of The Souls of Men* (Boston, 1707), 34; Burthogge's *Essay* was published in London in 1694.

[49] Increase Mather, *Disquisition Concerning . . . Souls,* 33.

[50] But not published in Boston until 1693.

[51] Cotton Mather made this statement in his life of Phips, *Pietas in Patriam* (London, 1697), reprinted in his *Magnalia* (London,1702), Book II, 62.

[52] Miller, *From Colony To Province,* 204.

[53] John Higginson, "An Epistle To The Reader," in John Hale, *A Modest Inquiry Into The Nature Of Witchcraft* (Boston, 1698), 6.

[54] *Ibid.* 166.

Mason I. Lowance, Jr. (essay date 1974)

SOURCE: "Science and Pseudoscience," in *Increase Mather,* Twayne Publishers, Inc., 1974, pp. 76-106.

[*In the following excerpt, Lowance analyzes Mather's attempts to combine scientific knowledge with theology to formulate explanations for occurrences in both nature and society, and also praises Mather for being forward-thinking and progressive in his scientific writings.*]

. . . Concomitant with the rise of interest in natural revelation was the growing awareness of the universe as a resource for scientific exploration. Although Increase Mather late in his life endorsed the scientific approach to inoculation against smallpox and even wrote a defense of the practice in *Several Reasons Proving that Inoculating or Transplanting the Small*

Pox is a Lawful Practice, and that it has been Blessed by God for the Saving of many a Life (1721), his actual explorations in science were limited and are not to be compared with those of his son, Cotton, who became a Fellow of the Royal Society in London. Rather, Increase Mather's concern with nature was focused on the employment of nature as a source for corroborating the evidences and truths already revealed to him through Scripture. But the modern reader should not be too cynical in his approach to Mather as a scientific thinker; for his time, Increase Mather was progressive and advanced rather than wholly conservative and backward-looking.

For example, in Mather's *An Essay for the Recording of Illustrious Providences,* we find quotations from the *Philosophical Transactions* (1678), a contemporary London journal well recognized for scientific discovery. He refers to the works of Sir Kenelm Digby, Sir Thomas Browne, and asserts in the preface that "I have often wished, that the *Natural History* of *New-England,* might be written and published to the World; the Rules and method described by that Learned and excellent person *Robert Boyle* Esq. being duely observed therein."[5] He refers to scientific discoveries throughout, indicating his familiarity with advances in those fields; and he devotes Chapter Four of the *Essay* to "Philosophical Meditations," which treat such natural phenomena as lightning, "its irresistible force, its being more speedy than the sound of its thunder, its fusible action on metals, while leaving wax unmelted; observations on the magnetic action and polarity of the loadstone under various conditions; of heat in relation to gravity; of 'fulminous stones or thunderbolts' then thought to be identical with meteors; of nitre, sulphur; of poisonous vapours, etc.; showing that 'There are Wonders in the Works of Creation as well as Providence.'"[6] If this posture seems to be an apologetic one for Mather's recording of some observations on the scientific aspects of the natural universe, his discussions of comets and astronomy are even more directly scientific.

In three separate works, Mather as a rudimentary scientist approaches the phenomena of comets. In 1680, he preached **Heavens Alarm to the World** during the appearance of a comet. This early work combines nature and Scripture effectively, and Mather's text is Genesis 1:14: "God said, Let there be lights in the Firmament of heaven, and let them be for Signs." How these signs are to be interpreted, of course, is to some extent left up to the exegete; and it seems that Mather was here concerned to show how "The stars of heaven are for natural signs. Their motions & appearances are significations that such and such things, will according to that course of nature which God hath setled, come to pass in the world.[7] Despite the emphasis on a scientific method of interpretation, Mather is too aware of the contemporary apostasy of New England from the "er-

rand into the wilderness" to allow an opportunity to slip by, and he chastises his countrymen with constant allusion to these "speaking Providences."

In 1682, he once again preached on comets in **The Latter Sign** during the appearance of what is now known as Halley's comet; however, it was the 1683 treatise called **Kometographia, or a Discourse Concerning Comets** that set forth Mather's most scientific statements about astronomy, and it is significant that the two earlier sermons were reprinted with this long document. His "To the Reader" makes clear the purpose of the statement: "My chief design, is to inform and edifie the ordinary sort of *Readers.* Yet considering that God hath made me a debter to the wise as well as to the weak, I have added some things of the *nature, place; motion of Comets,* which only such as have some skill in *Astronomy* can understand."[8]

The document itself is of little literary value, but it contains ten highly structured chapters that present the history of comets and a discussion of their nature and origin. A typical chapter title is that given the third, *"The History of* Comets *from the beginning of the World to the first coming of Christ, together with some remarkable Events attending them."* Theologically, the commentary is slight, and Kenneth Murdock remarks:

> Whatever one thinks of the theological compromise he proposes, his book quite defies classification as one which "supports the theological cometary theory fully." Instead, his doctrine is most cautiously expressed. Nor is it fair to say that the scientific view was a source of alarm to him, for, far from showing fear, he makes Kepler and Hevel two of his main authorities, cites Tycho Brahe, and Robert Hook, and makes repeated use of the publications of the Royal Society. He accepts some of the newest scientific tenets, and his attempt to combine them with his religious views results in a position held by others for a century after him, and not wholly abandoned to-day.

> One must admit, perhaps, that in the matter of comets, Mather was in the front rank of his time.[9]

Indeed, in **Kometographia** and in a later essay, **Angelographia,** the scientific method is employed to provide the strongest case possible for the operations of God's Providence in the natural universe.

Nevertheless, it is in the Mather works that bring together natural phenomena and scriptural revelation that we are able to see the writer at his most ingenious. Three works figure most prominently in developing this aspect of Mather's thinking: **The Doctrine of Divine Providence** (1684) tells clearly the theory of "Providences," and a methodology for the "determining" of Providences is provided in **An Essay for the Recording of Illustrious Providences**. In 1692, Mather published the now-famous *Cases of Conscience Concerning Evil Spirits,* in which he essentially argues that witches are not only possible but probable. This document has done much to affirm the modern impression of Mather as a witch-hunter, even though he was active in terminating the Salem trials on the grounds that the judges had relied too heavily on "spectral" evidence, or on evidence from accusers that the defendant had appeared to them in the form of a "specter" or santanic agent. These three documents, taken together, illustrate the principle on which Mather found the natural universe to be a servant of the spiritual world: that God was indeed working through His Providence to bring New England to an appointed end. Although the compromises between theology and science which he reaches in these documents might leave both theologians and scientists unsatisfied, the logic of his arguments from the premises he adopted cannot be questioned.

Natural and Scriptural Revelation

Doctrine of Divine Providence was published in the same year as ***An Essay for the Recording of Illustrious Providences*** (1684), but the degree to which the latter document develops Mather's theory of natural revelation is considerably greater than that suggested by the collection of sermons. ***The Doctrine of Divine Providence,*** however, suggests a relationship between the natural and spiritual worlds on which the more liberal attitudes rest. It consists of a series of five treatises written by Increase Mather and a sixth sermon by Nathaniel Mather, his brother. The persistent theme of the group is that "The God of Heaven has an overruling hand of Providence in whatever cometh to Pass in this world."[10] The immutable and eternal qualities of God's Providence are reaffirmed throughout the documents in a way that suggests predestination in such remarks as this: " . . . all Events of Providence are the issues and executions of an Ancient, Eternal, Unchangeable decree of Heaven" (8). Curiously, however, the emphasis is shifted away from the abstractions of theology to the *manner* in which this providential concern operates in the natural world. Beginning with the premise that "There is a Providence at work in every corner of the earth," and moving to specific notions like "The providence of God is extended to the least and most inconsiderable things that happen in the world" (9, 11), Mather employs biblical allusions to clarify his thesis that God's Divine governance extends to everyday life and to matters of little apparent significance.

The Calvinist sense of God's omniscience is everywhere stressed, as in Proposition I: *"The Lord in Heaven knows all that is done upon the Earth"* (3). But we are also told that "the providence of God is extended unto all Creatures. . . . Divine preservation is one thing in providence. And the providence of God is to

be admired in that all the several *species* or kinds of creatures which were made at the first Creation are still kept in Being. There are many creatures which haveing an Antipathy in their natures seek the destruction of each other; and there are many *individuals* that are destroyed every day; yet that sort of creature is kept living in the world ever since the Creation to this day. And God provides for all his creatures" (9-10).

The emphasis on God's operations in the natural universe, not the inaccuracy of Mather's scientific history, should be the concern here. These assertions are accompanied by numerous examples of God's providential provision for the faithful of the Bible, but contemporary examples are also supplied: "So if a man happen to kill another by meer Accident, it may be he is cutting wood, and the head of his ax flies off and kills his neighbour, the providence of God has for holy ends ordered that sad casualty" (11). If the early sermons contain a sense of God's foreordaining of the natural world, there is nevertheless a distinct attempt to correlate revelation in the universe with the truths understood through Scripture. Indeed, Mather argues very plainly that the natural world is a supreme expression of God's Providence and that the most logical proof of his existence is found in the investigations one makes of the universe:

> *Insasmuch as the world stands that's a sufficient Demonstration that there is a Providence.*
>
> For as the world could not give it self a Being at first, so neither can it continue it self in Being. If the same hand which made all creatures should not preserve them, they would all presently return to their first nothing. *Heb.* 1, 3. Now that is *Providence.* Creation giveth *Primo esse,* but Providence giveth *Porro esse,* as the schools express it. The frame of nature would be dissolved the next moment, if there were not an hand of Providence to uphold and govern all. To preserve and govern the world is too high a work for any meer creature to undertake. In asmuch then, as all creatures are preserved and kept in their order, it is because he that sitteth in Heaven ruleth over all. A Wheel must have an Hand to guide it or it will presently turn out of the way and fall to the ground; so if there were not a divine hand to manage the Wheel of Providence, all things would run into confusion, and the World would come to ruin in one day. (21-22)[11]

This important doctrine is perhaps the most significant portion of the entire work, because it clearly states the principles on which Mather's generation assumed the immanent presence of God in their everyday lives. God was separated from man in the distance created between them by the fact of sin; however, the immanence rather than the transcendence of God was stressed in these documents where scriptural and natural revelation were reconciled.

The Doctrine of Divine Providence was not composed without a substantial moral emphasis. Its sermons are structured in a relationship that chastises the sinner and illustrates the earthly opportunities of God's saints as their titles suggest: "Sins of Omission expose men to the Judgments of God," and "The Lord's servants whilst living in this world, have many Opportunities and Advantages to glorifie God which the Saints in Heaven have not" (82, 109). But Mather's strongest concern is obviously to demonstrate the creative power of God in establishing a natural world and the love of God in sustaining it through his Providence. The doctrine of the second sermon is, "The works of Divine Providence are great and wonderfull." In this document, orthodox examples of God's concern for the New English Israel are developed, such as the assurance that the Christian Church is sustained through the power of Providence. However, the most interesting portions are those in which Mather explores the work of Providence in the world of nature.

The central doctrine of natural Providence is stated in this way:

> That Law and Course of Nature which He hath Established in the world, is a great and marvellous work. His ordering of Times and Seasons, Heat and Cold, Seed-Time and Harvest, Summer and winter, Day and Night in their several Vicissitudes, These are wonderful works. The giving of rain and showers from Heaven is a work of ordinary Providence, yet a wonderful work. . . . The Causing of Clouds and vapours to ascend and descend, is mentioned amongst the wonderful works of God. . . . Some of the clouds are lifted up higher, others hang down lower, like unto *ballances;* God maketh those vapours to be higher or lower, according as he means to use them for the good or hurt of his Creatures, and that with as much exactness as if he weighed them all with a Ballance. These are marveilous works. The raising and allaying of mighty storms, is that which in the ordinary course of Providence is brought to pass, yet those are wonderful works. (45-46)

This unscientific explanation for the vicissitudes of weather was understood by Mather and his Puritan contemporaries to be a revealed expression of God's Will. Interpreted in the framework of Divine dispensation, it was therefore a kind of pseudoscientific rationalization of the natural phenomena that rendered the Puritan universe orderly and comprehensible.

To explain unusual natural phenomena, Mather developed the traditional idea of extraordinary Providences. The Puritans were strong believers in the specific application of God's power to express his pleasure or displeasure, and Mather is conventional when he asserts that "*there are Extraordinary providences.* These are by way of Eminency *great and marvellous works of God.* Such as Signs and Prodigies, which are more rarely seen in the world. These are called *wonders. Psal.* 135. 9. for that they cause wonderment in the world; And more especially when they are of a miraculous nature. . . . Works which are above and beyond the Constituted order of Nature. There are also extraordinary mercies and extraordinary judgements, which the Providence of God does sometimes dispense towards the children of men" (46-47).

These "works which are above and beyond the Constituted order of Nature" obviously fascinated Increase Mather, for he devoted an entire philosophical treatise to the study of such "remarkable Providences." The rules of the game were clear and unmistakable: God's Divine Will was revealed to man in the natural universe as well as in Scripture, and the orderly patterns of nature might reflect the goodness of his Providence in the glory and power of creation, but His mercies and judgments could also be expressed through daily occurrences and through His manipulation of natural phenomena. This attitude toward nature well suited the Federal or Covenant theology that the Mathers preached in which man's obedience or apostasy might play a role in determining his earthly fate as well as his afterlife. If the Puritans regarded their eternal destiny to be predetermined, they were sufficiently aware of God's immanence to conceive His response to their behavior in anthropomorphic terms. Man could never fully know God, but he could certainly determine something of the Divine Will by observing the way in which God managed the affairs of nature.

The innovation here was not one of theory, which was traditional and conventional with Christianity and especially with New England Puritanism. Rather, the new dimension was the emphasis given the natural world in developing a total picture of God's revelation. In Mather's ***Essay for the Recording of Illustrious Providences,*** this emphasis is so strong that it constitutes the foundation argument of the document. By the time of the Salem Witch Trials in 1692, the correspondences assumed between the natural and the spiritual worlds were sufficient to send young men and women to their deaths.

Those Remarkable or Illustrious Providences

Mather's ***Essay for the Recording of Illustrious Providences*** was possibly his most significant work. Its significance, however, lies not in doctrinal assertions or theological abstractions but in the way that it made clear the idea of Providence through a collection of examples that were to popularize the theological principle. It became, in effect, a handbook or manual of Providences; and it captured for the the popular imagination an extremely complex theological and philosophical notion. The "first edition" was printed in Boston in 1684 by Samuel Green, but it was soon reissued with a new title page. Another edition was issued in London by George Calvert, also in 1684. The second edition was issued in London in 1687, by Thomas Parkhurst, but the collation of this issue is identical with that of the three issues of 1684, "even to the minutiae of the errors in the running titles. . . . Variation seems to be in the title-pages only."[12] It was reprinted several times, viz., in London in 1856, with the title changed to *Remarkable Providences Illustrative of the Earlier Days of American Colonization*. In 1890, it was again reprinted, with the same changed title.

The original design of the work was not Mather's alone. In the preface, he remarks that "About six and twenty years ago, a *Design for the Recording of illustrious Providences,* was under serious consideration among some eminent Ministers in *England* and in *Ireland*. . . . But before any thing was brought to effect, the Persons to have been imployed, had their thoughts diverted another way. Nevertheless, there was a M.SS. (the Composer whereof is to me unknown) then written, wherein the Subjects proper for this *Record,* and some Rules for the better managing a design of this nature, are described" (i-ii).

Mather's personal aim in pursuing this project to its conclusion was stated in the preface: " . . . to publish a Discourse of *Miscellaneous observations, concerning things rare and wonderful; both as to the works of Creation and Providence*." But this broad topic was to be developed beyond the limits of the printed *Essay*. He notes the inadequacies of the present volume, but says "this must suffice for the present" (xviii). He had initially drawn up a proposal by which several ministers would contribute episodes to a general collection of Providences that could be used in the establishing of natural proof for scriptural truth. When the proposals were presented to a general meeting of the ministers of the Massachusetts Bay Colony in May, 1681, the objectives were clear: "*In Order to the Promoting of a design of this Nature, so as shall be indeed for Gods Glory, and the good of Posterity, it is necessary that utmost care shall be taken that All, and Only* Remarkable Providences *be Recorded and Published. . . . Such Divine Judgements, Tempests, Floods, Earthquakes, Thunders as are unusual, strange Apparitions, or what ever else shall happen that is Prodigious . . .*" (ix-x). But, at the same time, Mather seems equally concerned that the phenomena be representative of scientific as well as theological truth. Although the *Essay* is by no means a scientific or natural history, Increase Mather wished to think of it as such.

But *An Essay for the Recording of Illustrious Providences* is not a purely scientific document, even when it is assessed by seventeenth-century standards. Its scientific significance should be measured in terms of its contribution to the reconciliation of scientific method and theological conclusion, because Increase Mather was very careful to follow the method of a scientific procedure in assimilating his evidences for the glorification of God. First, the entire document is structured according to a systematic method of classification, so that one subject at a time is treated from its inception to its conclusion. The chapters of the volume suggest a collection of New England experiences with little theological overlay: "Remarkable Sea Deliverances"; "Remarkable Preservations"; "Remarkables about Thunder and Lightning"; "Philosophical Meditations"; "Things Preternatural which have hapned in New-England"; "Daemons and possessed persons"; "Apparitions"; "Several Cases of Conscience considered"; "The Dumb and Deaf . . . Ways to teach Deaf and Dumb persons to speak"; "Remarkable Tempests in New-England;" "Remarkable Judgements;" "Remarkables at Norwich in New England."

Although these topics do lend themselves to interpretation by a theological mind, Mather has carefully laid the groundwork for a pseudoscientific investigation in each chapter; and in each case or "Providence" that he examines, he rarely accepts as evidence information that he has obtained at second or third hand without making note of his source as though to caution the reader against his sources. Often he makes great efforts to establish the credibility of his reporting, and he takes most of his stories from eyewitness accounts, from letters sent him by sources he either questions for the reader or trusts as reliable. As modern readers, we are often suspicious of such relations, especially when they are accompanied by the writer's attempt to bring the narratives into a synthetic framework of God's Divine Providence; however, it is important to remember that, for the seventeenth-century reader, the "credibility gap" was not so pronounced as it is today. Indeed, Mather's readers would have found nothing in the *Illustrious Providences* inconsistent with their beliefs about what could possibly happen through natural circumstances. In this context, then, the document reflects a determined effort to reconcile prevailing scientific investigations with traditional theology to form a kind of theology of natural revelation. A process of selective adaptation is clearly at work, and Mather has ingeniously transformed some natural and abnormal phenomena into a curious combination of episode and interpretation.

As stories in themselves, the "Providences" are remarkable, and many of them make excellent narrative units. As a seventeenth-century compiler of providential narratives, Mather excels many of his contemporaries in unifying his sources around some central themes and in the sheer power of his storytelling art. Many of the episodes are too long to analyze here, and most are straightforward accounts of the event told in the third person with a concluding assessment of the work of God in bringing the event to a happy conclusion; however, there are several very brief accounts of which the following is a typical example:

> On *June* the sixth *A. D.* 1682. A Ship called the *Jamaica Merchant,* Captain *Joseph Wild* Commander, being then in the Gulph of *Florida,* Lat. 27 *gr.* about 1 *h. P.M.* was surprized with an amazing Thunder shower; the Lightning split the Main-mast, and knocked down one of the Seamen, and set the Ship on fire between Decks, in several places. They used utmost endeavour to extinguish the fire, but could not do it; seeing they were unable to overcome those Flames, they betook themselves to their Boat. The fire was so furious between the Cabbin and the Deck in the Steeridge, that they could not go to the relief of each other, insomuch that a Man and his Wife were parted. The Man leaped over-board into the Sea, and so swam to the Boat: his Wife and a Child were taken out of a Gallery Window into the Boat. Three Men more were saved by leaping out of the Cabbin Window. There were aboard this Vessel which Heaven thus set on fire, thirty four persons; yet all escaped with their lives: For the gracious providence of God so ordered, as that Captain *John Bennet* was then in company, who received these distressed and astonished Creatures into his Ship: so did they behold the Vessel burning, until about 8 *h. P. M.* when that which remained sunk to the bottom of the Sea. The Master with several of the Seamen were by Captain *Bennet* brought safe to *New-England,* where they declared how wonderfully they had been delivered from Death which God both by fire and water had threatened them with. (88-90)

All of the elements of consciously wrought narrative art are exhibited here: a third-person narrator whose distance from his subject is consistent throughout the narrative; the cosmic conflict of man and the natural elements, with a measure of the supernatural thrown in to add mystery and suspense to the drama; a touching domestic relationship that serves as the focus of distress in Mather's narration of the severity of the crisis; a dramatic unit with a beginning, middle, and end that moves swiftly to a conclusion while the reader is anxiously awaiting the resolution; factual details such as proper names and geographical location that add credibility to the story; a means of getting the story back to New England, so that the reader is not asked to believe reports second and third hand; and, finally, the immensely important intrigue of such an episode having occurred in a remote corner of the newly discovered world, off the coast of Florida aboard a ship exotically named the *Jamaica Merchant.* As narrative elements alone, these examples could not have failed to fascinate the seventeenth-century reader in England and New England, and they are but a fragment of the literary devices present in the whole book that lead the reader from one chapter to the next with alarming consistency.

But Mather was not a voyage narrator like Jonathan Swift, whose *Gulliver's Travels* had much of the same appeal, nor was he consciously attempting to deceive his readers into believing stories that he himself did not accept as true. Rather, he was simply relating *exempla* from a vast storehouse of narratives about God's Providence that would develop a strong argument for the acceptance of God's power and majesty by his readers. The assembling of some episodes that demonstrated the operations of God's power in natural phenomena was an immediate success because it brought together pseudoscientific assumptions and a scientific methodology for interpretation in the context of traditional scriptural conventions concerning God's presence in his created universe.

Mather and the Witches

One aspect of **An Essay for the Recording of Illustrious Providences** that has received an unusual amount of critical attention is the suggestion that the book was in part responsible for the Salem Witchcraft hysteria that occurred in 1692. To indict a popular book, or any single artifact of cultural significance, for direct influence on a major social movement is always risky at best. It is better, I believe, to acknowledge that those habits of mind by which the Puritan saw in nature the operations of the spiritual world were present both in Mather's book and in the Salem Witchcraft hysteria. **An Essay for the Recording of Illustrious Providences** is in fact a remarkably controlled book; what suggestions there are about the relations of witchcraft, the spirit world, and the natural world are rational and very credibly presented. Mather did popularize the prevailing notion of looking into nature as a source of revelation, but his emphasis was primarily on the *operations* of God's Providence in the natural universe, and in less than one-third of the book does he even approach the subject of Satan's manipulation of the natural world.

Moreover, when the subject of witchcraft is presented, Mather clearly states his skepticism about it and its influences, noting early that he accepts the idea that the supernatural can indeed proceed from the power of Satan as well as from the glory of God, but that men have often been mistaken in their finite interpretations so that superstitions rather than intelligent judgments have unfortunately prevailed. "I shall not suspect all those as guilty of Witchcraft, nor yet of Heresie, who call the received Opinion about Witches into question. There are four or five *English* Writers . . . and another Anonymous Author; who do with great vehemence affirm that never any did maintain that familiarity with the evil Spirits, which is commonly believed. . . . True it is, that many things have been looked upon as proceeding from Witchcraft, when it has not been so" (174-75). This caution, it must be remembered, was written eight years before the Salem episode, thereby indicating how clearly Mather perceived the liabilities in his own admission that the spirit world could be an influence for evil as well as good. The book is not in any way a defense of witchcraft, nor is it a condemnation of it; instead, it is a balanced account of episodes involving phenomena that were then interpreted to be indications of witchcraft.

Nevertheless, Mather does affirm the power of Satan to penetrate the natural world through masks and disguises that he manipulates for his devious ends. But Mather's examination is logical and rational; it is not delivered with a moral sense of indignation but with the firm belief that Satan's power is eternally at war with that of God. His readers are thus warned:

> It is not Heresie to believe that *Satan* has sometimes a great operation in causing Thunder-storms. I know this is vehemently denied by some. The late Witch-Advocates call it Blasphemy. And and old Council did *Anathematize* the men that are thus perswaded: but by their Favour; An orthodox & rational Man may be of the Opinion, that when the Devil has before him the Vapors and Materials out of which the Thunder and Lightning are generated, his Art is such as that he can bring them into form. If Chymists can make their *aurumfulminans,* what strange things may this *Infernal Chymist* effect? The Holy Scriptures intimate as much as this cometh to. In the Sacred Story concerning *Job,* we find that Satan did raise a great Wind which blew down the House where *Job's* Children were Feasting. (124-25)

Mather was certainly aware of the possibility that satanic powers were operating in the same universe that he conceived as being governed by Providence. What we as modern readers must remember in reviewing these theories from the past is that inexact correspondences between a book like **An Essay for the Recording of Illustrious Providences** and the historical event of the Salem hysteria are tempting to draw; what Mather says about witchcraft does indeed support a belief in its existence and its power over righteous people. However, it is quite another matter to conclude from these beliefs that the popularity of the book occasioned the later madness at Salem. It is more likely that Mather's work simply recorded currents in the popular imagination, which indicate how receptive the Salem community *might* have been to the suspicion of witchcraft in its midst.

Mather's account of witchcraft is nevertheless an interesting dimension of his view of the relation between nature and spirit. For example, he alludes to Christian history and even to Scripture to document his notion that the "Evil one" does operate in human time: "Accordingly we read in History, that some of the Popes have by their skill in the black Art, caused Balls of fire to be seen in the Air. So then it is not beyond Satans power to effect such things, if the great God give him

leave, without whose leave he cannot blow a Feather: much less raise a Thunder-storm. And as the Scriptures intimate Satan's Power in the Air to be great, so Histories do abundantly confirm it by remarkable Instances" (126). Once the frame of reference had been established, Mather proceeded with examples of witchcraft in operation.

The fifth chapter of this book is essentially a catalogue of Providences that the author labels "preternatural" (135). These narratives are united by their concern with the operations of satanic agents in the persons about whom they are told. Some accounts make very interesting reading as narrative units, but their significance is measured in light of the later accounts that emerged from the Salem trials. The stringent efforts of the authorities to determine the extent of the influence of Satan and, indeed, to confirm the presence of witchcraft, set the stage for the later examinations, though they certainly in no way determine the future experience. Domestic stories are most prominent in this group; Mather seems consciously aware of the effect his studies will have; the family unit is central, and each episode reflects the tensions of discovering a witch not only in the community of believers but within a specific family. This personal touch was not without its result: the book's immense popularity was no doubt partly occasioned by the way Mather made witchcraft "relevant" to everyman.

A particularly fascinating narrative concerns the house of "*William Morse* in *Newberry* in *New-England*" (142). Beginning on December 3, 1679, various troubles and instances of satanic molesting commenced at the Morse household, and Mather's account is rich with allusions to everyday chores which give seventeenth-century and modern readers a sense of identification with the subjects:

> The night following, they went to bed undressed, because of their late disturbances, and the Man, Wife, Boy, presently felt themselves pricked, and upon search found in the Bed a Bodkin, a knitting Needle, and two sticks picked at both ends. He received also a great blow, as on his Thigh, so on his Face, which fetched blood: and while he was writing a Candlestick was twice thrown at him, and a great piece of Bark fiercely smote him, and a pail of Water turned up without hands. On the 28 of the mentioned Moneth, frozen clods of Cow-dung were divers times thrown at the man out of the house in which they were; his Wife went to milk the Cow, and received a blow on her head, and sitting down at her Milking-work had Cow-dung divers times thrown into her Pail, the Man tried to save the Milk, by holding a Piggin side-wayes under the Cowes belly, but the Dung would in for all, and the Milk was only made fit for Hogs. On that night ashes were thrown into the porridge which they had made ready for their Supper, so as that they could not eat it; Ashes were likewise often thrown into the Man's Eyes, as he sat by the fire. (147-148)

The explanations Mather provides for these occurrences are, of course, "preternatural"; persons experienced in dairy farming would no doubt disagree, since in stories like this one the afflictions often associated with the manual milking of cows are common sources of anecdotes in agricultural folklore.

The most serious problem besetting the Morse family was the bewitching of its grandson. On December 29, "The Boy was violently thrown to and fro, only they carried him to the house of a Doctor in the Town, and there he was free from disturbances, but returning home at night, his former trouble began, and the Man taking him by the hand, they were both of them almost tript into the fire" (149-50). Whatever the malady affecting this child's diseased mind and body, the conventional interpretation given it provided Mather with clear evidence of the operations of preternatural spirits:

> Another time he was thrust out of his Chair and rolled up and down with out cries, that all things were on fire; yea, he was three times very dangerously thrown into the fire, and preserved by his Friends with much ado. The Boy also made for a long time together a noise like a Dog, and like an Hen with her Chickens, and could not speak rationally.

> Particularly, on *December* 26. He barked like a Dog, and clock't like an Hen, and after long distraining to speak, said, there's *Powel,* I am pinched; his Tongue likewise hung out of his mouth, so as that it could by no means be forced in till his Fit was over, and then he said 'twas forced out by *Powel* whom *Morse* looked upon as a Conjurer. (151)

These fits, probably epileptic seizures combined with other forms of psychological disorders, were given the usual single-minded interpretation by Mather as narrator:

> All this while the Devil did not use to appear in any visible shape, only they would think they had hold of the Hand that sometimes scratched them; but it would give them the slip. . . .

> Neither were there many Words spoken by Satan all this time, only once having put out their Light, they heard a scraping on the Boards, and then a Piping and Drumming on them, which was followed with a Voice, singing *Revenge! Revenge! Sweet is Revenge!* (153-54)

Perhaps the most telling aspect of this episode is the way it ends. Mather (or the original narrative account) introduces a *deus ex machina* in the form of a seaman, who is miraculously able to cure the boy of his illness. But the recovery from these bizarre fits is not terribly important in the narrative. Rather, it is subordinated to the concluding phase in the Morse account, the speculation as to which persons in the narrative were guilty of witchcraft:

> The Man does moreover affirm, that a Seaman (being a Mate of a Ship) coming often to visit him, told him that they wronged his Wife who suspected her to be guilty of Witchcraft; and that the Boy (his Grand-child) was the cause of this trouble; and that if he would let him have the Boy one day, he would warrant him his house should be no more troubled as it had been; to which motion he consented. The Mate came the next day betimes, and the Boy was with him until night; since which time his house he saith has not been molested with evil Spirits. (154-55)

Despite the concluding speculations concerning the locus of these terrors in the Morse family, Mather does dispel superstitions and spectral experiments in his summation. "It is sport to the Devils when they see silly Men thus deluded and made fools of by them," he remarks in criticizing the Morse neighbors who continued to seek a cause for the boy's illness by endowing horseshoes and other objects of superstition with powers of Satan's curse: " . . . it may be some other thing as yet kept hid in the secrets of providence might be the true original of all this Trouble" (156).

The sixth, seventh, and eighth chapters are elaborations of the witchcraft theme ("Daemons and possessed persons," "Apparitions," "Several Cases of Conscience considered"). Their significance is not so much that they develop more examples of "preternatural" disturbances, but that Mather has scattered throughout their pages theoretical justifications for his acceptance of witchcraft as a phenomenon, some of which are based on Scripture. As always, he is keenly aware of history, and he attempts to root his theories in examples from the past as well as the present. Consistent with his rigorous scriptural orthodoxy, Mather insists that "the Argument by many insisted on from the Scriptures is irrefragable. Therein Witch-crafts are forbidden." But he seems equally concerned to establish clearly the source and identity of witchcraft before rendering judgment forever in a specific case. "We often read in the Scripture of Metaphorical Bewitchings, *Nahum* 3.4. *Gal.* 3.1. which Similitudes are undoubtedly taken from things that have a real existence *in rerum natura*" (180). And he establishes early his position on hearsay evidence, including some of the stories that he has already incorporated into his own narrative: "I shall not suspect all those as guilty of Witchcraft, nor yet of Heresie, who call the received Opinion about Witches into question" (174). That "received Opinion" included a standard of measurement by which witches might be determined, and throughout Mather's narrative, there exists a tension between a theoretical acceptance of this standard and a willingness to reach firm conclusions based on its application.

The usual method for determining witchcraft in a person was as follows:

1. If the party concerned shall reveal secret things, either past or future, which without supernatural Assistance could not be known, it argueth Possession.

2. If he does speak with strange Languages, or discover skill in Arts and Sciences never learned by him.

3. If he can bear burthens, and do things which are beyond humane strength.

4. Uttering words without making use of the Organs of speech, when persons shall be heard speaking, and yet neither their Lips nor Tongues have any motion, tis a sign that an evil spirit speaketh in them.

5. When the Body is become inflexible.

6. When the Belly is on a sudden puft up, and instantly flat again. These are thought to be certain Arguments of an *Energumenical* person. (170-71)

But Mather throughout qualifies each dogmatic assertion with a balanced assertion that other signs of possession have been advanced and that sometimes the evidence is inconclusive in determining actual guilt in a witchcraft case.

The eighth chapter of *An Essay for the Recording of Illustrious Providences* is a loud appeal for moderation in judgment where these "Cases of conscience" are concerned. First, Mather argues against those who would resist witchcraft through superstition rather than through faith and prayer. "And as the Heathen learned such things from *Bel-zebub,* so have the Papists . . . from them learned to cure Diseases, and drive away Evil Spirits by Words and Spells, Exorcizations, &c." (258). Mather declares, condemning the superstitious almost as severely as the witches:

To use any Ceremonies invented by Satan, to attain a supernatural end, implies too great a concernment with him. Yea, such persons do honour and worship the Devil by hoping in his Salvation. They use means to obtain Health which is not natural, nor was ever appointed by God, but is wholly of the Devils Institution; which he is much pleased with, as being highly honoured thereby. Nay such practices do imply an invocation of the Devil for relief, and a pleading with him the Covenant which he hath made with the Witch, and a declaration of confidence that the Father of Lies will be as good as his word. (267)

This conservative attitude toward both the witches and the persons whose superstitions about witchcraft are

equally culpable is attended throughout the *Essay* by Mather's concern for innocent people both accused of witchcraft and actually bedeviled by preternatural spirits. He cautions that "Innocent persons have been extreamly wronged by such Diabolical tricks" as those perpetrated by the superstitious victims of witchcraft, thus compounding the initial injuries (269). Arguing against spectral evidence, the central form of evidence used in the Salem trials, he says that "sometimes . . . the Devil does not only himself inflict Diseases upon Men, but represent the visages of innocent persons to the phansies of the diseased, making them believe that they are tormented by them, when only himself does it. And in case they follow the Devils direction, by observing the Ceremonies which he has invented, hee'l afflict their Bodies no more. So does his malice bring the persons accused by him (though never so innocent) into great suspicion" (269).

Mather's apparent liberalism in dealing with persons suspected of witchcraft extends to the methods then employed to extract confessions from the accused. In a concluding "Case of conscience," he asks *Whether it be lawful to bind persons suspected for Witches, and so cast them into the Water, in order to making a discovery of their innocency or guiltiness; so as that if they keep above the Water, they shall be deemed as confoederate with the Devil, but if they sink they are to be acquitted from the crime of Witchcraft"* (280). His overwhelming response to this question is negative, and his arguments include scientific, pseudoscientific, and scriptural evidence, all drawn together in a synthesis of disapproval. "This practice has no Foundation in nature, nor in Scripture," he warns. "If the Water will bear none but Witches, this must need proceed either from some natural or some supernatural cause. No natural cause is or can be assigned why the bodies of such persons should swim rather than of any other. The Bodies of Witches have not lost their natural Properties, they have weight in them as well as others. Moral changes and viceousness of mind, make no alteration as to these natural proprieties which are inseparable from the body" (281-82).

This scientific analysis of the superstitious method for determining a witch is attended by Mather's vehement denunciation of all forms of punishment designed to extract confessions from those suspected of witchcraft: "Experience hath proved this to be a fallacious way of trying Witches, therefore it ought not to be practised. Thereby guilty persons may happen to be acquitted, and the innocent to be condemned" (283). These warnings add up to a balanced perspective on the problem of witchcraft, if we consider the historical circumstances of Mather's investigations, and the popular contemporary conceptions about the spirit world. Thus he summarizes his purposes in gathering together these Providences relating to witchcraft: " . . . my design in writing these things; that is so I might bear witness against the

Superstition, which some in this land of light have been found guilty of; and that (if God shall bless what has been spoken to convince men of the error of their way) the like evils may no more be heard of amongst us . . ." (276-77).

Unfortunately, those errors of superstition were to continue in New England, despite Mather's clear warnings against them in *An Essay for the Recording of Illustrious Providences*. Eight years later, nineteen persons were hanged in Salem in a single summer of witchcraft hysteria. In the middle of the hysteria, Increase Mather was on a ship returning from England, where he had been successfully negotiating with the King over the Charter. Accompanying him on the return voyage was Sir William Phips, the new governor of Massachusetts Bay. When the two men arrived on May 14, 1692, the jails in Salem were packed with accused witches who had been given no trials or hope of exoneration. Although posterity has incorrectly assigned both Cotton and Increase Mather the roles of witchhunters, it is clear that Increase Mather was in no way instrumental in generating the witchcraft hysteria and that he was quite effective in bringing the witch trials to a hasty close. His lifelong belief in the *possibility* of witchcraft and in its influence in human society has been misconstrued to indict him for participation in the Salem mania.

Governor Phips quickly formed a court, authorized as the Court of Oyer and Terminer, and trials were begun in early June. Of the fifty-two people slated for trial that summer, twenty were tried and hanged, of whom the first was Bridget Bishop. The story of the Salem trials is a long and complex one that is admirably told by David Levin in his study *What Happened in Salem*, a collection of documents relating to the trials. The significance of the explosion for Increase Mather's development as a writer and thinker has at least three dimensions. First, the trials occasioned his authorship of *Cases of Conscience Concerning Evil Spirits* (1693), a study of legal questions relating to the indictment of witches that developed from his earlier interest in the same problems in *An Essay for the Recording of Illustrious Providences*. Second, the trial procedures and Mather's legal investigation of them through *Cases of Conscience* show clearly his precise opposition to the witchcraft hysteria, and exonerate him from complicity even though his theories of revelation of the supernatural in the natural world might suggest some responsibility. Finally, Mather's clarification of the issues during the time of the trials made certain questionable aspects of the procedure well known, and led to the dissolution of the court before more damage had been done.

At the time of the trials, no one, including Mather, doubted the reality of witchcraft or the fear that Satan could manipulate the natural order against man just as

God could operate providentially on his behalf. What led to the legal confusion at Salem was a commonly accepted belief that God would not permit an innocent person to be accused by an afflcted one.[13] Obviously, one accused could easily be convicted simply by the polarities of argument. Ironically and unfortunately, a corollary of this view was that, through confession of one's guilt, the court should act mercifully, so that persons accused could further the hysteria about witchcraft by owning their sin as a means of saving their lives. Thus the accusations and the confessions fed one another.

The Cases of Conscience Concerning Evil Spirits

Although it would be incorrect to regard Increase Mather as an enlightened liberal on the matter of witchcraft, the *Cases of Conscience* did much to dispel some common superstitions of his day. Throughout its pages, there is a tacit assumption that witchcraft is a reality and that certain persons will inevitably become afflicted in a society tempted by Satan but devoted to God. The large question should be how one determines a witch from a sick person, and this question is precisely the one Mather's *Cases of Conscience* attempts to answer. The document is prefaced by a statement signed by fourteen ministers that contains these lines: "*So Odious and Abominable is the name of a Witch, to the Civilized, much more the Religious part of Mankind, that it is apt to grow up into a Scandal for any, so much as to enter some sober cautions against the over hasty suspecting, or too precipitant Judging of Persons on this account. But certainly, the more execrable the Crime is, the more Critical care is to be used in the exposing of Names, Liberties, and Lives of men (especially of a Godly Conversation) to the imputation of it.*"[14]

This apologia is a double-edged sword; on the one hand, it states the obvious revulsion that the ministers felt for the unjust conviction of an innocent person. However, it also states clearly the vengeance with which they were intent on pursuing witches if they could establish the means for obtaining legitimate convictions. *Cases of Conscience* did not wholly provide that means, but it did establish some ground rules for the exposing of witchcraft which were to have a significant influence in de-escalating the current hysteria. One of the ironies of the summer of 1692 is that the very ministers often accused of unfeeling vengeance on innocent girls were at work establishing a movement against the illegitimate practices of the trials, and Increase Mather was an effective, if late, voice of this group of men.

As early as June 15, a group of ministers had written a letter to establish some principles by which the trials were to be conducted, and one of the first problems they dealt with was the question of "spectral evidence."

This procedure enabled an afflicted person to allege that he had been bewitched by the accused in the form of a specter or spirit, by which of course anyone could be indicted for merely having appeared to another in a dream. The ministers' letter takes a firm stand against this practice: "Presumptions . . . *whereupon persons may be* Condemned *as Guilty of* Witchcrafts, *ought certainly to be more considerable, than barely the Accused Persons being Represented by a* Spectre *unto the Afflicted; inasmuch as 'tis an undoubted and a Notorious Thing, That a* Daemon *may, by Gods Permission, appear even to Ill purposes, in the Shape of an Innocent, yea, and a vertuous man. Nor can we esteem Alterations made in the Sufferers, by a* Look *or* Touch *of the Accused to be an Infallible Evidence of Guilt; but frequently Liable to be abused by the Devils* Legerdemains."[15] But their voices were unheeded. The trials did employ spectral evidence against the accused, and the so-called "witchcraft hysteria" that emerged from Salem that summer was not the consequence of a reasoned and faithful investigation into the possible presence of witches but of a frantic and reprehensible mania that resulted in a tragedy of human waste.

Mather wrote **Cases of Conscience** to sort the true from the false. He began by attacking the shibboleth about the devil appearing in the form of the accused to the bewitched, and he argued logically against this kind of evidence by showing an alternative possibility: that the devil could also distort the imagination of the bewitched so that he could no longer distinguish true witchcraft from fanciful imaginings: "The First Case that I am desired to express my Judgment in, is this, *Whether it is not Possible for the Devil to impose on the Imaginations of Persons Bewitched, and to cause them to Believe that an Innocent, yea that a Pious person do's torment them, when the Devil himself doth it, or whether Satan may not appear in the Shape of an Innocent and Pious, as well as a Nocent and Wicked Person to Afflict such as suffer by Diabolical Molestations?"[16]

On the heels of the hysteria, Mather responded to his own rhetorical question in the affirmative, and argued logically through six succeeding arguments to prove his case. He builds the argument step by step, just as he argued theological points from a scriptural text; and he then delivers a caustic summary that leaves no doubt as to his own position in the matter of spectral evidence.

> It is an awful thing which the Lord has done to convince some amongst us of their Error: This then I declare and testifie, that to take away the Life of any one, meerly because a *Spectre* or Devil, in a bewitched or possessed Person does accuse them, will bring the Guilt of Innocent Blood on the Land, where such a thing shall be done: Mercy forbid that it should, (and I trust that as it has not it never will be so) in *New-England*. What does such an Evidence

amount unto more than this: Either such an one did afflict such an one, or the Devil in his likeness, or his Eyes were bewitched. (19)

By raising this argument as more than a question of the trial's procedures, Mather was opening the floodgates for criticism of the principal form of evidence used in the convicting of the witches at Salem. But he was also positing logical and persuasive arguments against the kind of superstitious madness that had overcome sensible people at the time of the trials, and thereby he prevented a repetition of the Salem episode without there being at least one loud protest from a prominent figure that would give the perspective of opposing views.

The remaining two "cases" are similarly handled, but they are more specific, the larger issue having been dealt with immediately. The second asks: *"If one bewitched is struck down at the Look or cast of the Eye of another, and after that recovered again by a Touch from the same Person, Is not this an infallible Proof, that the Person suspected and complained of is in League with the Devil?"* (20). The response is less direct, but equally strong: "It must be owned that by such things as these Witchcrafts and Witches have been discovered more than once or twice: And that an ill Fame, or other Circumstances attending the suspected Party, this may be a Ground for Examination; but this alone does not afford sufficient Matter for Conviction. . . . " (20). The structured question and response would be mitigated by a common authorship if the "cases" themselves were not so prominent in the minds of Mather's audience. Each of these questions had been dealt with by the ministers in their letter of June 15, but this time, Mather writes in such a way that no future generation could mistake the conclusions developed.

The third and final "case" is perhaps the most important in view of contemporary feeling already generated against spectral evidence. Mather asks quietly, "If the things which have been mentioned are not infallible Proofs of Guilt in the accused Party, it is then Queried, *Whether there are any Discoveries of this Crime, which Jurors and Judges may with a safe Conscience proceed upon to the Conviction and Condemnation of the Persons under Suspicion?"* (29). And before delivering judgment forever, Mather cautiously states that the evidence for witchcraft should be as clear as that in any other crime of a capital type, of which there were many but for which the Puritans were exceedingly careful in their judgments. Rhetorically, his strategy is brilliant, for he makes his reader aware of the penalties for making a mistake *before* he supplies the authorized mechanism for discoving witchcraft. In the end, a personal confession not unlike that offered as evidence of regeneration is the only viable proof of witchcraft admissable as evidence, and even here, Mather is careful to spell out the conditions under which such a confession should be taken seriously:

> But then the Enquiry is, *What is sufficient Proof?* . . . 1. *That a free and voluntary Confession of the Crime made by the Person suspected and accused after Examination, is a sufficient Ground of Conviction.* Indeed, if Persons are Distracted, or under the Power of *Phrenetick Melancholy* that alters the Case; but the Jurors that examine them, and their Neighbours that know them, may easily determine that Case; or if Confession be extorted, the Evidence is not so clear and convictive; but if any Persons out of Remorse of Conscience, or from a Touch of God on their Spirits, confess and shew their Deeds, as the Coverted Magicians in *Ephesus* did . . . nothing can be more clear. (34)

Indeed, nothing was clearer to Mather and those who shared his views. **Cases of Conscience** was printed almost immediately, and its instantaneous and widespread popularity indicates that the people were skeptical of the methods employed at Salem and that they were anxious for something to be done about the court and the judgments. Mather's book was presented before its publication to the governor, and the clarification of the issues contained in his conclusions were spread around orally even before its release in a final, printed form. So there is justifiable cause in assuming that the dismissal of the court on October 26, 1692, was in part precipitated by Mather's emphatic **Cases of Conscience**.

Conclusion

Ultimately, of course, Increase Mather's epistemology was conservative and orthodox. He never dabbled in the scientific explorations of the natural universe that characterized his son's varied career, nor did he depart much from the employment of nature to corroborate truths he already knew from scriptural revelation. But he was more humane than many of his contemporaries in his understanding of human nature in and for itself by the way in which he plowed through the hysteria of the witchcraft episode to see the value of the individual on the other side. Scientifically, then, he was not even a pioneer; the allegorical habit of mind by which he read the book of nature was not unique to Puritanism, nor was it a particularly innovative feature in Mather's thinking.

What stands out in his career is the emphasis given natural revelation in his writing and actions. The political and social involvement that characterized Mather's career was often informed by his attempts to bring together those truths he knew from the Holy Word and those evidences of God's Will that he found manifest in nature. The skill and even brilliance with which he

resolved this tension show him not to be a man suspended between alternative modes of spiritual fulfilment, but that he was a thinker whose knowledge was certain, needing only to bring the new learning into focus with preordained truth, a synthetic process that he mastered beautifully in asserting the error he found at Salem. His conservatism in theology was constant, and the following chapter, which treats the scope of Mather's sermons, develops the central themes that pervade his orthodoxy from the beginning.

Notes

. . . [5] "The Preface," *An Essay for the Recording of Illustrious Providences* (Boston, 1684), p. [xviii].

[6] Thomas J. Holmes, *Increase Mather: A Bibliography of His Works,* 2 vols. (Cleveland, 1931), I, 244.

[7] *Heavens Alarm to the World* (Boston, 1681), p. 4.

[8] "To the Reader," *Kometographia* (Boston, 1683), p. [ii].

[9] Murdock, *Increase Mather,* pp. 146-47.

[10] *The Doctrine of Divine Providence* (Boston, 1684), p. 1.

[11] *The Doctrine of Divine Providence,* pp. 21 and 22 are misnumbered 23 and 20.

[12] Holmes, *Bibliography,* I, 238.

[13] *Ibid.,* I, 119.

[14] "To the Christian Reader," *Cases of Conscience Concerning Evil Spirits Personating Men; Witchcrafts, Infallible Proofs of Guilt in Such as Are Accused with that Crime* (Boston, 1693), p. i.

[15] As quoted by Holmes in *Increase Mather: A Bibliography of His Works,* I, p. 118.

[16] *Cases of Conscience,* p. 1. All subsequent references are indicated by parentheses in the text.

Mason I. Lowance, Jr. and David Watters (essay date 1977)

SOURCE: "Increase Mather's New Jerusalem: Millennialism in Late Seventeenth-Century New England," in *Proceedings of the American Antiquarian Society,* Vol. 87, 1978, pp. 343-408.

[*In the following essay, first presented as a lecture at the 1977 American Antiquarian Society annual meeting, Lowance and Watters maintain that "New Jerus-*

alem" reveals Mather's vision of life during the millennium—the thousand-year period that follows Christian Judgment, during which Christ will reign on earth. The authors also discuss Mather's language, use of symbolism, and his metaphorical and literal interpretations of the scriptures.]

In a recent issue of the *Proceedings of the American Antiquarian Society,* William L. Joyce and Michael G. Hall announced the identification of 'Three Manuscripts of Increase Mather,' housed in the Society's manuscript department.[1] We are pleased to present this edition of the most important of those manuscripts, the **'New Jerusalem,'** an account of the events of the last days as Increase Mather interpreted the Book of Revelation. This document is particularly important for several reasons, primarily 'because, unlike other Mather writings about the millennium, this book deals not with events preceding the second coming, but with what life itself will be like during the thousand years.'[2] It is also crucial because the interpretation of scripture not only reveals what Increase Mather believed about the chiliad, or the thousand-year period of peace that would follow the Judgment, but also because the **'New Jerusalem'** is a work of figural and symbolic significance. We may therefore gain from it an understanding of the metaphorical language employed to compose the vision as Mather conceived it, and this, in turn, offers many insights into the theologian's application of biblical figures to the events of his own time. This document is also critical for historians of ideas who have sought to unravel the mysteries of millennialism as they were understood by commentators of the late seventeenth century in old and New England, writers like Joseph Mede, Thomas Brightman, John Davenport, Increase and Cotton Mather, and Samuel Sewall. Moreover, Mather's **'New Jerusalem'** is filled with typological commentary, the systematic understanding of God's providential dispensations in cycles of historical prefiguration and fulfillment. Indeed, by correctly assessing the 'signs of the times' and relating current events to the patterns of biblical prophecy, a commentator was able to predict the future glory (or destruction) of New England by correlating type with antitype.

It is, perhaps, in Mather's chiliasm, his predictions of the future millennium, that his most concrete and specific contributions to the American imagination may be measured. Closely associated with the development of the jeremiad, the Mather chiliasm placed the coming of Christ before the millennium in traditional premillennial fashion and looked forward to a literal resurrection of the saints. Moreover, he persisted in a view of the flowering of the saints in millennial glory at a time when many ministers were more pessimistic in their assessments of the end of the world. Joyce and Hall write that

Increase Mather's chiliasm is an important key to the understanding of his complex and often paradoxical character. Mather grew to adulthood in years when revolutionary millennialism in England was at its height. Brightman, Mede, and John Cotton, the father of Mather's future bride, were all his heroes and all charismatic prophets of the imminent rule of the saints on earth. Increase was himself in the British Isles at the time of the last, fanatic effort by Fifth Monarchy rebels to overthrow Cromwell and anticipate the second coming. Then came the Restoration. For the rest of his life, Mather lived in a world of discourse where the literal promise of heaven on earth was steadily blurred over and made harmless. . . . John Eliot consented to having his blueprint of the radical millennium burned by the censor in Boston. The overthrow of Antichrist and the rule of the saints was no longer preached, Increase Mather, however, never gave up the vision.[3]

For Increase Mather, the literal and metaphorical meanings of scripture were fused in the working out of God's redemptive plan for mankind. Thus when other Puritan scholars were moving toward a wholly figural and metaphorical interpretation of those prophecies in Revelation and Isaiah, Mather held even more fervently to his view that there would be a literal restoration of the world following the Second Coming and Judgment. The conversion of the Jews, prophesied in Revelation and looked for as a sign of the imminent fulfillment of scripture promises, became for Mather a central symbol signifying the beginning of the end of the world. But if Mather viewed the millennium as imminent, he was more reluctant than some of his contemporaries to tie this vision to a particular date. 'Imminent, he explained on several occasions [writes Robert Middlekauff], meant sometime in the next few years; and one should not presume to calculate precisely the movement of the Lord.'[4]

In his early writings on the millennium, such as *The Mystery of Israel's Salvation* (London: John Allen, 1669) and *Diatriba de Signo Filii Hominis et de Secundo Messiae Adventu* (Amsterdam: Mercy Browning, 1682), Mather placed the coming Judgment and millennium in the future, and argued *'That there shall be a General conversion of the Tribes of* Israel, *is a truth which in some measure bath been known, and believed in all ages of the Church of God, since the Apostles days'.* (***Mystery of Israel's Salvation,*** C1.) Interpretations of Israel's salvation varied in Mather's time. Some commentators viewed the restoration of Israel as an event in the historical past, 'conceiving that there shall be no other calling of them, than what was at their return out of the *Babylonish Captivity.*' Like many of his contemporaries, Mather distinguished a 'spiritual *Israel h.e.*—such as in respect of faith and Religion'—from a 'carnal or natural *Israel, h.e.* those that are by generation of the seed of *Jacob,* who was afterwards called *Israel*' (pp. 6-7). But if Mather declared that 'We must know there is a double *Israel* spoken of in the Scripture,' he was emphatic in his assertion that the national conversion of the Jews which would precede the millennium was to be a literal, historical event. The 'doctrine' of **The Mystery of Israel's Salvation** argues *'That the time will surely come, when the body of the twelve tribes of* Israel *shall be brought out of their present condition of bondage and misery, into a glorious and wonderful state of salvation, not only spiritual but temporal'* (p. 12). This central doctrine, which places the millennium in the future and specifies that the Jewish nation will be converted prior to its arrival, is corroborated by Mather's insistence that the events of scripture are typological foreshadowings of contemporary events. 'That deliverance of the *Jews* by *Cyrus* out of *Babylon*,' he says, 'was very wonderful, yet nothing so wonderful as this will be, as is evident, because that was but a Type of this, and therefore it is, that in many places in the Scripture, the very same expressions are used to signifie both that deliverance out of *Babylon* and this which is to come . . .' (p. 77). And Mather's symbology is consistent with traditional views of exegetical hermeneutics; the type must remain inferior to the antitype, which succeeds it in historical time, and will eventually fulfill the promises implied in the typological adumbration:' . . . because that deliverance was a Type of this, therefore this will be the more eminent and wonderful, for the Type must needs come short of the Anti-type' (p. 78).

This identification of New England as the antitype of Old Israel was not original to Increase Mather's eschatology; the sustaining of this myth into the later seventeenth century, however, was a remarkable mythic, literary, and theological achievement. Since the formulation of the Half-Way Covenant in 1662, New England ministers had stressed the declension of the New English Israel from her original errand into the wilderness, and Samuel Danforth, the Boston minister who first employed the term in his election sermon of 1670, *A Briefe Recognition of New England's Errand into the Wilderness*, echoed a tradition of jeremiads that culminated in Mather's own **Ichabod: or, The Glory Departing**, preached and published in 1702. Thus the public acknowledgment that New England could possibly fulfill the promises of scripture by becoming the antitype to Old Israel's typological prefigurations was an affirmation of the vision of the first generation, conceived in traditional prophetic terms and articulated through the exegetical methods conventionally employed to assert the correspondences between New England and the cycles of ancient history. Danforth's relatively early work is important because it distinguished between a *literal* restoration of Israel and a *figurative* fulfillment of the scripture promises. But Mather is insistent that the imminent events will include the real, historical, *spiritual* transformation of the Jewish nation:

It is evident, that the Tribes of *Israel* shall partake of a spiritual salvation, if we consider the visible Church estate which they shall be in after their conversion.

Albeit now there is no Church amongst the *Jews,* but the time is at hand, when God will erect many glorious Churches amongst them, and upon every dwelling place of *Sion,* and upon all the glory he will be a defence. And the Church polity which *Israel* shall then be under, will not be a carnal one (such as was from *Moses* to Christ) but a very spiritual polity, for they shall be no more under Mosaical paedagogy, no more under the ceremonial Law (**Mystery of Israel's Salvation,** p. 113).

In the 1690s while other Puritan exegetes were beginning to view the millennium and Judgment as a metaphorical prophecy, suggesting that the times were too corrupt to provide an appropriate setting for the spiritual peace and harmony suggested in the eschatological passages of scripture, Increase Mather held firmly to his belief that God would commence the last days with a restoration of Israel as a nation, both spiritually and temporally. He dismissed the declension in piety—which he acknowledged and used to theological advantage in **Ichabod: or, The Glory Departing** (1702)—by showing that 'It is evident, that the salvation of *Israel* will be wonderful, if we compare it with those former deliverances which in the days of old have been vouchsafed unto the Tribes of *Israel*. It is indeed true, that God hath in former times bestowed more eminent and wonderful salvations upon the *Israelitish* Nation than upon any Nation in the world . . .' (**Mystery of Israel's Salvation,** 1669, p. 77). He knew that 'It will be in a time of very great trouble when *Israel* shall be saved' (p. 34), but he argued that

Isa. 65.25. *'The Wolf* and the Lamb shall feed together, and the Lion shall eat straw like the Bullock, and dust shall be the serpents meat, they shall not hurt nor destroy in all my holy mountain saith the *Lord*.' Before the fall, the Woolf and the Lamb, the Bullock and the Lion could live quietly by one another, man was not subject to hurt by serpents or venomous creatures, there was not that enmity in any of the creatures to seek the destruction of one another. Even thus shall it be again: as *Adam* was a Type of Christ, *Rom*. 5. 14. So was *Adams* world, a Type of Christ, the second *Adam* his world, when he shall come to judge the earth (**Mystery of Israel's Salvation,** pp. 124-25).

Thus Mather's anticipation of the forthcoming millennium is argued from the scripture types in a linear, historical movement toward the last days while his description, though brief, of the millennial period is couched in the language of Old Testament prophecy.

These positions are corroborated by his ***Dissertation Concerning the Future Conversion of the Jewish Nation*** (London: R. Tookey for Nath. Hillier, 1709), until recently the clearest known statement of Mather's millennial beliefs. Written between 1692 and 1695, the ***Dissertation*** affirms the Second Coming, the resurrection of the elect in bodily form, the thousand-year reign of the saints and angels on earth, to be concluded by a general resurrection. Moreover, the ***Dissertation,*** like much of Mather's eschatological writing, argues against the allegorizing of scripture as a way of predicting the future. As he wrote when speaking of Richard Baxter, 'if Men allow themselves this Liberty of *Allegorizing,* we may at last Allegorize Religion into nothing but Fancy, and say that the Resurrection is past already. How much safer it is to keep to the Letter of Scripture, when for us so to do is consistent with the Analogy of Faith?' (p. 27). Mather surveys the history of millennial interpretations and concludes that '*It is a known, received Maxim among Divines, that in the Interpretation of Scripture we may not depart from the Literal Sense, if it will stand with the Analogy of Faith.* For Men to make *Allegories* where there are none, is to obtrude their own Imaginations instead of Scripture. Now saith Mr. *Mede* (Fol. 943.) *The 20th of Apocalypse, of all the Narrations in that Book, seems to be the most plain and simple, most free of Allegory, and of the Involution of Prophetical Figures.* How can a Man then take a Passage of so plain, and ordinarily expressed Words as those about the *First Resurrection* are, in any other Sense than the usual and Literal' (***Dissertation,*** p. 19). Thus he adopts the typological reading of Revelation as an extension of the literal sense, not to be confused with the allegorizing of the Apocalypse that has confused scriptural interpretation since the early days of the church fathers. The millennium, or chiliad, he cites, is literal and future, not metaphorical and past. 'If the Millennial Reign began a Thousand Years ago, then Christ's Reign on Earth and Antichrist's would be at the very same time, which cannot be' (p. 25). The pastoral visions of peace prophesied in Isaiah and restated in Revelation will occur following the Second Coming and Judgment of the world, after which there will be a general or 'Second Resurrection.'

The doctrinal positions of the ***Dissertation*** are important because they indicate how strongly Increase Mather defended the literal reading of scripture promises, which he identified with the typological or figural instead of the allegorical. While the ***Dissertation*** treats a specific portion of the apocalyptic vision, two documents explore the whole range of millennial expectations, tracing the history of reformed interpretation and declaring authoritatively that the thousand-year reign is soon to be expected. Curiously, the first of these documents, the **'New Jerusalem,'** is a manuscript written in 1687 that has only recently come to light in the collections of the American Antiquarian Society.[5] The second is the well-known treatise ***A Discourse Concerning Faith and Fervency in Prayer and the Glorious Kingdom of the Lord Jesus Christ*** (Boston, 1710), which Perry Miller has described as 'the finest of his Chiliastic hymns.'[6] Both of these treatises affirm that Mather anticipated an imminent millennial kingdom and that he viewed the figures of scripture as types foreshadowing the Second Coming:

> When this Kingdom of our Lord Jesus Christ shall come and prevail over the World, *There will be Peace and Tranquility throughout the Earth.* Psal. 72.7 . . . Not only Peace, but *abundance of Peace.* Such happy tranquillity as the like was never yet known in the World. One of Christs glorious Titles is, *The Prince of Peace,* Isai. 9.6. *Solomon* was a Type of Christ in this respect: His Name has *Peace* in the signification of it; God said to his Father David, *A Son shall be born unto thee, who will be a man of rest. . . .* What happy days of Peace did the Children of Israel enjoy in his days, and under his Reign, Typifying the Peace of Christs Kingdom (***Discourse,*** pp. 51-52).

Throughout the ***Discourse,*** typological and prophetic figures abound. If they conform to the traditional linear and historical patterns established for typological exegesis, they incorporate into the *literal* reading of scripture a *figural* sense that derives from God's divine dispensation in scripture revelation. Mather makes this point extremely clear when he discusses the City of God, e.g.,

> *They of the City, viz.,* the Citizens of Jerusalem, who are by a *Synecdoche* put for all the Subjects of the Kingdom, *shall flourish like the grass of the Earth,* they shall increase and become very numerous and very happy. All these Expressions are used *Emblematically* to set forth the success of the Gospel, and the wonderful growth and flourishing Estate of Christ's Kingdom (***Discourse,*** p. 14).

Christ's Kingdom to come is everlasting, and the Mathers declared its imminence against alternative evidence provided by contemporary ministers of the jeremiad, who saw in the future a bleak judgment with little hope for the 'new heavens and new earth' prophesied by Isaiah. The chiliasm of Increase Mather, beautifully preached from his exegesis of scripture figures, made him unusual in New England at the close of the seventeenth century. Ironically, the Mather declarations were supported by some of the more scientific explanations of the coming of the end of the world, such as Thomas Burnet's *The Sacred Theory of the Earth* and William Whiston's *A New Theory of the Earth,* composed by a professor of mathematics at Cambridge, which argued that the world was about to be consumed by the advent of a comet.

The most intriguing of Increase Mather's chiliastic writings is the **'New Jerusalem'** manuscript, because it treats the actual sequence of events during the millennium rather than academic arguments about the timing of the Second Coming or the possibility that the millennium has already commenced. For the **'New Jerusalem,'** the future expectations of premillennialism are a given; 'the New Jerusalem, Mather wrote, would "excel the literl Jerusalem" in several ways: first, its maker and builder is God; second, only God's elect, members of the "mistical church," may inhabit Jerusalem and "miserable degenerates" would be excluded; third, unlike the Old Jerusalem which was destroyed, the New Jerusalem, the spiritual Jerusalem, "shall stand forever" as "an eternall excellence."'[7] The crucial point developed in the document is that the New Jerusalem shall be a restoration and renovation of the earth, a fulfillment of that prophecy in Isaiah that a 'new heavens and a new earth' shall be joined together. Nothing, Mather argues, can evolve from the contemporary scene to fulfill this prophecy. Rather, the millennial state, like salvation, must come from heaven in a divine dispensation. 'When the new Jerusalem comes downe from heaven, it is saide that the heaven and the earth that now are, shall be no more, but a new heaven and earth: Rev. 21: 1, 2. There will then be a *new world,* another world wonderfully differing from what this is at present where wee now live. And so will the resurrection world bee. It is in the Scripture saide to be another world. It is expressly distinguished from this present world' (**'New Jerusalem,'** p. 29).

The achievement of **'The New Jerusalem'** manuscript is that it establishes Mather's position on the specific conditions of the millennial paradise and shows clearly his premillennial faith in the future perfection of God's society of saints. To those postmillennial believers who thought that New England would evolve into the City of God without the assistance of grace, Mather declares, 'It is in Vaine for men to *think* or dream of perfection before that day. 1 John 1: 8, *If wee say wee have no sin wee deceive ourselves and the truth is not in us.* There are none that have more sin in them, than they that say or Imagine that They have none att all' (p. 33). He is emphatic about the process of the millennial dispensation; the 'new heavens and the new earth' result from the descent of the **'New Jerusalem'** from heaven to earth. On this point, Mather is insistent and repetitious: 'That the new Jerusalem doth Intend the resurrection world is further evident from severall things. First *In that when new Jerusalem doth come downe from heaven, there are such things to be done, as shall not be done untill the resurrection world shall begin'* (p. 28). '*Againe,* when new Jerusalem comes down from heaven it is saide that the heaven and the earth that now are, shall be no more, but a new heaven and earth: Rev. 21: 1, 2. There will then be a *New World,* another world wonderfully differing from what this is at present where wee now live. And so will the

resurrection world bee. It is in the Scripture saide to be another world. It is expressly distinguished from this present world, Luke 20: 34, 35. . . . *Wee look for a new heaven and a new earth* (a new world, that is for the Hebrews were wont to express the world by those tearmes of heaven and earth) *wherein righteousness shall dwell. Righteous ones shall be there'* (pp. 29-30).

The **'New Jerusalem'** is to be a perfect society, one in which '*all faithfull Christians shall one day partake in the glorious priviledges and happiness, of the New Jerusalem which comes downe from heaven'* (p. 25). In this respect, Mather takes John's vision quite literally, asserting that 'in Rev. 21: 2, 10, [John] had a vision wherein hee did behold the new Jerusalem descending from God out of heaven, whereas if it had intended the church triumphant in heaven only, it had been seen rather ascending to god in Heaven than descending and comming downe from god out of heaven' (p. 25). It is clear that the characteristics of the **'New Jerusalem'** differ from those of the Church Triumphant 'in heaven above'; namely, it is to be an earthly rather than heavenly church, 'compassed bout [by] the nations of the world,' and it is to be a national and visible church. Above all, it is to be a literal and historical expression of God's Providence, an earthly manifestation of His Divine Dispensation that appears in perfection at the end of human time. It is therefore eternal and immortal, a victorious figure of God's triumph over evil: 'But the day is coming when *all the world shall become christ's kingdome* Rev. 11: 15. When the seaventh angel doth sound the trumpett, a Voice is heard from heaven saying *the kingdomes of the world are become the kingdomes of our lord and of his christ.* That will be a glorious day when there shall not be a kingdome in all this world, but it shall be christs when all this world shall become christendome' (p. 55).

Doctrinally, this view is neither original to Mather nor unorthodox. However, that so affirmative a position on the coming of Christ's Kingdom should be expressed in 1687, when many of Mather's contemporaries were voicing the day of doom that would imminently arrive to destroy the corrupt world of Satan's kingdom, creates a paradox. Indeed, Mather's own jeremiads, such as *The Day of Trouble is Near* or *Ichabod,* would stress the other side of this future glory by emphasizing, in Jonathan Edwards's terms, that 'the future punishment is unavoidable and intolerable.' Mather even titled one of his denunciatory treatises *The Wicked Man's Portion* (Boston, 1675).

The **'New Jerusalem'** offers a superb view of Mather's use of figural language to prove his vision. We have seen that the literal interpretation of scripture provided his narrative with a descriptive authority, and that, following St. John's words, Mather anticipated a literal resurrection and a descent to the earth of the heavenly city. But several features of the treatise show that he followed closely the orthodox figuralism of typological exegesis in order to give his interpretation the authority of scripture prophecy and to ground his vision in the revelation of God's will. First, he is very specific about the origins of certain important words, as seen in his primitive etymology of the term 'Jerusalem' itself: 'The notation which some give of the Name *Jerusalem,* is, from the Hebrew word, *Jare,* which signifieth to *fear,* and *Salem,* the original name of that city, As much as to say, *Fear Ye Salem.* In Salem is gods Tabernacle, and his dwelling place in Sion. Be therefore afraid to sett yourselves against Salem, where God and his holy Angels are, able in a moment to destroy all Salems enemies' (p. 21n). This trope stands in the margin of the text, an emendation inscribed in Increase Mather's own hand, as he was rereading the copy transcribed by his son Cotton. The passage Increase thereby amplified reads: 'That the way to be secure and safe whatever may become of the world. . . . They shall repair thither as to a place of safty and security. The church of God is the securest place to be In, that possibly can be. So on the other hand, it is a dangerous thing for men to sett them selves against gods people. They sett them selves against Jerusalem and what be came of those that did so of old whilst It was a cittie beloved of God' (p. 21). The question of 'Jerusalem of Old' is answered through typological exegesis of the text, and Mather clearly shows how the early Jerusalem was but a figure of that which is to come. '*If Jerusalem The most glorious cittie in the whole world was a tipe and figure of the church of god, hence then the church must needs excell in glorie.* The antitipe must needs be more glorious than the *Tipe.* The substance must needs outdoe that which was but a figure and shadow of it' (p. 14).

This is conventional reformed doctrine concerning typology. The verifiable historical figure must foreshadow, imperfectly, that substance of which it was but a shade. When the veil is finally lifted, and all resurrected Saints view eternal glory with what Edward Taylor called 'bodilie eyes'—not those soul's eyes made more perfect through regeneration and grace but those resurrected in bodily form—then the magnificence of God's Holy City would be manifest to those elected for salvation. Mather is quite specific about the differences between the typological figure of the Old Jerusalem and the fulfilling antitype of the New Jerusalem:

> There are three things especially In which the church of god doth exceed and go beyond the old Jerusalem. The spirituall excels the Litterall Jerusalem. *First* in respect of the builder and founder of it. As for the old Jerusalem that was Built by men. There are disputes about the first founder of that cittie. Some think it was *Melchizedeck,* who is called the king of *Salem,* that was afterwards *Jerusalem.* To be sure it was some man. But as for the spiritual Jerusalem god hath laide the foundations Therof. Psalm 87.1.

> *His foundation is in the holy mountaines.* As for the church of god it is he that hath Laid the foundation therof. What shall one answer the messengers of the nations? That *god hath founded sion* (p. 15).

This proof is typical of mather's method. The scripture text is the foundation for a prophetic assessment of contemporary times, and the Old Testament figures are methodically explored as prophetic synecdoches of the coming of the future kingdom. And Mather is very clear about the abrogation of the type that prefigured the New Jerusalem: '*As for the old Jerusalem: that hath been destroyed long ago.* It was destroyed first by the Babylonians, and after it was rebuilt it was destroyed again by the Romans, and when about three hundred yeares after that Julian The Apostate out of his hatred of christ; and The christian name did Incourage the Jewes to build Jerusalem. . . . It was destroyed, by the Immediate hand of god from heaven . . . a mighty earthquake overturned all; so That there was not so much as a stone left upon a stone' (p. 18). The Old Jerusalem 'did miserably degenerate,' so that its godly perfection was no longer possible. Thus had New England degenerated in her 'errand into the wilderness,' so that now the saints could only hope for the coming of Christ's future kingdom, that 'new heavens and new earth' that would descend at the end of human time in fulfillment of the scripture promises. If the Puritans were to continue their imitation of Old Israel, a theocracy modeled on the revealed laws of God, then they could only, like Old Israel, look forward to the coming of the Messiah to redeem them and to establish a holy society out of the corruptions of contemporary life. Mather goes into great detail on this in both **Meditations on Death** and in **Meditations on the Glory of the Heavenly World**. He tells the saints it is obvious the millennium must come to rectify the present situation in which the church is downtrodden even in Boston.

Typology made this figural association possible; without it, the prophetic images of the Old Testament would be abrogated, condemned, pagan patterns of idolatrous degeneration. As Sacvan Bercovitch puts it, typology 'emphasizes the *imitatio,* it translates secular history, whether of individuals or of communities, into spiritual biography, and it recalls the tradition of the Saints' lives. . . . Typology recommended itself to the Reformers as an ideal method for regulating spiritualization, since it stressed the literal-historical (as opposed to a purely allegorical) level of exegesis, and then proceeded to impose the scriptural pattern. . . . '8

By extending the symbolic significance of scriptural typology to contemporary history, Increase Mather expanded the possibilities of biblical interpretation in New England. Although the typological method was used early in New England to assert the historical authority of the New English Israel, not all ministers were as convinced that New England would indeed usher in the long-awaited millennium. In fact, as an examination of Cotton Mather's uses of metaphor will show, the typological symbology of the late-seventeenth century was not fully shared even by this father and son. As Robert Middlekauff suggests, 'Cotton Mather never commented on this dream of his father. Typology remained for him a rhetorical device, not an instrument to be used in the analysis of history.'⁹ But for Increase Mather, writing of the **'New Jerusalem'** or *The Mystery of Israel's Salvation* only a few years earlier, 'Israel's future promised to be important in the end of the world: Christ's Second Coming and the destruction of Antichrist would be signalized by the salvation of the exiled Jews who would be gathered from the four corners of the world. Obviously New England would be affected by these last climactic events, and in the meantime she could profit much by Israel's example.'¹⁰

Mather's typological scheme was not inconsistent with the traditional premillennial reading of John's apocalyptic vision. But his insistence that a harmonious balance could be maintained between *litera* and *figura* continued the expanding possibilities of New England's sustained analogy between her experience and that of the Old Testament Israel. The typological method added prophetic dimension to the static figures of the First Dispensation and gave contemporary history a vital role in the continued history of the work of redemption.¹¹ Thus Mather's historiography pivoted on the typological reading of the Old Testament, and his vision of the future redemption of the world was presented in the prophetic language of Israel's eschatological fulfillment. It was not, of course, the progressive historiography that later developed among postmillennial Calvinists like Jonathan Edwards, but it shared with Edwards a view of America's promise that was rooted in the figural language of the scripture types. It is the fulfillment of these harmonious correspondences through the evolution of providential history that forms the center of Mather's **'New Jerusalem'** manuscript, and for those students of seventeenth-century millennialism and chiliasm, the publication of this important manuscript will be especially welcome.

EDITING PROCEDURE

The **'New Jerusalem'** manuscript is in the hand of Cotton Mather, who often transcribed his father's originals into his own more legible hand, and it was corrected throughout by Increase Mather after the transcription had been completed. We do not distinguish Increase Mather's emendations in our text, but we encourage students of Mather's style to view the original manuscript in the American Antiquarian

Society. It is difficult to distinguish upper- and lowercase 't' and 's' in Cotton Mather's hand, so we have been arbitrary in some cases. Also, we have eschewed the use of [*sic*], given the irregularity of both Mathers' spelling, and we have emended the text only when necessary to clarify the sense of a passage.

Increase Mather's use of scripture texts presents some interesting problems. The general inaccuracy of his citations seems to indicate a habit of quoting from memory or his own translations, and he often conflated wording from the King James Version and the Geneva Bible, while paraphrasing some texts to reinforce his arguments. Mather also translated many Old Testament texts from the future to the present tense, thus emphasizing the prophetic immediacy of the Scriptures. Where Mather misnumbered a text, we provide the correct citation in the text; where he misquoted or paraphrased, we call attention to this fact in a footnote. In modifying the text we have observed the following principles:

(1) Capitalization at the beginning of sentences and punctuation at the end of sentences have been regularized.

(2) Conventional abbreviations (Yᵉ, Yʳ, Oʳ, Wᵗʰ, Wᵉʰ,. . .) have been expanded.

(3) The ampersand and *e* become *and* and *et* unless occurring in the form &*c*.

(4) Catch words and running titles have been eliminated.

(5) Asterisks indicate an addition by Increase Mather which was probably intended for printing in the margin. Angle brackets <> indicate an emendation by the editors. To indicate pagination of the manuscript, a bracketed figure appears at the beginning of each new manuscript page, thus: [17].

The editors wish to acknowledge with gratitude the generous assistance and thorough work of William L. Joyce, curator of manuscripts at the American Antiquarian Society. Mr. Joyce and his staff have for several years been processing documents under a grant from the National Endowment for the Humanities, and they continue to bring to light previously unknown documents in the Society's rich collection of manuscript holdings, not the least of which are these seventeenth-century documents. Professor Lowance would also like to thank the Society and the Endowment for a six-month-long NEH Fellowship that he held in Worcester while editing the **'New Jerusalem.'**

Notes

¹ William L. Joyce and Michael G. Hall, 'Three Manuscripts of Increase Mather,' *Proceedings of the*

American Antiquarian Society 86 (1976): 113-23.

2 Ibid., pp. 122.

3 Ibid., pp. 120-21.

4 Robert Middlekauff, *The Mathers: Three Generations of Puritan Intellectuals, 1596—1728* (New York, 1971), p. 181. It is not central to an understanding of the 'New Jerusalem' to develop in detail the numerological scheme employed by the Mathers for predicting the date of the beginning of the millennium. However, both father and son relied heavily on William Whiston's *Essay on Revelation,* published in 1706 and reprinted many times thereafter.

5 See Joyce and Hall, 'Three Manuscripts,' pp. 113-23. The 'New Jerusalem' is in the hand of Cotton Mather, who was often the amanuensis for his father. In 'The Morning Star' (see pp. 64-84 in Mather, *The Excellency of a Publick Spirit* (Boston, 1702), Mather notes the exegetical difficulty confronting Reformation commentators who examined Revelation: 'There are many dark and difficult places in the *Scripture,* that formerly could not be understood, which of late have been opened with great clearness. And especially in this Book of *Revelations.* The first Reformers did very few of them search into it; and these few that did saw but a little. *Calvin,* though I believe he was the greatest interpreter that ever wrote on the Bible, yet he would not muddle with the Book of Revelations.' Increase Mather was less reticent, and he managed well a thorny exegetical problem in both the *Mystery of Israel's Salvation* and in the *Dissertation Concerning the Future Conversion of the Jewish Nation.* Most exegetes stumbled over the problem of two resurrections but only one Judgment Day in Revelation. This problem lent credence to those who said the first resurrection was either at the crucifixion when the graves opened, or whenever grace came to the individual. Then the second resurrection was the general resurrection at the Judgment Day. Mather resolved this problem by making the Judgment Day 1000 years long (thus tying into the tradition of sabbatism). The elect are resurrected in the morning; the damned rise in the afternoon and are judged by both Christ and the saints. This is significant because it avoids a static millennium—time, an essential adjunct of human experience, lasts through, the millennium only, ending with glorification in the third heaven.

6 Perry Miller, *The New England Mind: From Colony to Province* (Boston, 1963), p. 188.

7 Joyce and Hall, 'Three Manuscripts,' pp. 122-23.

8 Sacvan Bercovitch, *The Puritan Origins of the American Self* (New Haven, 1975), p. 36.

9 Middlekauff, *The Mathers,* p. 211.

10 Ibid., p. 105.

11 Ibid., pp. 107-8. Middlekauff puts the case for typology this way: 'In Increase's hand, typology became more than a technique for penetrating the puzzle of Scripture: it became a method for understanding the history of his own time. . . . Intended to solve so much, typology created an ambiguity that always resisted Mather's best efforts at resolution. Good typologist that he was, Increase insisted that two Israels were referred to in Scripture, and by an extension of thought easy to make, he was led almost unknowingly to think of two New Englands. By two Israels, Mather meant first historical Israel, or as he sometimes called it, "carnal" or "natural" Israel. This was the Israel of Jacob, national Israel, the covenanted people whose literal history was told in the Old Testament. But there was another Israel as well. This was spiritual Israel. Like most Puritan divines, Increase believed that the term sometimes served as a kind of shorthand for those chosen for salvation by God. The Scriptures worked back and forth between these two meanings and so, naturally, did he. In the same manner, he sometimes thought of New England as the entire people in covenant with God, and as that small body of saints who had been chosen for salvation.' See also Mason I. Lowance, Jr., *Increase Mather* (New York, 1975), ch. 2.

Richard Weisman (essay date 1984)

SOURCE: "The Salem Witchcraft Prosecutions: The Invisible World at the Vanishing Point," in *Witchcraft, Magic, and Religion in 17th-Century Massachusetts,* Amherst: The University of Massachusetts Press, 1984, pp. 160-83.

[*In the following excerpt, Weisman assesses Mather's* Cases of Conscience *as an attempt to end theological uncertainties about the accusations of witchcraft.*]

. . . Even before the Salem trials, there are ample indications that the clergy regarded the discovery of witchcraft as problematic. In the pre-Salem litigations, adherence to theological strictures had rendered the translation of popular suspicions into convictive proofs inoperational. During the Salem trials, the ecclasiastical recommendations of June 15 had advised against the use of spectral evidence without offering any alternative criteria for the validation of imputations of witchcraft. Now, in the aftermath of the Salem trials, some members of the clergy were prepared, however reluctantly, to reexamine the epistemological assumptions in terms of which acts of witchcraft and the identity of witches were believed to be humanly ascertainable.

It is in this context that Increase Mather's *Cases of*

Conscience may be appreciated as a final resolution to the long-standing theological uncertainties about witchcraft, for in spite of its conciliatory stance toward the magistrates, Mather's treatise was far more than an exercise in political diplomacy. The questions Mather raised about spectral evidence were questions that applied to other forms of evidence as well. *Cases* was a demonstration within the framework of orthodox doctrine that the workings of the invisible world were not available to human understanding and that, accordingly, errors in the discovery of witchcraft could be neither controlled nor eliminated.

As Mather formulated it, the testimony of the afflicted was unreliable not because it overestimated the powers of witchcraft but because it underestimated the powers of Satan. The use of spectral evidence was based upon an assumption that was crucial to the discovery of witchcraft in general, namely, that God imposed humanly recognizable limits upon Satan's capacity for evil. It followed from this assumption that God would make the activities of Satan and his confederates available to humanity, either by preventing a witch from reciting the Lord's Prayer or by refusing Satan the power to impersonate innocent men and women in spectral representations or by some other sign. It was this belief about the laws of supernatural causation that allowed courts of law to proceed with confidence in their determination of responsibility for acts of witchcraft.

Mather's work undermined this confidence by positing an inscrutable God who would permit Satan to act in ways that were too subtle for human comprehension. Thus, with regard to spectral evidence, Mather argued that it was entirely possible for Satan to represent the images of innocent and pious persons to the victims of bewitchment.[62] Indeed, Satan was so cunning that, in order to deceive the unwary, he could arrange for concomitances between empirically observable events. Accordingly, the recovery of afflicted persons when touched by their alleged assailants was as likely to be a diabolical trick as a providential sign.[63] Even the question of how to distinguish between possession and bewitchment could not be decided with certainty. It was quite conceivable that afflicted persons might only appear to be in conflict with the devil when, in fact, they were instruments of Satan's will. The outcome of Mather's critique was to suggest that human perceptions could not be trusted at all in matters relating to afflictions.

For Mather, however, the exclusion of spectral evidence as a method for the detection of witchcraft entailed the exclusion of all other forms of evidence in which it was assumed that the activities of Satan could be comprehended by humanity. The testimony of confessed witches was dismissed as the devil's testimony, and popular allegations of maleficia were not even

granted the status of presumptions. What remained as criteria for the validation of imputations of witchcraft were most unlikely to furnish a basis for successful convictions.

Mather allowed as sufficient proofs, first, the free and voluntary confessions of the defendant and, second, the sworn testimony of two credible witnesses that the accused party and not any spectral representation had performed supernatural feats. With respect to the second criterion, Mather urged extreme caution: "It were better that ten suspected Witches should escape, than that one innocent person should be condemned."[64] Henceforth, the criteria for the validation of imputations of witchcraft—confession and the two-person rule—would in no way differ from the criteria applied to the validation of other capital crimes.

In the course of formulating the theological grounds for the rejection of spectral evidence, Mather arrived at conclusions he himself was at pains to disclaim. Indeed, it is clear that he was no less ambivalent about the theological implications of his work than he had been about its political implications. The postscript to *Cases* included reassurances not only to the magistrates but to all believers in witchcraft. For those among his readers who might be troubled by possible deviations from orthodox doctrine, Mather promised to publish another discourse in which he would demonstrate the existence of witches and the need for decisive action against them.[65] Nevertheless, the promised sequel to *Cases* was not published, and Mather's drastic reformulation of the rules of evidence was left to stand as one of the final statements by a New England divine on the subject of witchcraft.

Ultimately, it was a later work by another minister that most directly confronted the epistemological problems relating to witchcraft. John Hale's *Modest Inquiry into the Nature of Witchcraft* made explicit the full theological implications of Mather's dissertation. Hale's work was published posthumously in 1702, some five years after it had been written. That the work evoked strong reactions from readers familiar with the manuscript may account for the delay. Despite his own public misgivings about the Salem trials, Sewall noted in his diary on November 19, 1697: "Mr. Hale and I lodg'd together; He discours'd me about writing a History of the Witchcraft; I fear lest he go into the other extream."[66]

Hale's critique of the evidences used in the Salem trials added little to what had already been articulated in *Cases of Conscience*. The criteria he recommended for the discovery of witchcraft were identical to those proposed by Mather.[67] What was distinctive about Hale's work was not its recommendations for future prosecutions but rather its analysis of past prosecutions, including the Salem trials. Hale's accomplishment was to formulate the problem of error in the Salem trials in such a way as to call into question the entire history of witchcraft prosecution in New England. Of all the contemporary commentators on witchcraft, it was Hale alone who dared to suggest that what made the Salem trials problematic made the discovery of witchcraft problematic altogether.

Certainly, by 1697, there were few inhabitants of Massachusetts Bay who would have challenged the claim that errors had been committed during the Salem trials. Far more controversial was the question of what errors had been committed. For some members, it was enough merely to note the consequences of judicial action. As the bill of October 26, 1692, had stated, the trials had resulted in the indictment and arrest of an extraordinarily large number of persons, many of whom were individuals of exemplary piety. Accordingly, the number and quality of the defendants were proof in themselves that mistakes had been made. More often, members pointed to the judicial reliance on spectral evidence. For some critics, the magistrates had violated the theological recommendations on the use of such testimony; for others, the court had confounded afflictions with possessions. In general, however, the tendency of contemporary postmortems was to rescue witchcraft from the Salem trials by conceiving of the errors of the Court of Oyer and Terminer as specific to the events of 1692 rather than as applicable to all witchfinding activities.

For Hale, the problem of error was more complex. He himself had been one of the most active supporters of witchcraft prosecutions among the clergy, and he had not offered this support on the basis of spectral evidence alone. The problem posed by the Salem trials was not that the rules of evidence were treated lightly but rather that they had been taken so seriously. The Court of Oyer and Terminer had organized the most cautiously empirical and systematic investigation into witchcraft ever to occur in New England. In addition to collecting spectral evidences as well as allegations of malefic harm, the magistrates had conducted searches for witch's marks, puppets, and special healing potions. Moreover, they had gathered testimony from confessed witches who implicated other suspects. They had even conducted experiments in the courtroom in order that the devil might reveal his confederates before witnesses.

The cumulative effect of this testimony was to corroborate in detail the magistrates' version of conspiracy. Indeed, during the trials, one of the best educated of the defendants, George Burroughs, conceded that the testimony against him was convictive in view of the fact that eight confessed witches had identified him as their leader.[68] Since he nevertheless claimed he was innocent because his accusers were false witnesses, Hale proceeded to question one of the confessors who had named him. She stood by her account even after Hale had urged her to reconsider her statement while Burroughs was still alive.

As Hale understood it, the Salem trials constituted a faithful and valid application of approved theological recommendations for the discovery of witchcraft. The failure of the Salem trials was the failure of a paradigm:

> If there were an Error in the proceedings in other places and in New England, it must be in the principles proceeded upon in the prosecuting of the suspected, or in the misapplication of the principles made use of. Now, as to the case at Salem, I conceive it proceeded from some mistaken principles made use of.[69]

That the identifications of the Court of Oyer and Terminer were in error was an anomaly that could not be explained in terms of the principles embodied either in earlier legal actions against witchcraft or in authoritative texts for the discovery of witchcraft. If the Salem trials had been based upon mistaken assumptions, then so also were the prosecutions against Margaret Jones, Ann Hibbins, and others in which an earlier generation of New England divines had participated.[70] If the policies followed by the Court of Oyer and Terminer were ill advised, then so also were the recommendations of Richard Bernard, Richard Baxter, and other revered authorities on witchcraft. For Hale, an acknowledgment of the errors of the Salem trials entailed an acknowledgment of past errors as well: "May we not say in this matter . . . We have sinned with our fathers?"[71]

While Hale's specific criticisms of the rules of evidence were primarily extensions of Mather's thesis on the inadequacy of human perceptions in understanding Satan's intentions, he went beyond *Cases* in another respect. Where Mather's work had expressed doubt about the possibility of objective criteria for the determination of witchcraft, there are intimations that Hale had arrived at an even more extreme attitude of disbelief. Various passages in *Modest Inquiry* verge on the radical interpretation that witchcraft might have no ontological basis apart from the perceptions of believers.

Thus Hale explained that the efficacy of charms, curses, and puppets as instruments of malefic harm had little to do with invisible forces:

> And probably the cause may be, that Satan, the Lord permitting him, may inflict his mischief on the person, the Spectators or Actors herein supposed to be concerned, suiting thereby his design to man's faith about it. And, if so, the reason why any

suspected person is hereby concerned is not because they are guilty but because they are suspected.[72]

Elsewhere he offered a similar interpretation of imputations of malefic witchcraft:

> Some persons will put an evil construction upon an innocent person, and so raise an evil fame against a person; and then others believing it, are apt to look upon other actions with a squint eye, and through the multiplying glass of their own jealosies, make a Molehill seem a mountain.[73]

Modest Inquiry was very nearly the work that Sewall had feared it might be. It was an indication that at least one member of the New England clergy had begun to reflect on witchcraft from outside the context of belief.

Cases of Conscience and *Modest Inquiry* articulate the theological closure around the problem of witchcraft. Together, the two works constitute an admission that witchcraft was no longer available as a demonstration of the existence of the invisible world. To be sure, Mather and Hale had met doctrinal requirements by acknowledging the reality of witchcraft, but such acknowledgments notwithstanding, both authors had served notice that, in the future, theological confirmation of imputations of witchcraft as real empirical events was most unlikely. The new rules of evidence virtually precluded the further production of witches. On the one hand, no provision had been made for the translation of popular suspicions into theologically acceptable proofs. On the other hand, the allowance for free and voluntary confessions as a sufficient proof was a condition that had been fulfilled by only a single earlier prosecution in Connecticut. In the aftermath of the Salem trials, witchcraft had become an impossible crime.

Symptomatic of the altered epistemological status of witchcraft was a proposal for the recording of special providences, signed by eight leading ministers on March 5, 1695.[74] The reasons for this undertaking were the same as those given in Increase Mather's earlier proposal of 1681: to help demonstrate the existence and agency of the invisible world. This time, however, there was a significant deletion in the list of unusual occurrences about which information was to be gathered. No mention was made of witchcraft. In this act of omission, the clergy tacitly acknowledged that witchcraft no longer had a place within orthodox doctrine. In the future, New England divines would look to other signs for the presence of God.

THE DECLINE OF WITCHCRAFT PROSECUTIONS

For all its apparent suddenness, the decline of witchcraft prosecutions after the Salem trials involved no marked discontinuities with the past. Apart from the events of 1692, popular allegations had formed the primary basis for legal action against witchcraft, and these testimonies had ceased to carry convictive weight after the last execution in 1656. Furthermore, though allegations of maleficia were included among the evidences gathered by the Court of Oyer and Terminer, there is no reason to believe that they were regarded with greater seriousness in 1692 than in the earlier prosecutions. Now, in the light of a further separation between popular and theological understandings of the problem of witchcraft and in view of the new rules of evidence, witchcraft soon disappeared entirely from the legal records of Massachusetts Bay.[75] Within two years after the Salem trials, witchcraft was no longer an actionable legal offense.

The final case to be recorded, that of Mary Watkins, well demonstrates that, by 1693, the legal possibilities for witchcraft as a valid form of deviant imputation had been exhausted. Mary, a Boston servant, confessed to witchcraft shortly after failing in an attempt at suicide.[76] She was brought before a magistrate, and a bill of indictment was presented to the grand jury of the Superior Court of Judicature on April 25, 1693. The jury refused the bill in spite of the confession. This time, when asked by the magistrates to reconsider their verdict, the jurors maintained their original finding of ignoramus. Although the grounds for the decision are not mentioned, it is likely that the defendant was judged to be distracted and therefore not competent to offer credible testimony. This possibility notwithstanding, the case of Mary Watkins was an indication that, after the Salem trials, not even voluntary confessions would be accepted as proof of witchcraft.

The decline of witchcraft prosecutions by no means coincided with the decline of witchcraft accusations. Despite official and ecclesiastical discouragement, villagers continued to believe in the efficacy of malefic witchcraft until well into the eighteenth century.[77] Indeed, fragmentary records indicate that, even without the benefit of legal authority, witchcraft allegations remained an effective weapon against suspected adversaries. An account in 1728 by a Massachusetts minister, the Reverend Mr. Turell of Medford, furnishes a detailed description of the local response in a small community in 1720 to three children believed to be afflicted. The report makes clear that the children and their supporters were able to mobilize local opinion against the woman whom they identified as responsible for their condition.[78] And, in the town of Colchester in neighboring Connecticut in 1724, one woman regarded the suspicions against her with sufficient seriousness to sue her accusers for 500 pounds in damages.[79]

At the same time, the outcome of these events suggests that if, in certain communities, popular beliefs in mystical harm had not changed greatly in the thirty years since the Salem trials, the response of civil and ecclesiastical authorities had nevertheless changed appreciably. In his narrative, Turell questioned not only the validity of the accusations but also the motives of the accusers. According to Turell, the afflictions were not only not genuine, they were deceitful strategies employed by the children to attract attention to themselves.[80] Similarly, the decision rendered in the Connecticut case also reveals an inclination to view as problematic not the behavior of the accused but the perceptions of the accuser. On appeal, the complainant was awarded a nominal compensation of one shilling in damages. More significantly, the same ruling included a judgment that the defendants were not insane. In the decades following the Salem trials, public attention began to focus less on the guilt of the accused and more on the credibility of the accuser.

Ultimately, the withdrawal of legal recognition from imputations of witchcraft entailed far more than the decriminalization of a category of deviant behavior. The loss of witchcraft as an actionable offense divested contemporary theories of supernatural causation of their last remaining claim to legal authority. With the decline of witchcraft prosecutions, questions about the availability of the invisible world ceased to be a matter of practical concern for the state.

Notes

. . . [62] Included with Cotton Mather's *Wonders,* pp. 255 ff.

[63] Ibid., p. 258 ff.

[64] Ibid., p. 283.

[65] Ibid., p. 285.

[66] Burr, *Narratives,* p. 389.

[67] Hale, *Modest Inquiry,* pp. 162-65.

[68] Burr, *Narratives,* p. 421.

[69] Hale, *Modest Inquiry,* p. 40.

[70] Hale may have overestimated the involvement of the clergy in these cases; see chapter 7, above.

[71] Burr, *Narratives,* p. 426.

[72] Hale, *Modest Inquiry,* p. 81.

[73] Ibid., p. 69.

[74] Calef, *More Wonders,* pp. 92-94.

[75] Interestingly, the only case in which the new rules of

evidence were applied occurred in Connecticut in 1693. A young woman who had been convicted on the basis of spectral evidence, the water test, popular allegations, and positive findings in the search for witch's marks, was reprieved by the governor of the colony. Increase Mather's *Cases of Conscience* was cited as part of the justification for reversing the decision of the court. See Taylor, *Witchcraft Delusion,* pp. 62-78.

[76] Burr, *Narratives,* pp. 383-84; also W. Watkins, "Mary Watkins," pp. 168-70.

[77] For further discussion of survivals of folk belief in witchcraft after the decline of prosecutions, see Herbert Leventhal, *In the Shadow of the Enlightenment,* pp. 66-125.

[78] Turell, "Detection of Witchcraft," pp. 10-11.

[79] Taylor, *Witchcraft Delusion,* p. 155.

[80] With regard to one of the afflicted, Turell wrote: "This little girl had observed what sort of treatment her sisters had met with during their disorders, viz., they seemed to be more the object of their parents' care and love, as well as pity, than ever . . . and, accordingly, she feigned herself afflicted, said and acted as they did, to the very last, without being found out"; Turell, "Detection of Witchcraft," p. 15.

David Levin (essay date 1985)

SOURCE: "Did the Mathers Disagree about the Salem Witchcraft Trials?," in *Proceedings of the American Antiquarian Society,* Vol. 95, 1985, pp. 19-38.

[*In the following essay, Levin questions whether Increase Mather and his son Cotton disagreed about the witch trials and studies the roles for which they are most remembered.*]

The question that I have posed may seem at first to be antiquarian in the narrowest sense. One of my colleagues suggested that I make the title more provocative by asking, Did the Mathers disagree about the Salem trials, and who cares? What could be more parochial than asking whether two embattled ministers, serving in the same congregation, disagreed toward the end of one of the most shameful episodes in early New England history? I could argue that this topic is worth thirty minutes of your time because the Salem trials have already held a disproportionately large place in American historical consciousness for nearly three centuries. Somehow we choose the historical topics that will become notorious. Everyone knows that twenty people were executed in Salem in 1692, whereas I had a doctorate in the History of American Civilization before I learned that in the city of New York, nearly half a century after the Salem trials, many black people were actually burned at the stake for an alleged conspiracy to revolt.[1] The question that I shall pursue instead concerns fairness to historical characters, and it asks us, in examining these recondite materials, to reconsider how it is that historical villains, and especially historical heroes, are made. The documentary evidence is small enough to be examined carefully in a brief space, and debatable enough to remind us that the answer to questions about such evidence often depends on our own desires. Learned historians and biographers, sophisticated in our self-awareness, we can still occasionally resemble Huckleberry Finn, the simple boy who decided to forgo 'borrowing' two of the fruits that he had been taking from people's trees. He decided to borrow no more crabapples or persimmons, so that he could believe that his borrowing of other fruits really did differ from stealing. 'I was glad the way it come out, too,' he says, 'because crabapples ain't ever good, and the p'simmons wouldn't be ripe for two or three months yet.'[2]

I cannot say that the scholars with whom I disagree are rationalizing quite so baldly as Huck Finn, but I shall try to show you why I believe that they have allowed their healthy skepticism about one kind of documentary evidence to betray them into credulous neglect or dismissal of other evidence that is equally explicit in the record. They put far too much emphasis on a postscript to Increase Mather's book on the Salem trials, and by shining their flashlights on one paragraph in that postscript itself, they leave other sections—and many of their trusting readers—in the darkness. Perry Miller, the most eminent of these scholars, and Kenneth Silverman, the most recent, have portrayed Increase Mather as a reasonable critic who belatedly demolished the reliability of the witchcraft court's procedures and verdicts in the autumn of 1692. The same scholars have argued that Cotton Mather, by persisting in defending the court, broke dramatically with his father and the other leading ministers of the colony;[3] that Cotton Mather thus tied to his own name the tin can that has rattled through history for nearly three centuries because he failed to stand with his father and their colleagues against the misguided judges, but chose instead to write a book in defense of the court.[4]

Let me warn you, too, against my own desire. Ever since I first studied these materials thirty-seven years ago, I have believed that Increase and Cotton Mather worked cooperatively in this crisis, as they did on nearly every other major and minor issue during their forty years as colleagues in the Second Church in Boston. Both father and son had written books in the 1680s to encourage the recording of 'illustrious' or 'remarkable providences,' and several nineteenth- and twentieth-century historians blamed those books as major causes of the Salem delusion. Modern scholarship has gener-

ally acknowledged that the lore, fear, and accusations of witchcraft were well known in Massachusetts through surer and earlier sources than the books of any ministers. Virtually nobody in Massachusetts denied, before it was much too late, that witches exist and that the state is obliged to execute them. I believe it is also fair to say that, although judgments of individual ministers range from severe criticism to praise, a modern consensus acknowledges the Boston clergy's efforts—equivocal and ineffective though they surely were—to protect the rights of the defendants and to warn judges against procedures that might convict defendants who were not guilty.[5] Cotton Mather wrote a long letter of this kind to one of the judges on May 31, 1692, three days before the first trial, and when Governor Phips asked the ministers for advice soon after that trial, Cotton Mather copied and paraphrased his letter in the document that he drafted and the other ministers, including his father, signed on June 15, 1692.[6]

This document is known to scholars as The Ministers' Return—that is, their answer to Governor Phips's request for advice. Five of its eight numbered paragraphs argue forcibly for great care. They urge 'a very critical and exquisite caution, lest by too much credulity for things received only upon the Devil's authority, there be a door opened for a long train of miserable consequences, and Satan get an advantage over us, for we should not be ignorant of his devices.' They insist that nobody should even be arrested, let alone convicted, on the mere testimony that a specter (or ghostly form) appeared to an afflicted person in the form of a real human being, for the ministers said it was both 'undoubted' and 'notorious' that a demon could appear to human beings in the shape of innocent and virtuous people. (Such evidence was called spectral evidence or specter evidence.) The ministers even went so far as to recommend that the people and the court try to insult the Devil by refusing to believe any evidence 'whose whole force and strength is from [the devils] alone'— evidence such as startling changes that seemed to be caused in 'the sufferers, by a look or touch of the accused.' Both Increase and Cotton Mather endorsed these warnings, and both also endorsed the final article of advice, which began with a big NEVERTHELESS and called for 'the speedy and vigorous prosecution of such as have rendered themselves obnoxious, according to the direction given in the laws of God, and the wholesome statutes of the *English* nation, for the detection of witchcrafts.'

My reason for reminding you that both Mathers signed this equivocal document is to underline Cotton's participation in the plea for caution and Increase's endorsement of vigorous prosecution. From the beginning of the crisis, they both expected, or at least hoped, to protect the innocent and prosecute the guilty. But as we all know, the door was indeed opened for a train of miserable consequences. By autumn, twenty men and women had been executed, others had been convicted, and many more were in jail awaiting trial. The accusations seemed to be spreading uncontrollably, and at the same time a growing feeling of doubt and resentment was questioning the fairness and the procedures of the special court, which had tried the cases without following the ministers' advice against spectral evidence. By the beginning of September, both Increase and Cotton Mather were writing books about the trials.

Increase Mather called his book *Cases of Conscience Concerning Evil Spirits Personating Men,* and he read it to a group of ministers early in October. This eloquent statement demolishes the validity of spectral evidence. Increase Mather not only establishes the truth that all the ministers had called notorious at the beginning of the summer. He declares that it would be better for ten guilty witches to go free than for one innocent person to be condemned.[7] He insists that 'the father of lies is never to be believed,' because that master of deceit will utter twenty truths in order to make us believe one of his lies (p. 40). And Increase Mather also demands that the court stop accepting testimony from the alleged victims of the witches, for these afflicted witnesses are admittedly possessed by the Devil, and therefore under his control in their testimony as well as in their dreadful fits.

Cotton Mather's book, *The Wonders of the Invisible World,* was completed no more than eight days after his father's *Cases of Conscience,* and the son's book was actually published first.[8] Here too one finds unmistakable acknowledgment that the Devil's purpose in the entire affair may have aimed at getting the Lord's people to maul one another 'hotly and madly . . . in the dark' (p. 43), and that spectral evidence may well have led the court into grave error. But Cotton Mather's *Wonders* has a purpose that more than one modern historian has called odious. This book sets out to 'countermine the whole PLOT of the Devil, against New-England, in every branch of it, as far as one of my *darkness* can comprehend such a *Work of Darkness*' (p. [vi]). Here Cotton Mather argues that, whatever their perplexities and errors, the judges acted in good faith and did convict a number of real witches—a position that Increase Mather's book stated just as clearly, though much more briefly. The theme of *The Wonders of the Invisible World* resounds in the five trials that Cotton Mather summarizes, with detailed quotation and paraphrase from the depositions and from transcripts of oral testimony before the magistrates and the special court. He tries to show that in every one of these five convictions spectral evidence was less important than reliable kinds of incriminating evidence, ranging from the defendant's perjury or self-contradiction to explicit curses, puppets with pins stuck in them, and feats that could not have been performed without supernatural aid. Cotton Mather also asked for the help of William Stoughton, the deputy-governor and chief justice of the special court, who returned the courtesy by writing a prefatory letter of commendation and signing (with Judge Samuel Sewall) an endorsement of the narratives.[9]

Here we have the essential division on which our little historical problem is based. Increase Mather, the father, presents a thorough argument, both scriptural and rational, for excluding all evidence that is in any way influenced by the Devil. Increase's son Cotton publishes a shrill, sometimes incoherent mixture of arguments, sermons, and narrative to show how the people became perplexed, why one should still believe in the Devil's power to set witches loose on human victims, and how a well-meaning, though fallible court could have justly convicted and condemned guilty defendants. Increase Mather demands an immediate, drastic change in procedure; Cotton Mather tries to persuade the people not to condemn the court.

The question for us to consider is whether these two books were complementary parts of a cooperative venture, or whether they represent an ill-concealed split between the Mathers. Besides the tones and themes of the two books themselves, the chief seventeenth-century evidence of a clear disagreement is of a negative kind: both Mathers explicitly deny that they disagree, and both explicitly say that others have attributed the disagreement to them. So far as I know, no documents survive that actually attribute disagreement to father and son. We cannot examine the rumors or any contemporaneous arguments for the existence of a disagreement. We have only the Mathers' denials. Let us consider them now.

Increase Mather had read his manuscript to the ministers on October 3, but by the time his book was published several weeks later, he already knew about rumors, presumably started by the publication of Cotton's *Wonders,* of a rift between himself and his son. Increase added a postscript to the first edition of his own book, and near the end of that addition he said, 'Some I hear have taken up a Notion, that the Book newly published by my Son, is contradictory to this of mine. 'Tis strange that such Imaginations should enter into the Minds of Men: I perused and approved of that book before it was printed, and nothing but my Relation to him hindered me from recommending it to the World: But myself and Son agreed unto the humble advice . . . which twelve Ministers concurringly presented . . . which let the World judge, whether there be anything in it dissentany from what is attested by either of us (p. [73]).' Increase then concluded his book by reprinting the entire eight articles of the Ministers' Return.

Cotton Mather's allusions to the rumors of disagreement appear in a letter and in his diary (or 'Reserved Memorials'), and his tone plainly indicates that he considers the minds of the rumormongers just as strange as his father says they were. When *The Wonders of the Invisible World* was printed, he writes in his diary at the end of the year, 'Many besotted People would not imagine any other, but that my Father's, *Cases of Conscience, about Witchcraft,* which came abroad just after it, were in opposition to it.'[10] Indeed, we have clear evidence that those besotted minds had put Cotton Mather on the defensive before either of these books had been written. At the outset, in his preface to *Wonders* (which he calls 'The Author's Defense'), he says that he has been 'driven' to defend himself 'by taking off the false Reports, and hard Censures about my Opinion in these Matters'—as if he had been trying to divide rather than reconcile the ministers, the court, and the people. He insists, too, that his 'unvaried Thoughts' about witchcraft trials 'will be owned by most of the Ministers of God in these Colonies; nor can amends be well made me, for the wrong done me, by other sorts of *Representations*' (p. [vi]).

But if Cotton Mather agreed with his father and the other ministers, why didn't he sign their preface endorsing his father's *Cases of Conscience?* Perry Miller and Kenneth Silverman have chosen to read the Mathers' protestations of agreement as insincere. In this reading of the evidence, Increase Mather's declaration that he had read and approved his son's manuscript is simply rejected as a polite lie—because neither one signed the preface to the other's book, because the two books differ in tone and emphasis, and because of a letter Cotton Mather wrote to his maternal uncle, John Cotton, a minister in Plymouth.[11] A close examination of that letter may yield a different interpretation.

The letter is dated October 20, 1692. Here Cotton Mather is evidently distressed, only a few days after the publication of his *Wonders,* by both the unfavorable response to his book and the claim that his book contradicts his father's. He begins by saying that he has never needed his favorite uncle's comforting thoughts more than he needs them now, but then he begs his uncle to read the book 'critically' and 'Lett mee know whether You think, I have served, as you know I have designed there in to serve, God and my generation.' The central issue is in the next three paragraphs, which I must quote in full:

> There are fourteen Worthy Minsters, that have newly sett their Hands, unto a Book now in the press, Containing, *Cases of Conscience* about Witchcrafts. I did, in *my* Conscience think, that as the Humours of this people now run, Such a Discorse going Alone, would not only Enable our Witch-Advocates, very Learnedly to Cavil & Nibble at the Late proceedings against the Witches, considered in parcels whilst things as

they Lay in Bulk, with their whole Dependences, were not exposed. but also ever-lastingly Stiffle any further proceedings of justice & more than so produce a public & open contest with the Judges, who would (tho beyond the intention of the Worthy Author & subscribers) find themselves brought unto the Bar before the Rashest *Mobile*[.] For such cause, & for one more, I did with all the modesty I could use, decline, Setting my Hand unto the Book: assigning the Reason, that I had already a Book in the press, which would sufficiently declare my opinion: and such a Book too, as had already passed the censure of the Hand which wrote what was then before us.

> With what Sinful & Raging Asperity, I have been since Treated, I had rather Forgett than Relate. Altho' I challeng'd the Fiercest of my Accusers, to find the Thousandth part of One wrong step taken by mee, in all these matters, Except it were my use of all Humble & Sober Endeavor, to prevent Such a bloody Quarrel between *Moses* and *Aaron,* as would bee *Bitterness in the Latter End;* no other Fault has yett been Laid before mee. At Last I have been driven to say *I will yett bee more vile!* and quoting, Math. 5. 9. I have concluded, *So, I shall not want a Father!*

> Since the Trial of these unworthy Treats, the persons that have used them, have Endeavoured such Expressions of sweetness towards mee, as may make mee satisfaction. But for the Great Slander, with which they have now fill'd the country against mee, *That I Run Against my own Father, & all the Ministers in the countrey,* meerly because I Run Between them, when they are Like mad men Running Against one another; they can make mee no Reparacon; However my God will!

It is easy to see why modern readers of this extraordinary letter would emphasize evidence of disagreement between the Mathers. Cotton Mather's allusions to the uses that 'Witch-Advocates' might make of his father's book, and his concern for what a mob might do to the judges—these combine with the tone of *Wonders,* the rumors of a rift, and the failure of either Mather to sign the other's book. Small wonder, then, that Miller and Silverman, though each in his own way, represent the postscript to *Cases of Conscience* as a belated, perfunctory gesture.

At least for the sake of argument, however, let us look at other language in the letter, and then at the corroborating evidence to which it leads us. Notice first that both father and son say explicitly not merely that Increase Mather failed to condemn his son's book, but that he had read the manuscript and approved it before it was published. Even if one believes that Increase Mather would lie publicly about such a question, we have no reason to believe that

Cotton Mather would lie about it in a private letter to his uncle.

Look, too, at the second sentence in the first paragraph, in which Cotton Mather worries about the effects of Increase's book: 'I did, in *my* Conscience think, that as the Humours of this people now run, Such a Discorse going Alone,' would have dire effects. If published in company with *The Wonders of the Invisible World,* however, Increase Mather's book would not bring a mob's wrath against the court that had tried the witches, nor would it necessarily 'Stiffle any further proceedings of justice.'

Precisely because historians have credited Increase Mather's book with everlastingly stifling further witchcraft proceedings, they have found it too easy to overlook the evidence that *Cases of Conscience* and *The Wonders of the Invisible World* concur. I have no doubt that Increase Mather's attack on spectral evidence did help to prevent further executions and convictions in Massachusetts and elsewhere. Yet no scholar known to me has met Increase Mather's challenge to find any disagreement between the Ministers' Return and his book. And in *Cases of Conscience* itself we find unmistakable declarations that it is still possible to convict a person justly of witchcraft. Even before the notorious postscript, which Messrs Miller and Silverman dismiss as a sop to Cotton Mather, *Cases of Conscience* describes two grounds for conviction: The first is 'a free and Voluntary Confession' (p. 59); the second, the sworn testimony of 'two Credible Persons . . . that they have seen the Person accused doing things which none but such as have Familiarity with the Devil ever did or can do.' That testimony, Increase Mather declares, is 'a sufficient Ground of Conviction' (p. 65). He then offers a list of rhetorical questions to show that 'Wizzards . . . have very often been known to do' supernatural tricks 'in the presence of credible witnesses.' 'How often,' he exclaims, have wizards 'been seen by others using Inchantments? Conjuring to raise Storms? . . . And to shew in a Glass or a Shew-stone persons absent? And to reveal Secrets which could not be discovered but by the Devil? And have not men been seen to do things which are above humane Strength that no man living could do, without Diabollical Assistances?' When two real, credible people—not specters—testify that a defendant has done such things, Mather says, 'it is proof enough' of witchcraft, and 'he or she, whoever they may be, ought to be exterminated from amongst men' (pp. 66-67).

Of course it is right here, just after his strongest endorsement of convictions and executions for witchcraft, that Increase Mather says 'It were better that Ten Suspected Witches should escape, than that one Innocent Person should be Condemned.' He even declares that he 'had rather judge a Witch to be an honest woman, than judge an honest woman as a Witch' (p. 67). But even in the main text of his book, before the postscript, his scruples concerning reasonable doubt do not cancel his plain rule that the sworn testimony of two credible witnesses to feats of superhuman strength or magic should suffice to justify the extermination of a defendant.

I have insisted that Increase Mather propounded this rule in the body of his text, before adding the postscript. The location is not merely academic, for the specific cases cited in the postscript satisfy the rules that he had prescribed and his fourteen colleagues had endorsed. Echoing his son's words, Mather begins the postscript by denying that he has ever wished to appear as 'an Advocate for Witches,' and he says he has written another essay, which he may well publish later, 'proving that there are such horrid Creatures as Witches in the World; and that they are to be extirpated and cut off from amongst the People of God.' He declares himself 'abundantly satisfied that there are still most cursed Witches in the Land,' for several persons 'now in prison have freely and credibly acknowledged' their guilt directly to him, including 'the Time and Occasion, with the particular circumstances of their Hellish Obligations and Abominations' (p. [70]).

But it is in the second paragraph of the postscript, disclaiming an intent to criticize the judges, that Increase Mather persuades me most conclusively of his agreement with his son. Here Increase Mather calls the judges 'wise and good men' who 'have acted with all Fidelity according to their Light, and have out of tenderness declined the doing of some things, which in their own Judgments they were satisfied about.' Because the cases were so difficult, Mather says, they deserve our 'Pity and Prayers rather than Censure. . . . On which Account I am glad that there is Published to the World (by my Son) a Breviate of the Trials of some who were lately Executed, whereby I hope the thinking part of mankind will be satisfied, that there was more than that which is called *Spectre Evidence* for the Conviction of the persons Condemned.' (p. [71]). Whether or not Increase Mather really believed that the convictions were based on better evidence than the spectral, he at least says here that he hopes his son's book will persuade the thinking part of mankind to the belief.[12] That statement in itself would suffice to endorse one major purpose, however insincere, of Cotton Mather's *Wonders:* to avoid attacks upon the court. But in my judgment Increase Mather's very next sentences, in the same paragraph, clinch the case. From the mere hope that we will see more than spectral evidence in Cotton Mather's narratives, Increase turns immediately to his own judgment of the one trial that he himself attended, the trial of George Burroughs, the only minister convicted of witchcraft and the first convict whose trial is summarized in *The Wonders of the Invisible World*. Even more important here than Increase Mather's statement that if he had been one of Burroughs' judges, 'I could not have acquitted him,' is the reason that he gives. It is precisely the same kind of evidence endorsed in the body of *Cases of Conscience*: 'For several persons did upon Oath Testify, that they saw him do such things as no Man that has not a Devil to be his Familiar could perform' (p. [71]). Not until two pages later, after more discussion of unacceptable ways of fighting the devils, does Increase Mather answer the rumor of disagreement between himself and his son.

When Increase Mather wrote his version of his own part in these events, several weeks or months after both books had been published, he retained for his autobiography only five or six lines, which condense everything into one entry, dated May 14, 1692—the day of his return from England with a copy of the new Massachusetts charter in one pocket and the new governor, nominated by himself, in another.[13] Here Increase Mather says not a word about having approved the extermination of every defendant whom two credible persons swear that they have seen doing things which only witches ever did or can do. He says nothing about having heard free and credible confessions in the prison, nothing about his belief in George Burroughs's guilt, nothing about having written another discourse to prove that witches exist and that they ought to be extirpated. Instead he remembers only his doubts and the humanitarian influence for which some contemporaries and many historians have justly given him credit. Increase Mather's selective memory has its counterpart in the selective narratives of Perry Miller and Kenneth Silverman. Miller does at least chide Increase Mather for neglecting to mention his endorsement of George Burroughs's conviction. Silverman not only fails to mention that endorsement, but actually declares that Increase Mather would not have approved of Burroughs's conviction. And then he declares that the Mathers 'undeniably' disagreed.[14]

Several lesser items remain to be examined before we turn to the significance of these recondite details. Cotton Mather's refusal to sign the fourteen ministers' preface to his father's book would be more important if the Mathers had been in the habit of endorsing each other's books. I see no reason to doubt Increase Mather's statement that only his relation to the author kept him from endorsing Cotton's *Wonders,* for (so far as I know) he endorsed none of Cotton's many other books in the 1690s, and he did not even join the other ministers who wrote testimonials to introduce Cotton's church history of New England, *Magnalia Christi Americana*. In 1693, meanwhile, both Mathers endorsed Charles Morton's *Spirit of Man,* for which Cotton Mather wrote the preface.[15]

If the Mathers were cooperating in the late summer and autumn of 1692, they wrote their books to serve complementary purposes. Although I admire Increase Mather's eloquent statements in *Cases of Conscience,* it seems clear to me that the book deliberately left room for further trials and convictions of witches. I cannot agree with Perry Miller that Increase Mather, 'and he alone,' stopped the executions (p. 195), or that by merely adding the postscript Increase Mather betrayed his conscience and the body of his book, turning what might have been 'a bold stroke' into 'a miserable species of doubletalk' (p. 199). Before either of the two Mathers' books was completed, a strong popular revulsion against the executions and the spreading accusations had alarmed the authorities. I agree with Robert Middlekauff that both father and son wanted to protect the innocent, slow down the rate of accusations and convictions, and yet give no comfort to the Devil, to scientific rationalists, or to political opponents of the court and the incumbent administration. Instead of doubletalk, I hear genuine perplexity.[16]

Just as overstating Increase Mather's criticism of the court makes him either too nearly heroic or at last too hypocritical, so overstating Cotton Mather's submission to William Stoughton and the other judges makes *The Wonders of the Invisible World* seem too simply obsequious. If the Mathers were cooperating with each other, the son certainly drew the nastier assignment. I do not mean to defend him. A wiser man would have argued at least that no sound basis for conviction could be found, and a better man would have written less defensively about himself, less fulsomely about the court, more charitably about the defendants, less shrilly about the Devil's threats. Yet insistence that the two Mathers disagreed, or that the two books about the witchcraft trials were both dishonest as they argued, respectively, for opposite conclusions, may neglect the complexity of Cotton Mather's *Wonders*.

The wonder about Cotton Mather's political achievement here, costly as it was to his later reputation, is not in his submission to William Stoughton but in his acquisition of Stoughton's support. Everybody who has looked into the story of the trials knows that Stoughton insisted on the value of spectral evidence, and that he even stormed out of the court one day in the winter of 1692-93 after his death sentence against three confessed witches had been overturned by Governor Phips.[17] Yet here is Stoughton in October 1692, less than three weeks after the last executions—and while he still hopes to send other convicts to the gallows—here is Stoughton endorsing a book that repeatedly admits to grave doubts about the value of both spectral evidence and the confessions of accused witches. In 'Enchantments Encountered,' the first section of the book after the 'Author's Defense,' Cotton Mather concedes that 'the Delusions of Satan' may well be mixed into some of the many confessions, even as he argues that we have little choice but to believe 'the *main Strokes* wherein' the 'many Voluntary Harmonious Confessions, made by Intelligent Persons of all Ages, in sundry Towns, at several Times, . . . all agree' (p. 7). Cotton Mather admits that some of the witches have actually confessed that they conspired to project spectral representations of innocent persons in order to save themselves (p. 9). And he insists that since 'the best man that ever lived' was denounced as a witch, specters must sometimes appear in the shape of 'a person that shall be none of the worst' (p. 9). Cotton Mather admits in a backhanded way that 'disputed Methods' have been used in the witch-hunt, and that 'there are very worthy Men, who are not a little dissatisfied at the Proceedings.'[18] He insists that the Devil's chief purpose is to inflame us 'one against another' (p. 13), and that hereafter the methods of trying the defendants must be 'unquestionably safe, *lest the latter end be worse than the beginning*' (p. 13).

Cotton Mather's success in gaining the endorsement of Stoughton and Sewall may well be connected to his decision not to join the other ministers in signing the preface to his father's book. Cotton Mather had been seeking Stoughton's approval for such a book ever since September 2, 1692, three weeks earlier than the date on which Thomas J. Holmes and Perry Miller say that Mather began to slap the book together. And the outline that Mather sent to Stoughton says plainly that the first part of the book had already been written more than a month before Increase Mather read *Cases of Conscience* to the ministers. Perry Miller is therefore mistaken in attributing the opening section to Cotton Mather's compulsive need to fill up pages while awaiting the transcripts of trials (promised around September 20) to arrive in Boston (p. 201). In the letter of September 2, Cotton Mather admits privately to Stoughton that in the manuscript 'I have Lett fall, . . . once or Twice, the Jealousies among us, of Innocent people being Accused.' But of course he promises 'humbly [to] Submitt all those Expressions unto your Honours Correction; that so there may not bee one word out of Joint.'[19]

After all this analysis, you may well ask the implicit question with which we began: 'What difference does it make whether the Mathers agreed or disagreed?' Aside from ironing out one wrinkle in the record, this little study may remind us that there were no heroes in 1692, except for Mary Easty and several of the other people who were executed—convicts who went to the gallows protesting their innocence, praying for the judges, and pleading for more charitable procedures that might save the lives of others who were wrongly accused. Increase Mather not only read and approved of his son's book, but prescribed two explicit and unqualified ways by which the court could still justly condemn witches. I believe Perry Miller is correct when he declares that the ministers who did not condemn the executions were betraying the best principles of Puritan tradition in their own time; they fell short of their own best standards. But Perry Miller does not advance our understanding of the characters or the time, then, when he proceeds on the assumption that both Mathers knew they were justifying 'murders' (p. 204). I see no reason to disbelieve Increase Mather's statement that he considered George Burroughs guilty and justly convicted. I see no reason to ignore Increase Mather's vehement denunciations of the Devil, no reason to ignore Increase Mather's participation in his son's examination of a bewitched young woman in Boston in the autumn of 1693, long after the last execution had taken place in Salem. Even if we reject Robert Calef's libelous claim that he saw both Mathers fumbling under that young woman's bedclothes in search of demons (and the pleasure of fondling her breast and belly),[20] and even if we reject the tradition that President Increase Mather had Calef's book burned in the Harvard College Yard, we should hesitate to portray Increase Mather as the voice of unqualified reason and charity. We should applaud Robert Middlekauff's perceptive reminder that Increase Mather continued to insist on the limits of human reason and the power of the supernatural.

If we recognize the major points of agreement in the two Mathers' books about the Salem trials, we may not only avoid the temptation to find heroes and villains. We may re-imagine minds that believed simultaneously in strengthening the Congregational ministers' power, in resisting the Devil during his last assault upon the people of God, in protecting the rights of the accused, in deploring the witchcraft court's unjust procedures, in the justice of many of the convictions, in sympathetic appreciation of the judges' difficulties, and in the grave necessity of maintaining popular respect for the newly established government. We cannot avoid judging those minds for the choices they made. We will judge them more fairly as we come closer to perceiving their full complexity.

Notes

[1] See John Hope Franklin, *From Slavery to Freedom: A History of Negro Americans,* 3d ed. (New York, 1969), pp. 93-94.

[2] Mark Twain, *Adventures of Huckleberry Finn,* ed. Leo Marx (Indianapolis, 1967), p. 82.

[3] Perry Miller, *The New England Mind from Colony to Province* (Cambridge, Mass., 1953), and Kenneth Silverman, *The Life and Times of Cotton Mather* (New York, 1984). Specific page numbers referring to these editions will be cited in parentheses in the text.

[4] It was Samuel Eliot Morison who wrote that Robert Calef had tied to Cotton Mather's tail a can that has rattled through the pages of popular history for three centuries. Perry Miller declares that 'the right can was tied to the proper tail, and through the pages of this volume it shall rattle and bang.' *From Colony to Province,* p. 204.

[5] One of the most sympathetic versions of this judgment is that of Chadwick Hansen, *Witchcraft at Salem* (New York, 1969).

[6] Cotton Mather to John Richards, May 31, 1692, *Collections of the Massachusetts Historical Society,* 4th ser. 8(1868):391-97. My quotations from *The Return of Several Ministers Consulted . . . by His Excellency . . . Upon the Present Witchcrafts in Salem Village* are taken from Thomas J. Holmes, *Cotton Mather: A Bibliography of His Works* 3 vols. (Cambridge, 1940), 3:913.

[7] Increase Mather, *Cases of Conscience Concerning Evil Spirits Personating Men, Witchcrafts, Infallible Proofs of Guilt in Such as Are Accused with That Crime* (Boston, 1693), p. 6. Further citations of this edition appear in parentheses in the text.

[8] On the dates of publication, see Holmes, *Cotton Mather,* 3:1257-58, and *Increase Mather: A Bibliography of His Works,* 2 vols. (Cleveland, 1931), 1:106, 123. Further citations from Cotton Mather, *The Wonders of the Invisible World* (London, 1693), will appear in parentheses in the text.

[9] Stoughton's letter is printed on p. [vii] of Mather's work, and the brief endorsement of factual accuracy, subscribed by Stoughton and Sewall, appears on p. 48.

[10] *The Diary of Cotton Mather,* 2 vols., ed. Worthington C. Ford (Boston, 1912), 1:153.

[11] The letter from Cotton Mather to his uncle, held in the Boston Public Library, is printed in Holmes, *Cotton Mather,* 2:551-52.

[12] Increase Mather's language here does not prove that he, rather than his son Cotton, is the person referred to as 'Mr. Mather' in an important entry (dated August 19) in *The Diary of Samuel Sewall,* 2 vols., ed. M. Halsey Thomas (New York, 1973),

1:294. But the diction is strikingly similar. Recording the execution of George Burroughs and others in Salem on a day when Sewall himself was in Watertown, Sewall says that 'All of them said they were innocent, [Martha] Carrier and all. Mr. Mather says they all died by a Righteous Sentence. Mr. Burrough by his Speech, Prayer, protestation of his Innocence, did much move unthinking persons, which occasions their speaking hardly concerning his being executed.'

Scholars have usually treated Sewall's entry as corroboration for Robert Calef's report (eight years later) that Cotton Mather, mounted on a horse, made an impromptu speech that prevented the unthinking persons from blocking the execution. Increase Mather's appeal to the thinking part of mankind may combine with Sewall's absence from Salem and Sewall's use of the past tense ('died') to undermine the corroborative value of Sewall's report.

[13] See the following passage taken from *The Autobiography of Increase Mather,* ed. M. G. Hall (Worcester, 1962), p. 344: 'I found the Countrey in a sad condition by reason of witchcrafts and possessed persons. The Judges and many of the people has espoused a notion, that the devill could not Represent Innocent persons as afflicting others. I doubt that Inocent blood was shed by mistakes of that nature. I therefore published my Cases of Conscience dé Witchcrafts etc—by which (it is sayed) many were enlightned, Juries convinced, and the shedding of more Innocent blood prevented.'

[14] See Miller, *From Colony to Province,* p. 200, and Silverman, *Life and Times,* pp. 110, 113-14, 117.

[15] See Holmes, *Cotton Mather,* 2:834.

[16] Robert Middlekauff, *The Mathers: Three Generations of Puritan Intellectuals 1596-1728* (New York, 1971), pp. 153-55.

[17] Letter of Sir William Phips to the Earl of Nottingham, February 21, 1693, David Levin, ed., *What Happened in Salem?,* (New York, 1960), p. 94.

[18] Here Mather quotes from the Ministers' Return. See Mather, *Wonders,* p. 12.

[19] This letter was available only in typescript when Kenneth Silverman edited *Selected Letters of Cotton Mather* (Baton Rouge, 1971) and when I wrote *Cotton Mather: The Young Life of the Lord's Remembrancer, 1663-1703* (Cambridge, Mass., 1978). But the original holograph has since been acquired by Boston College. The last word that I have quoted is misprinted as 'Point' in Silverman, *Letters,* p. 44. I am grateful to Boston College for permission to read

a photocopy of the manuscript, and for permission to quote it here.

[20] Robert Calef, coll., *Salem Witchcraft: Comprising More Wonders of the Invisible World* [London, 1700], reprinted as volume 2 in Samuel G. Drake, comp., *The Witchcraft Delusion in New England,* 3 vols. (Boston, 1866; reprint, 1970), p. 49.

Hall on Mather's conflict regarding spectral evidence:

On August 1 the ministerial association met again in the college hall at Cambridge. Only seven of the twenty-two members were present. They agreed among themselves that Increase Mather should compose a statement about the rules of evidence that should be adopted in cases of witchcraft. Going back to his study in Boston, Mather set to work with his usual thoroughness. Looking back on it now, Mather worked with painful, tragic slowness. Later that month four more were executed, three of them men, and on September 16 two more men. The executions quickened but could not catch up with the accusations. More than a hundred were in prison on September 22 when another multiple execution took the lives of six women and two men from a total of six towns, including Boston. At the center of each conviction was the issue of spectral evidence.

Increase Mather was pulled in two directions. At the assembly of ministers he had agreed to write out arguments against using spectral evidence in capital cases. But would there have been any case against the accused if spectral evidence were not used? Like the others, Mather was horrified at the outburst of accusations and the mounting executions. On the other hand, he was deeply troubled at the rising tide of atheism, which was widely thought to be connected to the growing disbelief in the world of spirits. . . .

Michael G. Hall, in The Last American Puritan: The Life of Increase Mather 1639-1723, *Wesleyan University Press, 1988.*

Daniel B. Shea (essay date 1988)

SOURCE: "The Mathers," in *Spiritual Autobiography in Early America,* The University of Wisconsin Press, 1988, pp. 152-63.

[*In the following excerpt, Shea examines the narrative style and some key terminology of Mather's autobiography.*]

Except for the Adamses, who came later, no American family rivaled the Mathers in an hereditary inclination toward biography and autobiography. The biography of the first American Mather, Richard (1596-1669), was written by his son Increase, who told his readers that although he would remain anonymous he wrote with the authority of one closely acquainted with his subject and aided by his subject's manuscripts, including an autobiography to age thirty-nine.[1] Shortly after he completed the monument to his father's life, Increase Mather (1639-1723) began the record of his own. His surviving diaries date from the early 1670's, and in 1685 he concluded the first portion of an autobiographical manuscript that continued to receive additions until eight years before his death. Cotton Mather (1663-1728) turned to these documents immediately after his father's death and in little more than a month had completed the biography published in 1724 as *Parentator: Memoirs of Remarkables in the Life and Death of the Ever-Memorable Dr. Increase Mather.* In his turn as biographer of a revered and learned parent, Samuel Mather (1706-1785) could consult an abundance of autobiographical materials beyond his needs or his devices to present them interestingly.[2] His father left more diaries, no doubt, than are preserved in the two substantial volumes of the modern edition, as well as an autobiography, "Paterna," based on the diaries and running to 356 manuscript pages.

The total volume of biographical materials represented in this grouping, and necessary distinctions among the persons who wrote them, stand as mute caution against multiplying generalizations about them. One can say at least that to be a Mather was to produce a eulogistic biography of one's father as well as the documents necessary to one's son for the same task. But it is not clear that the biographies resulting from this tradition may be combined uncritically into the composite biography of an idealized man of God—a Reverend and Learned Dr. Mather of Platonic dimensions—when we see, for example, that Samuel's biography passively accepts direction from the subject's manuscripts, while Cotton dominates the tone and shapes the materials of Increase Mather's *Life.* Simultaneous discussion of the autobiographies of Increase and Cotton Mather would involve even greater difficulties, including psychological speculations beyond the literary study of an autobiographical text. The two Mathers had similar autobiographical habits in some respects, but the autobiographies themselves require separate consideration

In what we have seen was a well-established tradition, both Mathers addressed their autobiographies to posterity, Increase specifying all his children ("[You] are all of you so many parts of myselfe"), Cotton singling out the first son who gave promise of living to maturity, then directing the manuscript to Samuel when the first son, Increase, was lost at sea. Both autobiographers make extensive verbatim use of other personal records, beginning with a continuous narrative but filling out their work over a period of several decades with gleanings from diaries or journals. The result, in both cases, is an almost total loss of the retrospective overview that helps distinguish autobiography from diary-keeping. Increase Mather's autobiography is described by its editor as falling into three sections: a narrative to Christmas Eve 1685, an account of Increase's political mission to England from 1688 to 1692, and miscellaneous entries from 1696 to 1715.[3] The middle section is self-justifying but not introspective, and the last section has the characteristics of a diary, with the exception of a long entry for June 2, 1711, which reviews the events and tendency of seventy-two years of completed life in thanksgiving to the Lord "for all his wonderful goodness towards me a most sinfull creature, throughout the whole course of my life."

Cotton Mather's "Paterna" is formally a somewhat more unified document than his father's autobiography. It also begins with a retrospective section on the author's youth and an account of his growth in learning and piety. Ten pages of sustained narrative carry him to age fifteen, but the next fifteen years require forty pages as narrative increasingly gives way to the setting forth of devices for the attainment of piety. After treating his thirty-fifth year, Mather relinquished the procedure of distinguishing his life into "lustres," or periods of five years. The time remaining to forge eternal bonds between his son and righteousness apparently seemed too little to permit leisurely composition. In the remaining half of the manuscript, Mather wills to his son the multitude of methods by which he had assaulted heaven's gates. Both autobiographies, then, are intended to instruct offspring, but even a cursory description of contents must note that Cotton pursued his task more single-mindedly and at much greater length.

The Autobiography *of Increase Mather*

In its subject matter alone, Increase Mather's spiritual narrative closely resembles that of Thomas Shepard, who had only recently arrived in New England when Mather was born there. Mather too acknowledges the debt he owed his pious parents, recalling especially his mother's deathbed exhortation that he devote himself to bringing others to righteousness. In Mather's account, also, conversion and university education coincide, and there is much foreshortening of the horrific experiences of conviction of sin which prepared the way for grace: "About which Time the Lord broke in upon my conscience with very terrible convictions and awakenings. . . . I was in extremity of anguish and horror in my soul." A symbolic gesture, writing down "all the sins which I could remember" and burning the paper they were written on "in way of confession," marks a new stage of spiritual development. After a day of secret prayer

and fasting, Mather continues, "I gave my selfe up to Jesus Christ," and "had ease and inward peace in my perplexed soul immediately" (pp. 279-280). Unquestionably, Mather counted this as his conversion, although the experience is contained entirely within a paragraph which lacks any detailed description of stages or special workings of the spirit.

Considerably more important in the early passages of the narrative are his recollections of attainment in learning, of his ambitious attempt to enter the ministry in England, and his difficulties as a Non-Conformist at the time of the Restoration. With Shepard he is able to claim the Puritan's badge of honor: "Thus was I persecuted out of two places Glocester and Guernsey, before I was 22 years of age." Unwilling to conform and read the Book of Common Prayer, Mather returned to New England in 1661, where for reasons he deprecates—"being by reason of my 4 years absence become like a stranger, and people are apt to run after strangers though they have little in them of real worth" (p. 286)—a dozen churches invited him to settle with them. In his review of the decade that followed his return, Mather continues to give generous space to vocational decisions, his father's death in 1669 marking their culmination and a new point of departure. His decision to write and publish a biography of his father introduces a group of resolutions that forecast Mather's entrance into the larger arena of the moral and theological life of New England. He had reminded himself that he would have to go about these things "with deep Humiliations and seekings of the face of God," an injunction implicitly obeyed in the narrative's punctuation of its subject's rise in career with grievous "Temptations to Atheisme" and Satanic assaults of melancholy. Mather's vantage point, in 1685, is that of a man who has seen the confirmation of a once troubled hope, "that by these terrible Temptations God would fit me for his service." From this perspective Mather has been able to integrate the materials of his public and spiritual affairs before he attaches the whole of the accomplishment to the theme of reliance on Providence. Mather concludes the first unit of the "Autobiography" by recalling that he had come at last to say, "yea, though I dy for it, I am resolved to Trust in God for his salvation; and let come on me what the Lord will" (p. 294).

Reliance on Providence, as we have seen, had been a thematic staple of Puritan autobiographies, especially those addressed to posterity. Essentially the parent argued that in his deliverance could be seen a Lord whose mercy inspired trust as His will demanded acceptance. Increase Mather's introductory declaration to this effect might be taken for any of a dozen others: "I have thought that the relation of what the Lord has done for your Father, and the wonderfull experience which hee has had of Gods Faithfullness towards him, might be a meanes to cause you to give yourselves entirely to the Lord Jesus and to endeavor to walk with God" (p. 277). Autobiographical arguments supporting this theme sometimes faltered as the writer, beguiled by other attractions in his evidence, spun a different pattern from its finer strands. Frequently, too, the autobiographical argument is logically weak. The experiences used by Anne Bradstreet, Thomas Shepard, or Solomon Mack to demonstrate the clemency and fidelity of Providence are not strongly persuasive, although the ardent fidelity of the autobiographer emerges nevertheless through an argument that cannot contain it.

Against this background, the autobiography of Increase Mather is remarkable for two things at once. It sustains an autobiographical argument for reliance on Providence with impressive evidence, logically employed. And it initiates another argument, carried on simultaneously, and continued at greater length in Cotton Mather's "Paterna," which suggests that Providence is a term an autobiographer may use in retrospect to describe God's recognition of good works.

Increase Mather's autobiographical glorification of Providence cannot be adequately discussed simply by reference to the language of his devotional expressions, if only because the language of many passages has a scriptural precedent. When Mather pauses to sum up the mercies extended to him in his first thirty years of life, "which I have cause forever to bless God for," it is natural that he should express thanks giving in a scriptural tradition: "Bless the Lord O my soul, and forget not all his benefits, who forgiveth all thine iniquities, who healeth all thi diseases, who Redeems thi life from destruction. . . . "[4] Indeed, Mather speaks of deliberately associating his experience with that of an Old Testament prototype when he reflects on the "sufferings" that ensued from a malicious forgery intended to represent him as treasonous. He had been able to read the Psalms "more feelingly than ever . . . before" because of the "particular application" they had acquired for him. "I could now say, princes have sat and spoken against me. I am filled with the contempt of them that are at ease. The proud have had me greatly in derision. . . . And innumerable other passages in the Psalmes could I then read and pray over so as never before nor since" (p. 310). The consolation of the Psalmist, too, Mather takes as his own in another passage, which he has excerpted from his diary: "If I be the Lords Servant, when I am gone, the Lord will make some of my people sensible of their neglects of me, though unworthy of any respect, in my selfe considered" (p. 298). So complete is the correspondence that at times the autobiographer appears subsumed in the prototype, even as Edward Taylor's "personal" and introspective *Preparatory Meditations* have as their speaker, not Taylor, but a generalized Every-soul, whose imagery comes to him in the broad stream of the history of salvation.

Mather's self-portrait from a scriptural model takes on personal significance only as he adapts the type to the particular events of his life. Experiences involving public service generally are made to conform to the outlines of two figures. Mather is either the Psalmist, reviled by men but remembered by God; or, in a close variation, he is the unheeded prophet, strangely persuaded that some calamity will befall Boston or New England at large. As autobiographer, of course, he can count among his historical materials the events in which God confirmed his warnings—King Philip's War, an epidemic, a fire in Boston. But momentarily setting aside finished fact, he recreates the emotions of the prophet whose warnings will be rejected by the very people he hopes to save: "O Lord God, I have told this people in thi Name that you are about to cut off dwellings, but they will not believe me. Lord who hath beleeved our report. Nevertheless, O Lord God, that you wouldst spare them, if it may stand with thi Holy pleasure" (p. 303). His own losses in the fire were not great, he notes, a mercy in the midst of judgment. The aims of the prophet and of the autobiographer are thus contradictory: the prophet is characterized as pleading to be heard, but the successful filling out of the figure Mather has in mind depends upon his not being heard.

It is not clear from Mather's reporting of this incident whether his congregation had before it an unambiguous statement of options. But in another instance, they are hard-hearted beyond a doubt when they ignore a specific prophecy: "During the warr Time, observing the murmurings of the people, and considering I Cor. 10.10. 'Neither murmur ye, as some of them also murmured, and were destroyed of the destroyer.' I was verily perswaded that God would punish that iniquity with some mortal disease, and accordingly I did in publick 3 times declare as much, which some were troubled at me for but the Lord confirmed the work spoken, by sending mortal feavors which were epidemical, and the small pox also whereby many dyed" (p. 302). The rebukes of the people illustrate how rigorously the man of faith will be tried, but only in theory does it seem possible that God may withdraw his consolations entirely and eternally. The autobiographer adheres undeviatingly to the notion that for the afflicted servant and rejected prophet, withdrawal of mercy is only temporary and apparent. Were it otherwise, autobiography would lose its reason for being and become an instrument of despair. The horror of this prospect leads Mather to say in effect that the auto-biographer's alacrity in adjusting his experience to exemplary scripture types must be matched by a similar readiness on the part of God to fulfill His exemplary role by rewarding faithful servants:

> Also, I that day begged of God, that Hee would give me leave to plead with him, (and with Tears and meltings of heart I did plead with him,) that if hee should not answer me graciously, others after my decease, that should see the papers which I had written and kept as remembrances of my walking before God, would be discouraged. For they would see and say, 'Here was one that prayed for bodily and spirituall Healing, yea and believed for it also, and yet hee perished in his affliction without that Healing which hee prayed and believed for; and if but one man should read those papers, Hee would tell others, and then they would conclude that there is not so much in prayer, and that Faith is not such a mighty thing as the word of God sayth it is, so that prayer, and Faith, and the Name of God will suffer if I should not be heard crying to him.' (p. 294)

The passage resembles some of the arguments Shepard offered for the members of his family, but Mather's plea is considerably more interesting in its explicit reference to autobiographical writing, its enlisting God on the side of successful autobiographical argument. The spiritual narrative of the American Puritans, beginning with the search for a pattern of experiences which would suggest the presence of saving grace, broadening at times into an edifying exhibition of all God's gracious and merciful dealings with the subject, here advances its didactic potential as a rather threatening argument for the favorable attention of Providence. Mather's prayer was followed, he recalls, by a resolution *"to Trust in God for his salvation: and let come on me what the Lord will,"* adequate testimony that his intentions were docile. The autobiographical text, on the other hand, suggests that Providence must be subservient to the highest aims of autobiography.

A tendency to invert the autobiographical relationship between man and Providence becomes more pronounced in Cotton Mather's "Paterna," but his father's narrative indicates just as clearly the meaning of the change. In that sequence of incidents Mather relates concerning his attempts to forewarn his people of calamitous judgments, one anecdote varies somewhat from those that surround it. After noting the confirmation of his warnings in Indian attacks and epidemics, Mather touches briefly on the success of his efforts to relieve a famine resulting from the war "amongst the poorer sort of people." More than proximity in time brings together the events of these two paragraphs. Both were attempts to perform service (the word is part of the basic vocabulary of the

autobiography) in his calling. By a habitual expression, Mather recognizes that, in such service, Providence is dominant: "it pleased God that some letters of mine to Ireland tooke such effect. . . . " Yet of all the incidents treated in this sequence, only this one closes with an explicit pointing of the moral, a lesson clasped ardently by at least one of Increase Mather's sons: "Let my children in this follow my example. Where they are not able to give and do good themselves let them excite others to do it" (p. 302). Between these two comments on his service, there is no great difficulty in discerning when Mather's voice relaxes in an idiomatic phrase and when its tone becomes strenuous, calling for attention. In the distance between them, the role of Providence diminishes, and autobiography becomes exemplary in its actions rather than its attitudes.

An epidemic of smallpox, especially when it has been forecast as a punishment for sins, preaches its own kind of sermon. As autobiographer, Mather adds that it was also a time when "divine providence put into my hands special advantages for service among his people." The opportunity was seized, he continues, in stirring up the General Court to pass "several wholesome laws for the suppressing of sin" (p. 302). Another turn of the screw—rather, an improvement of the lesson—could bring posterity to see that one need not wait for opportunities dispensed by Providence. With the aims of Providence securely in mind, one could make opportunities, indeed discover them lurking everywhere. When Increase Mather sets down a specimen week illustrating his method for the most "profitable improvement" of his time, he reveals his relation to his predecessors in spiritual autobiography by recording also the prayer by which he entrusted the success of method to the will of God: "Help a poor creatur, I earnestly beseech thee, to improve this Time as shall be most for thi glory. . . . " Yet, it seems equally important to acquaints his children with the pragmatic basis on which his methodism proceeded. They should not think he offered his schedule as an absolute, since he had always been prepared to refer it to circumstances, "or untill I should know a better method" (p. 304). One of the many ways in which Cotton Mather upheld and extended his father's work was by seeking out better methods and by recording a multitude of them in his autobiography. Providence may continue to be an ultimate mover in the autobiographical drama—so Benjamin Franklin will testify—but the stage will be filled with more proximate causes. . . .

Notes

[1] "Preface," *The Life and Death of That Reverend Man of God, Mr. Richard Mather* (Cambridge,

1670) p. 1r. The autobiography has not been preserved, but Richard Mather's sea-journal of the voyage to New England is available in Alexander Young, *Chronicles of the First Planters* (Boston, 1846).

[2] Samuel Mather, *The Life of the Very Reverend and Learned Cotton Mather* (Boston, 1729).

[3] M. G. Hall, ed., "The Autobiography of Increase Mather," *Proceedings of the American Antiquarian Society,* LXXI (October 1961), pp. 272-274.
[4] *Ibid.*, p. 300. Psalm 103 sets the theme again when Mather concludes the catalogue of thanksgiving he wrote in 1711, p. 358.

FURTHER READING

Biography

Hall, Michael G. *The Last American Puritan: The Life of Increase Mather, 1639-1723.* Middletown, Conn.: Wesleyan University Press, 1988, 428 p.
Examines Mather's life and his role in New England Puritanism.

Mather, Increase. *The Autobiography of Increase Mather,* edited by M. G. Hall. Worcester, Mass.: American Antiquarian Society, 1962, 360 p.
Incorporates writings Mather intended to include in his autobiography as well as journal entries from his later years.

Criticism

Eliot, Emory. "Storms of God's Wrath." In *Power and the Pulpit in Puritan New England,* pp. 88-135. Princeton: Princeton University Press, 1975.
Examines some metaphors in Mather's writings as well as the growth of his thought and style.

Gragg, Larry. "The End of the Trials." In *The Salem Witch Crisis,* pp. 161-80. New York: Praeger Publishers, 1992.
Discusses Mather's role in ending the Salem witch trials through using his *Cases of Conscience* to call for limited use of spectral evidence.

Hall, David D. "Beyond Conversionism." In *The Faithful Shepherd: A History of the New England Ministry in the Seventeenth Century,* pp. 249-69. Chapel Hill: University of North Carolina Press, 1972.
Examines the stances Mather took on issues of church policies throughout his life.

Mather, Cotton. *Magnalia Christi Americana; Or, The Ecclesiastical History of New-England.* Hartford: Silus Andrus and Son, 1855, 626 p.
Detailed description of the Puritan church in New England from 1620 to 1698.

Robinson, Enders A. *Salem Witchcraft and Hawthorne's House of Seven Gables.* Bowie, Md.: Heritage Books Inc., 1992.
Chronicles the events of the Salem witch trials and highlights some of the officials and families involved.

Ziff, Larzer. *Puritanism in America: New Culture in a New World.* New York: Viking Press, 1973, 338 p.
A study of the origins of Puritanism as well as its influence on nineteenth- and twentieth-century life.

Additional coverage of Mather's life and career is contained in the following source published by Gale Research: *Dictionary of Literary Biography*, Vol. 24.

The Special Judges:
John Hathorne, Samuel Sewall,
William Stoughton

JOHN HATHORNE (1641-1717)

INTRODUCTION

American politician and jurist.

Hathorne is thought to have been one of the most zealous witch hunters of the Salem witch trials. As one of the three magistrates in Salem in 1692, Hathorne carried out the preliminary examinations of the accused witches. He also served as a judge on the Court of Oyer and Terminer—the special court created by Governor William Phips to deal with the rising witch hysteria—which sentenced nineteen accused witches to death. An ancestor of the American author Nathaniel Hawthorne, he is thought to have been the inspiration for the character of the puritanical Colonel Pyncheon in *The House of Seven Gables* (1851).

Hathorne, son of one of the most powerful magistrates in Salem, was born in Salem Village, Massachusetts, in 1641. He married his fourteen-year-old bride at the age of thirty-three and built a mansion for his family in the center of Salem Village in 1675. Following in his father's footsteps, Hathorne was elected as a magistrate—assistant to the governor—in 1684. By age of forty-two he was a member of the Board of Assistants and was known as a tireless judge who followed the same Puritanical code as his father had before him. An influential politician in his own time, he held the position of Judge on the Supreme Court until two years before his death in 1717.

CRITICISM

Henry James (essay date 1879)

SOURCE: "Early Years," in *Hawthorne,* Macmillan, 1967, pp. 22-40.

[*In the following excerpt from a work originally published in 1879, James examines Nathaniel Hawthorne's Puritan ancestry and discusses the influence that John Hathorne had on his writings.*]

Nathaniel Hawthorne was by race of the clearest Puritan strain. His earliest American ancestor (who wrote the name 'Hathorne'—the shape in which it was transmitted to Nathaniel, who inserted the *w,*) was the younger son of a Wiltshire family, whose residence,

according to a note of our author's in 1837, was 'Wig-castle, Wigton'. Hawthorne, in the note in question, mentions the gentleman who was at that time the head of the family; but it does not appear that he at any period renewed acquaintance with his English kinsfolk. Major William Hathorne came out to Massachusetts in the early years of the Puritan settlement. . . .

He was one of the band of companions of the virtuous and exemplary John Winthrop, the almost lifelong royal Governor of the young colony, and the brightest and most amiable figure in the early Puritan annals. How amiable William Hathorne may have been I know not, but he was evidently of the stuff of which the citizens of the Commonwealth were best advised to be made. He was a sturdy fighting man, doing solid execution upon both the inward and outward enemies of the State. The latter were the savages, the former the Quakers; the energy expended by the early Puritans in resistance to the tomahawk not weakening their disposition to deal with spiritual dangers. They employed the same—or almost the same—weapons in both directions; the flintlock and the halberd against the Indians, and the cat-o'-nine-tails against the heretics. . . .

William Hathorne died in 1681; but those hard qualities that his descendant speaks of were reproduced in his son John, who bore the title of Colonel, and who was connected, too intimately for his honour, with that deplorable episode of New England history, the persecution of the so-called Witches of Salem. John Hathorne is introduced into the little drama entitled *The Salem Farms* in Longfellow's *New England Tragedies*. I know not whether he had the compensating merits of his father, but our author speaks of him, in the continuation of the passage I have just quoted, as having made himself so conspicuous in the martyrdom of the witches, that their blood may be said to have left a stain upon him. 'So deep a stain, indeed,' Hawthorne adds, characteristically, 'that his old dry bones in the Charter Street burial-ground must still retain it, if they have not crumbled utterly to dust.' Readers of *The House of the Seven Gables* will remember that the story concerns itself with a family which is supposed to be overshadowed by a curse launched against one of its earlier members by a poor man occupying a lowlier place in the world, whom this ill-advised ancestor had been the means of bringing to justice for the crime of witchcraft. Hawthorne apparently found the idea of the history of the Pyncheons in his own family annals. His witch-judging ancestor was reported to have incurred a malediction from one of his victims, in consequence of which the prosperity of the race faded utterly away. 'I know not,' the passage I have already quoted goes on, 'whether these ancestors of mine bethought themselves to repent and ask pardon of Heaven for their cruelties, or whether they are now groaning under the heavy consequences of them in another state of being. At all events, I, the present writer, hereby take shame upon myself for their sakes, and pray that any curse incurred by them—as I have heard, and as the dreary and unprosperous condition of the race for some time back would argue to exist—may be now and henceforth removed.' . . .

Julian Hawthorne (essay date 1884)

SOURCE: "Ancestral Matters," in *Nathaniel Hawthorne and His Wife: A Biography,* James R. Osgood and Company, 1885, pp. 1-38.

[In this excerpt from a work written in 1884, Julian Hawthorne (the son of Nathaniel Hawthorne) provides a short commentary on John Hathorne and reviews his career as a judge.]

[William Hathorne's] successor was his son John, the fifth of eight children, who lived to enjoy the sinister renown of having, in his capacity of Judge, examined and condemned to death certain persons accused of witchcraft,—one of whom, according to tradition, invoked a heavy curse upon him and upon his children's children. In the book of Court records of that period, under date of the 24th of March, 1691, there is entered a transcript of the examination of "Rebekah Nurse, at Salem village," from which I extract the following dialogue between John Hathorne, Rebekah, and others:—

> Mr. Hathorne.— 'What do you say?' (speaking to one afflicted.) 'Have you seen this woman hurt you?'

> 'Yes, she beat me this morning.'

> 'Abigail, have you been hurt by this woman?'

> 'Yes.'

> Ann Putnam in a grievous fit cried out that she hurt her.

> Mr. H.— 'Goody Nurse, here are now Ann Putnam, the child, and Abigail Williams complains of your hurting them. What do you say to it?'

> Nurse.— 'I can say before my Eternal Father I am innocent, and God will clear my innocency.'

> Mr. H.— 'You do know whether you are guilty, and have familiarity with the Devil; and now when

you are here present to see such a thing as these testify,—a black man whispering in your ear, and devils about you,—what do you say to it?'

> N.— 'It is all false. I am clear.'

> Mr. H.— 'Is it not an unaccountable thing, that when you are examined, these persons are afflicted?'

> N.— 'I have got nobody to look to but God.'

This passage in the Judge's career has thrown the rest of his life into the shade; but he was almost as able a man as his father, if less active and versatile. He began with being Representative; during the witchcraft cases he was "Assistant Judge," Jonathan Curwin being with him on the bench; ten years later, he was made Judge of the Supreme Court, and held that position until within two years of his death, which happened in 1717, in his seventy-seventh year. He also bore the title of Colonel, which was not, perhaps, a dignity so easily won then as now. In his will he describes himself as simply a "merchant." His brother William was a sea-captain, and the Judge probably invested a large part of his capital in commercial enterprises. He seems to have been an austere, painstaking, conscientious man, liable to become the victim of lamentable prejudices and delusions, but capable, also, of bitterly repenting his errors. He was a narrower man than his father, but probably a more punctiliously righteous person, according to the Puritan code of morality. He ended a poorer man than he began,—the witch's curse having taken effect on the worldly prosperity of the family. . . .

Vernon Loggins (essay date 1951)

SOURCE: "Witchcraft, Alas!," in *The Hawthornes,* Columbia University Press, 1951, pp. 130-37.

[Here, Loggins examines Hathorne's role in the Salem witchcraft trials and contends that, although Hathorne was involved in the preliminary hearings, he was not active in the sentencing of the accused.]

On at least one occasion Mr. Hathorne himself, in order to bring about an identification, resorted to magic. Certain afflicted girls and women were having difficulty in pointing out a man they were charging of wizardry. Mr. Hathorne ordered all to move into the yard in front of the meetinghouse. A great circle was drawn on the ground, and it was no sooner completed than one of the girls, in a trance, cried, "There's John Alden, a bold fellow, with his hat on before the judges! He sells powder and shot to the Indians and French, and lies with the Indian squaws, and has papooses!" Mr. Hathorne and Mr. Corwin a few days later committed as a wizard the man thus identified. He was an again well-to-do Boston merchant, son of the John

Alden and Priscilla Mullins who had brought romance into early Plymouth. Through breaking jail and fleeing he was to evade trial.

By May 14, when the frigate *Nonesuch,* bearing Sir William Phipps, the Reverend Increase Mather, and the new charter, arrived in Boston harbor, Mr. Hathorne and Mr. Corwin had the prisons of Essex and Suffolk Counties crowded with supposed witches and wizards. With the apprehension of each new suspect the country had become more alarmed. Nearly everybody was afraid of nearly everybody else. When two neighbors met, each was likely to be thinking, "Have you also signed the Fiend's book?" The new governor found Massachusetts Bay in unprecedented terror. He saw that something would have to be done immediately, and he knew that months would pass before the judicial machinery provided for in the new charter could be set up. Sir William therefore took advantage of an old English law and appointed a court of oyer and terminer to meet in the Salem town house at once and begin the trials of Their Majesties' subjects who were charged with witchcrafts.

The court consisted of nine magistrates, headed by Lieutenant Governor William Stoughton. He was a close friend of Increase and Cotton Mather, and held to the full their beliefs regarding witchcraft. Among the eight named to assist him were Samuel Sewall, Mr. Corwin, and Mr. Hathorne. Five, according to the governor's decree, constituted a quorum.

Certain historians were to make Mr. Hathorne a central figure in this court of oyer and terminer, the magistrate most assiduous in seeking death sentences for those on trial. The truth is that Mr. Hathorne rarely, if ever, took advantage of his right and sat as a member of the court. Not one of his contemporaries who wrote of the trials listed him among the judges. During the summer and early autumn he continued holding preliminary hearings, as he had done since March 1. With the trials at the town house attracting the curious, he questioned suspects at his own home, or at Deacon Ingersoll's tavern in Salem Village, or, more frequently, at Mr. Corwin's residence, which for this reason was one day to be known as the "witch house." Between the first of June and the middle of October as many as a hundred appeared before Mr. Hathorne and were committed. He could have had little time for other duties—except witnessing the executions of those whom Mr. Stoughton, Mr. Sewall, and others active in the court of oyer and terminer had condemned.

The first hanging, which came June 10, was that of Bridget Bishop, who twelve years before, when she was Bridget Oliver, had been sentenced to die for witchcraft and then, at the eleventh hour, had been pardoned by Governor Bradstreet. She had prospered as keeper of a tavern, where on occasion the merri-

ment was loud. She had moreover worn clothes such as most of her women neighbors could not afford. After her commitment by Mr. Hathorne a grand jury—sitting probably at Mr. Corwin's residence—returned a bill against her. Brought before the court of oyer and terminer, she was obliged to take care of her own defense. For there were still no lawyers, except counselors for the crown, in Massachusetts Bay. The woman's trial, on the upper floor of the town house, was a bedlam. Time and again the reading of the depositions stating her alleged acts of witchcraft were interrupted by the shricks of the stricken girls and women. But at last Bridget Bishop heard the clerk—Stephen Sewall, brother of Samuel Sewall—read the jury's verdict of guilty. Then she listened as Mr. Stoughton pronounced the sentence of death.

Mr. Hathorne, on horseback, was a prominent figure in the procession which followed her to the place of execution. She rode in a cart—standing, so that the hundreds of spectators could see her all the better. From the jail the procession moved south on Prison Lane, and then west on the main street. When the woman drew near the meetinghouse, she happened to cast her eyes in the direction of the sacred edifice. As she did so, said Mr. Cotton Mather, a board on the inside of the building broke from the heavy nails which held it and flew with the speed of a bullet to the opposite wall, hitting with a crash that could be heard throughout Salem. What more was needed to prove that Bridget Bishop had signed the Devil's book? At the corner of the Mill Pond farm—which for Mr. Hathorne and his family was a second home—the driver of the death cart turned from the main street into a narrow roadway which led northwest a short distance and then up a rocky mound, to be known in time as Gallows Hill. Mr. Hathorne, fulfilling his duty as a magistrate, looked on while Bridget Bishop was hanged, possibly from a gibbet, but more likely from the limb of a tree. When the hangman was sure that she was dead, the body was cut down and tossed into a shallow grave which had been dug at the foot of a rock.

On July 19 Mr. Hathorne witnessed the first mass execution. This time five women were hanged.

Among them was Sarah Good. When she came to Salem to be tried, she left in the Boston jail her little four-year-old daughter, Dorcas, also committed by Mr. Hathorne on a charge of witchcraft. He saw with his own eyes, he believed, the prints of her little teeth on the arms of two of the afflicted girls, bitten when the child's physical body was asleep in her own bed a mile or two away. The Boston jailer had to have special manacles made to fit the tiny wrists and ankles, and required the mother to pay for them. When Goody Good, sure of herself despite her fear and rancor, was about to be hanged, the Reverend Nicholas Noyes cried out, "You're a witch, and you know you are!" Turning upon him a look which in itself sent forth curses, she shouted, "You're a liar! I'm no more a witch than you're a wizard! And if you take my life God will give you blood to drink!"

Future commentators were to claim erroneously that this curse was addressed not to Mr. Noyes but to Mr. Hathorne and was spoken not by Sarah Good but by another woman hanged that day, Rebecca Nurse. This Christlike victim of the hysteria met death pitying her murderers rather than wishing evil upon them. Her husband was Francis Nurse, a large landholder and leader of influence in Salem Village. She was seventy-one, and all her life had been noted for her goodness and godliness. But because of disagreement over certain land boundaries she had won the enmity of Thomas Putnam's wife. Besides, Mrs. Nurse and her husband had never transferred their church membership from Salem to Salem Village, and were known to be in opposition to the scheme of Mr. Parris to obtain possession of the manse in which he was living. So Ann Putnam and two other girls cried out against Mrs. Nurse, and Mr. Hathorne committed her. She was so deaf that she missed most that was said at her trial. Mr. Stoughton, taking advantage of an equivocal answer she made to a question she failed to hear, finally succeeded in forcing from the trial jury a verdict of guilty. Then the Reverend Mr. Noyes, in a dread ceremony in the meetinghouse with Mrs. Nurse present in chains, pronounced upon her the doom of excommunication, and in doing so induced the politics-minded Governor Phipps to recall a reprieve he had issued. The passageway to hell freed of all churchly obstacles, Rebecca Nurse was crowded into the death cart with the four others and taken to the execution mound. Before she died she said, in complete resignation, "God will clear my innocency!"

On August 19, exactly one month later, Mr. Hathorne saw hanged four men, including the Reverend George Burroughs, and one woman, Martha Carrier, of Andover.

Mr. Burroughs was the short dark man, of great physical strength, whom the afflicted spoke often of seeing in their visions. The young woman who first identified him by name had been a servant in his house when he was the minister in Salem Village. Unable to bring about harmony in the quarrelsome parish, he had resigned, to return to his old home in Wells, Maine. He was in charge of the church in that settlement when Mr. Hathorne and Mr. Corwin issued the warrant for his arrest. Since he was a minister, his trial was specially sensational. Both the celebrated Mr. Mathers were in attendance. Even the ghosts of his two former wives, seen by the afflicted in their trances, came from their graves to testify against him, claiming that he had been their murderer! Mr. Stoughton had no trouble in getting the jury to agree at once on a conviction.

But at the execution mound, just before he was hanged, Mr. Burroughs proved that a man convicted of wizardry could, with great eloquence, repeat the Lord's Prayer. Then, in words so touching that many of his hearers were brought to tears, he addressed the crowd, avowing his innocence but dwelling more upon his fearlessness of death. Mr. Cotton Mather, present on horseback, in periwig and feathered hat, was quick to sense the effect of the speech, and as soon as he was sure that the body of Mr. Burroughs was lifeless, he too addressed the crowd. Unwilling in his piety to speak the name of a wizard, he called the hanged man G.B. Defending the action of Lieutenant Governor Stoughton and the rest of the court of oyer and terminer, he shot one thunderbolt of theological reasoning after another, each stronger than the preceding. The incontrovertible final discharge was, "This foul fiend G.B. preached from Christian pulpits—but never was he ORDAINED!"

When Mr. Mather saw the body of Martha Carrier dangling in the air, he shouted, "This is the hag whom the Devil promised to make the Queen of Hell!" She belonged to Andover, where the hysteria raged with a violence almost as great as in Salem Village. It was in Andover that a dog, supposed to have the power of bewitching, was by process of law executed. At Goody Carrier's preliminary examination Mr. Hathorne heard three of her children, among whom was a girl of eight, admit that they had yielded to their mother when she appeared in the likeness of a cat and threatened to tear them into pieces if they refused to sign Satan's book.

Mr. Hathorne let jailers and constables witness the next execution. The one victim this time was eighty-year-old Giles Corey. Because he stood dumb when he was asked to plead guilty or not guilty, he was sentenced by the court of oyer and terminer to suffer the ordeal of peine forte et dure until he admitted or denied being a wizard, or died. All he would say as he lay naked in jail while stone after stone was stacked on his chest was to be echoed in a song sung in eighteenth-century Massachusetts Bay, a ballad of the people bearing the refrain,

> "More weight! More weight!"
> Giles Corey he cried.

The ordeal, requiring three days, ended with the death of the old man on September 19.

The strength of character he showed in choosing to die an agonizing death rather than submit to trial by a court for which he had no respect was in time to make of him a popular hero. But the records credit him with little which his own age considered admirable. He and his middle-aged wife Martha, his third, inevitably became suspects as soon as the accusers began to look for victims. Though the Coreys in recent years had followed godly paths as church members, Salem could not forget that Giles had more than once been whipped for petty crimes and that Martha, who was of pure English origin, had some time previous to her marriage to Giles borne a mulatto son. Whether she had been wedded to the unidentified slave or freedman who was the child's father was not recorded.

She too, vowing to God her innocence as she prayed, was courageous when on September 22 she was taken with seven other women to the execution mound. As Mr. Hathorne sat on his horse looking at the swung bodies, he heard the Reverend Mr. Noyes cry out, "What a *sad* thing it is to see eight firebrands of hell hanging there!" Mr. Hathorne might have wondered whether the minister, who had pronounced excommunication on both the Coreys, was being ironic in his use of the adjective *sad*.

Seven more women were under sentence to die, and Mr. Hathorne expected to see them hanged in October. But after that September 22, 1692, no one was ever again to witness an execution for the crime of witchcraft in New England.

Not all the people in Massachusetts Bay had by any means fallen victim to the hysteria. It had seemed so at the start, so stunned were the clear-eyed at the quick penetration of the madness into the minds of men and women of every social level. But as the weeks passed and the frenzy grew in intensity, those who were still capable of rational thinking showed their stand by word and act. They granted that the Devil was busy in the land. But they refused to believe the silly tales told of him at the trials. They maintained rather that the Evil One was at work in the hearts of the promoters of the delusion, such as Mr. Cotton Mather, Mr. Parris, and Thomas Putnam's wife. First the Fiend had deadened their sensibilities to reality. Then, without their awareness perhaps, he had stirred up their personal hates, their neighborhood enmities, their passion to step up in the world, and their primitive instincts of cruelty for the sake of cruelty. . . .

Enders A. Robinson (essay date 1992)

SOURCE: "John Hawthorne, Magistrate," in *Salem Witchcraft and Hawthorne's House of the Seven Gables,* Heritage Books, Inc., 1992, pp. 64-75.

[*In the excerpt below, Robinson provides a short overview of Hathorne's life and examines the similarities between Hathorne and the fictional character of Colonel Pyncheon in Nathaniel Hawthorne's* The House of Seven Gables.]

. . . William Hathorne made full use of his position as magistrate to obtain wealth. During the Quaker perse-

cution the authorities took a yoke of oxen from the Quaker John Small to settle a fine. Small's wife came to court and asked the magistrates William Hathorne and Daniel Denison, "If her husband and the Friends were such an accursed people, how then did they meddle with their goods, for they must be accursed also?" Denison turned to the woman and said, "Woman, we have none of it, for we give it to the poor." As she was speaking, John Gedney, the rich Salem innkeeper in whose tavern the court was held, entered the room. "Is this man the poor you give it to? For it is this man that had my husband's oxen," she cried. "Woman," replied Hathorne, "would you have us starve, while we sit about your business?"[77] In 1692, John Hathorne, son of the magistrate, and Bartholomew Gedney, son of the innkeeper, would sit together as justices on the witchcraft court.

William Hathorne (1607-1681) had four sons, Eleazer Hathorne, born in 1636, Nathaniel Hathorne, born in 1639, John Hathorne, born in 1641, and William Hathorne, Jr., born in 1646. Nathaniel Hathorne died as a young man. As noted earlier, William Hathorne became a major in 1661, and became a magistrate, an assistant to the governor, in 1662. That year, John became twenty-one and his father gave him a portion of Mill Pond Farm on the outskirts of Salem Town. His father retained about sixty acres. John was employed in Salem Town to keep accounts for merchants. In 1668 Major William Hathorne turned over his downtown house on Main Street in Salem Town to his oldest son Eleazer, and returned to live permanently in his house on Mill Pond Farm.[78]

In March 1675, at age 33, John Hathorne married Ruth Gardner. The bride was only 14. She had been born when the Quaker persecution was at its height. Her mother was an open convert and her father was a sympathizer. Her parents were fined mercilessly for absence from Puritan church services, and persistently molested in other ways. Finally in 1673 her parents moved to Connecticut. But they left behind in Salem their daughter Ruth in the household of her childless uncle, Captain Joseph Gardner and his wife. John Hathorne received permission from the Gardners to court Ruth which led to their marriage.

In 1675 King Philip's War commenced, the only Indian war that nearly succeeded in driving the white man from New England. Throughout the war John Hathorne took advantage of the excellent opportunities it afforded for war profiteering. He entrenched himself in business, purchased a wharf, and secured a license to sell strong liquors. It was an auspicious time to build his permanent family seat.

John Hathorne wished to erect a mansion, framed in heavy oak timbers and designed to endure for many generations. He built his house in the center of Salem

Town, on the west side of School Lane near South River. John and his child-bride moved into the new mansion as soon as it was finished, at the end of 1675. But what would be the fate of this grand house and the Hathorne descendants destined to live in it? "What we call real estate—the solid ground to build a house on—is the broad foundation on which nearly all the guilt of this world rests. A man will commit almost any wrong—he will heap up an immense pile of wickedness, as hard as granite, and which will weigh as heavily upon his soul to eternal ages—only to build a great, gloomy, dark-chambered mansion, for himself to die in, and for his posterity to be miserable in."[79]

The first portent of disaster came quickly, December 1675. Captain Joseph Gardner, the uncle and guardian of John Hathorne's new bride, was killed in King Philip's War. "Here it comes, out of the same house whence we saw brave Captain Gardner go forth to the wars. What! A coffin, borne on men's shoulders, and six aged gentlemen as pall-bearers, and a long train of mourners, with black gloves and black hatbands, and everything black, save a white handkerchief in each mourner's hand, to wipe away the tears withal. Now, my kind patrons, you are angry with me. You were bidden to a bridal-dance, and find yourselves walking in a funeral procession.[80]

John Hathorne's younger brother, William Hathorne, Jr., was the lieutenant in Captain Gardner's company. When Gardner was killed in battle, his lieutenant succeeded him. William Hathorne, Jr., only 29 years old, attained the high military rank of captain. William Hathorne, Jr., one of the most dashing and one of the most ruthless officers in the army, was obsessed with fame. In 1676 he returned to Salem and married Sarah Ruck, daughter of John Ruck. In August 1676, Captain Hathorne was ordered with his company north to kill hostile Indians.

At Dover, New Hampshire, the captain met Richard Waldron, deputy magistrate of Dover. Waldron was the same man who, fourteen years earlier, had sentenced the three Quaker women to be stripped of their clothes and whipped in the snow on Christmas day. Together Hathorne and Waldron devised a plan. They would lead friendly neighborhood Indians into a trap by lying to them. The plan was neatly executed in September 1676, and by his treachery Captain Hathorne took four hundred captives. The strongest two hundred men were loaded into two waiting sloops and sold as slaves in Bermuda. Waldron was an old hand at the slave trade, and this transaction, the result of betrayal of the Indians' trust, brought great wealth to him and the young captain. All this was done with the approval of the Puritan leaders, the old guard. Cotton Mather later described the details in his history of King Philip's War, calling the devious affair

"the stunningest wound of all given to the Indians."[81] Puritan teaching maintained that the Indians were the Devil's children.

Two years later, in 1678, Captain William Hathorne, Jr., only 32 years old, died a mysterious death. Unsure of the cause of the captain's death, people blamed an old Indian wound. Some whispered that the wound was aggravated by the Devil because of the captain's treachery to his children, the Indians. Did the charms of some sorcerer carry out the Devil's will and cause a festering wound to inflict hideous torture? William's death dealt a major blow to his brother, John Hathorne. "The reserved and stately gentleman forgot his dignity; the gold-embroidered waistcoat flickered and glistened in the firelight with the convulsion of rage, terror, and sorrow of the human heart that was beating under it."[82]

In 1680 disaster struck the family again. Major William Hathorne's oldest son, Eleazer Hathorne, who had married a sister of Jonathan Corwin, died suddenly in Maine at age forty-three. His death was equally mysterious. The following year, 1681, Major William Hathorne died. John inherited his father's property at Mill Pond Farm. The future of the Hathorne family now rested in the hands of the only surviving son, John Hathorne.

In 1683, John Hathorne was elected to represent Salem as a deputy, and the following year as a magistrate, an assistant to the governor. At age 42, John Hathorne found himself a member of the Board of Assistants and a full inheritor of his father's privileges. He became a tireless judge who over the years adjudicated an endless number of cases in the Essex County Court.

As a young man, John Hathorne had entered into land speculation in Maine. He soon became obsessed with acquiring and owning land. At times he was obliged to go to sea in connection with his work; on one sea voyage he landed at a small settlement on the Maine coast. There for a few gold guineas he bought from a sagamore Indian called Robin Hood a vast and as yet unexplored and unmeasured tract. This Maine property, known to the Hathornes as the eastern land, embraced woods, lakes, and rivers. Apparently Robin Hood was aptly named, for he continued to sell the same land to other speculators. John Hathorne would spend a lifetime trying to track down these purchasers to buy back their deeds and give himself clear title. To later generations of Hathornes the eastern land offered dreams of great wealth. "When the pathless forest that still covered this wild principality should give place— as it inevitably must, though not perhaps till ages hence—to the golden fertility of human culture, it would be the source of incalculable wealth." In point of fact, it would bring nothing but bitter disappointment. "This impalpable claim, resulted in nothing more solid than to cherish, from generation to generation, an absurd delusion of family importance," wrote Nathaniel Hawthorne.[83]

In 1684 the English monarch, King Charles II, annulled the charter of the Massachusetts Bay Company under which the Puritans ruled. However the king's decree was blithely ignored in Boston, and things went on as before. With the death of King Charles II and the accession of King James II in 1685, the new king dismissed Simon Bradstreet as governor and appointed a temporary council to rule Massachusetts. Next the king named Sir Edmond Andros as the royal governor. On December 19, 1686, Andros landed in Boston and proclaimed himself captain general and governor-in-chief. With the complete abrogation of the old Massachusetts Bay charter, the colonists feared that the crown would demand ownership of all the land in the colony. They were all too familiar with the situation in England where the crown and the aristocracy owned the soil, and the common people were merely tenants. The colonists legitimately feared that the same feudal system might be imposed upon them.

The large landowners in New England had carefully used all possible means to substantiate their claims to the soil. Specifically they had implemented a scheme of persuading the descendants of the sagamores who had ruled New England to convey land deeds to them. This was an outlandish course of action; it was known that the crown held no regard for signatures of Indians. However, the colonists thought that the deeds signed by the Indians might embarrass the new royal governor just enough to prevent him from executing the king's plan. When Andros asked the senior minister of Salem, the Rev. John Higginson, Sr. whether New England was king's territory, Higginson replied that it belonged to the colonists because they held it by just occupation and purchase from the Indians.

Action taken by Salem to safeguard its vested interests resulted in a deed dated October 11, 1686. The grantees were John Ruck, John Higginson, Sr., Timothy Lindall, William Hirst, and Israel Porter, selectmen and trustees for the township of Salem.[84] The deed was signed, sealed and delivered by David Nonnuphanohow, Cicely Petaghuncksq, and eight other Indians. The consideration of release was £20 in current money. The Salem magistrate Bartholomew Gedney was present and the deed was acknowledged before him. The deed was written on parchment, a document of remarkable beauty and elaborateness of execution.[85]

The deed for Lynn, which includes the present city of Lynn and towns of Saugus, Lynnfield, Nahant, Swampscott, and a portion of Reading, was granted by David Kunkshamooshaw, who by credible intelligence was grandson to old sagamore George No Nose, so-called, alias Wenepawweekine, and by four other Indians. The land was obtained for a consideration of the sum of £16 of current sterling money of silver in hand paid to the Indians claiming, viz. David Kunkshamooshaw &c. The deed was executed on May 31, 1687. It was witnessed by John Hawkes and three other residents of Lynn and by Samuel Wardwell of Andover. The deed was acknowledged before Bartholomew Gedney, magistrate of Salem.[86]

The extensive and valuable Lynn land of the deceased Adam Hawkes was owned by his son, John Hawkes, and by his widow, Sarah (Hooper) Hawkes Wardwell. The value of Sarah's holdings was not lost on Bartholomew Gedney, aged 46, the magistrate acknowledging the deed. Gedney had become a magistrate, an assistant to the governor, in 1680. He was a captain in the militia at the time, and soon would be promoted to major. This crafty man was the son of John Gedney, the wealthy Salem innkeeper. Bartholomew Gedney lived all his life in Salem and owned a shipyard there. He is best known in history for his land speculations.

Bartholomew Gedney and his friend, John Hathorne, were two of the witchcraft judges who condemned the carpenter, Samuel Wardwell. This "pestilent wizard" was hanged and buried on Gallows Hill on September 22, 1692. In January 1693, Samuel's wife, Sarah Wardwell, was sentenced to death. Her grave was dug, but the governor, Sir William Phipps, reprieved her at the last minute. Yet the attainder—the loss of all civil rights legally consequent to a death sentence—remained in place and she could neither own nor pass down property. Her lands in Lynn were confiscated, falling into the hands of the assignees of Bartholomew Gedney, John Hathorne, John Corwin, and the others who divided the plunder of the witch hunt. They took "possession of the ill-gotten spoil—with the black stain of blood sunken deep into it. The wizard had been foully wronged out of his homestead, if not out of his life," wrote Nathaniel Hawthorne.[87]

John Hathorne was the most active and the most diligent government official in searching out and arresting those people accused of witchcraft in 1692. He rightly deserves the title of chief witch-hunter. "He is a determined and relentless man, with the genuine character of an inquisitor."[88] In *The Custom House*, Nathaniel Hawthorne wrote that John Hathorne "inherited the persecuting spirit, and made himself so conspicuous in the martyrdom of the witches, that their blood may fairly be said to have left a stain upon him. So deep a stain, indeed, that his old dry bones, in the Charter Street burialground, must still retain it." Again Hawthorne, with his ancestor, John Hathorne, in mind, wrote, "We shall only add, therefore, that the Puritan—so, at least, says chimney-corner tradition, which often preserves traits of character with marvelous fidelity—was bold, imperious, relentless, crafty; laying his purposes deep, and following them out with an inveteracy of pursuit that knew neither rest or con-science; trampling on the weak, and, when essential to his ends, doing the utmost to beat down the strong."[89]

Joseph Hathorne, a younger son of John Hathorne, inherited his father's house on Mill Pond Farm. The rocky outcrop of Gallows Hill, standing less than a couple of thousand feet from the house, shed an ominous shadow across the door. "It is not the less certain, however, that awe and terror brooded over the memories of those who died for this horrible crime of witchcraft. Their graves, in the crevices of the rocks, were supposed to be incapable of retaining the occupants who had been so hastily thrust into them."[90] Joseph, a small boy in 1692, had been too young to understand his father's prominent role in the witchcraft hangings. By the time of Joseph's death, however, the house had vanished. Had it burned to the ground? Or had Joseph ordered it torn down? Joseph's great-grandson would later write, "There is no such unwholesome atmosphere as that of an old home, rendered poisonous by one's defunct forefathers and relatives. It were a relief to me if that house could be torn down, and so the earth be rid of it, and grass be sown abundantly over its foundation."[91]

Nathaniel Hawthorne's *The House of the Seven Gables* is based upon the Salem witchcraft tragedy. The novel explores the question of inherited guilt. Hawthorne lays great emphasis upon a definite moral purpose at which he directs his work. He is obsessed with "the truth, namely, that the wrongdoing of one generation lives into the successive ones, and, divesting itself of every temporary advantage, becomes a pure and uncontrollable mischief."[92] The wrongdoing to which Hawthorne alludes in the novel refers to the crime perpetrated against the fictional Matthew Maule by the fictional Colonel Pyncheon during the Salem witchcraft affair. In 1692 the Puritan colonel accuses Matthew Maule of witchcraft. Before Maule is put to death, however, he curses the colonel. The colonel easily obtains the land of the dead wizard and builds the House of the Seven Gables on it. The carpenter who does the construction is Thomas Maule, none other than the dead wizard's son. As soon as the house is finished, however, the colonel meets with an untimely, mysterious death in it. The successive generations of the Pyncheon family who live in the seven-gabled house believe that their fortunes are blighted by the wizard's curse.

Many generations later, in 1850, the Pyncheon family has been reduced to only a few living members. Judge Pyncheon, a direct descendant of the Puritan colonel, is his "very image, in mind and body." Phoebe Pyncheon, a young cousin of the Judge, is "very pretty, as graceful as a bird, as pleasant about the house as a gleam of sunshine." Holgrave, a boarder in the house, is an artist, "a young man with so much faith in himself, and with so fair an appearance of admirable pow-

ers." Unknown to the Pyncheons, Holgrave is a descendant of the condemned Matthew Maule and inherited some of his magical powers. Judge Pyncheon meets his death in the house in the same manner as his seventeen-century ancestor, the colonel. The ancestral curse is finally lifted, however, when the young Phoebe Pyncheon falls in love with and agrees to marry Holgrave, who refused to exploit his magical powers over her.[93]

Despite Hawthorne's artistic license, some of the characters and events in his narrative may be linked to actual historical counterparts. In creating the fictional Pyncheon family, Hawthorne freely drew upon his knowledge of his own Hathorne ancestors. Literary critics generally accept that Hawthorne modelled the fictional seventeenth-century Colonel Pyncheon after his own great, great grandfather, John Hathorne. In turn, the nineteenth-century Judge Pyncheon embodies all of his ancestor's characteristics; "the Colonel Pyncheon of two centuries ago steps forward as the Judge of the passing moment!" Thus Hawthorne produced not one, but two fictional characters, Colonel Pyncheon and Judge Pyncheon, based upon the personal attributes of magistrate John Hathorne.[94]

"The similarity, intellectually and moral, between the Judge and his ancestor, appears to have been at least as strong as the resemblance of mien and feature would afford reason to anticipate. In old Colonel Pyncheon's funeral discourse, the clergyman absolutely canonized his deceased parishioner. So also, as regards the Judge Pyncheon of today, neither clergyman, nor legal critic, would venture a word against this eminent person's sincerity as a Christian, or respectability as a man, or integrity as a judge."[95]

The Salem witchcraft affair was sanctioned by the Puritan old guard: the most respectable magistrates and the most esteemed ministers in the colony. One was Hawthorne's ancestor, magistrate John Hathorne. In *The House of the Seven Gables,* Hawthorne's purpose was not merely to chronicle his ancestor's misdeeds, but to investigate the overriding question of why the witch hunt had occurred. What were the characteristics that permitted John Hathorne to condemn to death so many innocent people, and to escape with near total impunity? Hawthorne's explanation has been excerpted as follows (abbreviated with italics added for emphasis). In it he profiles his great, great grandfather with vivid immediacy as representative of the Puritan old guard who so eagerly propelled the witch hunt. Nathaniel Hawthorne supplies the strongest and most compelling answer offered before or since to the question which lies at the crux of the matter: Why was the witch hunt allowed to take place?

Like his fictional counterparts, magistrate John Hathorne was "a man of eminent respectability. The church acknowledged it; the state acknowledged it. It was denied by nobody. His conscience bore an accordant testimony with the world's laudatory voice. And yet, strong as this evidence may seem, we should hesitate to peril our own conscience on the assertion that the Judge and the consenting world were right. Hidden from mankind there may have lurked some evil or unsightly thing.

"Men of strong minds, great force of character, and a hard texture of sensibilities are very capable of falling into mistakes. They are ordinary men to whom forms are of paramount importance. They possess vast ability in grasping, and arranging, and appropriating to themselves the big, heavy, solid unrealities, such as gold, landed estate, offices of trust and emolument, and public honors. With these materials, and with deeds of goodly aspects, an individual of his class builds up, as it were, a tall and stately edifice, which in the view of other people is no other than the man's character, or the man himself. Behold, therefore, a palace! Its splendid halls are floored with a mosaic of costly marbles. Ah, but in some low and obscure nook—beneath the marble pavement, in a stagnant water puddle—may lie a corpse, half decayed, and still decaying, and diffusing its death scent all through the palace! *The inhabitant will not be conscious of it, for it has long been his daily breath! Neither will the visitors, for they smell only the rich odors which the master sedulously scatters through the palace.* Here then, we are to seek the true emblem of the man's character, and of the deed that gives whatever reality it possesses to his life. And beneath the show of the marble palace, that pool of stagnant water, foul with many impurities, and, perhaps, tinged with blood, is this man's miserable soul.

"The purity of his judicial character, while on the bench; the faithfulness of his public service; his remarkable zeal as president of Bible society; the cleanliness of his moral deportment; his prayers at morning and eventide; the studied propriety of his dress and equipment—what room could possibly be found for darker traits in a portrait made up of lineaments like these?

"A hard, cold man seldom or never looking inward, and resolutely taking his idea of himself from what purports to be his image as reflected in the mirror of public opinion, can scarcely arrive at true self-knowledge."[96] But Nathaniel Hawthorne withholds his most scathing indictment until the close of the book when he refers to the Judge as a man of "inward criminality."[97]

Hawthorne further probed the central issue when he asked "whether judges, clergymen, and other characters of that eminent stamp and respectability could really be otherwise than just and honorable men."

His answer was that "a wider scope of view, and a deeper insight, may see rank, dignity, and station all proved illusory, so far as regards their claim to human reverence."[98]

Notes

. . . [77] George Bishop, *New England Judged by the Spirit of the Lord, in two parts, Part First, The year 1656 to the year 1660, Second Part, Continued from Anno 1660 to Anno 1665,* Printed by T. Sowle, London, 1703, p. 245.

[78] Major William Hathorne had a brother, John Hathorne, who ran a tavern in Lynn and died in 1676. In 1652 this John Hathorne was charged with forgery and confessed himself guilty. In 1657, the peninsula of Nahant was purchased from an Indian sagamore for a suit of clothes; John Hathorne, Adam Hawkes, and a few others laid out the land for division. In 1663 John Hathorne complained that two residents of Lynn had given false testimony. They accused him of slander; he was found guilty and had to pay a fine and make a public acknowledgment in the meetinghouse. John Hathorne died in 1676 in Lynn, leaving sons and daughters.

[79] Nathaniel Hawthorne, *The House of the Seven Gables,* Tichnor, Reed, and Feilds, Boston, MA, 1851, Chapter 17.

[80] Nathaniel Hawthorne, *Main-Street,* in *The Snow-Image and Other Twice-told Tales,* 1852.

[81] Cotton Mather, *Magnalia Christi Americana,* or the *Ecclesiastical History of New England, in Seven Books,* London, 1702. Reprinted in 2 vols., Hartford, 1855.

[82] Hawthorne, *The House of the Seven Gables,* Chapter 13

[83] Hawthorne, *The House of the Seven Gables,* Chapter 1. Although most people today regard the state of Maine as being north of Boston, the colonists regarded it as being east of Boston. Actually it is northeast.

[84] John Ruck was the father of Sarah (Ruck) Hathorne Burroughs. She was the widow of the deceased Captain William Hathorne, Jr. She married the Rev. George Burroughs in Salem Village in 1682 and she died in Maine in 1690. John Higginson, Sr. was the senior minister of Salem and Israel Porter was the brother-in-law of John Hathorne.

[85] Sidney Perley, *Indian Land Titles of Essex County,* Salem, MA, 1912. pp. 64-87.

[86] Ibid.

[87] Hawthorne, *The House of the Seven Gables,* Chapter 1.

[88] Hawthorne, *The House of the Seven Gables.* Chapter 14.

[89] Hawthorne, *The House of the Seven Gables,* Chapter 8.

[90] Hawthorne, *The House of the Seven Gables,* Chapter 13.

[91] Hawthorne, *The House of the Seven Gables,* Chapter 17.

[92] Hawthorne, *The House of the Seven Gables,* Preface.

[93] Hawthorne, *The House of the Seven Gables.*

[94] John Hathorne was both a colonel and a judge.

[95] Hawthorne, *The House of the Seven Gables,* Chapter 8.

[96] Hawthorne, *The House of the Seven Gables,* Chapter 15.

[97] Hawthorne, *The House of the Seven Gables,* Chapter 21.

[98] Hawthorne, *The House of the Seven Gables,* Chapter 8.

Peter Charles Hoffer (essay date 1996)

SOURCE: "Accusations and Confessions," in *The Devil's Disciples: Makers of the Salem Witchcraft Trials,* Johns Hopkins University Press, 1966, pp. 102-30.

[*In the essay below, Hoffer analyzes Hawthorne's involvement in the preliminary hearings, or "examinations," of the Salem witchcraft trials.*]

. . . In the courthouse in Salem, [Jonathan] Corwin and [John] Hathorne had heard civil suits, appointed administrators of estates, and punished those presented for misdemeanors in the village. They knew all the men and women who would appear before them as witnesses, accusers, and defendants in the witchcraft cases.[21] Corwin had opposed the Dominion of New England and Andros; Hathorne briefly joined its political councils. Both men had served long as selectmen of the town and were familiar with the village's troubles. Both had opposed severing the village from the town, pitting them against the Putnams. Hathorne was related by marriage to the Porters, but the relation had deprived him of land (his father, William Hathorne,

had given it to the Porter girls as dower).[22]

The surviving legal record of these examinations [against the accused witches] preserves conversations: exchanges of words, signs, signals, and gestures. As in all such conversations, the speakers situated themselves in relation to one another, recalling talk that occurred in years past. For the speakers, conversation in these hearings was not easy talk—chatter—passing the time of day. For the girls, if they were truly afflicted, from whatever source, exposure to putative witches brought on new fits, hardly a pleasant experience. If they were shamming, they had to get it right, for exposure meant ridicule, punishment for lying, and perhaps suspicion that they were witches themselves. For the magistrates, the conversations were tests of their mettle as witch finders. They had to ferret out a deadly conspiracy before it struck at them or their children. Their target was not the witch only but the Great Adversary, hardly a being to be trifled with. They had to harden their hearts against instincts of mercy and sharpen their wits against fraud. They had to trap a wily foe.[23]

For the suspects, even more was at stake in this bartering of words. Some, particularly those against whom no prior accusation had been lodged, expressed bewilderment. They tried to persuade the girls to drop their accusations and the magistrates to lay aside their suspicions. Others, accustomed to such denunciation, retreated into hostility and cynicism. They professed their innocence with a hard-edged disregard for the whole proceeding. All of the suspects tried to talk their way out of the accusation, but none of the women and few of the men were practiced at public speech, and the record shows that they frequently misunderstood or could not keep up with the questions.

For witnesses, testifying literally hurt. It forced them to recall moments of terror when they came face to face with an apparition or a strange and horrifying animal, when they could not breathe or were paralyzed with fear. The memory was painful, and they trembled that its recital might arouse the dormant enmity of a witch. Witches were known to take revenge upon those who testified against witches. In general, the witnesses were not political figures, that is, their testimony was not a calculated ploy in some intravillage contest for power. Of course the Putnam clan hovered nearby, and although they did not speak much, they watched and listened. Everyone at the hearings had to run a gauntlet of Putnams. Other witnesses were friends, loved ones, and relatives of the suspects. Throughout the inquiry, they formed a quiet chorus, giving aid by their mere presence. On occasion, they offered character testimonials.

The examinations of the suspects began on the ground floor of Ingersoll's tavern house, but so many came to see the hearings that they were moved to the meeting house down the road. Thus what was to have been a civil event became a quasi-religious one.[24] Where might the two magistrates [Corwin and Hawthorne] have sat, to distance themselves from the throng and yet control it? They could not stand at the pulpit; that would have violated custom and embarrassed Parris. They could not sit in the pews, surrounded by the multitude. The only answer is that they sat on one side of the communion table, with their backs to the wall of the meeting house. Witnesses and accused milled about on the other side.[25] The communion table had great significance in its meeting house setting. In Salem Village's meeting house, as in many other New England churches, communion was the most important sacrament and defined Puritan piety. Entry to this sacrament was limited to those who could confess to the congregation their state of regeneracy, so confession in this physical setting gained greater force, raising the stakes, as it were, of the girls' accusations. Testifying before the communion table, the girls had a credibility they might not have had if they stood next to the dirty, knife-gouged tables in Ingersoll's tavern.

In the meeting house the two magistrates confronted for the first time the girls' physical convulsions. In one sense, these contortions were conventional, that is, they fit into an established niche. The Goodwin children had fits. Elizabeth Knapp had fits. Other women and men possessed or attacked by evil sprites had fits. In their physical and auditory manifestations these were chronicled with care and credulity by Increase and Cotton Mather, and as John Hale noted, the accounts were widely read. The girls were bitten and pinched by invisible agents. In visible and audible agony, the victims twisted their arms and backs and contorted their faces. Sometimes they could not speak; other times they could not stop speaking. Those who watched were filled with compassion and fully convinced that the girls were truly afflicted.

But were they afflicted by witches? And were those witches the ones they named? The reason that John Hale and others counseled Parris to wait and pray was that such identifications might be mistaken. Parris was convinced for a time, but the Putnams were not. All their anger at events in the village spurred their impatience. They did not see the witchcraft accusations as a way to get at their betters—not yet, for Good and Tituba were not related to their rivals in the village. Later suspects, possibly Osborn, and particularly the Nurse-Cloyse family, would match this profile, but the Putnams could not predict that turn of events, though they may have welcomed or even encouraged the girls to shift their attention to Rebecca Nurse and her sister Sarah Cloyse. At first, however, impatience motivated the Putnams. They wanted action, not reflection, punishment, not healing.[26]

In front of the magistrates, the girls' afflictions had passed into a second, also conventional, stage—but one from which there was no healing, no returning, no chance for regret short of the formal processes of law. Mere suffering whose origin was idiopathic changed into legally cognizable evidence. If the conventionality of the girls' fits allowed parents and other caretakers to reconfigure otherwise novel and frightening events as familiar ones, and so cope with them, the girls' tormented accusations turned illness into proof of wrongdoing. As Hale and Lawson averred in their first-hand accounts, and as the magistrates must have come to believe, the girls could not have been faking when they first accused Good, Osborn, and Tituba.

The magistrates heard the accusations under their commissions as justices of the peace. Their authority was written, based on textual models taken from English books of forms, but the informality of the hearing, the close physical proximity and intimate social relationships among all the participants, and the vividness of the girls' testimony gave substance to the accusations more than did any books of forms.

Imagine a theater-in-the-round wherein everyone—actors, writers, director, audience—could perform spontaneously, the plot merely sketched out, the actors improvising lines and gestures as they went along. And these were performances, as the girls soon realized. If they were not trained actors working from a script, they could and did borrow the language of countless tales of specters and spells. The absence of supporting physical evidence, particularly the invisibility of the spectral forms to all but the girls, did not diminish the impact of their performance. Recall Macbeth's soliloquy at King Duncan's door: "is this a dagger I see before me?" No one in the audience sees the dagger, but everyone believes it is there because they see it through Macbeth's eyes. So the girls convinced onlookers that specters of witches flew through the room. The girls used visible props as well. Pins, normally worn to keep dresses and bonnets together, became instruments of torture, as the girls accused defendants of pricking them. Mary Black, a slave of Nathaniel Putnam, accused by Ann Putnam and others, was made at her examination on April 22, 1692, to repin her neck cloth in front of the girls. They then complained of being pricked. Mary Walcott was able to show Hathorne and Corwin where blood came from a prick mark on her arm.[27] One can speculate that Mary Black was not the only one who brought pins to the examination. Witnesses for the defendants saw the act with pins. Sarah Nurse caught Sarah Bibber, one of the older women who had joined the accusers, pulling pins out of her clothing, hiding them in her hands, pricking herself, and then crying out against Rebecca Nurse.[28] Bruises were produced and bite marks displayed. Hathorne, like a director, could turn to the girls without warning and ask if the suspect afflicted them, and they, without missing a beat, would be struck dumb or fall into convulsions.[29]

Despite their familiarity with legal forms, neither Hathorne nor Corwin was a lawyer. Indeed, there was no lawyer present at these first hearings. Instead, they were gatherings of neighbors in which the conventions of ordinary social intercourse dominated the conversation. So it was in the first session when Sarah Good's husband blurted that she was "an enemy to all good."[30] William Good's public complaint about his wife illustrated the way in which informal, oral, vernacular usages penetrated the examinations and changed their course. In the middle of a formal legal proceeding in which words had (supposedly) precise and compelling, that is, categorical, meaning, he called his wife a witch. Did he mean that he knew she had committed the cognizable offense of witchcraft? No, he merely meant that she had not shown him the respect he thought he merited. Six months later, elderly Mary Bradbury of Salisbury and Andover stood before the magistrates, accused of witchcraft, and one of her accusers was a sailor, Samuel Endicott. He swore that eleven years earlier Bradbury had come down to the port to sell to his captain two tubs of butter. At sea the crew discovered that one of the tubs had gone rancid, "which made the men very much disturbed about it, and would often say that they heard that Mrs. Bradbury was a witch." If the butter had been sweet, would she have been as her neighbors later described her in a petition to the same magistrates—a loving and helpful model of Christian charity?[31] In such ways the vernacular culture—the nastiness of a bad marriage between ordinary New Englanders and a spoiled firkin of butter—intruded into the world of statutory definitions of crime, the learned world of law texts.

Before the Salem cases, neighbors had to be careful about what they said in such proceedings. Men and women who abused one another with assaultive speech were prosecuted in public forums and had to apologize. Such public confessions of error were an important ritual holding communities together.[32] In the heat of argument, Essex men and women did tell one another to go to the Devil, as Martha Cory shouted at a neighbor during a dispute over milk cows. Between 1672 and 1692, the Essex Country courts heard forty abusive charges and countercharges of devilment. How many more there must have been which did not end in litigation is anyone's guess.[33] When neighbors did not mean to cast aspersions, they took pains to say so. During the inquiry into the cases of Hugh and Mary Parsons, Jonathan Taylor deposed that he called Goody Merick "a witch" because she was able to open a beer keg tap that he, with all his might, could not budge, but he hastened to add, "[B]ut I would not have you think it was by witchery."[34] Taylor was well aware that the usage of ordinary people could be tak-

en quite differently when given in evidence in a criminal trial. . . .

The examinations began on the first of March and continued for three days. The accused had no legal counsel, but the form of the examination was not technically inquisitorial, for the suspects confronted their accusers and could summon their own witnesses.[41] Nevertheless, without formal legal advisors or patrons in the community, devoid of experience with the courts in matters of such moment, the first suspects must have found the examination inquisitorial whatever slender procedural rights they might have had. Good and Osborn stood firm—they were not witches. Good was bitter and mistrusted the magistrates. In counterpoint to her whining denials, the children, Betty, Abigail, Elizabeth Hubbard, and Ann Putnam Jr., screamed and writhed as if on cue. Hathorne may have been convinced of Good's guilt (for he knew her reputation), for he was harsh with her and she gave back venom. He belittled her and she became confused. Finally, she named Sarah Osborn as the tormentor of the children.[42]

Hathorne, the primary questioner, had pressed Good despite her repeated denials, from which fact historians have concluded that Hathorne believed that Good was guilty.[43] No doubt he did, but his persistent style of interrogation, repeating the same question over and over, was not uncommon or surprising. It had the imprimatur of John Winthrop, whose tenure as governor of Massachusetts spanned the colony's first three decades. Convinced of the charges upon evidence, Winthrop ordered that a magistrate was to press a suspect, examining "strictly." The suspect was not to be allowed to stand mute but had to respond.[44] In previous years, both Hathorne and his father had gained reputations as stern inquisitors, and their conduct was not different from that of modern prosecuting attorneys.[45]

Hathorne assumed that Good knew enough to be more forthcoming than she had been, but his real purpose was to elicit a confession, without which, despite all the testimony of neighbors and the girls' contortions, no conviction was sure. Good's final, exhausted concession rewarded Hathorne's persistence. Asked who it was, if not she, who pinched the children, Good said, "It was Sarah Osborn." The children concurred.[46]

Sarah Osborn was older than her fifty calendar years and sick, housebound for much of the winter. Confronted with the girls' torment, she denied that she had harmed them. Perhaps the Devil had assumed her form. Asked by Hathorne if she knew Good, she said she did not, plainly meaning that Good was nothing more than a casual acquaintance. Hathorne, always looking for a conspiracy of witches, asked when Osborn had seen Good last—as if the two had flown together to the most recent witches' sabbath. Osborn, obviously too ill to fly anywhere, replied that she had seen Good years earlier, in town. Well then, Hathorne sprung at her, what did you call Good then? "Sarah," replied Osborn. She was plainly tired but capable of some spunk. Were she not accused of witchcraft, Hathorne ought to have been properly abashed, for Puritanism valued the old and godly,[47] but he had learned that she did not attend church for more than a year. Why had she avoided going to meeting? The answer must have been written on her wretched face: she had been sick. A quarrelsome woman by all accounts, she was at the end of her tether. A mirror of the casual cruelty of these examinations: although she was not likely to flee the jurisdiction, the magistrates, upon the girls' testimony, remanded her to prison, where she died on May 10, denied the comfort of her own room and bed.[48]

Osborn's case raised a new question that Hathorne was unwilling or unable to confront. Her first husband was Robert Prince, a Salem Village man, and her in-laws were Lieutenant Thomas Putnam and Captain John Putnam. When her first husband died, he made his Putnam kin the executors of his estate. Sarah Prince broke the connection to the Putnam clan when she married her indentured servant, Alexander Osborn, an Irish immigrant. When the elder son of the first marriage reached his majority, the Putnams sought to settle him in his inheritance, but the Osborns resisted, and the parties grew quarrelsome. She had been an outsider when she married Prince, and now she threatened to disinherit two Salem Village lads.[49] Seen in this context, the accusation became a dispute over land waged by other means, in the same way that war is the continuation of failed diplomacy.

At last Tituba was called, and she at first denied any complicity. Had she remained adamant, Good and Osborn might well have been admonished and the affair ended. Hale opined that it was Tituba's confession, in which she named others as witches, which "encouraged those in authority to examine others that were suspected."[50] . . .

She had implicated others in the crime, which was exactly what the two justices of the peace wanted and feared to hear, for Hathorne and Corwin assumed that witches were always conspiratorial. Two years earlier, a runaway slave named Robert had testified that he was off to join a French and Indian expedition against the colony and he expected other Indians and blacks to join him. There was no expedition or general uprising, but because his story fed the authorities' worst fears of conspiracy, it was for a time believed.[61] Corwin and Hathorne put aside any hesitation they might have had in a less charged situation about crediting the testimony of a woman of color,[62] precisely because her story stoked their innermost concerns. . . .

For the time being, the magistrates were done, but Salem was not quiet. How could it be, when there were still witches (by Tituba's reckoning) unaccounted for? On March 11, Ann Putnam was afflicted by a new cadre of witches. Three days later, Abigail Williams was attacked by the same spectral forms. Soon the same accusers of Good, Osborn, and Tituba fastened upon Martha Cory and Rebecca Nurse, older women in the village who, unlike their predecessors, were members in good standing of churches and apparently led upright lives. Both Cory and Nurse, warned by their neighbors, regarded the girls' antics as the prattling of malice, but the men who went from house to house seeking evidence for the accusations, watching the faces and gestures of the new suspects, either did not see or would not credit the older women's view of the new accusations. Cory's sarcastic dismissal and Nurse's earnest bewilderment at the charges did not deter the activities of the growing number of unofficial witch finders in the village.

Deciding to put the girls in their place, Martha and Giles Cory challenged the investigation. Both had a reputation for being ornery.[65] Hearing through gossip that she was suspected, Martha told the constable that she had anticipated his arrival. He reported that comment to Hathorne, who took it as an evidence that she was a witch. At her examination, "a child" murmured to Cheever (and he dutifully recorded), "There is a man whispering in her ear." Alert to the presence of the Evil One, Hathorne increased the tempo of his questions, badgering the old woman. She denied all, but her denials became rote, no longer compelling Hathorne to take them or her seriously. He offered her "the out"—a technique that the police use to this day: "Why, confess" he suggested, and she would feel much better. She refused, maintaining her innocence. Then Abigail cried out, and as one the girls became distracted. Mercy Lewis saw Cory's specter swing an iron rod (a spectral one, presumably), and two of the other girls dodged it. When Cory laughed at their antics, they redoubled their efforts. Cory bit her lip; the girls produced bloody lips. She had an arthritis attack, clenching her hands, and they writhed, their hands twisted in a cruel but effective mockery of her pain. She was committed with her husband to Salem jail. . . .

Introduced with Cory, the melodrama could be reprised in the crucial case of Rebecca Nurse. Her husband, Francis, had been a constable and a juryman. Both had fine reputations in the town. If the girls could pull her down, their power to debase would be unstoppable. On March 24, after Lawson had preached, Goodwife Nurse was brought to the Ingersoll tavern, held for a time, and then transported up the steps to the meeting house. She had traveled this route so many times, in other circumstances, that she must have felt the irony of her new role. Did it also frighten her? Not from the evidence of her replies to the magistrates' questions.

At first, they were gentle, for the magistrates presiding over the interrogations did not want to believe all they heard. Hathorne turned to the girls and asked if they recognized Nurse, which they did. She was the afflicter. Putnam and Williams cried out, and a plainly bewildered but composed Nurse denied that she was the cause of their pain. "God will clear my innocency," she maintained. Hathorne for a moment might have wished it so, for he answered, "[T]here is never a one in the Assembly but desires it [more than I]"; yet if she were guilty, he was convinced that God would "discover" her.

Hathorne here revealed that he believed in the medieval idea of ordeals, in which God demonstrated who was innocent and who was guilty. He needed a sign, and Ann Putnam Sr. rushed to the aid of her daughter by accusing Nurse. She said, "Did you not bring the Black man with you, did you not bid me tempt God, and dye?" Goodwife Putnam verged on hysteria—she was not playacting—and her passion gave credibility to the girls' testimony. Her references to suicide must be taken seriously, for her daughter had exhibited the fits for almost two months, and the mother was beside herself with worry.[76] Williams and Ann Putnam Jr. began wailing, and Mary Walcott and Elizabeth Hubbard, hitherto quiet, added their voices to the clamor.[77]

Nurse was struck dumb by it all, and Hathorne, changing his tone, baited her: how could she have dry eyes when so much suffering poured out around her? What did Nurse say to the "grown persons" who joined the accusers? Hathorne again showed a little of his hand: he did not wholly credit the girls' accusations, but when their elders spoke—particularly Ann's mother—their words had to be weighed with care. Again, he offered Nurse an out: "Possibly you may apprehend you are no witch, but have you not been led aside by temptations that way[?]" She had not, she replied. Here was another refusal to help him, just like Cory's, but again he hesitated, moved perhaps by Nurse's friends, who had begun lamenting as well. Hathorne now tried a different tack, one he would repeat in later hearings: could the suspect help him explain the fits? "Do you think these suffer voluntarily or involuntarily?" he asked. Was it a trap? "I cannot tell," Nurse replied. He persisted, "That is strange[,] everyone can judge," and they had, but Nurse was at the end of her tether. "I cannot tell," she repeated. A good Puritan, she would not judge another. To have accused the girls of feigning was to charge them with perjury. To understand how the Devil worked was beyond her powers. Pressured, she finally guessed that the girls were not naturally afflicted but bewitched. Impressed by Nurse's calm, Hathorne gave her a last chance. Tituba loved Betty but affirmed that her specter, out of her control, must have afflicted the girl. Might not Nurse's apparition have done the same? Nurse was having none of it, however. "[Why do you] have me bely [belie]

myself," she retorted, but she did allow that the Devil might have taken her shape.

Exhausted, sick, and overcome, Nurse had nevertheless produced the one argument that was irrefutable in defense. Osborn had already assayed it. No one could stop the Devil from assuming the shape of a good person and using his powers to hurt others. Even Increase Mather had conceded as much, and he was a believer in the malign powers of witches.[78] Neither her defense nor her frailty deterred Hathorne from committing Nurse to jail, no doubt to chain her there (for chains, everyone knew, prevented the witch's specter from escaping her body), but the argument would continue to trouble everyone in authority. . . .

The examinations now convened on a regular basis, the episodic quality of the first month's revelations giving way to a continuous feature of Salem life. Seen for the first time, the hearings might have appeared to be disorderly affairs. In fact, they had a clear, discursive structure. In some, for example that of Good, and later Bridget Bishop, the examiners, notably Hathorne, directed the girls' performance, prompting them into their fits by asking them to identify the suspects, cuing the girls to interject their own voices and act out in chorus their afflictions. . . .

Over time, the girls' performance approached professional quality; there were no slips, no muffed lines, as when Sarah Buckley was brought before Corwin and Hathorne on May 18. Abigail said, "[T]his is the woman that hath bit me with her scragged teeth a great many times." . . .

By the beginning of the summer, the girls had only to fill in the blanks of the witch's name and make their own mark at the end of the deposition to secure an arrest. . . .

The speed of the process crippled the ability of neighbors and family to resist accusations against their friends and loved ones. The oral networks that had tied neighbors together now were frayed by suspicion and accusation. Adults' animosities and fears were loosed by the flood of accusations and flowed into the hearings. Husbands turned against wives and wives against husbands. Frightened, disoriented (and perhaps abused) children informed on parents.[86] The accusations radiated out from Salem. . . .

The tidal wave of accusations overwhelmed the institutions of criminal justice which had, until now, served the colony adequately. From a functional point of view, the purpose of a criminal justice system is to process those accused of crime. The key elements of colonial criminal justice—speed, inexpensiveness, social control—were adequately served in Massachusetts. But function did not dictate form. Rather, culture—the culture of a community of saints—shaped the laws and the institutions of criminal justice. The culture demanded that those whose conduct was hardly saintly conform to the norms laid down by the saints. The result was much contention but a remarkable degree of order.[88] The essence of Massachusetts criminal procedure, except in notorious cases, had been to force the accused to accept guilt and then to arrange for some punishment that permitted the accused to reinstate himor herself in the social web.[89] Thus most accusations of witchcraft had failed to lead to conviction, even when neighbors complained over many years. Instead, some admonition or threat by the magistrates forced the suspect to conform more closely to the expectations of neighborliness and quieted, for a time at least, the community's fears. In this way, witchcraft accusations served to "protect group life."[90] Salem's trials did not, however, perform this function. Something went wrong.

Hunted in their homes, the faces of their neighbors turned against them, confined to jail in conditions that were degrading and unhealthy, more of the suspects began to confess.[91] The first had been Tituba. The next was Abigail Hobbs, on April 19. "I will speak the truth," she told the magistrates. "I have seen many sights and been scared. I have been very wicked. I hope I shall be better, if God will help me." Hobbs did not have the opportunity, like Tituba, deliberately to misunderstand and then reconfigure the magistrates' questions. She admitted she had seen the Devil. She reported their conversations. She described her familiars. She confessed to pinching Putnam and Lewis at the Devil's command, that she might have fine things. The next day, she identified Sarah Good as another witch and described how she had eaten the red bread and wine at the witches' sabbath in Parris's pasture.[92]

It was nonsense, and she knew it, but she had become an informer and could not stop. Her safety, for the executions began on June 10 with Bridget Bishop, depended upon the verisimilitude and the appropriateness of her testimony. When the magistrates wanted confirmation that George Burroughs, then living in Maine, was the leader of the witches' coven (no woman would do for that role), Hobbs obliged. From the Salem jail, on May 12, she deposed that Burroughs had brought the poppets to the other witches and showed them how to stick pins in the dolls.[93] She testified against John Proctor as well, on June 29.[94] She, more than Tituba, gave the magistrates what they wanted—evidence of a conspiracy of witches which threatened the colony.

Now Mary Warren, Proctor's servant, was brought before the magistrates. At first she blurted out that the girls had dissembled, and they responded by falling into fits. She turned informer on the accusers, and the gang reacted by denouncing her. Accused of witchcraft, without aid—there were no parents or ministers or legal counsel to help her—she swooned. Coming to, she spoke wildly and then was taken outside for fresh air. She could not continue, but summoned privately before the two justices of the peace, she recognized that salvation in this world required confession and contrition, and she admitted that she had seen the Devil. More gently now, Hathorne and Corwin led Warren through her story. For two more days she provided the confirmation that they needed and sought of the conspiracy of witches. Later, like Hobbs, she would be brought periodically from jail to accuse some new suspect.[95]

The danger that Warren posed to the other young accusers went beyond breaking ranks with the gang. Bearing false witness, perjury in a felony case, was itself a felony, and children were early taught the evils of such acts. Indeed, was not the Devil the "father of lies"?[96] If Warren were believed, then the other girls had perjured themselves in a felony prosecution that could end in the execution of the accused. All their own necks would be exposed to the gallows. Did the girls know this? One assumes that they knew lying was a sin and that lying under oath was a crime. Warren recanted just in time for everyone on the prosecution side to breathe easier, and none more than the other girls.[97]

The magistrates did not warn Warren that her recantation could lead to her prosecution for lying or false witness. Rather, they were looking for evidence confirming their suspicion, verging now on certainty, that a conspiracy of witches threatened the colony. Tituba had told them that there were other witches, and sure enough, more witches appeared. Even the girls had to fear that others might name them—in effect, their accusations, like Warren's, alone kept them safe from others' accusations. All of this fed the magistrates' fears, for by this time they had committed themselves to the search for witches and sought all confirming evidence.

The more they heard which confirmed the work of the Devil, the more skeptical of contradictory evidence the magistrates became. It is a classic example of the avoidance of cognitive dissonance. Dissonant evidence was discarded or attacked; consonant evidence was believed and integrated into the story. When Sarah Churchill confessed on June 1 to signing the Devil's book brought her by Ann Pudeator and then sticking pins into dolls to hurt Mercy Lewis and the other girls, she was believed. She had already implicated her master, George Jacobs Sr., and Bridget Bishop, to whom she now added Pudeator.[98] What the magistrates expected was what fit into their increasingly detailed cognitive scheme of the conspiracy. Suspects could offer contrition—copious tears, signs of repentance, admissions of guilt—and would be believed and welcomed, but angry countercharges, repeated denials, and tearful insistence on innocence could not be credited without cognitive dissonance.

The magistrates' dogged resistance to inconsistency and recantation rested upon more than their aversion to dissonance. They shared the larger psychology of Puritanism, a state of mental tension and unease. Election—salvation—lay wholly in the hands of God. People could not save themselves, though they might search penitently for signs of grace and order their steps upon the straight and narrow.[99] In the gap between justification through God's unhindered grace and the orderly life every good Puritan was expected to lead lay days of worry and nights of yearning for signs that he or she was truly regenerate. The magistrates were not immune to agonies of uncertainty about their own souls' state, and the stakes were raised by the witchcraft accusations. These were no ordinary crimes of violence. The Devil was about, and to be uncertain about his intentions was to lay open all of God's commonwealth to the Great Deceiver's evil plan. Their own religious convictions thrust upon Hathorne and Corwin the need to be sure, certain, unwavering, and right. . . .

Notes

. . . [21] See, for example, Samuel Parris, "Meditations for Peace," November 1694, in *Salem-Village Witchcraft: A Documentary Record of Local Conflict in colonial New England,* rev. ed., ed. Paul Boyer and Stephen Nissenbaum (Boston, 1993), 152-53, (Hereafter cited as *SVP*).

[22] Enders A. Robinson, *The Devil Discovered: Salem Witchcraft, 1692* (New York, 1991) 33; Richard P. Gildrie, *Salem, Massachusetts, 1626-1683: A Covenanted Community* (Charlottesville, Va., 1986), 161-62; Christine Alice Young, *Good Order to the Glorious Revolution: Salem, Massachusetts, 1628-1689,* (Ann Arbor, 1981), 168.

[23] What, then, were the magistrates to do? The issue is still unresolved; we can take no comfort from our "modern" professional advances—for courts remain at a loss when they deal with children's evidence. See, for example, Veronica Serrato, "Expert Testimony in Child Abuse Cases: A Spectrum of Uses," *Boston University Law Review* 68 (1988): 155-64; J. Bulkley, ed., *Child Sexual Abuse and the Law* (Chicago, 1982); Hollida Wakefield and Ralph Underwager, *Accusations of Child Sexual Abuse* (Springfield, Ill., 1988); Steven I. Friedland, "On Common Sense and the Evaluation of Witness Credibility," *Case Western Reserve Law Review* 40 (1990): 165-87; Jean Montoya, "On Truth and Shielding in Child Abuse Trials," *Hastings Law Journal* 43 (1992): 1259-88. The key Supreme Court case is *Maryland v. Craig,* 110 S Ct 3157 (1990), which in effect ruled that children did not have to face the

cross-examination required of adults in open court. The children accusers at Salem were protected in ways similar to this, for the only challenge to them came from the defendants, themselves under duress and already placed in compromising positions.

[24] The warrants to the sheriff to bring Good, Osborn, and Tituba to the hearing specified that it would take place at Ingersoll's, but the locale was immediately shifted when the crowd and the noise made examination impossible. Paul Boyer and Stephen Nissenbaum, eds., *The Salem Witchcraft Papers: Verbatim Transcripts of the Legal Documents of the Salem Witchcraft Outbreak of 1692* (New York, 1977), 2:355 (hereafter cited as *SWP*). All dates in the text and the notes have been modernized. David C. Brown, *Guide to the Salem Witchcraft Hysteria of 1692* (Worcester, Mass., 1984), 12.

[25] As with so many surmises we make, I thought this insight was my own, until I happened across an Oxford University Press paperback edition of John Demos's *Entertaining Satan: Witchcraft and the Culture of Early New England* (New York, 1982) and looked closely at the cover illustration. The credit line thanks the Granger Collection, New York, for the wood engraving from which the illustration was reproduced. In it, the girls sit in a pew; the accused stand. Behind the accused to the left is what must be a pulpit, raised, with a large book on it. To the right, the magistrates and the clerk sit behind a low, solid, wide table. The magistrate in the center is a dead ringer for Nathaniel Hawthorne and must have been modeled upon him— thus John Hathorne came to resemble his descendant. If the scene is the meeting house, then the table must be the communion table.

[26] I have used the term *impatience* deliberately, for I just do not think that the Putnams had decided to use witchcraft accusations to bring down their village rivals. But *impatience* may be too diffuse. Boyer and Nissenbaum attribute stronger emotions to the Putnam clan: "Viewed thus schematically, the residential profile of the accused offers a vivid geographic metaphor for the anxieties of the 'Pro-Parris' [literally, the Putnam family] group: the regions beyond the Village bounds are dangerous 'enemy territory.' . . . The true Salem village has been driven westward and confined to a small enclave from which, back to the wall (or more literally, to the Ipswich River), it lashes out at the encircling enemy." Paul Boyer and Stephen Nissenbaum, eds., *Salem Possessed* (Cambridge, Mass., 1974) 192.

[27] *SWP,* 1:113-14.

[28] Ibid., 1:80.

[29] Ibid. 2:356-57. All exorcists knew that sudden in-

ability to speak was a symptom of possession. Fernando Cervantes, *The Devil in the New World: The Impact of Diabolism in New Spain* (New Haven, 1994), 116. On invisible props, see Michael Issachoroff, *Discourse as Performance* (Stanford, Calif., 1989), 9, 11.

[30] *SVW,* 6.

[31] *SWP,* 1:122.

[32] The forms by which "speech criminals" confessed in Massachusetts are discussed in Jane Kamensky, "Words, Witches, and Woman Trouble: Witchcraft, Disorderly Speech, and Gender Boundaries in Puritan New England," *Essex Institute Historical Collections* 128 (1992): 288-89, and Jane Kamensky, "Saying and Unsaying," paper read to the Philadelphia Center for Early American Studies/Institute of Early American History and Culture Conference, Philadelphia, June 4, 1994.

[33] David Thomas Konig, *Law and Society in Puritan Massachusetts: Essex County, 1629-1692* (Chapel Hill, 1979), 147, 149-50.

[34] David D. Hall, ed. *Witch-Hunting in Seventeenth Century New England: A Documentary History, 1638-1692* (Boston, 1991), 49-50. . .

[41] Smith, *Colonial Justice,* 145.

[42] *SWP,* 2:355-78. When the girls began to accuse people of higher station, merchants such as Philip English, ministers such as Samuel Willard, and eventually the magnates of the colony, Governor William Phips began to look for a way to terminate the proceedings. English and others like him were allowed to escape from custody (although the rich were not the only ones to flee), and Phips adjourned the court. Did social and economic status play a role in causing the crisis? I think not. Did social and economic status have some impact upon the fate of the accused: an emphatic yes.

[43] Larry Gragg, *Salem Witch Crisis* (New York, 1992), 51.

[44] John Winthrop, *History of New England,* ed. James Savage (Boston, 1826), 47. I am grateful to Eben Moglen for calling this reference to my attention.

[45] Gildrie, *Salem,* 135; John Murrin, "Magistrates, Sinners, and a Precarious Liberty: Trial by Jury in Seventeenth-Century New England," in Hall, Murrin, and Tate, *Saints and Revolutionaries,* 199; Wakefield and Underwager, *Accusations of Child Sexual Abuse,* 31.

[46] *SWP,* 2:358.

[47] David Hackett Fischer, *Albion's Seed: Four British*

Folkways in America (New York, 1989), 103-11.

[48] *SWP,* 2:609-13. The alternative was to take sureties for her good behavior and examine her again, later, if she was well enough. Witchcraft, a felony, was not a bailable offense.

[49] Robinson, *Devil Discovered,* 267; Boyer and Nissenbaum, *Salem Possessed,* 193-94.

[50] Hale, *Modest Inquiry,* in Burr, *Narratives,* 415. . . .

[61] ECCR (MS), 49: 57-2; Konig, *Law and Society,* 167.

[62] See, for example, Yasuhide Kawashima, *Puritan Justice and the Indian: White Man's Law in Massachusetts, 1630-1763* (Middletown, Conn., 1986), 130-31. . . .

[65] The Corys had the reputation of testing the honesty and the patience of their neighbors. It was Giles who had informed on John Proctor for selling liquor to the Indians in 1678, and the Corys often brought or defended slander suits. See, for example, *Essex County Court Records,* 7:123, 132.

[75] Deodat Lawson, *A Brief and True Narrative of Some Remarkable Passages...* [1692] in George Lincoln Burr, ed. *Narratives of the Witchcraft cases, 1648-1706* (New York, 1914), 160; *SWP,* 2:351-52; 3:994.

[76] In one recent California case of alleged child abuse, the supposed victim's mother not only seconded her son's claims but later charged that he had been molested by three witches and a member of the Los Angeles School Board. Lucy S. McGough, *Child Witnesses: Fragile Voices in the American Legal System* (New Haven, 1994), 15.

[77] *SWP,* 2:584-87.

[78] Increase Mather, *An Essay for the Recording of Illustrious Providences* [1684], ed. James A. Levernier (New York, 1977), 269. . . .

[86] I would guess that this might be true of little Dorcas Good, age four, who informed on her mother, Sarah, even if the latter was abusive. Dorcas Good confessed a week before she was scheduled to be executed. Much as those times differed from our own, I know of no other case of a small child hanged for such a crime, and surmise that the judges were eager to avoid that extremity, though I have no evidence for my surmise. . . .

[88] See, for example, William Nelson, *Dispute and Conflict Resolution in Plymouth County, Massachusetts, 1725-1825* (Chapel Hill, 1981).

[89] I should note that this is my reading of the way the system worked, much influenced by a rudimentary sociology of criminal law approach. A similar approach appears in the now classic study of deviance (including witchcraft) in the Bay Colony, Kai T. Erikson, *Wayward Puritans: A Study in the Sociology of Deviance* (New York, 1966), 137-59, but I do not mean to adopt the cynical pose of those who condemn the magistrates or the judges as simple woman haters, as in Lyle Koehler, *Search for Power: The "Weaker" Sex in Seventeenth-Century New England* (Urbana, Ill., 1980), 389-411.

[90] Demos, *Entertaining Satan,* 309.

[91] The modernist protests that such could not happen today, but the Ingram case in Olympia, and increasing numbers of child abuse cases elsewhere, contradict that smug confidence. Paul Ingram, unable to remember any of the incidents his daughters recalled, came to believe under stress and duress that he must have simply repressed the events and confessed to the charges. When this book was written, he was still serving a twenty-year sentence in a state penitentiary, although in a quieter time he recanted his confession. Lawrence Wright, *Remembering Satan: A Case of Recovered Memory and the Shattering of an American Family* (New York, 1994), 193.

[92] *SWP,* 2:405.

[93] Ibid., 2:411-12.

[94] Ibid., 2:413.

[95] Ibid., 3:793-804.

[96] Edmund S. Morgan, *Puritan Family: Religion and Domestic Relations in Seventeenth-Century New England*, rev. ed. (New York, 1966) 88; *The Diary of Michael Wigglesworth, 1653-1657: The Conscience of a Puritan,* ed. Edmund S. Morgan (New York, 1965), 17.

[97] *Lawes and Liberties,* 35, 6.

[98] *SWP,* 3:705.

[99] Perry Miller, *The New England Mind: The Seventeenth Century* (Cambridge, Mass., 1938), 26-27; Darrett Rutman, *American Puritanism: Faith and Practice* (Philadelphia, 1970), 15, 26, 99-100.

Additional coverage of Sewall's life and career is contained in the following source published by Gale Reseach: *Dictionary of Literary Biography,* Vol. 24.

SAMUEL SEWALL (1652-1730)

INTRODUCTION

English-born American diarist, essayist, politician, and jurist.

Sewall is best known for his *Diary* (1674-1729), a fifty-six- year account of his life as an influential Puritan magistrate in Boston, Massachusetts. The most comprehensive record available today about seventeenth-century New England life, Sewall's *Diary* is considered by many critics one of the best written in English. Sewall is also known for his role in the Salem witch trials. Appointed in 1692 to the Court of Oyer and Terminer—created by Governor William Phips in order to deal with the rising witch hysteria—Sewall was one of the judges responsible for the sentencing to death of nineteen accused witches. He is the only judge who ever publicly recanted, asking forgiveness from both man and God for his part in the Salem tragedy.

Biographical Information

Sewall was born in Hampshire, England, in 1652 and came to America at the age of nine. He attended Harvard College, where he met his first of three wives, Hannah Hull, with whom he had fourteen children. Although educated to be a minister, Sewall became involved in Boston's political life. As a wealthy merchant and landowner, he was also involved in banking and international trade. He held many public offices and advanced quickly; he became a member of the board of assistants, council, a judge of the supreme court, and finally, chief justice of the Superior Court of Judicature—a position he held until two years before his death in 1730.

Major Works

Sewall's first published book, *Phaenomena quaedam Apocalyptica Ad Aspectum Novi Orbis configurata* (1697; *Some few Lines towards a Description of the New Heaven, As It makes to those who stand upon the New Earth*), is an interpretation of the Book of Revelation in which he questions whether America is indeed the New Jerusalem. In his second published work, *The Selling of Joseph, A Memorial* (1700) Sewall makes a powerful case against slavery, calling it "the most atrocious of capital Crimes." Sewall wrote the three-page antislavery tract during a time in which the slave trade was not only acceptable, but considered a respected and legitimate business. Sewall was ahead of his time regarding other issues as well: in his *Talitha Cumi (An Invitation to Women to look after their Inheritance in the Heavenly Mansions)* he takes on the question of whether females will be allowed in heaven, and concludes that "without doubt all will." Sewall's numerous other writings include judicial decisions, business transactions, translations in English and Latin, essays, poems, and his most famous work—his *Diary*. Sewall began his *Diary* in 1673, shortly after he graduated from Harvard. His last entry, which relates the negotiation of a Puritan marriage match, was written several months before his death. His *Diary* is more than a source of information about New England history—it is the story of a man's life, filled with both his triumphs and tragedies. He writes about the small as well as the large details of his life—from petty gossip and news of the weather, to the deaths of his wives and children and his thoughts on religion and God. His *Diary* is particularly memorable for the humorous details of his courtship with Madam Winthrop, a lady whose affections he pursued but never won. However, for all of Sewall's excellent record-keeping, one major event is scantily covered in his *Diary*—the Salem witch trials. Critics remain disappointed by his insubstantial record of the trials, for such a record would be especially valuable in the continuing search for the causes of the witch hysteria of 1692.

Critical Reception

Criticism of Sewall's *Diary*, which was first published over a hundred years after his death, has been mixed. It has been credited by many scholars as being one of the best American diaries ever written, in addition to being the principal historical record of seventeenth-century New England. However, more recent assessments have deemed Sewall's *Diary* as lacking in literary merit. Steven Kagle, while not denying its intrinsic value as an historical document, has criticized Sewall's style and finds the work as a whole to be fragmented due to the length of time it covers. Similarly, others have criticized it for its concentration on trivial matters, a habit which contrasts with the deep reflection found in the personal writings of many other Puritans.

PRINCIPAL WORKS

Phaenomena quaedam Apocalyptica Ad Aspectum Novi Orbis configurata [*Some few Lines towards a Description of the New Heaven, As It makes to those who stand upon the New Earth*] (essay) 1697
The Selling of Joseph, A Memorial (essay) 1700
*Talitha Cumi [*An Invitation to Women to look after their Inheritance in the Heavenly Mansions*] (essay)
A Memorial Relating to the Kennebeck Indians (essay) 1721
Diary of Samuel Sewall (diary) 1674-1729

*The date of composition for this work is unknown.

CRITICISM

Moses Coit Tyler (essay date 1878)

SOURCE: "New England Traits in the Seventeenth Century," in *A History of American Literature,* G. P. Putnam's Sons, 1881, pp. 93-114.

[*In the following excerpt from a work originally published in 1878, Tyler praises Sewall's character and discusses his progressive his views on slavery and women.*]

A strong, gentle, and great man was Samuel Sewall, great by almost every measure of greatness,—moral courage, honor, benevolence, learning, eloquence, intellectual force and breadth and brightness. Both his father and his grandfather were among the pioneers of New England colonization; although his father, who founded the town of Newbury, Massachusetts, seems to have passed and repassed between England and America without bringing hither his wife and children, until 1661, when the boy, Samuel, was nine years old. This boy, destined to great usefulness and distinction in the new world, thus came to it in time to have that personal shaping for his life here, only to be got from early and direct contact with it. He had the usual education of a New England gentleman in those days. He was graduated at Harvard College. He tried his hand for a time at preaching,—a vocation for which he was well qualified, but from which he was diverted into a prosperous and benign secular career. He became a member of the board of assistants, then of the council, judge of the supreme court, and finally its chief-justice, holding the latter office until 1728, two years after which date he died. He was a man built, every way, after a large pattern. By his great wealth, his great offices, his learning, his strong sense, his wit, his warm human sympathy, his fearlessness, his magnanimity, he was a visible potentate among men in those days.

> Stately and slow, with thoughtful air,
> His black cap hiding his whitened hair,
> Walks the Judge of the great Assize,
> Samuel Sewall, the good and wise.
> His face with lines of firmness wrought,
> He wears the look of a man unbought,
> Who swears to his hurt and changes not;
> Yet, touched and softened nevertheless
> With the grace of Christian gentleness;
> The face that a child would climb to kiss;
> True and tender and brave and just,
> That man might honor and woman trust.[1]

He had the courage to rebuke the faults of other people; he had the still greater courage to confess his own. Having, in 1692, fallen into the witchcraft snare, and having from the bench joined in the sentence of condemnation upon the witches, five years later—when more light had broken into his mind—he made in church a public confession of his error and of his sorrow. The Indians of Massachusetts had then no wiser or more generous friend than he; and he was, perhaps, the first of Americans to see and renounce and denounce the crime of negro slavery as then practised in New England. In 1700, he spoke out plainly on this subject, publishing a tract named **"The Selling of Joseph;"**[2] an acute, compact, powerful statement of the case against American slavery, leaving, indeed, almost nothing new to be said a century and a half afterward, when the sad thing came up for final adjustment. In this pamphlet one sees traces both of his theological and his legal studies; it is a lawyer's brief, fortified by Scriptural texts, and illuminated by lofty ethical intuitions. Within those three pages he has left some strong and great words—immortal and immutable aphorisms of equity: "Liberty is in real value next unto life; none ought to part with it themselves or deprive others of it, but upon most mature consideration."[3] "All men, as they are the sons of Adam, are co-heirs, and have equal right unto liberty, and all other outward comforts of life."[4] "Originally and naturally there is no such thing as slavery."[5] "There is no proportion between twenty pieces of silver and liberty."[6]

All his lifetime he made the Biblical prophecies his favorite study,—a study out of which all manner of marvels, not always edifying, may be educed upon occasion; and the special marvel drawn from them by this sagacious Puritan judge was their palpable predictions of America as the final "rendezvous for Gog and Magog," and as the true seat of the New Jerusalem. In his **"Phaenomena Quaedam Apocalyptica; . . . or . . . a Description of the New Heaven as it makes to those who stand upon the New Earth,"** a book first published in 1697,[7] he unfolds this theory, going over the applicable prophecies clause by clause. Toward the end of his book, he replies to the objections that might be urged against his doctrine,—one of them being that in America the human race inevitably deteriorates, becomes barren, dies off early. The accusation he repels with an affluence of facts illustrating the productiveness and longevity of the human family here; and having done so, he rises into this rhythmical and triumphant passage, which in its quaint melody of learned phrase, and in a gentle humor that lurks and loses itself in the stiff folds of his own solemnity, has a suggestion of the quality of Sir Thomas Browne: "As long as Plum Island shall faithfully keep the commanded post, not withstanding all the hectoring words and hard blows of the proud and boisterous ocean; as long as any salmon or sturgeon shall swim in the streams of Merrimac, or any perch or pickerel in Crane Pond; as long as the sea-fowl shall know the time of their coming, and not neglect seasonably to visit the places of their acquaintance; as long as any cattle shall be fed with the grass growing in the meadows, which do humbly bow down themselves before Turkey-Hill; as long as any sheep shall walk upon Old-Town Hills, and shall from thence pleasantly look down upon the River Parker, and the fruitful marshes lying beneath; as long as any free and harmless doves shall find a white oak or other tree within the township, to perch, or feed, or build a careless nest upon, and shall voluntarily present themselves to perform the office of gleaners after barley-harvest; as long as Nature shall not grow old and dote, but shall constantly remember to give the rows of Indian corn their education by pairs; so long shall Christians be born there, and being first made meet, shall from thence be translated to be made partakers of the inheritance of the saints in light."[8]

It gives still another charm to the memory of this practical and hard-headed mystic of New England, this wide-souled and speculative

> Puritan,
> Who the halting step of his age outran,

to discover, that, in a matter of very serious concern, he had the chivalry to come forward as the champion of woman. He tells us that once, while "waiting upon a dear child in her last sickness," he took up a book to read. It was a book called "The British Apollo." Presently, his eye fell upon a startling question, worded thus: "Is there now, or will there be at the resurrection, any females in heaven; since there seems to be no need of them there?" Very likely he then closed the book; and there, by the death-bed of his daughter, over whose resurrection this question threw its cold shadow, his mind set to work upon the problem thus presented; and afterward he fully resolved it, in an essay bearing this delectable title: **"Talitha Cumi; or, An Invitation to Women to look after their Inheritance in the Heavenly Mansions."** He begins by quoting the question that he had met with; then he proceeds to say: "This malapert question had not patience to stay for an answer, as appears by the conclusion of it—'since there seems to be no need of them there.' 'Tis most certain there will be no needless, impertinent persons or things in heaven. Heaven is a roomy, a most magnificent palace, furnished with the most rich and splendid entertainments; and the noblest guests are invited to partake of them. But why should there seem to be no need of women in heaven? . . . To speak the truth, God has no need of any creature. His name is exalted far above all blessing and praise. But by the same argument there will be no angels nor men in heaven, because there is no need of them there." He then discusses, with judge-like care and fulness, all the arguments, on both sides, that may be drawn from reason, Scripture, and the ancient and modern theologians, reaching at last this assertion: "There are three women that shall rise again,—Eve, the mother of all living; Sarah, the mother of the faithful; and Mary, the mother of our Lord. And if these three rise again, without doubt all will." In the course of the discussion he meets the objection that, upon a certain branch of his subject, "the ancients are divided in their opinions." His answer to this objection comes edged by a flash of wit: "If we should wait till all the ancients are agreed in their opinions, neither men nor women would ever get to heaven."[9] . . .

Notes

[1] J. G. Whittier, "Prophecy of Samuel Sewall." Works, II. 141.

[2] First printed in a folio of three pages, at Boston, 1700. Reprinted in Mass. Iist. Soc. Proc. for 1863-1864, 161-165. I quote from the reprint.

[3] "The Selling of Joseph," 161.

[4] Ibid. 161.

[5] Ibid. 162.

[6] Ibid. 162.

[7] Reprinted, Boston, 1727.

[8] "Phaenomena," etc. 63. The reader will recall the use

of this passage made by Whittier in his delightful poem, "The Prophecy of Samuel Sewall." The old Puritan's prose in this case is more poetic than the poet's metrical paraphrase of it. Whittier speaks of Newbury as Sewall's "native town;" but Sewall was born at Horton, England. He also describes Sewall as an "old man," "propped on his staff of age" when he made this prophecy; but Sewall was then forty-five years old.

[9] Selections from Sewall MSS. Mass. Iist. Soc. Proc. for 1873, 380-384. . . .

Rev. N. H. Chamberlain (essay date 1897)

SOURCE: "Sewall and the Salem Witchcraft," in *Samuel Sewall and The World He Lived In*, second edition, De Wolfe, Fiske & Company, 1898, pp. 157-77.

[*In the essay that follows, originally published in 1897, Chamberlain discusses Sewall's role in the Salem witch trials and asserts that "a man with his large heart would never forget his hand in that strange misery until his death's day."*]

The Salem witchcraft business requires careful handling by those who would be just both to the sufferers and the offenders therein. Sewall's part in the matter was a brief though sad one, as one of the judges who pronounced sentence of death upon the innocent. A man with his large heart would never forget his hand in that strange misery until his death's day. Nor is it without a certain pathos of filial love towards the dead, that shortly after Sewall's decease his son moved in the General Court (1738) that inquiry should be made as to the condition of the victims' families, looking towards some sort of restitution, poor at best. The witches' "caldron" at Salem was as purely imaginary, so far as witches went, as the one that Shakespeare makes to bubble with ill-odored and poisoned ingredients on an imaginary moor in Scotland; yet into that Salem caldron, out of the hands of that Puritan age and people, were poured some of the most mixed, unreachable, and poisonous motives of which probably the human mind, in its most occult relationship to the human body, has as yet shown itself capable of emitting. Yet, sad to say, its bubbles turned to blood, and the smoke of this witches' incense creates a great sorrow among all lovers of New England folk until now.

There is, perhaps, no more valid canon of historical criticism than this, that the people of an age are to be judged as to conduct by the ethics and environment of that age, and by no other. Ancient Rome is not to be judged by the ethics of modern Italy. In judging the Salem witchcraft catastrophe, we must start with this postulate. But at that time the peoples of Christendom devoutly believed in actual witches, the English people being as stout devotees of that delusion as any.

English statute law declared witches and witchcraft to be verities by making so-called witchcraft a crime punishable with death. English judges had sentenced thousands of men and women for the offence, and European tribunals had destroyed by due process of law hundreds of thousands of accused persons for what we know to be a purely imaginary felony. Very few Englishmen in the Puritan age disbelieved in witches. Even as late as 1840, in West Dorsetshire, England, there were people who undertook to argue that a prevailing sickness there was brought about by witchcraft. It is needless to note, perhaps, what the Old Testament holds in this matter.

The Puritans held with the rest, only with a more tenacious grip. This was natural; we may well say, inevitable. This very attitude in church and state made them, more than most, doomed to the mistake. They held that they were God's chosen people in the wilderness just as actually as the Jews had been; that they had honored Him by founding institutions based on His revealed law; that they were His and He was theirs by a solemn compact; that He was therefore cognizant of their every word and deed; in minute oversight of His creatures, not even a sparrow fell to the ground unnoticed. When, therefore, an attack seemed to be in progress at Salem upon His church and people by His arch enemy the Devil, it was not simply an attack on them and their dearest aspirations, but on Him; and they were bound, on penalty of being held traitors to Him in the Judgment Day, not to stand neutral, but to fight His battle by destroying witchcraft from the land. They could logically, as New England Puritans, do nothing else. It is argued every now and then that their clergy were the chief malefactors in urging the people on to this wrong. That this point is not well taken ought to appear from the fact that in the Salem witchcraft, as indeed in everything else they put their hand to, as ought to appear in our whole colonial history, the Puritan clergy voiced and enforced with the power of an educated class the deliberate conscience and judgment of their own people, who fed them voluntarily and reverenced them greatly. If this were not so, how came it to pass that later on this same people parted from this same clergy both in politics and religion, and went their own way? With a few exceptions of the more fortunate-minded, the management at Salem was according to the consensus of the whole community. Cotton Mather is pointed to as one of the chief malefactors in inciting the Salem horrors. That Cotton Mather was a very human sort of man, and, therefore, sometimes blamable, may go without saying. But Cotton Mather actually agonized over the bewitched, or, as the ancient phrase went, "behagged," children, whom he took into his house in Boston in such a way as to remove all suspicion that he was juggling, or any way trying to do anything else than to probe to the bottom of the fact. To say that he was magnifying his office in order to hold his place in affairs,—an imputing of motives,—is not verified by the record. He, and most men about him, thought that any man who disbelieved in witches would disbelieve in the Devil; and that he who would disbelieve in the Devil would speedily come to disbelieve in God.

One thing more as a proviso. The times were ripe for such an outbreak as that at Salem. They were out of joint politically, the charter being lost, and people were sore and apprehensive of some great calamity. They were in the slough of an unknown transition. Besides, a new generation had sprung up, born here, wonted from youth to hardship and solitude, cruel from King Philip's War, less educated than their fathers, though of like faith, and actually falling backward into a barbarism bred from the wilderness. Add to this the fact that the Puritan mind, in spiritual things at least, was always high-strung, so that its vibrations were likely to be unnaturally acute, and it certainly looks as if no epoch in our history was so provocative of an honest but fierce outburst of fanaticism as the year 1692, when nineteen persons were put to death at Salem for witchcraft.

This is no place to tell the story, only to illustrate it, and narrate Judge Sewall's part in it. In brief, certain children and half-grown women at Salem, aided by a few base persons and an Indian, began the calamity by accusing some other persons—their neighbors, generally—of bewitching them. Their cries, contortions, and physical distresses and general absurdities, if stated, would seem incredible, if not impossible, to any one who had not read the record. Nothing shows like it in our history. The community rose *en masse* to inquire and to decide. It was trial by a mob, only the mob was pious. The accusations were in general, and, with a few exceptions, against respectable people, and finally reached far and wide, touching the best,—magistrates and ministers, or their wives. Then the fierce flame burned itself out, and there were graves, gallows, broken families, ruined fortunes, and misery for generations as a residuum. . . .

By the Provincial Charter of 1691 Sewall had been appointed one of the Council, an office to which he was annually chosen till 1725, when he was re-elected, but declined to serve, having outlived all the other councillors then appointed with him. All through March, 1692, the Salem fury had been gathering head; and on April 11, probably as a magistrate, he went down, in company with the lieutenant-governor and four others, to look into the matter.

> Went to Salem where in the meeting house the persons accused of witchcraft were examined: was a very great assembly; 'twas awful to see how the afflicted persons were agitated. Mr. Noyes prayed at the beginning and Mr. Higginson concluded.

A rather rustic event in the life of a rich man like Sewall, living in Boston, and noted down by him under date of Saturday, Feb. 27, may perhaps illustrate the abnormal excitement of men's minds, and apprehension of coming evil, running close upon a panic, before pointed out:—

> Between 4 and 5 morning we are startled at the roaring of a beast, which I conjectured to be an ox broken loose from a butcher, running along the street, but proved to be our own cow bitten by a dog, so that were forced to kill her; though calved but Jan. 4th and gives plenty of milk. Happy are they who have God for their spring and breast of supplies.

The men who could turn from a cow bit by a dog to God for mercy would be very likely to look out to Him and for Him in so strange a matter as the Salem misery.

There were now nearly one hundred accused persons in jail, and worse threatened. Governor Phipps, on his return from his Eastern expedition, found himself forced, by public opinion, to appoint a special commission of oyer and terminer to try these cases, of which Stoughton was chief-justice, with six associates, including Sewall. This court substantially was the government of the Province, so great was the solemnity thought to be. They were appointed June 13, 1692, and for the counties of Suffolk, Essex, and Middlesex. This court met at Salem in June and August, sending some nineteen persons to death. After the executions of Sept. 22, they adjourned to meet a few weeks later; but they met no more. In January, 1693, the grand jury brought in bills against some fifty persons; but all were acquitted except three, and they were reprieved. None who confessed were brought to trial. May, 1693, Governor Phipps, by proclamation, discharged all those in jail, and the delusion vanished as rapidly as it had spread.

With the exception of an entry April 11, there are no entries in Sewall's Diary for the three months of April, May, and June, when the excitement was at its height. The entries elsewhere in his journal touching this matter are few, and generally very brief. He evidently was ashamed, cast down, full of sorrow, and probably afraid of personal prosecution and loss of property at the hands of the survivors suing for damages. The court he belonged to was no doubt illegal, and its proceedings, as judged by the ethics of English law, more than questionable. From other sources, however, we can gain insight as to how things went on in court. First of all, neither he nor his associates were lawyers nor conversant with right legal procedure; although a high modern legal authority is of opinion that Sewall was the best of his associates. Indeed, as their law based itself on the Jewish Scriptures, ministers, not lawyers, were

the best expounders of the same, and the common law of England was at a discount. Therefore lawyers were systematically discountenanced, and orders are not wanting by which they were to be heavily fined if their plea was over an hour in length. The prosecuting attorney at Salem was a lawyer, and the court assisted. There was very much testimony before the court, but very little evidence. One of the rulings of Chief-Justice Stoughton ought to be remembered. He told the jury "that the Devil could not appear in the form of any one who was not in league with him. It followed, therefore, as the Devil had appeared in the form of many of the accused, according to the eye-witnesses there, the defendants must be guilty." But in this Stoughton must have forgotten his Scriptures, which speak of Satan sometimes appearing as "an angel of light." It was a fatal court to every one, though Stoughton stuck to it all his life that right had been done, and resigned his place on the bench rather than even tacitly allow the opposite.

Under date of July 20, Sewall writes: "Fast at the house of Capt. Alden," etc. Alden, the son of the Plymouth Pilgrim, "the tall man in Boston," as his accusers called him, for thirty years a respected member of the South Church, a brave seaman in command of the colony's armed vessels, doing noble service in the French and Indian wars, and seventy years of age, was now in jail for witchcraft. May 31 he had gone down and met his accusers at Salem,—"a group of wenches playing their juggling tricks," as he describes them, who charged him with afflicting, after the manner of witches, people whom he had never seen nor known. The honest indignation and "sea language" which he apparently used upon them did not save him from being sent to Boston jail, where he now was while Sewall, his fellow-parishioner and judge, was holding a fast with Revs. Cotton Mather and Willard, and a galaxy of Puritan church-members, at the captain's house for the latter's salvation. It is incredible that there should be hypocrisy of this quality on earth. But if we suppose them honest, then their Puritan behavior at Salem must at least have been honest also. After fifteen weeks in jail, Captain Alden escaped to Plymouth Colony, and probably died in his bed.

> July 30. Mrs. Cary makes her escape out of Cambridge prison who was committed for witchcraft. [That lady's story has been told before.]

> Aug. 19. This day George Burroughs, John Willard, Jn Procter, Martha Currier and George Jacobs were executed at Salem, a very great number of spectators being present. Mr. Cotton Mather was there, Mr. Sims, Hale, Noyes and Cheever, [ministers]. All of them said they were innocent, Currier and all. Mr. Mather says they all died by a righteous sentence. Mr. Burroughs by his speech, prayer, protestation of his innocence, did much move unthinking persons which

occasions their speaking hardly concerning his being executed.

Most of which is no doubt true, though Cotton Mather is wrong as usual. This day the victims had been hung; men and women, drawn a long way from jail in a big wagon which "stalled" or broke down, over a rough road to the highest hill thereabouts, with its jagged rocks thrust through the thin soil, clad in the gray mosses which grow there ever since, from that eminence overlooking the summer land and sea of their wild Essex, to go asking justice from some One, if there were justice either below or above the stars, and the charity which had been denied them here. They all died stoutly, as Sewall writes. Burroughs had been his friend, and had dined with him years before, as his Diary tells. Stripped of his prison clothes in that death whose majesty the rags they clad him in could not obscure,—uncoffined body flung into the shallow grave the rocky ledge allowed him, on that gallows' plot of shame,—his right arm stiffened until it rotted or dogs tore it, was seen as if pointing to those heavens where "the wicked cease from troubling and the weary are at rest." There are no witches that we know of. But if there were, there is perhaps no spot in all this West where they should be more at home in the weird desolation of their barren and uncanny lives than that same belt of rocky moorland, south of Salem city as it remains to-day; gray, mossy, rock-crested, with its long, narrow glens creeping in among the hills, yet seeming to have gone and going nowhere, down into which the scattered cedars of funeral plumage seem to speer as sentinels on watch for something which they never find—that land at whose west gate two centuries ago Puritan sincerity in a sad mistake built the Witches' Gallows.

> Monday, Sept. 19, 1692. About noon, at Salem Giles Corey was pressed to death for standing mute.

This execution is unique in American annals. By English law, a man might be pressed to death if he refused to plead yea or nay to his indictment. In case of a recalcitrant prisoner, he was brought three times into court and told the penalty. Remaining obstinate, he was then to be laid bound hand and foot on the floor of his prison cell, with heavy iron weights on his body. The first day he was to have three morsels of the worst bread for food, and the second day three draughts of standing water found nearest the prison walls; and so weights were added until he died. Giles Corey had a somewhat unsavory reputation, well or ill earned it is hard to say, and was a downright man in his will, and, when touched, in his heart. When his wife was accused of witchcraft he was first inclined to stand against her; but her piety and sad end brought him to flout the whole business as a wrong. Very naturally he had his turn as an accused wizard. If he pleaded not guilty he knew he was sure to be condemned, and to confess that he was a wizard was not in him. There was a dilemma here. For if he had pleaded and been condemned he expected his property would be confiscated and his heirs impoverished. He made his will in prison, and held his tongue. They pressed him to death,—somewhere, tradition has it, in the rocky fields of the others' doom; and the same tradition reports that in his agony he cried out to put on more rocks, as he would never plead. There is an old saw which says that time has two ages; one in which men of oak build houses of willow, and the other when men of willow build houses of oak. Giles Corey must have been a man of oak, however housed. There was a certain grim thrift which followed the Puritan even in his dealings with accused persons. He insisted that men should pay their own. Those who were released from jail paid their own charges,—for chains, board, and court fees. Many were ruined in consequence; and their descendants, counted now among the most respected, are entitled to cherish their memories.

Sewall cherished his memories thereof. Signs multiplied of a reaction. Oct. 26, 1692, he writes:—

> A bill is sent in about calling a fast and convocation of ministers that may be led in the right way as to the witchcrafts. The season and manner of doing it is such that the Court of Oyer and Terminer count themselves thereby dismissed, 29 noes and 33 yeas to the bill.

> Dec. 24. Sam recites to me in Latin Math. 12 from the 6th to the end of the 12th. The 7th verse did awfully bring to mind the Salem Tragedy.

That verse is this: "If ye had known what this meaneth, I will have mercy, and not sacrifice, ye would not have condemned the guiltless."

There were those who would have had the Salem court and its abettors pursued and punished for their mistake. How near they were to doing so cannot now be known, nor just why they failed. Their stand was at least stout enough to compel the legislature, in what looks like a penitence somewhat late, to appoint a fast Jan. 14, 1697, for what had been done amiss "in the late tragedy raised among us by Satan and his instruments, through the awful judgment of God." Since witchcraft times, Sewall had lost several little children; and at this fast, like the brave, honest-hearted man he was, he put up the following petition in his own parish meeting-house, "standing up at the reading of it and bowing when finished:"—

> Copy of the bill I put up on the fast day, giving it to Mr. Willard as he passed by, and standing up at the reading of it and bowing when finished; in the afternoon.

Samuel Sewall, sensible of the reiterated strokes of God upon himself and family and being sensible that as to the guilt contracted upon the opening of the late Commission of Oyer and Terminer at Salem (to which the order of this day relates.) he is upon many accounts, more concerned than any that he knows of, desires to take the blame and shame of it, asking pardon of men and especially desiring prayers that God who has an unlimited authority would pardon that sin and all other, his sins, personal and relative and according to his infinite benignity and sovereignty not visit the sin of him or of any other upon himself or any of his, nor upon the land; but that he would powerfully defend him against all temptations to sin for the future and vouchsafe him the efficacious, saving conduct of his word and Spirit. . . .

Vernon Louis Parrington (essay date 1927)

SOURCE: "Samuel Sewall:Yankee," in *Main Currents in American Thought, Vol. I,* Harcourt, Brace, Jovanovich, 1927, pp. 86-98.

[*In the essay below, Parrington examines Sewall's* Diary *and draws from it information on his political, intellectual, and personal characteristics.*]

By good fortune an intimate record of daily life in old New England has been preserved in abundant detail. The diary of Samuel Sewall not only narrates the homely activities of Boston in the evening of the theocracy, *antiquis moribus, prisca fide,* but it unconsciously reveals the transformation of the English Puritan into the New England Yankee. The sober Boston citizens who on the Sabbath droned Windsor and York tunes, and took notes of long sermons, on weekdays plied their gospel of thrift with notable success. They loved the meetinghouse as their fathers had loved it, but they were the sons and grandsons of tradesmen, and true to their English instincts they set about erecting a provincial mercantile society, dominated by the ideals of the little capitalist. Of this rising world of mercantilism, Samuel Sewall was a worthy representative. A Puritan magistrate and village capitalist, he made full use of his opportunities to worship God, to thrive and to rise. As the older ideal of theocratic stewardship is revealed in the career of John Winthrop, the newer practice of incipient capitalism is revealed in the life of Samuel Sewall.

The *Diary* is a fascinating book, with its petty gossip interwoven with matters of public concern, and its brisk activities set in a black border of innumerable funerals: the one among all the books of the time that is still quick with life after these two hundred years and more. In its meager entries we can trace the change that was coming to Massachusetts in the transition from a theocracy to a royal colony; and we can feel the strong emotions which that change aroused. The dry facts of history take on flesh and blood; forgotten names become living men walking the streets of Boston or arguing in the Council Chamber; Samuel Sewall himself becomes more real to us than our own contemporaries. He was the veritable embodiment of his serious, prudential Massachusetts, reflecting its changing fortunes with painstaking fidelity. In that petty world of conventional piety and shrewd self-interest, the kind-hearted Judge bustled about, a sermon in one hand to soothe the doubts of the troubled, and a bit of chocolate in the other to comfort the bedridden—as honest and friendly and prosaic a soul as Massachusetts ever bred. If one wishes to understand the first native New England generation, one cannot do better than linger over the daily jottings of this lawyer-tradesman, who knew his Calvin far better than his Coke, and who while busily adding new acres to his holdings strove to keep the younger generation uncontaminated by wigs and revels and other godless things, by the sweet ravishment of the psalms, in the singing of which the voice of the Judge was lifed up with pathetic earnestness.

For many years after his death fame dealt more than generously with Samuel Sewall. The prosperity that came to him during his earthly pilgrimage long provided for his memory, and made of him a greater figure than either nature or good fortune created. Who does not know Whittier's tribute?

> Stately and slow, with thoughtful air,
> His black cap hiding his whitened hair,
> Walks the Judge of the Great Assise,
> Samuel Sewall, the good and wise.
> His face with lines of firmness wrought,
> He wears the look of a man unbought,
> Who swears to his hurt and changes not;
> Yet touched and softened nevertheless
> With the grace of Christian gentleness;
> The face that a child would climb to kiss;
> True and tender and brave and just,
> That man might honor and woman trust.

And a hundred and forty-eight years after the cold January day when all that was mortal of him was "honorably Inter'd" in the Sewall tomb whither so many of his family had gone before,[1] a brilliant student of early American letters gave fresh currency to the stately Sewall of tradition. "He was a man built, every way, after a large pattern. By his great wealth, his great offices, his learning, his strong sense, his wit, his warm human sympathy, his fearlessness, his magnanimity, he was a visible potentate among men in those days."[2]

That was before the diary was published and the lay figure of tradition vanished in presence of the real man. We know Samuel Sewall now and see him as he was. That he was a great man it is impossible to make out; but that he was a small man by no means follows.

Behind the formal trappings of magistrate and councilor, we discover a capable, middle-class soul, honest, simple-hearted, serving himself yet not unmindful of his fellow townsmen, an excellent neighbor and citizen, to whom the strongest appeal of life was the economic. Like those kindred spirits, Defoe and Franklin, the dominant inspiration of his life was prudential, as befitted the descendant of generations of tradesmen. "Mr. Henry Sewall, my great Grandfather," wrote the Judge in old age, "was a Linen Draper in the City of Coventry in Great Britain. He acquired a great Estate, was a prudent Man, and was more than once chosen Mayor of the City."[3] In turning Puritan the English burgess did not change his nature, and Samuel Sewall was true to his breeding in fashioning his life upon that of his great grandfather. To acquire wealth and honors, to occupy a dignified position among his fellows, was the dominant ambition of his life. With excellent thrift he fixed his young affections upon the only child of a wealthy merchant, the richest heiress in the colony; no penniless "waiting-woman," for Samuel Sewall, such as had contented the unworldly Thomas Hooker. He understood how desirable it is to put money in one's purse; so he made a great alliance and proved himself a shrewd husbandman as well as a kind husband.[4] From commerce and land speculation and money lending and the perquisites of many offices, he accumulated steadily until his wealth entitled him to be regarded as one of the first citizens of Massachusetts. He did not forget his prudence even in his generosities, but set down carefully in his diary what his benefactions cost, that there might be no mistake when he came to make his reckoning with the Lord. He knew his rights and upheld them stoutly; and in the petty quarrels and litigations in which he found himself involved, he stuck to the letter of the law and usually won his point. He did not misuse his official position to feather his own nest, but what might be got legally from public office he took care to get.

With abundant wealth the path of preferment was easy to him. From his election to the privileges of a freeman in 1678, at the age of twenty-six, to the end of a long life, he was continuously engaged in public affairs. He sought office and was not backward in pushing his claims upon a desirable post;[5] and by careful attention to business rather than by exceptional parts, he rose to a place of very great influence in the commonwealth. Like a competent man of affairs, he was prompt in meeting engagements—"am, I think, the most constant attender of Councils," he remarked of himself approvingly. He carried out to the letter the early advice given him: "Mr. Reyner . . . Advised me not to keep overmuch within, but goe among men, and that thereby I should advantage myself."[6] Capable, industrious, public-spirited, he led a busy and useful life that justified more than commonly the responsibilities which came to him. His qualities might be middle-class, but they were sterling and worthy of honor. It was a fortunate star that led him out of Tory England, where he would never have been more than a prosperous tradesman, to the new world where kindred spirits were erecting a commonwealth after his own heart.[7]

Nevertheless with all his excellent qualities Samuel Sewall was not a great or original nature. The evidence is convincing that he was a capable executive and administrator rather than a creative thinker or forceful leader; a Puritan embodiment of Defoe's merchant ideal; an example of the man who rises to civic honors by simple business virtues. He was at home in the narrow round of routine, but for bold speculation he reveals the incapacity of the practical soul. His intellectual interests were few; his ready curiosity was that of the uncreative mind, concerning itself with persons and happenings rather than with ideas. To say that Sewall possessed either an economic or political philosophy would be too generous an interpretation of his opinions. The views which he upheld vigorously were little more than prejudices. Of the several economic questions which engaged the attention of the Council during his years of service, the most insistent was the question of issuing bills of credit to supplement the scanty currency. There was the usual class alignment, the wealthy opposing the issues, and the poor generally favoring them. The position of Sewall was clear. He vigorously opposed every issue, from the conviction that the only honest money was hard money, even going so far as to prefer barter to bills.[8] Nowhere does he reveal any intelligent grasp of the economics of the problem, nor was he aware that his judgment might have been influenced by his private interests as a money lender.

In his political views he was equally unconcerned with broad principles. He seems to have been wholly unread in political theory, and like his fellow magistrates he never examined fundamentals. He accepted without question the right of the godly to police society, and he would have no meddling with affairs of state by tavern and fireside politicians. As a member of the oligarchy he naturally approved oligarchic rule. Although he would turn to the democracy for support against the Lords of Trade, when the latter were moving to overturn the theocracy, he put no trust in the political wisdom of the common people. He was as magisterial as John Winthrop in his belief in the principle of the stewardship of the elders. Stability of government was the prime essential; there must be no criticism of government by private individuals or by newspapers. On an occasion when Dudley's administration had been sharply attacked in a London paper, a copy of which had been brought over and talked about, there was a great pother in Council. Although Sewall was not willing to defend Dudley, he was troubled.

> At last the Council voted, it tended to the disturbance
> of the Government. Lt. Govr. and Council order'd

me to Reprimand Mr. Dummer. . . . I told him how intolerable it was for privat persons to print Reflections and Censures on the highest Acts of Government. . . . Twas ill done of them who printed it in London, and twas ill done by them that carried it on here.[9]

His characteristic attitude then comes out in the phrase: "I said . . . I was for upholding Government whether in or out of it." Samuel Sewall was no rebel against authority. But if he was firm in support of the *de facto* government, he was insistent that it should be honest. He protested to Governor Dudley against padding the muster pay-rolls[10] and he dissented strongly against introducing the current English practice of buying commissions in the army.[11] The scandalous corruption of English politics must not be permitted to sully the government of Massachusetts.

Sewall enjoyed in his lifetime the repute of a scholar. He was Latinist enough to justify his Harvard degree of Master of Arts; he read a good deal, and wrote and published books. But he seems to have cared nothing for pure literature, and was unacquainted with the English classics. His intellectual interest was in things either occult or inconsequential. Biblical prophecy was his favorite study, and his most ambitious work, **Phaenomena Quaedam Apocalyptica,** essayed to prove that America was to be the final "rendezvous of Gog and Magog." Although long a magistrate and judge of the highest court, he was not a lawyer. He received no preliminary training in the law, and there are few indications in the **Diary** that he read the literature of the profession. His indifference seems to have given concern to his friends, for on January 13, 1696, four years after he had been chosen judge, he noted:

> When were there at first, Mr. Danforth bad me look on the Cupboard's head for a book; I told him I saw there a Law-book, Wingate on the Common Law. He said he would lend it me, I should speak to Amsden to call for it; and if he died, he would give it me. Again when took leave after prayer, He said he lent me that Book not to wrap up but to read, and if misliked it, should tell him of it.[12]

Primitive New England did not take kindly to lawyers, and in administering a patriarchal justice by rule of thumb, Sewall was like other New England magistrates. Neither did it take kindly to the spirit of free speculation. and in his potterings over occultisms he was confessing the sterility of intellectual interests.

If the kind-hearted Judge lacked capacity for bold and liberal thought, he lacked capacity as well for emotional fervor. He was quite without imagination. Despite his honest concern for his soul, and his sincere desire for the advancement of God's kingdom in New England, Sewall did not possess a deeply religious nature. In his religious life he was the same prudent, plodding soul, that stowed away in his strong-box deeds to ample possessions dur-

ing his pilgrimage through this vale of tears. The natural man was strong in his two hundred and odd pounds of flesh, and the religious mysticism that lurked in the heart of primitive Puritanism found no response in his phlegmatic soul. He was no Seeker, like Roger Williams, to be driven by a passionate fervor along untried paths; nor was he a philosopher, like John Wise, to concern himself with broad ecclesiastical principles. Instead, there is more than a hint of the tradesman's conception of religion—one has only to understand the profitableness of salvation to be led to invest in it. His religion must be orthodox; no untried methods or gambler's chances; a good business man will scrutinize title-deeds with due care, and the title-deeds to salvation are of the first importance. How characteristic are the following entries in the diary:

> Sabbath, March 2d. I Pray'd in the Family, that might have an interest in God, Signed, Sealed and Delivered, and that all that tended to make it sure, might be perfected.

> Febr. 6. [1718] This morning . . . I had a sweet and very affectionat Meditation Concerning the Lord Jesus; Nothing was to be objected against his Person, Parentage, Relations, Estate, House, Home! Why did I not resolutely, presently close with Him! And I cry'd mightily to God that He would help me so to doe!

> 23. 5. [1721] Mr. Prince preaches the Lecture, from Gen. 22. 18 . . . A very seasonable Discourse. One Fly was discovered in his Ointment: He asserted that the 1000. years Rev. 20. stood for Three Hundred and Sixty Thousand years; taking every day of the 1000. years for a year: as 365. days i.e. years. *Apage has nugas!* ["Away with this nonsense!"][13]

No higher criticism for Samuel Sewall. If we quibble over the plain words of Scripture, how shall we be certain of the terms of the contract?

A man so cautious by nature, and with so large a stake in the existing order, could not fail to be a conservative, content with a world that justified itself by the prosperity which it brought him, and which it would bring to others, he doubted not, if they governed their conduct with equal prudence. He desired no innovations in church or state; established forms answered his needs and filled the measure of his ideal. The existing system was approved by all the respectable people of the community; there was everything to gain in upholding it, and likelihood of loss in suffering power to pass into the hands of a royal governor or of the ignorant poor. And so, determined by complex motives, by habit, by class ties, by economic interest, and by honest liking, Samuel Sewall went with the stream of conventional orthodoxy, strong for the old theocratic principles, seeing no need for readjustments to meet changing conditions. The true principles of church and state had been laid down by the fathers, to which the common acceptance by the best people gave final sanction.

It is characteristic of the prosperous bourgeoisie, and the old Judge walked the streets of Boston, or sat in his pew, or took his place on the bench, as stubborn and unimaginative a conservative as any of his fellows. If his persistent opposition to change, whether in the matter of wigs, or Christmas keeping, or creed, or politics, was due in part to a phlegmatic love of use and wont, it was prompted also by an instinctive fear of innovation. The world doubtless is imperfect, but it answers to God's will and we understand its ways and can draw our contracts with open eyes. Whereas change, however desirable it may seem theoretically, entails too many disturbing uncertainties. Very likely it was this subconscious concern for his material interests that so often made the simple-minded Judge an unintelligent opponent of all popular movements looking to a freer and more liberal society. When his native kindliness was touched he spoke out frankly. His antislavery tract (*The Selling of Joseph*), slight in extent and somewhat overpraised by historians, was not only much in advance of his time, but it contains one sentence that should not be forgotten, "There is no proportion between twenty pieces of silver and liberty." Equally significant was his stand against capital punishment for counterfeiting.[14] Such acts as the following must also be set down to his credit: "I essay'd June 22 [1716], to prevent Indians and Negros being Rated with Horses and Hogs; but could not prevail."[15] His native sense of justice was as strong as his kindliness. Who does not know of his confession in regard to the witchcraft persecutions—an act that set all Boston tongues wagging. When he was convinced that he had made a grievous and sorrowful mistake, he rose in the congregation while the minister read his public acknowledgment of that mistake, and his repentance for his share in the unhappy business. Thereafter in commemoration he kept an annual day of prayer and fasting. We can forgive him much for that honest and manly act.

To the end of his life Sewall refused to go forward with the changing times, and his voluntary assumption of the office of *praefectura morum* laid him under a heavy responsibility to see that the primitive ways were upheld. He was magisterial in rebuke and few transgressors of the strict New England code escaped a censure. One would like to have James Franklin's private opinion of the sharp-eyed old Judge. To Franklin and other members of the Hell-fire Club—young fellows keenly interested in domesticating the new wit literature in homespun Boston, openly skeptical, inclining to Arianism and even to deism—he must have seemed a prosy old reactionary, upholding a decadent orthodoxy and an obsolete social order. No doubt many a sharp jibe was aimed at his back, for there were many to whom the older ways began to seem preposterous. It may very well have been that those who committed a certain prank which Sewall records may have had him in mind.

Aug. 3. [1717] . . . 'Tis said it should be so, but a virulent Libel was starch'd on the Three Doors of the Meeting House, containing the following Words:

TO ALL TRUE-HEARTED CHRISTIANS

Good people, within this House, this very day,
A Canting Crew will meet to fast, and pray.
Just as a miser fasts with greedy mind to spare;
So the glutton fasts, to eat a greater share.
But the sower-headed Presbyterians fast to seem more holy,
And their Canting Ministers to punish sinfull foley.[16]

Happily there is another and pleasanter side to the character of Samuel Sewall, and one that looked forward to the future instead of backward to the past. Despite the harshness of the Puritan creed and the bigotry of Puritan rule, the fields and meadows of New England, that sent a breath of the countryside through the crooked streets of Boston, were a wholesome influence in the lives of men and women. Magistrate and money-lender though he was, Samuel Sewall was a countryman and farmer also, a judge of milch cows and fat porkers as well as criminals, a lover of robins and flowers and fruitful orchards, one who sat his horse well, and when on circuit often drew up at a rail-fence to discuss the crops with some gossipy farmer. Above all, a lover of men, the most neighborly soul in the world, mingling freely with all classes, and although quite properly proud of a visit from the Governor or other great person, never above chatting with the carpenter, or doing a kindness to an old nurse. It was the friendly heart of the man that prompted so many little errands of helpfulness; and if sermons and tracts and good advice flowed from him like a spring freshet, if he was magisterial in petty rebuke, such little oddities of the man and the time did not detract from his sympathy or lessen his helpfulness. Men stood in awe of Cotton Mather, and children must have run from him, but neither awe nor fear threw their shadow across Sewall's path. We can make too much of the countless funerals that dot his pages, with their thrifty reckoning of gloves and scarfs and rings that were the queer perquisites of pallbearers. It was not an unwholesome world despite the smell of mortality that exudes from the old records, or the terrors of little children smitten with the fear of hell; and the homely round of Samuel Sewall's activities was very far from unwholesome.

It was his neighborliness that made him so representative of the leveling tendencies of a provincial village life—an easy comradeship with men of all conditions, unknown to the rigid class divisions of the old world. Going one day to visit the Jews' burial place at Mile-End, while on a visit to London, he invited the sexton to a pot of beer and a quiet chat, remarking in friendly fashion, "wisht might meet in Heaven: He answered, and drink a Glass of Beer together, which we were then doing."[17] His English friends would scarcely have understood that homely little scene, so natural to the colonial. Sewall is the first Yankee who reveals the native kindliness of the New England village. He was zealous to do good and to deal generously with others, because he had been generously dealt by. Growing more human with the ripening years, yet instinctively conservative, stubbornly intent on managing his own affairs in his own way and by his own agents, provincial to the core and strong in local pride, he reveals the special bent of the New England character, as it unconsciously differentiated itself from its English original. Not American as yet like Franklin, and no longer wholly English like Winthrop, far from democratic and yet no Tory, he was the progenitor of a practical race that was to spread the gospel of economic individualism across the continent.

Notes

[1] Two of his three wives and eleven of his fourteen children he had buried.

[2] Tyler, *History of American Literature during the Colonial Period,* Chapter XIII, Part IV.

[3] *Diary,* in *Massachusetts Historical Society Collections,* Fifth Series, Vol. 1, p. xi.

[4] Compare his haggling over the terms of settlement upon a later proposed marriage; see *Diary,* Vol. III, p. 205.

[5] See *Diary,* Vol. III, p. 168.

[6] *Diary,* Vol. I, p. 32.

[7] The following is part of an obituary notice by his son:

> In 1684, He was chosen a Magistrate of the *Massachusetts* Colony. . . . In 1692, He was appointed by King William and Queen Mary in their Royal Charter, one of the first Council for their Majesties in this Province, into which He was annually chosen and sat till 1725, when He resign'd his Election, having outlived all the others nominated in that Fundamental Constitution. In 1692 He was made one of the Judges, and in 1718, Chief Justice of our Superior Courts of Judicature thro' the Province, in which He sat till 1728, when his Infirmities growing on Him, He resign'd that Place also. In 1715, He was made Judge of Probates for this County of *Suffolk,* and continued in that Office till 1728, when He laid it down; it being the last Publick Post wherein He served and honoured his Country. *Diary,* Vol. III, pp. 409-410. In addition to the above, he was at times an overseer of Harvard College, censor of the press, and captain of the Ancient and Honourable Artillery Company; a frequent moderator of Boston town meeting, member of innumerable committees on church, parish and common-wealth matters, and adviser at large to whoever was in difficulties.

[8] See *Diary,* Vol. II, p. 366; Vol. III, pp. 87 and 345.

[9] *Diary,* Vol. III, pp. 84-85.

[10] *Diary,* Vol. II, p. 228.

[11] *Ibid.,* p. 214.

[12] *Diary,* Vol. 1, p. 419.

[13] *Diary,* Vol. I, p. 312; Vol. III, p. 165; Vol. III, pp 281-282.

[14] See *Diary,* Vo. III, p. 277.

[15] *Ibid.,* p. 87.

[16] *Diary,* Vol. III, pp. 116-117. Note the use of the word Presbyterian in these lines.

[17] *Diary,* Vol. I, p. 301.

Chamberlain examines the longevity of Sewall's *Diary*:

Sewall's ***Diary*** . . . will last because it is a rich mine of New England history; because it fulfils this cradle of so much gone into a nation's life, greater than its own, with the records and riches of its own unique and primitive life, as no other man ever has, or at this late day can. As a nation ages, it looks back, and to its monuments. When this is done, it will discover easily in the waste of its earlier days, certainly in its province of New England, that in Sewall's Diary there is more of its own history, on its human side, than in any other writing of the times. . . . Ilis performance in his ***Diary*** is in all ways suggestive and characteristic. It is very much as this land then was,—chaotic, migratory, rough, granite, actual, sincere. The barbaric wilderness, savage, cruel, vast, serves as the background of all his pictures, and not seldom, as an atmosphere, is often blown into them. While the ***Diary*** is rough, uncouth, and almost Gothic in its blunt, sometimes even coarse, downrightness, it is always sincere, confidential, and friendly. Sewall puts no gall in his ink, shows no malice, means to be just, with an intention that does not often fail him, and, in short, writes himself down as a strong-bodied, great-souled, honor-loving Puritan; not altogether above his age,— no genius, no saint except in intent, but withal as good "an all-round man" as New England has ever had. It is this man who has written our one great diary. . . .

Rev. N. H. Chamberlain, preface to Samuel Sewall and the World He Lived in, *De Wolfe, Fiske, & Company, 1898.*

Mark Van Doren (essay date 1963)

SOURCE: An introduction to *Samuel Sewall's Diary*, edited by Mark Van Doren, Russell & Russell, 1963, pp. 5-6.

[*In the excerpt that follows, Van Doren compares Sewall's* Diary *to that of his English contemporary Samuel Pepys and contends that "few such stories have ever been better told."*]

The **Diary** of Samuel Sewall . . . was first published in three volumes by the Massachusetts Historical Society (1878-1882). It is the most intimate record now available of life in New England during the important period which it covers, and indeed few segments of American experience, in whatever section or century, have been more satisfactorily set down for posterity to ponder.

The genius of the author for self-revelation, especially when he was unaware of what he revealed, has frequently won him the compliment of a comparison with Samuel Pepys, his English contemporary. One difference between the two Diaries, however, is that while that of Pepys was kept for only a decade, that of Sewall runs from 1674, three years after his graduation from Harvard College, to 1729, the year before his death: a total, that is to say, of fifty-five years. He was born in England in 1652, of parents who had emigrated to New England in 1634 but who returned soon after that. They came again when Samuel, the second of eight children, was nine years old, and settled in Boston, with which the rest of the diarist's long life is identified.

After further schooling in Boston, Sewall went through Harvard and for a while considered entering the ministry, but decided instead upon a mercantile career. His letters are a copious record of this career, which was basic to a life now of greater interest on other fronts: legal, political, and last of all—also likewise best of all—personal. Sewall held many public offices, and rose in the judicial system to be chief justice of the superior court of judicature, a position which he held from 1718 to 1728, two years before his death in 1730. He was imperfectly prepared to be a judge, yet his native probity and his strong sense of justice made him on the whole an ornament to the bench. His liberality was manifested on a number of occasions; and his own deep sense of responsibility expressed itself on the unforgettable day of January 14, 1697, when he stood up in the Old South Church while the Reverend Samuel Willard read at his request a moving confession of error and guilt because he had been one of the judges who in the witchcraft trials of 1692 condemned nineteen persons to death. He desired in this fashion "to take the blame and shame of it," and to ask pardon of both man and God, lest the sin of which he was guilty be visited upon him or his, or upon the land. He seems to have been no more in error than were his fellow judges in that terrible case, but on this occasion he chose to say so. He was the only one of them who ever publicly recanted.

Sewall's diary throughout is the diary of such a man. Its frankness, its simplicity of mind and heart, its willingness to tell the truth even at the expense of its author's dignity, and its consuming interest in the small as well as the large details of life—in food and drink, the weather, family quarrels, chance remarks by enemies or friends, sickness, death, and random misbehavior, no less than in commanding matters of church and state—these qualities do indeed justify its comparison with the immortal diary of Pepys, which is greater only because it is more complete for the years it preserves. The unique passion of Pepys for fixing on paper the events of a day lest they go the way of most days into oblivion led him to sit up many a night until the milkman came and the sun rose. Sewall was less obsessed than this; yet it is always evident that his commitment to the truth, the whole truth, and nothing but the truth was manly and strong. It is possible that he did not altogether understand himself, or see himself as others saw him. He was naive at times, and he could be inconsistent. The reader, however, may be glad that this is so. A more sophisticated document might have been less credible, and almost certainly it would have been less fascinating.

The women in Sewall's life, the three he married and the others whom as a widower he courted, are naturally of prime interest to any student of the diary. By his first wife, Hannah Hull, he had fourteen children. When she died in 1717 he waited two years to marry Abigail Tilley, and two years after her death in 1720 he married Mary Gibbs. But before Abigail Tilley there had been Mrs. Denison, and before Mary Gibbs there was Madam Katherine Winthrop. Both of these ladies he yearned for without reward, failing in each case to reach an understanding suitable on a mixture of personal and pecuniary grounds. His courtship of Madam Winthrop, reported in full and picturesque detail, is rightly the most famous item in all the work. Few such stories have ever been better told.

Ola Elizabeth Winslow (essay date 1964)

SOURCE: "On the Bench in Salem Village," in *Samuel Sewall of Boston*, The Macmillan Company, 1964, pp. 112-36.

[*In the essay that follows, Winslow provides an in-depth account of Sewall's involvement in the Salem witch trials.*]

The Hysteria of the witchcraft chapter was almost at hand, although to understand the "woeful chain of consequences" it would always be in our history, one must read the signs long backward. By the time Samuel Sewall returned from the English journey, it was already too late to check its course, and before he was appointed one of the judges to conduct the trials, time had quite run out. Salem jails were crowded with those condemned by their neighbors, hearings were already being held before local magistrates, and all New England was aroused. At this point legal action by the colony of Massachusetts, not the town of Salem, seemed the way out. By that path would come tragedy.

On May 14, 1692, Sir William Phips arrived with the new charter Massachusetts had waited for since 1684. He was immediately told what was happening in Salem, and on the advice of his Councillors, and as one of his first acts, he appointed seven Councillors of a Special Court of Oyer and Terminer to try those accused. William Stoughton was made Chief Justice and his associates, of whom any five were to constitute the Bench, were Jonathan Corwin, Bartholomew Gedney, John Hathorne, John Richards, Nathaniel Saltonstall, Peter Sergeant, Samuel Sewall, and Wait Still Winthrop. Nathaniel Saltonstall refused to serve, and Jonathan Corwin was put in his place. The first sitting having been arranged for June 2, Sir William Phips departed to the Indian wars in the north.

According to the provisions of the new charter, the General Court was to approve the Governor's appointments to any special courts such as this one. General Court was not in session until June 8th of this year, but in the urgency of the Salem situation, the judges held their first session prior to this date. Authority for so doing was the original Body of Liberties of the colony which had been the basis for court action during the period between one charter and the other. The first victim was executed on June 10th, two days before the General Court approved the judges appointed and voted in the phrasing of the original charter "to continue all laws not repugnant to England." The charge of illegality for the action of the first court session scarcely holds, since the Body of Liberties had been the authority invoked during the years of waiting for the issuing of the provincial charter.

Along with his fellow judges, Samuel Sewall brought to the trial sessions an almost unchallenged heritage of belief in the reality of witches as the devil's agents. To seventeenth century men and women of enlightenment, as well as to the ignorant, witches were willing agents of Satan, pledged to overthrow God's kingdom on earth. Their presence in any community was a *sign* the elect ignored at their peril. Every New England child had grown up knowing that Satan's dearest hope was to conquer New England for himself. This theme had been persistent in every pulpit since the first landing. In the Mother Land and in Europe the reality of witches was a belief centuries old. First arguments against so long-established a belief are impotent. Believers have no ears to hear them. To have denied the reality of these evil agents in 1692 would have meant to question also a literal heaven and hell, all angels, all devils, fire, brimstone, golden streets and even the Judgment Day itself. Witches were part of the total fabric of accepted truth, except to the very few as yet silent doubters, who were aware that across the sea this idea was just beginning to be challenged in print.

Massachusetts colony from the beginning had followed the specific statutes against witches from the reigns of Henry VI, Henry VIII, Elizabeth and James I, and had made witchcraft a capital offence. Mosaic law was the warrant. In stumbling human literalness they had obeyed Exodus 22, 18, "Thou shalt not suffer a witch to live," as God's own fiat. In the Massachusetts Body of Liberties this statute follows immediately after the provision for punishment of idolatry, which is article I. No II reads,

> If any man or woman be a witch (that is hath or consulteth with a familiar spirit) they shall be put to death.[1]

This legal definition of a witch was adhered to throughout the Salem trials.

Only rough estimates are possible, but the suggested figure of some 300,000 executions and burnings in Europe and the British Isles during the century of the Salem Village outbreak is perhaps an understatement. Against this towering figure, the nineteen deaths on the scaffold and one under heavy stones in New England, 1692, might seem a small total in proportion to the shame these deaths have spread over our colonial story, but as to the heaviness of that shame, let any history of New England testify. Our first century wrote no darker page.

There had been sporadic witchcraft cases in New England prior to 1692, but surprisingly few in comparison with the disasters that might so naturally have been attributed to evil spirits in human flesh. John Winthrop recorded the "malignant touch" of Margaret Jones, a practicing physcian in Charlestown, executed in 1648.[2] Her death was grimly remembered in Connecticut because of a "great tempest" that came at the hour she was on the gallows. Ann Hibbins, widow of a Representative to the General Court in Boston, and agent of the colony, had fallen victim to the malicious gossip of her neighbors and had been executed.[3] Her husband's services to Massachusetts colony, her own wit (was it in too great excess of wit belonging to those who maligned her?) and perhaps also her large estate had made her indictment and death for witchcraft the subject of some controversy and some denunciation, but 1655 was still too early for skepticism wide enough or healthy enough to call either the charge or the death penalty into question. There had been various other single cases, enough to keep witchcraft always in the foreground of one's fears and to account for the frequent mention of it in Sunday sermons. No one of these cases, however, had aroused widespread hysteria. In England a condemned witch had been burned as late as 1682, only ten years before the Salem panic. This seems to be the last witchcraft death on record in the British Isles.

Probable causes of the Salem hysteria are easy to assemble. Among them, Cotton Mather's printed account of the supposed "afflictions" of the four children of John Goodwin of Boston in 1688 is perhaps one of the most direct. In a time of depression and deep anxiety over loss of the charter and uncertainty as to New England's future government, this supposed tale of Satan in our midst gave concreteness to the feeling that something was very wrong with New England. To read such a book at such a time meant also to watch for similar manifestations in other families. The four "afflicted children" (two boys and two girls, the eldest thirteen), as reported by Cotton Mather, barked, purred, mewed, moved as though with wings, and took on many other strange behaviors. One girl rode herself up the stairs as though on horseback, simulated being in the oven—perspiration dropping from her face—or choking with an invisible noose around her neck. Most convincing of all her tricks, to the orthodox, was that she was struck senseless at the sight of the *Assembly's Catechism,* John Cotton's *Milk for Babes,* and other orthodox books, but could read the Book of Common Prayer, popish or Quaker books without a qualm. Surely Satan was within her. Parents, neighbors, physicians, ministers were in consternation and baffled to find any other cause than "bewitched" for such doings. Who was the witch? Goody Glover, the girl answered, and Goody Glover died on the gallows.

Cotton Mather's account was widely and immediately read. It was entitled, *Late Memorable Providences Relating to Witchcrafts and Possessions,*[4] for its day a title to invite readers. Richard Baxter, who wrote the recommendatory preface, testified that he had seen no reason to question these strange behaviors as proofs of demoniac power. Neither did many of the New England clergy who, fortified by Baxter's eminence, passed the book on to others. Its success lay in the circumstantial detail. Cotton Mather had taken the oldest girl, cleverest of the four children, into his home for a time, while he wrote his account of her antics, and for novelty alone, they are arresting. Read as "bewitchment" by her credulous contemporaries, they make a story of strange powers at work. Read today, against a heritage of disbelief in witches, they reveal on every page the adroit cleverness of this child, her flattery

of Cotton Mather, and his (to us) amazing blindness not to detect her trickery, while his pen was in his hand.

That other children, hearing about the Goodwins, might imitate their behaviors, apparently occurred to no one. However, that is precisely what happened in Salem Village, quickly becoming the first chapter in the sad "delusion." Irresponsible children had also been the "evidence" in the much publicized Bury St. Edmunds case in England, tried before Sir Matthew Hale twenty-eight years earlier.[5] Among the "marvels" those children had seen were invisible mice, which when caught and thrown into the fire had exploded with loud noises and flashes of fire. Amy Drury and Rose Callender were named as witches and tried on evidence such as this. Sir Matthew, eminent man of law, merciful beyond most, had been deeply affected by the testimony against them, and in his charge to the jury did not sum up the evidence, but left the room with a prayer that God "would direct their Heads." *Guilty* was the verdict and the two women had died. The eminence of Sir Matthew had made both his action and the jury's verdict in the case authoritative to other judges and juries. The Salem Village judges were well familiar with it.

"Afflicted children" had been the exciting cause of other witchcraft hysteria as well. In popular interpretation the assumed innocence of the very young made their supposed "affliction" a pitiable proof of the devil's dark designs, and the adult pursuit of their tormentors was swift and without mercy more often than not. As to the Salem children themselves, no doubt in the beginning they may have enjoyed the excitement of being central figures before an audience, and after they were all but forced to name their supposed tormentors, it was too late to stop what their antics had started. Perhaps sometimes they were frightened into keeping on, perhaps in the tumult which ensued, they half-believed their own supposed bewitchment. One had best leave three-century-old motives alone and keep to the facts. In the Salem story we also have the adult confession of Anne Putnam, the twelve-year-old leader of the "afflicted children."

Her two younger accomplices were Elizabeth Parris, nine-year-old daughter of Samuel Parris, the village minister, and Abigail Williams, his niece, who lived in the household. The parsonage was the place where it all started. Two older girls, Nancy Walcot, daughter of Deacon Walcot, and Mercy Lewis, employed in the household of the Rev. George Burroughs, one of those executed, were also members of the group. Four other young women, Elizabeth Booth, Susannah Sheldon, Nancy Warren and Sarah Churchill, were also part of the story. As it can be pieced together from many fragments of testimony, the children and young girls had apparently met together occasionally in the winter of

1691/92 in the parsonage parlor to read books about palmistry, magic and spiritism. The Parris bookshelves would very likely have held books on occult phenomena, and besides, such books were in circulation in any New England parish. William Perkins's *Discourse of the Damned Act of Witchcraft,* 1608, perhaps Joseph Glanvil's *Saducismus Triumphatus,* or *Full and Plain Evidence concerning Witches and Apparitions,* Richard Burton's *The Certainty of the World of Spirits,* were there also, as Cotton Mather had imported them. His *Memorable Providences,* telling of the Goodwin children, would hardly need the support of print; it was a conversation piece. If Samuel Parris knew of these meetings, he did not admit the knowledge, not even after the excitement put the parsonage in the center of everyone's thought.

Details of what went on at these meetings are too vague and scant for certain statement. They had probably begun in a natural curiosity about strange behaviors, fostered very likely by the contributions of Tituba, a West Indian servant in the house, and John Indian, her husband, both of whom would have been able to add bizarre details from their distant native land. It appeared at the trials that at the direction of Mary Sibley, Tituba had made a loathsome cake, supposedly possessing magic power. After the trials began, Mary Sibley was reprimanded in church meeting, and Tituba and John Indian were deported, but only after their testimony had done irreparable harm. The skill of the children in their muscular controls, bodily contortions, rigidity under pinpricking, pinching and other tests, their tongue-swallowing, apparent dislocation of joints, shrieking and moaning in strange keys need afford no mystery. Diligent practice and the desire to amaze others explain them easily enough, and suspicion of a devil's agent in such behaviors blinded the observer to any natural explanation. The best item of performance would seem to have been their ability to execute their tricks in perfect unison.

To later view, it would seem that Samuel Parris, father, uncle, and neighbor of the three principals, could hardly have failed to know what was going on in his own house and could have stopped it all, but he did not. Instead, he invited neighboring ministers to witness these strange "afflictions" of the children. Private fasts were held at the parsonage and guests spent hours in wondering parley and much prayer. Physicians were called in and admitted being baffled. The ministers departed, carrying the news to their own parishes and spreading the suspicion. Samuel Parris, who has been seriously accused for his part in the whole affair, was very probably only deluded.

He was not a minister by the usual training, but had been a merchant in the West Indies before deciding to preach and accepting the call to Salem Village. In terms of village peace, he had made sad mistakes before the

1692 crisis in his parish. He had been excessively concerned over a guaranteed salary increase for the future, had demanded title to the parsonage land as his own possession, and when refused, had instituted a lawsuit. He had also gone to law over his wood supply. The parish had been riven by party factions before his coming, and the intra-mural disputes over each of his demands had widened the breach between the parties. Perhaps a man of tact and Christian zeal could not have healed them; certainly one using such business methods to drive a hard bargain could not.[6] The congregation had grown deeply restive even before the suspicion of the devil's presence among them had precipitated a panic. All classes of members were involved in the previous unrest: half-way members, covenant members and even the unchurched of the village had taken sides, a condition which invited to crisis during the trials.

Excitement over the parsonage children had reached a pitch before March 24th, when Deodat Lawson, former pastor in the village, was announced as the preacher. Everyone came, including many from the country around. No one present would ever forget that sermon. The Rev. Mr. Lawson had been back in Salem Village for five days, had seen the apparent "sufferings" of the "afflicted children" demonstrated individually and in a group. They were present in the meetinghouse that morning and interrupted him by their strange outcries. His text was Zechariah 3, 2: "And the Lord said unto Satan, The Lord rebuke thee, O Satan; even the Lord that hath chosen Jerusalem rebuke thee: is not this a brand plucked out of the fire?" Truly the text was Zechariah, but the application was to Salem Village.

> You are therefore to be deeply humiliated, and sit in the dust, considering the signal hand of God is singling out this place, this poor village, for the first seat of Satan's tyranny, and to make it (as 'twere) the rendezvous of devils, where they muster their infernal force.

He addressed the local dignitaries who were present in their panoply of office.

> Let us admit no parley, give no quarter: let none of Satan's forces or furies be more vigilant to hurt us than we are to resist and repress them, in the name, and by the spirit, grace, and strength of our Lord Jesus Christ.

> Do all that in you lies to check and rebuke Satan; endeavoring, by all ways and means that are according to the rule of God, to discover his instruments in these horrid operations. [7]

The effect of these impassioned counsels, not from a stranger, but from one who had been pastor among them, was to add recklessness to action that had already gone past rational judgment. As to Deodat Lawson himself, one can only judge his unwisdom as that of a man in whom for the moment knowledge of human nature was forgotten, as he gave rein to his own irresponsible zeal. Those who heard were thus further prepared to act irresponsibly also.

Before Samuel Sewall and his fellow judges made their first journey empowered to conduct the trials, more than a hundred suspected persons were in jail, the town was obsessed by fear and torn apart with suspicion. Husbands wondered about wives, wives about husbands. Everyone watched everyone else, especially their own children, in search of evidence for bewitchment. On March 1st, Tituba confessed herself to be a witch. Two weeks later Martha Corey and Rebecca Nourse were named by the "afflicted children" and sent to prison. On April 3rd, Samuel Parris preached on the text, "Have I not chosen you twelve and one of you is a devil?" Sarah Cloyse, sister of Rebecca Nourse, left the meetinghouse. As she went out the door, it was slammed behind her, presumably by the wind. This was evidence. She too was taken to prison. All three of these women were eminent for their piety and godliness.

Not to ignore the local reasons for this state of affairs which are plain enough to see, or to quarrel with them, it is also well to place Salem Village at this hour of near tragedy within the provinciality of New England in 1692. Boston, its largest city, possibly had five thousand inhabitants. For all except the very few, especially in the towns and villages a day's journey by boat or horseback from Boston, local concerns, explained by local interpreters, had little chance to be placed in a wider perspective. At the right moment, some authoritative voice perhaps from Boston, from the throne of King William, or a voice from the Royal Society, searching for realistic answers to marvels of many sorts, could have brought an atmosphere in which the inquiry into the antics of the supposedly "afflicted children" might have been *What* instead of *Who,* but no such avenue was open to Salem Village in 1692, and no voice spoke. What was happening to the parsonage children filled the earth and sky of village thought. *Who* is hurting you was the first and the persistent question in trial after trial. The circumference of the parish became almost the boundary of the world. No wonder that local happenings gained gigantic size and importance within so limited a circumference. In part they can be understood when this tight boundary is taken into account.

It is well also to read the whole story against the current sermon background, familiar to any child in the village, as well as to their parents. So long as no name was named in the long list of *signs* that the devil is loose amongst us, witchcraft lay quietly among the other signs. But let a local name be named and the

teaching of a lifetime sprang into quick life. An unfamiliar sign in the preacher's list would have awakened no panic. It is what is already long familiar that becomes powerful when something immediate gives it fresh application. Proofs that God's smile had faded and that He was already punishing New England were numerous enough for every family in the village to have been touched by one woe or another. Locusts that ate the crops, smallpox that came again and again and was present that winter, wrecked vessels, burned houses and barns, drowned children, all were current. Most of all, the precious charter was gone and a new governor was in the chair. Spurred by Deodat Lawson's phrases, "the first seat of Satan's tyranny," the "rendezvous of devils," Salem Village became a concrete plan of action, not for herself alone, but to rid New England of their presence.

At the time of his appointment to the Court of Oyer and Terminer, Samuel Sewall was forty years old. Too much has been made of the assumption that he and his fellow judges were without legal training as a qualification for judging. Truly enough they had no formal training. Sewall had been a member of the General Court for seven years, and as a magistrate, he would have had considerable experience in dealing with those accused of misdemeanors. Under the colonial charter, the General Court exercised jurisdiction in all criminal cases for which a special court was not appointed. Later he imported books on English law and became one of the best equipped of Massachusetts judges in his day, but in 1692 this was still in the future. There was a strong vein of superstition in his nature, and he could accept as fact illogical details of supposed demoniac possession such as tradition had made familiar. So could his fellow judges.

To search his *Diary* for details of record for what he saw and heard during this fevered time is to be disappointed. His entries concerning Salem Village are few and brief. On April 11, 1692, more than a month before the arrival of Sir William Phips and his appointment as judge, he went to Salem with Thomas Danforth, Deputy Governor, and five members of his Council: James Russell, John Hathorne, Isaac Addington, Samuel Appleton and Jonathan Corwin. They went unofficially. The occasion was a hearing in the crowded meetinghouse, before local Salem authorities, at which Sarah Cloyse and Elizabeth Procter were being examined by Samuel Parris. The "afflicted children" were present. John Indian, Mary Walcott, Abigail Williams and Anne Putnam were asked questions, framed by Samuel Parris and recorded by him. Almost unfailingly, the question asked implied the answer.

(Of Anne Putnam)

"Anne Putnam, doth this woman hurt you?"
"Yes, Sir: a great many times."

Then the accused looked upon them, and they fell into fits.

> "She does not bring the book to you, does she?"
> "Yes, sir; often, and saith she hath made her maid set her hand to it."
>
> (Of Abigail Williams)
> "Abigail Williams, does this woman hurt you?"
> "Yes, sir, often."
> "Does she bring the book to you?"
> "Yes."
> "What would she have you do with it?"
> "To write in it, and I shall be well."
>
> (Of John Indian)
> "John, who hurt you?"
> "Goody Procter first, and then Goody Cloyse."
> "What did she do to you?"
> "She choked me, and brought the book."
> "How oft did she come to torment you?"
> "A good many times, she and Goody Cloyse."
> "Where did she take hold of you?"
> "Upon my throat, to stop my breath."
> "What did Goody Cloyse do to you?"
> "She pinched and bit me till the blood came."[8]

Asked similar questions, Mary Walcott fell into her fits at intervals. At each time of the fit she was carried near enough to the supposed witch to be able to touch her body at some point. Immediately the fit subsided, as according to belief, the diabolical fluid flowed back into the witch's body. The examination went on until the fit came again.

At the trial before Sir Matthew Hale in 1664 the "afflicted" ones were blindfolded at this point in the proceedings, and touched not the supposed witch, but the clerk of the court. Their suffering ceased immediately and their falseness was revealed. Had this test been applied in Salem Village, it might have brought the beginnings of skepticism to some on the bench, but apparently it occurred to no one to apply test of any sort to the witnesses or even to cross examine them.

When Samuel Parris had asked his quota of questions of each "afflicted" person, he turned to the accused women.

"What do you say, Goody Procter, to these things?"

Her reply is the only one of the afternoon, not implied in the question asked.

"I take God in heaven to be my witness, that I know nothing of it, no more than the child unborn." Similarly, the eloquence of Martha Carrier, at a later session, in her five words, "I have not done it." To the accusation that she had looked on the black man, "I know none."[9]

Samuel Sewall quotes none of this and supplies no details. His entry on the April 11th experience is a single sentence.

> "Went to Salem, where, in the Meeting-house, the persons accused of Witchcraft were examined; was a very great Assembly; 'twas awfull to see how the afflicted persons were agitated."[10] On July 30, 1692, he mentions the escape of Mrs. Cary from Salem jail, and on August 19th, the execution of five victims on Gallows Hill: Martha Carrier, George Burroughs, John Williard, John Procter, and George Jacob.
>
> "Mr. Mather says they all died by a Righteous Sentence. Mr. Burrough by his Speech, Prayer, protestation of his Innocence, did much move unthinking persons, which occasions their speaking hardly concerning his being executed."[11]

The Rev. George Burroughs had been a Harvard student with Sewall, had been a dinner guest at his home several years before his execution, on November 18, 1685 and on January 21, 1691, had preached at private meetings which Samuel Sewall attended. In the margin of this execution entry in the *Diary* are the words "Dolefull Witchcraft." These are the only references in his record to the witchcraft proceedings while they were taking place.

On July 20, 1692, in a letter to Cousin Hull in London, he wrote, "Am perplexed p[er] witchcrafts: six persons have already been condemned and executed in Salem."[12] He makes no mention of attending any of the executions and presumably did not, as he had done on other occasions. His silence in the *Diary* is not significant, as he makes many omissions of what might naturally seem to cry for a personal record. The phrase "Dolefull Witchcraft" might suggest a question in his own mind, but may of course have been added to the entry later.

The dogmatic insistence of Chief Justice Stoughton that the devil could not take the appearance of the spectre of an innocent person seems to have been openly contradicted by the other judges, as also by Increase and Cotton Mather and the larger body of ministers. Many words were spent on this controversial point, and had the majority prevailed against Stoughton, there would have been no limp bodies hanging from the scaffolds on Gallows Hill. It was the testimony of the "afflicted" that the spectres of the accused had appeared when they were far away, going about their daily tasks or asleep in their beds, that condemned them at the trials. The details are fantastic: spectres in the head of a blue boar, a cat, in the air, unbodied, recalled as seen even years before the trials which were going on. Read for this "spectre detail" through a dozen testimonies, conviction on these grounds passes all rational acceptance, except for a time when rational judgment on the bench as well as in the crowded assembly was laid to sleep.

One would think also that the duplication, time after time, of this flimsy spectral testimony in its limited range, of the little black man, the Red book, the little yellow bird sitting on the beam of the meetinghouse or on the rim of the minister's hat, wherever condemnation could be helped by it, would have lost its effectiveness and power to awe even those whose reason was elsewhere. Even more the precisely identical writhings, stiffenings, strange moanings and screamings, dislocation of joints of the "afflicted children" on the floor. But no. The condemned were prosecuted by the very judges who should have tested the evidence, but apparently the veracity of the children was never even questioned. A little of the seadog language of John Alden, son of John and Priscilla, might have opened some eyes, but when accused, he had the wit to escape from jail, and to be telling his friends, not the court, what he thought of being confronted by a "lot of wenches" he had never seen before, who were calling him a witch.

The drama of accusation, condemnation, execution lasted for four months. Court sessions were held in June, August and September. There were nineteen executions on Gallows Hill and one death in the open field under heavy stones, heaped on Giles Corey's chest. He had refused to speak, and for being "mute," met this almost unbelievably cruel fate. It had all been a brief chapter, measured in time, and small in total numbers, if put beside the scores of dying from other human causes in the length of a single day; but in New England history it was a story of tragedy lifetimes long, not only for the survivors of those who died, but for all the village and for all of New England so long as her history is written. A tale of human folly in a time of terror.

After the fever had cooled, it became apparent that there had been those in Salem, as well as all over the colony, who had believed in the innocence of the condemned. Testimonials had been submitted during the trials, but the judges would not consider them. There were also those who suspected the "afflicted children" of fraud and trickery, but speech in this direction was less open and confident. Cotton Mather's account of the Goodwin children was everyone's knowledge, and the Salem children were of the pastor's household. Samuel Parris was up there beside the bench taking down the testimony. In the trial sessions there appears to have been little doubt that the children were suffering, as they performed their tortures, while the WHO hurts you and WHY do you hurt these children were being asked over and over of the suspected. The presence of the five judges sitting high before the packed meetinghouse, redrobed, solemn, and their own pastor

as interrogator, was such a scene as had never been witnessed in Salem Village before, and was impressive in proportion. These judges in their panoply of office were the highest judicial authority in the colony. The drama of the scene itself offers plenteous explanation for the violence of the furor it created.

The whole episode, in the fact, in its blindness and hysteria, might have broken out in any equally self-contained and fairly remote New England village. In every detail except the speed with which it ended, it was typical and not unique. The court sat for the last time on September 17th, and on September 22nd, eight persons who had attested their innocence were executed on Gallows Hill. Eight more had been tried on September 9th and 17th, but by confessing that they were witches they saved their lives. Either to be an accuser or to confess were the two ways of safety. Confession, of course, had basic theological warrant, and was resorted to often. But not by such as Mary Easty. "I cannot, I dare not, belie my own soul," she said, and died for it.[13]

The Salem jail was full of those still awaiting trial, but by the January session that would hear them, many things had changed. The "afflicted persons" had over-reached themselves and named men and women in high places: the wife of Governor Phips, who had secured a pardon for one condemned; the Rev. Samuel Willard, one of the most outspoken against the trials and against spectral evidence, which he called "the devil's own testimony." The absurdity of such evidence, by which no one was safe anywhere, was beginning to be seen in a quite different light. Men and women, who had not dared to lift their voices in favor of the condemned, offered testimonials over their own signatures. Residents of Salem Village began to think what they had done. Godly Rebecca Nourse, aged, with a life of piety and kind deeds behind her; what had she done amiss? She had stayed away from meeting after one of the children had interrupted the pastor during prayer. Goody Cloyse, what had she done? Left the meetinghouse during the sermon on "One of you is a devil." At the trial she had fainted from either exhaustion or strain, when John Indian had said she had bitten him until the blood ran, drank it, and passed it on to others. "There is a yellow bird flying around her head," one of the children had screamed. Condemnation had followed and she had been executed. Ministers began to speak out more openly against such evidence as basis for a verdict of guilt.

When the court convened on January 3, 1692/93, it was difficult to get convictions without spectre testimony, but Chief Justice Stoughton had signed the warrant for the execution of eight more of the fifty prisoners under trial. Their graves were dug, when a messenger from Governor Phips arrived with reprieve for the eight and for three more. He also discharged all who were in jail, a number as large as the space of the jail could hold. Chief Justice Stoughton was indignant, and left the court, saying,

> We were in a way to have cleared the land of them; who is it that obstructs the cause of Justice, I know not; the Lord be merciful to the country.[14]

The "afflicted" children and young women suffered no more. They were not punished for their fraud, but Salem Village was not hospitable to them thereafter. Some of them sought oblivion elsewhere. Some changed their names in marriage. Years later Anne Putnam, leader of the children, now aged twenty-six, confessed and became a church member. As a confession, her statement is miscalled, since she did not really take the blame for what she had done, but said she was "deluded by Satan." This was on August 25, 1706, in a meeting-house packed to the doors. The Rev. Joseph Green, successor to Samuel Parris, read her statement, while she stood in her place and when he had finished, acknowledged it to be hers. Her denial of any belief in communications from the devil at the time of her deceit had its importance for her day, although to have been "deluded by the devil," as she stated, left him, in current belief, still free to delude others.[15]

One might expect that Samuel Sewall would have left some record in his *Diary* of his own change of view, but he disappoints us. The day before the Court adjourned, he noted the confession of Dorcas Hoar. "This is the first condemned person who has confess'd." The next day he spoke of five men who met at his house to discuss publishing "Some Trials of the Witches." On October 15th, he reported a discussion with "Mr. Danforth" at Cambridge, in which he said there could be no further procedure in the Court except there be "some better consent of Ministers and People."[16] The public mood was changing. On October 26th a bill was sent in calling for a "Fast and Convocation of Ministers to determine the right way as to the Witchcrafts." It failed to pass; there were twenty-nine Noes and thirty-three Yeas. Sewall's comment that the Court of Oyer and Terminer count themselves thereby dismissed was correct. On October 29th, Governor Phips said, "It must fall."

On November 22nd there is a hint of unease in his entry, as he prays that God would pardon his "Sinfull Wanderings . . . choose and assist our Judges, and vindicate the late Judges, consisting with his Justice and Holiness &c., with Fasting."[17] It is apparent in this entry that he knows he is in line for a Judgeship. On December 6th he was chosen a Justice of the Superior Court.

Four years later, when proposal for a fast was again being talked of, he recalled that when the proposal had been made in 1692, "I doe not know that ever I saw

the Council run upon with such a height of Rage before."[18] A second proposal had been made and also had failed to carry in the Council. A third attempt was made on December 11, 1696, and was concurred on December 17th. The date for the fast was set for Thursday, January 14th. A majority voted Yea. "I consent," said William Stoughton, hitherto an opposer.

This fast was held admittedly to ask God's forgiveness for what had been done about witches. This was four years after the last prisoners had been tried or freed. The proclamation mentioned specific calamities from which the province was suffering, and assumed there were specific sins for which God is angry and for which he expects forgiveness to be sought. Four years of course is a long time for any single event to hold the interest of the public, and the witchcraft trials did not, although there were few who had been old enough to share the intensity of excitement in 1692 who ever forgot that six-month panic. There was no need to remind them of the facts. After four years everything had been said and felt. Emotions had cooled long since, but everyone remembered.

From a few hints in his *Diary* and letters it is apparent that Samuel Sewall had been troubled. When on September 16th, the Governor, his Council and the Assembly had held a day of prayer in the Town-House, he wrote that Samuel Willard "spake smartly at last about the Salem Witchcrafts, and that an order had been suffer'd to come forth by Authority to ask God's pardon." There had been two deaths in Sewall's household during 1696, an abortive son on May 22nd, and little Sarah on December 23rd. She was buried on the 25th. Six of his children lay dead in the tomb. Wherein had he sinned? Was God angry with him? His thought of sin and disaster was always an equation. God kept unceasing watch over His children, punishing and rewarding them according to their deserts. Two more deaths; what did it mean? The simplicity of his reasoning seems childish indeed, but it was not his alone. It was a heritage as well as a current sermon view. He was finding the application of the text to his own life.

On December 24th, the day after little Sarah had died, Sam, his eldest son, was reading to his father in Latin, Matthew 12, 6-12. "The seventh verse did awfully bring to mind the Salem Tragedie,"[19] Sewall wrote down for the day. It was his only entry. The verse reads, "But if ye had known what this meaneth, I will have mercy, and not sacrifice, ye would not have condemned the guiltless." On the next day he wrote, "We bury our little daughter." He spent some time in the tomb, where Father and Mother Hull, Cousin Quincy, and his six children lay. He had given order that little Sarah's coffin be set at her grandmother's feet.

When the fast of Thursday, January 16th, was held, he was in his pew, and as Samuel Willard walked slowly up the aisle to the pulpit Samuel Sewall put in his hand the Bill of Contrition for his own error in the witchcraft trials. He included a copy in his *Diary,* with the heading,

> Copy of the Bill I put up on the Fast Day, giving it to Mr. Willard as he Pass'd by, and standing up as he read it, and bowing when finished; in the Afternoon.

It was a noble gesture, completely in line with the custom of the day, established for two generations. To express private joy in the birth of a child, sorrow for a death in the family, anxiety for a journey to come or thanks for one safely accomplished, this way was always open. Bills had been read almost every Sunday in nearly every meetinghouse in New England since the first one had been built. Samuel Sewall's acknowledgment of error on this occasion was a high point in personal courage, dignity and humility. The meetinghouse in which he had worshipped since his young manhood was the place in which

> To take the Blame and shame of it, asking pardon of men, and especially desiring prayers that God who has unlimited Authority, would pardon that sin and all his other sins; personal and Relative.

He did not oversay his contrition or understate the sin he acknowledged. The straight line of his simple statement must have been moving to the congregation of this Thursday fast. He was one of the leading men of Boston and known to all. One hopes that the burden in his mind and conscience for four years was eased as he sat down. At least in this statement of error he wrote the final word in the witchcraft chapter by those who had part in it. That none of the other judges took this chance makes his word no less history's than his own.

An act of penance can do nothing to right the wrong committed, but it can dignify a human life and possibly lift the man who performs it to higher ground and help him to expect more of himself. One thinks perhaps inevitably, of aging Samuel Johnson, standing with bared head for an hour on the site of the bookstall kept by his father in Uttoxeter many years before. As a sixteen-year-old boy Samuel Johnson had refused to keep the stall for a day when his father was ill, and now as an old man he had come back to the same spot, in inclement weather, and amid the jeers of bystanders "to do away with the sin of this disobedience." This was nearly a century after Samuel Sewall had been laid to sleep in the Old Granary Burying Ground. His Bill of error belongs in his life story, in his own words. Here it is.

> Samuel Sewall, sensible of the reiterated strokes of God upon himself and family; and being sensible,

that as to the Guilt contracted upon the opening of the late Commission of Oyer and Terminer at Salem (to which the order for this day relates) he is, upon many accounts, more concerned than any that he knows of, Desires to take the Blame and shame of it, asking pardon of men, And especially desiring prayers that God, who has an Unlimited Authority, would pardon that sin and all other his sins, personal and Relative; And according to his infinite Benignity, and Sovereignty, not Visit the sin of him, or of any other, upon himself or any of his, nor upon the land: But that He would powerfully defend him against all Temptations to Sin, for the future: and vouchsafe him the efficacious, saving Conduct of his Word and Spirit.[20]

To review this unhappy Salem episode in the life of a good man three centuries later calls for neither condemnation nor excuse. Both have been offered Samuel Sewall many times according to the perspective of historians who have told the story over once again. It is a story calling only for the interpretation of historical fact in the light of its own time and place, not of lifetimes later. Most men belong to their own times, and in their thinking they deserve to be understood through the overhanging ideas of that time and place, and the actions these ideas bring to pass. In no chapter of his seventy-eight years was Samuel Sewall more a seventeenth century Bostonian than in his share in the Salem Witchcraft Trials.

Notes

[1] In Plymouth's version of this law in 1671, the statute read, "If any *Christian* be a witch, ..." The insertion of the word *Christian* was intended to save the Indians who were regarded as devil worshippers.

[2] John Winthrop, *History of New England,* 2 vols., Savage edition, Boston, 1826, II, 326.

[3] *Ibid.,* I, 315, 321. Also Thomas Hutchinson, *The History of the Colony and Province of Massachusetts Bay,* 2 vols., edited by Lawrence Shaw Mayo, Harvard University Press, Cambridge, Mass., 1936, I, 160-161; II, 13.

[4] *Late Memorable Providences Relating to Witchcrafts and Possessions,* London, 1691; Hutchinson, *op. cit.,* II, 14-17.

[5] March 10, 1664. An account of these trials was printed in London in 1682.

[6] Samuel P. Fowler, *An Account of the Life, Character &c. of the Rev. Samuel Parris of Salem Village,* Salem. 1857.

[7] Charles Wentworth Upham, *Salem Witchcraft,* 2 vols., Boston, 1857, II, 85, 86. This sermon was immediately

published in London and reprinted in 1704.

[8] *Ibid.,* II, 102-103, 108. For more texts of the examinations, see also Hutchinson, *op. cit.,* II, 19-31. Other records are listed in Marion L. Starkey, *The Devil in Massachusetts,* New York, 1949, Statement of Primary Sources, pp. 301-302.

[9] *Op. cit.,* II, 107, 212.

[10] *Diary of Samuel Sewall,* Mass. Hist. Soc. Coll., Fifth Series, Boston, 1878-1882, 3 vols., Apr. 11, 1692; II, 358.

[11] *Diary,* July 30, 1692, II, 362.

[12] *Letter Book of Samuel Sewall,* Mass. Hist. Soc. Coll., Sixth Series, 1886-1888, 2 vols., July 20, 1692, I, 132.

[13] See also her "Humble Petition," Upham, *op. cit.,* II, 327-328.

[14] For a summary view from another century, see Perry Miller, *The New England Mind from Colony to Province,* Harvard University Press, Cambridge, Mass., 1953, Chap. XIII, "The judgement of the Witches," pp. 191-208.

[15] Upham, *op. cit.,* II, 509-512.

[16] *Diary,* Sept. 21, 1692, I, 365; Sept. 22, I, 367; Oct. 29, I, 368.

[17] *Ibid.,* Nov. 22, 1692, I, 369-370.

[18] *Ibid.,* Dec. 19, 1696, I, 441.

[19] *Ibid.,* Dec. 25, 1696, I, 443.

[20] *Ibid.,* Jan. 16, 1696, I, 445.

Harvey Wish (essay date 1967)

SOURCE: "Samuel Sewall and His *Diary*: An Introduction," in *The Diary of Samuel Sewall,* revised editon, G. P. Putnam's Sons, 1967, pp. 9-19.

[*In the essay below, Wish examines Sewall's Liary and maintains that, although it is important as an historical document, it is also valuable for showing "the secular side of this very human man . . . and his deep involvement in contemplation of the human condition."*]

The well-to-do Sewalls of England smoothed the path for Samuel to become a rich merchant, landowner, exporter and influential Boston magistrate. His great-grandfather, Henry, was a wealthy Coventry linendraper-merchant who had served as mayor repeatedly.

Another Henry, Samuel's father, migrated to New England in 1634, supplied with enough cattle and provisions to stock a plantation at Newbury. There young Henry Sewall married into the Dummer family, whose influential members figure prominently in the *Diary* as Boston officials. But when Henry's father-in-law complained of the climate, all returned to England in 1647. At their new home in Bishop-Stoke, in Hampshire, Samuel was born on March 28, 1652, later attending a local grammar school. After Henry returned to his Newbury plantation, the nine-year-old Samuel and his family followed on July 6, 1661.

Samuel continued his grammar school education under the erudite Dr. Thomas Parker, who had studied at Oxford and Leyden. It was Parker who shaped Samuel's lifelong interest in Biblical prophecies and speculations in the spirit of Biblical literalism. Fortunately, the Newbury environment also inspired Samuel's lifelong love of nature. Parker's preparatory school left Samuel well fitted for the orthodox atmosphere of Harvard under President Charles Chauncey during his student years of 1667-71. Sewall idealized this regime in later years when secularization was taking its toll. Closest to him among his classmates—quite literally since they shared the same bed—was the remarkable Edward Taylor, the future minister and poet, whose literary gifts remained a secret (except from Samuel who was to print his verses on solemn occasions). Only in the mid-twentieth century did a Harvard scholar discover the Taylor manuscripts and reveal their importance for Puritan literature.

Chauncey punished severely profaneness, cardplaying, and "filthy speaking." One student, as the *Diary* tells us, was punished for blasphemy by being compelled to sit alone by himself "uncovered at meals." Still the boys enjoyed many recreations that escaped condemnation—fishing, hunting, singing, some light reading as well as devotional tracts, vacations to nearby villages, the usual college pranks and, despite everything, an occasional riot. Of special interest to Samuel were Harvard's efforts, like those of Cambridge and Oxford, to stamp out the fashion of wearing long hair and wigs in the style of Cavaliers. The clear authority of the Bible (I Corinthians XI) was invoked against these fops: "Doth not even nature itself teach you that if a man have long hair, it is a shame unto him? But if a woman have long hair, it is a glory to her." This theme suggests many an entry in the *Diary.* With all his scriptural learning, it is not surprising that Sewall chose as a Master's thesis in theory, "Is Original Sin Both Sin and Punishment?" To this he answered in the affirmative. And always he deeply admired his orthodox contemporary, Michael Wigglesworth (1631-1705), the pastor-poet of Malden whose widely read *Day of Doom* supported metrically the difficult doctrine of infant damnation.

While a resident fellow at Harvard, Sewall met Hannah Hull, the only child of the wealthy Massachusetts mintmaster and colonial treasurer John Hull. Hannah had admittedly "set her affections" on Samuel and the elaborate marriage took place on February 28, 1675. For many decades, romantics have assumed that Nathaniel Hawthorne's story of the Sewall wedding, as told in *Grandfather's Chair,* is true, with its picture of John Hull determining the dowry by weighing his eighteen-year-old girl in a scale-balance with a pile of shining pine-tree shillings. Such an advantageous marriage assured the young man not only happiness, but a long step upward financially and in prestige. There was little danger now that Samuel would become a minister, as seemed to be his "calling" at first, and it was easy to foresee his future as a merchant-exporter and a member of the Boston magisterial class.

From his father-in-law, who had long shipped wheat, furs and fish abroad, Sewall learned much about international trade. From Hull also he acquired numerous accounts, exporting turpentine, fish and furs to the Caribbean and Europe and bringing back luxury goods, some intended for Hannah Sewall. But never did he share in the slave trade that was almost an integral part of the Triangular Trade between his fellow New England merchants, the West African slave traders, and the sugar planters of the West Indies. Like John Hull, he shared the old Puritan ethics that tempered the rising competitive capitalism, and politically he sympathized with the anti-Stuart views of the mercantile Whig dissenters in England. Among his enterprises were moneylending, banking, and the preparation of commercial documents—though he was never a lawyer—displaying a businesslike firmness toward borrowers while exercising philanthropy to many individuals and to causes such as the rights of Negroes and Indians.

He loved Harvard, which he served for many years on its Board of Overseers and aided by substantial gifts of land for the education of all youth, including Indians. He attended commencement ceremonies on numerous occasions, and accompanied his son Joseph to witness his oral examinations. When, in 1710, he feared that too much triviality had infected the College, he protested in a rather liberal vein to President Leverett, "The End of the College is that lovers of Learning may there meet; and be instructed, and have Sparks of Literature revived and enkindled. But this way of Faggoting discourages that and becomes an Extinguisher." While he was an investigator for the Board of Overseers into student morals, he refused to sustain the severe charges of the Comstockian pastor Cotton Mather, who insisted that he knew the boys to be reading plays, novels and "vicious pieces of poetry." Sewall noted only that there was too much drinking, visiting, and going to town on Sabbath mornings—altogether respectable vices. Yet he agreed with Increase and his son Cotton that the doctrinal decline of

Harvard required in 1701 a conservative antidote to liberalism in a new college—Yale.

Doctrinal orthodoxy was a lifelong concern of his. He even offended his Mather circle by going over to the faction that protested Increase Mather's residence near his Boston church, instead of amid his students at Harvard, where he was president. Increase was given the ultimatum of staying with the boys—actually a small enrollment—or resigning the presidency altogether, as he did. Furthermore, as a latter-day Puritan, Sewall scrutinized suspiciously President Leverett's high-church tendencies and he insisted, despite the protests of his associates, that the president revive the custom of making weekly expositions of scripture to the students.

In 1681, while operating a Boston bookshop, Sewall was appointed by the General Court to manage the Boston printing press, but he delegated the actual printing to Samuel Green, a well-known New London printer. The Sewall list reflected his Calvinist tastes, and included the first American edition of Bunyan's *Pilgrim's Progress,* as well as numerous sermons, almanacs, and scientific essays. He provided the Mathers with an assured literary outlet, though they had others, and when he admired a Mather sermon, such as "Horrid Crime of Self-Murder," he ordered it printed. Closest to Sewall's heart was the publication of John Eliot's Bible for the Indians, which reflected the Puritan hope for Indian conversion to Christianity. Not least of his publications were his own little pamphlets, such as **The Selling of Joseph,** dealing with slavery, a discussion of Indian problems, the fulfillment of Biblical prophecies, and the mystical meanings of the Book of Revelation.

Once he became a Freeman, in 1679, and manager of the Boston Press, he advanced quickly to Westfield Deputy to the General Court (1683) and membership in the colonial Council (1684). This influence must have been compounded by the marriage of Joseph Sewall to Governor Joseph Dudley's daughter, despite the uncertain course of their connubial bliss. Samuel as a judge used his official and informal influence to aid the harassed Dudley against the hostility of the Mather faction.

After Massachusetts was deprived of her charter by the Crown, Sewall went to England to assist Increase Mather to recover it, appearing before high Parliamentary leaders as well as lesser folk to argue the case for New England and to protect his own property interests. Actually the revolutionary regime of William and Mary acted solicitously for both imperial and colonial rights. Officialdom was resolved to protect Anglicans against extreme Congregationalists and to check the Boston theocracy. Conservative as he was, Sewall was no Tory, like his kinsman Governor Dudley, and he gloried in the revolution of 1688 that expelled the hated Governor Andros, even writing a pamphlet justifying Boston's revolution. While the new charter failed to give the orthodox Congregationalists their desired monopoly over the Massachusetts franchise, and even perpetuated the Church of England's "Romish" practices—which he assailed repeated in the *Diary*—the reactionary followers of Andros were replaced by more amenable friends of New England, like Governor William Phips, who even became a convert to Congregationalism.

Some of Sewall's neighbors, as he sadly noted, were greatly offended by what seemed to be his timidity in yielding so completely to the English demand for an official investigation and confirmation of land titles. Since in any frontier country it was obvious that the less said about land titles the better, such an official inquisition frightened many homeowners. Sewall's concern over such issues that involved his extensive landholdings led him to spend most of 1688-89 in England, aside from his desire to save the old charter.

Nothing hurt the prestige of the old Puritan theocracy—some have challenged this term as inapplicable to a community in which laymen carried such power—as much as the Salem witchcraft executions of 1692. Governor Phips had appointed Sewall and other special judges as "commissioners of the court of oyer and terminer" to try suspected witches. Sewall, like most judges, had no legal training and apparently he went along with the "spectral evidence" in which the acts of devils might be cited by witnesses as valid testimony. Though he was not as extreme as some of his associates, yet he felt that his personal guilt was unique and overwhelming in the decisions that sent nineteen persons to their death.

Only men of little faith doubted the existence of witches. Catholics as well as Protestants in both Europe and America did not usually question the Biblical injunction not to suffer a witch to live. Especially heavy was the guilt of the Mathers, whose pseudo-scientific writings about the invisible world accentuated pietistic curiosity about the recent infusion of witches. Increase Mather did make a belated protest against the use of spectral evidence to convict suspects, and convinced Governor Phips to suspend the executions. Some New Englanders believed that these witches were a divinely sent affliction for the laxness of the Chosen People in dealing with the heretical Quakers, who frequently invaded meetinghouses with dishevelled faces or even nudity as a sign of the wickedness of the Puritan rulers. One *Diary* item of July 8, 1677, reads as follows:

> Sabbath-Day. South-Meeting House. In Sermon-Time a female Quaker slipt in covered with a Canvas Frock, having her hair dishevelled and Loose, and powdered with Ashes resembling a flaxen or white

Perriwigg, her face as black as Ink, being led by two Quakers and followed by two more. It occasioned a great and amazing uproar.

But the *Diary* tells all too little about the celebrated Salem trials, though it relates the tragic deaths of Sewall's two children and his great contrition and open church confession of guilt based on the assumption that his acts as judge had aroused the vengeance of God. Yet it should be added that Sewall was far from a reactionary judge by contemporary standards, for he fought a strict miscegenation law, tried to moderate extreme treason laws, opposed capital punishment for counterfeiting, and felt deep pain when he had to sentence a slave. In one notable case, Judge Sewall (he was appointed a justice of the Superior Court in 1692, a judge of Probate in 1715, and chief justice of the Superior Court in 1718) rejected a master's insistence upon the letter of his contract and freed the bondsman. Readers of the *Diary* have warmed to his words in a case of 1716, "I essayed to prevent Indians and negroes being rated with horses and hogs, but could not prevail." Frequently in court he struck this theme of human equality.

Sewall expressed this concern for Negroes and Indians in his writings as well. At a time when slavery and the slave trade were respectable and Indians appeared to be the murderous wretches of the frontier, he published emphatic pamphlets in their defense. His essay *The Selling of Joseph* (1700) was the first antislavery tract in America. He united scriptural arguments for justice together with personal humane considerations. "It is most certain," he wrote, "that all men as they are the sons of Adam, are co-heirs; and have equal right unto liberty and all other outward comforts of life."

As for the Indians who destroyed so many settlements during King Philip's War (1676) and killed or carried off so many people he knew, Sewall did not conceal his deep compassion for the dispossessed tribesmen, and urged practical solutions to end the flagrant abuses practiced upon them. Too often their lands had been arbitrarily seized, their hunting guns confiscated, their fisheries damaged, and, after the war, many had been sold into slavery in the West Indies. Tame Indians survived as Christians in strictly segregated "praying villages" where they imitated unenthusiastically the Puritan inhibitions that they were taught through John Eliot's Bible and other means, especially the translations into Indian readers that Sewall provided. Sewall believed, as so many contemporaries did, that the Indians were descendants of the Ten Lost Tribes of Israel, hence their conversion was most important.

One of his major activities was serving as secretary and treasurer of the Missionary Society to the American Indians. Among his projects was the printing of a Psalter and a primer for the Indians and a new edition of the Bible in an Indian tongue. He urged the establishment of good English schools to assimilate the tribesmen to English ways and to curb drunkenness. A cherished idea of his was to set aside Indian reserves, marked off by natural boundaries, to protect their lands from white absorption. This plan, he hoped, would facilitate conversion and help to perpetuate peace, and he succeeded in persuading his fellow commissioners to purchase lands for needy Indians and to support Indian schools. But in the end, colonial greed and prejudices hampered such solutions. In one of his poems on the Indians, Sewall pleaded:

Give the poor Indians Eyes to see
The Light of Life; and set them free;
That they Religion may profess;
Denying all Ungodliness.

As a Councilor, he followed a cautious traditionalism, which aligned him with the old colonial families who were staunch Congregationalists and hostile to the aristocratic Papist Anglicanism of the King's officers. He resented the encroachments of the Stuarts and their successors upon the old charter privileges of Massachusetts. Psychologically, he built a moat around the Old South Meetinghouse where Samuel Willard and son Joseph Sewall preached their orthodox tenets. Sewall and his Calvinist friends resisted the efforts of the King's men to use the meetinghouses temporarily for Church of England services. When Puritans did share a meetinghouse with Anglicans, preaching in shifts, the Anglicans groaned over the long wait—lasting perhaps three hours—while the Calvinist divines struggled over an abstruse theological sermon.

As a merchant, an official, and a convinced economic conservative, he opposed all efforts to cheapen the rather scarce colonial currency by such devices as the issuance of large quantities of bills of credit during times of emergency. The *Diary* abounds with references to the use of miscellaneous foreign coins, such as the Spanish "pieces of eight," that supplemented English currency. In addition, he fought the legal-tender acts that would make bills of credit current for all transactions. As a creditor, involved in both mercantile transactions and loans, he had no sympathy for inflation and pointed out the disasters that had always followed the depreciation of currency.

Unlike his *Letter Book,* which is mainly concerned with affairs of trade, his *Diary* gives a strong if exaggerated impression that the man was ever concerned with prayers and religious speculations. Yet there is no doubt that Sewall was outraged by the smallest evidence of alleged Papist infiltrations by England's officials or garrison soldiers, and by the practices of Boston's Anglican institutions, such as the new King's Chapel. He notes occasionally the divine mission of the Puritans and their city on a hill that had to be kept pure of popery. The *Diary* is filled with adverse references to the use of the Cross in the colors of the Royal Governor, the increasing appearance of the Book of Common Prayer brought by the Anglicans, and the taking of oaths by kissing the Bible—an idolatrous act—instead of merely laying on hands. He apparently took special satisfaction in his annual entry on December 25 to point out how completely the Bostonians were ignoring Christmas, with its pagan connotations, by carrying on their daily tasks as on weekdays. Like Governor William Bradford of Plymouth, he regarded Christmas as an idler's holiday as well as a pagan festival.

Sewall disliked the anti-Puritan revelry of the Redcoats—their bloody duels; their violation of the Sabbath by drums and other noisy instruments; their boisterous stage spectacles; and their noisy diversions on midweek lecture days, which ranked next to Sunday as a holy day. He took a grim pleasure in recounting with disapproval the sharp increase in periwigs, the drinking of toasts, and Church of England services and rituals. He refused to sell land for Episcopalian churches, and led his fellow Congregationalists in Council in denying Governor Andros the use of the Town House for Anglican services, much to the anger of the King's men. Sewall saw the evils of the Restoration reflected in a general laxity of morals, drunkenness, cursing, street brawls, and even such old English customs as dancing around a maypole (recalling the scandal of Merrymount in Bradford's day).

Ever consistent in applying the standards of a Puritan, he criticized his own shortcomings as a Calvinist. "I pray'd this noon," he recorded on October 25, 1691, "that God would give me a pardon of my Sins under the Broad Seal of Heaven." He leaned hopefully upon the Covenant theology that conceded that God was absolute but not arbitrary since he had bound himself under a code—the Covenant of Grace—and no personal sins could outweigh the Savior's merits. His obsession with death was extreme, even by ascetic Puritan standards, suggesting neuroticism, and perhaps accounting for the hysterics that shook his children at the contemplation of death. He may have been partly motivated to record so many funerals because of their dramatic pageantry, but the contemplation of dread illnesses and man's short span was never far from his consciousnesses. Funerals also afforded him an occasion for writing a verse or two and attaching elegies to the coffin, printed copies of which were distributed by bookstores and country hawkers.

His contemporaries shared some of Sewall's fears, and would not have been surprised to learn that his diary recorded so many cases of fatal smallpox, as well as recoveries, even far from Boston. (Cotton Mather, his younger contemporary, has won favor in the eyes of modern historians for his courageous efforts to popularize the new practice of inoculation at a time when Boston mobs condemned its high rate of fatalities as murder.)

No abridgment of the *Diary* can conceal the intensive human interest in Sewall's courtship of the middle-aged widows Winthrop, Dennison, Tilley and Gibbs, which followed the death of Hannah Sewall after forty-four years of married life. Understandably, this December courtship was based on practical considerations, such as advantageous property settlements and the style in which Sewall proposed to live: e.g., would he purchase a carriage? Yet Sewall was too tender an individual to pursue callously the aim of remarriage without affection. Some modern readers may smile at Sewall's meticulous purchase list of chocolates, dates and other gifts with which he tried to soften the mind of an undecided widow, and others may be shocked to note how realistic he could be in frankly assessing the motives of both sides. But in Sewall's day it did not seem vulgar to retail careless personal habits, ailments, symptoms, and conjugal reactions as he did when his bride displayed alarming symptoms of a serious disease on their wedding night.

In evaluating Sewall's *Diary,* especially important is the wealth of social history that can be gleaned from it. At times, it seems as if no event in that Boston of 6,000 persons escaped Sewall's attention, though the doings of his own household are best told. Evidently he greatly enjoyed the family picnics, the lavish dinners, the sleigh rides, the cheerful Harvard commencement exercises, the various Thanksgivings and days of atonement, and the semifestive activities of the militia, of which he was a distinguished officer. At times, it is true, he had the Puritan habit of magnifying trivia and accidents into signs of divine intentions. On such occasions, he was apt to insert a host of Biblical citations (which are often omitted in this abridged edition); and he speculates upon the danger of divine retribution for the real or fancied failings of the Chosen People.

But the secular side of this very human man also emerges clearly, with its remarkable freedom from rationalization concerning his own defects and his deep involvement in contemplation of the human condition. . . .

M. Hasley Thomas

SOURCE: *The Diary of Samuel Sewall, Vol. I,* Farrar, Straus and Giroux, 1973, 612 p.

[*Here, Thomas examines Sewall's* Diary *and assesses the "scantiness of his record of the witchcraft episode."*]

Samuel Sewall, recent graduate and teaching fellow of Harvard College, began to keep a diary towards the end of 1673. His last entries were made fifty-six years later, three months before his death. Diary-keeping was common among the Puritans, and hundreds of these records have survived. Most of them are bare and factual, or documents of spiritual self-analysis, but Sewall set down the fullest existing record of how life was lived in his time, and it can read for pleasure after three centuries because he wrote of so much that interests us today. Nearly all the Puritan diaries were honest: under the eye of an all-seeing and all-knowing God it was useless to try to cheat. The idea of creating a favorable image of himself probably never occurred to Sewall; diaries of that sort came with more sophisticated times. Neither is it likely that Sewall ever envisioned publication, since no diary was printed until John Evelyn's appeared in 1818. Sewall undoubtedly kept his diary locked up, along with his business records, but its existence was no secret. Because of his devotion to record-keeping, more details and facts of his life are preserved than for most of his contemporaries, and we have nearly everything, even his weight. In fact, Sewall revealed himself so fully that those who have undertaken biographies have usually disclosed more about themselves than about him.

Sewall's diary meets the test of a good diary or book of memoirs of any period: he knew and had continuing and far from casual contacts with all the notable people of his place and time. For several decades Sewall was an important figure in Massachusetts-Bay, a man entrusted with numerous public offices, a man of wealth, and a member of the *in*-group. Though he lived in a small town and was conversant with all of its goings-on, lawful and otherwise, both as a recipient of gossip and officially in his capacity as magistrate, Sewall was by no means a small-town person. Throughout the diary there are constant references to the happenings of the great world. Every time a ship came into port Sewall eagerly received the corantos and gazettes with the news of the home and foreign countries, and lost no opportunities to question the captains and passengers. When a newspaper was finally established in Boston in 1704, he preserved his copies, annotated them, made rough indexes, and had them bound.

Boston was in its thirtieth year when Sewall landed there as a boy, and it was certainly the most learned and cultivated frontier town in history. He was raised in Newbury, however, and did not become a resident until his marriage in 1676. Exact figures on population are not available, and the estimates vary, but at no point in Sewall's lifetime did Boston exceed the present population of Plymouth, Massachusetts, or the borough of Princeton, New Jersey: some 13,000.

It is impossible not to be impressed with the many-sidedness of Samuel Sewall. He was a man of learning, full of the scholastic-cum-Renaissance lore discussed at length by Professor Morison in *Harvard College in the Seventeenth Century*. He was a linguist, retaining his mastery of Latin, Greek, and Hebrew throughout his life, and he wrote English with the exactitude of those trained in these languages. He never lost his interest in theology from college days, he liked nothing better than a good discussion with learned clerical friends, and he kept abreast of the subject as new books came out. When he was public printer in Boston he went so far as to learn to set type himself. As a merchant and private banker and landowner, the evidence is that he was efficient and businesslike, and in the tradition of Boston men of wealth and trustees, he held on to his money. Like businessmen from that day to this, he endeavored to get along with everyone, even if it meant appeasing Increase Mather on one occasion with a haunch of venison. As to his service as Councillor, it is only necessary to point out that he was re-elected annually thirty-three times without interruption. In a day when lawyers were forbidden or regarded with suspicion, and the requisite qualifications for judges were integrity, biblical knowledge, familiarity with the *Laws and Liberties* and subsequent statutes, plus *Coke upon Littleton* and books of procedure, Sewall was respected and well-informed and seems to have given entire satisfaction as justice and later chief justice of the Superior Court of Judicature. On the basis of the few surviving records, Emory Washburn felt that Sewall must have been altogether better read in the principles of the common law than any other judge upon the bench. Of his conscientiousness as a rider of the circuit, there can be no question; whatever the weather or conditions of travel, Sewall almost never missed one of his stated journeys. He enjoyed such music as was available to him, he served many years as precentor at the South Church, and when his failings obliged him to give up the office, he did so with regret. Concerning Sewall's literary efforts, his Latin and English poetry, his books and his tracts, this editor, lacking the recondite qualifications, offers no opinion.

Modern commentators have written of the monotony of Boston life in Sewall's time. That life might seem dull to those accustomed to the rat-race of the present day, but it is wrong to project the feeling. Sewall and his contemporaries were all busy people, and the Boston peninsula was a beehive of activity six days of the week. Sewall held so many jobs and had so many interests that he could hardly have spent a day of boredom in his adult life. Cotton Mather could not have found life monotonous when he was writing 468 books and pamphlets, battling Satan every day, preaching four hours every Sabbath, and sending off communications to the Royal Society; his time was so occupied that he had to put up, where his callers could see it, probably the earliest office sign on record: BE BRIEF Craftsmen led infinitely less monotonous lives than their counterparts today, since they began with raw materials and wrought them through all the stages to completion, whether the result was a pair of shoes, a house still standing and sound after three centuries, or a silver tankard or a chest of drawers highly treasured today. Life was anything but monotonous for the female population, who were given definite household duties as soon as they could amble about the kitchen, and had few dull moments after marriage, when they were producing and raising a dozen children and managing a household.

Sewall's diary entries relate to the days stated, although they may have been written up later; he was never without an interleaved almanac for immediate memoranda, particularly on his frequent journeys. He often skipped a day, sometimes months, in his record, and many times he failed to mention events of importance upon which we could reasonably expect his comment. Some of Sewall's omissions were inadvertent; this busy man just did not get around to making entries. Some omissions were unquestionably things he did not care to write about: if he had written as fully and frankly about the witchcraft trials as he did about other matters, it would be a record of the highest importance. We cannot avoid the feeling that he was dubious about the whole sorry business at the time, and he was the only one who publicly recanted his part in it, but then, there are the harsh words about his college-mate, George Burroughs. Because the happenings of his time and place were so fully recorded by others it has not been difficult to amplify Sewall's accounts———

> *April 11ᵗʰ 1692.* Went to Salem, where, in the Meeting-house, the persons accused of Witchcraft were examined; was a very great Assembly; 'twas awfull to see how the afflicted persons were agitated. Mr. Noyes pray'd at the beginning, and Mr. Higginson concluded. [*In the margin*], Væ, Væ, Væ, Witchcraft.

This is Sewall's first mention of the Salem witchcraft affair. Examinations of those accused or suspected had been going on for several weeks before the local magistrates, and many had been committed to jail. On this occasion the deputy governor, Thomas Danforth, and six members of his council were present: James Russell, John Hathorne, Isaac Addington, Samuel Appleton, Sewall, and Jonathan Corwin. The record is printed in Thomas Hutchinson's History of Massachusetts-Bay (1936), II, 21-23, and there is an account in Charles Wentworth Upham's Salem Witchcraft (1867), II, 101-113. John Proctor, his wife Elizabeth, and Sarah Cloyse were examined by Samuel Parris, and testimony was taken in all seriousness from the "afflicted"—the young girls whose wild imaginations, hysterical antics, and screaming fits had precipitated the delusion. Sewall's comment here is the reaction of a sensitive man who took the proceedings at their face value.

One of the major disappointments of the Sewall diary is the scantiness of his record of the witchcraft episode. Some diarists omit disagreeable occurrences from their pages, and Sewall's omissions may be accounted for by the revulsion of feelings of a man of warmth and kindness, and by doubts about the affair, doubts which ripened by the time of his recantation in 1697. Of Sewall's belief in witchcraft there can be no doubt: he was a man of his time, and the learned and the ignorant of 1692 no more questioned the existence of witchcraft than we question the passage of radio waves through the air today.

In the dismal and interminable winter of 1691-92, a group of bored teenage girls, and younger—the daughters, relatives, and neighbors of the Rev. Samuel Parris of Salem Village (now Danvers)—idled often in the kitchen of the parsonage to listen to the tales of Tituba, the half-Carib, half-Negro slave, and to learn voodoo tricks and spells from her. Before many of these forbidden gatherings had taken place they had worked themselves up into mass hysteria, and would put on an act of screaming, writhing, and swooning whenever there was an audience. The parents, the clergy, the doctors, had only one explanation: the girls were possessed. Next the girls accused various crones of bewitching them and torturing them by spectral means. A special court was convened in Salem to deal with this outbreak. Feeling their power as the venerable judges attended in all seriousness to their rantings, the girls went on to accuse scores of persons, some on the basis of family and church feuds which they heard about at home, and before the summer was over nineteen of the convicted had died on the gallows.

Salem and its environs, and indeed New England, were in a state of malaise at this time: the colony charter had been revoked, the Phips expedition had resulted in death, failure, and debt; from the frontier settlements constantly came news of fresh horrors perpetrated by the Indians; there were broken families, homeless children, footloose ex-soldiers. The stress and social disorganization finally produced a community hysteria which found its catharsis in the witch trials and executions.

Belief in witchcraft was once universal in western society, and is not totally unknown today. The English settlers carried it to the new world with the rest of their intellectual baggage. Church and civil law followed the biblical injunction that a witch must not be suffered to live (Exodus xxii, 18). Prior to 1692 there had been six executions for witchcraft in Massachusetts. In the seventeenth century in England the number is estimated in the hundreds; in Scotland the figure is 3,400 between 1580 and 1680; on the Continent, where a complicated and systematized doctrine formed the basis for inquisitorial proceedings, the victims from the fourteenth to the seventeenth century are reckoned at half a million. Most of these were burned; no witches were burned in English America—————

> *May 24th 1692.* First general Council, Saltonstall, Major Gedny, Walley, Hutchinson, Lothrop, Alcot, Sewall took their Oaths together, presently after Major Appleton took his. Justices of the Peace were nominated for the Province.

One of the first matters to come to the attention of the new governor was the witchcraft affair; already about a hundred of the accused were in jail awaiting trial. The Governor's Council met for the first time 24 May, as Sewall recorded. The next day Phips instituted a Court of Oyer and Terminer "to enquire, hear and determine all manner of crimes and offenses perpetrated within the counties of Suffolk, Essex and Middlesex . . ." The commissioners were William Stoughton (Harvard 1650), the lieutenant-governor, who presided; John Richards, Nathaniel Saltonstall (Harvard 1659). Wait Still Winthrop (Harvard ex-1662), Bartholomew Gedney, Samuel Sewall (Harvard 1671), John Hathorne, and Peter Sergeant, or any five of them. Saltonstall soon retired and was succeeded by Jonathan Corwin. The clerk was Sewall's brother Stephen. The court, sitting in the town house at Salem, met 2 June. Bridget Bishop was tried, convicted, and sentenced; she was hanged 10 June. On the 30th of June the court sat again, according to adjournment. Sarah Good, Elizabeth How, Sarah, the wife of John Wilds; Susanna Martin, and Rebecca Nurse were tried, convicted, and sentenced; they were executed 19 July—————

The Court of Oyer and Terminer sat 5 August and six were tried, convicted, and sentenced: Rev. George Burroughs (Harvard 1670), John Proctor and his wife Elizabeth; George Jacobs Sr., John Willard, and Martha Carrier. Thirty-five residents of Ipswich, headed by Rev. John Wise, sent a petition to the Court of Assistants at Boston, certifying the unblemished character of John Proctor and his wife, and twenty neighbors of Salem Village testified in their behalf; these actions saved the life of Elizabeth Proctor, who was enciente, but the other five were executed 19 August. Sewall made a record of this execution—————

> *Augt. 19th 1692.* This day the Lieut. Governor, Major Phillips, Mr. Russel, Capt. Lynde and my self went to Watertown. Advis'd the Inhabitants at their Town-Meeting to settle a Minister; and if could not otherwise agree, should first have a Town-Meeting to decide where the Meetinghouse should be set. Many say Whitney's Hill would be a convenient place.

> This day [*in the margin,* Dolefull! Witchcraft] George Burrough, John Willard, Jn° Procter, Martha Carrier and George Jacobs were executed at Salem, a very great number of Spectators being present.

Mr. Cotton Mather was there, Mr. Sims, Hale, Noyes, Chiever, &c. All of them said they were innocent, Carrier and all. Mr. Mather says they all died by a Righteous Sentence. Mr. Burrough by his Speech, Prayer, protestation of his Innocence, did much move unthinking persons, which occasions their speaking hardly concerning his being executed————

The special Court of Oyer and Terminer met again the 9th and 17th of September. On the first day six were tried, convicted, and sentenced, and on the second day nine were condemned. Of this number, eight were hanged 22 September on Gallows Hill: Martha, wife of Giles Corey; Mary Easty, Alice Parker, Mary Parker, Ann Pudeator, Willmot Reed, Margaret Scott, and Samuel Wardwell. There were no further executions for witchcraft————

Wish praises the underlying unity of Sewall's *Diary*:

The famous 56-year diary of Samuel Sewall, which contains entries from December 3, 1673, to October 13, 1729, except for an unexplained gap for 1677-84, is easily the most remarkable American personal account of its time—the era of the Salem witchcraft trials, the seizure of Captain Kidd, the brutality of King Philip's War, and the struggles of old-line Puritans like Sewall and the Mathers against Anglican imperial officials. There were in contemporary England more literary and frankly sensuous diaries; best known is that of Samuel Pepys, reflecting the bawdiness of the Restoration, and posterity has also prized the informative, if less intimate, diary of John Evelyn, the devout pro-Royalist Anglican. Unlike Pepys or Evelyn, Samuel Sewall liked to commune with himself and God, jotting down briefly both daily events and hurried impressions. Despite the scattered nature of this record, the reader soon discovers an underlying unity depicting the mood of the man and his times. . . .

Harvey Wish, preface to The Diary of Samuel Sewall, *L. P. Putnam's Sons, 1967.*

Steven E. Kagle (essay date 1979)

SOURCE: "Life Diaries," in *American Diary Literature: 1620-1799*, Twayne Publishers, 1979, pp. 142-82.

[*In the following excerpt, Kagle assesses the merit of Sewall's* Diary *as a work of literature.*]

. . . In discussing diary literature, especially American diary literature, it is frequently necessary to assert that the form and its individual works have been neglect-

ed. However, in the case of Sewall's diary we encounter a rare exception, a diary that has acquired a widespread reputation for excellence. Several respected critics have declared it to be one of the best diaries written in English, and no less a diary scholar than William Matthews has called it "probably the best American diary."[5] It would be a great comfort to accept the support of critical opinion; but, unfortunately, while I find much of value in Sewall's diary, I cannot endorse the widely accepted claim of its preeminent position.

The reason for this judgment is not so much a disagreement about the nature of the diary as it is a problem of criteria. In this volume I have asserted the primacy of intrinsic literary merit, and I have attempted to place the quality and unity of style, subject, and structure as the crucial determinants of that merit. Sewall's diary truly excels in the quality of its subject, but it is weaker in the other areas than its reputation would lead one to expect.

In the introduction to his excellent edition of Sewall's diary, Mr. Halsey Thomas wrote:

> Sewall's diary meets the test of a good diary or book of memoirs of any period: he knew and had continuing and far from casual contacts with all the notable people of his place and time. For several decades Sewall was an important figure in Massachusetts Bay, a man entrusted with numerous public offices, a man of wealth, and a member of the *in*-group. Though he lived in a small town and was conversant with all of its goings-on, lawful and otherwise, both as a recipient of gossip and officially in his capacity as magistrate, Sewall was by no means a small-town person. Throughout the diary there are constant references to the happenings of the great world. Every time a ship came into port Sewall eagerly received the corantos and gazettes with the news of the home and foreign countries, and lost no opportunities to question the captains and passengers. When a newspaper was finally established in Boston in 1704, he preserved his copies, annotated them, made rough indexes, and had them bound.[6]

This interest in and access to vital events can, and in the case of Sewall's work did, make a valuable diary; however, such content cannot by itself make a literarily valuable diary. Sewall's diary does not sufficiently impose or reveal a unity of event or character to supply a highly coherent pattern, and its style, though readable, has no special merit. Therefore, while Sewall's diary excels in several respects, an assessment of its merit as a work of literature must be more moderate.

One of the obstacles to such merit is the length of the period covered as compared to the amount of material written. In comparison with Pepys's diary, with which it is sometimes compared, Sewall's work attempted to cover fifty-six years in a fraction of the space that Pepys's covered ten. If Sewall's diary had been limited in focus, this situation might not have posed so great a problem. However, the very breadth of Sewall's interest, which produced so many items of value, fragmented the work as a whole. As a result, an appreciation of the diary depends on a sensitivity to the vitality of the society which Sewall revealed, rather than to any artistic control. Even some of the more coherent sets of entries depend for their full meaning on the reader's ability to link them to the general context of events in the diary.

Most anthologists have done an adequate job of portraying the strong points of Sewall's work, but because they cannot devote enough space to the context, they often give a distorted picture of the work as a whole. As an example, let us consider Sewall's recantation of his part in the Salem witchcraft trials included in the following entry:

> Copy of the Bill I put up on the Fast day; giving it to Mr. Willard as he pass'd by, and standing up at the reading of it, and bowing when finished; in the Afternoon.

> Samuel Sewall, sensible of the reiterated strokes of God upon himself and family; and being sensible, that as to the Guilt contracted, upon the opening of the late Commission of Oyer and Terminer at Salem (to which the order for this Day relates) he is, upon many accounts, more concerned than any that he knows of, Desires to take the Blame and Shame of it, Asking pardon of Men, And especially desiring prayers that God, who has an Unlimited Authority, would pardon that Sin and all other his Sins; personal and Relative: And according to his infinite Benignity, and Soveraignty, Not Visit the Sin of him, or of any other, upon himself or any of his, nor upon the Land: But that He would powerfully defend him against all Temptations to Sin, for the future; and vouchsafe him the Efficacious, Saving Conduct of his Word and Spirit. (pp. 366-67)

As readers of a diary we will be more concerned with the "reiterated strokes of God" than with the historically more significant witch trials. Sewall spent little time in the diary on the witch trials or on his decision to repent of them, but the diary is full of comments on the sufferings of his family and himself which he interpreted as divine warning or punishment. In the section just preceding the above entry Sewall wrote:

> Mr. Willard had the Meeting at his house to day, but We had no Invitation to be there as is usual.

On the 22th of May I buried my abortive son; so neither of us were then admitted of God to be there, and now the Owners of the family admit us not: It may be I must never more hear a Sermon there. The Lord pardon all my Sins of Omission and Commission: and by his Almighty power make me meet to be partaker of the Inheritance with the S^ts in Light. *Secund-day Jany 11, 169681/7* God helped me to pray more than ordinarily, that He would make up our Loss in the burial of our little daughter and other children, and that would give us a Child to Serve Him, pleading with Him as the Institutor of Marriage, and the Author of every good work. (p. 366)

To ignore either Sewall's concern about his ostracism from the Reverend Willard's meetings on earth or from God's "spiritual" church (symbolized by the misfortunes of his family) is to miss not only the full meaning of his bill of guilt, but also the dual nature of the diarist himself. Although Sewall's professions of lawyer and judge are today clearly secular, such was not the case in the late seventeenth century. Those accused of witchcraft in Salem were tried by laymen, not clergymen; those accused of civil offenses might be condemned from the pulpit.

For Sewall, spiritual forces acted in this world and had to be considered seriously. In one entry he noted having heard Increase Mather preaching "from Rev. 22. 16—bright and morning Star" and mentioning a "Sign in the Heaven," and that the following evening he "saw a large Cometical Blaze, someting fine and dim, pointing from the Westward, a little below Orion" (p. 462). The imputation was that these events were linked by more than coincidence. Even Sewall's dreams were treated as divine messages which should be recorded in the diary so that their message might be better understood. Like Winthrop, Sewall could see a theological lesson in a news item such as the following:

> Crabtree, a middle-aged woman, through some displeasure at her Son whom she beat, sat not down to Supper with her Husband and a Stranger at Table: when they had done, she took away, and in the Room where she set it, took a piece of grisly meat of a Shoulder of Mutton into her mouth which got into the top of the Larynx and stopt it fast, so she was presently choak'd. Tho. Pemberton and others found it so when they opened her Throat. She gave a stamp with her foot and put her finger in her mouth . . . and [she] di'd immediately. What need have all to Acknowledge God in whose Hand their breath is, &c. (p. 287)

One of the most unified sections of the diary is that covering Sewall's courtship period after the sudden death of his second wife. The common topic and cast of characters hold the group of entries together, but even here a full understanding of the group depends on an appreciation of diverse and often distant entries in the diary. For example, in their material on Sewall many anthologists include and literary historians cite entries in which Sewall carefully recorded giving a prospective bride "about 1/2 pounds of Sugar Almonds cost 3ˢ per £" (p. 965), or dickering about whether it would cost £40 or £100 a year to maintain a coach for her. Such passages make Sewall seem mercenary and devoid of romantic sentiment; however, there are other entries in which he wrote of his "flood of tears" at the death of his first wife (p. 864) or the way his "bowels yern towards" a woman who had rejected his suit (p. 911). Moreover, the reader of the whole diary will be aware that even eleven years and two marriages later Sewall could write of being "much affected" when he realized that it was "the same day of the week and Moneth that the Wife of my youth expired" (p. 1063). Such an understated assertion helps to put the courtship entries in a different light. Sewall the character is no longer seen as a comic fool, and Sewall the diarist can be given credit for recognizing the elements of humanity.

Another complex self-portrait emerges from a set of entries dealing with his conflict with Ebenezer Pemberton, then minister of the South Church. Sewall and Pemberton had argued before, but probably never with such emotion as was recorded in the diary for November 28, 1710. Pemberton began an attack in Sewall's own house, first with mocking sarcasm and then with open accusations of judicial favoritism:

> Mr. Pemberton quickly begun to say, What you have been holding a Court to day! Had it over again; I was a little amus'd at the word Court; however, I began to relate what had been done. Mr. Pemberton with extraordinary Vehemency said, (capering with his feet) If the Mathers order'd it, I would shoot him thorow. I told him he was in a passion. He said he was not in a Passion. I said, it was so much the worse. He said the Fire from the Altar was equal impartial. Upbraiding me, very plainly, as I understood, it with Partiality. The President said, The Governour was barbarously Treated (meaning Dr. Cotton Mather's Letter to his Excellency). I answered; That was put to the Council. Mr. Mayhew told me afterward, that I said his Carriage was neither becoming a Scholar nor Minister. The Truth is I was surpris'd to see my self insulted with such extraordinary Fierceness, by my Pastor, just when I had been vindicating two worthy Embassadors of Christ (his own usual Phrase) from most villanous Libels. (p. 646)

There, walking to dinner, Pemberton resumed his attack, revealing the imagined injustice that prompted it:

> In the Way Mr. Pemberton charg'd me again, I

was griev'd and said, What in the Street! He answer'd, No body hears. But Mr. Sergeant heard so much, that he turn'd back to still us. Mr. Pemberton told me that Capt. Martin, the Commadore, had abus'd him, yet I took no notice of it: I answer'd, you never laid it before me. He said, You knew it. I said, I knew it not. (For every Rumor is not ground sufficient for a Justice of Peace to proceed upon; and Mr. Pemberton never spake word of it to me before). He said Capt. Martin call'd him Rascal in the Street, and said had it not been for his coat, he would have can'd him. Mr. Pemberton said I excluded him, or he was excluded from Dining with the Superiour Court by the Invitation of Capt. Martin. (p. 646)

Sewall's crime in defending the Mathers against slander is here shown to be his failure to similarly defend Pemberton. Sewall's logical and judicial explanations were ignored, and Pemberton compounded his assault by having part of the Fifty-eighth Psalm sung in church the next Sunday, including the following verses:

> Speak, O ye Judges of the Earth
> 　if just your Sentence be:
> Or must not Innocence appeal
> 　to Heav'n from your Decree?
> Your wicked Hearts and Judgments are
> 　alike by Malice sway'd;
> Your griping Hands, by weighty Bribes,
> 　to Violence betrayed.
> To Virtue, strangers from the Womb
> 　their Infant Steps went wrong:
> They prattled Slander, and in Lyes
> 　employ'd their lisping Tongue.
>
> 　　　　　　　　　(p. 648n)

To this Sewall replied in the diary, "Tis certain, one may make Libels of David's Psalms; and if a person be abused, there is no Remedy: I desire to leave it to GOD who can and will Judge Righteously" (p. 649).

This was not the only incident in which Pemberton showed his hostility toward Sewall; yet, when finally Pemberton was on his deathbed it was Sewall he called for to be with him, speak to him, and to clasp his hand (p. 845). Such episodes are important to any assessment of Sewall's character.

As the product of such complex and far-reaching chains of entries, Sewall's is not an easy diary to grasp, but it will eventually yield its value to a persistent reader. It is clearly worth the effort, for even if the work is not the almost unequalled masterpiece it has often been considered to be, it is still a very fine diary. . . .

Notes

. . . [5] William Mathews, *American Diaries, An Annotated Bibliography of American Diaries Written Prior to the Year 1861* (Berkeley, 1945), p. 7.

[6] Samuel Sewall, *The Diary of Samuel Sewall,* ed. Halsey Thomas (New York, 1973), pp. v-vi. Hereafter all references to this work are from this edition and appear in parentheses in the text. . . .

FURTHER READING

Biography

Tiffany, Nina Moore. *Samuel E. Sewall: A Memoir.* Boston: Houghton, Mifflin and Company, 1898, 175 p.
     Standard biography of Sewall.

Criticism

Bailyn, Bernard. "The Merchant Group at the End of the Seventeenth Century." In *The New England Merchants in the Seventeenth Century*, pp. 168-200. Cambridge: Harvard University Press, 1955.
     Examines Sewall's role as a Bostonian merchant in the seventeenth century.

Hall, David D. "The Mental World of Samuel Sewall." In his *Worlds of Wonder, Days of Judgment: Popular Religious Belief in Early New England,* pp. 211-99. New York: Alfred A. Knopf, 1989.
     Thorough, scholarly discussion in which Hall emphasizes the unity of Sewall's *Diary.*

Murdock, Kenneth B. "The Personal Literature of the Puritans," in *Literature & Theology in Colonial New England,* pp. 99-136. Cambridge, Mass.: Harvard University Press, 1949.
     Discusses Sewall's *Diary,* contending that it contains "Both the confessional and the spiritual bookkeeping of a tormented soul in account with God."

Winship, George Parker. "Samuel Sewall and the New England Company." *Proceedings of the Massachusetts Historical Society* LXVII (October, 1941-May, 1944): 55-77.
     Discusses a manuscript which Sewall used in connection with his duties as active commissioner for the New England Company.

Additional coverage of Sewall's life and career is contained in the following source published by Gale Research: *Dictionary of Literary Biography,* Vol. 24.

WILLIAM STOUGHTON (1631?-1701)

INTRODUCTION

English-born American minister, politician, and jurist.

Stoughton, who is thought to have been born in England between the years 1631 and 1637, was a minister and political leader in New England. He is best known for his role as Chief Justice in the Salem witch trials. Stoughton was appointed to the Court of Oyer and Terminer, which was created in 1692 by Governor William Phips in order to deal with the rising witch hysteria. The trials which Stoughton presided over resulted in the execution of nineteen accused witches. Widely respected in his own time, Stoughton is remembered today as a notoriously stern and remorseless judge.

Stoughton studied divinity at Harvard College and received a master's degree at New College, Oxford, in 1653. He preached in Sussex and Dorchester, and is credited with writing *New England's True Interest* (1670), one of the most important jeremiads of the seventeenth century. After turning down a permanent position as a minister at both Dorchester and nent position as a minister at both Dorchester and Cambridge, Stoughton devoted the rest of his life to politics. He served as lieutenant governor and chief justice of Massachusetts from 1692 until shortly before his death. He became acting governor of Massachusetts in 1694, a post he served until his death in 1701.

PRINCIPAL WORKS

New England's True Interest; Not to Lie: Or, A Treatise declaring from the Word of Truth the Terms on which we stand, and the Tenure by which we hold our hitherto-continued Precious and Pleasant Things... (sermon) 1670

CRITICISM

Enders A. Robinson (essay date 1991)

SOURCE: "William Stoughton," in *The Devil Discovered: Salem Witchcraft 1692,* Hippocrene Books, 1991, pp. 19-36.

[*In the essay below, Robinson discusses the political conditions surrounding Stoughton's rise to power.*]

. . . In the decades of the 1620s and 1630s Massachusetts was settled as a Puritan commonwealth. Thousands of people, dissatisfied with conditions in England, flocked to the New England shore. The controlling minority of these immigrants were Puritans, who came because they were unable to express their religious sentiments in England. But the majority simply sought to escape the rigidity of the English class system and to build better lives for themselves in the New World. Virtually all were hard-working members of the emerging middle class. A new class system emerged, one in which priority of settlement and accumulated wealth played the greatest roles.

The Puritans held to the premise that everyone was a sinner. They believed that a regenerate (*born again*) person could become a *visible saint* by entering into a *covenant of grace,* a legal compact with God. They also believed that an entire nation could enter into such a covenant. The two covenants, personal and public, though branches of the same, were treated as distinct entities, Saints could dwell alone without a pledged society; a society could achieve this honor even though most of its citizens were not gracious. The doctrine of a national covenant allowed the rulers of New England to believe that they were the chosen people of God, even as the people of Israel in the Old Testament.

The government of Massachusetts, a theocracy, was based on the charter of the Massachusetts Bay Company. The charter was the very foundation of their Bible state. Upon it was based the right to government by God's elect, the right to exclude *error,* and the right to the established Congregational church.[14]

The Puritan, or Congregational, church, was comprised of individual, self-governing groups called congregations. The church in Salem was the first congregation in America. The members of each congregation elected their own minister; there were no bishops or other authorities to govern over them.

The only way to become a *church member* was to be elected by the members of a congregation. Anyone desiring admission had to first satisfy the minister and the elders that he or she was qualified, and then answer searching questions by the members on the floor of the meeting house. The church members were the visible saints of the Puritans. Only a select few were found worthy enough to attain this status. Significantly these were generally drawn from the middle and upper classes of Puritan society. Poor people, the large majority in New England, had little chance of ever becoming church members.

By limiting church membership to visible saints, the Puritan Church pretended to such excellence as the world had not witnessed since the time of Christ and the Apostles. Might this mean that other citizens had the right to worship in the church of their choice? Hardly! The Congregational church was the only legal church in New England, and by law all citizens were required to attend. Everyone, including children, was supposed to go to Sunday services, one in the morning and another in the afternoon, and a Thursday afternoon service as well. Each service was two or three hours long. However, in 1692 the seating capacity of all the churches in Boston would accommodate only about one-third of the population. Clearly, many in New England never entered a church, at least not on a regular basis.

The essence of the *congregational way* was the autonomous church, founded on the covenant of grace and limited to a few visible saints. This structure deliberately excluded most townspeople, who had both to submit to the rule of the *righteous* few, and to pay taxes for its support. Presbyterians in Britain denounced the Puritan covenant as an artificial notion, predicting civil war in any society that dared to unchurch the majority. Soon the debate was joined by Calvinists in Europe, who were alarmed at what appeared as the most sinister tendency of the Congregational church, *perfectionism.* Calvinists accepted regeneration as a genuine experience, but would not allow any person, even the most devout minister, to say to another, "You are infallibly elected."

Only male congregational members, the so-called freemen, were allowed to vote in political elections. The clergy, through their influence on church membership, were thus able to keep a tight control on the elected government. During the first great exodus to New England in the 1630's about 20 percent of the population were church members; by 1692 less than 4 percent of the much greater population held this status.[15] All others were disenfranchised; they could neither vote nor serve in other official capacities, such as jurors.

The freemen elected the governor. They also chose the magistrates who were the assistants to the governor. The assistants directed the general affairs of the land and dispensed justice to the people. In effect, the assistants made up both the upper legislative body and the highest judicial body of government. Also elected by the freemen were the deputies, who comprised the lower legislative body, and the justices of the peace, who settled minor cases.

The decade of the 1640s brought civil war to England, the royalists defending the crown against the Puritan roundheads. The Puritans resorted to a witch hunt to flush out perceived enemies, the heretics.[16] Since only those records favorable to the official side were preserved, the truth about the victims of this English witch hunt can only be imagined today.

After a series of bloody battles, the Puritan forces under Oliver Cromwell were victorious, and King Charles I was beheaded. The Puritans, holding the upper hand in England, proceeded to purify church buildings by destroying everything in them, the art of centuries past, leaving only bare walls and rubble. Without the religious motivation to leave England, the migration of Puritans to New England came to a standstill.

In the 1650s, England was subjected to rule of the austere Puritan Commonwealth. In the face of such strictures, many people, including some Puritans, longed for the good old days under the crown. Still, the intellectual contribution of many Puritans, notably the magnificent poet John Milton, deserve emphasis. The fruits of their principles, in the following generation, are seen in the political views of their scholar, John Locke. The Declaration of Independence is based on his writings. We are indebted today to the vision and courage of those Puritans who established many of the freedoms we take for granted. The leading New England Puritans were not among this group.

In 1660, the people of England had their way. The Puritan government fell, and the monarchy was restored. Charles II, son of the beheaded king, was placed on the throne; this event is called the *Restoration*. At this point, many of the most repressive English Puritans who had served under Cromwell fled to New England, the last bastion of Puritan safety. On the same tide were some returning New Englanders, who had lived in England during Puritan rule. Among them were the Rev. William Stoughton and the Rev. Increase Mather. (William Stoughton was the chief justice for the witchcraft trials in 1692.)

William Stoughton had been educated for the ministry at Harvard, graduating in the class of 1650. He then accepted the ministry of a church in England. While in England, he studied for, and received, his Master's degree at Oxford. Following his return to Massachusetts in 1660, he gave up the ministry in favor of politics. Before entering government service, he had preached in company with Increase Mather. Stoughton first became a magistrate, an assistant to the governor, in 1671. Stoughton leaned heavily on his religious training for guidance in determining guilt or innocence. A vigorous prosecutor, he was narrow and dogmatic in applying the most rigid Puritan doctrines. He never married.

The Restoration was the severest of setbacks for the Puritan orthodoxy. Charles II sent a letter in June 1662 expressing his desire that Congregational church membership would no longer be required for voting privileges, and that all landholders would be allowed to vote for civil and military officials. Yet New England officialdom turned a blind eye to the king's letter and carried on as before.

Economically, New England merchants had no cause for complaint, as the British exclusion of Dutch, French, and Spanish traders opened golden opportunities. Europe was entering an age of enlightenment, and new immigrants brought with them the seeds of change. Further, the majority of New Englanders eagerly hoped for freedom of religion, which would give the franchise to all citizens, making the elective process democratic.

Following the Restoration, the most important social development in New England was the emergence of a merchant class. This wealthy group found itself frequently clashing with the Puritan government. By the early 1680s, pressures from the increasingly diverse and restless population were seriously undermining the inflexible system imposed by the Puritan leaders, whose vulnerability was sensed by their opponents in England. The official downfall of the Puritan government of New England came in 1684 when Charles II annulled the charter of the Massachusetts Bay Company.

When the news reached Boston, the adherents of the old Puritan order were outraged. They well knew that the king's decree annulling the charter made the existing government in Massachusetts illegal. Undeterred, the Puritan rulers in Boston simply ignored the decree and continued to exercise power as before. The usual slowness of British administrators to take action provided leeway for the Puritans' defiance.

King Charles II died in 1685, and was succeeded by his brother King James II, a Roman Catholic and no friend of Puritanism. Finally, in May 1686, the elected governor of Massachusetts, Simon Bradstreet, was displaced and a temporary council appointed by the king began to rule Massachusetts. It was presided over by Joseph Dudley, and William Stoughton was deputy president, but most of the other Puritan leaders were excluded. The temporary council was composed almost exclusively of rich Massachusetts merchants. Relishing their newly found power, they went about satisfying their political desires. Free from the limitations of an elected legislature, they proceeded to enjoy a feast of executive privilege.

Sir Edmond Andros, the royal governor newly appointed by the king, arrived in Boston on December 19, 1686. At once he took over control from Dudley and Stoughton. Both, however, quickly accepted seats in his council. The council was expanded to include representatives from all the New England colonies, and later from New York. There still was no elected legislature. Andros' new government, the Dominion of New England, eventually extended from Maine to the Delaware River. It no longer embodied the interests of Massachusetts merchants alone, and in fact ruled against them on several important measures.

The Puritan faction of Massachusetts, now almost completely excluded from the direction of public affairs, began stirring up popular support against Andros' rule. More important, they found convenient new allies in most of the very merchants who previously had been their outspoken opponents. The Puritans' animosity against Andros turned to genuine hatred when he established an Anglican church, King's Chapel, in Boston.

In England royal authorities started the process of writing an entirely new charter for New England, a terrifying prospect for the old guard Puritans. A royal charter would forever put an end to their Puritan Commonwealth; their exclusive place in the world as the covenanted people of God would be lost. For the New England Puritans, these were unhappy times. Made of stern stuff, they were not about to give in.

In May 1688, the Rev. Increase Mather, the senior minister of the Second Church (Old North Church) in Boston, was sent to England, instructed by his cohorts to use his powers of negotiation to make the proposed royal charter as much like the old charter as possible. Upon arriving he found that the heart of the monarch was steeped in despotism, and not at all inclined to favor liberty in the colonies. However, in November 1688, King James II was forced to abdicate in a coup known as England's *Glorious Revolution.*

William of Orange, a Dutch stadholder, and his wife Mary, Protestant daughter of James II, succeeded to the throne of Great Britain as joint sovereigns. King William III and Queen Mary were to protect the Protestant religion in Britain. In March 1689, word of the Glorious Revolution reached Boston. The Puritans leaders, using the popular support that they had garnered, took their own action. On the morning of April 18, 1689 they revolted, and imprisoned Andros, the representative of the deposed king.

Regaining control of the government, the Puritans set up a provisional government, and ruled under the laws of the old charter. They dismissed Andros' council and happily reinstituted the Board of Assistants in its place. They brought back the respected, but now aged, Simon Bradstreet to serve as elected governor, largely as a figure head. The most striking effect of the "tyranny" of Andros was the disintegration of the party of moderate Puritans, and the emergence of a powerful group of conservative Puritans. This *old guard* was made up of hard-liners who had long defended the traditional Puritan ideals. The provisional government was in their hands. Because William Stoughton had served on the council under Andros, he had lost the confidence of the old guard, and they excluded him from the Board of Assistants. For the first time in his political life, Stoughton found himself in a precarious position.

Two new names were included in the Board of Assistants, Jonathan Corwin and Peter Sergeant. These men had not previously been high office-holders in the colony. Corwin was from Salem, and Sergeant from Boston; both were staunch members of the old guard. (Both of them were justices in the witchcraft trials of 1692.)

After their overthrow of Andros' government, the New England Puritans faced grave uncertainties about the permanence of their usurped rule. King William, although a Protestant, soon let it be known that he was not happy with their act of defiance. In fact, plain for all to see, their provisional government was nothing but an outlaw government.

At home, King William had his own troubles. His accession to the throne of Great Britain had started a war with France. Then in 1690 he met the former King James II in battle in Northern Ireland, the last military action in history in which two kings participated as combatants. The English war with France soon spread to America, where it was known as King William's War.

By the end of 1689, the French and the Indians had reduced American occupation of northern New England to a narrow coastal strip in New Hampshire and southern Maine. The front can be traced by a line beginning at the seaport town of Casco, Maine,[17] seventy-five miles northeast of Salem; running southwesterly along the Maine coast to York, Maine; from there inland to Exeter, New Hampshire; and then southwesterly to Andover, Groton, and Lancaster in Massachusetts. During 1690, the French kept the Indians supplied from Canada and encouraged them in further attacks on the northern settlements. In retaliation, in September and October 1690, New England ventured a military expedition to take Quebec, which ended in disaster. It was led by Sir William Phipps, a native of Maine. Phipps had been knighted for discovering and taking possession of the wealth of a sunken Spanish galleon for the English crown. By the end of 1690, all the remaining settlements in Maine had been destroyed by the Indians, except for three towns, Wells, York, and Kittery, in the extreme southwest corner of the province.

In their wartime plans, the Puritan old guard discounted the advice of the field commanders. In March 1690, in Andover, Captain John Osgood and Lieutenant John Barker resisted the reorganization of the Upper Regiment, the regiment of militia in northwestern Essex county. (John Osgood's wife, Mary, was arrested for witchcraft on September 8, 1692. John Barker's daughter, Mary Barker, and his brother, William Barker, were arrested for witchcraft on August 29, 1692, and three days later William's son, William Barker, Jr., was arrested.)[18]

The frontier towns in Massachusetts, under intermittent attack by the Indians, were hesitant to risk sending their ablebodied men as far away as Canada to fight a war. When towns balked at having their young men impressed for military duty, the Puritan rulers regarded their discontent as insubordination. After the surrender of Casco, Maine to the Indians on May 20, 1690, Major Bartholomew Gedney, went on a recruiting mission and found farmers from Salem Village reluctant to depart for the northeast. (Bartholomew Gedney was one of the justices in the witchcraft trials of 1692.) In July 1690 the Rev. John Emerson of Gloucester implored Major General Wait Still Winthrop to release members of the town's militia company which had been impressed into the army. (Wait Still Winthrop was one of the justices in the witchcraft trials of 1692.)

The war impoverished New England. In 1691 the French reorganized the Indians in New Hampshire and Maine, who renewed their attacks. The onslaught engendered fear throughout New England. As the frontier in Maine and New Hampshire was driven back by Indian raids, a steady stream of refugees and orphans fled south on the dirt tracks to Massachusetts.

Increase Mather, meanwhile, had stayed in England, waiting his chances. When attention again was directed to writing the new charter, he found himself unable to prevail. King William was an uncompromising defender of the Church of England. The new charter would include freedom of religion, and would give the right to vote to all citizens with property. Although the prospect was anathema to the Puritan leaders, ordinary citizens looked on it with favor. This group, led by wealthy traders and merchants, welcomed liberation from authoritarian Puritan rule, even if it meant a royal governor.

While the senior minister of Boston's Second Church (Old North) was in England, his son, the Rev. Cotton Mather, the assistant minister, served as acting minister. William Stoughton had always been close to the Mather family. As representative of the Dorchester church, Stoughton had attended Cotton Mather's ordination in 1685, a pivotal event in Cotton's life. Stoughton always liked Cotton Mather, and, in turn, Cotton Mather respected him. Their close friendship would never waver. Now, in 1691, William Stoughton, finding himself on the outside of the Puritan old guard, yet in full sympathy with its goals, made a fateful move to regain admittance. He appealed to Cotton Mather, his junior by many years. In response, Cotton Mather recommended to his father in England that he provide for Stoughton as "a real friend to New England, willing to make amendment for all his miscarriages," whom he desired his father "to restore to the favor of his country."[19] The Mathers, father and son, were both anxious to help Stoughton, a staunch Puritan who shared their particular philosophy and beliefs.

At Whitehall in England on October 7, 1691 the new charter for Massachusetts Bay was declared in force. The ministers of the crown regarded Increase Mather as the head of the clergy of Massachusetts. Knowing that the ecclesiastical was the predominant force in the colony, they were anxious to conciliate him. To this end, they allowed him to nominate the governor, the Council, and all the officers appointed under the new charter. He chose them, of course, from among his friends.

Increase Mather nominated Sir William Phipps as the new royal governor. Phipps was a good Congregationalist, and an admirer and follower of Increase Mather. However, he was not one of the old-guard Puritans. Why did Mather pick him instead of Stoughton? Phipps was a military man, well-regarded in England. The French were menacing, and King William wanted a military commander to govern New England. Had Mather not suggested Phipps, then the king might well have chosen an English military officer to be the royal governor. This, in Mather's view, would have been a calamity. As a result, he contented himself by choosing William Stoughton as the lieutenant governor. The crown accepted all of Increase Mather's recommendations.

The functions of the former Board of Assistants would be taken over by the Council of the new charter. Mather's recommendations insured that the members of the new Council were essentially the same as on the provincial board. Jonathan Corwin and Peter Sergeant were included. Thus, the old-guard Puritans would remain in control.

At the time of his appointment, October 1691, Sir William Phipps had been in England for a while. The new governor was to carry the royal charter with him over the ocean to New England, and begin his rule. As it happened, that process took half a year; Phipps was not to arrive in Boston until May 1692.

Increase Mather returned on the same ship. Back home again, he found himself in a dominant position. All the members of the executive branch of the new government were indebted to him for their nomination, including the governor and the lieutenant governor. To the Mathers, father and son, this was a family triumph.

In his diary, under the date of April 1692, Cotton Mather wrote, "The time for favor was now come! The set time was come! I am now to receive an answer of so many prayers. All the Councilors of the Province are of my own father's nomination and my father-in-law, with several related unto me, and several brethren of my own church, are among them. The Governor of the Province is not *my enemy,* but one whom I baptized, namely, Sir William Phipps, one of my own flock, and one of my dearest friends."[20]

William Stoughton found himself beholden to Cotton Mather, whose recommendation had made possible his re-emergence to political power. It cannot be doubted that the coincidence of Stoughton's passions, prejudices, and policy with those of the Mathers provided a decisive and driving force in what was to follow in the fateful year of 1692. In that year the Mathers were in the flush of their political influence. . . .

In October 1692, William Stoughton, serving as chief justice for the Salem witchcraft trials, wrote a thank you letter to the Rev. Cotton Mather. "Considering the place that I hold in the Court of Oyer and Terminer, still laboring and proceeding in the trial of persons accused and *convicted for witchcraft,* I express my obligation and thankfulness to you. Such is your design, your enmity to Satan, your compassion, such is your design, your enmity to Satan, your compassion, such your instruction and counsel, your care of truth, that all good men will greatly rejoice that the spirit of the Lord has thus enabled you to lift up a standard against the infernal enemy, that has been coming in like a flood upon us." At that point many accused witches were in jail awaiting trial. . . .

Notes

. . . [14] "There shall not be found among you any one that uses divination, or an enchanter, or a witch, or a charmer, or a consulter with familiar spirits, or a wizard, or a necromancer." Deut., 18:10-11.

[15] In 1692, there were less than 4,000 church members, about equally divided between men and women, in a population close to 100,000.

[16] Robbins, Rossell H. *The Encyclopedia of Witchcraft and Demonology.* New York, 1959. p. 249.

[17] Casco is the old name for the town later called Falmouth and now the city of Portland, Maine. In 1689, the population of Casco was about 600 persons.

[18] John Barker and William Barker are the writer's great, great, great, great, great, great, great-uncles.

[19] Hutchinson, Thomas. *The History of the Colony and Province of Massachusetts-Bay.* London, 1768. Reprint. 3 vols. Cambridge, MA, 1936. 1: 365.

[20] The Rev. Cotton Mather baptized the forty-year-old Phipps on March 23, 1690, and received him into membership in the Second Church (Old North) in Boston. . . .

Peter Charles Hoffer (essay date 1996)

SOURCE: "Trials," in *The Devil's Disciples: Makers of the Salem Witchcraft Trails,* Johns Hopkins University Press, 1996, pp. 154-78.

[*In the excerpt that follows, Hoffer attempts to make sense of the Salem witch trials "by reconstructing the surviving bits and pieces of the documentary [records]" and by examining the role that Stoughton and the other judges played in determining the outcomes of the trials.*]

. . . The absence of the crucial documentary records and the bitter, persistent divergence of the contemporary readings of what we, at this distance, cannot see provide some of the fascination of these cases—an enduring open-endedness that will continue to attract scholars to the trials just as it brings tourists to the "witch house" in modern Salem (actually Corwin's home). Yet we are not without our powers of conjuration. The trials are an empty space, but all around them the canvas is filled. The characters are more or less delineated for us by their conduct before and after the trials. The empty space becomes smaller as we move the characters into it and then capture their motion as they emerge.

Absent the transcript that Sewall gave Mather, we can try to make sense of the outcomes of the trials by reconstructing the surviving bits and pieces of the documentary as we did the pretrial hearings. Instead of just reading the record, we listen in it for the voices of the participants. Although the court met only five times, each time for a brief span of days, and compared with the trials, the conversation at the hearings was almost leisurely, nevertheless, at each trial, the Salem courthouse buzzed with sound. Indeed, the noise in the courtroom, combined with its primitive acoustics, the jostling and rustling of spectators, and the loud anguish of the victims, dictated the way in which the evidence was heard. As clerk Stephen Sewall later reported to the Nurse family about her trial: "In this trial are twenty papers, besides this judgment, and there were in this trial, as well as other trials of the same nature, several evidences *viva voce* which were not written so I can give no copies of them, some for and some against the parties. Some of the confessions did also mention this and other persons in their several declarations. Which being premised and considered, the said 20 papers herewith filed is the whole trial."[14] If we do not have the full text of this conversation—a verbatim stenographic "concordance," much less an electronic record—we can fill in gaps with the pretrial and other legal documents, the accounts of eyewitnesses, and the later recollections of participants.

As at the hearings, conversation in the courthouse was relational, gaining full meaning from the relationships among the speakers and the audience. The social distance between the performers was as important as the real space in which they performed. Thus the judges (like the magistrates before them) were almost certainly more courteous to those who had high status, which explains why the higher-status suspects were not brought to trial immediately, whereas the nineteen defendants tried first had, with two exceptions, low status in the communities where they resided. Higher-status suspects thus had more room to maneuver, to argue for themselves, and even to escape from custody.

Conversation in these face-to-face confrontations was temporally contexted. The exchanges could stretch back in time over weeks, months, even years, as speakers "remembered" incidents aloud or couched their recollections in terms of longstanding alliances, rivalries, attachments, and enmities. Memory and cultural convention scripted the conversation, and rules and customs of criminal procedure allowed the judges to direct the courtroom drama. Still, there were improvisations and unexpected twists. Over and over, popular culture triumphed over elite precept, folklore trumped erudition, and rumor became probative. The power of rumor in the trials confirms the efficacy of noise—for the rumors were longstanding ones, which changed their shape and became death sentences.[15]

Listening once again to the conversation at the trials helps us to understand their outcome. What was said and how it was said determined the verdict in cases far more than the dictates of any book of rules. Who spoke? The most imposing voices, the ones that commanded the attention of other speakers, belonged to the judges. Their place—the bench—was raised and at the front of the courtroom, and everyone could hear what they said. Their voices were loud, literally and figuratively, for they had on occasion to shout over the noise of the assemblage.

There is no mention of the participation of the bench in most surviving early American criminal court records, but over every defendant fell the long shadow of the judges. Unlike modern trials in America, the judge played a leading role in the colonial criminal court. Judges questioned witnesses and pressured jurors, although they might not punish the latter for their verdict unless it was corrupted. Judicial discretion in this area was framed by concepts of fairness on the one hand and political imperatives on the other. In England, during the "Popish Plot" and the "Rye House Plot" of the 1680s, judges had demanded that juries find the defendants guilty. On other occasions, judges were willing to let juries find their own verdicts.[16]

Did Stoughton, presiding, speak for the entire bench, as Hathorne had during the pretrial hearings? The record hints that Stoughton and his brethren did much of the questioning and spoke more frequently than anyone else, but unlike English judges, Stoughton was a politician, not a jurist. In England, the preeminence of the judge's voice in criminal trials was a tribute to the learning and professional status of the judges.[17] In Salem, the bench was experienced, but none of the judges were lawyers. These may have been, as some scholars argue, a group of able men in other walks of life, but no law was cited or debated in the court. Instead, the judges relied upon hearsay, spectral evidence, and folk witch-finding techniques like the touching test and examination for witch marks.[18]

Would a learned bench have made a difference in the outcome of the case? We must not ignore the force that legal formalism has upon those who practice law for a living. Professional lawyers and judges have audiences of other professionals at the bench and bar whose opinion is an important curb on discretion and misuse of power.[19] Such professionalism was doubly important in cases like these, in which questions of evidence were central, because the judges questioned witnesses and parties to the case. A defendant might ask a question of the accusers, and the accusers might add to their stories, but everything was initiated, generated, controlled, and limited by what the judges asked and where they wanted to go with the answers.[20] Matthew Hale, the most respected English jurist of the 1650s and 1660s, had credited spectral evidence, but more recently leading English jurists had become skeptical of such testimony.[21] The judges at Salem seemed unaware of the latter development.

A learned bench might have tried to protect the rights of defendants, although the concept of procedural guarantees in criminal proceedings, while a vital part of the Glorious Revolution in England, did not always seep down to the commoner slouching in the dock.[22] Mary Esty and Sarah Cloyse asked the judges to intervene for them and "direct" them wherein they stood "in neede."[23] They conceded that they had no right to assistance from the bench but seemed to have known that judges sometimes offered it to defendants, though only upon their own discretion, and only to remedy errors in law. In state trials, trials that were politically important to the authorities, judges rarely interceded for the defendants—quite the reverse was usually the case, as judges made the state's case plain to the jury.[24] There is no evidence that the Salem judges either helped or refused to help defendants when they faltered.

Could politics have combined with the relative lack of juridical sophistication to press the judges toward a sanguinary stance? The English high court judge, though he served at the pleasure of the Crown and was always aware of the Crown's displeasure, was not usually a politician. Stoughton and the others on the court of oyer and terminer were first and foremost partisans. It might have seemed to them that convictions in these cases would shore up the new government, but they were the same bench that presided over the conviction of old and addled Mary Glover three years before Phips and the new charter arrived. Where was the political motivation for conviction then?

The fact remains that the judges directed the course of these trials. The most striking example of judicial intervention—in part because it is the one best documented—occurred at the end of Rebecca Nurse's trial. The jury found her not guilty, a verdict that might have reached far beyond her own case, for she was, unlike those previously convicted, a woman of unblemished reputation and a church member in full communion. Her acquittal would have set a precedent that a good reputation could counter spectral evidence. The court intervened, in the person of Chief Judge Stoughton, according to the recollection of juryman Thomas Fisk, and directed the jury's attention to Nurse's words about Deliverance and Abigail Hobbs, two confessed witches who had turned informants. Nurse supposedly said, "'What, do these persons give in evidence against me now, they used to come among us.'" Stoughton told the jurors that such words could only mean Nurse admitted that she too was a witch. Some of the jurors asked the court's permission to retire to reconsider their verdict. When they retired, Fisk told his fellow jurors he was not certain what she meant, and he wanted her to have the chance to interpret her remarks for the jury. The jury returned and Nurse was asked what she meant, but old and hard of hearing, she missed the point. The jury then reversed itself and found her guilty. Informed of the change in her fortunes too late, she explained that she objected to being condemned by those who had admitted their miscarriages and weakness. Why should a jury believe such women and not her?[25] . . .

Notes

. . . [14] Samuel Parris, "Meditations for Peace," November 1694, in *Salem-Village Witchcraft: A Documentary Record of Local Conflict in Colonial New England,* rev. ed., ed. Paul Boyer and Stephen Nissenbaum (Boston, 1993), 34.

[15] Jeffrey S. Victor, *Satanic Panic: The Creation of a Contemporary Legend* (Chicago, 1993), 40-50.

[16] Edgar J. McManus, *Law and Liberty, in Early New England* (Amherst, Mass, 1993), 148 Thomas Andrew Green, *Verdict According to Conscience: Perspectives on the English Criminal Trial Jury, 1200-1800* (Chicago, 1985) 249-53.

[17] John H. Baker, *Introduction to English Legal History*, 3d. ed. (London, 1990), 189-93.

[18] Chadwick Hansen, *Witchcraft at Salem,* (New York, 1969) 122: "No more experienced or distinguished a court could have been assembled anywhere in English America." David C. Brown, "Forfeitures at Salem," *William and Mary Quarterly,* 3d. ser., 50 (1993): 86, agrees, citing as authority Richard Weisman, *Witchcraft, Magic, and Religion in Seventeenth-Century Massachusetts* (Amherst, Mass. 1984), 179. Brown writes, "[T]he judges conscientiously 'organized the most cautiously empirical and systematic investigation into witchcraft ever to occur in new England.'" The internal quote is from Weisman, true, but Weisman does not use the word conscientiously—that is Brown's own contribution. Nor does Weisman write "the judges." Instead, he wrote "the court." In fact there is no evidence that the judges set themselves a course of close reading of English tracts and precedents. Rather, in court, according to Weisman, they looked for witches' marks and forced suspects to look upon and touch their accusers. These tactics did reflect a systematic recovery of old, customary witch-finding devices but did not represent contemporary legal standards or empirical findings, and they hardly establish the legal acumen of the judges.

[19] See, for example, Owen Fiss, "Objectivity and Interpretation," *Stanford Law Review* 34 (1982): 739, 744.

[20] A nice recent summary is J. M. Beattie, "Scales of Justice: Defense Counsel and the English Criminal Trial in the Eighteenth and Nineteenth Centuries," *Law and History Review* 9 (1991): 221-67. There is no evidence that seventeenth-century Massachusetts procedure differed from this. See David C. Flaherty, "Criminal Prac-

Massachusetts, 1630-1800, ed. Daniel R. Coquillette (Boston, 1984), 191-242.

[21] Wallace Notestein, *A History of Witchcraft in England, from 1558 to 1718* (New York, 1911), 320.

[22] See, for example, John Langbein, "The Criminal Trial before the Lawyers," *University of Chicago Law Review* 45 (1978): 263-316.

[23] Paul Boyer and Stephen Nissenbaum, eds., *The Salem Witchcraft Papers: Verbatim Transcripts of the Legal Documents of the Salem Witchcraft Outbreak of 1692* (New York, 1977) 1:302 (hereafter cited as *SWP*). All dates in the text and the notes have been modernized.

[24] John Langbein, "The Historic Origins of the Privilege against Self-Incrimination at Common Law," *University of Michigan Law Review* 92 (1994): 1050-52.

[25] *SWP*, 2:607-8. The story is taken from Robert Calef's *More Wonders of the Invisible World* [1700], in George Lincoln Burr, ed. *Narratives of the Witchcraft cases, 1648-1706* (New York, 1914), 358-59. What reason might Calef have had for structuring the story in this way? Surely it makes Stoughton look like a bully at best and a demon at worst.

FURTHER READING

Elliott, Emory Elliott. "Storm's of God's Wrath," in *Power and the Pulpit in Puritan New England,* pp. 88-135. Princeton University Press, 1975.

> Examines Stoughton's sermons in order to "understand the powerful hold that the sermon had upon the imaginations of the New England Puritans."

Additional coverage of Stoughton's life and career is contained in the following source published by Gale Research: *Dictionary of Literary Biography*, Vol. 24.

Literature Criticism from 1400 to 1800

Cumulative Indexes

How to Use This Index

The main references

<pre>
Calvino, Italo
   1923-1985.....CLC 5, 8, 11, 22, 33, 39,
                                  73; SSC 3
</pre>

list all author entries in the following Gale Literary Criticism series:

BLC = *Black Literature Criticism*
CLC = *Contemporary Literary Criticism*
CLR = *Children's Literature Review*
CMLC = *Classical and Medieval Literature Criticism*
DA = *DISCovering Authors*
DC = *Drama Criticism*
HLC = *Hispanic Literature Criticism*
LC = *Literature Criticism from 1400 to 1800*
NCLC = *Nineteenth-Century Literature Criticism*
PC = *Poetry Criticism*
SSC = *Short Story Criticism*
TCLC = *Twentieth-Century Literary Criticism*
WLC = *World Literature Criticism, 1500 to the Present*

The cross-references

<pre>
See also CANR 23; CA 85-88;
   obituary CA 116
</pre>

list all author entries in the following Gale biographical and literary sources:

AAYA = *Authors & Artists for Young Adults*
AITN = *Authors in the News*
BEST = *Bestsellers*
BW = *Black Writers*
CA = *Contemporary Authors*
CAAS = *Contemporary Authors Autobiography Series*
CABS = *Contemporary Authors Bibliographical Series*
CANR = *Contemporary Authors New Revision Series*
CAP = *Contemporary Authors Permanent Series*
CDALB = *Concise Dictionary of American Literary Biography*
CDBLB = *Concise Dictionary of British Literary Biography*
DLB = *Dictionary of Literary Biography*
DLBD = *Dictionary of Literary Biography Documentary Series*
DLBY = *Dictionary of Literary Biography Yearbook*
HW = *Hispanic Writers*
JRDA = *Junior DISCovering Authors*
MAICYA = *Major Authors and Illustrators for Children and Young Adults*
MTCW = *Major 20th-Century Writers*
NNAL = *Native North American Literature*
SAAS = *Something about the Author Autobiography Series*
SATA = *Something about the Author*
YABC = *Yesterday's Authors of Books for Children*

Literary Criticism Series
Cumulative Author Index

Anderson, Robert (Woodruff)
1917- . . . . **CLC 23; DAM DRAM**
See also AITN 1; CA 21-24R; CANR 32;
DLB 7

Anderson, Sherwood
1876-1941 . . . . **TCLC 1, 10, 24; DA;**
DAB; DAC; DAM MST, NOV; SSC 1;
WLC
See also CA 104; 121; CDALB 1917-1929;
DLB 4, 9, 86; DLBD 1; MTCW

Andier, Pierre
See Desnos, Robert

Andouard
See Giraudoux, (Hippolyte) Jean

Andrade, Carlos Drummond de . . . . . . **CLC 18**
See also Drummond de Andrade, Carlos

Andrade, Mario de 1893-1945 . . . . . **TCLC 43**

Andreae, Johann V(alentin)
1586-1654 . . . . **LC 32**
See also DLB 164

Andreas-Salome, Lou 1861-1937 . . . **TCLC 56**
See also DLB 66

Andrewes, Lancelot 1555-1626 . . . . **LC 5**
See also DLB 151, 172

Andrews, Cicily Fairfield
See West, Rebecca

Andrews, Elton V.
See Pohl, Frederik

Andreyev, Leonid (Nikolaevich)
1871-1919 . . . . **TCLC 3**
See also CA 104

Andric, Ivo 1892-1975 . . . . **CLC 8**
See also CA 81-84; 57-60; CANR 43;
DLB 147; MTCW

Angelique, Pierre
See Bataille, Georges

Angell, Roger 1920- . . . . **CLC 26**
See also CA 57-60; CANR 13, 44; DLB 171

Angelou, Maya
1928- . . . . **CLC 12, 35, 64, 77; BLC; DA;**
DAB; DAC; DAM MST, MULT, POET,
POP
See also AAYA 7, 20; BW 2; CA 65-68;
CANR 19, 42; DLB 38; MTCW;
SATA 49

Annensky, Innokenty (Fyodorovich)
1856-1909 . . . . **TCLC 14**
See also CA 110; 155

Annunzio, Gabriele d'
See D'Annunzio, Gabriele

Anon, Charles Robert
See Pessoa, Fernando (Antonio Nogueira)

Anouilh, Jean (Marie Lucien Pierre)
1910-1987 . . . . . . **CLC 1, 3, 8, 13, 40, 50;**
DAM DRAM
See also CA 17-20R; 123; CANR 32;
MTCW

Anthony, Florence
See Ai

Anthony, John
See Ciardi, John (Anthony)

Anthony, Peter
See Shaffer, Anthony (Joshua); Shaffer,
Peter (Levin)

Anthony, Piers 1934- . . **CLC 35; DAM POP**
See also AAYA 11; CA 21-24R; CANR 28,
56; DLB 8; MTCW; SAAS 22; SATA 84

Antoine, Marc
See Proust, (Valentin-Louis-George-Eugene-)
Marcel

Antoninus, Brother
See Everson, William (Oliver)

Antonioni, Michelangelo 1912- . . . . . **CLC 20**
See also CA 73-76; CANR 45

Antschel, Paul 1920-1970
See Celan, Paul
See also CA 85-88; CANR 33; MTCW

Anwar, Chairil 1922-1949 . . . . **TCLC 22**
See also CA 121

Apollinaire, Guillaume
1880-1918 . . . . **TCLC 3, 8, 51;**
DAM POET; PC 7
See also Kostrowitzki, Wilhelm Apollinaris
de
See also CA 152

Appelfeld, Aharon 1932- . . . . **CLC 23, 47**
See also CA 112; 133

Apple, Max (Isaac) 1941- . . . . **CLC 9, 33**
See also CA 81-84; CANR 19, 54; DLB 130

Appleman, Philip (Dean) 1926- . . . . . **CLC 51**
See also CA 13-16R; CAAS 18; CANR 6,
29, 56

Appleton, Lawrence
See Lovecraft, H(oward) P(hillips)

Apteryx
See Eliot, T(homas) S(tearns)

Apuleius, (Lucius Madaurensis)
125(?)-175(?) . . . . **CMLC 1**

Aquin, Hubert 1929-1977 . . . . **CLC 15**
See also CA 105; DLB 53

Aragon, Louis
1897-1982 . . . . . **CLC 3, 22; DAM NOV,**
POET
See also CA 69-72; 108; CANR 28;
DLB 72; MTCW

Arany, Janos 1817-1882 . . . . **NCLC 34**

Arbuthnot, John 1667-1735 . . . . **LC 1**
See also DLB 101

Archer, Herbert Winslow
See Mencken, H(enry) L(ouis)

Archer, Jeffrey (Howard)
1940- . . . . **CLC 28; DAM POP**
See also AAYA 16; BEST 89:3; CA 77-80;
CANR 22, 52; INT CANR-22

Archer, Jules 1915- . . . . **CLC 12**
See also CA 9-12R; CANR 6; SAAS 5;
SATA 4, 85

Archer, Lee
See Ellison, Harlan (Jay)

Arden, John
1930- . . . . . **CLC 6, 13, 15; DAM DRAM**
See also CA 13-16R; CAAS 4; CANR 31;
DLB 13; MTCW

Arenas, Reinaldo
1943-1990 . . . . . . **CLC 41; DAM MULT;**
HLC
See also CA 124; 128; 133; DLB 145; HW

Arendt, Hannah 1906-1975 . . . . . **CLC 66, 98**
See also CA 17-20R; 61-64; CANR 26;
MTCW

Aretino, Pietro 1492-1556 . . . . **LC 12**

Arghezi, Tudor . . . . **CLC 80**
See also Theodorescu, Ion N.

Arguedas, Jose Maria
1911-1969 . . . . **CLC 10, 18**
See also CA 89-92; DLB 113; HW

Argueta, Manlio 1936- . . . . **CLC 31**
See also CA 131; DLB 145; HW

Ariosto, Ludovico 1474-1533 . . . . **LC 6**

Aristides
See Epstein, Joseph

Aristophanes
450B.C.-385B.C. . . . . **CMLC 4; DA;**
DAB; DAC; DAM DRAM, MST; DC 2
See also DLB 176

Arlt, Roberto (Godofredo Christophersen)
1900-1942 . . . . . **TCLC 29; DAM MULT;**
HLC
See also CA 123; 131; HW

Armah, Ayi Kwei
1939- . . . . **CLC 5, 33; BLC;**
DAM MULT, POET
See also BW 1; CA 61-64; CANR 21;
DLB 117; MTCW

Armatrading, Joan 1950- . . . . **CLC 17**
See also CA 114

Arnette, Robert
See Silverberg, Robert

Arnim, Achim von (Ludwig Joachim von
Arnim) 1781-1831 . . . . **NCLC 5**
See also DLB 90

Arnim, Bettina von 1785-1859 . . . . **NCLC 38**
See also DLB 90

Arnold, Matthew
1822-1888 . . . . . **NCLC 6, 29; DA; DAB;**
DAC; DAM MST, POET; PC 5; WLC
See also CDBLB 1832-1890; DLB 32, 57

Arnold, Thomas 1795-1842 . . . . . . **NCLC 18**
See also DLB 55

Arnow, Harriette (Louisa) Simpson
1908-1986 . . . . **CLC 2, 7, 18**
See also CA 9-12R; 118; CANR 14; DLB 6;
MTCW; SATA 42; SATA-Obit 47

Arp, Hans
See Arp, Jean

Arp, Jean 1887-1966 . . . . **CLC 5**
See also CA 81-84; 25-28R; CANR 42

Arrabal
See Arrabal, Fernando

Arrabal, Fernando 1932- . . . **CLC 2, 9, 18, 58**
See also CA 9-12R; CANR 15

Arrick, Fran . . . . **CLC 30**
See also Gaberman, Judie Angell

Artaud, Antonin (Marie Joseph)
1896-1948 . . . **TCLC 3, 36; DAM DRAM**
See also CA 104; 149

Arthur, Ruth M(abel) 1905-1979 . . . . **CLC 12**
See also CA 9-12R; 85-88; CANR 4;
SATA 7, 26

Artsybashev, Mikhail (Petrovich)
1878-1927 . . . . **TCLC 31**

Bailey, Paul 1937- .... **CLC 45**
See also CA 21-24R; CANR 16; DLB 14

Baillie, Joanna 1762-1851 .... **NCLC 2**
See also DLB 93

Bainbridge, Beryl (Margaret)
1933- .... **CLC 4, 5, 8, 10, 14, 18, 22, 62;
DAM NOV**
See also CA 21-24R; CANR 24, 55;
DLB 14; MTCW

Baker, Elliott 1922- .... **CLC 8**
See also CA 45-48; CANR 2

Baker, Jean H. .... **TCLC 3, 10**
See also Russell, George William

Baker, Nicholson
1957- .... **CLC 61; DAM POP**
See also CA 135

Baker, Ray Stannard 1870-1946 ... **TCLC 47**
See also CA 118

Baker, Russell (Wayne) 1925-...... **CLC 31**
See also BEST 89:4; CA 57-60; CANR 11,
41; MTCW

Bakhtin, M.
See Bakhtin, Mikhail Mikhailovich

Bakhtin, M. M.
See Bakhtin, Mikhail Mikhailovich

Bakhtin, Mikhail
See Bakhtin, Mikhail Mikhailovich

Bakhtin, Mikhail Mikhailovich
1895-1975 .... **CLC 83**
See also CA 128; 113

Bakshi, Ralph 1938(?)-........... **CLC 26**
See also CA 112; 138

Bakunin, Mikhail (Alexandrovich)
1814-1876 .... **NCLC 25, 58**

Baldwin, James (Arthur)
1924-1987 ...... **CLC 1, 2, 3, 4, 5, 8, 13,
15, 17, 42, 50, 67, 90; BLC; DA; DAB;
DAC; DAM MST, MULT, NOV, POP;
DC 1; SSC 10; WLC**
See also AAYA 4; BW 1; CA 1-4R; 124;
CABS 1; CANR 3, 24;
CDALB 1941-1968; DLB 2, 7, 33;
DLBY 87; MTCW; SATA 9;
SATA-Obit 54

Ballard, J(ames) G(raham)
1930- .... **CLC 3, 6, 14, 36; DAM NOV,
POP; SSC 1**
See also AAYA 3; CA 5-8R; CANR 15, 39;
DLB 14; MTCW

Balmont, Konstantin (Dmitriyevich)
1867-1943 .... **TCLC 11**
See also CA 109; 155

Balzac, Honore de
1799-1850 .... **NCLC 5, 35, 53; DA;
DAB; DAC; DAM MST, NOV; SSC 5;
WLC**
See also DLB 119

Bambara, Toni Cade
1939-1995 ...... **CLC 19, 88; BLC; DA;
DAC; DAM MST, MULT**
See also AAYA 5; BW 2; CA 29-32R; 150;
CANR 24, 49; DLB 38; MTCW

Bamdad, A.
See Shamlu, Ahmad

Banat, D. R.
See Bradbury, Ray (Douglas)

Bancroft, Laura
See Baum, L(yman) Frank

Banim, John 1798-1842 .... **NCLC 13**
See also DLB 116, 158, 159

Banim, Michael 1796-1874 ...... **NCLC 13**
See also DLB 158, 159

Banjo, The
See Paterson, A(ndrew) B(arton)

Banks, Iain
See Banks, Iain M(enzies)

Banks, Iain M(enzies) 1954-....... **CLC 34**
See also CA 123; 128; INT 128

Banks, Lynne Reid .... **CLC 23**
See also Reid Banks, Lynne
See also AAYA 6

Banks, Russell 1940- .... **CLC 37, 72**
See also CA 65-68; CAAS 15; CANR 19,
52; DLB 130

Banville, John 1945-.............. **CLC 46**
See also CA 117; 128; DLB 14; INT 128

Banville, Theodore (Faullain) de
1832-1891 .... **NCLC 9**

Baraka, Amiri
1934- .... **CLC 1, 2, 3, 5, 10, 14, 33;
BLC; DA; DAC; DAM MST, MULT,
POET, POP; DC 6; PC 4**
See also Jones, LeRoi
See also BW 2; CA 21-24R; CABS 3;
CANR 27, 38; CDALB 1941-1968;
DLB 5, 7, 16, 38; DLBD 8; MTCW

Barbauld, Anna Laetitia
1743-1825 .... **NCLC 50**
See also DLB 107, 109, 142, 158

Barbellion, W. N. P. .... **TCLC 24**
See also Cummings, Bruce F(rederick)

Barbera, Jack (Vincent) 1945-...... **CLC 44**
See also CA 110; CANR 45

Barbey d'Aurevilly, Jules Amedee
1808-1889 .... **NCLC 1; SSC 17**
See also DLB 119

Barbusse, Henri 1873-1935 .... **TCLC 5**
See also CA 105; 154; DLB 65

Barclay, Bill
See Moorcock, Michael (John)

Barclay, William Ewert
See Moorcock, Michael (John)

Barea, Arturo 1897-1957 .... **TCLC 14**
See also CA 111

Barfoot, Joan 1946-.............. **CLC 18**
See also CA 105

Baring, Maurice 1874-1945 .... **TCLC 8**
See also CA 105; DLB 34

Barker, Clive 1952- ... **CLC 52; DAM POP**
See also AAYA 10; BEST 90:3; CA 121;
129; INT 129; MTCW

Barker, George Granville
1913-1991 ..... **CLC 8, 48; DAM POET**
See also CA 9-12R; 135; CANR 7, 38;
DLB 20; MTCW

Barker, Harley Granville
See Granville-Barker, Harley
See also DLB 10

Barker, Howard 1946- .... **CLC 37**
See also CA 102; DLB 13

Barker, Pat(ricia) 1943-........ **CLC 32, 94**
See also CA 117; 122; CANR 50; INT 122

Barlow, Joel 1754-1812 .... **NCLC 23**
See also DLB 37

Barnard, Mary (Ethel) 1909-....... **CLC 48**
See also CA 21-22; CAP 2

Barnes, Djuna
1892-1982 ... **CLC 3, 4, 8, 11, 29; SSC 3**
See also CA 9-12R; 107; CANR 16, 55;
DLB 4, 9, 45; MTCW

Barnes, Julian (Patrick)
1946- .... **CLC 42; DAB**
See also CA 102; CANR 19, 54; DLBY 93

Barnes, Peter 1931- .... **CLC 5, 56**
See also CA 65-68; CAAS 12; CANR 33,
34; DLB 13; MTCW

Baroja (y Nessi), Pio
1872-1956 .... **TCLC 8; HLC**
See also CA 104

Baron, David
See Pinter, Harold

Baron Corvo
See Rolfe, Frederick (William Serafino
Austin Lewis Mary)

Barondess, Sue K(aufman)
1926-1977 .... **CLC 8**
See also Kaufman, Sue
See also CA 1-4R; 69-72; CANR 1

Baron de Teive
See Pessoa, Fernando (Antonio Nogueira)

Barres, Maurice 1862-1923 .... **TCLC 47**
See also DLB 123

Barreto, Afonso Henrique de Lima
See Lima Barreto, Afonso Henrique de

Barrett, (Roger) Syd 1946- .... **CLC 35**

Barrett, William (Christopher)
1913-1992 .... **CLC 27**
See also CA 13-16R; 139; CANR 11;
INT CANR-11

Barrie, J(ames) M(atthew)
1860-1937 .... **TCLC 2; DAB;
DAM DRAM**
See also CA 104; 136; CDBLB 1890-1914;
CLR 16; DLB 10, 141, 156; MAICYA;
YABC 1

Barrington, Michael
See Moorcock, Michael (John)

Barrol, Grady
See Bograd, Larry

Barry, Mike
See Malzberg, Barry N(athaniel)

Barry, Philip 1896-1949......... **TCLC 11**
See also CA 109; DLB 7

Bart, Andre Schwarz
See Schwarz-Bart, Andre

Barth, John (Simmons)
1930- ...... **CLC 1, 2, 3, 5, 7, 9, 10, 14,
27, 51, 89; DAM NOV; SSC 10**
See also AITN 1, 2; CA 1-4R; CABS 1;
CANR 5, 23, 49; DLB 2; MTCW

Belloc, (Joseph) Hilaire (Pierre Sebastien Rene Swanton)
1870-1953 ... **TCLC 7, 18; DAM POET**
See also CA 106; 152; DLB 19, 100, 141, 174; YABC 1

Belloc, Joseph Peter Rene Hilaire
See Belloc, (Joseph) Hilaire (Pierre Sebastien Rene Swanton)

Belloc, Joseph Pierre Hilaire
See Belloc, (Joseph) Hilaire (Pierre Sebastien Rene Swanton)

Belloc, M. A.
See Lowndes, Marie Adelaide (Belloc)

Bellow, Saul
1915- ...... **CLC 1, 2, 3, 6, 8, 10, 13, 15, 25, 33, 34, 63, 79; DA; DAB; DAC; DAM MST, NOV, POP; SSC 14; WLC**
See also AITN 2; BEST 89:3; CA 5-8R; CABS 1; CANR 29, 53; CDALB 1941-1968; DLB 2, 28; DLBD 3; DLBY 82; MTCW

Belser, Reimond Karel Maria de 1929-
See Ruyslinck, Ward
See also CA 152

Bely, Andrey .... **TCLC 7; PC 11**
See also Bugayev, Boris Nikolayevich

Benary, Margot
See Benary-Isbert, Margot

Benary-Isbert, Margot 1889-1979... **CLC 12**
See also CA 5-8R; 89-92; CANR 4; CLR 12; MAICYA; SATA 2; SATA-Obit 21

Benavente (y Martinez), Jacinto
1866-1954 ..... **TCLC 3; DAM DRAM, MULT**
See also CA 106; 131; HW; MTCW

Benchley, Peter (Bradford)
1940- ..... **CLC 4, 8; DAM NOV, POP**
See also AAYA 14; AITN 2; CA 17-20R; CANR 12, 35; MTCW; SATA 3, 89

Benchley, Robert (Charles)
1889-1945 .... **TCLC 1, 55**
See also CA 105; 153; DLB 11

Benda, Julien 1867-1956 .... **TCLC 60**
See also CA 120; 154

Benedict, Ruth 1887-1948 .... **TCLC 60**

Benedikt, Michael 1935- .... **CLC 4, 14**
See also CA 13-16R; CANR 7; DLB 5

Benet, Juan 1927- .... **CLC 28**
See also CA 143

Benet, Stephen Vincent
1898-1943 ..... **TCLC 7; DAM POET; SSC 10**
See also CA 104; 152; DLB 4, 48, 102; YABC 1

Benet, William Rose
1886-1950 ..... **TCLC 28; DAM POET**
See also CA 118; 152; DLB 45

Benford, Gregory (Albert) 1941-... **CLC 52**
See also CA 69-72; CANR 12, 24, 49; DLBY 82

Bengtsson, Frans (Gunnar)
1894-1954 .... **TCLC 48**

Benjamin, David
See Slavitt, David R(ytman)

Benjamin, Lois
See Gould, Lois

Benjamin, Walter 1892-1940 ..... **TCLC 39**

Benn, Gottfried 1886-1956 .... **TCLC 3**
See also CA 106; 153; DLB 56

Bennett, Alan
1934- ... **CLC 45, 77; DAB; DAM MST**
See also CA 103; CANR 35, 55; MTCW

Bennett, (Enoch) Arnold
1867-1931 .... **TCLC 5, 20**
See also CA 106; 155; CDBLB 1890-1914; DLB 10, 34, 98, 135

Bennett, Elizabeth
See Mitchell, Margaret (Munnerlyn)

Bennett, George Harold 1930-
See Bennett, Hal
See also BW 1; CA 97-100

Bennett, Hal .... **CLC 5**
See also Bennett, George Harold
See also DLB 33

Bennett, Jay 1912- .... **CLC 35**
See also AAYA 10; CA 69-72; CANR 11, 42; JRDA; SAAS 4; SATA 41, 87; SATA-Brief 27

Bennett, Louise (Simone)
1919- ..... **CLC 28; BLC; DAM MULT**
See also BW 2; CA 151; DLB 117

Benson, E(dward) F(rederic)
1867-1940 .... **TCLC 27**
See also CA 114; DLB 135, 153

Benson, Jackson J. 1930-......... **CLC 34**
See also CA 25-28R; DLB 111

Benson, Sally 1900-1972 .... **CLC 17**
See also CA 19-20; 37-40R; CAP 1; SATA 1, 35; SATA-Obit 27

Benson, Stella 1892-1933........ **TCLC 17**
See also CA 117; 155; DLB 36, 162

Bentham, Jeremy 1748-1832 ..... **NCLC 38**
See also DLB 107, 158

Bentley, E(dmund) C(lerihew)
1875-1956 .... **TCLC 12**
See also CA 108; DLB 70

Bentley, Eric (Russell) 1916-....... **CLC 24**
See also CA 5-8R; CANR 6; INT CANR-6

Beranger, Pierre Jean de
1780-1857 .... **NCLC 34**

Berdyaev, Nicolas
See Berdyaev, Nikolai (Aleksandrovich)

Berdyaev, Nikolai (Aleksandrovich)
1874-1948 .... **TCLC 67**
See also CA 120

Berendt, John (Lawrence) 1939-.... **CLC 86**
See also CA 146

Berger, Colonel
See Malraux, (Georges-)Andre

Berger, John (Peter) 1926- ...... **CLC 2, 19**
See also CA 81-84; CANR 51; DLB 14

Berger, Melvin H. 1927- .... **CLC 12**
See also CA 5-8R; CANR 4; CLR 32; SAAS 2; SATA 5, 88

Berger, Thomas (Louis)
1924-......... **CLC 3, 5, 8, 11, 18, 38; DAM NOV**
See also CA 1-4R; CANR 5, 28, 51; DLB 2; DLBY 80; INT CANR-28; MTCW

Bergman, (Ernst) Ingmar
1918-.................... **CLC 16, 72**
See also CA 81-84; CANR 33

Bergson, Henri 1859-1941 .... **TCLC 32**

Bergstein, Eleanor 1938-........... **CLC 4**
See also CA 53-56; CANR 5

Berkoff, Steven 1937-............. **CLC 56**
See also CA 104

Bermant, Chaim (Icyk) 1929- ...... **CLC 40**
See also CA 57-60; CANR 6, 31, 57

Bern, Victoria
See Fisher, M(ary) F(rances) K(ennedy)

Bernanos, (Paul Louis) Georges
1888-1948 .... **TCLC 3**
See also CA 104; 130; DLB 72

Bernard, April 1956- .... **CLC 59**
See also CA 131

Berne, Victoria
See Fisher, M(ary) F(rances) K(ennedy)

Bernhard, Thomas
1931-1989 .... **CLC 3, 32, 61**
See also CA 85-88; 127; CANR 32, 57; DLB 85, 124; MTCW

Berriault, Gina 1926-............. **CLC 54**
See also CA 116; 129; DLB 130

Berrigan, Daniel 1921-............ **CLC 4**
See also CA 33-36R; CAAS 1; CANR 11, 43; DLB 5

Berrigan, Edmund Joseph Michael, Jr.
1934-1983
See Berrigan, Ted
See also CA 61-64; 110; CANR 14

Berrigan, Ted .... **CLC 37**
See also Berrigan, Edmund Joseph Michael, Jr.
See also DLB 5, 169

Berry, Charles Edward Anderson 1931-
See Berry, Chuck
See also CA 115

Berry, Chuck .... **CLC 17**
See also Berry, Charles Edward Anderson

Berry, Jonas
See Ashbery, John (Lawrence)

Berry, Wendell (Erdman)
1934- .... **CLC 4, 6, 8, 27, 46; DAM POET**
See also AITN 1; CA 73-76; CANR 50; DLB 5, 6

Berryman, John
1914-1972 ...... **CLC 1, 2, 3, 4, 6, 8, 10, 13, 25, 62; DAM POET**
See also CA 13-16; 33-36R; CABS 2; CANR 35; CAP 1; CDALB 1941-1968; DLB 48; MTCW

Bertolucci, Bernardo 1940- .... **CLC 16**
See also CA 106

Bertrand, Aloysius 1807-1841 .... **NCLC 31**

Bertran de Born c. 1140-1215 ..... **CMLC 5**

Besant, Annie (Wood) 1847-1933 ... **TCLC 9**
See also CA 105

Bessie, Alvah 1904-1985.......... **CLC 23**
See also CA 5-8R; 116; CANR 2; DLB 26

Bethlen, T. D.
See Silverberg, Robert

Beti, Mongo.... **CLC 27; BLC; DAM MULT**
See also Biyidi, Alexandre

Betjeman, John
1906-1984 .... **CLC 2, 6, 10, 34, 43;**
DAB; DAM MST, POET
See also CA 9-12R; 112; CANR 33, 56;
CDBLB 1945-1960; DLB 20; DLBY 84;
MTCW

Bettelheim, Bruno 1903-1990 ...... **CLC 79**
See also CA 81-84; 131; CANR 23; MTCW

Betti, Ugo 1892-1953............. **TCLC 5**
See also CA 104; 155

Betts, Doris (Waugh) 1932-.... **CLC 3, 6, 28**
See also CA 13-16R; CANR 9; DLBY 82;
INT CANR-9

Bevan, Alistair
See Roberts, Keith (John Kingston)

Bialik, Chaim Nachman
1873-1934 .... **TCLC 25**

Bickerstaff, Isaac
See Swift, Jonathan

Bidart, Frank 1939- .... **CLC 33**
See also CA 140

Bienek, Horst 1930-........... **CLC 7, 11**
See also CA 73-76; DLB 75

Bierce, Ambrose (Gwinett)
1842-1914(?) .... **TCLC 1, 7, 44; DA;**
DAC; DAM MST; SSC 9; WLC
See also CA 104; 139; CDALB 1865-1917;
DLB 11, 12, 23, 71, 74

Biggers, Earl Derr 1884-1933 ..... **TCLC 65**
See also CA 108; 153

Billings, Josh
See Shaw, Henry Wheeler

Billington, (Lady) Rachel (Mary)
1942- .... **CLC 43**
See also AITN 2; CA 33-36R; CANR 44

Binyon, T(imothy) J(ohn) 1936- .... **CLC 34**
See also CA 111; CANR 28

Bioy Casares, Adolfo
1914- .... **CLC 4, 8, 13, 88;**
DAM MULT; HLC; SSC 17
See also CA 29-32R; CANR 19, 43;
DLB 113; HW; MTCW

Bird, Cordwainer
See Ellison, Harlan (Jay)

Bird, Robert Montgomery
1806-1854 .... **NCLC 1**

Birney, (Alfred) Earle
1904- .... **CLC 1, 4, 6, 11; DAC;**
DAM MST, POET
See also CA 1-4R; CANR 5, 20; DLB 88;
MTCW

Bishop, Elizabeth
1911-1979 ...... **CLC 1, 4, 9, 13, 15, 32;**
DA; DAC; DAM MST, POET; PC 3
See also CA 5-8R; 89-92; CABS 2;
CANR 26; CDALB 1968-1988; DLB 5,
169; MTCW; SATA-Obit 24

Bishop, John 1935-............... **CLC 10**
See also CA 105

Bissett, Bill 1939-.......... **CLC 18; PC 14**
See also CA 69-72; CAAS 19; CANR 15;
DLB 53; MTCW

Bitov, Andrei (Georgievich) 1937-... **CLC 57**
See also CA 142

Biyidi, Alexandre 1932-
See Beti, Mongo
See also BW 1; CA 114; 124; MTCW

Bjarme, Brynjolf
See Ibsen, Henrik (Johan)

Bjornson, Bjornstjerne (Martinius)
1832-1910 .... **TCLC 7, 37**
See also CA 104

Black, Robert
See Holdstock, Robert P.

Blackburn, Paul 1926-1971 ...... **CLC 9, 43**
See also CA 81-84; 33-36R; CANR 34;
DLB 16; DLBY 81

Black Elk
1863-1950 ..... **TCLC 33; DAM MULT**
See also CA 144; NNAL

Black Hobart
See Sanders, (James) Ed(ward)

Blacklin, Malcolm
See Chambers, Aidan

Blackmore, R(ichard) D(oddridge)
1825-1900 .... **TCLC 27**
See also CA 120; DLB 18

Blackmur, R(ichard) P(almer)
1904-1965 .... **CLC 2, 24**
See also CA 11-12; 25-28R; CAP 1; DLB 63

Black Tarantula
See Acker, Kathy

Blackwood, Algernon (Henry)
1869-1951 .... **TCLC 5**
See also CA 105; 150; DLB 153, 156

Blackwood, Caroline
1931-1996 .... **CLC 6, 9, 100**
See also CA 85-88; 151; CANR 32;
DLB 14; MTCW

Blade, Alexander
See Hamilton, Edmond; Silverberg, Robert

Blaga, Lucian 1895-1961 .... **CLC 75**

Blair, Eric (Arthur) 1903-1950
See Orwell, George
See also CA 104; 132; DA; DAB; DAC;
DAM MST, NOV; MTCW; SATA 29

Blais, Marie-Claire
1939- .... **CLC 2, 4, 6, 13, 22; DAC;**
DAM MST
See also CA 21-24R; CAAS 4; CANR 38;
DLB 53; MTCW

Blaise, Clark 1940-............... **CLC 29**
See also AITN 2; CA 53-56; CAAS 3;
CANR 5; DLB 53

Blake, Nicholas
See Day Lewis, C(ecil)
See also DLB 77

Blake, William
1757-1827 .... **NCLC 13, 37, 57; DA;**
DAB; DAC; DAM MST, POET; PC 12;
WLC
See also CDBLB 1789-1832; DLB 93, 163;
MAICYA; SATA 30

Blake, William J(ames) 1894-1969 ... **PC 12**
See also CA 5-8R; 25-28R

Blasco Ibanez, Vicente
1867-1928 .... **TCLC 12; DAM NOV**
See also CA 110; 131; HW; MTCW

Blatty, William Peter
1928- .... **CLC 2; DAM POP**
See also CA 5-8R; CANR 9

Bleeck, Oliver
See Thomas, Ross (Elmore)

Blessing, Lee 1949-............... **CLC 54**

Blish, James (Benjamin)
1921-1975 .... **CLC 14**
See also CA 1-4R; 57-60; CANR 3; DLB 8;
MTCW; SATA 66

Bliss, Reginald
See Wells, H(erbert) G(eorge)

Blixen, Karen (Christentze Dinesen)
1885-1962
See Dinesen, Isak
See also CA 25-28; CANR 22, 50; CAP 2;
MTCW; SATA 44

Bloch, Robert (Albert) 1917-1994... **CLC 33**
See also CA 5-8R; 146; CAAS 20; CANR 5;
DLB 44; INT CANR-5; SATA 12;
SATA-Obit 82

Blok, Alexander (Alexandrovich)
1880-1921 .... **TCLC 5**
See also CA 104

Blom, Jan
See Breytenbach, Breyten

Bloom, Harold 1930- .... **CLC 24**
See also CA 13-16R; CANR 39; DLB 67

Bloomfield, Aurelius
See Bourne, Randolph S(illiman)

Blount, Roy (Alton), Jr. 1941- ..... **CLC 38**
See also CA 53-56; CANR 10, 28;
INT CANR-28; MTCW

Bloy, Leon 1846-1917............. **TCLC 22**
See also CA 121; DLB 123

Blume, Judy (Sussman)
1938- ... **CLC 12, 30; DAM NOV, POP**
See also AAYA 3; CA 29-32R; CANR 13,
37; CLR 2, 15; DLB 52; JRDA;
MAICYA; MTCW; SATA 2, 31, 79

Blunden, Edmund (Charles)
1896-1974 .... **CLC 2, 56**
See also CA 17-18; 45-48; CANR 54;
CAP 2; DLB 20, 100, 155; MTCW

Bly, Robert (Elwood)
1926- .... **CLC 1, 2, 5, 10, 15, 38;**
DAM POET
See also CA 5-8R; CANR 41; DLB 5;
MTCW

Boas, Franz 1858-1942.......... **TCLC 56**
See also CA 115

Bobette
See Simenon, Georges (Jacques Christian)

Boccaccio, Giovanni
1313-1375 .... **CMLC 13; SSC 10**

Bochco, Steven 1943-............. **CLC 35**
See also AAYA 11; CA 124; 138

Bodenheim, Maxwell 1892-1954 ... **TCLC 44**
See also CA 110; DLB 9, 45

Broumas, Olga 1949- .... **CLC 10, 73**
See also CA 85-88; CANR 20

Brown, Alan 1951- .... **CLC 99**

Brown, Charles Brockden
1771-1810 .... **NCLC 22**
See also CDALB 1640-1865; DLB 37, 59, 73

Brown, Christy 1932-1981 .... **CLC 63**
See also CA 105; 104; DLB 14

Brown, Claude
1937- ..... **CLC 30; BLC; DAM MULT**
See also AAYA 7; BW 1; CA 73-76

Brown, Dee (Alexander)
1908- .... **CLC 18, 47; DAM POP**
See also CA 13-16R; CAAS 6; CANR 11, 45; DLBY 80; MTCW; SATA 5

Brown, George
See Wertmueller, Lina

Brown, George Douglas
1869-1902 .... **TCLC 28**

Brown, George Mackay
1921-1996 .... **CLC 5, 48, 100**
See also CA 21-24R; 151; CAAS 6; CANR 12, 37; DLB 14, 27, 139; MTCW; SATA 35

Brown, (William) Larry 1951- ...... **CLC 73**
See also CA 130; 134; INT 133

Brown, Moses
See Barrett, William (Christopher)

Brown, Rita Mae
1944- ..... **CLC 18, 43, 79; DAM NOV, POP**
See also CA 45-48; CANR 2, 11, 35; INT CANR-11; MTCW

Brown, Roderick (Langmere) Haig-
See Haig-Brown, Roderick (Langmere)

Brown, Rosellen 1939- .... **CLC 32**
See also CA 77-80; CAAS 10; CANR 14, 44

Brown, Sterling Allen
1901-1989 .... **CLC 1, 23, 59; BLC; DAM MULT, POET**
See also BW 1; CA 85-88; 127; CANR 26; DLB 48, 51, 63; MTCW

Brown, Will
See Ainsworth, William Harrison

Brown, William Wells
1813-1884 .... **NCLC 2; BLC; DAM MULT; DC 1**
See also DLB 3, 50

Browne, (Clyde) Jackson 1948(?)-... **CLC 21**
See also CA 120

Browning, Elizabeth Barrett
1806-1861 .... **NCLC 1, 16, 61; DA; DAB; DAC; DAM MST, POET; PC 6; WLC**
See also CDBLB 1832-1890; DLB 32

Browning, Robert
1812-1889 .... **NCLC 19; DA; DAB; DAC; DAM MST, POET; PC 2**
See also CDBLB 1832-1890; DLB 32, 163; YABC 1

Browning, Tod 1882-1962 .... **CLC 16**
See also CA 141; 117

Brownson, Orestes (Augustus)
1803-1876 .... **NCLC 50**

Bruccoli, Matthew J(oseph) 1931- .. **CLC 34**
See also CA 9-12R; CANR 7; DLB 103

Bruce, Lenny .... **CLC 21**
See also Schneider, Leonard Alfred

Bruin, John
See Brutus, Dennis

Brulard, Henri
See Stendhal

Brulls, Christian
See Simenon, Georges (Jacques Christian)

Brunner, John (Kilian Houston)
1934-1995 ...... **CLC 8, 10; DAM POP**
See also CA 1-4R; 149; CAAS 8; CANR 2, 37; MTCW

Bruno, Giordano 1548-1600 .... **LC 27**

Brutus, Dennis
1924- ..... **CLC 43; BLC; DAM MULT, POET**
See also BW 2; CA 49-52; CAAS 14; CANR 2, 27, 42; DLB 117

Bryan, C(ourtlandt) D(ixon) B(arnes)
1936- .... **CLC 29**
See also CA 73-76; CANR 13; INT CANR-13

Bryan, Michael
See Moore, Brian

Bryant, William Cullen
1794-1878 ..... **NCLC 6, 46; DA; DAB; DAC; DAM MST, POET**
See also CDALB 1640-1865; DLB 3, 43, 59

Bryusov, Valery Yakovlevich
1873-1924 .... **TCLC 10**
See also CA 107; 155

Buchan, John
1875-1940 .... **TCLC 41; DAB; DAM POP**
See also CA 108; 145; DLB 34, 70, 156; YABC 2

Buchanan, George 1506-1582 .... **LC 4**

Buchheim, Lothar-Guenther 1918- ... **CLC 6**
See also CA 85-88

Buchner, (Karl) Georg
1813-1837 .... **NCLC 26**

Buchwald, Art(hur) 1925- .... **CLC 33**
See also AITN 1; CA 5-8R; CANR 21; MTCW; SATA 10

Buck, Pearl S(ydenstricker)
1892-1973 .... **CLC 7, 11, 18; DA; DAB; DAC; DAM MST, NOV**
See also AITN 1; CA 1-4R; 41-44R; CANR 1, 34; DLB 9, 102; MTCW; SATA 1, 25

Buckler, Ernest
1908-1984 .. **CLC 13; DAC; DAM MST**
See also CA 11-12; 114; CAP 1; DLB 68; SATA 47

Buckley, Vincent (Thomas)
1925-1988 .... **CLC 57**
See also CA 101

Buckley, William F(rank), Jr.
1925- .... **CLC 7, 18, 37; DAM POP**
See also AITN 1; CA 1-4R; CANR 1, 24, 53; DLB 137; DLBY 80; INT CANR-24; MTCW

Buechner, (Carl) Frederick
1926- ...... **CLC 2, 4, 6, 9; DAM NOV**
See also CA 13-16R; CANR 11, 39; DLBY 80; INT CANR-11; MTCW

Buell, John (Edward) 1927- .... **CLC 10**
See also CA 1-4R; DLB 53

Buero Vallejo, Antonio 1916- ... **CLC 15, 46**
See also CA 106; CANR 24, 49; HW; MTCW

Bufalino, Gesualdo 1920(?)-........ **CLC 74**

Bugayev, Boris Nikolayevich 1880-1934
See Bely, Andrey
See also CA 104

Bukowski, Charles
1920-1994 .... **CLC 2, 5, 9, 41, 82; DAM NOV, POET**
See also CA 17-20R; 144; CANR 40; DLB 5, 130, 169; MTCW

Bulgakov, Mikhail (Afanas'evich)
1891-1940 .... **TCLC 2, 16; DAM DRAM, NOV; SSC 18**
See also CA 105; 152

Bulgya, Alexander Alexandrovich
1901-1956 .... **TCLC 53**
See also Fadeyev, Alexander
See also CA 117

Bullins, Ed
1935- .... **CLC 1, 5, 7; BLC; DAM DRAM, MULT; DC 6**
See also BW 2; CA 49-52; CAAS 16; CANR 24, 46; DLB 7, 38; MTCW

Bulwer-Lytton, Edward (George Earle Lytton)
1803-1873 .... **NCLC 1, 45**
See also DLB 21

Bunin, Ivan Alexeyevich
1870-1953 .... **TCLC 6; SSC 5**
See also CA 104

Bunting, Basil
1900-1985 .... **CLC 10, 39, 47; DAM POET**
See also CA 53-56; 115; CANR 7; DLB 20

Bunuel, Luis
1900-1983 .... **CLC 16, 80; DAM MULT; HLC**
See also CA 101; 110; CANR 32; HW

Bunyan, John
1628-1688 ...... **LC 4; DA; DAB; DAC; DAM MST; WLC**
See also CDBLB 1660-1789; DLB 39

Burckhardt, Jacob (Christoph)
1818-1897 .... **NCLC 49**

Burford, Eleanor
See Hibbert, Eleanor Alice Burford

Burgess, Anthony
. **CLC 1, 2, 4, 5, 8, 10, 13, 15, 22, 40, 62, 81, 94; DAB**
See also Wilson, John (Anthony) Burgess
See also AITN 1; CDBLB 1960 to Present; DLB 14

Burke, Edmund
1729(?)-1797 ...... **LC 7, 36; DA; DAB; DAC; DAM MST; WLC**
See also DLB 104

Burke, Kenneth (Duva)
1897-1993 . . . . CLC **2, 24**
See also CA 5-8R; 143; CANR 39; DLB 45, 63; MTCW

Burke, Leda
See Garnett, David

Burke, Ralph
See Silverberg, Robert

Burke, Thomas 1886-1945 . . . . TCLC **63**
See also CA 113; 155

Burney, Fanny 1752-1840 . . . . NCLC **12, 54**
See also DLB 39

Burns, Robert 1759-1796 . . . . PC **6**
See also CDBLB 1789-1832; DA; DAB; DAC; DAM MST, POET; DLB 109; WLC

Burns, Tex
See L'Amour, Louis (Dearborn)

Burnshaw, Stanley 1906- . . . . . CLC **3, 13, 44**
See also CA 9-12R; DLB 48

Burr, Anne 1937- . . . . CLC **6**
See also CA 25-28R

Burroughs, Edgar Rice
1875-1950 . . . . TCLC **2, 32; DAM NOV**
See also AAYA 11; CA 104; 132; DLB 8; MTCW; SATA 41

Burroughs, William S(eward)
1914- . . . . CLC **1, 2, 5, 15, 22, 42, 75;**
DA; DAB; DAC; DAM MST, NOV,
POP; WLC
See also AITN 2; CA 9-12R; CANR 20, 52; DLB 2, 8, 16, 152; DLBY 81; MTCW

Burton, Richard F. 1821-1890 . . . . NCLC **42**
See also DLB 55

Busch, Frederick 1941- . . . CLC **7, 10, 18, 47**
See also CA 33-36R; CAAS 1; CANR 45; DLB 6

Bush, Ronald 1946- . . . . CLC **34**
See also CA 136

Bustos, F(rancisco)
See Borges, Jorge Luis

Bustos Domecq, H(onorio)
See Bioy Casares, Adolfo; Borges, Jorge Luis

Butler, Octavia E(stelle)
1947- . . . . . CLC **38; DAM MULT, POP**
See also AAYA 18; BW 2; CA 73-76; CANR 12, 24, 38; DLB 33; MTCW; SATA 84

Butler, Robert Olen (Jr.)
1945- . . . . CLC **81; DAM POP**
See also CA 112; DLB 173; INT 112

Butler, Samuel 1612-1680 . . . . LC **16**
See also DLB 101, 126

Butler, Samuel
1835-1902 . . . . . . TCLC **1, 33; DA; DAB;**
DAC; DAM MST, NOV; WLC
See also CA 143; CDBLB 1890-1914; DLB 18, 57, 174

Butler, Walter C.
See Faust, Frederick (Schiller)

Butor, Michel (Marie Francois)
1926- . . . . CLC **1, 3, 8, 11, 15**
See also CA 9-12R; CANR 33; DLB 83; MTCW

Buzo, Alexander (John) 1944- . . . . . . CLC **61**
See also CA 97-100; CANR 17, 39

Buzzati, Dino 1906-1972 . . . . CLC **36**
See also CA 33-36R; DLB 177

Byars, Betsy (Cromer) 1928- . . . . . . CLC **35**
See also AAYA 19; CA 33-36R; CANR 18, 36, 57; CLR 1, 16; DLB 52; INT CANR-18; JRDA; MAICYA; MTCW; SAAS 1; SATA 4, 46, 80

Byatt, A(ntonia) S(usan Drabble)
1936- . . . CLC **19, 65; DAM NOV, POP**
See also CA 13-16R; CANR 13, 33, 50; DLB 14; MTCW

Byrne, David 1952- . . . . CLC **26**
See also CA 127

Byrne, John Keyes 1926-
See Leonard, Hugh
See also CA 102; INT 102

Byron, George Gordon (Noel)
1788-1824 . . . . . NCLC **2, 12; DA; DAB;**
DAC; DAM MST, POET; PC 16; WLC
See also CDBLB 1789-1832; DLB 96, 110

Byron, Robert 1905-1941 . . . . TCLC **67**

C. 3. 3.
See Wilde, Oscar (Fingal O'Flahertie Wills)

Caballero, Fernan 1796-1877 . . . . . NCLC **10**

Cabell, Branch
See Cabell, James Branch

Cabell, James Branch 1879-1958 . . . TCLC **6**
See also CA 105; 152; DLB 9, 78

Cable, George Washington
1844-1925 . . . . TCLC **4; SSC 4**
See also CA 104; 155; DLB 12, 74; DLBD 13

Cabral de Melo Neto, Joao
1920- . . . . CLC **76; DAM MULT**
See also CA 151

Cabrera Infante, G(uillermo)
1929- . . . . . CLC **5, 25, 45; DAM MULT;**
HLC
See also CA 85-88; CANR 29; DLB 113; HW; MTCW

Cade, Toni
See Bambara, Toni Cade

Cadmus and Harmonia
See Buchan, John

Caedmon fl. 658-680 . . . . CMLC **7**
See also DLB 146

Caeiro, Alberto
See Pessoa, Fernando (Antonio Nogueira)

Cage, John (Milton, Jr.) 1912- . . . . . CLC **41**
See also CA 13-16R; CANR 9; INT CANR-9

Cain, G.
See Cabrera Infante, G(uillermo)

Cain, Guillermo
See Cabrera Infante, G(uillermo)

Cain, James M(allahan)
1892-1977 . . . . CLC **3, 11, 28**
See also AITN 1; CA 17-20R; 73-76; CANR 8, 34; MTCW

Caine, Mark
See Raphael, Frederic (Michael)

Calasso, Roberto 1941- . . . . CLC **81**
See also CA 143

Calderon de la Barca, Pedro
1600-1681 . . . . LC **23; DC 3**

Caldwell, Erskine (Preston)
1903-1987 . . . . CLC **1, 8, 14, 50, 60;**
DAM NOV; SSC 19
See also AITN 1; CA 1-4R; 121; CAAS 1; CANR 2, 33; DLB 9, 86; MTCW

Caldwell, (Janet Miriam) Taylor (Holland)
1900-1985 . . . . CLC **2, 28, 39;**
DAM NOV, POP
See also CA 5-8R; 116; CANR 5

Calhoun, John Caldwell
1782-1850 . . . . NCLC **15**
See also DLB 3

Calisher, Hortense
1911- . . . . . CLC **2, 4, 8, 38; DAM NOV;**
SSC 15
See also CA 1-4R; CANR 1, 22; DLB 2; INT CANR-22; MTCW

Callaghan, Morley Edward
1903-1990 . . . . . CLC **3, 14, 41, 65; DAC;**
DAM MST
See also CA 9-12R; 132; CANR 33; DLB 68; MTCW

Callimachus
c. 305B.C.-c. 240B.C. . . . . CMLC **18**
See also DLB 176

Calvin, John 1509-1564 . . . . LC **37**

Calvino, Italo
1923-1985 . . . . . CLC **5, 8, 11, 22, 33, 39,**
73; DAM NOV; SSC 3
See also CA 85-88; 116; CANR 23; MTCW

Cameron, Carey 1952- . . . . CLC **59**
See also CA 135

Cameron, Peter 1959- . . . . CLC **44**
See also CA 125; CANR 50

Campana, Dino 1885-1932 . . . . TCLC **20**
See also CA 117; DLB 114

Campanella, Tommaso 1568-1639 . . . . LC **32**

Campbell, John W(ood, Jr.)
1910-1971 . . . . CLC **32**
See also CA 21-22; 29-32R; CANR 34; CAP 2; DLB 8; MTCW

Campbell, Joseph 1904-1987 . . . . CLC **69**
See also AAYA 3; BEST 89:2; CA 1-4R; 124; CANR 3, 28; MTCW

Campbell, Maria 1940- . . . . CLC **85; DAC**
See also CA 102; CANR 54; NNAL

Campbell, (John) Ramsey
1946- . . . . CLC **42; SSC 19**
See also CA 57-60; CANR 7; INT CANR-7

Campbell, (Ignatius) Roy (Dunnachie)
1901-1957 . . . . TCLC **5**
See also CA 104; 155; DLB 20

Campbell, Thomas 1777-1844 . . . . NCLC **19**
See also DLB 93; 144

Campbell, Wilfred . . . . TCLC **9**
See also Campbell, William

Campbell, William 1858(?)-1918
See Campbell, Wilfred
See also CA 106; DLB 92

Campion, Jane . . . . CLC **95**
See also CA 138

Campos, Alvaro de
See Pessoa, Fernando (Antonio Nogueira)

Camus, Albert
1913-1960 .... **CLC 1, 2, 4, 9, 11, 14, 32, 63, 69; DA; DAB; DAC; DAM DRAM, MST, NOV; DC 2; SSC 9; WLC**
See also CA 89-92; DLB 72; MTCW

Canby, Vincent 1924- .... **CLC 13**
See also CA 81-84

Cancale
See Desnos, Robert

Canetti, Elias
1905-1994 .... **CLC 3, 14, 25, 75, 86**
See also CA 21-24R; 146; CANR 23;
DLB 85, 124; MTCW

Canin, Ethan 1960-............... **CLC 55**
See also CA 131; 135

Cannon, Curt
See Hunter, Evan

Cape, Judith
See Page, P(atricia) K(athleen)

Capek, Karel
1890-1938 ...... **TCLC 6, 37; DA; DAB; DAC; DAM DRAM, MST, NOV; DC 1; WLC**
See also CA 104; 140

Capote, Truman
1924-1984 ...... **CLC 1, 3, 8, 13, 19, 34, 38, 58; DA; DAB; DAC; DAM MST, NOV, POP; SSC 2; WLC**
See also CA 5-8R; 113; CANR 18;
CDALB 1941-1968; DLB 2; DLBY 80, 84; MTCW; SATA 91

Capra, Frank 1897-1991............ **CLC 16**
See also CA 61-64; 135

Caputo, Philip 1941-.............. **CLC 32**
See also CA 73-76; CANR 40

Card, Orson Scott
1951- ...... **CLC 44, 47, 50; DAM POP**
See also AAYA 11; CA 102; CANR 27, 47;
INT CANR-27; MTCW; SATA 83

Cardenal, Ernesto
1925- .... **CLC 31; DAM MULT, POET; HLC**
See also CA 49-52; CANR 2, 32; HW;
MTCW

Cardozo, Benjamin N(athan)
1870-1938 .... **TCLC 65**
See also CA 117

Carducci, Giosue 1835-1907....... **TCLC 32**

Carew, Thomas 1595(?)-1640........ **LC 13**
See also DLB 126

Carey, Ernestine Gilbreth 1908- .... **CLC 17**
See also CA 5-8R; SATA 2

Carey, Peter 1943-......... **CLC 40, 55, 96**
See also CA 123; 127; CANR 53; INT 127;
MTCW

Carleton, William 1794-1869...... **NCLC 3**
See also DLB 159

Carlisle, Henry (Coffin) 1926-...... **CLC 33**
See also CA 13-16R; CANR 15

Carlsen, Chris
See Holdstock, Robert P.

Carlson, Ron(ald F.) 1947-........ **CLC 54**
See also CA 105; CANR 27

Carlyle, Thomas
1795-1881 ...... **NCLC 22; DA; DAB; DAC; DAM MST**
See also CDBLB 1789-1832; DLB 55; 144

Carman, (William) Bliss
1861-1929 .... **TCLC 7; DAC**
See also CA 104; 152; DLB 92

Carnegie, Dale 1888-1955 .... **TCLC 53**

Carossa, Hans 1878-1956........ **TCLC 48**
See also DLB 66

Carpenter, Don(ald Richard)
1931-1995 .... **CLC 41**
See also CA 45-48; 149; CANR 1

Carpentier (y Valmont), Alejo
1904-1980 .... **CLC 8, 11, 38; DAM MULT; HLC**
See also CA 65-68; 97-100; CANR 11;
DLB 113; HW

Carr, Caleb 1955(?)-.............. **CLC 86**
See also CA 147

Carr, Emily 1871-1945........... **TCLC 32**
See also DLB 68

Carr, John Dickson 1906-1977 ...... **CLC 3**
See also CA 49-52; 69-72; CANR 3, 33;
MTCW

Carr, Philippa
See Hibbert, Eleanor Alice Burford

Carr, Virginia Spencer 1929-....... **CLC 34**
See also CA 61-64; DLB 111

Carrere, Emmanuel 1957- .... **CLC 89**

Carrier, Roch
1937- ... **CLC 13, 78; DAC; DAM MST**
See also CA 130; DLB 53

Carroll, James P. 1943(?)-......... **CLC 38**
See also CA 81-84

Carroll, Jim 1951- .... **CLC 35**
See also AAYA 17; CA 45-48; CANR 42

Carroll, Lewis .... **NCLC 2, 53; WLC**
See also Dodgson, Charles Lutwidge
See also CDBLB 1832-1890; CLR 2, 18;
DLB 18, 163; JRDA

Carroll, Paul Vincent 1900-1968.... **CLC 10**
See also CA 9-12R; 25-28R; DLB 10

Carruth, Hayden
1921- ...... **CLC 4, 7, 10, 18, 84; PC 10**
See also CA 9-12R; CANR 4, 38; DLB 5, 165; INT CANR-4; MTCW; SATA 47

Carson, Rachel Louise
1907-1964 .... **CLC 71; DAM POP**
See also CA 77-80; CANR 35; MTCW;
SATA 23

Carter, Angela (Olive)
1940-1992 ...... **CLC 5, 41, 76; SSC 13**
See also CA 53-56; 136; CANR 12, 36;
DLB 14; MTCW; SATA 66;
SATA-Obit 70

Carter, Nick
See Smith, Martin Cruz

Carver, Raymond
1938-1988 .... **CLC 22, 36, 53, 55; DAM NOV; SSC 8**
See also CA 33-36R; 126; CANR 17, 34;
DLB 130; DLBY 84, 88; MTCW

Cary, Elizabeth, Lady Falkland
1585-1639 .... **LC 30**

Cary, (Arthur) Joyce (Lunel)
1888-1957 .... **TCLC 1, 29**
See also CA 104; CDBLB 1914-1945;
DLB 15, 100

Casanova de Seingalt, Giovanni Jacopo
1725-1798 .... **LC 13**

Casares, Adolfo Bioy
See Bioy Casares, Adolfo

Casely-Hayford, J(oseph) E(phraim)
1866-1930 .... **TCLC 24; BLC; DAM MULT**
See also BW 2; CA 123; 152

Casey, John (Dudley) 1939-........ **CLC 59**
See also BEST 90:2; CA 69-72; CANR 23

Casey, Michael 1947-.............. **CLC 2**
See also CA 65-68; DLB 5

Casey, Patrick
See Thurman, Wallace (Henry)

Casey, Warren (Peter) 1935-1988... **CLC 12**
See also CA 101; 127; INT 101

Casona, Alejandro................. **CLC 49**
See also Alvarez, Alejandro Rodriguez

Cassavetes, John 1929-1989........ **CLC 20**
See also CA 85-88; 127

Cassian, Nina 1924- .... **PC 17**

Cassill, R(onald) V(erlin) 1919-... **CLC 4, 23**
See also CA 9-12R; CAAS 1; CANR 7, 45;
DLB 6

Cassirer, Ernst 1874-1945 .... **TCLC 61**

Cassity, (Allen) Turner 1929- .... **CLC 6, 42**
See also CA 17-20R; CAAS 8; CANR 11;
DLB 105

Castaneda, Carlos 1931(?)-......... **CLC 12**
See also CA 25-28R; CANR 32; HW;
MTCW

Castedo, Elena 1937- .... **CLC 65**
See also CA 132

Castedo-Ellerman, Elena
See Castedo, Elena

Castellanos, Rosario
1925-1974 ...... **CLC 66; DAM MULT; HLC**
See also CA 131; 53-56; DLB 113; HW

Castelvetro, Lodovico 1505-1571..... **LC 12**

Castiglione, Baldassare 1478-1529 ... **LC 12**

Castle, Robert
See Hamilton, Edmond

Castro, Guillen de 1569-1631........ **LC 19**

Castro, Rosalia de
1837-1885 ...... **NCLC 3; DAM MULT**

Cather, Willa
See Cather, Willa Sibert

Cather, Willa Sibert
1873-1947 .... **TCLC 1, 11, 31; DA; DAB; DAC; DAM MST, NOV; SSC 2; WLC**
See also CA 104; 128; CDALB 1865-1917;
DLB 9, 54, 78; DLBD 1; MTCW;
SATA 30

Cato, Marcus Porcius
234B.C.-149B.C............. **CMLC 21**

Catton, (Charles) Bruce
    1899-1978 .... **CLC 35**
    See also AITN 1; CA 5-8R; 81-84;
        CANR 7; DLB 17; SATA 2;
        SATA-Obit 24

Catullus   c. 84B.C.-c. 54B.C. ..... **CMLC 18**

Cauldwell, Frank
    See King, Francis (Henry)

Caunitz, William J.   1933-1996 ..... **CLC 34**
    See also BEST 89:3; CA 125; 130; 152;
        INT 130

Causley, Charles (Stanley)   1917-.... **CLC 7**
    See also CA 9-12R; CANR 5, 35; CLR 30;
        DLB 27; MTCW; SATA 3, 66

Caute, David   1936-.... **CLC 29; DAM NOV**
    See also CA 1-4R; CAAS 4; CANR 1, 33;
        DLB 14

Cavafy, C(onstantine) P(eter)
    1863-1933 .... **TCLC 2, 7; DAM POET**
    See also Kavafis, Konstantinos Petrou
    See also CA 148

Cavallo, Evelyn
    See Spark, Muriel (Sarah)

Cavanna, Betty .... **CLC 12**
    See also Harrison, Elizabeth Cavanna
    See also JRDA; MAICYA; SAAS 4;
        SATA 1, 30

Cavendish, Margaret Lucas
    1623-1673 .... **LC 30**
    See also DLB 131

Caxton, William   1421(?)-1491(?)..... **LC 17**
    See also DLB 170

Cayrol, Jean   1911-................ **CLC 11**
    See also CA 89-92; DLB 83

Cela, Camilo Jose
    1916-..... **CLC 4, 13, 59; DAM MULT;**
                                        HLC
    See also BEST 90:2; CA 21-24R; CAAS 10;
        CANR 21, 32; DLBY 89; HW; MTCW

Celan, Paul ...... **CLC 10, 19, 53, 82; PC 10**
    See also Antschel, Paul
    See also DLB 69

Celine, Louis-Ferdinand
    .... **CLC 1, 3, 4, 7, 9, 15, 47**
    See also Destouches, Louis-Ferdinand
    See also DLB 72

Cellini, Benvenuto   1500-1571 .... **LC 7**

Cendrars, Blaise .... **CLC 18**
    See also Sauser-Hall, Frederic

Cernuda (y Bidon), Luis
    1902-1963 .... **CLC 54; DAM POET**
    See also CA 131; 89-92; DLB 134; HW

Cervantes (Saavedra), Miguel de
    1547-1616 .... **LC 6, 23; DA; DAB;**
        DAC; DAM MST, NOV; SSC 12; WLC

Cesaire, Aime (Fernand)
    1913- .... **CLC 19, 32; BLC;**
                                DAM MULT, POET
    See also BW 2; CA 65-68; CANR 24, 43;
        MTCW

Chabon, Michael   1963- .... **CLC 55**
    See also CA 139; CANR 57

Chabrol, Claude   1930- .... **CLC 16**
    See also CA 110

Challans, Mary   1905-1983
    See Renault, Mary
    See also CA 81-84; 111; SATA 23;
        SATA-Obit 36

Challis, George
    See Faust, Frederick (Schiller)

Chambers, Aidan   1934- .... **CLC 35**
    See also CA 25-28R; CANR 12, 31; JRDA;
        MAICYA; SAAS 12; SATA 1, 69

Chambers, James   1948-
    See Cliff, Jimmy
    See also CA 124

Chambers, Jessie
    See Lawrence, D(avid) H(erbert Richards)

Chambers, Robert W.   1865-1933... **TCLC 41**

Chandler, Raymond (Thornton)
    1888-1959 .... **TCLC 1, 7; SSC 23**
    See also CA 104; 129; CDALB 1929-1941;
        DLBD 6; MTCW

Chang, Jung   1952-............... **CLC 71**
    See also CA 142

Channing, William Ellery
    1780-1842 .... **NCLC 17**
    See also DLB 1, 59

Chaplin, Charles Spencer
    1889-1977 .... **CLC 16**
    See also Chaplin, Charlie
    See also CA 81-84; 73-76

Chaplin, Charlie
    See Chaplin, Charles Spencer
    See also DLB 44

Chapman, George
    1559(?)-1634 ..... **LC 22; DAM DRAM**
    See also DLB 62, 121

Chapman, Graham   1941-1989 ...... **CLC 21**
    See also Monty Python
    See also CA 116; 129; CANR 35

Chapman, John Jay   1862-1933 ..... **TCLC 7**
    See also CA 104

Chapman, Lee
    See Bradley, Marion Zimmer

Chapman, Walker
    See Silverberg, Robert

Chappell, Fred (Davis)   1936-.... **CLC 40, 78**
    See also CA 5-8R; CAAS 4; CANR 8, 33;
        DLB 6, 105

Char, Rene(-Emile)
    1907-1988 .... **CLC 9, 11, 14, 55;**
                                        DAM POET
    See also CA 13-16R; 124; CANR 32;
        MTCW

Charby, Jay
    See Ellison, Harlan (Jay)

Chardin, Pierre Teilhard de
    See Teilhard de Chardin, (Marie Joseph)
        Pierre

Charles I   1600-1649.............. **LC 13**

Charyn, Jerome   1937- .... **CLC 5, 8, 18**
    See also CA 5-8R; CAAS 1; CANR 7;
        DLBY 83; MTCW

Chase, Mary (Coyle)   1907-1981 ...... **DC 1**
    See also CA 77-80; 105; SATA 17;
        SATA-Obit 29

Chase, Mary Ellen   1887-1973 .... **CLC 2**
    See also CA 13-16; 41-44R; CAP 1;
        SATA 10

Chase, Nicholas
    See Hyde, Anthony

Chateaubriand, Francois Rene de
    1768-1848 .... **NCLC 3**
    See also DLB 119

Chatterje, Sarat Chandra   1876-1936(?)
    See Chatterji, Saratchandra
    See also CA 109

Chatterji, Bankim Chandra
    1838-1894 .... **NCLC 19**

Chatterji, Saratchandra .... **TCLC 13**
    See also Chatterje, Sarat Chandra

Chatterton, Thomas
    1752-1770 .... **LC 3; DAM POET**
    See also DLB 109

Chatwin, (Charles) Bruce
    1940-1989 .. **CLC 28, 57, 59; DAM POP**
    See also AAYA 4; BEST 90:1; CA 85-88;
        127

Chaucer, Daniel
    See Ford, Ford Madox

Chaucer, Geoffrey
    1340(?)-1400 .... **LC 17; DA; DAB;**
                                DAC; DAM MST, POET
    See also CDBLB Before 1660; DLB 146

Chaviaras, Strates   1935-
    See Haviaras, Stratis
    See also CA 105

Chayefsky, Paddy .... **CLC 23**
    See also Chayefsky, Sidney
    See also DLB 7, 44; DLBY 81

Chayefsky, Sidney   1923-1981
    See Chayefsky, Paddy
    See also CA 9-12R; 104; CANR 18;
        DAM DRAM

Chedid, Andree   1920-............. **CLC 47**
    See also CA 145

Cheever, John
    1912-1982 ...... **CLC 3, 7, 8, 11, 15, 25,**
        64; DA; DAB; DAC; DAM MST, NOV,
                        POP; SSC 1; WLC
    See also CA 5-8R; 106; CABS 1; CANR 5,
        27; CDALB 1941-1968; DLB 2, 102;
        DLBY 80, 82; INT CANR-5; MTCW

Cheever, Susan   1943-.......... **CLC 18, 48**
    See also CA 103; CANR 27, 51; DLBY 82;
        INT CANR-27

Chekhonte, Antosha
    See Chekhov, Anton (Pavlovich)

Chekhov, Anton (Pavlovich)
    1860-1904 ..... **TCLC 3, 10, 31, 55; DA;**
        DAB; DAC; DAM DRAM, MST; SSC 2;
                                        WLC
    See also CA 104; 124; SATA 90

Chernyshevsky, Nikolay Gavrilovich
    1828-1889 .... **NCLC 1**

Cherry, Carolyn Janice   1942-
    See Cherryh, C. J.
    See also CA 65-68; CANR 10

Cherryh, C. J. .... **CLC 35**
    See also Cherry, Carolyn Janice
    See also DLBY 80

Chesnutt, Charles W(addell)
1858-1932 .... **TCLC 5, 39; BLC;**
DAM MULT; SSC 7
See also BW 1; CA 106; 125; DLB 12, 50,
78; MTCW

Chester, Alfred 1929(?)-1971 ...... **CLC 49**
See also CA 33-36R; DLB 130

Chesterton, G(ilbert) K(eith)
1874-1936 .... **TCLC 1, 6, 64;**
DAM NOV, POET; SSC 1
See also CA 104; 132; CDBLB 1914-1945;
DLB 10, 19, 34, 70, 98, 149; MTCW;
SATA 27

Chiang Pin-chin 1904-1986
See Ding Ling
See also CA 118

Ch'ien Chung-shu 1910- .... **CLC 22**
See also CA 130; MTCW

Child, L. Maria
See Child, Lydia Maria

Child, Lydia Maria 1802-1880 .... **NCLC 6**
See also DLB 1, 74; SATA 67

Child, Mrs.
See Child, Lydia Maria

Child, Philip 1898-1978 .... **CLC 19, 68**
See also CA 13-14; CAP 1; SATA 47

Childers, (Robert) Erskine
1870-1922 .... **TCLC 65**
See also CA 113; 153; DLB 70

Childress, Alice
1920-1994 .... **CLC 12, 15, 86, 96; BLC;**
DAM DRAM, MULT, NOV; DC 4
See also AAYA 8; BW 2; CA 45-48; 146;
CANR 3, 27, 50; CLR 14; DLB 7, 38;
JRDA; MAICYA; MTCW; SATA 7, 48,
81

Chin, Frank (Chew, Jr.) 1940- .... **DC 7**
See also CA 33-36R; DAM MULT

Chislett, (Margaret) Anne 1943- .... **CLC 34**
See also CA 151

Chitty, Thomas Willes 1926- .... **CLC 11**
See also Hinde, Thomas
See also CA 5-8R

Chivers, Thomas Holley
1809-1858 .... **NCLC 49**
See also DLB 3

Chomette, Rene Lucien 1898-1981
See Clair, Rene
See also CA 103

Chopin, Kate
.... **TCLC 5, 14; DA; DAB; SSC 8**
See also Chopin, Katherine
See also CDALB 1865-1917; DLB 12, 78

Chopin, Katherine 1851-1904
See Chopin, Kate
See also CA 104; 122; DAC; DAM MST,
NOV

Chretien de Troyes
c. 12th cent. - .... **CMLC 10**

Christie
See Ichikawa, Kon

Christie, Agatha (Mary Clarissa)
1890-1976 ...... **CLC 1, 6, 8, 12, 39, 48;**
DAB; DAC; DAM NOV
See also AAYA 9; AITN 1, 2; CA 17-20R;
61-64; CANR 10, 37; CDBLB 1914-1945;
DLB 13, 77; MTCW; SATA 36

Christie, (Ann) Philippa
See Pearce, Philippa
See also CA 5-8R; CANR 4

Christine de Pizan 1365(?)-1431(?) .... **LC 9**

Chubb, Elmer
See Masters, Edgar Lee

Chulkov, Mikhail Dmitrievich
1743-1792 .... **LC 2**
See also DLB 150

Churchill, Caryl 1938- ... **CLC 31, 55; DC 5**
See also CA 102; CANR 22, 46; DLB 13;
MTCW

Churchill, Charles 1731-1764 .... **LC 3**
See also DLB 109

Chute, Carolyn 1947- .... **CLC 39**
See also CA 123

Ciardi, John (Anthony)
1916-1986 .... **CLC 10, 40, 44;**
DAM POET
See also CA 5-8R; 118; CAAS 2; CANR 5,
33; CLR 19; DLB 5; DLBY 86;
INT CANR-5; MAICYA; MTCW;
SATA 1, 65; SATA-Obit 46

Cicero, Marcus Tullius
106B.C.-43B.C. .... **CMLC 3**

Cimino, Michael 1943- .... **CLC 16**
See also CA 105

Cioran, E(mil) M. 1911-1995 .... **CLC 64**
See also CA 25-28R; 149

Cisneros, Sandra
1954- ..... **CLC 69; DAM MULT; HLC**
See also AAYA 9; CA 131; DLB 122, 152;
HW

Cixous, Helene 1937- .... **CLC 92**
See also CA 126; CANR 55; DLB 83;
MTCW

Clair, Rene .... **CLC 20**
See also Chomette, Rene Lucien

Clampitt, Amy 1920-1994 .... **CLC 32**
See also CA 110; 146; CANR 29; DLB 105

Clancy, Thomas L., Jr. 1947-
See Clancy, Tom
See also CA 125; 131; INT 131; MTCW

Clancy, Tom ..... **CLC 45; DAM NOV, POP**
See also Clancy, Thomas L., Jr.
See also AAYA 9; BEST 89:1, 90:1

Clare, John
1793-1864 .... **NCLC 9; DAB;**
DAM POET
See also DLB 55, 96

Clarin
See Alas (y Urena), Leopoldo (Enrique
Garcia)

Clark, Al C.
See Goines, Donald

Clark, (Robert) Brian 1932- .... **CLC 29**
See also CA 41-44R

Clark, Curt
See Westlake, Donald E(dwin)

Clark, Eleanor 1913-1996 .... **CLC 5, 19**
See also CA 9-12R; 151; CANR 41; DLB 6

Clark, J. P.
See Clark, John Pepper
See also DLB 117

Clark, John Pepper
1935- .... **CLC 38; BLC; DAM DRAM,**
MULT; DC 5
See also Clark, J. P.
See also BW 1; CA 65-68; CANR 16

Clark, M. R.
See Clark, Mavis Thorpe

Clark, Mavis Thorpe 1909- .... **CLC 12**
See also CA 57-60; CANR 8, 37; CLR 30;
MAICYA; SAAS 5; SATA 8, 74

Clark, Walter Van Tilburg
1909-1971 .... **CLC 28**
See also CA 9-12R; 33-36R; DLB 9;
SATA 8

Clarke, Arthur C(harles)
1917- .... **CLC 1, 4, 13, 18, 35;**
DAM POP; SSC 3
See also AAYA 4; CA 1-4R; CANR 2, 28,
55; JRDA; MAICYA; MTCW; SATA 13,
70

Clarke, Austin
1896-1974 ...... **CLC 6, 9; DAM POET**
See also CA 29-32; 49-52; CAP 2; DLB 10,
20

Clarke, Austin C(hesterfield)
1934- .... **CLC 8, 53; BLC; DAC;**
DAM MULT
See also BW 1; CA 25-28R; CAAS 16;
CANR 14, 32; DLB 53, 125

Clarke, Gillian 1937- .... **CLC 61**
See also CA 106; DLB 40

Clarke, Marcus (Andrew Hislop)
1846-1881 .... **NCLC 19**

Clarke, Shirley 1925- .... **CLC 16**

Clash, The
See Headon, (Nicky) Topper; Jones, Mick;
Simonon, Paul; Strummer, Joe

Claudel, Paul (Louis Charles Marie)
1868-1955 .... **TCLC 2, 10**
See also CA 104

Clavell, James (duMaresq)
1925-1994 .... **CLC 6, 25, 87;**
DAM NOV, POP
See also CA 25-28R; 146; CANR 26, 48;
MTCW

Cleaver, (Leroy) Eldridge
1935- ..... **CLC 30; BLC; DAM MULT**
See also BW 1; CA 21-24R; CANR 16

Cleese, John (Marwood) 1939- ..... **CLC 21**
See also Monty Python
See also CA 112; 116; CANR 35; MTCW

Cleishbotham, Jebediah
See Scott, Walter

Cleland, John 1710-1789 .... **LC 2**
See also DLB 39

Clemens, Samuel Langhorne 1835-1910
See Twain, Mark
See also CA 104; 135; CDALB 1865-1917;
DA; DAB; DAC; DAM MST, NOV;
DLB 11, 12, 23, 64, 74; JRDA;
MAICYA; YABC 2

Cleophil
See Congreve, William

Clerihew, E.
See Bentley, E(dmund) C(lerihew)

Clerk, N. W.
See Lewis, C(live) S(taples)

Cliff, Jimmy . . . . **CLC 21**
See also Chambers, James

Clifton, (Thelma) Lucille
1936- . . . . **CLC 19, 66; BLC; DAM MULT, POET; PC 17**
See also BW 2; CA 49-52; CANR 2, 24, 42; CLR 5; DLB 5, 41; MAICYA; MTCW; SATA 20, 69

Clinton, Dirk
See Silverberg, Robert

Clough, Arthur Hugh 1819-1861 . . **NCLC 27**
See also DLB 32

Clutha, Janet Paterson Frame 1924-
See Frame, Janet
See also CA 1-4R; CANR 2, 36; MTCW

Clyne, Terence
See Blatty, William Peter

Cobalt, Martin
See Mayne, William (James Carter)

Cobbett, William 1763-1835 . . . . . **NCLC 49**
See also DLB 43, 107, 158

Coburn, D(onald) L(ee) 1938- . . . . . . **CLC 10**
See also CA 89-92

Cocteau, Jean (Maurice Eugene Clement)
1889-1963 . . . . **CLC 1, 8, 15, 16, 43; DA; DAB; DAC; DAM DRAM, MST, NOV; WLC**
See also CA 25-28; CANR 40; CAP 2; DLB 65; MTCW

Codrescu, Andrei
1946- . . . . **CLC 46; DAM POET**
See also CA 33-36R; CAAS 19; CANR 13, 34, 53

Coe, Max
See Bourne, Randolph S(illiman)

Coe, Tucker
See Westlake, Donald E(dwin)

Coetzee, J(ohn) M(ichael)
1940- . . . . . . **CLC 23, 33, 66; DAM NOV**
See also CA 77-80; CANR 41, 54; MTCW

Coffey, Brian
See Koontz, Dean R(ay)

Cohan, George M. 1878-1942 . . . . . **TCLC 60**

Cohen, Arthur A(llen)
1928-1986 . . . . **CLC 7, 31**
See also CA 1-4R; 120; CANR 1, 17, 42; DLB 28

Cohen, Leonard (Norman)
1934- . . . . **CLC 3, 38; DAC; DAM MST**
See also CA 21-24R; CANR 14; DLB 53; MTCW

Cohen, Matt 1942- . . . . **CLC 19; DAC**
See also CA 61-64; CAAS 18; CANR 40; DLB 53

Cohen-Solal, Annie 19(?)- . . . . **CLC 50**

Colegate, Isabel 1931- . . . . **CLC 36**
See also CA 17-20R; CANR 8, 22; DLB 14; INT CANR-22; MTCW

Coleman, Emmett
See Reed, Ishmael

Coleridge, Samuel Taylor
1772-1834 . . . . . **NCLC 9, 54; DA; DAB; DAC; DAM MST, POET; PC 11; WLC**
See also CDBLB 1789-1832; DLB 93, 107

Coleridge, Sara 1802-1852 . . . . . . **NCLC 31**

Coles, Don 1928- . . . . **CLC 46**
See also CA 115; CANR 38

Colette, (Sidonie-Gabrielle)
1873-1954 . . . . **TCLC 1, 5, 16; DAM NOV; SSC 10**
See also CA 104; 131; DLB 65; MTCW

Collett, (Jacobine) Camilla (Wergeland)
1813-1895 . . . . **NCLC 22**

Collier, Christopher 1930- . . . . **CLC 30**
See also AAYA 13; CA 33-36R; CANR 13, 33; JRDA; MAICYA; SATA 16, 70

Collier, James L(incoln)
1928- . . . . **CLC 30; DAM POP**
See also AAYA 13; CA 9-12R; CANR 4, 33; CLR 3; JRDA; MAICYA; SAAS 21; SATA 8, 70

Collier, Jeremy 1650-1726 . . . . **LC 6**

Collier, John 1901-1980 . . . . **SSC 19**
See also CA 65-68; 97-100; CANR 10; DLB 77

Collingwood, R(obin) G(eorge)
1889(?)-1943 . . . . **TCLC 67**
See also CA 117; 155

Collins, Hunt
See Hunter, Evan

Collins, Linda 1931- . . . . **CLC 44**
See also CA 125

Collins, (William) Wilkie
1824-1889 . . . . **NCLC 1, 18**
See also CDBLB 1832-1890; DLB 18, 70, 159

Collins, William
1721-1759 . . . . **LC 4; DAM POET**
See also DLB 109

Collodi, Carlo 1826-1890 . . . . **NCLC 54**
See also Lorenzini, Carlo
See also CLR 5

Colman, George
See Glassco, John

Colt, Winchester Remington
See Hubbard, L(afayette) Ron(ald)

Colter, Cyrus 1910- . . . . **CLC 58**
See also BW 1; CA 65-68; CANR 10; DLB 33

Colton, James
See Hansen, Joseph

Colum, Padraic 1881-1972 . . . . **CLC 28**
See also CA 73-76; 33-36R; CANR 35; CLR 36; MAICYA; MTCW; SATA 15

Colvin, James
See Moorcock, Michael (John)

Colwin, Laurie (E.)
1944-1992 . . . . **CLC 5, 13, 23, 84**
See also CA 89-92; 139; CANR 20, 46; DLBY 80; MTCW

Comfort, Alex(ander)
1920- . . . . **CLC 7; DAM POP**
See also CA 1-4R; CANR 1, 45

Comfort, Montgomery
See Campbell, (John) Ramsey

Compton-Burnett, I(vy)
1884(?)-1969 . . . . . . **CLC 1, 3, 10, 15, 34; DAM NOV**
See also CA 1-4R; 25-28R; CANR 4; DLB 36; MTCW

Comstock, Anthony 1844-1915 . . . . **TCLC 13**
See also CA 110

Comte, Auguste 1798-1857 . . . . . . **NCLC 54**

Conan Doyle, Arthur
See Doyle, Arthur Conan

Conde, Maryse
1937- . . . . **CLC 52, 92; DAM MULT**
See also Boucolon, Maryse
See also BW 2

Condillac, Etienne Bonnot de
1714-1780 . . . . **LC 26**

Condon, Richard (Thomas)
1915-1996 . . . . . **CLC 4, 6, 8, 10, 45, 100; DAM NOV**
See also BEST 90:3; CA 1-4R; 151; CAAS 1; CANR 2, 23; INT CANR-23; MTCW

Confucius
551B.C.-479B.C. . . . . **CMLC 19; DA; DAB; DAC; DAM MST**

Congreve, William
1670-1729 . . . . **LC 5, 21; DA; DAB; DAC; DAM DRAM, MST, POET; DC 2; WLC**
See also CDBLB 1660-1789; DLB 39, 84

Connell, Evan S(helby), Jr.
1924- . . . . **CLC 4, 6, 45; DAM NOV**
See also AAYA 7; CA 1-4R; CAAS 2; CANR 2, 39; DLB 2; DLBY 81; MTCW

Connelly, Marc(us Cook)
1890-1980 . . . . **CLC 7**
See also CA 85-88; 102; CANR 30; DLB 7; DLBY 80; SATA-Obit 25

Connor, Ralph . . . . **TCLC 31**
See also Gordon, Charles William
See also DLB 92

Conrad, Joseph
1857-1924 . . . . **TCLC 1, 6, 13, 25, 43, 57; DA; DAB; DAC; DAM MST, NOV; SSC 9; WLC**
See also CA 104; 131; CDBLB 1890-1914; DLB 10, 34, 98, 156; MTCW; SATA 27

Conrad, Robert Arnold
See Hart, Moss

Conroy, Donald Pat(rick)
1945- . . . **CLC 30, 74; DAM NOV, POP**
See also AAYA 8; AITN 1; CA 85-88; CANR 24, 53; DLB 6; MTCW

Constant (de Rebecque), (Henri) Benjamin
1767-1830 . . . . **NCLC 6**
See also DLB 119

Conybeare, Charles Augustus
See Eliot, T(homas) S(tearns)

Cook, Michael 1933- . . . . **CLC 58**
See also CA 93-96; DLB 53

Cook, Robin 1940- . . . . **CLC 14; DAM POP**
See also BEST 90:2; CA 108; 111; CANR 41; INT 111

Cook, Roy
See Silverberg, Robert

Cooke, Elizabeth 1948- .... **CLC 55**
See also CA 129

Cooke, John Esten 1830-1886..... **NCLC 5**
See also DLB 3

Cooke, John Estes
See Baum, L(yman) Frank

Cooke, M. E.
See Creasey, John

Cooke, Margaret
See Creasey, John

Cook-Lynn, Elizabeth
1930- .... **CLC 93; DAM MULT**
See also CA 133; DLB 175; NNAL

Cooney, Ray .... **CLC 62**

Cooper, Douglas 1960-........... **CLC 86**

Cooper, Henry St. John
See Creasey, John

Cooper, J(oan) California
.... **CLC 56; DAM MULT**
See also AAYA 12; BW 1; CA 125;
CANR 55

Cooper, James Fenimore
1789-1851 ...... **NCLC 1, 27, 54**
See also CDALB 1640-1865; DLB 3;
SATA 19

Coover, Robert (Lowell)
1932- .... **CLC 3, 7, 15, 32, 46, 87;**
DAM NOV; SSC 15
See also CA 45-48; CANR 3, 37; DLB 2;
DLBY 81; MTCW

Copeland, Stewart (Armstrong)
1952- .... **CLC 26**

Coppard, A(lfred) E(dgar)
1878-1957 .... **TCLC 5; SSC 21**
See also CA 114; DLB 162; YABC 1

Coppee, Francois 1842-1908 ...... **TCLC 25**

Coppola, Francis Ford 1939-....... **CLC 16**
See also CA 77-80; CANR 40; DLB 44

Corbiere, Tristan 1845-1875 ..... **NCLC 43**

Corcoran, Barbara 1911-......... **CLC 17**
See also AAYA 14; CA 21-24R; CAAS 2;
CANR 11, 28, 48; DLB 52; JRDA;
SAAS 20; SATA 3, 77

Cordelier, Maurice
See Giraudoux, (Hippolyte) Jean

Corelli, Marie 1855-1924........ **TCLC 51**
See also Mackay, Mary
See also DLB 34, 156

Corman, Cid...................... **CLC 9**
See also Corman, Sidney
See also CAAS 2; DLB 5

Corman, Sidney 1924-
See Corman, Cid
See also CA 85-88; CANR 44; DAM POET

Cormier, Robert (Edmund)
1925- .... **CLC 12, 30; DA; DAB; DAC;**
DAM MST, NOV
See also AAYA 3, 19; CA 1-4R; CANR 5,
23; CDALB 1968-1988; CLR 12; DLB 52;
INT CANR-23; JRDA; MAICYA;
MTCW; SATA 10, 45, 83

Corn, Alfred (DeWitt III) 1943-.... **CLC 33**
See also CA 104; CAAS 25; CANR 44;
DLB 120; DLBY 80

Corneille, Pierre
1606-1684 .... **LC 28; DAB; DAM MST**

Cornwell, David (John Moore)
1931- .... **CLC 9, 15; DAM POP**
See also le Carre, John
See also CA 5-8R; CANR 13, 33; MTCW

Corso, (Nunzio) Gregory 1930-... **CLC 1, 11**
See also CA 5-8R; CANR 41; DLB 5, 16;
MTCW

Cortazar, Julio
1914-1984 ...... **CLC 2, 3, 5, 10, 13, 15,**
33, 34, 92; DAM MULT, NOV; HLC;
SSC 7
See also CA 21-24R; CANR 12, 32;
DLB 113; HW; MTCW

CORTES, HERNAN 1484-1547..... **LC 31**

Corwin, Cecil
See Kornbluth, C(yril) M.

Cosic, Dobrica 1921- .... **CLC 14**
See also CA 122; 138

Costain, Thomas B(ertram)
1885-1965 .... **CLC 30**
See also CA 5-8R; 25-28R; DLB 9

Costantini, Humberto
1924(?)-1987 .... **CLC 49**
See also CA 131; 122; HW

Costello, Elvis 1955-.............. **CLC 21**

Cotter, Joseph Seamon Sr.
1861-1949 .... **TCLC 28; BLC;**
DAM MULT
See also BW 1; CA 124; DLB 50

Couch, Arthur Thomas Quiller
See Quiller-Couch, Arthur Thomas

Coulton, James
See Hansen, Joseph

Couperus, Louis (Marie Anne)
1863-1923 .... **TCLC 15**
See also CA 115

Coupland, Douglas
1961- .... **CLC 85; DAC; DAM POP**
See also CA 142; CANR 57

Court, Wesli
See Turco, Lewis (Putnam)

Courtenay, Bryce 1933-........... **CLC 59**
See also CA 138

Courtney, Robert
See Ellison, Harlan (Jay)

Cousteau, Jacques-Yves 1910-...... **CLC 30**
See also CA 65-68; CANR 15; MTCW;
SATA 38

Coward, Noel (Peirce)
1899-1973 .... **CLC 1, 9, 29, 51;**
DAM DRAM
See also AITN 1; CA 17-18; 41-44R;
CANR 35; CAP 2; CDBLB 1914-1945;
DLB 10; MTCW

Cowley, Malcolm 1898-1989 ...... **CLC 39**
See also CA 5-8R; 128; CANR 3, 55;
DLB 4, 48; DLBY 81, 89; MTCW

Cowper, William
1731-1800 ...... **NCLC 8; DAM POET**
See also DLB 104, 109

Cox, William Trevor
1928- .... **CLC 9, 14, 71; DAM NOV**
See also Trevor, William
See also CA 9-12R; CANR 4, 37, 55;
DLB 14; INT CANR-37; MTCW

Coyne, P. J.
See Masters, Hilary

Cozzens, James Gould
1903-1978 .... **CLC 1, 4, 11, 92**
See also CA 9-12R; 81-84; CANR 19;
CDALB 1941-1968; DLB 9; DLBD 2;
DLBY 84; MTCW

Crabbe, George 1754-1832....... **NCLC 26**
See also DLB 93

Craddock, Charles Egbert
See Murfree, Mary Noailles

Craig, A. A.
See Anderson, Poul (William)

Craik, Dinah Maria (Mulock)
1826-1887 .... **NCLC 38**
See also DLB 35, 163; MAICYA; SATA 34

Cram, Ralph Adams 1863-1942.... **TCLC 45**

Crane, (Harold) Hart
1899-1932 .... **TCLC 2, 5; DA; DAB;**
DAC; DAM MST, POET; PC 3; WLC
See also CA 104; 127; CDALB 1917-1929;
DLB 4, 48; MTCW

Crane, R(onald) S(almon)
1886-1967 .... **CLC 27**
See also CA 85-88; DLB 63

Crane, Stephen (Townley)
1871-1900 .... **TCLC 11, 17, 32; DA;**
DAB; DAC; DAM MST, NOV, POET;
SSC 7; WLC
See also AAYA 21; CA 109; 140;
CDALB 1865-1917; DLB 12, 54, 78;
YABC 2

Crase, Douglas 1944-............. **CLC 58**
See also CA 106

Crashaw, Richard 1612(?)-1649...... **LC 24**
See also DLB 126

Craven, Margaret
1901-1980 .... **CLC 17; DAC**
See also CA 103

Crawford, F(rancis) Marion
1854-1909 .... **TCLC 10**
See also CA 107; DLB 71

Crawford, Isabella Valancy
1850-1887 .... **NCLC 12**
See also DLB 92

Crayon, Geoffrey
See Irving, Washington

Creasey, John 1908-1973 .... **CLC 11**
See also CA 5-8R; 41-44R; CANR 8;
DLB 77; MTCW

Crebillon, Claude Prosper Jolyot de (fils)
1707-1777 .... **LC 28**

Credo
See Creasey, John

Creeley, Robert (White)
1926- ..... **CLC 1, 2, 4, 8, 11, 15, 36, 78;**
DAM POET
See also CA 1-4R; CAAS 10; CANR 23, 43;
DLB 5, 16, 169; MTCW

Crews, Harry (Eugene)
1935- . . . . **CLC 6, 23, 49**
See also AITN 1; CA 25-28R; CANR 20,
57; DLB 6, 143; MTCW

Crichton, (John) Michael
1942- . . . . **CLC 2, 6, 54, 90; DAM NOV,**
POP
See also AAYA 10; AITN 2; CA 25-28R;
CANR 13, 40, 54; DLBY 81;
INT CANR-13; JRDA; MTCW; SATA 9,
88

Crispin, Edmund . . . . **CLC 22**
See also Montgomery, (Robert) Bruce
See also DLB 87

Cristofer, Michael
1945(?)- . . . . **CLC 28; DAM DRAM**
See also CA 110; 152; DLB 7

Croce, Benedetto 1866-1952 . . . . . . **TCLC 37**
See also CA 120; 155

Crockett, David 1786-1836 . . . . **NCLC 8**
See also DLB 3, 11

Crockett, Davy
See Crockett, David

Crofts, Freeman Wills
1879-1957 . . . . **TCLC 55**
See also CA 115; DLB 77

Croker, John Wilson 1780-1857 . . **NCLC 10**
See also DLB 110

Crommelynck, Fernand 1885-1970 . . **CLC 75**
See also CA 89-92

Cronin, A(rchibald) J(oseph)
1896-1981 . . . . **CLC 32**
See also CA 1-4R; 102; CANR 5; SATA 47;
SATA-Obit 25

Cross, Amanda
See Heilbrun, Carolyn G(old)

Crothers, Rachel 1878(?)-1958 . . . . . **TCLC 19**
See also CA 113; DLB 7

Croves, Hal
See Traven, B.

Crow Dog, Mary (Ellen) (?)- . . . . **CLC 93**
See also Brave Bird, Mary
See also CA 154

Crowfield, Christopher
See Stowe, Harriet (Elizabeth) Beecher

Crowley, Aleister . . . . **TCLC 7**
See also Crowley, Edward Alexander

Crowley, Edward Alexander 1875-1947
See Crowley, Aleister
See also CA 104

Crowley, John 1942- . . . . **CLC 57**
See also CA 61-64; CANR 43; DLBY 82;
SATA 65

Crud
See Crumb, R(obert)

Crumarums
See Crumb, R(obert)

Crumb, R(obert) 1943- . . . . **CLC 17**
See also CA 106

Crumbum
See Crumb, R(obert)

Crumski
See Crumb, R(obert)

Crum the Bum
See Crumb, R(obert)

Crunk
See Crumb, R(obert)

Crustt
See Crumb, R(obert)

Cryer, Gretchen (Kiger) 1935- . . . . . . **CLC 21**
See also CA 114; 123

Csath, Geza 1887-1919 . . . . **TCLC 13**
See also CA 111

Cudlip, David 1933- . . . . **CLC 34**

Cullen, Countee
1903-1946 . . . . . . **TCLC 4, 37; BLC; DA;**
DAC; DAM MST, MULT, POET
See also BW 1; CA 108; 124;
CDALB 1917-1929; DLB 4, 48, 51;
MTCW; SATA 18

Cum, R.
See Crumb, R(obert)

Cummings, Bruce F(rederick) 1889-1919
See Barbellion, W. N. P.
See also CA 123

Cummings, E(dward) E(stlin)
1894-1962 . . . . . . **CLC 1, 3, 8, 12, 15, 68;**
DA; DAB; DAC; DAM MST, POET;
PC 5; WLC 2
See also CA 73-76; CANR 31;
CDALB 1929-1941; DLB 4, 48; MTCW

Cunha, Euclides (Rodrigues Pimenta) da
1866-1909 . . . . **TCLC 24**
See also CA 123

Cunningham, E. V.
See Fast, Howard (Melvin)

Cunningham, J(ames) V(incent)
1911-1985 . . . . **CLC 3, 31**
See also CA 1-4R; 115; CANR 1; DLB 5

Cunningham, Julia (Woolfolk)
1916- . . . . **CLC 12**
See also CA 9-12R; CANR 4, 19, 36;
JRDA; MAICYA; SAAS 2; SATA 1, 26

Cunningham, Michael 1952- . . . . **CLC 34**
See also CA 136

Cunninghame Graham, R(obert) B(ontine)
1852-1936 . . . . **TCLC 19**
See also Graham, R(obert) B(ontine)
Cunninghame
See also CA 119; DLB 98

Currie, Ellen 19(?)- . . . . **CLC 44**

Curtin, Philip
See Lowndes, Marie Adelaide (Belloc)

Curtis, Price
See Ellison, Harlan (Jay)

Cutrate, Joe
See Spiegelman, Art

Czaczkes, Shmuel Yosef
See Agnon, S(hmuel) Y(osef Halevi)

Dabrowska, Maria (Szumska)
1889-1965 . . . . **CLC 15**
See also CA 106

Dabydeen, David 1955- . . . . **CLC 34**
See also BW 1; CA 125; CANR 56

Dacey, Philip 1939- . . . . **CLC 51**
See also CA 37-40R; CAAS 17; CANR 14,
32; DLB 105

Dagerman, Stig (Halvard)
1923-1954 . . . . **TCLC 17**
See also CA 117; 155

Dahl, Roald
1916-1990 . . . . . . **CLC 1, 6, 18, 79; DAB;**
DAC; DAM MST, NOV, POP
See also AAYA 15; CA 1-4R; 133;
CANR 6, 32, 37; CLR 1, 7, 41; DLB 139;
JRDA; MAICYA; MTCW; SATA 1, 26,
73; SATA-Obit 65

Dahlberg, Edward 1900-1977 . . . **CLC 1, 7, 14**
See also CA 9-12R; 69-72; CANR 31;
DLB 48; MTCW

Dale, Colin . . . . **TCLC 18**
See also Lawrence, T(homas) E(dward)

Dale, George E.
See Asimov, Isaac

Daly, Elizabeth 1878-1967 . . . . **CLC 52**
See also CA 23-24; 25-28R; CAP 2

Daly, Maureen 1921- . . . . **CLC 17**
See also AAYA 5; CANR 37; JRDA;
MAICYA; SAAS 1; SATA 2

Damas, Leon-Gontran 1912-1978 . . . **CLC 84**
See also BW 1; CA 125; 73-76

Dana, Richard Henry Sr.
1787-1879 . . . . **NCLC 53**

Daniel, Samuel 1562(?)-1619 . . . . **LC 24**
See also DLB 62

Daniels, Brett
See Adler, Renata

Dannay, Frederic
1905-1982 . . . . **CLC 11; DAM POP**
See also Queen, Ellery
See also CA 1-4R; 107; CANR 1, 39;
DLB 137; MTCW

D'Annunzio, Gabriele
1863-1938 . . . . **TCLC 6, 40**
See also CA 104; 155

Danois, N. le
See Gourmont, Remy (-Marie-Charles) de

d'Antibes, Germain
See Simenon, Georges (Jacques Christian)

Danticat, Edwidge 1969- . . . . **CLC 94**
See also CA 152

Danvers, Dennis 1947- . . . . **CLC 70**

Danziger, Paula 1944- . . . . **CLC 21**
See also AAYA 4; CA 112; 115; CANR 37;
CLR 20; JRDA; MAICYA; SATA 36,
63; SATA-Brief 30

Da Ponte, Lorenzo 1749-1838 . . . . **NCLC 50**

Dario, Ruben
1867-1916 . . . . . **TCLC 4; DAM MULT;**
HLC; PC 15
See also CA 131; HW; MTCW

Darley, George 1795-1846 . . . . **NCLC 2**
See also DLB 96

Darwin, Charles 1809-1882 . . . . . . **NCLC 57**
See also DLB 57, 166

Daryush, Elizabeth 1887-1977 . . . . **CLC 6, 19**
See also CA 49-52; CANR 3; DLB 20

Dashwood, Edmee Elizabeth Monica de la
Pasture 1890-1943
See Delafield, E. M.
See also CA 119; 154

Daudet, (Louis Marie) Alphonse
　1840-1897 .... **NCLC 1**
　See also DLB 123

Daumal, Rene 1908-1944 .... **TCLC 14**
　See also CA 114

Davenport, Guy (Mattison, Jr.)
　1927- .... **CLC 6, 14, 38; SSC 16**
　See also CA 33-36R; CANR 23; DLB 130

Davidson, Avram 1923-
　See Queen, Ellery
　See also CA 101; CANR 26; DLB 8

Davidson, Donald (Grady)
　1893-1968 .... **CLC 2, 13, 19**
　See also CA 5-8R; 25-28R; CANR 4;
　DLB 45

Davidson, Hugh
　See Hamilton, Edmond

Davidson, John 1857-1909 .... **TCLC 24**
　See also CA 118; DLB 19

Davidson, Sara 1943- .... **CLC 9**
　See also CA 81-84; CANR 44

Davie, Donald (Alfred)
　1922-1995 .... **CLC 5, 8, 10, 31**
　See also CA 1-4R; 149; CAAS 3; CANR 1,
　44; DLB 27; MTCW

Davies, Ray(mond Douglas) 1944- .. **CLC 21**
　See also CA 116; 146

Davies, Rhys 1903-1978 .... **CLC 23**
　See also CA 9-12R; 81-84; CANR 4;
　DLB 139

Davies, (William) Robertson
　1913-1995 ..... **CLC 2, 7, 13, 25, 42, 75,**
　91; DA; DAB; DAC; DAM MST, NOV,
　POP; WLC
　See also BEST 89:2; CA 33-36R; 150;
　CANR 17, 42; DLB 68; INT CANR-17;
　MTCW

Davies, W(illiam) H(enry)
　1871-1940 .... **TCLC 5**
　See also CA 104; DLB 19, 174

Davies, Walter C.
　See Kornbluth, C(yril) M.

Davis, Angela (Yvonne)
　1944- .... **CLC 77; DAM MULT**
　See also BW 2; CA 57-60; CANR 10

Davis, B. Lynch
　See Bioy Casares, Adolfo; Borges, Jorge
　Luis

Davis, Gordon
　See Hunt, E(verette) Howard, (Jr.)

Davis, Harold Lenoir 1896-1960 .... **CLC 49**
　See also CA 89-92; DLB 9

Davis, Rebecca (Blaine) Harding
　1831-1910 .... **TCLC 6**
　See also CA 104; DLB 74

Davis, Richard Harding
　1864-1916 .... **TCLC 24**
　See also CA 114; DLB 12, 23, 78, 79;
　DLBD 13

Davison, Frank Dalby 1893-1970 ... **CLC 15**
　See also CA 116

Davison, Lawrence H.
　See Lawrence, D(avid) H(erbert Richards)

Davison, Peter (Hubert) 1928- ..... **CLC 28**
　See also CA 9-12R; CAAS 4; CANR 3, 43;
　DLB 5

Davys, Mary 1674-1732 .... **LC 1**
　See also DLB 39

Dawson, Fielding 1930- .... **CLC 6**
　See also CA 85-88; DLB 130

Dawson, Peter
　See Faust, Frederick (Schiller)

Day, Clarence (Shepard, Jr.)
　1874-1935 .... **TCLC 25**
　See also CA 108; DLB 11

Day, Thomas 1748-1789 .... **LC 1**
　See also DLB 39; YABC 1

Day Lewis, C(ecil)
　1904-1972 .... **CLC 1, 6, 10;**
　DAM POET; PC 11
　See also Blake, Nicholas
　See also CA 13-16; 33-36R; CANR 34;
　CAP 1; DLB 15, 20; MTCW

Dazai, Osamu .... **TCLC 11**
　See also Tsushima, Shuji

de Andrade, Carlos Drummond
　See Drummond de Andrade, Carlos

Deane, Norman
　See Creasey, John

de Beauvoir, Simone (Lucie Ernestine Marie Bertrand)
　See Beauvoir, Simone (Lucie Ernestine
　Marie Bertrand) de

de Brissac, Malcolm
　See Dickinson, Peter (Malcolm)

de Chardin, Pierre Teilhard
　See Teilhard de Chardin, (Marie Joseph)
　Pierre

Dee, John 1527-1608 .... **LC 20**

Deer, Sandra 1940- .... **CLC 45**

De Ferrari, Gabriella 1941- .... **CLC 65**
　See also CA 146

Defoe, Daniel
　1660(?)-1731 .... **LC 1; DA; DAB; DAC;**
　DAM MST, NOV; WLC
　See also CDBLB 1660-1789; DLB 39, 95,
　101; JRDA; MAICYA; SATA 22

de Gourmont, Remy(-Marie-Charles)
　See Gourmont, Remy (-Marie-Charles) de

de Hartog, Jan 1914- .... **CLC 19**
　See also CA 1-4R; CANR 1

de Hostos, E. M.
　See Hostos (y Bonilla), Eugenio Maria de

de Hostos, Eugenio M.
　See Hostos (y Bonilla), Eugenio Maria de

Deighton, Len .... **CLC 4, 7, 22, 46**
　See also Deighton, Leonard Cyril
　See also AAYA 6; BEST 89:2;
　CDBLB 1960 to Present; DLB 87

Deighton, Leonard Cyril 1929-
　See Deighton, Len
　See also CA 9-12R; CANR 19, 33;
　DAM NOV, POP; MTCW

Dekker, Thomas
　1572(?)-1632 ..... **LC 22; DAM DRAM**
　See also CDBLB Before 1660; DLB 62, 172

Delafield, E. M. 1890-1943 .... **TCLC 61**
　See also Dashwood, Edmee Elizabeth
　Monica de la Pasture
　See also DLB 34

de la Mare, Walter (John)
　1873-1956 .... **TCLC 4, 53; DAB; DAC;**
　DAM MST, POET; SSC 14; WLC
　See also CDBLB 1914-1945; CLR 23;
　DLB 162; SATA 16

Delaney, Franey
　See O'Hara, John (Henry)

Delaney, Shelagh
　1939- .... **CLC 29; DAM DRAM**
　See also CA 17-20R; CANR 30;
　CDBLB 1960 to Present; DLB 13;
　MTCW

Delany, Mary (Granville Pendarves)
　1700-1788 .... **LC 12**

Delany, Samuel R(ay, Jr.)
　1942- .... **CLC 8, 14, 38; BLC;**
　DAM MULT
　See also BW 2; CA 81-84; CANR 27, 43;
　DLB 8, 33; MTCW

De La Ramee, (Marie) Louise 1839-1908
　See Ouida
　See also SATA 20

de la Roche, Mazo 1879-1961 ...... **CLC 14**
　See also CA 85-88; CANR 30; DLB 68;
　SATA 64

Delbanco, Nicholas (Franklin)
　1942- .... **CLC 6, 13**
　See also CA 17-20R; CAAS 2; CANR 29,
　55; DLB 6

del Castillo, Michel 1933- .... **CLC 38**
　See also CA 109

Deledda, Grazia (Cosima)
　1875(?)-1936 .... **TCLC 23**
　See also CA 123

Delibes, Miguel .... **CLC 8, 18**
　See also Delibes Setien, Miguel

Delibes Setien, Miguel 1920-
　See Delibes, Miguel
　See also CA 45-48; CANR 1, 32; HW;
　MTCW

DeLillo, Don
　1936- ..... **CLC 8, 10, 13, 27, 39, 54, 76;**
　DAM NOV, POP
　See also BEST 89:1; CA 81-84; CANR 21;
　DLB 6, 173; MTCW

de Lisser, H. G.
　See De Lisser, H(erbert) G(eorge)
　See also DLB 117

De Lisser, H(erbert) G(eorge)
　1878-1944 .... **TCLC 12**
　See also de Lisser, H. G.
　See also BW 2; CA 109; 152

Deloria, Vine (Victor), Jr.
　1933- .... **CLC 21; DAM MULT**
　See also CA 53-56; CANR 5, 20, 48;
　DLB 175; MTCW; NNAL; SATA 21

Del Vecchio, John M(ichael)
　1947- .... **CLC 29**
　See also CA 110; DLBD 9

de Man, Paul (Adolph Michel)
　1919-1983 .... **CLC 55**
　See also CA 128; 111; DLB 67; MTCW

Doctorow, E(dgar) L(aurence)
1931- ..... **CLC 6, 11, 15, 18, 37, 44, 65; DAM NOV, POP**
See also AITN 2; BEST 89:3; CA 45-48; CANR 2, 33, 51; CDALB 1968-1988; DLB 2, 28, 173; DLBY 80; MTCW

Dodgson, Charles Lutwidge 1832-1898
See Carroll, Lewis
See also CLR 2; DA; DAB; DAC; DAM MST, NOV, POET; MAICYA; YABC 2

Dodson, Owen (Vincent)
1914-1983 .... **CLC 79; BLC; DAM MULT**
See also BW 1; CA 65-68; 110; CANR 24; DLB 76

Doeblin, Alfred 1878-1957 .... **TCLC 13**
See also Doblin, Alfred
See also CA 110; 141; DLB 66

Doerr, Harriet 1910- .... **CLC 34**
See also CA 117; 122; CANR 47; INT 122

Domecq, H(onorio) Bustos
See Bioy Casares, Adolfo; Borges, Jorge Luis

Domini, Rey
See Lorde, Audre (Geraldine)

Dominique
See Proust, (Valentin-Louis-George-Eugene-) Marcel

Don, A
See Stephen, Leslie

Donaldson, Stephen R.
1947- .... **CLC 46; DAM POP**
See also CA 89-92; CANR 13, 55; INT CANR-13

Donleavy, J(ames) P(atrick)
1926- .... **CLC 1, 4, 6, 10, 45**
See also AITN 2; CA 9-12R; CANR 24, 49; DLB 6, 173; INT CANR-24; MTCW

Donne, John
1572-1631 .... **LC 10, 24; DA; DAB; DAC; DAM MST, POET; PC 1**
See also CDBLB Before 1660; DLB 121, 151

Donnell, David 1939(?)- .... **CLC 34**

Donoghue, P. S.
See Hunt, E(verette) Howard, (Jr.)

Donoso (Yanez), Jose
1924-1996 .... **CLC 4, 8, 11, 32, 99; DAM MULT; HLC**
See also CA 81-84; 155; CANR 32; DLB 113; HW; MTCW

Donovan, John 1928-1992 .... **CLC 35**
See also AAYA 20; CA 97-100; 137; CLR 3; MAICYA; SATA 72; SATA-Brief 29

Don Roberto
See Cunninghame Graham, R(obert) B(ontine)

Doolittle, Hilda
1886-1961 ..... **CLC 3, 8, 14, 31, 34, 73; DA; DAC; DAM MST, POET; PC 5; WLC**
See also H. D.
See also CA 97-100; CANR 35; DLB 4, 45; MTCW

Dorfman, Ariel
1942- .... **CLC 48, 77; DAM MULT; HLC**
See also CA 124; 130; HW; INT 130

Dorn, Edward (Merton) 1929-... **CLC 10, 18**
See also CA 93-96; CANR 42; DLB 5; INT 93-96

Dorsan, Luc
See Simenon, Georges (Jacques Christian)

Dorsange, Jean
See Simenon, Georges (Jacques Christian)

Dos Passos, John (Roderigo)
1896-1970 ...... **CLC 1, 4, 8, 11, 15, 25, 34, 82; DA; DAB; DAC; DAM MST, NOV; WLC**
See also CA 1-4R; 29-32R; CANR 3; CDALB 1929-1941; DLB 4, 9; DLBD 1; MTCW

Dossage, Jean
See Simenon, Georges (Jacques Christian)

Dostoevsky, Fedor Mikhailovich
1821-1881 ...... **NCLC 2, 7, 21, 33, 43; DA; DAB; DAC; DAM MST, NOV; SSC 2; WLC**

Doughty, Charles M(ontagu)
1843-1926 .... **TCLC 27**
See also CA 115; DLB 19, 57, 174

Douglas, Ellen .... **CLC 73**
See also Haxton, Josephine Ayres; Williamson, Ellen Douglas

Douglas, Gavin 1475(?)-1522 .... **LC 20**

Douglas, Keith 1920-1944 .... **TCLC 40**
See also DLB 27

Douglas, Leonard
See Bradbury, Ray (Douglas)

Douglas, Michael
See Crichton, (John) Michael

Douglas, Norman 1868-1952 ...... **TCLC 68**

Douglass, Frederick
1817(?)-1895 .... **NCLC 7, 55; BLC; DA; DAC; DAM MST, MULT; WLC**
See also CDALB 1640-1865; DLB 1, 43, 50, 79; SATA 29

Dourado, (Waldomiro Freitas) Autran
1926- .... **CLC 23, 60**
See also CA 25-28R; CANR 34

Dourado, Waldomiro Autran
See Dourado, (Waldomiro Freitas) Autran

Dove, Rita (Frances)
1952- .... **CLC 50, 81; DAM MULT, POET; PC 6**
See also BW 2; CA 109; CAAS 19; CANR 27, 42; DLB 120

Dowell, Coleman 1925-1985 .... **CLC 60**
See also CA 25-28R; 117; CANR 10; DLB 130

Dowson, Ernest (Christopher)
1867-1900 .... **TCLC 4**
See also CA 105; 150; DLB 19, 135

Doyle, A. Conan
See Doyle, Arthur Conan

Doyle, Arthur Conan
1859-1930 .... **TCLC 7; DA; DAB; DAC; DAM MST, NOV; SSC 12; WLC**
See also AAYA 14; CA 104; 122; CDBLB 1890-1914; DLB 18, 70, 156; MTCW; SATA 24

Doyle, Conan
See Doyle, Arthur Conan

Doyle, John
See Graves, Robert (von Ranke)

Doyle, Roddy 1958(?)- .... **CLC 81**
See also AAYA 14; CA 143

Doyle, Sir A. Conan
See Doyle, Arthur Conan

Doyle, Sir Arthur Conan
See Doyle, Arthur Conan

Dr. A
See Asimov, Isaac; Silverstein, Alvin

Drabble, Margaret
1939- .... **CLC 2, 3, 5, 8, 10, 22, 53; DAB; DAC; DAM MST, NOV, POP**
See also CA 13-16R; CANR 18, 35; CDBLB 1960 to Present; DLB 14, 155; MTCW; SATA 48

Drapier, M. B.
See Swift, Jonathan

Drayham, James
See Mencken, H(enry) L(ouis)

Drayton, Michael 1563-1631 .... **LC 8**

Dreadstone, Carl
See Campbell, (John) Ramsey

Dreiser, Theodore (Herman Albert)
1871-1945 .... **TCLC 10, 18, 35; DA; DAC; DAM MST, NOV; WLC**
See also CA 106; 132; CDALB 1865-1917; DLB 9, 12, 102, 137; DLBD 1; MTCW

Drexler, Rosalyn 1926- .... **CLC 2, 6**
See also CA 81-84

Dreyer, Carl Theodor 1889-1968.... **CLC 16**
See also CA 116

Drieu la Rochelle, Pierre(-Eugene)
1893-1945 .... **TCLC 21**
See also CA 117; DLB 72

Drinkwater, John 1882-1937 ..... **TCLC 57**
See also CA 109; 149; DLB 10, 19, 149

Drop Shot
See Cable, George Washington

Droste-Hulshoff, Annette Freiin von
1797-1848 .... **NCLC 3**
See also DLB 133

Drummond, Walter
See Silverberg, Robert

Drummond, William Henry
1854-1907 .... **TCLC 25**
See also DLB 92

Drummond de Andrade, Carlos
1902-1987 .... **CLC 18**
See also Andrade, Carlos Drummond de
See also CA 132; 123

Drury, Allen (Stuart) 1918- .... **CLC 37**
See also CA 57-60; CANR 18, 52; INT CANR-18

Eddison, E(ric) R(ucker)
1882-1945 . . . . TCLC 15
See also CA 109; 156

Edel, (Joseph) Leon 1907- . . . . . . CLC 29, 34
See also CA 1-4R; CANR 1, 22; DLB 103;
INT CANR-22

Eden, Emily 1797-1869 . . . . NCLC 10

Edgar, David
1948- . . . . CLC 42; DAM DRAM
See also CA 57-60; CANR 12; DLB 13;
MTCW

Edgerton, Clyde (Carlyle) 1944- . . . . CLC 39
See also AAYA 17; CA 118; 134; INT 134

Edgeworth, Maria 1768-1849. . . NCLC 1, 51
See also DLB 116, 159, 163; SATA 21

Edmonds, Paul
See Kuttner, Henry

Edmonds, Walter D(umaux) 1903- . . CLC 35
See also CA 5-8R; CANR 2; DLB 9;
MAICYA; SAAS 4; SATA 1, 27

Edmondson, Wallace
See Ellison, Harlan (Jay)

Edson, Russell . . . . CLC 13
See also CA 33-36R

Edwards, Bronwen Elizabeth
See Rose, Wendy

Edwards, G(erald) B(asil)
1899-1976 . . . . CLC 25
See also CA 110

Edwards, Gus 1939- . . . . CLC 43
See also CA 108; INT 108

Edwards, Jonathan
1703-1758 . . . . LC 7; DA; DAC;
DAM MST
See also DLB 24

Efron, Marina Ivanovna Tsvetaeva
See Tsvetaeva (Efron), Marina (Ivanovna)

Ehle, John (Marsden, Jr.) 1925- . . . . CLC 27
See also CA 9-12R

Ehrenbourg, Ilya (Grigoryevich)
See Ehrenburg, Ilya (Grigoryevich)

Ehrenburg, Ilya (Grigoryevich)
1891-1967 . . . . CLC 18, 34, 62
See also CA 102; 25-28R

Ehrenburg, Ilyo (Grigoryevich)
See Ehrenburg, Ilya (Grigoryevich)

Eich, Guenter 1907-1972 . . . . CLC 15
See also CA 111; 93-96; DLB 69, 124

Eichendorff, Joseph Freiherr von
1788-1857 . . . . NCLC 8
See also DLB 90

Eigner, Larry . . . . CLC 9
See also Eigner, Laurence (Joel)
See also CAAS 23; DLB 5

Eigner, Laurence (Joel) 1927-1996
See Eigner, Larry
See also CA 9-12R; 151; CANR 6

Einstein, Albert 1879-1955 . . . . TCLC 65
See also CA 121; 133; MTCW

Eiseley, Loren Corey 1907-1977 . . . . CLC 7
See also AAYA 5; CA 1-4R; 73-76;
CANR 6

Eisenstadt, Jill 1963- . . . . CLC 50
See also CA 140

Eisenstein, Sergei (Mikhailovich)
1898-1948 . . . . TCLC 57
See also CA 114; 149

Eisner, Simon
See Kornbluth, C(yril) M.

Ekeloef, (Bengt) Gunnar
1907-1968 . . . . CLC 27; DAM POET
See also CA 123; 25-28R

Ekelof, (Bengt) Gunnar
See Ekeloef, (Bengt) Gunnar

Ekwensi, C. O. D.
See Ekwensi, Cyprian (Odiatu Duaka)

Ekwensi, Cyprian (Odiatu Duaka)
1921- . . . . . . CLC 4; BLC; DAM MULT
See also BW 2; CA 29-32R; CANR 18, 42;
DLB 117; MTCW; SATA 66

Elaine . . . . TCLC 18
See also Leverson, Ada

El Crummo
See Crumb, R(obert)

Elia
See Lamb, Charles

Eliade, Mircea 1907-1986 . . . . CLC 19
See also CA 65-68; 119; CANR 30; MTCW

Eliot, A. D.
See Jewett, (Theodora) Sarah Orne

Eliot, Alice
See Jewett, (Theodora) Sarah Orne

Eliot, Dan
See Silverberg, Robert

Eliot, George
1819-1880 . . . . . NCLC 4, 13, 23, 41, 49;
DA; DAB; DAC; DAM MST, NOV;
WLC
See also CDBLB 1832-1890; DLB 21, 35, 55

Eliot, John 1604-1690 . . . . LC 5
See also DLB 24

Eliot, T(homas) S(tearns)
1888-1965 . . . . . CLC 1, 2, 3, 6, 9, 10, 13,
15, 24, 34, 41, 55, 57; DA; DAB; DAC;
DAM DRAM, MST, POET; PC 5;
WLC 2
See also CA 5-8R; 25-28R; CANR 41;
CDALB 1929-1941; DLB 7, 10, 45, 63;
DLBY 88; MTCW

Elizabeth 1866-1941 . . . . TCLC 41

Elkin, Stanley L(awrence)
1930-1995 . . . . . . CLC 4, 6, 9, 14, 27, 51,
91; DAM NOV, POP; SSC 12
See also CA 9-12R; 148; CANR 8, 46;
DLB 2, 28; DLBY 80; INT CANR-8;
MTCW

Elledge, Scott . . . . CLC 34

Elliot, Don
See Silverberg, Robert

Elliott, Don
See Silverberg, Robert

Elliott, George P(aul) 1918-1980 . . . . . CLC 2
See also CA 1-4R; 97-100; CANR 2

Elliott, Janice 1931- . . . . CLC 47
See also CA 13-16R; CANR 8, 29; DLB 14

Elliott, Sumner Locke 1917-1991 . . . CLC 38
See also CA 5-8R; 134; CANR 2, 21

Elliott, William
See Bradbury, Ray (Douglas)

Ellis, A. E. . . . . CLC 7

Ellis, Alice Thomas . . . . CLC 40
See also Haycraft, Anna

Ellis, Bret Easton
1964- . . . . CLC 39, 71; DAM POP
See also AAYA 2; CA 118; 123; CANR 51;
INT 123

Ellis, (Henry) Havelock
1859-1939 . . . . TCLC 14
See also CA 109

Ellis, Landon
See Ellison, Harlan (Jay)

Ellis, Trey 1962- . . . . CLC 55
See also CA 146

Ellison, Harlan (Jay)
1934- . . . . . . CLC 1, 13, 42; DAM POP;
SSC 14
See also CA 5-8R; CANR 5, 46; DLB 8;
INT CANR-5; MTCW

Ellison, Ralph (Waldo)
1914-1994 . . . . CLC 1, 3, 11, 54, 86;
BLC; DA; DAB; DAC; DAM MST,
MULT, NOV; WLC
See also AAYA 19; BW 1; CA 9-12R; 145;
CANR 24, 53; CDALB 1941-1968;
DLB 2, 76; DLBY 94; MTCW

Ellmann, Lucy (Elizabeth) 1956- . . . . CLC 61
See also CA 128

Ellmann, Richard (David)
1918-1987 . . . . CLC 50
See also BEST 89:2; CA 1-4R; 122;
CANR 2, 28; DLB 103; DLBY 87;
MTCW

Elman, Richard 1934- . . . . CLC 19
See also CA 17-20R; CAAS 3; CANR 47

Elron
See Hubbard, L(afayette) Ron(ald)

Eluard, Paul . . . . TCLC 7, 41
See also Grindel, Eugene

Elyot, Sir Thomas 1490(?)-1546 . . . . . LC 11

Elytis, Odysseus
1911-1996 . . . . CLC 15, 49, 100;
DAM POET
See also CA 102; 151; MTCW

Emecheta, (Florence Onye) Buchi
1944- . . CLC 14, 48; BLC; DAM MULT
See also BW 2; CA 81-84; CANR 27;
DLB 117; MTCW; SATA 66

Emerson, Ralph Waldo
1803-1882 . . . . . NCLC 1, 38; DA; DAB;
DAC; DAM MST, POET; WLC
See also CDALB 1640-1865; DLB 1, 59, 73

Eminescu, Mihail 1850-1889 . . . . . NCLC 33

Empson, William
1906-1984 . . . . CLC 3, 8, 19, 33, 34
See also CA 17-20R; 112; CANR 31;
DLB 20; MTCW

Enchi Fumiko (Ueda) 1905-1986. . . . CLC 31
See also CA 129; 121

Farren, Richard M.
See Betjeman, John

Fassbinder, Rainer Werner
1946-1982 . . . . **CLC 20**
See also CA 93-96; 106; CANR 31

Fast, Howard (Melvin)
1914- . . . . **CLC 23; DAM NOV**
See also AAYA 16; CA 1-4R; CAAS 18;
CANR 1, 33, 54; DLB 9; INT CANR-33;
SATA 7

Faulcon, Robert
See Holdstock, Robert P.

Faulkner, William (Cuthbert)
1897-1962 . . . . . **CLC 1, 3, 6, 8, 9, 11, 14,
18, 28, 52, 68; DA; DAB; DAC;
DAM MST, NOV; SSC 1; WLC**
See also AAYA 7; CA 81-84; CANR 33;
CDALB 1929-1941; DLB 9, 11, 44, 102;
DLBD 2; DLBY 86; MTCW

Fauset, Jessie Redmon
1884(?)-1961 . . . . **CLC 19, 54; BLC;
DAM MULT**
See also BW 1; CA 109; DLB 51

Faust, Frederick (Schiller)
1892-1944(?) . . . . **TCLC 49; DAM POP**
See also CA 108; 152

Faust, Irvin 1924- . . . . **CLC 8**
See also CA 33-36R; CANR 28; DLB 2, 28;
DLBY 80

Fawkes, Guy
See Benchley, Robert (Charles)

Fearing, Kenneth (Flexner)
1902-1961 . . . . **CLC 51**
See also CA 93-96; DLB 9

Fecamps, Elise
See Creasey, John

Federman, Raymond 1928- . . . . . . **CLC 6, 47**
See also CA 17-20R; CAAS 8; CANR 10,
43; DLBY 80

Federspiel, J(uerg) F. 1931- . . . . **CLC 42**
See also CA 146

Feiffer, Jules (Ralph)
1929- . . . . . . **CLC 2, 8, 64; DAM DRAM**
See also AAYA 3; CA 17-20R; CANR 30;
DLB 7, 44; INT CANR-30; MTCW;
SATA 8, 61

Feige, Hermann Albert Otto Maximilian
See Traven, B.

Feinberg, David B. 1956-1994 . . . . . . **CLC 59**
See also CA 135; 147

Feinstein, Elaine 1930- . . . . **CLC 36**
See also CA 69-72; CAAS 1; CANR 31;
DLB 14, 40; MTCW

Feldman, Irving (Mordecai) 1928- . . . . **CLC 7**
See also CA 1-4R; CANR 1; DLB 169

Fellini, Federico 1920-1993 . . . . . **CLC 16, 85**
See also CA 65-68; 143; CANR 33

Felsen, Henry Gregor 1916- . . . . **CLC 17**
See also CA 1-4R; CANR 1; SAAS 2;
SATA 1

Fenton, James Martin 1949- . . . . **CLC 32**
See also CA 102; DLB 40

Ferber, Edna 1887-1968 . . . . **CLC 18, 93**
See also AITN 1; CA 5-8R; 25-28R; DLB 9,
28, 86; MTCW; SATA 7

Ferguson, Helen
See Kavan, Anna

Ferguson, Samuel 1810-1886 . . . . . **NCLC 33**
See also DLB 32

Fergusson, Robert 1750-1774 . . . . **LC 29**
See also DLB 109

Ferling, Lawrence
See Ferlinghetti, Lawrence (Monsanto)

Ferlinghetti, Lawrence (Monsanto)
1919(?)- . . . . **CLC 2, 6, 10, 27;
DAM POET; PC 1**
See also CA 5-8R; CANR 3, 41;
CDALB 1941-1968; DLB 5, 16; MTCW

Fernandez, Vicente Garcia Huidobro
See Huidobro Fernandez, Vicente Garcia

Ferrer, Gabriel (Francisco Victor) Miro
See Miro (Ferrer), Gabriel (Francisco
Victor)

Ferrier, Susan (Edmonstone)
1782-1854 . . . . **NCLC 8**
See also DLB 116

Ferrigno, Robert 1948(?)- . . . . **CLC 65**
See also CA 140

Ferron, Jacques 1921-1985 . . . **CLC 94; DAC**
See also CA 117; 129; DLB 60

Feuchtwanger, Lion 1884-1958 . . . . . **TCLC 3**
See also CA 104; DLB 66

Feuillet, Octave 1821-1890 . . . . . . **NCLC 45**

Feydeau, Georges (Leon Jules Marie)
1862-1921 . . . . . **TCLC 22; DAM DRAM**
See also CA 113; 152

Ficino, Marsilio 1433-1499 . . . . **LC 12**

Fiedeler, Hans
See Doeblin, Alfred

Fiedler, Leslie A(aron)
1917- . . . . **CLC 4, 13, 24**
See also CA 9-12R; CANR 7; DLB 28, 67;
MTCW

Field, Andrew 1938- . . . . **CLC 44**
See also CA 97-100; CANR 25

Field, Eugene 1850-1895 . . . . **NCLC 3**
See also DLB 23, 42, 140; DLBD 13;
MAICYA; SATA 16

Field, Gans T.
See Wellman, Manly Wade

Field, Michael . . . . **TCLC 43**

Field, Peter
See Hobson, Laura Z(ametkin)

Fielding, Henry
1707-1754 . . . . . . **LC 1; DA; DAB; DAC;
DAM DRAM, MST, NOV; WLC**
See also CDBLB 1660-1789; DLB 39, 84,
101

Fielding, Sarah 1710-1768 . . . . **LC 1**
See also DLB 39

Fierstein, Harvey (Forbes)
1954- . . . . . **CLC 33; DAM DRAM, POP**
See also CA 123; 129

Figes, Eva 1932- . . . . **CLC 31**
See also CA 53-56; CANR 4, 44; DLB 14

Finch, Robert (Duer Claydon)
1900- . . . . **CLC 18**
See also CA 57-60; CANR 9, 24, 49;
DLB 88

Findley, Timothy
1930- . . . . . . **CLC 27; DAC; DAM MST**
See also CA 25-28R; CANR 12, 42;
DLB 53

Fink, William
See Mencken, H(enry) L(ouis)

Firbank, Louis 1942-
See Reed, Lou
See also CA 117

Firbank, (Arthur Annesley) Ronald
1886-1926 . . . . **TCLC 1**
See also CA 104; DLB 36

Fisher, M(ary) F(rances) K(ennedy)
1908-1992 . . . . **CLC 76, 87**
See also CA 77-80; 138; CANR 44

Fisher, Roy 1930- . . . . **CLC 25**
See also CA 81-84; CAAS 10; CANR 16;
DLB 40

Fisher, Rudolph
1897-1934 . . . . **TCLC 11; BLC;
DAM MULT; SSC 25**
See also BW 1; CA 107; 124; DLB 51, 102

Fisher, Vardis (Alvero) 1895-1968 . . . . **CLC 7**
See also CA 5-8R; 25-28R; DLB 9

Fiske, Tarleton
See Bloch, Robert (Albert)

Fitch, Clarke
See Sinclair, Upton (Beall)

Fitch, John IV
See Cormier, Robert (Edmund)

Fitzgerald, Captain Hugh
See Baum, L(yman) Frank

FitzGerald, Edward 1809-1883 . . . . **NCLC 9**
See also DLB 32

Fitzgerald, F(rancis) Scott (Key)
1896-1940 . . . . **TCLC 1, 6, 14, 28, 55;
DA; DAB; DAC; DAM MST, NOV;
SSC 6; WLC**
See also AITN 1; CA 110; 123;
CDALB 1917-1929; DLB 4, 9, 86;
DLBD 1; DLBY 81; MTCW

Fitzgerald, Penelope 1916- . . **CLC 19, 51, 61**
See also CA 85-88; CAAS 10; CANR 56;
DLB 14

Fitzgerald, Robert (Stuart)
1910-1985 . . . . **CLC 39**
See also CA 1-4R; 114; CANR 1; DLBY 80

FitzGerald, Robert D(avid)
1902-1987 . . . . **CLC 19**
See also CA 17-20R

Fitzgerald, Zelda (Sayre)
1900-1948 . . . . **TCLC 52**
See also CA 117; 126; DLBY 84

Flanagan, Thomas (James Bonner)
1923- . . . . **CLC 25, 52**
See also CA 108; CANR 55; DLBY 80;
INT 108; MTCW

Flaubert, Gustave
1821-1880 . . . . **NCLC 2, 10, 19; DA;
DAB; DAC; DAM MST, NOV; SSC 11;
WLC**
See also DLB 119

Flecker, Herman Elroy
See Flecker, (Herman) James Elroy

Fredro, Aleksander 1793-1876..... **NCLC 8**

Freeling, Nicolas 1927- .... **CLC 38**
See also CA 49-52; CAAS 12; CANR 1, 17, 50; DLB 87

Freeman, Douglas Southall
1886-1953 .... **TCLC 11**
See also CA 109; DLB 17

Freeman, Judith 1946-........... **CLC 55**
See also CA 148

Freeman, Mary Eleanor Wilkins
1852-1930 .... **TCLC 9; SSC 1**
See also CA 106; DLB 12, 78

Freeman, R(ichard) Austin
1862-1943 .... **TCLC 21**
See also CA 113; DLB 70

French, Albert 1943- .... **CLC 86**

French, Marilyn
1929- .... **CLC 10, 18, 60; DAM DRAM, NOV, POP**
See also CA 69-72; CANR 3, 31; INT CANR-31; MTCW

French, Paul
See Asimov, Isaac

Freneau, Philip Morin 1752-1832.. **NCLC 1**
See also DLB 37, 43

Freud, Sigmund 1856-1939 .... **TCLC 52**
See also CA 115; 133; MTCW

Friedan, Betty (Naomi) 1921-...... **CLC 74**
See also CA 65-68; CANR 18, 45; MTCW

Friedlander, Saul 1932-.......... **CLC 90**
See also CA 117; 130

Friedman, B(ernard) H(arper)
1926- .... **CLC 7**
See also CA 1-4R; CANR 3, 48

Friedman, Bruce Jay 1930-.... **CLC 3, 5, 56**
See also CA 9-12R; CANR 25, 52; DLB 2, 28; INT CANR-25

Friel, Brian 1929-.......... **CLC 5, 42, 59**
See also CA 21-24R; CANR 33; DLB 13; MTCW

Friis-Baastad, Babbis Ellinor
1921-1970 .... **CLC 12**
See also CA 17-20R; 134; SATA 7

Frisch, Max (Rudolf)
1911-1991 ..... **CLC 3, 9, 14, 18, 32, 44; DAM DRAM, NOV**
See also CA 85-88; 134; CANR 32; DLB 69, 124; MTCW

Fromentin, Eugene (Samuel Auguste)
1820-1876 .... **NCLC 10**
See also DLB 123

Frost, Frederick
See Faust, Frederick (Schiller)

Frost, Robert (Lee)
1874-1963 .... **CLC 1, 3, 4, 9, 10, 13, 15, 26, 34, 44; DA; DAB; DAC; DAM MST, POET; PC 1; WLC**
See also AAYA 21; CA 89-92; CANR 33; CDALB 1917-1929; DLB 54; DLBD 7; MTCW; SATA 14

Froude, James Anthony
1818-1894 .... **NCLC 43**
See also DLB 18, 57, 144

Froy, Herald
See Waterhouse, Keith (Spencer)

Fry, Christopher
1907- ..... **CLC 2, 10, 14; DAM DRAM**
See also CA 17-20R; CAAS 23; CANR 9, 30; DLB 13; MTCW; SATA 66

Frye, (Herman) Northrop
1912-1991 .... **CLC 24, 70**
See also CA 5-8R; 133; CANR 8, 37; DLB 67, 68; MTCW

Fuchs, Daniel 1909-1993 .... **CLC 8, 22**
See also CA 81-84; 142; CAAS 5; CANR 40; DLB 9, 26, 28; DLBY 93

Fuchs, Daniel 1934-............. **CLC 34**
See also CA 37-40R; CANR 14, 48

Fuentes, Carlos
1928-...... **CLC 3, 8, 10, 13, 22, 41, 60; DA; DAB; DAC; DAM MST, MULT, NOV; HLC; SSC 24; WLC**
See also AAYA 4; AITN 2; CA 69-72; CANR 10, 32; DLB 113; HW; MTCW

Fuentes, Gregorio Lopez y
See Lopez y Fuentes, Gregorio

Fugard, (Harold) Athol
1932-......... **CLC 5, 9, 14, 25, 40, 80; DAM DRAM; DC 3**
See also AAYA 17; CA 85-88; CANR 32, 54; MTCW

Fugard, Sheila 1932- .... **CLC 48**
See also CA 125

Fuller, Charles (H., Jr.)
1939- .... **CLC 25; BLC; DAM DRAM, MULT; DC 1**
See also BW 2; CA 108; 112; DLB 38; INT 112; MTCW

Fuller, John (Leopold) 1937-...... **CLC 62**
See also CA 21-24R; CANR 9, 44; DLB 40

Fuller, Margaret .... **NCLC 5, 50**
See also Ossoli, Sarah Margaret (Fuller marchesa d')

Fuller, Roy (Broadbent)
1912-1991 .... **CLC 4, 28**
See also CA 5-8R; 135; CAAS 10; CANR 53; DLB 15, 20; SATA 87

Fulton, Alice 1952-............. **CLC 52**
See also CA 116; CANR 57

Furphy, Joseph 1843-1912........ **TCLC 25**

Fussell, Paul 1924-.............. **CLC 74**
See also BEST 90:1; CA 17-20R; CANR 8, 21, 35; INT CANR-21; MTCW

Futabatei, Shimei 1864-1909 ...... **TCLC 44**

Futrelle, Jacques 1875-1912 ...... **TCLC 19**
See also CA 113; 155

Gaboriau, Emile 1835-1873 ...... **NCLC 14**

Gadda, Carlo Emilio 1893-1973 .... **CLC 11**
See also CA 89-92; DLB 177

Gaddis, William
1922- ...... **CLC 1, 3, 6, 8, 10, 19, 43, 86**
See also CA 17-20R; CANR 21, 48; DLB 2; MTCW

Gage, Walter
See Inge, William (Motter)

Gaines, Ernest J(ames)
1933- .... **CLC 3, 11, 18, 86; BLC; DAM MULT**
See also AAYA 18; AITN 1; BW 2; CA 9-12R; CANR 6, 24, 42; CDALB 1968-1988; DLB 2, 33, 152; DLBY 80; MTCW; SATA 86

Gaitskill, Mary 1954-............. **CLC 69**
See also CA 128

Galdos, Benito Perez
See Perez Galdos, Benito

Gale, Zona
1874-1938 ...... **TCLC 7; DAM DRAM**
See also CA 105; 153; DLB 9, 78

Galeano, Eduardo (Hughes) 1940-... **CLC 72**
See also CA 29-32R; CANR 13, 32; HW

Galiano, Juan Valera y Alcala
See Valera y Alcala-Galiano, Juan

Gallagher, Tess
1943- .. **CLC 18, 63; DAM POET; PC 9**
See also CA 106; DLB 120

Gallant, Mavis
1922- .... **CLC 7, 18, 38; DAC; DAM MST; SSC 5**
See also CA 69-72; CANR 29; DLB 53; MTCW

Gallant, Roy A(rthur) 1924- .... **CLC 17**
See also CA 5-8R; CANR 4, 29, 54; CLR 30; MAICYA; SATA 4, 68

Gallico, Paul (William) 1897-1976 ... **CLC 2**
See also AITN 1; CA 5-8R; 69-72; CANR 23; DLB 9, 171; MAICYA; SATA 13

Gallo, Max Louis 1932-........... **CLC 95**
See also CA 85-88

Gallois, Lucien
See Desnos, Robert

Gallup, Ralph
See Whitemore, Hugh (John)

Galsworthy, John
1867-1933 ...... **TCLC 1, 45; DA; DAB; DAC; DAM DRAM, MST, NOV; SSC 22; WLC 2**
See also CA 104; 141; CDBLB 1890-1914; DLB 10, 34, 98, 162

Galt, John 1779-1839........... **NCLC 1**
See also DLB 99, 116, 159

Galvin, James 1951-.............. **CLC 38**
See also CA 108; CANR 26

Gamboa, Federico 1864-1939...... **TCLC 36**

Gandhi, M. K.
See Gandhi, Mohandas Karamchand

Gandhi, Mahatma
See Gandhi, Mohandas Karamchand

Gandhi, Mohandas Karamchand
1869-1948 ..... **TCLC 59; DAM MULT**
See also CA 121; 132; MTCW

Gann, Ernest Kellogg 1910-1991.... **CLC 23**
See also AITN 1; CA 1-4R; 136; CANR 1

Garcia, Cristina 1958- .... **CLC 76**
See also CA 141

Green, Julian (Hartridge) 1900-
See Green, Julien
See also CA 21-24R; CANR 33; DLB 4, 72;
MTCW

Green, Julien . . . . **CLC 3, 11, 77**
See also Green, Julian (Hartridge)

Green, Paul (Eliot)
1894-1981 . . . . . . **CLC 25; DAM DRAM**
See also AITN 1; CA 5-8R; 103; CANR 3;
DLB 7, 9; DLBY 81

Greenberg, Ivan 1908-1973
See Rahv, Philip
See also CA 85-88

Greenberg, Joanne (Goldenberg)
1932- . . . . **CLC 7, 30**
See also AAYA 12; CA 5-8R; CANR 14,
32; SATA 25

Greenberg, Richard 1959(?)- . . . . **CLC 57**
See also CA 138

Greene, Bette 1934- . . . . **CLC 30**
See also AAYA 7; CA 53-56; CANR 4;
CLR 2; JRDA; MAICYA; SAAS 16;
SATA 8

Greene, Gael . . . . **CLC 8**
See also CA 13-16R; CANR 10

Greene, Graham
1904-1991 . . . . **CLC 1, 3, 6, 9, 14, 18, 27,
37, 70, 72; DA; DAB; DAC; DAM MST,
NOV; WLC**
See also AITN 2; CA 13-16R; 133;
CANR 35; CDBLB 1945-1960; DLB 13,
15, 77, 100, 162; DLBY 91; MTCW;
SATA 20

Greer, Richard
See Silverberg, Robert

Gregor, Arthur 1923- . . . . **CLC 9**
See also CA 25-28R; CAAS 10; CANR 11;
SATA 36

Gregor, Lee
See Pohl, Frederik

Gregory, Isabella Augusta (Persse)
1852-1932 . . . . **TCLC 1**
See also CA 104; DLB 10

Gregory, J. Dennis
See Williams, John A(lfred)

Grendon, Stephen
See Derleth, August (William)

Grenville, Kate 1950- . . . . **CLC 61**
See also CA 118; CANR 53

Grenville, Pelham
See Wodehouse, P(elham) G(renville)

Greve, Felix Paul (Berthold Friedrich)
1879-1948
See Grove, Frederick Philip
See also CA 104; 141; DAC; DAM MST

Grey, Zane
1872-1939 . . . . **TCLC 6; DAM POP**
See also CA 104; 132; DLB 9; MTCW

Grieg, (Johan) Nordahl (Brun)
1902-1943 . . . . **TCLC 10**
See also CA 107

Grieve, C(hristopher) M(urray)
1892-1978 . . . . **CLC 11, 19; DAM POET**
See also MacDiarmid, Hugh; Pteleon
See also CA 5-8R; 85-88; CANR 33;
MTCW

Griffin, Gerald 1803-1840 . . . . **NCLC 7**
See also DLB 159

Griffin, John Howard 1920-1980 . . . . **CLC 68**
See also AITN 1; CA 1-4R; 101; CANR 2

Griffin, Peter 1942- . . . . **CLC 39**
See also CA 136

Griffith, D(avid Lewelyn) W(ark)
1875(?)-1948 . . . . **TCLC 68**
See also CA 119; 150

Griffith, Lawrence
See Griffith, D(avid Lewelyn) W(ark)

Griffiths, Trevor 1935- . . . . **CLC 13, 52**
See also CA 97-100; CANR 45; DLB 13

Grigson, Geoffrey (Edward Harvey)
1905-1985 . . . . **CLC 7, 39**
See also CA 25-28R; 118; CANR 20, 33;
DLB 27; MTCW

Grillparzer, Franz 1791-1872 . . . . . . **NCLC 1**
See also DLB 133

Grimble, Reverend Charles James
See Eliot, T(homas) S(tearns)

Grimke, Charlotte L(ottie) Forten
1837(?)-1914
See Forten, Charlotte L.
See also BW 1; CA 117; 124; DAM MULT,
POET

Grimm, Jacob Ludwig Karl
1785-1863 . . . . **NCLC 3**
See also DLB 90; MAICYA; SATA 22

Grimm, Wilhelm Karl 1786-1859 . . **NCLC 3**
See also DLB 90; MAICYA; SATA 22

**Grimmelshausen, Johann Jakob Christoffel
von** 1621-1676 . . . . **LC 6**
See also DLB 168

Grindel, Eugene 1895-1952
See Eluard, Paul
See also CA 104

Grisham, John 1955- . . **CLC 84; DAM POP**
See also AAYA 14; CA 138; CANR 47

Grossman, David 1954- . . . . **CLC 67**
See also CA 138

Grossman, Vasily (Semenovich)
1905-1964 . . . . **CLC 41**
See also CA 124; 130; MTCW

Grove, Frederick Philip . . . . **TCLC 4**
See also Greve, Felix Paul (Berthold
Friedrich)
See also DLB 92

Grubb
See Crumb, R(obert)

Grumbach, Doris (Isaac)
1918- . . . . **CLC 13, 22, 64**
See also CA 5-8R; CAAS 2; CANR 9, 42;
INT CANR-9

Grundtvig, Nicolai Frederik Severin
1783-1872 . . . . **NCLC 1**

Grunge
See Crumb, R(obert)

Grunwald, Lisa 1959- . . . . **CLC 44**
See also CA 120

Guare, John
1938- . . . . **CLC 8, 14, 29, 67;
DAM DRAM**
See also CA 73-76; CANR 21; DLB 7;
MTCW

Gudjonsson, Halldor Kiljan 1902-
See Laxness, Halldor
See also CA 103

Guenter, Erich
See Eich, Guenter

Guest, Barbara 1920- . . . . **CLC 34**
See also CA 25-28R; CANR 11, 44; DLB 5

Guest, Judith (Ann)
1936- . . . . **CLC 8, 30; DAM NOV, POP**
See also AAYA 7; CA 77-80; CANR 15;
INT CANR-15; MTCW

Guevara, Che . . . . **CLC 87; HLC**
See also Guevara (Serna), Ernesto

Guevara (Serna), Ernesto 1928-1967
See Guevara, Che
See also CA 127; 111; CANR 56;
DAM MULT; HW

Guild, Nicholas M. 1944- . . . . **CLC 33**
See also CA 93-96

Guillemin, Jacques
See Sartre, Jean-Paul

Guillen, Jorge
1893-1984 . . . . . . **CLC 11; DAM MULT,
POET**
See also CA 89-92; 112; DLB 108; HW

Guillen, Nicolas (Cristobal)
1902-1989 . . . . **CLC 48, 79; BLC;
DAM MST, MULT, POET; HLC**
See also BW 2; CA 116; 125; 129; HW

Guillevic, (Eugene) 1907- . . . . **CLC 33**
See also CA 93-96

Guillois
See Desnos, Robert

Guillois, Valentin
See Desnos, Robert

Guiney, Louise Imogen
1861-1920 . . . . **TCLC 41**
See also DLB 54

Guiraldes, Ricardo (Guillermo)
1886-1927 . . . . **TCLC 39**
See also CA 131; HW; MTCW

Gumilev, Nikolai Stephanovich
1886-1921 . . . . **TCLC 60**

Gunesekera, Romesh . . . . **CLC 91**

Gunn, Bill . . . . **CLC 5**
See also Gunn, William Harrison
See also DLB 38

Gunn, Thom(son William)
1929- . . . . **CLC 3, 6, 18, 32, 81;
DAM POET**
See also CA 17-20R; CANR 9, 33;
CDBLB 1960 to Present; DLB 27;
INT CANR-33; MTCW

Gunn, William Harrison 1934(?)-1989
See Gunn, Bill
See also AITN 1; BW 1; CA 13-16R; 128;
CANR 12, 25

Gunnars, Kristjana 1948- . . . . **CLC 69**
See also CA 113; DLB 60

Gurganus, Allan
1947- . . . . **CLC 70; DAM POP**
See also BEST 90:1; CA 135

Gurney, A(lbert) R(amsdell), Jr.
1930- . . . . **CLC 32, 50, 54; DAM DRAM**
See also CA 77-80; CANR 32

Gurney, Ivor (Bertie) 1890-1937 . . . TCLC 33

Gurney, Peter
See Gurney, A(lbert) R(amsdell), Jr.

Guro, Elena 1877-1913 . . . . TCLC 56

Gustafson, James M(oody) 1925- . . CLC 100
See also CA 25-28R; CANR 37

Gustafson, Ralph (Barker) 1909-. . . . CLC 36
See also CA 21-24R; CANR 8, 45; DLB 88

Gut, Gom
See Simenon, Georges (Jacques Christian)

Guterson, David 1956-. . . . . CLC 91
See also CA 132

Guthrie, A(lfred) B(ertram), Jr.
1901-1991 . . . . CLC 23
See also CA 57-60; 134; CANR 24; DLB 6;
SATA 62; SATA-Obit 67

Guthrie, Isobel
See Grieve, C(hristopher) M(urray)

Guthrie, Woodrow Wilson 1912-1967
See Guthrie, Woody
See also CA 113; 93-96

Guthrie, Woody. . . . . CLC 35
See also Guthrie, Woodrow Wilson

Guy, Rosa (Cuthbert) 1928-. . . . . CLC 26
See also AAYA 4; BW 2; CA 17-20R;
CANR 14, 34; CLR 13; DLB 33; JRDA;
MAICYA; SATA 14, 62

Gwendolyn
See Bennett, (Enoch) Arnold

H. D. . . . . CLC 3, 8, 14, 31, 34, 73; PC 5
See also Doolittle, Hilda

H. de V.
See Buchan, John

Haavikko, Paavo Juhani
1931- . . . . CLC 18, 34
See also CA 106

Habbema, Koos
See Heijermans, Herman

Hacker, Marilyn
1942- . . . . CLC 5, 9, 23, 72, 91;
DAM POET
See also CA 77-80; DLB 120

Haggard, H(enry) Rider
1856-1925 . . . . TCLC 11
See also CA 108; 148; DLB 70, 156, 174;
SATA 16

Hagiosy, L.
See Larbaud, Valery (Nicolas)

Hagiwara Sakutaro 1886-1942 . . . . TCLC 60

Haig, Fenil
See Ford, Ford Madox

Haig-Brown, Roderick (Langmere)
1908-1976 . . . . CLC 21
See also CA 5-8R; 69-72; CANR 4, 38;
CLR 31; DLB 88; MAICYA; SATA 12

Hailey, Arthur
1920- . . . . CLC 5; DAM NOV, POP
See also AITN 2; BEST 90:3; CA 1-4R;
CANR 2, 36; DLB 88; DLBY 82; MTCW

Hailey, Elizabeth Forsythe 1938-. . . CLC 40
See also CA 93-96; CAAS 1; CANR 15, 48;
INT CANR-15

Haines, John (Meade) 1924-. . . . . . . CLC 58
See also CA 17-20R; CANR 13, 34; DLB 5

Hakluyt, Richard 1552-1616 . . . . LC 31

Haldeman, Joe (William) 1943-. . . . CLC 61
See also CA 53-56; CAAS 25; CANR 6;
DLB 8; INT CANR-6

Haley, Alex(ander Murray Palmer)
1921-1992 . . . . CLC 8, 12, 76; BLC; DA;
DAB; DAC; DAM MST, MULT, POP
See also BW 2; CA 77-80; 136; DLB 38;
MTCW

Haliburton, Thomas Chandler
1796-1865 . . . . NCLC 15
See also DLB 11, 99

Hall, Donald (Andrew, Jr.)
1928-. . CLC 1, 13, 37, 59; DAM POET
See also CA 5-8R; CAAS 7; CANR 2, 44;
DLB 5; SATA 23

Hall, Frederic Sauser
See Sauser-Hall, Frederic

Hall, James
See Kuttner, Henry

Hall, James Norman 1887-1951 . . . TCLC 23
See also CA 123; SATA 21

Hall, (Marguerite) Radclyffe
1886-1943 . . . . TCLC 12
See also CA 110; 150

Hall, Rodney 1935- . . . . CLC 51
See also CA 109

Halleck, Fitz-Greene 1790-1867 . . NCLC 47
See also DLB 3

Halliday, Michael
See Creasey, John

Halpern, Daniel 1945- . . . . CLC 14
See also CA 33-36R

Hamburger, Michael (Peter Leopold)
1924- . . . . CLC 5, 14
See also CA 5-8R; CAAS 4; CANR 2, 47;
DLB 27

Hamill, Pete 1935- . . . . CLC 10
See also CA 25-28R; CANR 18

Hamilton, Alexander
1755(?)-1804 . . . . NCLC 49
See also DLB 37

Hamilton, Clive
See Lewis, C(live) S(taples)

Hamilton, Edmond 1904-1977 . . . . . . CLC 1
See also CA 1-4R; CANR 3; DLB 8

Hamilton, Eugene (Jacob) Lee
See Lee-Hamilton, Eugene (Jacob)

Hamilton, Franklin
See Silverberg, Robert

Hamilton, Gail
See Corcoran, Barbara

Hamilton, Mollie
See Kaye, M(ary) M(argaret)

Hamilton, (Anthony Walter) Patrick
1904-1962 . . . . CLC 51
See also CA 113; DLB 10

Hamilton, Virginia
1936- . . . . CLC 26; DAM MULT
See also AAYA 2, 21; BW 2; CA 25-28R;
CANR 20, 37; CLR 1, 11, 40; DLB 33,
52; INT CANR-20; JRDA; MAICYA;
MTCW; SATA 4, 56, 79

Hammett, (Samuel) Dashiell
1894-1961 . . . . CLC 3, 5, 10, 19, 47;
SSC 17
See also AITN 1; CA 81-84; CANR 42;
CDALB 1929-1941; DLBD 6; MTCW

Hammon, Jupiter
1711(?)-1800(?) . . . . NCLC 5; BLC;
DAM MULT, POET; PC 16
See also DLB 31, 50

Hammond, Keith
See Kuttner, Henry

Hamner, Earl (Henry), Jr. 1923- . . . CLC 12
See also AITN 2; CA 73-76; DLB 6

Hampton, Christopher (James)
1946- . . . . CLC 4
See also CA 25-28R; DLB 13; MTCW

Hamsun, Knut . . . . TCLC 2, 14, 49
See also Pedersen, Knut

Handke, Peter
1942- . . . . CLC 5, 8, 10, 15, 38;
DAM DRAM, NOV
See also CA 77-80; CANR 33; DLB 85,
124; MTCW

Hanley, James 1901-1985 . . . CLC 3, 5, 8, 13
See also CA 73-76; 117; CANR 36; MTCW

Hannah, Barry 1942-. . . . . . . CLC 23, 38, 90
See also CA 108; 110; CANR 43; DLB 6;
INT 110; MTCW

Hannon, Ezra
See Hunter, Evan

Hansberry, Lorraine (Vivian)
1930-1965 . . . . . . CLC 17, 62; BLC; DA;
DAB; DAC; DAM DRAM, MST,
MULT; DC 2
See also BW 1; CA 109; 25-28R; CABS 3;
CDALB 1941-1968; DLB 7, 38; MTCW

Hansen, Joseph 1923-. . . . . CLC 38
See also CA 29-32R; CAAS 17; CANR 16,
44; INT CANR-16

Hansen, Martin A. 1909-1955 . . . . . TCLC 32

Hanson, Kenneth O(stlin) 1922- . . . . CLC 13
See also CA 53-56; CANR 7

Hardwick, Elizabeth
1916- . . . . CLC 13; DAM NOV
See also CA 5-8R; CANR 3, 32; DLB 6;
MTCW

Hardy, Thomas
1840-1928 . . . . . . TCLC 4, 10, 18, 32, 48,
53; DA; DAB; DAC; DAM MST, NOV,
POET; PC 8; SSC 2; WLC
See also CA 104; 123; CDBLB 1890-1914;
DLB 18, 19, 135; MTCW

Hare, David 1947- . . . . CLC 29, 58
See also CA 97-100; CANR 39; DLB 13;
MTCW

Harford, Henry
See Hudson, W(illiam) H(enry)

Hargrave, Leonie
See Disch, Thomas M(ichael)

Harjo, Joy 1951- . . . CLC 83; DAM MULT
See also CA 114; CANR 35; DLB 120, 175;
NNAL

Harlan, Louis R(udolph) 1922- . . . . . CLC 34
See also CA 21-24R; CANR 25, 55

Author Index

Harling, Robert 1951(?)- . . . . **CLC 53**
See also CA 147

Harmon, William (Ruth) 1938- . . . . . **CLC 38**
See also CA 33-36R; CANR 14, 32, 35;
SATA 65

Harper, F. E. W.
See Harper, Frances Ellen Watkins

Harper, Frances E. W.
See Harper, Frances Ellen Watkins

Harper, Frances E. Watkins
See Harper, Frances Ellen Watkins

Harper, Frances Ellen
See Harper, Frances Ellen Watkins

Harper, Frances Ellen Watkins
1825-1911 . . . . **TCLC 14; BLC;**
                    DAM MULT, POET
See also BW 1; CA 111; 125; DLB 50

Harper, Michael S(teven) 1938- . . **CLC 7, 22**
See also BW 1; CA 33-36R; CANR 24;
DLB 41

Harper, Mrs. F. E. W.
See Harper, Frances Ellen Watkins

Harris, Christie (Lucy) Irwin
1907- . . . . **CLC 12**
See also CA 5-8R; CANR 6; DLB 88;
JRDA; MAICYA; SAAS 10; SATA 6, 74

Harris, Frank 1856-1931 . . . . **TCLC 24**
See also CA 109; 150; DLB 156

Harris, George Washington
1814-1869 . . . . **NCLC 23**
See also DLB 3, 11

Harris, Joel Chandler
1848-1908 . . . . **TCLC 2; SSC 19**
See also CA 104; 137; DLB 11, 23, 42, 78,
91; MAICYA; YABC 1

Harris, John (Wyndham Parkes Lucas)
Beynon 1903-1969
See Wyndham, John
See also CA 102; 89-92

Harris, MacDonald . . . . **CLC 9**
See also Heiney, Donald (William)

Harris, Mark 1922- . . . . **CLC 19**
See also CA 5-8R; CAAS 3; CANR 2, 55;
DLB 2; DLBY 80

Harris, (Theodore) Wilson 1921- . . . **CLC 25**
See also BW 2; CA 65-68; CAAS 16;
CANR 11, 27; DLB 117; MTCW

Harrison, Elizabeth Cavanna 1909-
See Cavanna, Betty
See also CA 9-12R; CANR 6, 27

Harrison, Harry (Max) 1925- . . . . . . **CLC 42**
See also CA 1-4R; CANR 5, 21; DLB 8;
SATA 4

Harrison, James (Thomas)
1937- . . . . **CLC 6, 14, 33, 66; SSC 19**
See also CA 13-16R; CANR 8, 51;
DLBY 82; INT CANR-8

Harrison, Jim
See Harrison, James (Thomas)

Harrison, Kathryn 1961- . . . . **CLC 70**
See also CA 144

Harrison, Tony 1937- . . . . **CLC 43**
See also CA 65-68; CANR 44; DLB 40;
MTCW

Harriss, Will(ard Irvin) 1922- . . . . . . **CLC 34**
See also CA 111

Harson, Sley
See Ellison, Harlan (Jay)

Hart, Ellis
See Ellison, Harlan (Jay)

Hart, Josephine
1942(?)- . . . . **CLC 70; DAM POP**
See also CA 138

Hart, Moss
1904-1961 . . . . . . **CLC 66; DAM DRAM**
See also CA 109; 89-92; DLB 7

Harte, (Francis) Bret(t)
1836(?)-1902 . . . . **TCLC 1, 25; DA; DAC;**
            DAM MST; SSC 8; WLC
See also CA 104; 140; CDALB 1865-1917;
DLB 12, 64, 74, 79; SATA 26

Hartley, L(eslie) P(oles)
1895-1972 . . . . **CLC 2, 22**
See also CA 45-48; 37-40R; CANR 33;
DLB 15, 139; MTCW

Hartman, Geoffrey H. 1929- . . . . **CLC 27**
See also CA 117; 125; DLB 67

Hartmann von Aue
c. 1160-c. 1205 . . . . **CMLC 15**
See also DLB 138

Hartmann von Aue 1170-1210 . . . . **CMLC 15**

Haruf, Kent 1943- . . . . **CLC 34**
See also CA 149

Harwood, Ronald
1934- . . . . **CLC 32; DAM DRAM, MST**
See also CA 1-4R; CANR 4, 55; DLB 13

Hasek, Jaroslav (Matej Frantisek)
1883-1923 . . . . **TCLC 4**
See also CA 104; 129; MTCW

Hass, Robert
1941- . . . . **CLC 18, 39, 99; PC 16**
See also CA 111; CANR 30, 50; DLB 105

Hastings, Hudson
See Kuttner, Henry

Hastings, Selina . . . . **CLC 44**

Hathorne, John 1641-1717 . . . . **LC 38**

Hatteras, Amelia
See Mencken, H(enry) L(ouis)

Hatteras, Owen . . . . **TCLC 18**
See also Mencken, H(enry) L(ouis); Nathan,
George Jean

Hauptmann, Gerhart (Johann Robert)
1862-1946 . . . . . . **TCLC 4; DAM DRAM**
See also CA 104; 153; DLB 66, 118

Havel, Vaclav
1936- . . . . **CLC 25, 58, 65;**
                DAM DRAM; DC 6
See also CA 104; CANR 36; MTCW

Haviaras, Stratis . . . . **CLC 33**
See also Chaviaras, Strates

Hawes, Stephen 1475(?)-1523(?) . . . . . **LC 17**

Hawkes, John (Clendennin Burne, Jr.)
1925- . . . . . . **CLC 1, 2, 3, 4, 7, 9, 14, 15,**
                           27, 49
See also CA 1-4R; CANR 2, 47; DLB 2, 7;
DLBY 80; MTCW

Hawking, S. W.
See Hawking, Stephen W(illiam)

Hawking, Stephen W(illiam)
1942- . . . . **CLC 63**
See also AAYA 13; BEST 89:1; CA 126;
129; CANR 48

Hawthorne, Julian 1846-1934 . . . . . **TCLC 25**

Hawthorne, Nathaniel
1804-1864 . . . . . . **NCLC 39; DA; DAB;**
     DAC; DAM MST, NOV; SSC 3; WLC
See also AAYA 18; CDALB 1640-1865;
DLB 1, 74; YABC 2

Haxton, Josephine Ayres 1921-
See Douglas, Ellen
See also CA 115; CANR 41

Hayaseca y Eizaguirre, Jorge
See Echegaray (y Eizaguirre), Jose (Maria
Waldo)

Hayashi Fumiko 1904-1951 . . . . **TCLC 27**

Haycraft, Anna
See Ellis, Alice Thomas
See also CA 122

Hayden, Robert E(arl)
1913-1980 . . . . . . **CLC 5, 9, 14, 37; BLC;**
    DA; DAC; DAM MST, MULT, POET;
                         PC 6
See also BW 1; CA 69-72; 97-100; CABS 2;
CANR 24; CDALB 1941-1968; DLB 5,
76; MTCW; SATA 19; SATA-Obit 26

Hayford, J(oseph) E(phraim) Casely
See Casely-Hayford, J(oseph) E(phraim)

Hayman, Ronald 1932- . . . . **CLC 44**
See also CA 25-28R; CANR 18, 50;
DLB 155

Haywood, Eliza (Fowler)
1693(?)-1756 . . . . **LC 1**

Hazlitt, William 1778-1830 . . . . . . **NCLC 29**
See also DLB 110, 158

Hazzard, Shirley 1931- . . . . **CLC 18**
See also CA 9-12R; CANR 4; DLBY 82;
MTCW

Head, Bessie
1937-1986 . . . . **CLC 25, 67; BLC;**
                       DAM MULT
See also BW 2; CA 29-32R; 119; CANR 25;
DLB 117; MTCW

Headon, (Nicky) Topper 1956(?)- . . . **CLC 30**

Heaney, Seamus (Justin)
1939- . . . . . . **CLC 5, 7, 14, 25, 37, 74, 91;**
                    DAB; DAM POET
See also CA 85-88; CANR 25, 48;
CDBLB 1960 to Present; DLB 40;
DLBY 95; MTCW

Hearn, (Patricio) Lafcadio (Tessima Carlos)
1850-1904 . . . . **TCLC 9**
See also CA 105; DLB 12, 78

Hearne, Vicki 1946- . . . . **CLC 56**
See also CA 139

Hearon, Shelby 1931- . . . . **CLC 63**
See also AITN 2; CA 25-28R; CANR 18,
48

Heat-Moon, William Least . . . . **CLC 29**
See also Trogdon, William (Lewis)
See also AAYA 9

Hebbel, Friedrich
1813-1863 . . . . **NCLC 43; DAM DRAM**
See also DLB 129

Hebert, Anne
1916- .... CLC 4, 13, 29; DAC;
DAM MST, POET
See also CA 85-88; DLB 68; MTCW

Hecht, Anthony (Evan)
1923- ...... CLC 8, 13, 19; DAM POET
See also CA 9-12R; CANR 6; DLB 5, 169

Hecht, Ben 1894-1964 .... CLC 8
See also CA 85-88; DLB 7, 9, 25, 26, 28, 86

Hedayat, Sadeq 1903-1951....... TCLC 21
See also CA 120

Hegel, Georg Wilhelm Friedrich
1770-1831 .... NCLC 46
See also DLB 90

Heidegger, Martin 1889-1976 ...... CLC 24
See also CA 81-84; 65-68; CANR 34;
MTCW

Heidenstam, (Carl Gustaf) Verner von
1859-1940 .... TCLC 5
See also CA 104

Heifner, Jack 1946- .... CLC 11
See also CA 105; CANR 47

Heijermans, Herman 1864-1924 ... TCLC 24
See also CA 123

Heilbrun, Carolyn G(old) 1926-..... CLC 25
See also CA 45-48; CANR 1, 28

Heine, Heinrich 1797-1856 .... NCLC 4, 54
See also DLB 90

Heinemann, Larry (Curtiss) 1944- .. CLC 50
See also CA 110; CAAS 21; CANR 31;
DLBD 9; INT CANR-31

Heiney, Donald (William) 1921-1993
See Harris, MacDonald
See also CA 1-4R; 142; CANR 3

Heinlein, Robert A(nson)
1907-1988 ...... CLC 1, 3, 8, 14, 26, 55;
DAM POP
See also AAYA 17; CA 1-4R; 125;
CANR 1, 20, 53; DLB 8; JRDA;
MAICYA; MTCW; SATA 9, 69;
SATA-Obit 56

Helforth, John
See Doolittle, Hilda

Hellenhofferu, Vojtech Kapristian z
See Hasek, Jaroslav (Matej Frantisek)

Heller, Joseph
1923- .... CLC 1, 3, 5, 8, 11, 36, 63; DA;
DAB; DAC; DAM MST, NOV, POP;
WLC
See also AITN 1; CA 5-8R; CABS 1;
CANR 8, 42; DLB 2, 28; DLBY 80;
INT CANR-8; MTCW

Hellman, Lillian (Florence)
1906-1984 ...... CLC 2, 4, 8, 14, 18, 34,
44, 52; DAM DRAM; DC 1
See also AITN 1, 2; CA 13-16R; 112;
CANR 33; DLB 7; DLBY 84; MTCW

Helprin, Mark
1947- .... CLC 7, 10, 22, 32;
DAM NOV, POP
See also CA 81-84; CANR 47; DLBY 85;
MTCW

Helvetius, Claude-Adrien
1715-1771 .... LC 26

Helyar, Jane Penelope Josephine 1933-
See Poole, Josephine
See also CA 21-24R; CANR 10, 26;
SATA 82

Hemans, Felicia 1793-1835 ...... NCLC 29
See also DLB 96

Hemingway, Ernest (Miller)
1899-1961 .... CLC 1, 3, 6, 8, 10, 13, 19,
30, 34, 39, 41, 44, 50, 61, 80; DA; DAB;
DAC; DAM MST, NOV; SSC 25; WLC
See also AAYA 19; CA 77-80; CANR 34;
CDALB 1917-1929; DLB 4, 9, 102;
DLBD 1; DLBY 81, 87; MTCW

Hempel, Amy 1951- .... CLC 39
See also CA 118; 137

Henderson, F. C.
See Mencken, H(enry) L(ouis)

Henderson, Sylvia
See Ashton-Warner, Sylvia (Constance)

Henley, Beth .... CLC 23; DC 6
See also Henley, Elizabeth Becker
See also CABS 3; DLBY 86

Henley, Elizabeth Becker 1952-
See Henley, Beth
See also CA 107; CANR 32; DAM DRAM,
MST; MTCW

Henley, William Ernest
1849-1903 .... TCLC 8
See also CA 105; DLB 19

Hennissart, Martha
See Lathen, Emma
See also CA 85-88

Henry, O........ TCLC 1, 19; SSC 5; WLC
See also Porter, William Sydney

Henry, Patrick 1736-1799 .... LC 25

Henryson, Robert 1430(?)-1506(?).... LC 20
See also DLB 146

Henry VIII 1491-1547 .... LC 10

Henschke, Alfred
See Klabund

Hentoff, Nat(han Irving) 1925- ..... CLC 26
See also AAYA 4; CA 1-4R; CAAS 6;
CANR 5, 25; CLR 1; INT CANR-25;
JRDA; MAICYA; SATA 42, 69;
SATA-Brief 27

Heppenstall, (John) Rayner
1911-1981 .... CLC 10
See also CA 1-4R; 103; CANR 29

Heraclitus
c. 540B.C.-c. 450B.C........ CMLC 22
See also DLB 176

Herbert, Frank (Patrick)
1920-1986 ...... CLC 12, 23, 35, 44, 85;
DAM POP
See also AAYA 21; CA 53-56; 118;
CANR 5, 43; DLB 8; INT CANR-5;
MTCW; SATA 9, 37; SATA-Obit 47

Herbert, George
1593-1633 .... LC 24; DAB;
DAM POET; PC 4
See also CDBLB Before 1660; DLB 126

Herbert, Zbigniew
1924- .... CLC 9, 43; DAM POET
See also CA 89-92; CANR 36; MTCW

Herbst, Josephine (Frey)
1897-1969 .... CLC 34
See also CA 5-8R; 25-28R; DLB 9

Hergesheimer, Joseph
1880-1954 .... TCLC 11
See also CA 109; DLB 102, 9

Herlihy, James Leo 1927-1993 ...... CLC 6
See also CA 1-4R; 143; CANR 2

Hermogenes fl. c. 175- .... CMLC 6

Hernandez, Jose 1834-1886 ...... NCLC 17

Herodotus c. 484B.C.-429B.C..... CMLC 17
See also DLB 176

Herrick, Robert
1591-1674 ..... LC 13; DA; DAB; DAC;
DAM MST, POP; PC 9
See also DLB 126

Herring, Guilles
See Somerville, Edith

Herriot, James
1916-1995 .... CLC 12; DAM POP
See also Wight, James Alfred
See also AAYA 1; CA 148; CANR 40;
SATA 86

Herrmann, Dorothy 1941-......... CLC 44
See also CA 107

Herrmann, Taffy
See Herrmann, Dorothy

Hersey, John (Richard)
1914-1993 .... CLC 1, 2, 7, 9, 40, 81, 97;
DAM POP
See also CA 17-20R; 140; CANR 33;
DLB 6; MTCW; SATA 25;
SATA-Obit 76

Herzen, Aleksandr Ivanovich
1812-1870 .... NCLC 10, 61

Herzl, Theodor 1860-1904........ TCLC 36

Herzog, Werner 1942-............ CLC 16
See also CA 89-92

Hesiod c. 8th cent. B.C.- .... CMLC 5
See also DLB 176

Hesse, Hermann
1877-1962 .... CLC 1, 2, 3, 6, 11, 17, 25,
69; DA; DAB; DAC; DAM MST, NOV;
SSC 9; WLC
See also CA 17-18; CAP 2; DLB 66;
MTCW; SATA 50

Hewes, Cady
See De Voto, Bernard (Augustine)

Heyen, William 1940- .... CLC 13, 18
See also CA 33-36R; CAAS 9; DLB 5

Heyerdahl, Thor 1914-............ CLC 26
See also CA 5-8R; CANR 5, 22; MTCW;
SATA 2, 52

Heym, Georg (Theodor Franz Arthur)
1887-1912 .... TCLC 9
See also CA 106

Heym, Stefan 1913-.............. CLC 41
See also CA 9-12R; CANR 4; DLB 69

Heyse, Paul (Johann Ludwig von)
1830-1914 .... TCLC 8
See also CA 104; DLB 129

Heyward, (Edwin) DuBose
1885-1940 .... TCLC 59
See also CA 108; DLB 7, 9, 45; SATA 21

Jimenez Mantecon, Juan
See Jimenez (Mantecon), Juan Ramon

Joel, Billy .... **CLC 26**
See also Joel, William Martin

Joel, William Martin 1949-
See Joel, Billy
See also CA 108

John of the Cross, St. 1542-1591 .... **LC 18**

Johnson, B(ryan) S(tanley William)
1933-1973 .... **CLC 6, 9**
See also CA 9-12R; 53-56; CANR 9;
DLB 14, 40

Johnson, Benj. F. of Boo
See Riley, James Whitcomb

Johnson, Benjamin F. of Boo
See Riley, James Whitcomb

Johnson, Charles (Richard)
1948- .... **CLC 7, 51, 65; BLC;**
DAM MULT
See also BW 2; CA 116; CAAS 18;
CANR 42; DLB 33

Johnson, Denis 1949- .... **CLC 52**
See also CA 117; 121; DLB 120

Johnson, Diane 1934- .... **CLC 5, 13, 48**
See also CA 41-44R; CANR 17, 40;
DLBY 80; INT CANR-17; MTCW

Johnson, Eyvind (Olof Verner)
1900-1976 .... **CLC 14**
See also CA 73-76; 69-72; CANR 34

Johnson, J. R.
See James, C(yril) L(ionel) R(obert)

Johnson, James Weldon
1871-1938 .... **TCLC 3, 19; BLC;**
DAM MULT, POET
See also BW 1; CA 104; 125;
CDALB 1917-1929; CLR 32; DLB 51;
MTCW; SATA 31

Johnson, Joyce 1935- .... **CLC 58**
See also CA 125; 129

Johnson, Lionel (Pigot)
1867-1902 .... **TCLC 19**
See also CA 117; DLB 19

Johnson, Mel
See Malzberg, Barry N(athaniel)

Johnson, Pamela Hansford
1912-1981 .... **CLC 1, 7, 27**
See also CA 1-4R; 104; CANR 2, 28;
DLB 15; MTCW

Johnson, Robert 1911(?)-1938..... **TCLC 69**

Johnson, Samuel
1709-1784 ..... **LC 15; DA; DAB; DAC;**
DAM MST; WLC
See also CDBLB 1660-1789; DLB 39, 95,
104, 142

Johnson, Uwe
1934-1984 .... **CLC 5, 10, 15, 40**
See also CA 1-4R; 112; CANR 1, 39;
DLB 75; MTCW

Johnston, George (Benson) 1913- ... **CLC 51**
See also CA 1-4R; CANR 5, 20; DLB 88

Johnston, Jennifer 1930- .... **CLC 7**
See also CA 85-88; DLB 14

Jolley, (Monica) Elizabeth
1923- .... **CLC 46; SSC 19**
See also CA 127; CAAS 13

Jones, Arthur Llewellyn 1863-1947
See Machen, Arthur
See also CA 104

Jones, D(ouglas) G(ordon) 1929-.... **CLC 10**
See also CA 29-32R; CANR 13; DLB 53

Jones, David (Michael)
1895-1974 .... **CLC 2, 4, 7, 13, 42**
See also CA 9-12R; 53-56; CANR 28;
CDBLB 1945-1960; DLB 20, 100; MTCW

Jones, David Robert 1947-
See Bowie, David
See also CA 103

Jones, Diana Wynne 1934- .... **CLC 26**
See also AAYA 12; CA 49-52; CANR 4,
26, 56; CLR 23; DLB 161; JRDA;
MAICYA; SAAS 7; SATA 9, 70

Jones, Edward P. 1950- .... **CLC 76**
See also BW 2; CA 142

Jones, Gayl
1949- .... **CLC 6, 9; BLC; DAM MULT**
See also BW 2; CA 77-80; CANR 27;
DLB 33; MTCW

Jones, James 1921-1977.... **CLC 1, 3, 10, 39**
See also AITN 1, 2; CA 1-4R; 69-72;
CANR 6; DLB 2, 143; MTCW

Jones, John J.
See Lovecraft, H(oward) P(hillips)

Jones, LeRoi .... **CLC 1, 2, 3, 5, 10, 14**
See also Baraka, Amiri

Jones, Louis B. .... **CLC 65**
See also CA 141

Jones, Madison (Percy, Jr.) 1925- ... **CLC 4**
See also CA 13-16R; CAAS 11; CANR 7,
54; DLB 152

Jones, Mervyn 1922- .... **CLC 10, 52**
See also CA 45-48; CAAS 5; CANR 1;
MTCW

Jones, Mick 1956(?)- .... **CLC 30**

Jones, Nettie (Pearl) 1941- .... **CLC 34**
See also BW 2; CA 137; CAAS 20

Jones, Preston 1936-1979 .... **CLC 10**
See also CA 73-76; 89-92; DLB 7

Jones, Robert F(rancis) 1934- .... **CLC 7**
See also CA 49-52; CANR 2

Jones, Rod 1953- .... **CLC 50**
See also CA 128

Jones, Terence Graham Parry
1942- .... **CLC 21**
See also Jones, Terry; Monty Python
See also CA 112; 116; CANR 35; INT 116

Jones, Terry
See Jones, Terence Graham Parry
See also SATA 67; SATA-Brief 51

Jones, Thom 1945(?)- .... **CLC 81**

Jong, Erica
1942- .... **CLC 4, 6, 8, 18, 83;**
DAM NOV, POP
See also AITN 1; BEST 90:2; CA 73-76;
CANR 26, 52; DLB 2, 5, 28, 152;
INT CANR-26; MTCW

Jonson, Ben(jamin)
1572(?)-1637 ...... **LC 6, 33; DA; DAB;**
DAC; DAM DRAM, MST, POET;
DC 4; PC 17; WLC
See also CDBLB Before 1660; DLB 62, 121

Jordan, June
1936- ..... **CLC 5, 11, 23; DAM MULT,**
POET
See also AAYA 2; BW 2; CA 33-36R;
CANR 25; CLR 10; DLB 38; MAICYA;
MTCW; SATA 4

Jordan, Pat(rick M.) 1941- .... **CLC 37**
See also CA 33-36R

Jorgensen, Ivar
See Ellison, Harlan (Jay)

Jorgenson, Ivar
See Silverberg, Robert

Josephus, Flavius c. 37-100 ...... **CMLC 13**

Josipovici, Gabriel 1940- .... **CLC 6, 43**
See also CA 37-40R; CAAS 8; CANR 47;
DLB 14

Joubert, Joseph 1754-1824 .... **NCLC 9**

Jouve, Pierre Jean 1887-1976 ...... **CLC 47**
See also CA 65-68

Joyce, James (Augustine Aloysius)
1882-1941 .... **TCLC 3, 8, 16, 35, 52;**
DA; DAB; DAC; DAM MST, NOV,
POET; SSC 3; WLC
See also CA 104; 126; CDBLB 1914-1945;
DLB 10, 19, 36, 162; MTCW

Jozsef, Attila 1905-1937......... **TCLC 22**
See also CA 116

Juana Ines de la Cruz 1651(?)-1695 ... **LC 5**

Judd, Cyril
See Kornbluth, C(yril) M.; Pohl, Frederik

Julian of Norwich 1342(?)-1416(?) .... **LC 6**
See also DLB 146

Juniper, Alex
See Hospital, Janette Turner

Junius
See Luxemburg, Rosa

Just, Ward (Swift) 1935- .... **CLC 4, 27**
See also CA 25-28R; CANR 32;
INT CANR-32

Justice, Donald (Rodney)
1925- .... **CLC 6, 19; DAM POET**
See also CA 5-8R; CANR 26, 54;
DLBY 83; INT CANR-26

Juvenal c. 55-c. 127 .... **CMLC 8**

Juvenis
See Bourne, Randolph S(illiman)

Kacew, Romain 1914-1980
See Gary, Romain
See also CA 108; 102

Kadare, Ismail 1936- .... **CLC 52**

Kadohata, Cynthia. .... **CLC 59**
See also CA 140

Kafka, Franz
1883-1924 .... **TCLC 2, 6, 13, 29, 47, 53;**
DA; DAB; DAC; DAM MST, NOV;
SSC 5; WLC
See also CA 105; 126; DLB 81; MTCW

Kahanovitsch, Pinkhes
See Der Nister

Kahn, Roger 1927- .... **CLC 30**
See also CA 25-28R; CANR 44; DLB 171;
SATA 37

Kain, Saul
See Sassoon, Siegfried (Lorraine)

Kyprianos, Iossif
  See Samarakis, Antonis

La Bruyere, Jean de 1645-1696...... **LC 17**

Lacan, Jacques (Marie Emile)
  1901-1981...............**CLC 75**
  See also CA 121; 104

Laclos, Pierre Ambroise Francois Choderlos
  de 1741-1803.............. **NCLC 4**

La Colere, Francois
  See Aragon, Louis

Lacolere, Francois
  See Aragon, Louis

La Deshabilleuse
  See Simenon, Georges (Jacques Christian)

Lady Gregory
  See Gregory, Isabella Augusta (Persse)

Lady of Quality, A
  See Bagnold, Enid

La Fayette, Marie (Madelaine Pioche de la
  Vergne Comtes 1634-1693....... **LC 2**

Lafayette, Rene
  See Hubbard, L(afayette) Ron(ald)

Laforgue, Jules
  1860-1887........**NCLC 5, 53; PC 14;**
                  SSC 20

Lagerkvist, Paer (Fabian)
  1891-1974..........**CLC 7, 10, 13, 54;**
                DAM DRAM, NOV
  See also Lagerkvist, Par
  See also CA 85-88; 49-52; MTCW

Lagerkvist, Par.................... **SSC 12**
  See also Lagerkvist, Paer (Fabian)

Lagerloef, Selma (Ottiliana Lovisa)
  1858-1940................**TCLC 4, 36**
  See also Lagerlof, Selma (Ottiliana Lovisa)
  See also CA 108; SATA 15

Lagerlof, Selma (Ottiliana Lovisa)
  See Lagerloef, Selma (Ottiliana Lovisa)
  See also CLR 7; SATA 15

La Guma, (Justin) Alex(ander)
  1925-1985.......**CLC 19; DAM NOV**
  See also BW 1; CA 49-52; 118; CANR 25;
    DLB 117; MTCW

Laidlaw, A. K.
  See Grieve, C(hristopher) M(urray)

Lainez, Manuel Mujica
  See Mujica Lainez, Manuel
  See also HW

Laing, R(onald) D(avid)
  1927-1989.................**CLC 95**
  See also CA 107; 129; CANR 34; MTCW

Lamartine, Alphonse (Marie Louis Prat) de
  1790-1869.....**NCLC 11; DAM POET;**
                  PC 16

Lamb, Charles
  1775-1834.......**NCLC 10; DA; DAB;**
            DAC; DAM MST; WLC
  See also CDBLB 1789-1832; DLB 93, 107,
    163; SATA 17

Lamb, Lady Caroline 1785-1828.. **NCLC 38**
  See also DLB 116

Lamming, George (William)
  1927-.............**CLC 2, 4, 66; BLC;**
                  DAM MULT
  See also BW 2; CA 85-88; CANR 26;
    DLB 125; MTCW

L'Amour, Louis (Dearborn)
  1908-1988....**CLC 25, 55; DAM NOV,**
                    POP
  See also AAYA 16; AITN 2; BEST 89:2;
    CA 1-4R; 125; CANR 3, 25, 40;
    DLBY 80; MTCW

Lampedusa, Giuseppe (Tomasi) di
  1896-1957.................**TCLC 13**
  See also Tomasi di Lampedusa, Giuseppe
  See also DLB 177

Lampman, Archibald 1861-1899.. **NCLC 25**
  See also DLB 92

Lancaster, Bruce 1896-1963....... **CLC 36**
  See also CA 9-10; CAP 1; SATA 9

Lanchester, John.................. **CLC 99**

Landau, Mark Alexandrovich
  See Aldanov, Mark (Alexandrovich)

Landau-Aldanov, Mark Alexandrovich
  See Aldanov, Mark (Alexandrovich)

Landis, Jerry
  See Simon, Paul (Frederick)

Landis, John 1950-.............. **CLC 26**
  See also CA 112; 122

Landolfi, Tommaso 1908-1979... **CLC 11, 49**
  See also CA 127; 117; DLB 177

Landon, Letitia Elizabeth
  1802-1838................. **NCLC 15**
  See also DLB 96

Landor, Walter Savage
  1775-1864................. **NCLC 14**
  See also DLB 93, 107

Landwirth, Heinz 1927-
  See Lind, Jakov
  See also CA 9-12R; CANR 7

Lane, Patrick
  1939-...........**CLC 25; DAM POET**
  See also CA 97-100; CANR 54; DLB 53;
    INT 97-100

Lang, Andrew 1844-1912........ **TCLC 16**
  See also CA 114; 137; DLB 98, 141;
    MAICYA; SATA 16

Lang, Fritz 1890-1976........... **CLC 20**
  See also CA 77-80; 69-72; CANR 30

Lange, John
  See Crichton, (John) Michael

Langer, Elinor 1939-............ **CLC 34**
  See also CA 121

Langland, William
  1330(?)-1400(?)......**LC 19; DA; DAB;**
            DAC; DAM MST, POET
  See also DLB 146

Langstaff, Launcelot
  See Irving, Washington

Lanier, Sidney
  1842-1881......**NCLC 6; DAM POET**
  See also DLB 64; DLBD 13; MAICYA;
    SATA 18

Lanyer, Aemilia 1569-1645...... **LC 10, 30**
  See also DLB 121

Lao Tzu....................... **CMLC 7**

Lapine, James (Elliot) 1949-....... **CLC 39**
  See also CA 123; 130; CANR 54; INT 130

Larbaud, Valery (Nicolas)
  1881-1957..................**TCLC 9**
  See also CA 106; 152

Lardner, Ring
  See Lardner, Ring(gold) W(ilmer)

Lardner, Ring W., Jr.
  See Lardner, Ring(gold) W(ilmer)

Lardner, Ring(gold) W(ilmer)
  1885-1933................**TCLC 2, 14**
  See also CA 104; 131; CDALB 1917-1929;
    DLB 11, 25, 86; MTCW

Laredo, Betty
  See Codrescu, Andrei

Larkin, Maia
  See Wojciechowska, Maia (Teresa)

Larkin, Philip (Arthur)
  1922-1985....**CLC 3, 5, 8, 9, 13, 18, 33,**
          39, 64; DAB; DAM MST, POET
  See also CA 5-8R; 117; CANR 24;
    CDBLB 1960 to Present; DLB 27;
    MTCW

Larra (y Sanchez de Castro), Mariano Jose de
  1809-1837................. **NCLC 17**

Larsen, Eric 1941-............... **CLC 55**
  See also CA 132

Larsen, Nella
  1891-1964.............**CLC 37; BLC;**
                DAM MULT
  See also BW 1; CA 125; DLB 51

Larson, Charles R(aymond) 1938-.... **CLC 31**
  See also CA 53-56; CANR 4

Larson, Jonathan 1961(?)-1996..... **CLC 99**

Las Casas, Bartolome de 1474-1566.. **LC 31**

Lasker-Schueler, Else 1869-1945.. **TCLC 57**
  See also DLB 66, 124

Latham, Jean Lee 1902-........... **CLC 12**
  See also AITN 1; CA 5-8R; CANR 7;
    MAICYA; SATA 2, 68

Latham, Mavis
  See Clark, Mavis Thorpe

Lathen, Emma.................... **CLC 2**
  See also Hennissart, Martha; Latsis, Mary
    J(ane)

Lathrop, Francis
  See Leiber, Fritz (Reuter, Jr.)

Latsis, Mary J(ane)
  See Lathen, Emma
  See also CA 85-88

Lattimore, Richmond (Alexander)
  1906-1984.................... **CLC 3**
  See also CA 1-4R; 112; CANR 1

Laughlin, James 1914-............ **CLC 49**
  See also CA 21-24R; CAAS 22; CANR 9,
    47; DLB 48

Laurence, (Jean) Margaret (Wemyss)
  1926-1987.......**CLC 3, 6, 13, 50, 62;**
           DAC; DAM MST; SSC 7
  See also CA 5-8R; 121; CANR 33; DLB 53;
    MTCW; SATA-Obit 50

Laurent, Antoine 1952-........... **CLC 50**

Lauscher, Hermann
  See Hesse, Hermann

Lemann, Nancy 1956-............ **CLC 39**
See also CA 118; 136

Lemonnier, (Antoine Louis) Camille
1844-1913 .... **TCLC 22**
See also CA 121

Lenau, Nikolaus 1802-1850..... **NCLC 16**

L'Engle, Madeleine (Camp Franklin)
1918- .... **CLC 12; DAM POP**
See also AAYA 1; AITN 2; CA 1-4R;
CANR 3, 21, 39; CLR 1, 14; DLB 52;
JRDA; MAICYA; MTCW; SAAS 15;
SATA 1, 27, 75

Lengyel, Jozsef 1896-1975......... **CLC 7**
See also CA 85-88; 57-60

Lenin 1870-1924
See Lenin, V. I.
See also CA 121

Lenin, V. I. .... **TCLC 67**
See also Lenin

Lennon, John (Ono)
1940-1980 .... **CLC 12, 35**
See also CA 102

Lennox, Charlotte Ramsay
1729(?)-1804 .... **NCLC 23**
See also DLB 39

Lentricchia, Frank (Jr.) 1940-...... **CLC 34**
See also CA 25-28R; CANR 19

Lenz, Siegfried 1926-............ **CLC 27**
See also CA 89-92; DLB 75

Leonard, Elmore (John, Jr.)
1925- ...... **CLC 28, 34, 71; DAM POP**
See also AITN 1; BEST 89:1, 90:4;
CA 81-84; CANR 12, 28, 53; DLB 173;
INT CANR-28; MTCW

Leonard, Hugh .... **CLC 19**
See also Byrne, John Keyes
See also DLB 13

Leonov, Leonid (Maximovich)
1899-1994 .... **CLC 92; DAM NOV**
See also CA 129; MTCW

Leopardi, (Conte) Giacomo
1798-1837 .... **NCLC 22**

Le Reveler
See Artaud, Antonin (Marie Joseph)

Lerman, Eleanor 1952-............ **CLC 9**
See also CA 85-88

Lerman, Rhoda 1936-............ **CLC 56**
See also CA 49-52

Lermontov, Mikhail Yuryevich
1814-1841 .... **NCLC 47**

Leroux, Gaston 1868-1927....... **TCLC 25**
See also CA 108; 136; SATA 65

Lesage, Alain-Rene 1668-1747...... **LC 28**

Leskov, Nikolai (Semyonovich)
1831-1895 .... **NCLC 25**

Lessing, Doris (May)
1919- ..... **CLC 1, 2, 3, 6, 10, 15, 22, 40,
94; DA; DAB; DAC; DAM MST, NOV;
SSC 6**
See also CA 9-12R; CAAS 14; CANR 33,
54; CDBLB 1960 to Present; DLB 15,
139; DLBY 85; MTCW

Lessing, Gotthold Ephraim
1729-1781 .... **LC 8**
See also DLB 97

Lester, Richard 1932-............ **CLC 20**

Lever, Charles (James)
1806-1872 .... **NCLC 23**
See also DLB 21

Leverson, Ada 1865(?)-1936(?) .... **TCLC 18**
See also Elaine
See also CA 117; DLB 153

Levertov, Denise
1923- ...... **CLC 1, 2, 3, 5, 8, 15, 28, 66;
DAM POET; PC 11**
See also CA 1-4R; CAAS 19; CANR 3, 29,
50; DLB 5, 165; INT CANR-29; MTCW

Levi, Jonathan .... **CLC 76**

Levi, Peter (Chad Tigar) 1931-..... **CLC 41**
See also CA 5-8R; CANR 34; DLB 40

Levi, Primo
1919-1987 .... **CLC 37, 50; SSC 12**
See also CA 13-16R; 122; CANR 12, 33;
DLB 177; MTCW

Levin, Ira 1929- ..... **CLC 3, 6; DAM POP**
See also CA 21-24R; CANR 17, 44;
MTCW; SATA 66

Levin, Meyer
1905-1981 .... **CLC 7; DAM POP**
See also AITN 1; CA 9-12R; 104;
CANR 15; DLB 9, 28; DLBY 81;
SATA 21; SATA-Obit 27

Levine, Norman 1924- .... **CLC 54**
See also CA 73-76; CAAS 23; CANR 14;
DLB 88

Levine, Philip
1928- .... **CLC 2, 4, 5, 9, 14, 33;
DAM POET**
See also CA 9-12R; CANR 9, 37, 52;
DLB 5

Levinson, Deirdre 1931-.......... **CLC 49**
See also CA 73-76

Levi-Strauss, Claude 1908- .... **CLC 38**
See also CA 1-4R; CANR 6, 32, 57; MTCW

Levitin, Sonia (Wolff) 1934- .... **CLC 17**
See also AAYA 13; CA 29-32R; CANR 14,
32; JRDA; MAICYA; SAAS 2; SATA 4,
68

Levon, O. U.
See Kesey, Ken (Elton)

Levy, Amy 1861-1889.......... **NCLC 59**
See also DLB 156

Lewes, George Henry
1817-1878 .... **NCLC 25**
See also DLB 55, 144

Lewis, Alun 1915-1944........... **TCLC 3**
See also CA 104; DLB 20, 162

Lewis, C. Day
See Day Lewis, C(ecil)

Lewis, C(live) S(taples)
1898-1963 ..... **CLC 1, 3, 6, 14, 27; DA;
DAB; DAC; DAM MST, NOV, POP;
WLC**
See also AAYA 3; CA 81-84; CANR 33;
CDBLB 1945-1960; CLR 3, 27; DLB 15,
100, 160; JRDA; MAICYA; MTCW;
SATA 13

Lewis, Janet 1899- .... **CLC 41**
See also Winters, Janet Lewis
See also CA 9-12R; CANR 29; CAP 1;
DLBY 87

Lewis, Matthew Gregory
1775-1818 .... **NCLC 11**
See also DLB 39, 158

Lewis, (Harry) Sinclair
1885-1951 ..... **TCLC 4, 13, 23, 39; DA;
DAB; DAC; DAM MST, NOV; WLC**
See also CA 104; 133; CDALB 1917-1929;
DLB 9, 102; DLBD 1; MTCW

Lewis, (Percy) Wyndham
1884(?)-1957............**TCLC 2, 9**
See also CA 104; DLB 15

Lewisohn, Ludwig 1883-1955..... **TCLC 19**
See also CA 107; DLB 4, 9, 28, 102

Leyner, Mark 1956-............. **CLC 92**
See also CA 110; CANR 28, 53

Lezama Lima, Jose
1910-1976 .... **CLC 4, 10; DAM MULT**
See also CA 77-80; DLB 113; HW

L'Heureux, John (Clarke) 1934-.... **CLC 52**
See also CA 13-16R; CANR 23, 45

Liddell, C. H.
See Kuttner, Henry

Lie, Jonas (Lauritz Idemil)
1833-1908(?) .... **TCLC 5**
See also CA 115

Lieber, Joel 1937-1971............. **CLC 6**
See also CA 73-76; 29-32R

Lieber, Stanley Martin
See Lee, Stan

Lieberman, Laurence (James)
1935- .... **CLC 4, 36**
See also CA 17-20R; CANR 8, 36

Lieksman, Anders
See Haavikko, Paavo Juhani

Li Fei-kan 1904-
See Pa Chin
See also CA 105

Lifton, Robert Jay 1926-.......... **CLC 67**
See also CA 17-20R; CANR 27;
INT CANR-27; SATA 66

Lightfoot, Gordon 1938-.......... **CLC 26**
See also CA 109

Lightman, Alan P. 1948- .... **CLC 81**
See also CA 141

Ligotti, Thomas (Robert)
1953- .... **CLC 44; SSC 16**
See also CA 123; CANR 49

Li Ho 791-817.................. **PC 13**

Liliencron, (Friedrich Adolf Axel) Detlev von
1844-1909 .... **TCLC 18**
See also CA 117

Lilly, William 1602-1681.......... **LC 27**

Lima, Jose Lezama
See Lezama Lima, Jose

Lima Barreto, Afonso Henrique de
1881-1922 .... **TCLC 23**
See also CA 117

Limonov, Edward 1944-.......... **CLC 67**
See also CA 137

Lin, Frank
See Atherton, Gertrude (Franklin Horn)

Lincoln, Abraham 1809-1865..... **NCLC 18**

Lind, Jakov .... CLC **1, 2, 4, 27, 82**
   See also Landwirth, Heinz
   See also CAAS 4

Lindbergh, Anne (Spencer) Morrow
   1906- .... CLC **82; DAM NOV**
   See also CA 17-20R; CANR 16; MTCW;
   SATA 33

Lindsay, David 1878-1945 .... TCLC **15**
   See also CA 113

Lindsay, (Nicholas) Vachel
   1879-1931 .... TCLC **17; DA; DAC;**
                DAM MST, POET; WLC
   See also CA 114; 135; CDALB 1865-1917;
   DLB 54; SATA 40

Linke-Poot
   See Doeblin, Alfred

Linney, Romulus 1930- .... CLC **51**
   See also CA 1-4R; CANR 40, 44

Linton, Eliza Lynn 1822-1898 .... NCLC **41**
   See also DLB 18

Li Po 701-763 .... CMLC **2**

Lipsius, Justus 1547-1606 .... LC **16**

Lipsyte, Robert (Michael)
   1938- .... CLC **21; DA; DAC;**
                     DAM MST, NOV;
   See also AAYA 7; CA 17-20R; CANR 8,
   57; CLR 23; JRDA; MAICYA; SATA 5,
   68

Lish, Gordon (Jay) 1934-.. CLC **45; SSC 18**
   See also CA 113; 117; DLB 130; INT 117

Lispector, Clarice 1925-1977 ...... CLC **43**
   See also CA 139; 116; DLB 113

Littell, Robert 1935(?)- .... CLC **42**
   See also CA 109; 112

Little, Malcolm 1925-1965
   See Malcolm X
   See also BW 1; CA 125; 111; DA; DAB;
   DAC; DAM MST, MULT; MTCW

Littlewit, Humphrey Gent.
   See Lovecraft, H(oward) P(hillips)

Litwos
   See Sienkiewicz, Henryk (Adam Alexander
   Pius)

Liu E 1857-1909 .... TCLC **15**
   See also CA 115

Lively, Penelope (Margaret)
   1933- .... CLC **32, 50; DAM NOV**
   See also CA 41-44R; CANR 29; CLR 7;
   DLB 14, 161; JRDA; MAICYA; MTCW;
   SATA 7, 60

Livesay, Dorothy (Kathleen)
   1909- .... CLC **4, 15, 79; DAC;**
                   DAM MST, POET
   See also AITN 2; CA 25-28R; CAAS 8;
   CANR 36; DLB 68; MTCW

Livy c. 59B.C.-c. 17 .... CMLC **11**

Lizardi, Jose Joaquin Fernandez de
   1776-1827 .... NCLC **30**

Llewellyn, Richard
   See Llewellyn Lloyd, Richard Dafydd
   Vivian
   See also DLB 15

Llewellyn Lloyd, Richard Dafydd Vivian
   1906-1983 .... CLC **7, 80**
   See also Llewellyn, Richard
   See also CA 53-56; 111; CANR 7;
   SATA 11; SATA-Obit 37

Llosa, (Jorge) Mario (Pedro) Vargas
   See Vargas Llosa, (Jorge) Mario (Pedro)

Lloyd Webber, Andrew 1948-
   See Webber, Andrew Lloyd
   See also AAYA 1; CA 116; 149;
   DAM DRAM; SATA 56

Llull, Ramon c. 1235-c. 1316 ..... CMLC **12**

Locke, Alain (Le Roy)
   1886-1954 .... TCLC **43**
   See also BW 1; CA 106; 124; DLB 51

Locke, John 1632-1704 .... LC **7, 35**
   See also DLB 101

Locke-Elliott, Sumner
   See Elliott, Sumner Locke

Lockhart, John Gibson
   1794-1854 .... NCLC **6**
   See also DLB 110, 116, 144

Lodge, David (John)
   1935- .... CLC **36; DAM POP**
   See also BEST 90:1; CA 17-20R; CANR 19,
   53; DLB 14; INT CANR-19; MTCW

Loennbohm, Armas Eino Leopold 1878-1926
   See Leino, Eino
   See also CA 123

Loewinsohn, Ron(ald William)
   1937- .... CLC **52**
   See also CA 25-28R

Logan, Jake
   See Smith, Martin Cruz

Logan, John (Burton) 1923-1987 ..... CLC **5**
   See also CA 77-80; 124; CANR 45; DLB 5

Lo Kuan-chung 1330(?)-1400(?) ...... LC **12**

Lombard, Nap
   See Johnson, Pamela Hansford

London, Jack .. TCLC **9, 15, 39; SSC 4; WLC**
   See also London, John Griffith
   See also AAYA 13; AITN 2;
   CDALB 1865-1917; DLB 8, 12, 78;
   SATA 18

London, John Griffith 1876-1916
   See London, Jack
   See also CA 110; 119; DA; DAB; DAC;
   DAM MST, NOV; JRDA; MAICYA;
   MTCW

Long, Emmett
   See Leonard, Elmore (John, Jr.)

Longbaugh, Harry
   See Goldman, William (W.)

Longfellow, Henry Wadsworth
   1807-1882 ..... NCLC **2, 45; DA; DAB;**
               DAC; DAM MST, POET
   See also CDALB 1640-1865; DLB 1, 59;
   SATA 19

Longley, Michael 1939- .... CLC **29**
   See also CA 102; DLB 40

Longus fl. c. 2nd cent. - .... CMLC **7**

Longway, A. Hugh
   See Lang, Andrew

Lonnrot, Elias 1802-1884 .... NCLC **53**

Lopate, Phillip 1943- .... CLC **29**
   See also CA 97-100; DLBY 80; INT 97-100

Lopez Portillo (y Pacheco), Jose
   1920- .... CLC **46**
   See also CA 129; HW

Lopez y Fuentes, Gregorio
   1897(?)-1966 .... CLC **32**
   See also CA 131; HW

Lorca, Federico Garcia
   See Garcia Lorca, Federico

Lord, Bette Bao 1938- .... CLC **23**
   See also BEST 90:3; CA 107; CANR 41;
   INT 107; SATA 58

Lord Auch
   See Bataille, Georges

Lord Byron
   See Byron, George Gordon (Noel)

Lorde, Audre (Geraldine)
   1934-1992 .... CLC **18, 71; BLC;**
              DAM MULT, POET; PC 12
   See also BW 1; CA 25-28R; 142; CANR 16,
   26, 46; DLB 41; MTCW

Lord Houghton
   See Milnes, Richard Monckton

Lord Jeffrey
   See Jeffrey, Francis

Lorenzini, Carlo 1826-1890
   See Collodi, Carlo
   See also MAICYA; SATA 29

Lorenzo, Heberto Padilla
   See Padilla (Lorenzo), Heberto

Loris
   See Hofmannsthal, Hugo von

Loti, Pierre .... TCLC **11**
   See also Viaud, (Louis Marie) Julien
   See also DLB 123

Louie, David Wong 1954- .... CLC **70**
   See also CA 139

Louis, Father M.
   See Merton, Thomas

Lovecraft, H(oward) P(hillips)
   1890-1937 .... TCLC **4, 22; DAM POP;**
                      SSC 3
   See also AAYA 14; CA 104; 133; MTCW

Lovelace, Earl 1935- .... CLC **51**
   See also BW 2; CA 77-80; CANR 41;
   DLB 125; MTCW

Lovelace, Richard 1618-1657 .... LC **24**
   See also DLB 131

Lowell, Amy
   1874-1925 .... TCLC **1, 8; DAM POET;**
                    PC 13
   See also CA 104; 151; DLB 54, 140

Lowell, James Russell 1819-1891 .. NCLC **2**
   See also CDALB 1640-1865; DLB 1, 11, 64,
   79

Lowell, Robert (Traill Spence, Jr.)
   1917-1977 ... CLC **1, 2, 3, 4, 5, 8, 9, 11,**
       15, 37; DA; DAB; DAC; DAM MST,
             NOV; PC 3; WLC
   See also CA 9-12R; 73-76; CABS 2;
   CANR 26; DLB 5, 169; MTCW

Lowndes, Marie Adelaide (Belloc)
   1868-1947 .... TCLC **12**
   See also CA 107; DLB 70

Lowry, (Clarence) Malcolm
    1909-1957 . . . . **TCLC 6, 40**
    See also CA 105; 131; CDBLB 1945-1960;
    DLB 15; MTCW

Lowry, Mina Gertrude   1882-1966
    See Loy, Mina
    See also CA 113

Loxsmith, John
    See Brunner, John (Kilian Houston)

Loy, Mina . . . . **CLC 28; DAM POET; PC 16**
    See also Lowry, Mina Gertrude
    See also DLB 4, 54

Loyson-Bridet
    See Schwob, (Mayer Andre) Marcel

Lucas, Craig   1951- . . . . **CLC 64**
    See also CA 137

Lucas, George   1944- . . . . **CLC 16**
    See also AAYA 1; CA 77-80; CANR 30;
    SATA 56

Lucas, Hans
    See Godard, Jean-Luc

Lucas, Victoria
    See Plath, Sylvia

Ludlam, Charles   1943-1987 . . . . . **CLC 46, 50**
    See also CA 85-88; 122

Ludlum, Robert
    1927- . . . **CLC 22, 43; DAM NOV, POP**
    See also AAYA 10; BEST 89:1, 90:3;
    CA 33-36R; CANR 25, 41; DLBY 82;
    MTCW

Ludwig, Ken . . . . **CLC 60**

Ludwig, Otto   1813-1865 . . . . **NCLC 4**
    See also DLB 129

Lugones, Leopoldo   1874-1938 . . . . . **TCLC 15**
    See also CA 116; 131; HW

Lu Hsun   1881-1936 . . . . . . **TCLC 3; SSC 20**
    See also Shu-Jen, Chou

Lukacs, George . . . . **CLC 24**
    See also Lukacs, Gyorgy (Szegeny von)

Lukacs, Gyorgy (Szegeny von)   1885-1971
    See Lukacs, George
    See also CA 101; 29-32R

Luke, Peter (Ambrose Cyprian)
    1919-1995 . . . . **CLC 38**
    See also CA 81-84; 147; DLB 13

Lunar, Dennis
    See Mungo, Raymond

Lurie, Alison   1926- . . . . **CLC 4, 5, 18, 39**
    See also CA 1-4R; CANR 2, 17, 50; DLB 2;
    MTCW; SATA 46

Lustig, Arnost   1926- . . . . **CLC 56**
    See also AAYA 3; CA 69-72; CANR 47;
    SATA 56

Luther, Martin   1483-1546 . . . . **LC 9, 37**

Luxemburg, Rosa   1870(?)-1919 . . . . **TCLC 63**
    See also CA 118

Luzi, Mario   1914- . . . . **CLC 13**
    See also CA 61-64; CANR 9; DLB 128

Lyly, John   1554(?)-1606 . . . . **DC 7**
    See also DAM DRAM; DLB 62, 167

L'Ymagier
    See Gourmont, Remy (-Marie-Charles) de

Lynch, B. Suarez
    See Bioy Casares, Adolfo; Borges, Jorge
    Luis

Lynch, David (K.)   1946- . . . . **CLC 66**
    See also CA 124; 129

Lynch, James
    See Andreyev, Leonid (Nikolaevich)

Lynch Davis, B.
    See Bioy Casares, Adolfo; Borges, Jorge
    Luis

Lyndsay, Sir David   1490-1555 . . . . . . **LC 20**

Lynn, Kenneth S(chuyler)   1923- . . . . **CLC 50**
    See also CA 1-4R; CANR 3, 27

Lynx
    See West, Rebecca

Lyons, Marcus
    See Blish, James (Benjamin)

Lyre, Pinchbeck
    See Sassoon, Siegfried (Lorraine)

Lytle, Andrew (Nelson)   1902-1995 . . **CLC 22**
    See also CA 9-12R; 150; DLB 6; DLBY 95

Lyttelton, George   1709-1773 . . . . **LC 10**

Maas, Peter   1929- . . . . **CLC 29**
    See also CA 93-96; INT 93-96

Macaulay, Rose   1881-1958 . . . . . **TCLC 7, 44**
    See also CA 104; DLB 36

Macaulay, Thomas Babington
    1800-1859 . . . . **NCLC 42**
    See also CDBLB 1832-1890; DLB 32, 55

MacBeth, George (Mann)
    1932-1992 . . . . **CLC 2, 5, 9**
    See also CA 25-28R; 136; DLB 40; MTCW;
    SATA 4; SATA-Obit 70

MacCaig, Norman (Alexander)
    1910- . . . . . **CLC 36; DAB; DAM POET**
    See also CA 9-12R; CANR 3, 34; DLB 27

MacCarthy, (Sir Charles Otto) Desmond
    1877-1952 . . . . **TCLC 36**

MacDiarmid, Hugh
    . . . . **CLC 2, 4, 11, 19, 63; PC 9**
    See also Grieve, C(hristopher) M(urray)
    See also CDBLB 1945-1960; DLB 20

MacDonald, Anson
    See Heinlein, Robert A(nson)

Macdonald, Cynthia   1928- . . . . . . **CLC 13, 19**
    See also CA 49-52; CANR 4, 44; DLB 105

MacDonald, George   1824-1905 . . . . . **TCLC 9**
    See also CA 106; 137; DLB 18, 163;
    MAICYA; SATA 33

Macdonald, John
    See Millar, Kenneth

MacDonald, John D(ann)
    1916-1986 . . . . **CLC 3, 27, 44;**
    DAM NOV, POP
    See also CA 1-4R; 121; CANR 1, 19;
    DLB 8; DLBY 86; MTCW

Macdonald, John Ross
    See Millar, Kenneth

Macdonald, Ross . . . . . **CLC 1, 2, 3, 14, 34, 41**
    See also Millar, Kenneth
    See also DLBD 6

MacDougal, John
    See Blish, James (Benjamin)

MacEwen, Gwendolyn (Margaret)
    1941-1987 . . . . **CLC 13, 55**
    See also CA 9-12R; 124; CANR 7, 22;
    DLB 53; SATA 50; SATA-Obit 55

Macha, Karel Hynek   1810-1846 . . **NCLC 46**

Machado (y Ruiz), Antonio
    1875-1939 . . . . **TCLC 3**
    See also CA 104; DLB 108

Machado de Assis, Joaquim Maria
    1839-1908 . . . . . **TCLC 10; BLC; SSC 24**
    See also CA 107; 153

Machen, Arthur . . . . **TCLC 4; SSC 20**
    See also Jones, Arthur Llewellyn
    See also DLB 36, 156

Machiavelli, Niccolo
    1469-1527 . . . . **LC 8, 36; DA; DAB;**
    DAC; DAM MST

MacInnes, Colin   1914-1976 . . . . . . **CLC 4, 23**
    See also CA 69-72; 65-68; CANR 21;
    DLB 14; MTCW

MacInnes, Helen (Clark)
    1907-1985 . . . . . **CLC 27, 39; DAM POP**
    See also CA 1-4R; 117; CANR 1, 28;
    DLB 87; MTCW; SATA 22;
    SATA-Obit 44

Mackay, Mary   1855-1924
    See Corelli, Marie
    See also CA 118

Mackenzie, Compton (Edward Montague)
    1883-1972 . . . . **CLC 18**
    See also CA 21-22; 37-40R; CAP 2;
    DLB 34, 100

Mackenzie, Henry   1745-1831 . . . . **NCLC 41**
    See also DLB 39

Mackintosh, Elizabeth   1896(?)-1952
    See Tey, Josephine
    See also CA 110

MacLaren, James
    See Grieve, C(hristopher) M(urray)

Mac Laverty, Bernard   1942- . . . . **CLC 31**
    See also CA 116; 118; CANR 43; INT 118

MacLean, Alistair (Stuart)
    1922-1987 . . . . **CLC 3, 13, 50, 63;**
    DAM POP
    See also CA 57-60; 121; CANR 28; MTCW;
    SATA 23; SATA-Obit 50

Maclean, Norman (Fitzroy)
    1902-1990 . . . . **CLC 78; DAM POP;**
    SSC 13
    See also CA 102; 132; CANR 49

MacLeish, Archibald
    1892-1982 . . . . **CLC 3, 8, 14, 68;**
    DAM POET
    See also CA 9-12R; 106; CANR 33; DLB 4,
    7, 45; DLBY 82; MTCW

MacLennan, (John) Hugh
    1907-1990 . . . . **CLC 2, 14, 92; DAC;**
    DAM MST
    See also CA 5-8R; 142; CANR 33; DLB 68;
    MTCW

MacLeod, Alistair
    1936- . . . . . . **CLC 56; DAC; DAM MST**
    See also CA 123; DLB 60

MacNeice, (Frederick) Louis
1907-1963 . . . . . CLC 1, 4, 10, 53; DAB;
DAM POET
See also CA 85-88; DLB 10, 20; MTCW

MacNeill, Dand
See Fraser, George MacDonald

Macpherson, James 1736-1796 . . . . . LC 29
See also DLB 109

Macpherson, (Jean) Jay 1931- . . . . . CLC 14
See also CA 5-8R; DLB 53

MacShane, Frank 1927- . . . . CLC 39
See also CA 9-12R; CANR 3, 33; DLB 111

Macumber, Mari
See Sandoz, Mari(e Susette)

Madach, Imre 1823-1864 . . . . NCLC 19

Madden, (Jerry) David 1933- . . . . CLC 5, 15
See also CA 1-4R; CAAS 3; CANR 4, 45;
DLB 6; MTCW

Maddern, Al(an)
See Ellison, Harlan (Jay)

Madhubuti, Haki R.
1942- . . . . CLC 6, 73; BLC;
DAM MULT, POET; PC 5
See also Lee, Don L.
See also BW 2; CA 73-76; CANR 24, 51;
DLB 5, 41; DLBD 8

Maepenn, Hugh
See Kuttner, Henry

Maepenn, K. H.
See Kuttner, Henry

Maeterlinck, Maurice
1862-1949 . . . . . . TCLC 3; DAM DRAM
See also CA 104; 136; SATA 66

Maginn, William 1794-1842 . . . . . . NCLC 8
See also DLB 110, 159

Mahapatra, Jayanta
1928- . . . . CLC 33; DAM MULT
See also CA 73-76; CAAS 9; CANR 15, 33

Mahfouz, Naguib (Abdel Aziz Al-Sabilgi)
1911(?)-
See Mahfuz, Najib
See also BEST 89:2; CA 128; CANR 55;
DAM NOV; MTCW

Mahfuz, Najib . . . . CLC 52, 55
See also Mahfouz, Naguib (Abdel Aziz
Al-Sabilgi)
See also DLBY 88

Mahon, Derek 1941- . . . . CLC 27
See also CA 113; 128; DLB 40

Mailer, Norman
1923- . . . . . . CLC 1, 2, 3, 4, 5, 8, 11, 14,
28, 39, 74; DA; DAB; DAC; DAM MST,
NOV, POP
See also AITN 2; CA 9-12R; CABS 1;
CANR 28; CDALB 1968-1988; DLB 2,
16, 28; DLBD 3; DLBY 80, 83; MTCW

Maillet, Antonine 1929- . . . . . . CLC 54; DAC
See also CA 115; 120; CANR 46; DLB 60;
INT 120

Mais, Roger 1905-1955 . . . . TCLC 8
See also BW 1; CA 105; 124; DLB 125;
MTCW

Maistre, Joseph de 1753-1821 . . . . NCLC 37

Maitland, Frederic 1850-1906 . . . . . TCLC 65

Maitland, Sara (Louise) 1950- . . . . . . CLC 49
See also CA 69-72; CANR 13

Major, Clarence
1936- . . . . CLC 3, 19, 48; BLC;
DAM MULT
See also BW 2; CA 21-24R; CAAS 6;
CANR 13, 25, 53; DLB 33

Major, Kevin (Gerald)
1949- . . . . CLC 26; DAC
See also AAYA 16; CA 97-100; CANR 21,
38; CLR 11; DLB 60; INT CANR-21;
JRDA; MAICYA; SATA 32, 82

Maki, James
See Ozu, Yasujiro

Malabaila, Damiano
See Levi, Primo

Malamud, Bernard
1914-1986 . . . . . . CLC 1, 2, 3, 5, 8, 9, 11,
18, 27, 44, 78, 85; DA; DAB; DAC;
DAM MST, NOV, POP; SSC 15; WLC
See also AAYA 16; CA 5-8R; 118; CABS 1;
CANR 28; CDALB 1941-1968; DLB 2,
28, 152; DLBY 80, 86; MTCW

Malaparte, Curzio 1898-1957 . . . . . TCLC 52

Malcolm, Dan
See Silverberg, Robert

Malcolm X . . . . CLC 82; BLC
See also Little, Malcolm

Malherbe, Francois de 1555-1628 . . . . . LC 5

Mallarme, Stephane
1842-1898 . . . . NCLC 4, 41;
DAM POET; PC 4

Mallet-Joris, Francoise 1930- . . . . . . CLC 11
See also CA 65-68; CANR 17; DLB 83

Malley, Ern
See McAuley, James Phillip

Mallowan, Agatha Christie
See Christie, Agatha (Mary Clarissa)

Maloff, Saul 1922- . . . . CLC 5
See also CA 33-36R

Malone, Louis
See MacNeice, (Frederick) Louis

Malone, Michael (Christopher)
1942- . . . . CLC 43
See also CA 77-80; CANR 14, 32, 57

Malory, (Sir) Thomas
1410(?)-1471(?) . . . . . . LC 11; DA; DAB;
DAC; DAM MST
See also CDBLB Before 1660; DLB 146;
SATA 59; SATA-Brief 33

Malouf, (George Joseph) David
1934- . . . . CLC 28, 86
See also CA 124; CANR 50

Malraux, (Georges-)Andre
1901-1976 . . . . . . CLC 1, 4, 9, 13, 15, 57;
DAM NOV
See also CA 21-22; 69-72; CANR 34;
CAP 2; DLB 72; MTCW

Malzberg, Barry N(athaniel) 1939- . . . CLC 7
See also CA 61-64; CAAS 4; CANR 16;
DLB 8

Mamet, David (Alan)
1947- . . . . CLC 9, 15, 34, 46, 91;
DAM DRAM; DC 4
See also AAYA 3; CA 81-84; CABS 3;
CANR 15, 41; DLB 7; MTCW

Mamoulian, Rouben (Zachary)
1897-1987 . . . . CLC 16
See also CA 25-28R; 124

Mandelstam, Osip (Emilievich)
1891(?)-1938(?) . . . . . . TCLC 2, 6; PC 14
See also CA 104; 150

Mander, (Mary) Jane 1877-1949 . . . TCLC 31

Mandeville, John fl. 1350- . . . . CMLC 19
See also DLB 146

Mandiargues, Andre Pieyre de . . . . . . CLC 41
See also Pieyre de Mandiargues, Andre
See also DLB 83

Mandrake, Ethel Belle
See Thurman, Wallace (Henry)

Mangan, James Clarence
1803-1849 . . . . NCLC 27

Maniere, J.-E.
See Giraudoux, (Hippolyte) Jean

Manley, (Mary) Delariviere
1672(?)-1724 . . . . LC 1
See also DLB 39, 80

Mann, Abel
See Creasey, John

Mann, Emily 1952- . . . . DC 7
See also CA 130; CANR 55

Mann, (Luiz) Heinrich 1871-1950 . . . TCLC 9
See also CA 106; DLB 66

Mann, (Paul) Thomas
1875-1955 . . . . TCLC 2, 8, 14, 21, 35, 44,
60; DA; DAB; DAC; DAM MST, NOV,
SSC 5; WLC
See also CA 104; 128; DLB 66; MTCW

Mannheim, Karl 1893-1947 . . . . TCLC 65

Manning, David
See Faust, Frederick (Schiller)

Manning, Frederic 1887(?)-1935 . . . TCLC 25
See also CA 124

Manning, Olivia 1915-1980 . . . . . . CLC 5, 19
See also CA 5-8R; 101; CANR 29; MTCW

Mano, D. Keith 1942- . . . . CLC 2, 10
See also CA 25-28R; CAAS 6; CANR 26,
57; DLB 6

Mansfield, Katherine
. . TCLC 2, 8, 39; DAB; SSC 9, 23; WLC
See also Beauchamp, Kathleen Mansfield
See also DLB 162

Manso, Peter 1940- . . . . CLC 39
See also CA 29-32R; CANR 44

Mantecon, Juan Jimenez
See Jimenez (Mantecon), Juan Ramon

Manton, Peter
See Creasey, John

Man Without a Spleen, A
See Chekhov, Anton (Pavlovich)

Manzoni, Alessandro 1785-1873 . . NCLC 29

Mapu, Abraham (ben Jekutiel)
1808-1867 . . . . NCLC 18

Mara, Sally
See Queneau, Raymond

Marat, Jean Paul 1743-1793 . . . . **LC 10**

Marcel, Gabriel Honore
1889-1973 . . . . **CLC 15**
See also CA 102; 45-48; MTCW

Marchbanks, Samuel
See Davies, (William) Robertson

Marchi, Giacomo
See Bassani, Giorgio

Margulies, Donald . . . . **CLC 76**

Marie de France c. 12th cent. -. . . . **CMLC 8**

Marie de l'Incarnation 1599-1672. . . . **LC 10**

Marier, Captain Victor
See Griffith, D(avid Lewelyn) W(ark)

Mariner, Scott
See Pohl, Frederik

Marinetti, Filippo Tommaso
1876-1944 . . . . **TCLC 10**
See also CA 107; DLB 114

Marivaux, Pierre Carlet de Chamblain de
1688-1763 . . . . **LC 4; DC 7**

Markandaya, Kamala . . . . **CLC 8, 38**
See also Taylor, Kamala (Purnaiya)

Markfield, Wallace 1926-. . . . . **CLC 8**
See also CA 69-72; CAAS 3; DLB 2, 28

Markham, Edwin 1852-1940 . . . . . . **TCLC 47**
See also DLB 54

Markham, Robert
See Amis, Kingsley (William)

Marks, J
See Highwater, Jamake (Mamake)

Marks-Highwater, J
See Highwater, Jamake (Mamake)

Markson, David M(errill) 1927-. . . . **CLC 67**
See also CA 49-52; CANR 1

Marley, Bob . . . . **CLC 17**
See also Marley, Robert Nesta

Marley, Robert Nesta 1945-1981
See Marley, Bob
See also CA 107; 103

Marlowe, Christopher
1564-1593 . . . . . **LC 22; DA; DAB; DAC;**
DAM DRAM, MST; DC 1; WLC
See also CDBLB Before 1660; DLB 62

Marlowe, Stephen 1928-
See Queen, Ellery
See also CA 13-16R; CANR 6, 55

Marmontel, Jean-Francois
1723-1799 . . . . **LC 2**

Marquand, John P(hillips)
1893-1960 . . . . **CLC 2, 10**
See also CA 85-88; DLB 9, 102

Marques, Rene
1919-1979 . . . . . **CLC 96; DAM MULT;**
HLC
See also CA 97-100; 85-88; DLB 113; HW

Marquez, Gabriel (Jose) Garcia
See Garcia Marquez, Gabriel (Jose)

Marquis, Don(ald Robert Perry)
1878-1937 . . . . **TCLC 7**
See also CA 104; DLB 11, 25

Marric, J. J.
See Creasey, John

Marrow, Bernard
See Moore, Brian

Marryat, Frederick 1792-1848 . . . . **NCLC 3**
See also DLB 21, 163

Marsden, James
See Creasey, John

Marsh, (Edith) Ngaio
1899-1982 . . . . . . **CLC 7, 53; DAM POP**
See also CA 9-12R; CANR 6; DLB 77;
MTCW

Marshall, Garry 1934-. . . . . **CLC 17**
See also AAYA 3; CA 111; SATA 60

Marshall, Paule
1929- . . . . **CLC 27, 72; BLC;**
DAM MULT; SSC 3
See also BW 2; CA 77-80; CANR 25;
DLB 157; MTCW

Marsten, Richard
See Hunter, Evan

Marston, John
1576-1634 . . . . **LC 33; DAM DRAM**
See also DLB 58, 172

Martha, Henry
See Harris, Mark

Martial c. 40-c. 104 . . . . **PC 10**

Martin, Ken
See Hubbard, L(afayette) Ron(ald)

Martin, Richard
See Creasey, John

Martin, Steve 1945-. . . . . **CLC 30**
See also CA 97-100; CANR 30; MTCW

Martin, Valerie 1948-. . . . . **CLC 89**
See also BEST 90:2; CA 85-88; CANR 49

Martin, Violet Florence
1862-1915 . . . . **TCLC 51**

Martin, Webber
See Silverberg, Robert

Martindale, Patrick Victor
See White, Patrick (Victor Martindale)

Martin du Gard, Roger
1881-1958 . . . . **TCLC 24**
See also CA 118; DLB 65

Martineau, Harriet 1802-1876. . . . **NCLC 26**
See also DLB 21, 55, 159, 163, 166;
YABC 2

Martines, Julia
See O'Faolain, Julia

Martinez, Jacinto Benavente y
See Benavente (y Martinez), Jacinto

Martinez Ruiz, Jose 1873-1967
See Azorin; Ruiz, Jose Martinez
See also CA 93-96; HW

Martinez Sierra, Gregorio
1881-1947 . . . . **TCLC 6**
See also CA 115

Martinez Sierra, Maria (de la O'LeJarraga)
1874-1974 . . . . **TCLC 6**
See also CA 115

Martinsen, Martin
See Follett, Ken(neth Martin)

Martinson, Harry (Edmund)
1904-1978 . . . . **CLC 14**
See also CA 77-80; CANR 34

Marut, Ret
See Traven, B.

Marut, Robert
See Traven, B.

Marvell, Andrew
1621-1678 . . . . . . **LC 4; DA; DAB; DAC;**
DAM MST, POET; PC 10; WLC
See also CDBLB 1660-1789; DLB 131

Marx, Karl (Heinrich)
1818-1883 . . . . **NCLC 17**
See also DLB 129

Masaoka Shiki . . . . **TCLC 18**
See also Masaoka Tsunenori

Masaoka Tsunenori 1867-1902
See Masaoka Shiki
See also CA 117

Masefield, John (Edward)
1878-1967 . . . . **CLC 11, 47; DAM POET**
See also CA 19-20; 25-28R; CANR 33;
CAP 2; CDBLB 1890-1914; DLB 10, 19,
153, 160; MTCW; SATA 19

Maso, Carole 19(?)- . . . . **CLC 44**

Mason, Bobbie Ann
1940- . . . . **CLC 28, 43, 82; SSC 4**
See also AAYA 5; CA 53-56; CANR 11,
31; DLB 173; DLBY 87; INT CANR-31;
MTCW

Mason, Ernst
See Pohl, Frederik

Mason, Lee W.
See Malzberg, Barry N(athaniel)

Mason, Nick 1945-. . . . . **CLC 35**

Mason, Tally
See Derleth, August (William)

Mass, William
See Gibson, William

Masters, Edgar Lee
1868-1950 . . . . . . **TCLC 2, 25; DA; DAC;**
DAM MST, POET; PC 1
See also CA 104; 133; CDALB 1865-1917;
DLB 54; MTCW

Masters, Hilary 1928-. . . . . **CLC 48**
See also CA 25-28R; CANR 13, 47

Mastrosimone, William 19(?)- . . . . . . **CLC 36**

Mathe, Albert
See Camus, Albert

Mather, Cotton 1663-1728. . . . . **LC 38**
See also CDALB 1640-1865; DLB 24, 30,
140

Mather, Increase 1639-1723 . . . . **LC 38**
See also DLB 24

Matheson, Richard Burton 1926-. . . **CLC 37**
See also CA 97-100; DLB 8, 44; INT 97-100

Mathews, Harry 1930-. . . . . **CLC 6, 52**
See also CA 21-24R; CAAS 6; CANR 18,
40

Mathews, John Joseph
1894-1979 . . . . . . **CLC 84; DAM MULT**
See also CA 19-20; 142; CANR 45; CAP 2;
DLB 175; NNAL

Mathias, Roland (Glyn) 1915-. . . . . . **CLC 45**
See also CA 97-100; CANR 19, 41; DLB 27

Matsuo Basho 1644-1694. . . . . **PC 3**
See also DAM POET

Mattheson, Rodney
See Creasey, John

Matthews, Greg 1949- .... CLC 45
See also CA 135

Matthews, William 1942-......... CLC 40
See also CA 29-32R; CAAS 18; CANR 12, 57; DLB 5

Matthias, John (Edward) 1941-...... CLC 9
See also CA 33-36R; CANR 56

Matthiessen, Peter
1927- .... CLC 5, 7, 11, 32, 64;
                                    DAM NOV
See also AAYA 6; BEST 90:4; CA 9-12R;
CANR 21, 50; DLB 6, 173; MTCW;
SATA 27

Maturin, Charles Robert
1780(?)-1824 .... NCLC 6

Matute (Ausejo), Ana Maria
1925-...................... CLC 11
See also CA 89-92; MTCW

Maugham, W. S.
See Maugham, W(illiam) Somerset

Maugham, W(illiam) Somerset
1874-1965 .... CLC 1, 11, 15, 67, 93;
               DA; DAB; DAC; DAM DRAM, MST,
                                    NOV; SSC 8; WLC
See also CA 5-8R; 25-28R; CANR 40;
CDBLB 1914-1945; DLB 10, 36, 77, 100,
162; MTCW; SATA 54

Maugham, William Somerset
See Maugham, W(illiam) Somerset

Maupassant, (Henri Rene Albert) Guy de
1850-1893 ..... NCLC 1, 42; DA; DAB;
                 DAC; DAM MST; SSC 1; WLC
See also DLB 123

Maupin, Armistead
1944- .... CLC 95; DAM POP
See also CA 125; 130; INT 130

Maurhut, Richard
See Traven, B.

Mauriac, Claude 1914-1996........ CLC 9
See also CA 89-92; 152; DLB 83

Mauriac, Francois (Charles)
1885-1970 .... CLC 4, 9, 56; SSC 24
See also CA 25-28; CAP 2; DLB 65;
MTCW

Mavor, Osborne Henry 1888-1951
See Bridie, James
See also CA 104

Maxwell, William (Keepers, Jr.)
1908-...................... CLC 19
See also CA 93-96; CANR 54; DLBY 80;
INT 93-96

May, Elaine 1932- .... CLC 16
See also CA 124; 142; DLB 44

Mayakovski, Vladimir (Vladimirovich)
1893-1930 .... TCLC 4, 18
See also CA 104

Mayhew, Henry 1812-1887 ...... NCLC 31
See also DLB 18, 55

Mayle, Peter 1939(?)-............ CLC 89
See also CA 139

Maynard, Joyce 1953-............ CLC 23
See also CA 111; 129

Mayne, William (James Carter)
1928- .... CLC 12
See also AAYA 20; CA 9-12R; CANR 37;
CLR 25; JRDA; MAICYA; SAAS 11;
SATA 6, 68

Mayo, Jim
See L'Amour, Louis (Dearborn)

Maysles, Albert 1926- .... CLC 16
See also CA 29-32R

Maysles, David 1932-............ CLC 16

Mazer, Norma Fox 1931- .... CLC 26
See also AAYA 5; CA 69-72; CANR 12,
32; CLR 23; JRDA; MAICYA; SAAS 1;
SATA 24, 67

Mazzini, Guiseppe 1805-1872 .... NCLC 34

McAuley, James Phillip
1917-1976 .... CLC 45
See also CA 97-100

McBain, Ed
See Hunter, Evan

McBrien, William Augustine
1930-...................... CLC 44
See also CA 107

McCaffrey, Anne (Inez)
1926- ...... CLC 17; DAM NOV, POP
See also AAYA 6; AITN 2; BEST 89:2;
CA 25-28R; CANR 15, 35, 55; DLB 8;
JRDA; MAICYA; MTCW; SAAS 11;
SATA 8, 70

McCall, Nathan 1955(?)-.......... CLC 86
See also CA 146

McCann, Arthur
See Campbell, John W(ood, Jr.)

McCann, Edson
See Pohl, Frederik

McCarthy, Charles, Jr. 1933-
See McCarthy, Cormac
See also CANR 42; DAM POP

McCarthy, Cormac 1933-..... CLC 4, 57, 59
See also McCarthy, Charles, Jr.
See also DLB 6, 143

McCarthy, Mary (Therese)
1912-1989 ...... CLC 1, 3, 5, 14, 24, 39,
                                    59; SSC 24
See also CA 5-8R; 129; CANR 16, 50;
DLB 2; DLBY 81; INT CANR-16;
MTCW

McCartney, (James) Paul
1942-................... CLC 12, 35
See also CA 146

McCauley, Stephen (D.) 1955- ..... CLC 50
See also CA 141

McClure, Michael (Thomas)
1932-...................... CLC 6, 10
See also CA 21-24R; CANR 17, 46;
DLB 16

McCorkle, Jill (Collins) 1958-...... CLC 51
See also CA 121; DLBY 87

McCourt, James 1941-............. CLC 5
See also CA 57-60

McCoy, Horace (Stanley)
1897-1955 .... TCLC 28
See also CA 108; 155; DLB 9

McCrae, John 1872-1918........ TCLC 12
See also CA 109; DLB 92

McCreigh, James
See Pohl, Frederik

McCullers, (Lula) Carson (Smith)
1917-1967 .... CLC 1, 4, 10, 12, 48, 100;
               DA; DAB; DAC; DAM MST, NOV;
                                    SSC 9, 24; WLC
See also AAYA 21; CA 5-8R; 25-28R;
CABS 1, 3; CANR 18;
CDALB 1941-1968; DLB 2, 7, 173;
MTCW; SATA 27

McCulloch, John Tyler
See Burroughs, Edgar Rice

McCullough, Colleen
1938(?)- .... CLC 27; DAM NOV, POP
See also CA 81-84; CANR 17, 46; MTCW

McDermott, Alice 1953- .... CLC 90
See also CA 109; CANR 40

McElroy, Joseph 1930- .... CLC 5, 47
See also CA 17-20R

McEwan, Ian (Russell)
1948- .... CLC 13, 66; DAM NOV
See also BEST 90:4; CA 61-64; CANR 14,
41; DLB 14; MTCW

McFadden, David 1940-........... CLC 48
See also CA 104; DLB 60; INT 104

McFarland, Dennis 1950- .... CLC 65

McGahern, John
1934- .... CLC 5, 9, 48; SSC 17
See also CA 17-20R; CANR 29; DLB 14;
MTCW

McGinley, Patrick (Anthony)
1937-...................... CLC 41
See also CA 120; 127; CANR 56; INT 127

McGinley, Phyllis 1905-1978 ...... CLC 14
See also CA 9-12R; 77-80; CANR 19;
DLB 11, 48; SATA 2, 44; SATA-Obit 24

McGinniss, Joe 1942-............. CLC 32
See also AITN 2; BEST 89:2; CA 25-28R;
CANR 26; INT CANR-26

McGivern, Maureen Daly
See Daly, Maureen

McGrath, Patrick 1950-........... CLC 55
See also CA 136

McGrath, Thomas (Matthew)
1916-1990 .... CLC 28, 59; DAM POET
See also CA 9-12R; 132; CANR 6, 33;
MTCW; SATA 41; SATA-Obit 66

McGuane, Thomas (Francis III)
1939-................ CLC 3, 7, 18, 45
See also AITN 2; CA 49-52; CANR 5, 24,
49; DLB 2; DLBY 80; INT CANR-24;
MTCW

McGuckian, Medbh
1950- .... CLC 48; DAM POET
See also CA 143; DLB 40

McHale, Tom 1942(?)-1982....... CLC 3, 5
See also AITN 1; CA 77-80; 106

McIlvanney, William 1936-........ CLC 42
See also CA 25-28R; DLB 14

McIlwraith, Maureen Mollie Hunter
See Hunter, Mollie
See also SATA 2

McInerney, Jay
1955- . . . . **CLC 34; DAM POP**
See also AAYA 18; CA 116; 123;
CANR 45; INT 123

McIntyre, Vonda N(eel) 1948- . . . . . **CLC 18**
See also CA 81-84; CANR 17, 34; MTCW

McKay, Claude
. . . . **TCLC 7, 41; BLC; DAB; PC 2**
See also McKay, Festus Claudius
See also DLB 4, 45, 51, 117

McKay, Festus Claudius 1889-1948
See McKay, Claude
See also BW 1; CA 104; 124; DA; DAC;
DAM MST, MULT, NOV, POET;
MTCW; WLC

McKuen, Rod 1933- . . . . **CLC 1, 3**
See also AITN 1; CA 41-44R; CANR 40

McLoughlin, R. B.
See Mencken, H(enry) L(ouis)

McLuhan, (Herbert) Marshall
1911-1980 . . . . **CLC 37, 83**
See also CA 9-12R; 102; CANR 12, 34;
DLB 88; INT CANR-12; MTCW

McMillan, Terry (L.)
1951- . . . . . . **CLC 50, 61; DAM MULT,
NOV, POP**
See also AAYA 21; BW 2; CA 140

McMurtry, Larry (Jeff)
1936- . . . . **CLC 2, 3, 7, 11, 27, 44;
DAM NOV, POP**
See also AAYA 15; AITN 2; BEST 89:2;
CA 5-8R; CANR 19, 43;
CDALB 1968-1988; DLB 2, 143;
DLBY 80, 87; MTCW

McNally, T. M. 1961- . . . . **CLC 82**

McNally, Terrence
1939- . . . **CLC 4, 7, 41, 91; DAM DRAM**
See also CA 45-48; CANR 2, 56; DLB 7

McNamer, Deirdre 1950- . . . . **CLC 70**

McNeile, Herman Cyril 1888-1937
See Sapper
See also DLB 77

McNickle, (William) D'Arcy
1904-1977 . . . . . . **CLC 89; DAM MULT**
See also CA 9-12R; 85-88; CANR 5, 45;
DLB 175; NNAL; SATA-Obit 22

McPhee, John (Angus) 1931- . . . . . . **CLC 36**
See also BEST 90:1; CA 65-68; CANR 20,
46; MTCW

McPherson, James Alan
1943- . . . . **CLC 19, 77**
See also BW 1; CA 25-28R; CAAS 17;
CANR 24; DLB 38; MTCW

McPherson, William (Alexander)
1933- . . . . **CLC 34**
See also CA 69-72; CANR 28;
INT CANR-28

Mead, Margaret 1901-1978 . . . . **CLC 37**
See also AITN 1; CA 1-4R; 81-84;
CANR 4; MTCW; SATA-Obit 20

Meaker, Marijane (Agnes) 1927-
See Kerr, M. E.
See also CA 107; CANR 37; INT 107;
JRDA; MAICYA; MTCW; SATA 20, 61

Medoff, Mark (Howard)
1940- . . . . **CLC 6, 23; DAM DRAM**
See also AITN 1; CA 53-56; CANR 5;
DLB 7; INT CANR-5

Medvedev, P. N.
See Bakhtin, Mikhail Mikhailovich

Meged, Aharon
See Megged, Aharon

Meged, Aron
See Megged, Aharon

Megged, Aharon 1920- . . . . **CLC 9**
See also CA 49-52; CAAS 13; CANR 1

Mehta, Ved (Parkash) 1934- . . . . **CLC 37**
See also CA 1-4R; CANR 2, 23; MTCW

Melanter
See Blackmore, R(ichard) D(oddridge)

Melikow, Loris
See Hofmannsthal, Hugo von

Melmoth, Sebastian
See Wilde, Oscar (Fingal O'Flahertie Wills)

Meltzer, Milton 1915- . . . . **CLC 26**
See also AAYA 8; CA 13-16R; CANR 38;
CLR 13; DLB 61; JRDA; MAICYA;
SAAS 1; SATA 1, 50, 80

Melville, Herman
1819-1891 . . . . . **NCLC 3, 12, 29, 45, 49;
DA; DAB; DAC; DAM MST, NOV;
SSC 1, 17; WLC**
See also CDALB 1640-1865; DLB 3, 74;
SATA 59

Menander
c. 342B.C.-c. 292B.C. . . . . **CMLC 9;
DAM DRAM; DC 3**
See also DLB 176

Mencken, H(enry) L(ouis)
1880-1956 . . . . **TCLC 13**
See also CA 105; 125; CDALB 1917-1929;
DLB 11, 29, 63, 137; MTCW

Mendelsohn, Jane 1965(?)- . . . . **CLC 99**
See also CA 154

Mercer, David
1928-1980 . . . . **CLC 5; DAM DRAM**
See also CA 9-12R; 102; CANR 23;
DLB 13; MTCW

Merchant, Paul
See Ellison, Harlan (Jay)

Meredith, George
1828-1909 . . **TCLC 17, 43; DAM POET**
See also CA 117; 153; CDBLB 1832-1890;
DLB 18, 35, 57, 159

Meredith, William (Morris)
1919- . . **CLC 4, 13, 22, 55; DAM POET**
See also CA 9-12R; CAAS 14; CANR 6, 40;
DLB 5

Merezhkovsky, Dmitry Sergeyevich
1865-1941 . . . . **TCLC 29**

Merimee, Prosper
1803-1870 . . . . **NCLC 6; SSC 7**
See also DLB 119

Merkin, Daphne 1954- . . . . **CLC 44**
See also CA 123

Merlin, Arthur
See Blish, James (Benjamin)

Merrill, James (Ingram)
1926-1995 . . . . **CLC 2, 3, 6, 8, 13, 18, 34,
91; DAM POET**
See also CA 13-16R; 147; CANR 10, 49;
DLB 5, 165; DLBY 85; INT CANR-10;
MTCW

Merriman, Alex
See Silverberg, Robert

Merritt, E. B.
See Waddington, Miriam

Merton, Thomas
1915-1968 . . **CLC 1, 3, 11, 34, 83; PC 10**
See also CA 5-8R; 25-28R; CANR 22, 53;
DLB 48; DLBY 81; MTCW

Merwin, W(illiam) S(tanley)
1927- . . . . . . **CLC 1, 2, 3, 5, 8, 13, 18, 45,
88; DAM POET**
See also CA 13-16R; CANR 15, 51; DLB 5,
169; INT CANR-15; MTCW

Metcalf, John 1938- . . . . **CLC 37**
See also CA 113; DLB 60

Metcalf, Suzanne
See Baum, L(yman) Frank

Mew, Charlotte (Mary)
1870-1928 . . . . **TCLC 8**
See also CA 105; DLB 19, 135

Mewshaw, Michael 1943- . . . . **CLC 9**
See also CA 53-56; CANR 7, 47; DLBY 80

Meyer, June
See Jordan, June

Meyer, Lynn
See Slavitt, David R(ytman)

Meyer-Meyrink, Gustav 1868-1932
See Meyrink, Gustav
See also CA 117

Meyers, Jeffrey 1939- . . . . **CLC 39**
See also CA 73-76; CANR 54; DLB 111

Meynell, Alice (Christina Gertrude Thompson)
1847-1922 . . . . **TCLC 6**
See also CA 104; DLB 19, 98

Meyrink, Gustav . . . . **TCLC 21**
See also Meyer-Meyrink, Gustav
See also DLB 81

Michaels, Leonard
1933- . . . . **CLC 6, 25; SSC 16**
See also CA 61-64; CANR 21; DLB 130;
MTCW

Michaux, Henri 1899-1984 . . . . . . **CLC 8, 19**
See also CA 85-88; 114

Michelangelo 1475-1564 . . . . **LC 12**

Michelet, Jules 1798-1874 . . . . **NCLC 31**

Michener, James A(lbert)
1907(?)- . . . . **CLC 1, 5, 11, 29, 60;
DAM NOV, POP**
See also AITN 1; BEST 90:1; CA 5-8R;
CANR 21, 45; DLB 6; MTCW

Mickiewicz, Adam 1798-1855 . . . . . **NCLC 3**

Middleton, Christopher 1926- . . . . . . **CLC 13**
See also CA 13-16R; CANR 29, 54;
DLB 40

Middleton, Richard (Barham)
1882-1911 . . . . **TCLC 56**
See also DLB 156

Montesquieu, Charles-Louis de Secondat
1689-1755 .... **LC 7**

Montgomery, (Robert) Bruce 1921-1978
See Crispin, Edmund
See also CA 104

Montgomery, L(ucy) M(aud)
1874-1942 .... **TCLC 51; DAC;**
DAM MST
See also AAYA 12; CA 108; 137; CLR 8;
DLB 92; DLBD 14; JRDA; MAICYA;
YABC 1

Montgomery, Marion H., Jr. 1925- .. **CLC 7**
See also AITN 1; CA 1-4R; CANR 3, 48;
DLB 6

Montgomery, Max
See Davenport, Guy (Mattison, Jr.)

Montherlant, Henry (Milon) de
1896-1972 .... **CLC 8, 19; DAM DRAM**
See also CA 85-88; 37-40R; DLB 72;
MTCW

Monty Python
See Chapman, Graham; Cleese, John
(Marwood); Gilliam, Terry (Vance); Idle,
Eric; Jones, Terence Graham Parry; Palin,
Michael (Edward)
See also AAYA 7

Moodie, Susanna (Strickland)
1803-1885 .... **NCLC 14**
See also DLB 99

Mooney, Edward 1951-
See Mooney, Ted
See also CA 130

Mooney, Ted .... **CLC 25**
See also Mooney, Edward

Moorcock, Michael (John)
1939- .... **CLC 5, 27, 58**
See also CA 45-48; CAAS 5; CANR 2, 17,
38; DLB 14; MTCW

Moore, Brian
1921- ...... **CLC 1, 3, 5, 7, 8, 19, 32, 90;**
DAB; DAC; DAM MST
See also CA 1-4R; CANR 1, 25, 42; MTCW

Moore, Edward
See Muir, Edwin

Moore, George Augustus
1852-1933 .... **TCLC 7; SSC 19**
See also CA 104; DLB 10, 18, 57, 135

Moore, Lorrie .... **CLC 39, 45, 68**
See also Moore, Marie Lorena

Moore, Marianne (Craig)
1887-1972 .... **CLC 1, 2, 4, 8, 10, 13, 19,**
47; DA; DAB; DAC; DAM MST, POET;
PC 4
See also CA 1-4R; 33-36R; CANR 3;
CDALB 1929-1941; DLB 45; DLBD 7;
MTCW; SATA 20

Moore, Marie Lorena 1957-
See Moore, Lorrie
See also CA 116; CANR 39

Moore, Thomas 1779-1852 .... **NCLC 6**
See also DLB 96, 144

Morand, Paul 1888-1976 .. **CLC 41; SSC 22**
See also CA 69-72; DLB 65

Morante, Elsa 1918-1985 .... **CLC 8, 47**
See also CA 85-88; 117; CANR 35;
DLB 177; MTCW

Moravia, Alberto
1907-1990 .... **CLC 2, 7, 11, 27, 46**
See also Pincherle, Alberto
See also DLB 177

More, Hannah 1745-1833 .... **NCLC 27**
See also DLB 107, 109, 116, 158

More, Henry 1614-1687 .... **LC 9**
See also DLB 126

More, Sir Thomas 1478-1535 .... **LC 10, 32**

Moreas, Jean .... **TCLC 18**
See also Papadiamantopoulos, Johannes

Morgan, Berry 1919- .... **CLC 6**
See also CA 49-52; DLB 6

Morgan, Claire
See Highsmith, (Mary) Patricia

Morgan, Edwin (George) 1920- ..... **CLC 31**
See also CA 5-8R; CANR 3, 43; DLB 27

Morgan, (George) Frederick
1922- .... **CLC 23**
See also CA 17-20R; CANR 21

Morgan, Harriet
See Mencken, H(enry) L(ouis)

Morgan, Jane
See Cooper, James Fenimore

Morgan, Janet 1945- .... **CLC 39**
See also CA 65-68

Morgan, Lady 1776(?)-1859 ...... **NCLC 29**
See also DLB 116, 158

Morgan, Robin 1941- .... **CLC 2**
See also CA 69-72; CANR 29; MTCW;
SATA 80

Morgan, Scott
See Kuttner, Henry

Morgan, Seth 1949(?)-1990 .... **CLC 65**
See also CA 132

Morgenstern, Christian
1871-1914 .... **TCLC 8**
See also CA 105

Morgenstern, S.
See Goldman, William (W.)

Moricz, Zsigmond 1879-1942 ..... **TCLC 33**

Morike, Eduard (Friedrich)
1804-1875 .... **NCLC 10**
See also DLB 133

Mori Ogai .... **TCLC 14**
See also Mori Rintaro

Mori Rintaro 1862-1922
See Mori Ogai
See also CA 110

Moritz, Karl Philipp 1756-1793 ...... **LC 2**
See also DLB 94

Morland, Peter Henry
See Faust, Frederick (Schiller)

Morren, Theophil
See Hofmannsthal, Hugo von

Morris, Bill 1952- .... **CLC 76**

Morris, Julian
See West, Morris L(anglo)

Morris, Steveland Judkins 1950(?)-
See Wonder, Stevie
See also CA 111

Morris, William 1834-1896 .... **NCLC 4**
See also CDBLB 1832-1890; DLB 18, 35,
57, 156

Morris, Wright 1910- ... **CLC 1, 3, 7, 18, 37**
See also CA 9-12R; CANR 21; DLB 2;
DLBY 81; MTCW

Morrison, Chloe Anthony Wofford
See Morrison, Toni

Morrison, James Douglas 1943-1971
See Morrison, Jim
See also CA 73-76; CANR 40

Morrison, Jim .... **CLC 17**
See also Morrison, James Douglas

Morrison, Toni
1931- .... **CLC 4, 10, 22, 55, 81, 87;**
BLC; DA; DAB; DAM MST,
MULT, NOV, POP
See also AAYA 1; BW 2; CA 29-32R;
CANR 27, 42; CDALB 1968-1988;
DLB 6, 33, 143; DLBY 81; MTCW;
SATA 57

Morrison, Van 1945- .... **CLC 21**
See also CA 116

Morrissy, Mary 1958- .... **CLC 99**

Mortimer, John (Clifford)
1923- ...... **CLC 28, 43; DAM DRAM,**
POP
See also CA 13-16R; CANR 21;
CDBLB 1960 to Present; DLB 13;
INT CANR-21; MTCW

Mortimer, Penelope (Ruth) 1918- .... **CLC 5**
See also CA 57-60; CANR 45

Morton, Anthony
See Creasey, John

Mosher, Howard Frank 1943- ...... **CLC 62**
See also CA 139

Mosley, Nicholas 1923- .... **CLC 43, 70**
See also CA 69-72; CANR 41; DLB 14

Mosley, Walter
1952- ..... **CLC 97; DAM MULT, POP**
See also AAYA 17; BW 2; CA 142;
CANR 57

Moss, Howard
1922-1987 .... **CLC 7, 14, 45, 50;**
DAM POET
See also CA 1-4R; 123; CANR 1, 44;
DLB 5

Mossgiel, Rab
See Burns, Robert

Motion, Andrew (Peter) 1952- ...... **CLC 47**
See also CA 146; DLB 40

Motley, Willard (Francis)
1909-1965 .... **CLC 18**
See also BW 1; CA 117; 106; DLB 76, 143

Motoori, Norinaga 1730-1801 .... **NCLC 45**

Mott, Michael (Charles Alston)
1930- .... **CLC 15, 34**
See also CA 5-8R; CAAS 7; CANR 7, 29

Mountain Wolf Woman
1884-1960 .... **CLC 92**
See also CA 144; NNAL

Moure, Erin 1955- .... **CLC 88**
See also CA 113; DLB 60

Orwell, George
..... **TCLC 2, 6, 15, 31, 51; DAB; WLC**
See also Blair, Eric (Arthur)
See also CDBLB 1945-1960; DLB 15, 98

Osborne, David
See Silverberg, Robert

Osborne, George
See Silverberg, Robert

Osborne, John (James)
1929-1994 ..... **CLC 1, 2, 5, 11, 45; DA;**
DAB; DAC; DAM DRAM, MST; WLC
See also CA 13-16R; 147; CANR 21, 56;
CDBLB 1945-1960; DLB 13; MTCW

Osborne, Lawrence 1958- .... **CLC 50**

Oshima, Nagisa 1932- .... **CLC 20**
See also CA 116; 121

Oskison, John Milton
1874-1947 ..... **TCLC 35; DAM MULT**
See also CA 144; DLB 175; NNAL

Ossoli, Sarah Margaret (Fuller marchesa d')
1810-1850
See Fuller, Margaret
See also SATA 25

Ostrovsky, Alexander
1823-1886 .... **NCLC 30, 57**

Otero, Blas de 1916-1979......... **CLC 11**
See also CA 89-92; DLB 134

Otto, Whitney 1955-............. **CLC 70**
See also CA 140

Ouida .... **TCLC 43**
See also De La Ramee, (Marie) Louise
See also DLB 18, 156

Ousmane, Sembene 1923- .... **CLC 66; BLC**
See also BW 1; CA 117; 125; MTCW

Ovid
43B.C.-18(?) ... **CMLC 7; DAM POET;**
PC 2

Owen, Hugh
See Faust, Frederick (Schiller)

Owen, Wilfred (Edward Salter)
1893-1918 ...... **TCLC 5, 27; DA; DAB;**
DAC; DAM MST, POET; WLC
See also CA 104; 141; CDBLB 1914-1945;
DLB 20

Owens, Rochelle 1936-............. **CLC 8**
See also CA 17-20R; CAAS 2; CANR 39

Oz, Amos
1939- .... **CLC 5, 8, 11, 27, 33, 54;**
DAM NOV
See also CA 53-56; CANR 27, 47; MTCW

Ozick, Cynthia
1928- .... **CLC 3, 7, 28, 62; DAM NOV,**
POP; SSC 15
See also BEST 90:1; CA 17-20R; CANR 23;
DLB 28, 152; DLBY 82; INT CANR-23;
MTCW

Ozu, Yasujiro 1903-1963 .... **CLC 16**
See also CA 112

Pacheco, C.
See Pessoa, Fernando (Antonio Nogueira)

Pa Chin .... **CLC 18**
See also Li Fei-kan

Pack, Robert 1929-............. **CLC 13**
See also CA 1-4R; CANR 3, 44; DLB 5

Padgett, Lewis
See Kuttner, Henry

Padilla (Lorenzo), Heberto 1932-... **CLC 38**
See also AITN 1; CA 123; 131; HW

Page, Jimmy 1944-.............. **CLC 12**

Page, Louise 1955-.............. **CLC 40**
See also CA 140

Page, P(atricia) K(athleen)
1916- .... **CLC 7, 18; DAC; DAM MST;**
PC 12
See also CA 53-56; CANR 4, 22; DLB 68;
MTCW

Page, Thomas Nelson 1853-1922.... **SSC 23**
See also CA 118; DLB 12, 78; DLBD 13

Paget, Violet 1856-1935
See Lee, Vernon
See also CA 104

Paget-Lowe, Henry
See Lovecraft, H(oward) P(hillips)

Paglia, Camille (Anna) 1947-...... **CLC 68**
See also CA 140

Paige, Richard
See Koontz, Dean R(ay)

Pakenham, Antonia
See Fraser, (Lady) Antonia (Pakenham)

Palamas, Kostes 1859-1943 .... **TCLC 5**
See also CA 105

Palazzeschi, Aldo 1885-1974...... **CLC 11**
See also CA 89-92; 53-56; DLB 114

Paley, Grace
1922- .... **CLC 4, 6, 37; DAM POP;**
SSC 8
See also CA 25-28R; CANR 13, 46;
DLB 28; INT CANR-13; MTCW

Palin, Michael (Edward) 1943-..... **CLC 21**
See also Monty Python
See also CA 107; CANR 35; SATA 67

Palliser, Charles 1947-........... **CLC 65**
See also CA 136

Palma, Ricardo 1833-1919....... **TCLC 29**

Pancake, Breece Dexter 1952-1979
See Pancake, Breece D'J
See also CA 123; 109

Pancake, Breece D'J.............. **CLC 29**
See also Pancake, Breece Dexter
See also DLB 130

Panko, Rudy
See Gogol, Nikolai (Vasilyevich)

Papadiamantis, Alexandros
1851-1911 .... **TCLC 29**

Papadiamantopoulos, Johannes 1856-1910
See Moreas, Jean
See also CA 117

Papini, Giovanni 1881-1956....... **TCLC 22**
See also CA 121

Paracelsus 1493-1541............. **LC 14**

Parasol, Peter
See Stevens, Wallace

Pareto, Vilfredo 1848-1923 .... **TCLC 69**

Parfenie, Maria
See Codrescu, Andrei

Parini, Jay (Lee) 1948- .... **CLC 54**
See also CA 97-100; CAAS 16; CANR 32

Park, Jordan
See Kornbluth, C(yril) M.; Pohl, Frederik

Parker, Bert
See Ellison, Harlan (Jay)

Parker, Dorothy (Rothschild)
1893-1967 .... **CLC 15, 68;**
DAM POET; SSC 2
See also CA 19-20; 25-28R; CAP 2;
DLB 11, 45, 86; MTCW

Parker, Robert B(rown)
1932- .... **CLC 27; DAM NOV, POP**
See also BEST 89:4; CA 49-52; CANR 1,
26, 52; INT CANR-26; MTCW

Parkin, Frank 1940-.............. **CLC 43**
See also CA 147

Parkman, Francis, Jr.
1823-1893 .... **NCLC 12**
See also DLB 1, 30

Parks, Gordon (Alexander Buchanan)
1912- ... **CLC 1, 16; BLC; DAM MULT**
See also AITN 2; BW 2; CA 41-44R;
CANR 26; DLB 33; SATA 8

Parmenides
c. 515B.C.-c. 450B.C......... **CMLC 22**
See also DLB 176

Parnell, Thomas 1679-1718 .... **LC 3**
See also DLB 94

Parra, Nicanor
1914- ...... **CLC 2; DAM MULT; HLC**
See also CA 85-88; CANR 32; HW; MTCW

Parrish, Mary Frances
See Fisher, M(ary) F(rances) K(ennedy)

Parson
See Coleridge, Samuel Taylor

Parson Lot
See Kingsley, Charles

Partridge, Anthony
See Oppenheim, E(dward) Phillips

Pascal, Blaise 1623-1662 .... **LC 35**

Pascoli, Giovanni 1855-1912 ...... **TCLC 45**

Pasolini, Pier Paolo
1922-1975 .... **CLC 20, 37; PC 17**
See also CA 93-96; 61-64; DLB 128, 177;
MTCW

Pasquini
See Silone, Ignazio

Pastan, Linda (Olenik)
1932- .... **CLC 27; DAM POET**
See also CA 61-64; CANR 18, 40; DLB 5

Pasternak, Boris (Leonidovich)
1890-1960 ...... **CLC 7, 10, 18, 63; DA;**
DAB; DAC; DAM MST, NOV, POET;
PC 6; WLC
See also CA 127; 116; MTCW

Patchen, Kenneth
1911-1972 ... **CLC 1, 2, 18; DAM POET**
See also CA 1-4R; 33-36R; CANR 3, 35;
DLB 16, 48; MTCW

Pater, Walter (Horatio)
1839-1894 .... **NCLC 7**
See also CDBLB 1832-1890; DLB 57, 156

Paterson, A(ndrew) B(arton)
1864-1941 .... **TCLC 32**
See also CA 155

Paterson, Katherine (Womeldorf)
1932- .... **CLC 12, 30**
See also AAYA 1; CA 21-24R; CANR 28;
CLR 7; DLB 52; JRDA; MAICYA;
MTCW; SATA 13, 53, 92

Patmore, Coventry Kersey Dighton
1823-1896 .... **NCLC 9**
See also DLB 35, 98

Paton, Alan (Stewart)
1903-1988 ...... **CLC 4, 10, 25, 55; DA;
DAB; DAC; DAM MST, NOV; WLC**
See also CA 13-16; 125; CANR 22; CAP 1;
MTCW; SATA 11; SATA-Obit 56

Paton Walsh, Gillian 1937-
See Walsh, Jill Paton
See also CANR 38; JRDA; MAICYA;
SAAS 3; SATA 4, 72

Paulding, James Kirke 1778-1860.. **NCLC 2**
See also DLB 3, 59, 74

Paulin, Thomas Neilson 1949-
See Paulin, Tom
See also CA 123; 128

Paulin, Tom .... **CLC 37**
See also Paulin, Thomas Neilson
See also DLB 40

Paustovsky, Konstantin (Georgievich)
1892-1968 .... **CLC 40**
See also CA 93-96; 25-28R

Pavese, Cesare
1908-1950 ..... **TCLC 3; PC 13; SSC 19**
See also CA 104; DLB 128, 177

Pavic, Milorad 1929- .... **CLC 60**
See also CA 136

Payne, Alan
See Jakes, John (William)

Paz, Gil
See Lugones, Leopoldo

Paz, Octavio
1914- .... **CLC 3, 4, 6, 10, 19, 51, 65;
DA; DAB; DAC; DAM MST, MULT,
POET; HLC; PC 1; WLC**
See also CA 73-76; CANR 32; DLBY 90;
HW; MTCW

p'Bitek, Okot
1931-1982 .... **CLC 96; BLC;
DAM MULT**
See also BW 2; CA 124; 107; DLB 125;
MTCW

Peacock, Molly 1947-............. **CLC 60**
See also CA 103; CAAS 21; CANR 52;
DLB 120

Peacock, Thomas Love
1785-1866 .... **NCLC 22**
See also DLB 96, 116

Peake, Mervyn 1911-1968 .... **CLC 7, 54**
See also CA 5-8R; 25-28R; CANR 3;
DLB 15, 160; MTCW; SATA 23

Pearce, Philippa .... **CLC 21**
See also Christie, (Ann) Philippa
See also CLR 9; DLB 161; MAICYA;
SATA 1, 67

Pearl, Eric
See Elman, Richard

Pearson, T(homas) R(eid) 1956- .... **CLC 39**
See also CA 120; 130; INT 130

Peck, Dale 1967- .... **CLC 81**
See also CA 146

Peck, John 1941- .... **CLC 3**
See also CA 49-52; CANR 3

Peck, Richard (Wayne) 1934-...... **CLC 21**
See also AAYA 1; CA 85-88; CANR 19,
38; CLR 15; INT CANR-19; JRDA;
MAICYA; SAAS 2; SATA 18, 55

Peck, Robert Newton
1928- .. **CLC 17; DA; DAC; DAM MST**
See also AAYA 3; CA 81-84; CANR 31;
CLR 45; JRDA; MAICYA; SAAS 1;
SATA 21, 62

Peckinpah, (David) Sam(uel)
1925-1984 .... **CLC 20**
See also CA 109; 114

Pedersen, Knut 1859-1952
See Hamsun, Knut
See also CA 104; 119; MTCW

Peeslake, Gaffer
See Durrell, Lawrence (George)

Peguy, Charles Pierre
1873-1914 .... **TCLC 10**
See also CA 107

Pena, Ramon del Valle y
See Valle-Inclan, Ramon (Maria) del

Pendennis, Arthur Esquir
See Thackeray, William Makepeace

Penn, William 1644-1718........... **LC 25**
See also DLB 24

Pepys, Samuel
1633-1703 ..... **LC 11; DA; DAB; DAC;
DAM MST; WLC**
See also CDBLB 1660-1789; DLB 101

Percy, Walker
1916-1990 .... **CLC 2, 3, 6, 8, 14, 18, 47,
65; DAM NOV, POP**
See also CA 1-4R; 131; CANR 1, 23;
DLB 2; DLBY 80, 90; MTCW

Perec, Georges 1936-1982 .... **CLC 56**
See also CA 141; DLB 83

Pereda (y Sanchez de Porrua), Jose Maria de
1833-1906 .... **TCLC 16**
See also CA 117

Pereda y Porrua, Jose Maria de
See Pereda (y Sanchez de Porrua), Jose
Maria de

Peregoy, George Weems
See Mencken, H(enry) L(ouis)

Perelman, S(idney) J(oseph)
1904-1979 ...... **CLC 3, 5, 9, 15, 23, 44,
49; DAM DRAM**
See also AITN 1, 2; CA 73-76; 89-92;
CANR 18; DLB 11, 44; MTCW

Peret, Benjamin 1899-1959 .... **TCLC 20**
See also CA 117

Peretz, Isaac Loeb 1851(?)-1915... **TCLC 16**
See also CA 109

Peretz, Yitzkhok Leibush
See Peretz, Isaac Loeb

Perez Galdos, Benito 1843-1920... **TCLC 27**
See also CA 125; 153; HW

Perrault, Charles 1628-1703 .... **LC 2**
See also MAICYA; SATA 25

Perry, Brighton
See Sherwood, Robert E(mmet)

Perse, St.-John .... **CLC 4, 11, 46**
See also Leger, (Marie-Rene Auguste) Alexis
Saint-Leger

Perutz, Leo 1882-1957.......... **TCLC 60**
See also DLB 81

Peseenz, Tulio F.
See Lopez y Fuentes, Gregorio

Pesetsky, Bette 1932-............. **CLC 28**
See also CA 133; DLB 130

Peshkov, Alexei Maximovich 1868-1936
See Gorky, Maxim
See also CA 105; 141; DA; DAC;
DAM DRAM, MST, NOV

Pessoa, Fernando (Antonio Nogueira)
1888-1935 .... **TCLC 27; HLC**
See also CA 125

Peterkin, Julia Mood 1880-1961.... **CLC 31**
See also CA 102; DLB 9

Peters, Joan K. 1945-............. **CLC 39**

Peters, Robert L(ouis) 1924-........ **CLC 7**
See also CA 13-16R; CAAS 8; DLB 105

Petofi, Sandor 1823-1849........ **NCLC 21**

Petrakis, Harry Mark 1923-........ **CLC 3**
See also CA 9-12R; CANR 4, 30

Petrarch
1304-1374 .... **CMLC 20; DAM POET;
PC 8**

Petrov, Evgeny .... **TCLC 21**
See also Kataev, Evgeny Petrovich

Petry, Ann (Lane) 1908- .... **CLC 1, 7, 18**
See also BW 1; CA 5-8R; CAAS 6;
CANR 4, 46; CLR 12; DLB 76; JRDA;
MAICYA; MTCW; SATA 5

Petursson, Halligrimur 1614-1674 .... **LC 8**

Philips, Katherine 1632-1664........ **LC 30**
See also DLB 131

Philipson, Morris H. 1926- .... **CLC 53**
See also CA 1-4R; CANR 4

Phillips, Caryl
1958- .... **CLC 96; DAM MULT**
See also BW 2; CA 141; DLB 157

Phillips, David Graham
1867-1911 .... **TCLC 44**
See also CA 108; DLB 9, 12

Phillips, Jack
See Sandburg, Carl (August)

Phillips, Jayne Anne
1952- .... **CLC 15, 33; SSC 16**
See also CA 101; CANR 24, 50; DLBY 80;
INT CANR-24; MTCW

Phillips, Richard
See Dick, Philip K(indred)

Phillips, Robert (Schaeffer) 1938-... **CLC 28**
See also CA 17-20R; CAAS 13; CANR 8;
DLB 105

Phillips, Ward
See Lovecraft, H(oward) P(hillips)

Piccolo, Lucio 1901-1969......... **CLC 13**
See also CA 97-100; DLB 114

Pickthall, Marjorie L(owry) C(hristie)
1883-1922 .... **TCLC 21**
See also CA 107; DLB 92

Pico della Mirandola, Giovanni
    1463-1494 . . . . **LC 15**

Piercy, Marge
    1936- . . . . **CLC 3, 6, 14, 18, 27, 62**
    See also CA 21-24R; CAAS 1; CANR 13,
    43; DLB 120; MTCW

Piers, Robert
    See Anthony, Piers

Pieyre de Mandiargues, Andre 1909-1991
    See Mandiargues, Andre Pieyre de
    See also CA 103; 136; CANR 22

Pilnyak, Boris . . . . **TCLC 23**
    See also Vogau, Boris Andreyevich

Pincherle, Alberto
    1907-1990 . . . . . **CLC 11, 18; DAM NOV**
    See also Moravia, Alberto
    See also CA 25-28R; 132; CANR 33;
    MTCW

Pinckney, Darryl 1953- . . . . **CLC 76**
    See also BW 2; CA 143

Pindar 518B.C.-446B.C. . . . . **CMLC 12**
    See also DLB 176

Pineda, Cecile 1942- . . . . **CLC 39**
    See also CA 118

Pinero, Arthur Wing
    1855-1934 . . . . . **TCLC 32; DAM DRAM**
    See also CA 110; 153; DLB 10

Pinero, Miguel (Antonio Gomez)
    1946-1988 . . . . **CLC 4, 55**
    See also CA 61-64; 125; CANR 29; HW

Pinget, Robert 1919- . . . . **CLC 7, 13, 37**
    See also CA 85-88; DLB 83

Pink Floyd
    See Barrett, (Roger) Syd; Gilmour, David;
    Mason, Nick; Waters, Roger; Wright,
    Rick

Pinkney, Edward 1802-1828 . . . . . **NCLC 31**

Pinkwater, Daniel Manus 1941- . . . . **CLC 35**
    See also Pinkwater, Manus
    See also AAYA 1; CA 29-32R; CANR 12,
    38; CLR 4; JRDA; MAICYA; SAAS 3;
    SATA 46, 76

Pinkwater, Manus
    See Pinkwater, Daniel Manus
    See also SATA 8

Pinsky, Robert
    1940- . . **CLC 9, 19, 38, 94; DAM POET**
    See also CA 29-32R; CAAS 4; DLBY 82

Pinta, Harold
    See Pinter, Harold

Pinter, Harold
    1930- . . . . . **CLC 1, 3, 6, 9, 11, 15, 27, 58,**
    73; DA; DAB; DAC; DAM DRAM,
    MST; WLC
    See also CA 5-8R; CANR 33; CDBLB 1960
    to Present; DLB 13; MTCW

Piozzi, Hester Lynch (Thrale)
    1741-1821 . . . . **NCLC 57**
    See also DLB 104, 142

Pirandello, Luigi
    1867-1936 . . . . . . **TCLC 4, 29; DA; DAB;**
    DAC; DAM DRAM, MST; DC 5;
    SSC 22; WLC
    See also CA 104; 153

Pirsig, Robert M(aynard)
    1928- . . . . **CLC 4, 6, 73; DAM POP**
    See also CA 53-56; CANR 42; MTCW;
    SATA 39

Pisarev, Dmitry Ivanovich
    1840-1868 . . . . **NCLC 25**

Pix, Mary (Griffith) 1666-1709 . . . . **LC 8**
    See also DLB 80

Pixerecourt, Guilbert de
    1773-1844 . . . . **NCLC 39**

Plaidy, Jean
    See Hibbert, Eleanor Alice Burford

Planche, James Robinson
    1796-1880 . . . . **NCLC 42**

Plant, Robert 1948- . . . . **CLC 12**

Plante, David (Robert)
    1940- . . . . **CLC 7, 23, 38; DAM NOV**
    See also CA 37-40R; CANR 12, 36;
    DLBY 83; INT CANR-12; MTCW

Plath, Sylvia
    1932-1963 . . . . . **CLC 1, 2, 3, 5, 9, 11, 14,**
    17, 50, 51, 62; DA; DAB; DAC;
    DAM MST, POET; PC 1; WLC
    See also AAYA 13; CA 19-20; CANR 34;
    CAP 2; CDALB 1941-1968; DLB 5, 6,
    152; MTCW

Plato
    428(?)B.C.-348(?)B.C. . . . . . **CMLC 8; DA;**
    DAB; DAC; DAM MST
    See also DLB 176

Platonov, Andrei . . . . **TCLC 14**
    See also Klimentov, Andrei Platonovich

Platt, Kin 1911- . . . . **CLC 26**
    See also AAYA 11; CA 17-20R; CANR 11;
    JRDA; SAAS 17; SATA 21, 86

Plautus c. 251B.C.-184B.C. . . . . **DC 6**

Plick et Plock
    See Simenon, Georges (Jacques Christian)

Plimpton, George (Ames) 1927- . . . . . **CLC 36**
    See also AITN 1; CA 21-24R; CANR 32;
    MTCW; SATA 10

Plomer, William Charles Franklin
    1903-1973 . . . . **CLC 4, 8**
    See also CA 21-22; CANR 34; CAP 2;
    DLB 20, 162; MTCW; SATA 24

Plowman, Piers
    See Kavanagh, Patrick (Joseph)

Plum, J.
    See Wodehouse, P(elham) G(renville)

Plumly, Stanley (Ross) 1939- . . . . . . **CLC 33**
    See also CA 108; 110; DLB 5; INT 110

Plumpe, Friedrich Wilhelm
    1888-1931 . . . . **TCLC 53**
    See also CA 112

Poe, Edgar Allan
    1809-1849 . . . . **NCLC 1, 16, 55; DA;**
    DAB; DAC; DAM MST, POET; PC 1;
    SSC 1, 22; WLC
    See also AAYA 14; CDALB 1640-1865;
    DLB 3, 59, 73, 74; SATA 23

Poet of Titchfield Street, The
    See Pound, Ezra (Weston Loomis)

Pohl, Frederik 1919- . . . . . **CLC 18; SSC 25**
    See also CA 61-64; CAAS 1; CANR 11, 37;
    DLB 8; INT CANR-11; MTCW;
    SATA 24

Poirier, Louis 1910-
    See Gracq, Julien
    See also CA 122; 126

Poitier, Sidney 1927- . . . . **CLC 26**
    See also BW 1; CA 117

Polanski, Roman 1933- . . . . **CLC 16**
    See also CA 77-80

Poliakoff, Stephen 1952- . . . . **CLC 38**
    See also CA 106; DLB 13

Police, The
    See Copeland, Stewart (Armstrong);
    Summers, Andrew James; Sumner,
    Gordon Matthew

Polidori, John William
    1795-1821 . . . . **NCLC 51**
    See also DLB 116

Pollitt, Katha 1949- . . . . **CLC 28**
    See also CA 120; 122; MTCW

Pollock, (Mary) Sharon
    1936- . . . . **CLC 50; DAC; DAM DRAM,**
    MST
    See also CA 141; DLB 60

Polo, Marco 1254-1324 . . . . **CMLC 15**

Polonsky, Abraham (Lincoln)
    1910- . . . . **CLC 92**
    See also CA 104; DLB 26; INT 104

Polybius c. 200B.C.-c. 118B.C. . . . . **CMLC 17**
    See also DLB 176

Pomerance, Bernard
    1940- . . . . **CLC 13; DAM DRAM**
    See also CA 101; CANR 49

Ponge, Francis (Jean Gaston Alfred)
    1899-1988 . . . . . **CLC 6, 18; DAM POET**
    See also CA 85-88; 126; CANR 40

Pontoppidan, Henrik 1857-1943 . . . **TCLC 29**

Poole, Josephine . . . . **CLC 17**
    See also Helyar, Jane Penelope Josephine
    See also SAAS 2; SATA 5

Popa, Vasko 1922-1991 . . . . **CLC 19**
    See also CA 112; 148

Pope, Alexander
    1688-1744 . . . . . . **LC 3; DA; DAB; DAC;**
    DAM MST, POET; WLC
    See also CDBLB 1660-1789; DLB 95, 101

Porter, Connie (Rose) 1959(?)- . . . . . **CLC 70**
    See also BW 2; CA 142; SATA 81

Porter, Gene(va Grace) Stratton
    1863(?)-1924 . . . . **TCLC 21**
    See also CA 112

Porter, Katherine Anne
    1890-1980 . . . . . . **CLC 1, 3, 7, 10, 13, 15,**
    27; DA; DAB; DAC; DAM MST, NOV;
    SSC 4
    See also AITN 2; CA 1-4R; 101; CANR 1;
    DLB 4, 9, 102; DLBD 12; DLBY 80;
    MTCW; SATA 39; SATA-Obit 23

Porter, Peter (Neville Frederick)
    1929- . . . . **CLC 5, 13, 33**
    See also CA 85-88; DLB 40

Porter, William Sydney   1862-1910
See Henry, O.
See also CA 104; 131; CDALB 1865-1917;
DA; DAB; DAC; DAM MST; DLB 12,
78, 79; MTCW; YABC 2

Portillo (y Pacheco), Jose Lopez
See Lopez Portillo (y Pacheco), Jose

Post, Melville Davisson
1869-1930 . . . . **TCLC 39**
See also CA 110

Potok, Chaim
1929- . . . .   **CLC 2, 7, 14, 26; DAM NOV**
See also AAYA 15; AITN 1, 2; CA 17-20R;
CANR 19, 35; DLB 28, 152;
INT CANR-19; MTCW; SATA 33

Potter, Beatrice
See Webb, (Martha) Beatrice (Potter)
See also MAICYA

Potter, Dennis (Christopher George)
1935-1994 . . . . **CLC 58, 86**
See also CA 107; 145; CANR 33; MTCW

Pound, Ezra (Weston Loomis)
1885-1972 . . . . . . **CLC 1, 2, 3, 4, 5, 7, 10,
13, 18, 34, 48, 50; DA; DAB; DAC;
DAM MST, POET; PC 4; WLC**
See also CA 5-8R; 37-40R; CANR 40;
CDALB 1917-1929; DLB 4, 45, 63;
MTCW

Povod, Reinaldo   1959-1994 . . . . **CLC 44**
See also CA 136; 146

Powell, Adam Clayton, Jr.
1908-1972 . . . . **CLC 89; BLC;
DAM MULT**
See also BW 1; CA 102; 33-36R

Powell, Anthony (Dymoke)
1905- . . . . **CLC 1, 3, 7, 9, 10, 31**
See also CA 1-4R; CANR 1, 32;
CDBLB 1945-1960; DLB 15; MTCW

Powell, Dawn   1897-1965 . . . . **CLC 66**
See also CA 5-8R

Powell, Padgett   1952- . . . . **CLC 34**
See also CA 126

Power, Susan . . . . **CLC 91**

Powers, J(ames) F(arl)
1917- . . . . **CLC 1, 4, 8, 57; SSC 4**
See also CA 1-4R; CANR 2; DLB 130;
MTCW

Powers, John J(ames)   1945-
See Powers, John R.
See also CA 69-72

Powers, John R. . . . . **CLC 66**
See also Powers, John J(ames)

Powers, Richard (S.)   1957- . . . . **CLC 93**
See also CA 148

Pownall, David   1938- . . . . **CLC 10**
See also CA 89-92; CAAS 18; CANR 49;
DLB 14

Powys, John Cowper
1872-1963 . . . . **CLC 7, 9, 15, 46**
See also CA 85-88; DLB 15; MTCW

Powys, T(heodore) F(rancis)
1875-1953 . . . . **TCLC 9**
See also CA 106; DLB 36, 162

Prager, Emily   1952- . . . . **CLC 56**

Pratt, E(dwin) J(ohn)
1883(?)-1964 . . . . **CLC 19; DAC;
DAM POET**
See also CA 141; 93-96; DLB 92

Premchand . . . . **TCLC 21**
See also Srivastava, Dhanpat Rai

Preussler, Otfried   1923- . . . . **CLC 17**
See also CA 77-80; SATA 24

Prevert, Jacques (Henri Marie)
1900-1977 . . . . **CLC 15**
See also CA 77-80; 69-72; CANR 29;
MTCW; SATA-Obit 30

Prevost, Abbe (Antoine Francois)
1697-1763 . . . . **LC 1**

Price, (Edward) Reynolds
1933- . . . . **CLC 3, 6, 13, 43, 50, 63;
DAM NOV; SSC 22**
See also CA 1-4R; CANR 1, 37, 57; DLB 2;
INT CANR-37

Price, Richard   1949- . . . . **CLC 6, 12**
See also CA 49-52; CANR 3; DLBY 81

Prichard, Katharine Susannah
1883-1969 . . . . **CLC 46**
See also CA 11-12; CANR 33; CAP 1;
MTCW; SATA 66

Priestley, J(ohn) B(oynton)
1894-1984 . . . . **CLC 2, 5, 9, 34;
DAM DRAM, NOV**
See also CA 9-12R; 113; CANR 33;
CDBLB 1914-1945; DLB 10, 34, 77, 100,
139; DLBY 84; MTCW

Prince   1958(?)- . . . . **CLC 35**

Prince, F(rank) T(empleton)   1912- . . **CLC 22**
See also CA 101; CANR 43; DLB 20

Prince Kropotkin
See Kropotkin, Peter (Aleksieevich)

Prior, Matthew   1664-1721 . . . . **LC 4**
See also DLB 95

Pritchard, William H(arrison)
1932- . . . . **CLC 34**
See also CA 65-68; CANR 23; DLB 111

Pritchett, V(ictor) S(awdon)
1900- . . . . **CLC 5, 13, 15, 41;
DAM NOV; SSC 14**
See also CA 61-64; CANR 31; DLB 15,
139; MTCW

Private 19022
See Manning, Frederic

Probst, Mark   1925- . . . . **CLC 59**
See also CA 130

Prokosch, Frederic   1908-1989 . . . . **CLC 4, 48**
See also CA 73-76; 128; DLB 48

Prophet, The
See Dreiser, Theodore (Herman Albert)

Prose, Francine   1947- . . . . **CLC 45**
See also CA 109; 112; CANR 46

Proudhon
See Cunha, Euclides (Rodrigues Pimenta) da

Proulx, E. Annie   1935- . . . . **CLC 81**

Proust, (Valentin-Louis-George-Eugene-)
Marcel
1871-1922 . . . . **TCLC 7, 13, 33; DA;
DAB; DAC; DAM MST, NOV; WLC**
See also CA 104; 120; DLB 65; MTCW

Prowler, Harley
See Masters, Edgar Lee

Prus, Boleslaw   1845-1912 . . . . **TCLC 48**

Pryor, Richard (Franklin Lenox Thomas)
1940- . . . . **CLC 26**
See also CA 122

Przybyszewski, Stanislaw
1868-1927 . . . . **TCLC 36**
See also DLB 66

Pteleon
See Grieve, C(hristopher) M(urray)
See also DAM POET

Puckett, Lute
See Masters, Edgar Lee

Puig, Manuel
1932-1990 . . . . **CLC 3, 5, 10, 28, 65;
DAM MULT; HLC**
See also CA 45-48; CANR 2, 32; DLB 113;
HW; MTCW

Purdy, Al(fred Wellington)
1918- . . . . **CLC 3, 6, 14, 50; DAC;
DAM MST, POET**
See also CA 81-84; CAAS 17; CANR 42;
DLB 88

Purdy, James (Amos)
1923- . . . . **CLC 2, 4, 10, 28, 52**
See also CA 33-36R; CAAS 1; CANR 19,
51; DLB 2; INT CANR-19; MTCW

Pure, Simon
See Swinnerton, Frank Arthur

Pushkin, Alexander (Sergeyevich)
1799-1837 . . . . . **NCLC 3, 27; DA; DAB;
DAC; DAM DRAM, MST, POET;
PC 10; WLC**
See also SATA 61

P'u Sung-ling   1640-1715 . . . . **LC 3**

Putnam, Arthur Lee
See Alger, Horatio, Jr.

Puzo, Mario
1920- . . . . . **CLC 1, 2, 6, 36; DAM NOV,
POP**
See also CA 65-68; CANR 4, 42; DLB 6;
MTCW

Pygge, Edward
See Barnes, Julian (Patrick)

Pym, Barbara (Mary Crampton)
1913-1980 . . . . **CLC 13, 19, 37**
See also CA 13-14; 97-100; CANR 13, 34;
CAP 1; DLB 14; DLBY 87; MTCW

Pynchon, Thomas (Ruggles, Jr.)
1937- . . . . . **CLC 2, 3, 6, 9, 11, 18, 33, 62,
72; DA; DAB; DAC; DAM MST, NOV,
POP; SSC 14; WLC**
See also BEST 90:2; CA 17-20R; CANR 22,
46; DLB 2, 173; MTCW

Pythagoras
c. 570B.C.-c. 500B.C. . . . . **CMLC 22**
See also DLB 176

Qian Zhongshu
See Ch'ien Chung-shu

Qroll
See Dagerman, Stig (Halvard)

Quarrington, Paul (Lewis)   1953- . . . . **CLC 65**
See also CA 129

Author Index

Schiller, Friedrich
    1759-1805 . . . . **NCLC 39; DAM DRAM**
    See also DLB 94

Schisgal, Murray (Joseph) 1926-. . . . . **CLC 6**
    See also CA 21-24R; CANR 48

Schlee, Ann 1934-. . . . . **CLC 35**
    See also CA 101; CANR 29; SATA 44;
    SATA-Brief 36

Schlegel, August Wilhelm von
    1767-1845 . . . . **NCLC 15**
    See also DLB 94

Schlegel, Friedrich 1772-1829 . . . . **NCLC 45**
    See also DLB 90

Schlegel, Johann Elias (von)
    1719(?)-1749 . . . . **LC 5**

Schlesinger, Arthur M(eier), Jr.
    1917- . . . . **CLC 84**
    See also AITN 1; CA 1-4R; CANR 1, 28;
    DLB 17; INT CANR-28; MTCW;
    SATA 61

Schmidt, Arno (Otto) 1914-1979 . . . . **CLC 56**
    See also CA 128; 109; DLB 69

Schmitz, Aron Hector 1861-1928
    See Svevo, Italo
    See also CA 104; 122; MTCW

Schnackenberg, Gjertrud 1953-. . . . . **CLC 40**
    See also CA 116; DLB 120

Schneider, Leonard Alfred 1925-1966
    See Bruce, Lenny
    See also CA 89-92

Schnitzler, Arthur
    1862-1931 . . . . **TCLC 4; SSC 15**
    See also CA 104; DLB 81, 118

Schopenhauer, Arthur
    1788-1860 . . . . **NCLC 51**
    See also DLB 90

Schor, Sandra (M.) 1932(?)-1990 . . . **CLC 65**
    See also CA 132

Schorer, Mark 1908-1977 . . . . **CLC 9**
    See also CA 5-8R; 73-76; CANR 7;
    DLB 103

Schrader, Paul (Joseph) 1946-. . . . . . **CLC 26**
    See also CA 37-40R; CANR 41; DLB 44

Schreiner, Olive (Emilie Albertina)
    1855-1920 . . . . **TCLC 9**
    See also CA 105; DLB 18, 156

Schulberg, Budd (Wilson)
    1914- . . . . **CLC 7, 48**
    See also CA 25-28R; CANR 19; DLB 6, 26,
    28; DLBY 81

Schulz, Bruno
    1892-1942 . . . . **TCLC 5, 51; SSC 13**
    See also CA 115; 123

Schulz, Charles M(onroe) 1922- . . . . **CLC 12**
    See also CA 9-12R; CANR 6;
    INT CANR-6; SATA 10

Schumacher, E(rnst) F(riedrich)
    1911-1977 . . . . **CLC 80**
    See also CA 81-84; 73-76; CANR 34

Schuyler, James Marcus
    1923-1991 . . . . . **CLC 5, 23; DAM POET**
    See also CA 101; 134; DLB 5, 169; INT 101

Schwartz, Delmore (David)
    1913-1966 . . . **CLC 2, 4, 10, 45, 87; PC 8**
    See also CA 17-18; 25-28R; CANR 35;
    CAP 2; DLB 28, 48; MTCW

Schwartz, Ernst
    See Ozu, Yasujiro

Schwartz, John Burnham 1965- . . . . **CLC 59**
    See also CA 132

Schwartz, Lynne Sharon 1939-. . . . . **CLC 31**
    See also CA 103; CANR 44

Schwartz, Muriel A.
    See Eliot, T(homas) S(tearns)

Schwarz-Bart, Andre 1928-. . . . . . . **CLC 2, 4**
    See also CA 89-92

Schwarz-Bart, Simone 1938-. . . . . **CLC 7**
    See also BW 2; CA 97-100

Schwob, (Mayer Andre) Marcel
    1867-1905 . . . . **TCLC 20**
    See also CA 117; DLB 123

Sciascia, Leonardo
    1921-1989 . . . . **CLC 8, 9, 41**
    See also CA 85-88; 130; CANR 35;
    DLB 177; MTCW

Scoppettone, Sandra 1936-. . . . . **CLC 26**
    See also AAYA 11; CA 5-8R; CANR 41;
    SATA 9, 92

Scorsese, Martin 1942- . . . . **CLC 20, 89**
    See also CA 110; 114; CANR 46

Scotland, Jay
    See Jakes, John (William)

Scott, Duncan Campbell
    1862-1947 . . . . **TCLC 6; DAC**
    See also CA 104; 153; DLB 92

Scott, Evelyn 1893-1963. . . . . **CLC 43**
    See also CA 104; 112; DLB 9, 48

Scott, F(rancis) R(eginald)
    1899-1985 . . . . **CLC 22**
    See also CA 101; 114; DLB 88; INT 101

Scott, Frank
    See Scott, F(rancis) R(eginald)

Scott, Joanna 1960- . . . . **CLC 50**
    See also CA 126; CANR 53

Scott, Paul (Mark) 1920-1978 . . . . **CLC 9, 60**
    See also CA 81-84; 77-80; CANR 33;
    DLB 14; MTCW

Scott, Walter
    1771-1832 . . . . **NCLC 15; DA; DAB;**
    DAC; DAM MST, NOV, POET; PC 13;
    WLC
    See also CDBLB 1789-1832; DLB 93, 107,
    116, 144, 159; YABC 2

Scribe, (Augustin) Eugene
    1791-1861 . . . . **NCLC 16; DAM DRAM;**
    DC 5

Scrum, R.
    See Crumb, R(obert)

Scudery, Madeleine de 1607-1701. . . . . **LC 2**

Scum
    See Crumb, R(obert)

Scumbag, Little Bobby
    See Crumb, R(obert)

Seabrook, John
    See Hubbard, L(afayette) Ron(ald)

Sealy, I. Allan 1951- . . . . **CLC 55**

Search, Alexander
    See Pessoa, Fernando (Antonio Nogueira)

Sebastian, Lee
    See Silverberg, Robert

Sebastian Owl
    See Thompson, Hunter S(tockton)

Sebestyen, Ouida 1924-. . . . . **CLC 30**
    See also AAYA 8; CA 107; CANR 40;
    CLR 17; JRDA; MAICYA; SAAS 10;
    SATA 39

Secundus, H. Scriblerus
    See Fielding, Henry

Sedges, John
    See Buck, Pearl S(ydenstricker)

Sedgwick, Catharine Maria
    1789-1867 . . . . **NCLC 19**
    See also DLB 1, 74

Seelye, John 1931-. . . . . **CLC 7**

Seferiades, Giorgos Stylianou 1900-1971
    See Seferis, George
    See also CA 5-8R; 33-36R; CANR 5, 36;
    MTCW

Seferis, George . . . . **CLC 5, 11**
    See also Seferiades, Giorgos Stylianou

Segal, Erich (Wolf)
    1937- . . . . **CLC 3, 10; DAM POP**
    See also BEST 89:1; CA 25-28R; CANR 20,
    36; DLBY 86; INT CANR-20; MTCW

Seger, Bob 1945-. . . . . **CLC 35**

Seghers, Anna . . . . **CLC 7**
    See also Radvanyi, Netty
    See also DLB 69

Seidel, Frederick (Lewis) 1936-. . . . . **CLC 18**
    See also CA 13-16R; CANR 8; DLBY 84

Seifert, Jaroslav
    1901-1986 . . . . **CLC 34, 44, 93**
    See also CA 127; MTCW

Sei Shonagon c. 966-1017(?) . . . . . . **CMLC 6**

Selby, Hubert, Jr.
    1928- . . . . **CLC 1, 2, 4, 8; SSC 20**
    See also CA 13-16R; CANR 33; DLB 2

Selzer, Richard 1928-. . . . . **CLC 74**
    See also CA 65-68; CANR 14

Sembene, Ousmane
    See Ousmane, Sembene

Senancour, Etienne Pivert de
    1770-1846 . . . . **NCLC 16**
    See also DLB 119

Sender, Ramon (Jose)
    1902-1982 . . **CLC 8; DAM MULT; HLC**
    See also CA 5-8R; 105; CANR 8; HW;
    MTCW

Seneca, Lucius Annaeus
    4B.C.-65. . . . . . . **CMLC 6; DAM DRAM;**
    DC 5

Senghor, Leopold Sedar
    1906- . . . . . **CLC 54; BLC; DAM MULT,**
    POET
    See also BW 2; CA 116; 125; CANR 47;
    MTCW

Serling, (Edward) Rod(man)
    1924-1975 . . . . **CLC 30**
    See also AAYA 14; AITN 1; CA 65-68;
    57-60; DLB 26

Serna, Ramon Gomez de la
See Gomez de la Serna, Ramon

Serpieres
See Guillevic, (Eugene)

Service, Robert
See Service, Robert W(illiam)
See also DAB; DLB 92

Service, Robert W(illiam)
1874(?)-1958 ...... **TCLC 15; DA; DAC;**
DAM MST, POET; WLC
See also Service, Robert
See also CA 115; 140; SATA 20

Seth, Vikram
1952- .... **CLC 43, 90; DAM MULT**
See also CA 121; 127; CANR 50; DLB 120;
INT 127

Seton, Cynthia Propper
1926-1982 .... **CLC 27**
See also CA 5-8R; 108; CANR 7

Seton, Ernest (Evan) Thompson
1860-1946 .... **TCLC 31**
See also CA 109; DLB 92; DLBD 13;
JRDA; SATA 18

Seton-Thompson, Ernest
See Seton, Ernest (Evan) Thompson

Settle, Mary Lee 1918- .... **CLC 19, 61**
See also CA 89-92; CAAS 1; CANR 44;
DLB 6; INT 89-92

Seuphor, Michel
See Arp, Jean

Sevigne, Marie (de Rabutin-Chantal) Marquise
de 1626-1696 .... **LC 11**

Sewall, Samuel 1652-1730 .... **LC 38**
See also DLB 24

Sexton, Anne (Harvey)
1928-1974 .... **CLC 2, 4, 6, 8, 10, 15, 53;**
DA; DAB; DAC; DAM MST, POET;
PC 2; WLC
See also CA 1-4R; 53-56; CABS 2;
CANR 3, 36; CDALB 1941-1968; DLB 5,
169; MTCW; SATA 10

Shaara, Michael (Joseph, Jr.)
1929-1988 .... **CLC 15; DAM POP**
See also AITN 1; CA 102; 125; CANR 52;
DLBY 83

Shackleton, C. C.
See Aldiss, Brian W(ilson)

Shacochis, Bob .... **CLC 39**
See also Shacochis, Robert G.

Shacochis, Robert G. 1951-
See Shacochis, Bob
See also CA 119; 124; INT 124

Shaffer, Anthony (Joshua)
1926- .... **CLC 19; DAM DRAM**
See also CA 110; 116; DLB 13

Shaffer, Peter (Levin)
1926- ...... **CLC 5, 14, 18, 37, 60; DAB;**
DAM DRAM, MST; DC 7
See also CA 25-28R; CANR 25, 47;
CDBLB 1960 to Present; DLB 13;
MTCW

Shakey, Bernard
See Young, Neil

Shalamov, Varlam (Tikhonovich)
1907(?)-1982 .... **CLC 18**
See also CA 129; 105

Shamlu, Ahmad 1925- .... **CLC 10**

Shammas, Anton 1951-........... **CLC 55**

Shange, Ntozake
1948- .... **CLC 8, 25, 38, 74; BLC;**
DAM DRAM, MULT; DC 3
See also AAYA 9; BW 2; CA 85-88;
CABS 3; CANR 27, 48; DLB 38; MTCW

Shanley, John Patrick 1950-....... **CLC 75**
See also CA 128; 133

Shapcott, Thomas W(illiam) 1935-.. **CLC 38**
See also CA 69-72; CANR 49

Shapiro, Jane.................... **CLC 76**

Shapiro, Karl (Jay) 1913- .. **CLC 4, 8, 15, 53**
See also CA 1-4R; CAAS 6; CANR 1, 36;
DLB 48; MTCW

Sharp, William 1855-1905 .... **TCLC 39**
See also DLB 156

Sharpe, Thomas Ridley 1928-
See Sharpe, Tom
See also CA 114; 122; INT 122

Sharpe, Tom.................... **CLC 36**
See also Sharpe, Thomas Ridley
See also DLB 14

Shaw, Bernard.................... **TCLC 45**
See also Shaw, George Bernard
See also BW 1

Shaw, G. Bernard
See Shaw, George Bernard

Shaw, George Bernard
1856-1950 ... **TCLC 3, 9, 21; DA; DAB;**
DAC; DAM DRAM, MST; WLC
See also Shaw, Bernard
See also CA 104; 128; CDBLB 1914-1945;
DLB 10, 57; MTCW

Shaw, Henry Wheeler
1818-1885 .... **NCLC 15**
See also DLB 11

Shaw, Irwin
1913-1984 .... **CLC 7, 23, 34;**
DAM DRAM, POP
See also AITN 1; CA 13-16R; 112;
CANR 21; CDALB 1941-1968; DLB 6,
102; DLBY 84; MTCW

Shaw, Robert 1927-1978 .... **CLC 5**
See also AITN 1; CA 1-4R; 81-84;
CANR 4; DLB 13, 14

Shaw, T. E.
See Lawrence, T(homas) E(dward)

Shawn, Wallace 1943- .... **CLC 41**
See also CA 112

Shea, Lisa 1953-................. **CLC 86**
See also CA 147

Sheed, Wilfrid (John Joseph)
1930- .... **CLC 2, 4, 10, 53**
See also CA 65-68; CANR 30; DLB 6;
MTCW

Sheldon, Alice Hastings Bradley
1915(?)-1987
See Tiptree, James, Jr.
See also CA 108; 122; CANR 34; INT 108;
MTCW

Sheldon, John
See Bloch, Robert (Albert)

Shelley, Mary Wollstonecraft (Godwin)
1797-1851 .... **NCLC 14, 59; DA; DAB;**
DAC; DAM MST, NOV; WLC
See also AAYA 20; CDBLB 1789-1832;
DLB 110, 116, 159; SATA 29

Shelley, Percy Bysshe
1792-1822 .... **NCLC 18; DA; DAB;**
DAC; DAM MST, POET; PC 14; WLC
See also CDBLB 1789-1832; DLB 96, 110,
158

Shepard, Jim 1956-.............. **CLC 36**
See also CA 137; SATA 90

Shepard, Lucius 1947- .... **CLC 34**
See also CA 128; 141

Shepard, Sam
1943- .... **CLC 4, 6, 17, 34, 41, 44;**
DAM DRAM; DC 5
See also AAYA 1; CA 69-72; CABS 3;
CANR 22; DLB 7; MTCW

Shepherd, Michael
See Ludlum, Robert

Sherburne, Zoa (Morin) 1912-...... **CLC 30**
See also AAYA 13; CA 1-4R; CANR 3, 37;
MAICYA; SAAS 18; SATA 3

Sheridan, Frances 1724-1766 .... **LC 7**
See also DLB 39, 84

Sheridan, Richard Brinsley
1751-1816 .... **NCLC 5; DA; DAB;**
DAC; DAM DRAM, MST; DC 1; WLC
See also CDBLB 1660-1789; DLB 89

Sherman, Jonathan Marc.......... **CLC 55**

Sherman, Martin 1941(?)- .... **CLC 19**
See also CA 116; 123

Sherwin, Judith Johnson 1936-... **CLC 7, 15**
See also CA 25-28R; CANR 34

Sherwood, Frances 1940-.......... **CLC 81**
See also CA 146

Sherwood, Robert E(mmet)
1896-1955 ...... **TCLC 3; DAM DRAM**
See also CA 104; 153; DLB 7, 26

Shestov, Lev 1866-1938 .... **TCLC 56**

Shevchenko, Taras 1814-1861 .... **NCLC 54**

Shiel, M(atthew) P(hipps)
1865-1947 .... **TCLC 8**
See also CA 106; DLB 153

Shields, Carol 1935-......... **CLC 91; DAC**
See also CA 81-84; CANR 51

Shields, David 1956-.............. **CLC 97**
See also CA 124; CANR 48

Shiga, Naoya 1883-1971... **CLC 33; SSC 23**
See also CA 101; 33-36R

Shilts, Randy 1951-1994 .... **CLC 85**
See also AAYA 19; CA 115; 127; 144;
CANR 45; INT 127

Shimazaki, Haruki 1872-1943
See Shimazaki Toson
See also CA 105; 134

Shimazaki Toson................. **TCLC 5**
See also Shimazaki, Haruki

Sholokhov, Mikhail (Aleksandrovich)
1905-1984 .... **CLC 7, 15**
See also CA 101; 112; MTCW;
SATA-Obit 36

Sjowall, Maj
See Sjoewall, Maj

Skelton, Robin 1925- . . . . **CLC 13**
See also AITN 2; CA 5-8R; CAAS 5;
CANR 28; DLB 27, 53

Skolimowski, Jerzy 1938- . . . . **CLC 20**
See also CA 128

Skram, Amalie (Bertha)
1847-1905 . . . . **TCLC 25**

Skvorecky, Josef (Vaclav)
1924- . . . . **CLC 15, 39, 69; DAC;
DAM NOV**
See also CA 61-64; CAAS 1; CANR 10, 34;
MTCW

Slade, Bernard . . . . **CLC 11, 46**
See also Newbound, Bernard Slade
See also CAAS 9; DLB 53

Slaughter, Carolyn 1946- . . . . **CLC 56**
See also CA 85-88

Slaughter, Frank G(ill) 1908- . . . . . . **CLC 29**
See also AITN 2; CA 5-8R; CANR 5;
INT CANR-5

Slavitt, David R(ytman) 1935- . . . **CLC 5, 14**
See also CA 21-24R; CAAS 3; CANR 41;
DLB 5, 6

Slesinger, Tess 1905-1945 . . . . **TCLC 10**
See also CA 107; DLB 102

Slessor, Kenneth 1901-1971 . . . . **CLC 14**
See also CA 102; 89-92

Slowacki, Juliusz 1809-1849 . . . . . **NCLC 15**

Smart, Christopher
1722-1771 . . . **LC 3; DAM POET; PC 13**
See also DLB 109

Smart, Elizabeth 1913-1986 . . . . **CLC 54**
See also CA 81-84; 118; DLB 88

Smiley, Jane (Graves)
1949- . . . . **CLC 53, 76; DAM POP**
See also CA 104; CANR 30, 50;
INT CANR-30

Smith, A(rthur) J(ames) M(arshall)
1902-1980 . . . . **CLC 15; DAC**
See also CA 1-4R; 102; CANR 4; DLB 88

Smith, Adam 1723-1790 . . . . **LC 36**
See also DLB 104

Smith, Alexander 1829-1867 . . . . . **NCLC 59**
See also DLB 32, 55

Smith, Anna Deavere 1950- . . . . **CLC 86**
See also CA 133

Smith, Betty (Wehner) 1896-1972 . . . **CLC 19**
See also CA 5-8R; 33-36R; DLBY 82;
SATA 6

Smith, Charlotte (Turner)
1749-1806 . . . . **NCLC 23**
See also DLB 39, 109

Smith, Clark Ashton 1893-1961 . . . . **CLC 43**
See also CA 143

Smith, Dave . . . . **CLC 22, 42**
See also Smith, David (Jeddie)
See also CAAS 7; DLB 5

Smith, David (Jeddie) 1942-
See Smith, Dave
See also CA 49-52; CANR 1; DAM POET

Smith, Florence Margaret 1902-1971
See Smith, Stevie
See also CA 17-18; 29-32R; CANR 35;
CAP 2; DAM POET; MTCW

Smith, Iain Crichton 1928- . . . . **CLC 64**
See also CA 21-24R; DLB 40, 139

Smith, John 1580(?)-1631 . . . . **LC 9**

Smith, Johnston
See Crane, Stephen (Townley)

Smith, Joseph, Jr. 1805-1844 . . . . **NCLC 53**

Smith, Lee 1944- . . . . **CLC 25, 73**
See also CA 114; 119; CANR 46; DLB 143;
DLBY 83; INT 119

Smith, Martin
See Smith, Martin Cruz

Smith, Martin Cruz
1942- . . . . . **CLC 25; DAM MULT, POP**
See also BEST 89:4; CA 85-88; CANR 6,
23, 43; INT CANR-23; NNAL

Smith, Mary-Ann Tirone 1944- . . . . . **CLC 39**
See also CA 118; 136

Smith, Patti 1946- . . . . **CLC 12**
See also CA 93-96

Smith, Pauline (Urmson)
1882-1959 . . . . **TCLC 25**

Smith, Rosamond
See Oates, Joyce Carol

Smith, Sheila Kaye
See Kaye-Smith, Sheila

Smith, Stevie . . . . **CLC 3, 8, 25, 44; PC 12**
See also Smith, Florence Margaret
See also DLB 20

Smith, Wilbur (Addison) 1933- . . . . . **CLC 33**
See also CA 13-16R; CANR 7, 46; MTCW

Smith, William Jay 1918- . . . . **CLC 6**
See also CA 5-8R; CANR 44; DLB 5;
MAICYA; SAAS 22; SATA 2, 68

Smith, Woodrow Wilson
See Kuttner, Henry

Smolenskin, Peretz 1842-1885 . . . . **NCLC 30**

Smollett, Tobias (George) 1721-1771 . . **LC 2**
See also CDBLB 1660-1789; DLB 39, 104

Snodgrass, W(illiam) D(e Witt)
1926- . . . . **CLC 2, 6, 10, 18, 68;
DAM POET**
See also CA 1-4R; CANR 6, 36; DLB 5;
MTCW

Snow, C(harles) P(ercy)
1905-1980 . . . . . . **CLC 1, 4, 6, 9, 13, 19;
DAM NOV**
See also CA 5-8R; 101; CANR 28;
CDBLB 1945-1960; DLB 15, 77; MTCW

Snow, Frances Compton
See Adams, Henry (Brooks)

Snyder, Gary (Sherman)
1930- . . **CLC 1, 2, 5, 9, 32; DAM POET**
See also CA 17-20R; CANR 30; DLB 5, 16,
165

Snyder, Zilpha Keatley 1927- . . . . . . **CLC 17**
See also AAYA 15; CA 9-12R; CANR 38;
CLR 31; JRDA; MAICYA; SAAS 2;
SATA 1, 28, 75

Soares, Bernardo
See Pessoa, Fernando (Antonio Nogueira)

Sobh, A.
See Shamlu, Ahmad

Sobol, Joshua . . . . **CLC 60**

Soderberg, Hjalmar 1869-1941 . . . . **TCLC 39**

Sodergran, Edith (Irene)
See Soedergran, Edith (Irene)

Soedergran, Edith (Irene)
1892-1923 . . . . **TCLC 31**

Softly, Edgar
See Lovecraft, H(oward) P(hillips)

Softly, Edward
See Lovecraft, H(oward) P(hillips)

Sokolov, Raymond 1941- . . . . **CLC 7**
See also CA 85-88

Solo, Jay
See Ellison, Harlan (Jay)

Sologub, Fyodor . . . . **TCLC 9**
See also Teternikov, Fyodor Kuzmich

Solomons, Ikey Esquir
See Thackeray, William Makepeace

Solomos, Dionysios 1798-1857 . . . **NCLC 15**

Solwoska, Mara
See French, Marilyn

Solzhenitsyn, Aleksandr I(sayevich)
1918- . . . . . . **CLC 1, 2, 4, 7, 9, 10, 18, 26,
34, 78; DA; DAB; DAC; DAM MST,
NOV; WLC**
See also AITN 1; CA 69-72; CANR 40;
MTCW

Somers, Jane
See Lessing, Doris (May)

Somerville, Edith 1858-1949 . . . . . . **TCLC 51**
See also DLB 135

Somerville & Ross
See Martin, Violet Florence; Somerville,
Edith

Sommer, Scott 1951- . . . . **CLC 25**
See also CA 106

Sondheim, Stephen (Joshua)
1930- . . . . **CLC 30, 39; DAM DRAM**
See also AAYA 11; CA 103; CANR 47

Sontag, Susan
1933- . . . . **CLC 1, 2, 10, 13, 31;
DAM POP**
See also CA 17-20R; CANR 25, 51; DLB 2,
67; MTCW

Sophocles
496(?)B.C.-406(?)B.C. . . . . . **CMLC 2; DA;
DAB; DAC; DAM DRAM, MST; DC 1**
See also DLB 176

Sordello 1189-1269 . . . . **CMLC 15**

Sorel, Julia
See Drexler, Rosalyn

Sorrentino, Gilbert
1929- . . . . **CLC 3, 7, 14, 22, 40**
See also CA 77-80; CANR 14, 33; DLB 5,
173; DLBY 80; INT CANR-14

Soto, Gary
1952- . . . . **CLC 32, 80; DAM MULT;
HLC**
See also AAYA 10; CA 119; 125;
CANR 50; CLR 38; DLB 82; HW;
INT 125; JRDA; SATA 80

Steptoe, Lydia
See Barnes, Djuna

Sterchi, Beat   1949-............... **CLC 65**

Sterling, Brett
See Bradbury, Ray (Douglas); Hamilton, Edmond

Sterling, Bruce   1954-............. **CLC 72**
See also CA 119; CANR 44

Sterling, George   1869-1926....... **TCLC 20**
See also CA 117; DLB 54

Stern, Gerald   1925-.......... **CLC 40, 100**
See also CA 81-84; CANR 28; DLB 105

Stern, Richard (Gustave)   1928-... **CLC 4, 39**
See also CA 1-4R; CANR 1, 25, 52;
DLBY 87; INT CANR-25

Sternberg, Josef von   1894-1969..... **CLC 20**
See also CA 81-84

Sterne, Laurence
1713-1768 ...... **LC 2; DA; DAB; DAC;**
DAM MST, NOV; WLC
See also CDBLB 1660-1789; DLB 39

Sternheim, (William Adolf) Carl
1878-1942 .... **TCLC 8**
See also CA 105; DLB 56, 118

Stevens, Mark   1951-.............. **CLC 34**
See also CA 122

Stevens, Wallace
1879-1955 .... **TCLC 3, 12, 45; DA;**
DAB; DAC; DAM MST, POET; PC 6;
WLC
See also CA 104; 124; CDALB 1929-1941;
DLB 54; MTCW

Stevenson, Anne (Katharine)
1933-..................... **CLC 7, 33**
See also CA 17-20R; CAAS 9; CANR 9, 33;
DLB 40; MTCW

Stevenson, Robert Louis (Balfour)
1850-1894 ..... **NCLC 5, 14; DA; DAB;**
DAC; DAM MST, NOV; SSC 11; WLC
See also CDBLB 1890-1914; CLR 10, 11;
DLB 18, 57, 141, 156, 174; DLBD 13;
JRDA; MAICYA; YABC 2

Stewart, J(ohn) I(nnes) M(ackintosh)
1906-1994 .... **CLC 7, 14, 32**
See also CA 85-88; 147; CAAS 3;
CANR 47; MTCW

Stewart, Mary (Florence Elinor)
1916-..................... **CLC 7, 35; DAB**
See also CA 1-4R; CANR 1; SATA 12

Stewart, Mary Rainbow
See Stewart, Mary (Florence Elinor)

Stifle, June
See Campbell, Maria

Stifter, Adalbert   1805-1868...... **NCLC 41**
See also DLB 133

Still, James   1906-................ **CLC 49**
See also CA 65-68; CAAS 17; CANR 10,
26; DLB 9; SATA 29

Sting
See Sumner, Gordon Matthew

Stirling, Arthur
See Sinclair, Upton (Beall)

Stitt, Milan   1941-................ **CLC 29**
See also CA 69-72

Stockton, Francis Richard   1834-1902
See Stockton, Frank R.
See also CA 108; 137; MAICYA; SATA 44

Stockton, Frank R................ **TCLC 47**
See also Stockton, Francis Richard
See also DLB 42, 74; DLBD 13;
SATA-Brief 32

Stoddard, Charles
See Kuttner, Henry

Stoker, Abraham   1847-1912
See Stoker, Bram
See also CA 105; DA; DAC; DAM MST,
NOV; SATA 29

Stoker, Bram
1847-1912 .... **TCLC 8; DAB; WLC**
See also Stoker, Abraham
See also CA 150; CDBLB 1890-1914;
DLB 36, 70

Stolz, Mary (Slattery)   1920-....... **CLC 12**
See also AAYA 8; AITN 1; CA 5-8R;
CANR 13, 41; JRDA; MAICYA;
SAAS 3; SATA 10, 71

Stone, Irving
1903-1989 .... **CLC 7; DAM POP**
See also AITN 1; CA 1-4R; 129; CAAS 3;
CANR 1, 23; INT CANR-23; MTCW;
SATA 3; SATA-Obit 64

Stone, Oliver (William)   1946-...... **CLC 73**
See also AAYA 15; CA 110; CANR 55

Stone, Robert (Anthony)
1937-..................... **CLC 5, 23, 42**
See also CA 85-88; CANR 23; DLB 152;
INT CANR-23; MTCW

Stone, Zachary
See Follett, Ken(neth Martin)

Stoppard, Tom
1937-...... **CLC 1, 3, 4, 5, 8, 15, 29, 34,**
63, 91; DA; DAB; DAC; DAM DRAM,
MST; DC 6; WLC
See also CA 81-84; CANR 39;
CDBLB 1960 to Present; DLB 13;
DLBY 85; MTCW

Storey, David (Malcolm)
1933-..... **CLC 2, 4, 5, 8; DAM DRAM**
See also CA 81-84; CANR 36; DLB 13, 14;
MTCW

Storm, Hyemeyohsts
1935-................. **CLC 3; DAM MULT**
See also CA 81-84; CANR 45; NNAL

Storm, (Hans) Theodor (Woldsen)
1817-1888 .... **NCLC 1**

Storni, Alfonsina
1892-1938 ..... **TCLC 5; DAM MULT;**
HLC
See also CA 104; 131; HW

Stoughton, William   1631-1701....... **LC 38**
See also DLB 24

Stout, Rex (Todhunter)   1886-1975 ... **CLC 3**
See also AITN 2; CA 61-64

Stow, (Julian) Randolph   1935-.. **CLC 23, 48**
See also CA 13-16R; CANR 33; MTCW

Stowe, Harriet (Elizabeth) Beecher
1811-1896 ..... **NCLC 3, 50; DA; DAB;**
DAC; DAM MST, NOV; WLC
See also CDALB 1865-1917; DLB 1, 12, 42,
74; JRDA; MAICYA; YABC 1

Strachey, (Giles) Lytton
1880-1932 .... **TCLC 12**
See also CA 110; DLB 149; DLBD 10

Strand, Mark
1934-.. **CLC 6, 18, 41, 71; DAM POET**
See also CA 21-24R; CANR 40; DLB 5;
SATA 41

Straub, Peter (Francis)
1943-............ **CLC 28; DAM POP**
See also BEST 89:1; CA 85-88; CANR 28;
DLBY 84; MTCW

Strauss, Botho   1944-............... **CLC 22**
See also DLB 124

Streatfeild, (Mary) Noel
1895(?)-1986 .... **CLC 21**
See also CA 81-84; 120; CANR 31;
CLR 17; DLB 160; MAICYA; SATA 20;
SATA-Obit 48

Stribling, T(homas) S(igismund)
1881-1965 .... **CLC 23**
See also CA 107; DLB 9

Strindberg, (Johan) August
1849-1912 ...... **TCLC 1, 8, 21, 47; DA;**
DAB; DAC; DAM DRAM, MST; WLC
See also CA 104; 135

Stringer, Arthur   1874-1950....... **TCLC 37**
See also DLB 92

Stringer, David
See Roberts, Keith (John Kingston)

Strugatskii, Arkadii (Natanovich)
1925-1991 .... **CLC 27**
See also CA 106; 135

Strugatskii, Boris (Natanovich)
1933-..................... **CLC 27**
See also CA 106

Strummer, Joe   1953(?)-........... **CLC 30**

Stuart, Don A.
See Campbell, John W(ood, Jr.)

Stuart, Ian
See MacLean, Alistair (Stuart)

Stuart, Jesse (Hilton)
1906-1984 .... **CLC 1, 8, 11, 14, 34**
See also CA 5-8R; 112; CANR 31; DLB 9,
48, 102; DLBY 84; SATA 2;
SATA-Obit 36

Sturgeon, Theodore (Hamilton)
1918-1985 .... **CLC 22, 39**
See also Queen, Ellery
See also CA 81-84; 116; CANR 32; DLB 8;
DLBY 85; MTCW

Sturges, Preston   1898-1959....... **TCLC 48**
See also CA 114; 149; DLB 26

Styron, William
1925-.......... **CLC 1, 3, 5, 11, 15, 60;**
DAM NOV, POP; SSC 25
See also BEST 90:4; CA 5-8R; CANR 6, 33;
CDALB 1968-1988; DLB 2, 143;
DLBY 80; INT CANR-6; MTCW

Suarez Lynch, B.
See Bioy Casares, Adolfo; Borges, Jorge
Luis

Su Chien   1884-1918
See Su Man-shu
See also CA 123

Suckow, Ruth   1892-1960.......... **SSC 18**
See also CA 113; DLB 9, 102

Sudermann, Hermann 1857-1928 . . **TCLC 15**
See also CA 107; DLB 118

Sue, Eugene 1804-1857 . . . . **NCLC 1**
See also DLB 119

Sueskind, Patrick 1949- . . . . **CLC 44**
See also Suskind, Patrick

Sukenick, Ronald 1932- . . . . **CLC 3, 4, 6, 48**
See also CA 25-28R; CAAS 8; CANR 32;
DLB 173; DLBY 81

Suknaski, Andrew 1942- . . . . **CLC 19**
See also CA 101; DLB 53

Sullivan, Vernon
See Vian, Boris

Sully Prudhomme 1839-1907 . . . . . . **TCLC 31**

Su Man-shu . . . . **TCLC 24**
See also Su Chien

Summerforest, Ivy B.
See Kirkup, James

Summers, Andrew James 1942- . . . . . **CLC 26**

Summers, Andy
See Summers, Andrew James

Summers, Hollis (Spurgeon, Jr.)
1916- . . . . **CLC 10**
See also CA 5-8R; CANR 3; DLB 6

Summers, (Alphonsus Joseph-Mary Augustus)
Montague 1880-1948 . . . . **TCLC 16**
See also CA 118

Sumner, Gordon Matthew 1951- . . . . **CLC 26**

Surtees, Robert Smith
1803-1864 . . . . **NCLC 14**
See also DLB 21

Susann, Jacqueline 1921-1974 . . . . **CLC 3**
See also AITN 1; CA 65-68; 53-56; MTCW

Su Shih 1036-1101 . . . . **CMLC 15**

Suskind, Patrick
See Sueskind, Patrick
See also CA 145

Sutcliff, Rosemary
1920-1992 . . . . **CLC 26; DAB; DAC;**
DAM MST, POP
See also AAYA 10; CA 5-8R; 139;
CANR 37; CLR 1, 37; JRDA; MAICYA;
SATA 6, 44, 78; SATA-Obit 73

Sutro, Alfred 1863-1933 . . . . **TCLC 6**
See also CA 105; DLB 10

Sutton, Henry
See Slavitt, David R(ytman)

Svevo, Italo
1861-1928 . . . . **TCLC 2, 35; SSC 25**
See also Schmitz, Aron Hector

Swados, Elizabeth (A.) 1951- . . . . **CLC 12**
See also CA 97-100; CANR 49; INT 97-100

Swados, Harvey 1920-1972 . . . . **CLC 5**
See also CA 5-8R; 37-40R; CANR 6;
DLB 2

Swan, Gladys 1934- . . . . **CLC 69**
See also CA 101; CANR 17, 39

Swarthout, Glendon (Fred)
1918-1992 . . . . **CLC 35**
See also CA 1-4R; 139; CANR 1, 47;
SATA 26

Sweet, Sarah C.
See Jewett, (Theodora) Sarah Orne

Swenson, May
1919-1989 . . . . **CLC 4, 14, 61; DA; DAB;**
DAC; DAM MST, POET; PC 14
See also CA 5-8R; 130; CANR 36; DLB 5;
MTCW; SATA 15

Swift, Augustus
See Lovecraft, H(oward) P(hillips)

Swift, Graham (Colin) 1949- . . . . **CLC 41, 88**
See also CA 117; 122; CANR 46

Swift, Jonathan
1667-1745 . . . . . . **LC 1; DA; DAB; DAC;**
DAM MST, NOV, POET; PC 9; WLC
See also CDBLB 1660-1789; DLB 39, 95,
101; SATA 19

Swinburne, Algernon Charles
1837-1909 . . . . . . **TCLC 8, 36; DA; DAB;**
DAC; DAM MST, POET; WLC
See also CA 105; 140; CDBLB 1832-1890;
DLB 35, 57

Swinfen, Ann . . . . **CLC 34**

Swinnerton, Frank Arthur
1884-1982 . . . . **CLC 31**
See also CA 108; DLB 34

Swithen, John
See King, Stephen (Edwin)

Sylvia
See Ashton-Warner, Sylvia (Constance)

Symmes, Robert Edward
See Duncan, Robert (Edward)

Symonds, John Addington
1840-1893 . . . . **NCLC 34**
See also DLB 57, 144

Symons, Arthur 1865-1945 . . . . **TCLC 11**
See also CA 107; DLB 19, 57, 149

Symons, Julian (Gustave)
1912-1994 . . . . **CLC 2, 14, 32**
See also CA 49-52; 147; CAAS 3; CANR 3,
33; DLB 87, 155; DLBY 92; MTCW

Synge, (Edmund) J(ohn) M(illington)
1871-1909 . . . . **TCLC 6, 37;**
DAM DRAM; DC 2
See also CA 104; 141; CDBLB 1890-1914;
DLB 10, 19

Syruc, J.
See Milosz, Czeslaw

Szirtes, George 1948- . . . . **CLC 46**
See also CA 109; CANR 27

Szymborska, Wislawa 1923- . . . . **CLC 99**
See also CA 154

T. O., Nik
See Annensky, Innokenty (Fyodorovich)

Tabori, George 1914- . . . . **CLC 19**
See also CA 49-52; CANR 4

Tagore, Rabindranath
1861-1941 . . . . **TCLC 3, 53;**
DAM DRAM, POET; PC 8
See also CA 104; 120; MTCW

Taine, Hippolyte Adolphe
1828-1893 . . . . **NCLC 15**

Talese, Gay 1932- . . . . **CLC 37**
See also AITN 1; CA 1-4R; CANR 9;
INT CANR-9; MTCW

Tallent, Elizabeth (Ann) 1954- . . . . . **CLC 45**
See also CA 117; DLB 130

Tally, Ted 1952- . . . . **CLC 42**
See also CA 120; 124; INT 124

Tamayo y Baus, Manuel
1829-1898 . . . . **NCLC 1**

Tammsaare, A(nton) H(ansen)
1878-1940 . . . . **TCLC 27**

Tan, Amy (Ruth)
1952- . . . . **CLC 59; DAM MULT, NOV,**
POP
See also AAYA 9; BEST 89:3; CA 136;
CANR 54; DLB 173; SATA 75

Tandem, Felix
See Spitteler, Carl (Friedrich Georg)

Tanizaki, Jun'ichiro
1886-1965 . . . . . . **CLC 8, 14, 28; SSC 21**
See also CA 93-96; 25-28R

Tanner, William
See Amis, Kingsley (William)

Tao Lao
See Storni, Alfonsina

Tarassoff, Lev
See Troyat, Henri

Tarbell, Ida M(inerva)
1857-1944 . . . . **TCLC 40**
See also CA 122; DLB 47

Tarkington, (Newton) Booth
1869-1946 . . . . **TCLC 9**
See also CA 110; 143; DLB 9, 102;
SATA 17

Tarkovsky, Andrei (Arsenyevich)
1932-1986 . . . . **CLC 75**
See also CA 127

Tartt, Donna 1964(?)- . . . . **CLC 76**
See also CA 142

Tasso, Torquato 1544-1595 . . . . **LC 5**

Tate, (John Orley) Allen
1899-1979 . . . . **CLC 2, 4, 6, 9, 11, 14, 24**
See also CA 5-8R; 85-88; CANR 32;
DLB 4, 45, 63; MTCW

Tate, Ellalice
See Hibbert, Eleanor Alice Burford

Tate, James (Vincent) 1943- . . . **CLC 2, 6, 25**
See also CA 21-24R; CANR 29, 57; DLB 5,
169

Tavel, Ronald 1940- . . . . **CLC 6**
See also CA 21-24R; CANR 33

Taylor, C(ecil) P(hilip) 1929-1981 . . . **CLC 27**
See also CA 25-28R; 105; CANR 47

Taylor, Edward
1642(?)-1729 . . . . **LC 11; DA; DAB;**
DAC; DAM MST, POET
See also DLB 24

Taylor, Eleanor Ross 1920- . . . . **CLC 5**
See also CA 81-84

Taylor, Elizabeth 1912-1975 . . . **CLC 2, 4, 29**
See also CA 13-16R; CANR 9; DLB 139;
MTCW; SATA 13

Taylor, Henry (Splawn) 1942- . . . . . . **CLC 44**
See also CA 33-36R; CAAS 7; CANR 31;
DLB 5

Taylor, Kamala (Purnaiya) 1924-
See Markandaya, Kamala
See also CA 77-80

Tiptree, James, Jr. . . . . **CLC 48, 50**
See also Sheldon, Alice Hastings Bradley
See also DLB 8

Titmarsh, Michael Angelo
See Thackeray, William Makepeace

Tocqueville, Alexis (Charles Henri Maurice Clerel Comte) 1805-1859 . . . . . **NCLC 7**

Tolkien, J(ohn) R(onald) R(euel)
1892-1973 . . . . **CLC 1, 2, 3, 8, 12, 38;**
DA; DAB; DAC; DAM MST, NOV,
POP; WLC
See also AAYA 10; AITN 1; CA 17-18;
45-48; CANR 36; CAP 2;
CDBLB 1914-1945; DLB 15, 160; JRDA;
MAICYA; MTCW; SATA 2, 32;
SATA-Obit 24

Toller, Ernst 1893-1939 . . . . **TCLC 10**
See also CA 107; DLB 124

Tolson, M. B.
See Tolson, Melvin B(eaunorus)

Tolson, Melvin B(eaunorus)
1898(?)-1966 . . . . **CLC 36; BLC;**
DAM MULT, POET
See also BW 1; CA 124; 89-92; DLB 48, 76

Tolstoi, Aleksei Nikolaevich
See Tolstoy, Alexey Nikolaevich

Tolstoy, Alexey Nikolaevich
1882-1945 . . . . **TCLC 18**
See also CA 107

Tolstoy, Count Leo
See Tolstoy, Leo (Nikolaevich)

Tolstoy, Leo (Nikolaevich)
1828-1910 . . . . . . **TCLC 4, 11, 17, 28, 44;**
DA; DAB; DAC; DAM MST, NOV;
SSC 9; WLC
See also CA 104; 123; SATA 26

Tomasi di Lampedusa, Giuseppe 1896-1957
See Lampedusa, Giuseppe (Tomasi) di
See also CA 111

Tomlin, Lily . . . . **CLC 17**
See also Tomlin, Mary Jean

Tomlin, Mary Jean 1939(?)-
See Tomlin, Lily
See also CA 117

Tomlinson, (Alfred) Charles
1927- . . . . **CLC 2, 4, 6, 13, 45;**
DAM POET; PC 17
See also CA 5-8R; CANR 33; DLB 40

Tonson, Jacob
See Bennett, (Enoch) Arnold

Toole, John Kennedy
1937-1969 . . . . **CLC 19, 64**
See also CA 104; DLBY 81

Toomer, Jean
1894-1967 . . . . . . **CLC 1, 4, 13, 22; BLC;**
DAM MULT; PC 7; SSC 1
See also BW 1; CA 85-88;
CDALB 1917-1929; DLB 45, 51; MTCW

Torley, Luke
See Blish, James (Benjamin)

Tornimparte, Alessandra
See Ginzburg, Natalia

Torre, Raoul della
See Mencken, H(enry) L(ouis)

Torrey, E(dwin) Fuller 1937- . . . . . . **CLC 34**
See also CA 119

Torsvan, Ben Traven
See Traven, B.

Torsvan, Benno Traven
See Traven, B.

Torsvan, Berick Traven
See Traven, B.

Torsvan, Berwick Traven
See Traven, B.

Torsvan, Bruno Traven
See Traven, B.

Torsvan, Traven
See Traven, B.

Tournier, Michel (Edouard)
1924- . . . . **CLC 6, 23, 36, 95**
See also CA 49-52; CANR 3, 36; DLB 83;
MTCW; SATA 23

Tournimparte, Alessandra
See Ginzburg, Natalia

Towers, Ivar
See Kornbluth, C(yril) M.

Towne, Robert (Burton) 1936(?)- . . . . **CLC 87**
See also CA 108; DLB 44

Townsend, Sue 1946- . . **CLC 61; DAB; DAC**
See also CA 119; 127; INT 127; MTCW;
SATA 55; SATA-Brief 48

Townshend, Peter (Dennis Blandford)
1945- . . . . **CLC 17, 42**
See also CA 107

Tozzi, Federigo 1883-1920 . . . . **TCLC 31**

Traill, Catharine Parr
1802-1899 . . . . **NCLC 31**
See also DLB 99

Trakl, Georg 1887-1914 . . . . **TCLC 5**
See also CA 104

Transtroemer, Tomas (Goesta)
1931- . . . . **CLC 52, 65; DAM POET**
See also CA 117; 129; CAAS 17

Transtromer, Tomas Gosta
See Transtroemer, Tomas (Goesta)

Traven, B. (?)-1969 . . . . **CLC 8, 11**
See also CA 19-20; 25-28R; CAP 2; DLB 9,
56; MTCW

Treitel, Jonathan 1959- . . . . **CLC 70**

Tremain, Rose 1943- . . . . **CLC 42**
See also CA 97-100; CANR 44; DLB 14

Tremblay, Michel
1942- . . . . . . **CLC 29; DAC; DAM MST**
See also CA 116; 128; DLB 60; MTCW

Trevanian . . . . **CLC 29**
See also Whitaker, Rod(ney)

Trevor, Glen
See Hilton, James

Trevor, William
1928- . . . . . **CLC 7, 9, 14, 25, 71; SSC 21**
See also Cox, William Trevor
See also DLB 14, 139

Trifonov, Yuri (Valentinovich)
1925-1981 . . . . **CLC 45**
See also CA 126; 103; MTCW

Trilling, Lionel 1905-1975 . . . . **CLC 9, 11, 24**
See also CA 9-12R; 61-64; CANR 10;
DLB 28, 63; INT CANR-10; MTCW

Trimball, W. H.
See Mencken, H(enry) L(ouis)

Tristan
See Gomez de la Serna, Ramon

Tristram
See Housman, A(lfred) E(dward)

Trogdon, William (Lewis) 1939-
See Heat-Moon, William Least
See also CA 115; 119; CANR 47; INT 119

Trollope, Anthony
1815-1882 . . . . . **NCLC 6, 33; DA; DAB;**
DAC; DAM MST, NOV; WLC
See also CDBLB 1832-1890; DLB 21, 57,
159; SATA 22

Trollope, Frances 1779-1863 . . . . . **NCLC 30**
See also DLB 21, 166

Trotsky, Leon 1879-1940 . . . . **TCLC 22**
See also CA 118

Trotter (Cockburn), Catharine
1679-1749 . . . . **LC 8**
See also DLB 84

Trout, Kilgore
See Farmer, Philip Jose

Trow, George W. S. 1943- . . . . **CLC 52**
See also CA 126

Troyat, Henri 1911- . . . . **CLC 23**
See also CA 45-48; CANR 2, 33; MTCW

Trudeau, G(arretson) B(eekman) 1948-
See Trudeau, Garry B.
See also CA 81-84; CANR 31; SATA 35

Trudeau, Garry B. . . . . **CLC 12**
See also Trudeau, G(arretson) B(eekman)
See also AAYA 10; AITN 2

Truffaut, Francois 1932-1984 . . . . **CLC 20**
See also CA 81-84; 113; CANR 34

Trumbo, Dalton 1905-1976 . . . . **CLC 19**
See also CA 21-24R; 69-72; CANR 10;
DLB 26

Trumbull, John 1750-1831 . . . . . . **NCLC 30**
See also DLB 31

Trundlett, Helen B.
See Eliot, T(homas) S(tearns)

Tryon, Thomas
1926-1991 . . . . . . **CLC 3, 11; DAM POP**
See also AITN 1; CA 29-32R; 135;
CANR 32; MTCW

Tryon, Tom
See Tryon, Thomas

Ts'ao Hsueh-ch'in 1715(?)-1763 . . . . **LC 1**

Tsushima, Shuji 1909-1948
See Dazai, Osamu
See also CA 107

Tsvetaeva (Efron), Marina (Ivanovna)
1892-1941 . . . . **TCLC 7, 35; PC 14**
See also CA 104; 128; MTCW

Tuck, Lily 1938- . . . . **CLC 70**
See also CA 139

Tu Fu 712-770 . . . . **PC 9**
See also DAM MULT

Tunis, John R(oberts) 1889-1975 . . . **CLC 12**
See also CA 61-64; DLB 22, 171; JRDA;
MAICYA; SATA 37; SATA-Brief 30

Tuohy, Frank..................... **CLC 37**
See also Tuohy, John Francis
See also DLB 14, 139

Tuohy, John Francis 1925-
See Tuohy, Frank
See also CA 5-8R; CANR 3, 47

Turco, Lewis (Putnam) 1934- ... **CLC 11, 63**
See also CA 13-16R; CAAS 22; CANR 24,
51; DLBY 84

Turgenev, Ivan
1818-1883 .... **NCLC 21; DA; DAB;
DAC; DAM MST, NOV; DC 7; SSC 7;
WLC**

Turgot, Anne-Robert-Jacques
1727-1781 .... **LC 26**

Turner, Frederick 1943-.......... **CLC 48**
See also CA 73-76; CAAS 10; CANR 12,
30, 56; DLB 40

Tutu, Desmond M(pilo)
1931- ..... **CLC 80; BLC; DAM MULT**
See also BW 1; CA 125

Tutuola, Amos
1920- .... **CLC 5, 14, 29; BLC;
DAM MULT**
See also BW 2; CA 9-12R; CANR 27;
DLB 125; MTCW

Twain, Mark
.... **TCLC 6, 12, 19, 36, 48, 59; SSC 6;
WLC**
See also Clemens, Samuel Langhorne
See also AAYA 20; DLB 11, 12, 23, 64, 74

Tyler, Anne
1941-........ **CLC 7, 11, 18, 28, 44, 59;
DAM NOV, POP**
See also AAYA 18; BEST 89:1; CA 9-12R;
CANR 11, 33, 53; DLB 6, 143; DLBY 82;
MTCW; SATA 7, 90

Tyler, Royall 1757-1826.......... **NCLC 3**
See also DLB 37

Tynan, Katharine 1861-1931 .... **TCLC 3**
See also CA 104; DLB 153

Tyutchev, Fyodor 1803-1873 ..... **NCLC 34**

Tzara, Tristan
1896-1963 .... **CLC 47; DAM POET**
See also Rosenfeld, Samuel; Rosenstock,
Sami; Rosenstock, Samuel
See also CA 153

Uhry, Alfred
1936- ..... **CLC 55; DAM DRAM, POP**
See also CA 127; 133; INT 133

Ulf, Haerved
See Strindberg, (Johan) August

Ulf, Harved
See Strindberg, (Johan) August

Ulibarri, Sabine R(eyes)
1919- .... **CLC 83; DAM MULT**
See also CA 131; DLB 82; HW

Unamuno (y Jugo), Miguel de
1864-1936 ... **TCLC 2, 9; DAM MULT,
NOV; HLC; SSC 11**
See also CA 104; 131; DLB 108; HW;
MTCW

Undercliffe, Errol
See Campbell, (John) Ramsey

Underwood, Miles
See Glassco, John

Undset, Sigrid
1882-1949 .... **TCLC 3; DA; DAB;
DAC; DAM MST, NOV; WLC**
See also CA 104; 129; MTCW

Ungaretti, Giuseppe
1888-1970 .... **CLC 7, 11, 15**
See also CA 19-20; 25-28R; CAP 2;
DLB 114

Unger, Douglas 1952-............. **CLC 34**
See also CA 130

Unsworth, Barry (Forster) 1930-.... **CLC 76**
See also CA 25-28R; CANR 30, 54

Updike, John (Hoyer)
1932- ...... **CLC 1, 2, 3, 5, 7, 9, 13, 15,
23, 34, 43, 70; DA; DAB; DAC;
DAM MST, NOV, POET, POP;
SSC 13; WLC**
See also CA 1-4R; CABS 1; CANR 4, 33,
51; CDALB 1968-1988; DLB 2, 5, 143;
DLBD 3; DLBY 80, 82; MTCW

Upshaw, Margaret Mitchell
See Mitchell, Margaret (Munnerlyn)

Upton, Mark
See Sanders, Lawrence

Urdang, Constance (Henriette)
1922- .... **CLC 47**
See also CA 21-24R; CANR 9, 24

Uriel, Henry
See Faust, Frederick (Schiller)

Uris, Leon (Marcus)
1924- .... **CLC 7, 32; DAM NOV, POP**
See also AITN 1, 2; BEST 89:2; CA 1-4R;
CANR 1, 40; MTCW; SATA 49

Urmuz
See Codrescu, Andrei

Urquhart, Jane 1949-........ **CLC 90; DAC**
See also CA 113; CANR 32

Ustinov, Peter (Alexander) 1921- .... **CLC 1**
See also AITN 1; CA 13-16R; CANR 25,
51; DLB 13

Vaculik, Ludvik 1926- .... **CLC 7**
See also CA 53-56

Valdez, Luis (Miguel)
1940- ..... **CLC 84; DAM MULT; HLC**
See also CA 101; CANR 32; DLB 122; HW

Valenzuela, Luisa
1938- ... **CLC 31; DAM MULT; SSC 14**
See also CA 101; CANR 32; DLB 113; HW

Valera y Alcala-Galiano, Juan
1824-1905 .... **TCLC 10**
See also CA 106

Valery, (Ambroise) Paul (Toussaint Jules)
1871-1945 .... **TCLC 4, 15;
DAM POET; PC 9**
See also CA 104; 122; MTCW

Valle-Inclan, Ramon (Maria) del
1866-1936 ..... **TCLC 5; DAM MULT;
HLC**
See also CA 106; 153; DLB 134

Vallejo, Antonio Buero
See Buero Vallejo, Antonio

Vallejo, Cesar (Abraham)
1892-1938 .... **TCLC 3, 56;
DAM MULT; HLC**
See also CA 105; 153; HW

Vallette, Marguerite Eymery
See Rachilde

Valle Y Pena, Ramon del
See Valle-Inclan, Ramon (Maria) del

Van Ash, Cay 1918-.............. **CLC 34**

Vanbrugh, Sir John
1664-1726 .... **LC 21; DAM DRAM**
See also DLB 80

Van Campen, Karl
See Campbell, John W(ood, Jr.)

Vance, Gerald
See Silverberg, Robert

Vance, Jack...................... **CLC 35**
See also Vance, John Holbrook
See also DLB 8

Vance, John Holbrook 1916-
See Queen, Ellery; Vance, Jack
See also CA 29-32R; CANR 17; MTCW

**Van Den Bogarde, Derek Jules Gaspard Ulric
Niven** 1921-
See Bogarde, Dirk
See also CA 77-80

Vandenburgh, Jane .... **CLC 59**

Vanderhaeghe, Guy 1951- .... **CLC 41**
See also CA 113

van der Post, Laurens (Jan)
1906-1996 .... **CLC 5**
See also CA 5-8R; 155; CANR 35

van de Wetering, Janwillem 1931- .. **CLC 47**
See also CA 49-52; CANR 4

Van Dine, S. S. .... **TCLC 23**
See also Wright, Willard Huntington

Van Doren, Carl (Clinton)
1885-1950 .... **TCLC 18**
See also CA 111

Van Doren, Mark 1894-1972..... **CLC 6, 10**
See also CA 1-4R; 37-40R; CANR 3;
DLB 45; MTCW

Van Druten, John (William)
1901-1957 .... **TCLC 2**
See also CA 104; DLB 10

Van Duyn, Mona (Jane)
1921- .... **CLC 3, 7, 63; DAM POET**
See also CA 9-12R; CANR 7, 38; DLB 5

Van Dyne, Edith
See Baum, L(yman) Frank

van Itallie, Jean-Claude 1936-....... **CLC 3**
See also CA 45-48; CAAS 2; CANR 1, 48;
DLB 7

van Ostaijen, Paul 1896-1928 ..... **TCLC 33**

Van Peebles, Melvin
1932- .... **CLC 2, 20; DAM MULT**
See also BW 2; CA 85-88; CANR 27

Vansittart, Peter 1920-............. **CLC 42**
See also CA 1-4R; CANR 3, 49

Van Vechten, Carl 1880-1964 ...... **CLC 33**
See also CA 89-92; DLB 4, 9, 51

Van Vogt, A(lfred) E(lton) 1912-..... **CLC 1**
See also CA 21-24R; CANR 28; DLB 8;
SATA 14

Varda, Agnes 1928- .... **CLC 16**
See also CA 116; 122

Wakoski, Diane
1937- . . . . CLC 2, 4, 7, 9, 11, 40;
DAM POET; PC 15
See also CA 13-16R; CAAS 1; CANR 9;
DLB 5; INT CANR-9

Wakoski-Sherbell, Diane
See Wakoski, Diane

Walcott, Derek (Alton)
1930- . . . . CLC 2, 4, 9, 14, 25, 42, 67, 76;
**BLC; DAB; DAC; DAM MST, MULT,
POET; DC 7**
See also BW 2; CA 89-92; CANR 26, 47;
DLB 117; DLBY 81; MTCW

Waldman, Anne 1945- . . . . CLC 7
See also CA 37-40R; CAAS 17; CANR 34;
DLB 16

Waldo, E. Hunter
See Sturgeon, Theodore (Hamilton)

Waldo, Edward Hamilton
See Sturgeon, Theodore (Hamilton)

Walker, Alice (Malsenior)
1944- . . . . CLC 5, 6, 9, 19, 27, 46, 58;
**BLC; DA; DAB; DAC; DAM MST,
MULT, NOV, POET, POP; SSC 5**
See also AAYA 3; BEST 89:4; BW 2;
CA 37-40R; CANR 9, 27, 49;
CDALB 1968-1988; DLB 6, 33, 143;
INT CANR-27; MTCW; SATA 31

Walker, David Harry 1911-1992. . . . CLC 14
See also CA 1-4R; 137; CANR 1; SATA 8;
SATA-Obit 71

Walker, Edward Joseph 1934-
See Walker, Ted
See also CA 21-24R; CANR 12, 28, 53

Walker, George F.
1947- . . . . CLC 44, 61; DAB; DAC;
DAM MST
See also CA 103; CANR 21, 43; DLB 60

Walker, Joseph A.
1935- . . . . CLC 19; DAM DRAM, MST
See also BW 1; CA 89-92; CANR 26;
DLB 38

Walker, Margaret (Abigail)
1915- . . . CLC 1, 6; BLC; DAM MULT
See also BW 2; CA 73-76; CANR 26, 54;
DLB 76, 152; MTCW

Walker, Ted . . . . CLC 13
See also Walker, Edward Joseph
See also DLB 40

Wallace, David Foster 1962- . . . . CLC 50
See also CA 132

Wallace, Dexter
See Masters, Edgar Lee

Wallace, (Richard Horatio) Edgar
1875-1932 . . . . TCLC 57
See also CA 115; DLB 70

Wallace, Irving
1916-1990 . . . . . CLC 7, 13; DAM NOV,
POP
See also AITN 1; CA 1-4R; 132; CAAS 1;
CANR 1, 27; INT CANR-27; MTCW

Wallant, Edward Lewis
1926-1962 . . . . CLC 5, 10
See also CA 1-4R; CANR 22; DLB 2, 28,
143; MTCW

Walley, Byron
See Card, Orson Scott

Walpole, Horace 1717-1797 . . . . LC 2
See also DLB 39, 104

Walpole, Hugh (Seymour)
1884-1941 . . . . TCLC 5
See also CA 104; DLB 34

Walser, Martin 1927- . . . . CLC 27
See also CA 57-60; CANR 8, 46; DLB 75,
124

Walser, Robert
1878-1956 . . . . TCLC 18; SSC 20
See also CA 118; DLB 66

Walsh, Jill Paton . . . . CLC 35
See also Paton Walsh, Gillian
See also AAYA 11; CLR 2; DLB 161;
SAAS 3

Walter, Villiam Christian
See Andersen, Hans Christian

Wambaugh, Joseph (Aloysius, Jr.)
1937- . . . . CLC 3, 18; DAM NOV, POP
See also AITN 1; BEST 89:3; CA 33-36R;
CANR 42; DLB 6; DLBY 83; MTCW

Ward, Arthur Henry Sarsfield 1883-1959
See Rohmer, Sax
See also CA 108

Ward, Douglas Turner 1930- . . . . . . CLC 19
See also BW 1; CA 81-84; CANR 27;
DLB 7, 38

Ward, Mary Augusta
See Ward, Mrs. Humphry

Ward, Mrs. Humphry
1851-1920 . . . . TCLC 55
See also DLB 18

Ward, Peter
See Faust, Frederick (Schiller)

Warhol, Andy 1928(?)-1987 . . . . CLC 20
See also AAYA 12; BEST 89:4; CA 89-92;
121; CANR 34

Warner, Francis (Robert le Plastrier)
1937- . . . . CLC 14
See also CA 53-56; CANR 11

Warner, Marina 1946- . . . . CLC 59
See also CA 65-68; CANR 21, 55

Warner, Rex (Ernest) 1905-1986. . . . CLC 45
See also CA 89-92; 119; DLB 15

Warner, Susan (Bogert)
1819-1885 . . . . NCLC 31
See also DLB 3, 42

Warner, Sylvia (Constance) Ashton
See Ashton-Warner, Sylvia (Constance)

Warner, Sylvia Townsend
1893-1978 . . . . CLC 7, 19; SSC 23
See also CA 61-64; 77-80; CANR 16;
DLB 34, 139; MTCW

Warren, Mercy Otis 1728-1814. . . NCLC 13
See also DLB 31

Warren, Robert Penn
1905-1989 . . . . CLC 1, 4, 6, 8, 10, 13, 18,
39, 53, 59; DA; DAB; DAC; DAM MST,
NOV, POET; SSC 4; WLC
See also AITN 1; CA 13-16R; 129;
CANR 10, 47; CDALB 1968-1988;
DLB 2, 48, 152; DLBY 80, 89;
INT CANR-10; MTCW; SATA 46;
SATA-Obit 63

Warshofsky, Isaac
See Singer, Isaac Bashevis

Warton, Thomas
1728-1790 . . . . LC 15; DAM POET
See also DLB 104, 109

Waruk, Kona
See Harris, (Theodore) Wilson

Warung, Price 1855-1911. . . . . TCLC 45

Warwick, Jarvis
See Garner, Hugh

Washington, Alex
See Harris, Mark

Washington, Booker T(aliaferro)
1856-1915 . . . . TCLC 10; BLC;
DAM MULT
See also BW 1; CA 114; 125; SATA 28

Washington, George 1732-1799 . . . . . . LC 25
See also DLB 31

Wassermann, (Karl) Jakob
1873-1934 . . . . TCLC 6
See also CA 104; DLB 66

Wasserstein, Wendy
1950- . . . . CLC 32, 59, 90;
DAM DRAM; DC 4
See also CA 121; 129; CABS 3; CANR 53;
INT 129

Waterhouse, Keith (Spencer)
1929- . . . . CLC 47
See also CA 5-8R; CANR 38; DLB 13, 15;
MTCW

Waters, Frank (Joseph)
1902-1995 . . . . CLC 88
See also CA 5-8R; 149; CAAS 13; CANR 3,
18; DLBY 86

Waters, Roger 1944- . . . . CLC 35

Watkins, Frances Ellen
See Harper, Frances Ellen Watkins

Watkins, Gerrold
See Malzberg, Barry N(athaniel)

Watkins, Gloria 1955(?)-
See hooks, bell
See also BW 2; CA 143

Watkins, Paul 1964- . . . . CLC 55
See also CA 132

Watkins, Vernon Phillips
1906-1967 . . . . CLC 43
See also CA 9-10; 25-28R; CAP 1; DLB 20

Watson, Irving S.
See Mencken, H(enry) L(ouis)

Watson, John H.
See Farmer, Philip Jose

Watson, Richard F.
See Silverberg, Robert

Waugh, Auberon (Alexander) 1939- . . CLC 7
See also CA 45-48; CANR 6, 22; DLB 14

Wharton, James
    See Mencken, H(enry) L(ouis)

Wharton, William (a pseudonym)
    .... **CLC 18, 37**
    See also CA 93-96; DLBY 80; INT 93-96

Wheatley (Peters), Phillis
    1754(?)-1784 .... **LC 3; BLC; DA; DAC;**
        DAM MST, MULT, POET; PC 3; WLC
    See also CDALB 1640-1865; DLB 31, 50

Wheelock, John Hall 1886-1978 .... **CLC 14**
    See also CA 13-16R; 77-80; CANR 14;
    DLB 45

White, E(lwyn) B(rooks)
    1899-1985 .. **CLC 10, 34, 39; DAM POP**
    See also AITN 2; CA 13-16R; 116;
    CANR 16, 37; CLR 1, 21; DLB 11, 22;
    MAICYA; MTCW; SATA 2, 29;
    SATA-Obit 44

White, Edmund (Valentine III)
    1940- .... **CLC 27; DAM POP**
    See also AAYA 7; CA 45-48; CANR 3, 19,
    36; MTCW

White, Patrick (Victor Martindale)
    1912-1990 .. **CLC 3, 4, 5, 7, 9, 18, 65, 69**
    See also CA 81-84; 132; CANR 43; MTCW

White, Phyllis Dorothy James 1920-
    See James, P. D.
    See also CA 21-24R; CANR 17, 43;
    DAM POP; MTCW

White, T(erence) H(anbury)
    1906-1964 .... **CLC 30**
    See also CA 73-76; CANR 37; DLB 160;
    JRDA; MAICYA; SATA 12

White, Terence de Vere
    1912-1994 .... **CLC 49**
    See also CA 49-52; 145; CANR 3

White, Walter F(rancis)
    1893-1955 .... **TCLC 15**
    See also White, Walter
    See also BW 1; CA 115; 124; DLB 51

White, William Hale 1831-1913
    See Rutherford, Mark
    See also CA 121

Whitehead, E(dward) A(nthony)
    1933- .... **CLC 5**
    See also CA 65-68

Whitemore, Hugh (John) 1936- ..... **CLC 37**
    See also CA 132; INT 132

Whitman, Sarah Helen (Power)
    1803-1878 .... **NCLC 19**
    See also DLB 1

Whitman, Walt(er)
    1819-1892 ..... **NCLC 4, 31; DA; DAB;**
        DAC; DAM MST, POET; PC 3; WLC
    See also CDALB 1640-1865; DLB 3, 64;
    SATA 20

Whitney, Phyllis A(yame)
    1903- .... **CLC 42; DAM POP**
    See also AITN 2; BEST 90:3; CA 1-4R;
    CANR 3, 25, 38; JRDA; MAICYA;
    SATA 1, 30

Whittemore, (Edward) Reed (Jr.)
    1919- .... **CLC 4**
    See also CA 9-12R; CAAS 8; CANR 4;
    DLB 5

Whittier, John Greenleaf
    1807-1892 .... **NCLC 8, 59**
    See also DLB 1

Whittlebot, Hernia
    See Coward, Noel (Peirce)

Wicker, Thomas Grey 1926-
    See Wicker, Tom
    See also CA 65-68; CANR 21, 46

Wicker, Tom .... **CLC 7**
    See also Wicker, Thomas Grey

Wideman, John Edgar
    1941- .... **CLC 5, 34, 36, 67; BLC;**
        DAM MULT
    See also BW 2; CA 85-88; CANR 14, 42;
    DLB 33, 143

Wiebe, Rudy (Henry)
    1934- .... **CLC 6, 11, 14; DAC;**
        DAM MST
    See also CA 37-40R; CANR 42; DLB 60

Wieland, Christoph Martin
    1733-1813 .... **NCLC 17**
    See also DLB 97

Wiene, Robert 1881-1938 .... **TCLC 56**

Wieners, John 1934- .... **CLC 7**
    See also CA 13-16R; DLB 16

Wiesel, Elie(zer)
    1928- ...... **CLC 3, 5, 11, 37; DA; DAB;**
        DAC; DAM MST, NOV
    See also AAYA 7; AITN 1; CA 5-8R;
    CAAS 4; CANR 8, 40; DLB 83;
    DLBY 87; INT CANR-8; MTCW;
    SATA 56

Wiggins, Marianne 1947- .... **CLC 57**
    See also BEST 89:3; CA 130

Wight, James Alfred 1916-
    See Herriot, James
    See also CA 77-80; SATA 55;
    SATA-Brief 44

Wilbur, Richard (Purdy)
    1921- ... **CLC 3, 6, 9, 14, 53; DA; DAB;**
        DAC; DAM MST, POET
    See also CA 1-4R; CABS 2; CANR 2, 29;
    DLB 5, 169; INT CANR-29; MTCW;
    SATA 9

Wild, Peter 1940- .... **CLC 14**
    See also CA 37-40R; DLB 5

Wilde, Oscar (Fingal O'Flahertie Wills)
    1854(?)-1900 .... **TCLC 1, 8, 23, 41; DA;**
        DAB; DAC; DAM DRAM, MST, NOV;
        SSC 11; WLC
    See also CA 104; 119; CDBLB 1890-1914;
    DLB 10, 19, 34, 57, 141, 156; SATA 24

Wilder, Billy .... **CLC 20**
    See also Wilder, Samuel
    See also DLB 26

Wilder, Samuel 1906-
    See Wilder, Billy
    See also CA 89-92

Wilder, Thornton (Niven)
    1897-1975 ...... **CLC 1, 5, 6, 10, 15, 35,**
        82; DA; DAB; DAC; DAM DRAM,
        MST, NOV; DC 1; WLC
    See also AITN 2; CA 13-16R; 61-64;
    CANR 40; DLB 4, 7, 9; MTCW

Wilding, Michael 1942- .... **CLC 73**
    See also CA 104; CANR 24, 49

Wiley, Richard 1944- .... **CLC 44**
    See also CA 121; 129

Wilhelm, Kate .... **CLC 7**
    See also Wilhelm, Katie Gertrude
    See also AAYA 20; CAAS 5; DLB 8;
    INT CANR-17

Wilhelm, Katie Gertrude 1928-
    See Wilhelm, Kate
    See also CA 37-40R; CANR 17, 36; MTCW

Wilkins, Mary
    See Freeman, Mary Eleanor Wilkins

Willard, Nancy 1936- .... **CLC 7, 37**
    See also CA 89-92; CANR 10, 39; CLR 5;
    DLB 5, 52; MAICYA; MTCW;
    SATA 37, 71; SATA-Brief 30

Williams, C(harles) K(enneth)
    1936- .... **CLC 33, 56; DAM POET**
    See also CA 37-40R; CAAS 26; CANR 57;
    DLB 5

Williams, Charles
    See Collier, James L(incoln)

Williams, Charles (Walter Stansby)
    1886-1945 .... **TCLC 1, 11**
    See also CA 104; DLB 100, 153

Williams, (George) Emlyn
    1905-1987 ...... **CLC 15; DAM DRAM**
    See also CA 104; 123; CANR 36; DLB 10,
    77; MTCW

Williams, Hugo 1942- .... **CLC 42**
    See also CA 17-20R; CANR 45; DLB 40

Williams, J. Walker
    See Wodehouse, P(elham) G(renville)

Williams, John A(lfred)
    1925- ... **CLC 5, 13; BLC; DAM MULT**
    See also BW 2; CA 53-56; CAAS 3;
    CANR 6, 26, 51; DLB 2, 33;
    INT CANR-6

Williams, Jonathan (Chamberlain)
    1929- .... **CLC 13**
    See also CA 9-12R; CAAS 12; CANR 8;
    DLB 5

Williams, Joy 1944- .... **CLC 31**
    See also CA 41-44R; CANR 22, 48

Williams, Norman 1952- .... **CLC 39**
    See also CA 118

Williams, Sherley Anne
    1944- ..... **CLC 89; BLC; DAM MULT,**
        POET
    See also BW 2; CA 73-76; CANR 25;
    DLB 41; INT CANR-25; SATA 78

Williams, Shirley
    See Williams, Sherley Anne

Williams, Tennessee
    1911-1983 ..... **CLC 1, 2, 5, 7, 8, 11, 15,**
        19, 30, 39, 45, 71; DA; DAB; DAC;
        DAM DRAM, MST; DC 4; WLC
    See also AITN 1, 2; CA 5-8R; 108;
    CABS 3; CANR 31; CDALB 1941-1968;
    DLB 7; DLBD 4; DLBY 83; MTCW

Williams, Thomas (Alonzo)
    1926-1990 .... **CLC 14**
    See also CA 1-4R; 132; CANR 2

Williams, William C.
    See Williams, William Carlos

Wouk, Herman
    1915- .. CLC 1, 9, 38; DAM NOV, POP
    See also CA 5-8R; CANR 6, 33; DLBY 82;
    INT CANR-6; MTCW

Wright, Charles (Penzel, Jr.)
    1935- .... CLC 6, 13, 28
    See also CA 29-32R; CAAS 7; CANR 23,
    36; DLB 165; DLBY 82; MTCW

Wright, Charles Stevenson
    1932- .... CLC 49; BLC 3;
                    DAM MULT, POET
    See also BW 1; CA 9-12R; CANR 26;
    DLB 33

Wright, Jack R.
    See Harris, Mark

Wright, James (Arlington)
    1927-1980 .... CLC 3, 5, 10, 28;
                    DAM POET
    See also AITN 2; CA 49-52; 97-100;
    CANR 4, 34; DLB 5, 169; MTCW

Wright, Judith (Arandell)
    1915- .... CLC 11, 53; PC 14
    See also CA 13-16R; CANR 31; MTCW;
    SATA 14

Wright, L(aurali) R. 1939-........ CLC 44
    See also CA 138

Wright, Richard (Nathaniel)
    1908-1960 .... CLC 1, 3, 4, 9, 14, 21, 48,
    74; BLC; DA; DAB; DAC; DAM MST,
    MULT, NOV; SSC 2; WLC
    See also AAYA 5; BW 1; CA 108;
    CDALB 1929-1941; DLB 76, 102;
    DLBD 2; MTCW

Wright, Richard B(ruce) 1937- ...... CLC 6
    See also CA 85-88; DLB 53

Wright, Rick 1945-............... CLC 35

Wright, Rowland
    See Wells, Carolyn

Wright, Stephen Caldwell 1946- .... CLC 33
    See also BW 2

Wright, Willard Huntington 1888-1939
    See Van Dine, S. S.
    See also CA 115

Wright, William 1930-........... CLC 44
    See also CA 53-56; CANR 7, 23

Wroth, LadyMary 1587-1653(?) ..... LC 30
    See also DLB 121

Wu Ch'eng-en 1500(?)-1582(?)........ LC 7

Wu Ching-tzu 1701-1754 .... LC 2

Wurlitzer, Rudolph 1938(?)- ... CLC 2, 4, 15
    See also CA 85-88; DLB 173

Wycherley, William
    1641-1715 ..... LC 8, 21; DAM DRAM
    See also CDBLB 1660-1789; DLB 80

Wylie, Elinor (Morton Hoyt)
    1885-1928 .... TCLC 8
    See also CA 105; DLB 9, 45

Wylie, Philip (Gordon) 1902-1971... CLC 43
    See also CA 21-22; 33-36R; CAP 2; DLB 9

Wyndham, John.................. CLC 19
    See also Harris, John (Wyndham Parkes
    Lucas) Beynon

Wyss, Johann David Von
    1743-1818 .... NCLC 10
    See also JRDA; MAICYA; SATA 29;
    SATA-Brief 27

Xenophon
    c. 430B.C.-c. 354B.C........ CMLC 17
    See also DLB 176

Yakumo Koizumi
    See Hearn, (Patricio) Lafcadio (Tessima
    Carlos)

Yanez, Jose Donoso
    See Donoso (Yanez), Jose

Yanovsky, Basile S.
    See Yanovsky, V(assily) S(emenovich)

Yanovsky, V(assily) S(emenovich)
    1906-1989 .... CLC 2, 18
    See also CA 97-100; 129

Yates, Richard 1926-1992 ..... CLC 7, 8, 23
    See also CA 5-8R; 139; CANR 10, 43;
    DLB 2; DLBY 81, 92; INT CANR-10

Yeats, W. B.
    See Yeats, William Butler

Yeats, William Butler
    1865-1939 ..... TCLC 1, 11, 18, 31; DA;
    DAB; DAC; DAM DRAM, MST,
                    POET; WLC
    See also CA 104; 127; CANR 45;
    CDBLB 1890-1914; DLB 10, 19, 98, 156;
    MTCW

Yehoshua, A(braham) B.
    1936-................... CLC 13, 31
    See also CA 33-36R; CANR 43

Yep, Laurence Michael 1948-...... CLC 35
    See also AAYA 5; CA 49-52; CANR 1, 46;
    CLR 3, 17; DLB 52; JRDA; MAICYA;
    SATA 7, 69

Yerby, Frank G(arvin)
    1916-1991 .... CLC 1, 7, 22; BLC;
                    DAM MULT
    See also BW 1; CA 9-12R; 136; CANR 16,
    52; DLB 76; INT CANR-16; MTCW

Yesenin, Sergei Alexandrovich
    See Esenin, Sergei (Alexandrovich)

Yevtushenko, Yevgeny (Alexandrovich)
    1933- .... CLC 1, 3, 13, 26, 51;
                    DAM POET
    See also CA 81-84; CANR 33, 54; MTCW

Yezierska, Anzia 1885(?)-1970 ..... CLC 46
    See also CA 126; 89-92; DLB 28; MTCW

Yglesias, Helen 1915-........... CLC 7, 22
    See also CA 37-40R; CAAS 20; CANR 15;
    INT CANR-15; MTCW

Yokomitsu Riichi 1898-1947 ...... TCLC 47

Yonge, Charlotte (Mary)
    1823-1901 .... TCLC 48
    See also CA 109; DLB 18, 163; SATA 17

York, Jeremy
    See Creasey, John

York, Simon
    See Heinlein, Robert A(nson)

Yorke, Henry Vincent 1905-1974 ... CLC 13
    See also Green, Henry
    See also CA 85-88; 49-52

Yosano Akiko 1878-1942 .. TCLC 59; PC 11

Yoshimoto, Banana .... CLC 84
    See also Yoshimoto, Mahoko

Yoshimoto, Mahoko 1964-
    See Yoshimoto, Banana
    See also CA 144

Young, Al(bert James)
    1939- ..... CLC 19; BLC; DAM MULT
    See also BW 2; CA 29-32R; CANR 26;
    DLB 33

Young, Andrew (John) 1885-1971.... CLC 5
    See also CA 5-8R; CANR 7, 29

Young, Collier
    See Bloch, Robert (Albert)

Young, Edward 1683-1765.......... LC 3
    See also DLB 95

Young, Marguerite (Vivian)
    1909-1995 .... CLC 82
    See also CA 13-16; 150; CAP 1

Young, Neil 1945-................ CLC 17
    See also CA 110

Young Bear, Ray A.
    1950- .... CLC 94; DAM MULT
    See also CA 146; DLB 175; NNAL

Yourcenar, Marguerite
    1903-1987 .... CLC 19, 38, 50, 87;
                    DAM NOV
    See also CA 69-72; CANR 23; DLB 72;
    DLBY 88; MTCW

Yurick, Sol 1925-................ CLC 6
    See also CA 13-16R; CANR 25

Zabolotskii, Nikolai Alekseevich
    1903-1958 .... TCLC 52
    See also CA 116

Zamiatin, Yevgenii
    See Zamyatin, Evgeny Ivanovich

Zamora, Bernice (B. Ortiz)
    1938- ..... CLC 89; DAM MULT; HLC
    See also CA 151; DLB 82; HW

Zamyatin, Evgeny Ivanovich
    1884-1937 .... TCLC 8, 37
    See also CA 105

Zangwill, Israel 1864-1926........ TCLC 16
    See also CA 109; DLB 10, 135

Zappa, Francis Vincent, Jr. 1940-1993
    See Zappa, Frank
    See also CA 108; 143; CANR 57

Zappa, Frank.................... CLC 17
    See also Zappa, Francis Vincent, Jr.

Zaturenska, Marya 1902-1982.... CLC 6, 11
    See also CA 13-16R; 105; CANR 22

Zeami 1363-1443.................. DC 7

Zelazny, Roger (Joseph)
    1937-1995 .... CLC 21
    See also AAYA 7; CA 21-24R; 148;
    CANR 26; DLB 8; MTCW; SATA 57;
    SATA-Brief 39

Zhdanov, Andrei A(lexandrovich)
    1896-1948 .... TCLC 18
    See also CA 117

Zhukovsky, Vasily 1783-1852 .... NCLC 35

Ziegenhagen, Eric .... CLC 55

Zimmer, Jill Schary
    See Robinson, Jill

Zimmerman, Robert
See Dylan, Bob

Zindel, Paul
1936- . . . . . **CLC 6, 26; DA; DAB; DAC;**
DAM DRAM, MST, NOV; DC 5
See also AAYA 2; CA 73-76; CANR 31;
CLR 3, 45; DLB 7, 52; JRDA; MAICYA;
MTCW; SATA 16, 58

Zinov'Ev, A. A.
See Zinoviev, Alexander (Aleksandrovich)

Zinoviev, Alexander (Aleksandrovich)
1922- . . . . **CLC 19**
See also CA 116; 133; CAAS 10

Zoilus
See Lovecraft, H(oward) P(hillips)

Zola, Emile (Edouard Charles Antoine)
1840-1902 . . . . . . **TCLC 1, 6, 21, 41; DA;**
DAB; DAC; DAM MST, NOV; WLC
See also CA 104; 138; DLB 123

Zoline, Pamela 1941- . . . . **CLC 62**

Zorrilla y Moral, Jose 1817-1893 . . **NCLC 6**

Zoshchenko, Mikhail (Mikhailovich)
1895-1958 . . . . **TCLC 15; SSC 15**
See also CA 115

Zuckmayer, Carl 1896-1977 . . . . **CLC 18**
See also CA 69-72; DLB 56, 124

Zuk, Georges
See Skelton, Robin

Zukofsky, Louis
1904-1978 . . . . . . **CLC 1, 2, 4, 7, 11, 18;**
DAM POET; PC 11
See also CA 9-12R; 77-80; CANR 39;
DLB 5, 165; MTCW

Zweig, Paul 1935-1984 . . . . **CLC 34, 42**
See also CA 85-88; 113

Zweig, Stefan 1881-1942 . . . . **TCLC 17**
See also CA 112; DLB 81, 118

Zwingli, Huldreich 1484-1531 . . . . . . **LC 37**

Literary Criticism Series
Cumulative Topic Index

This index lists all topic entries in Gale's *Classical and Medieval Literature Criticism, Contemporary Literary Criticism, Literature Criticism from 1400 to 1800, Nineteenth-Century Literature Criticism,* and *Twentieth-Century Literary Criticism.*

Age of Johnson LC 15: 1-87
  Johnson's London, 3-15
  aesthetics of neoclassicism, 15-36
  "age of prose and reason," 36-45
  clubmen and bluestockings, 45-56
  printing technology, 56-62
  periodicals: "a map of busy life," 62-74
  transition, 74-86

AIDS in Literature CLC 81: 365-416

American Abolitionism NCLC 44: 1-73
  overviews, 2-26
  abolitionist ideals, 26-46
  the literature of abolitionism, 46-72

American Black Humor Fiction TCLC 54: 1-85
  characteristics of black humor, 2-13
  origins and development, 13-38
  black humor distinguished from related literary trends, 38-60
  black humor and society, 60-75
  black humor reconsidered, 75-83

American Civil War in Literature NCLC 32: 1-109
  overviews, 2-20
  regional perspectives, 20-54
  fiction popular during the war, 54-79
  the historical novel, 79-108

American Frontier in Literature NCLC 28: 1-103
  definitions, 2-12
  development, 12-17
  nonfiction writing about the frontier, 17-30
  frontier fiction, 30-45
  frontier protagonists, 45-66
  portrayals of Native Americans, 66-86
  feminist readings, 86-98

twentieth-century reaction against frontier literature, 98-100

American Humor Writing NCLC 52: 1-59
  overviews, 2-12
  the Old Southwest, 12-42
  broader impacts, 42-5
  women humorists, 45-58

American Popular Song, Golden Age of TCLC 42: 1-49
  background and major figures, 2-34
  the lyrics of popular songs, 34-47

American Proletarian Literature TCLC 54: 86-175
  overviews, 87-95
  American proletarian literature and the American Communist Party, 95-111
  ideology and literary merit, 111-7
  novels, 117-36
  Gastonia, 136-48
  drama, 148-54
  journalism, 154-9
  proletarian literature in the United States, 159-74

American Romanticism NCLC 44: 74-138
  overviews, 74-84
  sociopolitical influences, 84-104
  Romanticism and the American frontier, 104-15
  thematic concerns, 115-37

American Western Literature TCLC 46: 1-100
  definition and development of American Western literature, 2-7
  characteristics of the Western novel, 8-23
  Westerns as history and fiction, 23-34

critical reception of American Western literature, 34-41
  the Western hero, 41-73
  women in Western fiction, 73-91
  later Western fiction, 91-9

Art and Literature TCLC 54: 176-248
  overviews, 176-93
  definitions, 193-219
  influence of visual arts on literature, 219-31
  spatial form in literature, 231-47

Arthurian Literature CMLC 10: 1-127
  historical context and literary beginnings, 2-27
  development of the legend through Malory, 27-64
  development of the legend from Malory to the Victorian Age, 65-81
  themes and motifs, 81-95
  principal characters, 95-125

Arthurian Revival NCLC 36: 1-77
  overviews, 2-12
  Tennyson and his influence, 12-43
  other leading figures, 43-73
  the Arthurian legend in the visual arts, 73-6

Australian Literature TCLC 50: 1-94
  origins and development, 2-21
  characteristics of Australian literature, 21-33
  historical and critical perspectives, 33-41
  poetry, 41-58
  fiction, 58-76
  drama, 76-82
  Aboriginal literature, 82-91

Beat Generation, Literature of the TCLC 42: 50-102

Topic Index

theories, 293-8
and French Symbolism, 298-310
themes in poetry, 310-4
theater, 314-20
and the fine arts, 320-32

Symbolist Movement, French NCLC 20:
169-249
background and characteristics, 170-86
principles, 186-91
attacked and defended, 191-7
influences and predecessors, 197-211
and Decadence, 211-6
theater, 216-26
prose, 226-33
decline and influence, 233-47

Theater of the Absurd TCLC 38: 339-415
"The Theater of the Absurd," 340-7
major plays and playwrights, 347-58
and the concept of the absurd, 358-86
theatrical techniques, 386-94
predecessors of, 394-402
influence of, 402-13

Tin Pan Alley
See **American Popular Song, Golden Age of**

Transcendentalism, American NCLC 24:
1-99
overviews, 3-23
contemporary documents, 23-41
theological aspects of, 42-52
and social issues, 52-74
literature of, 74-96

Travel Writing in the Nineteenth Century NCLC 44: 274-392
the European grand tour, 275-303
the Orient, 303-47
North America, 347-91

Travel Writing in the Twentieth Century
TCLC 30: 407-56
conventions and traditions, 407-27
and fiction writing, 427-43
comparative essays on travel writers, 443-54

True-Crime Literature CLC 99: 333-433
history and analysis, 334-407
reviews of true-crime publications, 407-23

writing instruction, 424-29
author profiles, 429-33

***Ulysses* and the Process of Textual Reconstruction** TCLC 26: 386-416
evaluations of the new *Ulysses,* 386-94
editorial principles and procedures, 394-401
theoretical issues, 401-16

Utopian Literature, Nineteenth-Century
NCLC 24: 353-473
definitions, 354-74
overviews, 374-88
theory, 388-408
communities, 409-26
fiction, 426-53
women and fiction, 454-71

Utopian Literature, Renaissance LC-32:
1-63
overviews, 2-25
classical background, 25-33
utopia and the social contract, 33-39
origins in mythology, 39-48
utopia and the Renaissance country house, 48-52
influence of millenarianism, 52-62

Vampire in Literature TCLC 46: 391-454
origins and evolution, 392-412
social and psychological perspectives, 413-44
vampire fiction and science fiction, 445-53

Victorian Autobiography NCLC 40: 277-363
development and major characteristics, 278-88
themes and techniques, 289-313
the autobiographical tendency in Victorian prose and poetry, 313-47
Victorian women's autobiographies, 347-62

Victorian Fantasy Literature NCLC 60:
246-384
overviews, 247-91
major figures, 292-366
women in Victorian fantasy literature, 366-83

Victorian Novel NCLC 32: 288-454
development and major characteristics, 290-310
themes and techniques, 310-58
social criticism in the Victorian novel, 359-97
urban and rural life in the Victorian novel, 397-406
women in the Victorian novel, 406-25
Mudie's Circulating Library, 425-34
the late-Victorian novel, 434-51

Vietnam War in Literature and Film
CLC 91: 383-437
overview, 384-8
prose, 388-412
film and drama, 412-24
poetry, 424-35

Vorticism TCLC 62: 330-426
Wyndham Lewis and Vorticism, 330-8
characteristics and principles of Vorticism, 338-65
Lewis and Pound, 365-82
Vorticist writing, 382-416
Vorticist painting, 416-26

Women's Diaries, Nineteenth-Century
NCLC 48: 308-54
overview, 308-13
diary as history, 314-25
sociology of diaries, 325-34
diaries as psychological scholarship, 334-43
diary as autobiography, 343-8
diary as literature, 348-53

Women Writers, Seventeenth-Century
LC 30: 2-58
overview, 2-15
women and education, 15-9
women and autobiography, 19-31
women's diaries, 31-9
early feminists, 39-58

World War I Literature TCLC 34: 392-486
overview, 393-403
English, 403-27
German, 427-50
American, 450-66
French, 466-74
and modern history, 474-82

Topic Index

LC Cumulative Nationality Index

LC Cumulative Title Index

Title Index

Title Index

Title Index

Title Index

Title Index

Title Index

Title Index

Title Index

Title Index

Title Index

Title Index

ISBN 0-7876-1132-8

90000